# Microeconomics

8th Canadian Edition

**CAMPBELL R. McCONNELL**
University of Nebraska, Lincoln

**STANLEY L. BRUE**
Pacific Lutheran University

**THOMAS P. BARBIERO**
Ryerson Polytechnic University

Toronto Montréal New York Burr Ridge Bangkok
Bogotá Caracas Lisbon London Madrid Mexico City
Milan New Delhi Seoul Singapore Sydney Taipei

*McGraw-Hill*
***Ryerson Limited***

*A Subsidiary of The **McGraw·Hill** Companies*

Microeconomics: Scarcity, Wants, and Choices
Eighth Canadian Edition



ISBN: 0-07-560458-2

1 2 3 4 5 6 7 8 9 10 GTC 8 7 6 5 4 3 2 1 0 9

Printed and bound in Canada.



Senior Sponsoring Editor: *Lynn Fisher*
Editorial Consultant: *Joseph Gladstone*
Supervising Editor: *Jennifer Burnell*
Associate Editor: *Jenna Wallace*
Copy-editor: *Wendy Thomas*
Production Co-ordinator: *Nicla Dattolico*
Cover Design: *Liz Harasymczuk*
Cover Photo: *Mike Dobel/Masterfile*
Interior Design: *Liz Harasymczuk*
Typesetter: *Bookman Typesetting Co.*
Printer: *Transcontinental Printing*

**Canadian Cataloguing in Publication Data**
McConnell, Campbell R.
Microeconomics: scarcity, wants, and choices

8th Canadian ed.
Includes index.
ISBN 0-07-560458-2

1. Microeconomics. I. Brue, Stanley, L., 1945– . II. Barbiero, Thomas Paul, 1952– . III. Title
HB172.M115 1999 338.5 C98-932826-0

This book is dedicated to Elsa, Marta, Emilia and Robert.

# About the Authors

**Campbell R. McConnell** earned his Ph.D. from the University of Iowa after receiving degrees from Cornell College and the University of Illinois. He taught at the University of Nebraska-Lincoln from 1953 until his retirement in 1990. He is also co-author of *Contemporary Labor Economics*, 5th ed. (McGraw-Hill) and has edited readers for the principles and labour economics courses. He is a recipient of both the University of Nebraska Distinguished Teaching Award and the James A. Lake Academic Freedom Award, and is past-president of the Midwest Economics Association. Professor McConnell was awarded an honorary Doctor of Laws degree from Cornell College in 1973 and received its Distinguished Achievement Award in 1994. His primary areas of interest are labour economics and economic education. He has an extensive collection of jazz recordings and enjoys reading jazz history.

**Stanley L. Brue** did his undergraduate work at Augustana College (SD) and received his Ph.D. from the University of Nebraska-Lincoln. He teaches at Pacific Lutheran University, where he has been honoured as a recipient of the Burlington Northern Faculty Achievement Award. He has also received the national Leavey Award for excellence in economic education. Professor Brue is past president and a current member of the International Executive Board of Omicron Delta Epsilon International Economics Honorary. He is coauthor of *Economic Scenes*, 5th ed. (Prentice-Hall) and *Contemporary Labor Economics*, 5th ed. (McGraw-Hill) and author of *The Evolution of Economic Thought*, 5th ed. (HB/Dryden). For relaxation, he enjoys boating on Puget Sound and skiing trips with his family.

**Thomas P. Barbiero** received his Ph.D. from the University of Toronto after completing undergraduate studies at the same university. He has published papers on the role of the agricultural sector in the industrial development of northern Italy in the period 1861–1914. His research interests in the last few years have turned to economic methodology and the application of economic theory to explain social phenomena. Professor Barbiero spends part of his summer in Florence, where he teaches a European economic history course to Ryerson students. After the course is over, he and his wife search out good food and wine in the Tuscan countryside.

# About the Authors

# Contents

# Preface

Welcome to the eighth Canadian edition of *Macroeconomics* and *Microeconomics*. *Macroeconomics* and *Microeconomics* continue to be leading economics texts in both Canada and the United States; about 5 million students have used this book in the two countries. It has been adapted into Australian, Italian, and Russian editions and translated into French, Spanish, and several other languages.

The resurging Canadian economy, changes in the focus of monetary policy, economic turmoil in Southeast Asia, dynamic new technologies, swings in exchange rates, capitalism in Russia—what an interesting time to teach and learn economics! Clearly, those who undertstand economic principles will have a distinct advantage in making sense of the economy and successfully participating in it.

## WHAT'S NEW?

We thoroughly revised, polished, and updated this edition. (Using a software analogy, this is version 8.0, not 7.1 or 7.2.) The comments of reviewers and survey respondents motivated many of the changes and helped us create a text full of energy and innovation.

### New or "Mostly New" Chapters

One chapter is totally new to this edition, and four other chapters are "mostly new."

- Chapter 11 (Macroeconomics): Aggregate Demand and Aggregate Supply. We have introduced both the short-run and long-run aggregate supply curves, and connected the long-run aggregate supply curves with potential GDP.
- Chapter 13 (Microeconomics): Technology, R&D, and Efficiency. This entirely new chapter is an explicit and cohesive discussion of the microeconomics of technological advance. We think that topics such as invention, innovation, R&D decision making, and creative destruction are exciting and simply too important to ignore or set into sidebars, so we devote an entire chapter to them. (To make room for this new content, we consolidated the discussions of monopolistic competition and oligopoly into a single chapter [Chapter 12].)
- Chapter 16 (Macroeconomics): Long-Run Macroeconomic Adjustments. In this revised chapter we use the long-run aggregate demand-aggregate supply model to analyze demand-pull inflation, cost-push inflation, and recession. In the remainder of the chapter we look at other aggregate supply topics such as the Phillips Curve and supply-side economics.
- Chapter 17 (Macroeconomics): Disputes in Macro Theory and Policy. In this nearly new chapter we broaden the ideas developed in Chapter 16 to discuss modern disputes in macro theory and policy. We now use the classic Keynesian discussion of previous editions as a historical backdrop for an examination of modern debates on (1) the sources of macro instability, (2) the extent of "self-correction" in the economy, and (3) the debate over "rules" versus "discretion." The chapter systematically examines new classical economics and introduces ideas such as misperceptions theory, coordination failures, efficiency wages, and insider-outsider relationships.

- Chapter 23 (Macroeconomics): Transition Economies: Russia and China. We added a discussion of China to the previous edition's material on Russia. We look briefly at Marxian ideology and the institutions, goals, and major problems of central planning, and then turn to the collapse of the Soviet economy, the elements of the Russian reform, and contemporary outcomes. Finally, we discuss the main features of market reform in China, including rapid economic growth and remaining difficulties.

## New Pedagogy

- *Quick Quizzes.* We added four multiple-choice questions as Quick Quizzes to each of the 24 Key Graphs. Each quiz relates to the content of the specific Key Graph and is written in the same style and at the same level of difficulty as the test bank questions. The correct answers are provided upside down so students can instantly measure their understanding of key concepts.
- *Ten Key Concepts.* We have introduced the Ten Key Concepts in the first chapter of the text. These Key Concepts will help the student to better organize and understand the core materials of the text. The Ten Key Concepts are divided into three categories:

  1. those pertaining to the individual,
  2. concepts that explain the interaction among individuals; and
  3. concepts that deal with the economy as a whole.

  In Chapter 1, each concept is briefly identified with further elaboration of each of the Key Concepts provided as you progress through the text. Within a chapter, you will be notified in the "Big Picture" box each time a Key Concept is going to be discussed and an icon will be used to alert you when a Key Concept is about to be presented.
- *Chapter Learning Objectives.* We set out the learning objectives at the start of each chapter so the student can more easily organize the chapter's main concepts.
- *Internet Questions.* Each chapter contains one or two Web-Based Questions that require students to access specified Internet addresses. These questions help students apply specific economic concepts and introduce them to relevant *Economics* Internet sites.

## A Building-Block Approach to Macro

With the changes in this edition, we created a fully integrated building-block approach to macro theory, policy, and issues. Specifically, we

- Build the aggregate expenditures model (AE model)
- Derive aggregate demand from the AE model and develop the aggregate demand–aggregate supply model (AD-AS model)
- Introduce both the short-run and long-run AD-AS model.
- Use the AD-AS model to discuss fiscal policy
- Introduce monetary considerations into the AD-AS model
- Use the AD-AS model to discuss monetary policy
- Apply the long-run AD-AS model to macroeconomic instability, modern macroeconomic disputes, and economic growth

## Added Content on Women, Minorities, and Discrimination

In text and vignettes, this edition includes new information on women, minorities, and discrimination. For example, in Chapter 2 we added a Last Word on the rise of women's participation in the labour force. Chapter 16 in *Microeconomics* develops the taste for discrimination model, the idea of statistical discrimination, and the theory of occupational crowding. The new Last Word in Chapter 16 in *Microeconomics* looks at the effects of "blind" auditions on the gender composition of major symphony orchestras.

## Greater Emphasis on the Economic Perspective

Newly organized Chapter 1 now begins with a discussion of scarcity and choice, rational behaviour, and marginal analysis. In Chapter 2 we use the ideas of marginal benefits and marginal costs to determine the optimal position on the production possibilities curve. We continue to reinforce the economic perspective in the remainder of the book in a number of discussions, including those on investment decisions, sunk costs, rational R&D decisions, and immigration policy.

## Added Directness, Reduced Formalism, Extra Human Interest Material

Our line-by-line editing adds directness and reduces formalism, but we were careful to *not* reduce the thoroughness of our explanations. Where needed, the "extra sentence of explanation" remains a distinguishing characteristic of *Macroeconomics* and *Microeconomics*. Students will especially enjoy our new Last Word in *Microeconomics*, Chapter 13, On the Path to the Personal Computer and Internet. All 40 Last Words present interesting applications.

## Other New Topics and Revised Discussions

Along with the changes just discussed, there are many other revisions. Here are just a few examples in *Microeconomics*.

- ***Part 1.*** *Chapter 1:* Figure 1-1 and its discussion revised; new, livelier examples. *Chapter 2:* Improved discussion of the economic rationale for increasing costs; new applications (land-use controversies, devastation from war, and emerging technologies); consolidated discussion of economic systems. *Chapter 4:* New examples: increased demand for sports-utility vehicles; improved fuel efficiency of aircraft engines; increased demand for salsa; buyout of haddock fishing boats; the decline in the price of pink salmon. *Chapter 5:* New Global Perspective on the Index of Economic Freedom. New discussion of the principal-agent problem; new Global Perspective on government employment as a percentage of total employment for various countries. *Chapter 6:* Improved explanation of the most-favoured-nation clause.
- ***Part 2.*** *Chapter 7:* Revised discussion (based on new research) of the price elasticity of illegal drugs. *Chapter 8:* Figure 8-1 is now a Key Graph; new Figure 8-2 shows the demand curve derived from a change in product price in the utility-maximizing model. *Chapter 9:* Explicit definitions of marginal, average, and total product now precede the discussion of diminishing returns; substantially revised Table 9-1 and Figure 9-2; new example of scale economies ("extraordinarily large stamping machine"). *Chapter 10:* Figure 10-2 now includes the firm's total profit curve; the graphical discussion of the TR-TC approach is confined to profit maximization; section on qualifications of the pure competition model is consolidated. *Chapter 11:* New Table 11-2 lays out the steps for determining profit-maximizing output, price, and profit (if any) in pure monopoly; new graphical comparison of outcomes under pure monopoly and pure competition (Figure 11-6); "discount coupons" added as an example of price discrimination. *Chapter 12:* The discussion of monopolistic competition and oligopoly is now combined into a single chapter; kinked demand model as a Key Graph added; several new examples. *Chapter 13:* New chapter on technology, R&D, and efficiency.
- ***Part 3.*** *Chapter 15:* Table 15-3 summarizes the differences between substitute resources and complementary resources; updated labour demand examples; revised discussion of least-cost and profit-maximizing combinations of resources. Chapter 16: Discussions of real wage stagnation and pitfalls of pay-for-performance plans; rewritten section on labour market imperfections.
- ***Part 4.*** *Chapter 19:* New hypothetical example (enterprising artist and his public art) to highlight the free-rider problem and public goods characteristics; new discussion of the "tragedy of the commons." *Chapter 20:* Expanded discussion of pork-barrel politics and bureaucratic inefficiency; new material on VAT and flat tax proposals, including criticisms. *Chapter 22:* We have added this chapter on international trade to *Microeconomics* for the first time.

*Macroeconomics* has the following revisions:

- ***Part 2.*** *Chapter 7:* Changed terminology relating to Figure 7-2 (from "expanding, static, and declining economy" to "expanding, static, and declining production capacity"); simplification of the explanation of the GDP price index (new Tables 7-5 and 7-6); fuller discussion of the CPI. *Chapter 8:* Improved discussion of structural unemployment; revision of the discussion of Okun's law; addition to Table 8-2 of unemployment rates by level of education. *Chapter 9:* Figure 9-5 (investment demand) is now a Key Graph; new Figure 9-6 shows shifts in the investment-demand curve; new Figure 9-7 links the real interest rate, the investment-demand curve, and the economy's investment schedule. *Chapter 10:* Figure 10-8 on recessionary and inflationary gaps is now a Key Graph. *Chapter 11:* Introduction of both the short-run and long-run aggregate supply curves. *Chapter 12:* Clarified discussion of the crowding-out effect of fiscal policy, including criticisms of the idea.

- ***Part 3.*** *Chapter 13:* "Unit of account" replaces the term "measure of value"; new section on recent developments in money and banking (globalization of financial markets, and electronic money and smart cards). *Chapter 15:* New Global Perspective 15-1 lists the names (including nicknames) of the central banks of selected nations.
- ***Part 4.*** *Chapter 16:* Extends the analysis of aggregate supply. *Chapter 17:* "New" chapter contrasts contemporary views on macro theory and policy. *Chapter 18:* Covers economic growth (Chapter 19 in the seventh edition); discusses the weak productivity gains in services; discusses the controversial idea of a "new economy."
- ***Part 5.*** Chapter 20: Chapter on international trade tightened. *Chapter 21:* Improved explanation of the balance of payments; major consolidation of the discussion of past exchange-rate systems. *Chapter 22:* New world map indicating industrially advanced nations, middle-income developing nations, and low-income developing nations (Figure 22-1); revised discussion of international debt difficulties, including mention of the recent IMF bailouts of the Southeast Asian economies; entirely new policy section on development. *Chapter 23: Extensively revised chapter now includes discussion of the transition to markets in China as well as in Russia.*

### Last Words

We have brought back the Last Words, which were called Applying the Theory in previous editions. Several Last Words are new; others have been revised and updated. We have placed these boxes at the ends of chapters, where they are less likely to interrupt readers' concentration.

The new Last Word topics are women and production possibilities (Chapter 2); the irrelevancy of sunk costs (*Microeconomics* Chapter 9); maximization of consumer surplus in pure competition (*Microeconomics* Chapter 10); a brief history of the personal computer and Internet (*Microeconomics* Chapter 15); the impact of blind auditions on the employment of women in major orchestras (*Microeconomics* Chapter 16); enterprise transition to capitalism in Russia (*Microeconomics* Chapter 23).

## FUNDAMENTAL GOALS

Although the eighth edition only modestly resembles the first one, our intention remains the same: to introduce beginning economics students to principles essential to understanding the basic economizing problem, specific economic issues, and policy alternatives available for dealing with them. Two fortunate by-products of this objective are an ability to reason accurately and dispassionately about economic matters and a lasting interest in economics. As always, we present the principles and problems of economics in a straightforward, logical fashion. *We continue to stress clarity of presentation, step-by-step organization, and a consistent level of analysis.*

## DISTINGUISHING FEATURES

- ***Comprehensive Explanations at an Appropriate Level.*** *Microeconomics* and *Macroeconomics* are comprehensive, analytical, and challenging yet accessible to a wide range of students. Their thoroughness and accessibility enable instructors to select topics for special classroom emphasis with confidence that students can read and comprehend independently other assigned material in the book.
- ***Comprehensive Definition of Economics.*** Because students must first understand the fundamentals, we devote nearly all of Chapter 2 to a careful statement and development of the economizing problem and an exploration of its implications. This foundation will help put into proper perspective essential economic concepts.
- ***Fundamentals of the Market System.*** Economies throughout the world are making difficult transitions from planning to markets. Our detailed description of the institutions and operation of the *market system* in Chapter 3 is even more relevant than before. We pay particular attention to property rights, freedom of

enterprise and choice, competition, and the role of profits because these concepts are poorly understood by beginning students.

- ***Early Integration of International Economics.*** We give the principles and institutions of the global economy early treatment. Chapter 6 examines the growth of world trade, the major participants in world trade, specialization and comparative advantage, the foreign exchange market, tariffs and subsidies, and various trade agreements. This strong introduction to international economics permits "globalization" of later macroeconomics and microeconomics discussions.
- ***Early and Extensive Treatment of Government.*** Government is an integral component of modern capitalism. This book introduces the economic functions of government early and systematically treats them in Chapter 5. Chapter 19 in *Microeconomics* examines government and market failure in further detail, and Chapter 20 looks at salient facets of public choice theory and public finance. Both *Macroeconomics* and *Microeconomics* include problem- and policy-oriented chapters.
- ***Emphasis on Economic Growth.*** This edition continues to emphasize economic growth. Chapter 2 uses the production possibilities curve to show the basic ingredients of growth. Chapter 18 in *Macroeconomics* discusses the rate and causes of growth, in addition to some of the controversies surrounding it. Chapter 22 in *Macroeconomics* focuses on the developing countries and the growth obstacles they confront. Chapter 23 in *Macroeconomics* looks at growth in the transition economies of the Soviet Union and China. Our new micro chapter on technology, R&D, and efficiency lays the micro foundation for understanding economic growth.
- ***Emphasis on the Theory of the Firm.*** We give much attention to microeconomics in general and to the theory of the firm in particular, for two reasons. First, the concepts of microeconomics are difficult for most beginning students; too-brief expositions usually compound these difficulties by raising more questions than they answer. Second, we wanted to couple analysis of the various market structures with a discussion of the impact of each market arrangement on price, output levels, resource allocation, and the rate of technological advance.
- ***Emphasis on Economic Issues.*** For many students, Part 3 in *Macroeconomics* and Part 4 in *Microeconomics* are where the action is. We sought to guide that action along logical lines through the application of appropriate analytical tools. In these parts we favour inclusiveness; instructors can effectively omit whatever chapters they choose.

## ORGANIZATION AND CONTENT

*Microeconomics* and *Macroeconomics* reflect the challenge specific topics and concepts will likely pose for average students. For instance, the theory of the firm and macro output and price-level determination are carefully treated. Here, simplicity is correlated with comprehensiveness, not brevity.

Our experience suggests that in treating each basic topic—aggregate demand and aggregate supply, money and banking, theory of the firm, and international economics—it is desirable to couple analysis with policy. Generally, we use a three-step development of analytical tools: (1) verbal descriptions and illustrations, (2) numerical examples, and (3) graphical presentation based on these numerical illustrations.

## PEDAGOGICAL AIDS

*Microeconomics* and *Macroeconomics* have always been student-oriented. The To the Student statement at the beginning of Part 1 details the books' many pedagogical aids. The eighth edition is also accompanied by a variety of high-quality supplements. The supplements listed here may accompany *Microeconomics and Macroeconomics, Eighth Canadian Edition*. Please contact your local McGraw-Hill Ryerson representative for details concerning policies, prices, and availability as some restrictions may apply.

### The Supplements

- ***Study Guide.*** Torben Andersen (Ph.D. Economics, University of Washington), the current Chairperson of Humanities and Social Sciences at Red Deer College, has prepared the eighth Canadian edition of the *Study*

*Guide*, which many students will find indispensable. Each chapter has an introductory statement, a checklist of behavioural objectives, an outline, a list of important terms, fill-in questions, problems and projects, objective questions, and discussion questions. The answers to the end-of-chapter Key Questions appear at the end of the *Study Guide*.

- ***Instructor's Resource Manual.*** Text author Professor Tom Barbiero of Ryerson Polytechnic University has revised and updated the *Instructor's Resource Manual*. It includes chapter summaries, listings of "what's new" in each chapter, new teaching tips and suggestions, learning objectives, chapter outlines, data and visual aid sources with suggestions for classroom use, and questions and problems. Answers to the text's end-of-chapter Key Questions are also included.

## Computerized Test Banks

- ***Test Bank I.*** Completely Canadianized, this test bank includes more than 5,000 questions, most of them written by the text authors.

Also available:

- ***Test Bank II.*** Written by William Walstad, one of the world's foremost experts on economic education, this U.S. test bank contains more than 5,000 questions. All Test Bank II questions are now categorized according to level of difficulty: easy, moderate, or difficult.
- ***Test Bank III.*** Also prepared by William Walstad, the U.S. Test Bank III contains "constructive response" testing to evaluate student understanding in a manner different from conventional multiple-choice and true-false questions. Suggested answers to the essay and problem questions are included.
- ***PowerPoint Presentation.*** Sam Fefferman of the Northern Alberta Institute of Technology has created our PowerPoint slides.
- ***Student Software.*** The U.S. edition of DiscoverEcon is available for *Microeconomics and Macroeconomics*. This menu-driven software, which was developed by Gerald Nelson at the University of Illinois, gives students a complete tutorial linked to the text. Each chapter features two essay questions and a multiple-choice test. Whenever relevant, interactive graphing problems let students observe how the economic picture is altered when they select different data.

On the Web:

- **Online Learning Centre**
- **Internet Book Site**
- **McGraw-Hill Ryerson Web Communities** A dynamic Web site of resources, information, ideas, and opportunities, from Canadian faculty—for Canadian faculty. Instructors have the opportunity to use the Web communities to exchange ideas, news, issues, and insights on an ongoing basis. Content may include such topics as:
    - Current Events
    - Downloadables
    - Job Postings
    - Web Links
    - Lecture Suggestions
    - Site News

All linked to this text on a chapter-by-chapter basis!

Almost instantly, current issues can be connected to this text, improving the link between theory and practice. Classroom presentations and assignments will be enhanced by this access to the most up-to-date and relevant information related to what's being taught.

Contact your McGraw-Hill Ryerson representative for more information.

## ACKNOWLEDGEMENTS

The publication of this eighth edition will extend the life of *Microeconomics* well into its second decade. The acceptance of the parent text, *Economics*, which was generous from the outset, has expanded with each edition. This gracious reception has no doubt been fostered by the many teachers and students who have been kind enough to provide their suggestions and criticisms.

Our colleagues at the University of Nebraska-Lincoln, Pacific Lutheran University, and Ryerson Polytechnic University have generously shared knowledge of their specialties with us and have provided encouragement. We are especially indebted to Ryerson professors John Hughes, David Cape, Dagmar Rajagopal, Leo Michelis, Ingrid Bryan, Tom Tushingham, and Mark Lovewell, who have been most helpful in offsetting our comparative ignorance in their areas of specialty.

As indicated, the previous editions have benefited from a number of perceptive reviews. In both quality and quantity, they provided the richest possible source of suggestions for this revision. We wish to thank the following instructors who participated in the formal review process:

| | |
|---|---|
| T. Anderson | Red Deer College |
| B. Abbott | Northern Alberta Institute of Technology |
| M. Benarroch | University of Winnipeg |
| E. Black | Brandon University |
| D.Box | University College of the Fraser Valley |
| C. Burke | Lethbridge Community College |
| N. Clegg | Kwantlen College |
| B. Cook | University of New Brunswick |
| K. Dawson | Conestoga College |
| C. Dickhoff | British Columbia Institute of Technology |
| S. Dodaro | St. Francis Xavier University |
| M. Dore | Brock University |
| S. Fefferman | Northern Alberta Institute of Technology |
| P. Fortura | Algonquin College |
| B. Gayle-Amyiwe | Seneca College |
| C. Graham | Assiniboine College |
| P. Jacobs | Champlain Regional College |
| E. Jacobson | Northern Alberta Institute of Technology |
| S. Law | University of New Brunswick |
| M. Moy | University College of Cape Breton |
| V. Nallainayagam | Mount Royal College |
| J. Newark | Athabasca University |
| A. Nimarko | Vanier College |
| D. Pepper | British Columbia Institute of Technology |
| R. Schwindt | Simon Fraser University |
| J. Skuce | Georgian College |
| L. Smith | University of Waterloo |
| L. Swanson | Lakeland College |
| T. Tushingham | Ryerson Polytechnic University |

We also wish to thank the following instructors who participated in the formal review process of the eighth edition:

| | |
|---|---|
| Charles Burke | Lethbridge Community College |
| Ibrahim Hayani | Seneca College |
| Ron Kessler | British Columbia Institute of Technology |
| Judith Skuce | Georgian College |
| Terry Sulyma | Northern Alberta Institute of Technology |
| Campion Swartout | Saskatchewan Institute of Science and Technology |
| Bill Thomas | Sheridan College |

Throughout all editions of this text we have benefited from instructors who contributed in an informal manner their comments and suggestions to authors, editors, and McGraw-Hill Ryerson representatives we owe them a debt of gratitude. In this connection, I. Hayani of Centennial College, Sage Traviza of the International Centre for Tax Studies, Faculty of Management Studies, University of Toronto, Torben Andersen of Red Deer College, and Judith Skuce of Georgian College, were particularly helpful

We are greatly indebted to the many professionals at McGraw-Hill Ryerson—and in particular to Daphne Scriabin, Margaret Henderson, Jennifer Burnell, Jeff MacLean and Gary Bennett—for their publishing expertise. We thank Wendy Thomas for her thorough and sensitive editing.

We also strongly acknowledge the newly integrated Irwin/McGraw-Hill Ryerson sales staff, who greeted this edition with wholehearted enthusiasm.

Campbell R. McConnell
Stanley L. Brue
Thomas P. Barbiero

# Economics on the World Wide Web

## Part 1

**Bob Parks' A Random Walk Around Economics on the Net** wuecon.wustl.edu/~bob/econwalknet.html
**NetEc** netec.wustl.edu/local/NetEc.html
**Resources for Economists on the Internet** econwpa.wustl.edu/EconFAQ/EconFAQ.html
**Dismal Sciences** www.dismal.com/
**The Mining Company** economics.miningco.com/
**Classroom Expernomics** www.marietta.edu/~delemeeg/expernom.html
**Computer Aided Instruction in Economics** userwww.sfsu.edu/~bjblecha/cai.htm
**Economic Education, EcEdWeb** http://ecedweb.unomaha.edu/
**Econ Teaching Resources** woodrow.mpls.frb.fed.us/econed/class/econsite.html
**AmosWorld** amos.bus.okstate.edu/
**Economics Working Paper Archive (EconWPA)** econwpa.wustl.edu/wpawelcome.html
**Journal of Economic Literature and EconLit (JEL)** www.econlit.org/
**CARL's UnCover** uncweb.carl.org/
**sci.finance.abstracts** www.public.iastate.edu/~arnie/sci-finance-abstracts.htm
**Economics Research Network (ERN) (part of SSRN)** www.ssrn.Com/
**Student Economic Review** www.bess.tcd.ie/ser.html
**IDEAL (Academic Press)** www.apnet.com/www/ap/aboutid.htm
**Applied Economics** www.chapmanhall.com/ae/
**B>Quest (Business Quest)** www.westga.edu/~bquest/
**Roland's Overview of Conferences and Meetings on Economic Theory** www.wiwiss.fu-berlin.de/w3/w3bester/roland/econ_co.htm
**Economics Departments, Institutes and Research Centers in the World (EDIRC)—Associations and Societies** www.er.uqam.ca/nobel/r14160/economics/assocs.html
**American Economic Association (AEA)** www.vanderbilt.edu/AEA/
**History of Economics Society** cs.muohio.edu/~HisEcSoc/other_resources.shtml
**History of Economics Internet References** cfec.vub.ac.be/cfec/hope.htm
**Regional Science Association (RSA)** gopher://olymp.wu-wien.ac.at:70/11/.inst/.iir/.rsa
**International Association for Feminist Economics** www.bucknell.edu/~jshackel/iaffe
**International Economics and Philosophy Society** www.bath.ac.uk/Centres/Ethical/ieps.htm
**American Law and Economics Association (ALEA)** webserver.law.yale.edu/alea/alea.htm
**Southern Economic Association (SEA)** bubba.ucc.okstate.edu/economics/journal/south1.html
**Eastern Economic Association** www.iona.edu/orgs/eea.htm
**Western Economic Association International** www.weainternational.org/
**National Association of Business Economists (NABE)** www.nabe.com/
**Statistics Canada** www.statcan.ca/
**Canadian Economic Association** www.economics.ca
**Organization for Economic Cooperation and Development (OECD)** www.oecd.org

## Part 2

**Economic Science Association** www.econlab.arizona.edu/esa/
**Inter-university Consortium for Political and Social Research (ICPSR)** www.icpsr.umich.edu/
**Centre for Economic Learning and Social Evolution (ELSE)** ada.econ.ucl.ac.uk/
**Pool Listing Service in Game Theory** fismat.dima.unige.it/citg/citg.htm
**Economic Science Laboratory, Univ. of Arizona** www.econlab.arizona.edu/
**Center for Rationality** www.ma.huji.ac.il/~ranb
**The Information Economy (by Hal Varian)** www.sims.berkeley.edu/resources/infoecon

**Openair-Market Net: The World Wide Guide to Farmers' Markets, Street Markets, Flea Markets and Street Vendors** www.openair.org/
**Statistics Canada** www.statcan.ca/
**Canada Competition Bureau** www.strategis.ic.gc.ca

## Part 3

**Model User Group International (CGE Modeling)** watarts.uwaterloo.ca/~mug/index.html
**Communications for a Sustainable Future** csf.colorado.edu/
**Statistics Canada** www.statcan.ca
**Bank of Canada** www.bank-banque-canada.ca

## Part 4

**Government Information Sharing Project** govinfo.kerr.orst.edu/
**CIA Publications and Handbooks** www.odci.gov/cia/publications/pubs.html
**National Transportation Statistics** www.bts.gov
**Energy Resources Board (DOE)** www.eia.doe.gov/energy/
**Integrated Public Use Microdata Sample (IPUMS)** www.hist.umn.edu/~ipums
**International Society for Ecological Economics** kabir.umd.edu/ISEE/ISEEhome.html
**Centre for Economic and Social Studies for the Environment (CESSE)** www.ulb.ac.be/ceese/french/ceese.html
**Getting Around the Planet** www.olsen.ch/cgi-bin/exmenu/pathfinder/
**International Trade & Business WWW Reference Pages** pacific.commerce.ubc.ca/trade/
**The Global Trade Analysis Project (GTAP)** www.agecon.purdue.edu/gtap/index.htm
**Global Financial Data** www.globalfindata.com
**QuoteCom Data Service** www.quote.com/
**Australian Bureau of Statistics** www.statistics.gov.au/
**New Zealand Treasury** www.treasury.govt.nz/
**InTechTra's Hong Kong Stocks Reports** www.asiawind.com/pub/hksr/
**Turkish Economics Page** www.siue.edu/~itanris/econtr.html
**Israel Central Bureau of Statistics** www.cbs.gov.il/engindex.htm
**Finnish Society for Economic Research** www.hkkk.fi/~fecons/
**The Research Institute of the Finnish Economy (ETLA)** www.etla.fiEurostat europa.eu.int/eurostat.html
**European Economic Association** www.hec.unil.ch/prague/eea/premier.htm
**Euro Internet** fgr.wu-wien.ac.at/nentwich/euroint2.htm
**Central European Regional Research Organization (CERRO)** gopher://olymp.wu-wien.ac.at:70/11/.cerro.ind
**German Federal Statistical Office** www.statistik-bund.de/e_home.htm
**REESweb: Russian and East European Studies-Business, Economics, and Law Resources** www.pitt.edu/~cjp/rees.htm
**Statistics Canada** www.statcan.ca/
**Environment Canada** www.doe.ca
**World Trade Organization (WTO)** www.wto.org
**Revenue Canada** www.rc.gc.ca

# To the Student

Economics is concerned with efficiency—accomplishing goals using the best methods. Therefore, we offer some brief introductory comments on how to improve your efficiency—and your understanding and grade—in studying economics. Several features of this book will aid your learning.

- ***Appendix on graphs*** Being comfortable with graphical analysis and a few related quantitative concepts will be a big advantage to you in understanding principles of economics. The appendix to Chapter 1 reviews graphing, line slopes, and linear equations. Be sure not to skip it!
- ***The Big Picture*** The new Big Picture in each chapter is designed to stimulate interest, state the main objectives, and present an organizational overview of the chapter and its connection with previously covered chapters.
- ***Terminology*** A significant portion of any introductory course is terminology. To designate key terms, we have put them in boldface type, listed them at the end of each chapter, and provided a glossary of definitions at the end of the book.
- ***Reviews*** Important things should be said more than once. You will find a chapter summary at the conclusion of every chapter as well as two or three "Quick Reviews" within each chapter. These review statements will help you focus on the essential ideas of each chapter and also to study for exams. If any of these statements is unclear, you should reread the appropriate section of the text.
- ***Key Graphs*** We have labelled graphs having special relevance as "Key Graphs." Your instructor may or may not emphasize each of these figures, but pay special attention to those your instructor discusses in class. You can bet there will be exam questions on them!
- ***Ten Key Concepts*** There are Ten Key Concepts we have identified that will help you to organize the core materials of the text. The Ten Key Concepts are introduced in Chapter 1 and are reinforced throughout the textbook. You will be alerted to the concepts covered in each chapter in "The Big Picture" and an icon will further identify specific coverage in the text.
- ***Chapter Learning Objectives*** We set out the learning objectives at the start of each chapter so you can more easily organize the chapter's main concepts.
- ***Figure legends*** Economics is known for its many graphs. The legends accompanying the diagrams in this book are self-contained analyses of the concepts shown. Study these legends carefully—they are quick synopses of important ideas.
- ***Globalization*** Each nation functions increasingly in a global economy. To gain appreciation of this wider economic environment, be sure to take a look at the "Global Perspectives," which compare Canada to other selected nations.
- ***The Last Word*** While it is tempting to ignore these boxes, doing so is a mistake. Some "Last Word" boxes are revealing applications of economic concepts; some are short case studies; still others present views that contrast with mainstream thinking. All will deepen and broaden your grasp of economics.
- ***In the Media*** Interesting stories have been selected from the print media that show the real-world application of the economic theory

just learned. Each of these stories ends with a question to test your understanding of the chapter's materials.

- ***Questions*** A comprehensive list of questions is located at the end of each chapter. The old cliché that you "learn by doing" is very relevant to economics. Use of these questions will enhance your understanding. We designate several of them as "Key Questions" and answer them at the end of the book. You can immediately turn to these particular questions when they are cited in each chapter, or later after you have read the full chapter.
- ***Study Guide*** We enthusiastically recommend the *Study Guide* accompanying this text. This "portable tutor" contains not only a broad sampling of various kinds of questions, but a host of useful learning aids.

You will find in Chapter 1 that economics involves a special way of thinking—a unique approach to analyzing problems. The overriding goal of this book is to help you acquire that skill. If our cooperative efforts—yours, ours, and your instructor's—are successful, you will be able to comprehend a whole range of economic, social, and political problems that otherwise would have remained murky and elusive.

So much for the pep talk. Let's get on with the show.

Drabble reprinted by permission of United Feature Syndicate, Inc.

PART 1

# An Introduction to Economics and the Economy

## CHAPTER 1

# The Nature and Method of Economics

HUMAN BEINGS, THOSE UNFORTUNATE CREATURES, are plagued with desires. We want, among other things, love, social recognition, and the material necessities and comforts of life. Our efforts to meet our material wants, that is, to improve our well-being, are the concern of economics.

Biologically, we need only air, water, food, clothing, and shelter. But, in contemporary society, we also seek the many goods and services associated with a comfortable or affluent standard of living. Fortunately, society is blessed with productive resources—labour and managerial talent, tools and machinery, land and mineral deposits—that are used to produce goods and services. This production satisfies many of our material wants and occurs through the organizational mechanism called the *economic system* or, more simply, *the economy*.

The blunt reality, however, is that the total of all our material wants is many times greater than the productive capacity of our limited resources. Thus, the complete satisfaction of material wants is impossible. This unyielding reality provides our definition of **economics**—*the social science concerned with the efficient use of limited (scarce) resources to achieve maximum satisfaction of human material wants.*

Although it may not be evident, most of the headline-grabbing issues of our time—inflation, unemployment, health care, social security, budget deficits, discrimination, tax reform, poverty and inequality, pollution, and government regulation and deregulation of business—are rooted in the one challenge of using scarce resources efficiently.

**IN THIS CHAPTER YOU WILL LEARN:**

- The Ten Key Concepts to retain a lifetime.
- About the economic way of thinking.
- How economists construct theories.
- Six widely accepted economic goals.
- The distinction between microeconomics and macroeconomics.
- The pitfalls to objective thinking.

In this first chapter we will not plunge into problems and issues; instead, we will discuss some important preliminaries. Specifically, we first introduce what we consider the "Ten Key Concepts" of economics. We believe that these concepts will help you put the main issues in economics in their proper perspective. Hopefully, you will retain the Ten Key Concepts long after you finish the course and thus continue to use them to help understand economic events. Next, we state some of the benefits of studying economics. Then we consider the specific methods economists use to examine and explain economic behaviour and the economy, distinguishing between macroeconomics and microeconomics. Finally, we examine the problems, limitations, and pitfalls that hinder sound economic reasoning.

## The Big Picture

YOU ARE ABOUT TO EMBARK ON THE STUDY of economics, a discipline that can help you understand a vast array of human issues and problems. Economics is about *scarcity, wants,* and *choices.* Try to think of any goods or services of which there is such an abundance that *everyone* in the world has as much as he or she wants. You will not have much success! Even time must be carefully budgeted because there is less of it than we would like. As George Stigler, a Nobel Prize winner in economics, points out, "Anything that is an object of conscious desire must be scarce: One does not consciously desire the air breathed, or to hear bad jokes. Scarce things are costly. If they weren't, everyone would get so much of each that they would not be scarce anymore. So anything scarce, and worth having, has been costly for someone to obtain."*

* G.J. Stigler, *Memoirs of an Unregulated Economist* (New York: Basic Books, 1988).

If we wanted or needed very little in relation to available resources, the scarcity problem would be less pronounced. But because there are so many goods and services we need and want, we must make choices about which goods and services we most desire. Despite often being referred to as the "dismal science," economics is really about getting enjoyment out of life: getting as much enjoyment as possible out of the limited resources available to us; the study of economics may thus be your ticket to "happiness"! More realistically, you may come to better understand and appreciate the ubiquitous problem of scarcity in our daily lives.

You need to understand the scarcity problem if you are to succeed in the study of economics, particularly microeconomics. "The Big Picture" boxes have been written to continuously remind you of the raison d'être of economics, and to put the information in each chapter within the larger context of scarcity, wants, and choices. ■

## TEN KEY CONCEPTS TO RETAIN A LIFETIME

Suppose you unexpectedly meet your introductory economics professor on the street five or ten years after you complete this course. What will you be able to tell her you retained from the course? More than likely you will not be able to remember very much. To help you retain the main ideas that economics has to offer for many years after you complete it, we have come up with **Ten Key Concepts** we believe are essential to understand the world around you and help you in your chosen career. These key concepts will be reinforced throughout the textbook, and you will be alerted in the "Big Picture" box when each will be discussed. Also, an icon will alert you that a key concept is about to be discussed. The concepts will simply be listed here; elaboration on each of the key concepts will be found as we progress through the textbook. At the end of the course you should review these 10 key concepts. They will help you organize and better understand the materials you have studied. We have divided the 10 key concepts into three categories: (a) those pertaining to the individual; (b) concepts that explain the interaction among individuals; and (c) concepts that deal with the economy as a whole and the standard of living.

### The Individual

**CONCEPT 1:** Scarcity in relation to wants means you face **tradeoffs**; therefore you have to make **choices**.

**CONCEPT 2:** The **cost** of the choice you make is what you give up for it.

**CONCEPT 3:** Choices are usually made at the **margin**; we choose a "little" more or a "little" less of something.

**CONCEPT 4:** The choices you make are influenced by **incentives**.

### Interaction Among Individuals

**CONCEPT 5: Specialization** and **trade** will make everyone better off.

**CONCEPT 6: Markets** usually do a good job of coordinating trade among individuals, groups, and nations.

**CONCEPT 7: Governments** can occasionally improve the coordinating function of markets.

### The Economy as a Whole and the Standard of Living

**CONCEPT 8:** The **standard of living** of the average person in a particular country is dependent on its production of goods and services. A rise in the standard of living requires a rise in the output of goods and services.

**CONCEPT 9:** If the monetary authorities of a country annually print money in excess of the growth of output of goods and services it will eventually lead to **inflation**.

**CONCEPT 10:** In the short run, society faces a short-run **tradeoff** between **inflation** and its level of **unemployment**.

These concepts will be elaborated on throughout this textbook. Be sure to be on the lookout for the icon that alerts you that one of these concepts is being discussed. We now turn to our first topic, the economic way of thinking.

## THE ECONOMIC PERSPECTIVE

If you lived in a world in which human and property resources were unlimited, there would be no reason to study economics. In such a world every single individual would have as many goods and services as he or she desired. It is only because resources are scarce in relation to our wants that it is necessary to spend precious time on the study of economics. Thinking in terms of scarcity gives economists a unique perspective with which to view the world. This **economic perspective** or *economic way of thinking* has several interrelated features.

### Scarcity and Choice

2 KEY CONCEPT

From our definition of economics, it is easy to see why economists view the world through the lens of scarcity. Since human and property resources are scarce (limited), it follows that the goods and services we produce must also be scarce. Scarcity limits our options and necessitates that we make choices. Because we "can't have it all," we must decide what we will have.

At the core of economics is the idea that "there is no free lunch." You may get treated to lunch, making it "free" to you, but there is a cost to someone. Scarce inputs of land, equipment, farm labour, the labour of cooks and waiters, and managerial talent are required. Because these resources could be used in other production activities, they and the other goods and services they could have produced are sacrificed in making the "free" lunch available. Economists call these sacrifices *opportunity costs.*

### Rational Behaviour

Economics is grounded on the assumption of "rational self-interest." That is, individuals make rational decisions to achieve the greatest satisfaction or the maximum fulfilment of their goals. For instance, they spend their incomes to get the greatest benefit from the goods and services they can afford.

Rational behaviour implies that different people will make different choices because their preferences, circumstances, and available information differ. You may have decided that it is in your best interest to attend college or university before entering the full-time labour force, while a high school classmate has chosen to forgo additional schooling and go to work. Why the different choices? Your academic abilities, along with your family's income, may be greater than your classmate's. You may also know that college- or university-educated workers have better job opportunities and lower unemployment rates than less educated workers. Thus, you opted for more education, while your former classmate—the one with less academic ability, less money, and less information—chose a job. Both choices reflect the pursuit of self-interest and are rational, but they are based on differing circumstances and information.

Of course, rational decisions may change as circumstances change. Suppose the federal government decides it is in the national interest to increase the supply of college- and university-educated workers. It might offer two years of "free" post-secondary education to all low-income students. Under these new conditions, your high school classmate might now opt for college or university rather than a job.

Rational self-interest is *not* the same as selfishness. People make personal sacrifices to help family members or friends, and they contribute to charities because they derive pleasure from doing so. Parents help pay for their children's education for the same reason. These self-interested, but unselfish, acts help maximize the givers' satisfaction as much as any personal purchase of goods or services.

## Marginalism: Benefits and Costs 

The economic perspective focuses largely on **marginal analysis**—comparisons of marginal benefits and marginal costs. (Used this way, "marginal" means "extra," "additional," or "a change in.") Most choices or decisions involve changes in the status quo. Should you go to school for another year or not? Should you spend more or less money on compact discs each month? Similarly, businesses regularly must decide whether to employ more or fewer workers or to produce more or less output.

Each option involves marginal benefits and, because of scarcity, marginal costs. In making choices rationally, the decision maker must compare these two amounts. Example: Your time is scarce. What will you do with two "free" hours on a Saturday afternoon? You could watch Informed University's Fighting Aardvarks play hockey on television. The *marginal benefit* to you would be the pleasure of seeing the game. The *marginal cost* would be the benefit from the other things you have to sacrifice to watch the game, including perhaps studying, jogging, or taking a nap. If the marginal benefit exceeds the marginal cost, it is rational to watch the game. But if you determine that the marginal cost of watching the game is greater than the marginal benefit, you will select one of the other options.

On the national level, government regularly makes decisions involving marginal benefits and marginal costs. More spending on health care may mean less spending on libraries, aid to the poor, or military security. In a world of scarcity, the decision to obtain the marginal benefit associated with some specific option always includes the marginal cost of forgoing something else. Again, there is no free lunch.

One surprising implication of decisions based on marginal analysis is that there can be too much of a good thing. Although certain goods and services seem inherently desirable—education, health care, a clean environment—we can in fact have too much of them. "Too much" occurs when we keep producing them beyond the point where their marginal cost (the value of the forgone options) equals their marginal benefit.

If we choose to produce so much health care that its marginal cost to society exceeds its marginal benefit, we are providing "too much" of it even though we all agree that health care is a good thing. When the marginal costs of health care exceed the marginal benefits, we are sacrificing alternative products (for example, education and pollution reduction) that are more valuable than health care *at the margin*—the place where we consider the very last units of each. ***(Key Question 1)***

This chapter's In the Media and Last Word provide an everyday application of the economic perspective.

# WHY STUDY ECONOMICS?

Is studying economics worth your time and effort? More than half a century ago John Maynard Keynes (1883–1946)—one of the most influential economists of this century—said:

> The ideas of economists and political philosophers, both when they are right and when they are wrong, are more powerful than is commonly understood. Indeed the world is ruled by little else. Practical men, who believe themselves to be quite exempt from any intellectual influences, are usually the slaves of some defunct economist.

Most of the ideologies of the modern world have been shaped by prominent economists of the past—Adam Smith, David Ricardo, John Stuart Mill, Karl Marx, and John Maynard Keynes. And current world leaders routinely solicit the advice and policy suggestions of today's economists.

The Government of Canada has more than a thousand economists in its various ministries and agencies—and the advice of this army of economists is essential to the functioning of modern government. The areas economists advise on include unemployment and inflation, economic growth and productivity, taxation and public expenditures, poverty and income maintenance, the balance of payments and the international monetary system, labour-management relations, health care, pollution, immigration, discrimination, competition, and industrial regulation, among others.

## Economics for Citizenship

A basic understanding of economics is essential if we are to be well-informed citizens. Most of today's political problems have important economic aspects: How important is it that we balance the federal budget? How can we make the income security retirement program financially secure? How best can we reduce pollution? What must we do to keep inflation in check? What can be done to boost Canadian productivity and economic growth? Are existing welfare programs effective and justifiable? Do we need to reform our tax system? How should we respond to growing market dominance by a few firms in some high-technology sectors of the economy?

As voters, we can influence the decisions of our elected officials in responding to such questions. But intelligence at the polls requires a basic working knowledge of economics. And a sound grasp of economics is even more helpful to the politicians themselves.

### Professional and Personal Applications

Economics lays great stress on precise, systematic analysis. Thus, studying economics invariably helps students improve their analytical skills, which are in great demand in the workplace. Also, the study of economics helps us make sense of the everyday activity we observe around us. How is it that so many different people, in so many different places, doing so many different things, produce exactly the goods and services we want to buy? Economics provides an answer.

Economics is also vital to business. An understanding of the basics of economic decision making and the operation of the economic system enables business managers and executives to increase profit. The executive who understands when to use new technology, when to merge with another firm, when to expand employment, and so on, will outperform the executive who is less deft at such decision making. The manager who understands the causes and consequences of recessions (downturns in the overall economy) can make more intelligent business decisions during these periods.

Economics helps consumers and workers make better buying and employment decisions. How can you spend your limited money income to maximize your satisfaction? How can you hedge against the reduction in the dollar's purchasing power that accompanies inflation? Is it more economical to buy or lease a car? Should you use a credit card or pay cash? Which occupations pay well; which are most immune to unemployment?

Similarly, an understanding of economics makes for better financial decisions. Someone who understands the relationship between budget deficits and interest rates, between foreign exchange rates and exports, between interest rates and bond prices, is in a better position to successfully allocate personal savings. So, too, is someone who understands the business implications of emerging new technologies.

In spite of these practical benefits, however, you should know that economics is *mainly* an academic, not a vocational, subject. Unlike accounting, advertising, corporate finance, and marketing, economics is not primarily a how-to-make-money area of study. Knowledge of economics and mastery of the economic perspective will help you run a business or manage your personal finances, but that is not its primary objective. Instead, economics ultimately examines problems and decisions from the *social*, rather than the *personal*, point of view. The production, exchange, and consumption of goods and services are discussed from the viewpoint of society's best interest, not strictly from the standpoint of one's own pocketbook.

**1-1**

**QUICK REVIEW**

- Economics is concerned with obtaining maximum satisfaction through the efficient use of scarce resources.
- The economic perspective stresses **a** source scarcity and the necessity of making choices, **b** the assumption of rational behaviour, and **c** comparisons of marginal benefit and marginal cost.
- Your study of economics will help you as a voting citizen as well as benefit you professionally and personally.

## ECONOMIC METHODOLOGY

How do economists go about understanding economic phenomena, and how do they design economic policies that help reduce the scarcity problem? Figure 1-1 summarizes the methodology used by economists.

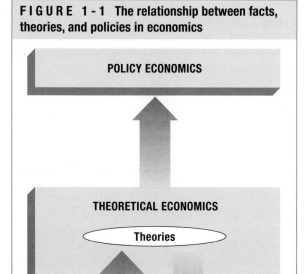

**FIGURE 1-1 The relationship between facts, theories, and policies in economics**

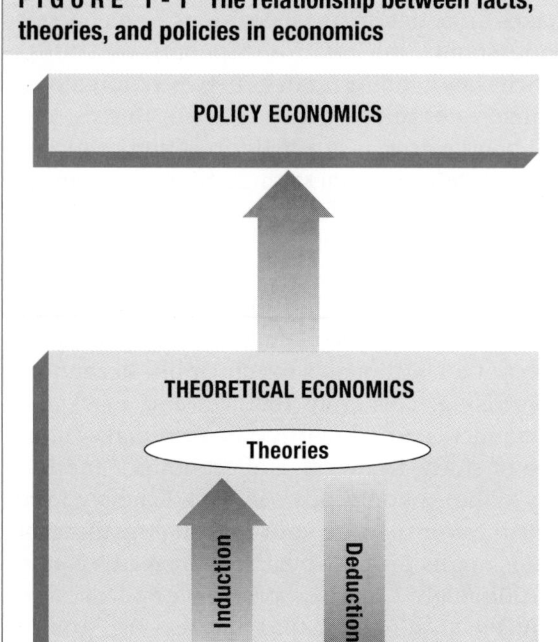


In constructing economic theories, economists may use the inductive method, through which they gather, systematically arrange, and generalize from facts. Alternatively, they may use the deductive method, in which they develop hypotheses that are then tested against facts. Generalizations derived from either method are useful not only in explaining economic behaviour but also as a basis for formulating economic policies.

## Theoretical Economics

The methodology used by economists to arrive at an understanding of economic phenomena is similar to that used in other social sciences and the natural sciences. It is generally referred to as the scientific method. All sciences are based on observable and verifiable behaviour, realities, or facts. As a social science, economics examines the observable and verifiable behaviour of individuals (consumers, workers) and institutions (business, government) engaged in the production, exchange, and consumption of goods and services.

But fact gathering about economic activity and economic outcomes can be a complex process. Because the world of reality is cluttered with millions of facts, economists, like all scientists, must be highly selective in gathering information. What they are looking for are regularities in the data that can give them an understanding of the economic event under investigation.

The economist thus seeks **principles** *or* **theories**—generalizations about the behaviour of individuals and institutions. Deriving principles or theories is called **theoretical economics** (see the lower box in Figure 1-1). *The role of economic theorizing is to systematically arrange facts, interpret them, and generalize from them to find regularities that give us an understanding of economic behaviour*. Theories, or principles, bring order to facts so that we can see the relationship between them. As the economist Kenneth Boulding states: "Theories without facts may be barren, but facts without theories are meaningless."[1]

**Terminology** Economists speak of *laws, principles, theories,* and *models*. These terms are sometimes confusing to students, but they all mean essentially the same thing: They are generalizations about the economic behaviour of individuals and institutions. The terms *economic laws* and *principles* are useful, but they are somewhat misleading because they imply a high degree of exactness, universal application, and even moral rightness that is rare in social science. The word *theory* is often used in economics even though many people incorrectly believe theories have nothing to do with real-world applications. Economists often use the term *model* instead of the term *theory*. Both refer to a simplified picture of reality, an abstract generalization of how relevant facts actually relate to one another.

In this book we will use these four terms synonymously. Custom or convenience will determine each particular choice. Thus, the relationship between the price of a product and the amount of the product consumers purchase will be called the *law of demand*, rather than the theory or principle of demand, simply because this is the custom.

## Deriving Theories

As Figure 1-1 shows, in deriving their theories economists are as likely to move from theory to facts in studying economic behaviour, as they are to move from facts to theory. That is, economists use both deductive and inductive methods.

[1] Kenneth Boulding, *Economic Analysis: Microeconomics*, 4th ed. (New York: Harper & Row, 1966), p. 5.

**Induction** moves from facts to theory, from the particular to the general. In this approach, facts are first gathered and then analyzed to derive the underlying theory. For example, suppose you collected data on the consumption and price of Pepsi at your college or university over time. As you study the data you start to see a pattern: As the price of Pepsi rises, the quantity purchased drops, and vice versa. You conclude that a generalization can be made about the relationship between the price of Pepsi and the amount of it purchased. The left upward arrow from "facts" to "theories" in the figure shows the inductive method.

More often, economists create generalization through **deduction**. They draw on casual observation, insight, logic, or intuition to frame a tenative, untested theory called a *hypothesis*. For example, they may conjecture, based on "armchair logic," that consumers will buy less of a product when its price rises. To test this hypothesis, economists collect the required data. Do real-world data confirm an inverse relationship between price and the amount purchased? If the data confirm that consumers buy less of a specific product when its price rises, we now have the basis on which to derive a theory. Of course, economists will want to subject this tentative theory to further testing before accepting it, just in case the initial testing process was flawed. The testing of a hypothesis is sometimes called *empirical economics* and is shown by the right downward arrow from "theories" to "facts" in Figure 1-1.

Deduction and induction are complementary, rather than opposing, techniques at deriving economic theories. A hypothesis formed by deduction provides a guideline for the economist in gathering and organizing data. Conversely, some understanding of factual, real-world, evidence is required to formulate meaningful hypotheses.

Derivation of economic principles requires a number of steps.

**Generalizations** As we have already mentioned, economic theories are **generalizations** relating to economic behaviour or to the economy itself. They are imprecise because economic facts are usually diverse; no two individuals or institutions act in exactly the same way. *Economic theories are expressed as the tendencies of typical, or average consumers, workers, or business firms.* For example, when economists say that consumer spending rises when personal income increases, they are well aware that some households may save *all* of an increase in their incomes. But, on average, and for the full economy, spending goes up when income increases. Similarly, economists say that consumers buy more of a particular product when its price falls. Some consumers may increase their purchases by a large amount, others by a small amount, and a few not at all. This "price-quantity" principle, however, holds for the *typical* consumer and for consumers as a group.

**Abstractions** Economic principles, or theories, are *abstractions*—simplifications that omit irrelevant facts and circumstances. These models do not mirror the full complexity of the real world. The very process of sorting out and analyzing facts requires simplification and removal of clutter. Unfortunately, this "abstraction" leads some people to consider economic theory impractical and unrealistic. This is nonsense! Economic theories are practical precisely because they *are* abstractions. The full scope of economic reality itself is too complex and bewildering to be understood as a whole. Economists abstract—that is, build models—to understand an otherwise overwhelming and confusing maze of facts. Theorizing for this purpose is highly practical.

**"Other-Things-Equal" Assumption** Like other scientists, economists use the *ceteris paribus*, or the **other-things-equal assumption**, to construct their theories. They assume that all other variables except those under immediate consideration are held constant for a particular analysis. For example, consider the relationship between the price of Pepsi and the amount purchased. It helps to assume that, of all the factors that might influence the amount of Pepsi purchased (for example, the price of Pepsi, the price of Coca-Cola, and consumer incomes and preferences), only the price of Pepsi varies. The economist can then focus on the "price of Pepsi–purchases of Pepsi" relationship without being confused by changes in other variables.

Natural scientists such as chemists or physicists can usually conduct controlled experiments where "all other things" are in fact held constant (or virtually so). They can test with great precision the assumed relationship between two variables. For example, they might examine the height from which an object is dropped and the length of time it takes to hit the ground. But economics is not a laboratory science. Economists test their theories using real-world data, which are generated by the actual operation of the economy. In this rather bewildering environment, "other things" *do* change. Despite the development of complex statistical techniques designed to hold other things equal, controls are less than perfect. As a result, economic principles are less certain and less precise than those of laboratory sciences.

**Graphical Expression** Many of the economic models in this book are expressed graphically; the most important are labelled "Key Graphs." We strongly urge you to read the appendix to this chapter as a review of graphs.

## Policy Economics

Applied economics or **policy economics** is the application of theories and data to formulate policies, as shown in the upper part of Figure 1-1. Economic theories are the foundation of economic policy—a course of action based on economic theories and intended to resolve a specific problem or further a nation's economic goals. Economic policy normally is applied to problems after they arise. However, if economic analysis can predict some undesirable event such as unemployment, inflation, or an increase in poverty, then it may be possible to avoid or moderate that event through economic policy.

**Formulating Economic Policy** Here are the basic steps in policymaking:

1. ***State the goal.*** The first step is to clearly state the economic goal. If we say that we want "full employment," do we mean that everyone between, say, 16 and 65 years of age should have a job? Or do we mean that everyone who wants to work should have a job? Should we allow for some unemployment caused by inevitable changes in the structure of industry and workers voluntarily changing jobs? The goal must be specific.
2. ***Determine the policy options.*** The next step is to formulate alternative policies designed to achieve the goal and determine the possible effects of each policy. This requires a detailed assessment of the economic impact, benefits, costs, and political feasibility of the alternative policies. For example, to achieve full employment, should government use fiscal policy (which involves changing government spending and taxes), monetary policy (which entails altering the supply of money), an education and training policy that enhances worker employability, or a policy of wage subsidies to firms that hire disadvantaged workers?
3. ***Implement and evaluate the policy that was selected.*** After implementing the policy, we need to evaluate how well it worked. Only through unbiased evaluation can we improve on economic policy. Did a specific change in taxes or the money supply alter the level of employment to the extent predicted? Did deregulation of a particular industry (for example, the airlines) yield the predicted beneficial results? If not, why not? ***(Key Question 5)***

**Economic Goals** If economic policies are designed to achieve certain economic goals, then we need to recognize a number of goals that are widely accepted in Canada and many other countries. They include:

1. ***Economic growth*** Produce more and better goods and services, or, more simply, develop a higher standard of living.
2. ***Full employment*** Provide suitable jobs for all citizens who are willing and able to work.
3. ***Economic efficiency*** Achieve the maximum fulfilment of wants using the available productive resources.
4. ***Price-level stability*** Avoid large upswings and downswings in the general price level; that is, avoid inflation and deflation.
5. ***Equitable distribution of income*** Ensure that no group of citizens faces stark poverty while others enjoy extreme luxury.
6. ***Balance of trade*** Seek a reasonable overall balance with the rest of the world in international trade and financial transactions.

Although most of us might accept these goals as generally stated, we might also disagree substantially on their specific meanings. What are "large" changes in the price level? What is an "equitable" distribution of income? These objectives are often the subject of spirited public debate.

Also, some of these goals are complementary; when one is achieved, some other one will also be realized. For example, achieving full employment means eliminating unemployment, which is a basic cause of inequitable income distribution. But other goals may conflict or even be mutually exclusive. They may entail **tradeoffs**, meaning that to achieve one we must sacrifice another. For example, efforts to equalize the distribution of income may weaken incentives to work, invest, innovate, and take business risks, all of which promote economic growth. Taxing high-income people heavily and transferring the tax revenues to low-income people is one way to equalize the distribution of income. But then the incentives to high-income individuals may diminish because higher taxes reduce their rewards for working. Similarly, low-income individuals may be less motivated to work when government stands ready to subsidize them.

When goals conflict, society must develop a system of priorities for the objectives it seeks. Society must assess the tradeoffs and decide on the optimal (best) balance between them.

1-2

**QUICK REVIEW**

- Economic theories (laws, principles, or models) are generalizations relating to the economic behaviour of individuals and institutions; good theories are supported by facts.
- There are two ways economists arrive at theories. Induction observes facts and generalizes from them; deduction uses logic to create hypotheses and then tests them with factual data.
- Policy making requires a clear statement of goals, a thorough assessment of options, and an unbiased evaluation of results.
- Some of society's economic goals are complementary while others conflict; where conflicts exist, tradeoffs arise.

## MACROECONOMICS AND MICROECONOMICS

Economists derive and apply theories about economic behaviour at two levels.

### Macroeconomics

**Macroeconomics** examines either the economy as a whole or its basic subdivisions or aggregates such as the government, household, and business sectors. An **aggregate** is a collection of specific economic units treated as if they were one unit. Therefore, we might lump together the millions of consumers in the Canadian economy and treat them as if they were one huge unit called "consumers."

In using aggregates, economists seek to obtain an overview, or general outline, of the structure of the economy and the relationships of its major aggregates. Macroeconomics deals with such economic measures as *total* output, *total* employment, *total* income, *aggregate* expenditures, and the *general* level of prices in analyzing various economic problems. No or very little attention is given to specific units making up the various aggregates. Macroeconomics examines the forest, not the trees.

### Microeconomics

**Microeconomics** looks at specific economic units. At this level of analysis, the economist observes the details of an economic unit, or very small segment of the economy, under the figurative microscope. In microeconomics we talk of an individual industry, firm, or household. We measure the price of a *specific* product, the number of workers employed by a *single* firm, the revenue or income of a *particular* firm or household, or the expenditures of a *specific* firm, government entity, or family. In microeconomics, we examine the trees, not the forest.

The macro-micro distinction does not mean that economics is so highly compartmentalized that every topic can be readily labelled as either macro or micro; many topics and subdivisions of economics are rooted in both. Example: While the problem of unemployment is usually treated as a macroeconomic topic (because unemployment relates to *aggregate* spending), the decisions made by *individual* workers in searching for jobs and the way *specific* product and labour markets operate are also critical in determining the unemployment rate. ***(Key Question 7)***

### Positive and Normative Economics

Both macroeconomics and microeconomics involve facts, theories, and policies. Each contains elements of *positive economics* and *normative economics*. **Positive economics** focuses on facts and avoids value judgements. It tries to establish statements about economic behaviour that can be verified by facts. Positive economics deals with what the economy is actually like. Such factually based analysis is critical to good policy analysis.

In contrast, **normative economics** involves value judgements about what the economy should be like or what particular policy actions should be recommended to get it to be that way. Normative statements cannot be verified by appealing to facts to determine if they are true or false. Normative economics looks at the desirability of certain aspects of the economy. It underlies expressions of support for particular economic policies.

Positive economics concerns *what is*, while normative economics embodies subjective feelings about *what ought to be*. Examples: Positive statement: "The unemployment rate in several European nations is higher than that in Canada." Normative statement: "European nations ought to undertake policies to reduce their unemployment rates." A second positive statement: "Other things equal, if tuition is increased, enrolment at Informed University (IU) will fall." Normative statement: "Tuition should be lowered at IU so that more students can obtain an education." Whenever words such as "ought" or "should" appear in a sentence, there is a strong chance you are encountering a normative statement.

As you can imagine, most of the disagreement among economists involves normative, value-based policy questions. Of course, there is often some disagreement about which theories or models best represent the economy and its parts. But most economic controversy reflects differing opinions or value judgements about what society itself should be like. ***(Key Question 8)***

**1-3**

**QUICK REVIEW**

- Macroeconomics examines the economy as a whole; microeconomics focuses on specific units of the economy.
- Positive economics deals with verifiable factual statements ("what is"); normative economics involves value judgements ("what ought to be").

## PITFALLS TO OBJECTIVE THINKING

Because they affect us so personally, we often have difficulty thinking objectively about economic issues. Here are some common pitfalls to avoid in successfully applying the economic perspective.

### Biases

Most people start out with a bundle of biases and preconceptions when thinking about economic issues. For example, you might think that corporate profits are excessive or that lending money is always superior to borrowing money. Perhaps you believe that government is necessarily less efficient than businesses or that more government regulation is always better than less. Biases cloud thinking and interfere with objective analysis. The student starting the study of economics must be willing to shed biases and preconceptions that are not supported by facts.

### Loaded Terminology

The economic terminology used in newspapers and popular magazines is sometimes emotionally biased, or loaded. The writer or the interest group he or she represents may have a cause to promote or an axe to grind and may slant an article accordingly. High profits may be labelled "obscene"; low wages may be called "exploitive"; or self-interested behaviour may be "greed." Government workers may be referred to as "mindless bureaucrats," and those favouring stronger government regulations may be called "socialists." To objectively analyze economic issues, you must be prepared to reject or discount such terminology.

### Definitions

Some of the terms used in economics have precise technical definitions that are quite different from those implied by their common usage. This is generally not a problem if everyone understands these definitions and uses them consistently. For example, "investment" to the average citizen means the purchase of stocks and bonds in security markets, as when someone "invests" in Bell Canada stock or government bonds. But to the economist, "investment" means the purchase of real capital assets such as machinery and equipment or the construction of a new factory building. It does not mean the purely financial transaction of swapping cash for securities.

### Fallacy of Composition

Another pitfall in economic thinking is the assumption that what is true for one individual is necessarily true for a group of individuals. This is a logical fallacy called the **fallacy of composition**;

it is *not* correct. A statement that is valid for an individual is *not* necessarily valid for the larger group.

Consider the following example from outside of economics. You are at a football game and the home team makes an outstanding play. In the excitement, you leap to your feet to get a better view. A valid statement: "If you, *an individual*, stand, your view of the game is improved." But is this also true for the group—for everyone watching the play? Not necessarily. If *everyone* stands to watch the play, everyone—including you—will probably have a worse view than when all remain seated.

A second example comes from economics: An *individual* farmer who reaps a particularly large crop is likely to realize a sharp gain in income. But this statement cannot be generalized to farmers as a *group*. The individual farmer's large or "bumper" crop will not influence (reduce) crop prices because each farmer produces a negligible fraction of the total farm output. But for *all* farmers as a group, prices decline when total output increases. Thus, if all farmers reap bumper crops, the total output of farm products will rise, depressing crop prices. If the price declines are relatively large, total farm income will actually *fall*.

Recall our earlier distinction between macroeconomics and microeconomics: *The fallacy of composition reminds us that generalizations valid at one of these levels of analysis may or may not be valid at the other.*

## Causation Fallacies

Causation is sometimes difficult to identify in economics. Two important fallacies often interfere with economic thinking.

**Post Hoc Fallacy** You must think very carefully before concluding that because event A precedes event B, A is the cause of B. This kind of faulty reasoning is known as the *post hoc, ergo propter hoc*, or **after this, therefore because of this fallacy**.

Example: Suppose that early each spring the medicine man of a tribe performs a special dance. A week or so later the trees and grass turn green. Can we safely conclude that event A, the medicine man's dance, has caused event B, the landscape's turning green? Obviously not. The rooster crows before dawn, but this does not mean the rooster is responsible for the sunrise!

Informed University hires a new hockey coach and the team's record improves. Is the new coach the cause? Maybe. But perhaps the presence of more experienced players or an easier schedule is the true cause.

**Correlation versus Causation** Do not confuse correlation, or connection, with causation. Correlation between two events or two sets of data indicates they are associated in some systematic and dependable way. For example, we may find that when variable X increases, Y also increases. But this correlation does not necessarily mean that there is causation—that an increase in X is the cause of an increase in Y. The relationship could be purely coincidental or dependent on some other factor, Z, not included in the analysis.

Here is an economic example: Economists have found a positive correlation between education and income. In general, people with more education earn higher incomes than people with less education. Common sense suggests education is the cause and higher incomes are the effect; more education implies a more knowledgeable and productive worker, and such workers receive larger salaries.

But causation could also partly run the other way. People with higher incomes could buy more education, just as they buy more furniture and steaks. Or is part of the relationship explainable in still other ways? Are education and income correlated because the characteristics—ability, motivation, personal habit—required to succeed in education are the same ones required to be a productive and highly paid worker? If so, then people with those traits will probably obtain more education *and* earn higher incomes. But greater education will not be the sole cause of the higher income. ***(Key Question 9)***

# A LOOK AHEAD

The ideas in this chapter will come into much sharper focus as you advance through Part 1, where we develop specific economic theories and models. Specifically, in Chapter 2 we build a model of the production choices facing an economy. In Chapter 3 we combine all markets in the economy to see how the so-called *market system* works. In Chapter 4 we develop a model that will help you understand how prices and quantities of goods and services are established in individual markets. Finally, in Chapters 5 and 6 we examine important sectors (components) of the economy, specifically, the private sector, the government sector, and the international sector.

## In The Media

4 KEY CONCEPT

# Smugglers go interprovincial

### Profits high, chances of getting caught low in the business of contraband cigarettes

BY PETER MOON
THE GLOBE AND MAIL

The federal government's sustained attack against the smuggling of contraband cigarettes into Canada has created a new multimillion-dollar crime problem.

Many smugglers are switching from international to interprovincial smuggling of cigarettes because the profits are high, the chances of getting caught are low, and even if they are caught the likelihood of going to prison is minimal.

"Interprovincial smuggling is costing millions and millions of dollars in lost taxes," Inspector John Ferguson, head of the RCMP's economic-crime unit in British Columbia, said in an interview. "It's a huge problem. People don't realize how serious it is."

He said British Columbia, where cigarette prices are among the highest in Canada, has been particularly hurt by the growth of interprovincial smuggling. Profits are so high it has attracted different organized-crime elements who are starting to fight among themselves for dominant positions in the trade.

"It's big business," he said. "And that's why they're in it, because it is such big business. When they get caught, they usually get fined, and that's it. They rarely go to jail."

British Columbia, because of its high tobacco taxes and large population, is a major market for smuggled cigarettes. Insp. Ferguson said it is hard to say what percentage of cigarettes reach the province through interprovincial smuggling compared to international smuggling, but added: "I sort of have the gut feeling that it is a 50–50 split."

A legal carton of cigarettes, for example, costs $26.40 in Ontario, compared with $48.55 in B.C. and $50.62 in Newfoundland. It is a problem that has captured the attention of the Auditor-General of Canada.

Source: *Globe and Mail*, July 28, 1997, p. A1 and A6. Reprinted with permission from the *Globe and Mail*.

## THE STORY IN BRIEF

Smugglers of contraband cigarettes have switched from smuggling cigarettes from the United States into Canada, to interprovincial smuggling. The smugglers buy cigarettes in provinces with low taxes and sell them on the black market in provinces with high taxes.

## THE ECONOMICS BEHIND THE STORY

- Economic decisions are based on marginal cost–marginal benefit considerations.
- The marginal cost–marginal benefit of smuggling cigarettes from abroad (primarily the United States) has changed. Costs have risen as the federal government crackdown intensifies.
- Compared with international cigarette smuggling, there are higher benefits and lower costs to smuggling cigarettes within Canada.
- The higher benefits to interprovincial smuggling have come about because some provinces, particularly Ontario and Quebec, lowered provincial taxes on a carton of cigarettes while others, such as British Columbia and Newfoundland, did not. The cost of interprovincial smuggling of cigarettes is lower than international smuggling because the probabilities of getting caught are much lower and the likelihood of going to prison is low.
- What should the federal and provincial governments do to stop interprovincial cigarette smuggling? ■

## The Last Word

1 KEY CONCEPT

### FAST-FOOD LINES: AN ECONOMIC PERSPECTIVE

**How can the economic perspective help us understand the behaviour of fast-food consumers?**

YOU ENTER A FAST-FOOD RESTAURANT. DO YOU immediately look to see which line is the shortest? What do you do when you are in the middle of a long line and a new station opens? Have you ever gone to a fast-food restaurant, seen very long lines, and then left? Have you ever become annoyed when someone in front of you in line placed an order that took a long time to fill?

The economic perspective is useful in analyzing the behaviour of fast-food customers. These customers are at the restaurant because they expect the marginal benefit from the food they buy to match or exceed its marginal cost. When customers enter the restaurant, they scurry to the *shortest* line, believing that the shortest line will reduce their time cost of obtaining their food. They are acting purposefully; time is limited and people prefer using it in some way other than standing in line.

If one fast-food line is temporarily shorter than other lines, some people will move towards that line. These movers apparently view the time saving associated with the shorter line to exceed the cost of moving from their present line. The line changing tends to equalize line lengths. No further movement of customers between lines occurs once all lines are about equal.

Fast-food customers face another cost-benefit decision when a clerk opens a new station at the counter. Should they move to the new station or stay put? Those who shift to the new line decide that the time saving from the move exceeds the extra cost of physically moving. In so deciding, customers must also consider just how quickly they can get to the new station compared with others who may be contemplating the same move. (Those who hesitate in this situation are lost!)

Customers at the fast-food establishment select lines without having perfect information. For example, they do not first survey those in the lines to determine what they are ordering before deciding which line to enter. There are two reasons for this. First, most customers would tell them "It's none of your business," and therefore no information would be forthcoming. Second, even if they could obtain the information, the amount of time necessary to get it (a cost) would most certainly exceed any time saving associated with finding the best line (the benefit). Because information is costly to obtain, fast-food patrons select lines without perfect information. Thus, not all decisions turn out as expected. For example, you might enter a short line and find that the person in front of you is ordering hamburgers and fries for 40 people in the Greyhound bus parked out back! Nevertheless, at the time you made your decision, you thought it was optimal.

Imperfect information also explains why some people who arrive at a fast-food restaurant and observe long lines decide to leave. These people conclude that the marginal cost (monetary plus time costs) of obtaining the fast food is too large relative to the marginal benefit. They would not have come to the restaurant in the first place had they known the lines would be so long. But getting that information by, say, employing an advance scout with a cellular phone would cost more than the perceived benefit.

Finally, customers must decide what to order when they arrive at the counter. In making their choices they again compare marginal costs and marginal benefits in attempting to obtain the greatest personal satisfaction or well-being for their expenditure.

Economists believe that what is true for the behaviour of customers at fast-food restaurants is true for economic behaviour in general. Faced with an array of choices, consumers, workers, and businesses rationally compare marginal costs and marginal benefits in making decisions. ■

## CHAPTER SUMMARY

1. Economics is the study of the efficient use of scarce resources in the production of goods and services to satisfy as many wants as possible.
2. The economic perspective includes three elements: scarcity and choice, rational behaviour, and marginalism. It sees individuals and institutions making rational decisions based on comparisons of marginal costs and marginal benefits.
3. A knowledge of economics contributes to effective citizenship and provides useful insights for politicians, consumers, and workers.
4. The tasks of empirical economics are (a) gathering economic facts relevant to a particular problem or specific segment of the economy, and (b) testing hypotheses against the facts to validate theories.
5. Generalizations stated by economists are called principles, theories, laws, or models. The derivation of these principles is the object of theoretical economics.
6. Induction distills theories from facts; deduction uses logic to derive hypotheses that are then tested against facts.
7. Economic principles are valuable predictors. They are the bases for economic policy, which is designed to identify and solve problems and control undesirable events.
8. Our society accepts certain shared economic goals, including economic growth, full employment, economic efficiency, price-level stability, equity in the distribution of income, and a reasonable balance in our international trade and finance. Some of these goals are complementary; others entail tradeoffs.
9. Macroeconomics looks at the economy as a whole or its major aggregates; microeconomics examines specific economic units or institutions.
10. Positive statements state facts ("what is"); normative statements express value judgements ("what ought to be").
11. In studying economics we encounter such pitfalls as biases and preconceptions, unfamiliar or confusing terminology, the fallacy of composition, and the difficulty of establishing clear cause-effect relationships.

## TERMS AND CONCEPTS

economics
tradeoff
inflation
unemployment
economic perspective
marginal analysis
principles
theoretical economics
induction
deduction
generalizations
other-things-equal assumption
policy economics
macroeconomics
aggregate
microeconomics
positive economics
normative economics
fallacy of composition
after this, therefore because of this fallacy

## STUDY QUESTIONS

1. KEY QUESTION *Use the economic perspective to explain why someone who is normally a light eater at a standard restaurant may become somewhat of a glutton at a buffet-style restaurant that charges a single price for all you can eat.*

2. Distinguish between the inductive and deductive methods for establishing economic theories. Why must both methods ultimately involve gathering facts?

3. Why is it significant that economics is not a laboratory science? What problems may be involved in deriving and applying economic principles?

4. Explain the following statements:
   a. Good economic policy requires good economic theory.
   b. Generalization and abstraction are nearly synonymous.
   c. Facts serve to sort out good and bad theories.
   d. The *other-things-equal* assumption helps isolate key economic relationships.

5. KEY QUESTION *Explain in detail the interrelationships between economic facts, theory, and policy. Critically evaluate this statement: "The trouble with economic theory is that it is not practical. It is detached from the real world."*

6. To what extent do you accept the six economic goals stated and described in this chapter? What priorities do you assign to them? It has been said that we seek simply four goals: progress, stability, justice, and freedom. Is this list of goals compatible with that given in the chapter?

7. KEY QUESTION *Indicate whether each of the following statements applies to microeconomics or macroeconomics:*
   a. *The unemployment rate in Canada was 8.4 percent in July of 1998.*
   b. *The Alpo dogfood plant in Bowser, Alberta, laid off 15 workers last month.*
   c. *An unexpected freeze in central Florida reduced the citrus crop and caused the price of oranges to rise.*
   d. *Our domestic output, adjusted for inflation, grew by about 4 percent in 1997.*
   e. *Last week the Royal Bank lowered its interest rate on business loans by one-half of 1 percentage point.*
   f. *The consumer price index rose by 1.6 percent in 1997.*

8. KEY QUESTION *Identify each of the following as either a positive or a normative statement:*
   a. *The high temperature today was 30 degrees.*
   b. *It was too hot today.*
   c. *The general price level rose by 4.4 percent last year.*
   d. *Inflation eroded living standards last year and should be reduced by government policies.*

9. KEY QUESTION *Explain and give an example of* **a** *the fallacy of composition, and* **b** *the "after this, therefore because of this" fallacy. Why are cause-and-effect relationships difficult to isolate in economics?*

10. Suppose studies show that students who study more hours receive higher grades. Does this relationship guarantee that any particular student who studies longer will get higher grades?

11. Studies indicate that married men on average earn more income than unmarried men of the same age. Why must we be cautious in concluding that marriage is the *cause* and higher income is the *effect*?

12. **(The Last Word)** Use the economic perspective to explain the behaviour of the *workers* (rather than the customers) observed at a fast-food restaurant. Why are these workers there, rather than, say, cruising around in their cars? Why do they work so diligently? Why do so many of them quit these jobs once they have graduated from high school?

13. WEB-BASED QUESTION **Economic Goals—Are They Being Achieved?** The three primary economic goals are economic growth, full employment, and price-level stability. Statistics Canada www.statcan.ca/english/Pgdb/Economy/econom.htm provides links to Canadian economic data. Visit their links for Output, Income, Expenditures (under National accounts), Prices and Employment, and Unemployment (Labour markets). How robust has economic growth (GDP) been? Has inflation remained steady? Has unemployment increased or decreased?

14. WEB-BASED QUESTION **Normative Economics—Canadian Politics.** Many economic policy statements made by the Liberal Party www.liberal.ca, the Reform Party www.reform.ca, the Progressive Conservative Party www.pcparty.ca, and the NDP www.ndp.ca can be considered normative rather than positive economic statements. Visit their Web sites and compare and contrast their views on how to achieve economic goals. How much of the rhetoric is based on positive statements and how much on normative statements?

# APPENDIX TO CHAPTER 1

## GRAPHS AND THEIR MEANING

If you glance quickly through this text, you will find many graphs. Some seem simple, while others seem more difficult. All are important. They are included to help you visualize and understand economic relationships. Physicists and chemists sometimes illustrate their theories by building arrangements of multicoloured wooden balls, representing protons, neutrons, and electrons, which are held in proper relation to one another by wires or sticks. Economists most often use graphs to illustrate their models. By understanding these "pictures," you can more readily comprehend economic relationships. Most of our principles or models explain relationships between just two sets of economic facts, which can be conveniently represented with two-dimensional graphs.

### Construction of a Graph

A graph is a visual representation of the relationship between two variables. Table A1-1 is a hypothetical illustration showing the relationship between income and consumption for the economy as a whole. Without even studying economics, we would expect intuitively that people would buy more goods and services when their incomes go up. Thus we are not surprised to find in Table A1-1 that total consumption in the economy increases as total income rises.

**TABLE A1-1 The relationship between income and consumption**

| Income (per week) | Consumption (per week) | Point |
|---|---|---|
| $ 0 | $ 50 | *a* |
| 100 | 100 | *b* |
| 200 | 150 | *c* |
| 300 | 200 | *d* |
| 400 | 250 | *e* |

The information in Table A1-1 is expressed graphically in Figure A1-1. Here is how it is done: We want to show visually or graphically how consumption changes as income changes. Since income is the determining factor, we represent it on the **horizontal axis** of the graph, as is customary. And because consumption depends on income, we represent it on the **vertical axis** of the graph, as is also customary. Actually, what we are doing is representing the *independent variable* on the horizontal axis and the *dependent variable* on the vertical axis.

Now we arrange the vertical and horizontal scales of the graph to reflect the ranges of values of consumption and income, and we mark the scales in convenient increments. As you can see, the values marked on the scales cover all the values in Table A1-1. The increments on both scales are $100 for approximately each 1.25 cm.

Because the graph has two dimensions, each point within it represents an income value and its associated consumption value. To find a point that represents one of the five income-consumption combinations in Table A1-1, we draw perpendiculars from the appropriate values on the vertical and horizontal axes. For example, to plot point *c*

**FIGURE A1-1 Graphing the direct relationship between consumption and income**

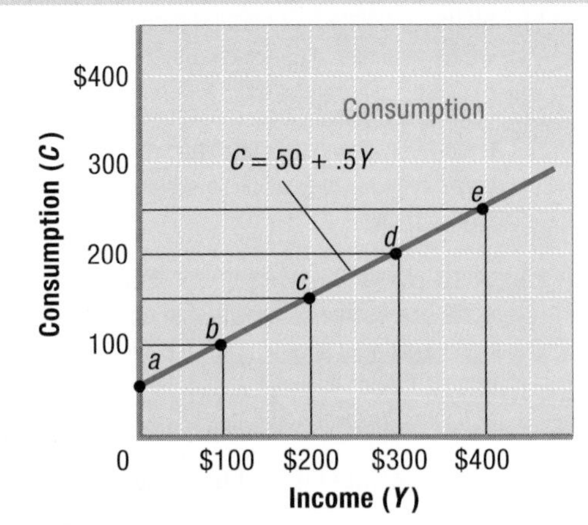


Two sets of data that are positively or directly related, such as consumption and income, graph as an upsloping line.

(the \$200 income–\$150 consumption point), perpendiculars are drawn up from the horizontal (income) axis at \$200 and across from the vertical (consumption) axis at \$150. These perpendiculars intersect at point *c*, which represents this particular income-consumption combination. You should verify that the other income-consumption combinations shown in Table A1-1 are properly located in Figure A1-1. Finally, by assuming that the same general relationship between income and consumption prevails for all other incomes, we draw a line or smooth curve to connect these points. That line or curve represents the income-consumption relationship.

If the graph is a straight line, as in Figure A1-1, we say the relationship is *linear.*

## Direct and Inverse Relationships

The line in Figure A1-1 slopes upward to the right, so it depicts a direct relationship between income and consumption. By a **direct relationship** (or positive relationship) we mean that two variables—in this case, consumption and income—change in the *same* direction. An increase in consumption is associated with an increase in income; a decrease in consumption accompanies a decrease in income. When two sets of data are positively or directly related, they always graph as an *upsloping* line, as in Figure A1-1.

In contrast, two sets of data may be inversely related. Consider Table A1-2, which shows the relationship between the price of basketball tickets and game attendance at Informed University. Here we have a negative or **inverse relationship** because the two variables change in *opposite* directions. When ticket prices decrease, attendance increases. When ticket prices increase, attendance decreases. The six data points in Table A1-2 are plotted in Figure A1-2. Observe that an inverse relationship always graphs as a *downsloping* line.

## Dependent and Independent Variables

Although it is not always easy, economists seek to determine which variable is the "cause" and which is the "effect." Or, more formally, they seek the independent variable and the dependent variable. The **independent variable** is the cause or source; it is the variable that changes first. The **dependent variable** is the effect or outcome; it is the variable that changes because of the change in the independent variable. As noted in our income-consumption example, income generally is the independent variable and consumption the dependent variable. Income causes consumption to be what it is rather than the other way around. Similarly, ticket prices determine attendance at IU hockey games; attendance does not determine ticket prices. Ticket price is the independent variable, and the quantity of tickets purchased is the dependent variable.

You may recall from your high school courses that mathematicians always put the independent variable (cause) on the horizontal axis and the dependent variable (effect) on the vertical axis.

**TABLE A1-2 The relationship between ticket prices and attendance**

| Ticket price | Attendance (thousands) | Point |
|---|---|---|
| \$25 | 0 | *a* |
| 20 | 4 | *b* |
| 15 | 8 | *c* |
| 10 | 12 | *d* |
| 5 | 16 | *e* |
| 0 | 20 | *f* |

**FIGURE A1-2 Graphing the inverse relationship between ticket prices and game attendance**

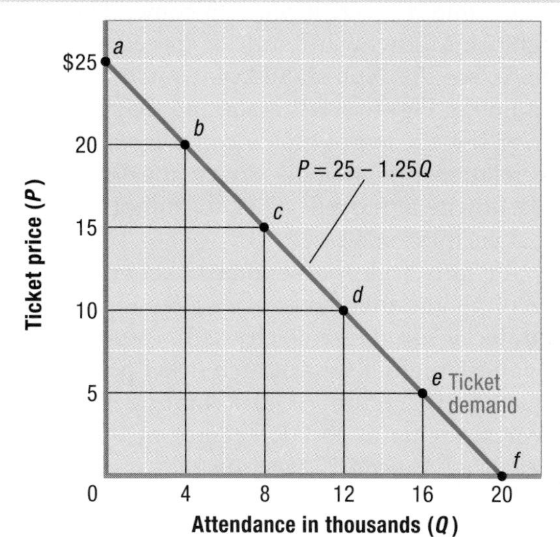


Two sets of data that are negatively or inversely related, such as ticket price and the attendance at basketball games, graph as a downsloping line.

Economists are less tidy; their graphing of independent and dependent variables is more arbitrary. Their conventional graphing of the income-consumption relationship is consistent with mathematical presentation, but economists put price and cost data on the vertical axis. Hence, economists' graphing of IU's ticket price–attendance data conflicts with normal mathematical procedure.

## Other Things Equal

Our simple two-variable graphs purposely ignore many other factors that might affect the amount of consumption occurring at each income level or the number of people who attend IU basketball games at each possible ticket price. When economists plot the relationship between any two variables, they invoke the *ceteris paribus* (other things equal) assumption. Thus, in Figure A1-1 all factors other than income that might affect the amount of consumption are presumed to be constant or unchanged. Similarly, in Figure A1-2 all factors other than ticket price that might influence attendance at IU hockey games are assumed constant. In reality, "other things" are not equal; they often change, and when they do, the relationship represented in our two tables and graphs will change. Specifically, the lines we have plotted would shift to new locations.

Consider a stock market "crash." The dramatic drop in the value of stocks might cause people to feel less wealthy and therefore less willing to consume at each level of income. The result might be a downward shift of the consumption line. To see this, you should plot a new consumption line in Figure A1-1, assuming that consumption is, say, $20 less at each income level. Note that the relationship remains direct; the line merely shifts downward to reflect less consumption spending at each income level.

Similarly, factors other than ticket prices might affect IU game attendance. If a professional hockey team locates in the same city as IU, attendance at IU games might be less at each ticket price. To see this, redraw Figure A1-2, assuming that 2,000 fewer students attend IU games at each ticket price. ***(Key Appendix Question 2)***

## Slope of a Line

Lines can be described in terms of their slopes. The **slope of a straight line** is the ratio of the vertical change (the rise or drop) to the horizontal change (the run) between any two points of the line.

### Positive Slope

Between point *b* and point *c* in Figure A1-1 the rise or vertical change (the change in consumption) is +\$50 and the run or horizontal change (the change in income) is +\$100. Therefore:

$$\text{Slope} = \frac{\text{vertical change}}{\text{horizontal change}} = \frac{+50}{+100} = \frac{1}{2} = .5$$

Note that our slope of $\frac{1}{2}$ or .5 is positive because consumption and income change in the same direction; that is, consumption and income are directly or positively related.

The slope of .5 tells us there will be a \$1 increase in consumption for every \$2 increase in income. Similarly, it indicates that for every \$2 decrease in income there will be a \$1 decrease in consumption.

### Negative Slope

Between any two of the identified points in Figure A1-2, say, point *c* and point *d*, the vertical change is –5 (the drop) and the horizontal change is +4 (the run). Therefore:

$$\text{Slope} = \frac{\text{vertical change}}{\text{horizontal change}} = \frac{-5}{+4} = -1\tfrac{1}{4} = -1.25$$

This slope is negative because ticket price and attendance have an inverse relationship.

Note that on the horizontal axis attendance is stated in thousands of people. So the slope of –5/+4 or –1.25 means that lowering the price by \$5 will increase attendance by 4,000 people. This is the same as saying that a \$1.25 price reduction will increase attendance by 1,000 persons.

### Slopes and Measurement Units

The slope of a line will be affected by the choice of units for either variable. If, in our ticket price illustration, we had chosen to measure attendance in individual people, our horizontal change would have been 4,000 and the slope would have been

$$\text{Slope} = \frac{-5}{+4000} = \frac{-1}{+800} = -.00125$$

The slope depends on the way the relevant variables are measured.

### Slopes and Marginal Analysis

Recall that economics is largely concerned with changes from the status quo. The concept of slope is important in economics because it reflects marginal changes—those involving 1 more (or 1 less) unit. For example, in Figure A1-1 the .5 slope shows that \$.50 of extra or marginal consumption is associated with each \$1 increase in income. In this example, people collectively will consume \$.50 of any \$1 increase in their incomes and reduce their consumption by \$.50 for each \$1 decline in income.

**Infinite and Zero Slopes** Many variables are unrelated or independent of one another. For example, the quantity of wristwatches purchased is not related to the price of bananas. In Figure A1-3(a) we represent the price of bananas on the vertical axis and the quantity of watches demanded on the horizontal axis. The graph of their relationship is the line parallel to the vertical axis, indicating that the same quantity of watches is purchased no matter what the price of bananas. The slope of such a line is *infinite.*

Similarly, aggregate consumption is completely unrelated to the nation's divorce rate. In Figure A1-3(b) we put consumption on the vertical axis and the divorce rate on the horizontal axis. The line parallel to the horizontal axis represents this lack of relatedness. This line has a slope of *zero.*

## Vertical Intercept

A line can be located on a graph (without plotting points) if we know its slope and its **vertical intercept**. The vertical intercept of a line is the point where the line meets the vertical axis. In Figure A1-1 the intercept is \$50. This intercept means that if current income were zero, consumers would still spend \$50. They might do this through borrowing or by selling off some of their assets. Similarly, the vertical intercept in Figure A1-2 shows that at a \$25 ticket price, IU's hockey team would be playing in an empty arena.

## Equation of a Linear Relationship

If we know the vertical intercept and slope, we can describe a line succinctly in equation form. In its general form, the equation of a line is

$$y = a + bx$$

where $y$ = dependent variable
$a$ = vertical intercept
$b$ = slope of the line
$x$ = independent variable.

For our income-consumption example, if $C$ represents consumption (the dependent variable) and $Y$ represents income (the independent variable), we can write $C = a + bY$. By substituting the known values of the intercept and the slope, we get

$$C = 50 + .5Y$$

This equation also allows us to determine the amount of consumption $C$ at any specific level of income. You should use it to confirm that at the \$250 income level, consumption is \$175.

When economists reverse mathematical convention by putting the independent variable on the vertical axis and the dependent variable on the horizontal axis, then $y$ stands for the independent variable, rather than the dependent variable in the general form. We noted previously that this case is relevant for our IU ticket price-attendance data. If $P$ represents the ticket price (independent vari-

**FIGURE A1-3 Infinite and zero slopes**

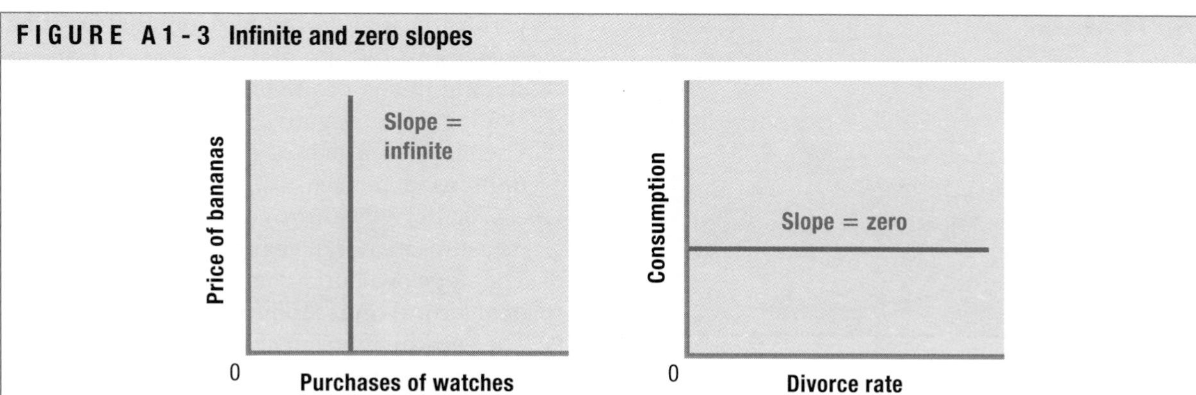


(a) A line parallel to the vertical axis has an infinite slope. Here, purchases of watches remain the same no matter what happens to the price of bananas. (b) A line parallel to the horizontal axis has a slope of zero. Here, consumption remains the same no matter what happens to the divorce rate. In both (a) and (b), the two variables are totally unrelated to one another.

able) and $Q$ represents attendance (dependent variable), their relationship is given by

$$P = 25 - 1.25Q$$

where the vertical intercept is 25 and the negative slope is $-1\frac{1}{4}$ or $-1.25$. Now, knowing the value of $P$ let's solve for $Q$, our dependent variable. You should use this equation to predict IU ticket sales when the ticket price is $7.50. ***(Key Appendix Question 3)***

## Slope of a Nonlinear Curve

We now move from the simple world of linear relationships (straight lines) to the more complex world of nonlinear relationships. The slope of a straight line is the same at all its points. The slope of a line representing a nonlinear relationship changes from one point to another. Such lines are referred to as curves. (It is also permissible to refer to a straight line as a "curve.")

Consider the downsloping curve in Figure A1-4. Its slope is negative throughout, but the curve flattens as we move down along it. Thus, its slope constantly changes; the curve has a different slope at each point.

To measure the slope at a specific point, we draw a straight line that is tangent to the curve at that point. A line is *tangent* at a point if it touches, but does not intersect, the curve at that point. Thus line *aa* is tangent to the curve in Figure A1-4 at point A. The slope of the curve at that point is equal to the slope of the tangent line. Specifically, the total vertical change (drop) in the tangent line *aa* is –20 and the total horizontal change (run) is +5. Because the slope of the tangent line *aa* is –20/+5, or –4, the slope of the curve at point *A* is also –4.

Line *bb* in Figure A1-4 is tangent to the curve at point *B*. Following the same procedure, we find the slope at *B* to be –5/+15, or –1/3. Thus, in this flatter part of the curve, the slope is less negative. ***(Key Appendix Question 6)***

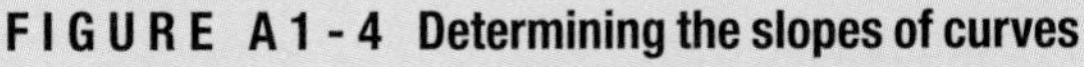

**FIGURE A1-4 Determining the slopes of curves**

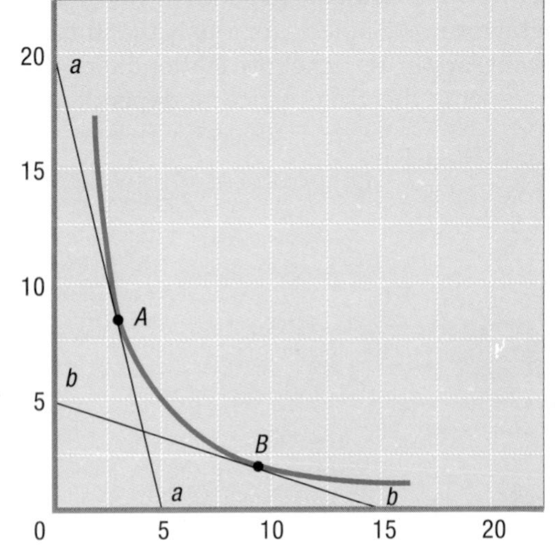


The slope of a nonlinear curve changes from point to point on the curve. The slope at any point (say, *B*) can be determined by drawing a straight line tangent to that point (line *bb*) and calculating the slope of that line.

## APPENDIX SUMMARY

1. Graphs are a convenient and revealing way to represent economic relationships.
2. Two variables are positively or directly related when their values change in the same direction. The line (curve) representing two directly related variables slopes upward.
3. Two variables are negatively or inversely related when their values change in opposite directions. The curve representing two inversely related variables slopes downward.
4. The value of the dependent variable (the "effect") is determined by the value of the independent variable (the "cause").
5. When the "other factors" that might affect a two-variable relationship are allowed to change, the graph of the relationship will likely shift to a new location.
6. The slope of a straight line is the ratio of the vertical change to the horizontal change between any two points. The slope of an upsloping line is positive; the slope of a downsloping line is negative.
7. The slope of a line or curve depends on the units used in measuring the variables. It is especially relevant for economics because it measures marginal changes.
8. The slope of a horizontal line is zero; the slope of a vertical line is infinite.
9. The vertical intercept and slope of a line determine its location; they are used in expressing the line—and the relationship between the two variables—as an equation.
10. The slope of a curve at any point is determined by calculating the slope of a straight line tangent to the curve at that point.

## APPENDIX TERMS AND CONCEPTS

horizontal axis
vertical axis
direct relationship
inverse relationship
independent variable
dependent variable
slope of a straight line
vertical intercept

## APPENDIX STUDY QUESTIONS

1. Briefly explain the use of graphs as a way to represent economic relationships. What is an inverse relationship? How does it graph? What is a direct relationship? How does it graph? Graph and explain the relationships you would expect to find between **a** the number of millimetres of rainfall per month and the sale of umbrellas, **b** the amount of tuition and the level of enrolment at a university, and **c** the size of a university's athletic scholarships and the number of games won by its football team.

   In each case cite and explain how variables other than those specifically mentioned might upset the expected relationship. Is your graph in part (b) consistent with the fact that, historically, enrolments and tuition have both increased? If not, explain any difference.

2. KEY APPENDIX QUESTION *Indicate how each of the following might affect the data shown in Table A1-2 and Figure A1-2 of this appendix:*
   **a.** *IU's athletic director schedules higher-quality opponents.*
   **b.** *IU's Fighting Aardvarks experience three losing seasons.*
   **c.** *IU contracts to have all its home games televised.*

3. KEY APPENDIX QUESTION *The following table contains data on the relationship between saving and income. Rearrange these data into a meaningful order and graph them on the accompanying grid. What is the slope of the line? The vertical intercept? Interpret the meaning of both the slope and the intercept. Write the equation that represents this line. What would you predict saving to be at the $12,500 level of income?*

| Income (per year) | Saving (per year) |
|---|---|
| $15,000 | $1,000 |
| 0 | –500 |
| 10,000 | 500 |
| 5,000 | 0 |
| 20,000 | 1,500 |

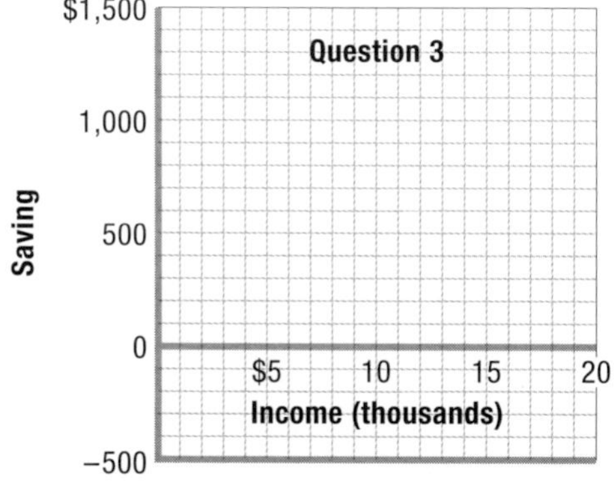

4. Construct a table from the data shown on the graph below. Which is the dependent variable and which the independent variable? Summarize the data in equation form.

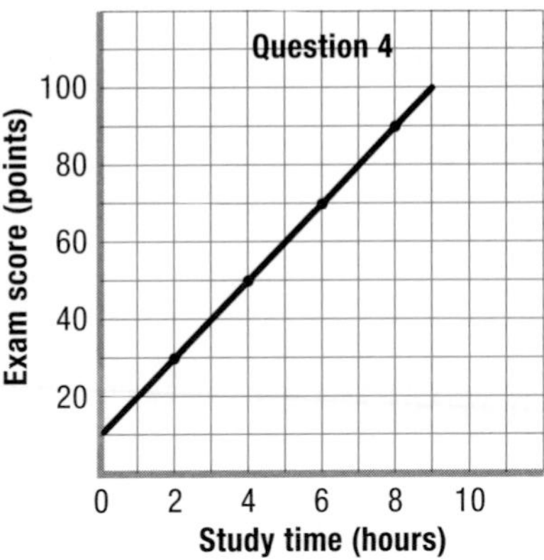


5. Suppose that when the interest rate that must be paid to borrow funds is 16 percent, businesses find it unprofitable to invest in machinery and equipment. However, when the interest rate is 14 percent, $5 billion worth of investment is profitable. At 12 percent interest, a total of $10 billion of investment is profitable. Similarly, total investment increases by $5 billion for each successive 2-percentage-point decline in the interest rate. Describe the relevant relationship between the interest rate and investment in words, in a table, graphically, and as an equation. Put the interest rate on the vertical axis and investment on the horizontal axis. In your equation use the form $i = a + bI$, where $i$ is the interest rate, $a$ is the vertical intercept, $b$ is the slope of the line (which is negative), and $I$ is the level of investment. Comment on the advantages and disadvantages of the verbal, tabular, graphical, and equation forms of description.

6. KEY APPENDIX QUESTION *The accompanying graph shows curve XX and tangents at points A, B, and C. Calculate the slope of the curve at these three points.*

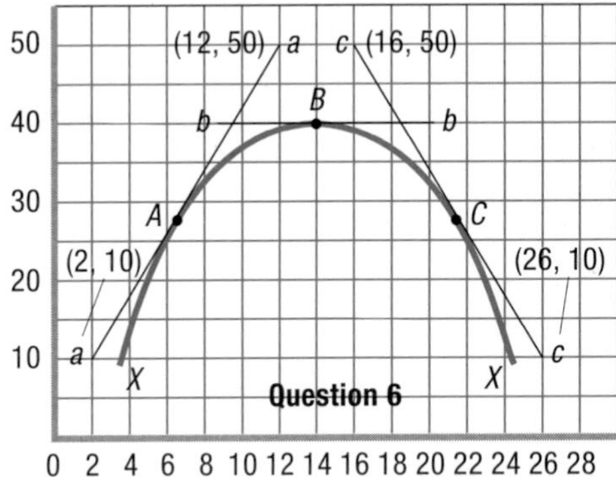


7. In the accompanying graph, is the slope of curve *AA′* positive or negative? Does the slope increase or decrease as we move along the curve from *A* to *A′*? Answer the same two questions for curve *BB′*.

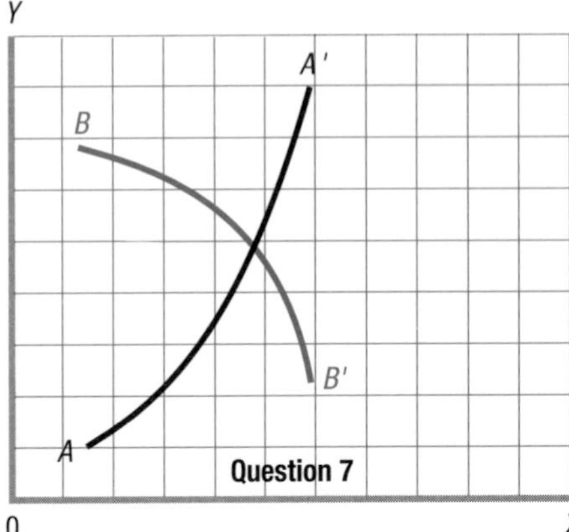

CHAPTER 2

# The Economic Problem: Scarcity, Wants, and Choices

YOU MAKE DECISIONS EVERY DAY THAT CAPTURE the essence of economics. Suppose you have $40 and are deciding how to spend it. Should you buy a pair of new jeans? Two or three compact discs? A ticket for a music concert?

Similarly, what should you do with your time between 3 and 6 o'clock on, say, a Thursday afternoon? Should you work extra hours at your part-time job? Do research on a term project? Prepare for an economics quiz? Watch TV? Take a nap?

Money and time are both scarce, and making decisions in the context of scarcity always means there are costs. If you choose the jeans, the cost is the forgone CDs or concert. If you nap or watch TV, the cost might be a low score on your quiz.

Scarcity, wants, and choices—these are the key elements of this chapter. Here we introduce and explore the fundamentals of economic science. We first illustrate, extend, and modify our definition of economics and explore the so-called *economizing problem* by means of a model. Next, we briefly survey the ways diverse economies respond to the economizing problem. Finally, we develop an overview of the market system in the form of the circular flow model.

**IN THIS CHAPTER YOU WILL LEARN:**

That economics is about choosing among alternative ends.

•

The distinction between allocative and productive efficiency.

•

What a production possibility curve is.

•

The meaning of opportunity cost.

•

The four different economic systems society can choose to coordinate production and consumption decisions.

•

What the circular model is.

## The Big Picture

THE ECONOMIZING PROBLEM ARISES FROM scarcity (or limited) resources and human unlimited wants. As a consequence, individuals and societies must make choices about what they want to produce and consume.

Consider the following scenario. Fall term has just ended and one weekend remains before the Christmas holiday begins. You must study for a final exam but you also need to do your Christmas shopping. Also, it just snowed and you are itching to ski for the first time of the season. Moreover, your friends have invited you to a Christmas party Friday night of the same weekend.

You need to make choices since it would be impossible for you to do all the things you want. And whatever choices you make entails giving something up. That, in short, captures the economizing problem, the result of limited resources and many wants.

As you read this chapter, keep the following points in mind:

- **Key Concepts 1, 2, 4,** and **8** are discussed.
- Resources to produce the goods and services we want are limited in relation to our wants.
- Even if a few very wealthy individuals have all the material things they desire, the vast majority of the human race certainly does not.
- In the face of limited resources, choices about what to produce and consume must be made.
- Limited resources imply that choosing more of one good or service means giving up some quantity of another good or service. ■

## THE FOUNDATION OF ECONOMICS

Two fundamental facts together constitute the **economizing problem** and provide a foundation for the field of economics:

1. *Society's material wants, that is, the material wants of its citizens and institutions, are virtually unlimited and insatiable.*
2. *Economic resources—the means of producing goods and services—are limited or scarce.*

You must fully understand these two facts because all that follows depends directly on them.

### Unlimited Wants 

In stating the first fact, what do we mean by "material wants"? We mean, first, the desires of consumers to obtain and use various goods and services that provide **utility**, meaning pleasure or satisfaction.[1] An amazingly wide range of products accomplishes this, from houses and automobiles to toothpaste, pizzas, sweaters, and hamburgers. Innumerable products sometimes classified as *necessities* (food, shelter, and clothing) and *luxuries* (perfumes, yachts, racecars) can satisfy human desires. Of course, what is a luxury to Smith may be a necessity to Jones, and what is a necessity today may have been a luxury a few years ago.

Services satisfy our wants as much as products do. Repair work on a car, the removal of an inflamed appendix, legal and accounting advice, and haircuts and hairstyling all satisfy human wants. Actually, we buy many goods—for example, automobiles and washing machines—for the services they render. Thus, the differences between goods and services are often smaller than they would appear to be.

"Wants" also include the desires of businesses and units of government to satisfy material goals. Businesses want factory buildings, machinery, trucks, warehouses, communication systems, and other things that help them achieve their production goals. Government, reflecting the collective wants of its citizenry or goals of its own, seeks highways, mass transit systems, schools, and military equipment.

We say that, as a group, these wants are *insatiable*, or *unlimited*, meaning that our desires for

[1] This definition leaves a variety of wants—recognition, status, love, and so forth—for the other social sciences to examine and study.

goods and services cannot be completely satisfied. Our desires for a *particular* good or service can be satisfied; over a short period of time we can surely get enough toothpaste or pasta. And one appendicitis operation is plenty.

But goods *in general* are another story. We do not, and presumably cannot, get enough. A simple mental experiment can help verify this: Suppose all members of society were asked to list the goods and services they would buy if they had unlimited income. Do you imagine that their list would ever end?

Furthermore, over time, wants multiply. As we fill some of the wants on the list, new ones pop up. Material wants have a high reproduction rate. The rapid introduction of new products whets our appetites, and extensive advertising persuades us that we need items we might not otherwise have desired. Not long ago, we did not want personal computers, Internet service, video recorders, fax machines, and compact discs because they did not exist. Also, we often cannot stop with simple satisfaction: The acquisition of an Escort or Geo has been known to whet the appetite for a Porsche or Mercedes.

At any specific time the individuals and institutions constituting society have innumerable unfulfilled material wants. Some wants—food, clothing, shelter—have biological roots. But some are also influenced by the conventions and customs of society. The specific kinds of food, clothing, and shelter we seek are frequently determined by the general social and cultural environment in which we live. Over time, wants change and multiply, fuelled by the development of new products and extensive promotion.

*The overall objective of all economic activity is to satisfy these diverse material wants.*

## Scarce Resources

In stating the second fundamental fact—*economic resources are limited or scarce*—what do we mean by **economic resources**? In general, we mean all natural, human, and manufactured resources that go into the production of goods and services. This covers a lot of ground: all the factory and farm buildings and all the equipment, tools, and machinery used to produce manufactured goods and agricultural products; all transportation and communication facilities; the innumerable types of labour; and land and mineral resources of all kinds. Economists broadly classify these as either *property* resources—land or raw materials and capital—or *human* resources—labour and entrepreneurial ability.

### Resource Categories

Let's examine four specific categories of resources.

**LAND** **Land** means much more to the economist than to most people. Land is all natural resources—all "gifts of nature"—usable in the production process. Such resources as arable land, forests, mineral and oil deposits, and water resources come under this classification.

**CAPITAL** **Capital** (or *capital goods* or *investment goods*) includes all manufactured aids to production, that is, all tools, machinery, equipment, and factory, storage, transportation, and distribution facilities used in producing goods and services and getting them to the ultimate consumer. The process of producing and purchasing capital goods is known as **investment**.

Two other points are pertinent. First, *capital goods* differ from *consumer goods* since the latter satisfy wants directly, while the former do so indirectly by aiding production of consumer goods. Second, the term "capital" as here defined does not refer to money. True, business executives and economists often talk of "money capital," meaning money available to purchase machinery, equipment, and other productive facilities. But money, as such, produces nothing, so it is not an economic resource. *Real capital*—tools, machinery, and other productive equipment—is an economic resource; *money* or *financial capital* is not.

**LABOUR** **Labour** is a broad term for all the physical and mental talents of individuals available and usable in producing goods and services. (This *excludes* a special set of talents—entrepreneurial ability—which, because of its special significance in a market economy, we consider separately.) The services of a logger, retail clerk, machinist, teacher, professional football player, and nuclear physicist all fall under the general heading "labour."

**ENTREPRENEURIAL ABILITY** Finally, there is the special human resource we label **entrepreneurial ability** or, simply, *enterprise*. The entrepreneur performs four related functions.

1. The entrepreneur *takes the initiative* in combining the resources of land, capital, and labour to produce a good or service. Both a sparkplug and a catalyst, the entrepreneur is the driving

force behind production and the agent who combines the other resources in what is hoped will be a successful business venture.

2. The entrepreneur *makes basic business-policy decisions*, that is, those nonroutine decisions that set the course of a business enterprise.
3. The entrepreneur *is an innovator*—the one who attempts to introduce on a commercial basis new products, new productive techniques, or even new forms of business organization.
4. The entrepreneur *is a risk taker*. This is apparent from a close examination of the other three entrepreneurial functions. The entrepreneur in a market economy has no guarantee of profit. The reward for his or her time, efforts, and abilities may be profits *or* losses and eventual bankruptcy. The entrepreneur risks not only time, effort, and business reputation but his or her invested funds and those of associates or stockholders.

Since these four resources—land, labour, capital, and entrepreneurial ability—are combined to *produce* goods and services, they are called the **factors of production**.

**Resource Payments** The income received from supplying raw materials and capital equipment (the property resources) is called *rental income* and *interest income*, respectively. The income accruing to those who supply labour is called *wages*, which includes salaries and all wage and salary supplements such as bonuses, commissions, and royalties. Entrepreneurial income is called *profits*, which may be negative—that is, losses.

### Relative Scarcity

The four types of economic resources, or factors of production, or *inputs*, have one fundamental characteristic in common: *They are scarce or limited in supply*. Our "spaceship earth" contains only limited amounts of resources to use in producing goods and services. Quantities of arable land, mineral deposits, capital equipment, and labour (time) are all limited; they are available only in finite amounts. Because of the scarcity of productive resources and the constraint that this scarcity puts on productive activity, output itself is limited. Society is not able to produce and consume all the goods and services it wants. Thus, in Canada—one of the most affluent nations—output per person was limited to $26,355 in 1997. In the poorest nations, annual output per person is as low as $200 or $300!

## ECONOMICS: GETTING THE MOST OUT OF AVAILABLE RESOURCES

The economizing problem is thus at the heart of the definition of economics, first stated in Chapter 1: *Economics is the social science concerned with the problem of using scarce resources to attain the maximum fulfilment of society's unlimited wants.* Economics is concerned with "doing the best with what we have." Because our resources are scarce, we cannot satisfy all our unlimited wants. The next best thing is to achieve the greatest possible satisfaction of those wants. Society wants to use its limited resources efficiently; it desires to produce as many goods and services as possible from its available resources, so that it maximizes total satisfaction. To realize this outcome, it must achieve both full employment and full production.

### Full Employment: Using Available Resources

By **full employment** we mean the use of all available resources. No workers should be involuntarily out of work; the economy should provide employment for all who are willing and able to work. Nor should capital equipment or arable land sit idle. But note that we say all *available* resources should be employed. Each society has certain customs and practices that determine what particular resources are available for employment. For example, in most countries legislation and custom provide that children and the very aged should not be employed. Similarly, to maintain productivity, it is desirable to allow farmland to lie fallow periodically. And it is desirable to "conserve" some resources for use by future generations.

### Full Production: Using Resources Efficiently

The employment of all available resources is not enough to achieve efficiency. Full production must also be realized. By **full production** we mean that all employed resources should be used so that they provide the maximum possible satisfaction of our material wants. If we fail to realize full production, economists say our resources are *underemployed*.

Full production implies two kinds of efficiency—productive and allocative efficiency:

1. **Productive efficiency** is the production of *any particular mix of goods and services in the least costly way*. When we produce, say, compact discs at the lowest achievable unit cost, we are expending the smallest amount of resources to produce CDs and therefore making available the largest amount of resources to produce other desired products. Suppose society has only $100 of resources available. If we can produce a CD for only $5 of resources, then $95 of resources will be available to produce other goods. This is clearly better than producing the CD for $10 and having only $90 of resources for alternative uses.

   In real-world terms, productive efficiency requires that Ford pickups and Dodge vans be produced with computerized and roboticized assembly techniques. It would be wasteful of scarce resources—that is, inefficient—to use the primitive assembly lines of the 1920s. Similarly, it would be inefficient to have farmers harvesting wheat with scythes or picking corn by hand since mechanical harvesting equipment is available to do the job at a much lower cost per unit.
2. **Allocative efficiency** is the production of *that particular mix of goods and services most wanted by society*. For example, society wants resources allocated to compact discs and cassettes, not to 45 rpm records. We want personal computers (PCs), not manual typewriters. Furthermore, we do not want to devote *all* our resources to producing CDs and PCs; we want to assign some of them to producing automobiles and office buildings. Allocative efficiency requires that the "right" mix of goods and services be produced—each item at the least unit cost. It means apportioning limited resources among firms and industries in such a way that society obtains the combination of goods and services that it wants the most. ***(Key Question 5)***

**2-1**

**QUICK REVIEW**

- Human material wants are virtually unlimited.
- Economic resources—land, capital, labour, and entrepreneurial ability—are scarce.
- Economics is concerned with the efficient allocation of scarce resources to achieve the maximum fulfilment of society's material wants.
- Economic efficiency requires full employment and full production; the latter requires both productive and allocative efficiency.

## Production Possibilities Table

Because resources are scarce, a full-employment, full-production economy cannot have an unlimited output of goods and services. Therefore, people must choose which goods and services to produce and which to forgo. The necessity and consequences of these choices can best be understood through a production possibilities model. Let's examine the model first as a table, then as a graph.

**Assumptions** We begin our discussion with four simplifying assumptions:

1. **FULL EMPLOYMENT AND PRODUCTIVE EFFICIENCY** The economy is employing all its available resources (full employment) and producing goods and services at least cost (productive efficiency). We will consider allocative efficiency later.
2. **FIXED RESOURCES** The available supplies of the factors of production are fixed in both quantity and quality. Nevertheless, they can be reallocated, within limits, among different uses; for example, land can be used for factory sites or for food production.
3. **FIXED TECHNOLOGY** The state of technology—the methods used to produce output—does not change during our analysis. This assumption and the previous one imply that we are looking at an economy at one specific time or over a very short period of time. Later in the analysis, we will examine the situation over a longer period.
4. **TWO GOODS** The economy is producing only two goods: pizzas and industrial robots. Pizza symbolizes **consumer goods**: products that satisfy our wants *directly*; industrial robots symbolize **capital goods**: products that satisfy our wants *indirectly* by enabling more efficient production of consumer goods.

**The Need for Choice** From our assumptions, we see that society must choose among alternatives. Limited resources mean limited outputs of pizza and robots. And since all available resources are fully employed, to increase the production of robots we must shift resources away from the production of pizza. The reverse is also true: To increase the production of pizza, we must take resources from the production of robots. There is no such thing as a free pizza. This, recall, is the essence of the economizing problem.

A **production possibilities table** lists the different combinations of two products that can be produced with a specific set of resources (and with full employment and productive efficiency). Table 2-1 is such a table for a pizza-robot economy; the data are, of course, hypothetical. At alternative A, this economy would be devoting all its available resources to the production of robots (capital goods); at alternative E, all resources would go to pizza production (consumer goods). Those alternatives are unrealistic extremes; an economy typically produces both capital and consumer goods, as in B, C, and D. As we move from alternative A to E, we increase the production of pizza at the expense of robot production.

Because consumer goods satisfy our wants directly, any movement towards E looks tempting. In producing more pizzas, society increases the current satisfaction of its wants. But there is a cost: fewer robots. This shift of resources to consumer goods catches up with society over time as the stock of capital goods dwindles—or at least ceases to expand at the current rate—with the result that some potential for greater production is lost. By moving towards alternative E, society chooses "more now" at the expense of "much more later."

By moving towards A, society chooses to forgo current consumption. The sacrifice of current consumption frees resources that can be used to increase the production of capital goods. By building up its stock of capital this way, society will have greater future production and, therefore, greater future consumption. By moving towards A, society is choosing "more later" at the cost of "less now."

Generalization: *At any point in time, an economy that is achieving full employment and productive efficiency must sacrifice some of one good to obtain more of another good. Scarce resources prohibit such an economy from having more of both goods.*

**TABLE 2-1 Production possibilities of pizza and robots with full employment and productive efficiency**

| | PRODUCTION ALTERNATIVES | | | | |
|---|---|---|---|---|---|
| **Type of product** | **A** | **B** | **C** | **D** | **E** |
| Pizza (in hundred thousands) | 0 | 1 | 2 | 3 | 4 |
| Robots (in thousands) | 10 | 9 | 7 | 4 | 0 |

## Production Possibilities Curve

The data and ideas of a production possibilities table can also be shown graphically. We use a simple two-dimensional graph, arbitrarily representing the output of capital goods (here, robots) on the vertical axis and the output of consumer goods (here, pizza) on the horizontal axis, as shown in ***Figure 2-1 (Key Graph)***. Following the procedure given in the appendix to Chapter 1, we graph a **production possibilities curve**.

Each point on the production possibilities curve represents some maximum output of the two products. The curve is a production *frontier* because it shows the limit of attainable outputs. To obtain the various combinations of pizza and robots that fall *on* the production possibilities curve, society must achieve both full employment and productive efficiency. Points lying *inside* (to the left of) the curve are also attainable but not as desirable as points on the curve. Points inside the curve imply that the economy could have more of both robots and pizza if it achieved full employment and productive efficiency. Points lying *outside* (to the right of) the production possibilities curve, like point *W*, would represent a greater output than that at any point on the curve, but such points are unattainable with the current supplies of resources and technology.

## Law of Increasing Opportunity Cost 

Because resources are scarce relative to the virtually unlimited wants that these resources can be used to satisfy, people must choose among alternatives. More of pizza means less of robots. The amount of other products that must be forgone or sacrificed to obtain 1 unit of a specific good is called the **opportunity cost** of that good. In our case, the amount of robots that must be given up to get another unit of pizza is the *opportunity cost*, or simply the *cost*, of that unit of pizza.

In moving from alternative A to B in Table 2-1, we find that the cost of 1 additional unit of pizza is 1 less unit of robots. But as we now pursue the concept of cost through the additional production possibilities—B to C, C to D, and D to E—an important economic principle is revealed: The opportunity cost of each additional unit of pizza is greater than that of the previous one. When we move from A to B, just 1 unit of robots is sacrificed for 1 more unit of pizza; but going from B to C sacrifices 2 additional units of robots for 1 more unit of pizza; then 3 more of robots for 1 more of pizza; and finally 4 for 1. Conversely, you should confirm that as we move from E to A, the cost of each additional robot is $\frac{1}{4}$, $\frac{1}{3}$, $\frac{1}{2}$, and 1 unit of pizza, respectively, for the four successive moves.

Note two points about these opportunity costs:

1. Our costs are measured in *real* terms, that is, in actual goods rather than money. We will shift to monetary comparisons in a moment.
2. We are discussing *marginal* (meaning "extra") opportunity costs, rather than cumulative or total opportunity costs. For example, the marginal opportunity cost of the third unit of pizza in Table 2-1 is 3 units of robots (= 7 – 4). But the *total* opportunity cost of 3 units of pizza is 6 units of robots (= 1 unit of robots for the first unit of pizza *plus* 2 units of robots for the second unit of pizza *plus* 3 units of robots for the third unit of pizza).

The **law of increasing opportunity costs** generalizes our example: The more of a product that is produced, the greater is its opportunity cost ("marginal" being implied).

**Concavity** The law of increasing opportunity costs is reflected in the shape of the production possibilities curve: The curve is *concave*, or bowed out, from the origin. In Figure 2-1, you can see that when the economy moves from *A* to *E*, it must give up successively larger amounts of robots (1, 2, 3, and 4) to acquire equal increments of pizza (1, 1, 1, and 1). This reality is shown by the slope of the production possibilities curve that becomes steeper as we move from *A* to *E*. A curve that gets steeper as you move down along it is always concave as viewed from the origin.

**Economic Rationale** What is the economic rationale for the law of increasing opportunity costs? Why does the sacrifice of robots increase as we produce more pizza? The answer is that *economic resources are not completely adaptable to alternative uses*. Many resources are better at producing one good than at producing others. Fertile farmland is highly conducive to producing the ingredients needed to make pizza, while land containing rich mineral deposits is highly suited to producing the materials needed to make robots. As we step up pizza production, resources that are less and less adaptable to making pizza must be "pushed" into pizza production. If we start at *A* and move to *B*, we can shift the resources whose productivity of pizza is greatest in relation to their productivity of robots. But as we move from *B* to *C*, *C* to *D*, and so on, resources highly productive of pizza become increasingly scarce. To get more pizza, resources whose productivity in robots is great in relation to their productivity in pizza will be needed. It will take more and more of such resources—and hence a greater sacrifice of robots—to achieve each increase of 1 unit in the production of pizza. This lack of perfect flexibility, or interchangeability, on the part of resources is the cause of increasing opportunity costs. ***(Key Question 6)***

## Allocative Efficiency Revisited

Our analysis has assumed full employment and productive efficiency, both of which are necessary to produce at *any point* on an economy's production possibilities curve. We now turn to allocative efficiency, which requires that the economy produce at the most valued, or *optimal*, point on the production possibilities curve. Of all the attainable combinations of pizza and robots on the curve in Figure 2-1, which is best? That is, what specific quantities of resources should be allocated to pizza and what specific quantities to robots?

Our discussion of the *economic perspective* in Chapter 1 puts us on the right track. Recall that economic decisions centre on comparisons of marginal benefits and marginal costs. Any economic activity—for example, production or consumption—should be expanded as long as marginal benefits exceed marginal costs and should be reduced if marginal costs are greater than marginal benefits. The optimal amount of the activity occurs where MB = MC.

Consider pizza. We already know from the law of increasing opportunity costs that the marginal cost (MC) of additional units of pizza will rise as

## KEY GRAPH

**FIGURE 2-1 The production possibilities curve**

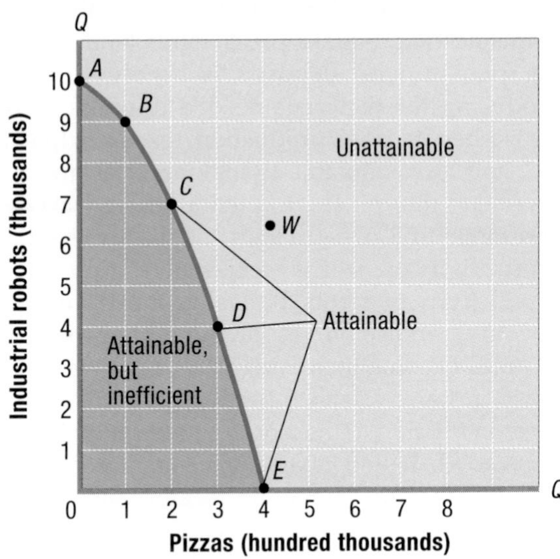


Each point on the production possibilities curve represents some maximum combination of two products that can be produced if full employment and full production are achieved. When operating on the curve, more robots mean less pizza, and vice versa. Limited resources and a fixed technology make any combination of robots and pizza lying outside the curve (such as at *W*) unattainable. Points inside the curve are attainable, but they indicate that full employment and productive efficiency are not being realized.

### 2-1 QUICK QUIZ

**1.** Production possibilities curve *ABCDE* is concave because:
**(a)** the marginal benefit of pizza declines as more pizza is consumed.
**(b)** the curve gets steeper as we move from *E* to *A*.
**(c)** it reflects the law of increasing opportunity costs.
**(d)** resources are scarce.

**2.** The *marginal* opportunity cost of the second unit of pizza is:
**(a)** 2 units of robots.
**(b)** 3 units of robots.
**(c)** 7 units of robots.
**(d)** 9 units of robots.

**3.** The *total* opportunity cost of 7 units of robots is:
**(a)** 1 unit of pizza.
**(b)** 2 units of pizza.
**(c)** 3 units of pizza.
**(d)** 4 units of pizza.

**4.** All points on this production possibilities curve necessarily represent:
**(a)** allocative efficiency.
**(b)** less than full use of resources.
**(c)** unattainable levels of output.
**(d)** productive efficiency.

**Answers:** 1. (c); 2. (a); 3. (b); 4 (d).

more units are produced. This can be shown with an upsloping MC curve, as in Figure 2-2. We are also aware that we obtain extra or marginal benefits (MB) from additional units of pizza. However, although material wants in the aggregate are insatiable, the second unit of a particular product yields less additional utility or benefit to you than the first. And a third will provide even less MB than the second. So it is for society as a whole. Therefore, we can portray the marginal benefits from pizza with a downsloping MB curve, as in Figure 2-2.

The optimal quantity of pizza production is indicated by the intersection of the MB and MC curves: 200,000 units in Figure 2-2. Why is this the optimal quantity? If only 100,000 pizzas were produced, the marginal benefit of pizza would exceed its marginal cost. In money terms, MB might be $15, while MC is only $5. This suggests that society would be *underallocating* resources to pizza production; more of it should be produced.

How do we know? Because society values an additional pizza as being worth $15, while the alternative products that the required resources could produce are worth only $5. Society benefits—it is better off in the sense of having a higher-valued output to enjoy—whenever it can gain something worth $15 by forgoing something worth only $5. A reallocating of resources from other products to pizza would mean society is using its resources more efficiently. Each addi-

**FIGURE 2-2 Allocative efficiency: MB = MC**

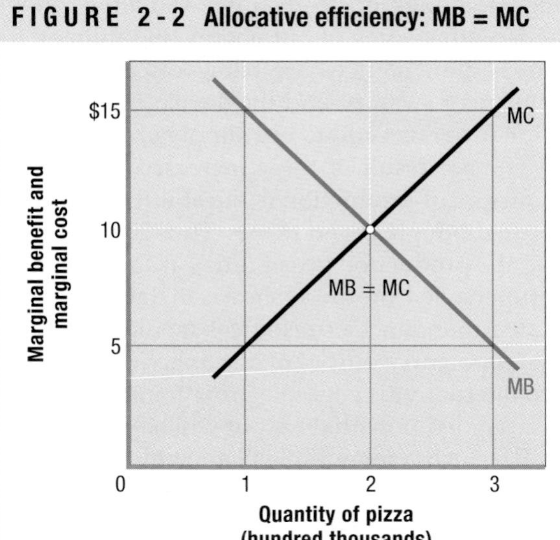


Resources are being allocated efficiently to a product when its output quantity is such that its marginal benefit (MB) equals its marginal cost (MC). Here, the optimal quantity of pizza is 200,000.

tional pizza up to 200,000 would provide such a gain, indicating that allocative efficiency would be improved by this production. But when MB = MC, the benefits of producing pizza or alternative products with the available resources are equal. Allocative efficiency is achieved where MB = MC.

The production of 300,000 pizzas would represent an *overallocation* of resources to their production. Here the MC of pizza is $15 and its MB is only $5. This means 1 unit of pizza is worth only $5 to society, while the alternative products that the required resources could otherwise produce are valued at $15. By producing 1 less unit, society loses a pizza worth $5. But by reallocating the freed resources, it gains other products worth $15. When society gains something worth $15 by forgoing something worth only $5, it is better off. In Figure 2-2, such net gains can be realized until pizza production has been reduced to 200,000.

Generalization: *Resources are being efficiently allocated to any product when its output is such that its marginal benefit equals its marginal cost (MB = MC).* Suppose that by applying the above analysis to robots, we find their optimal (MB = MC) output is 7,000. This would mean that alternative C on our production possibilities curve—200,000 pizzas and 7,000 robots—would result in allocative efficiency for our hypothetical economy. ***(Key Question 9)***

### 2-2 QUICK REVIEW

- The production possibilities curve illustrates four concepts: **a** *scarcity* of resources is implied by the area of unattainable combinations of output lying outside the production possibilities curve; **b** *choice* among outputs is reflected in the variety of attainable combinations of goods lying along the curve; **c** *opportunity cost* is illustrated by the downward slope of the curve; **d** the law of *increasing opportunity costs* is implied by the concavity of the curve.
- Full employment and productive efficiency must be realized for the economy to operate on its production possibilities curve.
- A comparison of marginal benefits and marginal costs is needed to determine allocative efficiency—the best or optimal output-mix on the curve.

## UNEMPLOYMENT, GROWTH, AND THE FUTURE

Let's now drop the first three assumptions underlying the production possibilities curve to see what happens.

### Unemployment and Productive Inefficiency

The first assumption was that our economy was achieving full employment and productive efficiency. Our analysis and conclusions change if some resources are idle (unemployment) or if least-cost production is not realized. The five alternatives in Table 2-1 represent maximum outputs; they illustrate the combinations of robots and pizzas that can be produced when the economy is operating at full capacity—with full employment and productive efficiency. With unemployment or inefficient production, the economy would produce less than each alternative shown in the table.

Graphically, situations of unemployment or productive inefficiency are represented by points *inside* the original production possibilities curve (reproduced in Figure 2-3). Point *U* is one such point. Here the economy is falling short of the various maximum combinations of pizza and robots

**FIGURE 2-3 Unemployment, productive inefficiency, and the production possibilities curve**

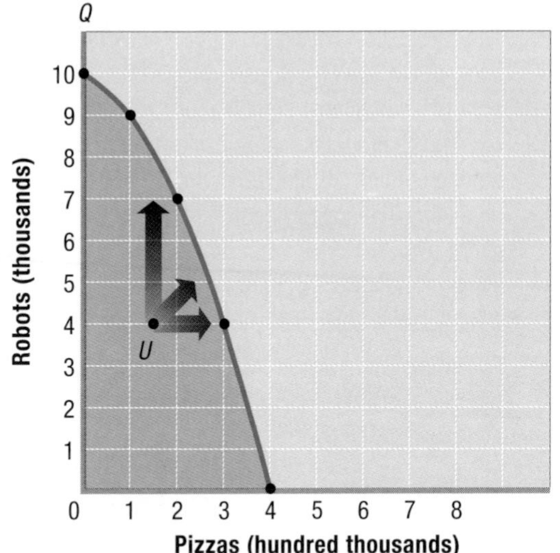


Any point inside the production possibilities curve, such as *U*, represents unemployment or a failure to achieve productive efficiency. The arrows indicate that, by realizing full employment and productive efficiency, the economy could operate on the curve. This means it could produce more of one or both products than it is producing at point *U*.

reflected by the points *on* the production possibilities curve. The arrows in Figure 2-3 indicate three possible paths back to full employment and least-cost production. A move towards full employment and productive efficiency would yield a greater output of one or both products.

## A Growing Economy 

When we drop the assumptions that the quantity and quality of resources and technology are fixed, the production possibilities curve shifts positions; that is, the potential maximum output of the economy changes.

**Increases in Resource Supplies** Let's first abandon the assumption that total supplies of land, labour, capital, and entrepreneurial ability are fixed in both quantity and quality. Common sense tells us that over time a nation's growing population will bring about increases in the supplies of labour and entrepreneurial ability. Also, labour quality usually improves over time. Historically, our stock of capital has increased at a significant, though unsteady, rate. And although we are depleting some of our energy and mineral resources, new sources are being discovered. The drainage of swamps and the development of irrigation programs add to our supply of arable land.

The net result of these increased supplies of the factors of production is the ability to produce more of both pizza and robots. Thus 20 years from now, the production possibilities in Table 2-1 may be superseded by those shown in Table 2-2. The greater abundance of resources would result in a greater potential output of one or both products at each alternative. Economic growth in the sense of an expanded potential output will have occurred.

But such a favourable change in the production possibilities data does not *guarantee* that the economy will actually operate at a point on its new production possibilities curve. Some 15 million jobs will give Canada full employment now, but 10 or 20 years from now its labour force will be larger, and 15 million jobs will not be sufficient for full employment. The production possibilities curve may shift, but at the future date the economy may fail to produce at a point on that new curve.

**Advances in Technology** Our second assumption is that we have constant or unchanging technology. Actually, though, technology has progressed greatly over time. An advancing technology involves both new and better goods *and* improved ways of producing them. For now, let's think of technological advances as being only improvements in capital facilities—more efficient machinery and equipment. Such technological advances alter our previous discussion of the economizing problem by improving productive efficiency, allowing society to produce more goods with fixed resources. As with increases in resource supplies, technological advances enable the production of more robots *and* more pizza.

**TABLE 2-2 Production possibilities of pizza and robots with full employment and productive efficiency**

| | PRODUCTION ALTERNATIVES | | | | |
|---|---|---|---|---|---|
| **Type of product** | **A′** | **B′** | **C′** | **D′** | **E′** |
| Pizza (in hundred thousands) | 0 | 2 | 4 | 6 | 8 |
| Robots (in thousands) | 14 | 12 | 9 | 5 | 0 |

Thus, when either supplies of resources increase or an improvement in technology occurs, the production possibilities curve in Figure 2-3 shifts outward and to the right, as illustrated by curve *A′*, *B′*, *C′*, *D′*, *E′* in Figure 2-4. Such an outward shift of the production possibilities curve represents growth of economic capacity or, simply, **economic growth**—*the ability to produce a larger total output.* This growth is the result of (1) increases in supplies of resources, (2) improvements in resource quality, and (3) technological advance.

The consequence of growth is that our full-employment economy can enjoy a greater output of both robots and pizza. *While a static, no-growth economy must sacrifice some of one product to get more of another, a dynamic, growing economy can have larger quantities of both products.*

Economic growth does *not* typically mean proportionate increases in a nation's capacity to produce all its products. Note in Figure 2-4 that at the maximums, the economy can produce twice as much pizza as before but only 40 percent more robots. You should sketch in two new production possibilities curves: one showing the situation where a better technique for producing robots has been developed while the technology for producing pizza is unchanged, and the other illustrating an improved technology for pizza while the technology for producing robots remains constant.

**FIGURE 2-4 Economic growth and the production possibilities curve**

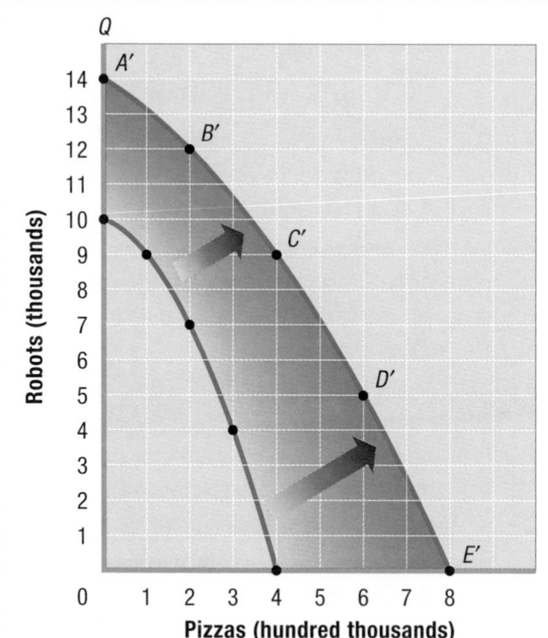


The expanding resource supplies, improved resource quality, and technological advances that occur in a dynamic economy move the production possibilities outward and to the right, allowing the economy to have larger quantities of both types of goods.

### Present Choices and Future Possibilities

An economy's current choice of positions on its production possibilities curve is a basic determinant of the future location of that curve. Let's designate the two axes of the production possibilities curve as *goods for the future* and *goods for the present*, as in Figure 2-5. Goods for the future are such things as capital goods, research and education, and preventive medicine. They increase the quantity and quality of property resources, enlarge the stock of technological information, and improve the quality of human resources. As we have already seen, goods for the future, like industrial robots, are the ingredients of economic growth. Goods for the present are pure consumer goods such as pizza, clothing, soft drinks, and boom boxes.

Now suppose there are two economies, Alta and Zorn, which are initially identical in every respect except one: Alta's current choice of positions on its production possibilities curve strongly favours present goods rather than future goods. Point *A* in Figure 2-5a indicates this choice. It is located quite far down the curve to the right, indicating a high priority for goods for the present, at the expense of fewer goods for the future. Zorn, in contrast, makes a current choice that stresses larger amounts of future goods and lesser amounts of present goods, as shown by point *Z* in Figure 2-5b.

Now, other things equal, we can expect the future production possibilities curve of Zorn to be farther to the right than Alta's curve. By currently choosing an output more favourable to technological advance and to increases in the quantity and quality of resources, Zorn will achieve greater economic growth than Alta. In terms of capital goods, Zorn is choosing to make larger current additions to its "national factory"—to invest more of its current output—than Alta. The payoff from this choice for Zorn is more rapid growth—greater future production capacity. The opportunity cost is fewer consumer goods in the present for Zorn to enjoy. ***(Key Questions 10 and 11)***

**FIGURE 2-5 An economy's present choice of positions on its production possibilities curve helps determine the curve's future location**

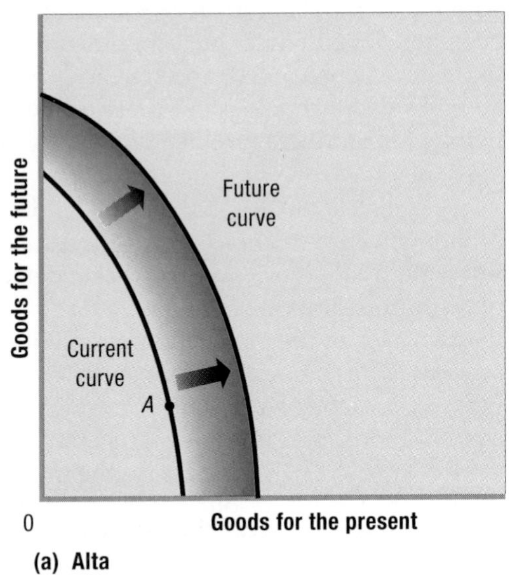


(a) Alta

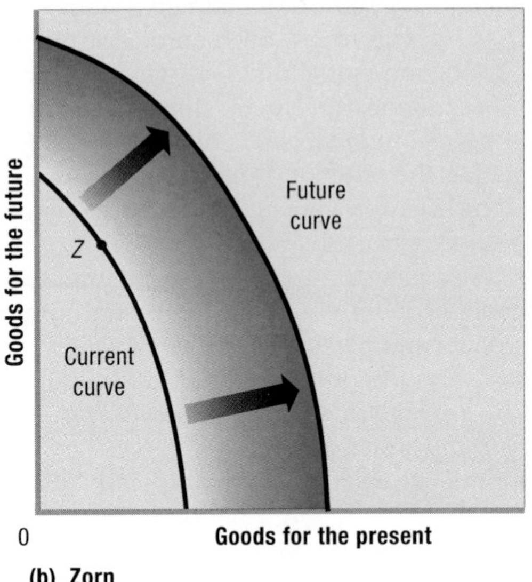


(b) Zorn

A nation's current choice favouring "present goods," as made by Alta in (a), will cause a modest outward shift of the curve in the future. A nation's current choice favouring "future goods," as made by Zorn in (b), will result in a greater outward shift in the curve in the future.

## A Qualification: International Trade

The message of the production possibilities curve is that an individual nation is limited to the combinations of output indicated by its production possibilities curve. *But this message must be modified when there is international specialization and trade.*

You will see in later chapters that a nation can avoid the output limits imposed by its domestic production possibilities curve through international specialization and trade. *International specialization* means directing domestic resources to output that a nation is highly efficient at producing. *International trade* involves the exchange of these goods for goods produced abroad. Specialization and trade enable a nation to get more of a desired good at less sacrifice of some other good. Rather than sacrifice 3 robots to get a third unit of pizza, as in Table 2-1, a nation might be able to obtain the third unit of pizza by trading only 2 units of robots for it. Specialization and trade have the same effect as having more and better resources or discovering improved production techniques; both increase the quantities of capital and consumer goods available to society. The output gains from greater international specialization and trade are the equivalent of economic growth.

### 2-3 QUICK REVIEW

- Unemployment and the failure to achieve productive efficiency cause the economy to operate at a point inside its production possibilities curve.
- Increases in resource supplies, improvements in resource quality, and technological advance cause economic growth, depicted as an outward shift of the production possibilities curve.
- An economy's present choice of output—particularly of capital and consumer goods—helps determine the future location of its production possibilities curves. (See Global Perspective 2-1.)
- International specialization and trade enable a nation to obtain more goods than indicated by its production possibilities curve.

## Applications

There are many possible applications of production possibilities analysis.

1. **GOING TO WAR** At the beginning of World War II (1939–45), Canada had considerable

## 2-1 GLOBAL PERSPECTIVE

### Investment and economic growth, selected countries

Nations that invest large portions of their national outputs tend to enjoy high growth rates, measured here by output per person. Additional capital goods make workers more productive and this means greater output per person.

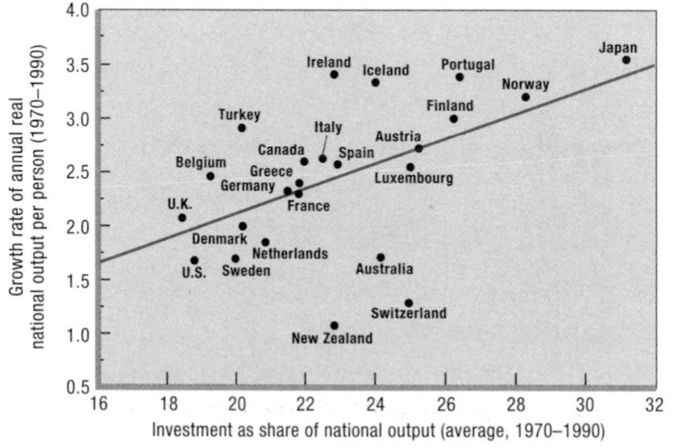


*Source:* International Monetary Fund data, as reported in *Economic Report of the President, 1994,* p. 37.

unemployment. By quickly employing its idle resources, the Canadian economy was able to produce an almost unbelievably large quantity of war goods and at the same time increase the output of consumer goods (as shown in Figure 2-3). The Soviet Union, in contrast, entered World War II at almost capacity production; it was operating close to full employment. An attempt to achieve simultaneously more pizza and more robots—or more guns and more butter—in a full-employment economy was doomed to failure. Its military preparations required considerable shifting of resources from the production of civilian goods, and its standard of living dropped substantially.

2. **DISCRIMINATION** Discrimination based on race, gender, age, sexual orientation, or ethnic background impedes the efficient employment of human resources, keeping the economy operating at some point inside its production possibilities curve. Discrimination prevents visible minorities, women, and others from obtaining jobs in which society can use their skills and talents efficiently. Elimination of discrimination would help move the economy from some point inside the production possibilities curve towards a point on the curve.

3. **LAND-USE CONTROVERSIES** The tradeoffs portrayed in the production possibilities curve are part of many controversies relating to alternative uses of publicly owned land.

   One example is the conflict between the logging industry in the U.S. Pacific Northwest and environmentalists trying to save that area's spotted owls. Envision a production possibilities curve with "lumber production" on one axis and "spotted owls" on the other. It so happens that the spotted owl depends on the mature trees in national forests for nests and survival. Increasing the output of lumber limits the owl's habitat, destroys the species, and thus reduces environmental quality. Maintaining the mature forests preserves the owl but destroys thousands of jobs in the logging and lumber industry.

   A second land-use example is the continuing debate over inclusion of more land in Canada's system of national parks. Some of these lands contain sizable oil, natural gas, and mineral deposits, and no drilling or mining is usually allowed. Here, the relevant production possibilities curve has "national parks" on one axis and "minerals" on the other. The concepts of resource scarcity, opportunity costs, and the necessity of choice again become quite apparent.

4. **MORE WOMEN IN THE WORKFORCE** An increase in the number of women who work outside the home has shifted the Canadian production possibilities curve outward. In 1970 about 35 percent of women worked in full-time or part-time jobs, compared to 68 percent today. As recently as 1980, only about 50 percent of married women were in the paid workforce. Today, that share is about 65 percent. This rise in the *quantity of labour* has contributed greatly to economic growth in Canada.

5. **FAMINE IN AFRICA** Modern industrial societies take economic growth—rightward shifts of the production possibilities curve—for granted. But periodic catastrophic famines in sub-Saharan nations of Africa show that in some circumstances the production possibilities curve may shift leftward. In addition to

drought, a cause of African famines is ecological degradation—poor land-use practices. Land has been deforested, overfarmed, and overgrazed, causing the production possibilities of these highly agriculturally oriented countries to diminish. In fact, the per-capita domestic outputs of most of these nations declined in the past decade or so.

6. **EMERGING TECHNOLOGIES** The world economies are experiencing a spurt of new technologies relating to computers, communications, and biotechnology. Technological advances have dropped the prices of computers and greatly enhanced their speed. Cellular phones, the Internet, and fax machines have increased communication capability, enhancing production and improving the efficiency of markets. Advances in biotechnology, specifically genetic engineering, have resulted in important agricultural and medical discoveries. Some observers believe that these new technologies are of such significance that they will ultimately contribute to faster economic growth than has occurred in the recent past (faster rightward shifts in nations' production possibilities curves).

## ECONOMIC SYSTEMS

A society needs to select an **economic system**—*a particular set of institutional arrangements and a coordinating mechanism*—to respond to the economizing problem. Economic systems can differ as to (1) who owns the factors of production and (2) the method used to coordinate and direct economic activity.

### Pure Capitalism

The private ownership of resources and the use of a system of markets and prices to coordinate and direct economic activity characterize *laissez-faire capitalism*, or **pure capitalism**. In such **market systems** each participant acts in his or her own self-interest; each individual or business seeks to maximize its satisfaction or profit through its own decisions regarding consumption or production. The system allows for the private ownership of capital, communicates through prices, and coordinates economic activity through *markets*—places where buyers and sellers come together. Goods and services are produced and resources are supplied by whomever is willing and able to do so. The result is competition among many small, independently acting buyers and sellers of each product and resource. Thus, economic power is widely dispersed.

Advocates of pure capitalism argue that such an economy promotes efficiency in the use of resources, stability of output and employment, and rapid economic growth. Hence, there is little or no need for government planning, control, or intervention. The term *laissez-faire* means "let it be," that is, keep government from interfering with the economy. The idea is that such interference will disturb the efficient working of the market system. Government's role is therefore limited to protecting private property and establishing an environment appropriate to the operation of the market system.

### The Command Economy

The polar alternative to pure capitalism is the **command economy**, or *communism*, characterized by public (government) ownership of virtually all property resources and economic decision making through central economic planning. All major decisions concerning the level of resource use, the composition and distribution of output, and the organization of production are determined by a central planning board appointed by government. Business firms are governmentally owned and produce according to government directives. The planning board determines production goals for each enterprise, and the plan specifies the amounts of resources to be allocated to each enterprise so that it can reach its production goals. The division of output between capital and consumer goods is centrally decided, and capital goods are allocated among industries on the basis of the central planning board's long-term priorities.

### Mixed Systems

Pure capitalism and the command economy are extremes; real-world economies fall between the two. The Canadian economy leans towards pure capitalism, but with important differences. Government actively participates in the economy by promoting economic stability and growth, providing certain goods and services that would be underproduced or not produced at all by the market system, and modifying the distribution of income. In contrast to wide dispersion of economic power among many small units, as implied by pure capitalism, the Canadian economy has spawned a number of very powerful economic organizations in the form of large corporations and labour unions. The ability of these power blocs to manipulate some markets to their advantage is a further reason for government involvement in the economy.

While the former Soviet Union historically approximated the command economy, it relied to some extent on market-determined prices and had some private ownership. Recent reforms in the former Soviet Union, China, and most of the eastern European nations have moved these economies toward more market-oriented systems. North Korea and Cuba are the best remaining examples of centrally planned economies.

But private ownership and reliance on the market system do not always go together, nor do state ownership and central planning. For example, the fascism of Hitler's Nazi Germany has been dubbed *authoritarian capitalism* because the economy had a high degree of governmental control and direction but property was privately owned. In contrast, the present economic system of China might be called *market socialism*. It has extensive government ownership of natural resources and capital coupled with considerable reliance on free markets to organize and coordinate some parts of economic activity. The Swedish economy is also a hybrid system. Although more than 90 percent of Sweden's business activity is in private hands, government is deeply involved in redistributing income. Similarly, the market-dominated Japanese economy involves much planning and coordination between government and the business sector.

### The Traditional Economy

Some developing countries have customary or **traditional economies**, in which production methods, exchange of goods, and distribution of income are all sanctioned by custom. Heredity and caste dictate the economic roles of individuals, and changes in socioeconomic status are rare. Technological change may also be constrained because it clashes with tradition and threatens the social fabric. Economic activity is often secondary to religious and cultural values and society's desire to perpetuate the status quo.

The main point here is that there is no unique or universally accepted way to respond to the economizing problem. Various societies, having different cultural and historical backgrounds, different mores and customs, and contrasting ideological frameworks—not to mention a great diversity of resources—use different institutions to deal with the reality of scarcity. The best method for responding to this reality in one society may or may not be appropriate in another society.

## THE CIRCULAR FLOW MODEL

Because market systems now dominate the world economy, our focus in the remainder of this chapter, and the two that follow, is on how nations use markets to respond to the economizing problem. Our goal in this last section is modest: We want to identify the major groups of decision makers and the major markets in the market system. Our tool is the circular flow diagram.

### Resource and Product Markets

***Figure 2-6 (Key Graph)*** shows two groups of decision makers—households and businesses. (Government will be added as a third decision maker in Chapter 5.) The coordinating mechanism that aligns the decisions of households and businesses is the market system, in particular resource and product markets.

The upper half of the diagram portrays the **resource market**—*the place where resources or the services of resource suppliers are bought and sold.* Households (that is, people) either own all economic resources directly or own them indirectly through their ownership of business corporations. These households *supply* their resources to businesses. Businesses *demand* resources because resources are necessary for producing goods and services. The interaction of the demand for and supply of the immense variety of human and property resources establishes the price of each resource. The payments that businesses make to obtain resources are costs to businesses, but those payments simultaneously are flows of wage, rent, interest, and profit income to the households supplying the resources. Thus resources flow from households to businesses, and money flows from businesses to households.

Now consider the **product market**—*the place where goods and services of businesses are bought and sold*—represented in the bottom half of the dia-

## KEY GRAPH

**FIGURE 2-6 The circular flow of output and income**

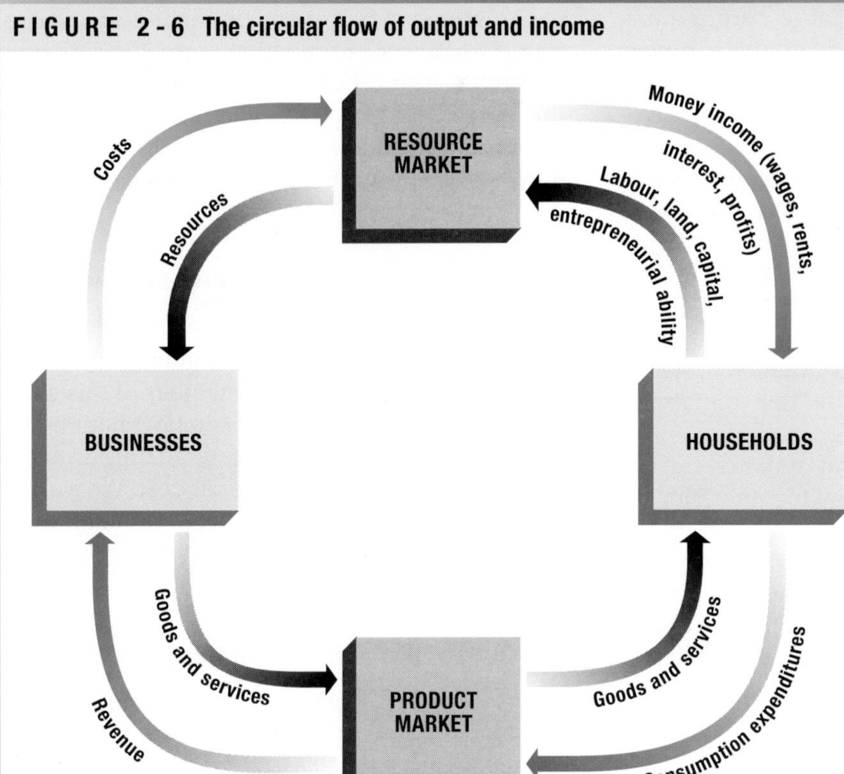


The prices paid for the use of labour, land, capital, and entrepreneurial ability are determined in the resource market shown in the upper loop. Businesses are on the demand side and households are on the supply side of this market. The prices of finished goods and services are determined in the product market shown in the lower loop. Households are on the demand side and businesses are on the supply side of this market.

### 2-6 QUICK QUIZ

1. The resource market is where:
   **(a)** households sell products and businesses buy products.
   **(b)** businesses sell resources and households sell products.
   **(c)** households sell resources and businesses buy resources (or the services of resources).
   **(d)** businesses sell resources and households buy resources (or the services of resources).
2. Which of the following would be determined in the product market?
   **(a)** a manager's salary.
   **(b)** the price of equipment used in a bottling plant.
   **(c)** the price of 80 hectares of farmland.
   **(d)** the price of a new pair of athletic shoes.
3. In this circular flow diagram:
   **(a)** money flows counterclockwise.
   **(b)** resources flow counterclockwise.
   **(c)** goods and services flow clockwise.
   **(d)** households are on the supply side of the product market.
4. In this circular flow diagram:
   **(a)** households spend income in the product market.
   **(b)** firms supply resources to households.
   **(c)** households receive income through the product market.
   **(d)** households produce goods.

**Answers:** 1. (c); 2. (d); 3. (b); 4. (a).

gram. The money income received by households from the sale of resources does not, as such, have real value. Consumers cannot eat or wear coins and paper money. But they can spend their money for goods and services. And by their willingness to spend money income, households express their *demand* for a vast variety of goods and services. Simultaneously, businesses combine the resources they have obtained to produce and *supply* these goods and services. The interaction of consumer demand and business supply decisions determines product prices. The flow of consumer expenditures for goods and services constitutes sales revenues for businesses.

This **circular flow model** suggests a complex, interrelated web of decision making and economic activity. Note that households and businesses participate in both basic markets, but on different sides of each. Businesses are on the buying or demand side of resource markets, and households (as resource owners and suppliers) are on the selling or supply side. In the product market, these positions are reversed; households are on the buying or demand side, and businesses on the selling or supply side. Each group of economic units both buys and sells.

Moreover, the spectre of scarcity haunts these transactions. Because households have only limited amounts of resources to supply to businesses, the money incomes of consumers are limited. This means that each consumer's income will go only so far. A limited amount of money income clearly will not permit the purchase of all the goods and services the consumer might like to buy. Similarly, because resources are scarce, the output of finished goods and services is also necessarily limited.

To summarize: In a monetary economy, households, as resource owners, sell their resources to businesses and, as consumers, spend the resource income by buying goods and services. Businesses must buy resources to produce goods and services; their finished products are then sold to households in exchange for consumption expenditures or, as business sees it, revenues. These revenues are used to purchase additional resources to maintain the circular flow. The net result is, in Figure 2-6, a counterclockwise *real flow* of economic resources and finished goods and services, and a clockwise *money flow* of income and consumption expenditures. These flows are simultaneous and repetitive.

## Limitations

Our model simplifies in many ways. Transactions between households and between businesses are concealed. Government and the "rest of the world" are ignored as decision makers. The model implies constant flows of output and income, while in fact these flows vary over time. Nor is the circular flow a perpetual-motion machine; production exhausts human energies and absorbs physical resources, the latter creating potential problems of environmental pollution. Finally, our model does not explain how product and resource prices are actually determined. We turn to this last topic in Chapter 4.

In The Media

1 KEY CONCEPT

## Down's Transplant Bid Poses Dilemma: Lung Recipients Face Long Odds

BY ALANNA MITCHELL

CALGARY—Terry Urquhart's request for a new lung has created a moral dilemma for the doctors and ethicists who decide who gets organ transplants.

Mr. Urquhart, 17, who has been placed on a waiting list and who reports for his medical assessment next week, is the first person with Down's syndrome in Canada, perhaps in the world, to be actively considered for a new lung, and the decision to put him on the list has raised an ethical storm that has shaken Alberta.

Some call it a moral victory and others say it is a waste of a scarce resource. To Mr. Urquhart, the medical miracle of a new lung means simply the chance to live out his last few years without gasping for air.

The people who run Canada's transplant programs say that since lung transplants became an option in Canada in the late 1980s, Mr. Urquhart is the first person with Down's to request one, despite the fact that severe lung problems are a common feature of that genetic disorder.

The case poses a problem for those who decide who gets which scarce organs, especially since costly transplant programs need to show success in order to survive. They also have a duty to use the scarce donated lungs in the best way possible.

In all of Canada, just 28 single-lung transplants were performed in 1993, the last year for which statistics are available. Between 20 per cent and 40 per cent of those who await a lung die during the wait.

Those who survive the operation face long odds. Roughly 14 per cent die within 30 days of the operation. About half are alive three years later. Doctors cannot offer recipients a guarantee of longer life, only the possibility of a life of better quality.

SOURCE: *Globe and Mail*, April 28, 1995, p. A1. Reproduced with permission from the *Globe and Mail*.

## THE STORY IN BRIEF

Scarcity often causes difficult moral dilemmas. There are not enough human organ donors to satisfy the need for organs. In this story, the issue is whether a person with Down's syndrome should receive one of the "scarce donated lungs."

## THE ECONOMICS BEHIND THE STORY

- The number of patients who want a lung transplant is greater than the number of donated lungs.
- A person with Down's syndrome has requested one of the scarce donated lungs. But giving a donated lung to one person necessarily means denying another patient one.
- The "moral" dilemma arises because of scarcity. If there were enough donated lungs to satisfy the demand for them, the "moral" dilemma would be resolved.
- Think of some other examples where "moral dilemmas" could be resolved by having more of any good or service so that painful tradeoffs are avoided. Is there a direct relationship between scarcity and moral dilemmas? ■

# The Last Word

## WOMEN AND EXPANDED PRODUCTION POSSIBILITIES

**A large increase in the number of employed women has shifted the Canadian production possibilities curve outward.**

ONE OF THE MORE REMARKABLE CANADIAN trends of the past half-century has been the substantial rise in the number of women working in the paid workforce. Today, nearly 70 percent of women work full- or part-time in paid jobs, compared to only 31 percent in 1965. There are many reasons for this increase.

1. **Rising Wage Rates of Women** Women have acquired more education and skill training, which have greatly increased their productivity in the workplace. As a result, the wages that women can earn in the labour market have increased rapidly over time. These higher wages have boosted women's opportunity costs—the forgone wage earnings—of staying at home. In response, women have substituted labour market employment for now more "expensive" home activities. This substitution has been particularly pronounced for married women.

   Higher wages for women have produced other reallocations of time and purchasing patterns to facilitate labour market work. Day-care services have partly replaced personal childcare. Restaurant meals, fast food, prepared take-home meals, and pizza delivery now substitute for elaborate home-made family meals. Convenience stores and catalogue sales have proliferated, as have lawn-care and in-home cleaning services. Shorter family vacations by airplane have replaced longer cross-country trips by car. Microwave ovens, dishwashers, automatic washers and dryers, and other household "capital goods" are now commonly used to enhance productivity in the home. These and similar household adjustments have helped make labour force participation more attractive for women.

2. **Expanded Job Accessibility** Greater accessibility to jobs, as distinct from higher pay, is a second factor boosting the employment of women. Service industries that traditionally have employed mainly women have expanded both absolutely and relatively in the past several decades. A growing demand for teachers, nurses, secretarial workers, salesclerks, and other service jobs has attracted many women to the labour market. Also, population has shifted from farms and rural regions to urban areas, where jobs for women are more abundant and geographically accessible. Finally, the decline in the average length of the workweek, together with an increased availability of part-time jobs, has made it easier for women to combine labour market employment with child-rearing and household activities.
3. **Changing Preferences and Attitudes** Women as a group have changed their preferences from household activities in favour of labour market employment. An increasing number of women have found personal fulfilment in jobs, careers, and earnings. More broadly, most industrial societies now widely accept and encourage labour force participation by married women, including women with preschool children. Today about 60 percent of Canadian mothers with preschool children participate in the labour force, compared to only 30 percent in 1970. More than half of today's employed mothers return to work before their youngest child is two years old.
4. **Declining Birthrates** While there were 3.8 lifetime births per woman in 1957 at the peak of the baby boom, that number is less than 2 today. This marked decline in the typical family size has freed up time for greater labour force participation since child rearing and associated homemaking activities are time-consuming. Not only do women now have fewer children, but these children are also spaced closer together in age. Thus, women who leave their jobs during their children's early years can return to the labour force sooner.

   The decline in birthrates has resulted from the widespread availability and use of birth control methods, coupled with changing lifestyles. But higher wage rates have also been at work. Women with relatively high wage earnings, on average, have fewer children than women with lower earnings. The opportunity cost of children—the income sacrificed by not being employed—rises as wage earnings rise. In the language of economics, the higher "price" associated with children has reduced the "quantity of children demanded."
5. **Rising Divorce Rates** Marital instability, as evidenced by high divorce rates in the 1970s and 1980s, may have motivated many women to establish and maintain labour-market ties. The economic impact of divorce on nonworking women is often disastrous because alimony and child support are not always forthcoming. Most previously nonworking women enter the labour force following divorce. And married women—perhaps even women contemplating marriage—may have increasingly participated in the labour force to protect themselves against the financial difficulties of potential divorce.
6. **Stagnating Male Earnings** A final factor explaining the rise in women's labour force participation rate is that men's real earnings have risen very slowly in the past two decades, particularly for men without university degrees. This stagnation has motivated many wives to enter the labour force to maintain family living standards. If wives had not entered the labour force in record numbers in the past two decades, many households would have suffered absolute or relative declines in their real incomes.

Together, these factors have produced a rapid rise in the availability of women workers in Canada. This increase in the *quantity of resources* has helped push the Canadian production possibilities curve outward. That is, it has greatly contributed to Canadian economic growth. ■

# CHAPTER SUMMARY

1. Economics is grounded on two basic facts: **a** human material wants are virtually unlimited; **b** economic resources are scarce.
2. Economic resources may be classified as property resources—raw materials and capital—or as human resources—labour and entrepreneurial ability. These resources (land, capital, labour, and entrepreneurial ability) are the factors of production.
3. Economics is concerned with the problem of using or managing scarce resources to produce goods and services that fulfil the material wants of society. Both full employment and efficient use of available resources are essential to maximize want satisfaction.
4. Efficient use of resources consists of productive efficiency (producing all output combinations in the least costly way) and allocative efficiency (producing the specific output mix most desired by society).
5. An economy that is achieving full employment and productive efficiency—that is, operating on its production possibilities curve—must sacrifice the output of some types of goods and services to achieve increased production of others. Because resources are not equally productive in all possible uses, shifting resources from one use to another brings the law of increasing opportunity costs into play. The production of additional units of a product entails the sacrifice of *increasing* amounts of the other product.
6. Allocative efficiency means operating at the optimal point on the production possibilities curve. That point represents the highest-valued mix of goods and is determined by expanding the production of each good until its marginal benefit (MB) equals its marginal cost (MC).
7. Over time, technological advance and increases in the quantity and quality of resources allow the economy to produce more of all goods and services—to experience economic growth. Society's choice as to the mix of consumer goods and capital goods in current output is a major determinant of the future location of the production possibilities curve and thus of economic growth.
8. The various economic systems of the world differ in their ideologies and also in their responses to the economizing problem. Basic differences centre on **a** whether most resources are owned by government or held privately and **b** whether economic activity is coordinated mainly by a market system or by central planning.
9. The circular flow model provides an overview of the operation of the market system. This simple model locates the product and resource markets and shows the major income-expenditure flows and resource-output flows that constitute the lifeblood of the market economy.

# TERMS AND CONCEPTS

economizing problem
utility
economic resources
land
capital
investment
labour
entrepreneurial ability
factors of production
full employment
full production
productive efficiency
allocative efficiency
consumer goods
capital goods
production possibilities table and curve
opportunity cost
law of increasing opportunity costs
economic growth
economic system
pure capitalism
market systems
command economy
traditional economies
resource market
product market
circular flow model

## STUDY QUESTIONS

1. Explain this statement: "If resources were unlimited and freely available, there would be no subject called *economics*."
2. Comment on the following statement from a newspaper article: "Our junior high school serves a splendid hot meal for $1 without costing the taxpayers anything, thanks in part to a government subsidy."
3. Critically analyze: "Wants aren't insatiable. I can prove it. I get all the coffee I want to drink every morning at breakfast." Explain: "Goods and services are scarce because resources are scarce." Analyze: "It is the nature of all economic problems that absolute solutions are denied to us."
4. What are economic resources? What are the major functions of the entrepreneur?
5. KEY QUESTION *Why is the problem of unemployment part of the subject matter of economics? Distinguish between productive efficiency and allocative efficiency. Give an illustration of achieving productive, but not allocative, efficiency.*
6. KEY QUESTION *Here is a production possibilities table for war goods and civilian goods:*

| TYPE OF PRODUCTION | PRODUCTION ALTERNATIVES | | | | |
|---|---|---|---|---|---|
| | A | B | C | D | E |
| Automobiles | 0 | 2 | 4 | 6 | 8 |
| Rockets | 30 | 27 | 21 | 12 | 0 |

   a. *Show these data graphically. Upon what specific assumptions is this production possibilities curve based?*
   b. *If the economy is at point C, what is the cost of one more automobile? One more rocket? Explain how the production possibilities curve reflects the law of increasing opportunity costs.*
   c. *What must the economy do to operate at some point on the production possibilities curve?*
7. What is the opportunity cost of attending college or university?
8. Suppose you arrive at a store expecting to pay $100 for an item but learn that a store two kilometres away is charging $50 for it. Would you drive there and buy it? How does your decision benefit you? What is the opportunity cost of your decision? Now suppose that you arrive at a store expecting to pay $6,000 for an item but learn that it costs $5,950 at the other store. Do you make the same decision as before? Perhaps surprisingly, you should! Explain why.
9. KEY QUESTION *Specify and explain the shapes of the marginal-benefit and marginal-cost curves. How are these curves used to determine the optimal allocation of resources to a particular product? If current output is such that marginal cost exceeds marginal benefit, should more or fewer resources be allocated to this product? Explain.*
10. KEY QUESTION *Label point G inside the production possibilities curve you drew in question 6. What does it indicate? Label point H outside the curve. What does that point represent? What must occur before the economy can attain the level of production shown by point H?*
11. KEY QUESTION *Referring again to question 6, suppose improvement occurs in the technology of producing rockets but not in the production of automobiles. Draw the new production possibilities curve. Now assume that a technological advance occurs in producing automobiles but not in producing rockets. Draw the new production possibilities curve. Now draw a production possibilities curve that reflects technological improvement in the production of both products.*
12. Explain how, if at all, each of the following affects the location of the production possibilities curve:
   a. Standardized examination scores of high school, university and college students decline.
   b. The unemployment rate falls from 9 to 6 percent of the labour force.
   c. Defence spending is reduced to allow government to spend more on health care.
   d. Society decides it wants compact discs rather than long-playing records.
   e. A new technique improves the efficiency of extracting copper from ore.
   f. A new baby boom increases the size of the nation's workforce.

13. Explain: "Affluence tomorrow requires sacrifice today."

14. Suppose that, based on a nation's production possibilities curve, an economy must sacrifice 10,000 pizzas domestically to get the one additional industrial robot it desires but that it can get the robot from another country in exchange for 9,000 pizzas. Relate this information to the following statement: "Through international specialization and trade, a nation can reduce its opportunity cost of obtaining goods and thus 'get outside its production possibilities curve.'"

15. Contrast how pure capitalism and a command economy try to cope with economic scarcity.

16. Explain this statement: "Although Canada has a capitalist economy, not a traditional economy, *traditions* (for example, weddings, Christmas, and Halloween) play an important role in determining what goods are produced."

17. Portray the major features of the circular flow model. In what way are businesses and households both *suppliers* and *demanders* in this model? Explain how scarcity enters the model.

18. **(The Last Word)** Which *two* of the six reasons listed in the Last Word do you think are the *most important* in explaining the rise of women's participation in the workplace? Explain your reasoning.

19. WEB-BASED QUESTION **Different Geographical Areas and Outputs—Japan and Canada** Compared to Japan, Canada has 26 times the geographical area and about 19 percent of its population. Other things equal, Canada should have approximately 19 percent of Japan's output. Visit the Web site of the OECD (Organization for Economic Cooperation and Development) www.oecd.org/std/gdp.htm and calculate the ratio of Canada's gross domestic product (a measure of national output) to the gross domestic product of Japan. Is the ratio above or below 19 percent? What might explain this difference?

20. WEB-BASED QUESTION **Increasing Productivity in Hong Kong** The Hong Kong Productivity Council hkpcms.hkpc.org/ was established in 1967 to promote increased productivity. Its mission is "to achieve a more effective utilization of available resources and to enhance the value-added content of products and services. The aim is to increase efficiency and competitiveness, thereby contributing to raising the standard of living of people in Hong Kong." How does the Council define productivity, and how does it try to increase it?

CHAPTER 3

# Overview of the Market System

IN THE PAST FEW YEARS THE MEDIA HAVE inundated us with stories of how Russian and other centrally planned economies are trying to alter their systems in the direction of capitalism, otherwise referred to as the market system or market economy. What are the features and institutions of a market system that these nations are trying to emulate?

Our initial task is to describe and explain how a pure market system, or laissez-faire capitalism, functions. Although a pure market system has never existed, a description of such an economy provides a useful approximation of how the economies of Canada and many other industrially advanced nations function. We will modify this approximation in later chapters to correspond more closely to the reality of modern economies.

In examining pure capitalism, we first discuss its basic assumptions and institutions. We then consider certain other institutions common to all advanced-industrial economies. Finally, we explain how a market system coordinates economic activity and contributes to the efficient use of scarce resources.

**IN THIS CHAPTER YOU WILL LEARN:**

The basic institutions required for a market economy.

•

The benefits of specialization and trade.

•

The Five Fundamental Questions any economy faces.

•

How the "invisible hand" helps to close the gap between private and public interests.

•

About the structure of the Canadian economy.

## The Big Picture

THE SCARCITY PROBLEM IS CONFRONTED BY all societies. Each society must choose a coordinating system that will determine how much of each product is produced, how it will be produced, and how output is divided among its population. This chapter offers an overview of one way to coordinate production and distribution: the market system—sometimes referred to as the capitalist system. A familiarity with the main features of a market system will greatly help you put the materials of this textbook in their proper perspective.

As you read this chapter, keep the following points in mind:

- **Key Concepts 4, 5,** and **6** are discussed.
- A market system does not arise automatically; it needs the proper institutions, such as private property.
- The driving force of the market system is "self-interest," not to be confused with selfishness. In a world of limited resources in relation to wants, competition follows automatically. In competing for the available resources, all participants in a market system—businesses and households—try to do the best they can for themselves.
- The distinguishing characteristics of the market system are **a** autonomous decision making by each participant, and **b** spontaneous coordination of production and consumption. ■

## THE MARKET SYSTEM

Let's begin by examining in some detail the basic tenets that define the market system of capitalism: (1) private property, (2) freedom of enterprise and choice, (3) self-interest as the dominant motive, (4) competition, (5) reliance on self-regulating markets, and (6) a limited role for government.

### Private Property

In a pure market system, property resources (land, capital) are usually owned by private individuals and firms, not by government. In fact, the private ownership of capital is what gives capitalism its name. This right of **private property**, coupled with the freedom to negotiate binding legal contracts, allows private persons or businesses to obtain, control, employ, and dispose of property resources as they see fit. The right to bequeath—the right of a property owner to designate who receives his or her property at the time of death—sustains the institution of private property.

Property rights are important because they encourage investment, innovation, exchange, and economic growth. Why would anyone stock a store, construct a factory, or clear land for farming if someone else, including government, could take that property for his or her own benefit?

Property rights also apply to intellectual property via patents and copyrights. These long-term protections encourage people to write books, music, and computer programs and to invent new products and production processes without fear that others will steal them and the rewards they may bring.

Another important role of property rights is that they facilitate exchange. A title to an automobile or deed to a cattle ranch assures the buyer that the seller is the legitimate owner. Finally, with property rights, people can spend their time, energy, and resources producing more goods and services, rather than using them to protect and retain the property they have already produced and acquired.

There are broad legal limits to this right of private ownership. For example, the use of private property to produce illegal drugs is prohibited. And even in pure capitalism, government ownership of certain property resources may be essential to produce "public goods": national defence, basic education, and courtrooms and prisons, for instance.

### Freedom of Enterprise and Choice

Closely related to private ownership of property is freedom of enterprise and choice. Capitalism requires that economic units make choices, which are expressed and implemented through the free markets of the economy.

**Freedom of enterprise** means that private businesses are free to obtain economic resources, to organize those resources in the production of goods and services of the firm's own choosing, and to sell them in the markets of their choice. In pure capitalism no artificial obstacles or restrictions imposed by government or other producers block an entrepreneur's decision to enter or leave a particular industry.

**Freedom of choice** means that owners can employ or dispose of their property and money as they see fit. It also means that workers are free to enter any lines of work for which they are qualified. Finally, it means that consumers are at liberty, within the limits of their incomes, to buy that collection of goods and services that best satisfies their wants.

Freedom of *consumer* choice in a capitalist economy is perhaps the most profound of these freedoms. The consumer is in a particularly strategic position; in a sense, the consumer is sovereign. Consumers ultimately decide via their choices what the market economy should produce. Businesses and resource suppliers then make their free choices within these constraints. They are not really "free" to produce goods and services consumers do not desire because producing such items would be unprofitable.

Again, all these choices are free only within broad legal limitations. Illegal choices are punished through fines and imprisonment. (The degree of economic freedom varies greatly from nation to nation, as indicated in Global Perspective 3-1.)

### 3-1 GLOBAL PERSPECTIVE

**Index of economic freedom, selected nations**

The Index of Economic Freedom measures economic freedom using 10 broad categories such as trade policy, property rights, and government intervention—with more than 50 specific economic criteria in each category. It then ranks 150 nations as to degree of economic freedom. Below are selected rankings for 1997.

FREE
1 Hong Kong
4 New Zealand
5 United States
MOSTLY FREE
11 Japan
15 Canada
20 Germany
MOSTLY UNFREE
78 Colombia
85 Poland
94 Brazil
REPRESSED
133 Haiti
143 Iran
148 Cuba


*Source:* Heritage Foundation and *Wall Street Journal*.

## Self-Interest

The primary driving force of capitalism is **self-interest**. Each economic unit strives to do what is best for itself. Entrepreneurs aim to maximize their firm's profit or, in adverse circumstances, minimize losses. Property owners attempt to get the highest price for the sale or rent of their resources. Workers attempt to maximize their satisfaction by finding jobs that offer the best combination of wages, fringe benefits, and working conditions. Consumers, in purchasing a specific product, seek to obtain it at the lowest possible price. Consumers also apportion their expenditures to maximize their satisfaction. In brief, capitalism presumes self-interest as the *modus operandi* for the various economic units as they express their free choices. The motive of self-interest gives direction and consistency to what might otherwise be an extremely chaotic economy.

Pursuit of self-interest should not be confused with selfishness. A stockholder may invest to receive the best available corporate dividends but then donate much of it to the United Way or give it to grandchildren. A worker may take a second job to help pay college or university tuition for her or his children. An entrepreneur may make a fortune and donate much of it to a charitable foundation.

## Competition

Freedom of choice exercised in promotion of one's own monetary returns is the basis for competition. In its pure form, **competition** requires:

1. Large numbers of independently acting buyers and sellers operating in the market for any particular product or resource.
2. Freedom of buyers and sellers to enter or leave any particular market, based on their economic self-interest.

**Large Numbers** The essence of competition is the widespread diffusion of economic power within the two major aggregates—businesses and households—that make up the economy. When many buyers and many sellers are in a particular market, no one buyer or seller is able to demand or supply a quantity of the product sufficiently large to affect its price. Let's examine this statement in terms of the supply side of the product market.

When a product becomes unusually scarce, its price rises. An unseasonable frost in Florida may seriously reduce the supply of citrus crops and sharply increase the price of oranges. Similarly, if a single producer or a small group of producers acting together can somehow restrict the total output of a product, then it can raise the price to the seller's advantage. By controlling supply, a firm can "rig the market" on its own behalf. In its purest form, competition means there are so many independently acting firms that each has virtually no influence over the market supply or, therefore, over price *because it is contributing an almost negligible fraction of the total output.*

Suppose there are 10,000 farmers, each producing and selling 100 bushels of corn in the Winnipeg grain market when the price of corn is $4 per bushel. Could a single farmer who is dissatisfied with that price cause an artificial scarcity of corn to boost the price above $4? The answer is no. Even if Farmer Jones withheld his output completely, he would reduce the total amount supplied only from 1,000,000 to 999,900 bushels. This is not much of a shortage! Supply would be virtually unchanged, and the $4 price would persist.

Competition means that each seller is providing a minuscule amount of the market supply. Individual sellers can make no noticeable impact on total output; thus a seller cannot as an individual producer manipulate product price, which is why economists say that an individual competitive seller is "at the mercy of the market."

The same reasoning applies to the demand side of the market. Buyers are plentiful and act independently. Thus single buyers cannot manipulate the market to their advantage by refusing to buy at the market price.

*The widespread diffusion of economic power underlying competition controls the use and limits the potential abuse of that power.* A producer charging more than the equilibrium price will lose sales to other producers. An employer paying less than the equilibrium wage rate will lose workers to other employers. Competition is the basic regulatory force in a market economy.

**Easy Entry and Exit** Competition also implies that it is simple for producers to enter or leave an industry; there are no artificial barriers to the expansion or contraction of specific industries. This freedom of an industry to expand or contract provides a competitive economy with the flexibility needed to remain efficient over time. Freedom of entry and exit allows the economy to adjust to changes in consumer tastes, technology, and resource availability.

## Markets and Prices

The basic coordinating mechanism of a capitalist economy is the market system. Without a market economy, there is no capitalism. Decisions made by buyers and sellers of products and resources become effective through a system of markets. A market is a mechanism or arrangement that brings buyers (demanders) and sellers (suppliers) into contact with one another. The preferences of sellers and buyers are registered on the supply and demand sides of various markets, and the outcome of these choices is a set of product and resource prices. These prices are guideposts on which resource owners, entrepreneurs, and consumers make and revise their free choices as they pursue their self-interests.

Just as competition is the controlling mechanism, so a system of markets and prices is the basic organizing force. The market system is an elaborate communication system through which innumerable individual free choices are recorded, summarized, and balanced against one another. Those who obey the dictates of the market system are rewarded; those who ignore them are penalized by the system. Through this communication system, society decides what the economy should produce, how production can be efficiently organized, and how the fruits of productive effort are distributed among the individual economic units that make up capitalism.

Not only is the market system the mechanism through which society decides how it allocates its resources and distributes the resulting output, but it is through the market system that these decisions are carried out.

## Limited Government

A competitive market economy promotes a high degree of efficiency in the use of its resources. There is little need for governmental intervention in the operation of such an economy beyond its role of imposing broad legal limits on the exercise of individual choices and the use of private property. The concept of pure capitalism as a self-regulating and self-adjusting economy precludes any extensive economic role for government. However, as you will find in Chapter 5, a number of limitations and potentially undesirable outcomes associated with the market system have resulted in active government participation in the economy.

**3-1**

**QUICK REVIEW**

- Pure capitalism rests on the private ownership of property and freedom of enterprise and choice.
- Pure capitalism permits economic entities—businesses, resource suppliers, and consumers—to pursue and further their own self-interests. Competition prevents any single economic entity from dictating product or resource prices.
- The coordinating mechanism of capitalism is a system of markets and prices.
- The efficient operation of the pure market system allegedly makes significant government intervention unnecessary.

# OTHER CHARACTERISTICS

Private property, freedom of enterprise and choice, self-interest as a motivating force, competition, and reliance on a market system are more or less exclusively associated with a pure market system.

But there are certain institutions and practices that are characteristic of all modern economies, including those with much central command: (1) the use of advanced technology and large amounts of capital goods, (2) specialization, and (3) the use of money. Advanced technology and specialization are prerequisites to efficient employment of an economy's resources. The use of money helps society specialize and use advanced technology.

## Extensive Use of Technology and Capital Goods

All advanced industrial economies are based on state-of-the-art technology and the extensive use of capital goods. In a market economy the opportunity and motivation for technological advance are created by competition, freedom of choice, self-interest, and the fact that monetary rewards for new products or production techniques accrue directly to the innovator. Pure capitalism therefore encourages extensive use and rapid development of complex capital goods: tools, machinery, large-scale factories, and facilities for storage, communication, transportation, and marketing. In the command economy, in contrast, the motivation for technological advance is weak; it must come through the directive of the central plan.

Why are advanced technology and capital goods important? Because the most direct method of producing a product is usually the least efficient. The inefficiencies of direct production can be avoided through **roundabout production**—the construction and use of capital to aid in the production of consumer goods. It would be ridiculous for a farmer to go at production with bare hands. There are huge benefits in the form of more efficient production and, therefore, a more abundant output, from creating tools of production (capital equipment) and using them in the production process. The farmer's output will increase with the use of a plough, a tractor, storage bins, and so on. There is a better way for the farmer to get water out of a well than to dive in after it!

But there is a hitch. Recall the main message of the production possibilities curve: For an economy operating on its production possibilities curve, resources used to produce capital goods must be diverted from the production of consumer goods. Society must sacrifice some consumer goods today to produce the capital goods that will give it more consumer goods tomorrow. Greater abundance tomorrow requires sacrifices today. ***(Key Question 2)***

## Specialization 

The extent to which society relies on **specialization** is astounding. The majority of consumers produce virtually none of the goods and services they consume, and they consume little or nothing of what they produce. The worker who spends most of a lifetime machining parts for marine engines may never "consume" an ocean cruise. The worker who devotes eight hours a day to installing windows in Fords may own a Honda. Few households seriously consider producing their own food, shelter, and clothing. Many farmers sell their milk to the local dairy and then buy margarine at the local general store. Society learned long ago that self-sufficiency breeds inefficiency. The jack-of-all-trades may be a very colourful individual but is certainly not efficient.

### Division of Labour

In what ways does human specialization—called the **division of labour**—enhance a society's output?

1. **MAKES USE OF ABILITY DIFFERENCES** Specialization enables individuals to take advantage of existing differences in their abilities and skills. If caveman A is strong, swift, and accurate with a spear, and caveman B is weak and slow but patient, their distribution of talents can be most efficiently used if A hunts and B fishes.

2. **ALLOWS LEARNING BY DOING** Even if the abilities of A and B are identical, specialization may be advantageous. By devoting all your time to a single task, you are more likely to develop the appropriate skills and to discover improved techniques than by apportioning your time among a number of diverse tasks. You learn to be a good hunter by hunting!

3. **SAVES TIME** Specialization—devoting all one's time to, say, a single task—avoids the loss of time involved in shifting from one job to another.

   For all these reasons the division of labour results in greater total output from society's limited human resources.

### Geographic Specialization

Specialization also works on a regional and international basis. Apples could be grown in Saskatchewan, but because of the unsuitability of the land, rainfall, and temperature, the costs would be very high. British Columbia could achieve some success in the production of wheat, but for similar reasons such production would be costly. That's why the farmers of Saskatchewan produce those products—wheat in particular—for which their resources are best adapted, and British Columbians (in the Okanagan valley) produce apples. In specializing, both produce more than is needed locally. Then, very sensibly, they swap some of their surpluses—wheat for apples. Specialization thus enables each area to make the goods it can most efficiently produce and it permits both to enjoy a larger amount of all goods than would otherwise be available.

Similarly, on an international basis Canada specializes in such items as telecommunication equipment and small commercial aircraft that it sells abroad in exchange for video recorders from Japan, bananas from Honduras, and woven baskets from Thailand. Both human specialization and geographical specialization are essential in achieving efficiency in the use of resources.

## Use of Money

Virtually all economies, advanced or primitive, use money. Money performs several functions, but first and foremost it is a **medium of exchange**; it makes trade easier.

In our example, Saskatchewan must exchange wheat for British Columbia's apples if both provinces are to share in the benefits of specialization. If trade were highly inconvenient or prohibited for some reason, the gains from their specialization would be lost. Saskatchewan and British Columbia would then be forced to be more self-sufficient—to produce both wheat and apples and whatever else their consumers desire. *A convenient means of exchanging goods is a prerequisite of specialization.*

Exchange can, and sometimes does, occur on the basis of **barter**, that is, swapping goods for goods, say, wheat for apples. But barter can pose serious problems for the economy because it requires a *coincidence of wants* between the two transactors. In our example, we assumed that Saskatchewan had excess wheat to trade and wanted apples. And we assumed British Columbia had excess apples to swap and wanted wheat. So exchange occurred. But if this coincidence of wants does not exist, trade is stymied.

Suppose Saskatchewan does not want any of B.C.'s apples but is interested in buying potatoes from Prince Edward Island. Ironically, Prince Edward Island wants B.C.'s apples but not Saskatchewan's wheat. And, to complicate matters, suppose that British Columbia wants some of Saskatchewan's wheat but none of Prince Edward Island's potatoes. The situation is summarized in Figure 3-1.

In no case do we find a coincidence of wants. Trade by barter clearly would be difficult. To overcome such a stalemate, economies use **money**, which is simply a convenient social invention to facilitate exchanges of goods and services. Historically, cattle, cigarettes, shells, stones, pieces of metal, and many other commodities have been used, with varying degrees of success, as a medium for facilitating exchange. But to be money, an item needs to pass only one test: *It must be generally acceptable to sellers in exchange for goods and services.* Money is socially defined; whatever society accepts as a medium of exchange *is* money.

Most economies use pieces of paper as money. This is true with the Saskatchewan–B.C.–P.E.I. economy; they use dollars as money. The use of dollars as a medium of exchange allows them to overcome their trade stalemate, as demonstrated in Figure 3-1.

**FIGURE 3-1 Money facilitates trade where wants do not coincide**

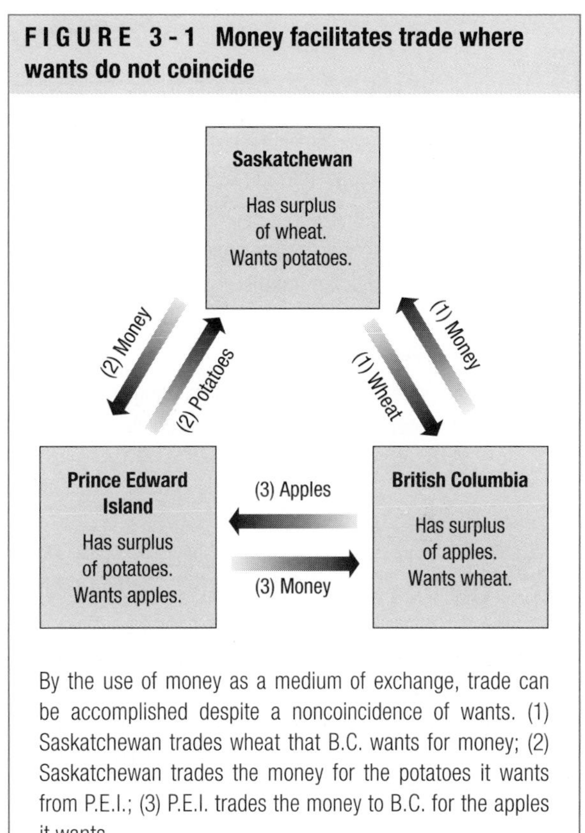


By the use of money as a medium of exchange, trade can be accomplished despite a noncoincidence of wants. (1) Saskatchewan trades wheat that B.C. wants for money; (2) Saskatchewan trades the money for the potatoes it wants from P.E.I.; (3) P.E.I. trades the money to B.C. for the apples it wants.

Specifically:

1. British Columbia exchanges money for some of Saskatchewan's wheat.
2. Saskatchewan exchanges the money earned from the sale of wheat for some of Prince Edward Island's potatoes.
3. Prince Edward Island then exchanges the money received from the sale of potatoes for some of B.C.'s surplus apples.

The willingness to accept paper money (or any other kind of money) as a medium of exchange has permitted a three-way trade that allows each province to specialize in one product and obtain the other product(s) its residents desire, despite the absence of a coincidence of wants between any two of the parties. Barter, resting as it does on a coincidence of wants, would not have permitted this exchange and so would not have allowed the three provinces to specialize. The efficiencies of specialization would then have been lost to those provinces.

On a global basis the fact that different nations have different currencies complicates international specialization and exchange. However, foreign exchange markets permit Canadians, Japanese, Germans, Britons, and Mexicans to exchange dollars, yen, marks, pounds, and pesos for one another to complete international exchanges of goods and services.

A final example: Imagine an Oshawa, Ontario, labourer producing crankshafts for Oldsmobiles. At the end of the week, instead of receiving a piece of paper endorsed by the company comptroller, or a few pieces of the paper we widely accept as money, the worker receives from the company paymaster four Oldsmobile crankshafts. With no desire to hoard crankshafts, the worker ventures into the Oshawa business district to spend this income on a bag of groceries, a pair of jeans, and a movie. Obviously, the worker is faced with some inconvenient and time-consuming trading, and may not be able to negotiate any exchanges at all. Finding a clothier with jeans who happens to be in the market for an Oldsmobile crankshaft can be a formidable task. And if the jeans do not trade evenly for crankshafts, how do the transactors "make change"? It is fair to say that money is one of the great social inventions of civilization.

**3-2**

**QUICK REVIEW**

- Advanced economies achieve greater efficiency in production through the use of large quantities of technologically advanced capital goods.
- Specialization enhances efficiency by allowing individuals, regions, and nations to produce those goods and services for which their resources are best suited.
- The use of money facilitates the exchange of goods and services, which specialization requires.

## THE COMPETITIVE MARKET SYSTEM

There are two primary *decision makers* in a market economy: **households** (consumers) and **firms** (businesses). Households are the ultimate suppliers of all economic resources and simultaneously the major spending group in the economy. Firms provide goods and services to the economy.

Consumers are at liberty to buy what they choose; firms to produce and sell what they choose; and resource suppliers to make their resources available in whatever endeavours or occupations they choose. We may wonder why such an economy does not collapse in chaos. If consumers want breakfast cereal, businesses choose to produce aerobic shoes, and resource suppliers want to offer their services in manufacturing computer software, production would be deadlocked because of the apparent inconsistency of these free choices.

In reality, the millions of decisions made by households and firms are highly consistent. Firms *do* produce those particular goods and services that consumers want. Households *do* provide the kinds of labour that businesses want to hire. What we want to explain is how a competitive market system constitutes a coordinating mechanism that overcomes the potential chaos of freedom of enterprise and choice. The competitive market system is a mechanism both for communicating the decisions of consumers, producers, and resource suppliers to one another and for synchronizing those decisions towards consistent production objectives.

## THE FIVE FUNDAMENTAL QUESTIONS

To understand the operation of a market economy, we must first recognize that every economy must respond to these **Five Fundamental Questions**:

1. *How much of a society's resources should be used?* What total amount of available resources should be used in producing goods and services?
2. *What is to be produced?* What collection of goods and services will best satisfy society's material wants?
3. *How is that output to be produced?* How should production be organized? What firms should do the producing, and what production techniques should they use?
4. *Who is to receive the output?* How should households share the output of the economy?
5. *Can the system adapt to change?* Can it adjust to changes in consumer wants, resource supplies, and technology?

The Five Fundamental Questions are merely an elaboration of the economic choices underlying Chapter 2's production possibilities curve. These questions would be irrelevant were it not for the economizing problem: scarce resources in a world of unlimited wants.

## THE MARKET SYSTEM AT WORK

Chapter 2's circular flow diagram (Figure 2-6) provides the setting for our discussion.

### What Is To Be Produced?

With product and resource prices established by competing buyers and sellers in both the product and resource markets, how would a market economy decide the types and quantities of goods to be produced? Since businesses seek profits and want to avoid losses, we can generalize that those goods and services that can be produced at a profit will be produced and those whose production leads to a loss will not. Those industries that are profitable usually expand, those that incur losses usually contract.

Consumers register their preferences on the demand side of the product market; producers and resource suppliers respond appropriately in seeking to further their own self-interests. The market system communicates the wants of consumers to businesses and resource suppliers and elicits appropriate responses.

### Organizing Production

How is production to be organized in a market economy? This Fundamental Question is composed of three subquestions:

1. How should resources be allocated among specific industries?
2. What specific firms should do the producing in each industry?
3. What combinations of resources—what technology—should each firm employ?

The market system steers resources to those industries whose products consumers want—simply because those industries survive, are profitable, and pay for resources. It simultaneously deprives unwanted industries of profits and hence of scarce resources.

The second and third subquestions are closely intertwined. In a competitive market economy, the firms that survive to do the producing are the ones willing and able to employ the most economically efficient technique of production. And the most efficient technique depends on:

1. The available technology, that is, the alternative combinations of resources that will produce the desired results
2. The prices of the needed resources.

### Distributing Total Output

The market system enters the picture in two ways in solving the problem of distributing total output. Generally, any specific product will be distributed to consumers on the basis of their ability and willingness to pay the existing market price for it. If the price of some product, say, a pocket calculator, is $15, then those buyers who are able and willing to pay that price will get a pocket calculator; those who are not, will not. This is the rationing function of equilibrium prices.

The sizes of consumers' money incomes determines their ability to pay the equilibrium prices for pocket calculators and other products. And consumers' money incomes depend on the quantities of the various property and human resources they supply and on the prices in the resource market. Resource prices are key in determining the size of each household's claim against the total output of society. Within the limits of a consumer's money income, however, it is a person's willingness to pay the equilibrium price for a pocket calculator that determines whether a unit of this product is distributed to her or him. And this willingness to buy the calculator depends on that consumer's preference for it compared with other available products and their relative prices. Thus, product price is not only key in determining how output is distributed, it also is central in determining the spending patterns of consumers.

There is nothing particularly ethical about the market system as a mechanism for distributing output. Households that accumulate large amounts of property resources by inheritance, through hard work and frugality, through business acumen, or by illegal activities will receive large incomes and thus command large shares of the economy's total output. Others, offering unskilled and relatively unproductive labour resources that elicit low wages, will receive meagre money incomes and small portions of total output.

### Accommodating Change

Industrial societies are dynamic: Consumer preferences, technology, and supplies of resources all change. This means that the particular allocation of resources that is *now* the most efficient for a *specific* pattern of consumer tastes, for a *specific* range of technological alternatives, and for *specific* supplies of resources will become obsolete and inefficient as consumer preferences change, new techniques of production are discovered, and resource supplies change over time. The market economy adjusts to these changes so that resources are still used efficiently.

## COMPETITION AND THE "INVISIBLE HAND"

In capitalism the market system is the organizational mechanism, and competition is the mechanism of control. Supply and demand communicate the wants of consumers (society) to businesses and, through businesses, to resource suppliers. It is competition, however, that forces businesses and resource suppliers to make appropriate responses.

But competition does more than guarantee responses appropriate to the wishes of society. It also forces firms to adopt the most efficient production techniques, keeping costs and prices at their lowest levels. In a competitive market, more efficient firms will eventually eliminate a firm that fails to use the least-costly production technique. And competition provides an environment conducive to such technological advance.

In 1776 Adam Smith, in his book *The Wealth of Nations*, first noted that the operation of a competitive market system creates a curious and important unity between private and social interests. Firms and resource suppliers, seeking to further their own self-interests and operating within the framework of a highly competitive market system, will simultaneously, as though guided by an **invisible hand**, promote the public or social interest. For example, we have seen that in a competitive environment, businesses use the least-costly combination of resources to produce a specific output because it is in their private self-interests to do so. To act otherwise would be to forgo profit or even to risk business failure. But, at the same time, it is clearly also in the social interest to use scarce resources in the least-costly (most efficient) way.

It is self-interest, awakened and guided by the competitive market system, that induces responses appropriate to the change in society's wants. Businesses seeking to make higher profits and to avoid losses, and resource suppliers pursuing greater monetary awards, negotiate changes in the allocation of resources and end up with the output that society demands. The force of competition controls or guides self-interest in such a way that it automatically, and quite unintentionally, furthers the best interests of society. The "invisible hand" tells us that when firms maximize their profits, society's domestic output is also maximized.

The virtues of the market system are thus implicit in our discussion. Three merit emphasis:

1. **EFFICIENCY** The basic economic argument for the market system is that it promotes the efficient use of resources. The competitive market system guides resources into the production of those goods and services most wanted by society. It forces the use of the most efficient techniques in organizing resources for production, and it leads to the development and adoption of new and more efficient production techniques.
2. **INCENTIVES** The market system provides incentives for improvement and innovation. Greater work effort means higher money incomes that can be translated into a higher standard of living. Similarly, the assuming of risks by entrepreneurs can result in substantial profit incomes. Successful innovations may also generate economic rewards.
3. **FREEDOM** The major noneconomic argument for the market system is its great emphasis on personal freedom. In contrast to central planning, the market system can coordinate economic activity without coercion. The market system permits—indeed, it thrives on—freedom of enterprise and choice. Entrepreneurs and workers are not herded from industry to industry by government directives to meet production targets established by some governmental agency. On the contrary, they are free to further their own self-interest, subject to the rewards and penalties imposed by the market system itself. ***(Key Question 9)***

### 3-3 QUICK REVIEW

- The output mix of the market system is determined by profits, which in turn depend heavily on consumer preferences. Profits cause preferred, efficient industries to expand; losses cause inefficient industries to contract.
- Competition forces industries to use the least-costly (most efficient) production methods.
- Consumer incomes and product prices determine the distribution of output among households in a market economy.
- Competitive markets reallocate resources in response to changes in consumer tastes, technological advances, and changes in supplies of resources.
- The "invisible hand" of the market system channels the pursuit of self-interest to the good of society.

## THE STRUCTURE OF THE CANADIAN ECONOMY AND ITS EVOLUTION OVER TIME

Table 3-1 sets out the contribution to Canadian domestic output (GDP) by each sector and industry. The major sectors of any economy are **primary,**

**TABLE 3-1 Production shares by sector, selected years 1870-1997**

| | % OF GROSS DOMESTIC PRODUCT AT FACTOR COST | | | | | | | |
|---|---|---|---|---|---|---|---|---|
| | 1870 | 1911 | 1926 | 1960 | 1970 | 1980 | 1986 | 1997 |
| PRIMARY | 46.2 | 39.4 | 23.4 | 10.4 | 8.3 | 11.2 | 10.0 | 7.4 |
| Agriculture | 34.3 | 30.8 | 18.1 | 4.9 | 3.3 | 3.3 | 3.3 | 1.8 |
| Forestry* | 9.9 | 4.6 | 1.3 | 1.3 | 0.8 | 0.9 | 0.7 | 1.5 |
| Fishing and trapping | 1.1 | 1.5 | 0.8 | 0.2 | 0.2 | 0.2 | 0.2 | 0.1 |
| Mining, quarrying, oil wells | 0.9 | 2.5 | 3.2 | 4.0 | 4.0 | 6.8 | 5.8 | 4.0 |
| SECONDARY | 22.6 | 29.7 | 38.7 | 44.8 | 41.4 | 38.3 | 36.7 | 34.0 |
| Manufacturing | na | 18.8 | 21.7 | 26.4 | 23.3 | 20.6 | 19.5 | 17.2 |
| Construction | na | 10.3 | 4.1 | 6.0 | 6.3 | 5.9 | 7.0 | 5.4 |
| Transportation and communication | na | na | 12.9 (Transportation and communication; Electric power, gas, and water utilities combined) | 9.6 | 8.9 | 8.3 | 7.3 | 7.7 |
| Electric power, gas, and water utilities | na | 0.6 | | 2.8 | 2.9 | 3.5 | 2.9 | 3.7 |
| TERTIARY | 31.2[a] | 30.8[a] | 37.9 | 44.8 | 50.2 | 50.5 | 53.3 | 58.6 |
| Trade (wholesale, retail) | na | na | 11.6 | 12.8 | 12.4 | 11.0 | 11.7 | 11.2 |
| Finance, insurance, real estate | na | na | 10.0 | 11.6 | 11.3 | 11.3 | 14.1 | 16.1 |
| Public administration, defence | na | na | 3.4 | 6.9 | 7.3 | 7.4 | 7.2 | 6.2 |
| Service | na | na | 12.9 | 13.5 | 19.2 | 20.8 | 20.3 | 25.1 |
| Total | 100.0 | 100.0 | 100.0 | 100.0 | 100.0 | 100.0 | 100.0 | 100.0 |

[a] Includes income generated by the railway and telephone industries.
* Figure for Forestry calculated as a residual.
Source: Data for 1870 to 1986 from C. Green, *Canadian Industrial Organization and Policy* (Toronto: McGraw-Hill Ryerson Ltd., 1990), p. 4. Data for 1997 calculated from Statistics Canada, *Canadian Economic Observer*, Statistical Summary, July 1998.

**secondary,** and **tertiary** (which is more commonly referred to as the service sector). Table 3-1 also breaks each sector into sub-sectors or industries.

The service sector has come to dominate in terms of its contributing share to Canadian domestic output, followed by the secondary sector, in which manufacturing dominates. The primary sector has experienced an almost continuous decline in GDP share over the last century.

Table 3-2, which shows employment shares by each sector and industry, reflects contribution to domestic output. For example, agriculture's employment share fell from about a quarter of the workforce in 1947 to just over 3 percent in 1997. Manufacturing has also experienced a decline in employment share, but a much less steep decline. The service sector, on the other hand, has almost doubled its employment share of the economy.

We noted earlier in this chapter that industries expand and contract on their profitability. The inter-sectoral shifts are due to a number of factors, of which technological improvements and accompanying productivity increases are dominant. For example, while there has been a continuous decline in agriculture's employment share, it has come about because of large labour (and land) productivity improvements. A large improvement in labour productivity means fewer people are needed in that sector, unless there is an accompanying increase in the demand for foodstuffs. Since there is a limit to our capacity to increase our food intake, the excess labour had to find work elsewhere. Throughout the nineteenth and early twentieth centuries, excess agricultural workers found jobs in the secondary sector, primarily in manufacturing.

Since World War II, the secondary sector has been losing employment share as productivity in that sector rose. Manufacturing in particular has seen a significant drop in its employment share.

**TABLE 3-2 Employment shares (%) by economic sector and industry**

| | 1891[a] | 1921[a] | 1947 | 1960 | 1970 | 1980 | 1987 | 1997 |
|---|---|---|---|---|---|---|---|---|
| PRIMARY | 49 | 36 | 27.5 | 14.3 | 9.3 | 7.3 | 6.4 | 6.5 |
| Agriculture | | | 24.1 | 11.3 | 6.5 | 4.5 | 4.0 | 3.1 |
| Forestry | | | 1.2 | 1.1 | 0.9 | 0.7 | 0.6 | 2.1 (Forestry, Fishing and trapping combined) |
| Fishing and trapping | | | 0.7 | 0.4 | 0.3 | 0.3 | 0.3 | |
| Mining, quarrying, oil wells | | | 1.5 | 1.5 | 1.6 | 1.8 | 1.5 | 1.3 |
| SECONDARY | 31 | 34 | 40.3 | 40.7 | 37.5 | 34.0 | 30.4 | 29.1 |
| Manufacturing | | | 26.7 | 24.9 | 22.7 | 19.7 | 17.1 | 16.0 |
| Construction | | | 5.2 | 7.2 | 6.0 | 5.8 | 5.7 | 5.5 |
| Transportation and communication | | | 7.7 | 7.5 | 7.7 | 7.3 | 6.6 | 7.6 (Transportation and communication, Public utilities combined) |
| Public utilities | | | 0.7 | 1.1 | 1.1 | 1.2 | 1.0 | |
| TERTIARY | 20 | 30 | 32.1 | 45.0 | 53.2 | 58.7 | 63.2 | 64.4 |
| Trade (wholesale, retail) | | | 12.3 | 16.2 | 16.7 | 17.2 | 17.7 | 17.6 |
| Finance, insurance, real estate | | | 2.7 | 3.8 | 4.6 | 5.7 | 5.8 | 5.9 |
| Community, business, personal services (including health, education) | | | 17.1 (Community services and Public administration combined) | 25.0 (Community services and Public administration combined) | 25.7 | 28.9 | 32.9 | 35.1 |
| Public administration | | | | | 6.2 | 6.9 | 6.8 | 5.8 |
| Total | 100.0 | 100.0 | 100.0 | 100.0 | 100.0 | 100.0 | 100.0 | 100.0 |

[a] Based on occupational data in which all clerical workers are allocated to the tertiary sector and all nonprimary sector labourers are allocated to the secondary sector.
Source: Data for 1891 to 1987 from C. Green, *op. cit.* (Toronto: McGraw-Hill Ryerson Ltd., 1990), p. 6. Data for 1997 calculated from Statistics Canada, *Canadian Economic Observer*, Statistical Summary, July 1998.

Table 3-1 shows manufacturing's GDP share dropped from a high of 26 percent in 1960, to just over 17 percent by 1997. Table 3-2 shows the employment share of manufacturing has fallen steadily since 1945 from over a quarter of the Canadian labour force to 16 percent in the late 1990s.

While it is true that natural resources are important to Canada's economy, the output and employment share of the primary sector continues to fall. Only the mining, quarrying, and oil wells category has maintained a relatively steady employment share, but a decreasing GDP share.

There is good evidence to suggest that some Canadian industries are highly concentrated in their market power. More will be said about this topic in Chapter 14. For now it will suffice to say that compared with the U.S. economy, many of our industries are dominated by a few firms that control a significant percentage of the market.

## Foreign Ownership

Another distinguishing characteristic of the Canadian economy is that a high percentage is **foreign owned**, particularly by Americans. The term "foreign owned" generally means outright ownership of a firm or at least owning 51 percent of the stocks, which means control of a firm.

Foreign ownership has costs and benefits. These have been extensively debated. Given the difficulties of measuring costs and benefits, it is not surprising that the issue of foreign ownership often arouses strong emotions. Perhaps the most serious accusation against foreign ownership is that it jeopardizes Canada's political autonomy. However, such an accusation is difficult to prove or disprove.

There are various explanations of the high incidence of foreign direct investment in Canada. Some attribute it to the relatively high Canadian tariffs instituted with the implementation of the National Policy in 1879. Since foreign firms, particularly American firms, couldn't compete by exporting here, they established production facilities. Our patent laws in the past, which allowed no protection to their foreign owner, also helped to stimulate foreign ownership as firms not wanting to have their technologies imitated quickly established themselves in Canada. Our country's proximity to the United States also has stimulated foreign ownership, as American firms often viewed Canada as an extension of their domestic market.

All these explanations have some merit. However, all that can be said with certainty is that if foreign firms decided to establish productive capacities in Canada, it must have been because it was the most profitable alternative.

## In The Media

# Rush for riches in Temagami

Prospectors raced across wild terrain yesterday, hoping for a toehold on mineral wealth as they staked claims in a vast region of northeastern Ontario

By Patrick Brethour
The Globe and Mail
Shining Tree, Ont.

It was a race for gold—or copper, or zinc or diamonds—Christmas and the Olympics rolled into 15 adrenalin-packed minutes.

Except that these sprints were run across slippery forest floors, through bogs and across lakes. And many of the racers carried axes, using them to notch trees and mark the line of their claims.

One of them, red-faced and wheezing, scrambled south through the bush toward Mitch Lavery—who greeted him with a grin.

The axe-carrying runner had just secured a mining claim for Strike Minerals Inc., which came out of yesterday's giant staking rush in the Temagami region of northeastern Ontario with 50 prime sites.

The rush may have been the province's largest ever, but the total number of claims staked won't be known for about a month. Earlier estimates put the number of prospectors at 600, and Strike Minerals alone spent $100,000 on its staking effort for the day.

However big it is, the rush is mining history in the making, said Mr. Lavery, vice-president of the Kirkland Lake, Ont., company. "This is a very unique situation that we won't ever likely see again."

Strike Minerals' red-faced runner was just one of the hundreds who swarmed over the vast tract that was opened up for staking after a 23-year land freeze.

Ontario's Progressive Conservative government, aiming to bring more economic development to the rural region, decided in June to allow mining and expanded logging.

The decision has elicited controversy as the area is also famed for its old-growth pines. Environmental groups did not disrupt the staking rush, but several people were arrested this week in protests against logging.

Still, environmentalists will target mining companies if large-scale exploration or exploitation occur, said Tim Gray, executive director of the Toronto-based Wildlands League. "We'll be there to make sure [big-scale mining is] not a good investment or a good business decision," he said on Sunday after an information session for prospectors in the town of Temagami before the rush.

The 617,500 hectares in 103 townships is the largest area in Ontario ever made available at one time for staking.

Mr. Lavery said he hopes Strike Minerals' sites—in Tyrell and Knight townships, about 120 kilometres northwest of Temagami—contain gold deposits that the junior gold explorer can exploit with the help of larger mining outfits.

For the prospectors—some working for themselves, some for industry giants—the rush is the chance of a lifetime. "There's no 10 per cent or anything else," Mr. Lavery said. "It's all or nothing."

The race for riches began yesterday at 9 a.m. Fifteen minutes later, winners were celebrating.

In between, the prospectors, including high-school track runners hired by the mining companies, raced around the 1.6-kilometre perimeter of each claim. One runner said he was being paid $100 a day and expenses plus a $100 bonus for each claim successfully staked.

To stake a claim, runners had to erect posts at the four corners of the claim, starting at the northeast and proceeding counterclockwise. Along the way, slipping across forest floors and through bogs, they had to mark trees with axes and inscribe the stakes to identify the claim.

As helicopters buzzed overhead just before the start, 18-year-old Derek Didyk braced himself for his run around a claim just off of Highway 560, in the northwestern tip of the staking area.

The terrain "is worse than I've ever seen it," Mr. Didyk said. He runs the 1,500-metre track event at his high school near Timmins, Ont.

Asked about the writing scrawled on his forearm and shirt, he explained that it was the information he would need to mark the posts of the claim. "You get the adrenalin pumping and you don't want to forget," he said.

At 9 a.m., he erected the first corner post and then ran off to the south, trailed by a second man who helped to notch trees.

Three minutes later, the red-faced runner from the claim to the north puffed his way to the corner post.

At 9:14, Mr. Didyk was back, muddy, huffing and jubilant, along with Mr. Lavery and the rest of the Strike Minerals prospectors.

Unexpectedly for the Strike Minerals crew, there was no competition for the four adjacent claims.

A few kilometres south, other Strike Minerals prospectors beat out teams from larger mining outfits for several hotly contested spots, pushing the company's total claims for the day to 50.

Sitting the night before in the crowded Lakeview Motel & Restaurant in Gowganda, a hamlet about 100 kilometres northwest of Temagami, Mr. Lavery explained the appeal of staking, which has changed little in the last 100 years.

"It is the last way the little guy can get a toehold onto the exploration business," he said, speaking over loud country music and louder strings of expletives. "It doesn't matter if you're big or small, everyone's on the same level playing field."

For Monday night at least, the more than 150 prospectors gathered at the Lakeview motel were anything but competitive as they recounted takes of past rushes —and the fervent hope that the Temagami one would be the richest.

Motel owners Erich and Inge Knies struck rich days before the rush. The couple, who have operated the Lakeview for 18 years, said they've never had a busier day than Monday.

They normally have room for 80 guests, and temporary quarters had to be set up in an elementary school.

*Source: Globe and Mail*, September 18, 1996, p. B5. Reprinted with permission from the *Globe and Mail.*

## THE STORY IN BRIEF

Ontario's government decided to allow mining and expanded logging in rural regions after a 23-year freeze. Many prospectors rushed to the Temagami area to try to stake claims.

## THE ECONOMICS BEHIND THE STORY

- Self-regulating markets work on the basis of self-interest. But by pursuing one's own individual self-interest, one is also serving the interest of society.
- Prospectors rushed out to stake their claim in the hope of "striking it rich." But such claims would be worthless unless there are people who want the commodities. Thus by an "invisible hand" the prospectors are serving the needs of society.
- While markets bring the interests of the individual and society closer to each other, it does not bring together the interests of the individual and every other individual of which society is composed. Environmental groups protested the development of the region.
- What drives markets? Explain in terms of producers and consumers. ■

## The Last Word

6 KEY CONCEPT

### THE MAGIC OF THE MARKET

MOST PEOPLE FIND IT HARD TO BELIEVE THAT self-regulating markets provide most of the goods and services we purchase every day. Our minds seem to be wired to believe that some authority is coordinating output and consumption. In a market economy, consumers are not forced to buy any particular product or service. Certainly, most producers are not told by anyone what to produce and in what quantities. By an "invisible hand" producers of goods and services come up with what consumers want.

Markets coordinate the decisions of consumer and producers. The signals used are prices. Consumers are constantly looking for lower prices, while producers hope for higher prices to add to their profit. Through the decisions of many buyers and sellers, a "market price" is arrived at. Some prices, such as those of stocks, can change every minute, while others, such as housing prices, change a lot less often.

One of the amazing attributes of the market is that it brings closer together the interest of the individual and the interest of other members of a society. The baker may bake bread to sell at a profit, but in doing so she is providing fellow citizens with bread that would not otherwise have been made available.

Prices transmit information about relative scarcities. If the price of wheat flour skyrockets, the baker will likely use less of it and more of a less costly flour. Consumers respond to higher prices of wheat flour by buying less wheat bread, and more of a less expensive bread, say rye.

The market system facilitates specialization and trade. Each person can specialize in producing a good and service and exchange some of it for other goods and service he or she needs. You may have a job selling popcorn at the local movie theatre. You then use your earnings to exchange for other goods and services, say a CD or music lessons. In a mature market economy, we often exchange with persons we do not know. You may travel to another country and rent a car from a complete stranger, except that the person happens to work for one of the large international car rental companies.

While it can appear a very complex system, the market is simply an institution through which individuals exchange the things each produces in return for goods and services that are desired. The complexity arises because there are billions of people engaged in exchange, each individual representing an extremely small part of the whole market system.

Not everyone finds the market a "magical" institution. Self-regulating markets can bring about an "unfair" distribution of income. Critics argue that one individual may become fabulously rich, such as Bill Gates of Microsoft, while others beg on street corners. Defenders of the market system point out that in the western industrialized nations where self-regulating markets dominate, most individuals are neither fabulously rich nor dirt poor, and the average person is materially much better off than citizens in countries with alternative economic systems.

Market economies need a central government to provide the institutional background for self-regulating markets to function efficiently. In the next chapter we will see that self-regulating markets do not work where collective decisions have to be made about providing certain goods and services, such as roads and airports, that no private company would find profitable to produce. ■

## CHAPTER SUMMARY

1. The capitalist, or market, system is characterized by private ownership of resources, including capital, and the freedom of individuals to engage in economic activities of their choice to advance their own material well-being. Self-interest is the driving force of such an economy, and competition functions as a regulatory or control mechanism.

2. In the capitalist system, markets and prices organize and make effective the many millions of individual decisions that determine what is produced, the methods of production, and the sharing of output. The pure market system assumes government plays a minor and relatively passive economic role.

3. Specialization and an advanced technology based on the extensive use of capital goods are common to all advanced industrial economies.

4. Functioning as a medium of exchange, money circumvents problems of bartering and thus permits easy trade and greater specialization, both domestically and internationally.

5. Every economy faces Five Fundamental Questions: **a** How much of available resources should be employed to produce goods? **b** What goods and services are to be produced? **c** How should they be produced? **d** To whom should the output be distributed? **e** Can the system adapt to changes in consumer tastes, resource supplies, and technology?

6. Consumer sovereignty means that both businesses and resource suppliers channel their efforts in accordance with the wants of consumers.

7. The competitive market system can communicate changes in consumer tastes to resource suppliers and entrepreneurs, prompting appropriate adjustments in the allocation of the economy's resources. The competitive market system also provides an environment conducive to technological advance and capital accumulation.

8. Competition, the primary mechanism of control in the market economy, promotes a unity of private and social interests; as though directed by an "invisible hand," competition harnesses the self-interest motives of businesses and resource suppliers to simultaneously further the social interest in using scarce resources efficiently.

9. In terms of both employment share and contribution to domestic production, the service sector dominates in the Canadian economy.

10. Compared to the U.S. economy, many of our industries are highly concentrated; a relatively few firms represent a high percentage of output and sales. A high proportion of our industries are foreign owned.

## TERMS AND CONCEPTS

private property
freedom of enterprise
freedom of choice
self-interest
competition
roundabout production
specialization
division of labour
medium of exchange
barter
money
households
firms
Five Fundamental Questions
invisible hand
primary, secondary, tertiary sectors
foreign owned

## STUDY QUESTIONS

1. Explain each of these statements:
   a. "Capitalism not only *accepts* self-interest as a fact of human existence; it *relies* on self-interest to achieve society's material goals."
   b. "Where there is private property, property rights, and economic freedom, there will be capitalism; unlike the command economy, capitalism emerges spontaneously."

2. KEY QUESTION *What advantages result from "roundabout" production? What problem is involved in increasing a full-employment economy's stock of capital goods? Illustrate this problem using the production possibilities curve. Does an economy with unemployed resources face the same problem?*

3. What are the advantages of specialization in the use of human and material resources? Explain: "Exchange is the necessary consequence of specialization."

4. What problems does barter entail? Indicate the economic significance of money as a medium of exchange. "Money is the only commodity that is good for nothing but to be gotten rid of. It will not feed you, clothe you, shelter you, or amuse you unless you spend or invest it. It imparts value only in parting." Explain this statement.

5. Briefly describe how the market system answers the Fundamental Questions. Why must economic choices be made?

6. Evaluate and explain the following statements:
   - **a.** "The market system is a profit and loss economy."
   - **b.** "Competition is the indispensable disciplinarian of the market economy."
   - **c.** "Production methods that are inferior in the engineering sense may be the most efficient methods in the economic sense."

7. Explain the meaning and implications of the following quotation.

   > The beautiful consequence of the market is that it is its own guardian. If output prices or certain kinds of remuneration stray away from their socially ordained levels, forces are set into motion to bring them back to the fold. It is a curious paradox which thus ensues: the market, which is the acme of individual economic freedom, is the strictest taskmaster of all. One may appeal the ruling of a planning board or win the dispensation of a minister; but there is no appeal, no dispensation, from the anonymous pressures of the market mechanism. Economic freedom is thus more illusory than at first appears. One can do as one pleases in the market. But if one pleases to do what the market disapproves, the price of individual freedom is economic ruination.[1]

8. Suppose the demand for bagels dramatically rises while the demand for breakfast cereal plummets. Explain how the competitive market economy will make the needed adjustments to reestablish an efficient allocation of society's scarce resources.

9. KEY QUESTION *Some large hardware stores such as Canadian Tire boast of carrying as many as 20,000 different products in each store. What motivated the producers of these particular items—everything from screwdrivers to ladders to water heaters—to make them and offer them for sale? How did producers decide on the best combinations of resources to use? Who made these resources available, and why? Who decides whether these specific hardware products should continue to get produced and offered for sale?*

10. In a single sentence, describe the meaning of the phrase "invisible hand."

11. **(The Last Word)** Describe how the market brings together public and private interest.

12. WEB-BASED QUESTION **The United Nations' Virtual Marketplace** The United Nations urgento.gse.rmit.edu.au/untpdc/eto has set up an Electronic Trade Opportunity (ETO), a large-scale virtual marketplace for trade offers (ETOs) from around the world. ETOs are received by millions of companies every week in one of several electronic forms. How does this new virtual marketplace improve the efficient use of resources and increase the freedom of enterprise and choice? Does it increase competition? How does it help firms in developing countries? Why would the United Nations set up such a virtual marketplace?

13. WEB-BASED QUESTION **Barter and Revenue Canada** Bartering occurs when goods or services are exchanged without the exchange of money. For some, barter's popularity is that it enables them to avoid paying taxes to the government. How might such avoidance occur? Does Revenue Canada www.rc.gc.ca/E/pub/tp/it490et/it490e.txt.html treat barter as taxable or nontaxable income? How is the value of a barter transaction determined? What are some of Revenue Canada's barter examples? What does Revenue Canada require of so-called barter exchanges with regard to their members?

[1] Robert L. Heilbroner, *The Worldly Philosophers*, 3d ed. (New York: Simon & Schuster, Inc., 1967), p. 42.

CHAPTER 4

# Demand and Supply

ACCORDING TO AN OLD JOKE, IF YOU TEACH A parrot to say "Demand and supply," you have an economist. There is an element of truth in this quip. The tools of demand and supply can take us far in understanding not only specific economic issues but also how the entire economy works.

Our circular flow model in Chapter 2 identified the participants in the product and resource markets. There, we asserted that prices were determined by the "interaction" between demand and supply in these markets. In this chapter we examine that interaction in detail, explaining how prices and output quantities are determined.

**IN THIS CHAPTER YOU WILL LEARN:**

- What demand is and what factors affect it.
- What supply is and what factors affect it.
- How demand and supply together determine price and quantity bought and sold.
- How prices allocate scarce resources in a market economy.

## The Big Picture

IN A WORLD OF SCARCITY IN RELATION TO unlimited wants, there is constant competition for the available goods and services. The supply and demand curves represent the self-interest of the producers and consumers respectively. Firms are willing to supply more of a specific product at successively higher prices, but consumers actually want less at successively higher prices. What quantities of a particular good or service and at what price it is exchanged are determined by the interaction of these two opposing forces. The price mechanism is at the heart of the market system because prices adjust in response to choices made by consumers, suppliers, and other actors in the economy. Price changes mediate the effects of these various choices, leading to a more or less coherent allocation of resources in our society.

As you read this chapter, keep the following points in mind:

- **Key Concepts 4** and **6** are discussed.
- Think of the supply and demand curves as independent of each other. Each of these curves shifts for different reasons. Remember that suppliers of goods and services and the consumers have diverging interests.
- Make sure you understand the distinction between movement along the curves and shifts of the curves.
- The supply and demand curves shift only when certain conditions change. It is imperative that you learn the causes of the demand and supply curve shifts, reproduced in Tables 4-4 and 4-7.
- Supply and demand analysis can appear deceptively easy at first glance. Whenever applying supply and demand analysis, be sure to use graphs; trying to figure out a problem in your head can quickly lead to errors. Supply and demand analysis is mastered by getting "your hands dirty"; you need lots of practice applying it, and graphing is an important part. ■

## MARKETS

Recall from Chapter 2 that a **market** *is an institution or mechanism that brings together buyers ("demanders") and sellers ("suppliers") of particular goods, services, or resources.* Markets exist in many forms. The corner gas station, the fast-food outlet, the local music store, a farmer's roadside stand—all are familiar markets. The Toronto Stock Exchange and the Chicago Board of Trade are markets where buyers and sellers of stocks and bonds and farm commodities from all over the world communicate with one another and buy and sell. Auctioneers bring together potential buyers and sellers of art, livestock, used farm equipment, and, sometimes, real estate. The professional hockey player and his agent bargain with the owner of an NHL team. A graduating finance major interviews with the Royal Bank or the Canadian Imperial Bank of Commerce at the university placement office.

All these situations that link potential buyers with potential sellers are markets. As our examples imply, some markets are local, while others are national or international. Some are highly personal, involving face-to-face contact between demander and supplier; others are impersonal, with buyer and seller never seeing or knowing each other.

To keep things simple, this chapter focuses on markets made up of large numbers of independently acting buyers and sellers exchanging a standardized product. These are the highly competitive markets such as a central grain exchange, a stock market, or a market for foreign currencies in which the equilibrium price is "discovered" by the interacting decisions of buyers and sellers. They are *not* the markets in which one or a handful of producers "set" prices, such as the markets for commercial airplanes or greeting cards.

## DEMAND

**Demand** *is a schedule or a curve showing the various amounts of a product consumers are willing and able to purchase at each of a series of possible prices during a* *specified period of time.*[1] Demand, therefore, shows the quantities of a product that will be purchased at various possible prices, *other things equal.* Demand can easily be shown in table form. Table 4-1 is a hypothetical **demand schedule** for a single consumer purchasing bushels of corn.

The portrayal of demand in Table 4-1 reflects the relationship between the possible prices of corn and the quantity of corn the consumer would be willing and able to purchase at each of these prices. We say willing and *able*, because willingness alone is not effective in the market. You may be willing to buy a Porsche, but if this willingness is not backed by the necessary dollars, it will not be effective and, therefore, not be reflected in the market. In Table 4-1, if the price of corn were $5 per bushel, our consumer would be willing and able to buy 10 bushels per week; if it were $4, the consumer would be willing and able to buy 20 bushels per week; and so forth.

The table showing demand does not tell us which of the five possible prices will actually exist in the corn market. This depends on demand *and supply*. Demand is simply a statement of a buyer's plans, or intentions, with respect to the purchase of a product.

To be meaningful, the quantities demanded at each price must relate to a specific period—a day, a week, a month. Saying "A consumer will buy 10 bushels of corn at $5 per bushel" is meaningless. Saying "A consumer will buy 10 bushels of corn *per week* at $5 per bushel" is clear and meaningful. Without a specific time period we would not know whether demand for a product was large or small.

## Law of Demand

A fundamental characteristic of demand is this: *All else equal, as price falls, the quantity demanded rises; and as price rises, the corresponding quantity demanded falls.* In short, there is a negative or *inverse* relationship between price and quantity demanded. Economists call this inverse relationship the **law of demand**.

The "other things equal" assumption is critical here. Many factors other than the price of the product being considered affect the amount purchased. The quantity of Nikes purchased will depend not

[1] This definition obviously is worded to apply to product markets. To adjust it to apply to resource markets, substitute the word "resource" for "product" and "businesses" for "consumers."

**TABLE 4-1 An individual buyer's demand for corn**

| Price per bushel | Quantity demanded per week |
|---|---|
| $5 | 10 |
| 4 | 20 |
| 3 | 35 |
| 2 | 55 |
| 1 | 80 |

only on the price of Nikes but also on the prices of such substitutes as Reeboks, Adidas, and Filas. The law of demand in this case says that fewer Nikes will be purchased if the price of Nikes rises *and the prices of Reeboks, Adidas, and Filas all remain constant*. In short, if the *relative price* of Nikes increases, fewer Nikes will be bought. However, if the price of Nikes and all other competing shoes increases by some amount—say, $5—consumers might buy more, less, or the same amount of Nikes.

What is the foundation for the law of demand? Why is it that as price falls, the quantity demanded of a good rises, and vice versa? There are several levels of analysis on which to argue the case. Let's look at two of them:

1. In any specific time period, each buyer of a product will derive less satisfaction (or benefit or utility) from each successive unit of the good consumed. The second Big Mac will yield less satisfaction to the consumer than the first, and the third still less satisfaction than the second. That is, consumption is subject to **diminishing marginal utility**. And because successive units of a particular product yield less and less marginal utility, consumers will buy additional units only if the price of those units is reduced.
2. The law of demand can also be explained in terms of income and substitution effects. The **income effect** indicates that a lower price increases the purchasing power of a buyer's money income, enabling the buyer to purchase more of the product than she or he could buy before. A higher price has the opposite effect.

   The **substitution effect** suggests that at a lower price, buyers have the incentive to substitute the now cheaper good for similar goods that are now relatively more expensive. Consumers tend to substitute less expensive products for dear products.

For example, a decline in the price of beef will increase the purchasing power of consumer incomes, enabling them to buy more beef (the income effect). At a lower price, beef is relatively more attractive and is substituted for pork, mutton, chicken, and fish (the substitution effect). The income and substitution effects combine to make consumers able and willing to buy more of a product at a low price than at a high price.

## The Demand Curve

The inverse relationship between price and quantity demanded for any product can be represented on a simple graph, in which, by convention, we measure *quantity demanded* on the horizontal axis and price on the vertical axis. In Figure 4-1 we have plotted the five price-quantity data points in Table 4-1 and connected them with a smooth curve, labelled *D*. Such a curve is called a **demand curve**. It slopes downward and to the right because the relationship it portrays between price and quantity demanded is inverse. The law of demand—people buy more at a low price than at a high price—is reflected in the downward slope of the demand curve.

Table 4-1 and Figure 4-1 contain exactly the same data and reflect the same relationship between price and quantity demanded. But the advantage of a graph is that it shows the relationship more simply and clearly than a table or a description in words. Moreover, graphs allow us to very easily show the effects of *changes* in variables. Graphs are thus valuable tools in economic analysis.

## Individual and Market Demand

Until now we have concentrated on just one consumer. But usually there are many buyers in each market. We can get from *individual* demand to *market* demand by adding the quantities demanded by all consumers at each of the various possible prices. If there are just three buyers in the market, as represented in Table 4-2, it is relatively easy to determine the total quantity demanded at each price. Figure 4-2 shows the graphical summing procedure: At each price we add the individual quantities demanded to obtain the total quantity demanded for that price; we then plot the price and total quantity as one point of the market demand curve.

**FIGURE 4-1 An individual buyer's demand for corn**

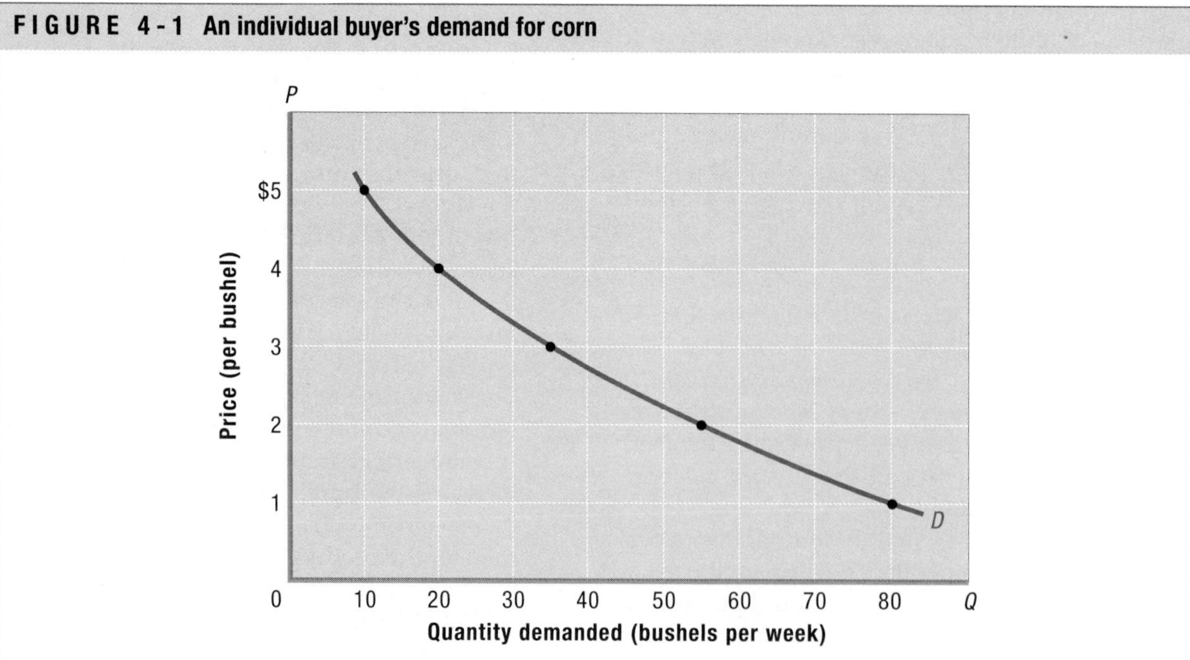


An individual's demand schedule graphs as a downsloping curve such as *D*, because price and quantity demanded are inversely related. Specifically, the law of demand generalizes that, other things equal, consumers will buy more of a product as its price declines. Here and in later figures, *P* stands for price, and *Q* stands for quantity (either demanded or supplied).

**FIGURE 4-2 Market demand for corn, three buyers**

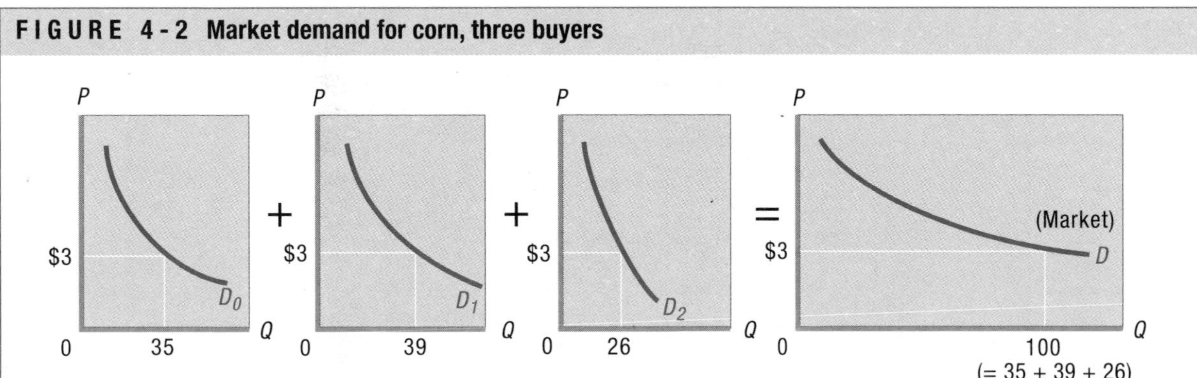


The market demand curve *D* (market) is found by adding horizontally the individual demand curves ($D_0$, $D_1$, and $D_2$) of all consumers in the market. At the price of $3, for example, the three individual curves yield a total quantity demanded of 100 bushels.

Of course, there are usually many more than three buyers of a product. To avoid hundreds or thousands or millions of additions, we suppose that all the buyers in a market are willing and able to buy the same amounts at each of the possible prices. Then we just multiply those amounts by the number of buyers to obtain the market demand. Curve $D_0$ in Figure 4-3 was obtained this way, for a market with 200 corn buyers whose demand is that in Table 4-1. Table 4-3 shows the calculations.

## Determinants of Demand

An economist constructing a demand curve such as $D_0$ in Figure 4-3 assumes that price is the most important influence on the amount of any product purchased. But the economist knows that other factors can and do affect purchases. These factors are called **determinants of demand**, and they are assumed to be constant when a demand curve like $D_0$ is drawn. They are the "other things equal" in the relationship between price and quantity demanded. When any of these determinants changes, the location of the demand curve will shift to the right or left. For this reason, determinants of demand are sometimes referred to as *demand shifters*.

The basic determinants of demand are (1) consumers' tastes and preferences, (2) the number of consumers in the market, (3) consumers' money incomes, (4) the prices of related goods, and (5) consumer expectations about future prices and incomes.

**TABLE 4-2 Market demand for corn, three buyers**

| | QUANTITY DEMANDED | | | | | | | Total quantity |
|---|---|---|---|---|---|---|---|---|
| Price per bushel | First buyer | | Second buyer | | Third buyer | | | demanded per week |
| $5 | 10 | + | 12 | + | 8 | = | | 30 |
| 4 | 20 | + | 23 | + | 17 | = | | 60 |
| 3 | 35 | + | 39 | + | 26 | = | | 100 |
| 2 | 55 | + | 60 | + | 39 | = | | 154 |
| 1 | 80 | + | 87 | + | 54 | = | | 221 |

## Change in Demand

A change in one or more of the determinants of demand will change the demand data (the *demand schedule*) of Table 4-3 and therefore the location of the demand curve in Figure 4-3. A change in the demand schedule or, graphically, a shift in the location of the demand curve is called a *change in demand*.

If consumers become willing and able to buy more corn at each possible price than is reflected in column 4 of Table 4-3, this *increase in demand* means a shift of the demand curve to the *right*, say, from $D_0$ to $D_1$. Conversely, *a decrease in demand* occurs when consumers buy less corn at each possible price than is indicated in column 4, Table 4-3. Graphically, a decrease in demand is shown as a shift of the demand curve to the *left*, say, from $D_0$ to $D_2$ in Figure 4-3.

Let's now examine how changes in each determinant affect demand.

**FIGURE 4-3 Changes in the demand for corn**

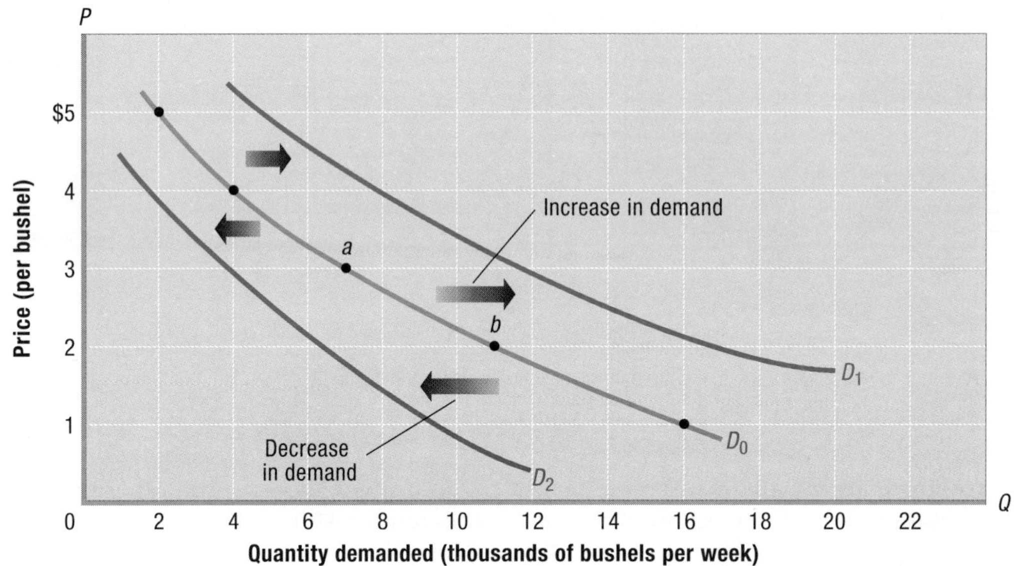


A change in one or more of the determinants of demand causes a change in demand. An increase in demand is shown as a shift of the demand curve to the right, as from $D_0$ to $D_1$. A decrease in demand is shown as a shift of the demand curve to the left, as from $D_0$ to $D_2$. These changes in demand are distinguished from a change in quantity demanded, which is caused by a change in the price of the product, as shown by a movement from, say, point *a* to point *b* on fixed demand curve $D_0$.

**Tastes** A favourable change in consumer tastes or preferences for a product—one that makes the product more desirable—means that more of it will be demanded at each price. Demand will increase; the demand curve will shift rightward. An unfavourable change in consumer preferences will decrease demand, shifting the demand curve to the left.

**TABLE 4-3 Market demand for corn, 200 buyers**

| (1) Price per bushel | (2) Quantity demanded per week, single buyer | | (3) Number of buyers in the market | | (4) Total quantity demanded per week |
|---|---|---|---|---|---|
| $5 | 10 | × | 200 | = | 2,000 |
| 4 | 20 | × | 200 | = | 4,000 |
| 3 | 35 | × | 200 | = | 7,000 |
| 2 | 55 | × | 200 | = | 11,000 |
| 1 | 80 | × | 200 | = | 16,000 |

New products can affect consumer tastes; for example, the introduction of compact discs has greatly decreased the demand for cassette tapes. Consumer concern about the health hazards of cholesterol and obesity have increased the demand for broccoli, low-calorie sweeteners, and fresh fruit while decreasing the demands for beef, veal, eggs, and whole milk. Over the past several years, the demands for light trucks and sports utility vehicles have greatly increased, driven by a change in tastes. So, too, has the demand for bagels.

**Number of Buyers** An increase in the number of consumers in a market increases demand. A decrease in the number of consumers decreases demand. For example, improvements in communications have given financial markets international range, increasing demand for stocks and bonds. And the baby boom after World War II increased demand for diapers, baby lotion, and the services of obstetricians. When the baby boomers reached their 20s in the 1970s, the demand for housing increased. Conversely, the aging of the baby boomers in the 1980s and 1990s has been a factor in the relative "slump" in housing demand.

Also, increasing life expectancy has increased demands for medical care, retirement communities, and nursing homes. And international trade agreements such as the North American Free Trade Agreement (NAFTA) and the General Agreement on Tariffs and Trade (GATT) have reduced foreign trade barriers to Canadian farm products, increasing the demands for those products.

**Income** How changes in money income affect demand is more complex. For most commodities, a rise in income causes an increase in demand. Consumers typically buy more steaks, sunscreen, and stereos as their incomes increase. Conversely, the demands for such products decline as incomes fall. Commodities whose demand varies *directly* with money income are called *superior*, or **normal, goods**.

Although most products are normal goods, there are a few exceptions. As incomes increase beyond some point, the amount of bread or lard or cabbages purchased at each price may diminish because higher incomes allow consumers to buy more high-protein foods, such as dairy products and meat. Rising incomes may also decrease the demands for used clothing and third-hand automobiles. Similarly, rising incomes may cause demands for hamburger and charcoal barbecues to decline as wealthier consumers switch to T-bones and gas barbecues. Goods whose demand varies *inversely* with money income are called **inferior goods**.

**Prices of Related Goods** A change in the price of a related good may increase or decrease the demand for a product, depending on whether the related good is a substitute or a complement. A **substitute good** is one that can be used in place of another good. A **complementary good** is one used together with another good.

**SUBSTITUTES** Beef and chicken are examples of substitute goods. When the price of beef rises, consumers buy less beef, increasing the demand for chicken. Conversely, as the price of beef falls, consumers buy more beef, decreasing the demand for chicken. *When two products are substitutes, the price of one and the demand for the other move in the same direction*. So it is with Nikes and Reeboks, sweaters and jackets, Toyotas and Hondas, and Coke and Pepsi.

**COMPLEMENTS** Complementary goods are used together and are usually demanded together. If the price of gasoline falls and, as a result, you drive your car more, this extra driving increases your demand for motor oil. Thus gas and oil are jointly demanded; they are complements. So it is with ham and eggs, movies and popcorn, and cameras and film. *When two products are complements, the price of one good and the demand for the other good move in opposite directions.*

**UNRELATED GOODS** Many goods are not related to one another; they are *independent goods*. Examples are such pairs of goods as butter and golf balls, potatoes and automobiles, bananas and wristwatches. A change in the price of one has little or no impact on the demand for the other.

**Expectations** Consumer expectations about future product prices, product availability, and future income can shift demand. Consumer expectations of higher future prices may prompt them to buy now to "beat" anticipated price rises, thus increasing today's demand. Similarly, the expectations of rising incomes may induce consumers to be freer in current spending. In contrast, the expectation of falling prices or falling income will decrease current demand for products.

First example: If freezing weather destroys much of Florida's citrus crop, consumers may reason that the price of orange juice will rise. Forthcoming shortages of frozen orange juice will escalate its price. They may stock up on orange juice by purchasing large quantities now.

Second example: A first-round NHL draft choice might splurge for a new Mercedes in anticipation of a lucrative professional hockey contract.

In summary, an *increase* in demand—the decision by consumers to buy larger quantities of a product at each possible price—can be caused by:

1. A favourable change in consumer tastes
2. An increase in the number of buyers
3. Rising incomes if the product is a normal good
4. Falling incomes if the product is an inferior good
5. An increase in the price of a substitute good
6. A decrease in the price of a complementary good
7. Consumer expectations of higher future prices and incomes

Be sure you can "reverse" these generalizations to explain a *decrease* in demand. Table 4-4 provides additional illustrations to reinforce your understanding of the determinants of demand. ***(Key Question 2)***

**TABLE 4-4 Determinants of demand: factors that shift the demand curve**

1. **Change in buyer tastes** Example: Physical fitness increases in popularity, increasing the demand for jogging shoes and bicycles
2. **Change in number of buyers** Examples: Japanese reduce import quotas on Canadian telecommunications equipment, increasing the demand for it; a birthrate decline reduces the demand for education
3. **Change in income** Examples: An increase in incomes increases the demand for such normal goods as butter, lobster, and filet mignon, while reducing the demand for such inferior goods as cabbage, turnips, retreaded tires, and used clothing
4. **Change in the prices of related goods** Examples: A reduction in airfares reduces the demand for bus transportation (substitute goods); a decline in the price of compact disc players increases the demand for compact discs (complementary goods)
5. **Change in expectations** Example: Inclement weather in South America causes the expectation of higher future coffee prices, thereby increasing the current demand for coffee

## Changes in Quantity Demanded

A *change in demand* must not be confused with a *change in quantity demanded*. A **change in demand** is a shift of the entire curve to the right (an increase in demand) or to the left (a decrease in demand). A change in demand occurs because the consumer's state of mind about purchasing the product has been altered. The cause is a change in one or more of the determinants of demand. Recall that *demand* is a schedule or curve; therefore, a *change in demand* means a change in the entire schedule and a shift of the entire curve.

In contrast, a **change in quantity demanded** is a movement from one point to another point—from one price-quantity combination to another—on a fixed demand schedule or demand curve. The cause of such a change is an increase or decrease in the price of the product being considered. In Table 4-3, for example, a decline in the price from $5 to $4 will increase the quantity of corn demanded from 2,000 to 4,000 bushels.

In Figure 4-3 the shift of the demand curve $D_0$ to either $D_1$ or $D_2$ is a change in demand. But the movement from point *a* to point *b* on curve $D_0$ represents a change in quantity demanded. Demand has not changed; it is the entire curve, and it remains fixed in place.

**4-1**

**QUICK REVIEW**

- A market is any arrangement that facilitates the purchase and sale of goods, services, and resources.
- Demand is a schedule or a curve showing the amount of a product buyers are willing and able to purchase at each potential price in a series of prices.
- The law of demand states that, other things equal, the quantity of a good purchased varies inversely with its price.
- The demand curve shifts because of changes in **a** consumer tastes, **b** the number of buyers in the market, **c** incomes, **d** the prices of substitute or complementary goods, and **e** expectations.
- A change in demand is a shift of the entire demand curve; a change in quantity demanded is a movement from one point to another on a firm's stable demand curve.

## SUPPLY

**Supply** *is a schedule or curve showing the amounts of a product a producer is willing and able to produce and make available for sale at each of a series of possible prices during a specific period.*[2] Table 4-5 is a hypothetical **supply schedule** for a single producer of corn. It shows the quantities of corn that will be supplied at various prices, other things equal.

## Law of Supply

Table 4-5 shows a positive or direct relationship between price and quantity supplied. *As price rises, the quantity supplied rises; as price falls, the quantity supplied falls.* This particular relationship is called the **law of supply**. A supply schedule tells us that firms will produce and offer for sale more of their product at a high price than at a low price. This, again, is basically common sense.

[2] This definition is worded to apply to product markets. To adjust it to apply to resource markets, substitute "resource" for "product," and "owner" for "producer."

**TABLE 4-5 An individual producer's supply of corn**

| Price per bushel | Quantity supplied per week |
|---|---|
| $5 | 60 |
| 4 | 50 |
| 3 | 35 |
| 2 | 20 |
| 1 | 5 |

Price is an obstacle from the standpoint of the consumer, who is on the paying end. The higher the price, the less the consumer will buy. But the supplier is on the receiving end of the product's price. To a supplier, price represents *revenue* and thus is an incentive to produce and sell a product. The higher the price, the greater this incentive and the greater the quantity supplied.

Consider a farmer who can shift resources among alternative products. As price moves up in Table 4-5, the farmer finds it profitable to take land out of wheat, oats, and soybean production and put it into corn. And the higher corn prices allow the farmer to cover the increased costs associated with more intensive cultivation and the use of more seed, fertilizer, and pesticides. The overall result is more corn.

Now consider a manufacturer. Beyond some production quantity, manufacturers usually encounter increasing costs per added unit of output. Certain productive resources—in particular, the firm's plant and machinery—cannot be expanded quickly. So the firm uses more of the other resources, such as labour, to produce more output. But at some point the existing plant becomes increasingly crowded and congested, meaning that each added worker produces less added output. As a result, the cost of successive units of output rises. The firm will not produce these more costly units unless it receives a higher price for them. Again, price and quantity supplied are directly related.

## The Supply Curve

As with demand, it is convenient to represent supply graphically. In Figure 4-4, curve $S_0$ is a graph of the market supply data in Table 4-6. Those data assume there are 200 suppliers in the market, each

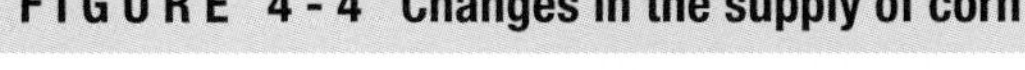

**FIGURE 4-4 Changes in the supply of corn**

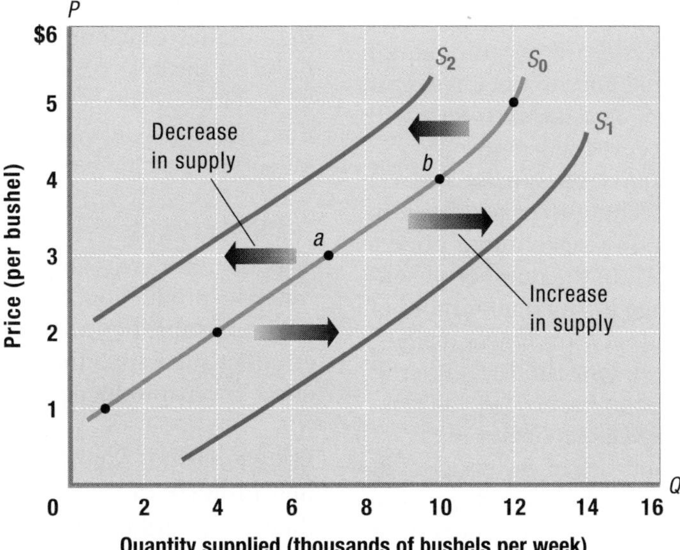


A change in one or more of the determinants of supply causes a change in supply. An increase in supply is shown as a rightward shift of the supply curve, as from $S_0$ to $S_1$. A decrease in supply is depicted as a leftward shift of the curve, as from $S_0$ to $S_2$. In contrast, a change in the quantity supplied is caused by a change in the product's price and is shown by a movement from one point to another—as from *a* to *b*—on a fixed supply curve.

**TABLE 4-6 Market supply of corn, 200 producers**

| (1) Price per bushel | (2) Quantity supplied per week, single producer | | (3) Number of sellers in the market | | (4) Total quantity supplied per week |
|---|---|---|---|---|---|
| $5 | 60 | × | 200 | = | 12,000 |
| 4 | 50 | × | 200 | = | 10,000 |
| 3 | 35 | × | 200 | = | 7,000 |
| 2 | 20 | × | 200 | = | 4,000 |
| 1 | 5 | × | 200 | = | 1,000 |

willing and able to supply corn according to Table 4-5. That is, we obtain the market **supply curve** by horizontally adding the supply curves of the individual producers. Note that the axes in Figure 4-4 are the same as those used in our graph of market demand, except for the change of "quantity demanded" to "quantity supplied" on the horizontal axis.

## Determinants of Supply

In constructing a supply curve, the economist assumes that price is the most significant influence on the quantity supplied of any product. But other factors (the *other things equal*) can and do affect supply. The supply curve is drawn assuming that these other things are fixed and do not change. If any of them does change, a *change in supply* will occur—the entire supply curve will shift.

The basic **determinants of supply** are (1) resource prices, (2) the technique of production, (3) taxes and subsidies, (4) prices of other goods, (5) price expectations, and (6) the number of sellers in the market. A change in any one or more of these determinants of supply, or *supply shifters*, will move the supply curve for a product either to the right or to the left. A shift to the *right*, as from $S_0$ to $S_1$ in Figure 4-4, is an *increase* in supply: Producers supply larger quantities of the product at each possible price. A shift to the *left*, as from $S_0$ to $S_2$, indicates a *decrease* in supply: Suppliers offer less output at each price.

## Changes in Supply

Let's consider how changes in each of the determinants affect supply. As our discussion proceeds, remember that costs are a major factor underlying supply curves; anything that affects costs (other than changes in output itself) usually shifts the supply curve.

**Resource Prices** The prices of the *resources* used in the production process help determine the costs of production incurred by firms. Higher *resource* prices raise production costs and, assuming a particular *product* price, squeeze profits. This reduction in profits reduces the incentive for firms to supply output at each product price. In contrast, lower resource prices induce firms to supply more output at each product price since production costs fall and profits expand.

It follows that a decrease in resource prices will increase supply, shifting the supply curve to the right. If prices of seed and fertilizer decrease, we can expect the supply of corn to increase. Conversely, an increase in resource prices will raise production costs and reduce supply, shifting the supply curve to the left. Increases in the prices of iron ore and coke will increase the cost of producing steel and reduce its supply.

**Technology** Improvements in technology enable firms to produce units of output with fewer resources. Because resources are costly, using fewer of them lowers production costs and increases supply. Example: Recent improvements in the fuel efficiency of aircraft engines have reduced the cost of providing passenger air service. Thus, airlines now offer more air service than previously at each ticket price; the supply of air service has increased.

**Taxes and Subsidies** Businesses treat most taxes as costs. An increase in sales or property taxes will increase production costs and reduce supply. In contrast, subsidies are "taxes in reverse." If government subsidizes the production of a good, it in effect lowers production costs and increases supply.

**Prices of Other Goods** Firms producing a particular product, say, soccer balls, can sometimes use their plant and equipment to produce alternative goods, say, basketballs and volleyballs. Higher prices of these "other goods" may entice soccer ball producers to switch production to them in order to increase profits. This *substitution in production* results in a decline in the supply of soccer balls. Alternatively, lower prices of basketballs and volleyballs may entice producers of these goods to produce more soccer balls, increasing their supply.

**Expectations** Expectations about the *future* price of a product can affect the producer's *current* willingness to supply that product. It is difficult, however, to generalize about how the expectation of higher prices affects the present supply of a product. Farmers anticipating a higher corn price in the future might withhold some of their current corn harvest from the market, which would cause a decrease in the current supply of corn. Similarly, if the price of Air Canada stock is expected to rise significantly in the near future, the supply offered for sale today might decrease. In contrast, in many types of manufacturing industries, expected price increases may induce firms to add another shift of workers or expand their production facilities, causing current supply to increase.

**Number of Sellers** Other things equal, the larger the number of suppliers, the greater the market supply. As more firms enter an industry, the supply curve shifts to the right. Conversely, the smaller the number of firms in the industry, the less the market supply. This means that as firms leave an industry, the supply curve shifts to the left. Example: Canada and the United States have imposed restrictions on haddock fishing to replenish dwindling stocks. As part of that policy, the federal government has bought the boats of some of the haddock fishermen as a way of putting them out of business and decreasing the catch. The result has been a decline in the market supply of haddock.

Table 4-7 is a checklist of the determinants of supply, along with further illustrations. ***(Key Question 5)***

**TABLE 4-7 Determinants of supply: factors that shift the supply curve**

1 **Change in resource prices** Examples: A decline in the price of fertilizer increases the supply of wheat; an increase in the price of irrigation equipment reduces the supply of corn

2 **Change in technology** Example: The development of a more effective insecticide for corn rootworm increases the supply of corn

3 **Changes in taxes and subsidies** Examples: An increase in the excise tax on cigarettes reduces the supply of cigarettes; a decline in subsidies to colleges and universities reduces the supply of higher education

4 **Change in prices of other goods** Example: A decline in the prices of mutton and pork increases the supply of beef

5 **Change in expectations** Example: Expectations of substantial declines in future oil prices cause oil companies to increase current supply

6 **Change in number of suppliers** An increase in the number of firms producing personal computers increases the supply of personal computers; formation of women's professional basketball leagues increases the supply of women's professional basketball games

## Changes in Quantity Supplied

The distinction between a *change in supply* and *change in quantity supplied* is the same as that between a change in demand and a change in quantity demanded. Because supply is a schedule or curve, a **change in supply** means a change in the entire schedule and a shift of the entire curve. An increase in supply shifts the curve to the right; a decrease in supply shifts it to the left. The cause of a change in supply is a change in one or more of the determinants of supply.

In contrast, a **change in quantity supplied** is a movement from one point to another on a fixed supply curve. The cause of such a movement is a change in the price of the specific product being considered. In Table 4-6, a decline in the price of corn from $5 to $4 decreases the quantity of corn supplied from 12,000 to 10,000 bushels. This is a change in quantity supplied, not a change in supply. Supply is the full schedule of prices and quantities shown, and this schedule does not change when price changes.

**4-2**

**QUICK REVIEW**

- A supply schedule or curve shows that, other things equal, the quantity of a good supplied varies directly with its price.
- The supply curve shifts because of changes in **a** resource prices, **b** technology, **c** taxes or subsidies, **d** prices of other goods, **e** expectations of future prices, and **f** the number of suppliers.
- A change in supply is a shift of the supply curve; a change in quantity supplied is a movement from one point to another on a fixed supply curve.

## SUPPLY AND DEMAND: MARKET EQUILIBRIUM

We can now bring together supply and demand to see how the buying decisions of households and the selling decisions of businesses interact to determine the price of a product and the quantity actually bought and sold. In Table 4-8, columns 1 and 2 repeat the market supply of corn (from Table 4-6), and columns 2 and 3 repeat the market demand for corn (from Table 4-3). Note that column 2 lists a common set of prices. We assume competition—a large number of buyers and sellers.

### Surpluses

We have limited our examples to only five possible prices. Of these, which will actually prevail as the market price for corn? We can find an answer through trial and error; for no particular reason, let's start with $5. We immediately see that this cannot be the prevailing market price. At the $5 price, producers are willing to produce and offer for sale 12,000 bushels of corn, but buyers are willing to buy only 2,000 bushels. The $5 price encourages farmers to produce lots of corn but discourages most consumers from buying it. The result is a 10,000-bushel **surplus** or *excess supply* of corn. This surplus, shown in column 4 in Table 4-8, is the excess of quantity supplied over quantity demanded at $5. Corn farmers would find themselves with 10,000 unsold bushels of output.

A price of $5—even if it existed temporarily in the corn market—could not persist over a period of time. The very large surplus of corn would prompt competing sellers to lower the price to encourage buyers to take the surplus off their hands.

**TABLE 4-8 Market supply of and demand for corn**

| (1) Total quantity supplied per week | (2) Price per bushel | (3) Total quantity demanded per week | (4) Surplus (+) or shortage (–) (arrows indicate effect on price) |
|---|---|---|---|
| 12,000 | $5 | 2,000 | +10,000↓ |
| 10,000 | 4 | 4,000 | + 6,000↓ |
| 7,000 | 3 | 7,000 | 0 |
| 4,000 | 2 | 11,000 | – 7,000↑ |
| 1,000 | 1 | 16,000 | –15,000↑ |

Suppose the price goes down to $4. The lower price encourages consumers to buy more corn and, at the same time, induces farmers to offer less of it for sale. The surplus diminishes to 6,000 bushels. Nevertheless, since there is still a surplus, competition among sellers will once again reduce the price. Clearly, then, the prices of $5 and $4 are unstable—they will not survive—because they are "too high." The market price of corn must be less than $4.

### Shortages

Let's jump now to $1 as the possible market price of corn. Observe in column 4 in Table 4-8 that at this price, quantity demanded exceeds quantity supplied by 15,000 units. The $1 price discourages farmers from devoting resources to corn production and encourages consumers to buy more than is available. The result is a 15,000-bushel **shortage** of, or *excess demand* for, corn. The $1 price cannot persist as the market price. Many consumers who are willing and able to buy at this price will not get corn. They will express a willingness to pay more than $1 to get some of the available output. Competition among these buyers will drive up the price to something greater than $1.

Suppose the competition among buyers boosts the price to $2. This higher price reduces, but does not eliminate the shortage of corn. For $2, farmers devote more resources to corn production, and some buyers who were willing to pay $1 per bushel choose not to buy corn at $2. But a shortage of 7,000 bushels still exists at $2. This shortage will push the market price above $2.

### Equilibrium Price and Quantity

By trial and error we have eliminated every price but $3. At $3, *and only at this price*, the quantity of corn that farmers are willing to produce and supply is identical with the quantity consumers are willing and able to buy. There is neither a shortage nor a surplus of corn at that price.

With no shortage or surplus at $3, there is no reason for the price of corn to change. Economists call this price the *market-clearing* or **equilibrium price**, equilibrium meaning "in balance" or "at rest." At $3, quantity supplied and quantity demanded are in balance at the **equilibrium quantity** of 7,000 bushels. So $3 is the only stable price of corn under the supply and demand conditions shown in Table 4-8.

The price of corn—or of any other product bought and sold in competitive markets—will be established where the supply decisions of producers and the demand decisions of buyers are mutually consistent. Such decisions are consistent only at the equilibrium price (here, \$3) and equilibrium quantity (here, 7,000 bushels). At a higher price, suppliers want to sell more than consumers want to buy and a surplus results; at any lower price, consumers want to buy more than producers make available for sale and a shortage results. Such discrepancies between the supply and demand intentions of sellers and buyers then prompt price changes that bring the two sets of intentions into accord.

A graphical analysis of supply and demand yields these same conclusions. ***Figure 4-5 (Key Graph)*** shows the market supply and demand curves for corn on the same graph. (The horizon-

## KEY GRAPH

**FIGURE 4-5 Equilibrium price and quantity**

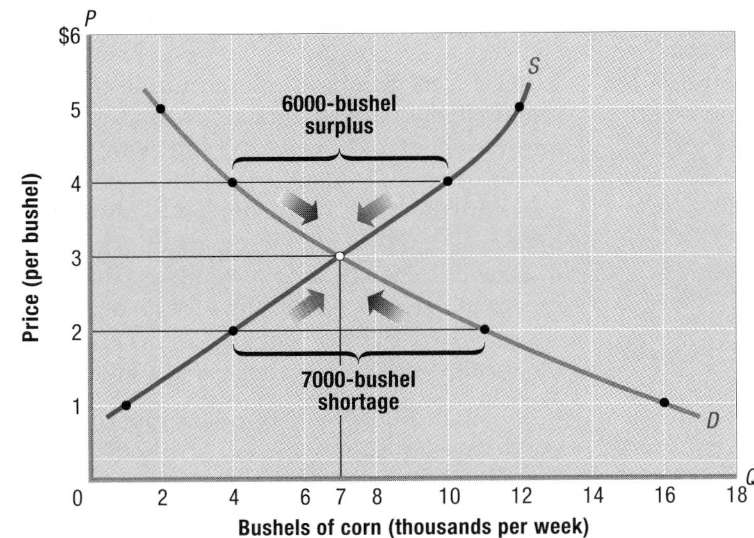


The intersection of the downsloping demand curve *D* and the upsloping supply curve *S* indicates the equilibrium price and quantity, here \$3 and 7,000 bushels of corn. The shortages of corn at below-equilibrium prices—for example, 7,000 bushels at \$2—drive up price. These higher prices increase the quantity supplied and reduce the quantity demanded until equilibrium is achieved. The surpluses caused by above-equilibrium prices—for example, 6,000 bushels at \$4—push price down. As price drops, the quantity demanded rises and the quantity supplied falls until equilibrium is established. At the equilibrium price and quantity, there are neither shortages nor surpluses of corn.

### 4-5 QUICK QUIZ

1. Demand curve *D* is downsloping because:
   - **(a)** producers offer less of a product for sale as the price of the product falls.
   - **(b)** lower prices of a product create income and substitution effects that lead consumers to purchase more of it.
   - **(c)** the larger the number of buyers in a market, the lower the product price.
   - **(d)** price and quantity demanded are directly (positively) related.
2. Supply curve *S*:
   - **(a)** reflects an inverse (negative) relationship between price and quantity supplied.
   - **(b)** reflects a direct (positive) relationship between price and quantity supplied.
   - **(c)** depicts the collective behaviour of buyers in this market.
   - **(d)** shows that producers will offer more of a product for sale at a low product price than at a high product price.
3. At the \$3 price:
   - **(a)** quantity supplied exceeds quantity demanded.
   - **(b)** quantity demanded exceeds quantity supplied.
   - **(c)** the product is abundant and a surplus exists.
   - **(d)** there is no pressure on price to rise or fall.
4. At price \$5 in this market:
   - **(a)** there will be a shortage of 10,000 units.
   - **(b)** there will be a surplus of 10,000 units.
   - **(c)** quantity demanded will be 12,000 units.
   - **(d)** quantity demanded will equal quantity supplied.

**Answers:** 1. (b); 2. (b); 3. (d); 4. (b)

tal axis now measures both quantity demanded and quantity supplied.)

*Graphically, the intersection of the supply curve and demand curve for a product indicates the market equilibrium.* Here, equilibrium price and quantity are $3 per bushel and 7,000 bushels. At any above-equilibrium price, quantity supplied exceeds quantity demanded. This surplus of corn causes price reductions by sellers who are eager to rid themselves of their surplus. The falling price causes less corn to be offered and simultaneously encourages consumers to buy more. The market moves to its equilibrium.

Any price below the equilibrium price creates a shortage; quantity demanded now exceeds quantity supplied. Buyers try to obtain the product by offering to pay more for it; this drives the price upward towards its equilibrium level. The rising price simultaneously causes producers to increase the quantity supplied and many buyers to leave the market, eliminating the shortage. Again the market moves to its equilibrium.

## Rationing Function of Prices

The ability of the competitive forces of supply and demand to establish a price at which selling and buying decisions are consistent is called the **rationing function of prices**. In our case, the equilibrium price of $3 clears the market, leaving no burdensome surplus for sellers and no inconvenient shortage for potential buyers. And it is the combination of freely made individual decisions that sets this market-clearing price. In effect, the market mechanism of supply and demand says that any buyer willing and able to pay $3 for a bushel of corn will be able to acquire one; those who are not, will not. Similarly, any seller willing and able to produce bushels of corn and offer them for sale at $3 will be able to do so; sellers who are not, will not. ***(Key Question 7)***

## Changes in Supply, Demand, and Equilibrium

We know that demand might change because of fluctuations in consumer tastes or incomes, changes in consumer expectations, or variations in the prices of related goods. Supply might change in response to changes in resource prices, technology, or taxes. What effects will such changes in supply and demand have on equilibrium price and quantity?

**Changes in Demand** Suppose that supply is constant and demand increases, as shown in Figure 4-6a. As a result, the new intersection of the supply and demand curves is at higher values on both the price and quantity axes. Clearly, an increase in demand raises both equilibrium price and equilibrium quantity. Conversely, a decrease in demand—such as that shown in Figure 4-6b—reduces both equilibrium price and equilibrium quantity. (The value of graphical analysis is now apparent: We need not fumble with columns of figures to determine the outcomes, but only compare the new and the old points of intersection on the graph.)

The explanation of the dynamics of how a shift in demand results in a new equilibrium price and quantity is similar to the shortage-surplus story in Figure 4-5. In the case of an increase in demand, there would be a shortage at the original equilibrium price, leading to a higher price. A higher price to producers results in more output offered for sale. To better understand the dynamics of an equilibrium change, draw a diagram with an equilbrium price and quantity and shift the demand curve to the right. Now, do an analysis of the dynamics. Go through the same exercise for a fall in demand. The key to understanding the dynamics of a change in equilibrium is to understand the shortage or surplus that occurs when there is excess demand or excess supply at a given price.

**Changes in Supply** Let's now suppose demand is constant but supply increases, as in Figure 4-6c. The new intersection of supply and demand is located at a lower equilibrium price but at a higher equilibrium quantity. An increase in supply reduces equilibrium price but increases equilibrium quantity. In contrast, if supply decreases, as in Figure 4-6d, the equilibrium price rises while the equilibrium quantity declines.

As in the case of a shift in demand, the explanation of the dynamics of a change in equilibrium when the supply curve shifts is the existence of a surplus or a shortage at the original equilibrium price. For example, if the supply curve shifts to the right, at the original equilibrium price there would be a surplus, therefore price drops. Draw a diagram and do the analysis of a change in equilibrium when the supply curve shifts to the right, and then repeat the analysis for a shift of the supply curve to the left.

As you do the above analysis, keep in mind that equilibrium price and quantity cannot spontaneously change; price and quantity change only as a result of a shift in demand and supply.

**Complex Cases** When both supply and demand change, the effect is a combination of the individ-

**FIGURE 4-6 Changes in demand and supply and the effects on price and quantity**

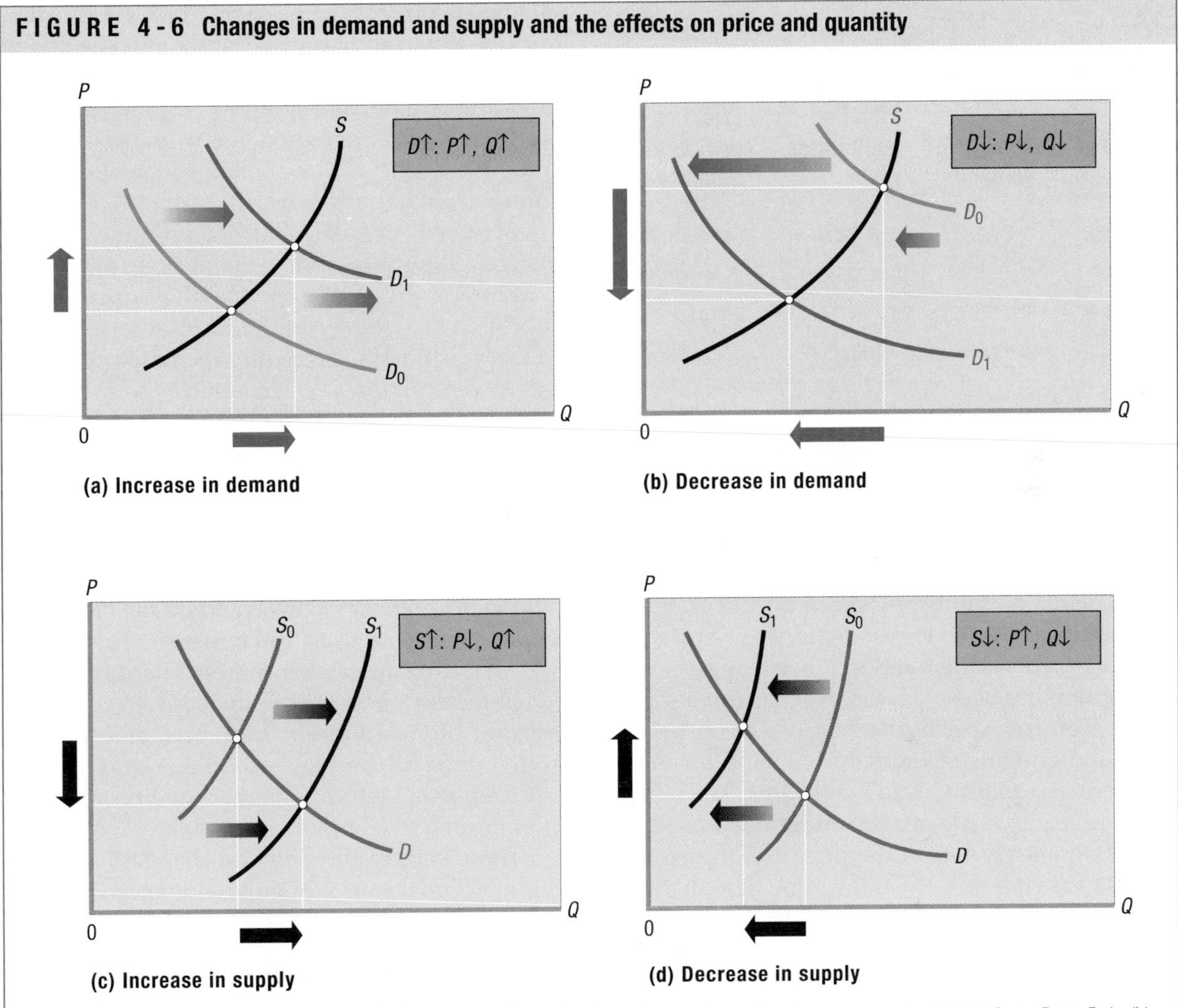


The increase in demand from $D_0$ to $D_1$ in (a) increases both equilibrium price and quantity. The decrease in demand from $D_0$ to $D_1$ in (b) decreases both equilibrium price and quantity. The increase in supply from $S_0$ to $S_1$ in (c) decreases equilibrium price and increases equilibrium quantity. The decline in supply from $S_0$ to $S_1$ in (d) increases equilibrium price and reduces equilibrium quantity. The boxes in the top right corners summarize the respective changes and outcomes. The upward arrows in the boxes signify increases in demand (D), supply (S), equilibrium price (P), and equilibrium quantity (Q); the downward arrows signify decreases in these items.

ual effects. There are four possibilities: (1) supply increases and demand decreases; (2) supply decreases and demand increases; (3) supply increases and demand decreases; and (4) supply decreases and demand decreases.

Table 4-9 summarizes these four cases. To understand them fully you should draw supply and demand diagrams for each case to confirm the effects listed in the table.

Special cases might arise where a decrease in demand and a decrease in supply, or an increase in demand and an increase in supply, exactly cancel out. In both cases, the net effect on equilibrium price will be zero; price will not change. ***(Key Question 8)***

## A Reminder: "Other Things Equal"

We stress once again that specific demand and supply curves—such as those in Figure 4-6—show relationships between prices and quantities demanded and supplied, *other things equal*. The downsloping demand curves tell us that price and quantity demanded are inversely related, other things equal. The upsloping supply curves imply that price and quantity supplied are directly related, *other things equal*.

If you forget the other-things-equal assumption, you can encounter situations that *seem* to be in conflict with these basic principles. For example,

**TABLE 4-9 Effects of changes in both supply and demand**

| Change in supply | Change in demand | Effect on equilibrium price | Effect on equilibrium quantity |
|---|---|---|---|
| 1 increase | decrease | decrease | indeterminate |
| 2 decrease | increase | increase | indeterminate |
| 3 increase | increase | indeterminate | increase |
| 4 decrease | decrease | indeterminate | decrease |

suppose salsa manufacturers sell 1 million bottles of salsa at $4 a bottle in one year; 2 million bottles at $5 in the next year; and 3 million at $6 in the year thereafter. Price and quantity purchased vary directly, and these data seem to be at odds with the law of demand. But there is no conflict here; these data do *not* refute the law of demand. The catch is that the law of demand's other-things-equal assumption has been violated over the three years in the example. Specifically, because of changing tastes and growing incomes, the demand for salsa has increased sharply, as in Figure 4-6a. The result is higher prices *and* larger quantities purchased.

As another example, the price of coffee occasionally has shot upward at the same time that the quantity of coffee produced has declined. These events seemingly contradict the direct relationship between price and quantity denoted by supply. The catch again is that the other-things-equal assumption underlying the upsloping supply curve was violated. Poor coffee harvests decreased supply, as in Figure 4-6d, increasing the equilibrium price of coffee and reducing the equilibrium quantity.

These examples also emphasize the importance of our earlier distinction between a change in quantity demanded (or supplied) and a change in demand (supply). In Figure 4-6a a change in demand caused a change in the quantity supplied. In Figure 4-6d a change in supply caused a change in quantity demanded.

## Application: Pink Salmon

To reinforce the concepts we just discussed, let's briefly examine the real-world market for pink salmon—a market in which price has dramatically changed.

In the early 1970s, fishermen earned today's equivalent of $1.20 for each kilogram of pink salmon delivered to the docks. This equilibrium price is shown in Figure 4-7 at the intersection of supply curve $S_0$ and demand curve $D_0$. The corresponding equilibrium quantity of pink salmon—the type most often used for canning—was $Q_0$ kilograms. (The actual "quantity numbers" are unimportant to our analysis.)

Between the early 1970s and late 1990s, changes in supply and demand occurred in the market for pink salmon. On the supply side, improved technology in the form of larger, more efficient fishing boats greatly increased the catch and lowered the cost of obtaining the fish. Also, the then-high profits at the $1.20 price encouraged many new fishermen to enter the industry. As a result of these changes, the supply of pink salmon greatly increased and the supply curve shifted to the right, as from $S_0$ to $S_1$ in Figure 4-7.

Over the same years, the demand for pink salmon declined, as represented by the shift from demand curve $D_0$ to $D_1$ in Figure 4-7. The decline in demand resulted mainly from changes in consumer tastes, together with increases in consumer income: Buyers shifted their preferences away from canned fish and towards higher-quality fresh or frozen fish, including higher-quality species of salmon such as Chinook and Coho.

These supply and demand changes had a sizable effect on the price of pink salmon, as shown in

**FIGURE 4-7 The market for pink salmon**

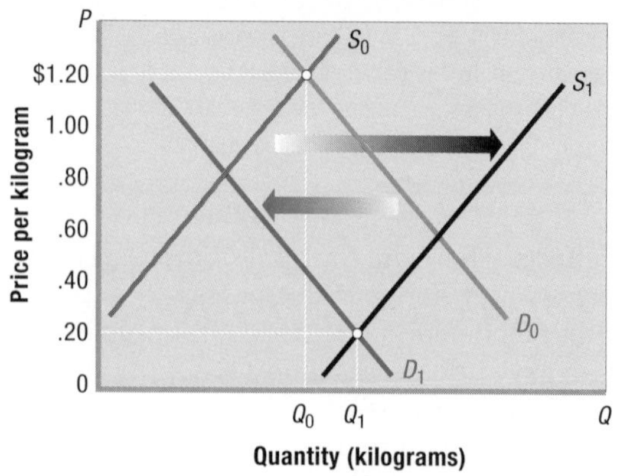

Since the early 1970s, the supply of pink salmon has increased and the demand for pink salmon has decreased. As a result, the price of pink salmon has declined, here from $1.20 to $.20 a kilogram. Since supply has increased more than demand has declined, the equilibrium quantity of pink salmon has increased, here from $Q_0$ to $Q_1$.

Figure 4-7. By 1997 the equilibrium price had fallen to just $.20 per kilogram—over 80 percent below the price in the early 1970s. Both the increase in supply and the decrease in demand helped reduce the equilibrium price. However, the equilibrium *quantity* of pink salmon increased, as represented by the increase from $Q_0$ to $Q_1$. This change in quantity occurred because the increase in the supply of pink salmon exceeded the decline in demand.

**4-3**

## QUICK REVIEW

- In competitive markets, prices adjust to the equilibrium level at which quantity demanded equals quantity supplied.
- The equilibrium price and quantity are those indicated by the intersection of the supply and demand curves for any product or resource.
- An increase in demand increases equilibrium price and quantity; a decrease in demand decreases equilibrium price and quantity.
- An increase in supply reduces equilibrium price but increases equilibrium quantity; a decrease in supply increases equilibrium price but reduces equilibrium quantity.
- Over time, equilibrium price and quantity may change in directions that seem at odds with the laws of demand and supply because the other-things-equal assumption is violated.

## In The Media

4 KEY CONCEPT

# London trader takes huge cocoa delivery

## Holds 212,500 tonnes after squeeze attempt

BY JALIL HAMID
REUTERS NEWS AGENCY

LONDON—A major commodity trader had to take virtually all the 212,500 tonnes of cocoa delivered on a London futures market yesterday after an attempt to squeeze the market failed.

The London Commodity Exchange said 21,250 original tenders representing 212,500 tonnes were registered, the largest delivery yet in one day. The LCE provided no further details, but market sources said a single large trader was believed to have received almost all the cocoa and has additional long positions of 8,000 to 9,000 10-tonne lots.

"It is an attempt to squeeze which didn't work because they underestimated the size of the crop and they underestimated the strength of other commodity traders," one trader said. "They never thought there would be enough cocoa that could be put on the market and they've been proved wrong."

The trader's position of about 300,000 tonnes of cocoa is equivalent to one-third of the crop produced by the world's top cocoa grower, Ivory Coast.

Yesterday's delivery marked the climax of a five-month war of nerves over the London September cocoa futures contract.

Although the tonnage came as no surprise, traders said the market is now watching the major trader's next move.

Traders estimated that it would cost the trader at least £1.25-million a year to store the cocoa.

"I don't suppose there's much else they can do in this moment in time," another trader said. "The market has given them cocoa ... and they have to carry [it] for the time being. There's nothing else they can do."

Any move to sell the cocoa—a fine, dark-brown powder made from pulverizing chocolate that's used to prepare beverages and as a flavouring ingredient—would put further pressure on a sliding market amid ample crops from producers and slack demand from the chocolate industry.

Cocoa delivered on the LCE has to have a grading certificate proving it is of acceptable quality. The certificate is valid for six months.

*Source*: *Globe and Mail*, September 3, 1996, p. B6. 

## THE STORY IN BRIEF

A commodity exchange is a market in which a trader can buy or sell a commodity to be delivered at a specified future date. A trader that tried to corner the cocoa market ended up having to take delivery of a very large quantity.

## THE ECONOMICS BEHIND THE STORY

- Commodity prices are determined by supply and demand. There is a futures market in which one can buy or sell a particular commodity. Buyers are those who need the commodity at some future time, sellers are the producers of a commodity who may wish to sell even before they produce the commodity. There are traders (speculators) who buy and sell commodities in the hope of making a profit by correctly predicting their prices at some future date. Such traders do not normally take delivery of commodities they trade.
- One trader bought large quantities of cocoa for future delivery in the expectation that there would be a shortage, thus the trader could sell the cocoa at a higher price than it was bought for.
- The trader was wrong. The crop was larger than expected, driving the supply curve for cocoa to the right.
- The trader in question could have sold the large position, but such a move would have driven the market supply curve further to the right, bringing the price down further. Thus the trader was left with the option of taking delivery of the cocoa and selling at a future date at possibly better prices, or taking an immediate very large loss.
- Can you explain why understanding supply and demand analysis will not easily make you rich? ■

# The Last Word

## TICKET SCALPING: A BUM RAP?

**Some market transactions get a bad name that's not warranted.**

TICKETS TO ATHLETIC AND ARTISTIC EVENTS are sometimes resold at higher-than-original prices—a market transaction known by the unsavoury term "scalping." For example, a $40 ticket to an NHL hockey game may be resold by the original buyer for $200, $250, or more. The media often denounce scalpers for "ripping off" buyers by charging "exorbitant" prices. Scalping and extortion are synonymous in some people's minds.

But is scalping really sinful? We must first recognize that such ticket resales are voluntary—not coerced—transactions. This implies that both buyer and seller expect to gain from the exchange or it would not occur. The seller must value the $200 more than seeing the game, and the buyer must value seeing the game more than the $200. So there are no losers or victims here: Both buyer and seller benefit from the transaction. The "scalping" market simply redistributes assets (game tickets) from those who value them less to those who value them more.

Does scalping impose losses or injury on other parties—in particular, the sponsors of the event? If the sponsors are injured, it is because they initially priced tickets below the equilibrium level. In so doing they suffer an economic loss in the form of less revenue and profit than they might have otherwise received. But the loss is self-inflicted because of their pricing error. That mistake is quite separate and distinct from the fact that some tickets were later resold at a higher price.

What about spectators? Does scalping somehow impose losses by deteriorating the quality of the game's audience? No! People who most want to see the game—generally those with the greatest interest in and understanding of the game—will pay the scalper's high prices. Ticket scalping also benefits the athletic teams and performing artists—they will appear before more dedicated and perhaps more appreciative audiences.

So, is ticket scalping undesirable? Not on economic grounds. Both seller and buyer of a "scalped" ticket benefit, and a more interested and appreciative audience results. Game sponsors may sacrifice revenue and profits, but that stems from their own misjudgement of the equilibrium price. ■

# CHAPTER SUMMARY

1. A market is any institution or arrangement that brings together buyers and sellers of a product, service, or resource.
2. Demand is a schedule or curve representing the willingness of buyers in a specific period to purchase a particular product at each of various prices. The law of demand says that consumers will buy more of a product at a low price than at a high price. Therefore, other things equal, the relationship between price and quantity demanded is negative or inverse and is graphed as a downsloping curve. Market demand curves are found by adding horizontally the demand curves of the many individual consumers in the market.
3. Changes in one or more of the determinants of demand—consumer tastes, the number of buyers in the market, the money incomes of consumers, the prices of related goods, and consumer expectations—shift the market demand curve. A shift to the right is an increase in demand; a shift to the left is a decrease in demand. A change in demand is different from a change in the quantity demanded, the latter being a movement from one point to another point on a fixed demand curve because of a change in the product's price.
4. Supply is a schedule or curve showing the amounts of a product that producers are willing to offer in the market at each possible price during a specific period. The law of supply states that, other things equal, producers will offer more of a product at a high price than at a low price. Thus, the relationship between price and quantity supplied is positive or direct, and supply is graphed as an upsloping curve. The market supply curve is the horizontal summation of the supply curves of individual producers of the product.
5. Changes in one or more of the determinants of supply—a change in resource prices, production techniques, taxes or subsidies, the prices of other goods, price expectations, or the number of sellers in the market—shift the supply curve of a product. A shift to the right is an increase in supply; a shift to the left is a decrease in supply. In contrast, a change in the price of the product being considered causes a change in the quantity supplied, which is shown as a movement from one point to another point on a fixed supply curve.
6. The equilibrium price and quantity are those indicated by the intersection of the supply and demand curves. The interaction of market demand and market supply adjusts the price to the point at which quantity demanded and quantity supplied are equal. This is the equilibrium price. The corresponding quantity is the equilibrium quantity.
7. The ability of market forces to synchronize selling and buying decisions to eliminate potential surpluses and shortages is known as the rationing function of prices.
8. A change in either demand or supply changes the equilibrium price and quantity. Increases in demand raise both equilibrium price and equilibrium quantity; decreases in demand reduce both equilibrium price and equilibrium quantity. Increases in supply reduce equilibrium price and increase equilibrium quantity; decreases in supply raise equilibrium price and reduce equilibrium quantity.
9. Simultaneous changes in demand and supply affect equilibrium price and quantity in various ways, depending on their direction and relative magnitudes.

# TERMS AND CONCEPTS

market
demand
demand schedule
law of demand
diminishing marginal utility
income and substitution effect
demand curve
substitution effect
demand curve
determinants of demand
normal good
inferior good
substitute good
complementary good
change in demand (or supply) versus change in quantity demanded (or supplied)
supply
supply schedule
law of supply
supply curve
determinants of supply
surplus
shortage
equilibrium price and quantity
rationing function of prices

## STUDY QUESTIONS

1. Explain the law of demand. Why does a demand curve slope downward? What are the determinants of demand? What happens to the demand curve when each of these determinants changes? Distinguish between a change in demand and a change in the quantity demanded, noting the cause(s) of each.

2. KEY QUESTION *What effect will each of the following have on the demand for product B?*
   a. *Product B becomes more fashionable.*
   b. *The price of substitute product C falls.*
   c. *Income declines and B is an inferior good.*
   d. *Consumers anticipate the price of B will be lower in the near future.*
   e. *The price of complementary product D falls.*
   f. *Foreign tariff barriers on B are eliminated.*

3. Explain the following news dispatch from Hull, England: "The fish market here slumped today to what local commentators called 'a disastrous level'—all because of a shortage of potatoes. The potatoes are one of the main ingredients in a dish that figures on almost every café-menu—fish and chips."

4. Explain the law of supply. Why does the supply curve slope upward? What are the determinants of supply? What happens to the supply curve when each of these determinants changes? Distinguish between a change in supply and a change in the quantity supplied, noting the cause(s) of each.

5. KEY QUESTION *What effect will each of the following have on the supply of product B?*
   a. *A technological advance in the methods of producing B.*
   b. *A decline in the number of firms in industry B.*
   c. *An increase in the prices of resources required in the production of B.*
   d. *The expectation that the equilibrium price of B will be lower in the future than it is currently.*
   e. *A decline in the price of product A, a good whose production requires substantially the same techniques and resources as does the production of B.*
   f. *The levying of a specific sales tax on B.*
   g. *The granting of a 50-cent per-unit subsidy for each unit of B produced.*

6. "In the corn market, demand often exceeds supply and supply sometimes exceeds demand." "The price of corn rises and falls in response to changes in supply and demand." In which of these two statements are the terms "supply" and "demand" used correctly? Explain.

7. KEY QUESTION *Suppose the total demand for wheat and the total supply of wheat per month in the Winnipeg grain market are as follows:*

| Thousands of bushels demanded | Price per bushel | Thousands of bushels supplied | Surplus (+) or shortage (–) |
|---|---|---|---|
| 85 | $3.40 | 72 | ______ |
| 80 | $3.70 | 73 | ______ |
| 75 | $4.00 | 75 | ______ |
| 70 | $4.30 | 77 | ______ |
| 65 | $4.60 | 79 | ______ |
| 60 | $4.90 | 81 | ______ |

   a. *What is the equilibrium price? What is the equilibrium quantity? Fill in the surplus-shortage column and use it to explain why your answers are correct.*
   b. *Graph the demand for wheat and the supply of wheat. Be sure to label the axes of your graph correctly. Label equilibrium price P and equilibrium quantity Q.*
   c. *Why will $3.40 not be the equilibrium price in this market? Why not $4.90? "Surpluses drive prices up; shortages drive them down." Do you agree?*

**d.** *Now suppose that the government establishes a ceiling (maximum legal) price of, say, $3.70 for wheat. Explain carefully the effects of this ceiling price. Demonstrate your answer graphically. What might prompt government to establish a ceiling price?*

**8.** KEY QUESTION *How will each of the following changes in demand and/or supply affect equilibrium price and equilibrium quantity in a competitive market; that is, do price and quantity rise, fall, or remain unchanged, or are the answers indeterminate because they depend on the magnitudes of the shifts? You should use supply and demand diagrams to verify the answers.*

**a.** *Supply decreases and demand is constant.*
**b.** *Demand decreases and supply is constant.*
**c.** *Supply increases and demand is constant.*
**d.** *Demand increases and supply increases.*
**e.** *Demand increases and supply is constant.*
**f.** *Supply increases and demand decreases.*
**g.** *Demand increases and supply decreases.*
**h.** *Demand decreases and supply decreases.*

**9.** "Prices are the automatic regulator that tends to keep production and consumption in line with each other." Explain.

**10.** Explain: "Even though parking meters may yield little or no net revenue, they should nevertheless be retained because of the rationing function they perform."

**11.** Critically evaluate: "In comparing the two equilibrium positions in Figure 4-6a, I note that a larger amount is actually purchased at a higher price. This refutes the law of demand."

**12.** Suppose you go to a recycling centre and are paid $.25 per kilogram for your aluminum cans. However, the recycler charges you $.20 per bundle to accept your old newspapers. Use demand and supply diagrams to portray both markets. Explain how different government policies with respect to the recycling of aluminum and paper might account for these different market outcomes.

**13.** **Advanced analysis:** Assume that demand for a commodity is represented by the equation $P = 10 - .2Q_d$ and supply by the equation $P = 2 + .2Q_s$, where $Q_d$ and $Q_s$ are quantity demanded and quantity supplied, respectively, and $P$ is price. Using the equilibrium condition $Q_s = Q_d$, solve the equations to determine equilibrium price. Now determine equilibrium quantity. Graph the two equations to substantiate your answers.

**14.** **(The Last Word)** Discuss the economic aspects of ticket scalping, specifying gainers and losers.

**15.** WEB-BASED QUESTION **Changes in Demand—Baby Diapers and Retirement Villages** Other things equal, an increase in the number of buyers for a product or service will increase demand. Baby diapers and retirement villages are two products designed for different population groups. The U.S. Census www.census.gov/ipc/www/idbpyr.html provides population pyramids (graphs which show the distribution of population by age and sex) for countries for the current year, 2025, and 2050. View the population pyramids for Mexico, Japan, and the United States. Which country would you expect to have the greatest percentage increase in demand for baby diapers in the year 2050? For retirement villages? Which country would you expect to have the greatest absolute increase in demand for baby diapers? For retirement villages?

# APPENDIX TO CHAPTER 4

## THE MATHEMATICS OF MARKET EQUILIBRIUM

A market equilibrium is the price and the quantity, denoted as the pair (Q*, P*), of a commodity bought or sold at price P*. The following mathematical note provides an introduction of how a market equilibrium (Q*, P*) is derived.

The market equilibrium is found by using the market demand (buyers' behaviour), the market supply (sellers' behaviour), and the negotiating process (to find the agreed upon price and quantity, namely P* and Q*, on which to transact). The market equilibrium is identified by the condition reached at the end of the negotiating process that at the price they negotiated, $P^*$, the quantity of the commodity that buyers are willing to buy, denoted as $Q_D$, and the quantity sellers are willing to sell, denoted as $Q_S$, matches exactly.

The equation describing the downward sloping demand, in which $Q_D$ represents the quantity demanded by buyers and P the price, is

$$P = a - bQ_d$$

The demand tells us that if the price is higher than $a$ then the buyers will not buy; thus, for a transaction to occur the price must be lower. The demand also tells us that at a price lower than $a$ the quantity demanded by the buyers increases. Buyers' behaviour, as described by the demand equation, is that at lower prices buyers buy more quantity.

The equation describing the upward sloping market supply function, in which $Q_S$ represents the quantity supplied by sellers and P the price is

$$P = c + dQ_s$$

For the sellers if the price is lower than $c$ then they will sell nothing. If the price is $c$ or higher, then the supply equation states that sellers facing higher prices sell more quantity. Sellers' behaviour, as described by the supply equation, is that at higher prices sellers sell more quantity.

The negotiating process (in which price and quantity or both adjust) provides the mechanism by which, eventually, buyers and sellers agree upon a price, $P^*$, and a quantity, $Q^*$, at which they can buy and sell and thus complete the transaction. At the end of the negotiating process, the quantity demanded by the buyers, $Q_D$, is equal to the quantity supplied by the sellers, $Q_S$ (at the agreed upon price), and thus the market is in equilibrium. The mathematical representation of such a negotiating process is described in the following paragraphs.

At the agreed price, $P^*$, the equilibrium condition of the negotiating process, the equality in the quantity demanded and supplied, is

$$D_d = Q_S$$

Having denoted $Q^*$ as the equilibrium quantity, then it must be that $Q^* = Q_d = Q_s$. To solve for the equilibrium quantity $Q^*$ and the equilibrium price $P^*$ the demand and supply functions are used. With $Q^*$ the equilibrium quantity, for the buyers

$$P^* = a - bQ^*,$$

and for the sellers

$$P^* = c + dQ^*.$$

Now, since $P^*$ is the same agreed upon price by both buyer and seller, then

$$a - bQ^* = c + dQ^*,$$

giving the equilibrium quantity, $Q^*$, as

$$Q^* = (a - c)/(b + d).$$

To find $P^*$ substitute $(a - c)/(b + d)$ in the supply (or demand) function.

$$P^* = c + d(a - c)/(b + d), \text{ thus}$$

$$P^* = (ad + bc)/(a + d).$$

The equilbrium is $(Q^*, P^*) = [(a - c)/(b + d), (ad + cb)/(a + d)]$.

The market equilibrium may also be represented diagrammatically, as follows:

**FIGURE A4-1**

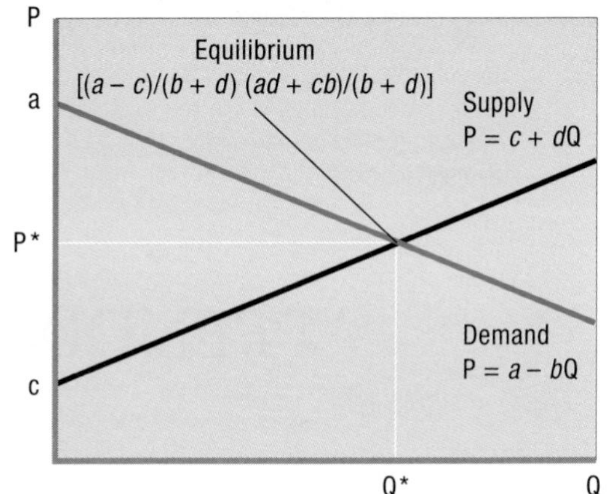


- Increase (decrease) in demand, $a$ increases (decreases) and both $Q^*$ and $P^*$ increase (decrease)
- Increase (decrease) in supply, $c$ decreases (increases) and $Q^*$ increases (decreases) and $P^*$ decreases (increases)

CHAPTER 5

# The Public Sector

WE NOTED IN CHAPTER 2 THAT A SOCIETY CAN choose various ways to deal with the economizing problem. A pure market system is one possibility; at the other extreme is a command economy, in which a central government makes the decisions as to what to produce, how much to produce, by what method to produce it, and how that production is distributed.

In fact, all economies are "mixed" to some extent; government and the market system share the responsibility of responding to the Five Fundamental Questions. In Canada, we have an economy dominated by markets, but government has played a significant role in the economic system of this country from the time of Confederation.

In this chapter we investigate several economic functions of the public sector in a market economy. Much emphasis is put on the crucial role of government when markets fail to fulfil their function of coordinating economic activity. The chapter ends with a discussion of the growth of government in recent decades and the ongoing debate on the extent of government involvement in self-regulating markets.

**IN THIS CHAPTER YOU WILL LEARN:**

- The five main economic functions of government in a market economy.
- What spillover benefits and costs are.
- What a public good is.
- The source of government revenues and expenditures in Canada.

## The Big Picture

PRIVATE MARKETS ARE VERY GOOD AT GETTING the most out of available resources. Markets also produce those goods and services that people with income to spend want most. But the market system does not arise instantaneously on its own. It requires certain institutions to function well. Among the most important of these is a central government that provides an environment conducive to a market economy.

Sometimes the market system fails to do its job of coordinating production and consumption decisions, or does it badly. We call these instances "market failures," and they require government intervention.

As you read this chapter, keep the following points in mind:

- **Key Concepts 1, 4,** and **7** are discussed.
- At times market participants have an effect on individuals not involved in market transactions. These effects can be negative, as in the case of a firm polluting the water supply of a village, or positive, as when a neighbour undertakes to beautify her house.
- Sometimes the market system does not produce enough of a specific good that is economically or socially justified. In such instances the government either produces the good itself or gives subsidies to private firms to supply it. ■

## ECONOMIC FUNCTIONS OF GOVERNMENT

All economies in the real world are "mixed": Government and the market system share the responsibility of responding to the Five Fundamental Questions. The Canadian economy is predominantly a market economy, yet the economic activities of government are of great significance.

In the next several sections we discuss the major economic functions of government—the public sector—in our economy. These functions are: (1) providing a legal and social framework; (2) maintaining competition within markets, (3) redistributing income as necessary for equity, (4) reallocating resources, and (5) stabilizing the economy.

The first two of these economic functions strengthen and facilitate the working of the market system; the last three modify pure capitalism to achieve economic and social goals.

## LEGAL AND SOCIAL FRAMEWORK

Government provides the legal framework and the services needed for a market economy to operate effectively. The legal framework sets the legal status of business enterprises, ensures the rights of private ownership, and allows the making and enforcement of contracts. Government also establishes the legal "rules of the game" governing the relationships of businesses, resource suppliers, and consumers with one another. Units of government can referee economic relationships, seek out foul play, and exercise authority in imposing appropriate penalties.

Services provided by government include police powers to maintain internal order, a system of standards for measuring the weight and quality of products, and a system of money to facilitate exchanges of goods and services.

The Food and Drug Act and Regulations of 1920 is an example of how government has strengthened the market system. This act sets rules of conduct governing producers in their relationships with consumers. It prohibits the sale of adulterated and misbranded foods and drugs, requires net weights and ingredients of products to be specified on their containers, establishes quality standards that must be stated on labels of packaged foods, and prohibits deceptive claims on patent-medicine labels. These measures are designed to prevent fraudulent activities by producers and to increase the public's confidence in the integrity of the market system. Similar legislation pertains to labour-management relations and relations of business firms to one another.

This type of government activity is presumed to improve resource allocation. Supplying a medium of exchange, ensuring product quality, defining ownership rights, and enforcing contracts increase the volume and safety of exchange. This widens markets and permits greater specialization in the use of property and human resources. Such specialization means a more efficient allocation of resources. However, some argue that government overregulates the interactions of businesses, consumers, and workers and say that this stifles economic incentives and impairs efficiency.

## MAINTAINING COMPETITION

Competition is the basic regulatory mechanism in a market economy. It is the force that subjects producers and resource suppliers to the dictates of consumer sovereignty. With competition, buyers are the boss, the market is their agent, and businesses are their servants.

It is a different story where there is only a single seller—a **monopoly**—or a small handful of sellers with *monopoly power*. Monopolists are not regulated by competition. When the number of sellers becomes so small that each seller can influence total supply, the seller or sellers have the power to set the product price. By restricting supply, these firms can charge above-competitive prices. Also, because entry to these industries is blocked, monopolists can enjoy persistent economic profits. The restricted output and the high prices and profits directly conflict with the interests of consumers. In fact, producer sovereignty supplants consumer sovereignty, and monopoly supplants competition. Where there is monopoly, the pursuit of self-interest does *not* lead to the social good. Rather, society's economic resources are *underallocated* to the monopolized product.

In Canada, government has attempted to control monopoly primarily in two ways:

1. **REGULATION AND OWNERSHIP** In a few situations, industries are *natural monopolies*—industries in which technology is such that only a single seller can achieve the lowest possible costs. Government has allowed these monopolies to exist but has also created public commissions to regulate their prices and set their service standards. Some aspects of transportation, communications, electricity, and other utilities are natural monopolies that government regulates in varying degrees. Sometimes, especially at the local level of government, public ownership replaces regulation.
2. **ANTI-MONOPOLY LAWS** In nearly all markets, efficient production can best be attained with a high degree of competition. The federal government has therefore enacted a series of anti-combines (anti-monopoly) laws, to maintain and strengthen competition.

## REDISTRIBUTION OF INCOME

The market system is impersonal. It may distribute income with more inequality than society desires. The market system yields very large incomes to those whose labour, by virtue of inherent ability and acquired education and skills, commands high wages. Similarly, those who—through hard work or easy inheritance—possess valuable capital and land receive large property incomes.

But others in society have less productive ability, have received only modest amounts of education and training, and have accumulated or inherited no property resources. Moreover, many of the aged, the physically and mentally handicapped, and female-headed families earn only very small incomes, or, like the unemployed, no incomes at all. Thus, in the market system there is considerable inequality in the distribution of income and therefore in the distribution of output among individual households. Poverty amidst overall plenty in the economy persists.

Thus, society chooses to redistribute income through a variety of government policies and programs:

1. **TRANSFERS** *Transfer payments,* for example, in the form of welfare cheques, provide relief to the destitute, the dependent, the handicapped, and older citizens; employment insurance payments provide aid to the unemployed.
2. **MARKET INTERVENTION** Government also alters the distribution of income by *market intervention*, that is, by acting to modify the prices that are or would be established by market forces. Providing farmers with above-market prices for their outputs and requiring that firms pay minimum wages are illustrations of government price fixing designed to raise incomes of specific groups.
3. **TAXATION** The personal income tax has been used historically to take a larger proportion of

the incomes of the rich than of the incomes of the poor, thus narrowing the after-tax income gap between high- and low-income earners.

The *extent* to which government should redistribute income is subject to many debates. Redistribution involves both benefits and costs. The alleged benefits are greater "fairness," or "economic justice"; the alleged costs are reduced incentives to work, save, invest, and produce, and therefore less total output and income.

## REALLOCATION OF RESOURCES

*Market failure* occurs when the competitive market system (1) produces the "wrong" amounts of certain goods and services or (2) fails to allocate any resources whatsoever to the production of certain goods and services whose output is economically justified. The first type of failure results from what economists call *spillovers*, and the second type involves *public goods*. Both kinds of market failure can be corrected by government action.

### Spillovers or Externalities

When we say that competitive markets automatically bring about efficient resource use, we assume that all the benefits and costs for each product are fully reflected in the market demand and supply curves. This is not always so in real markets; certain benefits or costs may escape the buyer or seller.

A spillover occurs when some of the costs or the benefits of a good are passed on to or "spill over to" parties other than the immediate buyer or seller. Spillovers are also called *externalities* because they are benefits or costs accruing to some third party that is external to the market transaction.

**Spillover Costs** Production or consumption costs that are inflicted on a third party without compensation are called **spillover costs**. Many spillover costs are in the form of environmental pollution. When a chemical manufacturer or meat-packing plant dumps its wastes into a lake or river, swimmers, fishermen, and boaters—and perhaps drinking-water supplies—suffer spillover costs. When a petroleum refinery pollutes the air with smoke or a paper mill creates distressing odours, the community bears spillover costs for which it is not compensated.

What are the economic effects? Recall that costs determine the position of the firm's supply curve. When a firm avoids some costs by polluting, its supply curve lies farther to the right than it does when the firm bears the full costs of production. This results in a larger output than is socially desirable—a market failure in the form of an *overallocation* of resources to the production of the good.

**Correcting for Spillover Costs** Government can do two things to correct the overallocation of resources. Both solutions are designed to internalize the external costs, that is, to make the offending firm pay the costs rather than shift them to others:

1. **LEGISLATION** In our examples of air and water pollution, the most direct action is legislation prohibiting or limiting pollution. Such legislation forces potential polluters to pay for the proper disposal of industrial wastes—here, by installing smoke-abatement equipment or water-purification facilities. The idea is to force potential offenders, under the threat of legal action, to bear all the costs associated with production.
2. **SPECIFIC TAXES** A less direct action is based on the fact that taxes are a cost and therefore a determinant of a firm's supply curve. Government might levy a *specific tax*—a tax confined to a particular product—on each unit of the polluting firm's output. The amount of this tax would roughly equal the estimated amount of the spillover cost arising from the production of each unit of output. Through this tax, government would pass back to the offending firm a cost equivalent to the spillover cost that the firm is avoiding. This would shift the firm's supply curve to the left, reducing equilibrium output and eliminating the overallocation of resources.

**Spillover Benefits** But spillovers may also appear as benefits. Production or consumption of certain goods and services may confer spillover or external benefits on third parties or on the community at large without compensating payment. Measles and polio immunization result in direct benefits to the immediate consumer of those vaccines. But immunization against contagious diseases yields widespread and substantial spillover benefits to the entire community. Discovery of an

AIDS vaccine would benefit society far beyond the persons vaccinated. Unvaccinated individuals would clearly benefit by the slowing of the spread of the disease.

Education is another example of **spillover benefits**. Education benefits individual consumers: "More educated" people generally achieve higher incomes than "less educated" people. But education also provides benefits to society. The economy as a whole benefits from a more versatile and more productive labour force, on the one hand, and smaller outlays for crime prevention, law enforcement, and welfare programs, on the other. There is evidence indicating that any worker with a *specific* educational or skill level will be more productive if associated workers have more education. In other words, worker Smith becomes more productive simply because coworkers Jones and Green are more educated.

Spillover benefits mean that the market demand curve, which reflects only private benefits, understates total benefits. The demand curve for the product lies farther to the left than it would if all benefits were taken into account by the market. This means that a smaller amount of the product will be produced or, alternatively, that there will be an *underallocation* of resources to the product—again a market failure.

**Correcting for Spillover Benefits** How might the underallocation of resources associated with spillover benefits be corrected? The answer is to either subsidize consumers (to increase demand), subsidize producers (to increase supply), or, in the extreme, have government produce the product.

1. **SUBSIDIZE CONSUMERS** To correct the underallocation of resources to higher education, the Canadian government provides low-interest loans to students so that they can afford more education. These loans increase the demand for higher education.
2. **SUBSIDIZE SUPPLIERS** In some cases government might find it more convenient and administratively simpler to correct an underallocation by subsidizing producers. This is done in higher education, where provincial governments provide substantial portions of the budgets of colleges and universities. These subsidies lower the costs of producing higher education and increase its supply. Publicly subsidized immunization programs, hospitals, and medical research are other examples.
3. **PROVIDE GOODS VIA GOVERNMENT** A third policy option may be used where spillover benefits are extremely large: Government may finance or, in the extreme, own and operate all industries that are involved.

## Public Goods and Services

Private goods, which are produced through the competitive market system, are said to be *divisible* because they are produced in units small enough to be purchased and used by individual buyers. Private goods are also subject to the **exclusion principle**. Buyers who are willing and able to pay the equilibrium price of the product obtain it, but those who are unable or unwilling to pay are *excluded* from the product and its benefits.

Certain other goods and services called **public goods** are not produced by the market system because they have the opposite characteristics. Public goods are indivisible; they must be produced in such large units that they cannot ordinarily be sold to individual buyers. Individuals can buy hamburgers, computers, and automobiles through the market, but not aircraft carriers, highways, space telescopes, and air-traffic control.

More important, *the exclusion principle does not apply to public goods*; there is no effective way of excluding individuals from their benefits once those goods come into existence. Obtaining the benefits of private goods requires that they be *purchased*; obtaining benefits from public goods requires only that they be *available*.

The classic public goods example is a proposed lighthouse on a treacherous coast. The construction of the lighthouse would be economically justified if its benefits (fewer shipwrecks) exceeded its cost. But the benefits accruing to one user would not be great enough to justify the purchase of such an indivisible product. Moreover, once it was in operation, the warning light would be a guide to all ships; there would be no practical way to exclude any captain from using the light. Economists call this the **free-rider-problem**: people receiving benefits from a good without contributing to its cost.

Because the exclusion principle does not apply to the lighthouse, private enterprises have no economic incentive to supply it. Since the services of the lighthouse cannot be priced and sold, it would be unprofitable for a private firm to devote resources to it. So here we have a service that could yield substantial benefits but to which the market would allocate no resources. It is a public good, much like national defence, flood control, public health, satellite navigation systems, and insect-abatement programs. If society requires such goods, they must be provided by the public sector and financed by compulsory charges in the form of taxes.

### Quasi-Public Goods

The applicability of the exclusion principle distinguishes private from public goods, and government may provide the latter. However, many other goods and services are provided by government even though they could be made exclusive. Such goods, called **quasi-public goods**, include education, streets and highways, police and fire protection, libraries and museums, preventive medicine, and sewage disposal. These goods or services could be produced and delivered in such a way that the exclusion principle applied. All could be priced and provided by private firms through the market system. But, as noted earlier, these services have substantial spillover benefits, so they would be underproduced by the market system. Therefore, government may provide them to avoid the underallocation of resources that would otherwise occur.

Since quasi-public goods can be produced in either the private or the public sector—and because spillover benefits are difficult to measure—we can understand the continuing controversy surrounding the status of medical care and low-income housing. Are these private goods to be produced through the market system, or are they quasi-public goods to be provided by government?

### Allocation of Resources to Public and Quasi-Public Goods

The market system fails to allocate resources for public goods and underallocates resources for quasi-public goods. What then is the mechanism by which such goods get produced?

Public and quasi-public goods are purchased through the government on the basis of group, or collective, choices. (Contrast this with private goods, which are purchased from private enterprises on the basis of individual choices.) The types and qualities of goods to be produced by government are determined in a democracy by political voting. That is, the members of a society vote for particular political candidates. Each candidate represents certain public policies, and those policies determine the quantities of the various public and quasi-public goods to be produced and consumed. The group choices made in the political arena supplement the choices of households and businesses in answering the Five Fundamental Questions.

How are resources reallocated from the production of private goods to the production of public and quasi-public goods? In an economy whose resources are fully employed, government must free resources from private goods production to make them available for production of public and quasi-public goods. The means of releasing resources from private uses is to reduce private demand for them. This is accomplished by levying taxes on households and businesses, taking some of their income out of the circular flow. With lower incomes and hence less purchasing power, households and businesses must curtail their consumption and investment spending. Taxes diminish the private demand for goods and services, which in turn reduce the private demand for resources. So by diverting purchasing power from private spenders to government, taxes remove resources from private uses. (Global Perspective 5-1 shows the extent to which various countries divert labour from private sector to public sector employment.)

Government expenditures of tax proceeds can then reallocate the resources to the provision of public and quasi-public goods and services. Personal and corporate income taxation releases resources from the production of consumer goods (food, clothing, television sets) and investment goods (printing presses, boxcars, warehouses). Government expenditures shift these resources to the production of public and quasi-public goods (post offices, submarines, parks). Government purposely reallocates resources to bring about significant changes in the composition of the economy's total output. ***(Key Questions 3 and 4)***

## STABILIZATION

Historically, the most recent function of government is that of stabilizing the economy—helping the private economy achieve full employment of resources and stable prices. Here we will only outline (rather than fully explain) how government tries to do this.

## 5-1 GLOBAL PERSPECTIVE

**Government employment as a percentage of total employment, selected nations**

The ratio of government employment to total employment measures the extent to which government diverts labour resources from the private sector in order to produce public goods and quasi-public goods. The ratio, or percentage, varies greatly among nations.

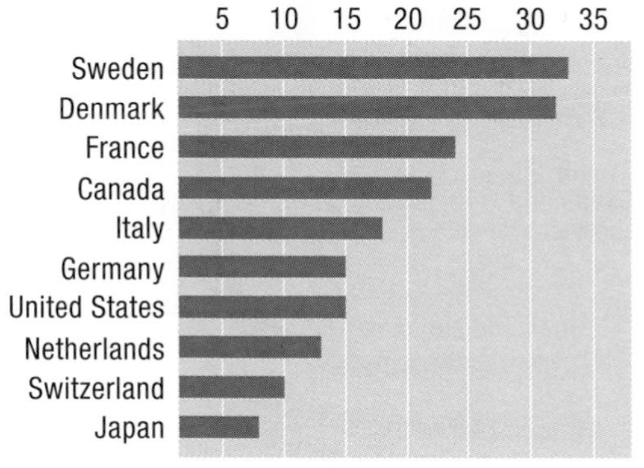


*Source:* Organization for Economic Cooperation and Development.

An economy's level of output depends directly on total or aggregate expenditure. A high level of total spending means it is profitable for industries to produce large outputs, which in turn ensures that both property and human resources will be employed at high levels. But aggregate spending may either fall short of or exceed the particular level necessary for full employment and price stability. Either of two possibilities, unemployment and inflation, may then occur:

1. **UNEMPLOYMENT** The level of total spending in the private sector may be too low to employ all available resources. Then government may choose to augment private spending so that total spending—private *plus* public—will be sufficient to generate full employment. Government can do this by adjusting government spending and taxation. Specifically, it might increase its own spending on public goods and services or reduce taxes to stimulate private spending. It might also reduce interest rates to promote more private borrowing and spending.
2. **INFLATION** Inflation is a rising general level of prices and is undesirable because it makes goods and services less attainable for many households. Prices of goods and services rise when the economy attempts to spend more than its capacity to produce. If aggregate spending exceeds the economy's output, prices will rise as consumers bid for available goods. That is, excessive aggregate spending is inflationary. Government's appropriate response is to eliminate the excess spending. It can do this by cutting its own expenditures, raising taxes to curtail private spending, or by increasing interest rates to reduce private borrowing and spending.

## 5-1 QUICK REVIEW

- Government enhances the operation of the market system by providing an appropriate legal foundation and promoting competition.
- Transfer payments, direct market intervention, and taxation are ways government can lessen income inequality.
- Government can correct for the overallocation of resources associated with spillover costs through legislation or specific taxes; the underallocation of resources associated with spillover benefits can be offset by government subsidies.
- Government (rather than private firms) must provide desired public goods because they are indivisible and the exclusion principle does not apply to them; government also provides many quasi-public goods because of their large spillover benefits.
- Government spending, tax revenues, and interest rates can be manipulated to stabilize the economy.

## THE CIRCULAR FLOW REVISITED

Government is thoroughly integrated into the real and monetary flows that make up the economy. In Figure 5-1 we have integrated government into the circular flow model of Chapter 2. In that figure flows (1) through (4) restate Figure 2-6. Flows (1) and (2) show business expenditures for the resources pro-

**FIGURE 5-1 The circular flow and the public sector**

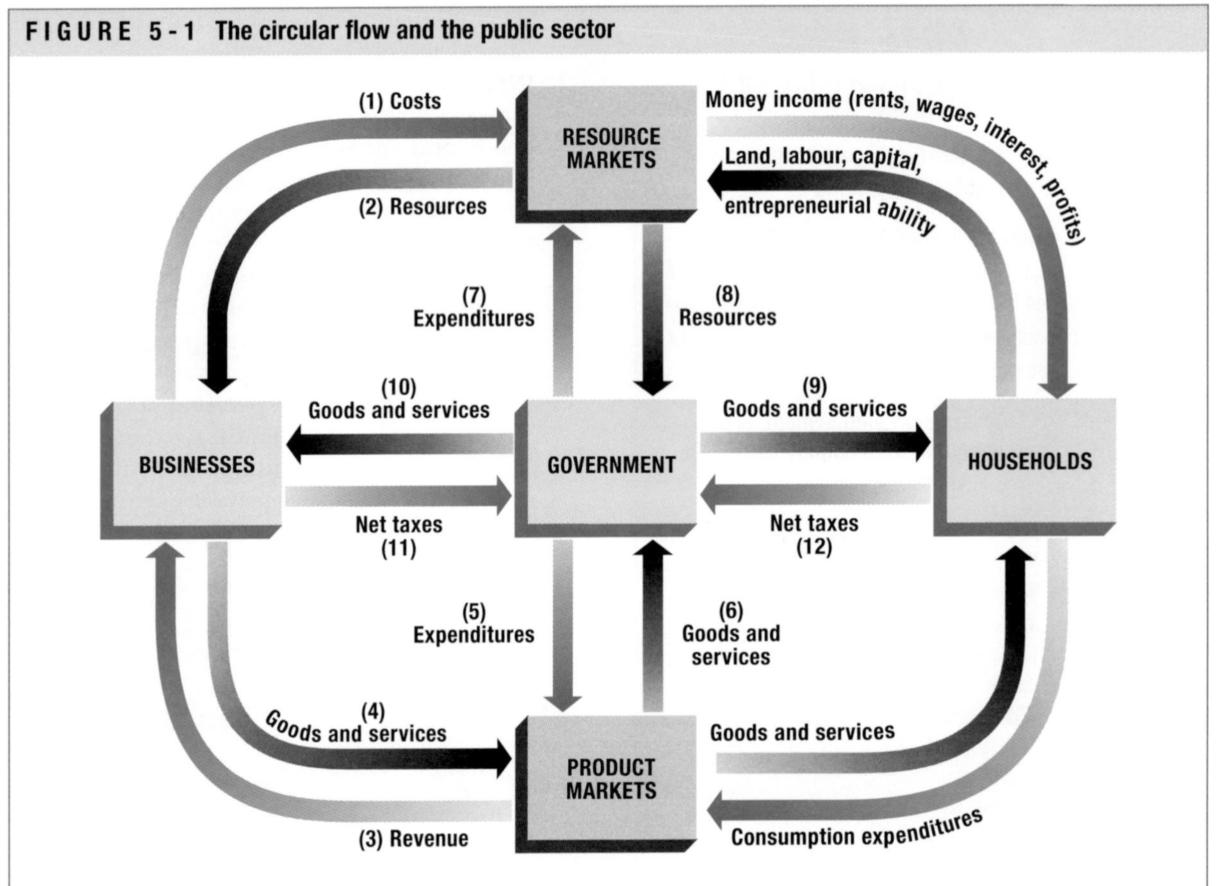


Government expenditures, taxes, and transfer payments affect the distribution of income, the allocation of resources, and the level of economic activity.

vided by households. These expenditures are costs to businesses but represent wage, rent, interest, and profit income to households. Flows (3) and (4) portray households' consumer expenditures for the goods and services produced by businesses.

Now consider the modifications resulting from the addition of government. Flows (5) through (8) tell us that government makes purchases in both product and resource markets. Specifically, flows (5) and (6) represent government purchases of such things as paper, computers, and military hardware from private businesses. Flows (7) and (8) reflect government purchases of resources. The federal government employs and pays salaries to members of Parliament, the armed forces, lawyers, meat inspectors, and so on. Provincial and municipal governments hire and pay teachers, bus drivers, police, and firefighters. The federal government might also lease or purchase land to expand a military base; a city may buy land on which to build a new elementary school.

Government then provides public goods and services to both households and businesses as shown by flows (9) and (10). Financing public goods and services requires tax payments by businesses and households as reflected in flows (11) and (12). These flows are labelled as *net* taxes to acknowledge that they also include "taxes in reverse" in the form of transfer payments to households and subsidies to businesses. Thus, flow (11) entails not merely corporate income, sales, and excise taxes flowing from businesses to government but also various subsidies to farmers, shipbuilders, and some airlines. Most business subsidies are "concealed" in the form of low-interest loans, loan guarantees, tax concessions, or public facilities provided at prices below their cost. Similarly, flow (12) includes both taxes (personal income taxes, payroll taxes) collected by government directly from households and transfer payments, for example, welfare payments and social insurance benefits, paid to households.

Our circular flow model shows how government can alter the distribution of income, reallocate resources, and change the level of economic activity. The structure of taxes and transfer payments can have a significant impact on income distribution. In flow (12) a tax structure that draws tax revenues primarily from well-to-do households, combined with a system of transfer payments to low-income households, will result in greater equality in the distribution of income.

Flows (6) and (8) imply an allocation of resources different from that of a purely private economy. Government buys goods and labour resources that differ from those purchased by households.

Finally, all the governmental flows suggest ways government might try to stabilize the economy. If the economy were experiencing unemployment, an increase in government spending with taxes and transfers held constant would increase total spending, output, and employment. Similarly, with the level of government expenditures constant, a decline in taxes or an increase in transfer payments would increase spendable incomes and boost private spending and employment. To fight inflation, the opposite policies would be in order: reduced government spending, increased taxes, and reduced transfers.

## THE SIZE OF GOVERNMENT

The size of governments has increased significantly since the end of World War II. Not only have the number of employees of the federal, provincial, and municipal governments increased, but the shares of the total output of goods and services governments take in taxes and spend have also risen significantly. In 1997 the expenditures of all three levels of governments in Canada collectively represented about 45 percent of the annual production of the country; this is more than double what it was in 1945. Figure 5-2 shows the growth of government expenditures and revenues of all three levels of governments in Canada since 1970. Expenditures have risen more rapidly than revenues, giving rise to persistent deficits. This trend reversed beginning in the mid-1990s as all levels of government cut back their expenditures.

**FIGURE 5-2 The growth of government**

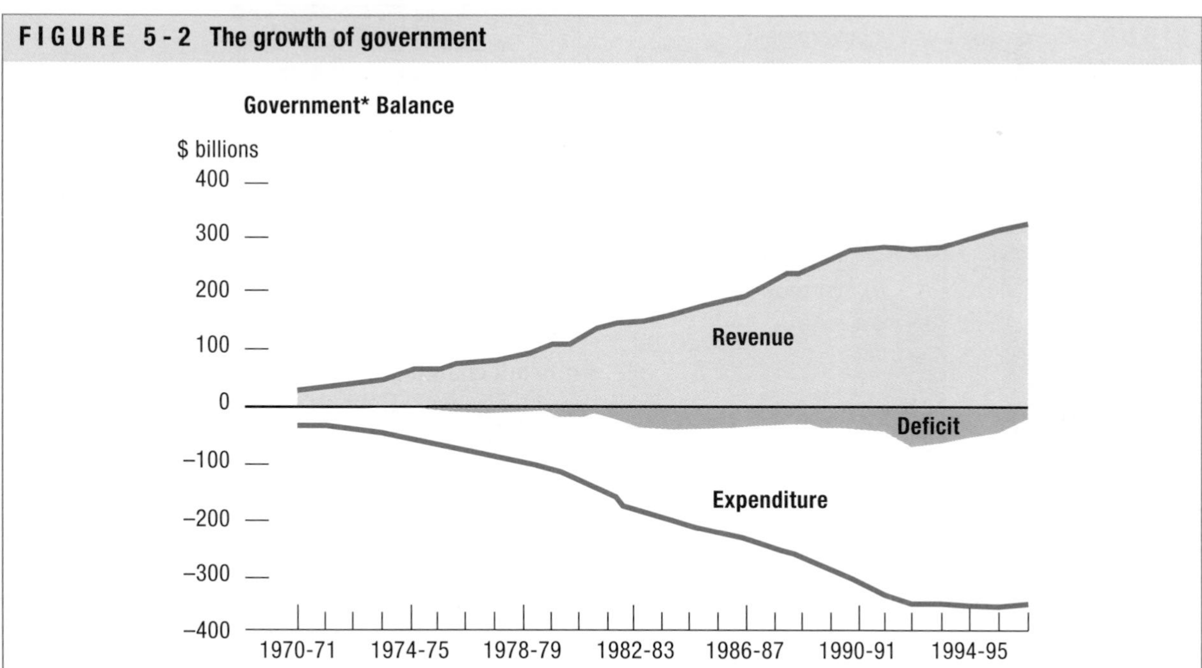


An indication of the increasing growth of government is the expanding combined expenditures and revenues of the federal, provincial, and municipal governments. Both government revenues and expenditures have increased rapidly since 1970, but levelled off in the mid-1990s.

*Consolidated federal, provincial, territorial and municipal governments.
*Source:* Data for 1970–71, adapted from Statistics Canada, *Canada Yearbook, 1994*, Catalogue No. 11-402; "Canadian Economic Observer," Catalogue No. 11-010; for the remaining years computed from data in Statistics Canada. CANSIM, Matrix 3315 and 3776.

## Growth of Government Outlays

We can get a general impression of the size and growth of government's economic role by examining government purchases of goods and services and government transfer payments. The distinction between these two types of outlays is significant.

1. **Government purchases** are "exhaustive"; they directly absorb or employ resources. For example, the purchase of a car absorbs the labour of engineers along with steel, plastic, and a host of other inputs.
2. **Transfer payments** are "nonexhaustive"; they do not directly absorb resources or account for production. Social and health benefits, welfare payments, veterans' benefits, and unemployment insurance payments are examples of transfer payments. Their key characteristic is that those who receive them make no current contribution to output in return for these payments.

Figure 5-3 shows the changing pattern of government expenditures between the mid-1980s and mid-1990s. The areas in which there have been significant changes are debt charges and spending on social services. Debt charges have doubled, while expenditure on social services has reached about a third of all government expenditure. Global Perspective 5-2 shows that total revenues as a percentage of GDP for the federal government are about 35 percent, closer to European countries than to the United States.

**FIGURE 5-3 The trend in government expenditure**

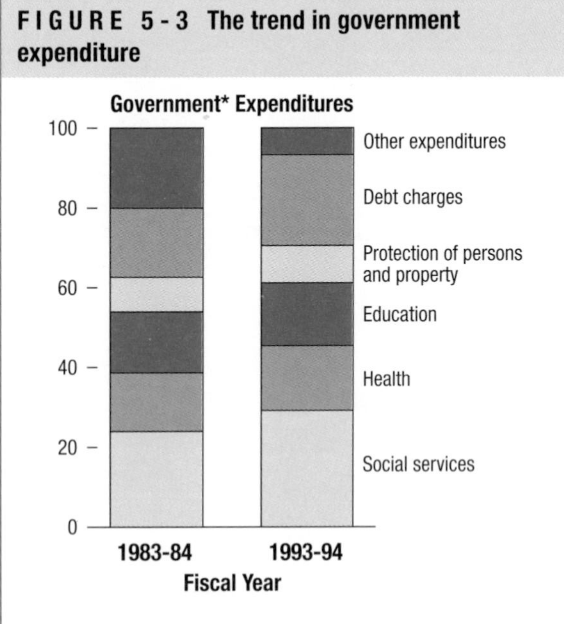


The two main changes in the pattern of government expenditures have been the increase in debt payment and spending on social services.

*Consolidated federal, provincial, territorial and municipal governments.
*Source:* Statistics Canada, *Canada Yearbook, 1997.*

**5-2**
**GLOBAL PERSPECTIVE**

**Total tax revenues as a percentage of domestic output**

The ratio of tax revenues to domestic output is one measure of a country's tax burden (level of taxes). Among the world's industrialized nations, Canada's tax burden is closer to those in western Europe, such as Italy and Germany, than those of our immediate neighbour to the south, the United States.

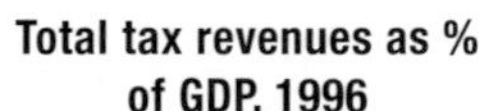


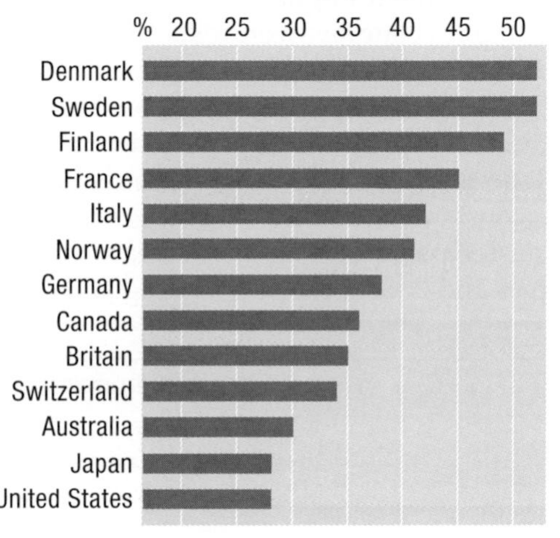


*Source:* Organization for Economic Cooperation and Development.

## SOURCES OF GOVERNMENT EXPENDITURES AND REVENUES

Now let's disaggregate the public sector into federal, provincial, and municipal units of govern-

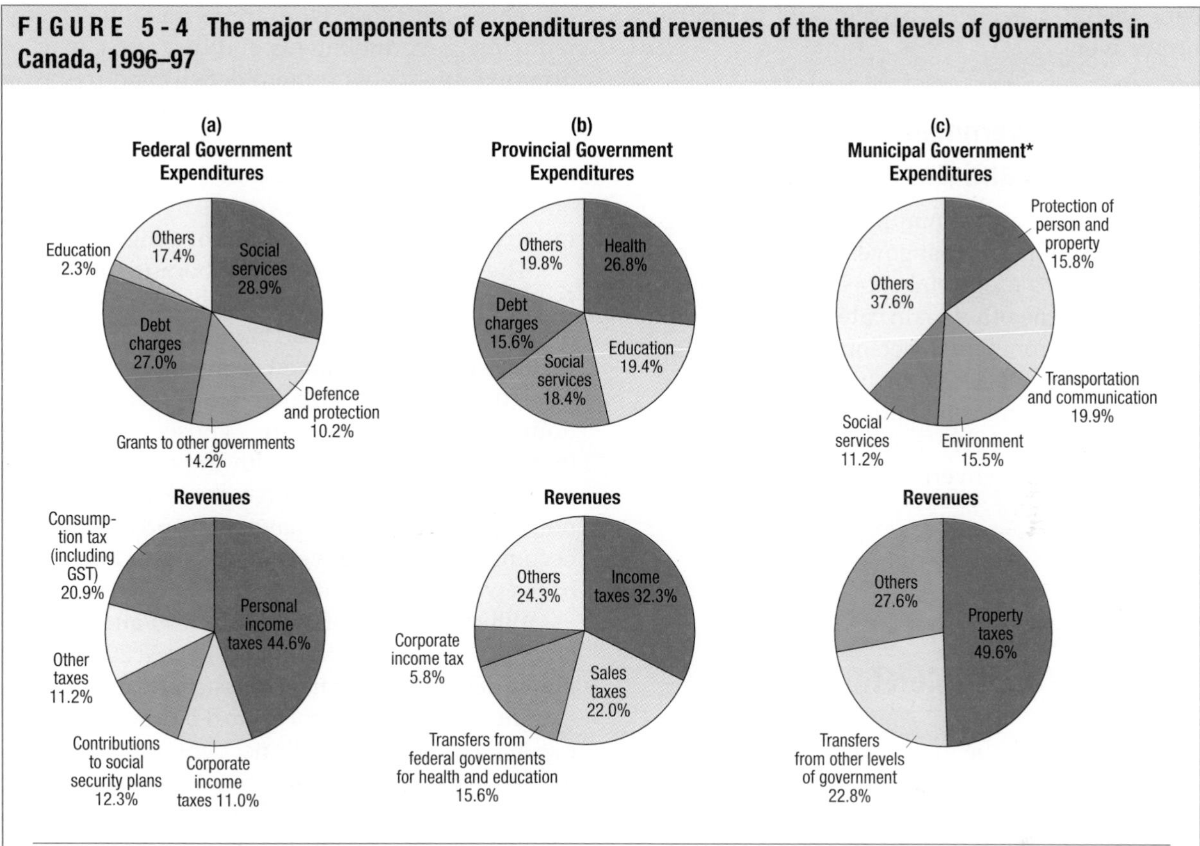


**FIGURE 5-4 The major components of expenditures and revenues of the three levels of governments in Canada, 1996–97**

*Source:* Statistics Canada, CANSIM, Matrix 3315, 3776, and 7093. More recent data are available from Statistics Canada www. statcan. ca/english/Pgdb/State/govern.htm.

*Municipal government data are for 1996.

ment to compare their expenditures. Figure 5-4a tells the story for the federal government.

## Federal Expenditures and Revenues

Figure 5-4a shows that three important areas of federal spending stand out: (1) social services, (2) protection of persons and property, and (3) interest on the public debt. The social services category, representing almost 30 percent of total expenditures, reflects the myriad income-maintenance programs for the aged, the disabled, the unemployed, the handicapped, and families with no breadwinner. *Transfers to other governments* constitute about 14 percent of the federal budget and underscore the fact that provinces and municipalities have constitutional responsibilities but inadequate sources of revenues. *Interest on the public debt* has risen steeply in recent years because the public debt itself has grown.

On the revenue side, **personal income taxes** continue to contribute the largest share of federal government revenues at about 45 percent; **corporate income taxes** represent 11 percent, while contributions to social security plans account for 12 percent. The remaining revenues are raised by a variety of taxes, including the Goods and Services Tax (GST), which contributes about 21 percent.

## Provincial Expenditures and Revenues

Health is the largest provincial and territorial outlay at an estimated 27 percent of total expenditures in 1996–97. Education was the second largest outlay at about 19 percent, and social services, the third largest expenditure, accounted for about the same percentage (18.4 percent).

Figure 5-4b shows that income taxes, general sales taxes, and transfers from other levels of governments represented the main generators of revenues at 32.3 percent, 22 percent, and 15.6 percent respectively.

### Municipal Government Expenditures and Revenues

Transportation and communication is the largest component of municipal government spending at almost 20 percent of total expenditures, as Figure 5-4c shows. The other main categories of expenditures are environmental, person and property protection, and social services outlays.

Municipal government revenues come primarily from **property taxes** (50 percent of the total); provincial government transfers make up about a quarter of the rest.

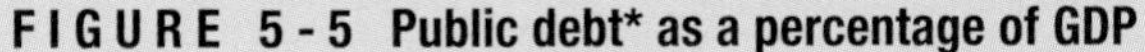

## THE DEBATE OVER THE SIZE OF GOVERNMENT

The debate over the appropriate size of government is a long-standing one, but it has received considerable attention in the last decade as government debt has spiralled upwards.

There are those who argue passionately for reducing government expenditure as a way of bringing down government deficits and reducing the size of government itself. Others maintain the government debt problem has been exaggerated and that if it is, or becomes, a problem the government ought to raise revenues by taxing corporations and well-off Canadians at a higher rate.

These differing views arise because of the different perceptions of the effectiveness of government policies in the past. Those in favour of reducing the size of government argue that instances of government success at alleviating social and economic problems are rare. Those who favour increasing taxes to deal with the mounting debt point out how much worse the social and economic problems would have been and are likely to become if drastic government expenditure cutbacks were implemented.

Whichever side of the debate you are on, there is no dispute over the fact that in the last 20 years the public debt in Canada has risen steeply, and more so than the OECD average. Figure 5-5 shows the steep rise in the Canadian public net debt compared with the OECD average between the mid-1980s and mid-1990s. Since then the growth of the public debt has levelled off and actually begun to fall.

**FIGURE 5-5 Public debt* as a percentage of GDP**

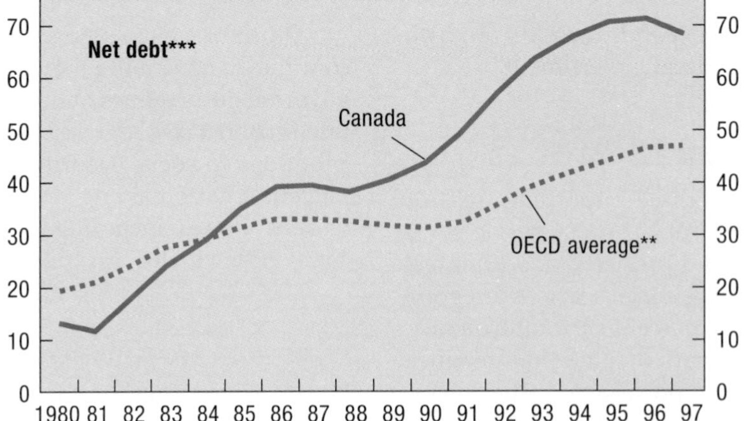


Since the mid-1980s, Canada's public debt has grown much more rapidly than the OECD average. Recently the public debt has levelled off and begun to fall compared to the OECD average.

*General government: National Accounts definitions. 1997 data are OECD projections.
**Weighted average using 1991 GDP weights and exchange rates.
***Financial liabilities less financial assets.
*Source:* OECD, National Accounts: Secretariat estimates.

In
The Media

1 KEY CONCEPT 4 KEY CONCEPT

# Blue-box Program not Huge Success*

## Leaked memo shows recycling cost far greater than disposal in landfills

BY GAY ABBATE
THE GLOBE AND MAIL

TORONTO—The blue-box recycling program in Toronto is far from the financial success that has been claimed, with 85 per cent of all residential garbage ending up at landfill sites, according to a leaked municipal works department document.

The document, leaked to The Globe and Mail and some Toronto city councillors, shows how poorly the blue-box program is doing 11 years after it was implemented.

The figures on the recycling program are on a one-page spreadsheet that Art Smith, a senior engineer in the waste reduction division of the former municipality of Metro Toronto, sent to a colleague in the old city of Toronto works department this month. The departments have since merged as part of the amalgamation of Toronto and other municipalities.

The data show that Torontonians produce about 859,262 tonnes of garbage annually, costing $89.8-million to collect and recycle or dump.

Among the details outlined in the document:

- About 39.5 per cent of the 5,818 tonnes of plastic containers used are deposited into blue boxes, but only 22 per cent of the total consumption ends up being recycled.
- About 25.8 per cent of the 6,654 tonnes of high-density polyethylene products are discarded into blue boxes but only 20 per cent is recycled.
- Only 23.31 per cent of the 6,620 tonnes of aluminum cans used are put into blue boxes, but only 22 per cent is recycled.
- About 112,600 tonnes of cardboard and corrugated products are generated, of which only 12.65 per cent is deposited in blue boxes, but all is recycled.

The figures are outrageous and shocking, said Councillor Judy Sgro, a strong advocate of recycling in the former municipality of North York, where she also was a councillor.

"It's costing us a fortune in dollars [to recycle], and most of the material is still ending up in landfill sites."

Ms. Sgro, who also received a copy of the document, said in an interview last night that the numbers are "significantly different from figures [Metro] staff gave me six weeks ago."

She said she was told that it cost about $55 a tonne to collect and recycle items in the blue boxes and $60 a tonne to put them into a dump site.

And last month, the group Corporations Supporting Recycling produced similar figures in a news release: $52 a tonne for recycling, compared with $87 a tonne for disposal in a landfill.

But according to the leaked figures, the net recycling cost per tonne is $136.89 and the cost for landfill disposal is $96.90 a tonne.

"Staff is telling us a major success story, but the numbers show otherwise," Ms. Sgro said.

Last year, Metro Toronto councillors approved construction of a recycling plant in the Dufferin Street and Allan Road area to sort all recyclable materials. The cost, between $4 million and $7 million, was approved because politicians believed the blue-box program was a success.

In light of the new figures, Toronto Council should halt the project immediately, Ms. Sgro said. She plans to demand that works department staff prepare a report for Mayor Mel Lastman, a strong advocate of recycling when he was mayor of North York.

*Source: Globe and Mail*, January 27, 1998, pp. A1 and A12. Reprinted with permission from the *Globe and Mail*.
*Subsequent stories on this subject suggested that recycling costs are not as high as this article reports.

## THE STORY IN BRIEF

The blue-box program in one large Canadian city seems to have failed. Most of the plastic containers, aluminum cans, and cardboard and corrugated products still end up in landfill sites, and the cost of recycling what is collected is much higher than dumping it in landfill sites.

## THE ECONOMICS BEHIND THE STORY

- Garbage can cause negative externalities by polluting landfill sites or taking up valuable farmland or potential residential building sites around urban areas. One way to reduce these negative externalities is to recycle some of the refuse.

- According to the report, many people are not separating their garbage; most of the recyclable refuse such as newspaper and plastic containers is thrown out with the rest of the garbage. This suggests that the marginal benefit of recycling to most people is less than the marginal cost associated with separating the garbage. It also appears that the cost of recycling is significantly higher than putting it in landfill sites.
- Can you think of a way to get households to reduce the amount of garbage they generate? ■

# The Last Word

7 KEY CONCEPT

## MARKET FAILURE AND THE NEED FOR GOVERNMENT

**Private markets fulfil individual desires very well, but where there is a need for collective action, they often fail.**

SUPPOSE A MUNICIPALITY REQUIRES NEW ROADS. In the absence of a government request that a private firm build it, it is unlikely that a private firm will build the required road on its own initiative. Or, to express it in another way, private markets will not make available public goods. The citizens of the municipality have to elect a government to either direct a private firm to build the road, or hire people to buy the capital equipment needed to construct the road on its own.

Why would a private firm not undertake to build a road on its own? The obstacle is common property rights. The land on which the road is to be built must be owned by the firm before it would consider building the road. Lands used by all citizens are most often held publicly. The firm would thus need to get the consent of all the citizens affected. Such unanimity would be difficult to achieve. Indeed, it is the difficulty of making collective decisions that makes governments essential to the creation of an infrastructure—such as roads and airports—necessary to facilitate the functioning of markets. Not only must a decision be made to build the road, but then the decision must be made as to who should bear the cost. The free-rider problem arises here. Every individual hopes someone will pay for the needed road. This way he or she can have the benefits without contributing to its cost. The free-rider problem can potentially arise in all situations where collective action must be taken. Unless we have a central authority—government—with the monopoly power to impose costs on all members of a society, many socially useful projects will not be undertaken.

In a pathbreaking book, *The Logic of Collective Action*,[1] Mancur Olson pointed out some 30 years ago that contrary to popular belief, groups of individuals with common interest do not necessarily attempt to further those common interests. In many instances group members attempt to further their own personal interests. A few years later, the political scientist Garrett Hardin popularized the term "the tragedy of the commons"[2] to describe the problems that arise when there are common property rights. For example, where there are common property rights to a natural resource, it is typically overexploited. The cod stocks on Canada's east coast have suffered just that fate.

Where collective action is required, or where there are common property rights, governments are needed because markets fail to bring together the interests of the individual and those of society. The federal government has had to impose mandatory fishing restrictions to save the cod stocks from dwindling further. Governments must make decisions to construct a road, otherwise the road might never get built. Clearly, markets work best where there are private property rights. ■

[1] Mancur Olson, *The Logic of Collective Action* (Cambridge: Cambridge University Press, 1965).

[2] Garret Hardin, "The Tragedy of the Commons," *Science* 162 (1968):1243–48.

## CHAPTER SUMMARY

1. Government enhances the operation of the market system by **a** providing an appropriate legal and social framework, and **b** acting to maintain competition.
2. Government alters the distribution of income through the tax-transfer system and market intervention.
3. Spillovers or externalities cause the equilibrium output of certain goods to vary from the socially efficient output. Spillover costs result in an overallocation of resources that can be corrected by legislation or specific taxes. Spillover benefits are accompanied by an underallocation of resources that can be corrected by subsidies to consumers or producers.
4. Only government is willing to provide public goods, because such goods are indivisible and entail benefits from which nonpaying consumers (free-riders) cannot be excluded; private firms will not produce these goods. Quasi-public goods have some characteristics of public goods and some of private goods; they are provided by government because the private sector would underallocate resources to their production.
5. Government can reduce unemployment or inflation by altering its taxation, spending, and interest-rate policies.
6. Government purchases use up or absorb resources; transfer payments do not. Government purchases have been rising as a percentage of domestic output since 1950. Transfers also have grown significantly, so that total government spending is now over 40 percent of domestic output.
7. The main categories of federal spending are for employment insurance, health, and interest on the public debt; revenues come primarily from personal income, payroll, and corporate income taxes.
8. The primary sources of revenue for the provinces are sales and excise taxes; public welfare, education, highways, and health and hospitals are their major expenditures.
9. At the local level, most revenue comes from property tax, and education is the largest expenditure.
10. Under our system of fiscal federalism, provincial and municipal tax revenues are supplemented by sizable revenue transfers from the federal government.

## TERMS AND CONCEPTS

monopoly
spillover costs
spillover benefits
exclusion principle
public goods
free-rider problem
quasi-public goods
government purchases
transfer payments
personal income taxes
corporate income taxes
property taxes

## STUDY QUESTIONS

1. List and briefly discuss the main economic functions of government. Which of these functions do you think is the most controversial? Explain your reasoning.
2. What divergences arise between equilibrium and an efficient output when **a** spillover costs and **b** spillover benefits are present? How might government correct for these discrepancies? "The presence of spillover costs suggests underallocation of resources to that product and the need for governmental subsidies." Do you agree? Why or why not? Explain how zoning and seat belt laws might be used to deal with a problem of spillover costs.
3. KEY QUESTION *What are the basic characteristics of public goods? Explain the significance of the exclusion principle. By what means does government provide public goods?*

4. KEY QUESTION *Draw a production possibilities curve with public goods on the vertical axis and private goods on the horizontal axis. Assuming the economy is initially operating on the curve, indicate how the production of public goods might be increased. How might the output of public goods be increased if the economy is initially operating at a point inside the curve?*

5. Use your understanding of the characteristics of private and public goods to determine whether the following should be produced through the market system or provided by government: **a** bread; **b** street lighting; **c** bridges; **d** parks; **e** swimming pools; **f** medical care; **g** mail delivery; **h** housing; **i** air-traffic control; **j** libraries. State why you answered as you did in each case.

6. Explain how government can manipulate its expenditures and tax revenues to reduce **a** unemployment and **b** the rate of inflation.

7. "Most government actions affect the distribution of income, the allocation of resources, and the levels of unemployment and prices." Use the circular flow model to confirm this assertion for each of the following: **a** the construction of a new high school in Huron County; **b** a 2 percent reduction in the corporate income tax; **c** an expansion of preschool programs for disadvantaged children; **d** a $50-million increase in spending for space research; **e** the levying of a tax on air polluters; and **f** a $1 increase in the legally required minimum wage.

8. What is the most important source of revenue and the major type of expenditure for the federal government? For provincial governments? For municipal governments?

9. **(The Last Word)** Why do private markets fail? In your answer, refer to the dwindling cod stocks on Canada's east coast.

10. WEB-BASED QUESTION **Federal Revenues and Expenditures** Look at Statistics Canada's Web site at www.statcan.ca/english/Pgdb/State/Government/govt026.htm and locate the federal government revenues and expenditures tables for the last five years. What has been the trend for expenditures? Revenues? What is the trend in the annual deficit or surplus?

CHAPTER 6

# Canada in the Global Economy

BACKPACKERS IN THE WILDERNESS LIKE TO THINK they are "leaving the world behind." Ironically, like Atlas, they carry the world on their shoulders. Much of their backpacking equipment is imported—knives from Switzerland, rain gear from South Korea, cameras from Japan, aluminum pots made in England, miniature stoves from Sweden, sleeping bags from China, and compasses from Finland. Some backpackers wear hiking boots from Italy, sunglasses made in France, and watches from Japan or Switzerland. Moreover, they may drive to the trailheads in Japanese-made Toyotas or Swedish-made Volvos, sipping coffee from Brazil or snacking on bananas from Honduras.

International trade and the global economy affect all of us daily, whether we are hiking in the wilderness, driving our cars, listening to music, or working at our jobs. We cannot "leave the world behind." We are enmeshed with the rest of the world in a complex web of economic relationships—trading of goods and services, multinational corporations, cooperative ventures among the world's firms, and ties among the world's financial markets. This web is so complex that it is difficult to determine just what is—or isn't—a Canadian product! Japanese auto companies have set up factories in Ontario, while many "Canadian" manufacturers have factories or outlets in other countries, particularly in the United States.

This chapter introduces the basic principles underlying the global economy. (A more advanced discussion of international economics is found in the last part of this book.) Here, we first look at world trade today, Canada's role in it, and some factors that have caused it to grow. Next, we modify Chapter 5's circular flow diagram to account for international trade flows, explore the basis for world trade, and look at the system of exchange rates that facilitates it. Finally, we describe several restrictive trade practices and discuss major efforts to implement freer trade.

**IN THIS CHAPTER YOU WILL LEARN:**

That trade is crucial to Canada's economic well-being.

•

The distinction between absolute advantage and comparative advantage.

•

That comparative advantage explains the gains from specialization and trade.

•

How the value of a currency is established on foreign exchange markets.

•

The economic costs of trade barriers.

•

About Canada's participation in the North American Free Trade Agreement (NAFTA), and the world's other trading blocs.

## The Big Picture

THE SCARCITY PROBLEM CAN BE LESSENED IF a society can produce more goods and services from its limited resources. One powerful way for all societies to produce more from the limited resources available to them is to specialize in producing specific goods. If all nations specialized in producing what each was especially good at, each could get its other needs by trading. If all nations specialized, the whole world would be materially better off since we would increase the total goods and services we could produce from available resources. As the twentieth century is coming to a close, this lesson is being followed by more and more nations. Not surprisingly, trade among nations is growing, and Canada is no exception in this trend.

As you read this chapter, keep the following points in mind:

- **Key Concept 5** is discussed.
- Opportunity cost plays a central role in specialization, and determines what products a nation ought to specialize in. Keep asking yourself what a particular good would cost to produce domestically compared to purchasing it from another nation. We could grow bananas in Canada (in greenhouses, of course), but could we purchase bananas at a lower price from a nation better suited to grow bananas?
- Specialization necessarily implies trade. Since nations have different currencies, there is a market for them called the foreign exchange market. As with any market, there are suppliers and those that demand a particular currency. The exchange rate is determined by supply and demand conditions at any given time period.
- Trade is reciprocal in nature: one nation's exports are another's imports, and a nation cannot import unless it also exports. ■

## GROWTH OF WORLD TRADE

The volume of world trade is so large and its characteristics so unique that it is difficult to describe except in some general terms.

### Volume and Pattern

Figure 6-1 provides a rough index of the importance of world trade for several selected countries. Many nations, such as Canada, with limited domestic markets cannot efficiently produce the variety of goods they want to consume. Such countries must import the goods they desire from other nations, which in turn means they must export, or sell abroad, some of their own products. In Canada exports make up about 38 percent of our national output. Other countries, the United States, for example, have rich and diversified resource bases and vast internal markets and are less dependent on world trade.

**Volume** For Canada and the world, the volume of international trade has been increasing both absolutely and relatively. A comparison of the boxed data within Figure 6-2 reveals the substantial growth in the absolute dollar volume of both Canadian exports and imports over the past several decades. The lines in the figure show the growth of exports and imports as a percentage of gross domestic product (GDP)—the dollar value of all goods and services produced within Canadian borders. Exports and imports currently are 38 and 37 percent of GDP respectively, up substantially from 1960.

**Dependence** Canada depends heavily on the world economy. Canada is almost entirely dependent on other countries for bananas, cocoa, coffee, spices, tea, raw silk, and natural rubber. Imported goods compete strongly in many of our domestic markets—for example, French and Italian wines, and Japanese autos. Foreign cars now account for about a third of the total automotive sales in Canada. Even the great Canadian pastime—hockey—relies heavily on imported equipment.

But world trade is a two-way street, and many Canadian industries are highly dependent on foreign markets. Almost all segments of agriculture rely heavily on foreign markets—wheat exports vary from one-fourth to more than one-half of

**FIGURE 6-1 Exports of goods and services as a percentage of GDP, selected countries, 1996**

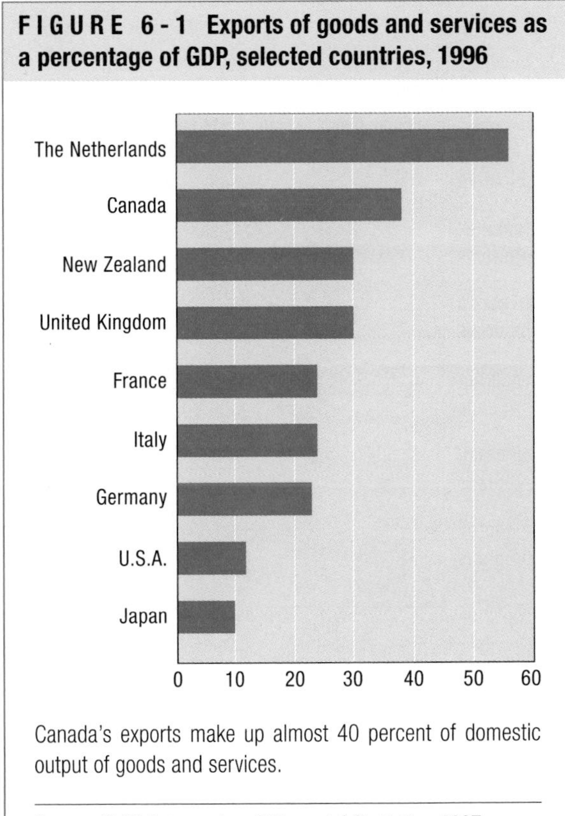


Canada's exports make up almost 40 percent of domestic output of goods and services.

Source: IMF, International Financial Statistics, 1997.

total output. The chemical, aircraft, automobile, machine tool, and forest industries are only a few of many Canadian industries that sell significant portions of their output in international markets. Figure 6-3 shows some of Canada's major commodity exports and imports.

**Trade Patterns** Figure 6-4 provides an overview of the pattern of Canada's international trade.

1. The bulk of our export and import trade is with other industrially advanced nations, not with the less developed nations or the countries of Eastern Europe.
2. The United States is our most important trading partner quantitatively. Over 80 percent of our exports are sold to Americans, who in turn provide us with three-quarters of our imports.
3. Canada imports some of the same categories of goods that it exports—specifically, automobiles, industrial machinery and materials, chemicals, and telecommunications equipment.

**Linkages** International trade means complex financial linkages among nations. A nation can have either an overall trade surplus or deficit. How does a nation—or a person—obtain more goods from others than it provides to them? The answer is either by borrowing or selling assets.

## Rapid Trade Growth

Several factors have facilitated the rapid growth of international trade since World War II.

**Transportation Technology** High transportation costs are a barrier to any type of trade, particularly trade between distance places. But improvements in transportation have shrunk the globe, fostering world trade. Airplanes now transport low-weight, high-value items such as diamonds and semiconductors quickly from one nation to another. We now routinely transport oil in massive tankers, greatly reducing the cost of transportation per barrel. Grain is loaded onto ocean-going ships at

**FIGURE 6-2 Canada's imports and exports as a percentage of GDP**

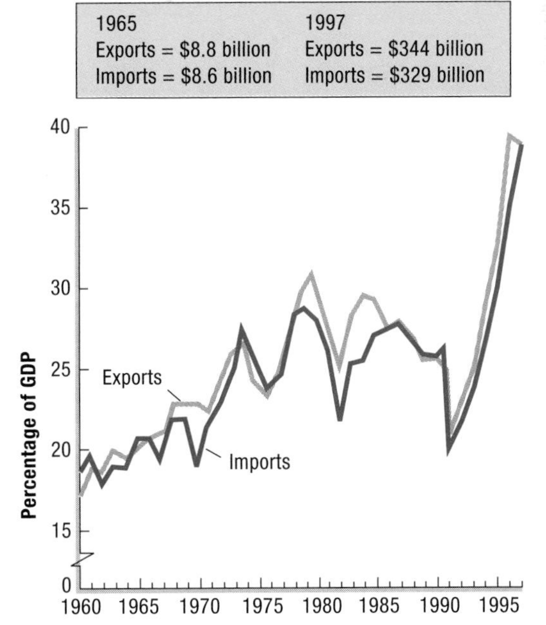


Canada's imports and exports have expanded since 1965, but have fluctuated over this period.

Source: Statistics Canada, CANSIM, Matrix 6548. Adapted from "Canadian International Merchandise Trade," Catalogue No. 65-001. More recent data are available from Statistics Canada www. statcan.ca/english/Pgdb/Economy/Economic/econ04.htm.

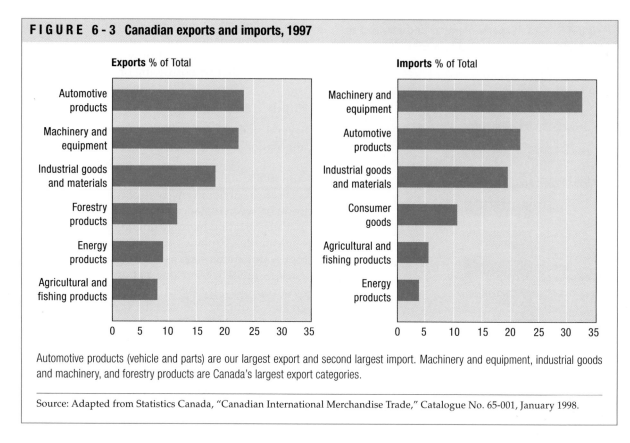

**FIGURE 6-3 Canadian exports and imports, 1997**

**Exports** % of Total
Automotive products
Machinery and equipment
Industrial goods and materials
Forestry products
Energy products
Agricultural and fishing products
0 5 10 15 20 25 30 35

**Imports** % of Total
Machinery and equipment
Automotive products
Industrial goods and materials
Consumer goods
Agricultural and fishing products
Energy products
0 5 10 15 20 25 30 35

Automotive products (vehicle and parts) are our largest export and second largest import. Machinery and equipment, industrial goods and machinery, and forestry products are Canada's largest export categories.

Source: Adapted from Statistics Canada, "Canadian International Merchandise Trade," Catalogue No. 65-001, January 1998.

modern, efficient grain silos located at Great Lakes ports and the coastal ports of Vancouver and Halifax. Container ships transport self-contained railroad boxes directly to foreign ports, where cranes place the containers onto railroad cars for internal shipment. Natural gas flows through large diameter pipelines from exporting to importing countries—for instance, from Russia to Germany and from this country to the United States. Workers clean fish on large processing ships located

**FIGURE 6-4 Canadian international trade by geographical areas, 1997**

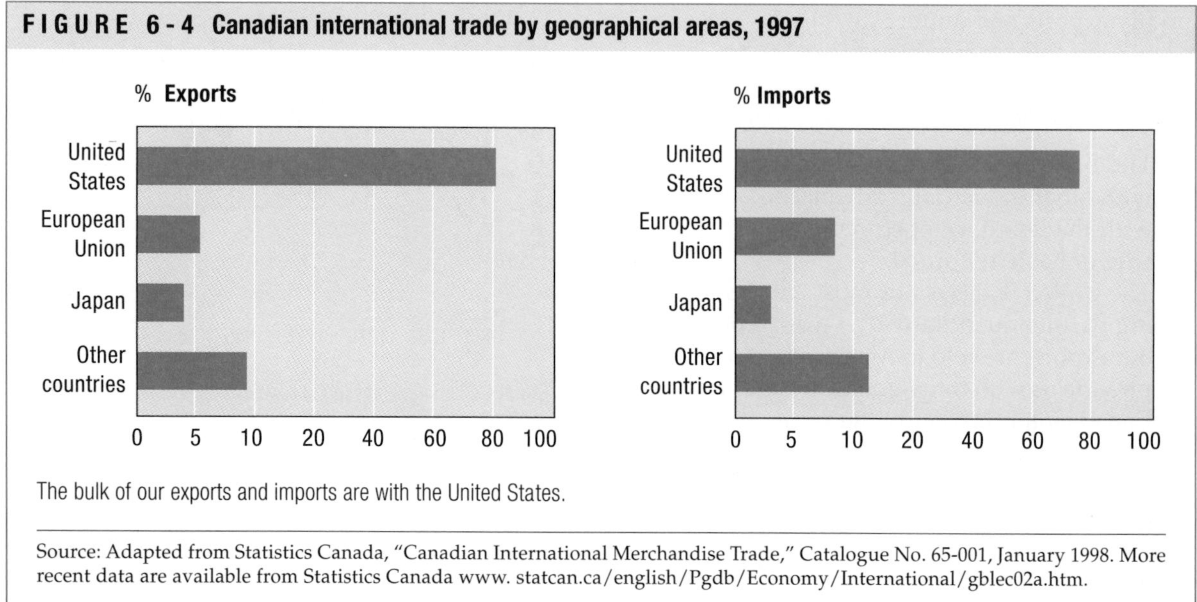


The bulk of our exports and imports are with the United States.

Source: Adapted from Statistics Canada, "Canadian International Merchandise Trade," Catalogue No. 65-001, January 1998. More recent data are available from Statistics Canada www. statcan.ca/english/Pgdb/Economy/International/gblec02a.htm.

directly on the fishing grounds. Refrigerated vessels then transport the fish to overseas ports.

**Communications Technology** World trade has expanded because of dramatic improvements in communications technology. Telephones, fax (facsimile) machines, and computers now directly link traders around the world, allowing exporters to assess overseas markets and to complete trade deals. New communications enable us to move money around the world in the blink of an eye. Exchange rates, stock prices, and interest rates flash onto computer screens nearly simultaneously in Vancouver, Toronto, London, and Lisbon.

In short, exporters and importers in today's world can as easily communicate between Sweden and Australia as between Calgary and Winnipeg. A distributor in Calgary can get a price quote on 1,000 thatched baskets in Thailand just as quickly as a quotation on 1,000 tonnes of steel in Hamilton.

**General Decline in Tariffs** Tariffs—excise taxes (duties) on imported products—have had their ups and downs, but since 1940 have generally fallen worldwide. A glance ahead to Figure 6-8 shows that Canada's tariff duties as a percentage of dutiable imports are now about 5 percent, down substantially from the highs of 1930. Many nations still have barriers to free trade, but on average, tariffs have fallen greatly, increasing international trade.

**Peace** World War II matched powerful industrial countries against one another and thus disrupted commercial international trade. Not only has trade been restored since World War II, but it has been greatly bolstered by peaceful relations and by trade agreements. In particular, Japan and Germany—two defeated World War II powers—now are major participants in world trade.

## Participants

All nations of the world participate to some extent in international trade.

**Canada, United States, Japan, and Western Europe** As implied in Global Perspective 6-1, the top participants in world trade are the United States, Germany, and Japan. In 1996 these three nations had combined exports of over U.S. $1.5 trillion. Along with Germany, other Western European nations such as France, Britain, and Italy are major exporters and importers. In fact, Canada, the United States, Japan, and the Western European nations now dominate world trade. These areas also are at the heart of the world's financial system and headquarter most of the world's large **multinational corporations**, which have sizable foreign production and distribution activities in other countries. Among the world's top 25 multinationals are Royal Dutch Shell and Unilever (Britain and the Netherlands); Ford Motor, General Motors, and IBM (United States); British Petroleum (Britain); Nestlé (Switzerland); Fiat (Italy); Siemens and Bayer Chemicals (Germany); Mitsubishi and Mitsui (Japan); and Elf Aquitaine (France).

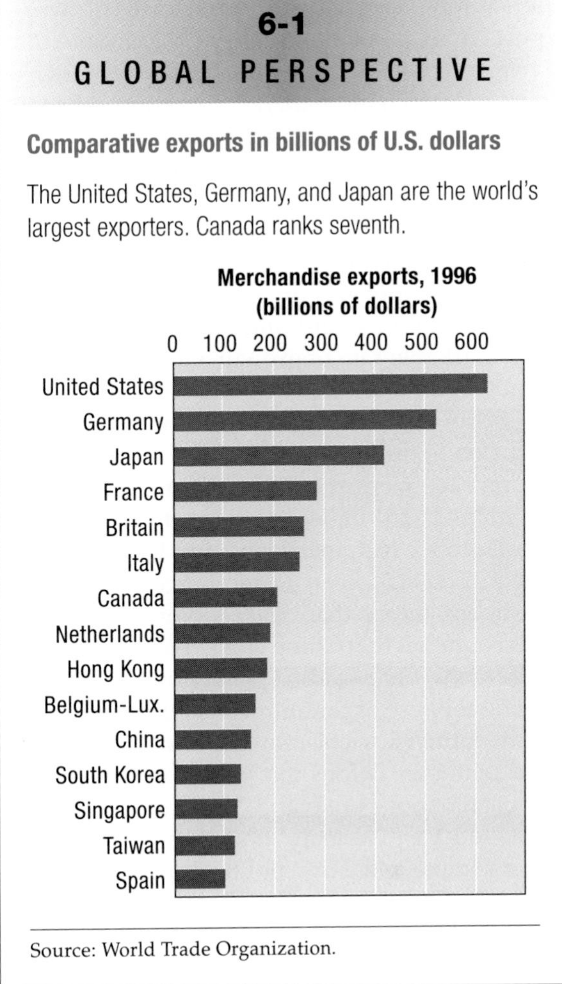

Source: World Trade Organization.

**New Players** New, important participants have arrived on the world trade scene. One group of such nations is the newly industrializing Asian economies of Hong Kong (now part of China), Singapore, South Korea, and Taiwan. These "**Asian**

**tigers**" have expanded their share of world exports from about 3 percent in 1972 to more than 10 percent today. Together they export as much as Japan and much more than either France, Britain, or Italy. Other countries in Southeast Asia, particularly Malaysia and Indonesia, have also expanded their international trade.

China is another emerging trading power. Since initiating market reforms in 1979, its annual growth of output has averaged 9 percent (compared to 2 to 3 percent annually in Canada). At this remarkable rate of growth, China's total output nearly doubles every eight years! An upsurge of exports and imports has accompanied this expansion of output. In 1989 Chinese exports and imports each were about $50 billion. In 1996 they each topped $151 billion, with about a third of the exports going to Canada and the United States. Also, China has been attracting much foreign investment (more than $600 billion since 1990). Experts predict that China will eventually become one of the world's leading trading nations.

The collapse of communism in Eastern Europe and the former Soviet Union has also altered world trade patterns. Before this collapse, the Eastern European nations of Poland, Hungary, Czechoslovakia, and East Germany traded mainly with the Soviet Union and such political allies as North Korea and Cuba. Today, East Germany is reunited with West Germany, and Poland, Hungary, and the Czech Republic have established new trade relationships with Western Europe and America.

Russia itself has initiated far-reaching market reforms, including widespread privatization of industry, and has consummated major trade deals with firms from across the globe. Although its transition to capitalism has been far from smooth, there is no doubt that Russia has the potential to be a major trading power. Other former Soviet republics—now independent nations—such as Ukraine and Estonia also are opening their economies to international trade and finance.

## BACK TO THE CIRCULAR FLOW MODEL

We can easily add "the rest of the World" to Chapter 5's circular flow model. We do so in Figure 6-5 via two adjustments.

1. Our previous "Resource Markets" and "Product Markets" now become "Canadian Resource Markets" and "Canadian Product Markets." Similarly, we add the modifier "Canadian" to the "Businesses," "Government," and "Households" sectors.
2. We place the foreign sector—the "Rest of the World"—so that it interacts with Canadian Product Markets. This sector designates all foreign nations that we deal with and the individuals, businesses, and governments that make them up.

Flow (13) in Figure 6-5 shows that people, businesses, and governments abroad buy Canadian products—our exports—from our product market. This goods and services flow of Canadian exports to foreign nations is accompanied by an opposite monetary revenue flow (14) from the rest of the world to us. In response to these revenues from abroad, Canadian businesses demand more domestic resources (flow 2) to produce the goods for export; they pay for these resources with revenues from abroad. Thus, the domestic flow (1) of money income (rents, wages, interest, and profits) to Canadian households rises.

But our exports are only half the picture. Flow (15) shows that Canadian households, businesses, and government spend some of their income on foreign products. These products, of course, are our imports (flow 16). Purchases of imports, say, autos and electronic equipment, contribute to foreign output and income, which in turn provides the means for foreign households to buy Canadian exports.

Our circular flow model is a simplification that emphasizes product market effects, but a few other Canada–Rest of the World relationships also require comment. Specifically, there are linkages between the Canadian resource markets and the rest of the world.

Canada imports and exports not only products, but also resources. For example, we import some crude oil and export raw logs. Moreover, some Canadian firms choose to engage in production abroad, which diverts spending on capital from our domestic resource market to resource markets in other nations. For instance, Nortel might build an assembly plant in Germany. Or flowing the other direction, Sony might construct a plant for manufacturing CD players in Canada.

There are also international flows of labour. About 250,000 immigrants enter Canada each year. These immigrants expand the availability of labour resources in Canada, raising our total output and income. On the other hand, immigration tends to increase the labour supply in certain Canadian labour markets, reducing wage rates for some types of Canadian labour.

The expanded circular flow model also demonstrates that a nation engaged in world trade faces potential sources of instability that would not affect a "closed" nation. Recessions and inflation can be highly contagious among nations. Suppose the nations of Western Europe experienced a rather severe recession. As their income declines, they curtail purchases of Canadian exports. As a result flows (13) and (14) in Figure 6-5 decline and inventories of unsold Canadian goods rise. Canadian firms would respond by limiting their production and employment, reducing the flow of money income to Canadian households (flow 1). Recession in Europe in this case contributed to a recession in Canada.

**FIGURE 6-5 The circular flow with the foreign sector**

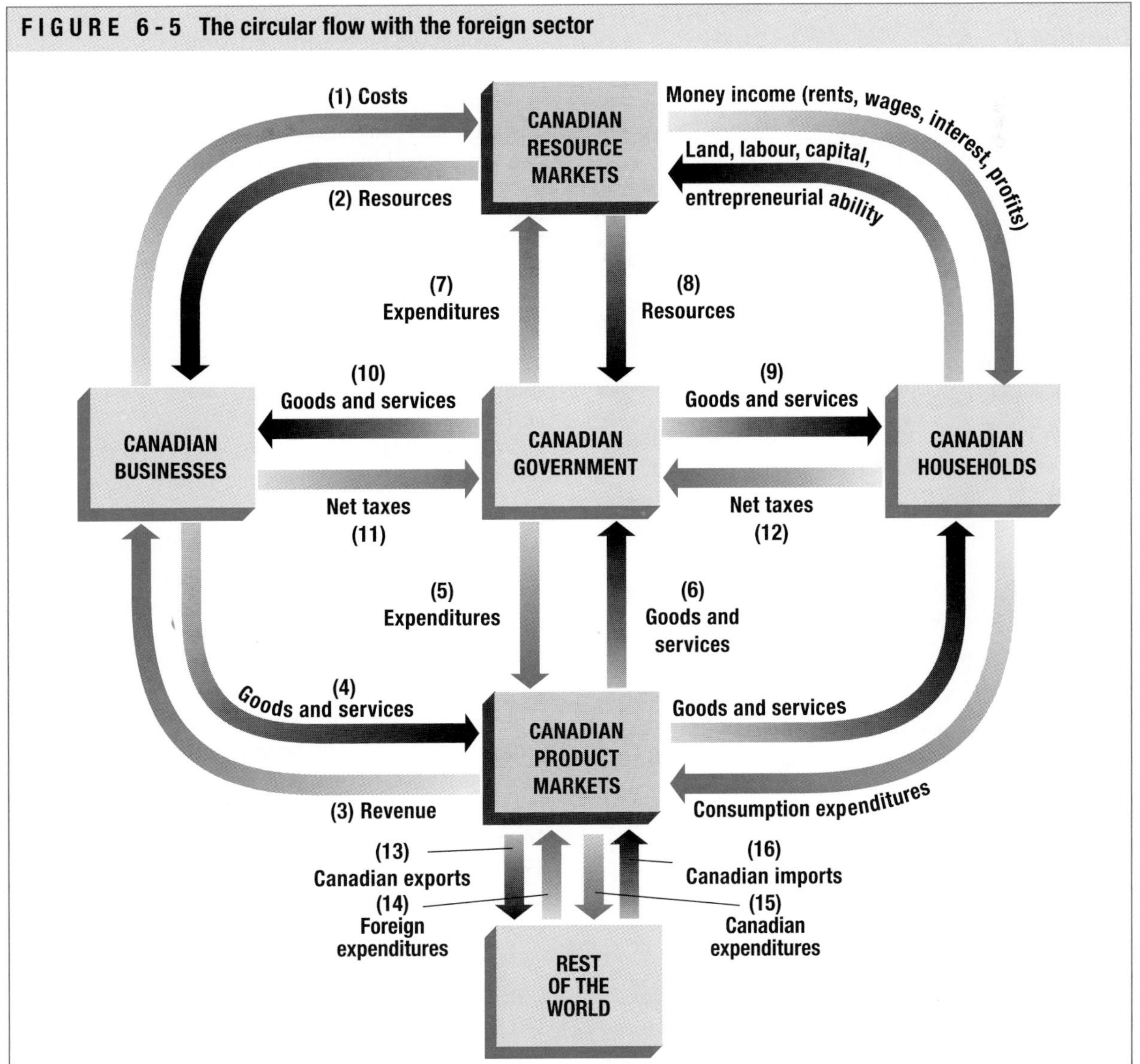


Flows 13-16 in the lower portion of the diagram show how the Canadian economy interacts with "The Rest of the World." People abroad buy Canadian exports, contributing to our business revenue and money income. Canadians, in turn, spend part of their incomes to buy imports from abroad. Income from a nation's exports helps pay for its imports.

Figure 6-5 also helps us to see that the foreign sector alters resource allocation and incomes in the Canadian economy. With a foreign sector, we produce more of some goods (our exports) and fewer of others (our imports) than we would otherwise. Thus, Canadian labour and other resources are shifted towards export industries and away from import industries. We use more of our resources to manufacture autos and telecommunication equipment. So we ask: "Do these shifts of resources make economic sense? Do they enhance our total output and thus our standard of living?" We look at some answers next. ***(Key Question 3)***

**6-1**

**QUICK REVIEW**

- World trade has increased globally and nationally. Canada is a leading international trader, with exports and imports about 38 percent and 37 percent of GDP.
- Advances in transportation and communications technology, declines in tariffs, and peaceful relations among major industrial countries all have helped to expand world trade.
- World trade is dominated by the United States, Japan, Canada, and the Western European nations, but has recently been bolstered by new participates such as the "Asian tigers" (Hong Kong, Singapore, South Korea, and Taiwan), China, the Eastern European nations, and the newly independent states formerly making up the Soviet Union.
- The circular flow model with foreign trade includes flows of exports from our domestic product market, imports to our domestic product market, and the corresponding flows of spending.

## SPECIALIZATION AND COMPARATIVE ADVANTAGE

*Specialization and trade increase the productivity of a nation's resources and allow for larger total output than otherwise.* This notion is not new! According to Adam Smith in 1776:

> It is the maxim of every prudent master of a family, never to attempt to make at home what it will cost him more to make than to buy. The taylor does not attempt to make his own shoes, but buys them from the shoemaker. The shoemaker does not attempt to make his own clothes, but employs a taylor. The farmer attempts to make neither the one or the other, but employs those different artificers....
>
> What is prudence in the conduct of every private family, can scarce be folly in that of a great kingdom. If a foreign country can supply us with a commodity cheaper than we can make it, better buy it of them with some part of the produce of our own industry, employed in a way in which we have some advantage.[1]

Nations specialize and trade for the same reasons as individuals: Specialization and exchange among individuals, regions, and nations result in greater overall output and income.

### Basic Principle

In the early 1800s British economist David Ricardo expanded Smith's idea, observing that it pays for a person or a country to specialize and exchange even if that person or nation is more productive than a potential trading partner in *all* economic activities.

Consider an example of a chartered accountant (CA) who is also a skilled house painter. Suppose the CA can paint her house in less time than the professional painter she is thinking of hiring. Also suppose the CA can earn $50 per hour doing her accounting and must pay the painter $15 per hour. Let's say that it will take the accountant 30 hours to paint her house; the painter, 40 hours.

Should the CA take time from her accounting to paint her own house or should she hire the painter? The CA's opportunity cost of painting her house is $1,500 (= 30 hours × $50 per hour of sacrificed income). The cost of hiring the painter is only $600 (40 hours × $15 per hour paid to the painter). The CA is better at both accounting and painting—she has an **absolute advantage** in both accounting and painting. But her relative or comparative advantage lies in accounting (more will be said about comparative advantage below). She will *lower the cost of getting her house painted* by specializing in accounting and using some of the earnings from accounting to hire a house painter.

[1] Adam Smith, *The Wealth of Nations* (New York: Modern Library, Inc., 1937), p. 424. [Originally published in 1776.]

Similarly, the house painter can reduce his cost of obtaining accounting services by specializing in painting and using some of his income to hire the CA to prepare his income tax forms. Suppose that it would take the painter ten hours to prepare his tax return, while the CA could handle this task in two hours. The house painter would sacrifice \$150 of income (= 10 hours × \$15 per hour of sacrificed time) to accomplish a task that he could hire the CA to do for \$100 (= 2 hours × \$50 per hour of the CA's time). By using the CA to prepare his tax return, the painter lowers *his cost of getting the tax return completed.*

What is true for our CA and house painter is also true for nations. Countries can reduce their cost of obtaining desirable goods by specializing.

## Comparative Costs

Our simple example clearly shows that specialization is economically desirable because it results in more efficient production. To understand the global economy, let's now put specialization in the context of trading nations, employing the familiar concept of the production possibilities table for our analysis. Suppose production possibilities for two products in Mexico and Canada are as shown in Tables 6-1 and 6-2. In these tables we assume constant costs. Each country must give up a constant amount of one product to secure a particular increment of the other product. (This assumption simplifies our discussion without impairing the validity of our conclusions.)

Specialization and trade are mutually beneficial or "profitable" to the two nations if the comparative costs of the two products within the two nations differ. What are the comparative costs of corn and soybeans in Mexico? By comparing production alternatives A and B in Table 6-1, we see that 5 tonnes of soybeans (= 15 – 10) must be sacrificed to produce 20 tonnes of corn (= 20 – 0). Or more simply, in Mexico it costs 1 tonne of soybeans (*S*) to produce 4 tonnes of corn (*C*); that is, 1*S* ≡ 4*C*. Because we assumed constant costs, this domestic *comparative-cost ratio* will not change as Mexico expands the output of either product. This is evident from looking at production possibilities B and C, where we see that 4 more tonnes of corn (= 24 – 20) cost 1 unit of soybeans (= 10 – 9).

**TABLE 6-1 Mexico's production possibilities table (in tonnes)**

| | PRODUCTION ALTERNATIVES | | | | |
|---|---|---|---|---|---|
| **Product** | **A** | **B** | **C** | **D** | **E** |
| Corn | 0 | 20 | 24 | 40 | 60 |
| Soybeans | 15 | 10 | 9 | 5 | 0 |

**TABLE 6-2 Canada's production possibilities table (in tonnes)**

| | PRODUCTION ALTERNATIVES | | | | |
|---|---|---|---|---|---|
| **Product** | **R** | **S** | **T** | **U** | **V** |
| Corn | 0 | 30 | 33 | 60 | 90 |
| Soybeans | 30 | 20 | 19 | 10 | 0 |

Similarly, in Table 6-2, comparing Canadian production alternatives R and S reveals that in Canada it costs 10 tonnes of soybeans (= 30 – 20) to obtain 30 tonnes of corn (= 30 – 0). That is, the domestic comparative-cost ratio for the two products in Canada is 1S ≡ 3C. Comparing production alternative S and T reinforces this; an extra 3 tonnes of corn (= 33 – 30) comes at the direct sacrifice of 1 tonne of soybeans (= 20 – 19).

The comparative costs of the two products within the two nations are clearly different. Economists say that Canada has a domestic comparative advantage or, simply, a **comparative advantage** over Mexico in soybeans. Canada must forgo only 3 tonnes of corn to get 1 tonne of soybeans, but Mexico must forgo 4 tonnes of corn to get 1 tonne of soybeans. In terms of domestic opportunity costs, soybeans are relatively cheaper in Canada. *A nation has a comparative advantage in some product when it can produce that product at a lower domestic opportunity cost than can a potential trading partner.* Mexico, in contrast, has a comparative advantage in corn. While 1 tonne of corn costs $\frac{1}{3}$ tonne of soybeans in Canada, it costs only $\frac{1}{4}$ tonne of soybeans in Mexico. Comparatively speaking, corn is cheaper in Mexico.

Because of these differences in domestic comparative costs, if both nations specialize, each according to its comparative advantage, each can achieve a larger total output with the same total input of resources. Together they will be using their scarce resources more efficiently.

## Terms of Trade

Canada can shift production between soybeans and corn at the rate of 1S for 3C. Thus, Canadians would specialize in soybeans only if they could obtain *more than* 3 tonnes of corn for 1 tonne of soybeans by trading with Mexico. Similarly, Mexico can shift production at the rate of 4C for 1S. So it would be advantageous to Mexico to specialize in corn if it could get 1 tonne of soybeans for *less than* 4 tonnes of corn.

Suppose that through negotiation the two nations agree on an exchange rate of 1 tonne of soybeans for $3\frac{1}{2}$ tonnes of corn. These **terms of trade** are mutually beneficial to both countries since each can "do better" through such trade than via domestic production alone. Canadians can get $3\frac{1}{2}$ tonnes of corn by sending 1 tonne of soybeans to Mexico, while they can get only 3 tonnes of corn by shifting resources domestically from soybeans to corn. Mexicans can obtain 1 tonne of soybeans at a lower cost of $3\frac{1}{2}$ tonnes of corn through trade with Canada, compared to the cost of 4 tonnes if Mexicans produce 1 tonne of corn themselves.

## Gains from Specialization and Trade

Let's pinpoint the size of the gains in total output from specialization and trade. Suppose that before specialization and trade, production alternative C in Table 6-1 and alternative T in Table 6-2 were the optimal product mixes for the two countries. These outputs are shown in column 1 of Table 6-3. That is, Mexicans preferred 24 tonnes of corn and 9 tonnes of soybeans (Table 6-1) and Canadians preferred 33 tonnes of corn and 19 tonnes of soybeans (Table 6-2) to all other alternatives available within their respective domestic economies.

Now assume both nations specialize according to comparative advantage, Mexico producing 60 tonnes of corn and no soybeans (alternative E) and Canada producing no corn and 30 tonnes of soybeans (alternative R). These outputs are reflected in column 2 of Table 6-3. Using our $1S = 3\frac{1}{2}C$ terms of trade, assume Mexico exchanges 35 tonnes of corn for 10 tonnes of Canadian soybeans. Column 3 of Table 6-3 shows the quantities exchanged in this trade. As indicated in Column 4, after trade Mexicans have 25 tonnes of corn and 10 tonnes of soybeans, while Canadians have 35 tonnes of corn and 20 tonnes of soybeans. Compared with their optimum product mixes before specialization and trade (column 1), *both* nations now enjoy more corn and more soybeans! Specifically, Mexico has gained 1 tonne of corn and 1 tonne of soybeans. Canada has gained 2 tonnes of corn and 1 tonne of soybeans. These gains are shown in column 5 where we have subtracted the *before*-specialization outputs of column (1) from the *after*-specialization outputs in column (4).

*Specialization based on comparative advantage improves resource allocation. The same total inputs of world resources result in a larger global output.* If Mexico and Canada allocate all their resources to corn and soybeans respectively, the same total inputs of resources can produce more output between them, indicating that resources are being used or allocated more efficiently.

We noted in Chapter 2 that through specialization and international trade a nation can overcome the production constraints imposed by its domestic production possibilities table and curve. Table 6-3 and its discussion show just how this is done. The domestic production possibilities data of the two countries have not changed, meaning that neither nation's production possibilities curve

**TABLE 6-3 Specialization according to comparative advantage and the gains from trade (in tonnes)**

| Country | (1) Outputs before specialization | (2) Outputs after specialization | (3) Amounts traded | (4) Outputs available after trade | (5) Gains from specialization and trade (4) – (1) |
|---|---|---|---|---|---|
| Mexico | 24 corn | 60 corn | −35 corn | 25 corn | 1 corn |
| | 9 soybeans | 0 soybeans | +10 soybeans | 10 soybeans | 1 soybeans |
| Canada | 33 corn | 0 corn | +35 corn | 35 corn | 2 corn |
| | 19 soybeans | 30 soybeans | −10 soybeans | 20 soybeans | 1 soybeans |

has shifted. But specialization and trade mean that citizens of both countries have enjoyed increased consumption. *Thus, specialization and trade have the same effect as an increase in resources or technological progress: they make more goods available to an economy.* ***(Key Question 4)***

## FOREIGN EXCHANGE MARKET

People, firms, or nations that specialize in the production of specific goods or services exchange those products for money and then use the money to buy other products or to pay for the use of resources. Within the economy, prices are stated in the domestic currency and buyers use that currency to purchase domestic products. In Mexico, for example, buyers possess pesos, exactly the currency that sellers want.

International markets are different. How many dollars does it take to buy a truckload of Mexican corn selling for 3,000 pesos, a German automobile selling for 90,000 marks, or a Japanese motorcycle priced at 300,000 yen? Producers in Mexico, Germany, and Japan want payment in pesos, marks, and yen, respectively, so they can pay their wages, rent, interest, dividends, and taxes. A **foreign exchange market**, a market in which various national currencies are exchanged for one another, serves this need. The equilibrium prices in these markets are called **exchange rates**—the rate at which the currency of one nation is exchanged for the currency of another nation. (See Global Perspective 6-2.) Two points about the foreign exchange market are particularly noteworthy:

1. **A COMPETITIVE MARKET** Real-world foreign exchange markets conform closely to the markets discussed in Chapter 4. They are competitive markets characterized by large numbers of buyers and sellers dealing in standardized products such as the Canadian dollar, the German mark, the British pound, the Swedish krona, and the Japanese yen.
2. **LINKAGES TO ALL DOMESTIC AND FOREIGN PRICES** The market price or exchange rate of a nation's currency is an unusual price; it links all domestic (say, Canadian) prices with all foreign (say, Japanese or German) prices. Exchange rates enable consumers in one country to translate prices of foreign goods into units of their own currency: They need only multiply the foreign product price by the exchange rate. If the dollar-yen exchange rate is $.01 (1 cent) per yen, a Sony television set priced at ¥20,000 will cost a Canadian $200 (= 20,000 × $.01) in the United States. If the exchange rate is $.02 (2 cents) per yen, it will cost a Canadian $400 (= 20,000 × $.02). Similarly, all other Japanese products would double in price to Canadian buyers. As you will see, a change in exchange rates has important implications for a nation's level of domestic production and employment.

### 6-2 GLOBAL PERSPECTIVE

**Exchange rates: foreign currency per Canadian dollar**

The amount of foreign currency that a dollar will buy varies greatly from nation to nation. These amounts are for May 1998 and fluctuate in response to supply and demand changes in the foreign exchange market.

**One Canadian dollar bought:**

- 1.25 German marks
- .42 British pounds
- .70 U.S. dollars
- 5.9 Mexican pesos
- 1.0 Swiss francs
- 4.1 French francs
- 91 Japanese yen
- 949 South Korean won
- 2.36 Polish zloty

### Dollar-Yen Market

How does the foreign exchange market work? Let's look briefly at the market for dollars and yen, leaving details to a later chapter. Canadian firms exporting to Japan want payment in dollars, not yen; but Japanese importers of Canadian goods possess yen, not dollars. So the Japanese importers are willing to supply their yen in exchange for dollars in the foreign exchange market. At the same time, there are Canadian importers of Japanese goods who need to pay Japanese exporters with yen, not dollars. These Canadians go to the foreign exchange market as demanders of yen. We then have a market in which the "price" is in dollars and the "product" is yen.

Figure 6-6 shows the supply of yen (by Japanese importers) and the demand for yen (by Canadian importers). The intersection of demand curve $D_y$ and supply curve $S_y$ establishes the equilibrium dollar price of yen. Here the equilibrium price of 1 yen—the dollar-yen exchange rate—is 1 cent per yen, or \$.01 = ¥1. At this price, the market for yen clears; there is neither a shortage nor a surplus of yen. The equilibrium \$.01 price of 1 yen means that \$1 will buy 100 yen or ¥100 worth of Japanese goods. Conversely, 100 yen will buy \$1 worth of Canadian goods.

## Changing Rates: Depreciation and Appreciation

What might cause the exchange rate to change? The determinants of the demand for and supply of yen are similar to the determinants of demand and supply for almost any product. In Canada, several things might increase the demand for—and therefore the dollar price of—yen. Incomes might rise in Canada, enabling Canadians to buy not only more domestic goods but also more Sony televisions, Nikon cameras, and Nissan automobiles from Japan. So Canadians would need more yen and the demand for yen would increase. Or a change in Canadian tastes might enhance their preferences for Japanese goods. When gas prices soared in the 1970s, many Canadian auto buyers shifted their demands from gas-guzzling domestic cars to gas-efficient Japanese compact cars. The result was an increased demand for yen.

The point is that an increase in the Canadian demand for Japanese goods will increase the demand for yen and raise the dollar price of yen. Suppose the dollar price of yen rises from \$.01 = ¥1 to \$.02 = ¥1. When the dollar price of yen increases, we say a **depreciation** of the dollar relative to the yen has occurred: It then takes more dollars (pennies in this case) to buy a single unit of the foreign currency (a yen). Alternatively stated, the *international value of the dollar* has declined. A depreciated dollar buys fewer yen and therefore fewer Japanese goods; the yen and all Japanese goods have become more expensive to Canadians. Result: Canadian consumers shift their expenditures from Japanese goods to now less expensive Canadian goods. The Ford Taurus becomes relatively more attractive than the Honda Accord to Canadian consumers. Conversely, because each yen buys more dollars—that is, because the international value of the yen has increased—Canadian goods become cheaper to people in Japan and Canadian exports to them rise.

If the opposite event occurred—if the Japanese demanded more Canadian goods—then they would supply more yen to pay for these goods. The increase in the supply of yen relative to the demand for yen would decrease the equilibrium price of yen in the foreign exchange market. For example, the dollar price of yen might decline from \$.01 = ¥1 to \$.005 = ¥1. A decrease in the dollar price of yen is called an **appreciation** of the dollar relative to the yen. It means that the international value of the dollar has increased. It then takes fewer dollars (or pennies) to buy a single yen; the dollar is worth more because it can purchase more yen and therefore more Japanese goods. Each Sony Walkman becomes less expensive in terms of dollars, so Canadians purchase more of them. In general, Canadian imports rise. Meanwhile, because it takes more yen to get a dollar, Canadian exports to Japan fall.

We summarize these currency relationships in Figure 6-7, which you should examine closely. ***(Key Question 6)***

**FIGURE 6-6 The market for yen**

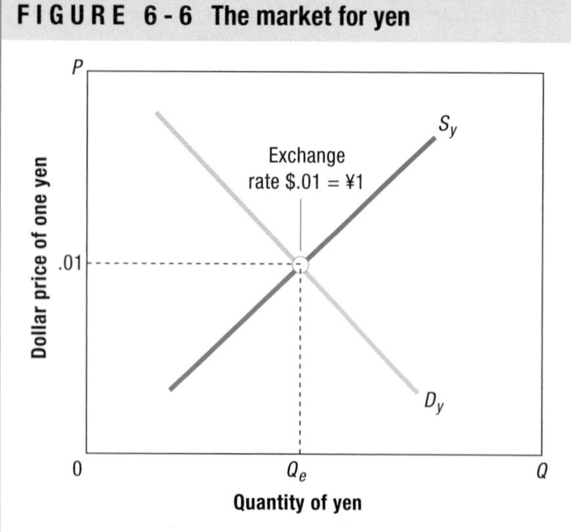


Canadian imports from Japan create a demand $D_y$ for yen, while Canadian exports to Japan create a supply $S_y$ of yen. The dollar price of one yen—the exchange rate—is determined at the intersection of the supply and demand curves. In this case the equilibrium price is \$.01, meaning that 1 cent will buy 1 yen.

**FIGURE 6-7 Currency appreciation and depreciation**

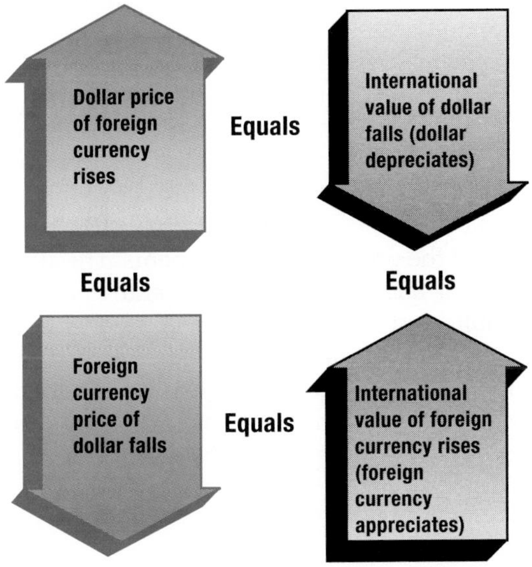

An increase in the dollar price of foreign currency is equivalent to a decline in the international value of the dollar (dollar depreciation). An increase in the dollar price of foreign currency also implies a decline in the foreign currency price of dollars. That is, the international value of foreign currency rises relative to the dollar (the foreign currency appreciates).

6-2

**QUICK REVIEW**

- A country has a comparative advantage in some product when it can produce it at a lower domestic opportunity cost than can a potential trading partner.
- Specialization based on comparative advantage increases the total output available for nations that trade with one another.
- The foreign exchange market is the market where the currencies of nations are exchanged for each other.
- An appreciation of the dollar is an increase in the international value of the dollar relative to the currency of some other nation; a dollar now buys more units of that currency. A depreciation of the dollar is a decrease in the international value of the dollar relative to another currency; a dollar now buys fewer units of that currency.

# GOVERNMENT AND TRADE

If people and nations benefit from specialization and international exchange, why do governments sometimes try to restrict the free flow of imports or to bolster exports? What kinds of world-trade barriers can governments erect, and why would they do so?

## Trade Impediments and Subsidies

There are four usual means by which governments might interfere with free trade:

1. **Protective tariffs** are excise taxes or duties placed on imported goods. Most are designed to shield domestic producers from foreign competition. They impede free trade by increasing the prices of imported goods, shifting demand towards domestic products. An excise tax on imported shoes, for example, would make domestically made shoes more attractive to consumers.
2. **Import quotas** are limits on the quantities or total value of specific items that may be imported. Once a quota is "filled," it chokes off imports of that product. Import quotas can be more effective than tariffs in retarding international commerce. A particular product could be imported in large quantities despite high tariffs; a low import quota completely prohibits imports once the quota is filled.
3. **Nontariff barriers** (and, implicitly, *nonquota* barriers) include licensing requirements, unreasonable standards pertaining to product quality, or simply unnecessary bureaucratic red tape in customs procedures. Some nations require their domestic importers of foreign goods to obtain licences. By restricting the issuance of licences, imports can be effectively impeded. Great Britain bars coal importation in this way. Also, some nations impede imports of fruit by insisting that *each* crate be inspected for worms and insects.
4. **Export subsidies** consist of governmental payments to domestic producers of export goods. The payments reduce their production costs, permitting them to charge lower prices and thus sell more exports in world markets. Two examples: Participating European governments have heavily subsidized Airbus Industries, which produces commercial aircraft. These subsidies have helped Airbus

compete against Boeing, an American firm with plants in Canada. Canada and other nations have subsidized domestic farmers, boosting domestic food supply. This has reduced the market price of food, artificially decreasing export prices on agricultural produce.

## Why Government Trade Interventions?

Why would a nation want to send more of its output for consumption abroad than it gains as imported output in return? Why the impulse to impede imports or boost exports through government policy when free trade is beneficial to a nation? There are several reasons—some legitimate, most not. We will look at two here, and examine others in a later chapter.

**Misunderstanding of the Gains from Trade** It is a commonly accepted myth that the fundamental benefit of international trade is greater domestic employment in the export sector. This suggests that exports are "good" because they increase domestic employment, whereas imports are "bad" because they deprive people of jobs at home. In reality, the true benefit from international trade is the *overall* increase in output obtained through specialization and exchange. A nation can fully employ its resources, including labour, with or without international trade. International trade, however, enables society to use its resources in ways that increase its total output and therefore its overall well-being.

A nation does not need international trade to locate *on* its production possibilities curve. A closed (nontrading) national economy can have full employment without international trade. But through world trade an economy can reach a point *beyond* its domestic production possibilities curve. The gain from trade is the extra output obtained from abroad—the imports got for less cost than if they were produced using domestic resources. The only valid reason for exporting part of our domestic output is to obtain imports that are of greater value to us. Specialization and international exchange make this possible.

**Political Considerations** While a nation as a whole gains from trade, trade may harm particular domestic industries and groups of resource suppliers. In our earlier comparative-advantage example, specialization and trade adversely affected the Canadian corn industry and the Mexican soybean industry. Those industries might seek to preserve their economic positions by persuading their respective governments to protect them from imports—perhaps with tariffs or import quotas.

Policymakers often see little public opposition to demands for *protectionism* because tariffs and quotas are buried in the prices of goods. Indeed, the public may be won over by the apparent plausibility ("Cut imports and prevent domestic unemployment") and patriotic ring ("Buy Canadian!") of the protectionist arguments. The alleged benefits of tariffs are immediate and clear-cut to the public, but the adverse effects cited by economists are obscure and dispersed over the entire economy. When political deal making is added in, the sum can be a network of protective tariffs, import quotas, and export subsidies.

## Costs to Society

Tariffs and quotas benefit domestic producers of the protected products, but they harm domestic consumers, who must pay higher than world prices for the protected goods. They also hurt those domestic firms that use the protected goods as inputs in their production processes. For example, a tariff on imported steel would boost the price of steel girders, hurting firms that construct large buildings. Also, tariffs and quotas reduce competition in the protected industries. With less competition from foreign producers, domestic firms may be slow to design and implement cost-saving production methods and introduce new and improved products.

Study after study has shown that the cost of trade protection to consumers and adversely affected input buyers exceeds the benefit to the protected firms. That is, there is a *net cost* (cost *minus* benefit) to society from trade protection. In Canada this net cost was as much as $5 billion a couple of decades ago but has dropped significantly in recent years along with declines in Canadian tariffs and quotas.

# MULTILATERAL TRADE AGREEMENTS AND FREE-TRADE ZONES

When one nation enacts barriers against imports, the nations whose exports suffer may retaliate with trade barriers of their own. In such a *trade war*, tariffs escalate, choking off world trade and reducing everyone's economic well-being. The raising of tariffs by many nations in the early 1930s to fight domestic unemployment is a classic example. Although Canada's action was meant to reduce imports and stimulate Canadian production, its high tariffs prompted affected nations to retaliate with equally high tariffs. International trade across the globe fell, lowering the output, income, and employment levels of all nations. Economic historians generally agree that the high tariffs were a contributing cause of the Great Depression. In view of this fact, the world's nations have worked to lower tariffs worldwide. Their pursuit of free trade has been aided by powerful domestic interest groups. Specifically, exporters of goods and services, importers of foreign components used in "domestic" products, and domestic sellers of imported products all strongly support lower tariffs worldwide.

Figure 6-8 makes clear that Canada has been a high-tariff nation over much of its history. But it also demonstrates that, in general, Canadian tariffs have declined during the past half-century.

**FIGURE 6-8 Canadian tariffs: 1930–1997**

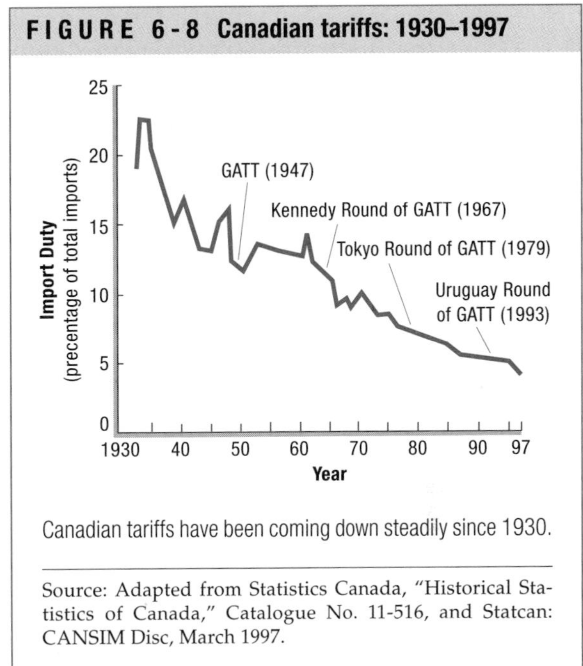


Canadian tariffs have been coming down steadily since 1930.

Source: Adapted from Statistics Canada, "Historical Statistics of Canada," Catalogue No. 11-516, and Statcan: CANSIM Disc, March 1997.

## BILATERAL AGREEMENTS AND GATT

The specific tariff reductions negotiated between Canada and any particular nation became generalized through **most-favoured-nation clauses**, which often accompanied these agreements. These clauses stipulate that any subsequently reduced Canadian tariff, resulting from negotiation with any other nation would apply equally to the nation signing the original agreement. So if Canada negotiates a reduction in tariffs with, say, France, the lower Canadian tariffs on French imports would also apply to the imports of other nations having the most-favoured-nation status, say, Sweden and Switzerland. This way, a new reduction in Canadian tariffs automatically applies to many other nations.

This approach was broadened in 1947 when 23 nations, including Canada, signed a **General Agreement on Tariffs and Trade (GATT).** GATT is based on three cardinal principles: (1) equal, nondiscriminatory trade treatment for all member nations; (2) the reduction of tariffs by multilateral negotiations; and (3) the elimination of import quotas.

Basically, GATT is a forum to negotiate reductions in trade barriers on a multilateral basis among nations. One hundred and twenty-five nations now belong to GATT, and there is little doubt that it has been a positive force in the trend towards liberalized world trade. Under its sponsorship, member nations have completed eight "rounds" of negotiations to reduce trade barriers in the post-World War II period.

**GATT's Uruguay Round** The eighth and most recent "round" of GATT negotiations began in Uruguay in 1986. After seven years of wrangling, in 1993 the participant nations reached a new agreement. The agreement took effect on January 1, 1995, and its provisions will be phased in through 2005.

Under this latest GATT agreement, tariffs will be eliminated or reduced on thousands of products, with tariffs dropping overall by 33 percent. The agreement will also liberalize government rules that in the past have impeded the global market for such services as advertising, legal services, tourist services, and financial services. Quotas on imported textiles and apparel will be phased out, to be replaced with tariffs. (Tariffs are preferable to quotas, since tariffs let in an unlimited amount of imported goods; in contrast, quotas block all imports beyond a specified quantity.)

Other important provisions will reduce agricultural subsidies paid to farmers and protect intellectual property (patents, trademarks, copyrights) against piracy. Finally, the Uruguay Round of GATT created the **World Trade Organization (WTO)** as GATT's successor. The WTO has judicial powers to mediate among members and rule on disputes involving the trade rules.

When fully implemented, the most recent GATT agreement is expected to boost the world's GDP by about $6 trillion, or 8 percent. Consumers in Canada will gain about $3 billion annually.

## European Union

Countries have also sought to reduce tariffs by creating regional free-trade zones or trade blocs. The most dramatic example is the **European Union (EU)**, formerly called the European Economic Community. Initiated as the Common Market in 1958, the EU now comprises 15 western European nations—France, Germany, Italy, Belgium, the Netherlands, Luxembourg, Denmark, Ireland, United Kingdom, Greece, Spain, Portugal, Austria, Finland, and Sweden.

**Goals** The original Common Market called for (1) gradual abolition of tariffs and import quotas on all products traded among the participating nations; (2) establishment of a common system of tariffs applicable to all goods received from nations outside the EU; (3) free movement of capital and labour within the Common Market; and (4) creation of common policies in other economic matters of joint concern, such as agriculture, transportation, and restrictive business practices. The EU has achieved most of these goals and is now a strong **trade bloc**: a group of countries having a common identity, set of economic interests, and trade rules.

**Results** The motives for creating the EU were political and economic. The main economic motive was liberalized trade for members. While it is difficult to determine how much of EU prosperity and growth has resulted from economic integration, that integration clearly has created large markets for EU industries. The resulting economies of large-scale production have enabled European industries to achieve much lower costs than they could in their small, single-nation markets.

The effects of EU success on nonmember nations, such as Canada, are mixed. A peaceful and increasingly prosperous EU makes its members better customers for Canadian exports. But Canadian and other nonmember firms encounter tariffs that make it difficult to compete against firms within the EU trade bloc. For example, before the establishment of the EU, North American, German, and French automobile manufacturers all faced the same tariff selling their products in, say, Belgium. However, with the establishment of free internal trading among EU members, Belgian tariffs on German Volkswagens and French Renaults fell to zero, but an external tariff still applies to North American Chevrolets and Fords. This puts Canadian and American firms at a serious disadvantage. Similarly, EU trade restrictions hamper Eastern European exports of metals, textiles, and farm products, goods that the Eastern Europeans produce in abundance.

By giving preferences to countries within their free-trade zone, trade blocs such as the EU tend to reduce their trade with nonbloc members. Thus, the world loses some of the benefits of a completely open global trading system. Eliminating this disadvantage has been one of the motivations for liberalizing global trade through the World Trade Organization.

## North American Free Trade Agreement

In 1993 Canada, Mexico, and the United States formed a trade bloc. The **North American Free Trade Agreement (NAFTA)** established a free-trade zone having about the same combined output of the EU, but covering a much larger geographical area. A 1989 free-trade agreement between Canada and the United States—the **Canada-U.S. Free Trade Agreement**—preceded NAFTA. NAFTA will eliminate tariffs and other trade barriers between Canada, Mexico, and the United States over a 15-year period.

Critics of the agreement fear that one result will be a loss of Canadian jobs as firms move to Mexico to take advantage of lower wages and weaker regulations on pollution and workplace safety. Also, there is concern that Japan and South Korea will build plants in Mexico to transport goods tariff-free to Canada and the United States, further hurting Canadian and American firms and workers.

Defenders of NAFTA reject these concerns. They contend that specialization according to comparative advantage will enable each nation to obtain more total output from its scarce resources. They also argue that NAFTA's free-trade zone will encourage worldwide investment in Mexico, enhancing Mexican productivity and national income. Mexican consumers will use some of that increased income to buy Canadian and American exports. Any loss of jobs, say defenders of NAFTA, most likely would have occurred anyway to other low-wage countries such as China.

### Hostile Trade Blocs or Further Integration?

With the formation of NAFTA, it may appear that the world's nations are separating into potentially hostile trade blocs. But NAFTA is also a means for negotiating reductions in trade barriers with the EU, Japan, and other trading countries. Access to the vast North American market is as important to the EU and Japan as is access to their markets by Canada, Mexico, and the United States. NAFTA gives its members leverage in future trade negotiations with the EU and Japan. Eventually, direct negotiations between the EU and NAFTA might link the two free-trade zones. Japan and other major trading nations, not wishing to be left out of the world's wealthiest trade markets, would be forced to eliminate their trade barriers—to open their domestic markets to additional imports. Nor do other nations and trade blocs want to be excluded from free-trade zones. Examples:

1. **APEC** Canada and several other nations have agreed to liberalize trade and open investment over the next few decades through the Asian-Pacific Economic Cooperation (APEC) forum. APEC members are Australia, Brunei, Canada, Chile, China (Hong Kong), Indonesia, Japan, Malaysia, Mexico, New Zealand, the Philippines, Papua New Guinea, Singapore, South Korea, Taiwan, Thailand, and the United States.
2. **CHILE'S POTENTIAL INCLUSION IN NAFTA** Canada, Mexico, and the United States are negotiating with Chile to become the fourth partner in NAFTA.
3. **MERCOSUR** The free-trade group encompassing Brazil, Argentina, Uruguay, and Paraguay—called Mercosur—has expressed interest in eventually linking up with NAFTA.

Economists generally agree that the ideal free-trade area would encompass the entire world. ***(Key Question 10)***

**6-3**

**QUICK REVIEW**

- Governments promote exports and reduce imports through tariffs, quotas, nontariff barriers, and export subsidies.
- The various "rounds" of the General Agreement on Tariffs and Trade (GATT) have established multinational reductions in tariffs and import quotas among the 125 member nations.
- The Uruguay Round of GATT, which went into effect in 1995 and will be fully implemented by 2005, **a** reduces tariffs worldwide; **b** liberalizes rules impeding barriers to trade in services; **c** reduces agricultural subsidies; **d** creates new protections for intellectual property; **e** phases out quotas on textiles and apparel; and **f** sets up the World Trade Organization.
- The European Union (EU) and the North American Free Trade Agreement (NAFTA) have reduced internal trade barriers among their members by establishing large free-trade zones.

## CANADIAN FIRMS IN THE WORLD ECONOMY

Freer international trade has brought with it intense competition in Canada and the world. Not long ago three large North American producers dominated the North American automobile industry. Imported autos were an oddity, accounting for a tiny portion of auto sales. But General Motors, Ford, and Chrysler now face intense competition as they struggle for sales against Nissan, Honda, Toyota, Hyundai, BMW, and others. Similarly, imports have gained major shares of the North American markets for automobile tires, clothing, sporting goods, electronics, motorcycles, outboard motors, and toys.

Nevertheless, thousands of Canadian firms—large and small—have thrived and prospered in the global marketplace. Nortel, Bombardier, Newbridge Networks, and Corel are just a few of them. These and many other firms have continued to retain high market shares at home and have dramatically expanded their sales abroad. Of course, not all firms have been so successful. Some corporations simply have not been able to compete; their international competitors make better-quality products, have lower production costs, or both. Not surprisingly, the Canadian firms that have been hurt most by foreign competition are precisely those that have long enjoyed the protection of tariffs and quotas. These barriers to imports have artificially limited competition, removing the incentive to improve production methods and products. Also, trade barriers have shielded some domestic firms from the gradual changes in output and employment resulting from national shifts in comparative advantage over time. As trade protection declines under WTO and NAFTA, some Canadian firms will surely discover that they are producing goods for which Canada clearly has a comparative *dis*advantage (perhaps some types of apparel, for example).

Is the greater competition that accompanies the global economy a good thing? Although some domestic producers and their workers do not like it, foreign competition clearly benefits consumers. Imports break down the monopoly power of existing firms, reducing product prices and providing consumers with a greater variety of goods. Foreign competition also forces domestic producers to become more efficient and to improve product quality; this has already happened in several Canadian industries, including steel and autos. Evidence shows that most—but clearly not all—Canadian firms *can* and *do* compete successfully in the global economy.

What about Canadian firms that cannot successfully compete in open markets? The harsh reality is that they should go out of business, much like an unsuccessful corner boutique. Persistent economic losses mean scarce resources are not being used efficiently. Shifting these resources to alternative, profitable uses will increase total Canadian output.

## In The Media

# Dollar Closes at Lowest Level Since 1858

### Bank of Canada appears reluctant to defend currency by raising rates

BY MARIAN STINSON
MONEY MARKETS REPORTER

The Canadian dollar ended trading yesterday at its lowest level since its creation in 1858, nine years before Confederation.

The 140-year low—69.20 cents (U.S.)—came despite buying efforts by the Bank of Canada to steady its value.

The dollar was hammered by hints from senior deputy Bank of Canada governor Bernard Bonin that interest rates may head lower because of turmoil in Asian markets.

"It could be less tightening or it could be more easing," he told reporters after a luncheon speech to financial analysts in Montreal.

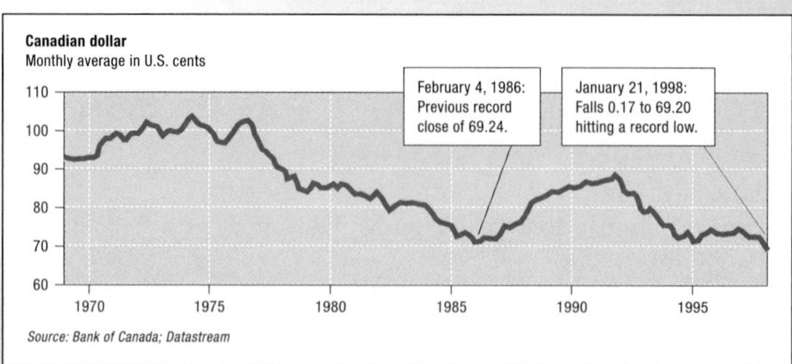


Such dismal days for the currency are a sharp departure from most of its history, when it traded above 90 cents (U.S.), and even above par with the U.S. dollar for brief periods, such as during the U.S. Civil War when the United States abandoned the gold standard, and during the 1970s, until a separist government was first elected in Quebec.

The only other time the dollar has traded as low as its current level was early 1986, when it fell as low as 69.13 cents (U.S.) on Feb. 3, but edged up to end that day at 69.24 cents.

The dollar first appeared in 1858 when a decimal currency system was introduced in Upper and Lower Canada to replace the mixture of coins and notes in circulation. After Confederation, the dollar became the currency in the new territories of the Dominion.

From 1870 to the beginning of the First World War in 1914, the dollar traded at par with the U.S. dollar, but depreciated sharply to 90 cents after the war and in the 1920s and during the Great Depression.

In 1940, it was pegged at 90.9 cents (U.S.) and was revalued at parity with the U.S. dollar in 1946. In October of 1950 it moved above par, but weakened again to 92.50 cents in 1961—and became known as the Diefenbuck—when then prime minister John Diefenbaker was in conflict with central bank governor James Coyne.

*Source: Globe and Mail,* January 22, 1998, p. A1. Reprinted with permission from the *Globe and Mail.*

## THE STORY IN BRIEF

In early 1998 the Canadian dollar reached its lowest level against the American dollar since the middle of the nineteenth century. (By August 1998 the Canadian dollar dropped below U.S.$ .64).

## THE ECONOMICS BEHIND THE STORY

- The value of a currency against other currencies is determined by supply and demand for that currency.
- In early 1998 the demand for the American dollar rose. As the demand for the U.S. dollar shifted to the right, the Canadian dollar price for one American dollar rose, at one point during the day in question reaching Can $ 1.445 for one U.S. dollar. (Later in 1998 the Canadian dollar declined to as low as $1.59 for one U.S. dollar.) The strong demand for the U.S. currency is partly explained by the turmoil on Asian equity and foreign exchange markets at the time. Investors were seeking the "safety" of the American currency.
- The Bank of Canada intervened in the foreign exchange market to slow the fall of the Canadian dollar. To achieve this end the Bank of Canada sold American dollars, thereby shifting the supply of the U.S. currency to the right.
- How would you expect Canadian imports and exports to the United States to be affected by a depreciating Canadian dollar? What about the effect on the number of American tourists to Canada? ■

# The Last Word

## PETITION OF THE CANDLEMAKERS, 1845

**The French economist Frédéric Bastiat (1801–1850) devastated the proponents of protectionism by satirically extending their reasoning to its logical and absurd conclusions.**

PETITION OF THE MANUFACTURERS OF CANDLES, Waxlights, Lamps, Candlesticks, Street Lamps, Snuffers, Extinguishers, and of the Producers of Oil Tallow, Rosin, Alcohol, and, Generally, of Everything Connected with Lighting.

**TO MESSIEURS THE MEMBERS OF THE CHAMBER OF DEPUTIES.**

Gentlemen—You are on the right road. You reject abstract theories, and have little consideration for cheapness and plenty. Your chief care is the interest of the producer. You desire to emancipate him from external competition, and reserve the national market for national industry.

We are about to offer you an admirable opportunity of applying your—what shall we call it? your theory? No; nothing is more deceptive than theory; your doctrine? your system? your principle? but you dislike doctrines, you abhor systems, and as for principles, you deny that there are any in social economy: we shall say, then, your practice, your practice without theory and without principle.

We are suffering from the intolerable competition of a foreign rival, placed, it would seem, in a condition so far superior to ours for the production of light, that he absolutely inundates our national market with it at a price fabulously reduced. The moment he shows himself, our trade leaves us—all consumers apply to him; and a branch of native industry, having countless ramifications, is all at once rendered completely stagnant. This rival ... is no other than the Sun.

What we pray for is, that it may please you to pass a law ordering the shutting up of all windows, skylights, dormerwindows, outside and inside shutters, curtains, blinds, bull's-eyes; in a word, of all openings, holes, chinks, clefts, and fissures, by or through which the light of the sun has been in use to enter houses, to the prejudice of the meritorious manufactures with which we flatter ourselves we have accommodated our country,—a country which, in gratitude, ought not to abandon us now to a strife so unequal.

If you shut up as much as possible all access to natural light, and create a demand for artificial light, which of our French manufactures will not be encouraged by it?

If more tallow is consumed, then there must be more oxen and sheep; and, consequently, we shall behold the multiplication of artificial meadows, meat, wool, hides, and, above all, manure, which is the basis and foundation of all agricultural wealth.

The same remark applies to navigation. Thousands of vessels will proceed to the whale fishery; and, in a short time, we shall possess a navy capable of maintaining the honor of France, and gratifying the patriotic aspirations of your petitioners, the undersigned candlemakers and others.

Only have the goodness to reflect, Gentlemen, and you will be convinced that there is, perhaps, no Frenchman, from the wealthy coalmaster to the humblest vender of lucifer matches, whose lot will not be ameliorated by the success of this our petition. ■

Source: Frédéric Bastiat, *Economic Sophisms* (Edinburgh: Oliver and Boyd, Tweeddale Court, 1873), pp. 49–53, abridged.

## CHAPTER SUMMARY

1. International trade is growing in importance globally and for Canada. World trade is vital to Canada in two respects. **a** Canadian imports and exports as a percentage of national output are significant. **b** Canada is completely dependent on trade for certain commodities and materials that cannot be obtained domestically.
2. Principal Canadian exports include automotive products, machinery and equipment, and grain; major Canadian imports are general machinery and equipment, automobiles, and industrial goods and machinery. Quantitatively, the United States is our most important trading partner.
3. Global trade has been greatly facilitated by **a** improvements in transportation technology; **b** improvements in communications technology; **c** general declines in tariffs; and **d** continuing peaceful relations among major industrial nations. Canada and the United States, Japan, and the Western European nations dominate the global economy. But the total volume of trade has been increased by several new trade participants, including the "Asian tigers" (Hong Kong, Singapore, South Korea, and Taiwan), China, the Eastern European countries, and the newly independent countries of the former Soviet Union.
4. The open economy circular flow model connects the domestic Canadian economy to the rest of the world. Customers from abroad enter our product market to buy some of our output. These Canadian exports create business revenues and generate income in Canada. Canadian households spend some of their money income on products made abroad and imported to Canada.
5. Specialization based on comparative advantage enables nations to achieve higher standards of living through exchange with other countries. A trading partner should specialize in products and services for which its domestic opportunity costs are lowest. The terms of trade must be such that both nations can get more of some output via trade than they can obtain by producing it at home.

6. The foreign exchange market sets exchange rates between nations' currencies. Foreign importers are suppliers of their currencies and domestic importers are demanders of foreign currencies. The resulting supply-demand equilibrium sets an exchange rate; these exchange rates link the price levels of all nations. Depreciation of a nation's currency reduces its imports and increases its exports; appreciation increases its imports and reduces exports.

7. Governments shape trade flows through **a** protective tariffs; **b** quotas; **c** nontariff barriers; and **d** export subsidies. These are impediments to free trade; they result from misunderstandings about the gains to be had from trade and also from political considerations. By increasing product prices, trade barriers cost Canadian consumers billions of dollars annually.

8. The post-World War period has seen a trend towards lower Canadian tariffs. In 1947 the General Agreement on Tariffs and Trade (GATT) was formed to **a** encourage nondiscriminatory treatment for all trading nations; **b** reduce tariffs; and **c** eliminate import quotas.

9. The Uruguay Round of GATT negotiations, completed in 1993 and to be implemented through 2005, **a** reduces tariffs, **b** liberalizes trade in services, **c** reduces agricultural subsidies, **d** reduces pirating of intellectual property, **e** phases out import quotas on textiles and apparel, and **f** establishes the World Trade Organization.

10. Free-trade zones (trade blocs) may liberalize trade within regions but may also impede trade with nonbloc members. Two examples of free-trade arrangements are the European Union (EU), formerly the European Community or "Common Market," and the North American Free Trade Agreement (NAFTA), comprising Canada, Mexico, and the United States.

11. The global economy has created intense foreign competition in many Canadian product markets, but most Canadian firms can compete well both at home and in global markets.

## TERMS AND CONCEPTS

multinational corporations
"Asian tigers"
absolute advantage
comparative advantage
terms of trade
foreign exchange market
exchange rates
depreciation
appreciation
protective tariffs
import quotas
nontariff barriers
export subsidies
most-favoured-nation clauses
General Agreement on Tariffs and Trade (GATT)
World Trade Organization
European Union (EU)
trade bloc
North American Free Trade Agreement (NAFTA)
Canada-U.S. Free Trade Agreement (FTA)

## STUDY QUESTIONS

1. How important is international trade to the Canadian economy? Who is Canada's most important trade partner? How can persistent trade deficits be financed? "Trade deficits mean we get more merchandise from the rest of the world than we provide them in return. Therefore, trade deficits are economically desirable." Do you agree? Why or why not?

2. What factors account for the rapid growth of world trade since World War II? Who are the major players in international trade today? Who are the "Asian tigers" and how important are they in world trade?

3. KEY QUESTION *Use the circular flow model (Figure 6-5) to explain how an increase in exports would affect the revenues of domestic firms, the money income of domestic households, and imports from abroad. Use Figure 6-3 to find the amounts (in 1997) of Canada's exports (flow 13) and imports (flow 16) in the circular flow model. What do these amounts imply for flows 14 and 15?*

4. **KEY QUESTION** *The following are production possibilities tables for South Korea and Canada. Assume that before specialization and trade the optimal product mix for South Korea is alternative B and for Canada alternative D.*

| PRODUCT | SOUTH KOREA'S PRODUCTION ALTERNATIVES | | | | | |
|---|---|---|---|---|---|---|
| | A | B | C | D | E | F |
| Radios (in thousands) | 30 | 24 | 18 | 12 | 6 | 0 |
| Chemicals (in tonnes) | 0 | 6 | 12 | 18 | 24 | 30 |

| PRODUCT | CANADA'S PRODUCTION ALTERNATIVES | | | | | |
|---|---|---|---|---|---|---|
| | A | B | C | D | E | F |
| Radios (in thousands) | 10 | 8 | 6 | 4 | 2 | 0 |
| Chemicals (in tonnes) | 0 | 4 | 8 | 12 | 16 | 20 |

**a.** *Are comparative-cost conditions such that the two areas should specialize? If so, what product should each produce?*
**b.** *What is the total gain in radio and chemical output that results from this specialization?*
**c.** *What are the limits of the terms of trade? Suppose actual terms of trade are 1 unit of radios for $1\frac{1}{2}$ units of chemicals and that 4 units of radios are exchanged for 6 units of chemicals. What are the gains from specialization and trade for each area?*
**d.** *Can you conclude from this illustration that specialization according to comparative advantage results in more efficient use of world resources? Explain.*

5. Suppose that the comparative-cost ratios of two products—baby formula and tuna fish—are as follows in the hypothetical nations of Canswicki and Tunata.
   Canswicki: 1 can baby formula ≡ 2 cans tuna fish
   Tunata: 1 can baby formula ≡ 4 cans tuna fish
   In what product should each nation specialize? Explain why terms of trade of 1 can baby formula = $2\frac{1}{2}$ cans tuna fish would be acceptable to both nations.

6. **KEY QUESTION** *"Canadian exports create a demand for foreign currencies; foreign imports of our goods generate supplies of foreign currencies." Do you agree? Other things being equal, would a decline in Canadian incomes or a weakening of Canadian preferences for foreign products cause the dollar to depreciate or appreciate? What would be the effects of that depreciation or appreciation on our exports and imports?*

7. If the French franc declines in value (depreciates) in the foreign exchange market, will it be easier or harder for the French to sell their wine in Canada? If you were planning a trip to Paris, how would the depreciation of the franc change the dollar cost of this trip?

8. True or false? "An increase in the Canadian dollar price of the German mark implies that the German mark has depreciated in value." Explain.

9. What tools do governments use to promote exports and restrict imports? Who benefits and who loses from protectionist policies? What is the net outcome for consumers?

10. **KEY QUESTION** *What is GATT? How does it affect nearly every person in the world? What were the major outcomes of the Uruguay Round of GATT? How is GATT related to the European Union (EU), the Canada-U.S. Free Trade Agreement (FTA), and the North American Free Trade Agreement (NAFTA)?*

11. Explain: "Free trade zones such as the EU and NAFTA lead a double life: They can promote free trade among members, but pose serious trade obstacles for nonmembers." Do you think the net effects of these trade blocs are good or bad for world trade? Why?

12. What do you see as the competitive strengths of Canadian firms? Competitive weaknesses? Explain: "Even if Japan captured the entire worldwide auto market, that simply would mean that Japan would have to buy a whole lot of other products from abroad. Thus, Canada and other industrial nations would necessarily experience an increase in exports to Japan."

13. **(The Last Word)** What point is Bastiat trying to make with his petition of the candlemakers?

14. WEB-BASED QUESTION **Trade Balances With Partner Countries.** Statistics Canada www.statcan.ca/english/Pgdb/Economy/International/gblec02a.htm sets out Canadian imports and exports to major trading partners and areas for the last five years. Do we have a trading surplus or deficit with the United States? What about with Japan and the European Union?

15. WEB-BASED QUESTION **Foreign Exchange Rates—the U.S. for Canadian Dollar.** Statistics Canada provides the exchange rate of the Canadian dollar against the U.S. dollar for the last five years at www.statcan.ca/english/Pgdb/Economy/Economic/econ07.htm. Assume you visited New York City every summer for the last five years and bought a Coney Island hotdog for U.S. $5. Convert this amount to Canadian dollars using the exchange rate for each year and plot the Canadian dollar price of the Coney Island hotdog. Has the Canadian dollar appreciated or depreciated against the U.S. dollar? What was the least amount in Canadian dollars your Coney Island hotdog cost? The most?

PART 2

# Microeconomics of Product Markets

CHAPTER 7

# Elasticities and Their Applications

SCARCE RESOURCES. UNLIMITED WANTS. THAT IS what economics is about. Because of its unlimited wants, society desires to use all its available resources fully and efficiently. The full employment of all available resources—and the long-run expansion of output—is the focus of *macroeconomics*. Efficiently using employed resources is the subject of *microeconomics*, to which we now turn.

We have seen that a market economy relies heavily on the self-interested behaviour of market participants to allocate resources efficiently. Our goal now is to examine this behaviour—and the resulting price, output, and efficiency outcomes—in much greater depth than in earlier chapters.

In this chapter we extend Chapter 4's discussion of demand and supply. Specifically, we now introduce and discuss the concept of *price elasticity*, a measure of consumers' and producers' responses to price changes. We then extend the elasticity concept by explaining the ideas of *cross* and *income* elasticity of demand. Finally, we apply our more detailed supply and demand analysis to markets in which government sets price ceilings and floors.

**IN THIS CHAPTER YOU WILL LEARN:**

- The concept of elasticity of demand and how to calculate it.
- The factors that determine the price elasticity of demand.
- The concept of the elasticity of supply and how to calculate it.
- The factors that determine the price elasticity of supply.
- The cross and income elasticity of demand and how to calculate them.
- To apply the concept of elasticity to various real-world situations.

## The Big Picture

YOU SHOULD THINK OF ELASTICITY AS A refinement of supply and demand analysis. In a world of scarcity, you must choose among alternative needs and wants every day. The choices you make are influenced by prices. As price changes, your choices about how much to purchase of each good or service change. But your response to price changes for each good or service you want will vary. The quantity demanded of antibiotics prescribed by your doctor is unlikely to change much even if there is a sizable change in price, either up or down! But if the price of chocolate bars were to rise to $10 each, you would undoubtedly consume fewer chocolate bars each year.

As you read this chapter, keep the following points in mind:

- Elasticity has important application to business decisions; it helps predict consumer response to price changes.
- Government policy choices are often made on the basis of elasticity. For example, if a government wants to raise its revenues from taxation, it should choose goods or services whose demand is relatively insensitive to a price change.
- Elasticity can help to explain some social phenomenon—for example, a change in drug-related crime due to a change in the price of drugs. ■

## PRICE ELASTICITY OF DEMAND

The law of demand tells us that consumers will respond to a decline in a product's price by buying more of that product. But how much more of it will they purchase? That amount can vary considerably by product and over different price ranges for the same product.

The responsiveness, or sensitivity, of consumers to a change in the price of a product is measured by the product's **price elasticity of demand**. Demand for some products is such that consumers are highly responsive to price changes; modest price changes lead to very large changes in the quantity purchased. Example: restaurant meals. The demand for such products is said to be *relatively elastic* or simply *elastic*. For other products, consumers are quite unresponsive to price changes; substantial price changes result only in small changes in the amount purchased. Example: salt. For such products, demand is *relatively inelastic* or simply *inelastic*.

### The Price Elasticity Coefficient and Formula

Economists measure the degree of price elasticity or inelasticity of demand with the coefficient $E_d$, defined as

$$E_d = \frac{\text{percentage change in quantity demanded of product X}}{\text{percentage change in price of product X}}$$

These *percentage* changes are calculated by dividing the change in price by the original price and the consequent change in quantity demanded by the original quantity demanded. Thus, our definition can be restated as the formula:

$$E_d = \frac{\text{change in quantity demanded of X}}{\text{original quantity demanded of X}} \div \frac{\text{change in price of X}}{\text{original price of X}}$$

**Use of Percentages** Why use percentages rather than absolute amounts in measuring consumer responsiveness? There are two reasons.

1. **CHOICE OF UNITS** If we use absolute changes, our impression of buyer responsiveness will be arbitrarily affected by the choice of units. To illustrate: If the price of product X falls from $3 to $2 and consumers increase their purchases from 60 to 100 kilograms, it may appear that consumers are quite sensitive to price changes and therefore that demand is elastic. After all, a price change of 1 unit has caused a change in the amount demanded of

40 units. But by changing the monetary unit from dollars to pennies (why not?), we find that a price change of 100 units causes a quantity change of 40 units, giving the impression of inelasticity. Using percentage changes avoids this problem. This particular price decline is 33 percent whether measured in dollars ($1/$3) or pennies (100¢/300¢).

2. **COMPARING PRODUCTS** By using percentages we can correctly compare consumer responsiveness to changes in the prices of *different* products. It makes little sense to compare the effects on quantity demanded of (1) a $1 increase in the price of a $10,000 auto with (2) a $1 increase in the price of a $1 can of cola. Here the price of the auto is rising by .01 percent while the price of the cola is up by 100 percent! If we increased the price of both products by 1 percent—$100 for the car and 1¢ for the cola—we could obtain a more sensible comparison of consumer sensitivity to the price changes.

**Ignore Minus Sign** We know from the downsloping demand curve that price and quantity demanded are inversely related. Thus, the price elasticity coefficient of demand $E_d$ will always be a *negative* number. As an example, if price declines, then quantity demanded will increase. This means that the numerator in our formula will be positive and the denominator negative, yielding a negative $E_d$. For an increase in price, the numerator will be negative but the denominator positive, again yielding a negative $E_d$.

Economists usually ignore the minus sign and simply present the *absolute value* of the elasticity coefficient to avoid an ambiguity that might otherwise arise. It can be confusing to say that an $E_d$ of –4 is greater than one of –2. This possible confusion is avoided when we say an $E_d$ of 4 reveals greater elasticity than one of 2. In what follows we thus ignore the minus sign in the coefficient of price elasticity of demand and show only the absolute value. Incidentally, the ambiguity does not arise with supply because price and quantity supplied are positively related.

## Interpretations of $E_d$

We can interpret the coefficient of price elasticity of demand as follows.

**Elastic Demand** Demand is said to be **elastic** if a specific percentage change in price results in a larger percentage change in quantity demanded. Then $E_d$ will be greater than 1. Example: If a 2 percent decline in price results in a 4 percent increase in quantity demanded, then demand is elastic and

$$E_d = \frac{.04}{.02} = 2$$

**Inelastic Demand** If a specific percentage change in price is accompanied by a smaller percentage change in quantity demanded, demand is said to be **inelastic**. Then $E_d$ will be less than 1. Example: If a 3 percent decline in price leads to only a 1 percent increase in quantity demanded, demand is inelastic and

$$E_d = \frac{.01}{.03} = .33$$

**Unit Elasticity** The case separating elastic and inelastic demands occurs where a percentage change in price and the accompanying percentage change in quantity demanded are equal. Example: A 1 percent drop in price causes a 1 percent increase in quantity demanded. This special case is termed **unit elasticity** because $E_d$ is exactly 1, or unity. In this example,

$$E_d = \frac{.01}{.01} = 1$$

**Extreme Cases** When we say demand is "inelastic," we do not mean that consumers are *completely* unresponsive to a price change. In that extreme situation, where a price change results in no change whatsoever in the quantity demanded, economists say that demand is **perfectly inelastic.** Examples include an acute diabetic's demand for insulin or an addict's demand for heroin. A line parallel to the vertical axis—such as $D_0$ in Figure 7-1—shows perfectly inelastic demand graphically.

Conversely, when we say demand is "elastic," we do not mean consumers are completely responsive to a price change. In that extreme situation, where a small price reduction would cause buyers to increase their purchases from zero to all they could obtain, economists say demand is **perfectly elastic**. A line parallel to the horizontal axis, such as $D_1$ in Figure 7-1, shows perfectly elastic demand. You will see in Chapter 10 that such a

**FIGURE 7-1 Perfectly inelastic and elastic demand**

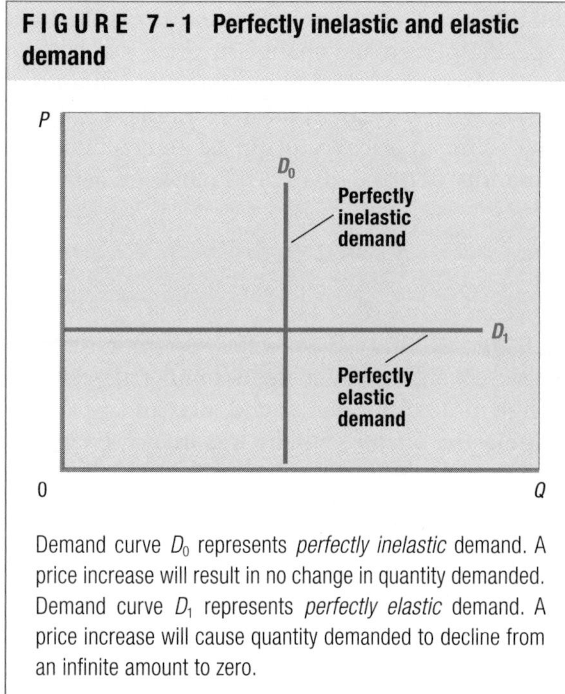


Demand curve $D_0$ represents *perfectly inelastic* demand. A price increase will result in no change in quantity demanded. Demand curve $D_1$ represents *perfectly elastic* demand. A price increase will cause quantity demanded to decline from an infinite amount to zero.

**TABLE 7-1 Price elasticity of demand as measured by the elasticity coefficient and the total revenue test**

| (1) Total quantity demanded per week | (2) Price per unit | (3) Elasticity coefficient, $E_d$ | (4) Total revenue (1) × (2) | (5) Total revenue test |
|---|---|---|---|---|
| 1 | $8 | | $ 8 | |
| | | 5.00 | | Elastic |
| 2 | 7 | | 14 | |
| | | 2.60 | | Elastic |
| 3 | 6 | | 18 | |
| | | 1.57 | | Elastic |
| 4 | 5 | | 20 | |
| | | 1.00 | | Unit elastic |
| 5 | 4 | | 20 | |
| | | 0.64 | | Inelastic |
| 6 | 3 | | 18 | |
| | | 0.38 | | Inelastic |
| 7 | 2 | | 14 | |
| | | 0.20 | | Inelastic |
| 8 | 1 | | 8 | |

demand applies to a firm, say, a raspberry grower, selling its product in a purely competitive market.

## Refinement: Midpoint Formula

The hypothetical demand data in Table 7-1 are useful for explaining an annoying problem that arises in computing the price elasticity coefficient: To calculate $E_d$ for, say, the $5-$4 price range, which price-quantity combination should we use as a point of reference? We have two choices: the $5-4 unit combination and the $4-5 unit combination, and our choice will influence the outcome.

For the $5-4 unit reference point, the price change is from $5 to $4, so the percentage decrease in price is 20 percent; the quantity change is from 4 to 5 units, so the percentage increase in quantity is 25 percent. Substituting in the formula, we get $E_d = 25/20$, or 1.25, indicating that demand is somewhat elastic.

But for the $4-5 unit reference point, the price change is from $4 to $5, making the percentage increase in price 25 percent; the quantity change is from 5 to 4 units, or a 20 percent decline in quantity. The elasticity coefficient is therefore 20/25, or 0.80, meaning demand is slightly inelastic. Which is it? Is demand elastic or inelastic?

A solution to this problem is to use *averages* of the two prices and two quantities as the reference point. For the same $5-$4 price-range, the price reference is $4.50, and the quantity reference 4.5 units. The percentage change in price is now $1/$4.50 or about 22 percent and the percentage change in quantity is 1/4.50 or also about 22 percent, providing an $E_d$ of 1. This solution estimates elasticity at the midpoint of the relevant price range. We now can restate the formula for $E_d$ as

$$E_d = \frac{\text{change in quantity}}{\text{sum of quantities}/2} \div \frac{\text{change in price}}{\text{sum of prices}/2}$$

Substituting data for the $5-$4 price range, we get

$$E_d = \frac{1}{9/2} \div \frac{1}{9/2} = 1$$

This indicates that *at* the $4.50-4.5 unit midpoint the price elasticity of demand is unity. Here a 1 percent price change would result in a 1 percent change in quantity demanded.

Assignment: Verify the elasticity coefficients for the $1-$2 and $7-$8 price ranges in Table 7-1. The interpretation of $E_d$ for the $1-$2 range is that a 1 percent change in price will change quantity demanded by 0.20 percent. For the \$7-\$8 range a 1 percent change in price will change quantity demanded by 5 percent.

## Graphical Analysis

Demand curve *D* in Figure 7-2a was plotted using the data in columns 1 and 2 of Table 7-1. It illustrates two important ideas.

1. **ELASTICITY VARIES WITH PRICE RANGE** Elasticity typically varies over the different price ranges of the same demand schedule or curve. For all straight-line and most other demand curves, demand is more elastic towards the upper left (the \$5-\$8 price range of *D*) than towards the lower right (the \$4-\$1 price range of *D*).

   This is the consequence of arithmetic properties of the elasticity measure. Specifically, in the upper left segment of the demand curve, the percentage change in quantity is large because the original reference quantity is small. Similarly, the percentage change in price is small in that segment because the original reference price is large. The relatively large percentage change in quantity divided by the relatively small change in price yields a large $E_d$—an elastic demand.

   The reverse holds true for the lower right segment of the demand curve. Here the percentage change in quantity is small because the original reference quantity is large; similarly, the percentage change in price is large because the original reference price is small. The relatively small percentage change in quantity divided by the relatively large percentage change in price results in a low $E_d$—an inelastic demand.
2. **SLOPE DOESN'T MEASURE ELASTICITY** The graphical appearance of a demand curve—its slope—is *not* a sound basis for judging elasticity. The catch is that the slope—the flatness or steepness—of a demand curve is computed from *absolute* changes in price and quantity, while elasticity involves *relative or percentage* changes in price and quantity.

   The demand curve in Figure 7-2a is linear, which by definition means the slope is constant throughout. But we have demonstrated that such a curve is elastic in its high-price (\$8-\$5) range and inelastic in its low-price (\$4-\$1) range. ***(Key Question 2)***

### 7-1 QUICK REVIEW

- Price elasticity of demand measures the sensitivity of consumers to changes in the price of a product.
- The price elasticity of demand coefficient $E_d$ is the ratio of the percentage change in quantity demanded to the percentage change in price. The average of the prices and quantities are used as references in calculating the percentage changes.
- When $E_d$ is greater than 1, demand is elastic; when $E_d$ is less than 1, it is inelastic; when $E_d$ is equal to 1, demand is of unit elasticity.
- Demand is typically elastic in the high-price (low-quantity) range of the demand curve and inelastic in the low-price (high-quantity) range of the curve.

## The Total-Revenue Test

**Total revenue** (TR) is the total amount the seller receives from the sale of a product; it is calculated by multiplying the product price (P) by the quantity *demanded and sold* (Q). In equation form:

$$\text{TR} = P \times Q$$

Total revenue and the price elasticity of demand are related. Indeed, perhaps the easiest way to infer whether demand is elastic or inelastic is to employ the **total-revenue test**, where we observe what happens to total revenue when product price changes.

**Elastic Demand** If demand is *elastic*, a *decrease* in price will *increase* total revenue. Even though a lesser price is received per unit, enough additional units are sold to more than make up for the lower price. For an example, look at demand curve *D* in Figure 7-2a, specifically the elastic-demand region at the upper left. (Disregard Figure 7-2b for the moment.) At point *a* on the curve, price is \$8 and quantity demanded is 1 unit. So total revenue, or price times quantity, is \$8.

If the price declines to \$7 (point *b*), the quantity demanded becomes 2 units, and total revenue is \$14 (= \$2 × 7 units). As a result of the price decline from \$8 to \$7, total revenue has increased from \$8 to \$14. This increase has occurred because the *loss* in revenue from the lower price per unit is *less* than the *gain* in revenue from the larger quan-

**FIGURE 7-2 Relation between price elasticity of demand and total revenue**

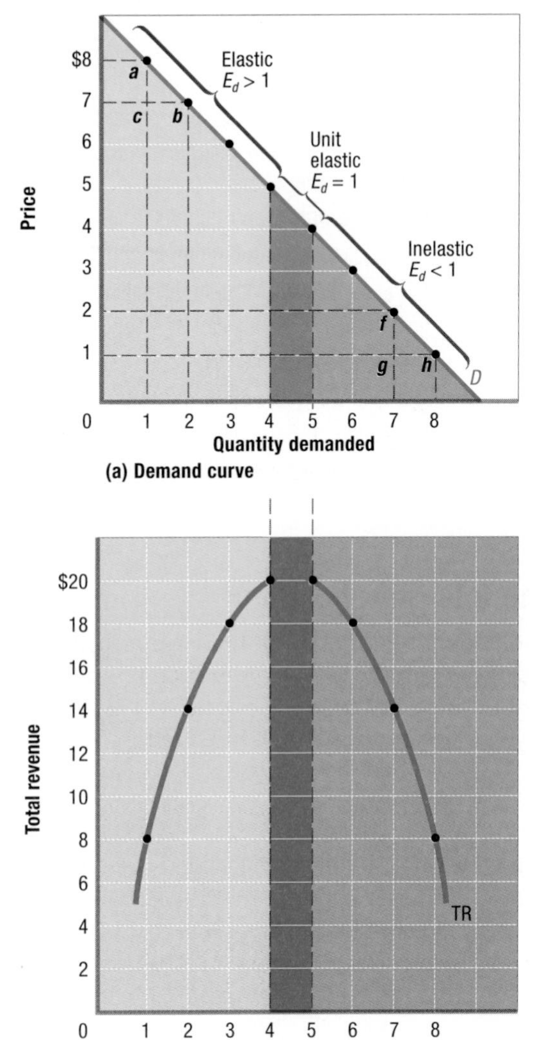


Demand curve *D* in (a) is based on Table 7-1 and marked to show that, typically, demand is elastic at higher price ranges and inelastic at lower price ranges. The total-revenue curve TR in (b) is derived from demand curve *D*. When price falls and TR increases, demand is elastic; when price falls and TR is unchanged, demand is unit-elastic; and when price falls and TR declines, demand is inelastic.

tity demanded accompanying the lower price. Specifically, the $1 price reduction applies to the original 1 unit for a loss of $1. But the lower price increases quantity demanded by 1 unit with a resulting gain in revenue of $7. Thus, there is a *net increase* in total revenue of $6 (= $7 – $1).

The reasoning is reversible: If demand is elastic, a price *increase* will *reduce* total revenue. If we shift from *b* to *a* on the demand curve, the gain in total revenue caused by the higher unit price is *less* than the *loss* in revenue from the drop in sales. Combining these results tells us that *demand is elastic if a price change causes total revenue to change in the opposite direction.*

**Inelastic Demand** If demand is inelastic, a price decrease will reduce total revenue. The modest increase in sales will not offset the decline in revenue per unit, and the net result is that total revenue declines. To see this, look towards the lower right of demand curve *D* in Figure 7-2a, specifically the inelastic-demand region. At point *f* on the curve, price is $2 and quantity demanded is 7 units. So total revenue is $14. If the price drops to $1 (point *h*), quantity demanded increases to 8 units. Total revenue becomes $8, which is clearly less than $14. Total revenue has declined because the loss of revenue from the lower unit price is larger than the gain in revenue from the accompanying increase in sales. The $1 decline in price applies to 7 units, with a consequent revenue loss of $7. The sales increase accompanying this lower price is 1 unit, which results in a revenue gain of $1. The overall result is a net decrease in total revenue of $6 (= $1 – $7).

Again our analysis is reversible: If demand is inelastic, a price *increase* will *increase* total revenue. Together, these results tell us that *demand is inelastic if a price change causes total revenue to change in the same direction.*

**Unit Elasticity** In the special case of *unit elasticity*, an increase or decrease in price leaves total revenue unchanged. The loss in revenue from a lower unit price is exactly offset by the gain in revenue from the accompanying increase in sales. Conversely, the gain in revenue from a higher unit price is exactly offset by the revenue loss associated with the accompanying decline in the amount demanded.

In Figure 7-2a we find that at the $5 price 4 units will be sold to yield total revenue of $20. At $4 a total of 5 units will be sold, again resulting in $20 of total revenue. The $1 price reduction causes the loss of $4 in revenue on the 4 units that could have been sold for $5 each. This is exactly offset by a $4 revenue gain that results from the sale of 1 more unit at the lower $4 price.

## Price Elasticity and the Total-Revenue Curve

In Figure 7-2b we graphed the total revenue corresponding to each price-quantity combination indicated in columns 1 and 4 in Table 7-1 and demand curve *D* in Figure 7-2a. The price-quantity demanded combination represented by point *a* on the demand curve yields total revenue of $8 (= $8 × 1 unit). In Figure 7-2b, we graphed this $8 amount vertically at 1 unit of quantity demanded. Similarly, the price-quantity demanded combination represented by point *b* yields total revenue of $14 (= $7 × 2 units). This amount is graphed vertically at 2 units of quantity demanded in the lower figure. The ultimate result of such graphing is total revenue curve TR, which initially slopes upward, reaches a maximum, and then turns downward.

Comparison of curves *D* and TR brings the relationship between elasticity and total revenue into sharp focus. Lowering the price in the elastic range of demand—say, from $8 to $5—increases total revenue. Conversely, increasing the price in that range reduces total revenue. In both cases, price and total revenue change in opposite directions, confirming that demand is elastic.

The $5–$4 price range of demand curve *D* is characterized by unit elasticity. When price either decreases from $5 to $4 or increases from $4 to $5, total revenue remains $20. In both cases, price has changed and total revenue has remained constant, confirming that demand is unit-elastic when we consider these particular price changes.

In the inelastic range of demand curve *D*, lowering the price—say, from $4 to $1—drops total revenue, as shown in the lower figure. Raising the price boosts total revenue. In both cases, price and total revenue move in the same direction, confirming that demand is inelastic.

So here again is the total revenue test: Note what happens to total revenue when the price of a product changes. If total revenue changes in the *opposite* direction from price, demand is elastic. If total revenue changes in the *same* direction as price, demand is inelastic. If total revenue *does not change* when price changes, demand is unit-elastic.

Table 7-2 summarizes the characteristics of price elasticity of demand, and you should study it carefully. ***(Key Questions 4 and 5)***

## Determinants of Price Elasticity of Demand

We cannot say just what will determine the price elasticity of demand in each individual situation. However, the following generalizations are often helpful.

**Substitutability** Generally, the larger the number of substitute goods that are available, the

**TABLE 7-2 Price elasticity of demand: a summary**

| Absolute value of elasticity coefficient | Demand is | Description | IMPACT ON TOTAL REVENUE OF A: Price increase | Price decrease |
|---|---|---|---|---|
| Greater than 1 ($E_d > 1$) | Elastic or relatively elastic | Quantity demanded changes by a larger percentage than does price | Total revenue decreases | Total revenue increases |
| Equal to 1 ($E_d = 1$) | Unit or unitary elastic | Quantity demanded changes by the same percentage as does price | Total revenue is unchanged | Total revenue is unchanged |
| Less than 1 ($E_d < 1$) | Inelastic or relatively inelastic | Quantity demanded changes by a smaller percentage than does price | Total revenue increases | Total revenue decreases |

greater the elasticity of demand. We will find later that in a purely competitive market, where by definition there are many perfect substitutes for the product of any specific seller, the demand curve seen by that single seller is perfectly elastic. If one competitive seller of carrots or potatoes raises its price, buyers will turn to the readily available perfect substitutes provided by its many rivals. Similarly, we would expect the lowering of world trade barriers to increase the elasticity of demand for most products by making more substitutes available. With unimpeded trade Hondas, Toyotas, Nissans, Mazdas, Volkswagens, and other foreign cars become effective substitutes for domestic autos. At the other extreme, we saw earlier that the diabetic's demand for insulin and the addict's demand for heroin are highly inelastic—there are no close substitutes.

The elasticity of demand for a product depends on how narrowly the product is defined. Demand for Petro-Canada motor oil is more elastic than is the overall demand for motor oil. Many other brands are readily substitutable for Petro-Canada's oil, but there are few, if any, good substitutes for motor oil.

**Proportion of Income** Other things equal, the higher the price of a good relative to people's income and hence to their budgets, the greater the good's price elasticity of demand. A 10 percent increase in the price of relatively low-priced pencils or chewing gum amounts to a few pennies, and quantity demanded will probably decline only slightly. Thus, price elasticity for such low-priced items will tend to be low. But a 10 percent increase in the price of relatively high-priced automobiles or housing means additional expenditures of perhaps $2,000 or $10,000, respectively. These price increases are significant fractions of the annual incomes and budgets of most families, and quantities demanded will likely diminish significantly. Price elasticity for such items tends to be high, meaning demand will be elastic.

**Luxuries versus Necessities** The demand for "necessities" tends to be price inelastic; that for "luxuries," price elastic. Bread and electricity are generally regarded as necessities; it is difficult to get along without them. A price increase will not significantly reduce the amount of bread consumed or the amounts of lighting and power used in a household. (Note the very low price elasticity coefficient of these goods in Table 7-3.) An extreme case: A person does not decline an operation for acute appendicitis because the physician has found a way to extra-bill!

On the other hand, Caribbean cruises and emeralds are luxuries that, by definition, can be forgone. If the price of cruises or emeralds rises, an individual need not buy them and will suffer no great hardship without them.

What about the demand for a common product like salt? It is highly inelastic on three counts: There are few good substitutes available; salt is a negligible item in the family budget; and it is a "necessity" rather than a luxury.

**Time** Generally, product demand is more elastic the longer the time period under consideration. Many consumers are creatures of habit. When the price of a product rises, it takes time to find and experiment with other products to see if they are acceptable. Consumers may not immediately reduce their purchases very much when the price of beef rises by 10 percent, but in time they may shift to chicken or fish, for which they will "develop a taste."

Another consideration is product durability. Studies show that "short-run" demand for gasoline is more inelastic ($E_d$ = 0.2) than is "long-run" demand ($E_d$ = 0.7). In the long run, large, gas-guzzling automobiles wear out and, with rising gasoline prices, are replaced by smaller, more fuel-efficient cars.

Table 7-3 shows estimated price elasticity coefficients for a number of products. You should be able to explain each coefficient with the elasticity determinants just discussed. ***(Key Question 6)***

### 7-2
### QUICK REVIEW

- When the price of a good changes, total revenue will change in the opposite direction if demand for the good is price elastic; in the same direction if demand is price inelastic; and not at all if demand is unit elastic.
- Price elasticity of demand is greater **a** the larger the number of substitutes available; **b** the higher the price of a product relative to one's budget; **c** the greater the extent to which the product is a luxury; and **d** the longer the time period involved.

**TABLE 7-3 Selected price elasticities of demand***

| Product or service | Coefficient of price elasticity of demand, $E_d$ | Product or service | Coefficient of price elasticity of demand, $E_d$ |
|---|---|---|---|
| Housing | .01 | Gasoline | .60 |
| Electricity (household) | .13 | Milk | .63 |
| Bread | .15 | Household appliances | .63 |
| Major league baseball tickets | .23 | Movies | .87 |
| Telephone service | .26 | Beer | .90 |
| Sugar | .30 | Shoes | .91 |
| Medical care | .31 | Motor vehicles | 1.14 |
| Eggs | .32 | Beef | 1.27 |
| Legal services | .37 | China, glassware, tableware | 1.54 |
| Automobile repair | .40 | Restaurant meals | 2.27 |
| Clothing | .49 | Lamb and mutton | 2.65 |

*Compiled from numerous studies and sources reporting price elasticity of demand. Adapted from "National Income and Expenditure Accounts, First Quarter 1995," Catalogue No. 11-210.

## Applications of Price Elasticity of Demand

The concept of price elasticity of demand has great practical significance, as seen in the following examples.

**Bumper Crops** The demand for most farm products is highly inelastic; $E_d$ is perhaps 0.20 or 0.25. As a result, increases in the output of farm products arising from a good growing season or from increased productivity tend to depress both the prices of farm products and the total revenues (incomes) of farmers. For farmers as a group, the inelastic nature of the demand for their products means a bumper crop may be undesirable. For policy makers it means higher total farm income requires that farm output be restricted.

**Automation** The impact of technological advances on employment depends in part on the elasticity of demand for the product or service that is involved. Suppose a firm installs new labour-saving machinery, replacing 500 of its workers who are then laid off. Assume too that part of the cost reduction from this technological advance is passed on to consumers as reduced product prices. The effect of this price reduction on the firm's sales will depend on the price elasticity of demand for the product. If demand is elastic, sales might increase greatly, so that some of, all of, or even more than the 500 displaced workers must be rehired. If demand is inelastic, the price reduction will result in only a small increase in sales, and few, if any, displaced workers will be rehired.

**Excise Taxes** Government pays attention to the elasticity of demand when selecting goods and services on which to levy excise taxes. If a $1 tax is levied on some product, and $10,000 units are sold, tax revenue will be $10,000. If the tax will be raised to $1.50 and the consequent higher price causes sales to decline to 5,000 because of an elastic demand, tax revenue will *decline* to $7,500. A higher tax on a product with an elastic demand will bring in less tax revenue. Therefore, legislatures will seek out products with inelastic demand—for example, liquor, gasoline, and cigarettes—when levying excises.

**Drugs and Street Crime** The fact that the demand for crack cocaine and heroin by addicts is highly inelastic poses some awkward tradeoffs in law enforcement. The approach typically used to reduce drug addiction is to restrict supply by intercepting shipment into Canada.

But if this policy is successful, given the highly inelastic demand for drugs, the street price to addicts will rise sharply while the amount purchased will decrease only slightly. For the drug dealers this means increased revenues and profits. For the addicts it means greater total expenditures on heroin. Because much of the income that addicts spend on drugs comes from crime—shoplifting, burglary, prostitution, and muggings—these crimes will increase as addicts increase their total expenditures for drugs. Thus, the effort of law-enforcement authorities to control the spread of drug addiction may increase the amount of crime committed by addicts.

In recent years proposals to legalize drugs have been widely debated. Proponents contend drugs should be treated like alcohol, should be made legal for adults, and regulated for purity and potency. The current war on drugs, it is argued, has been unsuccessful and the associated costs—including enlarged police forces, an overburdened court system, and untold human costs—have increased markedly. Legalization would allegedly reduce drug trafficking greatly by taking the profit out of it. Crack cocaine and heroin, for example, are cheap to produce and could be sold at low prices in legal markets. Because the demand of addicts is highly inelastic, the amounts consumed at the lower price increase only modestly. Total expenditures for cocaine and heroin by addicts would decline and so would the street crime that finances these expenditures.

Opponents of legalization say that the overall demand for cocaine and heroin is much more elastic than proponents of legalization think. In addition to the inelastic demand of addicts, there is another market segment whose demand is relatively elastic. This segment consists of the occasional users or "dabblers," who use hard drugs when their prices are low but abstain or substitute, say, alcohol when their prices are high. Thus, the lower prices associated with legalization of these drugs would increase consumption by dabblers. Also, removal of the legal prohibitions against using drugs might make drug use more socially acceptable, shifting the demand curve for cocaine and heroin to the right.

Many economists predict that the legalization of cocaine and heroin would reduce their street prices by 60 percent. According to a recent study, price declines of that size would increase the number of occasional users of heroin by 54 percent and the number of occasional users of cocaine by 33 percent. The total quantity of heroin demanded would rise by an estimated 100 percent; the quantity of cocaine demanded, by 50 percent.[1] Moreover, many existing and new dabblers might in time become addicts. The overall result, say the opponents of legalization, would be higher social costs associated with drug use, possibly including an *increase* in street crime.

**Minimum Wage** Minimum wage legislation prohibits employers from paying covered workers less than a specified amount per hour. Critics say that a minimum wage, if it is above the equilibrium market wage, moves employers upward along their downsloping labour demand curves towards lower quantities of labour demanded. In this way it causes unemployment, particularly among teenage workers. On the other hand, workers who remain employed at the minimum wage receive higher incomes than otherwise. The amount of income lost by the newly unemployed and the amount of income gained by those who keep their jobs depend on the elasticity of demand for teenage labour. Research suggests the demand for teenage labour is quite inelastic, with $E_d$ possibly as low as 0.15 or 0.25. If correct, this means income gains associated with the minimum wage exceed income losses. The "unemployment argument" made by critics of the minimum wage would be stronger if the demand for teenage workers were elastic.

## PRICE ELASTICITY OF SUPPLY

The concept of price elasticity also applies to supply. If producers are relatively responsive to price changes, supply is elastic. If they are relatively insensitive to price changes, supply is inelastic.

We measure the degree of price elasticity or inelasticity of supply with the coefficient $E_s$, defined almost like $E_d$ except that we substitute "percentage change in quantity *supplied*" for "percentage change in quantity *demanded*":

$$E_s = \frac{\text{percentage change in quantity supplied of product X}}{\text{percentage change in price of product X}}$$

[1] Henry Saffer and Frank Chaloupka, "The Demand for Illegal Drugs," National Bureau of Economic Research, Working Paper 5238.

For reasons explained earlier, the averages—or midpoints—of the before and after quantities supplied and prices are used as reference points for the percentage changes. Suppose the price of a good increases from \$4 to \$6, increasing the quantity supplied from 10 units to 14 units. The percentage change in price would be 2/5, or 40 percent, and the percentage change in quantity would be 4/12, or 33 percent:

$$E_s = \frac{.33}{.40} = .83$$

In this case, supply is inelastic, since the price elasticity coefficient is less than 1. If $E_s$ is greater than 1, supply is elastic. If it is equal to 1, supply is unit-elastic. Also, $E_s$ is never negative; price and quantity supplied are *directly* related. Thus, there are no minus signs to drop, as was necessary with elasticity of demand.

The main determinant of **price elasticity of supply** is the amount of time available to producers for responding to a change in product price. A firm's response to, say, an increase in the price of Christmas trees depends on its ability to shift resources from the production of other products (whose prices we assume remain constant) to the production of trees. And shifting resources takes time: the longer the time, the greater the resource "shiftability." Thus, we can expect a greater response—and therefore greater elasticity of supply—the longer a firm has to adjust to a price change.

In analyzing the impact of time on elasticity, economists distinguish among the immediate market period, the short run, and the long run.

## Supply Elasticity: The Market Period

The **market period** is the time immediately after a change in market price during which producers cannot respond with a change in quantity supplied. Suppose the owner of a small farm brings an entire season's output of tomatoes—one truckload—to market. The supply curve for these tomatoes is perfectly inelastic (vertical); the farmer will sell the truckload whether the price is high or low. Why? Because the farmer can offer only one truckload of tomatoes even if the price of tomatoes is much higher than anticipated. He or she might like to offer more tomatoes, but tomatoes cannot be produced overnight. Another full growing season is needed to respond to a higher-than-expected price by producing more than one truckload. Similarly, because the product is perishable, the farmer cannot withhold it from the market. If the price is lower than anticipated, he or she will still sell the entire truckload.

The farmer's costs of production, incidentally, will not enter into this decision to sell. Though the price of tomatoes may fall far short of production costs, the farmer will nevertheless sell out to avoid a total loss through spoilage. So during this time period—the market period—our farmer's supply of tomatoes is fixed; only one truckload is offered no matter how high or low the price.

Figure 7-3a shows the farmer's vertical supply curve in the market period. Supply is perfectly inelastic because the farmer does not have time to respond to a change in demand, say from $D_0$ to $D_1$. The resulting price increase from $P_o$ to $P_m$ simply determines which buyers get the fixed quantity supplied; it elicits no increase in output.

However, not all supply curves need be perfectly inelastic immediately after a price change. If the product is not perishable and the price rises, producers may choose to increase quantity supplied by drawing down their inventories of unsold, stored goods. This will cause the market supply curve to have some positive slope. For our tomato farmer, the market period may be a full growing season; for producers of goods that can be inexpensively stored, there may be no market period at all.

## Supply Elasticity: The Short Run

In the **short run,** the plant capacity of individual producers and the industry is fixed. But firms *do* have time to use their fixed plants more or less intensively. Thus in the short run, our farmer's plant—made up land and farm machinery—is fixed, but the farmer does have time to cultivate tomatoes more intensively by applying more labour and more fertilizer and pesticides to the crop. The result is a somewhat greater output in response to a presumed increase in demand; this greater output is reflected in a more elastic supply of tomatoes, as shown by $S_s$ in Figure 7-3b. Note now that the increase in demand from $D_0$ to $D_1$ is met by an increase in quantity (from $Q_o$ to $Q_s$) so there is a smaller price adjustment (from $P_o$ to $P_s$) than in the market period. The equilibrium price is therefore lower in the short run than in the market period.

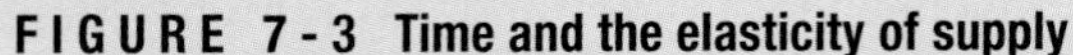

**FIGURE 7-3 Time and the elasticity of supply**

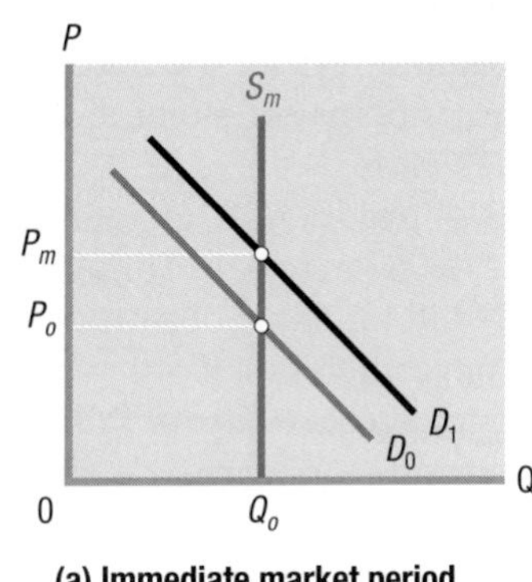


(a) Immediate market period

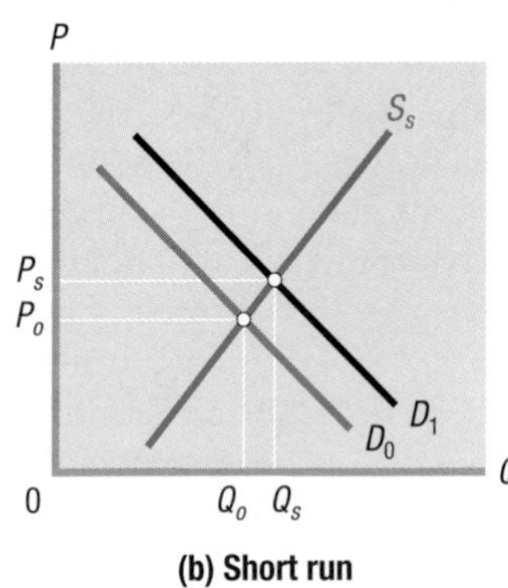


(b) Short run

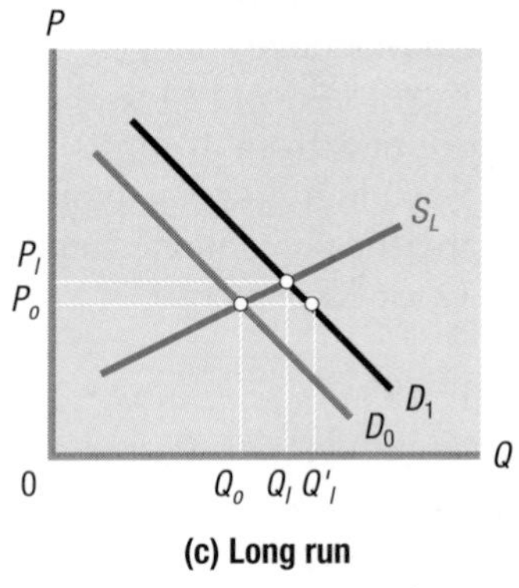


(c) Long run

The greater the amount of time producers have to adjust to a change in demand, here from $D_0$ to $D_1$, the greater will be their output response. In the immediate market period (a) there is insufficient time to change output, and so supply is perfectly inelastic. In the short run (b) plant capacity is fixed, but output can be altered by changing the intensity of its use; supply is therefore more elastic. In the long run (c) all desired adjustments—including changes in plant capacity—can be made, and supply becomes still more elastic.

## Supply Elasticity: The Long Run

The **long run** is a time period sufficiently long that firms can make all desired resource adjustments; individual firms can expand (or contract) their plant capacities; and new firms can enter (or existing firms can leave) the industry. In the "tomato industry," our farmer can acquire additional land and buy more machinery and equipment. Furthermore, more farmers may be attracted to tomato production by the increased demand and higher price. These adjustments mean an even greater supply response, that is, the even more elastic supply curve $S_L$. In Figure 7-3c, the result, is a smaller price rise ($P_0$ to $P_l$) and a larger output increase ($Q_0$ to $Q_1$) in response to the assumed increase in demand from $E_0$ to $D_1$. ***(Key Question 10)***

There is no total-revenue test for elasticity of supply. Supply shows a positive or direct relationship between price and amount supplied; the supply curve is upsloping. Regardless of the degree of elasticity, or inelasticity, price and total revenue always move together.

# CROSS AND INCOME ELASTICITY OF DEMAND

The price elasticities measure the responsiveness of the quantity of a product demanded or supplied when its price changes. It is also useful to know how the consumption of a good is affected by a change in the price of a *related product* or by a change in *income*.

## Cross Elasticity of Demand

Suppose Coca-Cola is considering a reduction in the price of its Sprite brand. Not only will it want to know something about the price elasticity of demand for Sprite (will the price cut increase or decrease total revenue?), but it will also be interested in knowing if the increased sales of Sprite will come at the expense of Coke itself. How sensitive is the quantity demanded of one product (Coke) to a change in the price of a second product (Sprite)? To what extent will the lower price and increased sales of Sprite reduce the sales of Coke?

Or suppose government is trying to assess whether a proposed merger between two large firms will substantially reduce competition and therefore should be blocked. One question it needs to answer is this: Are the two firms' products highly substitutable for one another, or are they largely unrelated to one another? If the former, then competition might be reduced; if the latter, there is probably no cause for concern.

The concept of **cross elasticity of demand** sheds light on such questions from firms and government. It does so by measuring how sensitive consumer purchases of *one* product (say, X) are to a change in the price of some *other* product (say, Y). We calculate a coefficient of $E_{xy}$ cross elasticity of demand by relating the percentage change in the consumption of X to the percentage change in the price of Y:

$$E_{xy} = \frac{\text{percentage change in quantity demanded of product X}}{\text{percentage change in price of product X}}$$

This cross elasticity concept allows us to quantify and more fully understand substitute and complementary goods, introduced in Chapter 4.

**Substitute Goods** If cross elasticity of demand is positive—that is, the quantity demanded of X moves in the same direction as a change in the price of Y—then X and Y are *substitute goods*. An example is Kodak film (X) and Fuji film (Y). An increase in the price of Kodak film causes consumers to buy more Fuji film. The larger the positive cross elasticity coefficient, the greater the substitutability between the two products.

**Complementary Goods** When cross elasticity is negative, we know that X and Y "go together"; an increase in the price of one decreases the demand for the other. So the two are *complementary goods*. For example, an increase in the price of cameras will decrease the amount of film purchased. The larger the negative cross elasticity coefficient, the greater the complementarity between the two goods.

**Independent Goods** A zero or near-zero cross elasticity suggests that the two products are unrelated or *independent goods*. An example is walnuts and film: We would not expect a change in the price of walnuts to have any effect on purchases of film.

## Income Elasticity of Demand

**Income elasticity of demand** measures the degree to which consumers respond to a change in their *incomes* by buying more or less of a particular good. The coefficient of income elasticity of demand $E_i$ is found as

$$E_i = \frac{\text{percentage change in quantity demanded}}{\text{percentage change in income}}$$

**Normal Goods** For most goods the income elasticity coefficient $E_i$ is *positive*, meaning that more of them is demanded as incomes increase. Such goods are called *normal* or *superior goods*, which we first described in Chapter 4. But the value of $E_i$ varies greatly among normal goods. For example, the income elasticity of demand for automobiles is about +3.00, while income elasticity for most farm products is only about +0.20.

**Inferior Goods** A negative income elasticity coefficient designates an *inferior good*. Retreaded tires, cabbage, long-distance bus tickets, and used clothing, are likely candidates. Consumers *decrease* their purchases of such products as incomes *increase*.

**Insights** Income elasticity of demand coefficients provide insights about the economy. Here are two examples:

1. Income elasticity helps explain the relative expansion and contraction of industries in Canada. On average, total income in the economy has grown 2 to 3 percent annually. As income has expanded, industries producing products for which demand is quite income elastic have expanded their outputs. Thus automobiles ($E_i = 3$), housing ($E_i = +1.5$), books ($E_i = +1.4$), and restaurant meals ($E_i = +1.4$) have all experienced strong growth of output. Meanwhile, industries producing products for which income elasticity is low or negative have tended to grow less rapidly or to decline. For example, agriculture ($E_i = +0.20$) has grown far more slowly than has the economy's total output.
2. Some estimates of the coefficient of the income elasticity of demand for health care are about +1.0, indicating that spending on health care rises proportionately with incomes. This coefficient tells policy makers that the inordinate rise in health care spending in Canada over the past two or three decades is caused by factors other than just income growth. ***(Key Questions 12 and 13)***

Table 7-4 is a convenient synopsis of the cross and income elasticity concepts.

## APPLICATIONS

Supply and demand analysis and the elasticity concept are applied repeatedly in the remainder of this book. Let's strengthen our understanding of

**TABLE 7-4 Cross and income elasticities of demand**

| Value of coefficient | Description | Type of good(s) |
|---|---|---|
| Cross elasticity: | | |
| Positive ($E_{wz} > 0$) | Quantity demanded of W changes in same direction as change in price of Z | Substitutes |
| Negative ($E_{xy} < 0$) | Quantity demanded of X changes in opposite direction as change in price of Y | Complements |
| Income elasticity: | | |
| Positive ($E_i > 0$) | Quantity demanded of the product changes in same direction as change in income | Normal or superior |
| Negative ($E_i < 0$) | Quantity demanded of the product changes in opposite direction as change in income | Inferior |

**FIGURE 7-4 The incidence of an excise tax**

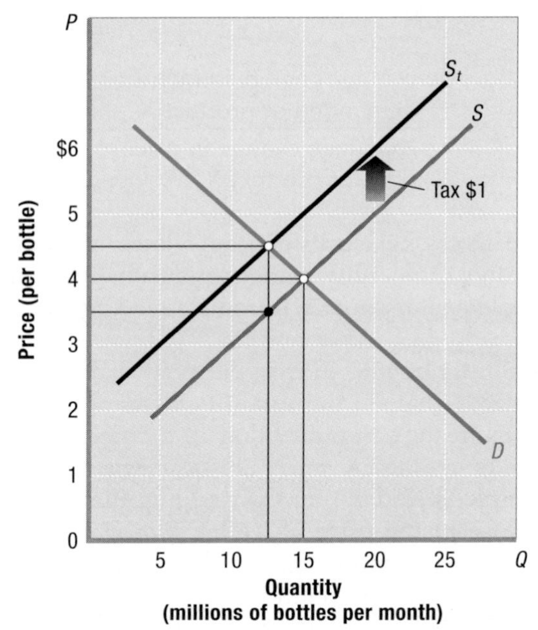


An excise tax of a specified amount, per unit: here $1 per unit, shifts the supply curve upward by the amount of the tax per unit: the vertical distance between *S* and $S_t$. This results in a higher price (here $4.50) to the consumer and a lower after-tax price (here $3.50) to the producer. Thus, consumers and producers share the burden of the tax in some proportion (here equally at $.50 per unit).

these analytical tools and their significance by examining (a) elasticity and tax incidence, and (b) some of the implications of prices fixed by law.

## Elasticity and Tax Incidence

In Figure 7-4, *S* and *D* represent the pretax market for a certain domestic wine; the no-tax equilibrium price and quantity are $4 per bottle and 15 million bottles. If government levies an excise tax of $1 per bottle at the winery, who actually pays it?

**Division of Burden** Since government places the tax on the sellers (suppliers), the tax can be viewed as an addition to the marginal cost of the product. Now sellers must get $1 more for each bottle to receive the same per-unit profit they were getting before the tax. While sellers are willing to offer, for example, 5 million bottles of untaxed wine at $2 per bottle, they must now receive $3 per bottle—$2 plus the $1 tax—to offer the same 5 million bottles. The tax shifts the supply curve upward (leftward) as shown in Figure 7-4, where $S_t$ is the "after-tax" supply curve.

The after-tax equilibrium price is $4.50 per bottle, whereas the before-tax price was $4.00. So, in this case, half the $1 tax is paid by consumers as a higher price; the other half must be paid by producers in the form of a lower after-tax per-unit revenue. That is, after remitting the $1 tax per unit to government, producers receive $3.50, or 50¢ less than the $4.00 before-tax price. In this instance, consumers and producers share the burden of this tax equally; producers shift half the tax to consumers in the form of a higher price and bear the other half themselves.

Note also that the equilibrium quantity decreases as a result of the tax levy and the higher price it imposed on consumers. In Figure 7-4, that decline in quantity is from 15 million bottles to 12.5 million bottles per month.

**Elasticities** If the elasticities of demand and supply were different from those shown in Figure 7-4, the incidence of tax would also be different. Two generalizations are relevant.

1. *With a specific supply, the more inelastic the demand for the product, the larger the portion of the tax shifted to consumers.* To verify this, sketch graphically the extreme cases where demand is perfectly elastic and perfectly inelastic. In the first case, the incidence of the tax is entirely on sellers; in the second, the tax is shifted entirely to consumers.

   Figure 7-5 contrasts the more usual cases where demand is either relatively elastic or relatively inelastic in the relevant price range. With elastic demand (Figure 7-5a), a small portion of the tax ($P_e - P_1$) is shifted to consumers and most of the tax ($P_1 - P_2$) is borne by the producers. With inelastic demand (Figure 7-5b), most of the tax ($P_i - P_1$) is shifted to consumers and only a small amount ($P_1 - P_b$) is paid by producers. In both graphs the per-unit tax is represented by the *vertical* distance between $S_t$ and $S$.

   Note also that the decline in equilibrium quantity ($Q_1 - Q_2$) is smaller when demand is more inelastic. This is the basis of our previous applications of the elasticity concept: Revenue-seeking legislatures place heavy excise taxes on liquor, cigarettes, automobile tires, telephone service, and other products whose demands are thought to be inelastic. Since demand for these products is relatively inelastic, the tax does not reduce sales much, so the tax revenue stays high.

2. *With a specific demand, the more inelastic the supply, the larger the portion of the tax borne by producers.* When supply is elastic (Figure 7-6a) most of the tax ($P_e - P_1$) is shifted to consumers and only a small portion ($P_1 - P_a$) is borne by sellers. But where supply is inelastic (Figure 7-6b), the reverse is true; the major portion of the tax ($P_1 - P_b$) falls on sellers, and a relatively small amount ($P_i - P_1$) is shifted to buyers. The equilibrium quantity also declines less with an inelastic supply than it does with an elastic supply.

   Gold is an example of a product with an inelastic supply and therefore one where the burden of an excise tax would mainly fall on producers. On the other hand, because the supply of baseballs is elastic, producers would pass on to consumers much of an excise tax on baseballs. ***(Key Question 14)***

## Price Ceilings and Floors

On occasion the general public and government conclude that supply and demand result in prices either unfairly high to buyers or unfairly low to sellers. In such instances government may intervene by limiting by law how high or low the price may go.

**FIGURE 7-5 Demand elasticity and the incidence of an excise tax**

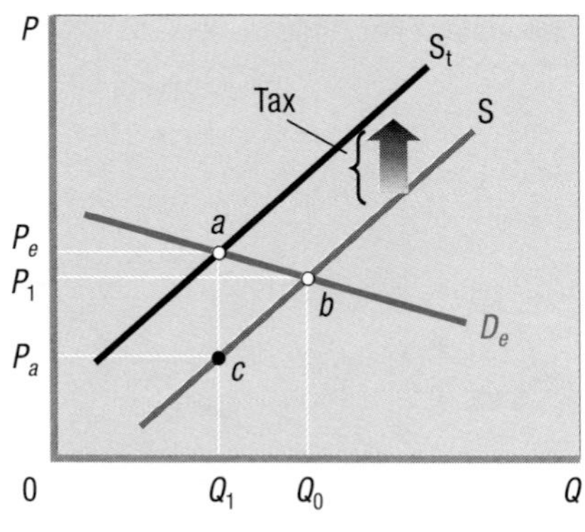


**(a) Tax incidence and elastic demand**

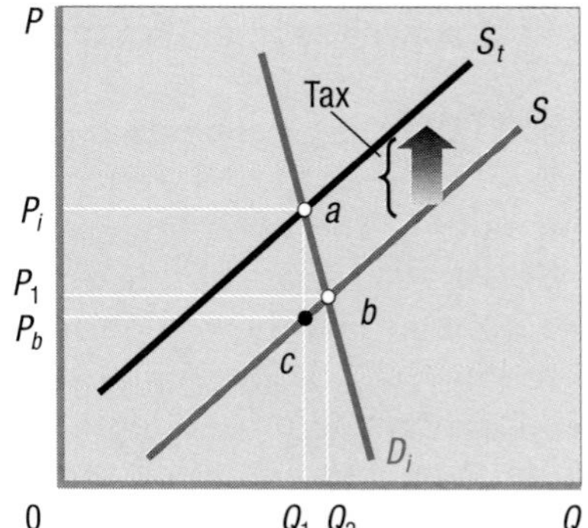


**(b) Tax incidence and inelastic demand**

(a) If demand is elastic in the relevant price range, price rises modestly ($P_1$ to $P_e$) when an excise tax is levied. Hence, the producer bears most of the tax burden. (b) If demand is inelastic, the price to the buyer will increase substantially ($P_1$ to $P_i$) and most of the tax is shifted to consumers.

**FIGURE 7-6 Supply elasticity and the incidence of an excise tax**

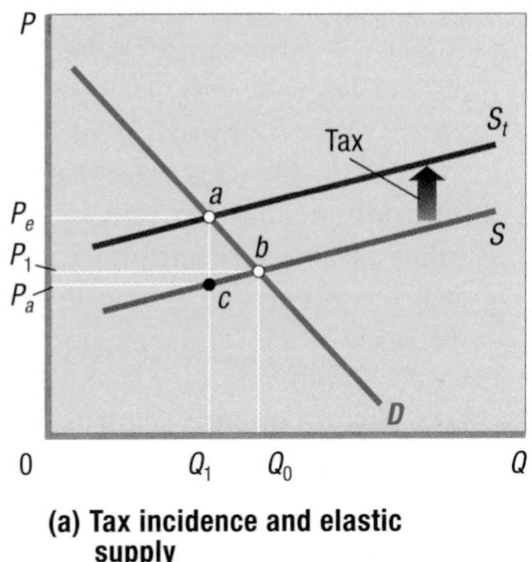


**(a) Tax incidence and elastic supply**

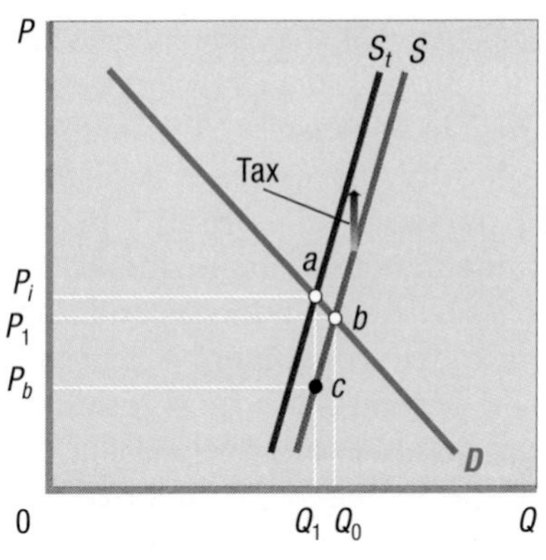


**(b) Tax incidence and inelastic supply**

(a) With an elastic supply an excise tax results in a large price increase ($P_1$ to $P_e$) and the tax is therefore paid mainly by consumers. (b), If supply is inelastic, the price rise is small ($P_1$ to $P_i$) and sellers will have to bear most of the tax.

## Price Ceilings and Shortages

A **price ceiling** is *the maximum legal price that a seller may charge for a product or service.* The rationale for price ceilings on specific products is that they supposedly allow consumers to obtain some "essential" good or service they could not afford at the equilibrium price. Rent controls and usury laws (which specify maximum interest rates that may be charged to borrowers) are examples. Price ceilings or general price controls have been used in attempting to restrain the overall rate of inflation in the economy. Wage and price controls were invoked during World War II, as well as from 1975 to 1979.

### World War II Price Controls

Let's turn back the clock to World War II and analyze the effects of a price ceiling on butter. The booming wartime prosperity of the early 1940s was shifting demand for butter to the right so that the equilibrium or market price $P_0$ reached, say, \$1.20 per pound as in Figure 7-7. The rapidly rising price of butter was contributing to inflation and excluding from the butter market those families whose money incomes were not keeping pace with the soaring cost of living. To help stop inflation and to keep butter on the tables of the poor, government imposed a price ceiling $P_c$, of, say, \$0.90 per pound. To be effective a ceiling price must be *below* equilibrium price. A price ceiling of \$1.50 would have no immediate effect on the butter market.

What are the effects of this \$0.90 price ceiling? The rationing ability of the free market is ineffective. At the price ceiling, there is a lasting shortage of butter. The quantity of butter demanded at $P_c$ is $Q_d$ and the quantity supply is only $Q_s$; a persistent excess demand or shortage in the amount $Q_d - Q_e$ occurs. The actual size of such a shortage varies directly with the price elasticities of supply and

**FIGURE 7-7 Price ceiling results in a persistent shortage**

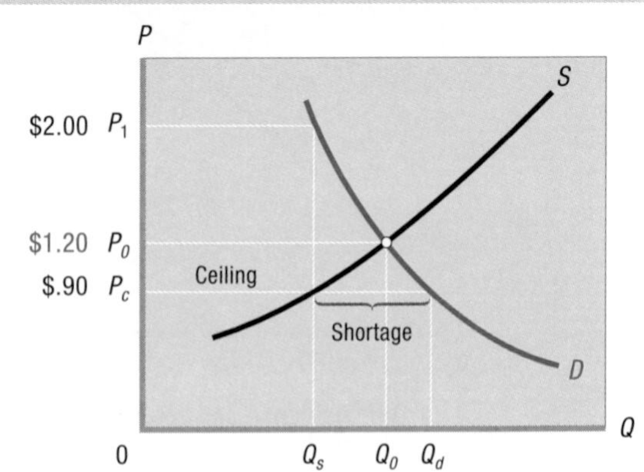


A price ceiling—a maximum legal price—such as $P_c$ results in a persistent product shortage, here equal to the horizontal distance between $Q_d$ and $Q_s$.

demand. The greater these elasticities, the greater the shortage.

The important point is that the price ceiling $P_c$ prevents the usual market adjustment, where competition among buyers bids up price, inducing more production and rationing some buyers out of the market. This process would continue until the shortage disappears at the equilibrium price and quantity, $P_0$ and $Q_0$.

1. **RATIONING PROBLEM** How is the available supply, $Q_s$, to be apportioned among buyers who want amount $Q_d$? Should supply be distributed on a first-come, first-served basis? Or should the grocer distribute butter on the basis of favouritism? An unregulated shortage does not lead to an equitable distribution of butter. Instead, the government must establish some formal system of rationing it to consumers. This was done during World War II by issuing ration coupons to individuals. The rationing system entailed, first, printing of ration coupons equal to $Q_s$ pounds of butter and, then, their equitable distribution among consumers so that the wealthy family of four and the poor family of four both received the same number of coupons.
2. **BLACK MARKETS** But ration coupons do not prevent a second problem from arising. The demand curve in Figure 7-7 tells us there are many buyers willing to pay more than the ceiling price. And of course it is more profitable for grocers to sell at a price above the ceiling. Thus, despite the sizable enforcement bureaucracy that accompanied World War II price controls, illegal *black markets*—markets where products were bought and sold at prices above the legal limits—flourished for many goods. Counterfeiting of ration coupons was also a problem. As Figure 7-7 indicates, there is an excess demand of butter at the ceiling price of \$0.90. Since only quantity $Q_s$ is available, a black market price of $P_1$ (\$2) would result. The black market would be given impetus by coupon holders willing to forgo part of their ration to get \$2 cash for each pound of butter they would be willing to part with.

**Rent Controls** Rent controls are another example of attempts to intervene in the functioning of the market to achieve a well-intentioned social goal. Rent control legislation has been passed in Canada in the past few decades as some provincial governments have attempted to maintain existing stocks of "affordable" rental housing. In a few provinces these laws have since been phased out.

When controls are first imposed they usually restrict increases in rents above current levels. The short-run supply curve for rental accommodation is inelastic because it takes landlords some time to react to price changes and bring new units on the market. Most tenants benefit, since the quantity of rental accommodation currently on the market or under construction is not significantly affected. Thus the program appears to be successful even if shortages begin to appear. Figure 7-8 portrays a market for rental accommodation with rents fixed at $R_c$ and a short-run supply curve, $S_s$. A shortage $Q_1 - Q_2$ exists in the short run.

In the long run the shortage of rental accommodation will worsen since the supply of rental accommodation becomes more elastic. Construction of new units decreases and landlords try to convert existing units to other uses or allow them to deteriorate. The supply curve becomes more elastic in the long run, shown by $S_L$ in Figure 7-8b, making the shortage worse, and increasing it to $Q_1 - Q_3$.

The gradually worsening shortage in the long run leads to several related problems. As in the case of controls on food prices, a black market will emerge. The black market in rental accommodation is often characterized by the charging of "key money." Prospective tenants will often be forced to bribe a landlord or a subletting tenant to acquire a particular rental unit. The acceptance of key money is illegal in most jurisdictions with rent controls, but the practice is difficult to stamp out because it is to the advantage of both parties. Those desperate for rental accommodation will have to pay the black market rate of as much as $R_1$, shown in Figure 7-8b.

Another problem that results from controls is the emergence of a dual rental market if new buildings are exempt from controls. Apartment units whose rents are below market levels are almost always rented informally or with some form of key money attached. The units that have recently come on the market will be offered at rents above the levels that would exist without controls as landlords attempt to compensate for future restrictions on rent increases. Because of discrimination by landlords and the ability to pay key money, middle-class tenants will find it easier to secure units in the controlled market, while the poor will be forced to

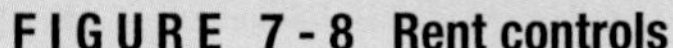

**FIGURE 7-8 Rent controls**

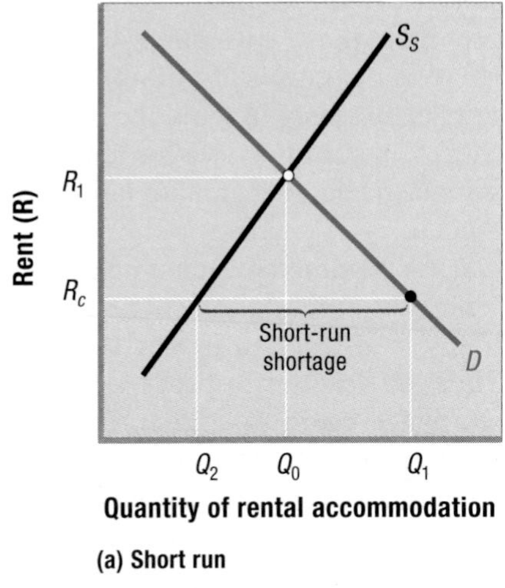


(a) Short run

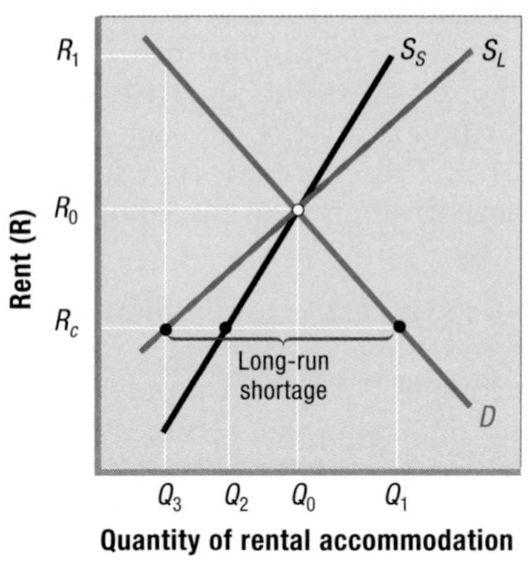


(b) Long run

In the short run the supply for rental accommodation is inelastic. If rent controls are set at $R_c$ a shortage of $Q_1 - Q_2$ will occur in the short run. In the long run, supply becomes more elastic as landlords are able to add or withdraw rental units from the market. In the long run the shortage will worsen to $Q_3 - Q_2$. On the black market, rents of as much as $R_1$ will be charged.

seek units in the uncontrolled market. Perversely, tenants with higher incomes can be the major beneficiaries of the program.

Rent controls distort market signals and misallocate resources. Too few resources are allocated to rental housing, too many to alternative uses. Ironically, although rent controls are often legislated to lessen the effects of perceived housing shortages, in fact, controls are a primary cause of such shortages.

**Rock Concerts** Below-equilibrium pricing should not be associated solely with government policies. Rock superstars frequently price their concert tickets below the market-clearing price. Tickets are usually rationed on a first-come, first-served basis, and ticket "scalping" is common. Why should these stars want to subsidize their fans—at least those who are fortunate enough to obtain tickets—with below-equilibrium prices? Why not set ticket prices at a higher, market-clearing level and realize more income from a tour?

The answer is that long lines of fans waiting hours or days for bargain-priced tickets catch the attention of the press, as does an occasional attempt by those who do not get tickets to crash a sold-out concert. The millions of dollars worth of free publicity that result undoubtedly stimulates cassette and CD sales, from which much of any musician's income is derived. Thus, the "gift" of below-equilibrium ticket prices from a rock star to fans also benefits the star. The gift also imposes costs to fans—the opportunity cost of the time spent waiting in line to buy tickets.

Incidentally, many people regard the ticket scalping often associated with musical or athletic events as a form of extortion, where the extortionist's (seller's) gain is the victim's (buyer's) loss. But the fact that scalping is a voluntary transaction suggests that both seller and buyer gain or the exchange would not occur. Such exchanges redistribute assets (tickets) from those who value them less to those who value them more.

## Price Floors and Surpluses

**Price floors** *are minimum prices fixed by government that are above equilibrium prices.* Price floors have been implemented when society has believed the free functioning of the market system was not providing a sufficient income for certain groups of resource suppliers or producers. Minimum-wage legislation and the support of agricultural prices are the two most widely discussed examples of government price floors. Let's examine price floors as applied to a specific farm commodity.

Suppose the equilibrium price for oats is $2 per bushel, and because of this low price, many

**FIGURE 7-9 Price floors result in persistent surpluses**

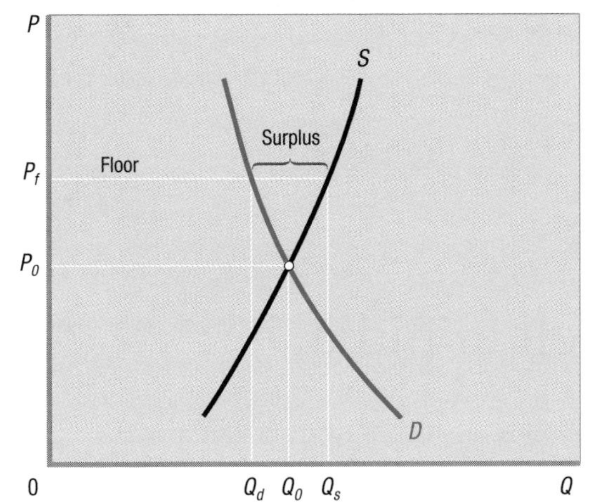


A price floor—a minimum legal price—such as $P_f$ results in a persistent product surplus, here equal to the horizontal distance between $Q_s$ and $Q_d$.

farmers have low incomes. Government decides to help out by establishing a price fixed by law or *price support* of $3 per bushel.

What will be the effects? At any price above the equilibrium price, quantity supplied will exceed quantity demanded. There will be a persistent excess supply or *surplus* of the product. Farmers will be willing to produce and offer for sale more than private buyers are willing to purchase at the price floor. The size of this surplus will vary directly with the elasticity of demand and supply. The greater the elasticity of demand and supply, the greater the surplus. As we saw with a price ceiling, the rationing ability of the free market is disrupted by an imposed ceiling price.

Figure 7-9 illustrates the effect of a price floor. Let *S* and *D* be the supply and demand curves for corn. Equilibrium price and quantity are $P_0$ and $Q_0$, respectively. If government imposes a price floor of $P_f$, farmers will produce $Q_s$, but private buyers will purchase only $Q_d$. The surplus is the excess of $Q_s$ over $Q_d$.

Government may cope with the surplus resulting from a price floor in two ways.

1. It can restrict supply (for example, by acreage allotments by which farmers agree to take a certain amount of land out of production) or increase demand (for example, by researching new uses for agricultural products). These actions may reduce the difference between the equilibrium price and the price floor and reduce the size of the resulting surplus.
2. If these efforts are not successful, then government must purchase the surplus output (thereby subsidizing farmers) and store or otherwise dispose of it.

## Controversial Tradeoffs

In a free market, the forces of supply and demand bring the supply decisions of producers and demand decisions of buyers into accord. But price ceilings and floors interfere with this outcome. Government must step in and provide a rationing system to handle product shortages stemming from price ceilings and devise ways to eliminate product surpluses arising from price floors. Legal maximum and minimum prices thus entail controversial tradeoffs. The alleged benefits of price ceilings and floors to consumers and producers, respectively, must be balanced against the costs associated with the consequent shortages and surpluses.

Furthermore, our discussion of price controls and rent controls shows that government interference with the market can have unintended, undesirable side effects. Price controls, for example, create illegal black markets. Rent controls may discourage housing construction and repair and hurt the very low-income families they were intended to help.

### 7-3 QUICK REVIEW

- Price elasticity of supply measures the sensitivity of suppliers to changes in the price of a product. The price elasticity of supply coefficient $E_s$ is the ratio of the percentage change in quantity supplied to the percentage change in price. The elasticity of supply varies directly with the amount of time producers have to respond to the price change.
- The cross elasticity of demand coefficient $E_{xy}$ is computed as the percentage change in the quantity demanded of product X divided by the percentage change in the price of product Y. If the cross elasticity coefficient is positive, the two products are substitutes; if negative, they are complements.
- The income elasticity coefficient $E_i$ is computed as the percentage change in quantity demanded

divided by the percentage change in income. A positive coefficient indicates a normal or superior good. The coefficient is negative for an inferior good.

- Government-controlled prices—ceilings and floors—stifle the rationing function of prices and cause unintended side effects.

In The Media

# Organ Racket Alive and Well in India

Illegal Transplants/Despite a government crackdown, destitute donors can always be found.

BY JOHN STACKHOUSE
THE GLOBE AND MAIL

DELHI—Ashiq Ali was desperate for money when he met an agent in Delhi's old city and agreed to sell part of his body.

Unable to replay a loan for his small shop, Mr. Ali agreed to a series of medical tests, closed shop and travelled to Bombay for a mysterious operation that he still does not understand. "I had no other means to survive," the young man said.

Not any longer. Mr. Ali returned to Delhi with 30,000 rupees, or $1,200, which represents a year's income for most city residents. He also returned with only one kidney. His other one (people have two kidneys but can survive with only one) was transplanted in a man he never met from the Middle East.

Mr. Ali's operation was conducted before a 1995 government crackdown in India on the commercial sale of organs, but according to many reports, India's cash-for-kidneys business continues apace, mainly in small private hospitals where regulations are weak and medical technology is plentiful.

"I won't deny that it still goes on, but it is mostly in private hospitals," said S. C. Dash, the leading transplant surgeon at New Delhi's All-India Institute of Medical Science. "The number has been reduced by 75 to 80 per cent, I would guess."

The kidney racket is the most active segment of India's illegal organ trade because, doctors say, the transplant is quick and relatively risk-free, and thus hard for health officials to control. With many recipients willing to come to India from abroad, especially from the Middle East, the cash incentives also can be a windfall for impoverished organ donors.

Before the transplant law was introduced, about 5,000 operations were carried out every year. But now the number runs only in the hundreds.

*Source: Globe and Mail*, Aug 16, 1997, p. A1. Reprinted with permission from the *Globe and Mail*.

## THE STORY IN BRIEF

The buying and selling of human body organs in India continues despite a government crackdown against the practice.

## THE ECONOMICS BEHIND THE STORY

- A market will materialize anywhere there are willing buyers and sellers. The progress made in organ transplantation in recent years has decreased the potential risk of death (the potential cost), while increasing the potential benefits for both buyers and sellers of certain organs, particularly human kidneys. Thus a market for human organs materialized.
- Most people find the buying and selling of body parts unethical. Because of public pressure, the Indian government banned the buying and selling of human organs. As predicted by supply-demand analysis, a black market for human organs replaced the

previously legal exchange. Given the presumed inelastic demand for human organs, we would expect the black market prices to be higher than those prevailing prior to the introduction of legislation banning the buying and selling of human organs.

- Are you in favour of or against a market for human organs? Do you think you would change your mind if you were in need of, say, a kidney? On the assumption there were a legal market in kidneys, what would be your guess about the price elasticity of demand for a kidney to someone whose life depended on a transplant? What about the income elasticity of demand? ■

## The Last Word

### MARKET FORCES AND THE VALUE OF EDUCATION

**Recent growth in the earnings of university-educated workers relative to less-educated workers in Canada reflects the fact that the supply of highly educated workers has not kept pace with a rapidly growing demand for their skills.**

COMPARISONS OF THE AVERAGE (MEDIAN) real incomes of university and high-school graduates show that the gap between the two—what can be called "university premium"—has risen sharply since 1980. To a lesser extent this differential also exists for those holding college diplomas. In other words, the value of education has been increasing. This widening income disparity can be understood in terms of the changing demand and supply for the services of college- and high-school-educated workers.

The vertical axis of the graph gives the ratio of the median income of university graduates to the median income of high-school graduates (a measure of the university premium). A ratio of 1.5 would indicate that university graduates earn 50 percent more than high school graduates. The horizontal axis indicates the percentage of young people (aged 25–34) with four years or more of university. The vertical (perfectly inelastic) supply curves *S* reflect the fact that the quantity of university graduates does not respond quickly to a change in the income ratio. For example, if the ratio rises today, it will take four or five years for the additional university enrollees to earn their degrees and enter the labour market. The downsloping demand curves *D* indicate that as the university premium decreases, employers will choose to hire more university-trained workers.

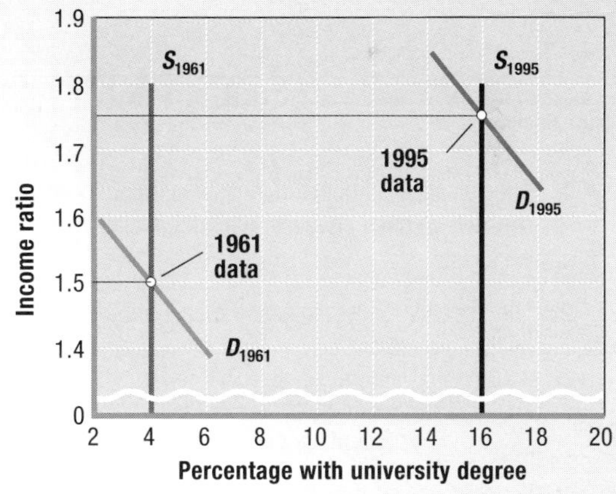


The 1961 data show an earnings ratio of 1.5, indicating that in that year university graduates earned about 50 percent more than high school graduates. But by 1995 this gap had risen to over 70 percent. Explanation: Despite the increase in the supply of university graduates (from about 4 to about 16 percent of the 25–34 age group), demand increased by a relatively greater amount.

Why? It appears that technological advance since about 1980 has been increasingly "skill-biased." Innovation has raised the productivity of (and therefore the demand for) more educated workers to a greater degree than that of less educated workers. Computerization of the workplace alone may explain one-third to two-thirds of the increased returns to education. Greater use of high-tech capital goods in manufacturing is also relevant.

The demand side of the market has also been affected by the lowering of world trade barriers. Lower barriers have increased the demand for the high-tech products that Canadian firms export and for the more educated workers producing them. Conversely, freer trade has expanded domestic demand for low-cost imports made by less skilled workers abroad. Such imports have effectively increased the competition faced by less educated workers in Canada, stifling their earnings growth. A rise in the number of low-skilled immigrants to Canada in the 1980s and 1990s has also slowed the earnings growth of less-educated workers.

Why didn't the supply of university graduates increase more than shown in the graph and thereby keep the university premium from rising? Why didn't increases in the earnings gap in the 1980s induce more people to enter and eventually graduate from university? Other factors—in particular, the rising real costs of a university education—have restricted growth in the supply of university graduates. In the 1980s the cost of university rose. At the same time, government grants and loans to students fell behind the inflation rate.

Some implications: First, an individual's economic well-being is now more closely tied to her or his educational attainment than in the past. Second, wage differences between more and less educated workers have been growing and contribute to greater income inequality in the economy as a whole. Third, the prosperity of any city, province, or region depends increasingly on its commitment to education. ■

## CHAPTER SUMMARY

1. Price elasticity of demand measures the responsiveness of consumers to price changes. If consumers are relatively sensitive to price changes, demand is elastic. If consumers are relatively unresponsive to price changes, demand is inelastic.
2. The price elasticity coefficient measures the degree of elasticity or inelasticity of demand. The coefficient is found by the formula

$$E_d = \frac{\text{percentage change in quantity demanded of X}}{\text{percentage change in price of X}}$$

Economists use the averages of the prices and quantities under consideration as reference points in determining the percentage changes in price and quantity. If $E_d$ is greater than 1, demand is elastic. If $E_d$ is less than 1, demand is inelastic. Unit elasticity is the special case in which $E_d$ equals 1.
3. Perfectly inelastic demand is graphed as a line parallel to the vertical axis: perfectly elastic demand is shown by a line above and parallel to the horizontal axis.
4. Elasticity varies at different price ranges on a demand curve, tending to be elastic in the upper left segment and inelastic in the lower right segment. Elasticity cannot be judged by the steepness or flatness of a demand curve.
5. If total revenue changes in the opposite direction from price, demand is elastic. If price and total revenue change in the same direction, demand is inelastic. In the case where demand is of unit elasticity, a change in price leaves total revenue unchanged.
6. The number of available substitutes, the size of an item's price relative to one's budget, whether the product is a luxury or necessity, and the time period involved are all determinants of elasticity of demand.
7. The elasticity concept also applies to supply. The coefficient of price elasticity of supply is found by the formula

$$E_S = \frac{\text{percentage change in quantity supplied of X}}{\text{percentage change in price of X}}$$

Elasticity of supply depends on the ease of shiftability of resources between alternative uses. This shiftability in turn varies directly with the time producers have to adjust to a particular price change.

**8.** Cross elasticity of demand indicates how sensitive the purchase of one product is to changes in the price of another product. The coefficient of cross elasticity of demand is found by the formula

$$E_{xy} = \frac{\text{percentage change in quantity demanded of X}}{\text{percentage change in price of Y}}$$

Positive cross elasticity of demand identifies substitute goods; negative cross elasticity identifies complementary goods.

**9.** Income elasticity of demand indicates the responsiveness of consumer purchases to a change in income. The coefficient of income elasticity of demand is found by the formula

$$E_i = \frac{\text{percentage change in quantity demanded of X}}{\text{percentage change in income}}$$

The coefficient is positive for normal goods and negative for inferior goods.

**10.** Excise taxes affect demand or supply and therefore equilibrium price and quantity. The more inelastic the demand for a product the greater the portion of the tax shifted to consumers. The greater the inelasticity of supply, the larger portion of the tax borne by the seller.

**11.** Prices fixed by law upset the rationing function of equilibrium prices. Effective price ceilings result in persistent product shortages and, if an equitable distribution of the product is sought, government will have to ration the product to consumers. Price floors lead to product surpluses; government must purchase these surpluses or eliminate them by imposing restrictions on production or by increasing private demand.

## TERMS AND CONCEPTS

price elasticity of demand
elastic demand
inelastic demand
unit elasticity
perfectly inelastic demand
perfectly elastic demand
total revenue
total-revenue test
price elasticity of supply
market period
short run
long run
cross elasticity of demand
income elasticity of demand
price ceiling
price floor

## STUDY QUESTIONS

**1.** Review questions 1, 4, and 8 at the end of Chapter 4.

**2.** KEY QUESTION *Graph the accompanying demand data and then use the midpoint formula for $E_d$ to determine price elasticity of demand for each of the four possible \$1 price changes. What can you conclude about the relationship between the slope of a curve and its elasticity? Explain in a nontechnical way why demand is elastic in the upper left segment of the demand curve and inelastic in the lower right segment.*

| Product price | Quantity demanded |
|---|---|
| $5 | 1 |
| 4 | 2 |
| 3 | 3 |
| 2 | 4 |
| 1 | 5 |

3. Draw two linear demand curves parallel to one another. Demonstrate that for any specific price change demand is more elastic on the curve closer to the origin.

4. KEY QUESTION *Calculate total revenue data from the demand schedule in question 2. Graph total revenue below your demand curve. Generalize in the relationship between price elasticity and total revenue.*

5. KEY QUESTION *How would the following changes in price affect total revenue—that is, would total revenue increase, decline, or remain unchanged?*
   **a.** *Price falls and demand is inelastic.*
   **b.** *Price rises and demand is elastic.*
   **c.** *Price rises and supply is elastic.*
   **d.** *Price rises and supply is inelastic.*
   **e.** *Price rises and demand is inelastic.*
   **f.** *Price falls and demand is elastic.*
   **g.** *Price falls and demand is of unit elasticity.*

6. KEY QUESTION *What are the major determinants of price elasticity of demand? Use these determinants in judging whether demand for each of the following products is elastic or inelastic:* **a.** *oranges;* **b.** *cigarettes;* **c.** *Export cigarettes;* **d.** *gasoline;* **e.** *butter;* **f.** *salt;* **g.** *automobiles;* **h.** *football games;* **i.** *diamond bracelets; and* **j.** *this textbook.*

7. What effect would a rule stating that university students must live in university dormitories have on the price elasticity of demand for dormitory space? What impact might this in turn have on room rates?

8. "If the demand for farm products is highly price inelastic, a bumper crop may reduce farm incomes." Evaluate and illustrate graphically.

9. You are chairperson of a provincial tax commission responsible for establishing a program to raise new revenue through sales taxes. Would elasticity of demand be important to you in determining those products on which sales taxes should be levied? Explain.

10. KEY QUESTION *In May 1990 Vincent van Gogh's painting "Portrait of Dr. Gachet" sold at auction for $82.5 million. Portray this sale in a demand and supply diagram and comment on the elasticity of supply.*

11. In the 1950s the local Boy Scout troop in Kamloops, British Columbia, decided to gather and sell at auction elk antlers shed by thousands of elk wintering in the area. Buyers were mainly local artisans who used the antlers to make belt buckles, buttons, and tie clasps. Price per kilogram was 6¢ and the troop took in $500 annually. In the 1970s a fad developed in Asia that involved grinding antlers into powder to sprinkle on food for purported aphrodisiac benefits. In 1979 the price per kilogram of elk antlers in the Kamloops auction was $6 per kilogram and the Boy Scouts earned $51,000! Show graphically and explain these dramatic increases in price and total revenue. Assuming no shift in the supply curve of elk antlers, use the midpoints formula to calculate the coefficient for the elasticity of supply.

12. KEY QUESTION *Suppose the cross elasticity of demand for products A and B is +3.6 and for products C and D it is –5.4. What can you conclude about how products A and B are related? Products C and D?*

13. KEY QUESTION *The income elasticities of demand for movies, dental services, and clothing have been estimated to be +3.4, +1.0, and +0.5, respectively. Interpret these coefficients. What does it mean if an income elasticity coefficient is negative?*

14. KEY QUESTION *What is the incidence of an excise tax when demand is highly inelastic? Elastic? What effect does the elasticity of supply have on the incidence of an excise tax?*

15. Why is it desirable for price ceiling to be accompanied by government rationing? And for price floors to be accompanied by surplus-purchasing or output-restricting or demand-increasing programs? Show graphically why price ceilings entail shortages and price floors result in surpluses. What effect, if any, does elasticity of demand and supply have on the size of these shortages and surpluses? Explain.

16. **(The Last Word)** What has happened to the earnings gap between university-educated and high-school educated workers in recent years? Use demand and supply-side factors to explain this change.

17. WEB-BASED QUESTION **K mart-Determinants of Demand Elasticities and "Blue Light Specials"** Generally, the elasticity of demand for a product will be greater **a** the larger the number of substitutes, **b** the greater the proportion of income an item takes, and **c** the more the item is a nonnecessity. K mart www.kmart.com/ posts

a weekly sales circular on selected merchandise. K mart must conclude that demand for these Blue Light Specials is elastic: The decrease in price will increase total revenue. Check out this week's specials and, for each item, score 1 point for meeting the criterion of each determinant above. How many specials score a 3? Do any score 0? Why would K mart include any item that scored less than a 3?

18. WEB-BASED QUESTION **New York Apartments—The Impact of Price Ceilings** In New York City rent control was enacted during World War II and then maintained by New York City. In 1997, there were approximately 71,000 rent-controlled apartments in New York City. Visit Tenant Net www.tenant.net/ and NYC Rent Guidelines Board www.nycrgb.com/ and find out the difference between "rent control" and "rent stabilization" in New York City. Are both price ceilings? What has been the impact of such controls? Are rent controls increasing or decreasing?

CHAPTER 8

# The Theory of Consumer Choice

WE NOW LEAVE GENERAL SUPPLY-DEMAND ANALYSIS behind to focus exclusively on the demand curve. Because resources are scarce in relation to our wants, all of us have to choose among the vast array of available goods and services. This chapter investigates how consumers decide which goods and services to purchase.

If you were to compare the shopping carts of two consumers, you would observe striking differences. Why does Paula have potatoes, parsnips, plums, and Pepsi in her cart, while Sam has sugar, saltines, soap, and 7-Up in his? Why didn't Paula also buy pork and pimentos? Why didn't Sam have soup and spaghetti on his grocery list? In this chapter, you will see how individual consumers allocate their money incomes among the various goods and services available to them. Why does a consumer buy a certain bundle of goods rather than any of the other possible bundles? As we examine these issues, you will also strengthen your understanding of the law of demand.

**IN THIS CHAPTER YOU WILL LEARN:**

- The two explanations for why the demand curve is downward sloping.
- The distinction between total and marginal utility.
- How marginal utility theory explains consumer choice.
- How to derive the demand curve.
- To apply marginal utility theory to real world situations.

## The Big Picture

WE NOW LEAVE GENERAL SUPPLY-DEMAND analysis behind to focus exclusively on the details of the demand curve. What motivates consumer choice; why do consumers buy more of a specific good or service when its price falls and buy less of it when its price rises (*ceteris paribus*)? Recall that the economizing problem has two components: limited resources and unlimited wants. Faced with this, consumers try to do the best they can—buy those goods and services that will yield the greatest satisfaction—with the money income at their disposal.

As you read this chapter, keep the following points in mind:

- **Key Concept 3** is discussed.
- We assume individuals maximize satisfaction automatically; they don't have to be told how to do it.
- Consumers could always do with a few more goods and services to make life a little easier. Because of unlimited wants, money income is never quite enough, and consumers try to stretch that money income as far as it can go. Thus, consumers prefer lower prices to higher prices for a specific good or service. (When was the last time you heard someone say they were disgusted at how *low* prices were for a specific good or service?) ■

## TWO EXPLANATIONS OF THE LAW OF DEMAND

The law of demand is based on common sense. A high price discourages consumers from buying; a low price encourages them to buy. We now explore two complementary explanations of the downsloping demand curve. (A third explanation, based on indifference curves, is summarized in the appendix of this chapter.)

### Income and Substitution Effects

Our first explanation of the downward slope of the demand curve—introduced in Chapter 4—involves the income and substitution effects.

1. INCOME EFFECT The *income effect* is the impact a change in the price of a product has on a consumer's real income and consequently on the quantity demanded of that good. If the price of a product—say, steak—declines, the real income or purchasing power of anyone buying that product increases. The increase in real income will be reflected in increased purchases of many normal goods, including steak. For example, with a constant money income of $40 per week you can buy 5 kilograms of steak at $8 per kilogram. But if the price of steak falls to $4 per kilogram and you buy 5 kilograms, $20 per week is freed to buy more of both steak and other commodities. A decline in the price of steak increases the consumer's real income, enabling him or her to purchase more steak. This is called the **income effect**.
2. SUBSTITUTION EFFECT The *substitution effect* is the impact a change in a product's price has on its relative expensiveness, and consequently on the quantity demanded. When the price of a product falls, that product becomes cheaper relative to all other products. Consumers will substitute the cheaper product for other products that are now relatively more expensive. In our example, as the price of steak falls—prices of other products being unchanged—steak becomes more attractive to the buyer. At $4 per kilogram it is a "better buy" than at $8. The lower price will induce the consumer to substitute steak for some of the now relatively less attractive items in the budget—perhaps pork, chicken, veal, fish, or other foods. Because a lower price increases the relative attractiveness of a product, the consumer buys more of it. This is the **substitution effect**.

The income and substitution effects combine to make a consumer able and willing to buy more of a specific good at a lower price than at a higher price.

## Law of Diminishing Marginal Utility 

A second explanation of the downsloping demand curve is that, although consumer wants in general may never be completely satisfied, wants for specific commodities can be fulfilled. In a specific span of time over which buyers' tastes are unchanged, consumers can get as much of a particular good or service as they want. The more of that product consumers obtain, the less they want more units of the same product.

This can be readily seen for durable goods. A consumer's want for an automobile, when he or she has none, may be very strong. But the desire for a second car is less intense; for a third or fourth, very weak. Even the wealthiest families rarely have more than a half-dozen cars, although their incomes would allow them to purchase a whole fleet of vehicles.

**Terminology** Economists theorize that specific consumer wants can be fulfilled with succeeding units of a commodity but that each unit provides less utility than the previous unit. Recall that a product has utility if it can satisfy a want: **Utility** *is want-satisfying power*. The utility of a good or service is the satisfaction or pleasure one gets from consuming it. Three characteristics of this concept must be emphasized.

1. "Utility" and "usefulness" are not synonymous. Paintings by Picasso may be useless functionally and yet offer great utility to art connoisseurs.
2. Implied in the first characteristic is the fact that utility is subjective. The utility of a specific product will vary widely from person to person. A bottle of inexpensive muscatel wine may yield substantial utility to the alcoholic but zero or negative utility to a nondrinker. Eyeglasses have great utility to someone who is extremely far- or near-sighted, but no utility to a person with 20-20 vision.
3. Because utility is subjective, it is difficult to quantify. But for purposes of illustration, we assume that people can measure satisfaction with units called *utils* (units of utility). For example, a particular consumer may get 100 utils of satisfaction from an ice cream cone, 10 utils of satisfaction from a candy bar, and 1 util of satisfaction from a single stick of gum. These mythical units of satisfaction are convenient for quantifying consumer behaviour.

**Total Utility and Marginal Utility** We must carefully distinguish between total utility and marginal utility. **Total utility** is the total amount of satisfaction or pleasure a person derives from consuming some specific quantity—say, 10 units—of a good or service. **Marginal utility** is the *extra* satisfaction a consumer realizes from an additional unit of that product—say, from the eleventh unit. Alternatively, we can say marginal utility is the *change* in total utility resulting from the consumption of one more unit of a product.

Figure 8-1 and the accompanying table reveal the relation between total utility and marginal utility. The curves are drawn from the data in the table. Column 2 shows the total utility associated with each level of hamburger consumption; column 3, the marginal utility—the change in total utility—resulting from the consumption of each successive hamburger. Starting at the origin in Figure 8-1a, we observe that each of the first five units increases total utility (TU), but by a diminishing amount. Total utility reaches a maximum at the sixth unit, and then declines. Hence, in Figure 8-1b we find that marginal utility (MU) remains positive but diminishes through the first five units (because total utility increases at a declining rate). Marginal utility is zero for the sixth unit (because that unit doesn't change total utility). Marginal utility then becomes negative with the seventh unit and beyond (because total utility is falling). Figure 8-1b and table column 3 tell us that each successive hamburger yields less extra utility—fewer utils—than the previous one as the consumer's want for hamburgers comes closer and closer to fulfilment.[1] The principle that marginal utility declines as the consumer acquires additional units of a specific product is known as the **law of diminishing marginal utility**. ***(Key Question 2)***

**Relation to Demand and Elasticity** How does this law explain why the demand curve for a specific product is downsloping? If successive units of a good yield smaller and smaller amounts of mar-

[1] Technical footnote: For a time the marginal utility of successive units of a product may increase. A second glass of lemonade on a hot day may yield more extra satisfaction than the first. But beyond some point we can expect the marginal utility of additional glasses to decline. Also, note in Figure 8-1b that marginal utility is graphed at half-units. For example, we graph the marginal utility of 4 utils at $3\frac{1}{2}$ units because the 4 utils refers neither to the third nor the fourth unit per se but to the *addition* of the fourth unit.

## KEY GRAPH

**FIGURE 8-1 Total and marginal utility**

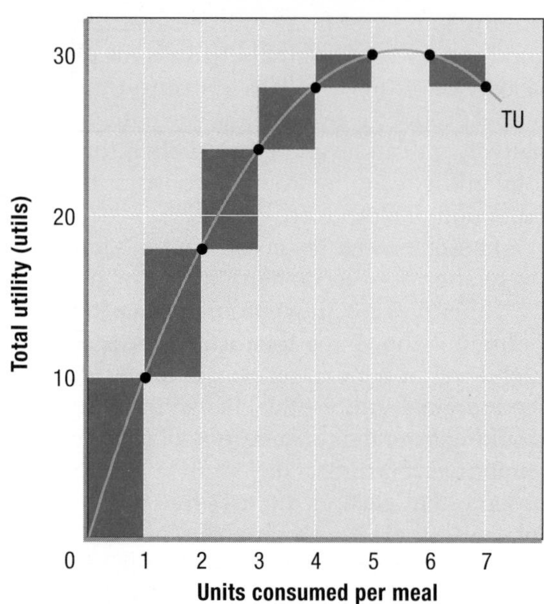


**(a) Total utility**

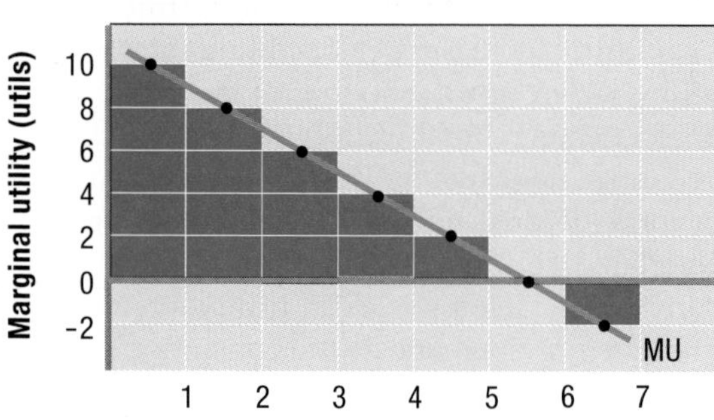


**(b) Marginal utility**

| (1) Hamburgers consumed per meal | (2) Total utility, utils | (3) Marginal utility, utils |
|---|---|---|
| 0 | 0 | |
| 1 | 10 | 10 |
| 2 | 18 | 8 |
| 3 | 24 | 6 |
| 4 | 28 | 4 |
| 5 | 30 | 2 |
| 6 | 30 | 0 |
| 7 | 28 | -2 |

Curves TU and MU are graphed from the data in the table. (a) As more of a product is consumed, total utility increases at a diminishing rate, reaches a maximum, and then declines. (b) Marginal utility, by definition, reflects the changes in total utility. Thus marginal utility diminishes with increased consumption, becomes zero when total utility is at a maximum, and is negative when total utility declines. As shown by the solid green rectangles in (a) and (b), marginal utility is the change in total utility associated with each added hamburger. Or, alternatively, each new level of total utility is found by adding marginal utility to the previous level of total utility.

### 8-1 QUICK QUIZ

1. Marginal utility:
   **(a)** is the extra output a firm obtains when it adds another unit of labour.
   **(b)** explains why product supply curves are upsloping.
   **(c)** typically rises as successive units of a good are consumed.
   **(d)** is the extra satisfaction from the consumption of 1 more unit of some good or service.
2. Marginal utility in graph (b) is positive, but declining, when total utility in graph (a) is positive and:
   **(a)** rising at an increasing rate.
   **(b)** falling at an increasing rate.
   **(c)** rising at a decreasing rate.
   **(d)** falling at a decreasing rate.
3. When marginal utility is zero in graph (b), total utility in graph (a) is:
   **(a)** also zero.
   **(b)** neither rising nor falling.
   **(c)** negative.
   **(d)** rising, but at a declining rate.
4. Suppose the person represented by these graphs experienced a diminished taste for hamburgers. As a result the:
   **(a)** TU curve would get steeper.
   **(b)** MU curve would get flatter.
   **(c)** TU and MU curves would shift downward.
   **(d)** MU curve, but not the TU curve, would collapse to the horizontal axis.

**Answers:** 1. (d); 2. (c); 3. (b); 4. (c).

ginal, or extra, utility, then the consumer will buy additional units of a product only if its price falls. The consumer for whom Figure 8-1 is relevant may buy two hamburgers at a price of $1 each. But, because he or she obtains less marginal utility from additional hamburgers, the consumer will choose *not* to buy more at this price. The consumer would rather spend additional dollars on products that provide more (or equal) utility, not less utility. Therefore, additional hamburgers with less utility are not worth buying unless the price declines. (When marginal utility becomes negative, McDonald's or Burger King would have to pay *you* to consume another hamburger!) Thus, diminishing marginal utility supports the notion that price must decrease for quantity demanded to increase—that is, that the demand curve slopes downward.

The amount by which marginal utility declines as more units of a product are consumed will help determine that product's price elasticity of demand. Other things equal, if marginal utility falls sharply as successive units of a product are consumed, demand will be inelastic. A particular decline in price would elicit only a relatively small increase in quantity demanded, since the MU of extra units drops off so rapidly. Conversely, modest declines in marginal utility as consumption increases imply an elastic demand. A particular decline in price will entice consumers to buy considerably more units of the product since the MU of the additional units declines so slowly.

### 8-1 QUICK REVIEW

- The law of demand can be explained by the income effect (a decline in price raises the consumer's purchasing power) and the substitution effect (a product whose price falls is substituted for other products).
- Utility is the benefit or satisfaction a person receives from consuming a good or service.
- The law of diminishing marginal utility indicates that gains in satisfaction become smaller as successive units of a specific product are consumed.
- Diminishing marginal utility provides another rationale for the law of demand, as well as one for differing price elasticities.

## THEORY OF CONSUMER CHOICE

In addition to explaining the law of demand, the idea of diminishing marginal utility explains how consumers allocate their money incomes among the many goods and services available for purchase.

### Consumer Choice and Budget Constraint

The typical consumer's situation has four dimensions.

1. **RATIONAL BEHAVIOUR** The consumer is a rational person, trying to use his or her money income to derive the greatest amount of satisfaction, or utility, from it. Consumers want to get "the most for their money" or, technically, to maximize their total utility.
2. **PREFERENCES** Each consumer has clear-cut preferences for certain goods and services available in the market. We assume buyers also have a good idea of how much marginal utility they will get from successive units of the various products they might purchase.
3. **BUDGET CONSTRAINT** At any point in time the consumer has a fixed, limited amount of money income. Each consumer supplies a finite amount of human and property resources to businesses or government. Therefore, he or she earns only limited income payments. Thus, all consumers face a *budget constraint*, even those who earn millions of dollars each year. Of course, this income limitation is more severe for typical consumers with average incomes than for those with extraordinarily high incomes.
4. **PRICES** Goods and services are scarce in relation to the demand for them, or, stated differently, producing them involves opportunity costs. Thus every good and service carries a price tag. We assume that the product prices are not affected by the amounts of specific goods that the individual consumer buys. Each consumer's purchase is such a small part of total demand that it does not affect a product's price.

If a consumer has limited dollars and the products he or she wants have price tags on them, the consumer can purchase only a limited amount of goods. The consumer cannot buy everything wanted when each purchase exhausts a portion of a fixed money income. It is precisely this point that brings the economic fact of scarcity home to the individual consumer.

The consumer must therefore compromise; he or she must choose among alternative goods to obtain, with limited money income, the most satisfying mix of goods and services. Different individuals will choose different mixes of goods. And, as is shown in Global Perspective 8-1, mixes of goods will vary among nations.

## Utility-Maximizing Rule

Of all the different combinations of goods and services a consumer can obtain within his or her budget, which specific combination will yield the maximum utility or satisfaction? To maximize satisfaction *the consumer should allocate his or her money income so that the last dollar spent on each product yields the same amount of extra (marginal) utility.* We call this the **utility-maximizing rule.** When the consumer has "balanced his or her margins" using this rule, there is no incentive to alter the expenditure pattern. The consumer is in *equilibrium* and would be worse off—total utility would decline—if there was any alteration in the bundle of goods purchased, providing there is no change in taste, income, products, or prices.

### 8-1 GLOBAL PERSPECTIVE

**Shares of household budgets spent on food, selected nations**

Consumer spending patterns differ not only among individuals but among nations. One striking feature is that, although households in rich countries spend larger absolute amounts on food than those in poor countries, households in poor nations spend a much larger proportion of their budgets on food.

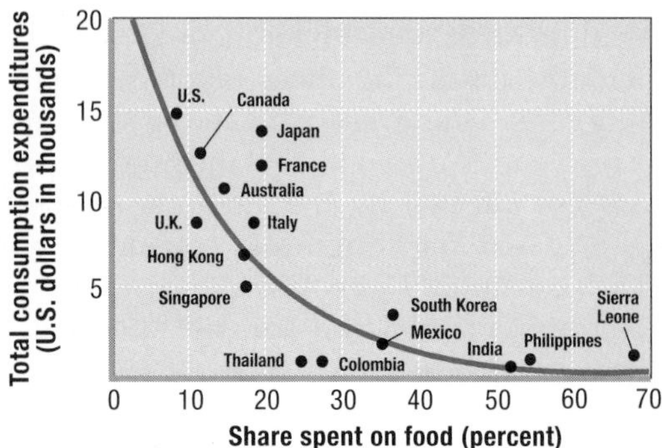


Source: Judith Jones Putnam and Jane E. Allhouse, *Food Consumption, Prices, and Expenditures*, 1970–92 (U.S. Department of Agriculture, 1993, Economic Research Service Statistical Bulletin 867).

## Numerical Example

An illustration will help explain the utility-maximizing rule. For simplicity our discussion is limited to two products, but the analysis applies as well if there are more. Suppose consumer Holly is trying to decide which combination of two products—A and B—she should purchase with her fixed daily income of $10. Holly's preferences for products A and B and their prices determine the combination that will maximize her satisfaction. Table 8-1 summarizes those data, with column 2a showing the amount of marginal utility she will derive from each successive unit of A and column 3a showing the same thing for product B. Both columns reflect the law of diminishing marginal utility, which in this case begins with the second units of each product purchased.

**Marginal Utility per Dollar** Before applying the utility-maximizing rule to these data, we must put the marginal utility information in columns 2a and 3a on a per-dollar-spent basis. A consumer's choices are influenced not only by the extra utility that successive units of product A will yield but also by how many dollars (and therefore how many units of alternative good B) she must give up to obtain those added units of A.

The rational consumer must compare the extra utility from each product with its added cost (that is, its price). Suppose you prefer a pizza whose marginal utility is, say, 36 utils to a movie whose marginal utility is 24 utils. But if the pizza's price is $12 and the movie costs only $6, you would choose the movie rather than the pizza! Why? Because the marginal utility per dollar spent would be 4 utils for the movie (= 24 utils ÷ $6) compared to only 3 utils for the pizza (= 36 utils ÷ $12). You could buy two movies for $12 and, assuming the marginal utility of the second movie is, say, 16 utils, your total utility would be 40 utils. Clearly, 40 units of satisfaction from two movies is superior to 36 utils from the same $12 expenditure on one pizza. *To make the amounts of extra utility derived from differently priced goods comparable, marginal utilities must be put on a per-dollar-spent basis.* This is done in columns 2b and 3b by dividing the mar-

**TABLE 8-1 The utility-maximizing combination of products A and B obtainable with an income of $10***

| (1) UNIT OF PRODUCT | (2) PRODUCT A: PRICE $1 | | (3) PRODUCT B: PRICE = $2 | |
|---|---|---|---|---|
| | (a) Marginal utility, utils | (b) Marginal utility per dollar (MU/price) | (a) Marginal utility, utils | (b) Marginal utility per dollar (MU/price) |
| First | 10 | 10 | 24 | 12 |
| Second | 8 | **8** | 20 | 10 |
| Third | 7 | 7 | 18 | 9 |
| Fourth | 6 | 6 | 16 | **8** |
| Fifth | 5 | 5 | 12 | 6 |
| Sixth | 4 | 4 | 6 | 3 |
| Seventh | 3 | 3 | 4 | 2 |

*It is assumed in this table that the amount of marginal utility received from additional units of each of the two products is independent of the quantity of the other product. For example, the marginal-utility schedule for product A is independent of the amount of B obtained by the consumer. Adapted from "Canadian Economic Observer, Historical Statistical Supplement," Catalogue No. 11-210.

ginal utility data of columns 2a and 3a by the prices of A and B—$1 and $2, respectively.

**Decision-Making Process** Now we have Holly's preferences—on a unit and a per-dollar basis—and the price tags of A and B before us. With $10 to spend, in what order should Holly allocate her dollars on units of A and B to achieve the highest degree of utility within the $10 limit imposed by her income? And what specific combination of A and B will she have obtained at the time she exhausts her $10?

Concentrating on columns 2b and 3b in Table 8-1, we find that Holly should first spend $2 on the first unit of B, because its marginal utility per dollar of 12 utils is higher than A's 10 utils. But now Holly finds herself indifferent about whether she should buy a second unit of B or the first unit of A because the marginal utility per dollar of both is 10 utils. So she buys both of them. Holly now has 1 unit of A and 2 units of B. Also, the last dollar she spent on each good yielded the same marginal utility per dollar (10 utils). But this combination of A and B does not represent the maximum amount of utility that Holly can obtain. It cost her only $5 [= (1 × $1) + (2 × $2)], so she has $5 remaining, which she can spend to achieve a still higher level of total utility.

Examining columns 2b and 3b again, we find that Holly should spend the next $2 on a third unit of B because marginal utility per dollar for the third unit of B is 9 compared with 8 for the second unit of A. But now, with 1 unit of A and 3 units of B, we find she is again indifferent between a second unit of A and a fourth unit of B; both provide 8 utils/dollar. So Holly purchases one more unit of each. Now, the last dollar spent on each product provides the same marginal utility per dollar (8 utils), and Holly's money income of $10 is exhausted. *The utility-maximizing combination of goods attainable by Holly is 2 units of A and 4 of B.* By summing marginal utility information from columns 2a and 3a we find that Holly is realizing 18 (= 10 + 8) utils of satisfaction from the 2 units of A and 78 (= 24 + 20 + 18 + 16) utils of satisfaction from the 4 units of B. Her $10, optimally spent, yields 96 (= 18 + 78) utils of satisfaction.

Table 8-2 summarizes our step-by-step process for maximizing Holly's utility and it merits careful study. Note that we have implicitly assumed that Holly spends her entire income; she neither borrows nor saves. However, saving can be regarded as a utility-yielding good and incorporated into our analysis. It is treated that way in question 4 at the end of this chapter. ***(Key Question 4)***

**Inferior Options** Other combinations of A and B can be obtained with $10. But none will yield as great a total utility as do 2 units of A and 4 of B. As an example, 4 units of A and 3 of B can be obtained for $10. However, this combination yields only 93

**TABLE 8-2 Sequence of purchases to achieve consumer equilibrium, given the data in Table 8-1**

| Choice number | Potential choices | Marginal utility per dollar | Purchase decision | Income remaining |
|---|---|---|---|---|
| 1 | First unit of A<br>First unit of B | 10<br>12 | First unit of B for $2 | $8 = $10 – $2 |
| 2 | First unit of A<br>Second unit of B | 10<br>10 | First unit of A for $1<br>and second unit of B for $2 | $5 = $8 – $3 |
| 3 | Second unit of A<br>Third unit of B | 8<br>9 | Third unit of B for $2 | $3 = $5 – $2 |
| 4 | Second unit of A<br>Fourth unit of B | 8<br>8 | Second unit of A for $1<br>and fourth unit of B for $2 | $0 = $3 – $3 |

utils, clearly inferior to the 96 utils provided by 2 of A and 4 of B. Furthermore, there are other combinations of A and B (such as 4 of A and 5 of B *or* 1 of A and 2 of B) where the marginal utility of the last dollar spent is the same for both A and B. But all such combinations are either unobtainable with Holly's limited money income (as 4 of A and 5 of B) or fail to exhaust her income (as 1 of A and 2 of B) and therefore do not yield the maximum utility attainable.

Problem: Suppose Holly's income is $14 rather than $10. What now is the utility-maximizing combination of A and B? Are A and B normal or inferior goods?

## Algebraic Restatement

Our allocation rule says that a consumer will maximize her satisfaction when she allocates her money income so that the last dollar spent on product A, the last on product B, and so forth, yield equal amounts of additional, or marginal, utility. The marginal utility per dollar spent on A is indicated by MU of product A divided by the price of A (column 2b in Table 8-1) and the marginal utility per dollar spent on B by MU of product B divided by the price of B (column 3b in Table 8-1). Our utility-maximizing rule merely requires that these ratios be equal. Algebraically,

$$\frac{\text{MU of product A}}{\text{price of A}} = \frac{\text{MU of product B}}{\text{price of B}}$$

and, of course, the consumer *must* exhaust her available income. Table 8-1 shows us that the combination of 2 units of A and 4 of B fulfils these conditions in that

$$\frac{8 \text{ utils}}{\$1} = \frac{16 \text{ utils}}{\$2}$$

and the consumer's $10 income is spent.

If the equation is not fulfilled, then some reallocation of the consumer's expenditures between A and B (from the low to the high marginal-utility-per-dollar product) will increase the consumer's total utility. For example, if the consumer spent $10 on 4 of A and 3 of B, we would find that

$$\frac{\text{MU of A: 6 utils}}{\text{price of A: \$1}} < \frac{\text{MU of B: 18 utils}}{\text{price of B: \$2}}$$

Here the last dollar spent on A provides only 6 utils of satisfaction, and the last dollar spent on B provides 9 (= 18 ÷ $2). Hence, the consumer can increase total satisfaction by purchasing more of B and less of A. As dollars are reallocated from A to B, the marginal utility per dollar of A will increase while the marginal utility per dollar of B will decrease. At some new combination of A and B—specifically, 2 of A and 4 of B—the two will be equal and consumer equilibrium will be achieved.

## UTILITY MAXIMIZATION AND THE DEMAND CURVE

Once you understand the utility-maximizing rule, you can easily see why the demand curve is downsloping. Recall that the basic determinants of an individual's demand for a specific product are (1) preferences or tastes, (2) money income, and (3) the prices of other goods. The utility data in Table 8-1 reflect our consumer's preferences. We continue to suppose that her money income is $10. And, concentrating on the construction of a simple demand curve for product B, we assume that the price of A—representing "other goods"—is still $1.

**FIGURE 8-2 Deriving an individual demand curve**

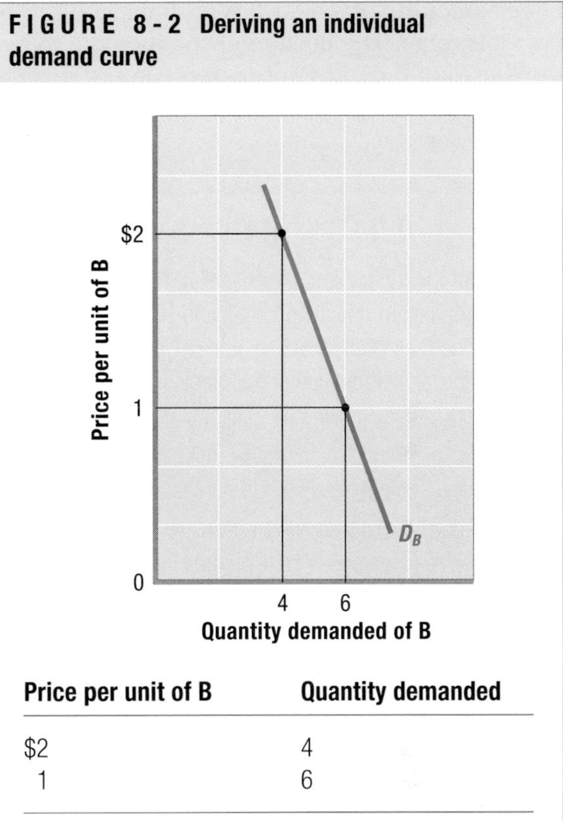


| Price per unit of B | Quantity demanded |
|---|---|
| $2 | 4 |
| 1 | 6 |

At a price of $2 for B, the consumer represented by the data in the table maximizes utility by purchasing 4 units of product B. The decline in the price of B to $1 upsets the consumer's initial utility-maximizing equilibrium. The person restores equilibrium by purchasing 6 rather than 4 units of B. Thus, a simple price-quantity schedule emerges, which locates two points on a downsloping demand curve.

## Deriving the Demand Schedule and Curve

We can derive a single consumer's demand schedule for product B by considering alternative prices at which B might be sold and then determining the quantity the consumer will purchase. We have already determined one such price-quantity combination in the utility-maximizing example: Given tastes, income, and prices of other goods, our rational consumer will purchase 4 units of B at $2.

Now let's assume the price of B falls to $1. The marginal-utility-per-dollar data of column 3b in Table 8-1 will double because the price of B has been halved; the new data for column 3b are in fact identical to those in column 3a. But the purchase of 2 units of A and 4 of B is no longer an equilibrium combination. By applying the same reasoning we used in the initial utility-maximizing example, we now find that Holly's utility-maximizing combination is 4 units of A and 6 units of B. As summarized in the table in Figure 8-2, Holly will purchase 6 units of B when the price of B is $1. The data in this table are then used to sketch the downsloping demand curve $D_B$ shown in Figure 8-2. This exercise, then, clearly links the utility-maximizing behaviour of a consumer and that person's demand curve for a particular product.

**Income and Substitution Effects Revisited** At the beginning of this chapter we indicated that the law of demand can be understood in terms of the substitution and income effects. Our analysis does not let us sort out these two effects quantitatively. However, we can see through utility maximization how each is involved in the increased purchase of product B when the price of B falls.

To see the *substitution effect*, recall that before the price of B declined, Holly was in equilibrium when purchasing 2 units of A and 4 units of B in that $MU_A(8)/P_A(\$1) = MU_B(16)/P_B(\$2)$. But after B's price falls from $2 to $1, we have $MU_A(8)/P_A(\$1) < MU_B(16)/P_B(\$1)$; more simply stated, the last dollar spent on B now yields more utility (16 utils) than does the last dollar spent on A (8 utils). This indicates that a switching of purchases from A to B is needed to restore equilibrium; that is, a *substitution* of now cheaper B for A will occur when the price of B drops.

What about the *income effect*? The assumed decline in the price of B from $2 to $1 increases Holly's real income. Before the price decline, Holly was in equilibrium when buying 2 of A and 4 of B. But at the lower $1 price for B, Holly would have to spend only $6 rather than $10 on this same combination of goods. She has $4 left over to spend on more of A, more of B, or more of both. In short, the price decline of B has caused Holly's *real* income to increase so that she can now obtain larger amounts of A and B with the same $10 of *money* income. The portion of the increase in her purchases of B due to this increase in *real* income is the income effect. ***(Key Question 5)***

**8-2**

**QUICK REVIEW**

- The theory of consumer behaviour assumes that, with limited money incomes and a set of product prices, consumers make rational choices on the basis of well-defined preferences.
- A consumer maximizes utility by allocating money income so that the marginal utility per dollar spent is the same for every good purchased.
- A downsloping demand curve can be derived by changing the price of one product in the consumer-behaviour model and noting the change in the utility-maximizing quantity of that product demanded.

## APPLICATIONS AND EXTENSIONS

Many real-world phenomena can be explained by applying the theory of consumer choice.

### The Compact Disc Takeover

Compact discs made their Canadian debut in 1983. The CD revolutionized the retail music industry, pushing the vinyl long-playing record to virtual extinction. In 1983 fewer than 1 million CDs were sold in North America as compared to over 200 million LP discs. But by 1997 over 500 million CDs were sold in North America, while the sales of LPs plummeted to less than 2 million. Two events caused this swift turnabout.

1. **PREFERENCE CHANGES** The quality of CDs prompted a massive shift of consumer preferences from LPs to CDs. CDs are played with a laser beam, not a phonograph needle, and therefore are virtually impervious to the scratches and wear that plague LPs. CDs also provide a wider range of sound and greater brilliance of tone. They can also hold much more music than LPs. All these features make CDs preferable to LPs for most consumers.
2. **DECREASES IN THE PRICES OF CD PLAYERS** While prices of CDs themselves have not fallen significantly, prices of CD players have. Costing $1,000 or more a decade ago, most players currently sell for under $200. While CDs and LPs are substitute goods, CD players and CDs are complementary goods. The lower prices for players have increased the demand for CDs.

In short, a technologically based change in consumer tastes coupled with a sharp drop in the prices of CD players has revolutionized the retail music market.

### The Diamond-Water Paradox

Before economists understood the distinction between total utility and marginal utility, they were puzzled by the fact that some "essential" goods had much lower prices than other "unimportant" goods. Why would water, essential to life, be less expensive than diamonds, which have much less usefulness? The paradox is resolved when we first acknowledge that water is in great supply relative to demand and thus has a very low price per litre. Diamonds, in contrast, are rare and are costly to mine, cut, and polish. Because their supply is small relative to demand, their price is very high per caret.

The large supply of water and its low price means that the *marginal* utility of the last unit of water consumed is very low. The reason follows from our utility-maximizing rule. Consumers (and producers) respond to the very low price of water by using a great deal of it—for electrical generation, irrigating crops, drinking, hot-water heating, watering lawns, and so on. Consumption is expanded until marginal utility—which declines as more water is consumed—equals this low price. In contrast, relatively few diamonds are purchased because of their prohibitively high price, meaning that their marginal utility remains high. In equilibrium:

$$\frac{\text{MU of water (low)}}{\text{Price of water (low)}} = \frac{\text{MU of diamonds (high)}}{\text{Price of diamonds (high)}}$$

Although the *marginal* utility of the last unit of water consumed is low and the marginal utility of the last diamond purchased is high, the *total* utility of water is very high and the *total* utility of diamonds quite low. The total utility derived from the consumption of water is so large because of the enormous amounts of water we consume. Total utility is the sum of the marginal utilities of *all* the litres of water consumed, including the trillions of litres which have far higher marginal utilities than the last unit consumed. In contrast, the total utility derived from diamonds is low, since their high price means that relatively few of them are bought. Thus the water-diamond paradox is solved: Water has much more total utility (roughly, usefulness) than diamonds even though the price of diamonds greatly exceeds the price of water. These relative prices reflect marginal utility, not total utility.

## The Value of Time

The theory of consumer behaviour has been generalized to account for the economic value of *time*. Both consumption and production activities take time. Time is a valuable economic commodity; by working—by using an hour in productive activity—a person may earn $6, $10, $50, or more, depending on her or his education and skills. By using that hour for leisure or in consumption activities, the individual incurs the opportunity cost of forgone income; she or he sacrifices the $6, $10, or $50 that could have been earned by working.

Imagine a consumer who is considering buying a round of golf, on the one hand, and a concert, on the other. The market price of the golf game is $15 and that of the concert is $20. But the golf game takes more time than the concert. Suppose this consumer will spend four hours on the golf course but only two hours at the concert. If her time is worth $7 per hour—as evidenced by the $7 wage rate she can obtain by working—then the "full price" of the golf game is $43 (the $15 market price *plus* $28 worth of time). Similarly, the full price of the concert is $34 (the $20 market price *plus* $14 worth of time). We find that, contrary to what market prices alone indicate, the full price of the concert is really *less* than the full price of the golf game.

If we now assume that the marginal utilities derived from successive golf games and concerts are identical, our consumer should consume more golf games than concerts because the market price of the former ($15) is lower than that of the latter ($20). But when time is taken into account, the situation is reversed and golf games ($43) are more expensive than concerts ($34). Thus, it is rational in this case for this person to consume more concerts than golf games.

By accounting for time, we can explain certain observable phenomena that traditional theory does not. It may be rational for the unskilled worker or retiree whose time has little market value to ride a bus from Halifax to Fredericton. But the corporate executive, whose time is very valuable, will find it cheaper to fly, even though bus fare is only a fraction of plane fare. It is sensible for the retiree, living on a modest pension cheque and having ample time, to spend many hours shopping for bargains. It is equally intelligent for the highly paid physician, working 55 hours per week, to have lunch at the hospital cafeteria and to buy a new television set over the phone.

People in other nations feel affluent Canadians are "wasteful" of food and other material goods but "overly economical" in the use of time. Canadians who visit developing countries find that time is used casually or "squandered," while material goods are very highly prized and carefully used. These differences are not a paradox or a case of radically different temperaments. The differences reflect the high productivity of labour in an industrially advanced society, which gives time a high market value, or opportunity cost, whereas the opposite is true in a low-income developing country.

## Transfers and Gifts

Government provides to eligible households both *cash transfers* (such as welfare payments and employment insurance benefits) and in-kind or *noncash transfers* that specify particular purchases (for examples, subsidies for housing). Most economists contend that noncash transfers are less efficient than cash transfers because the government-specified uses may not match the recipient's preferences. Stated differently, consumers know their own preferences better than does the government.

Look back to Table 8-2. Suppose Holly has zero earned income, but is given the choice of a $2 cash transfer or a noncash transfer of 2 units of A. Because 2 units of A can be bought with $2, these two transfers are of equal monetary value. But by spending the $2 *cash* transfer on the first unit of B, Holly could obtain 24 utils. The *noncash* transfer of the first 2 units of A would yield only 18 (= 10 + 8) units of utility. Conclusion: The noncash transfer is less efficient (it yields less utility) than the cash transfer.

As this chapter's Last Word demonstrates, the same reasoning applies to private gifts. Research suggests that noncash gifts to others can result in a substantial loss of efficiency or utility. Of course, there may be other perceived *benefits* of providing noncash gifts that offset this efficiency loss.

In The Media

# Buying Mania Greets VW's Bug

## Sight-unseen orders for Beetle rolling in, dealers say

By Gregg Keenan
Auto Industry Reporter

The waiting lists are growing for the new Volkswagen Beetle, Canadian dealers say, even though they don't have any of the cars yet and the Bug's price was announced only last week.

It's not quite the buying frenzy that Mercedes-Benz Canada Inc. and BMW Canada Inc. faced when they brought a luxury sport utility vehicle and a new roadster to Canadian dealerships, respectively, but it's unusual for a car that's going to sell for less than $20,000.

"Do we have orders? We're drowning in orders," said Peter Menzel, owner of Agincourt Autohaus Inc. in Toronto, who will receive 13 of the new Beetles in March, compared with 31 orders from customers.

"These sales are, of course, nostalgia-laden in the beginning," he said, but so far, those ordering the car are spread through several age groups and demographics.

At Clarkdale Motors Ltd. in Vancouver, general sales manager Rick Applegath received more than a dozen orders last weekend after the Beetle was shown off at the Vancouver Auto Show.

He now has between 45 and 50 orders, but expects to receive about 200 of the total Canadian allocation of 8,000 Beetles.

Steve Leightoff, sales manager of Norden Autohaus in Calgary, has taken $500 deposits from nine buyers so far, with many of them place before the car made its debut last week at the North American International Auto Show in Detroit.

Mr. Leightoff has been told to expect 50 Beetles this year. "It's going to be about half of what we need," he said, adding that many buyers are existing owners of Volkswagen cars.

In the Beetle's heyday in the late 1960s and 1970s, sales routinely topped 20,000 annually and exceeded 40,000 in 1968.

Whether nostalgia for an up-to-date version of a car that Volkswagen Canada Inc. stopped selling in 1979 will generate sustained sales is difficult to predict.

Source: The Globe and Mail, January 19, 1998, p. B5. Reprinted with permission from the *Globe and Mail.*

### THE STORY IN BRIEF

The German automaker Volkswagen is resuming the production of the "Beetle," a car the company stopped selling in Canada some 20 years ago. Advanced orders for the new Beetle were quite brisk as consumers tried to snap up the limited number allocated to Canada.

### THE ECONOMICS BEHIND THE STORY

- Value for the consumer is determined by his or her subjective evaluation. The story reports the popularity of a new version of a Volkswagen Beetle recently introduced to the car market. Advance orders for the new Beetle signal that it may be very popular among some consumers.
- The consumers who have put in advance orders must get at least $20,000—its approximate price—worth of utility from the new Beetle. That we know for sure. More difficult to explain is the Beetle's renewed popularity. For some consumers the fact that few others have the new car may give it special appeal. We know that diminishing marginal utility sets in with the additional consumption of a given good or service. When none of the new models were on the road in Canada, some consumers would get much utility from being one of the first to drive the new version of the Beetle. The excitement may wear off (marginal utility will fall) as more Beetles appear on Canadian roads.
- Would you pay $20,000 for a new Beetle? On what basis have you made your decision? ■

# The Last Word

## THE INEFFICIENCY OF CHRISTMAS GIFT-GIVING

**The theory of consumer choice assumes that individual consumers know their product preferences better than anyone else. This raises a question as to whether gift-giving—consumer choices rendered by someone other than the ultimate consumer—is inefficient.**

A RECENT STUDY BY YALE'S JOEL WALDFOGEL* suggests that Christmas gift-giving is inefficient to the extent that between one-tenth and one-third of the value of Christmas gifts is lost because they do not match their recipients' tastes. Professor Waldfogel surveyed two groups of his students, asking them to compare the estimated price of each Christmas gift with what they would be willing to pay for it. For example, Aunt Flo may have paid $13 for the Barry Manilow CD she gave you, but you would pay only $6.50 for it. Thus, a $6.50, or 50 percent, value loss is involved.

In one of the surveys, students estimated that while family and friends paid an average of $438 for a recipient's total gifts, the recipient would be willing to pay only $313 for the same gifts, reflecting a value loss of $125. Conclusion: Christmas gift-giving destroyed more than one-quarter of the gift value.

Two other questions were explored. First, does the value loss vary with the social distance between giver and recipient? Second, which givers are most likely to give cash?

On the first question it was found that noncash gifts from more distant relatives such as grandparents, aunts, and uncles entail greater value loss than gifts received from friends, siblings, parents, and "significant others." Furthermore, gifts from grandparents, aunts, and uncles are much more likely to be exchanged. The most probable reason is that more distant relatives are less likely to be aware of the recipient's consumption preferences.

The answer to the second question entails an offsetting consideration. Many grandparents, aunts, and uncles apparently realize they are uninformed about the receiver's tastes and therefore are more likely to give cash. The survey found that 42 percent of grandparents gave cash, while only about 10 percent of parents and no significant others did so. Cash gifts, of course, can be spent by the recipient as he or she wishes and therefore entail no efficiency loss.

Conclusions: There is a value loss or inefficiency in noncash gift-giving. Noncash gifts from more distant relatives result in greater value losses than do gifts from those "close" to the recipient. Those more socially distant are more likely to give cash, which avoids any value loss. ■

*Joel Waldfogel, "The Deadweight Loss of Christmas," *American Economic Review*, December 1993, pp. 1328-1336.

## CHAPTER SUMMARY

1. The law of demand can be explained in terms of the income and substitution effects or the law of diminishing marginal utility.
2. The income effect implies that a decline in the price of a product increases the consumer's real income and enables the consumer to buy more of that product with a fixed money income. The substitution effect implies that a lower price makes a product relatively more attractive and therefore increases the consumer's willingness to substitute it for other products.

3. The law of diminishing marginal utility states that beyond some quantity, additional units of a specific good will yield declining amounts of extra satisfaction to a consumer.
4. We assume the typical consumer is rational and acts on the basis of well-defined preferences. Because income is limited and goods have prices, the consumer cannot purchase all the goods and services he or she might want. The consumer therefore selects that attainable combination of goods that maximizes his or her utility or satisfaction.
5. A consumer's utility is maximized when income is allocated so that the last dollar spent on each product purchased yields the same amount of extra satisfaction. Algebraically, the utility-maximizing rule is fulfilled when

$$\frac{\text{MU of product A}}{\text{price of A}} = \frac{\text{MU of product B}}{\text{price of B}}$$

and the consumer's total income is spent.

6. The utility-maximizing rule and the demand curve are logically consistent. Because marginal utility declines, a lower price is needed to induce the consumer to buy more of a particular product.

## TERMS AND CONCEPTS

income effect
substitution effect
utility
total utility
marginal utility
law of diminishing marginal utility
utility-maximizing rule

## STUDY QUESTIONS

1. Explain the law of demand through the income and substitution effects, using a price increase as a point of departure for your discussion. Explain the law of demand in terms of diminishing marginal utility.
2. KEY QUESTION *Complete the following table and answer the questions below.*

| Units consumed | Total utility | Marginal utility |
|---|---|---|
| 0 | 0 | — |
| 1 | 10 | 10 |
| 2 | — | 8 |
| 3 | 25 | — |
| 4 | 30 | — |
| 5 | — | 3 |
| 6 | 34 | — |

   a. *At which rate is total utility increasing: a constant rate, a decreasing rate, or an increasing rate? How do you know?*
   b. *"A rational consumer will purchase only 1 unit of the product represented by these data, since that amount maximizes marginal utility." Do you agree? Explain why or why not.*
   c. *"It is possible that a rational consumer will not purchase any units of the product represented by these data." Do you agree? Explain why or why not.*

3. Mrs. Wilson buys loaves of bread and litres of milk each week at prices of $1 and 80¢ respectively. At present she is buying these two products in amounts such that the marginal utilities from the last units purchased of the two products are 80 and 70 utils, respectively. Is she buying the utility-maximizing combination of bread and milk? If not, how should she reallocate her expenditures between the two goods?

4. KEY QUESTION *Columns 1 through 4 in the table below show the marginal utility, measured in utils, which Ricardo would get by purchasing various amounts of products A, B, C, and D. Column 5 shows the marginal utility Ricardo gets from saving. Assume that the prices of A, B, C, and D are $18, $6, $4, and $24, respectively, and that Ricardo has a money income of $106.*

| COLUMN 1 | | COLUMN 2 | | COLUMN 3 | | COLUMN 4 | | COLUMN 5 | |
|---|---|---|---|---|---|---|---|---|---|
| Units of A | MU | Units of B | MU | Units of C | MU | Units of D | MU | Number of dollars saved | MU |
| 1 | 72 | 1 | 24 | 1 | 15 | 1 | 36 | 1 | 5 |
| 2 | 54 | 2 | 15 | 2 | 12 | 2 | 30 | 2 | 4 |
| 3 | 45 | 3 | 12 | 3 | 8 | 3 | 24 | 3 | 3 |
| 4 | 36 | 4 | 9 | 4 | 7 | 4 | 18 | 4 | 2 |
| 5 | 27 | 5 | 7 | 5 | 5 | 5 | 13 | 5 | 1 |
| 6 | 18 | 6 | 5 | 6 | 4 | 6 | 7 | 6 | $\frac{1}{2}$ |
| 7 | 15 | 7 | 2 | 7 | $3\frac{1}{2}$ | 7 | 4 | 7 | $\frac{1}{4}$ |
| 8 | 12 | 8 | 1 | 8 | 3 | 8 | 2 | 8 | $\frac{1}{8}$ |

**a.** *What quantities of A, B, C, and D will Ricardo purchase in maximizing his utility?*
**b.** *How many dollars will Ricardo choose to save?*
**c.** *Check your answers by substituting them into the algebraic statement of the utility-maximizing rule.*

5. KEY QUESTION *You are choosing between two goods, X and Y, and your marginal utility from each is as shown below. If your income is $9 and the prices of X and Y are $2 and $1, respectively, what quantities of each will you purchase to maximize utility? What total utility will you realize? Assume that, other things remaining unchanged, the price of X falls to $1. What quantities of X and Y will you now purchase? Using the two prices and quantities for X, derive a demand schedule for X.*

| Units of X | $MU_x$ | Units of Y | $MU_y$ |
|---|---|---|---|
| 1 | 10 | 1 | 8 |
| 2 | 8 | 2 | 7 |
| 3 | 6 | 3 | 6 |
| 4 | 4 | 4 | 5 |
| 5 | 3 | 5 | 4 |
| 6 | 2 | 6 | 3 |

6. How can time be incorporated into the theory of consumer behaviour? Foreigners frequently point out that Canadians are very wasteful of food and other material goods and very conscious of, and overly economical in, their use of time. Can you explain this observation?

7. Explain:
**a.** "Before economic growth, there were too few goods; after growth, there is too little time."
**b.** "It is irrational for an individual to take the time to be completely rational in economic decision making."

8. In the last decade or so there has been a dramatic expansion of small retail convenience stores—such as Mac's Milk, 7-Elevens, Beckers—although their prices are generally much higher than those in the large supermarkets. Can you explain their success?

9. "Nothing is more useful than water: but it will purchase scarce any thing; scarce any thing can be had in exchange for it. A diamond, on the contrary, has scarce any value in use; but a very great quantity of goods may frequently be had in exchange for it."[2] Explain.

10. Many owners of apartment complexes are installing water meters for each individual apartment and billing the occupants according to the amount of water they use. This is in contrast to formerly having a central meter for the entire

[2] Adam Smith, *The Wealth of Nations* (New York: Modern Library, Inc., originally published in 1776), p. 28.

complex and dividing up the water expense as part of the rent. Where individual meters have been installed, water usage has declined 10 to 40 percent. Explain this drop, referring to price and marginal utility.

11. **Advanced analysis:** Let $MU_A = z = 10 - x$ and $MU_B = z = 21 - 2y$, where $z$ is marginal utility per dollar measured in utils, $x$ is the amount spent on product A, and $y$ is the amount spent on B. Assume the consumer has $10 to spend on A and B; that is, $x + y = 10$. How is the $10 best allocated between A and B? How much utility will the marginal dollar yield?
12. **(The Last Word)** Explain why private and public gift-giving might entail economic inefficiency. Distinguish between cash and noncash gifts in your answer.
13. WEB-BASED QUESTION **The ESPN Sportszone—To Fee or Not to Fee** The ESPN Sportszone www.espn.sportszone.com/ is a major sports information site. Most of the content is free, but ESPN has a Premium Membership available for a monthly or an annual fee. Similar, but fee-free, sports content can be found at USA Today Sports www.usatoday.com/, CNN/Sports Illustrated, and the Canadian Broadcasting Corporation www.cbc.ca. Since ESPN has put a price tag on some of its sports content, it implies that the utility of a premium membership cannot be found at a no-fee site and is therefore worth the price. Is this the case? Use the utility maximization rule to justify your subscription or nonsubscription to the Premium Membership.
14. WEB-BASED QUESTION **Visit Wal-Mart On line—Here's $500, Go Spend It** Assume that you and several classmates each receive a $500 credit voucher (good for today only) from Wal-Mart Online. Go to www.wal-mart.com/ and select $500 worth of merchandise. You may use the Add to Cart feature or a pen and paper to keep a running total. Compare your list with your classmates' lists. What explains the differences? How many of your items were on sale? Would you have purchased these items if you had received $500 in cash?

# APPENDIX TO CHAPTER 8

## INDIFFERENCE CURVE ANALYSIS

A more advanced explanation of consumer behaviour and equilibrium is based on (1) budget lines and (2) indifference curves.

### The Budget Line: What Is Attainable

A **budget line** *is a schedule or curve that shows various combinations of two products a consumer can purchase with a specific money income.* If the price of product A is $1.50 and the price of B is $1.00, then a consumer could purchase all the combinations of A and B shown in Table A8-1 with $12 of money income. At one extreme the consumer might spend all of his or her income on 8 units of A and have nothing left to spend on B. Or, by giving up 2 units of A and thereby "freeing" $3, the consumer could have 6 units of A and 3 of B. And so on to the other extreme, at which the consumer could buy 12 units of B at $1.00 each, spending his

**IN THIS APPENDIX YOU WILL LEARN:**

What a budget line is and what factors shift it.

•

What an indifference curve and indifference map are.

•

The explanation of consumer choice using indifference curves and budget lines.

•

How to derive the demand curve.

**TABLE A8-1 The budget line: whole-unit combinations of A and B attainable with an income of $12**

| Units of A (price = $1.50) | Units of B (price = $1.00) | Total expenditure |
|---|---|---|
| 8 | 0 | $12 (= $12 + $0) |
| 6 | 3 | $12 (= $9 + $3) |
| 4 | 6 | $12 (= $6 + $6) |
| 2 | 9 | $12 (= $3 + $9) |
| 0 | 12 | $12 (= $0 + $12) |

or her entire money income on B with nothing left to spend on A.

Figure A8-1 shows the same budget line graphically. Note that the graph is not restricted to whole units of A and B as is the table. Every point on the graph represents a possible combination of A and B, including fractional quantities. The slope of the graphed budget line measures the ratio of the price of B to the price of A; more precisely, the absolute value of the slope is $P_B/P_A = \$1.00/\$1.50 = 2/3$. This is the mathematical way of saying that the consumer must forgo 2 units of A (measured on the vertical axis) to buy 3 units of B (measured on the horizontal axis). In moving down the budget or price line, 2 of A (at $1.50 each) must be given up to obtain 3 more of B (at $1.00 each). This yields a slope of $\frac{2}{3}$.

**FIGURE A8-1 A consumer's budget line**

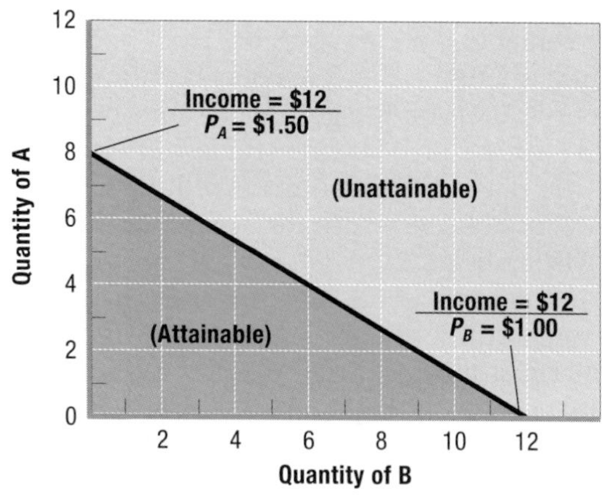

The budget line shows all the combinations of any two products that can be purchased, given the prices of the products and the consumer's money income.

There are two other characteristics of the budget line you should know about:

1. **INCOME CHANGES** The location of the budget line varies with money income. An *increase* in income shifts the budget line to the *right*; a *decrease* in income moves it to the *left*. To verify this, recalculate Table A8-1 assuming income is (a) $24 and (b) $6 and plot the new budget lines in Figure A8-1.
2. **PRICE CHANGES** A change in product prices also shifts the budget line. A decline in the prices of both products—the equivalent of a real income increase—shifts the curve to the right. (You can verify this by recalculating Table A8-1 and replotting Figure A8-1 assuming that $P_A = \$.75$ and $P_B = \$.50$.) Conversely, an increase in the prices of A and B shifts the curve to the left. (Assume $P_A = \$3$ and $P_B = \$2$ and rework Table A8-1 and Figure A8-1 to substantiate this statement.)

Note what happens if $P_B$ changes while $P_A$ and income remain constant. In particular, if $P_B$ drops, say, from $1.00 to $.50, the lower end of the budget line fans outward to the right. Conversely, if $P_B$ increases, say, from $1.00 to $1.50, the lower end of the line fans inward to the left. In both instances the line remains "anchored" at 8 units on the vertical axis because $P_A$ has not changed.

## Indifference Curves: What Is Preferred

Budget lines reflect "objective" market data, specifically income and prices. The budget line reveals combinations of products A and B that can be purchased, given current income and prices.

Indifference curves, on the other hand, reflect "subjective" information about consumer preferences for A and B. An **indifference curve** *shows all combinations of two products A and B that will yield the same total satisfaction or total utility to a consumer.* Table A8-2 and Figure A8-2 present a hypothetical indifference curve for products A and B. The consumer's subjective preferences are such that he or she will realize the same total utility from each combination of A and B shown in the table or on the curve. Thus, the consumer will be *indifferent* as to which combination is actually obtained.

Several characteristics of indifference curves are important.

**TABLE A8-2 An indifference schedule (whole units)**

| Combination | Units of A | Units of B |
|---|---|---|
| *j* | 12 | 2 |
| *k* | 6 | 4 |
| *l* | 4 | 6 |
| *m* | 3 | 8 |

**They Are Downsloping** An indifference curve slopes downward because more of one product means less of the other, if total utility is to remain unchanged. Suppose the consumer moves from one combination of A and B to another, say, from *j* to *k* in Figure A8-2. In so doing, the consumer gets more of product B, increasing his or her total utility. But because total utility is the same everywhere on the curve, the consumer must give up some of the other product, A, to reduce total utility by a precisely offsetting amount. Thus "more of B" necessitates "less of A," and the quantities of A and B are inversely related. A curve that reflects inversely related variables is downsloping.

**FIGURE A8-2 A consumer's indifference curve**

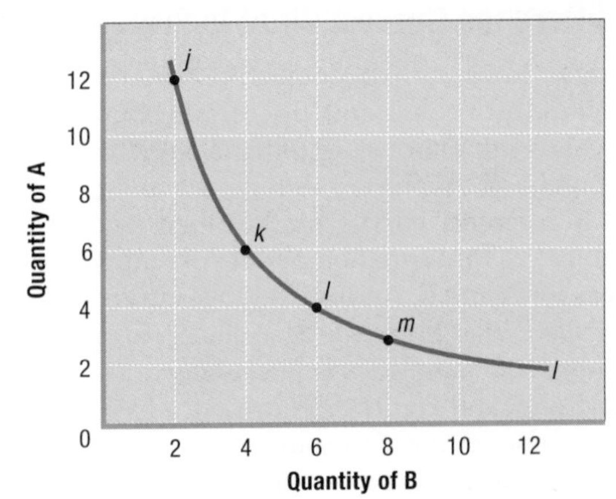


Every point on indifference curve *I* represents some combination of products A and B, and all those combinations are equally satisfactory to the consumer. That is, each combination of A and B on the curve yields the same total utility.

**They Are Convex from the Origin** As viewed from the origin, a downsloping curve can be *concave (bowed outward)* or *convex (bowed inward)*. A concave curve has an increasing (steeper) slope as one moves down the curve, while a convex curve has a diminishing (flatter) slope as one moves down it. Note in Figure A8-2 that *the indifference curve is convex as viewed from the origin.* Its slope diminishes or becomes flatter as we move from *j* to *k* to *l*, and so on down the curve. Technically, the slope of the indifference curve at each point measures the **marginal rate of substitution** (*MRS*) of the combination represented by that point. The slope or *MRS* shows the rate at which the consumer will substitute one good for the other (say, B for A) and remain equally satisfied. The diminishing slope of the indifference curve means the willingness to substitute B for A diminishes as one moves down the curve.

The rationale for a diminishing *MRS* is that a consumer's willingness to substitute B for A (or A for B) will depend on the amounts of B and A he or she has to begin with. Consider Table A8-2 and Figure A8-2 again, beginning at point *j*. Here, in relative terms, the consumer has a substantial amount of A and very little of B. Within this combination, a unit of B is very valuable (that is, its marginal utility is high), while a unit of A is less valuable (its marginal utility is low). The consumer will then be willing to give up a substantial amount of A to get, say, 2 more units of B. In this case, the consumer is willing to forgo 6 units of A to get 2 more units of B; the *MRS* is $\frac{6}{2}$, or 3.

But at point *k* the consumer has less A and more B. Here A is somewhat more valuable, and B less valuable, "at the margin." In a move from point *k* to point *l*, the consumer is willing to give up only 2 units of A to get 2 more units of B, so the *MRS* is only $\frac{2}{2}$, or 1. Having still less of A and more of B at point *l*, the consumer is willing to give up only 1 unit of A in return for 2 more units of B and the *MRS* falls to $\frac{1}{2}$.

In general, as the amount of B *increases*, the marginal utility of additional units of B *decreases*. Similarly, as the quantity of A *decreases*, its marginal utility *increases*. In Figure A8-2 we see that in moving down the curve, the consumer will be willing to give up smaller and smaller amounts of A to offset acquiring each additional unit of B. The result is a curve with a diminishing slope, a curve that is convex viewed from the origin. The *MRS* declines as one moves lower right along the indifference curve.

## The Indifference Map

The single indifference curve of Figure A8-2 reflects some constant (but unspecified) level of total utility or satisfaction. It is possible—and useful—to sketch a whole series of indifference curves or an **indifference map** as shown in Figure A8-3. Each curve reflects a different level of total utility. Specifically, each curve to the *right* of our original curve (labelled $I_2$ in Figure A8-3) reflects combinations of A and B that yield *more* utility than $I_2$. Each curve to the *left* of $I_2$ reflects *less* total utility than $I_2$. *As we move out from the origin, each successive indifference curve represents a higher level of utility.* To demonstrate this fact, draw a line in an upper right direction from the origin; note that its points of intersection with successive curves entail larger amounts of *both* A and B and therefore higher levels of total utility.

## Equilibrium at Tangency

Since the axes in Figures A8-1 and A8-3 are identical, we can superimpose a consumer's budget line on his or her indifference map, as shown in Figure A8-4. By definition, the budget line indicates all combinations of A and B the consumer can attain with his or her income, given the prices of A and B. Of these attainable combinations, the consumer will most prefer that combination that yields the greatest satisfaction or utility. Specifically, *the utility-maximizing combination will be the one lying on the highest attainable indifference curve.* That utility-maximizing combination is called the consumer's **equilibrium position**.

In Figure A8-4 the consumer's utility-maximizing or equilibrium combination of A and B is at point $X$, where the budget line is *tangent* to $I_2$. Why not point $Y$? Because $Y$ is on a lower indifference curve, $I_1$. By moving "down" the budget line—by shifting dollars from purchases of A to purchases of B—the consumer can attain an indifference curve farther from the origin and increase total utility from the same income. Why not point $Z$? Same reason: Point $Z$ is on a lower indifference curve, $I_0$. By moving "up" the budget line—by reallocating dollars from B to A—the consumer can get on higher indifference curve $I_2$ and increase total utility.

**FIGURE A8-3 An indifference map**

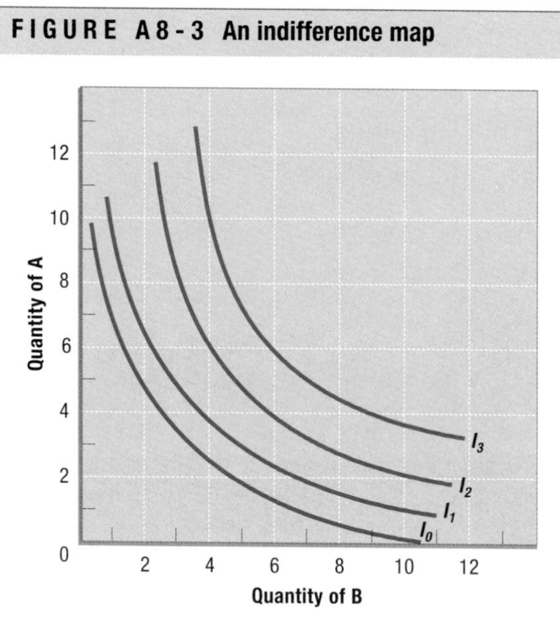


An indifference map is a set of indifference curves. Curves farther from the origin indicate higher levels of total utility. Thus any combination of products A and B represented by a point on $I_3$ has greater total utility than any combination of A and B represented by a point on $I_2$, $I_1$, and $I_0$.

**FIGURE A8-4 The consumer's equilibrium position**

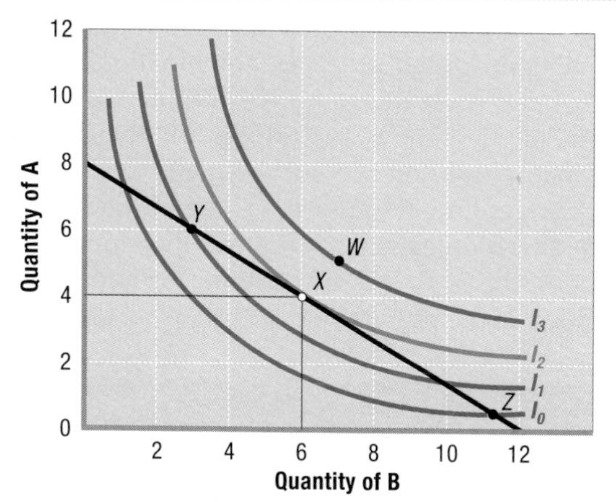


The consumer's equilibrium position is represented by point $X$, where the black budget line is tangent to indifference curve $I_2$. The consumer buys 4 units of A at $1.50 per unit and 6 of B at $1.00 per unit with a $12 money income. Points $Z$ and $Y$ represent attainable combinations of A and B but yield less total utility, as is evidenced by the fact that they are on lower indifference curves. Point $W$ would entail more utility than $X$, but it requires a greater income than the $12 represented by the budget line.

How about point *W* on indifference curve $I_3$? While *W* would yield a greater total utility than X, point *W* is beyond (outside) the budget line and thus *not* attainable by the consumer. Point X represents the optimal *attainable* combination of products A and B. At this point we note that, by definition of tangency, the slope of the highest attainable indifference curve equals the slope of the budget line. Because the slope of the indifference curve reflects the *MRS* and the slope of the budget line is $P_B/P_A$, the optimal or equilibrium position is the point where

$$MRS = \frac{P_B}{P_A}$$

*Appendix Key Question 3* is recommended at this point.

## The Measurement of Utility

There is an important difference between the marginal-utility theory of consumer demand and the indifference curve theory. The marginal utility theory assumes that utility is *numerically* measurable. The consumer is assumed to be able to say *how much* extra utility he or she derives from each extra unit of A or B. The consumer needs that information to realize the utility-maximizing (equilibrium) position, as indicated by

$$\frac{\text{Marginal utility of A}}{\text{Price of A}} = \frac{\text{Marginal utility of B}}{\text{Price of B}}$$

The indifference curve approach poses a less stringent requirement for the consumer. He or she need only specify whether a specific combination of A and B yields more, less, or the same amount of utility than some other combination of A and B. The consumer need only say, for example, that 6 of A and 7 of B yield more (or less) satisfaction than 4 of A and 9 of B. Indifference curve theory does *not* require that the consumer specify *how much* more (or less) satisfaction will be realized.

When the equilibrium situations in the two theories are compared, we find that in the indifference curve analysis the *MRS* equals $P_B/P_A$ at equilibrium; however, in the marginal utility approach the ratio of marginal utilities equals $P_B/P_A$. We therefore deduce that at equilibrium the *MRS* is equivalent in the marginal utility approach to the ratio of the marginal utilities of the last purchased units of the two products.[3]

## The Derivation of the Demand Curve

We noted earlier that with a fixed price for A, an increase in the price of B will cause the bottom of

**FIGURE A8-5 Deriving the demand curve**

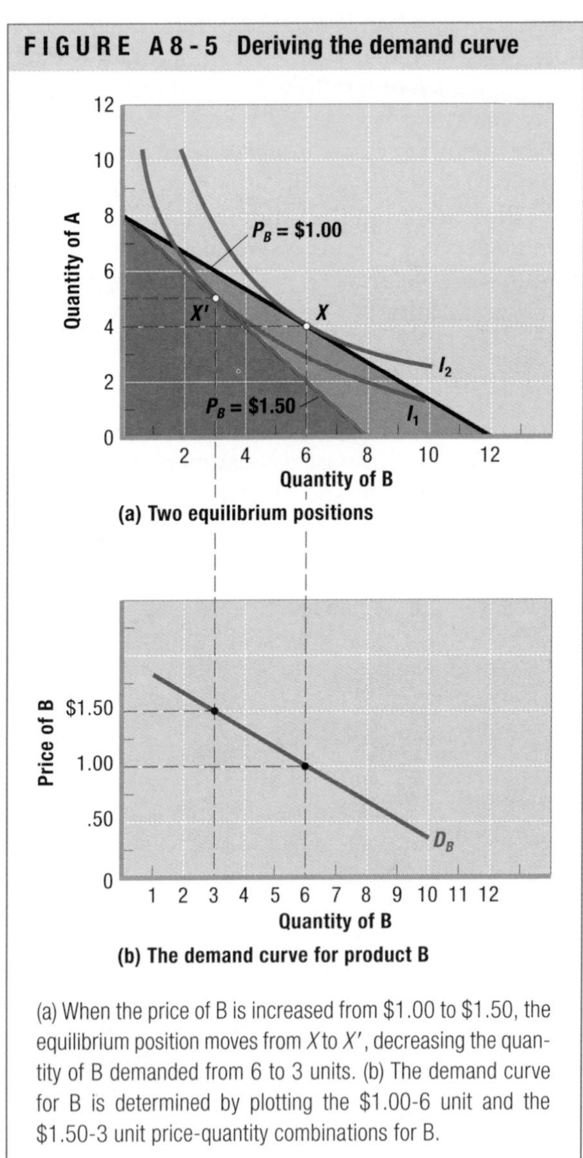


(a) When the price of B is increased from $1.00 to $1.50, the equilibrium position moves from *X* to *X'*, decreasing the quantity of B demanded from 6 to 3 units. (b) The demand curve for B is determined by plotting the $1.00-6 unit and the $1.50-3 unit price-quantity combinations for B.

[3] Technical footnote: If we begin with the utility-maximizing rule, $MU_A/P_A = MU_B/P_B$, and then multiply through by $P_B$ and divide through by $MU_A$, we obtain $P_B/P_A = MU_B/MU_A$. In indifference curve analysis we know that at the equilibrium position $MRS = P_B/P_A$. Hence, at equilibrium *MRS* also equals $MU_B/MU_A$.

the budget line to fan inward to the left. This fact can be used to derive a demand curve for product B. In Figure A8-5a we reproduce the part of Figure A8-4 that shows our initial consumer equilibrium at point X. The budget line determining this equilibrium position assumes that an income is $12 and that $P_A = \$1.50$ and $P_B = \$1.00$. Let's examine what happens to the equilibrium position if we increase $P_B$ to $1.50, holding money income and the price of A constant.

The result is also shown in Figure A8-5a. The budget line fans to the left, yielding a new equilibrium point X′ where it is tangent to lower indifference curve $I_2$. At X′ the consumer buys 3 units of B and 5 of A compared with 4 of A and 6 of B at X. Our interest is in B, and we now have sufficient information to locate two points on the demand curve for product B. We know that at equilibrium point X the price of B is $1.00 and 6 units are purchased; at equilibrium point X′ the price of B is $1.50 and 3 units are purchased.

These data are shown graphically in Figure A8-5a as points on the consumer's demand curve for B. Note that the horizontal axes of Figure A8-5a and A8-5b are identical; both measure the quantity demanded of B. We can therefore drop vertical reference lines from Figure A8-5a down to the horizontal axis of Figure A8-5b. On the vertical axis of Figure A8-5b we locate the two chosen prices of B. Knowing that these prices yield the relevant quantities demanded, we locate two points on the demand curve for B. By simple manipulation of the price of B in an indifference curve-budget line context, we have obtained a downsloping demand curve for B. We have thus again derived the law of demand assuming "other things equal" since only the price of B was changed (the price of A and the consumer's income and tastes remained constant). But, in this case, we have derived the demand curve without resorting to the questionable assumption that consumers can measure utility in units called "utils." In this indifference-curve approach, consumers simply compare combinations of products A and B and determine which combination they prefer, given their incomes and the prices of the two products.

## APPENDIX SUMMARY

1. The indifference curve approach to consumer behaviour is based on the consumer's budget line and indifference curves.
2. The budget line shows all combinations of two products that the consumer can purchase, given his or her money income and product prices.
3. A change in product prices or money income moves the budget line.
4. An indifference curve shows all combinations of two products that yield the same total utility to a consumer. Indifference curves are downsloping and convex from the origin.
5. An indifference map consists of a number of indifference curves; the farther from the origin, the higher the total utility associated with a curve.
6. The consumer is in equilibrium (utility is maximized) at that point on the budget line which lies on the highest attainable indifference curve. At that point the budget line and indifference curve are tangent.
7. Changing the price of one product shifts the budget line and determines a new equilibrium point. A downsloping demand curve can be derived by plotting the price-quantity combinations associated with two or more equilibrium points.

## APPENDIX TERMS AND CONCEPTS

budget line
indifference curve
marginal rate of substitution
indifference map
equilibrium position

# APPENDIX STUDY QUESTIONS

1. What information is embodied in a budget line? What shifts occur in the budget line when money income **a** increases and **b** decreases? What shifts occur in the budget line when the price of the product shown on the vertical axis **a** increases and **b** decreases?

2. What information is contained in an indifference curve? Why are such curves **a** downsloping and **b** convex from the origin? Why does total utility increase as the consumer moves to indifference curves farther from the origin? Why can't indifference curves intersect?

3. APPENDIX KEY QUESTION *Using Figure A8-4, explain why the point of tangency of the budget line with an indifference curve is the consumer's equilibrium position. Explain why any point where the budget line intersects an indifference curve is not equilibrium. Explain: "The consumer is in equilibrium where $MRS = P_B/P_A$."*

4. Assume that the data in the accompanying table give an indifference curve for Mr. Chen. Graph this curve, putting A on the vertical axis and B on the horizontal axis. Assuming that the prices of A and B are \$1.50 and \$1.00, respectively, and that Chen has \$24 to spend, add his budget line to your graph. What combination of A and B will Chen purchase? Does your answer meet the $MRS = P_B/P_A$ rule for equilibrium?

| Units of A | Units of B |
|---|---|
| 16 | 6 |
| 12 | 8 |
| 8 | 12 |
| 4 | 24 |

5. Explain graphically how indifference analysis can be used to derive a demand curve.

6. **Advanced analysis:** Demonstrate mathematically that the equilibrium condition $MRS = P_B/P_A$ is the equivalent of the utility-maximizing rule $MU_A/P_A = MU_B/P_B$.

## CHAPTER 9

# The Organization and Costs of Production

IN THE PREVIOUS CHAPTER WE LOOKED AT THE behaviour of *consumers* and how that behaviour relates to product demand. Now we turn to the behaviour of *producers*, asking how it relates to product supply. As we observed in Chapter 4, the basic factor underlying the ability and willingness of firms to supply a product is the cost of making that product. Production requires using economic resources that, because of their relative scarcity, bear price tags. The amount of a product a firm is willing to supply depends on:

- the prices (costs) and productivity of the resources required for its production, and
- the price the product sells for in the market.

These two components determine the firm's profit, its main goal.

In this chapter we consider the organization of production and the general nature of *production costs*. Then, in the next several chapters we bring product demand, product prices, and revenue back into the picture, explaining how firms compare revenues and costs in setting their profit-maximizing levels of output. Our ultimate purpose is to show how these decisions relate to economic efficiency.

**IN THIS CHAPTER YOU WILL LEARN:**

The various organizational forms a firm can take.

•

The nature of economic costs.

•

The law of diminishing returns.

•

The connection between a firm's output and costs in the short run.

•

The link between a firm's size and costs in the long run.

## The Big Picture

LET'S PUT THE DEMAND CURVE ON THE BACK burner for the moment and concentrate on the supply curve. What is behind the supply curve? Why is it upward sloping?

Firms are organizations that bring together the factors of production (land, labour, capital, and entrepreneurial talent) to produce goods and services consumers want. Firms function in a world of scarcity, thus competing for available resources. In the last chapter, we noted that the goal of the consumer is to get as much satisfaction as possible from the income he or she has. The aim of the firm is to make as much profit as possible.

In trying to maximize their profits in a world of scarcity, business owners must make a number of choices. These include **a** what form of organizational structure to adopt (proprietorship, partnership, or corporation); **b** what combination of resources to use; and **c** whether to continue operating in their current line of production. Over the next number of chapters, we will delve deeper into various constraints or limitations the firm must operate under. These range from the time frame within which the firm is making choices, to policy and legal constraints, to the extent and type of competition that the firm faces from other businesses trying to maximize their profits in the same market.

As you read this chapter, keep the following points in mind:

**Key Concepts 2** and **3** are discussed.

- A firm will choose the form of organization most conducive to its goal of maximizing profit.
- Whatever your normative stance (opinion) on profit, it is the prime motivating drive of firms. It is imperative you accept this fact.
- A firm will stay in a specific line of production or service as long as it cannot make more profits elsewhere.
- In the short run, there are fixed plant and equipment that can't be altered. In the long run, all input variables can be changed.
- The bulk of this chapter is concerned with often tedious details about production and costs. It is crucial you take the time to master the concepts. Unless you do so, the following chapters will be much more difficult for you to comprehend. ■

## THE NEED FOR FIRMS

Businesses, or firms, make up one of the two major players in the private sector; the other is the household, or consumption, sector.

Why is there a need for the firm in a market economy? Could people not work in their own homes? While this is possible, it would greatly decrease the efficiency of an economy. Production and distribution are much more efficiently carried out at a centralized location. The task of organizing production and distribution at a centralized location is easier and less costly.

### The Main Goal of the Firm

The main goal of a firm is to maximize profits. The firm may have many objectives—behaving in a socially responsible manner, giving to charities, offering scholarships, etc.—but the overriding goal is to maximize profit.

## THE BUSINESS SECTOR

A firm can be organized in a number of ways. To avoid confusion, we must start by distinguishing among a plant, a firm, and an industry.

A **plant** is a physical establishment—a factory, farm, mine, store, or warehouse that performs one or more functions in fabricating and distributing goods and services.

A business **firm** is a business organization that owns and operates plants. Most firms operate only one plant, but many own and operate several. Multiplant firms may own "horizontal," "vertical," or "conglomerate" combinations of plants. A **vertical combination** of plants is a group of plants that each performs a different function in the various stages of the production process. As an example, a large steel firm—Stelco or Dofasco—owns iron ore and coal mines, limestone quarries, metal refineries, rolling mills, foundries, and, in some cases, fabricating shops.

A **horizontal combination** of plants is one in which all plants perform the same function. The large chain stores in the retail field—The Bay, Foot Locker, Toys R Us, Eaton's—are examples.

A **conglomerate combination** is made up of plants that operate across several different markets and industries. For example, Canadian Pacific operates in such diverse fields as pulp and paper, railroad transportation, and hotels. Firms such as these are called *conglomerates.*

An **industry** is a group of firms producing the same, or similar, products. This seems to be a simple concept, but industries are usually difficult to identify in practice. For example, how do we identify the automobile industry? The simplest answer is "All firms producing automobiles." But how should we account for small trucks? Certainly, small pickup trucks are similar in many respects to vans and station wagons. And what about firms that make parts for cars, say, airbags? What industry are they in? Is it better to speak of the "motor vehicle industry" rather than the "automobile industry?" If so, where should we place motorcycles?

Delineating an industry becomes even more complex because most businesses are multiproduct firms. North American automobile manufacturers also make such diverse products as diesel locomotives, buses, refrigerators, guided missiles, and air conditioners. For these reasons, industry classifications are usually somewhat arbitrary.

## Legal Forms of Businesses

The business population is extremely diverse, ranging from giant corporations like Bell Canada Enterprises (BCE) with 1996 sales of $28.6 billion and 121,000 employees to neighbourhood specialty shops and "mom-and-pop" groceries with one or two employees and sales of only $200 to $300 per day. This diversity makes it necessary to classify business firms by some criterion such as legal structure, industry or product, or size.

### Sole Proprietorship

A **sole proprietorship** is a business owned and operated by one person. Usually, the proprietor (the owner) personally supervises its operation.

**Advantages** This simple type of business organization has two major advantages:

1. A sole proprietorship is easy to organize—there is virtually no red tape or expense.
2. The proprietor is his or her own boss and has substantial freedom of action. Since the proprietor's profit income depends on the enterprise's success, there is a strong and immediate incentive to manage the business efficiently.

**Disadvantages** The disadvantages of this form of business organization are several:

1. With rare exceptions, the financial resources of a sole proprietorship are insufficient to permit the firm to grow into a large enterprise. Finances are usually limited to what the proprietor has in the bank and to what he or she can borrow. Since proprietorships often fail, banks are not eager to extend them credit.
2. Being in complete control of an enterprise forces the proprietor to carry out all management functions. A proprietor must make decisions concerning buying, selling, and the hiring and training of personnel, as well as producing, advertising, and distributing the firm's product. In short, the potential benefits of specialization in business management are not available to the typical small-scale proprietorship.
3. Most important, the proprietor is subject to *unlimited liability*. Individuals in business for themselves risk not only the assets of the firm but also their personal assets. If the assets of an unsuccessful sole proprietorship are insufficient to pay the firm's bills, creditors can file claims against the proprietor's personal property.

### Partnership

The **partnership** form of business organization is a natural outgrowth of the sole proprietorship. Partnerships were developed to overcome some of the shortcomings of proprietorships. In a partnership, two or more individuals (the partners) agree to own and operate a business together. Usually they pool their financial resources and business skills. Similarly, they share the risks and the profits or losses.

**Advantages** What are the advantages of a partnership?

1. Like the sole proprietorship, it is easy to organize. Although a written agreement is almost invariably involved, there is not much red tape.
2. Greater specialization in management is possible because there are more participants.

3. Because there are several owners the odds are that the financial resources of a partnership are greater than those of a sole proprietorship. Partners can pool their financial capital and are usually somewhat better risks in the eyes of lending institutions.

**Disadvantages** Partnerships may have some of the shortcomings of the proprietorship and some of their own as well:

1. Whenever several people participate in management, the division of authority can lead to inconsistent policies or to inaction when action is required. Worse, partners may disagree on basic policy.
2. The finances of partnerships are still limited, although they are generally superior to those of a sole proprietorship. But the financial resources of three or four partners may still not be enough to ensure the growth of a successful enterprise.
3. The continuity of a partnership is precarious. Generally, when a partner dies or withdraws, the partnership must be dissolved and completely reorganized, which can disrupt its operations.
4. Unlimited liability plagues a partnership, just as it does a proprietorship. In fact, each partner is liable for all business debts incurred, not only as a result of each partner's own management decisions but also as a consequence of the actions of any other partner. A wealthy partner risks money on the prudence of less affluent partners.

## Corporation

A **corporation** is a legal creation that can acquire resources, own assets, produce and sell products, incur debts, extend credit, sue and be sued, and perform the functions of any other type of enterprise. This "legal person" is distinct and separate from the individuals who own it. Hired managers operate most corporations.

**Advantages** The advantages of the corporate form of business enterprise have catapulted it into a dominant position in the modern market economy. Although corporations are relatively small in number, they are frequently large in size and scale of operations. Although corporations make up less than 20 percent of all businesses, they account for roughly 80 percent of all business sales.

1. The corporation is by far the most effective form of business organization for raising financial capital (money). As this chapter's Last Word reveals, the corporation features unique methods of finance—the selling of stocks and bonds—which allow the firm to pool the financial resources of extremely large numbers of people.

   Financing via sales of stocks and bonds also provides advantages to the purchasers of these securities. **Stocks** are shares of ownership of a corporation. **Bonds** are promises to repay a loan, usually with a set rate of interest. Financing through stocks and bonds allows households to participate in business and share the expected monetary reward without actively engaging in management. In addition, an individual can spread any risks by buying the securities of several corporations. Finally, it is usually easy for holders of corporate securities to sell those holdings. Organized stock exchanges simplify the transfer of securities from sellers to buyers. This "ease of sale" increases the willingness of savers to make financial investments in corporate securities.

   In addition, corporations have easier access to bank credit than other types of business organizations. Corporations are better risks and are more likely to become profitable clients of banks.
2. Corporations have the distinct advantage of **limited liability**. The owners (stockholders) of a corporation risk *only* what they paid for their stock. Their personal assets are not at stake if the corporation cannot pay its debts. Creditors can sue the corporation as a legal person but cannot sue the owners of the corporation as individuals. Limited liability clearly makes it easier for the corporation to sell its stock.
3. Because of their advantage in attracting financial capital, successful corporations find it easier to expand the size and scope of their operations and to realize the benefits of expansion. They can take advantage of mass-production technologies and greater specialization in the use of human resources. While the manager of a sole proprietorship may be forced to share her or his time among production, accounting,

and marketing functions, a corporation can hire specialists in each of these areas and achieve greater efficiency.

4. As a legal entity, the corporation has a life independent of its owners and its officers. Sole proprietorships and partnerships are subject to sudden and unpredictable demise, but legally at least, corporations are immortal. The transfer of corporate ownership through inheritance or the sale of stock does not disrupt the continuity of the corporation. Corporations have a permanence, lacking in other forms of business organization, which is conducive to long-range planning and growth.

**Disadvantages** The corporation's advantages are of tremendous significance and typically override any accompanying disadvantages. Yet there are drawbacks to the corporate form:

1. Some red tape and legal expenses are involved in obtaining a corporate charter.
2. From the social point of view, the corporate form of enterprise lends itself to certain abuses. Because the corporation is a legal entity, unscrupulous business owners sometimes can avoid personal responsibility for questionable business activities by adopting the corporate form of enterprise.
3. A further disadvantage of corporations is the **double taxation** of some corporate income. Corporate profit that is shared among stockholders as *dividends* is taxed twice—once as corporate profit and again as stockholders' personal income.
4. In sole proprietorships and partnerships, the owners of the real and financial assets of the firm also directly control those assets. In large corporations in which ownership is widely diffused over tens or hundreds of thousands of stockholders, there is *separation of ownership and control*. That is, the people who own a corporation usually do not manage it—others are hired to do so.

   This reality may create a so-called **principal-agent problem**. The *principals*, in this case, are the stockholders who own the corporation. These owners hire managers as their *agents* to run the business on their behalf. But the interests of the managers (agents) and the wishes of the owners (principals) are not always in accord. The owners typically want maximum profit. Management, however, seeking the power and prestige that accompany control over a large enterprise, may favour unprofitable expansion of the firm's operations. Or a conflict of interest can develop over dividend policies, such as what portion of corporate earnings after taxes should be paid out as dividends and what portion reinvested by the firm. And corporation officials may vote themselves large salaries, pensions, and so forth out of corporate earnings that might otherwise be used for increased dividend payments. ***(Key Question 2)***

### 9-1 QUICK REVIEW

- A plant is a physical establishment that contributes to the production of goods and services; a firm is a business organization that owns and operates plants; plants may be arranged in vertical, horizontal, or conglomerate combinations.
- The three basic legal forms of business are the sole proprietorship, the partnership, and the corporation; while sole proprietorships make up nearly three-fourths of all firms, corporations account for about 80 percent of total sales.
- The major advantages of corporations that have led to their popularity are a superior ability to raise financial capital, the limited liability they convey to owners, and their life beyond that of their owners and officers.
- Very large corporations dominate many Canadian industries.

## ECONOMIC COSTS

Costs exist because resources are scarce and have alternative uses. When we use a bundle of resources to produce some particular good, all alternative production opportunities relating to those specific resources are forgone. Production costs in economics arise from forgoing the opportunity to produce other goods or services. The **economic cost,** or **opportunity cost**, of any resource used in producing a good is measured as its value or worth in its best alternative use.

This view of costs is that stressed in the production possibilities analysis in Chapter 2. The opportunity cost of producing more pizzas is the industrial robots that must be forgone. Similarly, steel used for constructing office buildings is not available for manufacturing automobiles or refrigerators. Paper used for economics textbooks is not available for encyclopedias or romance novels. And if an assembly line worker can assemble either personal computers or washing machines, then the cost to society of employing this worker in a personal-computer plant is the contribution the worker would have made in producing washing machines.

## Explicit and Implicit Costs

Let's now consider costs from the firm's viewpoint. Keeping in mind the notion of opportunity costs, we can say that *economic costs are those payments a firm must make, or incomes it must provide, to resource suppliers to attract the resources away from alternative production opportunities.* These payments or incomes may be either explicit or implicit.

The monetary payments—the "out-of-pocket" or cash expenditures a firm makes to "outsiders" who supply labour services, materials, fuel, transportation services, and the like—are called **explicit costs**. Explicit costs are money payments to nonowners of the firm for the resources they supply.

But, in addition, a firm may use certain resources the firm itself owns. Our concept of opportunity costs tells us that, regardless of whether a resource is owned by an enterprise or hired, there is a cost incurred in using that resource in a specific employment. The costs of such self-owned, self-employed resources are called **implicit costs**. To the firm, implicit costs are the money payments the self-employed resources could have earned in their best alternative use.

Example: Suppose you are earning $20,000 a year as a sales representative for a compact disc manufacturer. You decide to open a store to sell CDs at the retail level. You invest $20,000 of savings that has been earning you $1,000 per year in interest. Also, you decide your new firm will occupy a small store you own and have been renting out for $5,000 per year. One clerk is hired to help you in the store.

After a year's operations you total up your accounts and find the following:

| | | |
|---|---|---|
| Total sales revenue | | $120,000 |
| Cost of CDs | $40,000 | |
| Clerk's salary | 20,000 | |
| Utilities | 5,000 | |
| Total (explicit) costs | | 65,000 |
| Accounting profit | | 55,000 |

But this accounting profit does not accurately reflect the economic status of your venture because it ignores implicit costs. What is significant here is the total amount of resources used (as opposed to dollars expended) in your enterprise. By providing your own financial capital, building, and labour, you incur implicit costs (forgone incomes) of $1,000 in interest, $5,000 in rent, and $20,000 in wages. Also, let's suppose that your entrepreneurial talent is worth $5,000 annually in other similar business endeavours. Then:

| | | |
|---|---|---|
| Accounting profit | | $55,000 |
| Forgone interest | $ 1,000 | |
| Forgone rent | 5,000 | |
| Forgone wages | 20,000 | |
| Forgone entrepreneurial income | 5,000 | |
| Total implicit costs | | 31,000 |
| Economic profit | | 24,000 |

## Normal Profit as a Cost

The $5,000 implicit cost of your entrepreneurial talent in the above example is called a **normal profit**. As is true of the forgone rent and forgone wages, the payment you could otherwise receive for performing entrepreneurial functions is indeed an implicit cost. If you did not realize at least this minimum, or normal, payment for your effort, you could withdraw from this line of production and shift to a more attractive business endeavour.

*The economist includes as costs of production all the costs—explicit and implicit, including a normal profit—required to attract and retain resources in a specific line of production.*

## Economic, or Pure, Profit

Obviously, then, economists and accountants use the term "profit" differently. *Accounting profit is the firm's total revenue less its explicit costs.* But economists define profit in another way. **Economic profit** *is total revenue less all costs (explicit and implicit, the latter including a normal profit to the* *entrepreneur)*. Therefore, when an economist says a particular firm is earning only enough revenue to cover its costs, it means all explicit and implicit costs are being met and the entrepreneur is receiving a payment just large enough to retain his or her talents in the present line of production.

If a firm's total revenue *exceeds* all its economic costs, this residual is called an *economic*, or *pure, profit*. In short:

$$\text{Economic profit} = \text{total revenue} - \text{opportunity costs of all inputs}$$

In our example, the economic profit is $24,000 (= $120,000 of revenue minus $96,000 of explicit and implicit costs). An economic profit is not a cost, because by definition it is a return in excess of the normal profit required to retain the entrepreneur in this particular line of production. Even if the economic profit is zero, the entrepreneur is still covering all explicit and implicit costs, including a normal profit. In our example, as long as accounting profit is $31,000 or more (so that economic profit is zero or more), you will be earning the $5,000 normal profit and will continue to operate your CD store.

Figure 9-1 shows the relationship among various cost and profit concepts. To test yourself, you might want to enter cost data from our example in the appropriate blocks. ***(Key Question 5)***

## Short Run and Long Run

When the demand for a firm's product changes, the firm's profitability may depend on how quickly it can adjust the amounts of the various resources it employs. The quantities employed of many resources—most labour, raw materials, fuel, and power—can be varied easily and quickly. Capital resources, however, require more time for adjustment. The capacity of a manufacturing plant, that is, the size of the factory building and the amount of machinery and equipment in it, can be varied only over a considerable period of time. In some heavy industries it may take several years to alter plant capacity. Because of these differences in adjustment time, economists find it useful to distinguish between the *short run* and the *long run*.

**Short Run: Fixed Plant** The **short run** is a period too brief for a firm to alter its plant capacity, yet long enough to permit a change in the degree to which the fixed plant is used. The firm's plant capacity is fixed in the short run. However, it can vary its output by applying larger or smaller amounts of labour, materials, and other resources to that plant. Existing plant capacity can be used more or less intensively in the short run.

**Long Run: Variable Plant** From the viewpoint of an existing firm, the **long run** is a period long enough for that firm to adjust the quantities of *all* the resources it employs, including plant capacity. From the industry's viewpoint, the long run also encompasses enough time for existing firms to dissolve and leave the industry or for new firms to be created and enter the industry. *While the short run is a "fixed-plant" period, the long run is a "variable-plant" period.*

**Illustrations** If Bombardier hires 100 extra workers for one of its Ski-doo plants or adds an entire shift of workers, we are speaking of the short run. If it adds a new production facility and installs more equipment, we are referring to the long run. The first situation is a *short-run adjustment*; the second is a *long-run adjustment*.

Note that the short run and the long run are *conceptual* periods rather than calendar time periods. In light-manufacturing industries, changes in plant capacity may be accomplished almost overnight. A small T-shirt firm can increase its plant capacity in days by ordering and installing a couple of new cutting tables and several extra

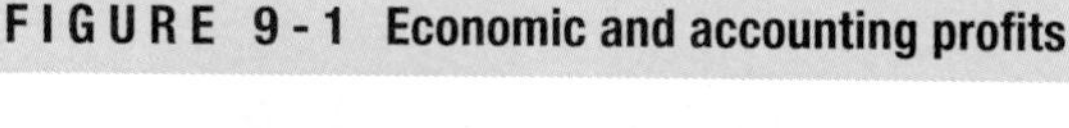
**FIGURE 9-1 Economic and accounting profits**

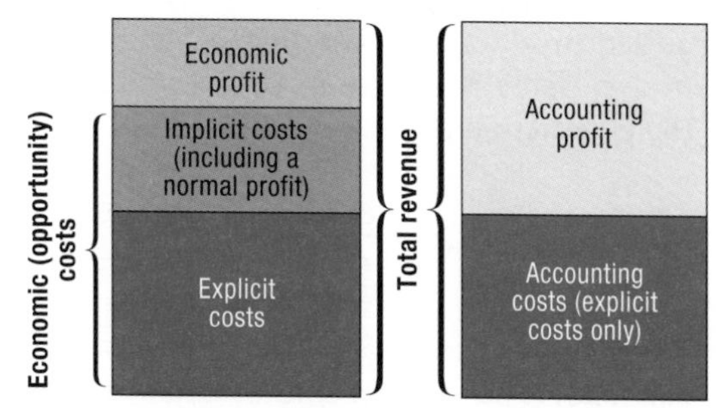


Economic profit is equal to total revenue less opportunity costs. Economic or opportunity costs are the sum of explicit and implicit costs, the latter including a normal profit to the entrepreneur. Accounting profit is equal to total revenue less accounting (explicit) costs.

sewing machines. But for heavy industry, the long run is a different story. Petro-Canada may require several years to construct a new oil refinery.

**9-2**

**QUICK REVIEW**

- Explicit costs are money payments a firm makes to outside suppliers of resources; implicit costs are the opportunity costs associated with a firm's use of resources it owns.
- Normal profit is the implicit cost of entrepreneurship. Economic profit is total revenue less all explicit and implicit costs, including normal profit.
- In the short run a firm's plant capacity is fixed; in the long run a firm can vary its plant size and firms can enter or leave the industry.

## SHORT-RUN PRODUCTION RELATIONSHIPS

A firm's costs of producing a specific output depend not only on the *prices* of needed resources but also on the *quantities* of resources (inputs) needed to produce that output. These quantities are determined by technological aspects of production, specifically, relationships between inputs and output. Before examining these relationships, we need to define three terms:

1. **Total product** (TP) is the total quantity, or total *output*, of a particular good produced.
2. **Marginal product** (MP) is the *extra* output or added product associated with adding a unit of a variable resource, in this case labour, in the production process. Thus,

$$\text{Marginal product} = \frac{\text{change in total product}}{\text{change in labour input}}$$

3. **Average product** (AP), also called *labour productivity*, is output per unit of labour input.

$$\text{Average product} = \frac{\text{total product}}{\text{units of labour}}$$

In the short run, a firm can combine a variable resource (labour) with its fixed resource (plant) to produce output. For a time, it can increase its output by adding units of labour to its fixed plant. But by how much will output rise when it adds this labour? Why do we say "for a time"?

### Law of Diminishing Returns 

The answers are provided in general terms by the **law of diminishing returns**, also called the *law of diminishing marginal product* and the *law of variable proportions*. This law assumes that technology is fixed, meaning that the techniques of production do not change. It states that *as successive units of a variable resource (say, labour) are added to a fixed resource (say, capital or land), beyond some point the extra, or marginal, product attributable to each additional unit of the variable resource will decline.* If additional workers are applied to a constant amount of capital equipment, output will eventually rise by smaller and smaller amounts as more workers are employed.

**Rationale** Suppose a farmer has a fixed amount of land—80 hectares—planted in corn. If the farmer does not cultivate the cornfields (clear the weeds) at all, the yield will be 40 bushels per hectare. If the land is cultivated once, output may rise to 50 bushels per hectare. A second cultivation may increase output to 57 bushels per hectare, a third to 61, and a fourth to 63. Succeeding cultivations would add less and less to the land's yield. If this were not so, the world's needs for corn could be fulfilled by extremely intense cultivation of this single 80-hectare plot of land. Indeed, if diminishing returns did not occur, the world could be fed out of a flowerpot.

The law of diminishing returns also holds true in nonagricultural industries. Assume a wood shop is manufacturing wooden furniture frames. It has a specific amount of equipment—lathes, planers, saws, sanders. If this firm hired just one or two workers, total output and productivity (output per worker) would be very low. These workers would perform many different jobs, and the advantages of specialization would not be realized. Time would be lost in switching from one job to another, and machines would stand idle much of the time. In short, the plant would be understaffed, and production inefficient because there was too much capital relative to labour.

These difficulties would disappear if more workers were added. Equipment would be more fully used, and workers could now specialize on a single job. Time would no longer be lost from job switching. Thus as more workers were added to the initially understaffed plant, the marginal product of each succeeding worker would rise, as the operation became more efficient.

But this cannot go on indefinitely. If still more workers are added, problems of overcrowding arise. Workers would have to wait in line to use the machinery, so now *workers* would be underused. Total output would increase at a diminishing rate because, with the fixed plant size, each worker has less capital equipment to work with as more and more labour is hired. The marginal product of additional workers would decline because the plant was more intensively staffed; there would be more labour in proportion to the fixed amount of capital. Eventually, adding still more workers would cause so much congestion in the plant that marginal product would become negative—total product would decline. In the extreme, the continuous addition of labour would use up all the standing room, and total product would fall to zero.

Note that the law of diminishing returns assumes all units of variable inputs—workers in this case—are of equal quality. Each successive worker is presumed to have the same innate ability, motor coordination, education, training, and work experience. Marginal product ultimately diminishes not because successive workers are qualitatively inferior but because more workers are being used relative to the amount of plant and equipment available.

**Tabular Example** Table 9-1 presents a numerical illustration of the law of diminishing returns. Column 2 shows the total product, or total output, resulting from combining each level of variable input, labour, in column 1 with a fixed amount of capital.

Column 3 shows the marginal product, the change in total product associated with each additional unit of labour. Note that with no labour input, total product is zero; a plant with no workers in it will produce no output. The first 3 units of labour reflect increasing marginal returns, their marginal products being 10, 15, and 20 units, respectively. But beginning with the fourth unit of labour, marginal product diminishes continuously, actually becoming zero with the seventh unit of labour and negative with the eighth.

Average product or output per labour unit is shown in column 4. It is calculated by dividing

**TABLE 9-1 Total, Marginal, and Average Product: The Law of Diminishing Returns**

| (1) Units of the variable resource (labour) | (2) Total product (TP) | (3) Marginal product (MP), change in (2)/change in (1) | | (4) Average product (AP), (2)/(1) |
|---|---|---|---|---|
| 0 | 0 | | | — |
| | | 10 | Increasing marginal returns | |
| 1 | 10 | | | 10.00 |
| | | 15 | | |
| 2 | 25 | | | 12.50 |
| | | 20 | | |
| 3 | 45 | | | 15.00 |
| | | 15 | Diminishing marginal returns | |
| 4 | 60 | | | 15.00 |
| | | 10 | | |
| 5 | 70 | | | 14.00 |
| | | 5 | | |
| 6 | 75 | | | 12.50 |
| | | 0 | | |
| 7 | 75 | | | 10.71 |
| | | −5 | Negative marginal returns | |
| 8 | 70 | | | 8.75 |

total product (column 2) by the number of labour units needed to produce it (column 1). At 5 units of labour, for example, AP is 14 (= 70/5).

**Graphical Portrayal** *Figure 9-2 (Key Graph)* shows the diminishing returns data in Table 9-1 graphically and further clarifies the relationships between total, marginal, and average products. (Marginal product in Figure 9-2b is plotted halfway between the units of labour, since it applies to the *addition* of each labour unit.)

Note first in Figure 9-2a that total product, TP, goes through three phases: It rises initially at an increasing rate; then it increases, but at a dimin-

## KEY GRAPH

**FIGURE 9-2 The law of diminishing returns**

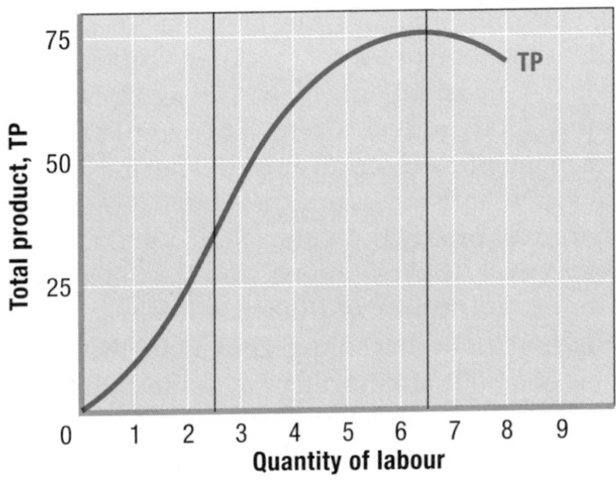


**(a) Total product**

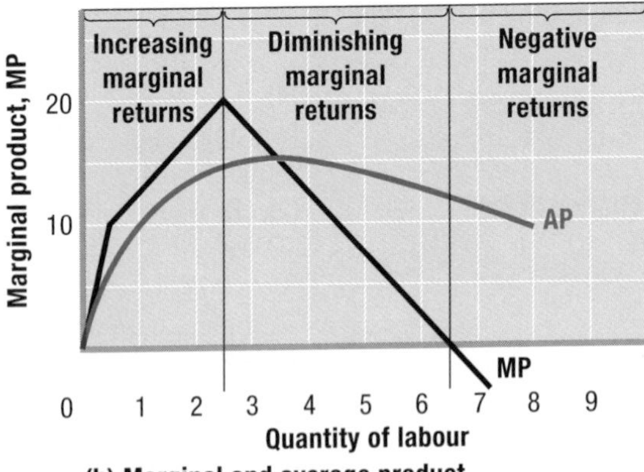


**(b) Marginal and average product**

As a variable resource (labour) is added to fixed amounts of other resources (land or capital), the resulting total product will eventually increase by diminishing amounts, reach a maximum, and then decline. Marginal product is the change in total product associated with each new unit of labour. Average product is simply output per labour unit. Note that marginal product intersects average product at the maximum average product.

### 9-2 QUICK QUIZ

1. Which of the following is an assumption underlying these figures?
   **(a)** Firms first hire "better" workers and then hire "poorer" workers.
   **(b)** Capital and labour are both variable, but labour increases more rapidly than capital.
   **(c)** Consumers will buy all the output (total product) produced.
   **(d)** Workers are of equal quality.
2. Marginal product is:
   **(a)** the change in total product divided by the change in the quantity of labour.
   **(b)** total product divided by the quantity of labour.
   **(c)** always positive.
   **(d)** unrelated to total product.
3. Marginal product in graph (b) is zero when:
   **(a)** average product in graph (b) stops rising.
   **(b)** the slope of the marginal-product curve in graph (b) is zero.
   **(c)** total product in graph (a) begins to rise at a diminishing rate.
   **(d)** the slope of the total-product curve in graph (a) is zero.
4. Average product in graph (b):
   **(a)** rises when it is less than marginal product.
   **(b)** is the change in total product divided by the change in the quantity of labour.
   **(c)** can never exceed marginal product.
   **(d)** falls whenever total product in graph (a) rises at a diminishing rate.

**Answers:** 1. (d); 2. (a); 3. (d); 4. (a)

ishing rate; finally, after reaching a maximum, it declines.

Geometrically, marginal product—shown by the MP curve in Figure 9-2b—is the slope of the total product curve. Marginal product measures the change in total product associated with each succeeding unit of labour. Thus, the three phases of total product are also reflected in marginal product. Where total product is increasing at an increasing rate, marginal product is necessarily rising. Here, extra units of labour are adding larger and larger amounts to total product. Similarly, where total product is increasing but at a decreasing rate, marginal product is positive but falling. Each additional unit of labour adds less to total product than did the previous unit. When total product is at a maximum, marginal product is zero. When total product declines, marginal product becomes negative.

Average product, AP (Figure 9-2b), displays the same tendencies as marginal product. It increases, reaches a maximum, and then decreases as more and more units of labour are added to the fixed plant. But note the relationship between marginal product and average product: Where marginal product exceeds average product, average product rises. And where marginal product is less than average product, average product declines. It follows that marginal product intersects average product where average product is at a maximum.

This relationship is a mathematical necessity. If you add to a total a number that is greater than the current average of that total, the average must rise. And if you add to a total a number that is less than the current average of that total, the average must fall. You raise your average examination grade only when your score on an additional (marginal) examination is greater than the average of all your past scores. You lower your average when your grade on an additional exam is below your current average. In our production example, when the amount an extra worker adds to total product exceeds the average product of all workers already employed, average product will rise. Conversely, when an extra worker adds to total product an amount that is less than the present average product, then average product will decrease.

The law of diminishing returns is embodied in the shapes of all three curves. But, as our definition of the law of diminishing returns indicates, economists are most concerned with its effects on marginal product. The regions of increasing, diminishing, and negative marginal product (returns) are shown in Figure 9-2b. ***(Key Question 7)***

## SHORT-RUN PRODUCTION COSTS

Production information such as that provided in Table 9-1 and Figures 9-2a and b must be coupled with resource prices to determine the total and per-unit costs of producing various levels of output. We know that in the short run some resources—those associated with the firm's plant—are fixed. Others are variable. This means that in the short run costs can be classified as either fixed or variable.

### Fixed, Variable, and Total Cost

**Fixed Costs** **Fixed costs** *are those costs that in total do not vary with changes in output.* Fixed costs are associated with the very existence of a firm's plant and therefore must be paid even if its output is zero. Such costs as interest on a firm's debts, rental payments, a portion of depreciation on equipment and buildings, and insurance premiums are generally fixed costs. In column 2 in Table 9-2 we assume that the firm's total fixed cost is $100. By definition, this fixed cost is incurred at all levels of output, including zero. Fixed costs cannot be avoided in the short run.

**Variable Costs** **Variable costs** *are those costs that change with the level of output.* They include payments for materials, fuel, power, transportation services, most labour, and similar variable resources. In column 3 of Table 9-2 we find that the total of variable costs changes directly with output. But note that *the increases in variable cost associated with succeeding one-unit increases in output are not equal.* As production begins, variable cost will for a time increase by a *decreasing* amount; this is true through the fourth unit of output in Table 9-2. Beyond the fourth unit, however, variable cost rises by *increasing* amounts for succeeding units of output.

The reason for this lies in the shape of the marginal product curve. At first, as in Figure 9-2b, we have increasing marginal product; so smaller and smaller increases in the amounts of variable resources are needed to produce successive units of output. Hence the variable cost of successive units of output decreases. But when marginal product begins to decline as diminishing returns are encountered, larger and larger additional

**TABLE 9-2 Total-, average-, and marginal-cost schedules for an individual firm in the short run**

| TOTAL-COST DATA | | | | AVERAGE-COST DATA | | | MARGINAL COST |
|---|---|---|---|---|---|---|---|
| (1) Total product (Q) | (2) Total fixed cost (TFC) | (3) Total variable cost (TVC) | (4) Total cost (TC) | (5) Average fixed cost (AFC) | (6) Average variable cost (AVC) | (7) Average total cost (ATC) | (8) Marginal cost (MC) |
| | | | TC = TFC + TVC | $AFC = \frac{TFC}{Q}$ | $AVC = \frac{TVC}{Q}$ | $ATC = \frac{TC}{Q}$ | $MC = \frac{\text{change in TC}}{\text{change in Q}}$ |
| 0 | $100 | $ 0 | $ 100 | | | | |
| | | | | | | | $ 90 |
| 1 | 100 | 90 | 190 | $100.00 | $90.00 | $190.00 | |
| | | | | | | | 80 |
| 2 | 100 | 170 | 270 | 50.00 | 85.00 | 135.00 | |
| | | | | | | | 70 |
| 3 | 100 | 240 | 340 | 33.33 | 80.00 | 113.33 | |
| | | | | | | | 60 |
| 4 | 100 | 300 | 400 | 25.00 | 75.00 | 100.00 | |
| | | | | | | | 70 |
| 5 | 100 | 370 | 470 | 20.00 | 74.00 | 94.00 | |
| | | | | | | | 80 |
| 6 | 100 | 450 | 550 | 16.67 | 75.00 | 91.67 | |
| | | | | | | | 90 |
| 7 | 100 | 540 | 640 | 14.29 | 77.14 | 91.43 | |
| | | | | | | | 110 |
| 8 | 100 | 650 | 750 | 12.50 | 81.25 | 93.75 | |
| | | | | | | | 130 |
| 9 | 100 | 780 | 880 | 11.11 | 86.67 | 97.78 | |
| | | | | | | | 150 |
| 10 | 100 | 930 | 1030 | 10.00 | 93.00 | 103.00 | |

amounts of variable resources are needed to produce successive units of output. Total variable cost therefore increases by increasing amounts.

**Total Cost** **Total cost** is the *sum of fixed cost and variable cost at each level of output.* It is shown in column 4 in Table 9-2. At zero units of output, total cost is equal to the firm's fixed cost. Then for each unit of production—1 through 10—total cost varies by the same amounts as does variable cost.

Figure 9-3 shows graphically the fixed-, variable-, and total-cost data in Table 9-2. Note that total variable cost is measured vertically from the horizontal axis, and total costs added vertically to total variable cost to obtain points on the total-cost curve.

The distinction between fixed and variable costs is significant to the business manager. Variable costs can be controlled or altered in the short run by changing production levels. Fixed costs are beyond the business executive's present control; they are incurred in the short run and must be paid regardless of output level.

## Per-Unit, or Average, Costs

Producers are certainly interested in their total costs, but they are equally concerned with *per unit,* or *average, costs.* In particular, average-cost data are more meaningful for making comparisons with product price, which is always stated on a per-unit basis. Average fixed cost, average variable cost, and average total cost are shown in columns 5 to 7, Table 9-2.

**AFC** **Average fixed cost** (AFC) for any output level is found by dividing total fixed costs (TFC) by that output ($Q$). That is,

**FIGURE 9-3 Total cost is the sum of fixed cost and variable cost**

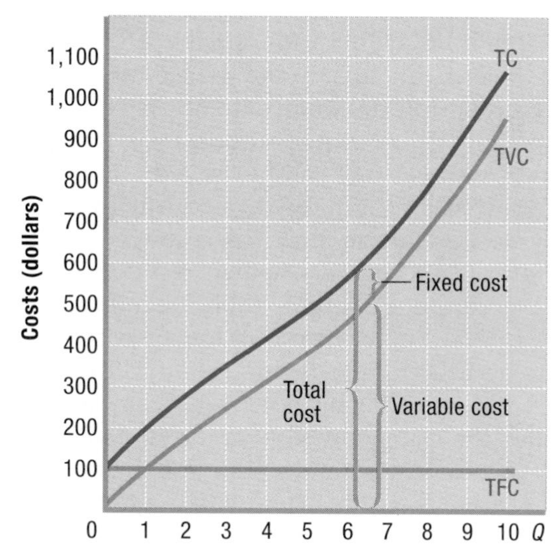


Total variable cost (TVC) changes with output. Fixed cost (TFC) is independent of the level of output. The total cost (TC) at any output is the vertical sum of the fixed cost and variable cost at that output.

$$AFC = \frac{TFC}{Q}$$

Because the total fixed cost is, by definition, the same regardless of output, AFC must decline as output increases. As output rises, the total fixed cost is spread over a larger and larger output. When output is just 1 unit in Table 9-2, TFC and AFC are the same at $100. But at 2 units of output, the total fixed cost of $100 becomes $50 of AFC or fixed cost per unit; then it becomes $33.33 per unit as $100 is spread over 3 units, and $25 per unit when spread over 4 units. This process is sometimes referred to as "spreading the overhead." Figure 9-4 shows that AFC graphs as a continuously declining curve as total output is increased.

**AVC** **Average variable cost** (AVC) for any output level is calculated by dividing total variable costs (TVC) by that output ($Q$):

$$AVC = \frac{TVC}{Q}$$

As output is increased by adding variable resources, AVC declines initially, reaches a minimum, and then increases again. A graph of AVC is a U-shaped or saucer-shaped curve, as shown in Figure 9-4.

Because total variable costs reflect the law of diminishing returns, so must AVC, which is derived from total variable costs. Due to initially increasing marginal returns, it takes fewer and fewer additional variable resources to produce each of the first 4 units of output. As a result, variable cost per unit declines. AVC hits a minimum with the fifth unit of output, and beyond this point AVC rises as diminishing returns require more and more variable resources to produce each additional unit of output.

In simpler terms, at very low levels of output production is relatively inefficient and costly. Because the firm's fixed plant is understaffed, average variable cost is relatively high. As output expands, however, greater specialization and better use of the firm's capital equipment yield more efficiency, and variable cost per unit of output declines. As still more variable resources are added, a point is reached where diminishing returns are incurred. The firm's capital equipment is now staffed more intensively, and therefore each added input unit does not increase output by as much as preceding inputs. This means AVC eventually increases.

You can verify the U or saucer shape of the AVC curve by returning to Table 9-1. Assume the

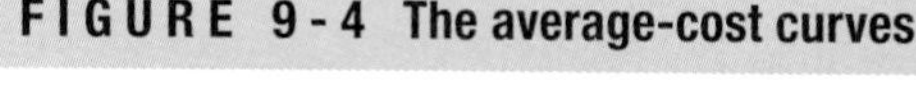

**FIGURE 9-4 The average-cost curves**

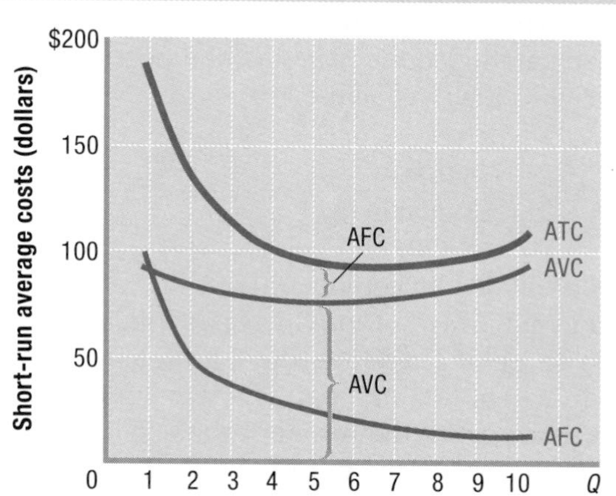


AFC falls as a given amount of fixed costs is apportioned over a larger and larger output. AVC initially falls because of increasing marginal returns but then rises because of diminishing marginal returns. Average total cost (ATC) is the vertical sum of average variable cost (AVC) and average fixed cost (AFC).

price of labour is $10 per unit. By dividing average product (output per labour unit) into $10 (price per labour unit), we determine the labour cost per unit of output. Because we have assumed labour to be the only variable input, the labour cost per unit of output is the variable cost per unit of output or AVC. When average product is initially low, AVC is high. As workers are added, average product rises and AVC falls. When average product is at its maximum, AVC is at its minimum. Then, as still more workers are added and average product declines, AVC rises. The "hump" of the average-product curve is reflected in the saucer or U shape of the AVC curve. As you will soon see, the two are mirror images of each other.

**ATC** **Average total cost** (ATC) for any output level is found by dividing total cost (TC) by that output ($Q$) or by adding AFC and AVC at that output:

$$\text{ATC} = \frac{\text{TC}}{Q} = \text{AFC} + \text{AVC}$$

Graphically ATC can be found by adding vertically the AFC and AVC curves, as in Figure 9-4. Thus the vertical distance between the ATC and AVC curves measures AFC at any level of output.

## Marginal Cost

3 KEY CONCEPT

One final and very crucial cost concept remains—marginal cost. **Marginal cost** (MC) *is the extra, or additional, cost of producing 1 more unit of output.* MC can be determined for each added unit of output by noting the *change* in total cost that that unit's production entails:

$$\text{MC} = \frac{\text{change in TC}}{\text{change in } Q}$$

**Calculations** In column 4, Table 9-2, production of the first unit of output increases total cost from $100 to $190. Therefore, the additional, or marginal, cost of that first unit is $90 (column 8). The marginal cost of the second unit is $80 (= $270 – $190); the MC of the third is $70 (= $340 – $270); and so forth. The MC for each of the 10 units of output is shown in column 8.

MC can also be calculated from the total-variable-cost column because the only difference between total cost and total variable cost is the constant amount of fixed costs ($100). Thus, the *change* in total cost and the *change* in total variable cost associated with each additional unit of output are always the same.

**Marginal Decisions** Marginal costs are costs that the firm can directly and immediately control. Specifically, MC designates all the cost incurred in producing the last unit of output. Thus, it also designates the cost that can be "saved" by not producing that last unit. Average-cost figures do *not* provide this information. For example, suppose the firm is undecided whether to produce 3 or 4 units of output. At 4 units Table 9-2 indicates that ATC is $100. But the firm does not increase its total costs by $100 by producing the fourth unit, nor does it save $100 by not producing that unit. Rather, the change in costs involved here is only $60, as the MC column in Table 9-2 reveals.

A firm's decisions as to what output level to produce are typically marginal decisions, that is, decisions to produce a few more or a few less units. Marginal cost is the change in costs when 1 more or 1 less unit of output is produced. When coupled with marginal revenue (which we will find in Chapter 10 indicates the change in revenue from 1 more or 1 less unit of output), marginal cost allows a firm to determine if it is profitable to expand or contract its production. The analysis in the next three chapters centres on these marginal calculations.

**Graphical Portrayal** Marginal cost is shown graphically in ***Figure 9-5 (Key Graph)***. Marginal cost at first declines sharply, reaches a minimum, and then rises rather abruptly. This reflects the fact that variable costs, and therefore total cost, increase first by decreasing amounts and then by increasing amounts (see columns 3 and 4, Table 9-2).

**MC and Marginal Product** The marginal-cost curve's shape is a consequence of the law of diminishing returns. The relationship between marginal product and marginal cost can be seen by looking back to Table 9-1. If all units of a variable resource (here labour) are hired at the same price, the marginal cost of each extra unit of output will *fall* as long as the marginal product of each additional worker is *rising*. This is so because marginal cost is the (constant) cost of an extra worker divided by his or her marginal product. Therefore, in Table 9-1, suppose each worker can be hired for $10. Because the first worker's mar-

KEY GRAPH

**FIGURE 9-5 The relationship of marginal cost to average total cost and average variable cost**

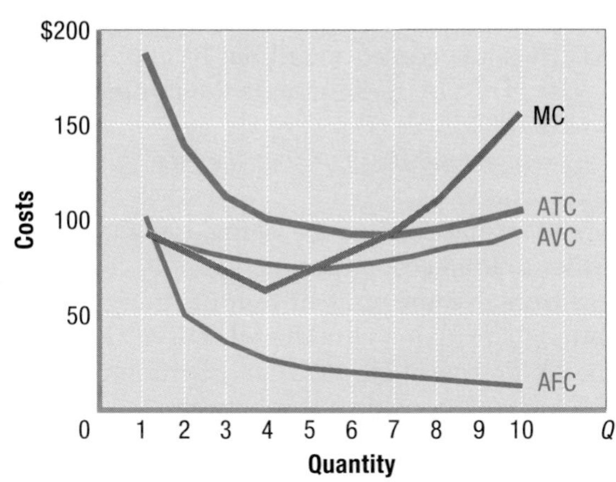


The marginal cost (MC) curve cuts through the average total cost (ATC) curve and the average variable cost (AVC) curve at their minimum points. When MC is below average total cost, ATC falls; when MC is above average total cost, ATC rises. Similarly, when MC is below average variable cost, AVC falls; when MC is above average variable cost, AVC rises.

9-5

QUICK QUIZ

1. The marginal-cost curve first declines and then increases because of:
   **(a)** increasing, then diminishing, marginal utility.
   **(b)** the decline in the gap between ATC and AVC as output expands.
   **(c)** increasing, then diminishing, marginal returns.
   **(d)** constant marginal revenue.
2. The vertical distance between ATC and AVC measures:
   **(a)** marginal cost.
   **(b)** total fixed cost.
   **(c)** average fixed cost.
   **(d)** economic profit per unit.
3. ATC is:
   **(a)** AVC − AFC.
   **(b)** MC + AVC.
   **(c)** AFC + AVC.
   **(d)** (AFC + AVC) × Q.
4. When the marginal-cost curve lies:
   **(a)** above the ATC curve, ATC rises.
   **(b)** above the AVC curve, ATC rises.
   **(c)** below the AVC curve, total fixed cost increases.
   **(d)** below the ATC curve, total fixed cost falls.

**Answers:** 1. (c); 2. (c); 3. (c); 4. (a)

ginal product is 10 output units and hiring this worker increases the firm's costs by $10, the marginal cost of each of these 10 extra units of output is $1 (= $10 ÷ 10 units). The second worker also increases costs by $10, but the marginal product is 15, so the marginal cost of each of these 15 extra units of output is $.67 (= $10 ÷ 15 units). Similarly, the MC of each of the 20 extra units of output contributed by the third worker is $.50 (= $10 ÷ 20 units). In general, as long as marginal product is rising, marginal cost will fall.

But as diminishing returns set in—in this case, with the fourth worker—marginal cost will begin to rise. Thus, for the fourth worker, marginal cost is $.67 (= $10 ÷ 15 units); for the fifth worker, MC is $1.00 ($10 ÷ 10 units); for the sixth, MC is $2.00 (= $10 ÷ 5 units), and so on. *If the price (cost) of the variable resource remains constant, increasing marginal returns will be reflected in a declining marginal cost, and diminishing marginal returns in a rising marginal cost.* The MC curve is a mirror reflection of the marginal-product curve. As you can see in Figure 9-6, when marginal product is rising, marginal cost is necessarily falling. When marginal product is at its maximum, marginal cost is at its minimum. And when marginal product is falling, marginal cost is rising.

**Relation of MC to AVC and ATC** Figure 9-5 shows that the marginal-cost curve MC intersects both the AVC and ATC curves at their minimum points. As noted earlier, this marginal-average relationship is a mathematical necessity, which a simple illustration will reveal. Suppose a professional baseball pitcher has allowed his opponents an average of 3 runs per game in the first three

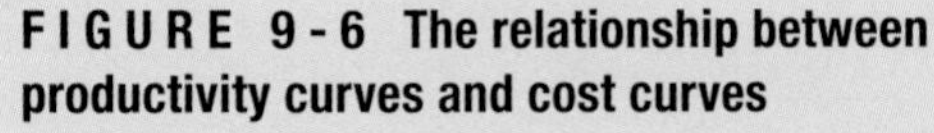

**FIGURE 9-6 The relationship between productivity curves and cost curves**

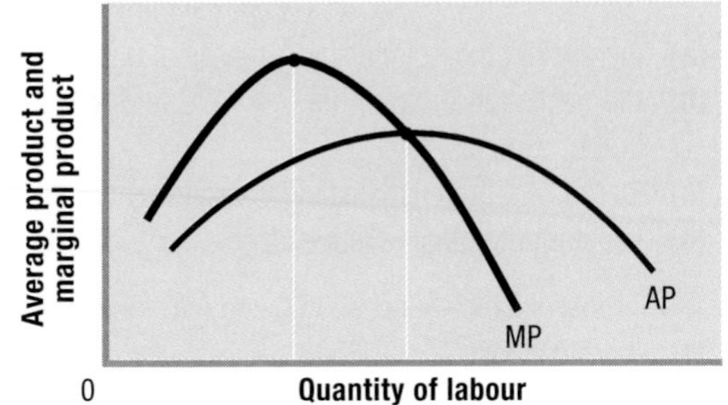


**(a) Product curves**

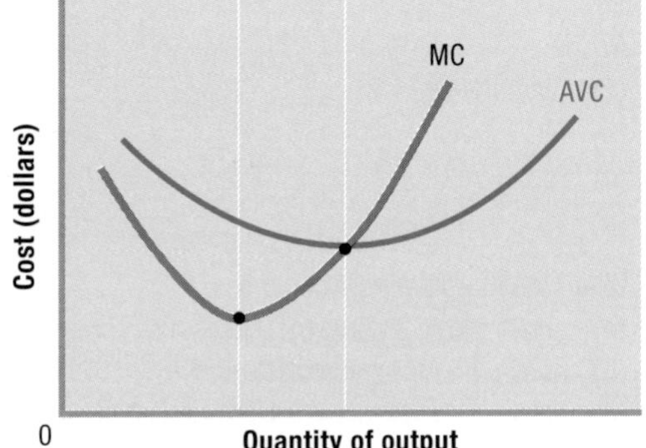


**(b) Cost curves**

The marginal-cost (MC) curve and average-variable-cost curve in (b) are mirror images of the marginal product (MP) and average product (AP) curves in (a). Assuming that labour is the only variable input and that its price (the wage rate) is constant, then when MP is rising, MC is falling and when MP is falling, MC is rising. Under the same assumptions, when AP is rising, AVC is falling and when AP is falling, AVC is rising.

games he has pitched. Now, whether his average falls or rises as a result of pitching a fourth (marginal) game will depend on whether the additional runs he allows in that extra game are fewer or more than his current 3-run average. If he allows fewer than 3 runs—for example, 1—in the fourth game, his total runs will rise from 9 to 10, and his average will fall from 3 to $2\frac{1}{2}$ (= 10 ÷ 4). Conversely, if he allows more than 3 runs—say, 7 —in the fourth game, his total will increase from 9 to 16 and his average will rise from 3 to 4 (= 16 ÷ 4).

So it is with costs. When the amount (the marginal cost) added to total cost is less than the current average total cost, ATC will fall. Conversely, when the marginal cost exceeds ATC, ATC will rise. This means in Figure 9-5 that as long as MC lies below ATC, ATC will fall, and whenever MC is above ATC, ATC will rise. Therefore, at the point of intersection where MC equals ATC, ATC has just ceased to fall but has not yet begun to rise. This, by definition, is the minimum point on the ATC curve. *The marginal-cost curve intersects the average-total-cost curve at the ATC curve's minimum point.*

Marginal cost can be defined as the addition either to total cost *or* to total variable costs resulting from 1 more unit of output; thus this same rationale explains why the MC curve also crosses the AVC curve at the AVC curve's minimum point. No such relationship exists between the MC curve and the average-fixed-cost curve, because the two are not related; marginal cost includes only those costs that change with output, and fixed costs by definition are those that are independent of output. ***(Key Question 10)***

## Shifting the Cost Curves

Changes in either resource prices or technology will shift the cost curves. If fixed costs rose—say, to $200 rather than the $100 we assumed in Table 9-2—then the AFC curve in Figure 9-5 would be shifted upward. The ATC curve would also move upward because AFC is a component of ATC. But the positions of the AVC and MC curves would be unaltered because their locations are based on the prices of variable rather than fixed resources. However, if the price (wage) of labour or some other variable input rose, the AVC, ATC, and MC curves would all shift upward, but the position of AFC would remain unchanged. Reductions in the prices of fixed or variable resources would entail cost curve shifts exactly opposite those just described.

If a more efficient technology were discovered, then the productivity of all inputs would increase. The cost figures in Table 9-2 would all be lower. To illustrate, if labour is the only variable input, wages are $10 per hour, and average product is 10 units, then AVC would be $1. But if a technological improvement increases the average product of labour to 20 units, then AVC will decline to $.50. More generally, an upward shift in the productivity curves shown in Figure 9-6a will mean a downward shift in the cost curves portrayed in Figure 9-6b. (See Global Perspective 9-1.)

9-1

GLOBAL PERSPECTIVE

**Relative changes in labour costs in manufacturing since 1992, selected nations**

Labour costs are a large percentage of ATC for most firms. Average labour costs in Canadian manufacturing have been falling since 1992. But labour costs (in dollars) have risen in some nations and declined in others, shifting ATC curves upward or downward.

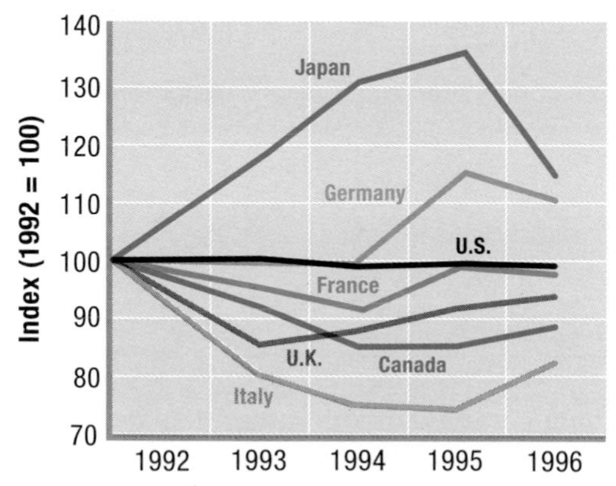


*Source:* U.S. Bureau of Labour Statistics.

9-3

QUICK REVIEW

- The law of diminishing returns indicates that, beyond some point, output will increase by diminishing amounts as more units of a variable resource (labour) are added to a fixed resource (capital).
- In the short run the total cost of any level of output is the sum of fixed and variable cost (TC = TFC + TVC).
- Average fixed, average variable, and average total cost are fixed, variable, and total costs per unit of output; marginal cost is the extra cost of producing 1 more unit of output.
- Average fixed cost declines continuously as output increases; average-variable-cost and average-total-cost curves are U-shaped, reflecting increasing and then diminishing returns; the marginal-cost curve falls but then rises, intersecting both the average-variable- and the average-total-cost curves at their minimum points.

## LONG-RUN PRODUCTION COSTS

In the long run individual firms in an industry can undertake all desired resource adjustments. The firm can alter its plant capacity; it can build a larger plant or revert to a smaller plant than assumed in Table 9-2. The industry can also change its plant size; the long run allows sufficient time for new firms to enter or existing firms to leave an industry. We will discuss the impact of the entry and exit of firms to and from an industry in the next chapter; here we are concerned only with changes in plant capacity made by a single firm. We will couch our analysis in terms of average total cost (ATC), making no distinction between fixed and variable costs because all resources, and therefore all costs, are variable in the long run.

### Firm Size and Costs

Suppose a single-plant manufacturer begins on a small scale and, as the result of successful operations, expands to successively larger plant sizes with larger output capacities. What happens to average total cost as this occurs? For a time successively larger plants will lower average total cost. However, eventually the building of a still larger plant may cause ATC to rise.

Figure 9-7 illustrates this situation for five possible plant sizes. ATC-1 is the short-run average-total-cost curve for the smallest of the five plants, and ATC-5 that for the largest. Constructing larger plants will lower the minimum average total costs through plant size 3. But then larger plants will mean higher minimum average total costs.

### The Long-Run Cost Curve

The vertical lines perpendicular to the output axis in Figure 9-7 indicate those outputs at which the firm should change plant size to realize the lowest attainable average total cost of production. These are the outputs at which the per-unit cost for a larger plant drops below that for the current, smaller plant. For all outputs up to 20 units, the lowest average total per-unit costs are attainable with plant size 1. However, if the firm's volume of sales expands to some level greater than 20 units but less than 30, it can achieve lower per-unit costs by constructing a larger plant—plant size 2. Although *total* cost will be higher at the greater lev-

**FIGURE 9-7 The long-run average-total-cost curve: five possible plant sizes**

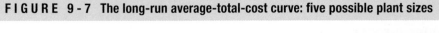

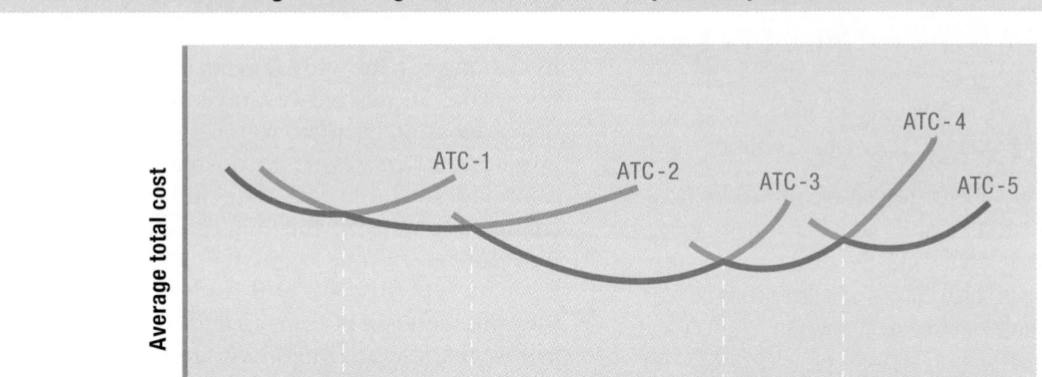


The long-run average-total-cost curve is made up of segments of the short-run cost curves (ATC-1, ATC-2, etc.) of the various-sized plants from which the firm might choose. Each point on the bumpy planning curve shows the least unit cost attainable for any output when the firm has had time to make all desired changes in its plant size.

els of production, the cost *per unit* of output will be less. For any output between 30 and 50 units, plant size 3 will yield the lowest average total cost. From 50 to 60 units of output, plant size 4 must be built to achieve the lowest unit costs. Lowest average total cost for any output over 60 units demands construction of the still larger plant size 5.

Tracing these adjustments, we find that the long-run ATC curve for the enterprise is made up of segments of the short-run ATC curves for the various plant sizes that can be constructed. *The long-run ATC curve shows the least average total cost at which any output can be produced after the firm has had time to make all appropriate adjustments in its plant size.* In Figure 9-7 the dark green, bumpy curve is the firm's long-run ATC curve or, as it is often called, the firm's *planning curve*.

In most lines of production the choice of plant sizes is much wider than in our illustration. In many industries the number of possible plant sizes is virtually unlimited, and in time quite small changes in the volume of output will lead to changes in plant size. Graphically, this implies an unlimited number of short-run ATC curves, one for each output level, as suggested by ***Figure 9-8 (Key Graph)***. Then, rather than being made up of *segments* of short-run ATC curves as in Figure 9-7, the long-run ATC curve is made up of all the *points of tangency* of the unlimited number of short-run ATC curves from which the long-run ATC curve is derived. Therefore, the planning curve is smooth rather than bumpy. Each point on it tells us the minimum ATC of producing the corresponding level of output.

## Economies and Diseconomies of Scale

We have assumed that for a time larger and larger plant sizes will lead to lower unit costs, but that beyond some point successively larger plants will mean higher average total costs. That is, we have assumed the long-run ATC curve is U-shaped. But why should this be? Note, first, that the law of diminishing returns does *not* apply in the long run. That's because diminishing returns presumes one resource is fixed in supply while the long run means all resources are variable. Also, our discussion assumes resource prices are constant. We can explain the U-shaped long-run average-total-cost curve in terms of economies and diseconomies of large-scale production.

### Economies of Scale

**Economies of scale**, meaning economies of mass production, explain the downsloping part of the long-run ATC curve, as indicated in Figures 9-9a, b, and c. As plant size increases, a number of factors will for a time lead to lower average costs of production.

1. **LABOUR SPECIALIZATION** Increased specialization in the use of labour becomes more possible as a plant increases in size. Hiring

## KEY GRAPH

**FIGURE 9-8 The long-run average-total-cost curve: unlimited number of plant sizes**

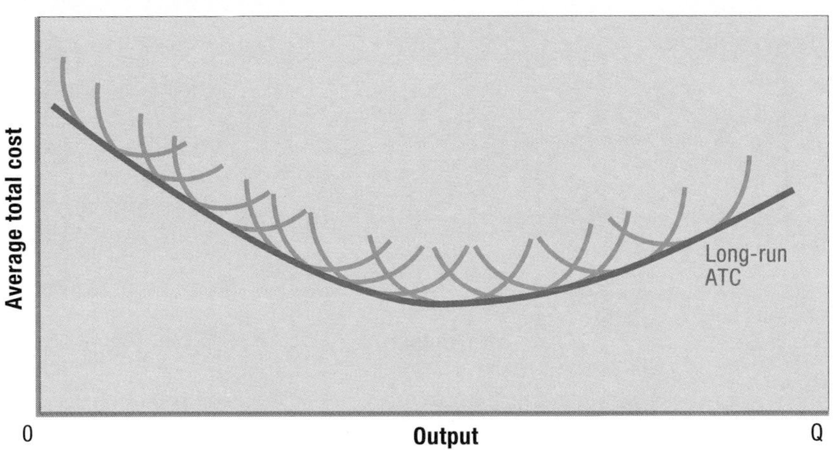


If the number of possible plant sizes is very large, the long-run average-total-cost curve approximates a smooth curve. Economies of scale, followed by diseconomies of scale, cause the curve to be U-shaped.

### 9-8
### QUICK QUIZ

1. The unlabelled tinted curves in this figure illustrate the:
   **(a)** long-run average-total-cost curves of various firms constituting the industry.
   **(b)** short-run average-total-cost curves of various firms constituting the industry.
   **(c)** short-run average-total-cost curves of various plant sizes available to a particular firm.
   **(d)** short-run marginal-cost curves of various plant sizes available to a particular firm.
2. The unlabelled tinted curves in this figure derive their shapes from:
   **(a)** decreasing, then increasing, short-run returns.
   **(b)** increasing, then decreasing, short-run returns.
   **(c)** economies, then diseconomies, of scale.
   **(d)** diseconomies, then economies, of scale.
3. The long-run ATC curve in this figure derives its shape from:
   **(a)** decreasing, then increasing, short-run returns.
   **(b)** increasing, then decreasing, short-run returns.
   **(c)** economies, then diseconomies, of scale.
   **(d)** diseconomies, then economies, of scale.
4. The long-run ATC curve is often called the firm's:
   **(a)** planning curve.
   **(b)** capital-expansion path.
   **(c)** total-product curve.
   **(d)** production possibilities curve.

**Answers:** 1. (c); 2. (b); 3. (c); 4. (a).

more workers means jobs can be divided and subdivided. Each worker may now have just one task to perform instead of five or six. Workers can work full time on those particular tasks for which they have special skills. In a small plant, skilled machinists may spend half their time performing unskilled tasks, leading to higher production costs.

Further, by working at fewer tasks, workers become proficient at those tasks. The jack-of-all-trades doing five or six jobs will not likely be efficient in any of them. Concentrating on one task, the same worker may become highly efficient.

Finally, greater labour specialization eliminates the loss of time that accompanies each shift of a worker from one task to another.

2. **MANAGERIAL SPECIALIZATION** Large-scale production also means better use of, and greater specialization in, management. A supervisor who can handle 20 workers is underused in a small plant that employs only 10 people. The

**FIGURE 9-9 Various possible long-run average-total-cost curves**

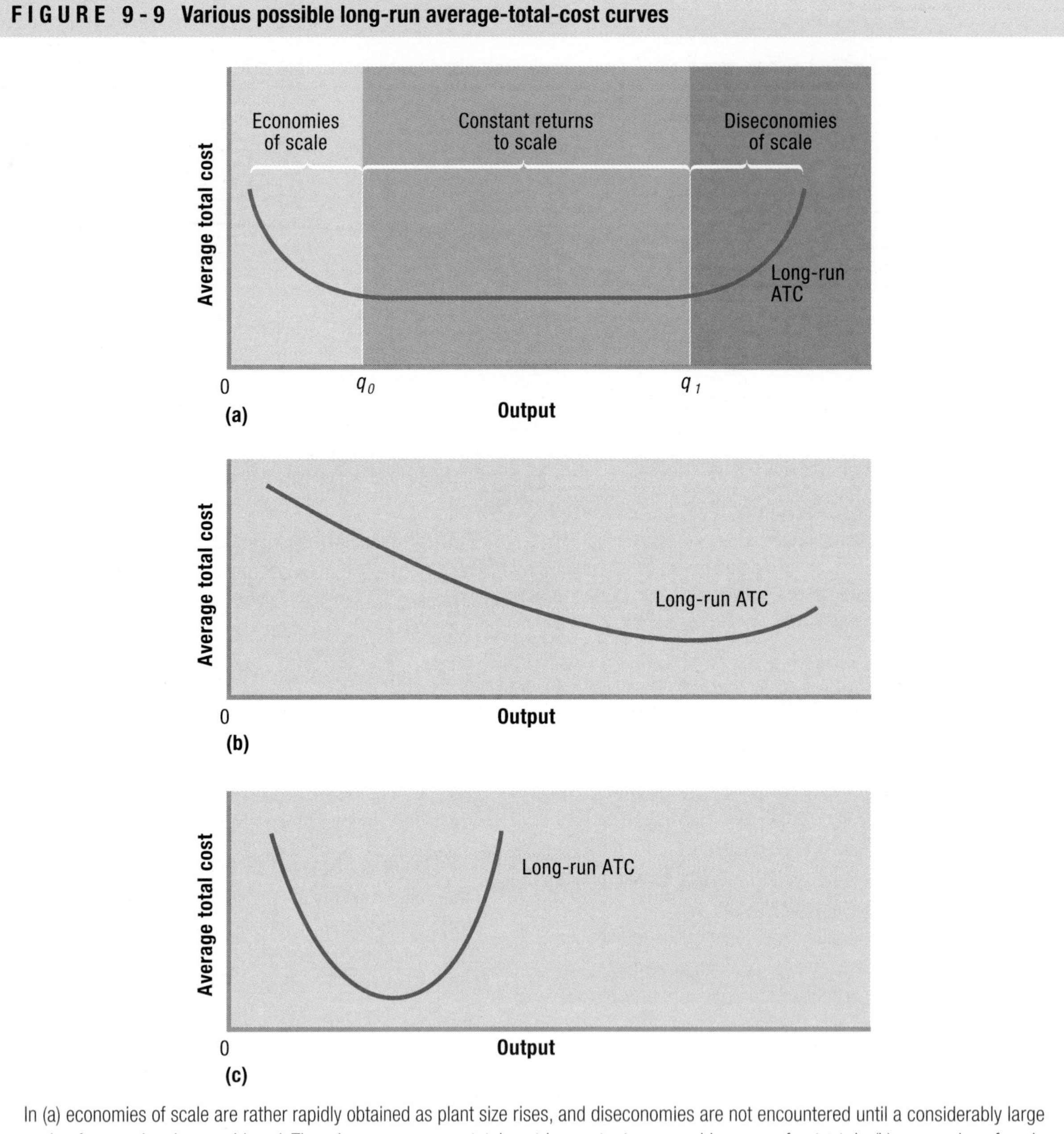


In (a) economies of scale are rather rapidly obtained as plant size rises, and diseconomies are not encountered until a considerably large scale of output has been achieved. Thus, long-run average total cost is constant over a wide range of output. In (b) economies of scale are extensive and diseconomies occur only at very large outputs. Average total cost therefore declines over a broad range of output. In (c) economies of scale are exhausted quickly, followed immediately by diseconomies. Minimum ATC thus occurs at a relatively low output.

production staff could be doubled with no increase in supervisory costs.

Small firms cannot use management specialists to best advantage. In a small plant a sales specialist may have to divide his or her time between several executive functions—for example, marketing, personnel, and finance. A larger scale of operations will mean that the marketing expert can supervise marketing full time, while appropriate specialists perform other managerial functions. Greater efficiency and lower unit costs are the net result.

3. **EFFICIENT CAPITAL** Small firms often cannot afford the most efficient capital equipment. In many lines of production this machinery is available only in very large and extremely expensive

units. Furthermore, effective use of this equipment demands a high volume of production, and that again requires large-scale producers.

In the automobile industry the most efficient fabrication method employs robotics and elaborate assembly line equipment. Effective use of this equipment demands an annual output of perhaps 200,000 to 400,000 automobiles. Only very large-scale producers can afford to purchase and use this equipment efficiently. The small-scale producer is faced with a dilemma. To fabricate automobiles using other equipment is inefficient and therefore more costly per unit. The alternative of purchasing the efficient equipment and underusing it at low levels of output is also inefficient and costly.

4. **OTHER FACTORS** Many products require design and development costs, as well as other "start-up" costs, which must be incurred irrespective of projected sales. These costs decline per unit as output is increased. Similarly, advertising costs decline per auto, per computer, per stereo system, and per case of beer as more units are produced.

All these factors contribute to lower average total cost for the producer able to expand its scale of operations. Where economies of scale are possible, an increase in *all* resources of, say, 10 percent will cause a more-than-proportionate increase in output of, say, 20 percent. The result will be a decline in ATC.

In many Canadian manufacturing industries, economies of scale have been of great significance. Firms that have expanded their scale of operations to obtain economies of mass production have survived and flourished. Those unable to expand became relatively high-cost producers, doomed to a struggle to survive.

**Diseconomies of Scale** In time the expansion of a firm *may* lead to diseconomies and therefore higher average total cost.

The main factor causing **diseconomies of scale** is the difficulty of efficiently controlling and coordinating a firm's operations as it becomes a large-scale producer. In a small plant a single key executive may make all the basic decisions for the plant's operation. Because of the firm's small size, the executive is close to the production line, understands the firm's operations, and can digest information and make efficient decisions.

This neat picture changes as a firm grows. There are now many management levels between the executive suite and the assembly line; top management is far removed from the actual production operations of the plant. One person cannot assemble, digest, and understand all the information essential to decision making on a large scale. Authority must be delegated to many vice-presidents, second vice-presidents, and so forth. This expansion of the management hierarchy leads to problems of communication and cooperation, bureaucratic red tape, and the possibility that decisions will not be coordinated. Similarly, decision making may be slowed down to the point that decisions fail to quickly reflect changes in consumer tastes or technology. The result is impaired efficiency and rising average total costs.

Also, in massive production facilities workers may feel alienated from their employers and care little about working efficiently. Opportunities to shirk—to avoid work in favour of on-the-job leisure—may be greater in large plants than in small ones. Countering worker alienation and shirking may require additional worker supervision, which increases costs.

Where diseconomies of scale are operative, an increase in all inputs of, say, 10 percent will cause a less-than-proportionate increase in output of, say, 5 percent. As a consequence, ATC will increase. Diseconomies of scale are illustrated by the rising portion of the long-run cost curves in Figure 9-9.

**Constant Returns to Scale** In some industries there may exist a rather wide range of output between the output at which economies of scale and the output at which diseconomies of scale begin. That is, there may be a range of **constant returns to scale** over which long-run average cost does not change. The $q_0q_1$ output range of Figure 9-9a is an example. Here a given percentage increase in *all* inputs of, say, 10 percent will cause a proportionate 10 percent increase in output. Thus, in this range ATC is constant.

## Applications and Illustrations

The business world contains many examples relating to economies and diseconomies of scale. Here are just a few.

**Textbooks** Next semester when you buy texts at your bookstore, compare the prices of introductory or basic texts with the prices of more specialized, advanced books. You may be surprised that the price of a two-semester principles of economics text is not much more—and perhaps less—than that of a one-semester advanced text. This is true even if the principles text is 200 pages longer and has a multicolour format, while the advanced book is in mundane black and white. Economies of scale are at work here. Both introductory and advanced texts require design, editing, and typesetting costs that are about the same per page whether 5,000 copies (of the advanced text) or 100,000 copies (of the introductory text) are printed. With introductory books these costs are spread over many more units of output, meaning lower unit costs and a comparatively low price per book.

**A "Monster Machine"** We pointed out that the use of the most technologically efficient equipment—and thus achievement of economies of scale—often demands a high volume of output. Specific example: In 1996 Verson (an American firm located in Chicago) introduced a new stamping machine—a 49-foot-tall metal stamping machine that is the size of a house and weighs as much as 12 locomotives. This $30-million machine, which cuts and sculpts raw sheets of steel into automobile hoods and fenders, enables automakers to make new parts in just five *minutes* compared with eight *hours* for older stamping presses. A single so-called "monster machine" is designed to make 5 million auto parts a year. A firm desiring to achieve the cost saving delivered by this machine must have sufficient auto production to use all these parts.

**General Motors** Monster machines aside, executives of General Motors—the world's largest auto producer—are well aware of the realities of *diseconomies* of scale. In a classic statement relating to diseconomies of scale, a former GM president commented thus on GM's Chevrolet division:

> Chevrolet is such a big monster that you twist its tail and nothing happens at the other end for months and months. It is so gigantic that there isn't any way to really run it. You just sort of try to keep track of it.[1]

Experts on the auto industry have concluded that GM's large size is a liability; the company is one-third larger than Ford, more than three times larger than Chrysler, and larger than Toyota and Nissan combined. Compared with these domestic and foreign competitors, GM has a substantial cost disadvantage and a declining long-term market share. To try to reduce scale diseconomies, GM has taken several actions. It has established joint ventures (combined projects) with smaller foreign rivals such as Toyota to reduce its production costs. It has created Saturn, a separate, stand-alone auto-manufacturing company. It has given each of its five automotive divisions (Chevrolet, Buick, Pontiac, Oldsmobile, and Cadillac) greater autonomy with respect to styling, engineering, and marketing decisions to reduce the layers of managerial approval required in decision making. Finally, GM has reorganized into a small-car group and a midsize and luxury group to try to cut costs and bring new cars to the market faster. Whether these actions can overcome GM's diseconomies of scale remains to be seen.

## Minimum Efficient Scale and Industry Structure

Economies and diseconomies of scale are an important determinant of an industry's structure. Here it is helpful to introduce the concept of **minimum efficient scale** (MES), which is the lowest level of output at which a firm can minimize long-run average costs. In Figure 9-9a this occurs at $q_0$ units of output. Because of the extended range of constant returns to scale, firms producing substantially greater outputs could also realize the minimum attainable average costs. Specifically, firms would be equally efficient within the $q_0$ to $q_1$ range. We would therefore not be surprised to find an industry with such cost conditions to be populated by firms of quite different sizes. The apparel, food processing, furniture, wood products, and small-appliance industries provide approximate examples. With an extended range of constant returns to scale, relatively large and relatively small firms could coexist in an industry and be equally successful.

Compare this with Figure 9-9b, where economies of scale occur over a wide range of output, and diseconomies of scale appear only at very high levels of output. This pattern of declining long-run average total cost occurs over an extended range of output, as is the case in the automobile, aluminum, steel, and other heavy industries. Given consumer demand, efficient production will be achieved with a few large-scale

[1] As quoted in Walter Adams (ed.), *The Structure of American Industry*, eighth edition. (New York: Macmillan, 1990), p. 115.

producers. Small firms cannot realize the minimum efficient scale and will not be able to compete. In the extreme, economies of scale might extend beyond the market's size, resulting in what is termed **natural monopoly**: a market situation in which average total cost is minimized when only one firm produces the particular good or service.

Where economies of scale are few and diseconomies come into play quickly, the minimum efficient size occurs at a low level of output, as shown in Figure 9-9c. In such industries a particular level of consumer demand will support a large number of relatively small producers. Many retail trades and some types of farming fall into this category. So do certain types of light manufacturing, such as the baking, clothing, and shoe industries. Fairly small firms are as efficient as, or more efficient than, large-scale producers in such industries.

Our point here is that the shape of the long-run average-total-cost curve is determined by technology and resulting economies and diseconomies of scale. The shape of the long-run ATC curve, in turn, can be significant in determining whether an industry is populated by a relatively large number of small firms or dominated by a few large producers, or is somewhere between the two.

But we must be cautious because industry structure does not depend on cost conditions alone. Government policies, the geographic size of markets, managerial ability, and other factors must be considered in explaining the structure of a particular industry. ***(Key Question 13)***

## 9-4 QUICK REVIEW

- Most firms have U-shaped long-run average-total-cost curves, reflecting economies and then diseconomies of scale.
- Economies of scale are the consequence of greater specialization of labour and management, more efficient capital equipment, and the spreading of start-up costs among more units of output.
- Diseconomies of scale are caused by problems of coordination and communication that arise in large firms.
- Minimum efficient scale is the lowest level of output at which a firm's long-run average total cost is at a minimum.

## In The Media

# New Era in Banking

### Royal, Bank of Montreal say merger needed to compete internationally

BY LES WHITTINGTON
BUSINESS REPORTER

A new era in Canadian financial business arrived yesterday as the Royal Bank of Canada and the Bank of Montreal announced plans to join forces and create the third-biggest company of its kind in North America.

Citing the threat from increasingly huge global financial competitors, the two banks decided to push ahead with a $40 billion merger blueprint without waiting for the federal government to make up its mind about the future shape of the industry.

The deal would rank as the second-largest ever in North America, upstaged only by WorldCom Inc.'s takeover of MCI Communications in November for $51 billion.

With assets of $453 billion, the as-yet-unnamed Canadian financial giant would be larger than every other North American bank except U.S. titans Chase Manhattan, with $551 billion in assets, and Citicorp, with $469 billion.

The new Canadian institution would also have 17 million customers and a market capitalization (the total value of outstanding stock) of $40 billion.

"In today's market for financial services, achieving size matters," Royal Bank chairman John Cleghorn told a hastily assembled news conference after the surprise announcement yesterday morning.

He and Bank of Montreal chairman Matthew Barrett appeared unfazed by a warning from Finance Minister Paul Martin that Ottawa was concerned about the proposed deal and would not make a decision on the union until a federal task force on the industry completes its work in September.

"I see that as normal," Barrett told reporters. "There's no point in setting up a task force and not asking its opinion."

*Source:* Toronto Star, January 24, 1998, p. C1. Reprinted with permission—The Toronto Star Syndicate.

## THE STORY IN BRIEF

The Royal Bank of Canada and the Bank of Montreal announce their intention to merge, creating the third largest financial institution in North America.

## THE ECONOMICS BEHIND THE STORY

- The two banks claim that they are merging because of the threat of international competition. Implicitly the two banks are saying that by merging they can get their costs down. Such cost reduction will presumably come from capturing the economies of scale of bringing the two banks together to form one entity.
- Such a large merger will require the permission of the federal government because of possible reduction of competition.
- Is the merger likely to translate into fewer jobs? If the same number of employees remain, what will have to occur to output per person for average costs to fall? ■

# The Last Word

## IRRELEVANCY OF SUNK COSTS

**Sunk costs should be disregarded in decision making.**

THERE IS AN OLD SAYING: DON'T CRY OVER spilt milk. The message is that once you have spilled a glass of milk, there is nothing you can do to recover it, so you should forget about it and "move on from there." This saying has great relevance to what economists call *sunk* costs. Such costs are like sunken ships on the ocean floor: Once these costs are incurred, they cannot be recovered.

Let's gain an understanding of this idea by initially applying it to consumers and then to businesses. Suppose you bought an expensive ticket to an upcoming football game, but the morning of the game you wake up with a bad case of the flu. Feeling miserable, you step outside to find that the wind chill is about –20 degrees. You absolutely do not want to go to the game, but you remind yourself that you paid a steep price for the ticket. You call several people to try to sell the ticket, but you soon discover that no one is interested in it, even at a discounted price. You conclude that everyone who wants a ticket has one.

Should you go to the game? Economic analysis says that you should not take actions for which marginal cost exceeds marginal benefit. And, in this situation, the price you paid for the ticket is irrelevant to the decision. Both marginal or additional cost and marginal or additional benefit are forward looking. If the marginal cost of going to the game is greater than the marginal benefit, the best decision is to go back to bed. This decision should be the same whether you paid \$2, \$20, or \$200 for the game ticket because the price that you pay for something does not affect its marginal benefit. Once the ticket has been purchased and cannot be resold, its cost is irrelevant to the decision to attend the game. Since "you absolutely do not want to go," clearly the marginal cost exceeds the marginal benefit of the game.

Here is a helpful second consumer example. Suppose a family is on vacation and stops at a roadside stand to buy some apples. The kids get back into the car and bite into their apples, immediately pronouncing them "totally mushy" and unworthy of another bite. Both parents agree that the apples are "terrible," but the father continues to eat his, because, as he says, "we paid a premium price for them." One of the older children replies, "Dad, that is irrelevant." Although it wasn't stated very diplomatically, the child, of course, is exactly right. In making a new decision, you should ignore all costs that are not affected by the decision. The prior bad decision (in retrospect) to buy the apples should not dictate a second decision for which marginal benefit is less than marginal cost.

Now let's apply the idea of sunk costs to firms. Some of a firm's costs are not only fixed (recurring, but unrelated to the level of output), but sunk (unrecoverable). For example, a nonrefundable annual lease payment for the use of a store cannot be recouped once it has been paid. A firm's decision about whether to move from the store to a more profitable location does not depend on the amount of time remaining on the lease. If moving means greater profit, it makes sense to move whether there are 300 days, 30 days, or 3 days left on the lease.

Or, as another example, suppose a firm spends $1 million on R&D to bring out a new product, only to discover that the product sells very poorly. Should the firm continue to produce the product at a loss even when there is no realistic hope for future success? Obviously, it should not. In making this decision, the firm realizes that the amount it has spent in developing the product is irrelevant; it should stop production of the product and cut its losses. In fact, many firms have dropped products after spending millions of dollars on their development. Examples are the quick decision by Coca-Cola to drop its New Coke and the eventual decision by McDonald's to drop its McLean Burger.

Consider a final real-world example. For decades, Boeing and McDonnell Douglas were keen rivals in the worldwide sale of commercial airplanes. Each company spent billions of dollars on R&D and marketing in an attempt to gain competitive advantages over each other. Then, in 1996 they suddenly merged. Many observers wondered how two fierce rivals who had spent such huge amounts to compete could suddenly forget the past and agree to merge. But these past efforts and expenditures were irrelevant to the decision; they were sunk costs. The forward-looking decision led both companies to conclude, each for its own reasons, that the marginal benefit of a merger would outweigh the marginal cost.

In short, if a cost has been incurred and cannot be partly or fully recouped by some other choice, a rational consumer or firm should ignore it. Sunk costs are irrelevant. Or, as the saying goes, Don't cry over spilt milk. ■

## CHAPTER SUMMARY

1. The firm is the most efficient form of organizing production and distribution. The main goal of a firm is to maximize profit.
2. Sole proprietorships, partnerships, and corporations are the major legal forms that business enterprises may assume. Though proprietorships dominate numerically, the bulk of total output is produced by corporations. Corporations have grown to their position of dominance in the business sector primarily because they are **a** characterized by limited liability and **b** can acquire money capital for expansion more easily than other firms.
3. Economic costs include all payments that must be received by resource owners to ensure a continued supply of needed resources to a particular line of production. This includes explicit costs, which flow to resources owned and supplied by others, and implicit costs, which are payments for the use of self-owned and self-employed resources. One implicit cost is a normal profit to the entrepreneur. Economic profit occurs when total revenue exceeds total cost (= explicit costs + implicit costs, including a normal profit).
4. In the short run a firm's plant capacity is fixed. The firm can use its plant more or less intensively by adding or subtracting units of variable resources, but the firm does not have sufficient time in the short run to alter plant size.

5. The law of diminishing returns describes what happens to output as a fixed plant is used more intensively. As successive units of a variable resource such as labour are added to a fixed plant, beyond some point the marginal product associated with each additional worker declines.

6. Because some resources are variable and others fixed, costs can be classified as variable or fixed in the short run. Fixed cost is independent of the level of output; variable cost varies with output. The total cost of any output is the sum of fixed and variable cost at that output.

7. Average fixed, average variable, and average total cost are fixed, variable, and total cost per unit of output. Average fixed cost declines continuously as output increases because a fixed sum is being spread over a larger and larger number of units of production. A graph of average variable cost is U-shaped, reflecting the law of diminishing returns. Average total cost is the sum of average fixed and average variable costs; its graph is also U-shaped.

8. Marginal cost is the extra, or additional, cost of producing 1 more unit of output. It is the amount by which total cost and total variable cost change when 1 more or 1 less unit of output is produced. Graphically, the marginal-cost curve intersects the ATC and AVC curves at their minimum points.

9. Lower resource prices shift cost curves downward, as does technological progress. Higher input prices shift cost curves upward.

10. The long run is a period of time sufficiently long for a firm to vary the amounts of all resources used, including plant size. In the long run all costs are variable. The long-run ATC, or planning, curve is composed of segments of the short-run ATC curves, and it represents the various plant sizes a firm can construct in the long run.

11. The long-run ATC curve is generally U-shaped. Economies of scale are first encountered as a small firm expands. Greater specialization in the use of labour and management, the ability to use the most efficient equipment, and the spreading of start-up costs among more units of output all contribute to economies of scale. As the firm continues to grow, it will encounter diseconomies of scale stemming from the managerial complexities that accompany large-scale production. The output ranges over which economies and diseconomies of scale occur in an industry are often an important determinant of the structure of that industry.

## TERMS AND CONCEPTS

plant
firm
vertical combination
horizontal combination
conglomerate combination
industry
sole proprietorship
partnership
corporation
stocks
bonds
limited liability
double taxation
principal-agent problem
economic (opportunity) cost
explicit costs
implicit costs
normal profit
economic profit
short run
long run
total product
marginal product
average product
law of diminishing returns
fixed costs
variable costs
total cost
average fixed cost
average variable cost
average total cost
marginal cost
economies of scale
diseconomies of scale
constant returns to scale
minimum efficient scale
natural monopoly

# STUDY QUESTIONS

1. Distinguish between a plant, a firm, and an industry. Why is an "industry" often difficult to define in practice?

2. KEY QUESTION *What are the major legal forms of business organization? Briefly state the advantages and disadvantages of each. How do you account for the dominant role of corporations in our economy?*

3. "The legal form of an enterprise is dictated primarily by the financial requirements of its particular line of production." Do you agree?

4. Distinguish between explicit and implicit costs, giving examples of each. What are some explicit and implicit costs of attending college? Why does the economist classify normal profit as a cost? Is economic profit a cost of production?

5. KEY QUESTION *Gomez runs a small pottery firm. He hires one helper at $12,000 per year, pays annual rent of $5,000 for his shop, and spends $20,000 per year on materials. Gomez has $40,000 of his own funds invested in equipment (pottery wheels, kilns, and so forth), which could earn him $4,000 per year if alternatively invested. Gomez has been offered $15,000 per year to work as a potter for a competitor. He estimates his entrepreneurial talents are worth $3,000 per year. Total annual revenue from pottery sales is $72,000. Calculate the accounting profit and economic profit for Gomez's pottery.*

6. Which of the following are short-run and which are long-run adjustments? **a** McDonald's builds a new restaurant; **b** Acme Steel Corporation hires 200 more workers; **c** A farmer increases the amount of fertilizer used on his corn crop; **d** An Alcan plant adds a third shift of workers.

7. KEY QUESTION *Complete the following table by calculating marginal product and average product from the data given.*

| Inputs of labour | Total product | Marginal product | Average product |
|---|---|---|---|
| 0 | 0 | ______ | |
| 1 | 15 | ______ | ______ |
| 2 | 34 | ______ | ______ |
| 3 | 51 | ______ | ______ |
| 4 | 65 | ______ | ______ |
| 5 | 74 | ______ | ______ |
| 6 | 80 | ______ | ______ |
| 7 | 83 | ______ | ______ |
| 8 | 82 | | ______ |

*Plot the total, marginal, and average products and explain in detail the relationship between each pair of curves. Explain why marginal product first rises, then declines, and ultimately becomes negative. What bearing does the law of diminishing returns have on short-run costs? Be specific. "When marginal product is rising, marginal cost is falling. And when marginal product is diminishing, marginal cost is rising." Illustrate and explain graphically.*

8. Why can the distinction between fixed and variable costs be made in the short run? Classify the following as fixed or variable costs: advertising expenditures, fuel, interest on company-issued bonds, shipping charges, payments for raw materials, real estate taxes, executive salaries, insurance premiums, wage payments, depreciation and obsolescence charges, sales taxes, and rental payments on leased office machinery. "There are no fixed costs in the long run; all costs are variable." Explain.

9. List several fixed and variable costs associated with owning and operating an automobile. Suppose you are considering whether to drive your car or fly 1,000 km for spring break. Which costs—fixed, variable, or both—would you take into account in making your decision? Would any implicit costs be relevant? Explain.

10. KEY QUESTION *A firm has $60 fixed costs and variable costs as indicated in the table below. Complete the table; check your calculations by referring to question 4 at the end of Chapter 10.*

| Total product | Total fixed cost | Total variable cost | Total cost | Average fixed cost | Average variable cost |
|---|---|---|---|---|---|
| 0 | $_____ | $ 0 | $_____ | $_____ | $_____ |
| 1 | _____ | 45 | _____ | _____ | _____ |
| 2 | _____ | 85 | _____ | _____ | _____ |
| 3 | _____ | 120 | _____ | _____ | _____ |
| 4 | _____ | 150 | _____ | _____ | _____ |
| 5 | _____ | 185 | _____ | _____ | _____ |
| 6 | _____ | 225 | _____ | _____ | _____ |
| 7 | _____ | 270 | _____ | _____ | _____ |
| 8 | _____ | 325 | _____ | _____ | _____ |
| 9 | _____ | 390 | _____ | _____ | _____ |
| 10 | _____ | 465 | _____ | _____ | _____ |

**a.** *Graph total fixed cost, total variable cost, and total cost. Explain how the law of diminishing returns influences the shapes of the variable-cost and total-cost curves.*

**b.** *Graph AFC, AVC, ATC, and MC. Explain the derivation and shape of each of these four curves and their relationships to one another. Specifically, explain in nontechnical terms why the MC curve intersects both the AVC and ATC curves at their minimum points.*

**c.** *Explain how the location of each curve graphed in question 7b would be altered if (1) total fixed cost had been $100 rather than $60, and (2) total variable cost had been $10 less at each level of output.*

**11.** Indicate how each of the following would shift the **a** marginal-cost curve, **b** average-variable-cost curve, **c** average-fixed-cost curve, and **d** average-total-cost curve of a manufacturing firm. In each case specify the direction of the shift.

**(1)** A reduction in business property taxes
**(2)** An increase in the nominal wages of production workers
**(3)** A decrease in the price of electricity
**(4)** An increase in insurance rates on plant and equipment
**(5)** An increase in transportation costs

**12.** Suppose a firm has only three possible plant size options, represented by the ATC curves shown in the accompanying figure. What plant size will the firm choose in producing **a** 50, **b** 130, **c** 160, and **d** 250 units of output? Draw the firm's long-run average-cost curve on the diagram and describe this curve.

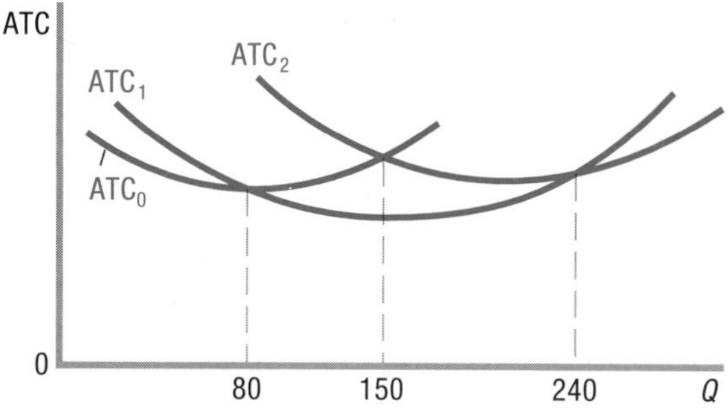


**13.** KEY QUESTION *Use the concepts of economies and diseconomies of scale to explain the shape of a firm's long-run ATC curve. What is the concept of minimum efficient scale? What bearing can the shape of the long-run ATC curve have on the structure of an industry?*

**14.** **(The Last Word)** What is a sunk cost? Why are such costs irrelevant in making decisions about future actions?

**15.** WEB-BASED QUESTION **Economies/ Diseconomies of Scale—Internal versus External** Search Yahoo www.yahoo.com/ (select Options, then choose "An exact phrase match" for "diseconomies of scale" or "economies of scale") and answer the following: What is the difference between internal and external economies or diseconomies of scale? What are the factors that cause internal diseconomies of scale? What are the factors that cause external economies and diseconomies of scale? Would these internal/external factors affect small and large firms the same way?

16. WEB-BASED QUESTION **Corporate Annual Reports—Identify Fixed and Variable Costs** Every year, major corporations publish their annual reports, which show how well they performed financially during the past year. Part of the annual report is the income statement, which shows revenues, costs, and profit. Use one of the major search engines—www.yahoo.com, www.infoseek.com, www.aol.com/netfind/, www.excite.com, or www.lycos.com—to locate the company of your choice. Review the company's income statement in its annual report and classify the nonrevenue items as either fixed or variable costs. Are all costs clearly identifiable as either fixed or variable? What item would be considered accounting profit? Would economic profit be higher or lower than this accounting profit? Explain. Note: Most annual reports on the Web are in Acrobat PDF file formats. Download the free PDF reader at www.adobe.com/prodindex/acrobat/readstep.htm.

## CHAPTER 10

# Pure Competition

CHAPTERS 7 TO 9 PROVIDED THE BASIC TOOLS OF analysis for understanding how product price and output are determined. But a firm's decisions concerning price and production will depend greatly on the character of the industry in which it is operating. There is no "average" or "typical" industry. At one extreme we can find a single producer that dominates the market; at the other extreme are industries in which thousands of firms each supply a minute fraction of total output. And between these extremes lies an unlimited variety of market structures.

We cannot possibly hope to examine each industry individually. Therefore, in the next three chapters we will focus on several basic *models* of market structures. Together, these models will help you understand, in a general way, how price and output are determined in the many product markets in our economy. They will also help you assess the extent of efficiency or inefficiency in those markets.

**IN THIS CHAPTER YOU WILL LEARN:**

- The four basic market structures and how they determine the degree of competition among firms.
- The four conditions required for perfectly competitive markets.
- The profit maximizing output for a firm in pure competition.
- The point at which a firm will shut down production in the short run.
- That profits and losses lead firms to enter or exit an industry.
- That in competitive markets firms attain both allocative and productive efficiency.

## The Big Picture

THE GOAL OF THE FIRM IS TO MAKE AS MUCH profit as possible. Scarcity *automatically* brings about competition among firms as each tries to do the best it can for itself.

But competing for scarce resources in the input (or factor) market and customers in the product market is hard work; the more firms compete, the harder each firm has to work, in some cases just to survive. For a firm, an ideal world is one in which it would have no competition and lots of profits. Alas, the probability that such an ideal situation could persist in a world pervaded by scarcity is small. There will always be competitors—or at least potential competitors—unless a firm is protected from competition, a topic we will take up in the next chapter.

With this chapter we begin to examine firm behaviour under different market structures. Note that we are now focusing on the product market—the market for goods and services; the factor market is analyzed in later chapters. The main goal of the firm never changes, but its behaviour will be influenced by the amount of competition (or lack of it) it has, and this is dictated by the market structure. There are almost limitless shades of competition possible. To get an idea of the amount of competition between firms, we study four models: the two extremes, pure competition and monopoly, and the much more prevalent forms found in the real world, monopolistic competition and oligopoly.

As you read this chapter, keep the following points in mind:

- **Key Concepts 3** and **6** are discussed.
- Pure competition is the ideal system against which to compare the other market structures. In this market structure, firms produce the most out of the available resources, and produce the goods and services most wanted by society.
- The pure competitive model stresses the underlying force in a market economy: competition. Never lose sight of the fact that in a market economy there are constant competitive, or potentially competitive, forces at work no matter what the market structure.
- Be sure to clearly distinguish between the firm and the industry.
- The dynamics of the pure competitive model will be easier to understand if you distinguish between the short and long run. Long-run losses mean firms leave the industry; short-run economic profits attract firms to the industry; in the long run, only normal profits are possible. ■

## FOUR MARKET MODELS

Economists group the many industries into four distinct market structures: pure competition, pure monopoly, monopolistic competition, and oligopoly. These four market models differ as to the number of firms in the industry, whether those firms produce a standardized product or try to differentiate their products from those of other firms, and how easy or difficult it is for firms to enter the industry.

The main characteristics of the four models are summarized in Table 10-1. Briefly, we can describe them as follows:

1. **Pure competition** requires a very large number of firms producing a standardized product (one identical to that of other producers, such as corn or cucumbers). New firms can enter the industry very easily.
2. **Pure monopoly** is a market structure in which one firm is the sole seller of a product or service (a local utility company). Entry of additional firms is blocked so that the one firm *is* the industry. Because the monopolist produces a unique product, it makes no effort to differentiate its product.
3. **Monopolistic competition** is characterized by a relatively large number of sellers producing differentiated products (clothing, furniture, books). There is much *nonprice competition*, a selling strategy in which one firm tries to distinguish its product or service from all competing products on the basis of attributes like design and workmanship (an approach called *product differentiation*). Entry to these monopolistically competitive industries is quite easy.

**TABLE 10-1 Characteristics of the four basic market models**

| | MARKET MODEL | | | |
|---|---|---|---|---|
| **Characteristic** | **Pure competition** | **Monopolistic competition** | **Oligopoly** | **Pure monopoly** |
| Number of firms | A very large number | Many | Few | One |
| Type of product | Standardized | Differentiated | Standardized or differentiated | Unique; no close substitutes |
| Control over price | None, price taker | Some, but within rather narrow limits | Limited by mutual interdependence; considerable with collusion | Considerable, price maker |
| Conditions of entry | Very easy, no obstacles | Relatively easy | Significant obstacles present | Blocked |
| Nonprice competition | None | Considerable emphasis on advertising, brand names, trademarks | Typically a great deal, particularly with product differentiation | Mostly public relations advertising ("goodwill") |
| Examples | Agriculture | Retail trade, dresses, shoes | Steel, automobiles, farm implements, many household appliances | Local utilities |

4. **Oligopoly** is a market structure with only a few sellers; this "fewness" means that each firm is affected by the decisions of rivals and must take those decisions into account in determining its own price and output.

These descriptions and the characteristics outlined in Table 10-1 will come into sharper focus as we examine each model in detail. In discussing these four market models, we will occasionally distinguish the characteristics of a purely competitive market from those of the other basic market structures—pure monopoly, monopolistic competition, and oligopoly. To facilitate such comparisons we will employ the generic term **imperfect competition** to designate all those market structures that deviate from the purely competitive model.

## PURE COMPETITION: CHARACTERISTICS AND OCCURRENCE

Let's expand our description of pure competition—the subject of this chapter:

1. **VERY LARGE NUMBERS** A basic feature of a purely competitive market is the presence of a large number of independently acting sellers, often offering their products in large national or international markets. Markets for farm commodities, the stock market, and the foreign exchange market are examples.
2. **STANDARDIZED PRODUCT** Purely competitive firms produce a standardized or homogenous product. If the price is the same, consumers will be indifferent about which seller to buy the product from. Buyers view the products of firms B, C, D, and E as perfect substitutes for firm A's product. Because purely competitive firms sell standardized products, they make no attempt to differentiate their products and do not engage in other forms of nonprice competition.
3. **"PRICE TAKERS"** In a purely competitive market *individual firms* exert no significant control over product price. This characteristic follows from the preceding two. Under pure competition each firm produces such a small fraction of total output that increasing or decreasing its output will not perceptibly

influence total supply or, therefore, product price.

Assume there are 10,000 competing firms, each currently producing 100 units of output. Total supply is therefore 1,000,000. Now suppose one of these firms cuts its output to 50 units. This reduces the total quantity supplied from 1,000,000 to 999,950—not nearly enough of a change to affect product price noticeably. In short, the individual competitive producer is a **price taker**: the competitive firm cannot change market price but can only adjust to it.

That means the individual competitive producer is at the mercy of the market; product price is a given fact over which the producer exerts no influence. The firm gets the same price per unit for a large output as it does for a small output. To ask a price higher than the going market price would be futile. Consumers will not buy from firm A at $2.05 when its 9,999 competitors are selling an identical product, and therefore a perfect substitute, at $2 per unit. Conversely, because firm A can sell as much as it chooses at $2 per unit, there is no reason for it to charge a lower price, say, $1.95, for to do so would shrink its profit.

4. **EASY ENTRY AND EXIT** New firms can freely enter and existing firms can freely leave purely competitive industries. No significant obstacles—legal, technological, financial, or other—prohibit new firms from forming and selling their output in any competitive market.

### Relevance of Pure Competition

Although pure competition is rare in practice, this market model is highly relevant.

1. A few industries more closely approximate pure competition than any other market structure. In particular, much can be learned about markets for agricultural produce (wheat, rice), foreign exchange (pesos, yen), and seafood (salmon, lobsters) by understanding the pure competition model.
2. Pure competition provides the simplest context in which to apply the revenue and cost concepts developed in previous chapters.
3. The operation of a purely competitive economy gives us a standard against which the efficiency of the real-world economy can be compared and evaluated.

Pure competition is thus a market model that will help us observe and evaluate what goes on in the real world.

## DEMAND AS SEEN BY A PURELY COMPETITIVE SELLER

In developing a tabular and graphical model of pure competition, let's first examine demand from a competitive seller's viewpoint and see how it affects revenue. Because each purely competitive firm offers a negligible fraction of total supply, it cannot influence the market price established by the forces of supply and demand. The purely competitive firm does not have a pricing strategy—it cannot *choose* the price for its product. Rather, it must accept the price determined by the market. The competitive seller is a *price taker*, not a *price maker*.

### Perfectly Elastic Demand

Stated technically, the demand curve of the individual competitive firm is *perfectly elastic*. Columns 1 and 2 in Table 10-2 show perfectly elas-

**TABLE 10-2 The demand and revenue schedules for an individual purely competitive firm**

| FIRM'S DEMAND OR AVERAGE-REVENUE SCHEDULE | | REVENUE DATA | |
|---|---|---|---|
| (1) Product price, $P$ (average revenue) | (2) Quantity demanded, $Q$ | (3) Total revenue, TR (1) × (2) | (4) Marginal revenue, MR |
| $131 | 0 | $ 0 | |
| | | | $131 |
| 131 | 1 | 131 | |
| | | | 131 |
| 131 | 2 | 262 | |
| | | | 131 |
| 131 | 3 | 393 | |
| | | | 131 |
| 131 | 4 | 524 | |
| | | | 131 |
| 131 | 5 | 655 | |
| | | | 131 |
| 131 | 6 | 786 | |
| | | | 131 |
| 131 | 7 | 917 | |
| | | | 131 |
| 131 | 8 | 1048 | |
| | | | 131 |
| 131 | 9 | 1179 | |
| | | | 131 |
| 131 | 10 | 1310 | |

tic demand where the market price is assumed to be $131. The firm cannot obtain a higher price by restricting its output; nor does it have to lower its price to increase its sales volume.

We are *not* saying that *market* demand is perfectly elastic in a competitive market. Instead, it graphs as a downsloping curve, as a glance ahead at Figure 10-7b reveals. In fact, the total-demand curves for most agricultural products are quite *in*elastic, even though agriculture is the most competitive industry in our economy. However, the demand schedule faced by the *individual firm* in a purely competitive industry is perfectly elastic.

The distinction comes about in this way: An entire industry—all firms producing a particular product—can affect price by changing industry output. For example, all firms, acting independently but simultaneously, can increase price by restricting supply. But not so for the individual firm. If a single producer increases or decreases output, and the outputs of all other competing firms are constant, the effect on total supply and market price is negligible. Demand as seen by the single firm is therefore perfectly elastic—that is, horizontal, as in Figures 10-1 and 10-7a. This is the fallacy of composition at work. What is true for the industry or group of firms (a downsloping, less than perfectly elastic demand curve) is *not* true for the individual, purely competitive firm (a perfectly elastic demand curve).

## Average, Total, and Marginal Revenue

The firm's demand schedule is also a revenue schedule. What appears in column 1, Table 10-2 as price per unit to the purchaser is also revenue per unit, or **average revenue**, to the seller. To say that all buyers must pay $131 per unit is to say that the revenue per unit, or average revenue, received by the seller is $131. Price and average revenue are the same thing seen from different points of view.

The **total revenue** for each sales level is calculated by multiplying price by the corresponding quantity the firm can sell. Multiply column 1 by column 2, and the result is column 3. In this case, total revenue increases by a constant amount, $131, for each additional unit of sales. Each unit sold adds exactly its constant price to total revenue.

When a firm is pondering a change in its output, it will consider how its revenue will *change* as

**FIGURE 10-1 Demand, marginal revenue, and total revenue of a purely competitive firm**

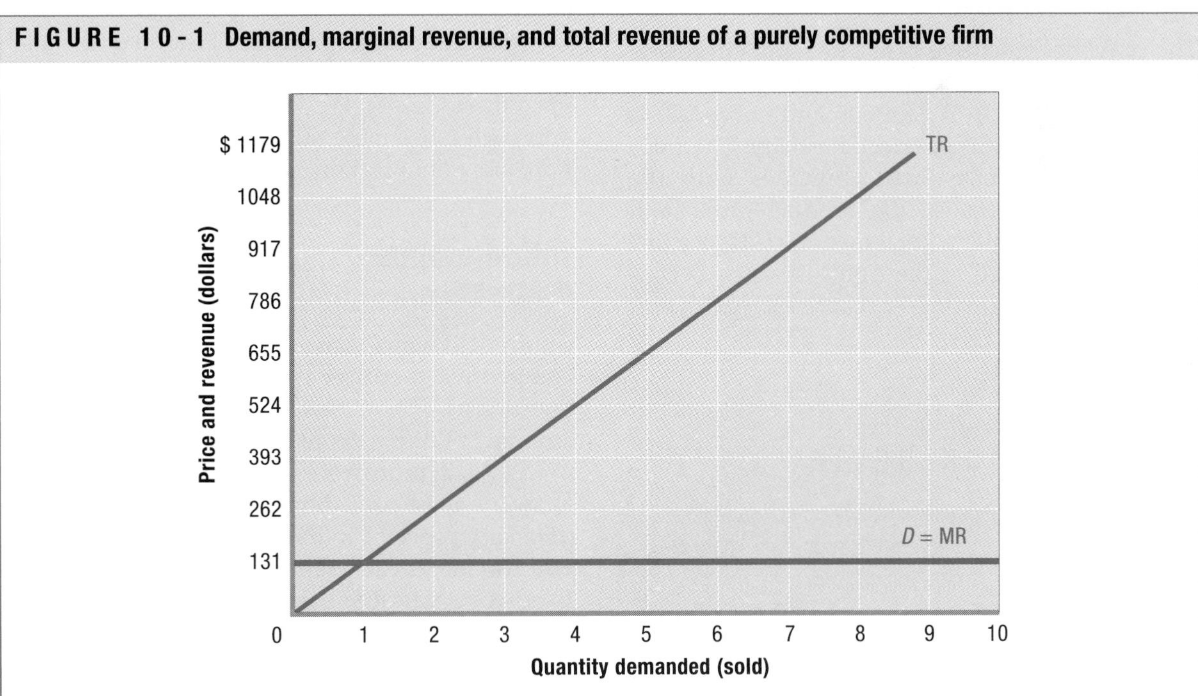


Because a purely competitive firm can sell additional units of output at the market price, its marginal-revenue curve (MR) coincides with its perfectly elastic demand curve (*D*). The firm's total-revenue curve (TR) is a straight upsloping line.

a result of that change in output. What will be the additional revenue from selling another unit of output? **Marginal revenue** is the change in total revenue, that is, the extra revenue, which results from selling 1 more unit of output. In column 3, Table 10-2, total revenue is zero when zero units are sold. The first unit of output sold increases total revenue from zero to $131. Marginal revenue—the increase in total revenue from the sale of the first unit of output—is therefore $131. The second unit sold increases total revenue from $131 to $262, so marginal revenue is again $131. Note in column 4 that marginal revenue is a constant $131, because total revenue increases by a constant amount with every extra unit sold.

Under purely competitive conditions, product price is constant to the individual firm. Added units of output therefore can be sold without lowering product price. Each additional unit of sales contributes exactly its price ($131) to total revenue, and marginal revenue ($131) is precisely this addition to total revenue. So marginal revenue *equals* price in pure competition; it is constant because additional units can be sold at the constant price. ***(Key Question 3)***

### Graphical Portrayal

The purely competitive firm's demand curve and total-revenue and marginal-revenue curves are shown in Figure 10-1. The demand curve (*D*) is horizontal, indicating perfect elasticity. The marginal-revenue curve (MR) coincides with the demand curve because the product price (and hence MR) is constant. Total revenue (TR) is a line that slopes upward to the right. Its slope is constant—it is a straight line—because each extra unit of sales increases TR by the same $131.

**10-1**

**QUICK REVIEW**

- In a purely competitive industry a large number of firms produce a standardized product and there are no significant barriers to entry.
- The demand seen by a competitive firm is perfectly elastic—horizontal on a graph—at the market price.
- Marginal and average revenues for a competitive firm coincide with the firm's demand curve; total revenue rises by the product price for each additional unit sold.

## PROFIT MAXIMIZATION IN THE SHORT RUN

Because the purely competitive firm is a price taker, it can maximize its economic profit (or minimize its loss) only by adjusting its *output*. And, in the short run, the firm has a fixed plant. Thus it can adjust its output only through changes in the amount of variable resources (materials, labour) it uses. The economic profit it seeks by adjusting its variable resources is the difference between *total revenue* and *total cost*. That fact gives us our direction. We will combine the revenue data of the previous section and the cost data of Chapter 9 to determine the profit-maximizing output of the competitive firm.

There are two ways to determine the level of output at which a competitive firm will realize maximum profit or loss. One way is to compare total revenue and total cost; the other is to compare marginal revenue and marginal cost. Both approaches apply not only to a purely competitive firm but also to firms operating in any of the other three basic market structures. To make sure you understand these approaches, we will apply both of them to output determination under pure competition. But since we want to *emphasize* the marginal approach, we will limit our graphical application of the total-revenue approach to a situation where the firm maximizes profits. We will then use the marginal approach to examine three cases: profit maximization, loss minimization, and shutdown.

### Total-Revenue–Total-Cost Approach: Profit-Maximization Case

Confronted with the market price of its product, the competitive producer is faced with three related questions: (1) Should we produce? (2) If so, in what amount? (3) What profit (or loss) will we realize?

Let's demonstrate how a pure competitor answers these questions, given particular cost data and a specific market price. The cost data we will use are already familiar to you. They are the fixed-cost, variable-cost, and total-cost data in Table 9-2, repeated in columns 1 to 4, Table 10-3. Assuming that the market price is $131, we can obtain the total revenue for each output level by multiplying output (total product) by price. These data are presented in column 5. Then in column 6 the profit or loss at each output level is found by subtracting total cost, TC (column 4), from total

**TABLE 10-3 The profit-maximizing output for a purely competitive firm: total-revenue–total-cost approach (prices: $131, $81, $71)**

| | | | | PRICE: $131 | |
|---|---|---|---|---|---|
| (1) Total product (output), Q | (2) Total fixed cost, TFC | (3) Total variable cost | (4) Total cost, TC | (5) Total revenue, TR | (6) Profit (+) or loss (–) |
| 0 | $100 | $ 0 | $ 100 | $ 0 | $–100 |
| 1 | 100 | 90 | 190 | 131 | –59 |
| 2 | 100 | 170 | 270 | 262 | –8 |
| 3 | 100 | 240 | 340 | 393 | +53 |
| 4 | 100 | 300 | 400 | 524 | +124 |
| 5 | 100 | 370 | 470 | 655 | +185 |
| 6 | 100 | 450 | 550 | 786 | +236 |
| 7 | 100 | 540 | 640 | 917 | +277 |
| 8 | 100 | 650 | 750 | 1048 | +298 |
| 9 | 100 | 780 | 880 | 1179 | +299 |
| 10 | 100 | 930 | 1030 | 1310 | +280 |

revenue, TR (column 5). Now we have all the data needed to answer the three questions.

Should the firm produce? Definitely. It can realize a profit by doing so. How much should it produce? Nine units, because column 6 tells us this is the output at which total economic profit will be at a maximum. What will the size of that profit be? It will be $299, the difference between total revenue ($1,179) and total cost ($880).

Figure 10-2a compares total revenue and total cost graphically for this *profit-maximizing case*. Total revenue is a straight line because under pure competition each additional unit adds the same amount—its price—to total revenue (Table 10-2). Total cost increases with output; more production requires more resources. But the rate of increase in total cost varies with the relative efficiency of the firm. Specifically, the cost data reflect Chapter 9's law of diminishing marginal returns. From zero to 4 units of output, total cost increases at a decreasing rate as the firm uses its fixed resources more efficiently. With additional output, total cost begins to rise by ever-increasing amounts because of the diminishing returns accompanying more intensive use of the plant.

Where the two curves in Figure 10-2a intersect (at roughly 2 units of output), total revenue and total cost are equal. All costs (including a normal profit) are covered by revenues, but there is no economic profit. For this reason economists call this output a **break-even point**: an output at which a firm makes only a *normal profit*. If we extended the data beyond 10 units of output, another break-even point would occur where total cost would catch up with total revenue somewhere between 13 and 14 units of output in Figure 10-2a. Any output within the two break-even points identified in the figure will produce an economic profit. The firm achieves maximum profit

**FIGURE 10-2 Total-revenue–total-cost approach to profit maximization for a purely competitive firm**

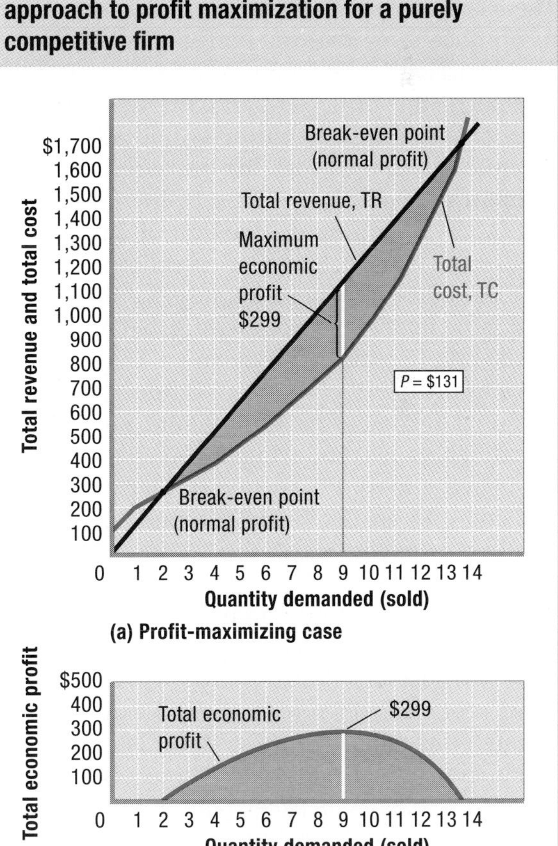


(a) The firm's profit is maximized at that output (9 units) where total revenue, TR, exceeds total cost, TC, by the maximum amount. (b) The vertical distance between TR and TC in (a) is plotted as a total-economic-profit curve. Maximum economic profit is $299 at 9 units of output.

where the vertical distance between the total-revenue and total-cost curves is greatest. For our particular data, this is at 9 units of output, where maximum profit is $299.

The profit-maximizing output is easily seen in Figure 10-2b, where we have graphed total profit for each level of output. Where the total-revenue and total-cost curves intersect in Figure 10-2a, economic profit is zero, as shown by the total-profit line in Figure 10-2b. Where the vertical distance between TR and TC is greatest in the upper graph, economic profit is at its peak ($299), as shown in the lower graph. This firm will choose to produce 9 units, since that output maximizes its profit.

## Marginal-Revenue–Marginal-Cost Approach

There is another way a firm can decide how much to produce—one that fits perfectly with Chapter 1's discussion of the economic perspective. In this approach, the firm compares the amounts that each *additional* unit of output would add to total revenue and to total cost. In other words, the firm compares the *marginal revenue* (MR) and *marginal cost* (MC) of each successive unit of output. Any unit whose marginal revenue exceeds its marginal cost should be produced because the firm would gain more in revenue from selling that unit than it would add to costs by producing it. Conversely, if the marginal cost of a unit of output exceeds its marginal revenue, the firm should not produce that unit because producing it would reduce profit (or increase loss). Production of that unit would add more to costs than to revenue; such a unit would not "pay its way."

**MR = MC Rule** In the initial stages of production, where output is relatively low, marginal revenue will usually (but not always) exceed marginal cost. It is therefore profitable to produce through this range of output. But at later stages of production, where output is relatively high, rising marginal costs will exceed marginal revenue. Obviously, a profit-maximizing firm will want to avoid output levels in this range. Separating these two production ranges is a unique point at which marginal revenue equals marginal cost. This point is the key to the output-determining rule: *In the short run, the firm will maximize profit or minimize loss by producing that output at which marginal revenue equals marginal cost.* We call this profit-maximizing guide the **MR = MC rule**. For most sets of MR and MC data, MR and MC will be precisely equal at a fractional level of output. In such instances the firm should produce the last complete unit of output whose MR exceeds its MC.

**Three Characteristics** There are three features of the MR = MC rule that you should know:

1. The rule assumes the firm will choose to produce rather than shut down. Shortly, we will note that marginal revenue must equal or exceed average variable cost or the firm will prefer to shut down rather than produce the MR = MC output.
2. The rule is an accurate guide to profit maximization for all firms—purely competitive, monopolistic, monopolistically competitive, or oligopolistic. The rule is *not* limited to the special case of pure competition.
3. The rule can be restated in a slightly different form when applied to a purely competitive firm. We have noted that the purely competitive firm can sell as much or as little as it chooses at the market price, but cannot manipulate the price itself. In technical terms the demand, or sales, schedule faced by a competitive seller is perfectly elastic at the going market price. The result is that product price and marginal revenue are equal; that is, each extra unit sold adds precisely its price to total revenue, as shown in Table 10-2 and Figure 10-1. Thus, under pure competition—and *only* under pure competition—we may substitute price for marginal revenue in the rule, so that it reads as follows: *To maximize profit or minimize loss, the competitive firm should produce at that point where price equals marginal cost* ($P$ = MC).

Now let's apply the MR = MC rule or, because we are considering pure competition, the $P$ = MC rule, first using the same price as in our total-revenue–total-cost approach to profit maximization. Then, by considering other prices, we can demonstrate two additional cases: loss minimization and shutdown. *It is crucial that you understand the MR = MC analysis that follows; it is used not only in the remainder of this chapter but in the two chapters that follow.*

**Profit-Maximizing Case** The first five columns in Table 10-4 reproduce the AFC, AVC, ATC, and MC data derived for our product in Table 10-2. It

**TABLE 10-4 The profit-maximizing output for a purely competitive firm: marginal-revenue-equals-marginal-cost approach (price = $131)**

| (1) Total product (output) | (2) Average fixed cost, AFC | (3) Average variable cost, AVC | (4) Average total cost, ATC | (5) Marginal cost, MC | (6) Price = marginal revenue, MR | (7) Total economic profit (+) or loss (–) |
|---|---|---|---|---|---|---|
| 0 | | | | | | $–100 |
| 1 | $100.00 | $90.00 | $190.00 | $ 90 | $131 | –59 |
| 2 | 50.00 | 85.00 | 135.00 | 80 | 131 | –8 |
| 3 | 33.33 | 80.00 | 113.33 | 70 | 131 | +53 |
| 4 | 25.00 | 75.00 | 100.00 | 60 | 131 | +124 |
| 5 | 20.00 | 74.00 | 94.00 | 70 | 131 | +185 |
| 6 | 16.67 | 75.00 | 91.67 | 80 | 131 | +236 |
| 7 | 14.29 | 77.14 | 91.43 | 90 | 131 | +277 |
| 8 | 12.50 | 81.25 | 93.75 | 110 | 131 | +298 |
| 9 | 11.11 | 86.67 | 97.78 | 130 | 131 | +299 |
| 10 | 10.00 | 93.00 | 103.00 | 150 | 131 | +280 |

is the marginal-cost data of column 5 that we will compare with price (equals marginal revenue) for each unit of output. Suppose first that the market price, and therefore marginal revenue, is $131, as shown in column 6.

What is the profit-maximizing output? Every unit of output up to and including the ninth unit represents a greater marginal revenue than marginal cost of output. Each of the first 9 units therefore adds to the firm's profit and should be produced. The tenth unit, however, should not be produced. It would add more to cost ($150) than to revenue ($131).

**Profit Calculations** The economic profit realized by producing 9 units can be calculated from the average-total-cost data. Multiplying price ($131) by output (9), we find that total revenue is $1,179. Multiplying average total cost ($97.78) by output (9) gives us total cost of $880.[1] The difference of $299 (= $1,179 – $880) is the economic profit.

Another way to calculate the economic profit is to determine the profit *per unit* by subtracting the average total cost ($97.78) from the product price ($131) and multiplying the difference (a per-unit profit of $33.22) by output (9). Take some time now to verify the figures in column 7 in Table 10-4. You will find that any output other than that adhering to the MR = MC rule will mean either losses or profits below $299.

**Graphical Portrayal** *Figure 10-3 (Key Graph)* shows price (= MR) and marginal cost graphically. They are equal at the profit-maximizing output of 9 units. There the per-unit economic profit is $P – A$, where $P$ is the market price and $A$ is the average total cost for an output of 9 units. The total economic profit is $9 \times (P – A)$, shown by the grey rectangular area.

Note that the firm wants to maximize its total profit, not its per-unit profit. Per-unit profit is greatest at 7 units of output, where price exceeds average total cost by $39.57 (= $131 – $91.43). But by producing only 7 units, the firm would be forgoing the production of 2 additional units of output that would clearly contribute to total profit. The firm is happy to accept lower per-unit profits for additional units of output because they nonetheless add to total profit.

[1] Most of the unit-cost data are rounded figures. Therefore, economic profits calculated from them will typically vary by a few cents from the profits determined in the total-revenue–total-cost approach. We here ignore the few-cents differentials to make our answers consistent with the results of the total-revenue–total-cost approach.

## KEY GRAPH

**FIGURE 10-3 The short-run profit-maximizing position of a purely competitive firm**

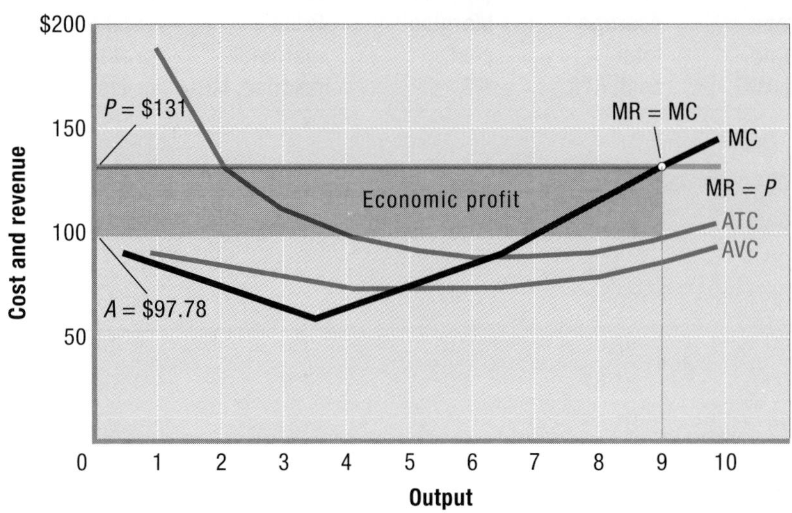


The MR = MC output allows the purely competitive firm to maximize profits or minimize losses. In this case MR (= *P* in pure competition) and MC are equal at an output *Q* of 9 units. There *P* exceeds the average total cost *A* = $97.78, so the firm realizes an economic profit of *P* – *A* per unit. The total economic profit is represented by the grey rectangle and is 9 × (*P* – *A*).

### 10-3 QUICK QUIZ

1. Curve MR is horizontal because:
   **(a)** product price falls as output increases.
   **(b)** the law of diminishing marginal utility is at work.
   **(c)** the *market* demand for this product is perfectly elastic.
   **(d)** this firm is a "price taker."

2. At a price of $131 and 7 units of output:
   **(a)** MR exceeds MC, and the firm should expand its output.
   **(b)** total revenue is less than total cost.
   **(c)** AVC exceeds ATC.
   **(d)** the firm would earn only a normal profit.

3. In maximizing profits at 9 units of output, this firm is adhering to which of the following decision rules?
   **(a)** Produce where MR exceeds MC by the greatest amount.
   **(b)** Produce where *P* exceeds ATC by the greatest amount.
   **(c)** Produce where total revenue exceeds total cost by the greatest amount.
   **(d)** Produce where average fixed costs are zero.

4. Suppose price declined from $131 to $100. This firm's:
   **(a)** marginal-cost curve would shift downward.
   **(b)** economic profit would fall to zero.
   **(c)** profit-maximizing output would decline.
   **(d)** total cost would fall by more than its total revenue.

**Answers:** 1. (d); 2. (a); 3. (c); 4. (c).

**Loss-Minimizing Case** Now let's assume that the market price is $81 rather than $131. Should the firm still produce? If so, how much? And what will be the resulting profit or loss? The answers, respectively, are "Yes," "Six units," and "A loss of $64."

The first five columns in Table 10-5 are the same as those in Table 10-4. Column 6 shows the new price (equal to MR), $81. Comparing columns 5 and 6, we find that the first unit of output adds $90 to total cost but only $81 to total revenue. One might conclude: "Don't produce—close down!" But this would be hasty. Remember that in the very early stages of production, marginal product is low, making marginal cost unusually high. The price–marginal-cost relationship improves with increased production. For the next 5 units—units 2 through 6—price exceeds marginal cost. Each of these 5 units adds more to revenue than to cost. Column 7 shows that each of these units decreases the total loss. They more than compensate for the "loss" taken on the first unit. Beyond 6 units, however, MC exceeds MR (= *P*). The firm should therefore produce 6 units. In general, the profit-seeking producer should always compare marginal revenue (or price under pure competition) with the *rising* portion of the marginal-cost schedule or curve.

**TABLE 10-5 The loss-minimizing outputs for a purely competitive firm: marginal-revenue-equals-marginal-cost approach (prices = $81 and $71)**

| (1) Total product (output) | (2) Average fixed cost, AFC | (3) Average variable cost, AVC | (4) Average total cost, ATC | (5) Marginal cost, MC | (6) $81 price = marginal revenue, MR | (7) Profit (+) or loss (–), $81 price | (8) $71 price = marginal revenue, MR | (9) Profit (+) or loss (–), $71 price |
|---|---|---|---|---|---|---|---|---|
| 0 | | | | | | $–100 | | $–100 |
| 1 | $100.00 | $90.00 | $190.00 | $ 90 | $81 | –109 | $71 | –119 |
| 2 | 50.00 | 85.00 | 135.00 | 80 | 81 | –108 | 71 | –128 |
| 3 | 33.33 | 80.00 | 113.33 | 70 | 81 | – 97 | 71 | –127 |
| 4 | 25.00 | 75.00 | 100.00 | 60 | 81 | – 76 | 71 | –116 |
| 5 | 20.00 | 74.00 | 94.00 | 70 | 81 | – 65 | 71 | –115 |
| 6 | 16.67 | 75.00 | 91.67 | 80 | 81 | – 64 | 71 | –124 |
| 7 | 14.29 | 77.14 | 91.43 | 90 | 81 | – 73 | 71 | –143 |
| 8 | 12.50 | 81.25 | 93.75 | 110 | 81 | –102 | 71 | –182 |
| 9 | 11.11 | 86.67 | 97.78 | 130 | 81 | –151 | 71 | –241 |
| 10 | 10.00 | 93.00 | 103.00 | 150 | 81 | –220 | 71 | –320 |

**Loss Determination** Will production be profitable? No, because at 6 units of output the average total cost of $91.67 exceeds the price of $81 by $10.67 per unit. If we multiply that by the 6 units of output, we find the firm's total loss is $64. Alternatively, comparing the total revenue of $486 (= 6 × $81) with the total cost of $550 (= 6 × $91.67), we see again that the firm's loss is $64.

Then why produce? Because this loss is less than the firm's $100 of fixed costs—the $100 loss the firm would incur in the short run by closing down. The firm receives enough revenue per unit ($81) to cover its average variable costs of $75 and also provide $6 per unit, or a total of $36, to apply against fixed costs. Therefore, the firm's loss is only $64 (= $100 – $36), rather than $100.

**Graphical Portrayal** This loss-minimizing case is shown graphically in Figure 10-4. Wherever price $P$ exceeds average variable cost AVC, the firm can pay part, but not all, of its fixed costs by producing. The loss is minimized by producing the output at which MC = MR (here, 6 units). At that output, each unit contributes $P - V$ to covering fixed cost, where $V$ is the AVC at 6 units of output. The per-unit loss is $A - P$ = $10.67, and the total loss is $6 \times (A - P)$, or $64, as shown by the white area.

**Shutdown Case** Suppose now that the market price is only $71. Should the firm produce? No, because at every output the firm's average variable cost is greater than the price (compare columns 3 and 8 in Table 10-5). The smallest loss it can incur by producing is greater than the $100 fixed cost it will lose by shutting down (as shown by column 9). The best action is to shut down.

This shutdown situation can be seen in Figure 10-5. Price comes closest to covering average variable costs at the MR (= $P$) = MC output of 5 units. But even here, price or revenue per unit would fall short of average variable cost by $3 (= $74 – $71). By producing at the MR (= $P$) = MC output, the firm would lose its $100 worth of fixed cost *plus* $15 ($3 of variable cost on each of the 5 units), for a total loss of $115. This compares unfavourably with the $100 fixed-cost loss the firm would incur by shutting down and producing no output. Hence, it will pay the firm to shut down rather than produce at a $71 price—or at any price less than the minimum average variable cost of $74.

The shutdown case obligates us to modify our MR (= $P$) = MC rule. *A competitive firm will maximize profit or minimize losses in the short run by producing that output at which* MR (= $P$) = MC, *provided that market price exceeds minimum average variable cost.*

**FIGURE 10-4 The short-run loss-minimizing position of a purely competitive firm**

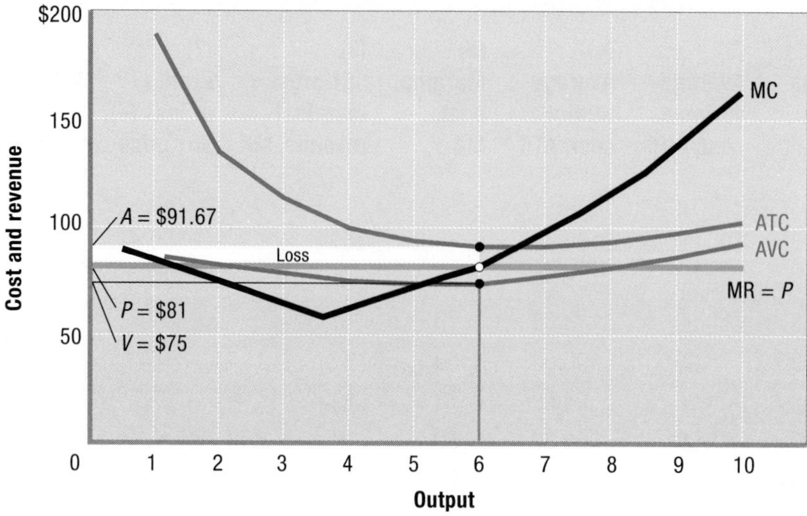


If price $P$ exceeds the minimum AVC (here \$74 at $Q = 5$) but is less than ATC, the MR = MC output (here 6 units) will permit the firm to minimize its losses. In this instance the loss is $A - P$ per unit, where $A$ is the average total cost at 6 units of output. The total loss is shown by the white area and is equal to $6 \times (A - P)$.

## MARGINAL COST AND SHORT-RUN SUPPLY

You will recognize that in the preceding section we simply selected three different prices and asked what quantity the profit-seeking competitive firm, faced with certain costs, would choose to offer in the market at each of these prices. This information—product prices and corresponding quantities supplied—constitutes the supply schedule for the competitive firm.

**FIGURE 10-5 The short-run shutdown position of a purely competitive firm**

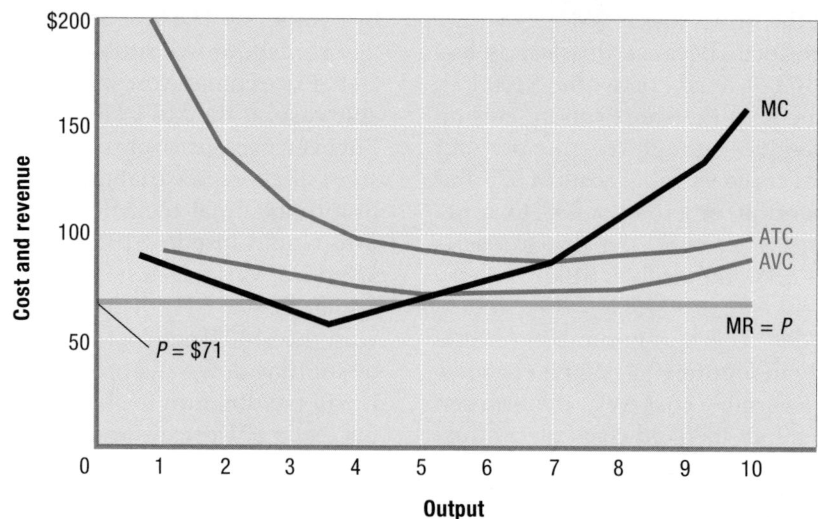


If price $P$ falls below the minimum AVC (here \$74 at $Q = 5$), the competitive firm will minimize its losses in the short run by shutting down. There is no level of output at which the firm can produce and realize a loss smaller than its total fixed cost.

Table 10-6 summarizes the supply-schedule data for those three prices—$131, $81, and $71—and four others. This table confirms the direct relationship between product price and quantity supplied that we identified in Chapter 4. Note first that the firm will not produce at price $61 or $71, because both are less than the $74 minimum AVC. Then note that quantity supplied increases as price increases. Observe finally that economic profit is higher at higher prices.

## Generalized Depiction

*Figure 10-6 (Key Graph)* generalizes the MR = MC rule and the relationship between short-run production costs and the firm's supply behaviour. The ATC, AVC, and MC curves are shown, along with several marginal-revenue lines drawn at possible market prices. Let's observe quantity supplied at each of these prices:

1. Price $P_0$ is below the firm's minimum average variable cost, so at this price the firm won't operate at all. Quantity supplied will be zero, as it will be at all other prices below $P_1$.
2. Price $P_1$ is just equal to the minimum average variable cost. The firm will supply $Q_1$ units of output (where $MR_1$ = MC) and just cover its total variable cost. Its loss will equal its total fixed cost. (Actually, the firm would be indifferent as to shutting down or supplying $Q_1$ units of output, but we assume it produces.)
3. At price $P_2$ the firm will supply $Q_2$ units of output to minimize its short-run losses. At any other price between $P_1$ and $P_3$ the firm will minimize its losses by producing and supplying the quantity at which MR (= $P$) = MC.

**TABLE 10-6 The supply schedule of a competitive firm confronted with the cost data in Table 10-4**

| Price | Quantity supplied | Maximum profit (+) or minimum loss (–) |
|---|---|---|
| $151 | 10 | $+480 |
| 131 | 9 | +299 |
| 111 | 8 | +138 |
| 91 | 7 | –3 |
| 81 | 6 | –64 |
| 71 | 0 | –100 |
| 61 | 0 | –100 |

4. The firm will break even at price $P_3$. There it will supply $Q_3$ units of output (where $MR_3$ = MC), earning a normal profit but not an economic profit. Total revenue will cover total cost, including a normal profit, because the revenue per unit ($MR_3 = P_3$) and the total cost per unit (ATC) are the same.
5. At price $P_4$ the firm will realize an economic profit by producing and supplying $Q_4$ units of output. In fact, at *any* price above $P_3$ the firm will obtain economic profit by producing to the point where MR (= $P$) = MC.

Note that each of the MR (= $P$) = MC intersection points labelled *b*, *c*, *d* and *e* in Figure 10-6 indicates a possible product price (on the vertical axis) and the corresponding quantity that the firm would supply at that price (on the horizontal axis). Thus, points such as these are on the upsloping supply curve of the competitive firm. Note too that quantity supplied would be zero at any price below the minimum average variable cost (AVC). *We can conclude that the portion of the firm's marginal-cost curve lying above its average-variable-cost curve is its* **short-run supply curve**. In Figure 10-6, the solid segment of the marginal-cost curve MC *is* this firm's short-run supply curve. It tells us the amount of output the firm will supply at each price in a series of prices.

## Diminishing Returns, Production Costs, and Product Supply

We have now identified the links between *the law of diminishing returns* (Chapter 9), *production costs*, and *product supply* in the short run. Because of the law of diminishing returns, marginal cost eventually rises as more units of output are produced. And because marginal cost rises with output, a purely competitive firm must get successively higher prices to entice it to produce additional units of output.

Viewed alternatively, higher product prices and marginal revenue encourage a purely competitive firm to expand output. As its output increases, its marginal cost of output rises as a result of the law of diminishing returns. At some now greater output, this higher MC equals the new product price and MR. Profit once again is maximized, but now at a greater total amount. Quantity supplied has increased in direct response to an increase in product price and the desire to maximize profit.

## KEY GRAPH

**FIGURE 10-6 The $P = MC$ rule and the competitive firm's short-run supply curve**

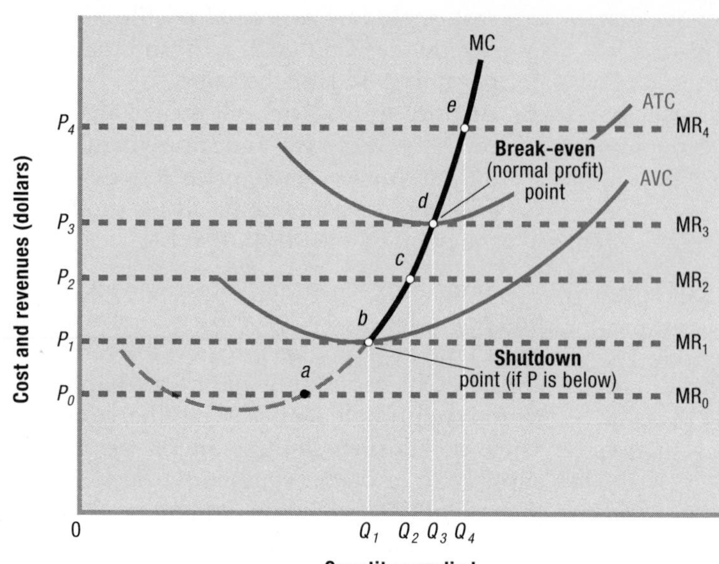


Application of the $P = MC$ rule, as modified by the shutdown case, reveals that the (solid) segment of the firm's MC curve that lies above AVC is the firm's short-run supply curve. More specifically, at price $P_0$, $P = MC$ at point *a*, but the firm will produce no output because $P_0$ is less than minimum AVC. At price $P_1$ the firm will operate at point *b*, where it produces $Q_1$ units and incurs a loss equal to its total fixed cost. With the price at $P_3$ the firm operates at point *d*. In this case the firm earns a normal profit because at output $Q_3$ price equals ATC. At price $P_3$ the firm operates at point *e* and maximizes its economic profit by producing $Q_4$ units.

### 10-6 QUICK QUIZ

1. Which of the following might increase product price from $P_2$ to $P_4$?
   **(a)** An improvement of production technology
   **(b)** A decline in the price of a substitute good
   **(c)** An increase in the price of a complementary good
   **(d)** Rising incomes if the product is a normal good
2. An increase of price from $P_2$ to $P_4$ would:
   **(a)** shift this firm's MC curve to the right.
   **(b)** mean that $MR_4$ exceeds MC at $Q_2$ units, inducing the firm to expand output to $Q_4$.
   **(c)** decrease this firm's average variable costs.
   **(d)** enable this firm to obtain a normal, but not an economic, profit.
3. At $P_3$:
   **(a)** this firm has no economic profit.
   **(b)** this firm will earn only a normal profit and thus will shut down.
   **(c)** $MR_3$ will be less than MC at the profit-maximizing output.
   **(d)** the profit-maximizing output will be $Q_4$.
4. Suppose $P_3$ is \$10, $P_4$ is \$15, $Q_3$ is 8 units, and $Q_4$ is 10 units. This firm's:
   **(a)** supply curve is elastic over the $Q_3 - Q_4$ range of output.
   **(b)** supply curve is inelastic over the $Q_3 - Q_4$ range of output.
   **(c)** total revenue will decline if price goes up from $P_3$ to $P_4$.
   **(d)** marginal-cost curve will shift downward if price falls from $P_4$ to $P_3$.

**Answers:** 1. (d); 2. (b); 3. (a); 4. (b).

## Supply Curve Shifts

In Chapter 9 we saw that changes in such factors as the prices of variable inputs or in technology will shift the marginal-cost or short-run supply curve to a new location. All else equal, for example, a wage increase would shift the supply curve in Figure 10-6 to the left, indicating a decrease in supply. Similarly, technological progress that increases the productivity of labour would shift the marginal-cost or supply curve to the right. This represents an increase in supply.

## Firm and Industry: Equilibrium Price

In the preceding section we developed the competitive firm's short-run supply curve by applying the MR (= *P*) = MC rule. We now determine which

**TABLE 10-7 Firm and market supply and market demand**

| (1) Quantity supplied, single firm | (2) Total quantity supplied, 1,000 firms | (3) Product price | (4) Total quantity demanded |
|---|---|---|---|
| 10 | 10,000 | $151 | 4,000 |
| 9 | 9,000 | 131 | 6,000 |
| 8 | 8,000 | 111 | 8,000 |
| 7 | 7,000 | 91 | 9,000 |
| 6 | 6,000 | 81 | 11,000 |
| 0 | 0 | 71 | 13,000 |
| 0 | 0 | 61 | 16,000 |

of the various possible prices will actually be the market equilibrium price.

From Chapter 4 we know that in a purely competitive market, equilibrium price is determined by *total*, or market, supply and total demand. To derive total supply, the supply schedules or curves of the individual competitive sellers must be summed. Columns 1 and 3 in Table 10-7 repeat the supply schedule for the individual competitive firm, as derived in Table 10-6. We now assume that there are 1,000 competitive firms in this industry, all having the same total and unit costs as the single firm we discussed. This lets us calculate the market-supply schedule (columns 2 and 3) by multiplying the quantity-supplied figures of the single firm (column 1) by 1,000.

**Market Price and Profits** To determine the equilibrium price and output, these total-supply data must be compared with total-demand data. Let's assume total demand is as shown in columns 3 and 4 in Table 10-7. By comparing the total quantity supplied and total quantity demanded at the seven possible prices, we determine that the equilibrium price is $111 and the equilibrium quantity 8,000 units for the industry—8 units for each of the 1,000 identical firms.

Will these conditions of market supply and demand make this a profitable or an unprofitable industry? Multiplying produce price ($111) by output (8 units), we find the total revenue of each firm is $888. The total cost is $750, found by looking at column 4 in Table 10-3. The $138 difference is the economic profit of each firm. For the industry, total economic profit is $138,000. This, then, *is* a profitable industry.

Another way of calculating economic profit is to determine per-unit profit by subtracting average total cost ($93.75) from product price ($111) and multiplying the difference (per-unit profit of $17.25) by the firm's equilibrium level of output (8). Again we obtain an economic profit of $138 per firm and $138,000 for the industry.

**Graphical Portrayal** Figure 10-7 shows this analysis graphically. The individual supply curves of each of the 1,000 identical firms—one of which is shown as $s$ = MC in Figure 10-7a—are summed horizontally to get the total-supply curve $S$ = MC of Figure 10-7b. With total-demand curve $D$, it yields the equilibrium price $111 and equilibrium quantity (for the industry) 8,000 units. This equilibrium price is given and unalterable to the individual firm; that is, each firm's demand curve is perfectly elastic at the equilibrium price, as indicated by $d$ in Figure 10-7a. Because the individual firm is a "price taker," the marginal-revenue curve coincides with the firm's demand curve $d$. This $111 price exceeds the average total cost at the firm's equilibrium MR = MC output of 8 units, so the firm earns an economic profit represented by the grey area in Figure 10-7a.

Assuming no changes in costs or market demand, these diagrams reveal a genuine equilibrium in the short run. There are no shortages or surpluses in the market to cause price or total quantity to change. Nor can any of the firms in the industry increase its profit by altering its output. Note, too, that higher unit and marginal costs, on the one hand, or weaker market demand, on the other, could change the situation so that Figure 10-7a resembles Figure 10-4 or Figure 10-5. You are urged to sketch, in Figure 10-7a and b, how higher costs or decreased demand could produce short-run losses.

**Firm versus Industry** Figure 10-7 underscores a point made earlier: Product price is a given fact to the *individual* competitive firm, but the supply plans of all competitive producers *as a group* are a basic determinant of product price. If we recall the fallacy of composition, we find there is no inconsistency here. Though one firm, supplying a negligible fraction of total supply, cannot affect price, the sum of the supply curves of all the firms in the

**FIGURE 10-7 Short-run competitive equilibrium for (a) a representative firm and (b) the industy**

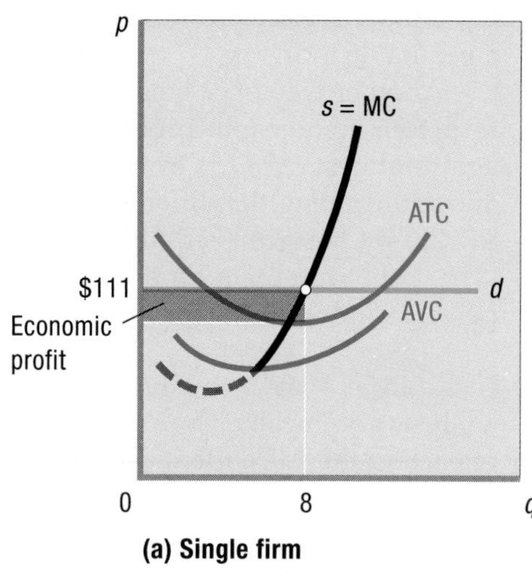


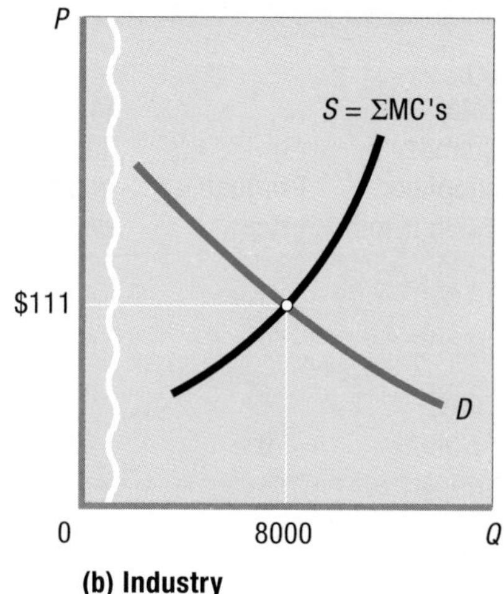


The horizontal sum of the 1,000 firms' individual supply curves (*S*) determines the industry supply curve (*S*). Given industry demand (*D*), the short-run equilibrium price and output for the industry are $111 and 8,000 units. Taking the equilibrium price as given datum, the individual firm establishes its profit-maximizing output at 8 units and, in this case, realizes the economic profit shown by the shaded area.

industry constitutes the industry supply curve, and this curve does have an important bearing on price. ***(Key Question 4)***

**10-2**

**QUICK REVIEW**

- Profit is maximized, or loss minimized, at that output at which marginal revenue (or price in pure competition) equals marginal cost.
- If the market price is below the minimum average variable cost, the firm will minimize its losses by shutting down.
- The segment of the firm's marginal-cost curve that lies above the average-variable-cost curve is its short-run supply curve.
- Table 10-8 summarizes the MR = MC approach to determining the competitive firm's profit-maximizing output. It also shows the equivalent analysis in terms of total revenue and total cost.
- Under competition, equilibrium price is a given to the individual firm and simultaneously is the result of the production (supply) decisions of all firms as a group.

## PROFIT MAXIMIZATION IN THE LONG RUN

In the short run there are a specific number of firms in an industry, each with a fixed, unalterable plant. Firms may shut down in the sense that they can

**TABLE 10-8 Short-run output determination in pure competition**

| Question | Answer |
|---|---|
| Should this firm produce? | Yes, if price is equal to, or greater than, minimum average variable cost. This means that the firm is profitable or that its losses are less than its fixed cost. |
| What quantity should this firm produce? | Produce where MR (= *P*) = MC; there, profit is maximized (TR exceeds TC by a maximum amount) or loss is minimized. |
| Will production result in economic profit? | Yes, if price exceeds average total cost (TR will exceed TC). No, if average total cost exceeds price (TC will exceed TR). |

produce zero units of output in the short run, but they do not have sufficient time to liquidate their assets and go out of business. By contrast, in the long run firms have sufficient time either to expand or to contract their plant capacities. More important, the number of firms in the industry may either increase or decrease as new firms enter or existing firms leave. We now examine how these long-run adjustments modify our conclusions concerning short-run output and price determination.

## Assumptions

We make three simplifying assumptions, none of which affects our conclusions:

1. **ENTRY AND EXIT ONLY** The only long-run adjustment is the entry or exit of firms. Moreover, we ignore all short-run adjustments to concentrate on the effects of the long-run adjustments.
2. **IDENTICAL COSTS** All firms in the industry have identical cost curves. This assumption lets us discuss an "average," or "representative," firm knowing that all other firms in the industry are similarly affected by any long-run adjustments that occur.
3. **CONSTANT-COST INDUSTRY** The industry under discussion is a constant-cost industry. This means that the entry and exit of firms does *not* affect resource prices or, therefore, the locations of the average-total-cost curves of individual firms.

## Goal

The basic conclusion we seek to explain is this: *After all long-run adjustments are completed, product price will be exactly equal to, and production will occur at, each firm's minimum average total cost.*

This conclusion follows from two basic facts: (1) Firms seek profits and shun losses, and (2) under pure competition, firms are free to enter and leave industries. If market price initially exceeds average total costs, the resulting economic profits will attract new firms to the industry. But this industry expansion will increase supply until price is brought back down to equality with minimum average total cost. Conversely, if price is initially less than average total cost, resulting losses will cause firms to leave the industry. As they leave, total supply will decline, bringing the price back up to equality with minimum average total cost.

## Long-Run Equilibrium

Consider the average firm in a purely competitive industry that is initially in long-run equilibrium. This firm is represented in Figure 10-8a,

**FIGURE 10-8 Temporary profits and the re-establishment of long-run equilibrium in (a) a representative firm and (b) the industry**

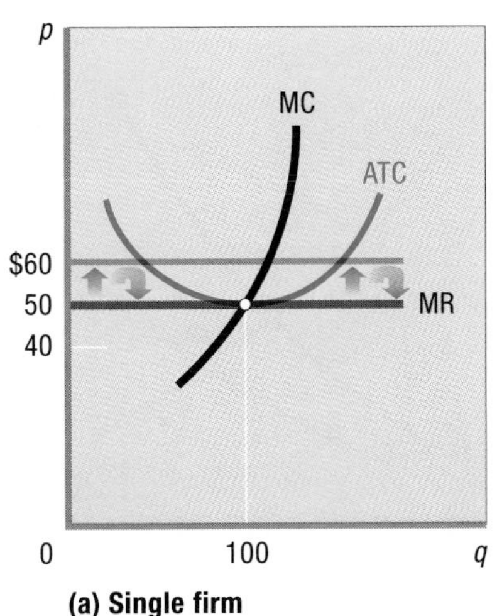


(a) Single firm

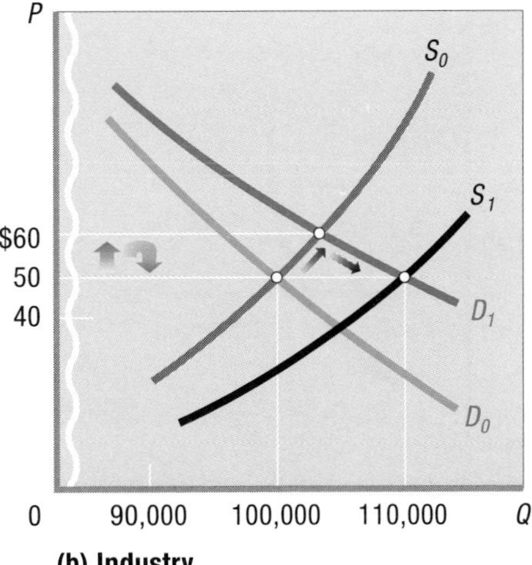


(b) Industry

A favourable shift in demand ($D_0$ to $D_1$) will upset the original industry equilibrium and cause economic profits. But those profits will cause new firms to enter the industry, increasing supply ($S_0$ to $S_1$) and lowering product price until economic profits are once again zero.

where MR = MC and price and minimum average total cost are equal at $50. Economic profit here is zero; the industry is in equilibrium or "at rest" because there is no tendency for firms to enter or to leave. The existing firms are earning normal profits, which, recall, are included in their cost curves. The $50 market price is determined in Figure 10-8b by market or industry demand $D_0$ and supply $S_0$. ($S_0$ is a short-run supply curve; we will develop the long-run industry supply curve in our discussion.)

As shown on the quantity axes of the two graphs, equilibrium output in the industry is 100,000 while equilibrium output for the single firm is 100. If all firms in the industry are identical, there must be 1,000 firms (= 100,000/100).

**Entry Eliminates Economic Profits** Let's upset the long-run equilibrium in Figure 10-8 and see what happens. Suppose a change in consumer tastes increases product demand from $D_0$ to $D_1$. Price will rise to $60, as determined at the intersection of $D_1$ and $S_0$, and the firm's marginal-revenue curve will shift upward to $60. This $60 price exceeds the firm's average total cost of $50 at output 100, creating an economic profit of $10 per unit. This economic profit will lure new firms into the industry. Some entrants will be newly created firms; others will shift from less prosperous industries.

As firms enter, the market supply of the product increases, pushing the product price below $60. Economic profits persist, and entry continues until short-run supply increases to $S_1$. Market price falls to $50, as does marginal revenue for the firm. Price and minimum average total cost are again equal at $50. The economic profits caused by the boost in demand have been eliminated, and as a result, the previous incentive for more firms to enter the industry has disappeared. Long-run equilibrium has been restored.

**Exit Eliminates Losses** Now let's consider a shift in the opposite direction. We begin in Figure 10-9a with curves $S_0$ and $D_0$ setting the same initial long-run equilibrium situation as in our previous analysis, including the $50 price.

Suppose consumer demand declines from $D_0$ to $D_2$. This forces the market price and marginal revenued down to $40, making production unprofitable at the minimum ATC of $50. In time the resulting losses will induce some firms to leave the industry. Their owners will seek a normal profit elsewhere rather than accept the below-normal profits (loss) now confronting them. And as capital equipment wears out, some firms will simply go out of business. As this exodus of firms proceeds, however, industry supply decreases, push-

**FIGURE 10-9 Temporary losses and the re-establishment of long-run equilibrium in (a) a representative firm and (b) the industry**

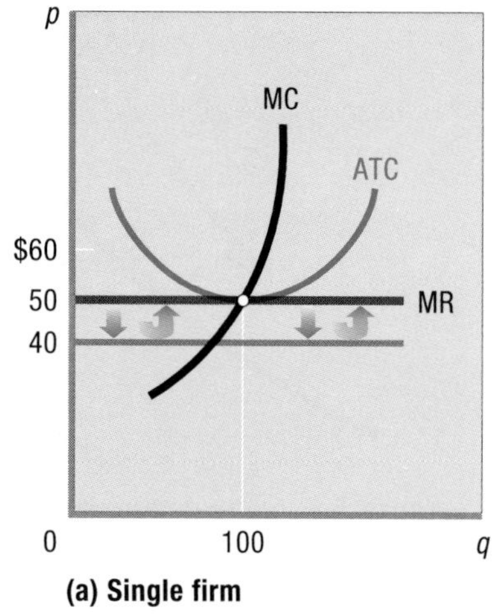

(a) Single firm

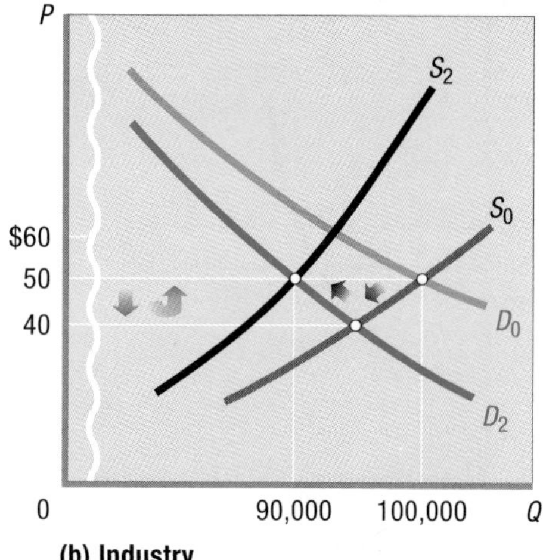

(b) Industry

An unfavourable shift in demand ($D_0$ to $D_2$) will upset the original industry equilibrium and cause losses. But those losses will cause firms to leave the industry, decreasing supply ($S_0$ to $S_2$) and increasing product price until all losses have disappeared.

ing the price up from $40 towards $50. Losses continue and more firms leave the industry until the supply curve shifts to $S_2$. Once this happens, price is again $50, just equal to the minimum average total cost. Losses have been eliminated and long-run equilibrium is restored.

Observe in Figure 10-9a and b that total quantity supplied is now 90,000 units and each firm is producing 100 units. The industry is populated by only 900 firms rather than the original 1,000; losses have forced 100 firms out of the industry.

You may have noted that we have sidestepped the question of which firms will leave the industry when losses occur by assuming all firms have identical cost curves. In the "real world" entrepreneurial talents differ. Even if resource prices and technology are the same for all firms, inferior entrepreneurs tend to incur higher costs and therefore are the first to leave an industry when demand declines. Similarly, firms with less productive labour forces will be higher-cost producers and likely candidates to quit an industry when demand decreases.

We have now reached an intermediate goal: Our analysis verifies that competition, reflected in the entry and exit of firms, eliminates economic profits or losses by adjusting price to equal minimum long-run average total cost. In addition, this competition forces firms to select output levels at which average total cost is minimized.

## Long-Run Supply for a Constant-Cost Industry

Although our analysis has dealt with the long run, we have noted that the market supply curves in Figures 10-8b and 10-9b are short-run curves. What then is the character of the **long-run supply curve** of a competitive industry? The analysis points us towards an answer. The crucial factor here is the effect, if any, that changes in the number of firms in the industry will have on costs of the individual firms in the industry.

### Constant-Cost Industry

In our analysis of long-run competitive equilibrium we assumed the industry under discussion was a **constant-cost industry**. This means that industry expansion or contraction will not affect resource prices and therefore production costs. Graphically, it means the entry or exit of firms does not shift the long-run ATC curves of individual firms. This is the case when the industry's demand for resources is small in relation to the total demand for those resources. Then the industry can expand or contract without significantly affecting resource prices and costs.

### Perfectly Elastic Long-Run Supply

What does the long-run supply curve of a constant-cost industry look like? The answer is contained in our previous analysis. There we saw that the entry and exit of firms changes industry output but always brings the product price back to its original level, where it is just equal to the constant minimum ATC. Specifically, we discovered that the industry would supply 90,000, 100,000, or 110,000 units of output, all at a price of $50 per unit. In other words, the long-run supply of a constant-cost industry is perfectly elastic.

This is demonstrated graphically in Figure 10-10, which uses data from Figures 10-8 and 10-9. Suppose industry demand is originally $D_0$, industry output is $Q_0$ (100,000 units), and product price is $P_0$ ($50). This situation, from Figure 10-8, is one of long-run equilibrium. We saw that when demand increases to $D_1$, upsetting this equilibrium, the resulting economic profits attract new

**FIGURE 10-10 The long-run supply curve for a constant-cost industry is horizontal**

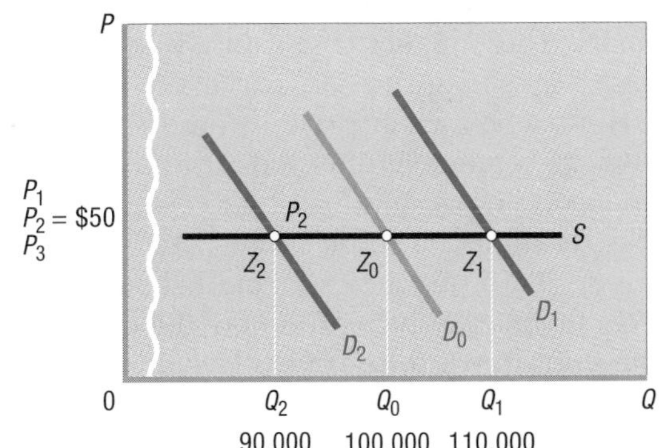


Because the entry or exodus of firms does not affect resource prices or therefore unit costs, an increase in demand ($D_0$ to $D_1$) causes an expansion in industry output ($Q_0$ to $Q_1$) but no alteration in price ($50). Similarly, a decrease in demand ($D_0$ to $D_2$) causes a contraction of output ($Q_0$ to $Q_2$) but no change in price. This means that the long-run industry supply curve ($S$) is horizontal through points $Z_0$, $Z_1$, and $Z_2$.

firms. Because this is a constant-cost industry, entry continues and industry output expands until the price is driven back down to the level of the unchanged minimum ATC. This is at price $P_1$ ($50) and output $Q_1$ (110,000).

From Figure 10-9, we saw that a decline in market demand from $D_0$ to $D_2$ causes an exit of firms and ultimately restores equilibrium at price $P_2$ ($50) and output $Q_2$ (90,000 units). The points $Z_0$, $Z_1$, and $Z_2$ in Figure 10-10 represent these three price-quantity combinations. A line or curve connecting all such points shows the various price-quantity combinations that firms would produce if they had enough time to make all desired adjustments to changes in demand. This line or curve is the industry's long-run supply curve. In a constant-cost industry this curve (straight line) is horizontal, as in Figure 10-10, thus representing perfectly elastic supply.

## Long-Run Supply for an Increasing-Cost Industry

Constant-cost industries are a special case. Most industries are **increasing-cost industries**, in which firms' ATC curves shift upward as the industry expands and downward as the industry contracts. Usually, the entry of new firms will increase resource prices, particularly so in industries using specialized resources whose supplies are not readily increased in response to an increase in resource demand. Higher resource prices result in higher long-run average total costs for all firms in the industry. These higher costs cause upward shifts in each firm's long-run ATC curve.

Thus, when an increase in product demand results in economic profits and attracts new firms to an increasing-cost industry, a two-way squeeze works to eliminate those profits. As before, the entry of new firms increases market supply and lowers the market price. But now the entire ATC curve shifts upward. The overall result is a higher-than-original equilibrium price. The industry produces a larger output *at a higher product price* because the industry expansion has increased resource prices and the minimum average total cost. We know that, in the long run, the product price must cover ATC.

Since greater output will be supplied at a higher price, the long-run industry supply curve is upsloping. Instead of supplying either 90,000, 100,000, or 110,000 units at the same price of $50, an increasing-cost industry might supply 90,000 units at $45, 100,000 units at $50, and 110,000 units at $55. A higher price is required to induce more production because costs per unit of output increase as production rises.

We show this in Figure 10-11. Original market demand is $D_0$ and industry price and output are $P_0$ ($50) and $Q_0$ (100,000 units), respectively, at equilibrium point $Y_0$. An increase in demand to $D_1$ upsets this equilibrium and leads to economic profits. New firms enter the industry, increasing both market supply and production costs of individual firms. A new price is established at point $Y_1$, where $P_1$ is $55 and $Q_1$ is 110,000 units.

Conversely, a decline in demand from $D_0$ to $D_2$ makes production unprofitable and causes firms to leave the industry. The resulting decline in resource prices reduces the minimum average total cost of production for firms that stay. A new equilibrium price is established at some level below the original price, say, at point $Y_2$, where $P_2$ is $45 and $Q_2$ is 90,000 units. Connecting these three equilibrium positions, we derive the upsloping long-run supply curve $S$ in Figure 10-11.

## Long-Run Supply for a Decreasing-Cost Industry

In industries known as **decreasing-cost industries**, firms may experience lower costs as the industry

**FIGURE 10-11 The long-run supply curve for an increasing-cost industry is upsloping**

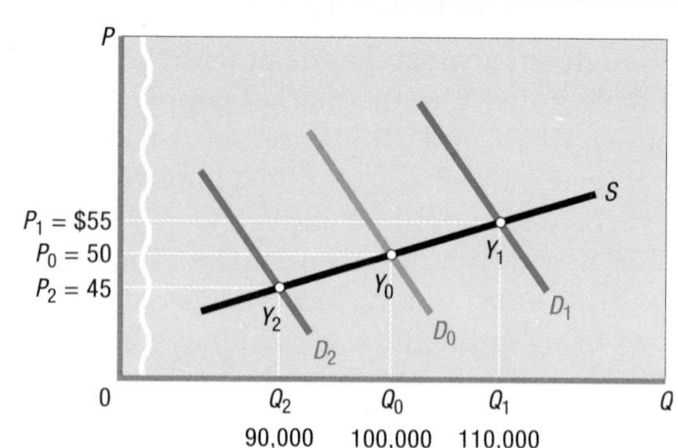


In an increasing-cost industry, the entry of firms in response to increases in demand ($D_2$ to $D_0$ to $D_1$) will bid up resource prices and thereby increase unit costs. As a result, an increased industry output ($Q_2$ to $Q_0$ to $Q_1$) will be forthcoming only at higher prices ($55 > $50 > $45). The long-run industry supply curve ($S$) therefore slopes upward through points $Y_2$, $Y_0$ and $Y_1$.

expands. Classic example: As more mines are established in a particular locality, each firm's costs of pumping out water seepage decline because with more mines pumping, seepage into each is less. Moreover, with only a few mines in an area, industry output might be so small that only relatively primitive and therefore costly transportation facilities are available. But as the number of firms and their output expand, a railroad might build a spur into the area and thereby significantly reduce transportation costs.

We urge you to rework the analysis underlying Figure 10-11 to show that the long-run supply curve of a decreasing-cost industry is *downsloping*. ***(Key Question 6)***

## PURE COMPETITION AND EFFICIENCY

Our final goal in this chapter is to relate pure competition to efficiency. Whether a purely competitive industry is a constant-cost industry or an increasing-cost industry, the final long-run equilibrium position of all firms has the same basic characteristics relating to economic efficiency. As shown in ***Figure 10-12 (Key Graph)***, price (and

### KEY GRAPH

**FIGURE 10-12 The in long-run equilibrium position of a competitive firm: *P* = MC = minimum ATC**

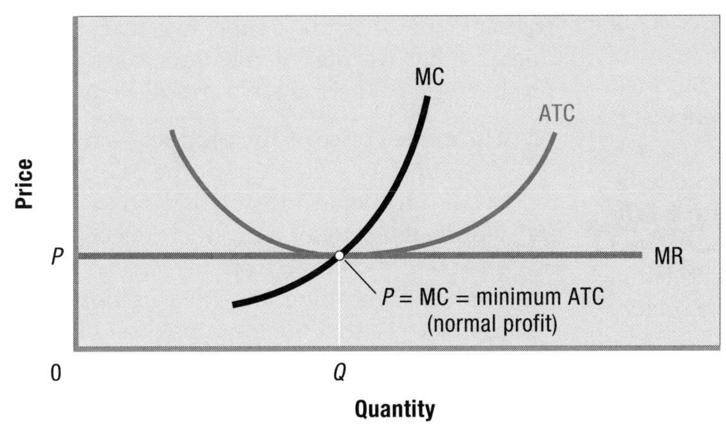


The equality of price and minimum average total cost indicates that the firm is using the most efficient known technology and is charging the lowest price, *P*, and producing the greatest output, *Q*, consistent with its costs. The equality of price and marginal cost indicates that resources are being allocated in accordance with consumer preferences.

### 10-12 QUICK QUIZ

**1.** We know this firm is a "price taker" because:
- **(a)** its MC curve slopes upward.
- **(b)** its ATC curve is U-shaped.
- **(c)** its MR curve is horizontal.
- **(d)** MC and ATC are equal at the profit-maximizing output.

**2.** This firm's MC curve is rising because:
- **(a)** it is a "price taker."
- **(b)** of the law of diminishing marginal utility.
- **(c)** wage rates rise as output expands.
- **(d)** of the law of diminishing marginal returns.

**3.** At this firm's profit-maximizing output:
- **(a)** total revenue equals total cost.
- **(b)** it is earning an economic profit.
- **(c)** allocative, but not necessarily productive, efficiency is achieved.
- **(d)** productive, but not necessarily allocative, efficiency is achieved.

**4.** The equality of *P*, MC, and minimum ATC:
- **(a)** occurs only in constant cost industries.
- **(b)** encourages entry of new firms.
- **(c)** means that the "right goods" are being produced in the "right ways."
- **(d)** results in a zero accounting profit.

**Answers:** 1. (c); 2. (d); 3. (a); 4. (c).

marginal revenue) will settle where it is equal to minimum average total cost: *P* (and MR) = minimum ATC. Moreover, since the marginal-cost curve intersects the average-total-cost curve at its minimum point, marginal cost and average total cost are equal: MC = minimum ATC. Thus in long-run equilibrium there is a multiple equality: *P* (and MR) = MC = minimum ATC.

This triple equality tells us that although a competitive firm may realize economic profit or loss in the short run, it will earn only a normal profit by producing in accordance with the MR (= *P*) = MC rule in the long run. Also, this triple equality suggests certain conclusions of great social significance concerning the efficiency of a purely competitive economy.

Economists agree that, subject to certain qualifications discussed shortly, a purely competitive economy leads to an efficient use of society's scarce resources. *A competitive market economy uses the limited amounts of resources available to society in a way that maximizes the satisfaction of consumers.* As we discussed in Chapter 2, efficient use of limited resources requires both productive efficiency and allocative efficiency.

**Productive efficiency** requires that goods be produced in the least costly way. **Allocative efficiency** requires that resources be apportioned among firms and industries so as to yield the mix of products and services most wanted by society (consumers). Allocative efficiency has been realized when it is impossible to change the composition of total output and achieve a net gain for society. Let's look at how productive and allocative efficiency would be achieved under purely competitive conditions.

## Productive Efficiency: *P* = Minimum ATC

In the long run, pure competition forces firms to produce at the minimum average total cost of production and to charge a price that is just consistent with that cost, a highly favourable situation from the consumer's point of view. It means that firms must use the best-available (least-cost) production methods and combinations of inputs or they will not survive. Stated differently, it means the minimum amount of resources will be used to produce any particular output.

For an example, in the final equilibrium position shown in Figure 10-9a, each firm in the industry is producing 100 units of output by using $5,000 (equal to average total cost of $50 times 100 units) worth of resources. If one firm produced that same output at a total cost of, say, $7,000, its resources would be used inefficiently. Society would be faced with a net loss of $2,000 worth of alternative products. But this cannot happen in pure competition; this firm would incur a loss of $2,000, requiring it either to reduce its costs or quit its business.

Note, too, that consumers benefit from productive efficiency by paying the lowest product price possible under the prevailing technology and cost conditions.

## Allocative Efficiency: *P* = MC

Productive efficiency alone does not ensure the efficient allocation of resources. Productive efficiency must be used to provide society with the "right goods"—the goods consumers want most. Before we can show that the competitive market system does just that, we must discuss the social meaning of product prices. There are two critical elements here:

1. The money price of any product—say, product X—is society's measure of the relative worth of an additional unit of that good. In other words, the price of a product reflects the *marginal benefit* derived from the good.
2. Similarly, recalling the idea of opportunity cost, we see that the marginal cost of product X measures the value, or relative worth, of the other goods that the resources used in producing an extra unit of X could otherwise have produced. In short, the *marginal cost* of producing a unit of X measures society's sacrifice of goods that could have been produced instead of X.

To understand why *P* = MC defines allocative efficiency, let's first look at situations where this is not the case.

**Underallocation: *P* > MC** In pure competition, a firm will realize the maximum possible profit only by producing where price equals marginal cost (Figure 10-12). Producing less of X, so that MR (and thus *P*) exceeds MC, yields less than maximum profit. It also entails an *underallocation* of resources to this product from society's standpoint. The fact that price still exceeds marginal cost indicates that society values additional units of X more highly than the alternative products the resources could otherwise produce.

To illustrate, if the price or marginal benefit of a shirt is $20 and its marginal cost is $16, producing an additional shirt will cause a net increase in total well-being of $4. Society will gain a shirt valued at $20, while the alternative products sacrificed by allocating more resources to shirts would be valued at only $16. Whenever society can gain something valued at $20 by giving up something valued at $16, the initial allocation of resources must have been inefficient.

**Overallocation: *P* < MC** For similar reasons, the production of X should not go beyond the output at which price equals marginal cost. To produce where MR (and thus *P*) is less than MC would yield less than the maximum profit for the producer and entail an *overallocation* of resources to X from the standpoint of society. Producing X where its marginal costs exceed its price or marginal benefit means that X is being produced by sacrificing alternative goods that society values more highly than added units of X.

For example, if the price of a shirt is $20 and its marginal cost is $26, then the production of one less shirt would result in a net increase in society's total well-being of $6. Society would lose a shirt valued at $20, but reallocating the freed resources to their best alternative uses would increase the output of some other good valued at $26. Whenever society is able to give up something of lesser value in return for something of greater value, the original allocation of resources must have been inefficient.

**Efficient Allocation** Our conclusion is that in pure competition, when profit-motivated firms produce each good or service to the point where price (marginal benefit) and marginal cost are equal, society's resources are being allocated efficiently. Each item is being produced to the point at which the value of the last unit is equal to the value of the alternative goods sacrificed by its production. To alter the production of product X would reduce consumer satisfaction. To produce X beyond the *P* = MC point would sacrifice alternative goods whose value to society exceeds that of the extra units of X. To produce X short of the *P* = MC point would sacrifice units of X that society values more than the alternative goods its resources can produce.

**Dynamic Adjustments** A further attribute of purely competitive markets is their ability to restore efficiency when disrupted by changes in the economy. A change in consumer tastes, resource supplies, or technology will automatically set in motion the appropriate realignments of resources. We have already explained what happens when a change in consumer tastes increases the demand for product X. First, its price will increase so that, at its present output, the price of X will exceed its marginal cost. At this point efficiency will be lost, but the higher price will create economic profits in industry X and stimulate its expansion. The profitability of X will permit the industry to bid resources away from now less pressing uses. Expansion of this industry will end only when the price of X and its marginal cost are equal, that is, when allocative efficiency has been restored.

Similarly, a change in the supply of a particular resource or in a production technique will upset an existing price-marginal-cost equality by either raising or lowering marginal cost. The resulting inequality will cause business executives, in either pursuing profit or avoiding loss, to reallocate resources until price once again equals marginal cost. In so doing, they will correct any inefficiency in the allocation of resources that the original change may have temporarily imposed on the economy.

**"Invisible Hand" Revisited** A final point: The highly efficient allocation of resources that a purely competitive economy promotes comes about because businesses and resource suppliers seek to further their own self-interests. The "invisible hand" (Chapter 3) is at work in a competitive market system. The competitive system not only maximizes profits for individual producers but simultaneously results in a pattern of resource allocation that maximizes consumer satisfaction. The "invisible hand" thus organizes the *private interests* of producers in a way that is fully in accord with *society's interest* in using scarce resources efficiently. ***(Key Question 7)***

**10-3**

**QUICK REVIEW**

- In the long run, the entry of firms into an industry will compete away any economic profits, and the exit of firms will eliminate losses so that price and minimum average total cost are equal.
- The long-run supply curves of constant-, or increasing-, and decreasing-cost industries are horizontal, upsloping, and downsloping, respectively.
- In purely competitive markets both productive efficiency (price equals minimum average total cost) and allocative efficiency (price equals marginal cost) are achieved in the long run.

## Qualifications

Our conclusion that a purely competitive market system results in both productive and allocative efficiency must be qualified in several respects.

**Market Failure: Spillovers and Public Goods** In the market system, each producer will assume only those costs that it *must* pay. In some lines of production there are significant costs producers can and do avoid, usually by polluting the environment. Recall from Chapter 5 that these avoided costs accrue to society and are aptly called *spillover* or *external costs*. On the other hand, when individuals consume certain goods and services, such as education and measles vaccinations, widespread benefits accrue to society as a whole. These satisfactions are called *external* or *spillover benefits*.

The profit-seeking activities of pure competitors will bring about an allocation of resources that is efficient from society's point of view only if (1) marginal cost embodies *all* the costs that production entails and (2) product price accurately reflects *all* the benefits that society gets from a good. Only then will competitive production at the MR (= $P$) = MC point balance the *total* sacrifices and satisfactions of society and result in an efficient allocation of resources. If price and marginal cost are not accurate indexes of sacrifices and satisfactions—if sizable spillover costs and benefits exist—production at the MR (= $P$) = MC point will *not* signify an efficient allocation of resources.

Remember, too, the point of the lighthouse example in Chapter 5: The market system does not provide for social or public goods, that is, for goods to which the exclusion principle does *not* apply. Despite its other virtues, the competitive price system ignores an important class of goods and services—national defence, flood control, public parks, and so forth—that can and do yield satisfaction to consumers but that cannot be priced and sold through the market system.

**Economies of Scale** In developing the pure competition model, we assumed that all producers were operating at their optimal size. But in certain lines of production, existing technology may be such that a firm must be a large-scale producer to realize the lowest per-unit costs of production. Given consumer demand, this suggests that in some industries a relatively small number of large-scale producers are needed if production is to be carried out efficiently. If the large number of small-scale producers needed for pure competition populated those industries, then major efficiencies would be lost.

**Technological Advance** Some economists believe that a purely competitive economy would not foster a very rapid rate of technological progress. The incentive for research and development may be weak under pure competition since profit—even that resulting from a technological improvement—is at best only temporary because of ease of entry. Also, the small size of the typical competitive firm and the fact that it tends to "break even" in the long run make it difficult for producers to finance substantial research and development programs. Thus, pure competition may not motivate the development of new production techniques or lead to improvements in existing products or the creation of new ones. We will return to the question of technological progress after our discussion of the other market structures.

**Range of Consumer Choice** A purely competitive economy might not provide a sufficient range of product choice for consumers. Pure competition means product standardization, whereas other market structures—for example, monopolistic competition and, frequently, oligopoly—promote a wide range of types, styles, and quality levels of products. This product variety widens the range of free choice available to consumers and simultaneously allows them to more completely fulfil their preferences.

In The Media

# Small-dish satellite firms fighting price war

## Slashing the cost of the equipment and service to attract new business and entice grey market customers to turn in their U.S. dishes

BY ROBERT BREHL
MEDIA REPORTER

Canada's small-dish satellite companies are fighting a price war aimed at attracting new customers and enticing owners of grey market dishes to turn in their U.S. equipment.

For the first time, prices for Canadian dishes and set-top digital boxes have fallen below $500 in many parts of the country. And those who turn in their grey market dishes are being offered up to $800 worth of free programming.

But company officials say prices will likely go back up in the new year.

There are an estimated 300,000 grey market customers in Canada. It is called grey market because the services are not authorized for distribution in Canada. Customers must have a U.S. billing address set up to pay their monthly programming charges.

Star Choice Communications Inc., controlled by Calgary-based cable giant Shaw Communications Inc., this week slashed the price of a digital set-top receiver and dish to $549, with $50 worth of free programming tossed in for a net price of $499. When Fredericton-based Star Choice launched earlier this year, its hardware, alone, retailed for $999.

The move is in direct response to competitor ExpressVu Inc., which is 91 per cent owned by Montreal-based telecommunications titan BCE Inc.

ExpressVu's lowest-priced set-top box and dish is selling for $499 in the retail outlets of its sister firm Bell Mobility across Ontario and Quebec. Bell Mobility is 65 per cent owned by BCE. At other locations selling the ExpressVu dish, the suggested retail price is $599, but it has fallen in these stores to $549 or lower.

"Bell Mobility disrupted the marketplace but it's a temporary blip," said ExpressVu president Michael Neuman.

Star Choice officials said temporary or not, their product will not be undersold.

"This is our response to Bell Mobility's price," said Star Choice vice-president Guy Skipworth. "We've always said we'll be competitive."

As for the grey market, Star Choice doubled its so-called amnesty program. It now gives away $800 worth of programming for anyone who returns a DirecTV or EchoStar dish. Put another way, turn in a U.S. dish and get free Canadian satellite service for up to two years. The company's previous amnesty was a combination of a $250 rebate on hardware and $150 of free programming for a total of $400.

*Source: Globe and Mail*, December 17, 1997, p. B7. Reprinted with permission from the *Globe and Mail*.

## THE STORY IN BRIEF

A price war breaks out among Canada's small dish satellite companies. To lure customers using "grey market dishes" originating in the United States, Canadian companies are offering them some free programming.

## THE ECONOMICS BEHIND THE STORY

- Not many years ago, urban consumers wanting TV programming had two alternatives: cable TV or an antenna; the latter was a very poor substitute. Rural consumers could choose between very large and expensive satellite dishes or a regular antenna. Technological progress has shrunk the size of satellite dishes, while new competitors providing both satellite dishes and programming have entered the market.
- Given more firms and a more or less standardized product and service, firms are competing on the basis of price, in this case primarily by lowering the price of satellite dishes, a necessity to receive satellite TV programming. The lower price for a satellite dish is likely to attract more consumers to use satellite firms' programming.
- What will be the likely effect on the number of cable TV subscribers as the cost of satellite dishes and programming falls? ■

# The Last Word

## PURE COMPETITION AND CONSUMER SURPLUS

**Pure competition provides consumers with the largest utility surplus that is consistent with keeping the product in production.**

IN ALMOST ALL MARKETS, CONSUMERS collectively obtain more utility (total satisfaction) from their purchases than the amount of their expenditures (product price × quantity). This surplus of utility arises because some consumers are willing to pay more than the equilibrium price but need not do so.

Consider the market for oranges depicted in the accompanying figure. The demand curve *D* tells us that some consumers of oranges are willing to pay more than the $4 equilibrium price per bag. For example, assume Bob is willing to pay $9; Barb, $8; Bill, $7; Bart, $6; and Brent, $5. Betty, in contrast, is *un*willing to pay one penny more than the $4 equilibrium price.

There are many other consumers besides Bob, Barb, Bill, Bart, and Brent in this market who are willing to pay prices above $4. Only Betty pays exactly the price she is willing to pay; the others receive some amount of utility beyond their expenditures. The difference between that utility value (measured by the vertical height of the points on the demand curve) and the $4 price is called *consumer surplus.* When we add together each buyer's utility surplus, we obtain the consumer surplus for all the consumers in the market. To get the $Q_1$ bags of oranges, consumers collectively are *willing* to pay the sum of the amounts represented by the green triangle and grey rectangle. However, they only *have to pay* the amount represented by the grey rectangle. The green triangle thus represents consumer surplus.

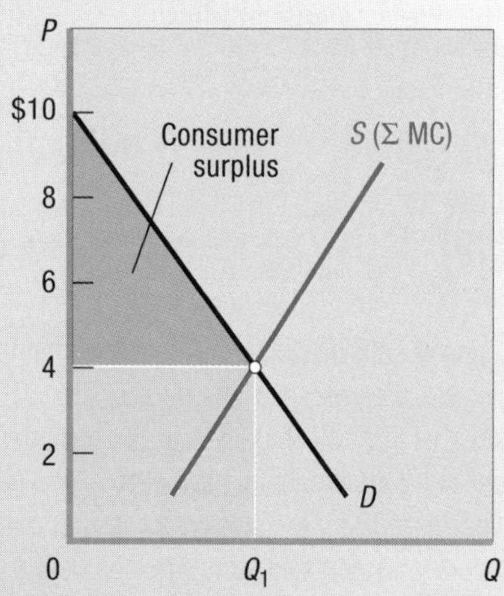


A glance at the figure shows that the amount of consumer surplus—the size of the green triangle—would be less if the sellers could charge some price above $4. As just one example, at a price of $8, only a very small triangle of consumer surplus would exist. But purely competitive firms cannot charge $8 because they are price takers. Any firm that charged a price above $4 would immediately lose all its business to the other firms.

Moreover, we know that in pure competition the equilibrium price equals the marginal cost of the $Q_1$ bags of oranges. And, since we are assuming that entry and exit have resulted in this price being equal to lowest average total cost, each seller is earning only a normal profit. By definition, this profit is just sufficient to continue production of oranges.

The principle that emerges is this: By establishing the lowest price consistent with continued production, pure competition yields the largest sustainable amount of consumer surplus. ■

# CHAPTER SUMMARY

1. Economists group industries into four models based on their market structures: **a** pure competition, **b** pure monopoly, **c** monopolistic competition, and **d** oligopoly.

2. A purely competitive industry consists of a large number of independent firms producing a standardized product. Pure competition assumes that firms and resources are mobile among different industries.

3. No single firm can influence market price in a competitive industry; the firm's demand curve is perfectly elastic and price therefore equals marginal revenue.

4. Short-run profit maximization by a competitive firm can be analyzed by comparing total revenue and total cost or applying marginal analysis. A firm maximizes its short-run profit by producing that output at which total revenue exceeds total cost by the greatest amount.

5. Provided price exceeds minimum average variable cost, a competitive firm maximizes profit or minimizes loss in the short run by producing that output at which price or marginal revenue equals marginal cost. If price is less than average variable cost, the firm minimizes its loss by shutting down. If price is greater than average variable cost but less than average total cost, the firm minimizes its loss by producing the $P =$ MC output. If price also exceeds average total cost, the firm maximizes its economic profit at the $P =$ MC output.

6. Applying that MR ($= P$) = MC rule at various possible market prices leads to the conclusion that the segment of the firm's short-run marginal-cost curve lying above its average-variable-cost curve is its short-run supply curve.

7. In the long run, the market price of a product will equal the minimum average total cost of production. At a greater price, economic profits would cause firms to enter the competitive industry until those profits had been competed away. At a lesser price, losses would force the exit of firms from the industry until the product price rose to equal average total cost.

8. The long-run supply curve is horizontal for a constant-cost industry, upsloping for an increasing-cost industry, and downsloping for a decreasing-cost industry.

9. The long-run equality of price and minimum average total cost means that competitive firms will use the most efficient known technology and charge the lowest price consistent with their production costs.

10. The long-run equality of price and marginal cost implies that resources will be allocated in accordance with consumer tastes. The competitive price system will reallocate resources in response to a change in consumer tastes, technology, or resource supplies to maintain allocative efficiency over time.

11. Economists recognize four possible deterrents to allocative efficiency in a competitive economy. **a** There is no reason why the competitive market system will result in an optimal distribution of income. **b** In allocating resources, the competitive model does not allow for spillover costs and benefits or for the production of public goods. **c** A purely competitive industry may preclude the large-scale production needed for individual firms to achieve economies of scale and therefore obtain the lowest possible per-unit production costs. **d** Pure competition may not motivate the development of new and improved production techniques and new and improved products. **e** The product standardization associated with pure competition limits product variations that provide consumers with a wide range of choice.

## TERMS AND CONCEPTS

pure competition
pure monopoly
monopolistic competition
oligopoly
imperfect competition
price taker
average revenue
total revenue
marginal revenue
break-even point
MR = MC rule
short-run supply curve
long-run supply curve
constant-cost industry
increasing-cost industry
decreasing-cost industry
productive efficiency
allocative efficiency

# STUDY QUESTIONS

1. Briefly indicate the basic characteristics of pure competition, pure monopoly, monopolistic competition, and oligopoly. Under which of these market classifications does each of the following most accurately fit? **a** a supermarket in your home town; **b** the steel industry; **c** a Manitoba wheat farm; **d** the commercial bank in which you or your family has an account; **e** the automobile industry. In each case justify your classification.

2. Strictly speaking, pure competition has never existed and probably never will. Then why study it?

3. KEY QUESTION *Use the following demand schedule to determine total and marginal revenue for each possible level of sales:*

| Product price | Quantity demanded | Total revenue | Marginal revenue |
|---|---|---|---|
| $2 | 0 | $_____ | |
| | | | $_____ |
| 2 | 1 | _____ | |
| | | | _____ |
| 2 | 2 | _____ | |
| | | | _____ |
| 2 | 3 | _____ | |
| | | | _____ |
| 2 | 4 | _____ | |
| | | | _____ |
| 2 | 5 | _____ | |

   **a.** *What can you conclude about the structure of the industry in which this firm is operating? Explain.*
   **b.** *Graph the demand, total-revenue, and marginal-revenue curves for this firm.*
   **c.** *Why do the demand and marginal-revenue curves coincide?*
   **d.** *"Marginal revenue is the change in total revenue associated with additional units of output." Explain verbally and graphically, using the data in the table.*

4. KEY QUESTION *Assume the following unit-cost data are for a purely competitive producer:*

| Total product | Average fixed cost | Average variable cost | Average total cost | Marginal cost |
|---|---|---|---|---|
| 0 | | | | |
| | | | | $45 |
| 1 | $60.00 | $45.00 | $105.00 | |
| | | | | 40 |
| 2 | 30.00 | 42.50 | 72.50 | |
| | | | | 35 |
| 3 | 20.00 | 40.00 | 60.00 | |
| | | | | 30 |
| 4 | 15.00 | 37.50 | 52.50 | |
| | | | | 35 |
| 5 | 12.00 | 37.00 | 49.00 | |
| | | | | 40 |
| 6 | 10.00 | 37.50 | 47.50 | |
| | | | | 45 |
| 7 | 8.57 | 38.57 | 47.14 | |
| | | | | 55 |
| 8 | 7.50 | 40.63 | 48.13 | |
| | | | | 65 |
| 9 | 6.67 | 43.33 | 50.00 | |
| | | | | 75 |
| 10 | 6.00 | 46.50 | 52.50 | |

   **a.** *At a product price of $32, will this firm produce in the short run? Why or why not? If it does produce, what will be the profit-maximizing or loss-minimizing output? Explain. What economic profit or loss will the firm realize per unit of output?*
   **b.** *Answer the questions of 4a assuming product price is $41.*
   **c.** *Answer the questions of 4a assuming product price is $56.*
   **d.** *Complete the short-run supply schedule for the firm (columns 1 and 2) and indicate the profit or loss incurred at each output (column 3).*

| (1) Price | (2) Quantity supplied, single firm | (3) Profit (+) or loss (–) | (4) Quantity supplied, 1500 firms |
|---|---|---|---|
| $26 | ______ | $______ | ______ |
| 32 | ______ | ______ | ______ |
| 38 | ______ | ______ | ______ |
| 41 | ______ | ______ | ______ |
| 46 | ______ | ______ | ______ |
| 56 | ______ | ______ | ______ |
| 66 | ______ | ______ | ______ |

**e.** *Explain: "That segment of a competitive firm's marginal-cost curve that lies above its average-variable-cost curve constitutes the short-run supply curve for the firm." Illustrate graphically.*

**f.** *Now assume that are 1,500 identical firms in this competitive industry; that is, there are 1,500 firms, each of which has the cost data shown in the table. Complete the industry supply schedule (column 4).*

**g.** *Suppose the market demand data for the product are as follows:*

| Price | Total quantity demanded |
|---|---|
| $26 | 17,000 |
| 32 | 15,000 |
| 38 | 13,500 |
| 41 | 12,000 |
| 46 | 10,500 |
| 56 | 9,500 |
| 66 | 8,000 |

*What will be the equilibrium price? What will be the equilibrium output for the industry? For each firm? What will profit or loss be per unit? Per firm? Will this industry expand or contract in the long run?*

**5.** Why is the equality of marginal revenue and marginal cost essential for profit maximization in all market structures? Explain why price can be substituted for marginal revenue in the MR = MC rule when an industry is purely competitive.

**6.** KEY QUESTION *Using diagrams for both the industry and a representative firm, illustrate competitive long-run equilibrium. Employing these diagrams, show how* **a** *an increase, and* **b** *a decrease in market demand will upset this long-run equilibrium. Trace graphically and describe verbally the adjustment processes by which the long-run equilibrium is restored. Assume the industry is one of constant costs. Now rework your analysis for increasing and decreasing cost industries and compare the three long-run supply curves.*

**7.** KEY QUESTION *In long-run equilibrium, P = minimum ATC = MC. Of what significance for the allocation of resources is the equality of P and minimum ATC? The equality of P and MC? Distinguish between productive and allocative efficiency in your answer.*

**8.** **(The Last Word)** Suppose that improved technology causes the supply curve for oranges to shift rightward in the market discussed in this Last Word (see the figure there). Assuming no change in the location of the demand curve, what will happen to consumer surplus? Explain why.

**9.** WEB-BASED QUESTION **Pure Competition—Locate Some Real-World Examples** Pure competition is rare in practice. However, Yahoo www.yahoo.ca/Regional/Countries/Canada/Business_and_Economy/Companies/ includes a collection of firms in various industries. Find three industries that have the characteristics of pure competition: very large number of firms, standardized products, price taker, and free entry and exit. Hint: Start by looking at the number of firms in each industry link. In Ergonomics there are fewer than 10 companies, while Internet Services lists more than 200 firms.

10. WEB-BASED QUESTION **Agricultural Commodities—Examples of Purely Competitive Markets** In a purely competitive market, individual firms produce homogeneous products and exert no significant control over product price. The Alberta government www.agric.gov.ab.ca/economic/market/mpmod05.html provides a brief overview of how a commodity exchange functions and has links to the main commodity exchanges in North America. Visit the Winnipeg Commodity Exchange and select "Daily Market Summary." Which of the main crops has had the largest price movement and why?

CHAPTER 11

# Pure Monopoly

WE NOW JUMP FROM PURE COMPETITION TO PURE monopoly, which is at the opposite end of the spectrum of industry structures listed previously in Table 10-1. You deal with monopolies—sole sellers of products and services—more often than you might think. When you mail a letter, you are using the services of Canada Post, a government-sponsored monopoly. Similarly, when you make a local telephone call, turn on your lights, or subscribe to cable TV, you are patronizing a monopoly.

We begin by defining what we mean by "pure monopoly," and then we discuss some of the conditions that allow a monopoly to arise and persist. Then we get to the core of the chapter: the determination of price and output for a monopolistic firm. We also ask whether monopoly can achieve the productive and allocative efficiency associated with pure competition and, if not, whether government policies can improve the pricing and output practices of a pure monopolist.

**IN THIS CHAPTER YOU WILL LEARN:**

- The necessary conditions required for monopoly to arise.
- How the monopolist determines the profit-maximizing price and output.
- About the inefficiencies of monopoly.
- Why a monopolist prefers to charge different prices in different markets.
- What a natural monopoly is and why governments often choose to regulate natural monopolies.

## The Big Picture

IF YOU OWNED A FIRM PRODUCING A PRODUCT or providing a service, you would prefer it to be the only firm of its type, and the demand for its product to be strong and price inelastic. Under these conditions, your firm would probably make economic profits. You would undoubtedly attract envy from competitors and potential competitors; in a world pervaded by scarcities, others would want a piece of the (your) action.

But consumers would not be happy; they would have to pay a higher price for your firm's product compared to a situation where your firm had many competitors. Thus, there is a serious conflict between what is good for your firm and what is good for society (consumers). Monopoly—what you wish for your firm—stands much in contrast to pure competition, where the conflict between the firm and consumers is mitigated. Recall that the pure competitive model ensures firms produce at the lowest possible price (productive efficiency) and also produce those goods and services consumers want most (allocative efficiency). To this end, the pure competitive model ensures a society is getting the most out of its limited resources. The monopoly model serves to demonstrate two important points: **a** the inefficiencies of a one-firm industry—neither productive nor allocative efficiencies are achieved—and **b** the difficulty of maintaining a monopoly. A monopoly is difficult to maintain because economic profits attract other firms to the industry. Only if it is impossible for others to enter the industry will a monopoly persist.

As you read this chapter, keep the following points in mind:

- **Key Concept 7** is discussed.
- Despite what you may believe, a monopolist cannot charge any price it wants; a monopolist is constrained by the demand curve.
- There is no industry supply curve. Whatever is supplied by the monopolist is also the industry supply curve.
- A natural monopoly is one in which the average total cost falls continuously over a significant range as the size of the firm increases. Examples of natural monopolies are utility companies—water, gas, hydro. Since natural monopolies can produce at the lowest possible unit cost, they are beneficial. But in the absence of competition, a natural monopoly could make economic profits; thus to protect consumers' interests, natural monopolies are regulated by governments. ■

## PURE MONOPOLY: INTRODUCTION

**Pure monopoly** exists when *a single firm is the sole producer of a product for which there are no close substitutes.* Let's examine first the characteristics of pure monopoly and then provide some examples.

### Characteristics

1. **SINGLE SELLER** A pure, or absolute, monopoly is a one-firm industry. A single firm is the only producer of a specific product or the sole supplier of a service; the firm and the industry are synonymous.
2. **NO CLOSE SUBSTITUTES** The monopolist's product is unique in that there are no good, or close, substitutes. From the buyer's viewpoint, there are no reasonable alternatives. The consumer who does not buy the product from the monopolist has no alternative but to do without it.
3. **"PRICE MAKER"** The individual firm operating under pure competition exercises no influence over product price; it is a "price taker." This is so because it contributes only a negligible portion of total supply. In contrast, the pure monopolist is a *price maker;* the firm exercises considerable control over price because it is responsible for, and therefore controls, the total quantity supplied. Confronted with the usual downsloping demand curve for its product, the monopolist can change product price by changing the quantity of the product supplied. The monopolist will use this power whenever there is an advantage to doing so.
4. **BLOCKED ENTRY** A pure monopolist has no immediate competitors because there are bar-

riers that keep potential competitors from entering the industry. These barriers may be economic, technological, legal, or of some other type. But under conditions of pure monopoly, entry is totally blocked.

### Examples of Monopoly

In most cities government-owned or -regulated public utilities—gas and electric companies, the water company, the cable TV company, and local telephone service—are all monopolies or virtually so. There are no close substitutes for services provided by these public utilities. Of course, there is almost always *some* competition. Candles or kerosene lights are imperfect substitutes for electricity; telegrams, letters, and courier services can be substituted for the telephone. But such substitutes are either costly, less convenient, or unappealing.

The classic example of a private, unregulated monopoly is the De Beers diamond syndicate, which effectively controls 70 percent of the world's diamond supply (see this chapter's Last Word). But in Canada, major manufacturing monopolies are rare and usually short-lived; eventually competitors emerge to destroy the single-producer status.

Professional sports teams are, in a sense, monopolies because they are the sole suppliers of specific services in large geographic areas. Each large Canadian city is served by a single major-league team in each sport. If you want to see a live major-league baseball game in Toronto or Montreal, you must patronize the Blue Jays or the Expos, respectively.

Other geographic monopolies exist. A small town may be served by only one airline or railroad. The local bank branch, movie theatre, or bookstore may approximate a monopoly in a small, isolated community.

### Importance of Monopoly and Its Study

You should understand the workings of pure monopoly for two reasons.

1. A significant amount of economic activity—perhaps 5 or 6 percent of domestic output—is carried out under conditions approaching pure monopoly.
2. A study of pure monopoly will help you understand the more common market structures of monopolistic competition and oligopoly, discussed in Chapter 12. These two market structures combine, in differing degrees, characteristics of pure competition and pure monopoly.

## BARRIERS TO ENTRY

The obstacles that prohibit firms from entering an industry are called **barriers to entry**. In pure monopoly, strong barriers to entry effectively block all potential competition. Barriers that are a bit weaker may permit the existence of oligopoly, a market dominated by a few firms. Still weaker barriers allow the fairly large number of competing firms that characterize monopolistic competition. And the absence of entry barriers permits the very large number of firms that is the basis of pure competition. Hence, barriers to entry are pertinent not only to the extreme case of pure monopoly but also to many other markets in which there is some degree of monopoly-like conditions.

### Economies of Scale

Modern technology in some industries is such that efficient, low-cost production can be achieved only if producers are extremely large both absolutely and in relation to the market. Where economies of scale are very significant, a firm's long-run average-cost schedule will decline over a wide range of output. Given market demand, achieving low unit costs and therefore low unit prices for consumers depends on the existence of a few large firms or, in the extreme case, only one firm.

Figure 11-1 indicates the presence of economies of scale—declining average total cost—throughout a wide range of outputs. If total consumer demand is within that output range, then demand can be satisfied at least cost when there is a single producer—a monopoly. Note, for example, that a monopolist can produce 200 units at a per-unit cost of \$10 and a total cost of \$2,000. If there are two firms in the industry and each produces 100 units, the unit cost is \$15 and total cost rises to \$3,000 (= 200 units × \$15). A still more competitive situation with four firms each producing 50 units would boost unit and total cost to \$20 and \$4,000, respectively. Conclusion: When ATC is declining, only a single producer—a monopolist—can produce any particular output at minimum total cost.

If a pure monopoly exists in such an industry, economies of scale will be an entry barrier and

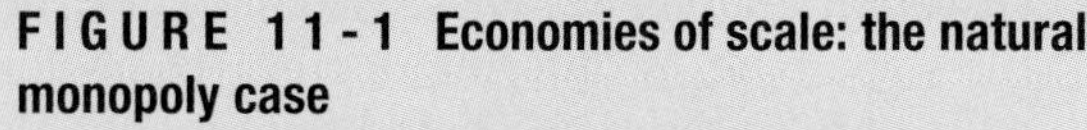

**FIGURE 11-1 Economies of scale: the natural monopoly case**

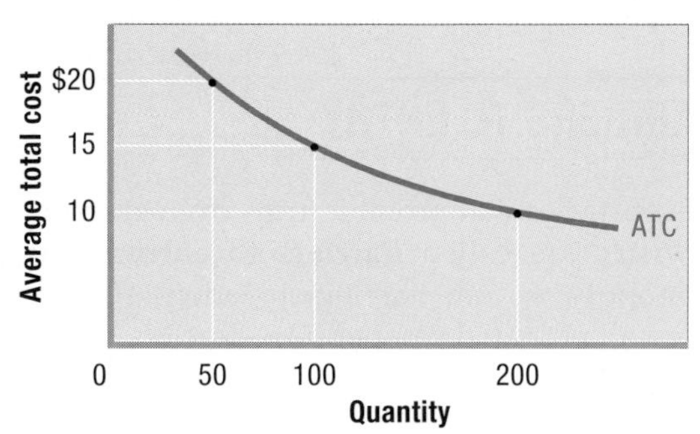


A declining average-total-cost curve over a wide range of output quantities indicates extensive economies of scale. A single monopoly firm can produce, say, 200 units of output at lower cost ($10 each) than could two or more firms whose combined output is 200 units.

will protect the monopolist from competition. New firms attempting to enter the industry as small-scale producers cannot realize the cost economies of the monopolist and therefore obtain the profits necessary for survival or growth. A new firm might try to start out big, that is, to enter the industry as a large-scale producer so as to achieve the necessary economies of scale. But the massive plant facilities would necessitate huge amounts of financing, which a new and untried enterprise would find difficult to secure. The financial obstacles and risks to "starting big" are so great in most cases that they are prohibitive. This explains why efforts to enter such industries as the manufacturing of automobiles, commercial aircraft, and basic steel are very rare.

In the extreme circumstance, in which the market demand curve cuts the long-run ATC curve where average total costs are still declining, the single firm is called a *natural monopoly*. Our discussion implies that a natural monopolist's lower unit cost allows it to charge a lower price than if the industry were more competitive. But this won't happen. As you will see, a pure monopolist may set its price far above ATC and obtain substantial economic profit. Then the lowest-unit-cost advantage of a natural monopolist may accrue to the monopolist as profit and not to consumers in the form of lower prices. For this reason government typically regulates natural monopolies, specifying the price they may charge.

Most of the so-called public utilities—electric and gas companies, bus firms, local water and telephone companies—are regulated natural monopolies. It would be wasteful if a community had several firms supplying water or electricity when a single firm can do so at least cost. Technology is such in these industries that extensive capital expenditures on generators, pumping and purification equipment, water mains, and transmission lines are required. Duplicating this equipment would waste society's scarce resources.

So single producers are given exclusive distribution rights—so-called franchises—by government. But in return for the sole right to supply electricity, water, or bus transportation to a particular geographic area, government reserves the right to regulate prices and services to prevent abuses of the monopoly power it has granted.

## Legal Barriers to Entry: Patents and Licences

We have just noted that government frequently allows and regulates natural monopolies. Government also creates legal entry barriers by awarding patents and licences.

**Patents** A patent is the exclusive right of an inventor to use, or allow another to use, her or his invention. Patents and patent laws aim to protect the inventor from rivals who would use the invention without having shared in the effort and expense of its development. At the same time, patents provide the inventor with a monopoly position for the life of the patent. Historically, patents have extended for 17 years in Canada. But in the 1995 GATT agreement (Chapter 6), the world's nations agreed on a uniform patent length of 20 years from the time of application.

Patents figured prominently in the growth of modern-day industrial giants such as NCR Corporation (formerly National Cash Register), General Motors, Xerox, Polaroid, General Electric, and Du Pont. The United Shoe Machinery Company in the United States is a notable example of a firm that abused patents to achieve monopoly power. United Shoe became the exclusive supplier of certain essential shoemaking machines through its control of patents for those machines. The firm leased, but did not sell, its machines. It extended its monopoly power to other types of shoemaking machinery by requiring all lessees of its patented machines to sign a "tying agreement" in which shoe manufacturers also agreed to lease all other shoemaking machinery from United Shoe. This allowed United Shoe to monopolize the market until anti-trust action was taken by the United States government in 1955.

Research and development (R&D) is what leads to patentable inventions and products. Firms that gain monopoly power through their own research or by purchasing the patents of others can use patents to strengthen their market position. The profit from one patent can finance the research required to develop new patentable products. In the pharmaceutical industry, patents on prescription drugs have produced large monopoly profits that have helped finance the discovery of new patentable medicines. Monopoly power achieved through patents may well be self-sustaining.

**Licences** Entry into an industry or occupation may be limited by government and the limit enforced through licensing. At the national level the Canadian Radio-television Telecommunications Commission licenses only so many radio and television stations in each geographic area. In many large cities you need a municipal licence to drive a taxicab. The consequent restriction of the supply of cabs creates economic profit for cab owners and drivers. New cabs cannot enter the industry to drive down prices and profit. In a few instances government might "license" itself to provide some product and thereby create a public monopoly. For example, in some provinces liquor is sold only through province-owned retail outlets. Similarly, many provinces have "licensed" themselves to run lotteries.

## Ownership or Control of Essential Resources

Private property can be used by a monopolist as an obstacle to potential rivals. A firm owning or controlling a resource essential to the production process can prohibit the creation of rival firms. The Aluminum Company of America allegedly maintained its monopoly position in the aluminum industry for many years through its control of developed sources of bauxite, the ore from which aluminum is refined. At one time the International Nickel Company of Canada (now called Inco) controlled 90 percent of the world's known nickel reserves. As this chapter's Last Word details, most of the world's known diamond mines are owned or effectively controlled by the De Beers Company of South Africa. Similarly, it is very difficult for new professional sports leagues to evolve when existing leagues have contracts with the best players and leases on the major stadiums and arenas.

## Pricing and Other Strategic Barriers

Even if a firm is not protected from entry by, say, extensive economies of scale or ownership of essential resources, entry may effectively be blocked by the way the monopolist responds to attempts by rivals to enter the industry. Confronted with a new entrant, the monopolist may "create an entry barrier" by slashing its price, greatly increasing its advertising, or taking other strategic actions to make it difficult for the entrant to succeed. The very *threat* of price cuts and other retaliatory actions by the monopolist may dissuade firms from attempting to enter a monopolized industry. Monopolists have been known to purposely create excess production capacity to warn potential entrants that they can quickly lower price and expand output if a new firm tries to enter.

## Two Implications

Our discussion of barriers to entry suggests two important points about monopoly.

**Rarity** Barriers to entry are seldom complete—meaning pure monopoly is relatively rare. Although research and technological advance may strengthen the market position of a firm, technology may also undermine existing monopoly power. Over time the creation of new technologies can destroy existing monopoly positions. The development of courier delivery systems, fax machines, and electronic mail has eroded the monopoly power of the postal service. Cable television monopolies are now challenged by satellite TV and by new technologies that permit the transmission of audio and visual signals through telephone lines.

Similarly, existing patent advantages may be eroded by the development of new and distinct, yet substitutable, products. New sources of major resources may be found. It is probably only a modest overstatement to say that monopoly in the sense of a one-firm industry persists over time only with the sanction or aid of government, as with the postal service's monopoly on the delivery of first-class mail.

**Desirability** Monopolies may be desirable or undesirable from the standpoint of economic efficiency. Where economies of scale are available, market demand may be such that monopoly can yield efficient low-cost production. But, for reasons we discuss later, to benefit fully from the lower costs, society may need to limit the prices the monopolists charge.

On the other hand, where ownership of resources, patents, licensing, and entry-deterring actions are sources of monopoly, the result may be inefficient and undesirable.

## MONOPOLY DEMAND

We begin our analysis of the price and output decisions of a pure monopolist by making three assumptions:

1. Our monopolist's status is secured by patents, economies of scale, or resource ownership.
2. The firm is *not* regulated by any unit of government.
3. The firm is a *single-price* monopolist; it charges the same price for all units of output.

The crucial difference between a pure monopolist and a purely competitive seller is on the demand side of the market. Recall from Chapter 10 that the purely competitive seller faces perfectly elastic demand at the price determined by market supply and demand. The competitive firm is a "price taker" that can sell as much or as little as it wants at the going market price. Each additional unit sold will add a constant amount—its price—to the firm's total revenue. That means marginal revenue for the competitive seller is constant and equal to product price. (Refer to Table 10-2 and Figure 10-1 for price, marginal-revenue, and total-revenue relationships for the purely competitive firm.)

The monopolist's demand curve—indeed, the demand curve of any imperfectly competitive seller—is very different. Because the pure monopolist *is* the industry, its demand curve *is* the market demand curve. And because market demand is not perfectly elastic, its demand curve is downsloping. Columns 1 and 2 in Table 11-1 illustrate this concept; note that quantity demanded increases as price decreases.

Recall that in Chapter 10 we drew separate demand curves for the purely competitive industry and for a single firm in the industry. But only a single demand curve is needed in pure monopoly because the firm and the industry are one and the same. Part of the demand data in Table 11-1 is graphed as demand curve *D* in Figure 11-2.

**TABLE 11-1 Revenue and cost data of a pure monopolist**

| REVENUE DATA | | | | COST DATA | | | |
|---|---|---|---|---|---|---|---|
| (1) Quantity of output | (2) Price (average revenue) | (3) Total revenue | (4) Marginal revenue | (5) Average total cost | (6) Total cost | (7) Marginal cost | (8) Profit (+) or loss (–) |
| 0 | $172 | $ 0 | | | $ 100 | | $–100 |
| | | | $162 | | | $ 90 | |
| 1 | 162 | 162 | | $190.00 | 190 | | –28 |
| | | | 142 | | | 80 | |
| 2 | 152 | 304 | | 135.00 | 270 | | +34 |
| | | | 122 | | | 70 | |
| 3 | 142 | 426 | | 113.33 | 340 | | +86 |
| | | | 102 | | | 60 | |
| 4 | 132 | 528 | | 100.00 | 400 | | +128 |
| | | | 82 | | | 70 | |
| 5 | 122 | 610 | | 94.00 | 470 | | +140 |
| | | | 62 | | | 80 | |
| 6 | 112 | 672 | | 91.67 | 550 | | +122 |
| | | | 42 | | | 90 | |
| 7 | 102 | 714 | | 91.43 | 640 | | +74 |
| | | | 22 | | | 110 | |
| 8 | 92 | 736 | | 93.75 | 750 | | –14 |
| | | | 2 | | | 130 | |
| 9 | 82 | 738 | | 97.78 | 880 | | –142 |
| | | | –18 | | | 150 | |
| 10 | 72 | 720 | | 103.00 | 1030 | | –310 |

**FIGURE 11-2 Price and marginal revenue in pure monopoly**

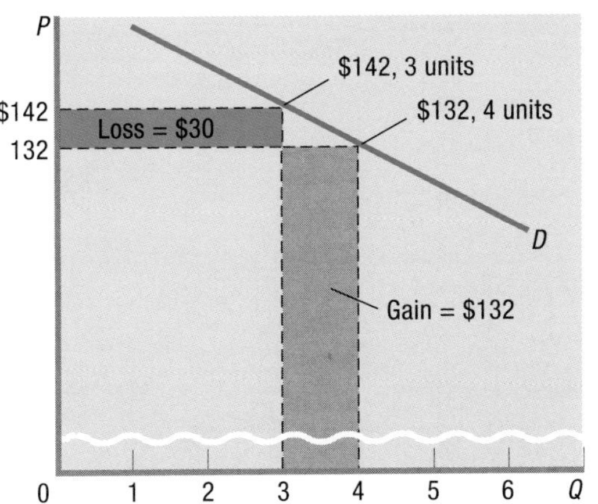


A pure monopolist—or any other imperfect competitor with a downsloping demand curve such as *D*—must set a lower price to sell more output. Here, by charging $132 rather than $142, the monopolist sells an extra unit (the fourth unit) and gains $132 from that sale. But from this gain must be subtracted $30, which reflects the $10 less the monopolist charged for each of the first 3 units. Thus, the marginal revenue of the fourth unit is $102 (= $132 – $30), considerably less than its $132 price.

The downsloping demand curve has three implications that you must understand in order to understand the monopoly model.

## Marginal Revenue Is Less Than Price

The downsloping demand curve faced by a pure monopolist means it can increase sales only by charging a lower price. *Because the monopolist must lower its price to increase sales, marginal revenue is less than price (average revenue) for every level of output except the first.* The reason is that the lower price applies not only to the extra output sold but also to all prior units of output. Each additional unit of output sold increases total revenue by an amount equal to its own price *less* the sum of the price cuts that apply to all prior units of output.

Figure 11-2 confirms this point. There, we have highlighted two price-quantity combinations from the monopolist's demand curve. The monopolist can sell 1 more unit at $132 than it can at $142 and thereby obtain $132 of extra revenue. But to sell this fourth unit for $132, the monopolist must also sell the first 3 units at $132 rather than $142. This $10 reduction in revenue on 3 units results in a $30 revenue loss. The *net* difference in total revenue from selling a fourth unit is $102, the $132 gain minus the $30 loss. This net gain of $102—the *marginal revenue* of the fourth unit—is obviously less than the $132 *price* of the fourth unit.

Column 4 in Table 11-1 shows that marginal revenue is always less than the corresponding product price in column 2, except for the first unit of output. Because marginal revenue is the change in total revenue associated with each additional unit of output, the declining amounts of marginal revenue in column 4 mean that total revenue increases at a diminishing rate (as shown in column 3.

The relationship between the monopolist's marginal-revenue curve and total-revenue curve is shown in Figure 11-3. For this figure the demand and revenue data of columns 1 through 4 in Table 11-1 were extended assuming that successive $10 price cuts will each bring about 1 additional unit of sales. That is, 11 units can be sold at a price of $62, 12 at $52, and so on.

Note that the monopolist's MR curve lies below the demand curve, indicating that marginal revenue is *less than* price at every output quantity but the very first unit. Observe also the special relationship between total revenue and marginal revenue. Because marginal revenue is the change in total revenue, marginal revenue is positive while total revenue is increasing. When total revenue reaches its maximum, marginal revenue is zero. When total revenue is diminishing, marginal revenue is negative.

## The Monopolist Is a "Price Maker"

In all imperfectly competitive markets with downsloping demand curves—that is, in pure monopoly, oligopoly, and monopolistic competition—firms can to one degree or another influence total supply through their own output decisions. In changing market supply, they can also affect product price. Rather than being price takers, as are pure competitors, firms with downsloping demand curves are "price makers."

This is most evident in pure monopoly, where one firm controls total output. The monopolist faces a downsloping demand curve in which each output is associated with some unique price. Thus, in deciding on what volume of output to

**FIGURE 11-3 Demand, marginal revenue, and total revenue for an imperfectly competitive firm**

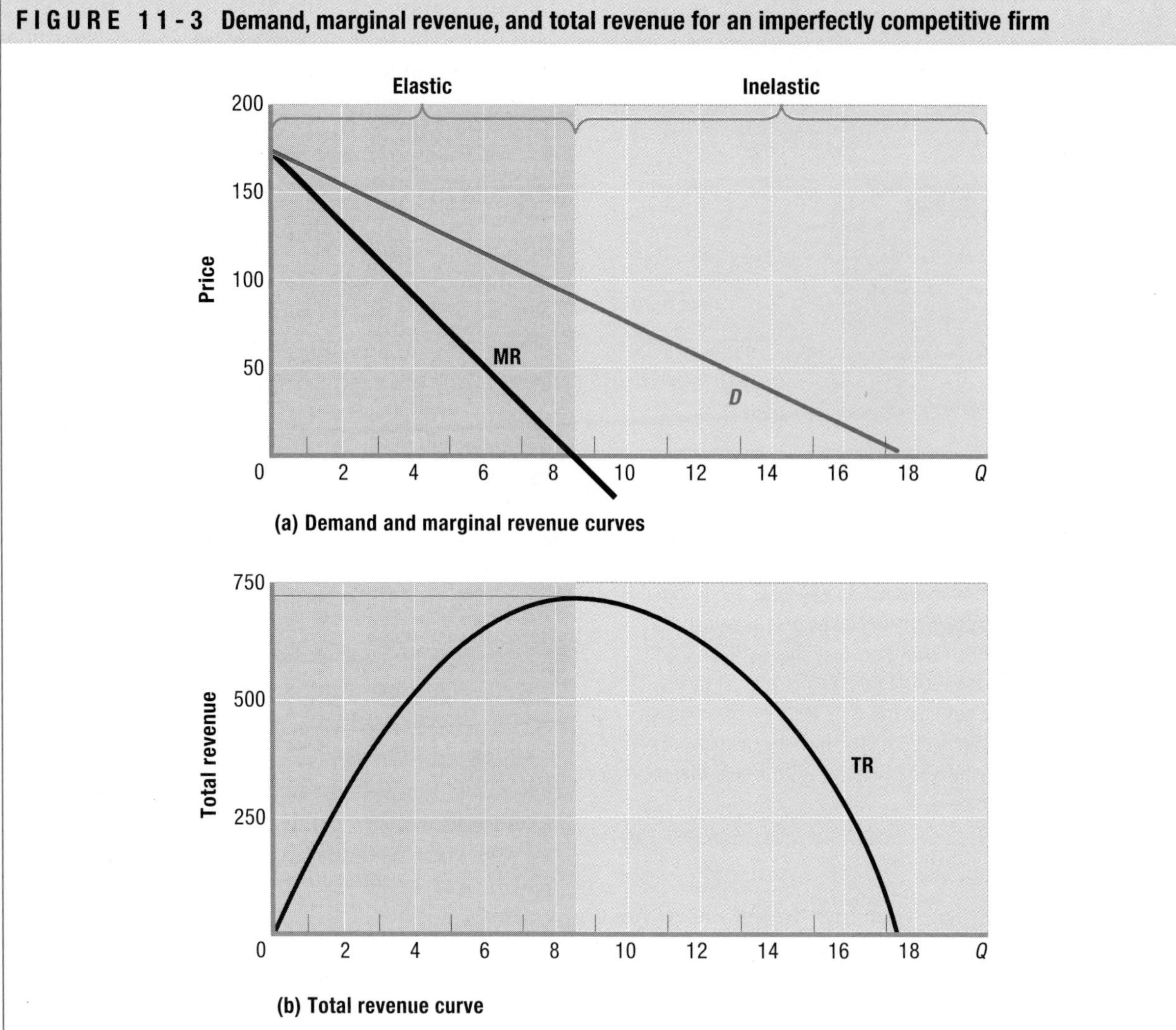


(a) Because it must lower price on all units sold to increase its sales, an imperfectly competitive firm's marginal-revenue curve (MR) lies below its downsloping demand curve (*D*). The elastic and inelastic regions of demand are highlighted. (b) Total revenue (TR) increases at a decreasing rate, reaches a maximum, and then declines. Note that in the elastic region, TR is increasing and hence MR is positive. When TR reaches its maximum, MR is zero. In the inelastic region of demand, TR is declining, so MR is negative.

produce, the monopolist is also determining the price it will charge. Through control of output, it can "make the price." From columns 1 and 2 in Table 11-1 we find that the monopolist can charge a price of $72 if it produces and offers for sale 10 units. It can charge a price of $82 if it produces and offers for sale 9 units, and so forth.

## The Monopolist Prices in the Elastic Region of Demand

The total-revenue test for price elasticity of demand is the basis for our third implication. Recall from Chapter 7 that the total-revenue test reveals that when demand is elastic, a decline in price will increase total revenue. Similarly, when demand is inelastic, a decline in price will reduce total revenue. Beginning at the top of demand curve *D* in Figure 11-3a, observe that as the price declines from $172 to approximately $82, total revenue increases (and marginal revenue therefore is positive). This means that demand is elastic in this price range. Conversely, for price declines below $82, total revenue decreases (marginal revenue is negative), which indicates that demand is inelastic there.

The implication is that a monopolist will never choose a price-quantity combination where price declines cause total revenue to decrease (marginal revenue to be negative). *The profit-maximizing monopolist will always want to avoid the inelastic segment of its demand curve in favour of some price-quantity combination in the elastic region.* Here's why: To get into the inelastic region, the monopolist must lower the price and increase output. In the inelastic region a lower price means less total revenue. And increased output always means increased total cost. Less total revenue and higher total cost yield diminished profit. ***(Key Question 4)***

**11-1**

**QUICK REVIEW**

- A pure monopolist is the sole supplier of a product or service for which there are no close substitutes.
- Monopolies exist because of entry barriers such as economies of scale, patents and licences, and the ownership of essential resources.
- The monopolist's demand curve is downsloping, and its marginal-revenue curve lies below its demand curve.
- The downsloping demand curve means that the monopolist is a "price maker."
- The monopolist will operate in the elastic region of demand, because it can increase total revenue and reduce total cost—thereby increasing profits—by reducing output, moving it to the elastic region.

## OUTPUT AND PRICE DETERMINATION

At what specific price-quantity combination will a profit-maximizing monopolist choose to operate? To answer this question, we must add production costs to our analysis.

### Cost Data

On the cost side, we will assume that although the firm is a monopolist in the product market, it hires resources competitively and employs the same technology as our competitive firm in the preceding chapter. This lets us use the cost data we developed in Chapter 9 and we applied in Chapter 10, so we can compare the price-output decisions of a pure monopoly with those of a pure competitor. Columns 5 through 7 in Table 11-1 restate the pertinent cost data in Table 9-2.

### MR = MC Rule

A monopolist seeking to maximize total profit will employ the same rationale as a profit-seeking firm in a competitive industry. It will produce another unit of output as long as that unit adds more to total revenue than it adds to total cost. The firm will increase output up to that output at which marginal revenue equals marginal cost (MR = MC).

A comparison of columns 4 and 7 in Table 11-1 indicates that the profit-maximizing output is 5 units; the fifth unit is the last unit of output whose marginal revenue exceeds its marginal cost. What price will the monopolist charge? The demand schedule shown as columns 1 and 2 in Table 11-1 indicates that there is only one price at which 5 units can be sold: $122.

This analysis is shown in ***Figure 11-4 (Key Graph)***, where the demand, marginal-revenue, average-total-cost, and marginal-cost data in Table 11-1 have been graphed. The profit-maximizing output occurs where MR = MC. We see that the marginal-revenue (MR) and marginal-cost (MC) curves intersect—that is, MR = MC—at 5 units of output, which we call $Q_m$. What price will the monopolist charge? This price is found by extending a vertical line from $Q_m$ up to the demand curve *D*. The unique price $P_m$ at which $Q_m$ units can be sold is the price corresponding to 5 units on demand curve *D*. In this case, the profit-maximizing price is $122.

Columns 2 and 5 in Table 11-1 indicate that, at 5 units of output, the product price ($122) exceeds the average total cost ($94). An economic profit of $28 per unit is therefore earned; the total economic profit is then $140 (= 5 units × $28). In Figure 11-4, per-unit profit is $P_m - A$ where *A* is the average total cost of producing $Q_m$ units. Total economic profit is found by multiplying this per-unit profit by the profit-maximizing output $Q_m$.

The profit-maximizing output can also be determined by comparing total revenue and total cost at each possible level of production and choosing the output with the greatest positive difference. You should use columns 3 and 6 in Table 11-1 to verify our conclusion that 5 units is the profit-maximizing output. Accurately graphing total revenue and total cost against output will also show the

## KEY GRAPH

**FIGURE 11-4 The profit-maximizing position of a pure monopolist**

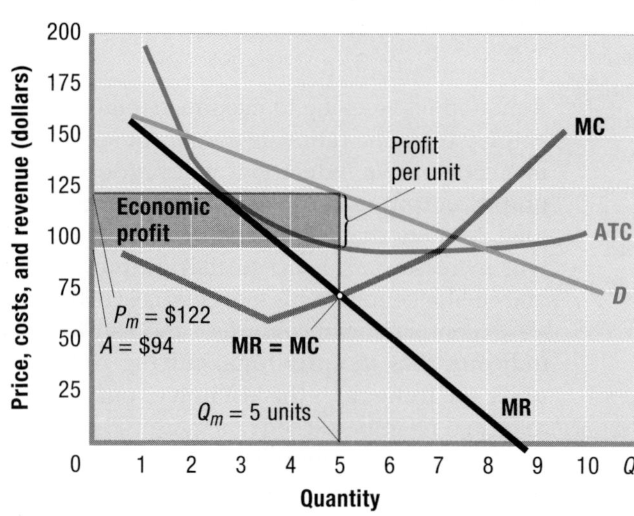


The pure monopolist maximizes profit by producing the MR = MC output, here $Q_m = 5$ units. Then, as seen from the demand curve, it will charge price $P_m = \$122$. Average total cost will be $A = \$94$, meaning that per-unit profit is $P_m - A$ and total profit is $5 \times (P_m - A)$. Total economic profit is thus represented by the grey rectangle.

### 11-4 QUICK QUIZ

1. The MR curve lies below the demand curve in this figure because the:
   **(a)** demand curve is linear (a straight line).
   **(b)** demand curve is highly inelastic throughout its full length.
   **(c)** demand curve is highly elastic throughout its full length.
   **(d)** gain in revenue from an extra unit of output is less than the price charged for that unit of output.
2. The area labelled "Economic profit" can be found by multiplying the difference between *P* and ATC by quantity. It also can be found by:
   **(a)** dividing profit per unit by quantity.
   **(b)** subtracting total cost from total revenue.
   **(c)** multiplying the coefficient of demand elasticity by quantity.
   **(d)** multiplying the difference between *P* and MC by quantity.
3. This pure monopolist:
   **(a)** charges the highest price it can get.
   **(b)** earns only a normal profit in the long run.
   **(c)** restricts output to create an insurmountable entry barrier.
   **(d)** restricts output to increase its price and total economic profit.
4. At this monopolist's profit-maximizing output:
   **(a)** price equals marginal revenue.
   **(b)** price equals marginal cost.
   **(c)** price exceeds marginal cost.
   **(d)** profit per unit is maximized.

**Answers:** 1. (d); 2. (b); 3. (d); 4. (c).

greatest difference (the maximum profit) at 5 units of output. Table 11-1 is a step-by-step summary of the process for determining the profit-maximizing output, the profit-maximizing price, and economic profit in pure monopoly. ***(Key Question 5)***

## No Monopoly Supply Curve

Recall that MR equals *P* in pure competition and that the supply curve of a purely competitive firm is determined by applying the MR (= *P*) = MC profit-maximizing rule. At any specific market-determined price the purely competitive seller will maximize profit by supplying the quantity at which MC is equal to that price. When the market price increases or decreases, the competitive firm produces more or less output. Each market price is thus associated with a specific output, and all such price-output pairs define the supply curve. This supply curve turns out to be that portion of the firm's MC curve that lies above the average-variable-cost curve (Figure 10-6 shows it).

At first glance we would suspect that the pure monopolist's marginal-cost curve would also be its supply curve. But this is *not* the case. *The pure monopolist has no supply curve.* The reason is that there is no unique relationship between price and quantity supplied for a monopolist. Like the competitive firm, the monopolist equates marginal revenue and marginal cost to determine output, but for the monopolist marginal revenue is less than price. Because the monopolist does not equate marginal cost to price, it is possible for different demand conditions to bring about different prices for the same output. To convince yourself of this, refer to Figure 11-4 and pencil in a new, steeper marginal-revenue curve that intersects the marginal-cost curve at the same point as does the present marginal-revenue curve. Then draw in a new demand curve that roughly corresponds with your new marginal-revenue curve. With the new curves, the same MR = MC output of 5 units now corresponds with a higher profit-maximizing price. Conclusion: There is no single, unique price associated with each output level $Q_m$, and so there is no supply curve for the pure monopolist.

## Misconceptions Concerning Monopoly Pricing

Our analysis explodes two fallacies concerning monopoly behaviour.

**Not Highest Price** Because a monopolist can manipulate output and price, people often believe it "will charge the highest price it can get." This is incorrect. There are many prices above $P_m$ in Figure 11-4, but the monopolist shuns them because they yield a smaller-than-maximum total profit. The monopolist seeks maximum total profit, not maximum price. Some high prices that could be charged would reduce sales and total revenue too severely to offset any decrease in total cost.

**Total, Not Unit, Profit** The monopolist seeks maximum *total* profit, not maximum *unit* profit. In Figure 11-4 a careful comparison of the vertical distance between average total cost and price at various possible outputs indicates that per-unit profit is greater at a point slightly to the left of the profit-maximizing output $Q_m$. This is seen in Table 11-1, where unit profit at 4 units of output is $32 (= $132 – $100) compared with $28 (= $122 – $94) at the profit-maximizing output of 5 units. Here the monopolist accepts a lower-than-maximum per-unit profit because additional sales more than compensate for the lower unit profit. A profit-seeking monopolist would rather sell 5 units at a profit of $28 per unit (for a total profit of $140) than 4 units at a profit of $32 per unit (for a total profit of only $128).

## Possibility of Monopolist Losses

The likelihood of economic profit is greater for a pure monopolist than for a pure competitor. In the long run the latter is destined to have only a normal profit, whereas barriers to entry mean that any economic profit realized by the monopolist can persist. In pure monopoly there are no entrants to increase supply, drive down price, and eliminate economic profit.

But pure monopoly does not guarantee profit. The monopolist is not immune from changes in tastes that reduce the demand for its product. Nor is it immune from upward-shifting cost curves due to escalating resource prices. If the demand and cost situation faced by the monopolist is far less favourable than that in Figure 11-4, the monopolist will incur losses in the short run. Despite its dominance in the market, the monopoly in Figure 11-5 suffers a loss, as shown, because of weak demand and relatively high costs. Yet it continues to operate for the time being because its total loss is less than its fixed cost. More precisely, at output $Q_m$ the monopolist's price $P_m$ exceeds its average variable cost $V$. Its loss per unit is $A - P_m$, and the total loss is shown by the grey rectangle.

Like the pure competitor, the monopolist will not persistently operate at a loss. Faced with continuing losses, in the long run the firm's owners will move their resources to alternative industries offering better profit opportunities. Thus we can expect the monopolist to realize a normal profit or better in the long run.

# ECONOMIC EFFECTS OF MONOPOLY

Let's now evaluate pure monopoly from the standpoint of society as a whole. Our reference for this evaluation will be the long-run efficiency outcome in a purely competitive market, identified by the triple equality $P$ = MC = minimum ATC.

## Price, Output, and Efficiency

Figure 11-6 graphically contrasts the price, output, and efficiency outcomes of pure monopoly and a

**FIGURE 11-5 The loss-minimizing position of a pure monopolist**

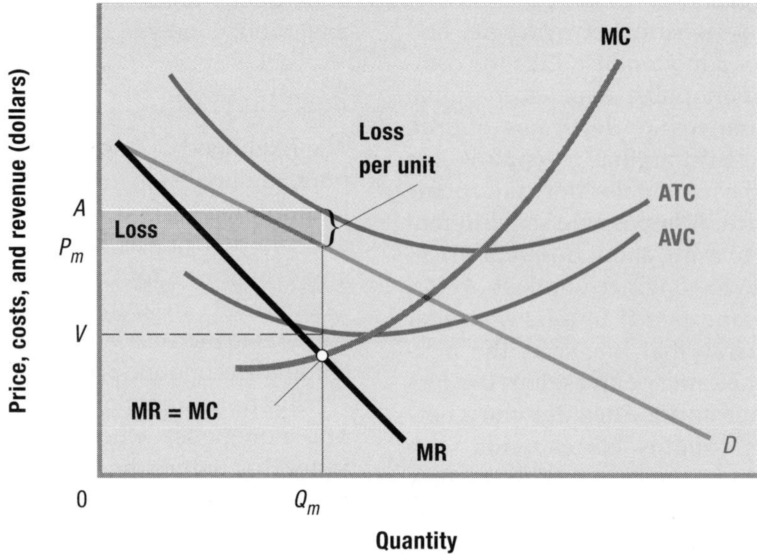


If demand $D$ is weak and costs are high, the pure monopolist may be unable to make a profit. Because $P_m$ exceeds $V$, the average variable cost at the MR = MC output $Q_m$, the monopolist will minimize losses in the short run by producing at that output. The loss per unit is $A - P_m$, and the total loss is indicated by the grey rectangle.

purely competitive *industry* graphically. Starting with Figure 11-6a, we are reminded that the purely competitive industry's market supply curve $S$ is the horizontal sum of the marginal-cost curves of all the firms in the industry. Let's suppose there are 1,000 such firms. Comparing their combined supply curves $S$ with market demand $D$, we get the purely competitive price and output of $P_c$ and $Q_c$.

Recall that this price-output combination results in both productive efficiency and allocative efficiency. *Productive efficiency* is realized because easy entry and exit force firms to operate where average total cost is at a minimum. The sum of the minimum-ATC outputs of the 1,000 pure competitors is the industry output, here, $Q_c$. Product price is at the lowest level consistent with minimum average total cost. The *allocative efficiency* of pure competition results because production occurs up to that output at which price (the measure of a product's value or marginal benefit to society) equals marginal cost (the worth of the alternative products forgone by society in producing any given commodity). In short: $P = \text{MC} = \text{minimum ATC}$.

Now let's suppose this industry becomes a pure monopoly (Figure 11-6b) as a result of one firm buying out all its competitors. We also assume that no changes in costs or market demand result from this dramatic change in the industry structure. What were formerly 1,000 competing firms are now a single pure monopolist consisting of 1,000 noncompeting branches.

The competitive market supply curve $S$ has become the marginal-cost curve (MC) of the monopolist, the summation of the MC curves of its many branch plants. (Since the monopolist does not have a supply curve, as such, we have removed the $S$ label.) The important change, however, is on the demand side. From the viewpoint of each of the 1,000 individual competitive firms, demand was perfectly elastic, and marginal revenue was therefore equal to price. Each firm equated MR (= price) and MC in maximizing profits. But market demand and individual demand are the same to the pure monopolist. The firm *is* the industry, and thus the monopolist sees the downsloping demand curve $D$ shown in Figure 11-6b.

This means that marginal revenue is less than price, that graphically the MR curve lies below demand curve $D$. In using the MR = MC rule, the monopolist selects output $Q_m$ and price $P_m$. A comparison of both graphs in Figure 11-6 reveals that the monopolist finds it profitable to sell a smaller

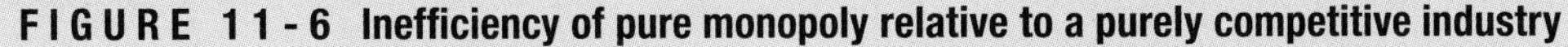

**FIGURE 11-6 Inefficiency of pure monopoly relative to a purely competitive industry**

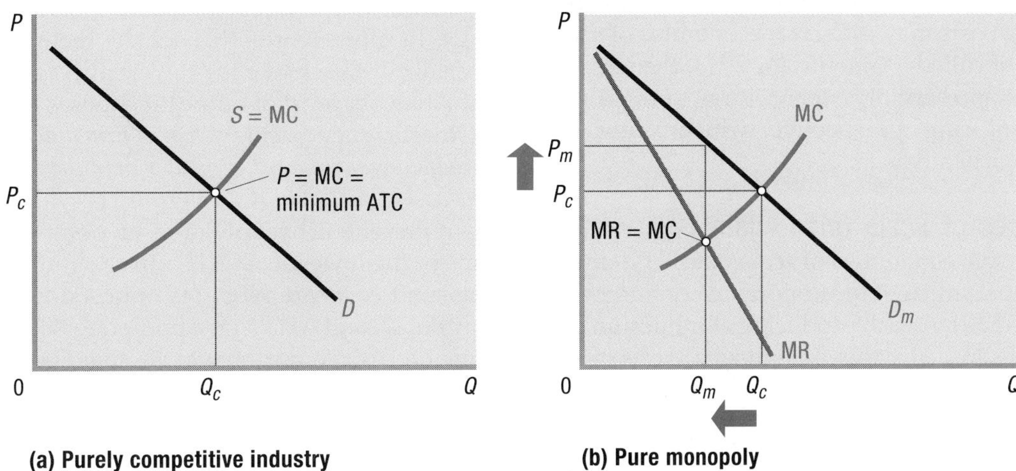


**(a) Purely competitive industry**

**(b) Pure monopoly**

(a) In a purely competitive industry, entry and exit of firms ensures that price ($P_c$) equals marginal cost (MC) and that the minimum average-total-cost output ($Q_c$) is produced. Both productive efficiency ($P$ = minimum ATC) and allocative efficiency ($P$ = MC) are obtained. (b) In pure monopoly, the MR curve lies below the demand curve. The monopolist maximizes profit at output $Q_m$, where MR = MC, and charges price $P_m$. Thus, output is lower ($Q_m$ rather than $Q_c$) and price is higher ($P_m$ rather than $P_c$) than they would be in a purely competitive industry. Monopoly is inefficient, since output is less than that required to achieve minimum ATC (here at $Q_c$) and because price exceeds MC.

output at a higher price than do the competitive producers. Monopoly yields neither productive nor allocative efficiency. The monopolist's output is less than $Q_c$, the output at which average total cost is lowest. And price is higher than the competitive price $P_c$, which in long-run equilibrium pure competition equals minimum average total cost. Thus the monopoly price *exceeds* minimum average total cost. Also, at the monopolist's $Q_m$ output, product price is considerably higher than marginal cost, which means that society values additional units of this monopolized product more highly than it values the alternative products the resources could otherwise produce. So the monopolist's profit-maximizing output results in an underallocation of resources. The monopolist finds it profitable to restrict output and therefore employ fewer resources than are justified from society's standpoint. Hence the monopolist does not achieve allocative efficiency.

In monopoly, then, $P >$ MC and $P >$ minimum ATC.

## Income Distribution

In general, monopoly contributes to inequality in income distribution. By virtue of their market power, monopolists charge a higher price than would a purely competitive firm with the same costs; monopolists in effect can levy a "private tax" on consumers and obtain substantial economic profits. These monopolistic profits are not widely distributed because corporate stock ownership is largely concentrated in the hands of upper-income groups. The owners of monopolistic enterprises thus tend to be enriched at the expense of the rest of society.

Exception: If the buyers of a monopoly product are wealthier than the owners of the monopoly, the monopoly may *reduce* income inequality. But, in general, this is not the case, and we thus conclude that monopoly contributes to income inequality.

## Cost Complications

Our evaluation of pure monopoly has led us to conclude that, *given identical costs*, a pure monopolist will charge a higher price, produce a smaller output, and allocate economic resources less efficiently than a purely competitive industry. These inferior results are rooted in the entry barriers characterizing monopoly.

Now we must recognize that costs may *not* be the same for purely competitive and monopolistic producers. The unit cost incurred by a monopolist may be either larger or smaller than that incurred by a purely competitive firm. There are four reasons why costs may differ: (1) economies of scale, (2) a factor called "X-inefficiency," (3) the need for monopoly-preserving expenditures, and (4) the "very long-run" perspective, which allows for technological advance.

**Economies of Scale Once Again** Where there are extensive economies of scale, market demand may not be sufficient to support a large number of competing firms, each producing at minimum efficient scale. In such cases, an industry of one or two firms would have a lower average total cost than would the same industry made up of numerous competitive firms. At the extreme, only a single firm—a natural monopoly—might be able to achieve the lowest long-run average total cost.

Most economists, however, conclude that natural monopoly is rare. And, in the more usual cases of monopoly, it is unlikely that cost reduction arising from monopoly is sufficient to offset the inefficiencies caused by the monopolist's reduced output and higher price. That is, the possibility of some cost reduction from size does not change our general conclusion that, compared with more competitive industries, monopolies yield more inferior overall efficiency results.

**X-Inefficiency** All the average-total-cost curves used in this book are based on the assumption that the firm uses the most efficient existing technology. In other words, it uses the technology that permits it to achieve the lowest average total cost of whatever level of output it chooses to produce. **X-inefficiency** occurs *when a firm's actual cost of producing any output is greater than the lowest possible cost of that output.* In Figure 11-7 X-inefficiency is represented by operation at points $X$ and $X'$ above the lowest-cost ATC curve. At these points, per-unit costs are $ATC_x$ (as opposed to $ATC_1$) for output $Q_1$ and $ATC'_{x'}$ (as opposed to $ATC_2$) for output $Q_2$. Any point above the average-total-cost-curve in Figure 11-7 is possible but reflects inefficiency or "bad management" by the firm.

Why is X-inefficiency allowed to occur if it reduces profits? The answer is that managers may have goals—firm growth, an easier work life, avoidance of business risk, giving jobs to incompetent friends and relatives—that conflict with cost minimization. Or X-inefficiency may arise because a firm's workers are poorly motivated or ineffectively supervised. Or a firm may simply become lethargic and inert, relying on rules of thumb in decision making as opposed to relevant calculations of costs and revenues.

For our purposes the relevant question is whether monopolistic firms tend more to X-ineffi-

**FIGURE 11-7 X-inefficiency**

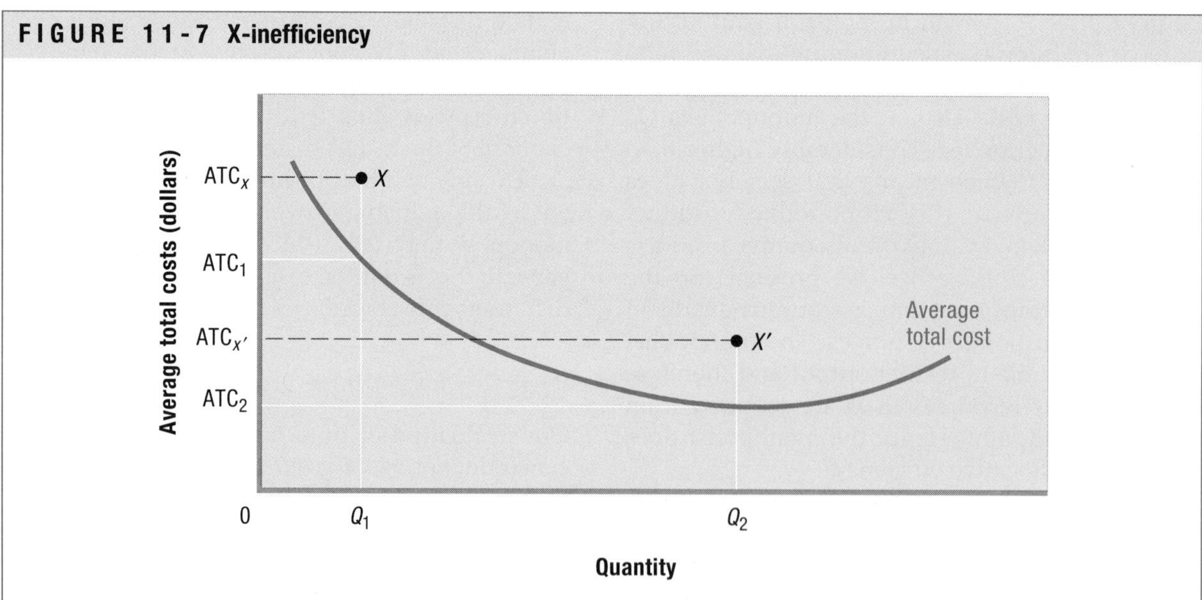


The average-total-cost curve (ATC) is assumed to reflect the minimum cost of producing each particular unit of output. Any point above this "lowest-cost" ATC curve, such as $X$ or $X'$, implies X-inefficiency: operation at greater than lowest cost for a particular level of output.

ciency than competitive producers. Presumably they do. Firms in competitive industries are continually under pressure from rivals, forcing them to be internally efficient to survive. But monopolists are sheltered from such competitive forces by entry barriers, and this lack of pressure leads to X-inefficiency.

There is no indisputable evidence of X-inefficiency, but what we have suggests than X-inefficiency increases as the amount of competition decreases. A reasonable estimate is that X-inefficiency may be 10 percent or more of costs for monopolists but only 5 percent for an "average" oligopolistic industry in which the four largest firms produce 60 percent of total output.[1] In the words of one authority: "The evidence is fragmentary, but it points in the same direction. X-inefficiency exists, and it is more apt to be reduced when competitive pressures are strong than when firms enjoy insulated market positions."[2]

**Rent-Seeking Expenditures** **Rent-seeking behaviour** is any activity designed to transfer income or wealth to a particular firm or resource supplier at someone else's, or even society's, expense. We have seen that a monopolist can earn an economic profit even in the long run. Therefore, it is no surprise that a firm may go to great expense to acquire or maintain a monopoly granted by government through legislation or an exclusive licence. Such rent-seeking expenditures add nothing to the firm's output, but they clearly increase its costs. They imply that monopoly involves higher costs and less efficiency than suggested in Figure 11-6b.

**Technological Advance** In the very long run, firms can reduce their costs through discovery and implementation of new technology. If monopolists are more likely than competitive producers to develop more efficient production techniques over time, then the inefficiency of monopoly might be overstated. Since research and development (R&D) is the topic of Chapter 15, we will provide only a brief assessment here.

The general view of economists is that a pure monopolist will not be technologically progressive. Although its economic profit provides ample means to finance research and development, it has little incentive to implement new techniques (or products). The absence of competitors means there is no external pressure for technological advance in a monopolized market. Because of its sheltered market position, the pure monopolist can afford to be inefficient and lethargic; there simply is no penalty for being so.

One caveat: Research and technological advance may be one of the monopolist's barriers to entry. Thus, the monopolist may continue to seek technological advance or fall prey to new rivals. In this case technological advance is essential to the maintenance of monopoly. But it is then potential *competition*, not the monopoly market structure, that is driving the technological advance. In theory, there is no such competition in the pure monopoly model; entry is completely blocked.

## Policy Options

Our overall conclusion is that pure monopoly is economically inefficient. What then should society do about monopoly when it arises in the real world? Three general policy options are available:

1. If the monopoly creates substantial economic inefficiency and appears to be long-lasting, government can file charges against the monopoly under the anti-combines laws, seeking to break up the monopoly into several competing firms. (Anti-combines action is the subject of Chapter 14.)
2. If the monopoly is a natural monopoly, society can allow it to continue but directly regulate its prices and operations.
3. If the monopoly appears to be relatively short-lived, say, because of emerging new technology, society can simply choose to ignore it. (The potential for real-world monopoly to collapse in the very long run is discussed in Chapter 13.)

**11-2**

**QUICK REVIEW**

- The monopolist maximizes profit (or minimizes loss) at the output where MR = MC and charges the price that corresponds to this output on its demand curve.

[1] William G. Shepherd, *The Economics of Industrial Organization*, 4th ed. (Englewood Cliffs, NJ: Prentice-Hall, 1997), p. 107. For a rather extensive review of case study evidence of X-inefficiency, see F.M. Scherer and David Ross, *Industrial Market Structure and Economic Performance*, 3rd ed. (Chicago: Rand McNally College Publishing, 1990), pp. 668–672.

[2] Scherer and Ross, op. cit., p. 672.

- The monopolist has no supply curve since any of several prices can be associated with a specific quantity of output supplied.
- Assuming identical costs, a monopolist will be less efficient than a purely competitive industry because the monopolist produces less output and charges a higher price.
- The inefficiencies of monopoly may be offset or lessened by economies of scale and, less likely, technological progress, but intensified by the presence of X-inefficiency and rent-seeking expenditures.

## PRICE DISCRIMINATION

We have assumed in this chapter that the monopolist charges a single price to all buyers. But under certain conditions the monopolist can increase its profit by charging different prices to different buyers. In so doing, the monopolist is engaging in **price discrimination**, *the practice of selling a specific product or service at more than one price when the price differences are not justified by cost differences.*

### Conditions

The opportunity to engage in price discrimination is not readily available to all sellers. Price discrimination is possible when three conditions are realized:

1. **MONOPOLY POWER** The seller must be a monopolist or, at least, possess some degree of monopoly power, that is, some ability to control output and price.
2. **MARKET SEGREGATION** The seller must be able to segregate buyers into distinct classes, each of which has a different willingness or ability to pay for the product. This separation of buyers is usually based on different elasticities of demand, as the illustrations below will make clear.
3. **NO RESALE** The original purchaser cannot resell the product or service. If buyers in the low-price segment of the market could easily resell in the high-price segment, the monopolist's price discrimination strategy would create competition in the high-price segment. This competition would reduce the price in the high-price segment and undermine the monopolist's price discrimination policy. This condition suggests that service industries such as the transportation industry or legal and medical services, where resale is impossible, are candidates for price discrimination.

### Examples

Price discrimination is widely practised in the Canadian economy:

1. The sales representative who must communicate important information to corporate headquarters has a highly inelastic demand for long-distance telephone service and pays the high daytime rate. The university or college student "reporting in" to the folks at home has an elastic demand and can wait to take advantage of lower evening or weekend rates.
2. Electric utilities frequently segment their markets by end uses, such as lighting and heating. The absence of reasonable lighting substitutes means the demand for electricity for illumination is inelastic and the price per kilowatt-hour for this use is high. But the availability of natural gas and petroleum for heating makes the demand for electricity less inelastic for this purpose and the price charged is lower.
3. Movie theatres and golf courses vary their charges on the basis of time (higher rates in the evening and on weekends when demand is strong) and age (ability to pay).
4. Railroads vary the rate charged per tonne kilometre of freight according to the market value of the product being shipped. The shipper of 10 tonnes of television sets or costume jewellery is charged more than the shipper of 10 tonnes of gravel or coal.
5. Airlines charge high fares to travelling executives, whose demand for travel is inelastic, and offer lower fares such as "family rates" and "14-day advanced purchase fares" to attract vacationers and others whose demands are more elastic.
6. The issuance of discount coupons, redeemable at purchase, is a form of price discrimination. It permits firms to give price discounts to their most price-sensitive customers—those with elastic demand. Less price-sensitive consumers—those with less elastic demand—are not as likely to undertake the clipping and redeeming of coupons. The firm thus makes a

larger profit than if it had used a single-price, no-coupon strategy.

7. In international trade, price discrimination is often called "dumping." A South Korean electronics manufacturer, for example, might sell a particular TV set for $100 less in Canada than in South Korea. In Canada, this seller faces an elastic demand because several substitute brands are available. But in South Korea, where the manufacturer dominates the market, consumers have fewer choices and thus demand is less elastic.

## Consequences of Price Discrimination

As you will see shortly, a monopolist can increase its profit by practising price discrimination. At the same time, perfect price discrimination results in greater output than that occurring with a single monopoly price.

**More Profit** The simplest way to understand why price discrimination can yield additional profit is to look again at our monopolist's downsloping demand curve in Figure 11-4. There we saw that the profit-maximizing single price is $P_m$ = $122. However, the segment of the demand curve lying above the grey economic profit area tells us some buyers are willing to pay *more than* $122 rather than forgo the product.

If the monopolist can identify and segregate these buyers and charge the maximum price each would pay, total revenue—and hence profit—would increase. In columns 1 and 2 in Table 11-1 we note that buyers of the first 4 units of output would be willing to pay $162, $152, $142, and $132, respectively, for those units. If the seller could practise perfect price discrimination by charging the maximum price for each unit, total revenue would increase from $610 (= $122 × 5) to $710 (= $122 + $132 + $142 + $152 + $162) and profit would increase from $140 (= $610 – $470) to $240 (= $710 – $470).

**More Production** Other things equal, the discriminating monopolist will choose to produce a larger output than the nondiscriminating monopolist. Recall that when the nondiscriminating monopolist lowers its price to sell additional output, the lower price applies not only to the additional output but also to *all prior* units of output. As a result, marginal revenue is less than price and, graphically, the marginal-revenue curve lies below the demand curve. The fact that marginal revenue is less than price acts as a disincentive to increased production.

But when a perfectly discriminating monopolist lowers price, the reduced price applies *only* to the additional unit sold and *not* to prior units. Thus, price and marginal revenue are equal for each unit of output. For the perfectly discriminating monopolists, the marginal-revenue curve coincides with the demand curve, so the disincentive to increase production is removed.

Table 11-1 shows that, because marginal revenue now equals price, the discriminating monopolist finds it profitable to produce 7, rather than 5, units of output. The additional revenue from the sixth and seventh units is $214 (= $112 + $102). Thus total revenue for 7 units is $924 (= $710 + $214). Total cost for 7 units is $640, so profit is $284.

Ironically, although price discrimination increases the monopolist's profit compared with that of a nondiscriminating monopolist, it also results in greater output and thus less allocative inefficiency. In our example, the output level of 7 units matches the output that would occur in pure competition. That is, allocative efficiency ($P$ = MC) is achieved.

**Graphical Portrayal** Figure 11-8 shows the effects of price discrimination. Figure 11-8a merely restates Figure 11-4 in a generalized form to show the position of a nondiscriminating monopolist as a benchmark. The nondiscriminating monopolist produces output $Q_1$ (where MR = MC) and charges a price of $P_1$. Total revenue is area *0bce* and economic profit is area *abcd*.

The monopolist in Figure 11-8b engages in perfect price discrimination, charging each buyer the highest price he or she is willing to pay. Starting at the very first unit, each additional unit is sold for the price indicated by the corresponding point on the demand curve. This monopolist's demand and marginal-revenue curves coincide because it does *not* cut price on preceding units to sell more output. Thus, the most profitable output is $Q_2$ (where MR = MC), which is greater than $Q_1$. Total revenue is area *0fgk* and total cost is area *0hjk*. The discriminating monopolist's economic profit of *hfgj* is clearly larger than the single-price monopolist's profit of *abcd*.

The impact of discrimination on consumers is mixed. Those buying each unit out to $Q_1$ will pay more than the nondiscriminatory price of $P_1$. But those additional consumers brought into the mar-

**FIGURE 11-8 Single-price versus perfectly discriminating monopolist pricing**

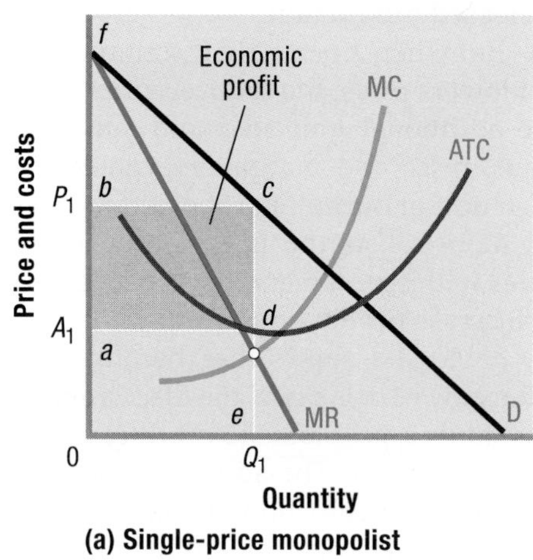


(a) Single-price monopolist

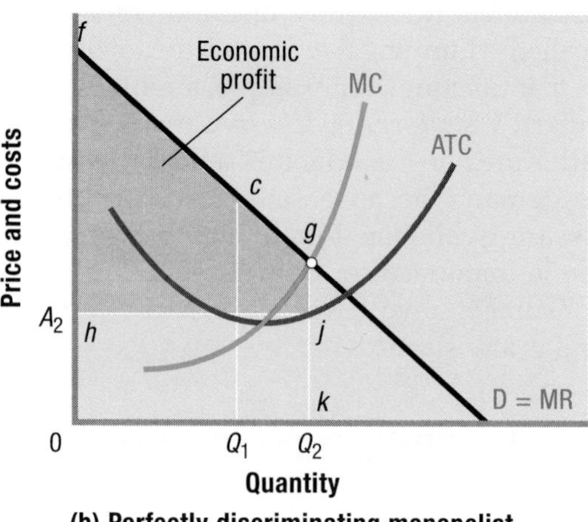


(b) Perfectly discriminating monopolist

(a) The single-price monopolist produces output $Q_1$ at which MR = MC, charges price $P_1$ for all units, incurs an average total cost of $A_1$, and realizes an economic profit represented by area *abcd*. (b) The perfectly discriminating monopolist has MR = *D* and, as a result, produces output $Q_2$ (where MR = MC). It then charges the maximum price for each unit of output, incurs average total cost $A_2$, and realizes an economic profit represented by area *hfgj*.

ket by discrimination will pay less than $P_1$. Specifically, they will pay the various prices shown on segment *cg* of the *D* = MR curve.

Overall, then, as compared with uniform pricing, perfect price discrimination results in greater profit, greater output, and higher prices for many consumers but lower prices for those purchasing the extra output. ***(Key Question 6)***

## NATURAL MONOPOLIES AND THEIR REGULATION

Anti-combines policy assumes society will benefit if monopoly is prevented from evolving or is dissolved where it already exists. We now return to a special situation in which there is an economic reason for an industry to be organized monopolistically.

### Natural Monopoly

A **natural monopoly** exists when economies of scale are so extensive that a single firm can supply the entire market at lower unit cost than could a number of competing firms. Such conditions exist for the *public utilities*, such as electricity, water, gas, and local telephone service. In these cases, large-scale operations are necessary if low unit costs—and a low price—are to be obtained. Where there is natural monopoly, competition is uneconomical. If the market were divided among many producers, economies of scale would not be achieved, unit costs would be high, and high prices would be necessary to cover those costs.

There are two possible alternatives for promoting socially acceptable behaviour on the part of a natural monopoly. One is public ownership, and the other is public regulation.

*Public ownership* has been established in some instances; Canada Post, CN and the St. Lawrence Seaway come to mind at the national level. All the provinces except Alberta and Prince Edward Island have Crown corporations producing their electricity, while mass transit, the water system, and garbage collection are typically public enterprises at the local level.

But *public regulation*, or what economists call *industrial regulation*, has been the preferred option in Canada. In this type of regulation, government commissions regulate the prices (or rates) charged by natural monopolists. Because of deregulation over the past two decades, such control is on the wane. Table 11-2 lists the major federal regulatory agencies.

**TABLE 11-2 The main federal regulatory agencies**

Atomic Energy Control Board
Canadian Dairy Commission
Canadian Grain Commission
Canadian Radio-television and Telecommunications Commission
Canadian Wheat Board
National Energy Board
National Farm Products Marketing Council
National Harbours Board
National Transport Agency of Canada

## Setting Price in a Regulated Monopoly

Monopolies that are natural monopolies normally are subject to regulation. The public utilities are all natural monopolies, and the prices they charge are determined by a federal, provincial, or municipal regulatory commission.

Figure 11-9 shows the demand faced by, and long-run costs of, a natural monopoly. Because of extensive economies of scale, the demand curve cuts the long-run average-total-cost curve at a point where it is still falling. It would be inefficient to have several firms in such an industry. Each would produce a much smaller output, operating well to the left on the average-total-cost curve, so that its per-unit cost would be substantially higher. Attaining the lowest per-unit cost in such a situation requires a single producer.

We know by application of the MR = MC rule that $Q_m$ and $P_m$ are the profit-maximizing output and price an unregulated monopolist would choose. Because price exceeds average total cost at output $Q_m$, the monopolist enjoys a substantial economic profit. Furthermore, price exceeds marginal cost, indicating an underallocation of resources to this product or service. Can government regulation bring about better results from society's point of view?

### Optimal Social Price: *P* = MC

If the objective of a regulatory commission is to achieve allocative efficiency, it should attempt to establish a legal (ceiling) price for the monopolist that is equal to *marginal cost*. Since each point on the market demand curve designates a price-quantity combination, the marginal-cost curve

**FIGURE 11-9 Regulated monopoly**

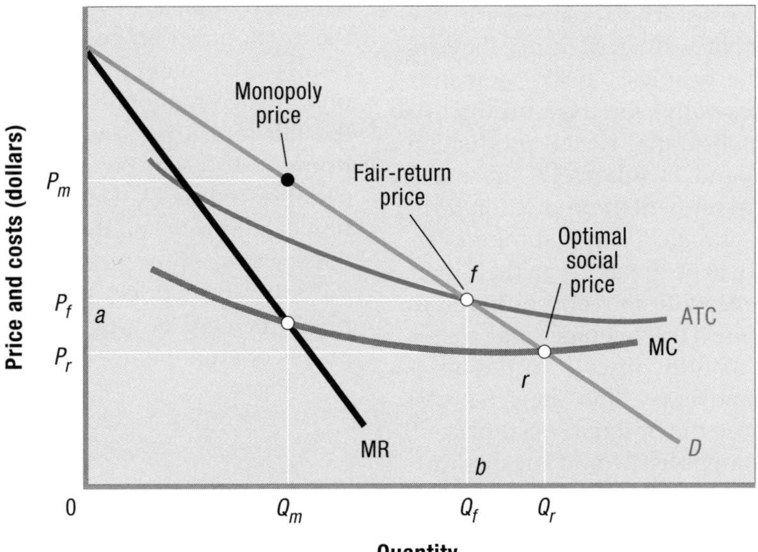


The optimal social price $P_r$, found where *D* and MC intersect, will result in an efficient allocation of resources but may entail losses to the monopoly. The fair-return price $P_f$ will allow the monopolist to break even but will not fully correct the underallocation of resources.

cuts the demand curve only at point *r*, and we see that $P_r$ is the only price on the demand curve equal to marginal cost. The maximum or price ceiling effectively causes the monopolist's demand curve to become horizontal (indicating perfectly elastic demand) from zero out to point *r*, where the regulated price ceases to be effective. Also, out to point *r* we have MR = $P_r$.

Confronted with the ceiling price $P_r$, the monopolist will maximize profit or minimize loss by producing $Q_r$ units of output, because it is at this output that MR (= $P_r$) = MC. By making it illegal to charge more than $P_r$ per unit, the regulatory agency has removed the monopolist's incentive to restrict output to $Q_m$ to obtain a higher price and greater profit.

In short, by imposing the price ceiling $P_r$ and letting the monopolist choose its profit-maximizing or loss-minimizing output, the allocative forces of pure competition can be simulated. Production takes place where $P_r$ = MC, and this equality indicates an efficient allocation of resources to this product or service. The price, which achieves allocative efficiency, is called the **optimal social price**.

## Fair-Return Price: *P* = ATC

But the optimal social price $P_r$ may pose a problem of losses for the regulated firm. The price that equals marginal cost may be so low that average total costs are not covered, as is the case in Figure 11-9. The result is losses. The reason lies in the basic character of public utilities. Because they are required to meet the heaviest "peak" demands (both daily and seasonally) for their product or service, they have substantial excess production capacity when demand is relatively "normal." Their high level of investment in production facilities and economies of scale mean that their average total cost is likely to be greater than their marginal cost over a very wide range of outputs. In particular, as in Figure 11-9, average total cost is likely to be greater than the price $P_r$ at the intersection of the demand curve and marginal-cost curve. Then, to impose the optimal social price $P_r$ on the regulated monopolist would mean short-run losses and long-run bankruptcy for the utility.

What to do? One option is to provide a public subsidy to cover the loss that marginal-cost pricing would entail. Another possibility is to condone price discrimination and hope that the additional revenue gained will permit the firm to cover costs.

In practice, regulatory commissions have pursued a third option: they modify the objective of allocative efficiency and *P* = MC pricing. Most regulatory agencies in Canada establish a **fair-return price**. They do so because, as the courts have seen it, an optimal social price leading to losses and bankruptcy would deprive the monopoly's owners of their private property without "due process of law."

Remembering that total cost includes a normal or "fair" profit, we see in Figure 11-9 that a fair-return price should be on the average-total-cost curve. Because the demand curve cuts average total cost only at point *f*, clearly $P_f$ is the only price on the demand curve that permits a fair return. The corresponding output at regulated price $P_f$ will be $Q_f$. Total revenue of 0*afb* will equal the utility's total cost of the same amount, and the firm will realize a normal profit.

## Dilemma of Regulation

Comparing results of the optimal social price (*P* = MC) and the fair-return price (*P* = ATC) suggests a policy dilemma, sometimes termed the **dilemma of regulation**. When its price is set to achieve the most efficient allocation of resources (*P* = MC), the regulated monopoly is likely to suffer losses. Survival of the firm would presumably depend on permanent public subsidies out of tax revenues. On the other hand, although a fair-return price (*P* = ATC) allows the monopolist to cover costs, it only partially resolves the underallocation of resources that the unregulated monopoly price would foster. That is, the fair-return price would increase output only from $Q_m$ to $Q_f$ in Figure 11-9, while the optimal social output is $Q_r$. Despite this dilemma, regulation can improve on the results of monopoly from the social point of view. Price regulation (even at the fair-return price) can simultaneously reduce price, increase output, and reduce the economic profits of monopolies. ***(Key Question 11)***

**11-3**

**QUICK REVIEW**

- Price discrimination occurs when a firm sells a product at different prices that are not based on cost differences.

- The conditions necessary for price discrimination are **a** monopoly power, **b** the ability to segregate buyers on the basis of demand elasticities, and **c** the inability of buyers to resell the product.
- Compared with single pricing by a monopolist, perfect price discrimination results in greater profit and greater output. Many consumers pay higher prices, but other buyers pay prices below the single price.
- Natural monopoly occurs where economies of scale are so extensive that only a single firm can produce the product at minimum average total cost.
- Monopoly price can be reduced and output increased through government regulation.
- The optimal social price (*P* = MC) achieves allocative efficiency but may result in losses; the fair-return price (*P* = ATC) yields a normal profit but falls short of allocative efficiency.

## THE EFFECTIVENESS OF NATURAL MONOPOLY REGULATION

The intent of legislation that regulates a natural monopoly is embodied in the **public interest theory of regulation**. This theory says that such an industry should be regulated for the benefit of the public so that consumers may be ensured quality service at reasonable rates. If competition is inappropriate or impractical, monopoly should be established but *regulated* to avoid possible abuses of uncontrolled monopoly power. Regulation should guarantee that *consumers* benefit from the economies of scale—the lower per-unit costs—that natural monopolists are able to achieve. In practice, regulators seek to establish rates that will cover production costs and yield a "fair" or "reasonable" return to the enterprise.

### Problems

There is considerable disagreement on the effectiveness of regulation. Let's examine three criticisms.

**Costs and Inefficiency** An unregulated firm has great incentive to reduce its production costs because doing so will increase profit. A regulated firm, however, is confined to a normal profit or a "fair return" on the value of its assets. If a regulated firm lowers its operating costs, the rising profit will lead the regulatory commission to require that the firm lower its rates so only a normal profit is earned. The regulated firm therefore has little or no incentive to reduce such costs. Worse yet, higher costs do not result in lower profits. Because the regulatory commissions must allow the public utility a fair return, higher production costs simply get passed through to consumers in the form of higher rates. A regulated firm may reason that it might as well have high salaries for its workers, nice working conditions for management, and the like since the "return" is the same whether costs are minimized or not. So although natural monopoly reduces cost through economies of scale, industrial regulation fosters considerable X-inefficiency.

There is still another potential for inefficiency. Since the regulated firm receives a certain rate of return on the value of its assets (real capital), the firm may make uneconomical substitutions of capital for labour. This, too, would contribute to X-inefficiency.

**Commission Deficiencies** Some critics say that regulatory commissions function inadequately because they and their staffs are often populated by people who were once in the industries they are now supposed to control. Therefore, regulation may not be in the public interest but, rather, may protect and nurture the comfortable position of the natural monopolist. Regulation allegedly becomes a way to guarantee profits and protect the regulated industry from new competition that technological change might create.

**Regulation of Competitive Industries** Perhaps the most severe criticism of industrial regulation is that it has sometimes been applied to industries that are not natural monopolies and that, without regulation, would be quite competitive. Specifically, regulation has been used in industries such as trucking and airlines, where economies of scale are not great and entry barriers are relatively weak. In such instances regulation itself, by limiting entry, may create the monopoly. The result is higher prices and less output than without regulation. Contrary to the public interest theory of regulation, the beneficiaries of regulation are then the regulated firms and their employees. The losers are the public and potential competitors barred from entering the industry.

Example: Regulation of the railroads was justified in the late 1800s and early 20th century. But by the 1930s the nation had developed a network of highways and the trucking industry had seriously undermined the monopoly power of the railroads. At that time it would have been desirable to dismantle the regulatory agency and let railroads and truckers, along with barges and airlines, compete with one another. Instead, the regulatory net of what is now the National Transport Agency of Canada was cast wider in the 1930s to include the airlines, while each province created its own trucking oligopoly. ***(Key Question 12)***

## Legal Cartel Theory

The regulation of potentially competitive industries has produced the **legal cartel theory of regulation.** In place of socially minded officials *forcing* regulation on natural monopolies to protect consumers, this view sees practical politicians as supplying the "service" of regulation to firms that *want* to be regulated. Regulation is desired by these firms because it yields a legal cartel that can be highly profitable to regulated firms. Specifically, the regulatory commission performs such functions as dividing up the market and restricting potential competition by enlarging the cartel. While private cartels are unstable and often break down, the special attraction of a government-sponsored cartel under the guise of regulation is that it endures. The legal cartel theory of regulation suggests that regulation results from rent-seeking activities.

Occupational licensing is a labour-market application of the legal cartel theory. Certain occupational groups—barbers, interior designers, dietitians—demand licensing because it protects the public from charlatans and quacks. But the real reason may be to limit occupational entry so that practitioners may receive monopoly incomes.

### 11-4 QUICK REVIEW

- The public interest theory of regulation says that government must regulate natural monopolies to prevent abuses arising from monopoly power.
- The legal cartel theory of regulation suggests that some firms seek government regulation to reduce price competition and ensure stable profits.

## In The Media

### Wheat Board Strips Farmers of Rights, Economists Tells Trial

By Scott Edmonds
Canadian Press

Winnipeg—Using its monopoly, the Canadian Wheat Board effectively strips farmers of ownership rights over wheat and barley, a farm economist told a court yesterday.

Al Loyns was testifying on the opening day of a constitutional challenge of the board's powers backed by the Canadian Farm Enterprise Network and the National Citizens' Coalition.

Mr. Loyns, co-author of a controversial Alberta-commissioned report critical of the board released in 1996, said the board takes control over grain and makes all major decisions, including when a farmer can deliver and how much he'll get paid.

"The individual loses marketing options, marketing choices, simply by delivering grain to a Canadian Wheat Board account," said Mr.

Loyns, who recently retired from the University of Manitoba.

In 1996, Mr. Loyns and Colin Carter of the University of California concluded farmers lose $20 a tonne because of the board.

The findings were attacked by board supporters and contradicted by another study that said farmers make an additional $20 a tonne because of the board's single-desk system.

The court case centres on Dave Bryan, a Saskatchewan farmer charged with failing to report the grain he was trucking across the border to export and failing to provide a wheat-board export permit.

Mr. Bryan is one of about 100 farmers across Western Canada facing similar charges for border-busting efforts in the past few years to draw attention to their claims that the wheat-board system is unfair.

Under the Canadian Wheat Board Act, the board has control over all wheat and barley grown in the West for human consumption or export.

*Source: Globe and Mail,* February 10, 1998, p. A7. By Scott Edmonds, February, 1998. Reprinted with permission of the Canadian Press.

## THE STORY IN BRIEF

The Canadian Wheat Board (CWB) has complete control over all wheat and barley sales in western Canada. Individual farmers have to sell their wheat (or barley) to the CWB. A farmer who tried to sell his wheat directly to a customer in the United States was charged. One economist argues that the monopoly power of the CWB is costing farmers $20 a tonne and claims that the Wheat Board is stripping farmers of their ownership rights.

## THE ECONOMICS BEHIND THE STORY

- The CWB has a legal monopoly to sell wheat and barley grown in the west. No other agency is allowed to sell the wheat or barley, including farmers. One farmer broke the law and is being prosecuted.
- An economist tells the trial that the monopoly of the CWB both strips the farmers of ownership right and causes farmers to lose $20 a tonne. The argument is that if allowed to sell on their own farmers could fetch a better price and would not have to pay for the cost of running the CWB. Another study contradicted the loss to farmers.
- A monopolist achieves neither productive nor allocative efficiency. Except in the case of a natural monopoly, more competition will improve the welfare of consumers, and in this case perhaps also the welfare of producers.
- According to the materials in this chapter, is there a compelling economic argument for the CWB monopoly? Elaborate. ■

# The Last Word

## DE BEERS' DIAMONDS: ARE MONOPOLIES FOREVER?

**De Beers Consolidated Mines of South Africa is one of the world's strongest and most enduring monopolies, having dominated the diamond market for over 60 years.**

DE BEERS PRODUCES ABOUT 50 PERCENT OF all rough-cut diamonds in the world and buys for resale a large portion of the diamonds produced by other mines worldwide. As a result, it markets about 70 percent of the world's diamonds to a select group of diamond cutters and dealers.

**Monopoly Behaviour** De Beers' behaviour and results are well represented by the unregulated monopoly model in Figure 11-4. It sells only that quantity of diamonds that will yield an "appropriate" (monopoly) price. This price bears little relationship to production costs, and profits have been enormous. In "good" years profits are 60 percent of total revenues and rates of return on equity (ownership) capital are 30 percent or more.

When demand falls, De Beers restricts sales to maintain price. The excess of production over sales is then reflected in growing diamond stockpiles held by De Beers. It also attempts to bolster demand through advertising ("diamonds are forever"). When demand is strong, it increases sales by reducing its diamond inventories.

De Beers controls the production of mines it does not own in several ways. First, it tries to convince independent producers that "single-channel" or monopoly marketing through De Beers is in their best interests in that it maximizes profit. Second, mines that circumvent De Beers are likely to find that the market is suddenly flooded from De Beers' stockpiles with the particular kind of diamonds that the "rogue" mine produces. The resulting price decline and loss of profit are likely to bring the mine into the De Beers fold. Finally, De Beers will simply purchase and stockpile diamonds produced by independent mines so their added supply will not "spoil" the market.

**Threats and Problems** But even such an enduring monopoly as De Beers faces threats and problems. New diamond discoveries have resulted in a growing leakage of diamonds into world markets outside De Beers' control. For example, wildcat prospecting and trading in Angola have forced De Beers to spend as much as $500 million per year to keep such diamonds off the market. The recent diamond supplies discovered in Canada's northwest territories pose a future threat. Similarly, although Russia is part of the De Beers' monopoly, this cash-strapped country has been selling about $300 million in diamonds per year directly into the world markets. When new Siberian mines are brought into production, the additional output will pose a further threat to De Beers. Russia's estimated $4-to-$8-billion stockpile of diamonds is another potential source of uncontrolled supply.

Of more immediate concern to De Beers, Australian diamond producer Argyle has opted to withdraw from the De Beers' monopoly. Its annual production of mostly low-grade industrial diamonds accounts for about 6 percent of the global $6-billion diamond market.

De Beers' diamond inventories now exceed $5 billion, an amount greater than its annual sales. Observers wonder whether De Beers' capacity to absorb future unregulated production will reach a breaking point. They also speculate that Argyle will team up with Canadian producers to directly market the diamonds mined in the northwest territories. This one-two punch may cause the De Beers' monopoly to unravel. Although diamonds may be forever, the De Beers' monopoly may soon be history. ■

## CHAPTER SUMMARY

1. A pure monopolist is the sole producer of a commodity for which there are no close substitutes.
2. Barriers to entry, in the form of **a** economies of scale, **b** patent ownership and research, **c** ownership or control of essential resources, and **d** pricing and other strategic behaviour, help explain the existence of pure monopoly and other imperfectly competitive market structures.
3. The pure monopolist's market situation differs from a competitive firm's in that the monopolist's demand curve is downsloping, causing the marginal-revenue curve to lie below the demand curve. Like the competitive seller, the pure monopolist will maximize profit by equating marginal revenue and marginal cost. Barriers to entry may permit a monopolist to acquire economic profit even in the long run. However, **a** the monopolist does not charge "the highest price it can get"; **b** the price that yields maximum total profit to the monopolist rarely coincides with the price that yields maximum unit profit; **c** high costs and a weak demand may prevent the monopolist from realizing any profit at all; and **d** the monopolist avoids the inelastic region of its demand curve.
4. With the same costs, the pure monopolist will find it profitable to restrict output and charge a higher price than would sellers in a purely competitive industry. This restriction of output causes resources to be misallocated, as is evidenced by the fact that price exceeds marginal cost in monopolized markets.
5. In general, monopoly increases income inequality.

6. The costs monopolists and competitive producers face may not be the same. On the one hand, economies of scale may make lower unit costs available to monopolists but not to competitors. Also, pure monopoly may be more likely than pure competition to reduce costs via technological advance because of the monopolist's ability to realize economic profit that can be used to finance research. On the other hand, X-inefficiency—the failure to produce with the least costly combination of inputs—is more common to monopolists than to competitive firms. Also, monopolists may make costly expenditures to maintain monopoly privileges that are conferred by government. Finally, the blocked entry of rival firms weakens the monopolist's incentive to be technologically progressive.

7. A monopolist can increase its profit by practising price discrimination, provided **a** it can segregate buyers on the basis of elasticities of demand and **b** its product or service cannot be readily transferred between the segregated markets. Other things equal, the perfectly discriminating monopolist will produce a larger output than the nondiscriminating monopolist.

8. Price regulation can be invoked to eliminate wholly or partially the tendency of monopolists to underallocate resources and to earn economic profits. The optimal social price is determined where the demand and marginal-cost curves intersect; the "fair-return" price is determined where the demand and average-total-cost curves intersect.

9. The objective of industrial regulation is to protect the public from the market power of natural monopolies by regulating prices and quality of service. Critics contend that industrial regulation is conducive to inefficiency and rising costs and that, in many instances, it constitutes a legal cartel for the regulated firms.

## TERMS AND CONCEPTS

pure monopoly
barriers to entry
X-inefficiency
rent-seeking behaviour
price discrimination
natural monopoly
optimal social price
fair-return price
dilemma of regulation
public interest theory of regulation
legal cartel theory of regulation

## STUDY QUESTIONS

1. "No firm is completely sheltered from rivals; all firms compete for consumer dollars. If that is so, then pure monopoly does not exist." Do you agree? Explain. How might you use Chapter 10's concept of cross elasticity of demand to judge whether monopoly exists?

2. Discuss the major barriers to entry into an industry. Explain how each barrier can foster monopoly or oligopoly. Which barriers, if any, do you feel give rise to monopoly that is socially justifiable?

3. How does the demand curve faced by a purely monopolistic seller differ from that confronting a purely competitive firm? Why does it differ? Of what significance is the difference? Why is the pure monopolist's demand curve not perfectly inelastic?

4. KEY QUESTION *Use the demand schedule that follows to calculate total revenue and marginal revenue at each quantity. Plot the demand, total-revenue, and marginal-revenue curves and carefully explain the relationships between them. Explain why the marginal revenue of the fourth unit of output is $3.50, even though its price is $5.00. Use Chapter 10's total-revenue test for price elasticity to designate the elastic and inelastic segments of your graphed demand curve. What generalization can you make as to the relationship between marginal revenue and elasticity of demand? Suppose the marginal cost of successive units of output were zero. What output would the profit-seeking firm produce? Finally, use your analysis to explain why a monopolist would never produce in the region of inelastic demand.*

| Price ($P$) | Quantity demanded ($Q$) | Price ($P$) | Quantity demanded ($Q$) |
|---|---|---|---|
| $7.00 | 0 | $4.50 | 5 |
| 6.50 | 1 | 4.00 | 6 |
| 6.00 | 2 | 3.50 | 7 |
| 5.50 | 3 | 3.00 | 8 |
| 5.00 | 4 | 2.50 | 9 |

5. **KEY QUESTION** *Suppose a pure monopolist is faced with the demand schedule shown below and the same cost data as the competitive producer discussed in question 4 at the end of Chapter 10. Calculate the missing total- and marginal-revenue amounts, and determine the profit-maximizing price and output for this monopolist. What is the monopolist's profit? Verify your answer graphically and by comparing total revenue and total cost.*

| Price | Quantity demanded | Total revenue | Marginal revenue |
|---|---|---|---|
| $115 | 0 | $_____ | |
| | | | $_____ |
| 100 | 1 | _____ | |
| | | | _____ |
| 83 | 2 | _____ | |
| | | | _____ |
| 71 | 3 | _____ | |
| | | | _____ |
| 63 | 4 | _____ | |
| | | | _____ |
| 55 | 5 | _____ | |
| | | | _____ |
| 48 | 6 | _____ | |
| | | | _____ |
| 42 | 7 | _____ | |
| | | | _____ |
| 37 | 8 | _____ | |
| | | | _____ |
| 33 | 9 | _____ | |
| | | | _____ |
| 29 | 10 | _____ | |

6. **KEY QUESTION** *If the firm described in question 5 could engage in perfect price discrimination, what would be the level of output? Of profits? Draw a diagram showing the relevant demand, marginal-revenue, average-total-cost, and marginal-cost curves and the equilibrium price and output for a nondiscriminating monopolist. Use the same diagram to show the equilibrium position of a monopolist able to practise perfect price discrimination. Compare equilibrium outputs, total revenues, economic profits, and consumer prices in the two cases. Comment on the economic desirability of price discrimination.*

7. Assume a pure monopolist and a purely competitive firm have the same unit costs. Contrast the two with respect to **a** price, **b** output, **c** profits, **d** allocation of resources, and **e** impact on the distribution of income. Since both monopolists and competitive firms follow the MC = MR rule in maximizing profits, how do you account for the different results? Why might the costs of a purely competitive firm and a monopolist be different? What are the implications of such a cost difference?

8. Critically evaluate and explain:
   - **a.** "Because they can control product price, monopolists are always assured of profitable production by simply charging the highest price consumers will pay."
   - **b.** "The pure monopolist seeks that output which will yield the greatest per-unit profit."
   - **c.** "An excess of price over marginal cost is the market's way of signalling the need for more production of a good."
   - **d.** "The more profitable a firm, the greater its monopoly power."
   - **e.** "The monopolist has a pricing policy; the competitive producer does not."
   - **f.** "With respect to resource allocation, the interests of the seller and of society coincide in a purely competitive market but conflict in a monopolized market."
   - **g.** "In a sense the monopolist makes a profit for not producing; the monopolist produces profit more than it does goods."

CHAPTER 12

# Monopolistic Competition and Oligopoly

PURE COMPETITION AND PURE MONOPOLY ARE the exceptions, not the rule, in the Canadian economy. Most market structures fall somewhere between these two extremes. Two examples are:

- If you want to go out to eat, you have an amazing variety of choices. You can get a meal at a fast-food place such as McDonald's, Subway, or Taco Bell. Or you can go to a restaurant with a fuller menu and with table service. For a special meal you can choose an Italian, French, or Japanese fine-food restaurant where your bill may be $30 or more per person. Each of these establishments serves food and beverages, but all have different menus and prices. Competition among them is based not only on price but also on product quality, location, service, and advertising.
- Do you plan to buy a new car once you graduate from a community college or university and land a good job? Although you will have many choices of brands and models, most likely you will buy your new car from one of a handful of auto producers—General Motors, Ford, Honda, Chrysler, or Toyota. In many of our manufacturing, mining, and wholesaling industries there are only a few dominant firms, not the thousands of producers presumed in pure competition or the single producer characterizing monopoly.

In this chapter we examine two market structures that more closely approximate "real-world" markets: *monopolistic competition* and *oligopoly*. You will see that monopolistic competition implies a considerable amount of competition mixed with a small dose of monopoly power, as in our restaurant example. Oligopoly, in contrast, has a blend of greater monopoly power and less competition; there are only a few firms in an oligopolistic industry, and entry is difficult, as is the case in the automobile industry.

**IN THIS CHAPTER YOU WILL LEARN:**

- The necessary conditions required for monopolistic competition and oligopoly to arise.
- How the profit-maximizing price and output are determined in monopolistic competition and oligopoly.
- That game theory can help explain the behaviour of oligopolists.
- About the debate of the impact of advertising on consumers and firms.
- Why neither monopolistic competition nor oligopoly achieves productive and allocative efficiency.

Our discussion proceeds as follows: First, we define monopolistic competition, detail its characteristics, and examine its occurrence. Then, we evaluate the price, output, and efficiency outcomes of monopolistic competition. Next, we turn to oligopoly, surveying the possible courses of price, output, and advertising behaviour that oligopolistic industries might follow. Finally, we assess whether oligopoly is an efficient or inefficient market structure.

## The Big Picture

THE PURE COMPETITIVE MARKET STRUCTURE is the ideal against which we measure other market structures. The monopoly model demonstrates the other extreme, the inefficiencies of a one-firm industry. But most industries do not approach either extreme. We now use what you learned in the last two chapters to investigate market structures prevalent in the real world.

Monopolistic competition: the term tells us a great deal about this market structure. There are elements of monopoly and elements of competition. The monopoly part applies because each firm produces a unique product. There may be close substitutes—for example, Coke and Pepsi—but each product has a quality (or qualities) that makes its producer the "only" supplier. The competition part comes in because there are close substitutes and many firms in the industry.

Oligopoly refers to a market structure in which there are a few large firms that dominate the market. The fact that there are a few firms makes it difficult to come up with one model that adequately explains an oligopolist's price and output behaviour. We lack one good model of oligopoly because each firm's price and output behaviour depends on what its rivals do, or expect to do. If all firms think in this way, it is far from certain what price or quantity will materialize in an oligopolistic market structure. Because we do not have one good model, we have to look at more than one.

As you read this chapter, keep the following points in mind:

- A pivotal distinguishing feature of monopolistic competition is product differentiation—each firm produces a variation of a particular good or service. There are also a relatively large number of firms in any industry competing with each other.
- In the monopolistic competition model, losses in the short run will lead to firms leaving the industry and economic profits will attract firms to the industry. In the long run, firms generally earn normal profits.
- Because an oligopolist's move depends on what its competitors do, there is a tendency for firms to agree, overtly or covertly, to coordinate output and price.
- If oligopolists do cooperate to set price and output, the result will be the same as that of a pure monopolist.
- There are anti-combines laws against collusion. But even in the absence of such laws, collusive agreements are unstable in the long run. In a world of scarce resources in relation to wants, participants in the collusion game will be tempted. ■

## MONOPOLISTIC COMPETITION: CHARACTERISTICS AND OCCURRENCE

The defining characteristics of **monopolistic competition** are (1) a relatively large number of sellers; (2) differentiated products (often accompanied by heavy advertising); and (3) easy entry to, and exit from, the industry. The first and third characteristics provide the "competitive" aspect of monopolistic competition; the second characteristic contributes the "monopolistic" aspect.

### Relatively Large Number of Sellers

Monopolistic competition does not require hundreds or thousands of firms, as does pure competition, but only a fairly large number, say, 25, 35, 60, or 70 firms in each industry. Several characteristics of monopolistic competition follow from the presence of these relatively large number of firms.

1. **SMALL MARKET SHARE** Each firm has a comparatively small percentage of the total market, so each has limited control over market price.
2. **NO COLLUSION** The presence of a relatively large number of firms ensures that collusion—action by a group of firms to restrict output and set prices—is very unlikely.
3. **INDEPENDENT ACTION** With numerous firms in an industry, there is little interdependence among them; each firm can determine its own pricing policy without considering the possible reactions of rival firms. Firm X

may realize a 10 or 15 percent increase in sales by cutting its price, but the effect on competitors' sales will be spread so thinly over the 20, 40, or 60 other firms that it will be nearly imperceptible. And if rivals cannot feel the impact of firm X's actions, they will have no reason to react to those actions.

## Differentiated Products

In contrast to pure competition, monopolistic competition has the fundamental feature of **product differentiation**. Purely competitive firms produce a standardized or homogeneous product; monopolistically competitive producers turn out variations of a particular product. That is, monopolistic competitors provide products that are slightly different from competing products with regard to product attributes, services to customers, location and accessibility, or other qualities, real or imagined.

Let's examine these aspects of product differentiation in more detail.

**Product Attributes** Product differentiation may take the form of physical or qualitative differences in the products themselves. Real differences in functional features, materials, design, and workmanship are vital aspects of product differentiation. Personal computers, for example, differ in their storage capacity, speed, graphic displays, and user-friendliness. There are scores of competing principles of economics texts that differ in content, organization, presentation and readability, pedagogical aids, and graphics and design. Most cities have a variety of retail stores selling men's and women's clothing varying greatly in styling, materials, and quality of work. Similarly, one fast-food hamburger chain may feature curly fries, while a competitor stresses its traditional fries.

Credit cards may seem like homogeneous "products," differing only in annual fees and interest-rate charges. Not so. Some provide rebates on purchases; others offer free airline travel miles; and still others offer extended warranties on products purchased on credit.

**Service** Service and the conditions surrounding the sale of a product are forms of product differentiation. One grocery store may stress the helpfulness of its clerks who bag your groceries and carry them to your car. A warehouse competitor may leave bagging and carrying to its customers but feature lower prices. One-day cleaning may be preferred to cleaning of equal quality that takes three days. The prestige appeal of a store, the courteousness and helpfulness of clerks, the firm's reputation for servicing or exchanging its products, and credit availability are all service aspects of product differentiation.

**Location** Products may also be differentiated through location and accessibility. Minigroceries or convenience stores successfully compete with large supermarkets, even though they have a more limited range of products and charge higher prices. They compete on the basis of location—being close to customers and on busy streets—and in some cases by being open 24 hours a day. A gas station's proximity to a major highway gives it a locational advantage that may allow it to sell gasoline at a higher price than gas stations farther away from the main highway.

**Brand Names and Packaging** Product differentiation may also be created through the use of brand names and trademarks, packaging, and celebrity connections. Most aspirin tablets are very much alike, but many headache sufferers feel that one brand—Bayer, or Anacin, or Bufferin—is superior and worth a higher price than a generic substitute. A celebrity's name associated with jeans, perfume, or athletic equipment may enhance those products in the minds of buyers. Many consumers prefer toothpaste in a pump container to the same toothpaste in a conventional tube. Environment-friendly "green" packaging or "natural spring" bottled water is used to attract additional customers.

**Some Control over Price** One implication of product differentiation is that, despite the relatively large number of firms, monopolistically competitive producers do have some control over the prices of their products. If consumers prefer the products of specific sellers, then *within limits* they will pay more to satisfy their preferences. Sellers and buyers are not linked randomly, as in a purely competitive market. But the monopolistic competitor's control over price is very limited since there are numerous potential substitutes for its product.

## Easy Entry and Exit

Entry into monopolistically competitive industries is relatively easy. Because monopolistic competitors are typically small firms, both absolutely and relatively, economies of scale are few and capital requirements are low. On the other hand, compared with pure competition, financial barriers may result from the need to develop a product different from rivals' products and the need to advertise it. Some existing firms may hold patents on their products and copyrights on their brand names and trademarks, increasing the difficulty and cost of successfully imitating them.

Exit from monopolistically competitive industries is also relatively easy. Nothing prevents an unprofitable monopolistic competitor from holding a going-out-of-business sale and permanently shutting down.

### Nonprice Competition and Advertising

The expense and effort involved in product differentiation would be wasted if consumers were not made aware of product differences. Thus, monopolistic competitors advertise their products, often heavily. The goal of product differentiation and advertising—so-called **nonprice competition**—is to make price less of a factor in consumer purchases, and product differences a greater factor. If successful, the firm's demand curve will shift to the right and become less elastic.

### Monopolistically Competitive Industries

Sectors in the Canadian economy approximating monopolistically competive conditions include retail stores in metropolitan areas, grocery stores, gasoline stations, barber shops, dry cleaners, clothing stores, and restaurants.

## MONOPOLISTIC COMPETITION: PRICE AND OUTPUT DETERMINATION

We now analyze the price and output decisions of a monopolistically competitive firm. We assume initially that each firm in the industry is producing a specific differentiated product and engaging in a particular amount of advertising. Later we'll see how changes in the product and the amount of advertising modify our conclusions.

### The Firm's Demand Curve

Our explanation begins with Figure 12-1 ***(Key Graph)***. The basic feature of this diagram is the elasticity of demand, as shown by the individual firm's demand curve. *The demand curve faced by a monopolistically competitive seller is highly, but not perfectly, elastic.* This feature distinguishes monopolistic competition from pure monopoly and pure competition. The monopolistic competitor's demand is more elastic than the demand faced by a pure monopolist because the monopolistically competitive seller has many competitors producing close substitutes. The pure monopolist has no rivals at all. Yet, for two reasons, the monopolistically competitive seller's demand is not perfectly elastic like the purely competitive producer's. First, the monopolistically competitive firm has fewer rivals; second, the products of monopolistic competitors are differentiated, so they are not perfect substitutes.

The degree of price elasticity of demand the monopolistically competitive firm sees will depend on the exact number of rivals and the degree of product differentiation. The larger the number of rivals and the weaker the product differentiation, the greater the elasticity of each seller's demand; that is, the closer monopolistic competition will be to pure competition.

### The Short Run: Profit or Loss

The monopolistically competitive firm maximizes its profit or minimizes its loss in the short run just as do the other firms we have discussed: by producing the output at which marginal revenue equals marginal cost (MR = MC). In Figure 12-1a the firm produces output $Q_1$, where MR = MC. As shown by demand curve $D_1$, it then can charge price $P_1$. Here, it realizes an economic profit shown by the grey area [$= (P_1 - A_1) \times Q_1$].

But with less favourable demand or costs, the firm may incur a loss in the short run. This possibility is shown in Figure 12-1b, where the firm's best strategy is to minimize its loss. It does this by producing output $Q_2$ (where MR = MC) and, as determined by demand curve $D_2$, charging price $P_2$. Because price $P_2$ is less than average total cost $A_2$, the firm incurs the loss shown by the grey area [$= (A_2 - P_2) \times Q_2$].

### The Long Run: Only a Normal Profit

In the long run, firms will enter a profitable monopolistically competitive industry and leave an unprofitable one. As a result, in the long run a monopolistically competitive firm will earn

## KEY GRAPH

**FIGURE 12-1 A monopolistically competitive firm: short run and long run**

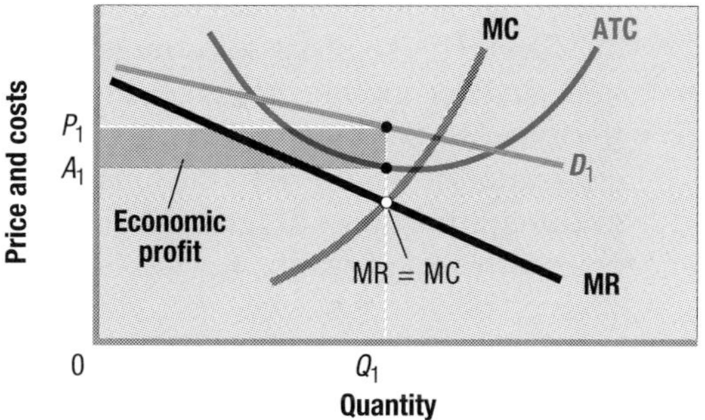


(a) Short-run profits

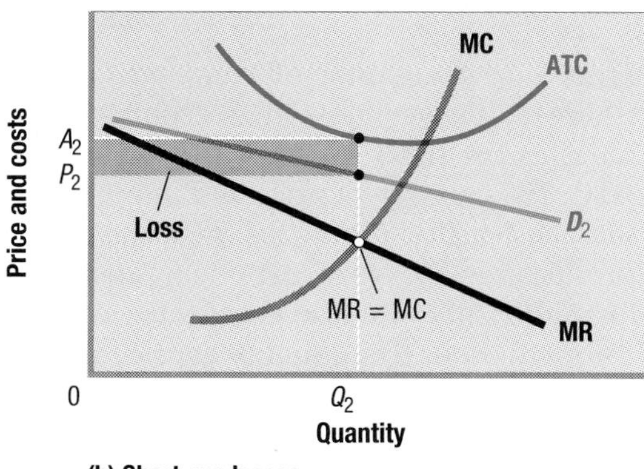


(b) Short-run losses

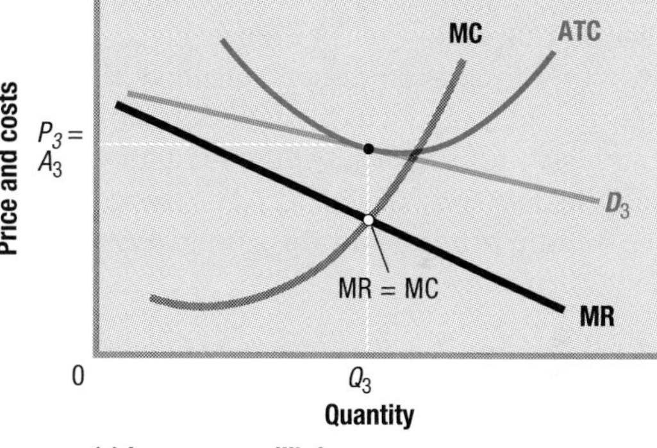


(c) Long-run equilibrium

The monopolistic competitor maximizes profit or minimizes loss by producing the output at which MR = MC. The economic profit shown in (a) will induce new firms to enter, eventually eliminating economic profit. The loss shown in (b) will cause an exit of firms until normal profit is restored. After such entry and exit, the price will settle in (c) to where it just equals average total cost at the MR = MC output. At this price $P_3$ and output $Q_3$, the monopolistic competitor earns only a normal profit and the industry is in long-run equilibrium.

## 12-1 QUICK QUIZ

**1.** Price exceeds MC in:
- **(a)** graph (a) only.
- **(b)** graph (b) only.
- **(c)** graphs (a) and (b) only.
- **(d)** graphs (a), (b), and (c).

**2.** Price exceeds ATC in:
- **(a)** graph (a) only.
- **(b)** graph (b) only.
- **(c)** graphs (a) and (b) only.
- **(d)** graphs (a), (b), and (c).

**3.** The firm represented by Figure 12-1c is:
- **(a)** making a normal profit.
- **(b)** incurring a loss, once opportunity costs are considered.
- **(c)** producing at the same level of output as a purely competitive firm.
- **(d)** producing a standardized product.

**4.** Which of the following pairs are both "competition-like elements" in monopolistic competition?
- **(a)** Price exceeds MR; standardized product.
- **(b)** Entry is relatively easy; only a normal profit in the long run.
- **(c)** Price equals MC at the profit-maximizing output; economic profits are likely in the long run.
- **(d)** The firms' demand curve is downsloping; differentiated products.

**Answers:** 1. (d); 2. (a); 3. (a); 4. (b).

only a normal profit or, in other words, only break even.

**Profits: Firms Enter** In the case of short-run profit (Figure 12-1a), economic profits attract new rivals because entry to the industry is easy. As new firms enter, the demand curve faced by the typical firm will shift to the left (fall). Why? Because each firm has a smaller share of total demand and now faces a larger number of close-substitute products. This decline in the firm's demand reduces its economic profit. When entry of new firms has caused the demand curve to fall to the degree that it is tangent to the average-total-cost curve at the profit-maximizing output, the firm is just making a normal profit. This situation is shown in Figure 12-1c, where demand is $D_3$ and the firm's long-run equilibrium output is $Q_3$. As Figure 12-1c clearly indicates, any greater or lesser output will entail an average total cost that exceeds product price $P_3$, meaning losses for the firm. At the tangency point between the demand curve and ATC, there are no more economic profits, and thus no incentive for additional firms to enter.

**Losses: Firms Leave** When the industry suffers short-run losses—as in Figure 12-1b—some firms will exit in the long run. Faced with fewer substitute products and an expanding share of total demand, surviving firms will see their demand curves shift to the right (rise), as to $D_3$, and their losses disappear and give way to normal profits (Figure 12-1c). (For simplicity we have assumed constant costs; shifts in the cost curves as firms enter or leave would complicate our discussion slightly but would not alter the conclusions.)

**Complications** The representative firm in the monopolistic competition model earns only a *normal* profit in the long run. This outcome may not always occur, however, in the real world of small firms for two reasons.

1. Some firms may achieve product differentiation to an extent that other firms cannot duplicate, even over time. A hotel in a major city may have the best location relative to business and tourist activities. Or a firm may hold a patent giving it a slight but more or less permanent advantage over imitators. Such firms may have sufficient monopoly power to realize a sliver of economic profits even in the long run.
2. Entry to some monopolistically competitive industries may not be as easy as in others. Because of product differentiation, there are likely to be greater financial barriers to entry than there would be if the product were standardized. This suggests some monopoly power, with small economic profits continuing even in the long run. Despite these exceptions, our generalization still holds that the long-run normal profit equilibrium of Figure 12-1c is a reasonable portrayal of reality.

## MONOPOLISTIC COMPETITION AND ECONOMIC EFFICIENCY

From our evaluation of competitive pricing in Chapter 10, we know that economic efficiency requires the triple equality $P$ = MC = minimum ATC. The equality of price and minimum average total cost yields *productive efficiency*. The good is produced in the least costly way, and the price is just sufficient to cover average total cost, including a normal profit. The equality of price and marginal cost yields *allocative efficiency*. The right amount of output is being produced, and thus the right amount of society's scarce resources is being devoted to this specific use.

How efficient is monopolistic competition, as measured with this triple equality?

### Neither Productive nor Allocative Efficiency

In monopolistic competition, neither productive nor allocative efficiency is achieved in long-run equilibrium. Figure 12-2, which includes an enlargement of part of Figure 12-1c, shows this fact. First note that the profit-maximizing price $P_3$ slightly exceeds the lowest average total cost, $A_4$. Therefore, in producing the profit-maximizing output $Q_3$, the firm's average total cost is slightly higher than optimal from society's perspective—productive efficiency is not achieved. Also note that the profit-maximizing price $P_3$ exceeds marginal cost (here $M_3$), which means the monopolistic element in monopolistic competition causes a small underallocation of resources. Society values each unit of output between $Q_3$ and $Q_4$ more highly than the goods it would have to forgo to produce these units. Thus, to a modest extent,

**FIGURE 12-2 The inefficiency of monopolistic competition**

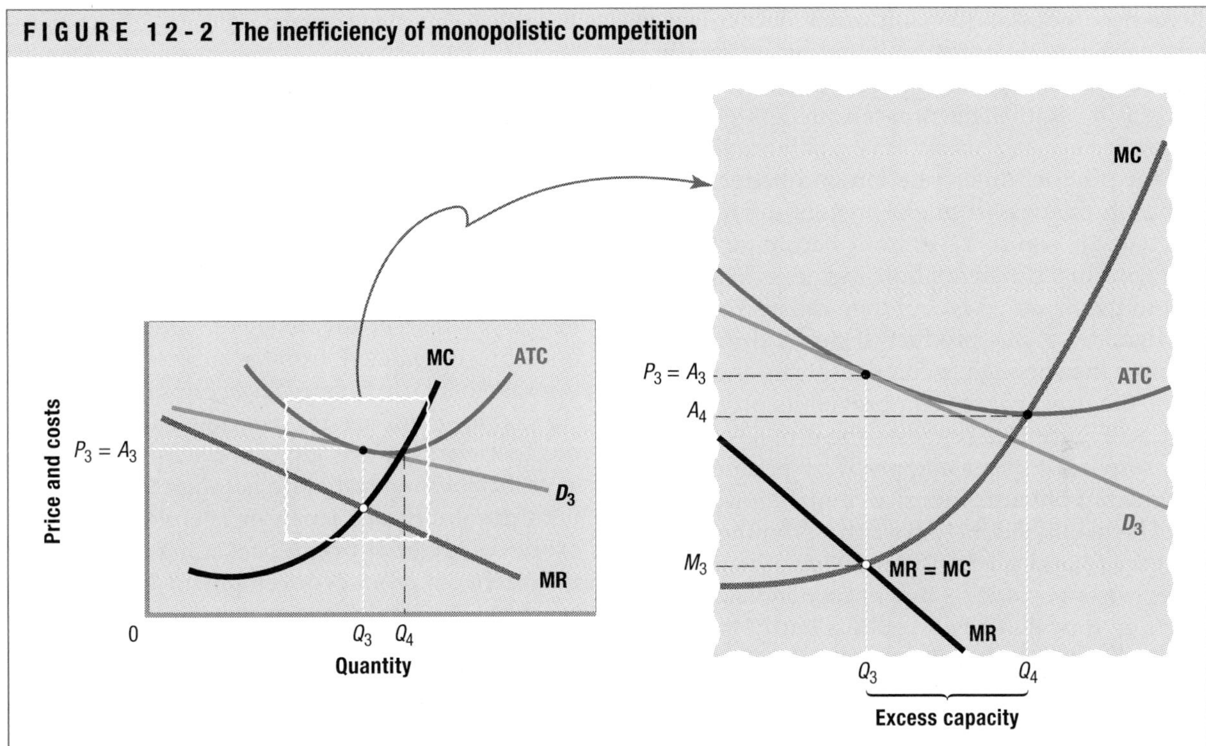


In long-run equilibrium a monopolistic competitor achieves neither productive nor allocative efficiency. Productive efficiency is not realized because production occurs where the average total cost $A_3$ exceeds the minimum average total cost $A_4$. Allocative efficiency is not realized because the product price $P_3$ exceeds the marginal cost $M_3$. The result is an underallocation of resources and excess productive capacity of $Q_4 - Q_3$.

monopolistic competition also fails the allocative-efficiency test. Consumers pay a higher-than-competitive price and obtain a less-than-optimal output. Indeed, monopolistic competitors *must* charge a higher-than-competitive price in the long run to achieve a normal profit.

## Excess Capacity

In monopolistic competition, the output gap $Q_4$ to $Q_3$ in Figure 12-2 identifies **excess capacity**: *plant and equipment that are underused because firms are producing less than the minimum-ATC output.* If each monopolistic competitor could profitably produce at the minimum-ATC output, fewer firms could produce the same total output, and the product could be sold at a lower price. Monopolistically competitive industries thus tend to be overcrowded with firms, each operating below its optimal capacity, that is, without achieving productive efficiency. This situation is typified by many kinds of retail establishments. Another example is the numerous small motels, many operating with excess capacity, that are found in most cities. ***(Key Question 2)***

# MONOPOLISTIC COMPETITION: NONPRICE COMPETITION

The situation portrayed in Figures 12-1c and 12-2 is not very satisfying to monopolistic competitors since it foretells only a normal profit. These producers would like to improve on that long-run situation.

How can they do this? It can be accomplished through nonprice competition in the form of product differentiation and advertising. Each firm has a product distinguishable in some way from those of the other producers. Developing or improving it can presumably further differentiate the product. And advertising can be used to emphasize real product differences and help create perceived differences. So the profit-realizing firm of Figure

12-1a need not stand by and watch new competitors eliminate its profit by imitating its product, matching its customer service, and copying its advertising. Rather, the firm can attempt to sustain its profit and stay ahead of competitors through further product differentiation and better advertising. In this way it might prevent the long-run outcome of Figure 12-1c from becoming reality. True, product differentiation and advertising will add to the firm's costs, but they can also increase the demand for its product. If demand increases by more than enough to compensate for the added costs, the firm will have improved its profit position. As Figure 12-2 suggests, the firm has little or no prospect of increasing profit by price cutting. So why not practise nonprice competition?

The likelihood that easy entry promotes product variety and product improvement is to some observers a positive feature of monopolistic competition—one that offsets, at least partly, its inefficiency. In fact, product differentiation is at the centre of a tradeoff between consumer choice and productive efficiency. The stronger the product differentiation, the greater the excess capacity and, hence, the greater the productive *in*efficiency. But the greater the product differentiation, the more likely the variety of diverse consumer tastes will be fully satisfied. The greater the excess capacity problem, the wider the range of consumer choice.

There are two considerations here: (1) product differentiation at a point in time, and (2) product development over a period of time.

## Product Differentiation

If a product is differentiated, the consumer will be offered a wide range of types, styles, brands, and quality gradations of that product. Compared with pure competition, this suggests possible advantages to the consumer. The range of choice is widened, and variations in consumer taste are more fully met by producers.

But skeptics warn that product differentiation may reach the point where the consumer becomes confused and rational choice becomes time-consuming and difficult. Variety may add spice to the consumer's life, but only up to a point. Worse, some observers fear that the consumer, faced with a myriad of similar products, may judge product quality by price; the consumer may irrationally assume that price is always a measure of product quality.

## Product Development

Product development is the process that, over time, leads to product changes and thus to most product differentiation. Its purpose usually is to develop a more useful or otherwise improved product. Product development may cause still more product development in two ways. First, a successful product improvement by one firm obligates rivals to imitate or improve on that firm's temporary market advantage or suffer losses. Second, profit realized from a successful product improvement can finance *further* improvements.

Again, there are critics. They say that many product changes are more apparent than real—superficial changes that do *not* improve the product's durability, efficiency, or usefulness. A more exotic container or bright packaging is frequently the extent of "product development." It is argued, too, that particularly with durable and semi-durable consumer goods, development may follow a pattern of "planned obsolescence," with firms improving a product only by the amount necessary to make the average consumer dissatisfied with last year's model.

## Monopolistic Competition and Economic Analysis

The ability to engage in nonprice competition makes the market situation of a monopolistically competitive firm more complex than Figure 12-1 indicates. That figure assumes a *given* (unchanging) product and *given* level of advertising expenditures. But we know that, in practice, product attributes and advertising are not fixed. The monopolistically competitive firm juggles three factors—price, product, and advertising—in seeking maximum profit. It must determine what variety of product, selling at what price, and supplemented by what level of advertising activity will result in the greatest profit. This complex situation is not easily expressed in a simple, meaningful economic model. At best, we can say that each possible combination of price, product, and advertising poses a different demand and cost (production cost plus advertising cost) situation for the firm, and one of them will yield the maximum profit.

In practice, this optimal combination cannot be readily forecast but must be found by trial and error. Even then, in some instances certain limitations may be imposed by the actions of rivals: A firm may not be free to eliminate its advertising for fear its share of the market will decline sharply, benefiting rivals that do advertise. Similarly, patents held by rivals may rule out certain desirable product improvements.

**12-1**

**QUICK REVIEW**

- Monopolistic competition involves a relatively large number of firms operating noncollusively and producing differentiated products with easy entry and exit.
- In the short run, a monopolistic competitor will maximize profit or minimize loss by producing that output at which marginal revenue equals marginal cost.
- In the long run, easy entry and exit of firms cause monopolistic competitors to earn only a normal profit.
- A monopolistic competitor's long-run equilibrium output is such that price exceeds the minimum average total cost (implying that consumers do not get the product at the lowest price attainable) and price exceeds marginal cost (indicating that resources are underallocated to the product).

## OLIGOPOLY: CHARACTERISTICS AND OCCURRENCE

In terms of competitiveness, the spectrum of market structures moves from pure competition, to monopolistic competition, to oligopoly, to pure monopoly (review Table 10-1). We now direct our attention to **oligopoly**, *a market dominated by a few large producers of a homogeneous or differentiated product*. Because of their "fewness," oligopolists have considerable control over their prices, but each must consider the possible reaction of rivals to its own pricing, output, and advertising decisions.

### A Few Large Producers

What does "a few large producers" mean? This term is necessarily vague because the market model of oligopoly covers much ground, ranging between pure monopoly, on the one hand, and monopolistic competition, on the other. Thus oligopoly encompasses the Canadian steel industry, in which two large firms dominate an entire national market, and the situation in which four or five gasoline stations may enjoy roughly equal shares of the market in a medium-sized town. Generally, when you hear a term such as "Big Three," "Big Four," or "Big Six," you can be sure it refers to an oligopolistic industry.

### Homogeneous or Differentiated Products

An oligopoly may be either a **homogeneous oligopoly** or a **differentiated oligopoly**, depending on whether the firms in the oligopoly produce standardized or differentiated products. Many industrial products—steel, zinc, copper, aluminum, lead, cement, industrial alcohol—are virtually standardized products that are produced in oligopolies. Alternatively, many consumer goods industries—automobiles, tires, household appliances, electronics equipment, breakfast cereals, cigarettes, and many sporting goods—are differentiated oligopolies. These differentiated oligopolies typically engage in considerable nonprice competition, supported by heavy advertising.

### Control over Price, but Mutual Interdependence

Because firms are few in oligopolistic industries, each firm is a "price maker"; like the monopolist, it can *set* its price and output levels to maximize its profit. But unlike the monopolist, which has no rivals, the oligopolist must consider how its rivals will react to any change in its price, output, product characteristics, or advertising. Oligopoly is thus characterized by **mutual interdependence**: *a situation in which each firm's profit depends not on its own price and sales strategies but on those of its rivals.* Example: In deciding whether to increase the price of its baseball gloves, Rawlings will try to predict the response of the other major producers, such as Wilson. Second example: In deciding on its advertising strategy, Burger King will take into consideration how McDonald's might react.

### Entry Barriers

The same barriers to entry that create pure monopoly also explain the existence of oligopoly. Economies of scale are important entry barriers in a number of oligopolistic industries such as the aircraft, automobile, and cement industries. In these industries, three or four firms can each have sufficient sales to achieve economies of scale, but new firms would have such a small market share that they could not do so. They would then be high-cost producers, and they could not survive. A closely related barrier is the large expenditure for capital—the cost of obtaining necessary plant and equipment—required to enter certain industries. The jet engine, automobile, and petroleum-refining industries, for example, are all characterized by very high capital requirements.

The ownership and control of raw materials explain the oligopoly that exists in many mining industries, including gold, silver, and copper. In the electronics, chemical, photographic equipment, office machine, and pharmaceutical industries, patents have served as entry barriers. Also, oligopolists have been known to deter entry of potential new competitors through preemptive and retaliatory pricing and advertising strategies. In the 1980s, for example, a major attempt to enter the soft-drink industry in North America by a new producer (King Cola) allegedly was thwarted by price discounts and heavy advertising by Coca-Cola and Pepsi.

## Mergers

Some oligopolies have emerged mainly through *internal* growth of the dominant firms (examples: breakfast cereals, chewing gum, candy bars). But for other industries the route to oligopoly has been *external*, specifically via mergers (examples: automobiles, in their early history, and, more recently, airlines, banking, and entertainment). The merging, or combining, of two or more formerly competing firms may substantially increase their market share, enabling the new and larger producer to achieve greater economies of scale. Global Perspective 12-1 sets out the world's largest banks. If the proposed mergers among some of Canada's banks go through, some of them will be large even by international standards.

Another motive underlying the "urge to merge" is monopoly power. A larger firm may have greater ability to control market supply and thus the price of its product. Also, since it is a larger buyer of inputs, it may be able to demand and obtain lower prices (costs) on its production inputs.

## Measures of Industry Concentration

Several means are used to measure the degree to which oligopolistic industries are concentrated in the "hands" of their largest firms. We will discuss the most-often-used measures here: concentration ratios and the Herfindahl index.

**12-1 GLOBAL PERSPECTIVE**

**An international comparison of Canada's six major banks**

Each of Canada's major banks is not very large when compared with the biggest in the world. The proposed merger of the Royal Bank and the Bank of Montreal will make the new bank one of the largest in North America.

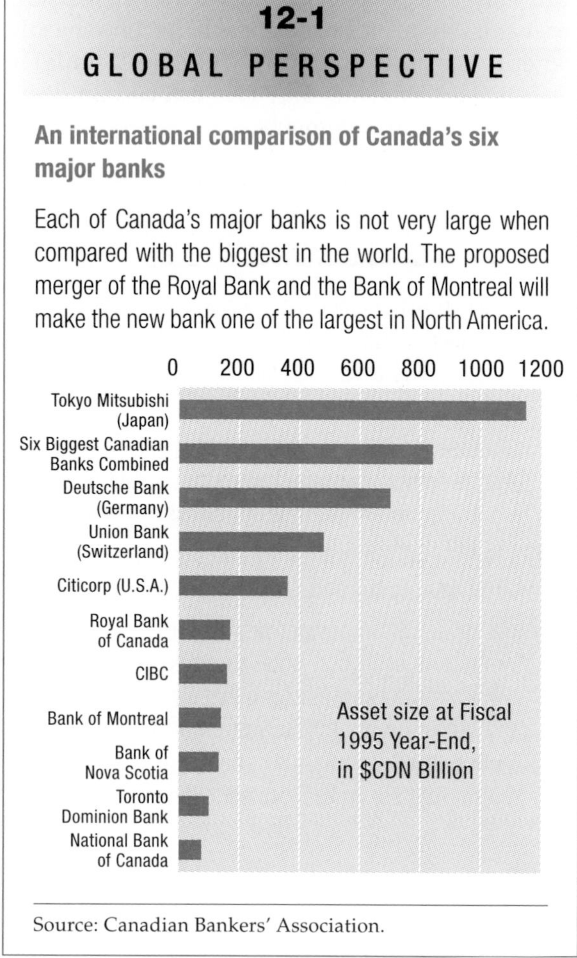


Source: Canadian Bankers' Association.

**Concentration Ratio** A **concentration ratio** gives the percentage of an industry's total sales represented by its largest firms. Column 2 in Table 12-1 lists the *four-firm concentration ratio*—the percentage of total industry sales accounted for by the four largest firms—for a number of oligopolistic industries. For example, the four largest Canadian producers of cigarettes manufacture 99 percent of all cigarette brands produced in Canada.

When the largest four firms in an industry control 40 percent or more of the market, that industry is considered oligopolistic. Using this benchmark, about one-half of all Canadian manufacturing industries are oligopolies.

While concentration ratios provide useful insights into the competitiveness or monopoly

**TABLE 12-1 Four-firm concentration ratios***

| Industry | Percent of revenue of four largest firms |
|---|---|
| Tobacco products | 98.9 |
| Motor vehicles | 95.1** |
| Petroleum and coal products | 74.5 |
| Beverages | 59.2 |
| Primary metals | 63.3 |
| Rubber products | 51.2 |
| Paper and allied industries | 38.9 |
| Textile mills | 32.5 |
| Chemical products | 25.5 |
| Concrete products | 22.7** |
| Food | 19.6 |
| Machinery | 11.3 |
| Construction | 2.2 |

*Data refers to 1988, the last year for which they are available.
**Data are for 1985.
*Source:* Statistics Canada.

power of various industries, they have three shortcomings, discussed below.

**LOCALIZED MARKETS** Concentration ratios pertain to a nation as a whole, while the relevant markets for some products are actually highly localized because of high transportation costs. For example, the four-firm concentration ratio for concrete products is only 23 percent, suggesting a competitive industry. But the sheer bulk of this product limits the relevant market to a specific town or metropolitan area, and in such localized markets we often find oligopolistic suppliers. At the local level, some aspects of the retail trade—particularly in small- and medium-sized towns—are characterized by oligopoly.

**INTERINDUSTRY COMPETITION** Definitions of industries are somewhat arbitrary, and we must be aware of **interindustry competition**, that is, competition between two products associated with different industries. Table 12-1's high concentration ratio for primary metals understates competition. Aluminum competes with copper in many applications—for example, in the market for electrical transmission lines. Similarly, steel and aluminum are in intense competition for use in some components of automobiles, for instance, exterior body panels and engines.

**WORLD TRADE** The data in Table 12-1 are for products produced in Canada only and may overstate concentration because they do not account for the **import competition** of foreign suppliers. The automobile industry is a good example. Although Table 12-1 shows that four firms produce 95 percent of the domestic output, it ignores the fact that a large portion of the cars bought in Canada are imports. Many of the world's largest corporations are foreign, and many of these firms do business in Canada.

## Herfindahl Index

The shortcomings listed above actually apply to many measures of concentration, but one shortcoming can be eliminated: Suppose that in some industry, say, industry X, one firm produces all the market output. In a second industry, say, industry Y, there are four firms and each has 25 percent of the market. The concentration ratio is 100 percent for both these industries. But industry X is a pure monopoly, while industry Y is an oligopoly that may be facing significant economic rivalry. Most economists would concur that monopoly power (or market power) is substantially greater in industry X than in industry Y, a fact disguised by their identical 100 percent concentration ratios.

The **Herfindahl index** addresses this problem. This index is the *sum of the squared percentage market shares of all firms in the industry.* In equation form:

$$\text{Herfindahl index} = (\%S_1)^2 + (\%S_2)^2 + (\%S_3)^2 \ldots + (\%S_n)^2$$

where $\%S_1$ is the percentage market share of firm 1, $\%S_2$ is the percentage market share of firm 2, and so on for each firm in the industry. By squaring the percentage market shares of all firms in the industry, the Herfindahl index gives much greater weight to larger—and thus more powerful—firms than to smaller ones. In the case of the single-firm industry X, the index would be at its maximum of $100^2$ (100 percent squared), or 10,000, indicating an industry with complete monopoly power. For our supposed four-firm industry Y, the index would be $25^2 + 25^2 + 25^2 + 25^2$, or 2,500, indicating much less market power. (For a purely competitive industry, the index would approach zero since each firm's market share—$\%S$ in the equation—is extremely small.) To generalize, the larger the

Herfindahl index, the greater the market power within an industry. ***(Key Question 7)***

## OLIGOPOLY BEHAVIOUR: A GAME THEORY OVERVIEW

Oligopoly pricing behaviour has the characteristics of a game of strategy such as poker, chess, or bridge. The best way to play such a game depends on the way opponents play. Players (and oligopolists) must pattern their actions according to the actions and expected reactions of rivals. The science of strategy is called *game theory*, and we will use a simple **game theory model** to analyze the pricing behaviour of oligopolists. We assume a *duopoly*, or two-firm oligopoly, producing athletic shoes. Each of the two firms—let's call them RareAir and Uptown—has a choice of two pricing strategies: price high or price low. The profit each firm earns will depend on the strategy it chooses and the strategy its rival chooses.

**FIGURE 12-3 Profit payoff (in millions) for a two-firm oligopoly**

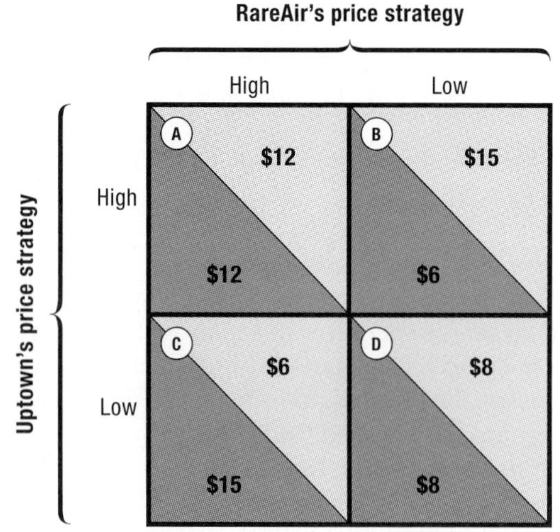


Each firm has two possible pricing strategies. RareAir's strategies are shown in the top margin, and Uptown's in the left margin. Each lettered cell of this four-cell payoff matrix represents one combination of a RareAir strategy and an Uptown strategy and shows the profit that combination would earn for each firm.

There are four possible combinations of strategies for the two firms, and a lettered cell in Figure 12-3 represents each. For example, cell C represents a low-price strategy for Uptown along with a high-price strategy for RareAir. Figure 12-3 is called a *payoff matrix* because each cell shows the payoff (profit) to each firm that would result from each combination of strategies. Cell C shows that if Uptown adopts a low-price strategy and RareAir a high-price strategy, then Uptown will earn $15 million (dark green portion) and RareAir will earn $6 million (light green portion).

### Mutual Interdependence Revisited

The data in Figure 12-3 are hypothetical, but their relationships are typical of real situations. Recall that oligopolistic firms can increase their profits, and affect rivals' profits, by changing their pricing strategies. Each firm's profit depends on its own pricing strategy and that of its rivals. This mutual interdependence of oligopolists is the most obvious point demonstrated by Figure 12-3. If Uptown adopts a high-price strategy, its profit will be $12 million *provided* RareAir also employs a high-price strategy (cell A). But if RareAir uses a low-price strategy against Uptown's high-price strategy (cell B), RareAir will increase its market share and boost its profit from $12 to $15 million. RareAir's higher profit will come at the expense of Uptown, whose profit will fall from $12 to $6 million. Uptown's high-price strategy is a good strategy only if RareAir also employs a high-price strategy.

### Collusive Tendencies

A second point of Figure 12-3 is that oligopolists can increase their profit through **collusion**, meaning cooperation among rivals. To see the benefits of collusion, first suppose that both firms in Figure 12-3 are acting *independently* and following high-price strategies. Each realizes a $12 million profit (cell A).

Note that either RareAir or Uptown could increase its profit by switching to a low-price strategy (cell B or C). The low-price firm would increase its profit to $15 million, and the high-price firm's profit would fall to $6 million. The high-price firm would be better off if it, too, adopted a low-price policy. Doing so would increase its profit from $6 million to $8 million (cell D). The upshot is that all this independent strategy shifting would have the effect of reducing both firms' profits from $12 million (cell A) to $8 million (cell D).

In real situations, too, independent action by oligopolists may lead to mutual "competitive" low-price strategies: Independent oligopolists compete with respect to price, which leads to lower prices *and* lower profits. This is clearly beneficial to consumers but not to the oligopolists, whose profits decrease.

How can oligopolists avoid the low-profit outcome of cell D? The answer is that they could collude, rather than establish prices competitively or independently. In our example, the two firms would be better off if they agree to establish and maintain a high-price policy. Each firm thus will increase its profit from $8 million (cell D) to $12 million (cell A).

### Incentive to Cheat

The payoff matrix also explains why an oligopolist might be strongly tempted to cheat on a collusive agreement. Suppose Uptown and RareAir agree to maintain high-price policies, with each earning $12 million in profit (cell A). Both are tempted to cheat on this collusive pricing agreement because either firm can increase its profit to $15 million by lowering its price. If Uptown secretly cheats on the agreement by charging low prices, the payoff moves from cell A to cell C. Uptown's profit rises to $15 million, and RareAir's falls to $6 million. If RareAir cheats, the payoff moves from cell A to cell B and RareAir gets the $15 million. ***(Key Question 8)***

**12-2**

**QUICK REVIEW**

- An oligopolistic industry is made up of relatively few firms producing either homogeneous or differentiated products; these firms are mutually interdependent.
- Barriers to entry such as scale economies, control of patents or strategic resources, or the ability to engage in retaliatory pricing characterize oligopolies. Oligopolies can result from internal growth of firms, mergers, or both.
- The four-firm concentration ratio shows the percentage of an industry's sales accounted for by its four largest firms; the Herfindahl index measures the degree of market power in an industry by summing the squares of the percentage market shares held by the individual firms in the industry.
- Game theory reveals that **a** oligopolies are mutually interdependent in their pricing policies; **b** collusion enhances oligopoly profits; and **c** there is a temptation for oligopolists to cheat on a collusive agreement.

## THREE OLIGOPOLY MODELS

To gain further insights into oligopolistic pricing and output behaviour, we will examine three distinct pricing models: (1) the kinked demand curve, (2) collusive pricing, and (3) price leadership.

Why not a single model as in our discussions of the other market structures? There is no standard portrait of oligopoly for two reasons:

1. **DIVERSITY OF OLIGOPOLIES** Oligopoly encompasses a greater range and diversity of market situations than other market structures. It includes the *tight oligopoly*, in which two or three firms dominate an entire market, and the *loose oligopoly*, in which six or seven firms share, say, 70 or 80 percent of a market while a "competitive fringe" of firms shares the remainder. It includes both differentiated and standardized products. It includes cases in which firms act in collusion and those in which they act independently. It embodies situations in which barriers to entry are very strong and those in which they are not quite so strong. In short, the diversity of oligopoly does not allow us to explain all oligopolistic behaviours with a single market model.
2. **COMPLICATIONS OF INTERDEPENDENCE** The mutual interdependence of oligopolistic firms complicates matters significantly. Because firms cannot predict the reactions of their rivals with certainty, they cannot estimate their own demand and marginal-revenue data. Without such data, firms cannot determine their profit-maximizing price and output.

Despite these analytical difficulties, two interrelated characteristics of oligopolistic pricing have been observed. First, if the macroeconomy is generally stable, oligopolistic prices are typically inflexible (or "rigid" or "sticky"). Prices change less frequently under oligopoly than under pure competition, monopolistic competition and, in some instances, pure monopoly. Second, when oligopolistic prices do change, firms are likely to change their prices together; this suggests there is a tendency to act in concert, or collusively, in setting and changing prices (as we discussed in the preceding section). The diversity of oligopolies and the presence of mutual interdependence are reflected in the models that follow.

## Noncollusive Oligopoly: Kinked-Demand Theory

Imagine an oligopolistic industry made up of three firms, A, B, and C, each having about one-third of the total market for a differentiated product. Assume the firms are "independent," meaning they do not engage in collusive price practices. Suppose, too, that the going price for firm A's product is $P_0$ and its current sales are $Q_0$, as shown in ***Figure 12-4a (Key Graph)***.

Now the question is "What does the firm's demand curve look like?" Mutual interdependence *and* the uncertainty about rivals' reactions make this question difficult to answer. The location and shape of an oligopolist's demand curve depend on how the firm's rivals will react to a price change introduced by A. There are two plausible assumptions about the reactions of A's rivals.

1. **MATCH PRICE CHANGES** One possibility is that firms B and C will exactly match any price change initiated by A. In this case, A's demand and marginal-revenue curves will look like the straight lines labelled $D_1$ and $MR_1$ in Figure 12-4a. Why are they so steep? Reason: If A cuts its price, its sales will increase only modestly because its two rivals will also cut their prices to prevent A from gaining an advantage over them. The small increase in sales that A (and its two rivals) will realize is at the expense of other industries; A will gain no sales from B and C. If A raises its price, its sales will fall only modestly because B and C will match its price increase. The industry will lose sales to other industries, but A will lose no customers to B and C.
2. **IGNORE PRICE CHANGES** The other possibility is that firms B and C will ignore any price change by A. In this case, the demand and marginal-revenue curves faced by A will resemble the straight lines $D_2$ and $MR_2$ in Figure 12-4a. Demand in this case is considerably more elastic than under the previous assumption. The reasons are clear: If A lowers its price and its rivals do not, A will gain sales significantly at the expense of its two rivals because it will be underselling them. Conversely, if A raises its price and its rivals do not, A will lose many customers to B and C, which will be underselling it. Because of product differentiation, however, A's sales will not fall to zero when it raises its price; some of A's customers will pay the higher price because they have strong preferences for A's product.

**A Combined Strategy** Now, which is the most logical assumption for A to make about how its rivals will react to any price change it might initiate? The answer is "some of each." Common sense and observation of oligopolistic industries suggest that price declines below $P_0$ will be matched as a firm's rivals act to prevent the price-cutter from taking its customers. But price increases above $P_0$ will be ignored because rivals of the price-increasing firm stand to gain the business lost by the price booster. In other words, the dark green left-hand segment of the "rivals ignore" demand curve $D_2$ seems relevant for price increases, and the dark green right-hand segment of the "rivals follow" demand curve $D_1$ seems relevant for price cuts. It is logical, then, or at least a reasonable assumption, that the noncollusive oligopolist faces the **"kinked" demand curve** $D_2eD_1$, as shown in Figure 12-4b. Demand is highly elastic above the going price $P_0$ but much less elastic or even inelastic below that price.

Note also that if rivals will follow a price cut but ignore an increase, the marginal-revenue curve of the oligopolist will also have an odd shape. It, too, will be made up of two segments—the black left-hand part of marginal-revenue curve $MR_2$ in Figure 12-4a and the black right-hand part of marginal-revenue curve $MR_1$. Because of the sharp difference in elasticity of demand above and below the going price, there is a gap, or what we can treat as a vertical segment, in the marginal-revenue curve. This gap is shown by the dashed segment in the combined marginal-revenue curve $MR_2fgMR_1$ in Figure 12-4b.

**Price Inflexibility** This analysis goes far to explain why prices are generally stable in noncollusive oligopolistic industries.

**ON THE DEMAND SIDE** The kinked demand curve gives each oligopolist reason to believe that any change in price will be for the worse. If it raises its price, many of its customers will desert

## KEY GRAPH

**FIGURE 12-4 The kinked demand curve**

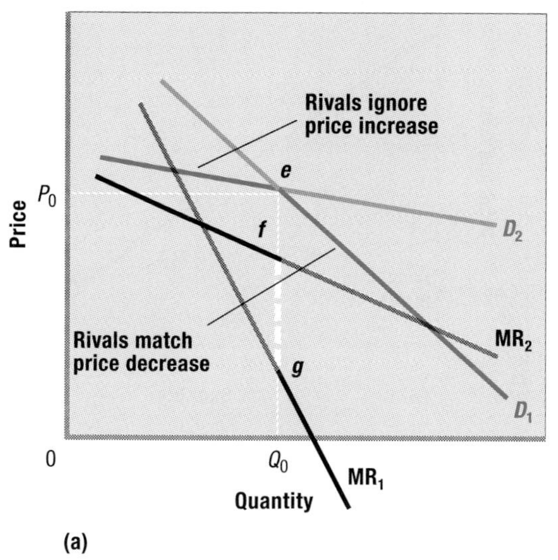


(a)

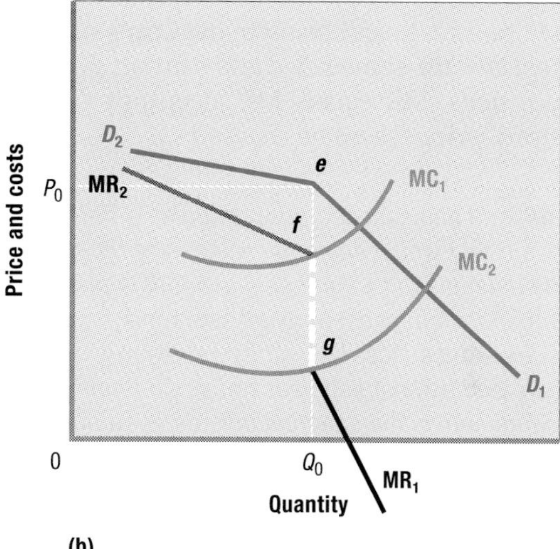


(b)

(a) The slope of a noncollusive oligopolist's demand and marginal-revenue curves depends on whether its rivals match (straight lines $D_1$ and $MR_1$) or ignore (straight lines $D_2$ and $MR_2$) any price changes that it may initiate from the current price $P_0$. (b) In all likelihood an oligopolist's rivals will ignore a price increase but follow a price cut. This causes the oligopolist's demand curve to be kinked ($D_2eD_1$) and the marginal-revenue curve to have a vertical break, or gap (*fg*). Because any shift in marginal costs between $MC_1$ and $MC_2$ will cut the vertical (dashed) segment of the marginal-revenue curve, no change in either price $P_0$ or output $Q_0$ will result from such a shift.

### 12-4 QUICK QUIZ

**1.** Suppose $Q_0$ in this figure represents annual sales of 5 million units for this firm. The other two firms in this three-firm industry sell 3 million and 2 million units, respectively. The Herfindahl index for this industry is:
- **(a)** 100 percent.
- **(b)** 400.
- **(c)** 10.
- **(d)** 3800.

**2.** The $D_2e$ segment of the demand curve $D_2eD_1$ in graph (b) implies that:
- **(a)** this firm's total revenue will fall if it increases its price above $P_0$.
- **(b)** other firms will match a price increase above $P_0$.
- **(c)** the firm's relevant marginal-revenue curve will be $MR_1$ for price increases above $P_0$.
- **(d)** the product in this industry is necessarily standardized.

**3.** By matching a price cut, this firm's rivals can:
- **(a)** increase their market shares.
- **(b)** increase their marginal revenues.
- **(c)** maintain their market shares.
- **(d)** lower their total costs.

**4.** A shift of the marginal-cost curve from $MC_2$ to $MC_1$ in graph (b) would:
- **(a)** increase the "going price" above $P_0$.
- **(b)** leave price at $P_0$, but reduce this firm's total profit.
- **(c)** leave price at $P_0$, but reduce this firm's total revenue.
- **(d)** make this firm's demand curve more elastic.

**Answers:** 1. (d); 2. (a); 3 (c); 4. (b).

it. If it lowers its price, its sales at best will increase very modestly since rivals will match the lower price. Even if a price cut increases the oligopolist's total revenue somewhat, its costs may well increase by a greater amount. And if its demand is inelastic to the right of $Q_0$, as it may well be, then the firm's profit will surely fall. A price decrease in the inelastic region lowers the firm's total revenue, and the production of a larger output increases its total cost.

**ON THE COST SIDE** The broken marginal-revenue curve suggests that even if an oligopolist's costs change substantially, the firm may have no reason to change its price. In particular, all positions of the marginal-cost curve between $MC_1$ and $MC_2$ in Figure 12-4b will result in the firm's deciding on exactly the same price and output. For all those positions, MR equals MC at output $Q_0$; at that output, price $P_0$ will be charged.

**Criticisms** The kinked-demand analysis has two shortcomings. First, *it does not explain how the going price gets to be at $P_0$ in Figure 12-4 in the first place.* It only helps explain why oligopolists tend to stick with an existing price. The kinked demand curve explains price inflexibility but not price itself.

Second, when the macroeconomy is unstable, oligopoly prices are not as rigid as the kinked-demand theory implies. During inflationary periods, many oligopolists have raised their prices often and substantially. And during downturns (recessions) in the macroeconomy, some oligopolists have cut prices. In some instances these price reductions have set off a **price war**: *successive and continuous rounds of price cuts by rivals as they attempt to maintain their market shares.* ***(Key Question 9)***

## Cartels and Other Collusion

Our game theory model suggests that oligopoly is conducive to collusion. We can say that *collusion occurs whenever firms in an industry reach an agreement to fix prices, divide up the market, or otherwise restrict competition among themselves.* The disadvantages and uncertainties of noncollusive, kinked-demand oligopoly are obvious. There is always the danger of a price war breaking out—especially during a general business recession. Then each firm finds itself with unsold goods and excess capacity and can reduce per-unit costs by increasing market share. Then, too, a new firm may surmount entry barriers and initiate aggressive price cutting to gain a foothold in the market. In addition, the kinked demand curve's tendency towards rigid prices may adversely affect profits if general inflationary pressures increase costs. However, by controlling price through collusion, oligopolists may be able to reduce uncertainty, increase profits, and perhaps even prohibit the entry of new rivals.

**Price and Output** Assume once again that there are three oligopolistic firms—A, B, and C—producing, in this instance, homogeneous products. All three firms have identical cost curves. Each firm's demand curve is indeterminate unless we know how its rivals will react to any price change. Therefore, we suppose each firm assumes its two rivals will match either a price cut or a price increase. In other words, each firm has a demand curve like the straight line $D_1$ in Figure 12-4a. And since they have identical cost data, and the same demand and thus marginal-revenue data, we can say that Figure 12-5 represents the position of each of our three oligopolistic firms.

**FIGURE 12-5 Collusion and the tendency towards joint-profit maximization**

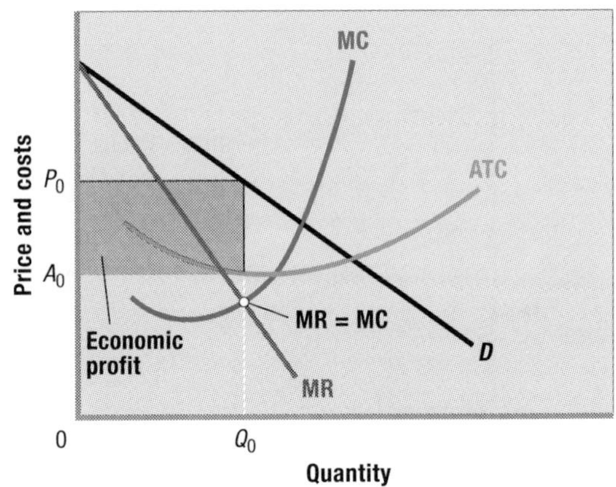


If oligopolistic firms face identical or highly similar demand and cost conditions, they may collude to limit their joint output and to set a single, common price. Thus each firm acts as if it were a pure monopolist, setting output at $Q_0$ and charging price $P_0$. This price and output combination maximizes each oligopolist's profit (grey area) and thus their combined or joint profit.

What price and output combination should, say, A choose? If A were a pure monopolist, the answer would be clear: Establish output at $Q_0$, where marginal revenue equals marginal cost, charge the corresponding price $P_0$, and enjoy the maximum profit attainable. However, firm A *does* have two rivals selling identical products, and if A's assumption that its rivals will match its price of $P_0$ proves to be incorrect, the consequences could be disastrous for A. Specifically, if B and C actually charge prices below $P_0$ then A's demand curve *D* will shift sharply to the left as its potential customers turn to its rivals, which are now selling the same product at a lower price. Of course, firm

A can retaliate by cutting its price too, but this will move all three firms down their demand curves, lowering their profits. It may even drive them to a point where average total cost exceeds price and losses are incurred.

So the question becomes "Will B and C want to charge a price below $P_0$?" Under our assumptions, and recognizing that A has little choice except to match any price they may set below $P_0$, the answer is "no." Faced with the same demand and cost circumstances, B and C will find it in their interest to produce $Q_0$ and charge $P_0$. This is a curious situation; each firm finds it most profitable to charge the same price, $P_0$, but only if its rivals actually do so! How can the three firms ensure the price $P_0$ and quantity $Q_0$ solution in which each is keenly interested? How can they avoid the less profitable outcomes associated with either higher or lower prices?

The answer is evident: Collusion—get together, talk it over, and agree to charge the same price, $P_0$. In addition to reducing the possibility of price wars, this will give each firm the maximum profit. And for society, the result will be the same as would occur if the industry were a pure monopoly composed of three identical plants.

**Overt Collusion: The OPEC Cartel** Collusion may assume a variety of forms. The most comprehensive form is the **cartel**, *a group of producers that typically develops a formal written agreement as to how much each member will produce and charge.* Output must be controlled—the market must be divided up—to maintain the agreed-upon price. The collusion is *overt*, or open to be seen.

The most spectacularly successful international cartel of recent decades has been the Organization of Petroleum Exporting Countries (OPEC). Made up of 13 oil-producing nations, OPEC was extremely effective in the 1970s in restricting the oil supply and raising prices. The cartel was able to raise world oil prices from $2.50 to $11.00 per barrel within a 6-month period in 1973–74. By early 1980, price hikes had brought the per-barrel price into the $32 to $34 range. The result was enormous profits for cartel members, a substantial stimulus to worldwide inflation, and serious international trade deficits for oil importers.

OPEC was highly effective in the 1970s for several reasons. First, it dominated the world market for oil. If a nation imported oil, it was almost obligated to do business with OPEC. Second, world demand for oil was strong and expanding in the 1970s. Finally, the short-run demand for oil was highly inelastic because the economies of oil-importing nations such as Canada were locked into low-gas-mileage automobiles and energy-intensive housing and capital equipment. This inelastic demand meant that a small restriction of output by OPEC would result in a relatively large price increase. As shown in Figure 12-6, between 1973 and 1980 OPEC was able to achieve an enormous increase in oil price by reducing output only very modestly. With inelastic demand, higher prices meant greatly increased total revenues to OPEC members. The accompanying smaller output meant lower total costs. The combination of increased total revenues and lower total costs resulted in greatly expanded profits. (We discuss the serious weakening of the OPEC cartel later in this chapter.)

### Covert Collusion: Quebec City Cement Industry

Cartels are illegal in Canada, and hence what collusion there is has been *covert* or secret. A recent example of covert collusion is provided by the case of four cement firms in the Quebec City Region. In 1996 St. Lawrence Cement Inc., Lafarge

**FIGURE 12-6 The OPEC cartel and the world oil market**

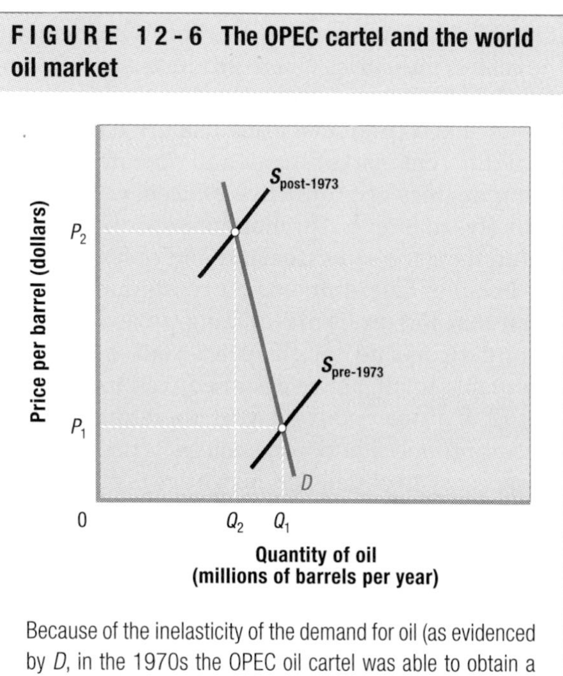


Because of the inelasticity of the demand for oil (as evidenced by $D$, in the 1970s the OPEC oil cartel was able to obtain a dramatic increase in the price of oil ($P_1$ to $P_2$) by means of only a very modest decline in production and sales ($Q_1$ to $Q_2$).

Canada Inc., Cement Quebec Inc., and Beton Orleans Inc. were fined a total of $5.8 million for price fixing. The conspiracy was discovered by a Quebec City newspaper that reported the cost of the city's new convention centre was higher than anticipated mostly because of higher cement costs. The first three of these companies had previously been fined in 1983 for a similar violation of the Competition Act.

In many other instances collusion is even more subtle. **Tacit understandings** (historically called *gentlemen's agreements*) are frequently made at cocktail parties, on golf courses, by phone calls, or at trade association meetings. In such agreements, competing firms reach a verbal understanding on product price, leaving market shares to be decided by nonprice competition. Although they too violate anti-combines laws—and can result in severe personal and corporate penalties—their elusive character of tacit understandings makes them more difficult to detect.

**Obstacles to Collusion** Normally, cartels and similar collusive arrangements are difficult to establish and maintain. Let's briefly consider several important barriers to collusion.

**DEMAND AND COST DIFFERENCES** When oligopolists face different costs and demand curves, it is difficult to agree on a price. This is particularly the case in industries where products are differentiated and change frequently. Even with highly standardized products, firms usually have somewhat different market shares and operate with differing degrees of productive efficiency. Thus it is unlikely that even homogeneous oligopolists would have the same demand and cost curves.

In either case, differences in costs and demand mean that the profit-maximizing price will differ among firms; no single price will be readily acceptable to all, as we assumed was true in Figure 12-5. Price collusion will therefore depend on compromises and concessions. These are not always easy to obtain and hence act as an obstacle to collusion.

**NUMBER OF FIRMS** Other things equal, the larger the number of firms, the more difficult it is to achieve a cartel or other form of price collusion. Agreement on price by three or four producers that control an entire market may be relatively easy to accomplish. But such agreement is more difficult to secure where there are, say, 10 firms, each with roughly 10 percent of the market, or where the Big Three have 70 percent of the market while a "competitive fringe" of 8 or 10 smaller firms battles for the remainder.

**CHEATING** As is clear from the game theory model, there is a constant temptation for collusive oligopolists to engage in secret price-cutting to increase sales and profit. The difficulty with such cheating is that buyers paying a high price may become aware of the lower-priced sales and demand similar treatment. Or buyers receiving a price concession (decrease) from one producer may use the concession as a wedge to get even larger price concessions from that producer's rival. Buyers' attempts to play producers against one another may precipitate price wars among the producers. Although they are potentially profitable, secret price concessions threaten collusive oligopolies over time. Collusion is more likely to be successful when cheating is easy to detect and punish. In those circumstances, the conspirators are less likely to cheat on the price agreement.

**RECESSION** Long-lasting recession is usually an enemy of collusion because slumping markets increase average total cost. In technical terms, as the oligopolists' demand and marginal-revenue curves shift to the left in Figure 12-5 due to a recession, each firm moves leftward and upward to a higher operating point on its average-total-cost curve. Firms find they have substantial excess production capacity, sales are down, unit costs are up, and so profits are being squeezed. Under these conditions, businesses may feel they can avoid serious profit reductions (or even losses) by cutting price and thus gaining sales at the expense of rivals.

**POTENTIAL ENTRY** The higher prices and profits that result from collusion may attract new entrants, including foreign firms. This would increase market supply and reduce prices and profits. Therefore, successful collusion requires that colluding oligopolists block the entry of new producers.

**LEGAL OBSTACLES: ANTI-COMBINES LAW** Canadian anti-combines law prohibits cartels and the kind of price-fixing collusion we have been discussing. So less obvious means of price control have evolved in Canada.

**OPEC in Disarray** The highly successful OPEC oil cartel of the 1970s fell into disarray in the

1980s. The reasons for OPEC's decline relate closely to the obstacles to collusion just examined.

**NEW SUPPLIERS** The dramatic surge of oil prices in the 1970s stimulated the search for new oil reserves, and soon non-OPEC nations, which OPEC could not block from entering world markets, became part of the world oil industry. Great Britain, Norway, Mexico, and Russia have all become major oil suppliers. As a result, OPEC's share of world oil production has declined.

**DECLINING DEMAND** On the demand side, oil conservation, worldwide recession in the early 1980s, and expanded use of alternative energy sources (such as coal, natural gas, and nuclear power) all reduced the demand for oil. The combination of greater production by non-OPEC nations and decline in world demand generated an "oil glut" and seriously impaired OPEC's ability to control world oil prices.

**CHEATING** OPEC has had a serious cheating problem stemming from the relatively large number of members (13) and the diversity of their economic circumstances. Saudi Arabia is the dominant cartel member; it has the largest oil reserves and is probably the lowest-cost producer. Saudi Arabia has favoured a "moderate" pricing policy because it has feared that very high oil prices would hasten the development of more alternative energy sources (such as solar power and synthetic fuels) and increase the attractiveness of existing substitutes such as coal and natural gas. These developments would greatly reduce the value of its vast oil reserves. Saudi Arabia also has a small population and a very high per-capita domestic output. But other OPEC members—for example, Nigeria and Venezuela—are relatively poor, have large populations, and are burdened with large external debts. Still others—Iran, Iraq, and Libya—have had large military commitments. All these members have immediate needs for cash. Thus, there has been substantial cheating, and some members have exceeded assigned production quotas and have sold oil at prices below those agreed to by the cartel. Result: Although OPEC's official oil price reached $34 per barrel in 1979, it is currently only about $19 per barrel.

## Price Leadership

Another method by which firms can act in cconcert is **price leadership**, an implicit understanding by which oligopolists can coordinate prices without engaging in outright collusion. Formal agreements and secret meetings are not involved. Rather, a practice evolves whereby the "dominant firm"—usually the largest or most efficient in the industry—initiates price changes and all other firms more or less automatically follow that lead. Many industries, including farm machinery, cement, copper, newsprint, glass containers, steel, beer, fertilizer, cigarettes, and tin, are practising, or have in the recent past practised, price leadership.

**Leadership Tactics** An examination of price leadership in a variety of industries suggests that the price leader is likely to observe the following tactics.

**INFREQUENT CHANGES** Because price changes always carry some risk that rivals will not follow the lead, price adjustments are made infrequently. The price leader does not respond to minuscule day-to-day changes in costs and demand. Price is changed only when cost and demand conditions have been altered significantly and on an industrywide basis as the result of, for example, industrywide wage increases, an increase in excise taxes, or an increase in the price of some basic input such as energy. In the automobile industry, price adjustments traditionally have been made when new models are introduced each fall.

**COMMUNICATIONS** The price leader often communicates impending price adjustments to the industry through speeches by major executives, trade publication interviews, and so forth. By publicizing "the need to raise prices," the price leader can seek agreement among its competitors regarding the actual increase.

**LIMIT PRICING** The price leader does not necessarily choose the price that maximizes short-run profits for the industry because the industry may want to discourage new firms from entering. If the cost advantages (economies of scale) of existing firms are a major barrier to entry, this barrier could be surmounted by new entrants if product price were set high enough by the existing firms: New firms that are relatively inefficient because of their small size might survive and grow if the industry's price were very high. So, to discourage new competitors and maintain the current oligopolistic structure of the industry, price may be kept below the short-run profit-maximizing level. The strategy of establishing a price that prevents the entry of new firms is called *limit pricing*.

### Breakdowns in Price Leadership: Price Wars

Price leadership in oligopoly occasionally breaks down, at least temporarily, and sometimes results in a price war. A recent disruption of price leadership occurred in the breakfast cereal industry, in which Kellogg traditionally had been the price leader. General Mills countered Kellogg's leadership in 1995 by reducing the prices of its cereals by 11 percent. In 1996 Post responded with a 20 percent price cut, which Kellogg then followed. Not to be outdone, Post reduced its prices by another 11 percent.

Most price wars eventually run their course. When all firms recognize that low prices are severely reducing their profits, they again cede price leadership to one of the industry's leading firms. That firm begins to increase prices, and the other firms willingly follow.

**12-3**

**QUICK REVIEW**

- In the kinked-demand theory of oligopoly, price is relatively inflexible because a firm contemplating a price change assumes that rivals will follow a price cut and ignore a price increase.
- Cartels agree on production limits and set a common price to maximize the joint profit of their members as if each were a unit of a single pure monopoly.
- Collusion among oligopolists is difficult because of **a** demand and cost differences among sellers, **b** the complexity of output coordination among producers, **c** the potential for cheating, **d** a tendency for agreements to break down during recessions, **e** the potential entry of new firms, and **f** anti-combines laws.
- Price leadership involves an informal understanding among oligopolists to match any price change initiated by a designated firm (often the industry's dominant firm.)

## OLIGOPOLY AND ADVERTISING

We noted that oligopolists would rather not compete via price and may become involved in price collusion. Nonetheless, each firm's share of the total market is typically determined through product development and advertising. This emphasis has its roots in two facts:

1. Product development and advertising campaigns are less easily duplicated than price cuts. Price cuts can be quickly and easily matched by a firm's rivals to cancel any potential gain in sales from that strategy. Product improvements and successful advertising, however, can produce more permanent gains in market share. They cannot be duplicated as quickly and completely as price reductions.
2. Oligopolists have sufficient financial resources to engage in product development and advertising. For most oligopolists, the economic profits earned in the past can help finance current advertising and product development.

Product development (or, more broadly, "research and development") is the subject of the next chapter, so we will confine our present discussion to advertising. In recent years, Canadian advertising has exceeded $20 billion annually, and worldwide advertising, over $400 billion. Both monopolistic competitors and differentiated oligopolists engage in advertising.

Advertising can affect prices, competition, and efficiency both positively and negatively, depending on the circumstances. While our focus here is on advertising by oligopolists, the analysis is equally applicable to advertising by monopolistic competitors.

### Positive Effects of Advertising

Consumers need information about product characteristics and prices to make rational (efficient) decisions. Advertising can be a low-cost means of providing that information. Suppose you are in the market for a high-quality camera and there is no newspaper or magazine advertising of this product. To make a rational choice, you have to spend several days visiting stores to determine the prices and features of various brands. This search entails both direct costs (gasoline, parking fees) and indirect costs (the value of your time). Advertising reduces your *search time* and minimizes these costs.

By providing information about the various competing goods that are available, advertising diminishes monopoly power. In fact, advertising is frequently associated with the introduction of new products designed to compete with existing brands. Could Toyota and Honda have so strongly challenged North American auto producers without advertising? Could Federal Express have sliced market share away from UPS and the Canadian Postal Service without advertising? How about upstart Mentadent toothpaste, which recently has gained market share from long-time leaders Crest and Colgate?

Viewed this way, advertising is an efficiency-enhancing activity. It is a relatively inexpensive means of providing useful information to consumers and thus lowering their search costs. By enhancing competition, advertising results in greater economic efficiency. By facilitating the introduction of new products, advertising speeds up technological progress. And by increasing output, advertising can reduce long-run average total cost by enabling firms to obtain economies of scale.

## Potential Negative Effects of Advertising

Not all the effects of advertising are positive. Much advertising is designed to persuade consumers, that is, to alter their preferences in favour of the advertiser's product. A television commercial indicating that a popular personality drinks a particular brand of soft drink—and therefore that you should too—conveys little or no information to consumers about price or quality. In addition, advertising is sometimes based on misleading and extravagant claims that confuse consumers rather than enlighten them. Indeed, in some cases advertising may well persuade consumers to pay high prices for much-acclaimed but inferior products, forgoing better but unadvertised products selling at lower prices. Example: *Consumer Reports* recently found that heavily advertised premium motor oils and fancy additives provide no better engine performance and longevity than do cheaper brands.

Firms often establish substantial brand-name loyalty and thus monopoly power via their advertising (see Global Perspective 12-2). As a consequence, they are able to increase their sales, expand their market shares, and enjoy greater profits. Larger profit permits still more advertising and further enlargement of a firm's market share and profit. In time, consumers may lose the advantages of competitive markets and face the disadvantages of monopolized markets. Moreover, potential new entrants to the industry need to incur large advertising costs to establish their products in the marketplace; thus, advertising costs may be a barrier to entry.

Advertising can also be self-cancelling. The advertising campaign of one fast-food hamburger chain may be offset by equally costly campaigns waged by rivals, so each firm's demand is actually unchanged. Few, if any, extra burgers will be purchased, and each firm's market share will stay the same. But because of the advertising, the cost and hence the price of hamburgers will be higher.

When advertising either leads to increased monopoly power or is self-cancelling, economic inefficiency results.

### 12-2 GLOBAL PERSPECTIVE

**The world's top 10 brand names***

Here are the world's top 10 brands, based on four criteria: the brand's market share within its category, the brand's world appeal across age groups and nationalities, the loyalty of customers to the brand, and the ability of the brand to "stretch" to products beyond the original product.

- McDonald's
- Coca-Cola
- Disney
- Kodak
- Sony
- Gillette
- Mercedes-Benz
- Levi's
- Microsoft
- Marlboro

*Source:* Interbrand, as reported in the *Economist*, Nov. 16, 1996, p. 75. Data are for 1996.

## Graphical Analysis

Two of the efficiency aspects of advertising are shown in Figure 12-7, which focuses on the idea that advertising usually has two effects. First, it increases demand, output, and sales; and second, it adds an extra expense to the firm.

Through successful advertising, a firm increases its demand, permitting it to expand output and sales from, say, $Q_1$ to $Q_2$. Despite the fact that advertising outlays will shift the firm's long-run ATC curve upward, per-unit cost declines from $A_1$ to $A_2$ as the firm moves from point *a* to point *b*.

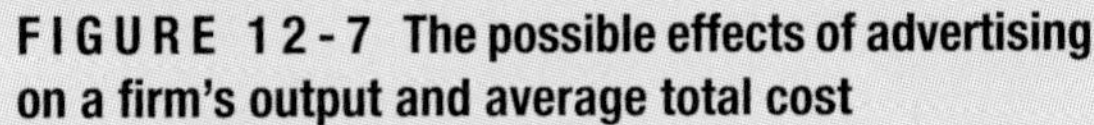
**FIGURE 12-7 The possible effects of advertising on a firm's output and average total cost**

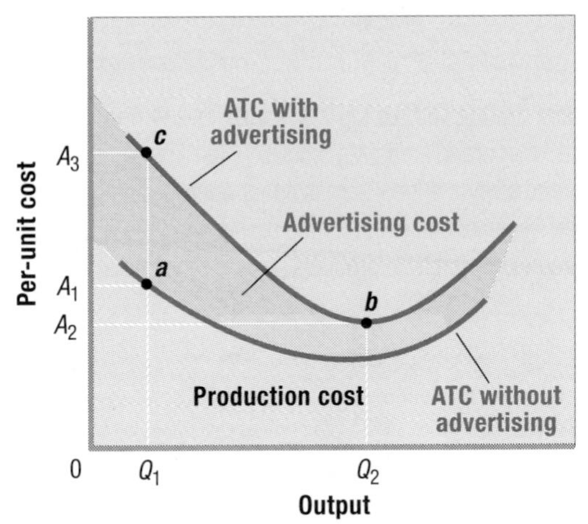


In some cases, advertising may expand the firm's production from, say, point *a* to *b* and lower average total cost from $A_1$ to $A_2$ through economies of scale. But in other instances, it may be self-cancelling, increase average total cost, and leave output largely unchanged. If so, the firm may move from, say, *a* to *c*, experiencing an increase in average total cost from $A_1$ to $A_3$.

Greater productive efficiency from economies of scale more than offsets the increase in per-unit cost from advertising. Assuming no increase in monopoly power, consumers therefore get the product at a lower price with advertising than they would without.

But what if the advertising efforts of all firms are self-cancelling? Then output may stay at $Q_1$ while the long-run ATC curve shifts upward. Instead of moving the firm from *a* to *b*, self-cancelling advertising moves it from *a* to *c*. In this case, per-unit cost rises to $A_3$, and the consumer pays a higher price because of advertising.

As this analysis indicates, no *general* conclusion can be reached as to the impact of advertising on price, competition, and efficiency. There are possibilities for positive and negative outcomes, and the net impact may well vary by industry and by particular situation. ***(Key Question 11)***

## OLIGOPOLY AND EFFICIENCY

Is oligopoly, then, an efficient market structure from society's standpoint? How do the price and output decisions of the oligopolist measure up to the triple equality $P = \text{MC} = \text{minimum ATC}$ occurring in pure competition?

### Productive and Allocative Efficiency

Many economists believe that the outcome of some oligopolistic markets is approximated by the collusive model shown in Figure 12-5. This view is bolstered by evidence that many oligopolists sustain sizable economic profits year after year. In that case, the oligopolist's production occurs where price exceeds marginal cost and average total cost. Moreover, production is below the output at which average total cost is minimized. In this view, neither productive efficiency ($P$ = minimum ATC) nor allocative efficiency ($P$ = MC) is likely to occur under oligopoly.

A few observers assert that oligopoly is actually less desirable than pure monopoly because pure monopoly in Canada is usually regulated by government to guard against abuses of monopoly power. Informal collusion among oligopolists may yield price and output results similar to those under pure monopoly yet give the outward appearance of competition involving independent firms.

### Qualifications

We should note, however, three qualifications to this view:

1. **INCREASED FOREIGN COMPETITION** In the past decade, foreign competition has increased rivalry in a number of oligopolistic industries—steel, automobiles, photographic film, electric shavers, outboard motors, and copy machines, for example. This has helped break down such cozy arrangements as price leadership and stimulate more competitive pricing.
2. **LIMIT PRICING** Recall that some oligopolists may purposely keep prices below the short-run profit-maximizing level to bolster entry barriers. In essence, consumers and society may get some of the benefits of competition—prices closer to marginal cost and minimum average total cost—even without the competition that easy entry would provide.
3. **TECHNOLOGICAL ADVANCE** Over time, oligopolistic industries may foster more rapid product development and greater improvement of production techniques than would be possible if they were purely competitive. Oli-

gopolists have large economic profits from which they can fund expensive research and development (R&D). Moreover, the existence of barriers to entry may give the oligopolist some assurance that it will reap the rewards of successful R&D. Thus, short-run economic inefficiencies of oligopolists may be partly or wholly offset by oligopolists' contributions to better products, lower prices, and lower costs over time. We will have more to say about these more dynamic aspects of rivalry in Chapter 13.

## In The Media

# Film Feud Hits New Peaks

### Kodak and Fuji take their rivalry to the Nagano Olympics

BY LAURA JOHANNES AND NORIHIKO SHIROUZU
THE WALL STREET JOURNAL

NAGANO, Japan—This town of 400,000, host to the Winter Olympics, is at the centre of a high-stakes international battle between the world's top two makers of photographic film. In theory, it's a Kodak moment, since the U.S. company paid $44-million (U.S.) to become an official sponsor, with exclusive rights to the Olympic name and the cachet of its five-ring symbol.

But Fuji Photo Film Co., which first gained a toehold in the United States by outbidding Eastman Kodak Co. for sponsorship of the Los Angeles summer games in 1984, isn't sitting idle while Kodak attempts to reverse the feat on its home turf. The market for film in Japan is about $2-billion a year, compared with about $2.7-billion in the United States, according to analyst Jonathan Rosenzweig at Salomon Smith Barney Inc.

Kodak says its pre-Olympics marketing blitz has doubled its market share in the Nagano area to 20 per cent since September, 1996, when its sponsorship began. Its efforts include snazzy outdoor advertising with an Olympic theme, price discounts, in-store displays and a fleet of buses shrink-wrapped with photos of its products.

To bypass distributors loyal to Fuji, Kodak is trucking in film to Nagano. And when Nagano's oldest Fuji retailer declined to convert to Kodak, the U.S. company convinced local entrepreneur Ichimi Kitamura to open a Kodak shop right next door. Kodak picked up half the cost, a total of 15 million yen ($117,000 U.S.).

The Olympics, which begin Friday, are expected to draw as many as 1.2 million visitors—half of them Japanese—to Nagano. "This is a fabulous opportunity, since the Japanese treat the Olympics with some reverence," says Michael Tette, Kodak's brand manager for the games.

Fuji disputes that Kodak's market share has shot up in Nagano, and says it isn't planning Olympics-related marketing to counter Kodak. "Our best defence, we believe, is to carry out our business activities as usual," says spokesman Ken Sugiyama.

Fuji also says it isn't cutting wholesale prices in Japan. But in Nagano and elsewhere, store owners say the opposite. Hoey Arai, manager of the Koshina Color photo shop in Nagano, says Fuji has been matching Kodak's price cuts "blow-by-blow," something he says the company has never done before. "It's pretty astounding to see what Olympic sponsorship can do to rock the status quo," he says.

Fuji is setting up a film-processing lab so sports photographers loyal to Fuji have an alternative to the official Kodak-run lab, which will only process film that comes in yellow boxes. Fuji will not, however, match Kodak's other big perk: unlimited free film to all 650 accredited photographers.

But the home team won't be outdone when it comes to road signs. Early last year, as Kodak's pre-Olympic publicity shifted into high gear, Fuji struck back with billboards that read: "Fuji Cheers for Nagano at the Center of the World." The Japanese Olympic Committee cried foul, and asked Fuji to ditch the slogan. "Obviously Fuji knew what they were doing with the billboard. It was a case of free-riding when they weren't an official sponsor," said Toru Watanabe, a Japan Olympic Committee Official.

Fuji denies that its billboard was intended to ambush Kodak's sponsorship, but agreed to change it in August. Even its new "Captures the Moment of Truth" version seems also to evoke the Olympics, according to Kodak. "Would you call this business as usual?" asks Kodak regional manager Shigehiro Maeda.

Kodak has long struggled to raise its market share in Japan, which had been stuck at under 10 per cent for years. In 1996, the U.S. government filed a case on Kodak's behalf with the World Trade Organization, alleging that the Japanese government effectively shut foreign film makers out of the distribution system. But last week, the international arbitration body ruled that the United States hadn't proved its case.

*Source: Globe the Mail,* February 3, 1998, p. B16. Reprinted by permission of the Wall Street Journal © 1998, Dow Jones & Company, Inc.

## THE STORY IN BRIEF

The Winter Olympics of 1998 saw fierce competition for market share between Kodak and Fuji, the two largest photographic film makers in the world.

## THE ECONOMICS BEHIND THE STORY

- The world photographic film-making industry is an oligopoly dominated by Kodak of the United States and Fuji of Japan. Kodak paid $44 million (U.S.) to be the official sponsors at the 1998 Winter Olympics in Nagano, Japan, in an attempt to raise its market share not only worldwide but particularly in Japan.
- The article reports that the two giant photographic film makers engaged in both price and nonprice competition, Fuji matching Kodak's price cuts "blow by blow." Kodak in turn paid half the cost of opening a retail shop next to one selling Fuji photographic film. Each company's large advertising outlay is an attempt to differentiate its product from its competitor's.
- Is there mutual interdependence between Kodak and Fuji? Explain. ■

# The Last Word

## MEGA-BANKS TO FACE LITTLE COMPETITION, WATCHDOG TOLD

**By Shawn McCarthy**
**Parliamentary Bureau**

OTTAWA—FOREIGN BANKS OR OTHER FINANCIAL institutions will be unable to offset a serious lack of competition that will occur if major Canadian banks are allowed to merge, business and consumer groups have told the federal Competition Bureau.

As part of its review of proposed bank mega-mergers, the competition watchdog asked Canadians to comment on the guidelines it proposes to use to assess the impact of the deal on the financial services market.

While the banks argue that the bureau's merger guidelines underestimate the impact of emerging competitors, groups representing insurance companies, small business and even foreign banks have warned that serious barriers remain for those who would take on the Canadian giants.

And the resulting impact on small businesses and consumers could be devastating, they argue. Their submissions were posted on a government Web site on the weekend.

Royal Bank of Canada and Bank of Montreal stunned the country with their announcement in January that they planned to merge in order to reduce costs and prepare themselves for growing global competition. Fearing they would be left behind, Canadian Imperial Bank of Commerce and Toronto-Dominion Bank announced last month that they, too, would join forces.

Those proposed mergers must be approved by the Competition Bureau, as well as by Finance Minister Paul Martin.

The Canadian Life and Health Insurance Association said foreign banks and trust companies have failed to mount any serious competition to the banks, which in the past decade have gained an increasing market share for a wide range of financial products.

Past experience of the banks' competitors suggests that, even with regulatory changes, they would have trouble filling the competitive void resulting from big bank mergers, said the association, which represents Canada's largest insurance companies.

The bureau should be extremely careful in allowing efficiency gains that could result from the mergers to outweigh the impact of lessening competition, the association said.

Under the Competition Act, the bureau must approve a deal—despite any resulting substantial lessening of competition—if the merger will have a positive impact on the Canadian economy.

"If a proposed merger would limit such [small] business from starting up or expanding because they cannot afford a loan or cannot obtain one, either as a result of higher loan costs or...rationing, negative effects could extend very broadly to workers, communities and the country in general," the insurance association said.

The Atlantic Canada Opportunities Agency, a federal regional developmental body, urged the bureau to consider not only the price impact of reduced competition, but also its effect on credit availability for small business, particularly in rural areas.

The banks' limited presence in rural Canada already results in higher loan-rejection rates and limited alternatives there, the agency said. Bank mergers would exacerbate a problem that is already a major barrier to business success.

William Loewen, president of Tel-Pay, a bill payment unit of CTI-Com-Tel Inc. of Winnipeg, said banks have a stranglehold over some key aspects of the financial system, such as the Interac debit system and the Canadian Payments Association, which runs the clearing system for cheques. "The talk of creating competition by inviting foreign banks into Canada is nothing but hot air."

U.S.-based Capital One Financial Corp., which now offers credit cards and consumer instalment loans in Canada, said it faces an uphill battle for a share of the market. ■

# CHAPTER SUMMARY

1. The distinguishing features of monopolistic competition are **a** there are enough firms in the industry so that each has only limited control over price, mutual interdependence is absent, and collusion is nearly impossible; **b** products are characterized by real or perceived differences so that economic rivalry entails both price and nonprice competition; and **c** entry to the industry is relatively easy. Many aspects of retailing, and some manufacturing industries where economies of scale are few, approximate monopolistic competition.

2. Monopolistically competitive firms may earn economic profits or incur losses in the short run. The easy entry and exit of firms results in only normal profits in the long run.

3. The long-run equilibrium position of firms in the monopolistic competition is less socially desirable than that attainable under a purely compettive market structure. Under monopolistic competition, price exceeds marginal cost, suggesting an underallocation of resources to the product, and price exceeds minimum average total cost, indicating that consumers do not get the product at the lowest price that cost conditions allow.

4. Nonprice competition provides a means by which monopolistically competitive firms can offset the long-run tendency for economic profit to fall to zero. Through product differentiation and advertising, a firm may strive to increase the demand for its product more than enough to cover the added cost of such nonprice competition.

5. In practice, the monopolistic competitor seeks that specific combination of price, product, and advertising that will maximize profit.

6. Oligopolistic industries are characterized by the presence of few firms, each having a significant fraction of the market. Firms are mutually interdependent: the behaviour of any one firm directly affects, and is affected by, the actions of rivals. Products may be virtually uniform or significantly differentiated. Various barriers to entry, including economies of scale, underlie and maintain oligopoly.

7. Concentration ratios help measure oligopoly (monopoly) power. By giving more weight to larger firms, the Herfindahl index is designed to measure market dominance in an industry.

8. Game theory **a** shows the mutual interdependence of oligopolists' pricing policies; **b** reveals the tendency of oligopolists to collude; and **c** explains the temptation of oligopolists to cheat on collusive arrangements.

9. Noncollusive oligopolists face a kinked demand curve. This curve and the accompanying marginal-revenue curve help explain the price rigidity that often characterizes oligopolies; they do not, however, explain how the actual prices of products were first established.

10. The uncertainties inherent in oligopoly promote collusion. Collusive oligopolists such as cartels maximize joint profits—that is, they behave like pure monopolists. Demand and cost differences, a "large" number of firms, cheating through secret price concessions, recessions, and the anti-trust laws are all obstacles to collusive oligopoly.

11. Price leadership is an informal means of collusion whereby one firm, usually the largest or most efficient, initiates price changes and other firms in the industry follow.

12. Market shares in oligopolistic industries are usually determined on the basis of product development and advertising. Oligopolists emphasize nonprice competition because **a** advertising and product variations are less easy for rivals to match and **b** oligopolists frequently have ample resources to finance nonprice competition.

13. Advertising can affect prices, competition, and efficiency either positively or negatively. Positive: It can provide consumers with low-cost information about competing products, help introduce new competing products into concentrated industries, and generally reduce monopoly power and its attendant inefficiencies. Negative: It can promote monopoly power via persuasion and the creation of entry barriers. Moreover, it can be self-cancelling when engaged in by rivals; then it boosts costs and increases economic inefficiency while accomplishing little else.

14. Neither productive nor allocative efficiency is realized in oligopolistic markets, but oligopoly may be superior to pure competition in promoting research and development and technological progress.

# TERMS AND CONCEPTS

monopolistic competition
product differentiation
nonprice competition
excess capacity
oligopoly
homogeneous oligopoly
differentiated oligopoly
mutual interdependence
concentration ratio
interindustry competition
import competition
Herfindahl index
game theory model
collusion
kinked demand curve
price war
cartel
tacit understandings
price leadership

# STUDY QUESTIONS

1. How does monopolistic competition differ from pure competition in its basic characteristics? From pure monopoly? Explain fully what product differentiation may involve. Explain how the entry of firms into its industry affects the demand curve facing a monopolistic competitor and how that, in turn, affects its economic profit.

2. KEY QUESTION *Compare the elasticity of the monopolistic competitor's demand with that of a pure competitor and a pure monopolist. Assuming identical long-run costs, compare graphically the prices and outputs that would result in the long run under pure competition and monopolistic competition. Contrast the two market structures in terms of productive and allocative efficiency. Explain: "Monopolistically competitive industries are characterized by too many firms, each of which produces too little."*

3. "Monopolistic competition is monopolistic up to the point at which consumers become willing to buy close-substitute products and competitive beyond that point." Explain.

4. "Competition in quality and service may be just as effective as price competition in giving buyers more for their money." Do you agree? Why? Explain why monopolistically competitive firms frequently prefer nonprice competition to price competition.

5. Critically evaluate and explain:
   - **a.** "In monopolistically competitive industries economic profits are competed away in the long run; hence, there is no valid reason to criticize the performance and efficiency of such industries."
   - **b.** "In the long run, monopolistic competition leads to a monopolistic price but not to monopolistic profits."

6. Why do oligopolies exist? List five or six oligopolists whose products you own or regularly purchase. What distinguishes oligopoly from monopolistic competition?

7. KEY QUESTION *Answer the following questions, which relate to measures of concentration:*
   - **a.** *What is the meaning of a four-firm concentration ratio of 60 percent? 90 percent? What are the shortcomings of concentration ratios as measures of monopoly power?*
   - **b.** *Suppose that the five firms in industry A have annual sales of 30, 30, 20, 10, and 10 percent of total industry sales. For the five firms in industry B the figures are 60, 25, 5, 5, and 5 percent. Calculate the Herfindahl index for each industry and compare their likely competitiveness.*

8. KEY QUESTION *Explain the general meaning of the following profit payoff matrix for oligopolists C and D. All profit figures are in thousands.*

| | | **C's possible prices** | |
|---|---|---|---|
| | | $40 | $35 |
| **D's possible prices** | $40 | $57 / $60 | $59 / $55 |
| | $35 | $50 / $69 | $55 / $58 |

   - **a.** *Use the payoff matrix to explain the mutual interdependence that characterizes oligopolistic industries.*
   - **b.** *Assuming no collusion between C and D, what is the likely pricing outcome?*
   - **c.** *In view of your answer to 8b, explain why price collusion is mutually profitable. Why might there be a temptation to cheat on the collusive agreement?*

9. KEY QUESTION *What assumptions about a rival's response to price changes underlie the kinked demand curve for oligopolists? Why is there a gap in the oligopolist's marginal-revenue curve? How does the kinked demand curve explain price rigidity in oligopoly? What are the shortcomings of the kinked-demand model?*

10. Why might price collusion occur in oligopolistic industries? Assess the economic desirability of collusive pricing. What are the main obstacles to collusion? Discuss the weakening of OPEC in the 1980s in terms of these obstacles.

11. KEY QUESTION *Advertising can have two effects: It can increase a firm's output, and it can shift a firm's average-total-cost curve upward. Explain how the relative sizes of these two effects may affect consumers.*

12. **(The Last Word)** What is the main criticism of the proposed mega-banks' mergers? Do the critics have an interest in seeing the bank mergers derailed?

13. WEB-BASED QUESTION **Bookselling on the Internet—How Do Sellers Differentiate Identical Books?** An upstart company called Amazon www.amazon.com introduced bookselling to the Web. Amazon's success enticed

a long-time bookseller, Barnes and Noble www.barnesandnoble.com/ to go online with a major Web site. Search both sites for Viktor Frankl's *Man's Search for Meaning* (paperback). Find the price delivered to your address. Is one cheaper? Identify the nonprice competition that would lead you to order from one company rather than the other.

14. WEB-BASED QUESTION **Grocery Stores—Can You Buy Spuds Online?** Grocery stores are now using the Web for advertising and sales promotion. Examples can be found at Yahoo www.yahoo.ca/Regional/Countries/Canada/Business_and_Economy/Companies/Food/Retail/Grocers/Online_Shopping/. How are the large national and regional grocery chains using the Web for advertising and sales promotion? Several small companies have set up virtual grocery stores. Consumers put together a shopping list over the Internet and select a payment method, and then the groceries are delivered to their door. Are any of the large chains doing this? Is there anything preventing them from doing this?

CHAPTER 13

# Technology, R&D, and Efficiency

"JUST DO IT!" IN 1968 TWO ENTREPRENEURS IN Oregon developed a lightweight sport shoe and formed a new company called Nike, incorporating a "swoosh" logo (designed by a graduate student for $35). Today, Nike employs 14,200 workers and sells $5.9 billion worth of athletic shoes, hiking boots, and sports apparel annually.

"Intel inside." Intel? In 1967 neither this company nor its product existed. Today it is the world's largest producer of microprocessors for personal computers, with 40,500 employees and more than $16 billion of annual sales.

In 1986 Terrence Matthews founded Newbridge Networks in Kanata, just outside Ottawa. The company employs a new telecommunications technology, ATM—asynchronous transfer mode. The technology allows networks to transmit voice, data images, and video. Today the company, based in Ottawa, has over 6,000 employees worldwide and has clients in more than 100 countries throughout the world.

These brief descriptions involve elements of **technological advance**, broadly defined as *new and better goods and services and new and better ways of producing or distributing them.* For economists, technological advance involves the very long run. Recall that in our four market models (pure competition, monopolistic competition, oligopoly, and pure monopoly), the *short run* is a period in which technology and plant and equipment are fixed. Also recall that in the *long run*, technology is constant but firms can change their plant sizes and are free to enter or exit industries. In contrast, the **very long run** is *a period in which technology can change and in which firms can introduce entirely new products.*

In this chapter we first define several terms relating to technological advance and then examine how it is motivated and implemented. One way to realize technological advance is through research and development (R&D), so we explain how a firm determines its optimal amount of R&D spending and how innovation can expand profit by enhancing revenue or reducing cost. Then we discuss the extent and implications of the possible imitation problem facing innovators. Finally, we assess whether particular market structures are conducive to technological advance and how technological advance, in turn, relates to economic efficiency.

**IN THIS CHAPTER YOU WILL LEARN:**

The definition of technological advance.

•

To distinguish between an invention, an innovation, and technological diffusion.

•

A firm's optimal amount of R&D.

•

How technological advance enhances both productive and allocative efficiency.

## The Big Picture

WE HAVE BEEN STRESSING THE ESSENCE OF THE economizing problem: scarce resources and unlimited wants. The economizing problem can be alleviated if society can get more output of goods and services from its scarce resources. Technological advance has been the main driving force behind the large increase of outputs of goods and services in industrialized nations in the last two hundred years. Canada's production possibility curve has shifted by many fold in this century. The main method of bringing about technological advance is through research and development (R&D). But technological advance is not enough; entrepreneurs needed to take risks to turn new technologies into marketable ideas.

As you read this chapter, keep the following points in mind:

- **Key Concept 8** is discussed.
- Technological advance also includes improving the quality of existing goods and services and finding new ways of organizing production and consumption.
- In a market economy, profit is the most powerful force driving technological advance.
- Entrepreneurs undertake the risks associated with R&D based on expected marginal cost and marginal benefit.
- With some exceptions, technological advance enhances both productive and allocative efficiency. ■

## TECHNOLOGICAL ADVANCE: INVENTION, INNOVATION, AND DIFFUSION

In Chapter 2 we saw that technological advance shifts an economy's production possibilities curve outward, enabling the economy to obtain more goods and services. Technological advance is a three-step process of invention, innovation, and diffusion. Let's see what these steps entail.

### Invention

The most basic element of technological advance is **invention**: *the first discovery of a product or process through the use of imagination, ingenious thinking, and experimentation and the first proof that it will work.* While invention is a process, the result of the process, unfortunately, is also called an invention. The first prototype (basic working model) of the telephone, the automobile, the television set, the microchip—each of these is an invention. Invention is usually based on scientific knowledge and is the product of individuals, either working on their own or as members of corporate R&D staffs. Later on you will see how governments encourage invention by providing the originator with a **patent**: *an exclusive right to sell any new and useful process, machine, or product for a set period of time.*

### Innovation

Innovation, a second element of technological change, draws directly on invention. While invention is "first discovery and proof of workability," **innovation** *is the first successful commercial introduction of a new product, the first use of a new method, or the creation of a new form of business enterprise.* Innovation is of two broad types: **product innovation**, which involves new and improved products or services; and **process innovation**, which involves new and improved production or distribution methods.

Unlike inventions, innovations, as such, cannot be patented. Nevertheless, innovation is a major factor in competition since it sometimes enables a firm to "leapfrog" competitors by making their products or processes obsolete. For example, personal computers coupled with software for word processing unceremoniously pushed some typewriter manufacturers into relative obscurity. More recently, innovations in hardware retailing (large warehouse stores such as Home Depot) have threatened the very existence of smaller, more traditional hardware stores.

But innovation need not destroy existing firms. Aware that new products and processes can threaten their survival, existing firms have a powerful incentive to engage continuously in R&D of their own. Innovative new products and processes often enable these firms to maintain or increase their profit. The introduction of aluminum cans by Reynolds, disposable contact lenses by Johnson & Johnson, and scientific calculators by Hewlett-Packard are good examples. Thus, innovation can either diminish or strengthen existing market power.

## Diffusion

The spread of an innovation through imitation or copying is known as **diffusion**. To take advantage of new profit opportunities or slow the erosion of their profit, new and existing firms emulate the successful innovations of others. Years ago McDonald's successfully introduced the fast-food hamburger; Burger King, Wendy's, and other firms soon copied that idea. Alamo greatly increased its auto rentals by offering renters unlimited mileage, but Hertz, Avis, Budget, and others eventually followed. More recently, a relatively new restaurant chain, Swiss Chalet, has popularized oven-roasted chicken. KFC, the chicken-market leader, has responded by adding this menu item, too. Chrysler Corporation profitably introduced a luxury version of its Jeep Grand Cherokee; other manufacturers including Ford, Acura, and Mercedes have countered with luxury sport-utility vehicles of their own. In each of these cases, innovation has led eventually to widespread imitation—that is, diffusion.

### 13-1 GLOBAL PERSPECTIVE

**Total R&D expenditures as a percentage of GDP, selected nations**

In 1995, Japan and the United States led the seven leading industrial nations in spending on R&D relative to the sizes of their economies. Canada was second last. From a microeconomic perspective, R&D helps promote economic efficiency; from a macroeconomic perspective, R&D helps promote economic growth.

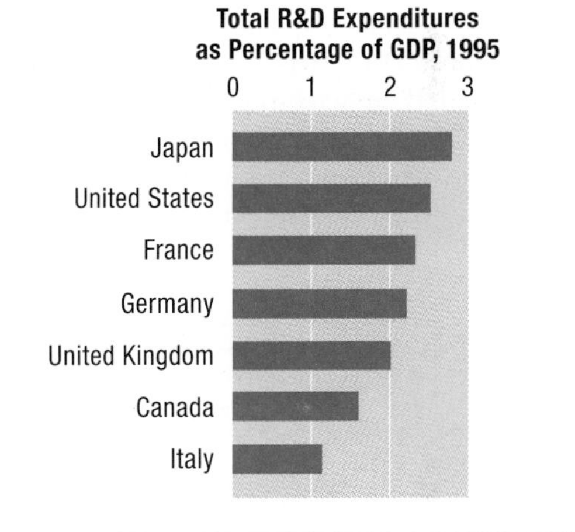


Source: *National Science Foundation.*

## R&D Expenditures

As it relates to *businesses*, the term "research and development" is used loosely to include direct efforts towards invention, innovation, and diffusion. However, *government* also engages in R&D, particularly that related to national defence. In 1996 *total* Canadian R&D expenditures (business *plus* government) were approximately $12 billion. This amount was about 1.5 percent of Canadian GDP and is a reasonable measure of the emphasis an economy puts on technological advance. As shown in Global Perspective 13-1, this is a low percentage relative to that in several other nations.

Canadian *businesses* spent $6 billion on R&D in 1995. Canadian firms collectively channelled the bulk of their R&D expenditures to "development" (innovation and imitation, the route to diffusion). They used much less for applied research, roughly equivalent to pursuing invention. For reasons we will address later, only a very small percentage of business R&D expenditures went for basic research—the search for general scientific principles. Of course, different industries, and different firms within industries, vary greatly in the amounts of emphasis they place on these three processes.

## Modern View of Technological Advance

For decades most economists envisioned technological advance as being *external* to the economy—a random *outside* force to which the economy adjusted. From time to time fortuitous advances in scientific and technological knowledge occurred, paving the way for major new products (automobiles, airplanes) and new production processes (assembly lines). Firms and industries—each at its own pace—then incorporated the new technology into products or processes, to enhance or maintain their profit. After making the appropriate adjustments, industries settled back into new long-run equilibrium positions. Although technological advance is vitally important to the economy, economists thought it was rooted in the independent advance of science, an element largely external to the market system.

Most contemporary economists have a different view. They see the market economy itself as the driving force of technological advance. In this view, invention, innovation, and diffusion occur in response to incentives within the economy, meaning that technological advance is an *internal* process. Specifically, technological advance arises from intense rivalry among individuals and firms which motivates them to seek and exploit new profit opportunities or to expand existing opportunities. This rivalry occurs both among existing firms and between them and new firms. Moreover, many advances in "pure" scientific knowledge are also motivated, at least in part, by the prospect of commercial applicability and eventual profit. In the modern view, entrepreneurs and other innovators are at the heart of technological advance.

## ROLE OF ENTREPRENEURS AND OTHER INNOVATORS

It will be helpful to distinguish between "entrepreneurs" and "other innovators."

1. **ENTREPRENEURS** Recall that the entrepreneur is an initiator, innovator, and risk bearer —the catalyst who combines land, labour, and capital resources in new and unique ways to produce new goods and services. Historically, a single individual carried out the entrepreneurial role—a Hart Massey in farm machinery, a Henry Ford in automobiles, or a Levi Strauss in blue jeans. Such substantial advances as air conditioning, power steering, the ballpoint pen, cellophane, the jet engine, insulin, xerography, the helicopter, and the refining of petroleum all have an individualistic heritage. But in today's more technologically complex economy, entrepreneurship is just as likely to be carried out by *entrepreneurial teams.* Such collaborative teams may include only two or three people working "as their own bosses" on some new product idea or may consist of larger groups of entrepreneurs who have pooled their resources.
2. **OTHER INNOVATORS** This designation includes the other key people involved in the pursuit of innovation, but unlike entrepreneurs, other innovators do not bear personal financial risk. These people include key executives, scientists, and other salaried employees engaged in commercial R&D activities. (They are sometimes referred to as *intrapreneurs,* since they provide the spirit of entrepreneurship *within* existing firms.)

### Forming Start-Ups

Quite often, entrepreneurs form small new companies called **start-ups**: *firms focused on creating and introducing a particular new product or employing a specific new production or distribution technique.* Two people, working out of their garages, founded one such start-up in the mid-1970s. Neither of their employers—Hewlett-Packard and Atari, the developer of Pong (the first video game)—was interested in their prototype personal computer. So they founded their own company: Apple Computers. More recent examples of successful start-ups are Amgen, a biotechnology firm specializing in new medical treatments; Second Cup, a seller of gourmet coffee; and Corel, which has developed innovative graphics software.

### Innovating Within Existing Firms

Innovators are also found within *existing* corporations, large and small. While such innovators are salaried workers, many firms have pay systems that provide them with substantial bonuses or shares of the profit. Examples of firms known for their skilful internal innovators are Canada's Nortel, developer of digital switching technology; America's 3M Corporation, the developer of Scotch tape, Post-it Note Pads, and Thinsulate insulation, and Canon, the Japanese developer of the "laser engine" for personal copiers and printers. R&D work in major corporations has produced significant technological improvements in such products as television sets, home appliances, automobiles, automobile tires, and sporting equipment.

Many large firms are aware that excessive bureaucracy can stifle creative thinking and technological advance. A few such firms have actually separated part of their R&D and manufacturing divisions to form new, more flexible, innovative firms. Two recent and significant examples of such "spinoff firms" are Lucent Technologies, a telephone equipment and R&D firm created by AT&T, and Imation, a new high-technology firm spun off by 3M Corporation.

### Anticipating the Future

In 1949 a writer for *Popular Mechanics* magazine boldly predicted that "computers in the future may weigh no more than 1.5 tonnes." Today's notebook computers weigh less than three *kilograms*. It is difficult to anticipate the future, but that is what innovators try to do. Those with strong anticipatory ability and determination have a knack for introducing new and improved products or services at just the right time. The rewards are both nonmonetary and monetary. Product innovation and development are creative endeavours, with attendant intangible rewards of personal satisfaction. Also, many people simply enjoy participating in the competitive "contest." But arguably of greatest importance, the "winners" can reap large monetary rewards in the form of economic profits, stock appreciation, or large bonuses. Extreme example: Bill Gates—one of the founders of Microsoft in 1975—had a net worth in 1997 of $40 billion, mainly in the form of Microsoft stock.

Past successes often give entrepreneurs and innovative firms access to *more* resources for further innovation—further actions that anticipate consumer wants. They may or may not again succeed, but in general, the market entrusts the production of goods and services to businesses that have consistently succeeded in filling consumer wants. And the market does not care whether these "winning" entrepreneurs and innovative firms are Canadian, American, Brazilian, Japanese, German, or Swiss. Entrepreneurship and innovation are global in scope.

### Exploiting University and Government Scientific Research

Only a small percentage of business R&D spending in Canada is for basic scientific research. This percentage is so small because scientific principles, as such, cannot be patented, nor do they usually have immediate commercial uses. Yet new scientific knowledge is highly important to technological advance. For that reason, entrepreneurs actively study the scientific output of university and government laboratories to find discoveries with commercial applicability.

In fact, government and university labs have been fertile ground for many technological breakthroughs. Entire new high-tech industries—computers and biotechnology, for example—have sprung up close to major research universities and government laboratories. And nations with strong scientific communities tend to have the most technologically progressive firms and industries.

Also, firms increasingly help fund university research that relates to their products. Business-funded R&D at universities has grown rapidly. Today, the separation between university scientists and innovators is narrowing; scientists increasingly realize their work may have commercial value and are teaming with innovators to share in the potential profit. A few firms, of course, *do* find it profitable to conduct basic scientific research on their own. New scientific knowledge can give them a major head-start in creating an invention or new product. This is particularly true in the pharmaceutical industry, where it is not uncommon for firms to parlay new scientific knowledge from their corporate labs into new, patentable drugs.

**13-1**

**QUICK REVIEW**

- Broadly defined, technological advance means new or improved products and services and new or improved production and distribution processes.
- Invention is the *discovery* of a new product or method; innovation is the *successful commercial application* of some invention; and diffusion is the *widespread imitation* of the innovation.
- Many economists view technological advance as mainly a response to profit opportunities arising within a market economy.
- Technological advance is fostered by entrepreneurs and other innovators and is supported by the scientific research of universities and government-sponsored laboratories.

## A FIRM'S OPTIMAL AMOUNT OF R&D

How does a firm decide on its optimal amount of research and development? This amount will depend on the firm's perception of the marginal benefit and marginal cost of R&D activity. The decision rule here flows from basic economics: *To earn the greatest profit, expand a particular activity until its marginal benefit (MB) equals its marginal cost (MC).* A firm that sees the marginal benefit of a particular

R&D activity, say, innovation, as exceeding the marginal cost should expand that activity. In contrast, an activity whose marginal benefit is less than its marginal cost should be cut back. But the R&D spending decision is complex since it involves a present sacrifice for a future expected gain. While the cost of R&D is immediate, the expected benefits occur at some future time and are highly uncertain. So estimating these benefits is often more art than science. Nevertheless, the MB = MC framework remains relevant for analyzing R&D decisions and provides direction to our discussion.

## Interest-Rate Cost of Funds

Firms have several means available for obtaining the funds needed to finance their R&D activities:

1. **BANK LOANS** Some firms may be able to obtain a loan from a chartered bank or other financial institution. Then the cost of using the funds is the interest paid to the lender. The marginal cost is the cost per extra dollar borrowed, which is simply the market interest rate for borrowed funds.
2. **BONDS** Established, profitable firms may be able to borrow funds for R&D by issuing bonds and selling them in the bond market. In this case, the cost is the interest paid to the lenders—the bondholders. Again the marginal cost of using the funds is the interest rate.
3. **RETAINED EARNINGS** A larger, more established firm may be able to draw on its own corporate saving to finance R&D. Typically, such a firm retains part of its profit rather than paying it all out as dividends to its corporate owners. Some of the undistributed corporate profit, called *retained earnings*, can be used to finance R&D activity. The marginal cost is the rate at which these funds could have earned interest as deposits in a financial institution.
4. **VENTURE CAPITAL** A smaller start-up firm might be able to attract venture capital to finance its R&D projects. **Venture capital** is financial capital—that is, *money*—not real capital. It consists *of that part of household saving used to finance high-risk business ventures in exchange for shares of the profit if the ventures succeed*. The marginal cost of venture capital is the share of expected profit that the firm will have to pay to those who provided the money. This can be stated as a percentage of the venture capital, so it has the basic nature of an interest rate.
5. **PERSONAL SAVINGS** Finally, individual entrepreneurs might draw on their own savings to finance the R&D for a new venture. The marginal cost of the financing is again the forgone interest rate.

Thus, whatever the source of the R&D funds, we can state the marginal cost of these funds as an interest rate *i*. For simplicity, let's assume this interest rate is the same no matter how much financing is required. Further, we suppose that a certain firm called MedTech must pay an interest rate of 8 percent, the least expensive funding available to it. Then a graph of the marginal cost of each funding amount for this firm is a horizontal line at the 8 percent interest rate, as shown in Figure 13-1. Such a graph is called an **interest-rate cost-of-funds curve**. This one tells us that MedTech can borrow $10, $10,000, $10,000,000 or more at the 8 percent interest rate. The table accompanying the graph contains the data used to construct the graph and tells us much the same thing.

With these data in hand, MedTech wants to determine how much R&D to finance in the coming year.

## Expected Rate of Return

A firm's marginal benefit from R&D is its expected profit (or return) from the last (marginal) dollar spent on R&D. That is, the R&D is expected to result in a new product or production method that will increase revenue, reduce production costs, or both (in ways we will soon discuss). This return is expected, *not* certain; that is, there is risk in R&D decisions. Let's suppose that after considering such risks, MedTech anticipates that an R&D expenditure of $1 million will result in a new product that will yield a one-time added profit of $1.2 million a year later. The expected rate of return *r* on the $1 million R&D expenditure (after $1 million is repaid) is 20 percent (= $200,000/$1,000,000). This is the marginal benefit of the first $1 million of R&D. (Stretching the return over several years complicates the computation of *r*, but it does not alter the basic analysis.)

MedTech can use this same method to estimate the expected rates of return for R&D expenditures of $2 million, $3 million, $4 million, and so on. Suppose those marginal rates of return are the ones indicated in the table in Figure 13-2, where they are also graphed as the **expected-rate-of-return curve**. This curve shows the expected rate

**FIGURE 13-1 The interest-rate cost-of-funds schedule and curve**

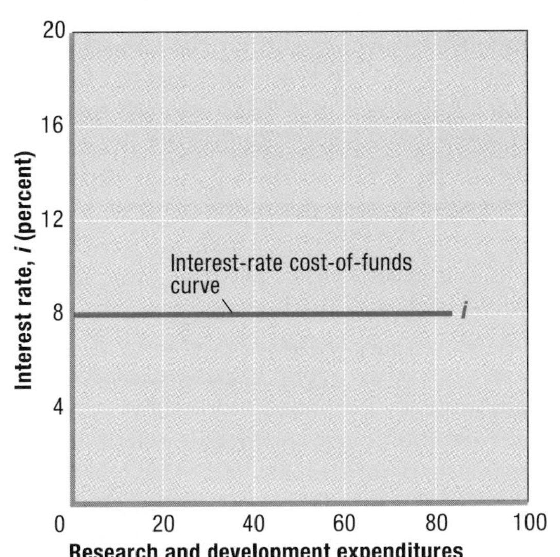


| R&D, millions | Interest-rate cost of funds, % |
|---|---|
| $10 | 8 |
| 20 | 8 |
| 30 | 8 |
| 40 | 8 |
| 50 | 8 |
| 60 | 8 |
| 70 | 8 |
| 80 | 8 |

As it relates to R&D, a firm's interest-rate cost-of-funds schedule (the table) and curve (the graph) show the interest rate the firm must pay to obtain any particular amount of funds to finance R&D. Curve *i* indicates the firm can finance as little or as much R&D as it wants at a constant 8 percent rate of interest.

of return—the marginal benefit—of each dollar of expenditure on R&D. The curve slopes downward because of diminishing returns to R&D expenditures. A firm will direct its initial R&D expenditures to the highest expected-rate-of-return activities and then use additional funding for activities with successively lower expected rates of return. That is, as R&D spending is increased, it is used to finance R&D activities with lower and lower expected rates of return.

## Optimal R&D Expenditures

Figure 13-3 combines the interest-rate-cost-of-funds curve (Figure 13-1) and the expected-rate-of-return curve (Figure 13-2). The curves intersect at MedTech's **optimal amount of R&D**, which is $60 million. This amount can also be determined from the table as the amount of funding for which the expected rate of return and the interest cost of borrowing are equal (here, 8 percent). Both the curve and the table tell us that at $60 million of R&D

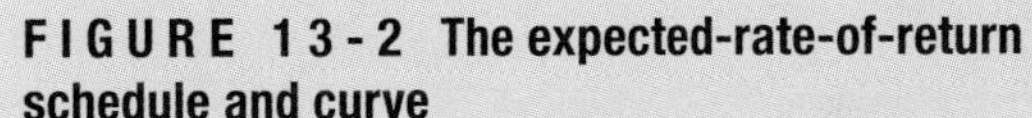

**FIGURE 13-2 The expected-rate-of-return schedule and curve**

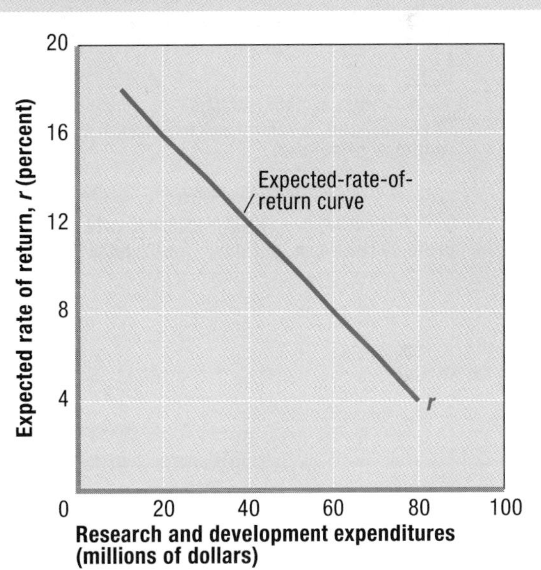


| R&D, millions | Expected rate of return, % |
|---|---|
| $10 | 18 |
| 20 | 16 |
| 30 | 14 |
| 40 | 12 |
| 50 | 10 |
| 60 | 8 |
| 70 | 6 |
| 80 | 4 |

As it relates to R&D, a firm's expected-rate-of-return schedule (the table) and curve (the graph) show its expected gain in profit, as a percentage of R&D spending, for each level of R&D spending. Curve *r* slopes downward because the firm assesses its potential R&D projects in descending order of expected rates of return.

**FIGURE 13-3 A firm's optimal level of R&D expenditures**

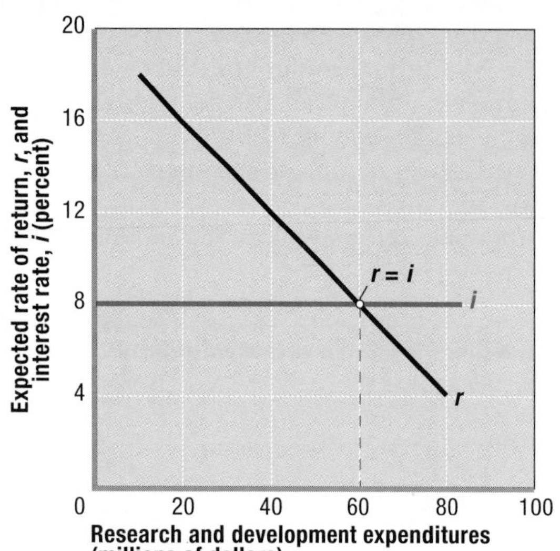


| Expected rate of return, % | R&D, millions | Interest-rate cost of funds, % |
|---|---|---|
| 18 | $10 | 8 |
| 16 | 20 | 8 |
| 14 | 30 | 8 |
| 12 | 40 | 8 |
| 10 | 50 | 8 |
| **8** | **60** | **8** |
| 6 | 70 | 8 |
| 4 | 80 | 8 |

The firm's optimal level of R&D expenditures ($60 million) occurs where its expected rate of return equals the interest-rate cost of funds, as shown in both the table and the graph. At $60 million of R&D spending, the firm has taken advantage of all R&D opportunities for which the expected rate of return, *r*, exceeds or equals the 8 percent interest cost of borrowing, *i*.

expenditures, the marginal benefit and marginal cost of the last dollar spent on R&D are equal. This firm should undertake all R&D expenditures up to $60 million, since these outlays yield a higher marginal benefit or expected rate of return, *r*, than the 8 percent marginal cost or interest-rate cost of borrowing, *i*. But it should not undertake R&D expenditures beyond $60 million; for these outlays, *r* (marginal benefit) is less than *i* (marginal cost). Only at $60 million do we have $r = i$, telling us that MedTech will spend $60 million on R&D.

Our analysis reinforces two important points:

1. **OPTIMAL VERSUS AFFORDABLE R&D** From previous discussions we know there can be too much, as well as too little, of a "good thing." So it is with R&D and technological advance. Figure 13-3 shows that R&D expenditures make sense to a firm only as long as the expected return from the outlay equals or exceeds the cost of obtaining the funds needed to finance it. Many R&D expenditures may be affordable but not worthwhile, because their marginal benefit is less than their marginal cost.
2. **EXPECTED, NOT GUARANTEED, RETURNS** The outcomes from R&D are *expected*, not guaranteed. With 20-20 hindsight, a firm can always look back and decide whether a particular expenditure for R&D was worthwhile. But this assessment is irrelevant to the original decision. At the time of the decision, the expenditure was thought to be worthwhile, based on existing information and expectations. Some R&D decisions may be more like an informed gamble rather than the typical business decision. Invention and innovation, in particular, carry with them a great deal of risk. For every successful outcome, there are scores of costly disappointments. ***(Key Questions 4 and 5)***

## INCREASED PROFIT VIA INNOVATION

In discussing how a firm determines its optimal amount of R&D spending, we sidestepped the question of how technological change can increase a firm's profit. Although the answer may seem obvious—by increasing revenue or reducing production cost—there are insights to be gained by exploring these two potential outcomes in some detail.

### Increased Revenue via Product Innovation

Firms have profitably introduced hundreds of new products in the past two or three decades. Examples include in-line skates, laser pointers, cordless drills, laser printers, "snake" lights, camcorders, fibre-optic cable, compact discs, projection TVs, and microwave popcorn. Other new products are gourmet coffee, cellular phones, notebook computers, telephone pagers, automobile airbags, mountain bikes, new artificial sweeteners, "breathable" waterproof fabrics, and snowboards. All these reflect technological advance in the form of *product innovation.*

It will be useful to see how such new products gain consumer acceptance. As you know from Chapter 7, to maximize their satisfaction, consumers purchase products having the highest marginal utility per dollar. They determine which products to buy in view of their limited money incomes by comparing the ratios of MU/price for the various goods. They first select the unit of the good with the highest MU/price ratio, then the one with the next highest, and so on, until their income is used up.

The first five columns of Table 13-1 repeat some of the information in Table 8-1. Before the introduction of new product C, the consumer maximized total utility from $10 of income by buying 2 units of A at $1 per unit and 4 units of B at $2 per unit. The total $10 budget was thus expended, with $2 spent on A and $8 on B. As shown in columns 2b and 3b, the marginal utility per dollar spent on the last unit of each product was 8 (= 8/$1 = 16/$2). The total utility, derived from columns 2a and 3a, was 96 utils (= 10 + 8 from the first 2 units of A *plus* 24 + 20 + 18 + 16 from the first 4 units of B). (If you are uncertain about this outcome, please review the discussion of Table 8-1.)

Now suppose an innovative firm offers new product C (columns 4a and 4b in Table 13-1), priced at $4 per unit. Note that the first unit of C has a *higher* marginal utility per dollar (13) than any unit of A and B and that the second unit of C and the first unit of B have equal MU/price ratios of 12. To maximize satisfaction, the consumer now buys 2 units of C at $4 per unit, 1 unit of B at $2 per unit, and zero units of A. Our consumer has spent the entire $10 of income ($8 on C and $2 on B), and the MU/price ratios of the last units of B and C are equal at 12. But as determined via columns 3a and 4a, the consumer's total utility is now 124 utils (= 24 from the first unit of B *plus* 52 + 48 from the first 2 units of C). Total utility has increased by 30 utils (+ 124 utils – 96 utils)—and that is why product C was purchased. *Consumers will buy a new product only if it increases the total utility they obtain from their limited incomes.*

From the innovating firm's perspective, these "dollar votes" represent new product demand that yields increased revenue. When per-unit revenue exceeds per-unit cost, the product innovation creates per-unit profit. Total profit rises by the per-unit profit multiplied by the number of units sold. As a percentage of the original R&D expenditure, the rise in total profit is the return on that R&D expenditure. It was the basis for the expected-rate-of-return curve *r* in Figure 13-2.

**TABLE 13-1 Utility maximization with the introduction of a new product (income = $10)**

| (1) UNIT OF PRODUCT | (2) PRODUCT A: PRICE = $1 | | (3) PRODUCT B: PRICE = $2 | | (4) NEW PRODUCT C: PRICE = $4 | |
|---|---|---|---|---|---|---|
| | (a) Marginal utility, utils | (b) Marginal utility per dollar (MU/price) | (a) Marginal utility, utils | (b) Marginal utility per dollar (MU/price) | (a) Marginal utility, utils | (b) Marginal utility per dollar (MU/price) |
| First | 10 | 10 | 24 | 12 | 52 | 13 |
| Second | 8 | **8** | 20 | 10 | 48 | 12 |
| Third | 7 | 7 | 18 | 9 | 44 | 11 |
| Fourth | 6 | 6 | 16 | **8** | 36 | 9 |
| Fifth | 5 | 5 | 12 | 6 | 32 | 8 |

*It is assumed in this table that the amount of marginal utility received from additional units of each of the three products is independent of the quantity purchased of the other products. For example, the marginal-utility schedule for product C is independent of the amount of A and B purchased by the consumer.

Three other points:

1. **IMPORTANCE OF PRICE** Consumer acceptance of a new product depends on both its marginal utility *and* its price. You should confirm that the consumer represented in Table 13-1 would buy zero units of new product C if its price were \$8 rather than \$4. To be successful, a new product must not only deliver utility to consumers but do so at an acceptable price.
2. **UNSUCCESSFUL NEW PRODUCTS** For every successful new product, there are hundreds of others that do not succeed; the *expected* return that motivates product innovation is not always realized. Examples of colossal product flops are Ford's Edsel automobile, 3-D movies, quadraphonic stereo, New Coke by Coca-Cola, Kodak disc cameras, and McDonald's McLean burger. In each of these cases, millions of dollars of R&D and promotion expense ultimately resulted in loss, not profit.
3. **PRODUCT IMPROVEMENTS** Most product innovation consists of incremental improvements to existing products rather than radical inventions. Examples: more fuel-efficient automobile engines, new styles of pizza, lighter-weight shafts for golf clubs, more flavourful bubblegum, "rock shocks" for mountain bikes, and clothing made of wrinkle-free fabrics. ***(Key Question 6)***

## Reduced Cost via Process Innovation

The introduction of better methods of producing products—*process innovation*—is also a path towards enhanced profit and a positive return on R&D expenditures. Suppose a firm introduces a new and better production process, say, assembling its product by teams rather than by a standard assembly line. Alternatively, suppose this firm replaces old equipment with more productive equipment embodying technological advance. In either case, the innovation yields an upward shift in the firm's total-product curve from $TP_1$ to $TP_2$ in Figure 13-4a. Now more units of output can be produced *at each level of resource usage.* Note from the figure, for example, that this firm can now produce 2,500 units of output, rather than 2,000 units, when using 1,000 units of labour. So its average product has increased from 2 (= 2,000 units of output ÷ 1,000 units of labour) to 2.5 (= 2,500 units of output ÷ 1,000 units of labour).

**FIGURE 13-4 Process innovation, total product, and average total cost**

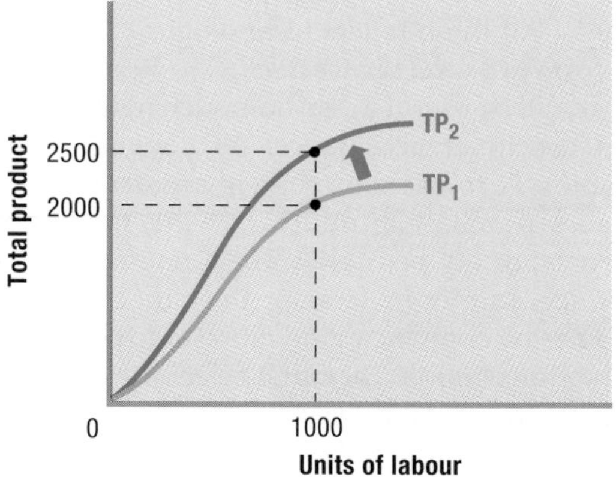


**(a) Upward shift of the total-product curve**

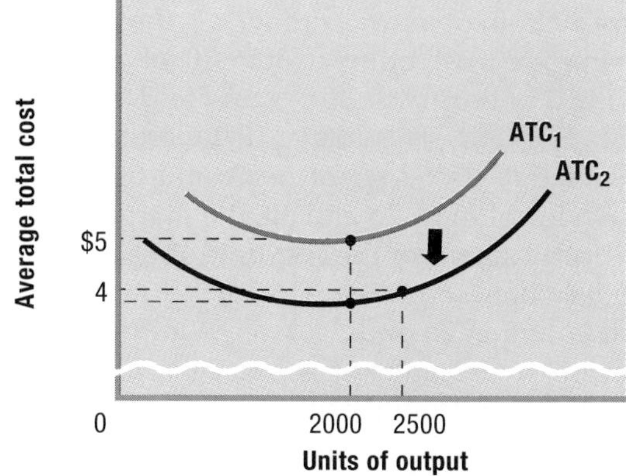


**(b) Downward shift of the average-total-cost curve**

(a) Process innovation shifts a firm's total-product curve upward from $TP_1$ to $TP_2$, meaning that the firm can produce more output at each level of labour input. As shown, with 1,000 units of labour it can produce 2,500 rather than 2,000 units of output. (b) The upward shift in the total-product curve results in a downward shift in the firm's average-total-cost curve, from $ATC_1$ to $ATC_2$. This means the firm can produce any particular unit of output at a lower average total cost than it could previously. For example, the original 2,000 units can be produced at less than \$4 per unit, versus \$5 per unit originally. Or 2,500 units can now be produced at \$4 per unit.

The result is a downward shift in the firm's average-total-cost curve, from $ATC_1$ to $ATC_2$ in Figure 13-4b. To understand why, let's assume this firm pays \$1,000 for the use of its capital and \$9 for each unit of labour. Since it uses 1,000 units of labour, its labour cost is $9,000 (= $9 × 1,000); its capital cost is $1,000; and thus its total cost is $10,000. When its output increases from 2,000 to 2,500 units due to the process of innovation, its total cost remains $10,000; however, its average total cost declines from $5 (= $10,000/2,000) to $4 (= $10,000/2,500). Alternatively, the firm could produce the original 2,000 units of output with fewer units of labour at an even lower average total cost.

This reduction in average total cost enhances the firm's profit. As a percentage of the R&D expenditure that fostered it, this extra profit is the expected return $r$, the basis for the rate-of-return-curve in Figure 13-2. In this case, the expected rate of return arose from the prospect of lower production costs through process innovation.

Approximate example: Computer-based inventory control systems, such as those pioneered by the American department store Wal-Mart, enabled innovators to reduce the number of people keeping track of inventories and placing reorders of sold goods. They have also enabled firms to keep goods arriving "just in time," reducing the cost of storing inventories. The consequence? Significant increases in sales per worker, declines in average total cost, and increased profit. ***(Key Question 8)***

## IMITATION AND R&D INCENTIVES

Our analysis of product and process innovation explains how technological advance can enhance a firm's profit, but it also hints at a potential **imitation problem**: a firm's rivals may be able to imitate its new product or process, greatly reducing the originator's profit from its R&D effort. As just one example, in the 1980s North American auto firms took apart Japanese Honda Accords, piece by piece, to discover the secrets of their high quality. This *reverse engineering*—which ironically was perfected earlier by the Japanese—helped the North American firms incorporate innovative features into their own cars. This type of imitation is perfectly legitimate and fully anticipated; it is often the main path to widespread diffusion of an innovation.

In fact, a dominant firm that is making large profits from its existing products may let smaller firms in the industry incur the high costs of product innovation while it closely monitors their successes and failures. The dominant firm then moves quickly to imitate any successful new product; its goal is to become the *second* firm to embrace the innovation. In using this so-called **fast-second strategy**, the dominant firm counts on its own product-improvement abilities, marketing prowess, or economies of scale to prevail.

Examples abound: Royal Crown introduced the first diet cola, but Diet Coke and Diet Pepsi dominate diet-cola sales today. Gillette moved quickly with its own stainless-steel razor blade only after a smaller firm, Wilkinson, introduced this product innovation.

### Benefits of Being First

Imitation and the fast-second strategy raise an important question: What incentive is there for *any* firm to bear the expenses and risks of innovation if competitors can imitate its new or improved products? Why not let others bear the costs and risks of product development and then just imitate the successful innovations? Although we have seen that this may be a plausible strategy in some situations, there are several protections for, and potential advantages to, taking the lead.

**Patents** Some technological breakthroughs, specifically inventions, can be patented. Then they cannot be legally imitated for two decades. The purpose of patents is, in fact, to reduce imitation and its negative effect on the incentive for engaging in R&D. Example: Polaroid's patent of its instant camera enabled it to earn high economic profits for many years. When Kodak "cloned" the camera, Polaroid won a patent-infringement lawsuit against its rival. Kodak not only had to stop producing its version of the camera but also had to buy back the Kodak instant cameras it had sold and pay millions of dollars of damages to Polaroid.

**Copyrights and Trademarks** *Copyrights* protect publishers of books, computer software, movies, videos, and musical compositions from having their works copied. *Trademarks* give the original innovators of products the exclusive right to use a particular product name ("M&Ms," "Barbie Doll," "Wheaties"). By reducing the problem of direct copying, these legal protections increase the incentive for product innovation. They have been strengthened worldwide through recent international trade agreements.

**Brand-Name Recognition** Along with trademark protection, brand-name recognition may give the original innovator a major marketing advantage for years or even decades. Consumers often identify a new product with the firm first introducing and popularizing it in the mass market. Examples: *Levi's* blue jeans, *Kleenex* soft tissues, Johnson and Johnson's *Band-Aids*, Sony's *Walkman*, and Kellogg's *Corn Flakes*.

**Trade Secrets and Learning by Doing** Some innovations involve *trade secrets*, without which competitors cannot imitate the product or process. Example: Coca-Cola has successfully kept its formula for Coke a secret from potential rivals. Many other firms have perfected special production techniques known only to them. In a related advantage, a firm's head-start with a new product often allows it to achieve substantial cost reductions through *learning by doing*. The innovator's lower cost may enable it to continue to profit even after imitators have entered the market.

**Time Lags** Time lags between innovation and diffusion often permit innovating firms to realize a substantial economic profit. It takes time for an imitator to gain knowledge of the properties of a new innovation. And once it has that knowledge, the imitator must design a substitute product, gear up a factory for its production, and conduct a marketing campaign. Various entry barriers—large financial requirements, economies of scale, and price cutting—may extend the time lag between innovation and imitation. In practice, it may take years or even decades before rival firms can successfully imitate a profitable new product and cut into the market share of the innovator. In the meantime, the innovator continues to profit.

**Profitable Buyouts** A final advantage of being first arises from the potential of a *buyout*—an outright purchase—of the innovating firm by a larger firm. Here, the innovative entrepreneurs take their rewards immediately—as cash or as shares in the buying firm, rather than waiting for perhaps uncertain long-run profits from their own production and marketing efforts.

In short, even with the imitation problem, there are significant protections and advantages that enable most innovating firms to profit from their R&D efforts. The continuing high levels of R&D spending by firms year after year imply this fact. As shown in Figure 13-5, business R&D spending in Canada has grown over the past quarter-century. The growth of spending simply would not continue if imitation consistently and severely depressed actual rates of return on R&D expenditures.

**FIGURE 13-5 The growth of business R&D expenditures in Canada 1975-1996**

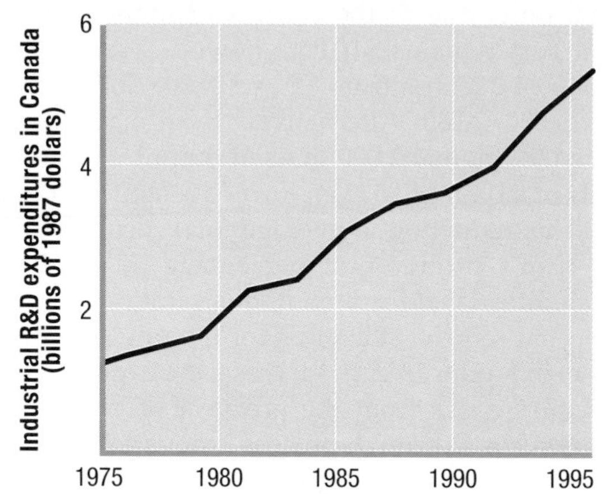


R&D expenditures by firms are substantial and growing, suggesting that R&D continues to pay off for firms, even in the face of possible imitation.

Source: Statistics Canada, Industrial Research and Development, 1997 (Ottawa, 1997), Cat. 88-202.

### 13-2 QUICK REVIEW

- A firm's optimal R&D expenditure is that amount at which the expected rate of return (marginal benefit) from the R&D expenditure just equals the interest-rate cost of borrowing (marginal cost) required to finance it.
- Product innovation can entice consumers to substitute a new product for existing products to increase their total utility, thereby increasing the innovating firm's revenue and profit.
- Process innovation can lower a firm's production costs and increase its profit by increasing total product and decreasing average total cost.
- A firm faces reduced profitability from R&D if competitors can successfully imitate its new product or

process. Nevertheless, there are significant potential protections and benefits to being first, including patents, copyrights, and trademarks; brand-name recognition, trade secrets, and cost reductions from learning by doing; and major time lags between innovation and imitation.

## ROLE OF MARKET STRUCTURE

In view of our discussion of market structures in the last three chapters, it is logical to ask whether there is some particular market structure or firm size that spurs technological progress. Is a highly competitive industry in the traditional sense of pure competition preferable to an industry comprising only two or three large firms? Or is some intermediate structure best?

### Market Structure and Technological Advance

As a first step towards answering these questions, let's survey our four market models, evaluating their strengths and shortcomings in regard to technological advance.

**Pure Competition** The willingness and ability of purely competitive firms to undertake R&D is debatable. On the positive side, strong competition provides a reason for these firms to innovate; competitive firms tend to be less complacent than monopolists. If a pure competitor does not seize the initiative, one or more rivals may introduce a new product or cost-reducing production technique that could drive it from the market. As a matter of short-term profit and long-term survival, pure competitors are under continual pressure to improve products and lower costs through innovation. Also, where there are many competing firms, there is a reduced chance that an idea for improving a product or process will be overlooked by a single firm.

On the negative side, the expected rate of return on R&D may be low or even negative for a pure competitor. Because of easy entry, its profit rewards from innovation may quickly be competed away by existing or entering firms that also produce the new product or adopt the new technology. Also, the small size of competitive firms and the fact that they earn only a normal profit in the long run lead to serious questions as to whether such producers can finance substantial R&D programs. Observers have noted that the high rate of technological advance in the purely competitive agricultural industry, for example, has come not from the R&D of individual farmers but from government-sponsored research and oligopolistic firms' development of fertilizers, hybrid seed, and farm implements.

**Monopolistic Competition** Like pure competitors, monopolistic competitors cannot afford to be complacent. But unlike pure competitors that sell standardized products, monopolistic competitors have a strong profit incentive to engage in product development. This incentive to differentiate products from those of competitors stems from the fact that sufficiently novel products may create monopoly power and thus economic profit. There are many examples of innovative firms (McDonald's, Blockbuster Video) that started out as monopolistic competitors in localized markets but soon gained considerable national market power, with the attendant economic profit.

For the typical firm, however, the shortcomings of monopolistic competition in relation to technological advance are the same as those of pure competition. Most monopolistic competitors remain small, which limits their ability to secure inexpensive financing for R&D. In addition, monopolistic competitors find it very difficult to extract large profits from technological advances. Any economic profits from innovation are usually temporary, because entry to monopolistically competitive industries is relatively easy. In the long run, new entrants with similar goods reduce the demand for the innovator's product, leaving the innovator with only a normal profit. Monopolistic competitors therefore usually have relatively low expected rates of return on R&D expenditures.

**Oligopoly** Many of the characteristics of oligopoly are conducive to technological advance. First, the large size of oligopolists enables them to finance the often very expensive R&D costs associated with major product or process innovation. In particular, the typical oligopolist realizes ongoing economic profits, a part of which is retained. This undistributed profit serves as a major source of readily available, relatively low-cost funding for R&D. Moreover, the existence of barriers to entry gives the oligopolist some assurance that it can maintain any economic profit it gains from innovation. Then, too, the large sales volume of the oligopolist allows it to spread the cost of specialized R&D equipment and teams of specialized researchers over a great many units of output. Finally, the broad scope of R&D activity within oligopolistic firms helps them offset the inevitable R&D "misses" with more than compensating R&D "hits." Thus, oligopolists clearly have the means and incentive to innovate.

But there is also a negative side to R&D in oligopoly. In many instances, the oligopolist's incentive to innovate may be far less than we have implied above because oligopoly tends to breed complacency. An oligopolist may reason that it makes little sense to introduce costly new technology and produce new products when it currently is earning a sizable economic profit without them. The oligopolist wants to maximize its profit by exploiting fully all its capital assets. Why rush to develop a new product (say, batteries for electric automobiles) when that product's success will render obsolete much of the firm's current equipment designed to produce its existing product (say, gasoline engines)? It is not difficult to cite oligopolistic industries in which the largest firms' interest in R&D has been quite modest. Examples: the steel, cigarette, and aluminum industries.

**Pure Monopoly** In general, the pure monopolist has little incentive to engage in R&D; its high profit is maintained by entry barriers that, in theory, are complete. The only incentive for the monopolist to engage in R&D is defensive—to reduce the risk of being blindsided by some new product or production process that destroys its monopoly. If such a product is out there to be discovered, the monopolist may have an incentive to find it. By so doing, it can either exploit the new product or process for continued monopoly profit or suppress the product until it has extracted the maximum profit from its present capital assets. But, in general, economists agree that pure monopoly is the market structure *least* conducive to innovation.

## Inverted-U Theory

Analysis like this has led some experts on technological progress to postulate a so-called **inverted-U theory** of the relationship between market structure and technological advance. This theory is illustrated in Figure 13-6, which relates R&D spending as a percentage of a firm's sales (vertical axis) with the industry's four-firm concentration ratio (horizontal axis). The "inverted-U" shape of the curve suggests that R&D effort is at best weak in both very low concentration industries (pure

**FIGURE 13-6 The inverted-U theory of R&D expenditures**

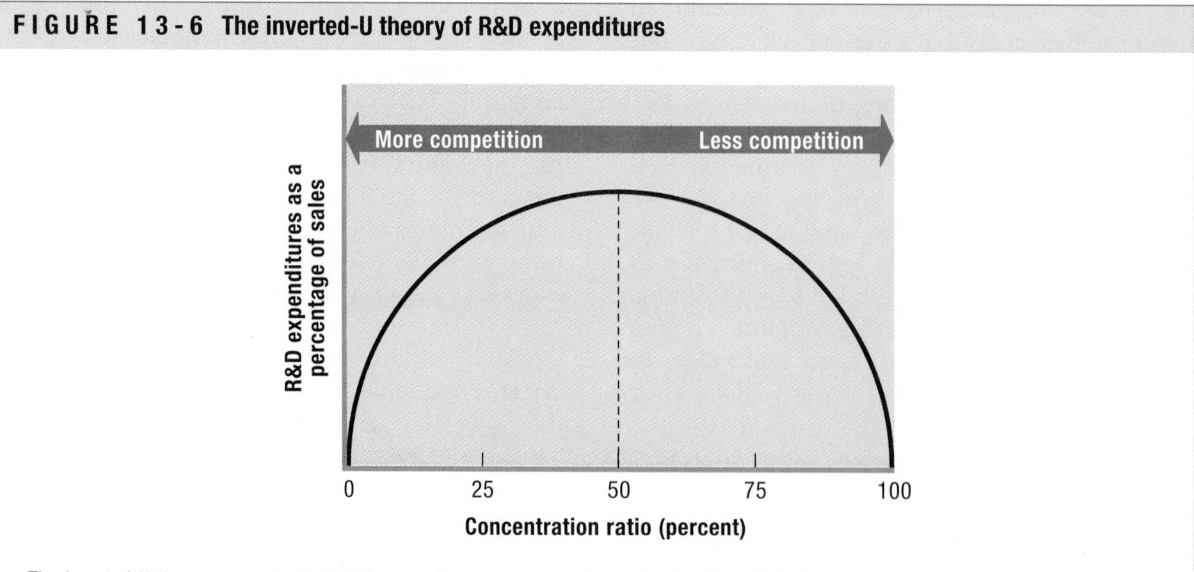


The inverted-U theory suggests that R&D expenditures as a percentage of sales rise with industry concentration until the four-firm concentration ratio reaches about 50 percent. Further increases in industry concentration are associated with lower relative R&D expenditures.

competition) *and* very high-concentration industries (pure monopoly). Starting from the lowest concentrations, R&D spending as a percentage of sales rises with concentration until a concentration ratio of 50 percent or so is reached, meaning that the four largest firms account for about one-half the total industry output. Beyond that, relative R&D spending decreases as concentration rises.

The logic of the inverted-U theory follows from our discussion. Firms in industries with very low concentration ratios are mainly competitive firms. They are small, which makes it difficult for them to finance R&D. Moreover, entry to these industries is easy, making it difficult to sustain economic profit from innovations that are not supported by patents. As a result, firms in these industries spend little on R&D relative to their sales. At the other end (far right) of the curve, where concentration is exceptionally high, monopoly profit is already high and innovation will not add much more profit. Furthermore, innovation often requires costly retooling of very large factories, which will cut into whatever additional profit is realized. As a result, the expected rate of return from R&D is quite low, as are expenditures for R&D relative to sales. Finally, the lack of rivals makes the monopolist quite complacent about R&D.

The optimal industry structure for R&D is one in which expected returns on R&D spending are high and funds to finance it are readily available and inexpensive. From our discussion, these factors seem to occur in industries where a few firms are absolutely and relatively large but where the concentration ratio is not so high as to prohibit vigorous competition by smaller rivals. Rivalry among the larger oligopolistic firms and competition between the larger and smaller firms then provide a strong incentive for R&D. The inverted-U theory, as represented by Figure 13-6, also points towards this "loose" oligopoly as the optimal structure for R&D spending.

## Market Structure and Technological Advance: The Evidence

Dozens of actual industry studies have tried to pin down the relationship between market structure and technological advance. Because these studies involved different industries, time periods, and methodologies, they are not easily compared and summarized. Nevertheless, the overall evidence provides general support for the inverted-U theory.[1] Other things equal, the optimal market structure for technological advance seems to be an industry in which there is a mix of large oligopolistic firms (a 40 to 60 percent concentration ratio), with several highly innovative smaller firms.

But our "other things equal" qualification is quite important here. The technical nature of a particular industry may well be a more important determinant of R&D than its structure. While some concentrated industries (electronics, aircraft, and petroleum) devote large quantities of resources to R&D and are very innovative, others (cigarettes, aluminum, gypsum products) are not. *The level of R&D spending within an industry seems to result as much from an industry's scientific character and "technological opportunities" as from its market structure.* There simply may be more opportunities to innovate in the computer and pharmaceutical industries than in the brick-making and coal-mining industries.

Conclusion: The inverted-U curve shown in Figure 13-6 is a useful depiction of the general relationship between R&D spending and market structure, *other things equal.*

# TECHNOLOGICAL ADVANCE AND EFFICIENCY

Technological advance plays an important role in enhancing economic efficiency. New and better processes and products enable society to produce more output, as well as a higher-valued mix of output.

## Productive Efficiency

Technological advance as embodied in *process* innovation improves *productive efficiency* by increasing the productivity of inputs (as indicated in Figure 13-4a) and by reducing average total costs (as in Figure 13-4b). This means that society can produce any particular good or service using fewer of its scarce resources, thereby freeing the unneeded resources to produce other desired goods and services. Alternatively, process innovation means that society can produce a greater

[1] Douglas F. Greer, *Industrial Organization and Public Policy,* 3d ed. (New York: Macmillan, 1992), pp. 680–87.

quantity of any particular good using the same number of resources as it used previously. Viewed either way, process innovation enhances productive efficiency: it reduces society's per-unit cost of whatever mix of goods and services it chooses. It thus is an important means of shifting an economy's production possibilities curve rightward.

**Allocative Efficiency** Technological advance as embodied in *product* (or service) innovation enhances *allocative efficiency* by giving society a more preferred mix of goods and services. Recall from our previous discussion that consumers buy a new product rather than an old product only when purchasing the new one increases the utility obtained from their limited incomes. Obviously, then, the new product—and the new mix of products that it implies—creates a higher level of total utility for society.

In terms of markets, the demand for the new product rises and the demand for the old product declines. The high economic profit of the new product attracts resources away from less valued uses and to the production of the new product. In theory, such shifting of resources continues until the price of the new product equals its marginal cost.

There is a caveat here, however. Innovation (product or process) can create monopoly power through patents or through the many advantages of being first. When new monopoly power results from innovation, society may lose *part* of the improved efficiency it otherwise would have gained from the innovation. The reason is that the profit-maximizing monopolist restricts output to keep its product price above marginal cost. Possible example: Microsoft has used its early innovation in computer software (its DOS operating system) to achieve a commanding presence in some parts of the software industry. It has built its monopoly power partly on a strategy of continual, identifiable product upgrades—from MS-DOS to Windows to Windows 95, with new versions in between. These product improvements are often announced well in advance and contain more and more features of competing software. Moreover, Microsoft has extended some of its monopoly power to related software products (Word, PowerPoint). So although society has greatly benefited from the surge of product improvements flowing from Microsoft, another result has been rising entry barriers in the software industry. Also, Microsoft continues to have economic profit far above the long-run normal profit associated with allocative efficiency.

On the other hand, innovation can reduce or even disintegrate existing monopoly power by providing competition where there was none. Economic efficiency is enhanced when this results, because the new competition helps push prices down closer to marginal cost and minimum average total cost. Innovation that leads to greater competition within an industry reduces the inefficiency associated with reduced output restriction and monopoly prices. In the Microsoft example, the new technology of the Internet has, at least temporarily, reduced Microsoft's dominance in some emerging areas of the software industry. Specifically, firms such as Sun Microsystems and Netscape have pioneered new software relating to the Internet (Java programming language, Netscape Navigator browser), leaving Microsoft working hard to catch up. Thus far, there are no signs that Microsoft's monopoly power has resulted in complacency towards innovation; currently it spends $2 billion per year on research.

## Creative Destruction

At the extreme, innovation may generate **creative destruction**, where the *creation* of new products and production methods simultaneously *destroys* the monopoly market positions of firms committed to existing products and old ways of doing business. As stated many years ago by Joseph Schumpeter, who championed this view:

> In capitalist reality ... it is ... competition from the new commodity, the new technology, the new source of supply, the new type of business organization—competition which commands a decisive cost or quality advantage and which strikes not at the margins of profits of the existing firms but at their foundation and their very lives. This kind of competition is ... so ... important that it becomes a matter of comparative indifference whether competition in the ordinary sense functions more or less promptly; the powerful lever that in the [very] long run expands output and brings down prices is in any case made of other stuff.[2]

There are many examples of creative destruction: In the 1800s wagons, ships, and barges were the only means of transporting freight until the

[2] Joseph A. Schumpeter, *Capitalism, Socialism, and Democracy*, 3d ed. (New York: Harper & Row, 1950), pp. 84–85.

railroads broke up their monopoly; the dominant market position of the railroads was, in turn, undermined by trucks, and later, by airplanes. Movies brought new competition to live theatre, at one time the "only show in town," but were later challenged by television. Vinyl long-playing records supplanted acetate 78-rpm phonograph records; cassettes then challenged LP records, and now compact discs have undermined cassettes. Aluminum cans and plastic bottles have displaced glass bottles in many uses. Cable television has assaulted the networks, and now satellite dishes threaten cable. Fax machines, overnight delivery services, and e-mail have challenged the postal service.

According to Schumpeter, any monopolist that no longer delivers superior performance will *automatically* be displaced by a new innovator. But many contemporary economists think this notion reflects more wishful thinking than fact. In this view, the idea that creative destruction is automatic

> ... neglects the ability of powerful established firms to erect private storm shelters—or lobby government to build public storm shelters for them—in order to shield themselves from the Schumpeterian gales of creative destruction. It ignores the difference between the legal freedom of entry and the economic reality deterring the entry of potential newcomers into concentrated industries.[3]

That is, some dominant firms may be able to use such strategies as selective price cutting, buyouts, and massive advertising to block competition from even the most innovative new firms and existing rivals. Moreover, dominant firms have been known to collude to fix prices and to persuade government to give them tax breaks, subsidies, and tariff protection that strengthen their market power.

In short, while innovation in general enhances economic efficiency, in some cases it can lead to entrenched monopoly power. Further innovation may eventually destroy this monopoly power, but the process of creative destruction is neither automatic nor inevitable. On the other hand, our discussion has made it clear that rapid technological change, innovation, and efficiency are not *necessarily* inconsistent with monopoly power.

[3] Walter Adams and James Brock, *The Structure of American Industry*, 9th ed. (Englewood Cliffs, NJ: Prentice-Hall, 1995), p. 310.

## In The Media

# Huge merger will hit Canadian drug firms

### Blockbuster research budget aim of deal

BY ERIC REGULY
THE GLOBE AND MAIL

The proposed merger of two British drug giants—the largest corporate deal in history—is set to trigger a wave of takeovers around the world that will ultimately reshape the Canadian pharmaceuticals industry.

If British rivals Glaxo Wellcome PLC and SmithKline Beecham PLC merge, the new entity would be able to commit the equivalent of almost $5 billion a year to research and development, much of it devoted to hunting for the genes that make people susceptible to various diseases. No company would be able to match the new group's R&D firepower.

Genetic technology is the industry's fastest-growing scientific pursuit and the one with the greatest potential to maintain earnings momentum into the next century. The blockbuster R&D budget would allow the new company to take better advantage of scientific breakthroughs that are spewing out of laboratories.

"This whole thing is R&D driven," said Martin Sutton, a Glaxo spokesman in London. "You need critical mass to take advantage of the huge number of opportunities."

Boosting research-and-development, resources is driving the mergers, R&D is fantastically expensive. Drug companies estimate that it takes about eight years and about $500 million to bring a new drug to market. A SmithKline spokesman said a medium-sized drug company needs to launch 22 products every 10 years to maintain a 10-per-cent growth rate. Large companies have to move even faster.

Cost cutting, of course, allows R&D budgets to be preserved and expanded. Steven Gerber, an analyst in Los Angeles with CIBC Oppenheimer Inc., said drug-company mergers generate savings of no less than 10 per cent as operations such as sales forces are combined and overlapping jobs are shed.

*Source: Globe and Mail*, February 3, 1998, pp. A1 and A2. Reprinted with permission from the *Globe and Mail*.

## THE STORY IN BRIEF

A proposed merger between two multinational drug giants will affect their Canadian operation. Driving the merger is R&D costs.

## THE ECONOMICS BEHIND THE STORY

- R&D is "fantastically expensive"; a company needs some $500 million to bring a new drug to market. The proposed merger would pool the financial resource of two already large companies and would allow the new company to capture economies of scale in both its operations and R&D.
- Lower costs would allow the new company to compete more effectively with its rivals. If the proposed merger goes through, other companies may be forced to merge in order to compete with the new company.
- Pharmaceuticals companies now have a 20-year monopoly on a new drug. Is such a long period justified? Why or why not? ■

# The Last Word

## ON THE PATH TO THE PERSONAL COMPUTER AND INTERNET

**Technological advance is clearly evident in the development of the modern personal computer and the emergence of the Internet. Here is a brief history of these events.**

**1945** Grace Murray Hopper finds a dead moth between relay contacts in the experimental Mark II computer at Harvard University. Whenever the computer subsequently malfunctions, workers set out to "debug" the device.

**1946** ENIAC is revealed. This precursor to the modern-day computer relies on 18,000 vacuum tubes and fills 3,000 cubic feet of space.

**1947** AT&T scientists invent the "transfer resistance device," later known as the transistor. It replaces the less reliable vacuum tubes in computers.

**1961** Bob Noyce (who later founded Intel Corporation) and Jack Kilby invent the first integrated circuit, which miniaturizes electronic circuitry onto a single silicon chip.

**1964** IBM introduces the System/360 computer. Configured as a system, it takes up nearly the same space as two tennis courts.

**1965** Digital Equipment Corporation unveils its PDP-8, the first relatively small-sized computer (a "minicomputer").

**1969** A networking system called ARPANET is born; it is the beginning of the Internet.

**1971** Intel introduces its 4004 processor (a "microprocessor"). The $200 chip is the size of a thumbnail and has as much computing capability as the earlier ENIAC.

**1975** Xerox markets Alto, the first personal computer (a "microcomputer"). Bill Gates and Paul Allen found Microsoft. MITS Corporation's Altair 8800 arrives on the scene. It contains Intel's 8080 microprocessor that Intel developed a year earlier to control traffic lights.

**1977** Apple II, Commodore's PET, and Tandy Radio Shack TRS-80 go on sale, setting the stage for the personal computer revolution.

**1981** IBM enters the market with its personal computer powered by the Intel 8800 chip and operated by the Microsoft Disc Operating System (MS-DOS). Osborne Computer markets the Osborne 1, the first self-contained microcomputer, but within two years the firm declares bankruptcy. Logitech commercializes the "X-Y Position Indicator for a Display System," invented earlier by Douglas Engelbart in a U.S. government-funded research lab. Someone dubs it a "computer mouse" because it appears to have a tail.

**1982** Compaq Computer "clones" the IBM machines; others do the same. Eventually Compaq becomes the leading seller of personal computers.

**1984** Apple introduces its Macintosh computer, with its "user-friendly" icons, attached mouse, and preloaded software. College student Michael Dell founds Dell Computers, which builds personal computers and sells them through mail order. IBM, Sears Roebuck, and CBS team up to launch Prodigy Services, the first on-line computer business.

**1985** Microsoft releases its Windows graphical interface operating system that improves upon MS-DOS.

**1990** Microsoft introduces Windows 3.0, which, like Macintosh, features windows, icons, and pull-down menus. Apple sues Microsoft for copyright infringement.

**1991** The World Wide Web (an Internet system) is invented.

**1993** Intel introduces its first of several Pentium chips, which greatly speed up computing. The courts reject Apple's claim that Microsoft violated its copyrights on its Macintosh operating system.

**1994** Marc Andreessen starts up Netscape Communications and markets Netscape Navigator, which quickly becomes the leading software browser for the emerging Internet. David Filo and Jerry Yang develop Yahoo, a system for locating material stored on the Internet.

**1995** Microsoft releases Windows 95 operating system, and it becomes the dominant operating system of personal computers (90 percent market share). Microsoft is now well established as the world's leading software producer. Sun Microsystems introduces Java, an Internet programming language.

**1996** Playing catch-up with Netscape, Microsoft develops Microsoft Internet Explorer and gives it away free. More than 40 million personal computers are manufactured worldwide during this year alone.

**1997** Oracle Computers introduces a relatively inexpensive "network" computer that bypasses Windows and goes directly to the Internet. More than one out of four Canadian households has a personal computer, and the use of the Internet explodes. ■

# CHAPTER SUMMARY

1. Technological advance consists of new and improved goods and services and new and improved production or distribution processes. In economists' models, technological advance occurs only in the *very long run.*

2. *Invention* is the first discovery of a product or process through the use of imagination, ingenious thinking, and experimentation. *Innovation* is the first successful commercial introduction of a new product, the first use of a new method, or the creation of a new form of business enterprise. *Diffusion* is the spread of an earlier innovation among competing firms. Firms channel a majority of their R&D expenditures to innovation and imitation, rather than to basic scientific research and invention.

3. Historically, most economists viewed technological advance as a random, *external* force to which the economy adjusted. Many contemporary economists see technological advance as an *internal* element of the market economy, occurring in response to profit incentives within the economy.

4. Entrepreneurs and other innovators attempt to anticipate the future, thus playing central roles in technological advance by initiating changes in products and processes. Entrepreneurs often form start-ups that focus on creating and introducing new products. In other cases, innovators are located in the R&D labs of major corporations. Entrepreneurs and innovative firms often rely heavily on the basic research done by university and government scientists.

5. A firm's optimal amount of R&D spending occurs where its expected return (marginal benefit) from the R&D equals its interest-rate cost of funds (marginal cost) to finance the R&D. Entrepreneurs and firms use several sources to finance R&D, including **a** bank loans, **b** bonds, **c** venture capital (funds loaned in return for a share of the profits if the business succeeds), **d** undistributed corporate profits (retained earnings), and **e** personal savings.

6. *Product innovation*, the introduction of new products, succeeds when it provides consumers with higher marginal utility per dollar spent than do existing products. The new product enables consumers to obtain greater total utility from a given income. From the firm's perspective, product innovation increases revenue and, net of production cost, yields a positive rate of return on the R&D spending that produced it.

7. *Process innovation* can lower a firm's production costs by improving its internal production techniques. This increases the firm's total product, lowering its average total cost and increasing its profit. This added profit provides a positive rate of return on the R&D spending that produced the process innovation.

8. Imitation poses a potential problem for innovators since it threatens their returns on R&D expenditures. Some dominant firms use a fast-second strategy, letting smaller firms initiate new products and then quickly imitating the successes. Nevertheless, there are significant protections and potential benefits for firms that take the lead with R&D and innovation, including **a** patent protection, **b** copyrights and trademarks, **c** lasting brand-name recognition, **d** benefits from trade secrets and learning by doing, **e** high economic profits during the time lag between a product's introduction and its imitation, and **f** the possibility of lucrative buyout offers from larger firms.

9. Each of the four basic market structures has potential strengths and weaknesses regarding the likelihood of R&D and innovation. The *inverted-U theory* holds that a firm's R&D spending as a percentage of its sales rises with its industry four-firm concentration ratio, reaches a peak at a 50 percent concentration ratio, and then declines as concentration increases further. Empirical evidence is not clear-cut but lends general support to this theory. For any specific industry, however, the technological opportunities that are available may count more than market structure in determining R&D spending and innovation.

10. In general, technological advance enhances both productive and allocative efficiency. But in some situations patents and the advantages of being first with an innovation can increase monopoly power. While in some cases *creative destruction* eventually destroys monopoly, most economists doubt that this process is either automatic or inevitable.

## TERMS AND CONCEPTS

technological advance
very long run
invention
patent
innovation (product and process)
diffusion
start-ups
venture capital
interest-rate cost-of-funds curve
expected-rate-of-return curve
optimal amount of R&D
imitation problem
fast-second strategy
inverted-U theory of R&D
creative destruction

## STUDY QUESTIONS

1. What is meant by technological advance, as broadly defined? How does technological advance enter into the definition of the very long run? Which of the following are examples of technological advance, and which are not: an improved production process; entry of a firm into a profitable purely competitive industry; the imitation of a new production process by another firm; an increase in a firm's advertising expenditures?

2. Listed below are several possible actions by firms. Write INV beside those that reflect invention, INN beside those that reflect innovation, and DIF beside those that reflect diffusion.
   - **a.** An auto manufacturer adds "heated seats" as a standard feature in its luxury cars to keep pace with a rival firm whose luxury cars already have this feature.
   - **b.** A television production company pioneers the first music video channel.
   - **c.** A firm develops and patents a working model of a self-erasing whiteboard for classrooms.
   - **d.** A maker of light bulbs becomes the first firm to produce and market lighting fixtures using halogen lamps.
   - **e.** A rival toy maker introduces a new Jenny doll to compete with Mattel's Barbie doll.

3. Contrast the older and modern views of technological advance as they relate to the economy. What is the role of entrepreneurs and other innovators in technological advance? How does research by universities and government affect innovators and technological advance? Why do you think some university researchers are increasingly becoming more like entrepreneurs and less like "pure scientists"?

4. KEY QUESTION *Suppose a firm expects that a $20 million expenditure on R&D will result in a new product that will increase its revenue by a total of $30 million one year from now. The firm also estimates that the production cost of the new product will be $29 million.*
   a. *What is the expected rate of return on this R&D expenditure?*
   b. *Suppose the firm can get a bank loan at 6 percent interest to finance its $20 million R&D project. Will the firm undertake the project? Explain why or why not.*
   c. *Now suppose the interest-rate cost of borrowing, in effect, falls to 4 percent because the firm decides to use its own retained earnings to finance the R&D. Will this lower interest rate change the firm's R&D decision? Explain.*

5. KEY QUESTION *Answer the lettered questions below on the basis of the information in this table:*

| Amount of R&D, millions | Expected rate of return on R&D, % |
|---|---|
| $10 | 16 |
| 20 | 14 |
| 30 | 12 |
| 40 | 10 |
| 50 | 8 |
| 60 | 6 |

   a. *If the interest-rate cost of funds is 8 percent, what will be the optimal amount of R&D spending for this firm?*
   b. *Explain why $20 million of R&D spending will not be optimal.*
   c. *Why won't $60 million be optimal either?*

6. KEY QUESTION *Refer to Table 13-1 and suppose the price of new product C is $2 instead of $4. How does this affect the optimal combination of products A, B, and C for the person represented by the data? Explain: "The success of a new product depends not only on its marginal utility but also on its price."*

7. Learning how to use software takes time. So once customers have learned to use a particular software package, it is easier to sell them software upgrades than to convince them to switch to new software. What implications does this have for expected rates of return on R&D spending for software firms developing upgrades versus those developing imitative products?

8. KEY QUESTION *Answer the following questions on the basis of this information for a single firm: total cost of capital = $1,000; price paid for labour = $12 per labour unit; price paid for raw materials = $4 per raw-material unit.*
   a. *Suppose the firm can produce 5,000 units of output by combining its fixed capital with 100 units of labour and 450 units of raw materials. What are the total cost and average total cost of producing the 5,000 units of output?*
   b. *Now assume the firm improves its production process so that it can produce 6,000 units of output by combining its fixed capital with 100 units of labour and 450 units of raw materials. What are the total cost and average cost of producing the 6,000 units of output?*
   c. *In view of your answers to 8a and 8b, explain how process innovation can improve economic efficiency.*

9. Why might a firm making a large economic profit from its existing product employ a fast-second strategy in relationship to new or improved products? What risks does it run in pursuing this strategy? What incentive does a firm have to engage in R&D when rivals can imitate its new product?

10. Do you think the overall level of R&D would increase or decrease over the next 20 to 30 years if the lengths of new patents were extended from 20 years to, say, "forever"? What if the duration were reduced from 20 years to, say, 3 years?

11. Make a case that neither pure competition nor pure monopoly is very conducive to a great deal of R&D spending and innovation. Why is oligopoly more favourable to R&D spending and innovation than either pure competition or pure monopoly? What is the inverse-U theory and how does it relate to your answers to these questions?

12. Evaluate: "Society does not need laws outlawing monopolization and monopoly. Inevitably, monopoly causes its own self-destruction, since its high profit is the lure for other firms or entrepreneurs to develop substitute products."

13. **(The Last Word)** Identify a specific example of each of the following in this Last Word: **a** entrepreneurship, **b** invention, **c** innovation, and **d** diffusion.

14. WEB-BASED QUESTION **NASA—What Are the Commercial Spinoffs?** NASA (the U.S. National Aero-nautics and Space Administration) maintains that its research and development over the past three decades has had a favourable impact on individuals, firms, and industries. Canadian companies have contributed to NASA's success. Visit NASA's Technology Transfer Office www.sti.nasa.gov/tto to determine if there have been significant commercial benefits from secondary use of NASA technology. Are there any that have been inconsequential? How does the NASA Commercial Technology Network nctn.hq.nasa.gov/ move technology from the lab to the marketplace?

CHAPTER 14

# Competition Policy, Regulation, and Industrial Policy

HERE ARE SEVERAL TRIVIAL PURSUIT QUESTIONS and answers for you:

- Why did a Quebec Superior Court judge impose a fine of almost $6 million on four cement companies for conspiring to fix prices in the Quebec City area? Such lawsuits are based on **anti-combines policy**: laws and government actions designed to promote competition.
- How are electricity, natural gas, and local phone calls related? All are produced by so-called *public utilities* and are subject to **industrial regulation**: government regulation of prices (or rates) within selected industries.
- What do workplace safety standards, air bags, affirmative action, access for the disabled, antipollution laws, and auto fuel standards have in common? All are the objects of **social regulation**: government regulation of the conditions under which goods are produced, the physical characteristics of goods, and the impact of goods' production and consumption on society.
- And what do government subsidies to promote fuel-efficient automobiles and enhance exports have in common? Both are components of **industrial policy**: government policies to promote selected industries, products, or technologies.

Anti-combines policy, industrial regulation, social regulation, and industrial policy are government interventions that relate to the structure, conduct, and performance of industry. This chapter examines the purposes and effects of these interventions but first defines and clarifies the debate over industrial concentration.

**IN THIS CHAPTER YOU WILL LEARN:**

The costs and benefits of industrial concentration.

•

About the evolution of Canadian competition (anti-combines) policy and its current aims.

•

What social regulations are and what their goals are.

•

The pros and cons of industrial policy.

## The Big Picture

WHEN WE STUDIED MARKET STRUCTURES WE concluded that in a world of scarce resources, pure competition is the market structure that produces the most out of limited resources, and produces those goods and services society wants most. While pure competition itself is rare in the real world, the model tells us that more competition is better than less.

Because competition is desirable, governments encourage it—and discourage the opposite: restriction of competition. That's also the aim of anti-combines laws. But make no mistake; there are tradeoffs between regulated versus unregulated markets. The desire for more competition is a societal goal; a firm with a monopoly will not lobby a government for more competition—that would not be in its interest. On the other hand, recall that there are instances when a natural monopoly may deliver the lowest costs for consumers. Thus, it is not easy to find the right balance between regulated and unregulated markets. It is no surprise that governments continually revisit their policy in this regard.

As you read this chapter, keep the following points in mind:

- **Key Concepts 6** and **7** are discussed.
- Some industrial concentration may be beneficial to consumers because of the lower unit costs it can bring about.
- Natural monopolies are desirable because they can produce goods at the lowest possible unit cost. But in the absence of competition the benefits of the scale economies achieved are unlikely to be passed on to consumers. Thus, governments regulate them to ensure the benefits of scale economies are passed on to consumers.
- The aim of deregulation is to promote competition. Deregulation is desirable if it brings about more competition, thus lower prices for consumers. But deregulation can bring about the opposite result: a few firms can come to dominate the industry.
- Government often imposes regulations on firms for perceived beneficial social ends. The regulations sometimes lessen competition.
- Social regulations attempt to lessen undesirable social side effects of a competitive market economy. There are pros and cons to social regulations.
- Industrial policy seeks to intervene in the market system to improve the social and economic outcome in particular sectors of the economy. Industrial policy has its supporters and detractors. ■

## DEFINITION OF INDUSTRIAL CONCENTRATION

In Chapter 11 we developed and applied a strict definition of monopoly. A *pure monopoly*, we said, is a one-firm industry—a situation whereby a unique product is being produced entirely by a single firm and entry to the industry is totally blocked.

In this chapter we will use the term *industrial concentration* to include pure monopoly and markets in which there is much potential monopoly power. **Industrial concentration** *exists whenever a single firm or a small number of firms control the major portion of the output of an industry.* One, two, or three firms dominate the industry, potentially resulting in higher-than-competitive prices and profits. This definition, which is closer to how the general public understands the "monopoly problem," includes many industries we have previously designated as oligopolies.

"Industrial concentration" in this chapter thus refers to industries in which firms are large in absolute terms and in relation to the total market. Examples are the telephone equipment industry, in which Nortel, large by any standard, dominates the market; the automobile industry, where General Motors of Canada, Ford of Canada, and Chrysler of Canada are dominant; the chemical industry, dominated by Petro-Canada, Imperial Oil (Exxon), and Shell Canada; the aluminum industry, where industrial giant Alcan Aluminum reigns supreme; and the steel industry, where the two large producers, Dominion Foundries & Steel (Dofasco) and Steel Company of Canada (Stelco), command the lion's share of the market.

## INDUSTRIAL CONCENTRATION: BENEFICIAL OR HARMFUL?

Does industrial concentration help or hinder the working of our economy? There are contrasting arguments for and against industrial concentration.

### The Case Against Industrial Concentration

We stated the case against monopoly and oligopoly in previous chapters. Here we simply review and extend those arguments.

**Inefficient Resource Allocation** Monopolists and oligopolists find it possible and profitable to produce less output and charge higher prices than they could if their industries were competitive. With pure competition, production occurs where $P$ = MC. This equality represents an efficient allocation of resources because price $P$ measures the marginal benefit to society of an extra unit of output, while marginal cost MC reflects the cost of an extra unit. When $P$ = MC, society cannot gain by producing 1 more or 1 less unit of the product. In contrast, a monopolist maximizes profit by equating marginal revenue (not price) with marginal cost. At this MR = MC point, price exceeds marginal cost, meaning that society would obtain more benefit than it would incur cost by producing extra units. There is an underallocation of resources to the monopolized product, and thus the economic well-being of society is less than it would be with pure competition.

**Unnecessary for Economies of Scale and Technological Progress** Critics say industrial concentration normally is not needed to achieve either economies of scale or technological progress. In most industries, they contend, less than 5 percent of the market is necessary for achieving minimum average total cost; industrial concentration is *not* a prerequisite for productive efficiency.

Furthermore, most technological efficiency is attained, not in a firm, but in each individual plant. You can correctly argue that productive efficiency requires, say, a large-scale integrated auto-manufacturing plant. But it would be perfectly consistent to argue that there is no technological justification for a huge firm such as General Motors, which is composed of many geographically separate production plants, none of which increases the other's efficiency. In this view, many existing firms have become far larger than necessary for achieving full economies of scale.

Nor does technological progress require huge firms with substantial monopoly power. Large firms with great market power are not necessarily the ones that create new products and better methods of production. Instead, the sheltered positions of such firms may promote lethargy; there is no competition to spur innovation. Furthermore, monopolists and oligopolists may resist or suppress technological advances that cause sudden obsolescence of their existing machinery and equipment.

**Income Inequality** Industrial concentration is criticized as a contributor to income inequality. Because of entry barriers, monopolists and oligopolists can charge a price above average total cost and consistently obtain economic profits. These profits go to corporate stockholders and executives who are generally among the upper-income groups.

**Political Dangers** Because economic power and political clout go hand in hand, it is argued that giant corporations exert undue influence over government. This is reflected in legislation and government policies that are less suited to the public interest than to the preservation and growth of large firms. Large corporations allegedly have exerted political power to become primary beneficiaries of defence contracts, tax loopholes, patent policy, tariff and quota protection, and other subsidies and privileges.

### Defences of Industrial Concentration

Industrial concentration, however, *does* have significant defences.

**Superior Products** One defence is that monopolists and oligopolists have gained their market dominance by offering superior products. Large firms cannot *coerce* consumers to buy, say, Colgate or Crest toothpaste, soft drinks from Coca-Cola and Pepsi, greeting cards from Hallmark, ketchup from Heinz, or soup from Campbell. Consumers have collectively decided that these products are more desirable than those offered by other producers. Monopoly profits and large market shares have been "earned," according to this view.

**Underestimated Competition** Another defence of industrial concentration rests on the assertion that economists often view competition too narrowly. While there may be only a few firms producing a specific product, those firms may face **interindustry competition**. That is, large firms may have competition from other industries producing different but highly substitutable products. There may be only a handful of firms responsible for the nation's output of aluminum. But aluminum faces competition from steel, copper, wood, plastics, and a host of other products, depending on the specific market.

**Foreign competition** must also be taken into account. While General Motors (GM), Ford, and Chrysler dominate domestic automobile production, strong import competition affects all their pricing and output decisions. While there are only a handful of steel producers in Canada, they still face stiff competition from foreign producers.

Furthermore, the large profit that would result from the full use of a monopolist's market power would attract potential competitors to the industry. This **potential competition** moderates the price and output decisions of firms now possessing market power. These firms wish to deter entry, and one way to do that is to keep prices low.

**Economies of Scale** Where economies of scale are extensive, only producers that are large both absolutely and in relation to the market can obtain low unit costs and therefore sell their output to consumers at low prices. The traditional anti-monopoly contention that industrial concentration means less output, higher prices, and an inefficient allocation of resources assumes that cost economies would be equally available to firms whether the industry's structure were highly competitive or quite monopolistic. This is frequently not so; minimum average total cost may require such high levels of output that competition *in the sense of a large number of firms* is inefficient. Society is clearly better off with say, 3 firms producing 1 million units of X at a per-unit cost of $50 and charging $70 per unit than with 1,000 firms producing X at a per-unit cost of $100 and charging $100 per unit. In this situation, the fact that the three firms are obtaining large economic profits is irrelevant; consumers and society benefit from the industrial concentration.

**Technological Progress** In direct rebuttal to the critics, defenders of industrial concentration assert that large oligopolistic industries tend to be technologically progressive because they have both the financial resources *and* the incentive to undertake technological research. The financial resources derive from retained earnings, while the strong incentive for R&D results from entry barriers which allow oligopolists to sustain high returns from these efforts.

**14-1**
**QUICK REVIEW**

- Industrial concentration exists where a single firm or a small number of firms control the major portion of an industry's output.
- The case against industrial concentration is that it creates allocative inefficiency, impedes technological progress, promotes income inequality, and poses political dangers.
- Those who defend industrial concentration say it results from superior performance and economies of scale; is countered by interindustry, foreign, and potential competition; and provides both the wherewithal and the incentives for technological progress.

## ANTI-COMBINES LEGISLATION

The sharp conflict of opinion over the merits of industrial concentration is reflected in Canadian anti-combines policy, which has been neither clear-cut nor consistent.

### Historical Background

The Canadian economy has been a fertile ground for development of a suspicious, fearful public attitude towards industrial concentration. This distrust of big business bloomed in the decades following Confederation. The widening of local markets into national markets as transportation facilities improved, the ever-increasing mechanization of production, and the widespread adoption of the corporate form of business enterprise contributed to the development of industrial concentration between the 1880s and World War I.

Not only were questionable tactics used in the concentration of these industries, the resulting market power was exerted to the detriment of all who did business with them. Farmers and owners of small businesses were particularly vulnerable to the growth of monopoly power and were among the first to oppose them. Consumers and labour unions were not far behind in their opposition.

In these monopolized industries, market forces no longer provided adequate control to ensure socially tolerable outcomes. In response, opponents adopted two techniques of control as substitutes for, or supplements to, the market forces.

1. **REGULATORY AGENCIES** In the few markets where the nature of the product precludes effective working of the market—where there is "natural monopoly"—Canada has established public regulatory agencies to control economic behaviour.
2. **ANTI-COMBINES LAWS** In most other markets, where economic and technological conditions have not made monopoly essential, social control has taken the form of **anti-combines legislation** designed to inhibit or prevent the growth of monopoly.

Let's consider the anti-combines legislation that, as refined and extended by various amendments, constitutes the basic law of the land with respect to corporate size and concentration. Before we do, let's examine merger types.

## Merger Types

There are three basic types of mergers, as shown in Figure 14-1. This diagram shows two stages of production, one the input stage, the other the final-good stage of two distinct final-good industries: autos and beer. Each rectangle (A, B, C ... X, Y, Z) represents a particular firm.

A **horizontal merger** *is a merger between two competitors selling similar products in the same market.* In Figure 14-1 this type of merger is shown as a combination of glass producers T and U. Examples of horizontal mergers would be the Bay's merger with K-Mart and the Royal Bank's merger with the Bank of Montreal.

A **vertical merger**—*the merging of firms at different stages of the production process in the same industry*—is shown in Figure 14-1 as a merger between firm Z, a hops producer, and firm F, a brewery. Vertical mergers involve firms having buyer-seller relationships. Examples of mergers of this type are PepsiCo's mergers with Pizza Hut, Taco Bell, and Kentucky Fried Chicken. PepsiCo supplies soft drinks to each of these fast-food outlets.

A **conglomerate merger** is officially defined as *any merger that is not horizontal or vertical; in general, it is the combination of firms in different industries or firms operating in different geographical areas.* Conglomerate mergers can extend the line of products

**FIGURE 14-1 Types of mergers**

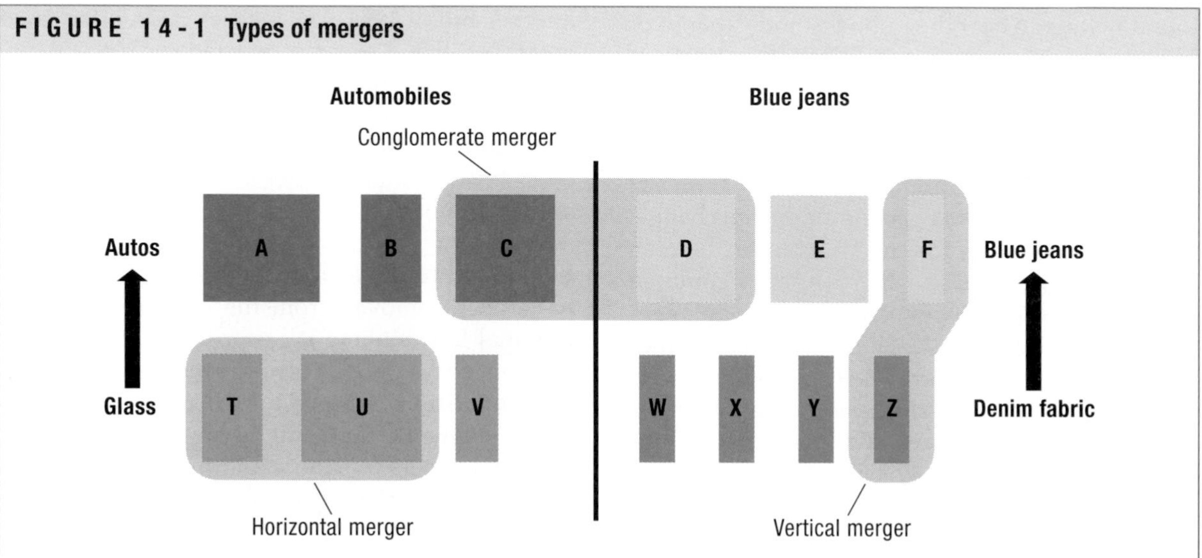


Horizontal mergers (T + U) bring together firms selling the same product in the same geographical market; vertical mergers (F + Z) connect firms having a buyer-seller relationship; and conglomerate mergers (C + D) join firms in different industries or firms operating in different geographical areas.

sold, or combine totally unrelated companies. In Figure 14-1, the merger between firm C, an auto manufacturer, and firm D, a blue jeans producer, is a conglomerate merger.

We now turn to look at the evolution of anti-combines legislation in Canada.

## The Act of 1889

Canadian anti-combines legislation began in 1889 with the passage of an Act that made it a misdemeanour to conspire to restrict either trade or output, or competition. Three years later, the Act of 1889 became a section of the Criminal Code and the offence became an indictable one. In the first ten years of this century there were *six* prosecutions under the section, resulting in four convictions. Securing evidence to get a conviction under the Criminal Code was particularly difficult, and further changes became necessary.

## Combines Investigation Act, 1910

The result was the passing of the **Combines Investigation Act** in 1910, an Act whose name was with us in successive Acts until June 1986, when it became the Competition Act. The 1910 Act authorized a judge, on receiving an application by six persons, to order an investigation into an alleged combine.

The 1910 Act was hardly a success, for two reasons: (1) Rarely could six private citizens be found willing to bear the publicity and expense of initiating an investigation. (2) Each investigation, if and when ordered by a judge, started afresh; there was no person or body to administer the Act continuously. Thus, there was only *one* investigation under the Act before World War I.

The next 50 years saw no fundamental change. Of note were the 1952 amendments to the Act, which split the duties of the combines commissioner and assigned them to two separate agencies—one for investigation and research, the other for appraisal and report. Thus were established a director of investigation and research and a Restrictive Trade Practices Commission, the latter being superseded in June 1986 by the Competition Tribunal (see below).

In 1960, the Combines Investigation Act was at last amended to include the provisions relating to combinations that had been laid down in the Criminal Code since 1892. As well, mergers and monopolies now were deemed unlawful only if a "detriment or against the interest of the public."

In 1967, the newly formed Department of Consumer and Corporate Affairs took over responsibility for combines, mergers, monopolies, and restraint of trade. Shortly thereafter, in 1969, the Economic Council of Canada reported that the provisions of the Combines Investigation Act making mergers and monopolies criminal offences were "all but inoperative" because a criminal offence had to be proved "beyond a shadow of a doubt"—a very difficult task. However, the Economic Council did *not* recommend barriers be placed in the way of a company achieving dominance through internal growth or superior efficiency. The Economic Council's whole approach then was based on the goal of economic efficiency. It was this same approach that led the Economic Council to recommend that competition policy be extended to services.

On January 1, 1976, new amendments to the Combines Investigation Act became effective, with the result that it became applicable to services as well.

## The Competition Act, 1986

Successive governments in Ottawa have attempted to bring about changes to Canada's law governing monopolies. Three attempts, Bills brought before Parliament in 1971, 1977, and 1977–79, met with organized opposition from business. Extensive consultations with the private sector and provincial governments preceded the introduction of yet another Bill in 1984. The 1984 election intervened and this Bill, too, was not enacted.

Finally, in June 1986, Parliament passed the Competition Tribunal Act and the **Competition Act**, the latter being the new name for the Combines Investigation Act. Some of the major changes are worth noting.

### Civil Law Framework

Mergers and monopolies have been removed from the jurisdiction of the criminal law, making it easier to prosecute those mergers and monopolies not in the public interest. A **Competition Tribunal** adjudicates under a civil law framework that will permit the issuing of remedial orders to restore and maintain competition in the market. The tribunal is made up of judges of the Federal Court and lay persons, with a judge as chairperson. The Restrictive Trade Practices Commission is abolished as a result.

### Merger

Only those mergers resulting in an unacceptable lessening of competition could be prohibited or modified by the Competition Tribunal. Mergers that result in gains in efficiency—through, for example, economies of scale—that more than offset the costs stemming from the lessening of competition are allowed.

**Abuse of Dominant Position** The abuse-of-dominance provision is designed to ensure that dominant firms compete with other firms on merit, not through the abuse of their market power.

**Conspiracy** The conspiracy provision in the old Combines Investigation Act is considerably tightened by adding that the existence of a conspiracy may be proven from circumstantial evidence with or without direct evidence of communication among the parties. The maximum fine has been increased from $1 million to $10 million.

**Export Agreements** Export consortia—combines—are permitted, provided they relate only to the export of products from Canada, even should they have the unintended, ancillary effect of lessening domestic competition.

**Specialization Agreements** Many of our industries are composed of firms with short production runs of several different products. Efficiency could be gained through greater specialization and longer production runs. Thus, the Competition Tribunal may approve a specialization agreement if the promised gains in efficiency are likely to more than offset the costs caused by the lessening of competition.

**Banks** Banking agreements and bank mergers are subject to the Competition Act. In early 1998 the Royal Bank and the Bank of Montreal announced their intention to merge; a few months later the Canadian Imperial Bank of Commerce and the Toronto-Dominion Bank also announced a proposed merger. The main justification given was that their merger would help them "compete" with larger foreign banks.

**Crown Corporations** All Crown corporations, both federal and provincial, in commercial activity and in competition with other firms, are subject to the Act.

The thrust of the latest version of the Competition Act is the surveillance of all firms providing goods and services in our economy, but the Act recognizes that some mergers may be warranted from an efficiency viewpoint. This is important because under the North American Free Trade Agreement (NAFTA), firms must compete with Mexican and American competitors. Any advantage that may be gained through mergers that increase efficiency would be beneficial.

## Exemptions to Anti-Combines Legislation

Over the years, government has enacted certain laws that have either exempted certain specific industries or, alternatively, have excluded certain trade practices from anti-combines prosecution. In doing so, the government has fostered the growth of monopoly power.

Labour unions, co-operatives, **caisses populaires,** and credit unions have been exempt—subject to limitations—from the competition law. Legislation and policy have provided some measure of monopolistic power for agriculture and kept agricultural prices above competitive levels. Since 1945, federal and provincial legislation has generally facilitated the growth of labour unions. According to some authorities, the government-sponsored growth has resulted in the formation of union monopolies, whose goal is above-competitive wage rates. At provincial and local levels, a wide variety of occupational groups have succeeded in establishing licensing requirements that arbitrarily restrict entry to certain occupations, keeping wages and earnings above competitive levels. Finally, as we saw in Chapter 11, **patent laws** may encourage monopolies into research and development.

## Other Desirable Goals

Achieving economic efficiency through competition is only one of society's goals. Strict enforcement of anti-combines laws occasionally may conflict with some other worthy goal. Examples:

1. **BALANCE OF TRADE** Governments seek ways to increase exports to pay for imports. Anti-combines actions to undo a merger of, for example, two chemical suppliers, break up a dominant aircraft manufacturer, or dissolve an emerging software monopolist might weaken the targeted firms, reducing their competitiveness and sales abroad. Our total exports might therefore decline and a trade deficit could result or an existing trade deficit worsen.

Should government strictly enforce anti-combines laws, even when significant amounts of exports are potentially at stake? Should the anti-combines goal of efficiency supersede the goal of balancing exports and imports?

2. **EMERGING NEW TECHNOLOGIES** Occasionally, new technologies combine to create new products and services. A current example is the meshing of computers and communications technologies to create the "information superhighway," a generic name for the hookups of computers, telephones, television sets, and other communications devices. This interactive "highway" is improving communications capabilities of households, businesses, and governments across the globe. It also allows them to access unprecedented amounts of information via a click of a "mouse" and directly buy and sell goods and services. This technology has set off a spate of mergers involving companies from diverse areas. Should government strictly enforce Canada's anti-combines laws to block some of those mergers that increase industrial concentration and threaten to reduce competition? Or should government temporarily "suspend the anti-combines rules" to encourage the major restructuring of industries that followed the introduction of this new technology? The continuing development of the information superhighway may also increase our exports of these services.

These tradeoffs have stirred controversy. The issue of anti-combines enforcement is more complex when it conflicts with other desirable social goals. Some argue that the gains from an anti-combines policy must be weighed against the effects of the policy on these conflicting objectives. Others contend that selective enforcement of the anti-combines laws is a facet of government industrial policy (discussed later) that interferes with the efficient market process. Different policy makers may well view these considerations and tradeoffs differently. ***(Key Question 3)***

**14-2**

**QUICK REVIEW**

- There are three types of mergers: horizontal, vertical, and conglomerate.
- The first Canadian anti-combines legislation was passed in 1889. Its purpose was to make it unlawful to restrict competition unduly.
- The original anti-combines legislation subsequently came under the Criminal Code, making successful prosecution difficult.
- The Competition Act, passed in 1986, removed anti-combines activity from the Criminal Code, making prosecution easier. This Act also stressed that even if some mergers lessened competition, they should be allowed if such mergers bring about significant efficiency gains.
- Some government legislation lessens competitive forces, for example, patent laws. But patent laws may encourage research and development.

## SOCIAL REGULATION

Industrial regulation focuses on the regulation of prices (or rates) in natural monopolies. But in the early 1960s a new type of regulation began to evolve and grow. This *social regulation* is concerned with the conditions under which goods and services are produced, the impact of production on society, and the physical qualities of the goods themselves.

The federal government carries out most social regulation, although provinces also play a role.

### Distinguishing Features

Social regulation differs from industrial regulation in several ways:

1. Social regulation applies to far more firms than industrial regulation. Social regulation is often applied "across the board" to all industries and directly affects far more producers. While the Air Transport Committee of the National Transport Agency of Canada controls only the air transport industry, the rules and regulations of the Canada Labour (Safety) Code and its provincial counterparts apply to every employer.
2. Social regulation intrudes into the day-to-day production process to a greater extent than industrial regulation. While industrial regulation focuses on rates and costs, and profits, social regulation often dictates the design of

products, the conditions of employment, and the nature of the production process. Social regulation involves government in the details of the production process. For example, rather than specify safety standards for vehicles, the Motor Vehicle Safety Act includes, among many others, six standards limiting motor vehicle exhaust and noise emissions.

3. Social regulation has expanded rapidly during the same period in which industrial regulation has waned.

## Overregulation?

While economists agree on the need for social regulation, they disagree on whether the current level of such regulation is optimal. Recall that *no* activity should be expanded to such an extent that its marginal cost exceeds its marginal benefit. Critics of social regulation contend that this is precisely what has happened in Canada. In this view, society would achieve net benefits by cutting back on social regulation. In contrast, defenders of social regulation argue that it has achieved notable successes and, overall, has greatly enhanced society's well-being. They say that cutbacks are unwarranted.

Let's look at the costs and criticisms of social regulation and then examine some counter-arguments.

**Costs** The costs of social regulation are *administrative costs*, such as salaries paid to employees of the commissions, office expenses, and the like, and *compliance costs*, the costs incurred by businesses and provincial and local governments in meeting the requirements of regulatory commissions.

**Criticisms** Critics of social regulation argue that our economy is now subject to overregulation.

**UNECONOMICAL GOALS** First, critics say that many social regulation laws are poorly written, so that regulatory objectives and standards are difficult to understand. As a result, regulators pursue goals well beyond the original intent of the legislation. Businesses complain that regulators often press for additional increments of improvement, unmindful of costs. For example, once certain pollution has been reduced by, say, 60 percent, a requirement to reduce it by an added 5 percent may cost much more than did the first 60 percent reduction. The marginal cost of that last 5 percent reduction, critics argue, may far exceed the marginal benefit.

**INADEQUATE INFORMATION** Decisions must often be made and rules formed on the basis of inadequate information. For example, the federal Health Protection Branch officials may make decisions about certain cancer-causing ingredients in products on the basis of limited laboratory experiments with animals. Or government agencies may establish costly pollution standards to attack the global-warming problem without knowing for certain whether pollution is the main cause of the problem. These efforts, say critics, tend to overregulate business.

**UNINTENDED SIDE EFFECTS** Critics argue that social regulations produce many unintended and costly side effects. For example, the gas mileage standard for automobiles has been blamed for hundreds of traffic deaths a year because auto manufacturers have reduced the weight of vehicles to meet the higher kilometres-per-litre standards. Other things equal, drivers of lighter cars have a higher fatality rate than drivers of heavier vehicles.

**Overzealous Personnel** Critics also say that the regulatory agencies may attract overzealous personnel who "believe" in regulation. It is argued that the bureaucrats of the new statutory regulatory agencies may be overly sensitive to criticism by some special interest group—for example, environmentalists. The result is bureaucratic inflexibility and the establishment of extreme or nonsensical regulations so that no watchdog group will question the agency's commitment to its social goal.

**Economic Implications of Overregulation** If overregulation exists—and that is subject to debate—what are its consequences?

**HIGHER PRICES** Social regulation increases product prices in two ways. It does this directly because compliance costs normally get passed on to consumers, and it does so indirectly by reducing labour productivity. Resources invested in antipollution equipment, for example, are not available for investment in new machinery designed to increase output per worker. Where the wage rate is fixed, a drop in labour productivity increases the marginal and average total costs of production. In effect, the supply curve for the product shifts leftward, causing its price to rise.

**SLOWER INNOVATION** Social regulation may have a negative impact on the rate of innovation. Technological advance may be stifled by, say, the fear that a new plant will not meet federal guidelines or that a new medicine will require years of testing before being approved.

**REDUCED COMPETITION** Social regulation may have an anti-competitive effect since it usually places a relatively greater burden on small firms than on large ones. The costs of complying with social regulation are, in effect, fixed costs. Because smaller firms produce less output over which to distribute these costs, their compliance costs per unit of output put them at a competitive disadvantage with their larger rivals. Social regulation is more likely to force smaller firms out of business, thus contributing to the increased concentration of industry.

**In Support of Social Regulation** Supporters of social regulation strongly defend it. They point out that the problems that social regulation confront are serious and substantial. Nearly 1,000 workers die annually in job-related accidents. Air pollution continues to cloud major Canadian cities, imposing large costs in reduced property values and increased health care expense. Numerous children and adults die each year in accidents involving poorly designed products or tainted food. Discrimination against visible minorities, women, persons with disabilities, and older workers reduces their earnings and imposes heavy costs on society.

The proponents of social regulation correctly point out that a high "price" for something does not necessarily mean that it should not be purchased. They say the relevant economic test should be not whether costs of social regulation are high or low but, rather, whether the benefits of social regulation *exceed* the costs. After years of neglect, they further assert, society cannot expect to cleanse the environment, enhance the safety of the workplace, and promote economic opportunity for all without substantial costs. So statements about the huge costs of social regulation are irrelevant, say defenders, since the benefits are even greater. These benefits are often underestimated by the public since they are more difficult to measure than costs and often become apparent only after some time has passed.

Proponents of social regulation point to its many specific benefits. Here are just a few examples: It is estimated that highway fatalities would be 40 percent greater annually without auto safety features mandated through regulation. Compliance with child safety-belt laws has significantly reduced the auto fatality rate for small children. The national air-quality standards set by law have been reached in nearly all parts of the nation for sulphur dioxide, nitrogen dioxide, and lead. Affirmative action regulations have increased the labour demand for visible minorities and females. The use of childproof lids has resulted in a 90 percent decline in child deaths caused by accidental swallowing of poisonous substances.

Defenders say these and many other benefits are well worth the costs of social regulation. The costs are simply the "price" we must pay to create a hospitable, sustainable, and just society. ***(Key Question 7)***

**14-3**

**QUICK REVIEW**

- Social regulation is concerned with conditions under which goods and services are produced, the effects of production on society, and physical characteristics of goods themselves.
- Critics of social regulation say uneconomical policy goals, inadequate information, unintended side effects, and overzealous personnel create overregulation and regulatory costs that exceed regulatory benefits.
- Defenders of social regulation point to the benefits arising from policies that keep dangerous products from the marketplace, reduce workplace injuries and deaths, contribute to clean air and water, and reduce employment discrimination.

## INDUSTRIAL POLICY

In recent years industrial policy has joined anti-combines activities, industrial regulation, and social regulation as a distinct form of government involvement with business. Industrial policy *consists of governmental actions to promote the economic vitality of specific firms or industries.* The other forms of government involvement alter the structure or restrict the conduct of private firms, generally reducing their revenues or increasing their costs. Industrial policy *promotes* the interests of selected firms and industries, usually adding to their profitability.

## Antecedents

Governmental promotion of industries has a long, controversial history. In the 1600s and 1700s European governments practised an economic policy known as mercantilism. At the heart of mercantilism was the belief that a nation's wealth consisted of its precious metals. Because merchants received inflows of gold in return for their exports, governments established elaborate policies to promote exports and reduce imports. Such policies included tariffs on imports of finished goods, free importation of resources, and the granting of monopoly trading privileges to selected companies (such as the East India Company and the Hudson Bay Company). Governments also regulated production techniques to ensure the quality of exports and, in general, subsidized production in their exporting industries.

Canada's history is replete with examples of industrial policy. In the 1800s government granted free land to railroads to promote their westward expansion. This expansion hastened economic development, increased productivity, and helped raise national output and employment. Government has heavily subsidized Canadian agriculture over the decades, boosting profits in that industry.

## Recent Emphasis

In the past decade or so there has been a growing concern that Canada's industrial strength has been seriously eroded. Our domestic markets have been flooded with foreign steel, automobiles, motorcycles, cameras, watches, sporting goods, and electronic equipment. Some suggest that the growing imports mean we have lost our competitive edge.

Noting apparent Japanese export success, many politicians, union, and business leaders—but very few economists—feel Canada needs a strong industrial policy to maintain its industrial strength. They argued that government should take a more active and direct role in determining the structure and composition of Canadian industry. Government, they say, should use low-interest loans, loan guarantees, favourable tax treatment, research and development subsidies, anti-combines immunity, and even protection against foreign goods to accelerate the development of "high-tech" industries and to revitalize basic core manufacturing industries such as steel. Presumably the result will be that the Canadian economy will enjoy a higher average level of productivity and be more competitive in world markets.

Although the federal government has not committed itself to a comprehensive industrial policy, there are many examples of specific programs consistent with this concept.

1. **AUTO INDUSTRY** The surge of Japanese auto imports during the 1970s and 1980s placed tremendous financial pressure on Canadian auto producers. Governments responded with a series of actions to promote the domestic auto industry. For example, in 1979 the Ontario provincial government "bailed out" both Massey-Ferguson and Chrysler Corporation by providing loan guarantees to financial institutions lending to the two corporations. Second example: In the mid-1980s the government negotiated "voluntary" export restrictions on automobiles imported from Japan. In these agreements the Japanese government and auto firms agreed to limit auto exports to North America to no more than a set number of cars.
2. **ALTERNATIVE FUEL PROGRAM** In response to the "oil crisis" of the mid-1970s, the government established a subsidy program to promote the development of alternative fuels. Also, much money went into the development to recover oil from oil shale and the Alberta tar sands. Overall, this government effort has not worked out as well as hoped.
3. **EXPORT DEVELOPMENT CORPORATION** This federal entity subsidizes interest rates on loans taken out by foreign buyers of Canadian exports. These subsidies directly benefit Canadian exporters of goods bought on credit. In effect, the subsidies reduce the total price (product price plus interest on loan) to the foreign buyer.

## Controversy

Advocates of industrial policy—or what some now label "technology policy"—point out that several leading Canadian products were developed with direct government support. They argue that well-targeted government industrial policy enhances private-sector entrepreneurial forces and, ultimately, expands economic growth. By subsidizing R&D efforts, industrial policy purportedly reduces the risk of exploring and applying new technologies. In this view, these technologies often spur complementary products and entire new industries, boosting a nation's productivity, standard of living, and international competitiveness.

Proponents of industrial policy cite Japan's Ministry of International Trade and Industry (MITI) as a model. Since World War II, Japan has achieved rapid economic growth because it has been highly successful in penetrating world markets. During this time, MITI has had a much-publicized industrial policy. Yet the role of industrial policy in Japan's industrial success is not at all clear. Subsidies to some of Japan's industries have surely succeeded (in particular, the semiconductor, machine tool, steel, and ship-building industries). In others, Japan's industrial policy has failed (in the aluminum-smelting, petrochemical, and high-definition-television industries). Still other Japanese industries (autos, electronics, and motorcycles) have developed successfully without government support.

Critics of industrial policy point out that Japan's MITI has made major errors in judgement. Two examples: It tried to block Honda from entering its auto industry; Honda now is one of Japan's most successful and innovative auto manufacturers. MITI pushed Japanese industry to develop an analog version of high-definition television. But U.S. producers, with minimal government support, have implemented a far superior digital technology. Japan, in essence, spent $8.3 billion for naught, mainly because MITI decided on analog.

European industrial policy has also had mixed results. Europe's subsidizing of Airbus Industries, a manufacturer of commercial aircraft, was successful but its subsidization of a supersonic transport aircraft was an economic failure.

"Short-circuiting" the market mechanism by promoting selected technologies and industries sounds appealing, but critics question any government's ability to identify the technologies and industries that will be winners and losers. The question is who can better determine where R&D and investment funds ought to be channelled. Critics say that private investors, who invest their *own* funds, have a greater incentive to obtain accurate information about technologies and industries than bureaucrats investing *taxpayers'* funds.

They also argue that government might be tempted to use investment funds to buy the political support of subsidized industries. If that were to happen, the economic goals of enhanced industrial efficiency and increased exports might become secondary to the political goal of collecting campaign contributions and getting re-elected. In addition, the expansion of industrial policy might lead to "lemon socialism": government support or ownership of declining industries, dying companies and inefficient technologies. ***(Key Question 18)***

## In The Media

7 KEY CONCEPT

# Quebec Cement Firms Socked

### $5.8-million fine over price-fixing

BY KONRAD YAKABUSKI
QUEBEC BUREAU

MONTREAL—A Quebec Superior Court judge has slapped a $5.8 million fine on four cement companies, including three of the industry's largest players, for conspiring to fix prices in the Quebec City area.

Mr. Justice Louis de Blois said one of the reasons he imposed such a hefty fine—the second largest ever levied on a group convicted of violating the Competition Act—was because all but one of the companies had pleaded guilty to a similar charge in 1983.

Yesterday, all four companies admitted to having entered into an agreement and "collaborated with other persons to share the sales of ready-mix concrete" produced for public building projects in the Quebec City region.

St. Lawrence Cement Inc. and Lafarge Canada Inc., both based in Montreal, were each ordered to pay $1.88-million. Ciment Quebec Inc. of Saint-Basile, Que., was fined $1.73-million, Béton Orléans Inc.—a wholly-owned subsidiary of St. Lawrence Cement—was hit with a $300,000 penalty.

The fines are the culmination of a year-long investigation by the federal Bureau of Competition Policy triggered when the Quebec City daily Le Soleil uncovered the price-fixing arrangement in mid-1995.

The conspiracy came to light when the cost of one of the projects, the city's new convention centre, was inflated by about $400,000 because of higher cement prices, the newspaper reported.

In addition to the fine, Judge de Blois imposed a 15-year prohibition order on the companies warning them against doing the same thing again.

The cement industry—both in Canada and abroad—has long been the focus of charges of anti-competition behaviour. In 1983, St. Lawrence, Lafarge, Ciment Québec and a fourth company, Les Constructions Pilot & Frères Inc., were fined $456,000 for conspiring to set prices in the same region in the late 1970s.

And in 1991, the European Commission hit 33 cement companies and nine trade associations with a $509 million fine for colluding to keep prices high.

Lafarge Canada is an indirect subsidiary of Paris-based Lafarge S.A., while Ciment Québec is a wholly owned unit of Ciments Français S.A. of France.

The Competition Bureau meanwhile said yesterday it is continuing its investigation into the Quebec City region regarding allegations of conspiracy and bid-rigging by other producers of ready-mix concrete.

Yesterday's fine was exceeded only by a $6.15-million penalty imposed in 1991 on five companies in the compressed-gas industry. Union Carbide Canada Ltd., Canadian Liquid Air Ltd., and Liquid Carbonic Inc., each paid $1.7-million, while two other companies paid lesser fines.

The largest penalty paid by a single company convicted of violating the Competition Act was the $2.5-million fine imposed in 1995 on Canada Pipe of Hamilton, Ont.

*Source: Globe and Mail*, August 20, 1996, pp. A1 and A7. Reprinted with permission from the *Globe and Mail.*

## THE STORY IN BRIEF

A Quebec superior court imposes a fine on four cement companies for conspiring to fix prices.

## THE ECONOMICS BEHIND THE STORY

- In Chapter 12, we saw that there is a constant temptation for oligopolists to conspire to collude to raise profits. In this case, a local oligopoly in ready-mix concrete conspired to fix prices, violating Canada's Competition Act. The four companies were fined a total of $5.8 million.
- The cement industry has a history of violating anti-combines laws in Canada. Ready-mix cement producers do not have effective competition because of the large transport costs incurred by potential competitors from outside the immediate area. Thus, local cement producers have the market to themselves. Such an environment is conducive to collusion.
- What would the likely outcome have been in the Quebec City ready-mix cement market had one of the four firms broken the price-fixing agreement and undercut its competitors? ■

# The Last Word

## DEREGULATION OF THE AIRLINES

ALTHOUGH THE AIRLINE INDUSTRY WAS deregulated more than a decade ago, it is still adjusting to deregulation. Nevertheless, some of the effects of deregulation have become clear.

**Fares** Deregulation has exerted downward pressure on fares, with overall fares rising less rapidly than the general price level. Discount air tickets, in particular, have increased in availability and declined in price.

Today, fares generally are about one-third lower in real terms than before deregulation. Of course, fare reductions have not been uniform in all markets and some fares have decreased more than others. Passengers flying from some cities have enjoyed greater decreases in fares than passengers originating their flights elsewhere.

Deregulation has produced lower fares for two reasons. First, competition among air carriers has driven down prices. Before regulation, ticket prices greatly exceeded the average total cost (ATC) of passenger service. Competition has reduced fares and economic profits; prices are closer to ATC. Second, competition has pressured firms to reduce costs. The industry's "hub and spoke" route system—analogous to a bicycle wheel—has reduced costs by allowing airlines to use smaller planes on the spoke routes and wide-bodied craft between the major hub airports. Wide-body aircraft cost less to operate per seat mile than smaller aircraft.

Also, some airlines have established two-tier wage systems paying new workers less than current employees. Union work rules have been made more flexible to increase worker productivity and reduce wage costs. Airlines are increasingly leasing work such as airline maintenance to lower-cost outside companies.

**Service and Safety** While some major airlines have withdrawn service to and from a few smaller cities, commuter airlines usually fill the resulting void. The hub and spoke system has increased flight frequencies at most airports. It has also reduced the amount of airline switching required of passengers.

On the negative side, the hub system's added stopovers have increased average travel time between cities. Also, by increasing the volume of traffic, deregulation has contributed to greater airport congestion, resulting in more frequent and longer flight delays.

There is mixed evidence whether deregulation has reduced the safety margin of air transportation. The greater volume of air traffic has resulted in higher reported instances of near collisions in midair. But the accident and fatal accident rates of airlines are much lower today than before deregulation. Furthermore, deregulation has prevented an estimated 80 deaths annually on the nation's highways, because lower fares have enticed people to substitute air travel for more dangerous automobile travel.

**Industry Structure** Airline deregulation initially induced the entry of new chartered carriers. But in the past several years the industry has gone through a "shakeout" in which some chartered airlines have failed and others have merged with stronger competitors.

Growing concentration in the airlines industry is of some concern. Air Canada and Canadian International Airlines now dominate the industry. Some think consolidation of the industry eventually may be detrimental to the very goals of deregulation itself. Studies in the United States show that fares at airports dominated by one or two airlines are as much as 25 percent higher than at airports where competition is greater. Moreover, entry of new carriers into the industry is more difficult than many economists predicted. The lack of airport capacity—at least in the short term—means that airline markets are far from being perfectly competitive. A firm wishing to enter a particular market because existing carriers are earning economic profits cannot do so if long-term leases allow existing carriers to control the airline gates.

Airline tactics also make successful entry difficult. Airline reservation systems developed by the major carriers often give their own flights priority listings on the computers used by travel agents. Frequent-flyer programs—discounts based on accumulated flight mileage—encourage passengers to use dominant existing carriers rather than new entrants. Also, price matching by existing carriers makes it difficult for new entrants to lure customers through lower ticket prices.

**Conclusion** Although it is too soon for a definitive assessment of airline deregulation, most economists see a positive outcome to date. Although lasting entry has proved difficult, there are some success stories. In particular, chartered airlines such as Canada 3000 and Air Transat have been able to compete successfully with the two major Canadian airlines, Air Canada and Canadian Airlines International. ■

# CHAPTER SUMMARY

1. The case against industrial concentration contends that it **a** causes a misallocation of resources; **b** retards the rate of technological advance; **c** promotes income inequality; and **d** creates undue political influence by large firms.
2. The defence of industrial concentration maintains: **a** firms have obtained their large market shares by offering superior products; **b** interindustry and foreign competition, along with potential competition from new industry entrants, makes Canadian industries more competitive than generally believed; **c** some degree of monopoly may be essential to realize economies of scale; and **d** monopolies and oligopolies may be technologically progressive.
3. Mergers can be of three types: horizontal, vertical, and conglomerate.
4. The cornerstone of anti-combines policy consists of amendments to the Criminal Code in 1892 and the Combines Investigation Acts of 1910 and 1923, as subsequently frequently amended. On the fifth attempt since 1971, the Competition Act was finally passed in mid-1986, supplanting the Combines Investigation Act.
5. Issues in applying anti-combines laws include: **a** the problem of determining whether an industry should be judged by its structure or its behaviour; **b** defining the scope and size of the dominant firm's market; and **c** balancing the gains from anti-combines against other desirable goals such as balancing exports and imports and encouraging new technologies.
6. Social regulation is concerned with product safety, safer working conditions, less pollution, and greater economic opportunity. Critics contend that businesses are overregulated in that marginal costs exceed marginal benefits, while defenders dispute that contention.
7. Industrial policy consists of government actions promoting the economic vitality of specific industries or firms. Proponents of industrial policy see it as a way to strengthen the industrial sector, speed development of new technologies, increase productivity, and increase international competitiveness. Critics charge that industrial policy substitutes the whims of politicians and bureaucrats for the hard scrutiny of entrepreneurs and business executives in allocating society's resources.

# TERMS AND CONCEPTS

anti-combines policy
industrial regulation
social regulation
industrial policy
industrial concentration
interindustry competition
foreign competition
potential competition
anti-combines legislation
horizontal merger
vertical merger
conglomerate merger
Combines Investigation Act
Competition Act
Competition Tribunal
caisses populaires
patent laws

# STUDY QUESTIONS

1. Suppose you are president of General Motors or Ford. Discuss critically the case *against* industrial concentration. Now suppose you are a representative for a consumer organization and are attempting to convince a parliamentary committee that the presence of industrial concentration is a significant factor contributing to high prices. Critically evaluate the case *for* industrial concentration.

2. Explain how strict enforcement of the anti-combines laws might conflict with **a** promoting exports to achieve a balance of trade; and **b** encouraging new technologies. Do you see any dangers of using selective anti-combines enforcement as part of an industrial policy?

3. KEY QUESTION *How would you expect anti-combines authorities to react to* **a** *a proposed merger of the Canadian subsidiaries of Ford and Chrysler;* **b** *evidence of secret meetings by contractors to rig bids for highway construction projects;* **c** *a proposed merger of a large shoe manufacturer and a chain of retail shoe stores; and* **d** *a proposed merger of a small life insurance company and a regional candy manufacturer?*

4. Suppose a proposed merger of firms will simultaneously lessen competition and reduce unit costs through economies of scale. Do you think such a merger should be allowed?

5. "The anti-combines laws serve to penalize efficiently managed firms." Do you agree?

6. "The social desirability of any particular firm should be judged not on the basis of the structure of the industry in which it finds itself, but rather on the basis of the market performance and behaviour of that firm." Analyze critically.

7. KEY QUESTION *How does social regulation differ from industrial regulation? What types of costs and benefits are associated with social regulation?*

8. KEY QUESTION *What is industrial policy and how does it differ from anti-combines policy, industrial regulation, and social regulation? Why might businesses look more favourably on industrial policy than these other policies? Cite an example of industrial policy. What are the pros and cons of industrial policy?*

9. **(The Last Word)** What is meant by saying that the airline industry has been deregulated? What have been the impacts of deregulation on fares, service and safety, and industry structure? Some say, "The jury is still out on airline deregulation." Speculate on what they may mean.

10. WEB-BASED QUESTION **Canada's Competition Bureau** Visit Canada's Competition Bureau's Web site at www.strategis.ic.gc.ca/SSG/etooolle.html. How many branches are there? What are their functions?

11. WEB-BASED QUESTION **Industrial Policy Example—Japan's Ministry of International Trade and Industry** Canada does not have a comprehensive industrial policy. The most extensive industrial policy among developed countries is carried out by Japan's Ministry of International Trade and Industry (MITI) www.miti.go.jp/index-e.html. What is the structure of MITI, and how does MITI carry out its industrial policy? What are the Current Topics that relate to an industrial policy? MITI's current emphasis is "economic structural reform." What does this mean? What industries have been chosen as "new and growth fields"?

PART 3

# Microeconomics of Resource Markets and the Distribution of Income

## CHAPTER 15

# The Demand for Resources

IN THE PRECEDING CHAPTERS WE EXPLORED THE pricing and output of goods and services under four product market structures: pure competition, monopolistic competition, oligopoly, and pure monopoly. Although firms operating under these four market structures differ greatly, they have something in common: In producing their products, they need productive resources. A purely competitive cucumber farmer needs land, tractors, fertilizers, and pickers. A monopolistically competitive restaurant buys kitchen equipment and hires cooks and waiters. An oligopolistic auto producer buys machinery and hires executives, accountants, engineers, and assembly-line workers. A regional natural gas monopolist leases land, builds pipelines and storage tanks, and hires billing clerks.

We now turn from the pricing and production of goods and services to the pricing and employment of *resources*. Land, labour, capital, and entrepreneurial resources indirectly or directly are owned and supplied by households. In terms of the circular flow model (Chapters 2, 5, and 6), we shift attention from the bottom loop of the diagram (where firms supply products that households demand) to the top loop (where households supply resources that businesses demand).

In this chapter we examine the factors underlying the *demand* for all economic resources. We will at times couch our discussion in terms of labour, but the principles developed also apply to land, capital, and entrepreneurial ability. In Chapter 16 we will combine resource (labour) demand with labour *supply* to analyze wage rates. Then in Chapter 17 resource demand and resource supply will be used to analyze the prices of, and returns to, the other productive resources.

**IN THIS CHAPTER YOU WILL LEARN:**

- How resource prices are determined.
- What determines the demand for a resource.
- What determines the elasticity of resource demand.
- How to arrive at the optimal combination of resources used in the production process.

## The Big Picture

UP TO THIS POINT WE HAVE BEEN FOCUSING on the product market—the market for goods and services. But to produce goods and services we require inputs of the factors of production. Recall these are labour, land, capital and entrepreneurial talent. The factors of production are available in limited quantities, thus the economizing problem—scarcity, unlimited wants, and the need for choices—also applies to the factor market. In the product market, allocation of goods and services is determined by prices; in the factor market, the allocation of land, labour, capital, and entrepreneurial ability is also determined by "price," although "price" for each of the factors goes by a different name. The "price" for labour is wages; the "price" for capital is the interest rate; the "price" for land is rent; and the "price" for entrepreneurial talent is profit. This chapter focuses on the demand for the factors of production in general. Chapter 16 looks at the labour markets and the determinants of wages (and salaries). Chapter 17 analyzes the determinants of the "prices" for the other factors: rent, interest, and profits.

As you read this chapter, keep the following points in mind:

- **Key Concept 3** is discussed.
- The price of factors is determined by supply and demand conditions.
- The demand for any factor, for example, labour, is determined by the demand for the product the factor is used in making.
- The demand for any factor also depends on its contribution to output.
- As in the product market, the amount of competition in the factor market depends on the relative market power of factor owners and factor sellers. ■

## SIGNIFICANCE AND COMPLEXITY OF RESOURCE PRICING

There are several reasons to study resource pricing:

1. **MONEY-INCOME DETERMINATION** The elemental fact about resource prices is that they are a major factor in determining households' money incomes. The expenditures firms make in acquiring economic resources flow as wage, rent, interest, and profit incomes to those households that supply these human and property resources.
2. **RESOURCE ALLOCATION** Just as product prices ration finished goods and services to consumers, so do resource prices allocate resources among industries and firms. In a dynamic economy, where technology and tastes change often, the efficient allocation of resources over time requires continuing shifts in resources among alternative uses. The role of resource pricing in bringing about those shifts is particularly significant.
3. **COST MINIMIZATION** To the firm, resource prices are costs; to realize maximum profit, it must produce the profit-maximizing output with the most efficient (least costly) combination of resources. Given technology, resource prices play the major role in determining the quantities of land, labour, capital, and entrepreneurial ability that will be combined in producing each good or service.
4. **POLICY ISSUES** Many ethical questions and public policy issues surround the resource market. In a market economy, some households may receive a disproportionate share of the income generated in an economy. What degree of income inequality is acceptable? Should government levy a special tax on "excess" pay of corporate executives? Is it desirable for government to establish a legal minimum wage? Does it make sense for government to provide subsidies to farmers? The facts, ethics, and debates relating to income distribution are based on resource pricing.

Economists generally agree on the basic principles of resource pricing. Yet they disagree on how these principles vary when they are applied to particular resource markets. Economists agree, for example, that the pricing and employment of economic resources are supply-and-demand-based; however, they also recognize that in particular markets, resource supply and demand may assume unique dimensions. Further complications result when supply and demand are altered or even replaced by the policies and practices of government, business firms, or labour unions.

## MARGINAL PRODUCTIVITY THEORY OF RESOURCE DEMAND

To keep things simple, let's initially assume that a firm hires a certain resource in a purely competitive resource market and sells its output in a purely competitive product market. The simplicity of this situation is twofold: In a competitive product market the firm is a "price taker" and can dispose of as little or as much output as it chooses at the market price. The firm is selling such a negligible fraction of total output that it exerts no influence on product price. Similarly, in the competitive resource market, the firm is a "wage taker," hiring such a small fraction of the total supply of the resource that it cannot affect the resource price.

### Resource Demand as a Derived Demand

The demand for resources is a **derived demand**; it is derived from the products that those resources help produce. Resources usually do not directly satisfy customer wants but do so indirectly by producing goods and services. No one wants to consume a hectare of land, a tractor, or the labour services of a farmer, but households do want to consume the food and fibre products these resources help produce. Similarly, the demand for automobiles generates a demand for automobile workers and the demands for such services as income tax preparation, haircuts, and child care create derived demands for accountants, barbers, and child-care workers. Global Perspective 15-1 shows emphatically that the global demand for labour is derived.

**15-1**

**GLOBAL PERSPECTIVE**

**Labour demand and allocation: developing countries, industrially advanced countries, and Canada**

The idea of derived demand implies that the composition of a country's product market demand will determine the allocation of its labour force among agricultural products, industrial goods, and services. Because poor nations must spend most of their incomes for food and fibre, the bulk of their labour is allocated to agriculture. The much-richer industrially advanced economies allocate most of their labour to industrial products and services.

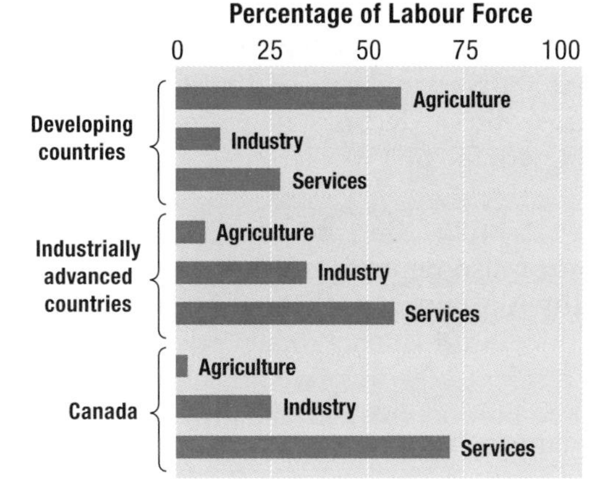


### Marginal Revenue Product (MRP)

The derived nature of resource demand means that the strength of the demand for any resource will depend on (1) the productivity of the resource in helping to create a good, and (2) the market value or price of the good it is producing. A resource that is highly productive in turning out a highly valued commodity will be in great demand. On the other hand, demand will be very weak for a relatively unproductive resource that is capable only of producing a good that few households demand. And there will be *no* demand for a resource that is phenomenally efficient in producing something *no one* wants to buy.

**Productivity** The roles of productivity and product price in determining resource demand is clearly seen in Table 15-1. Here we assume a firm adds one variable resource—labour—to its fixed plant. Columns 1 and 2 give the number of units of the resource applied to production and the resulting total product (output). Column 3 provides the marginal product (MP), or additional output, due to each additional resource unit. Columns 1 through 3 remind us that the law of diminishing returns applies here, causing the **marginal prod-**

**TABLE 15-1 The demand for labour: pure competition in the sale of the product**

| (1) Units of resource | (2) Total product (output) | (3) Marginal product, (MP) | (4) Product price | (5) Total revenue, or (2) × (4) | (6) Marginal revenue product, (MRP) |
|---|---|---|---|---|---|
| 0 | 0 | | $2 | $ 0 | |
| 1 | 7 | 7 | 2 | 14 | $14 |
| 2 | 13 | 6 | 2 | 26 | 12 |
| 3 | 18 | 5 | 2 | 36 | 10 |
| 4 | 22 | 4 | 2 | 44 | 8 |
| 5 | 25 | 3 | 2 | 50 | 6 |
| 6 | 27 | 2 | 2 | 54 | 4 |
| 7 | 28 | 1 | 2 | 56 | 2 |

**uct** (MP) of labour to fall beyond some point. For simplicity, we assume these diminishing marginal returns—these declines in marginal product—begin with the first worker hired.

**Product Price** But the derived demand for a resource also depends on the price of the commodity it produces. Column 4 in Table 15-1 adds this price information. Product price is constant, in this case at $2, because we are supposing a competitive product market. The firm is a price taker and will sell units of output only at this market price.

Multiplying column 2 by column 4 gives us the total-revenue data of column 5. These are the amounts of revenue the firm realizes from the various levels of resource usage. From these total-revenue data we can compute **marginal revenue product** (MRP)—*the change in total revenue resulting from the use of each additional unit of a resource* (labour, in this case). In equation form,

$$\text{Marginal revenue product} = \frac{\text{Change in total revenue}}{\text{Change in resource quantity}}$$

The MRPs are listed in column 6 in Table 15-1.

## Rule for Employing Resources: MRP = MRC

*The MRP schedule—columns 1 and 6—is the firm's demand schedule for labour.* To explain why, we must first discuss the rule that guides a profit-seeking firm in hiring any resource: *To maximize profit, a firm should hire additional units of a specific resource as long as each successive unit adds more to the firm's total revenue than it adds to total cost.*

Economists have special terms designating what each additional unit of labour or other variable resource adds to total cost and what it adds to total revenue. We already saw that MRP measures how much each successive unit of a resource adds to total revenue. The amount that each additional unit of a resource adds to the firm's total (resource) cost is called its **marginal resource cost** (MRC).

In equation form,

$$\text{Marginal resource cost} = \frac{\text{Change in total (resource) cost}}{\text{Change in resource quantity}}$$

Thus we can restate our rule for hiring resources as follows: *It will be profitable for a firm to hire additional units of a resource up to the point at which that resource's MRP is equal to its MRC.* If the number of workers a firm is currently hiring is such that the MRP of the last worker exceeds his or her MRC, the firm can profit by hiring more workers. But if the number being hired is such that the MRC of the last worker exceeds the MRP, the firm is hiring workers who are not "paying their way," and it can increase its profit by discharging some workers. You may have recognized that this **MRP = MRC rule** is similar to the MR = MC profit-maximizing rule employed throughout our discussion of price and output determination. The rationale of the two rules is the same, but the point of reference is now *inputs* of a resource, rather than *outputs* of a product.

## MRP as Resource Demand Schedule

In a purely competitive labour market, the wage rate is established by market supply and market demand. Because each firm hires such a small fraction of market supply, it cannot influence the market wage rate; it is a "wage taker" not a "wage maker." This means that for each additional unit of labour hired, total resource cost increases by exactly the same amount—the market wage rate. Or put another way, the MRC of labour exactly equals the constant market wage rate. Thus, resource "price" (the market wage rate) and resource "cost" (marginal resource cost) are equal for a firm hiring a resource in a competitive labour market. Then the MRP = MRC rule tells us that in pure competition, the firm will hire workers to the point at which the market *wage rate* (its MRC) is equal to its MRP.

In terms of the data in columns 1 and 6 in Table 15-1, if the market wage rate is, say, $13.95, the firm will hire only one worker. This is so because the first worker adds $14 to total revenue and slightly less—$13.95—to total cost. In other words, because MRP exceeds MRC for the first worker, it is profitable to hire that worker. For each successive worker, however, MRC (= $13.95) exceeds MRP (= $12 or less), indicating that it will not be profitable to hire any of those workers. If the wage rate is $11.95, by the same reasoning we discover that it will pay the firm to hire both the first and second workers. Similarly, if the wage rate is $9.95, three will be hired. If $7.95, four. If $5.95, five. And so forth. Hence *the MRP schedule constitutes the firm's demand for labour, because each point on this schedule (or curve) indicates the number of workers the firm would hire at each possible wage rate.* The $D$ = MRP curve for the data in Table 15-1 is shown in Figure 15-1.

The logic here should be familiar to you: In Chapter 10 we applied the price-equals-marginal-cost ($P$ = MC) rule for the profit-maximizing output to discover that the portion of the purely competitive firm's short-run marginal-cost curve lying above the AVC curve is the short-run *product supply* curve. Here, we are applying the MRP = MRC (= resource price) rule for the profit-maximizing input to discover that the purely competitive firm's MRP curve is its *resource demand* curve.

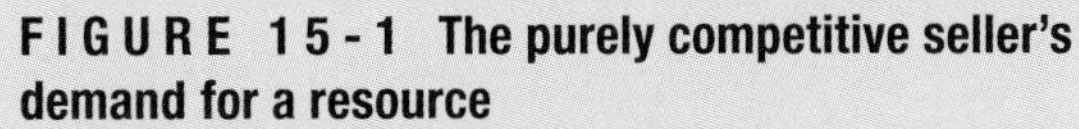

**FIGURE 15-1 The purely competitive seller's demand for a resource**

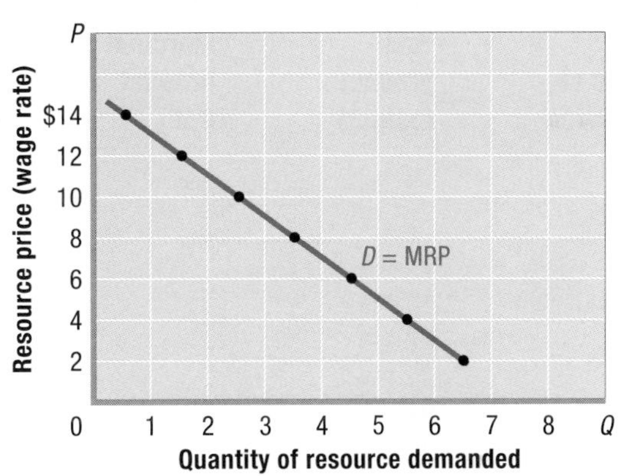


The MRP curve *is* the resource demand curve; each of its points relates a particular resource price (= MRP when profit is maximized) with a corresponding quantity of the resource demanded. Under pure competition, product price is constant; therefore, the downward slope of the $D$ = MRP curve is due solely to the decline in the resource's marginal product (law of diminishing marginal returns).

## Resource Demand Under Imperfect Product Market Competition

Our analysis of labour demand becomes more complex when the firm is selling its product in an imperfectly competitive market: one in which the firm is a "price maker." Pure monopoly, oligopoly, and monopolistic competition in the product market all mean that the firm's product demand curve is downsloping; the firm must lower its price to increase sales.

The productivity data in Table 15-1 are retained in columns 1 to 3 in Table 15-2. But here we show in column 4 that product price must be lowered to sell the marginal product of each successive worker. The MRP of the purely competitive seller of Table 15-1 falls for one reason: marginal product diminishes. But the MRP of the imperfectly competitive seller of Table 15-2 falls for two reasons: marginal product diminishes *and* product price falls as output increases.

We emphasize that the lower price accompanying each increase in output (total product) applies not only to the marginal product of each successive worker but also *to all prior output units that otherwise could have been sold at a higher price.* Note that the second worker's marginal product is

**TABLE 15-2 The demand for labour: imperfect competition in the sale of the product**

| (1) Units of resource | (2) Total product (output) | (3) Marginal product, (MP) | (4) Product price | (5) Total revenue, or (2) × (4) | (6) Marginal revenue product, (MRP) |
|---|---|---|---|---|---|
| 0 | 0 | | $2.80 | $ 0 | |
| 1 | 7 | 7 | 2.60 | 18.20 | $18.20 |
| 2 | 13 | 6 | 2.40 | 31.20 | 13.00 |
| 3 | 18 | 5 | 2.20 | 39.60 | 8.40 |
| 4 | 22 | 4 | 2.00 | 44.00 | 4.40 |
| 5 | 25 | 3 | 1.85 | 46.25 | 2.25 |
| 6 | 27 | 2 | 1.75 | 47.25 | 1.00 |
| 7 | 28 | 1 | 1.65 | 46.20 | −1.05 |

6 units. These 6 units can be sold for $2.40 each, or, as a group, for $14.40. But this is *not* the MRP of the second worker. To sell these 6 units, the firm must take a 20-cent price cut on the 7 units produced by the first worker—units that otherwise could have been sold for $2.60 each. Thus, the MRP of the second worker is only $13.00 [= $14.40 – (7 × 20 cents)], as shown.

Similarly, the third worker adds 5 units to total product, and these units are worth $2.20 each, or $11.00 total. But to sell these 5 units the firm must take a 20-cent price cut on the 13 units produced by the first two workers. So the third worker's MRP is only $8.40 [= $11.00 – (13 × 20 cents)]. The other figures in column 6 are derived similarly.

The result is that the MRP curve—the resource demand curve—of the imperfectly competitive producer is less elastic than that of the purely competitive producer. At a wage rate or MRC of $11.95, both the purely competitive and the imperfectly competitive seller will hire two workers. But at $9.95 the competitive firm will hire three, and the imperfectly competitive firm only two. And at $7.95 the purely competitive firm will employ four employees, and the imperfect competitor only three. This difference in resource demand elasticity can be seen by graphing the MRP data in Table 15-2 and comparing the graph with Figure 15-1, as is done in Figure 15-2.[1]

It is not surprising that the imperfectly competitive producer is less responsive to resource price cuts than the purely competitive producer. The imperfect competitor's relative reluctance to employ more resources, and produce more output, when resource prices fall reflects the imperfect competitor's tendency to restrict output in the

**FIGURE 15-2 The imperfectly competitive seller's demand curve for a resource**

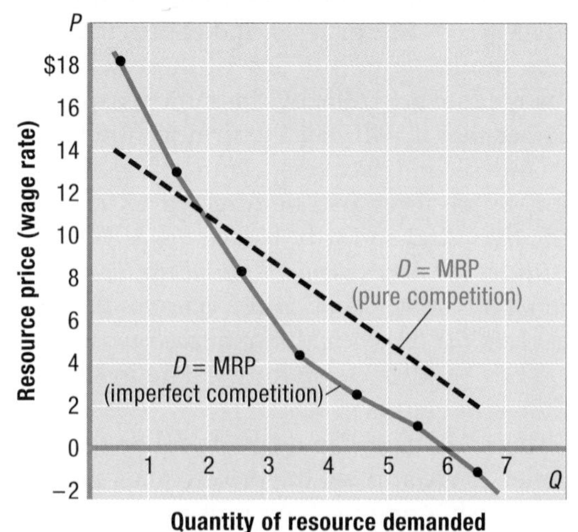


An imperfectly competitive seller's resource demand curve *D* (solid) slopes downward because *both* marginal product *and* product price fall as resource employment and output rise. This downward slope is greater than that for a purely competitive seller (dashed resource demand curve) because the pure competitor can sell the added output at a constant price.

[1] Note the points in Figures 15-1 and 15-2 are plotted halfway between succeeding numbers of resource units because MRP is associated with the *addition* of 1 *more* unit. Thus, in Figure 15-2, for example, the MRP of the second unit ($13.00) is plotted not at 1 or 2, but rather at 1 1/2. This "smoothing" allows us to sketch a continuously downsloping curve rather than one that moves downward in discrete steps as each new unit of labour is hired.

product market. Other things equal, the imperfectly competitive seller produces less of a product than a purely competitive seller. In producing this smaller output, it demands fewer resources.

But one important qualification exists. We noted in Chapter 12 that the market structure of oligopoly *might* lead to technological progress and greater production, more employment, and lower prices in the very long run than would a purely competitive market. The resource demand curve in these cases would lie farther to the right than it would if output were restricted due to monopoly power. ***(Key Question 2)***

## Market Demand for a Resource

We have now explained the individual firm's demand curve for a resource. Recall that the total, or market, demand curve for a *product* is found by summing horizontally the demand curves of all individual buyers in the market. The market demand curve for a particular *resource* is derived in essentially the same way—by summing the individual demand or MRP curves for all firms hiring that resource.

### 15-1
### QUICK REVIEW

- To maximize profit a firm will use a resource in an amount at which the resource's marginal revenue product equals its marginal resource cost (MRP = MRC).
- Application of the MRP = MRC rule to a firm's MRP curve demonstrates that the MRP curve is the firm's resource demand curve. In a purely competitive resource market, resource price (the wage rate) equals MRC.
- The resource demand curve of a purely competitive seller is downsloping solely because the marginal product of the resource diminishes; the resource demand curve of an imperfectly competitive seller is downsloping because marginal product diminishes and product price falls as output is increased.

# DETERMINANTS OF RESOURCE DEMAND

What will alter the demand for a resource, that is, shift the resource demand curve? The fact that resource demand is derived from *product demand* and depends on *resource productivity* suggests two "resource demand shifters." Also, our analysis of how changes in the prices of other products can shift a product's demand curve (Chapter 4) suggests another factor: changes in the prices of other *resources*.

## Changes in Product Demand

Other things equal, a change in the demand for a product will change the demand for the resource used to make the product. *More precisely, a change in the demand for a product that uses a particular resource will change the demand for the resource in the same direction.*

Let's see how this works. The first thing to recall is that a change in the demand for a product will change its price. In Table 15-1, let's assume an increase in product demand occurs that boosts product price from $2 to $3. You should calculate the new resource demand schedule (columns 1 and 6) that would result, and plot it in Figure 15-1 to verify that the new resource demand curve lies to the right of the old demand curve. Similarly, a decline in the product demand (and price) will shift the resource demand curve to the left. This effect—resource demand changing along with product demand—demonstrates that resource demand is derived from product demand.

## Productivity Changes

*Other things equal, a change in the productivity of a resource will change the demand for the resource in the same direction.* If we doubled the MP data of column 3 in Table 15-1, the MRP data of column 6 would also double, indicating an increase (rightward shift) in the resource demand curve.

The productivity of any resource can be altered in several ways:

1. **QUANTITIES OF OTHER RESOURCES** The marginal productivity of any resource will vary with the quantities of the other resources used with it. The greater the amount of capital and land resources used with, say, labour, the greater will be labour's marginal productivity and, thus, labour demand.
2. **TECHNOLOGICAL PROGRESS** Technological improvements that increase the *quality* of other resources, say, capital, have the same effect. The better the quality of capital, the greater the productivity of labour used with it.

Dockworkers employed with a specific amount of real capital in the form of unloading cranes are more productive than dockworkers with the same amount of real capital embodied in older conveyor-belt systems.

3. **QUALITY OF THE VARIABLE RESOURCE** Improvements in the quality of the variable resource itself, say, labour, will increase its marginal productivity and therefore its demand. In effect, there will be a new demand curve for a different, more skilled, kind of labour.

All these considerations help explain why the average level of (real) wages is higher in industrially advanced nations (Canada, Germany, Japan, France, and so forth) than in developing nations (India, Ethiopia, Angola, Cambodia, and so on). Workers in industrially advanced nations are generally healthier, more educated, and better trained than are workers in developing countries. Also, in most industries they work with a larger and more efficient stock of capital goods and more abundant natural resources. For all these reasons there is a strong demand for labour in these countries. On the supply side of the market, labour is *relatively* scarce compared with that in most developing nations. A strong demand and a relatively scarce supply of labour result in high wage rates in nations like Canada, Japan, and Germany.

## Changes in the Prices of Other Resources

Just as changes in the prices of other products will change the demand for a specific product, changes in the prices of other resources will change the demand for a specific resource. Also recall that the effect of a change in the price of product X on the demand for product Y depends on whether X and Y are substitute or complementary goods *in consumption*. Similarly, the effect of a change in the price of resource A on the demand for resource B depends on their substitutability or their complementarity *in production.*

**Substitute Resources** Suppose the technology in a certain production process is such that labour and capital are substitutable. A firm can produce some specific amount of output using a relatively small amount of labour and a relatively large amount of capital, or vice versa. Now assume the price of machinery (capital) falls. The effect on the demand for labour will be the net result of two opposed effects: the substitution effect and the output effect.

1. **SUBSTITUTION EFFECT** The decline in the price of machinery prompts the firm to substitute machinery for labour. This allows the firm to produce its output at lower cost. So, at the fixed wage rate, smaller quantities of labour are now employed. This **substitution effect** decreases the demand for labour. More generally, the substitution effect indicates that a firm will purchase more of an input whose relative price has declined and, conversely, use less of an input whose relative price has increased.
2. **OUTPUT EFFECT** Because the price of machinery has fallen, the costs of producing various outputs must also decline. With lower costs, the firm finds it profitable to produce and sell a greater output. The greater output increases the demand for all resources, including labour. So this **output effect** increases the demand for labour. More generally, the output effect means that the firm will purchase more of one particular input when the price of the other input falls and less of that particular input when the price of the other input rises.
3. **NET EFFECT** The substitution and output effects are both present when the price of an input changes, but they work in opposite directions. For a decline in the price of capital, the substitution effect decreases the demand for labour and the output effect increases it. The net change in labour demand depends on the relative sizes of the two effects. (This is analogous to a boat drifting on the ocean, being pushed in one direction by the tide and in the opposite direction by the wind. The actual course of the boat will depend on which of the two effects is strongest.)

In terms of resource demand, *if the substitution effect outweighs the output effect, a change in the price of a resource changes the demand for a substitute resource in the same direction. If the output effect exceeds the substitution effect, a change in the price of a resource changes the demand for a substitute resource in the opposite direction.*

**Complementary Resources** Recall from Chapter 4 that certain products, such as cameras and film or computers and software, are complementary goods; they "go together" and are jointly demanded. Resources may also be complementary; an increase in the quantity of one of them used in the production process requires an increase in the amount used of the other as well, and vice versa. Suppose a small manufacturer of metal products uses punch presses as its basic piece of capital equipment. Each press is designed to be operated by one worker; the machine is not automated—it will not run itself—and a second worker would have nothing to do.

Now assume that technological advance in the production of these presses substantially reduces their price. There can be no substitution effect because labour and capital must be used in *fixed proportions*, one person for one machine. Capital cannot be substituted for labour. But there *is* an output effect. Other things equal, the reduction in the price of capital goods means lower production costs. It will therefore be profitable to produce a larger output. In doing so, the firm will use both more capital and more labour. When labour and capital are complementary, a decline in the price of capital increases the demand for labour through the output effect. Conversely, when there is an increase in the price of capital, the output effect reduces the demand for labour. *A change in the price of a resource will cause the demand for a complementary resource to change in the opposite direction.*

We have cast our analysis of substitute resources and complementary resources mainly in terms of a decline in the price of capital. Table 15-3 summarizes the effects of an increase in the price of capital on the demand for labour. You should study this table carefully.

Now that we have discussed the full list of the determinants of labour demand, let's again review their effects. Stated in terms of the labour resource, the demand for labour will *increase* (the labour demand curve will shift *rightward*) when:

1. The demand for (and therefore the price of) the product produced by that labour *increases.*
2. The productivity (MP) of labour *increases.*
3. The price of a substitute input *decreases,* provided the output effect exceeds the substitution effect.
4. The price of a substitute input *increases,* provided the substitution effect exceeds the output effect.
5. The price of a complementary input *decreases.*

Be sure that you can "reverse" these effects to explain a *decrease* in labour demand.

## Real-World Applications

The determinants of labour demand have much significance, as seen by the following examples.

**Restaurant Workers** In the past decade, the demand for fast-food and other restaurant workers has increased significantly. One reason is that more and more women are working outside the home, causing families to substitute restaurant

**TABLE 15-3 The effect of an increase in the price of capital on the demand for labour, $D_L$**

| (1) RELATIONSHIP OF INPUTS | (2) INCREASE IN THE PRICE OF CAPITAL | | |
|---|---|---|---|
| | (a) Substitution effect | (b) Output effect | (c) Combined effect |
| Substitutes in production | Labour substituted for capital | Production costs up, output down, and less of both capital and labour used | $D_L$ increases if the substitution effect exceeds the output effect; $D_L$ decreases if the output effect exceeds the substitution effect |
| Complements in production | No substitution of labour for capital | Production costs up, output down, and less of both capital and labour used | $D_L$ decreases |

meals for home-prepared meals. Also, incomes have increased, and with this increase has come greater demand for restaurant meals. Both factors have resulted in increases in the derived demand for restaurant workers.

**Computer-Related Workers** In the last decade or so there has been a remarkable drop in the average price of personal computers and an equally impressive rise in the computing power of the typical personal computer. These developments have increased the demand for some kinds of labour and decreased it for other kinds.

Demand for software designers and computer-assembly workers has rocketed. So, too, has the demand for salesclerks in computer stores. But the effect on the demand for office workers has been mixed. In some offices, computers and labour (keyboard personnel) are complementary inputs. There, the decline in computer prices has reduced production costs, increased the number of computers purchased, and increased the demand for computer operators. In other offices the decline in computer prices has caused computers to be substituted for labour, reducing the demand for labour and allowing these offices to use fewer workers to produce their goods and services.

**Defence Personnel** The end of the Cold War, and the resulting reductions in Canadian defence spending, has reduced labour demand by the military and by firms supplying military equipment. An estimated 16,500 Canadian Forces jobs were lost between 1994 and 1998. Also, the demand for labour in industries producing military hardware has declined, reducing employment in defence-related industries.

**Part-Time Workers** One of the biggest labour market changes of recent years has been that many employers have reduced the size of their full-time "core" workforces and simultaneously increased their use of part-time workers. Why has the demand for part-time workers increased? First, increasingly expensive fringe benefits such as extra health insurance, pension plans, paid vacations, and sick leave are typically not provided for part-time workers, making their employment less costly. Second, part-time workers give firms more flexibility in responding to changing economic conditions. As product demand changes, firms can readily increase or decrease the sizes of their workforces by employing more or fewer part-time workers. This flexibility allows firms to compete more effectively, especially in international markets.

Table 15-4 provides additional illustrations of the determinants of labour demand.

**TABLE 15-4 Determinants of labour demand: factors that shift the labour demand curve**

1. *Changes in product demand*
   Examples: Gambling increases in popularity, increasing the demand for workers at casinos; consumers increase their demand for leather coats, increasing the demand for tanners.
2. *Productivity changes*
   Examples: An increase in the skill levels of glass blowers increases the demand for their services; computer-assisted graphic design increases the productivity of, and demand for, graphic artists.
3. *Changes in the prices of other resources*
   Examples: An increase in the price of electricity increases the cost of producing aluminum and reduces the demand for aluminum workers; the price of security equipment used by businesses to protect against illegal entry falls, decreasing the demand for night guards; the price of telephone switching equipment decreases, greatly reducing the cost of telephone service, which in turn increases the demand for telemarketers.

## ELASTICITY OF RESOURCE DEMAND

The demand changes we have just discussed are shifts in the location of a resource demand curve. These changes in demand must be distinguished from a change in the quantity of a resource demanded. The latter is not a shift of the demand curve. Rather, it is a movement from one point to another on a fixed resource demand curve because of a change in the price of the specific resource under consideration. Example: In Figure 15-1 we note that an increase in the wage rate from \$5 to \$7 will reduce the quantity of labour demanded from 5 to 4 units. This is a change in the quantity of labour demanded.

The sensitivity of producers to changes in resource prices is measured by the **elasticity of resource demand.** In coefficient form:

$$E_{rd} = \frac{\text{Percentage change in resource quantity}}{\text{Percentage change in resource price}}$$

When $E_{rd}$ is greater than 1, resource demand is elastic; when $E_{rd}$ is less than 1, resource demand is inelastic; and when $E_{rd}$ equals 1, resource demand is unit-elastic. What determines the elasticity of resource demand? There are several factors at work.

**Rate of MP Decline** A purely technical consideration is the rate at which the marginal product of the particular resource declines. If the marginal product of one resource declines slowly as it is added to a fixed amount of other resources, the demand (MRP) curve for that resource declines slowly and tends to be highly elastic. A small decline in the price of such a resource will yield a relatively large increase in the amount demanded. Conversely, if the marginal product of the resource declines sharply as more of it is added, the resource demand curve also declines rapidly. This means that a relatively large decline in the wage rate will be accompanied by a modest increase in the amount of labour hired; labour demand is inelastic.

**Ease of Resource Substitutability** The degree to which resources are substitutable is also a determinant of elasticity. *The larger the number of good substitute resources available, the greater the elasticity of demand for a particular resource.* If a furniture manufacturer finds that five or six different types of wood are equally satisfactory in making coffee tables, a rise in the price of any one type of wood may cause a sharp drop in the amount demanded as the producer substitutes other woods. At the other extreme, there may be no reasonable substitutes; bauxite is absolutely essential in the production of aluminum ingots. Thus, the demand for bauxite by aluminum producers is inelastic.

*Time* can play a role in the input substitution process. For example, a firm's truck drivers may obtain a substantial wage increase with little or no immediate decline in employment. But over time, as the firm's trucks wear out and are replaced, that wage increase may motivate the company to purchase larger trucks and in that way deliver the same total output with fewer drivers. As a second example, new commercial aircraft have been specifically designed to require only two cockpit personnel rather than the customary three, again indicating some substitutability between labour and capital if there is enough time.

**Elasticity of Product Demand** The elasticity of demand for any resource depends on the elasticity of demand for the product it helps produce. *The greater the elasticity of product demand, the greater the elasticity of resource demand.* The derived nature of resource demand leads us to expect this relationship. A small rise in the price of a product with great elasticity of demand will sharply reduce output, bringing about a relatively large decline in the amounts of various resources demanded. This means that the demand for the resource is elastic.

Remember that the resource demand curve of Figure 15-1 is more elastic than the resource demand curve shown in Figure 15-2. The difference arises because in Figure 15-1 we assume a perfectly elastic product demand curve, while Figure 15-2 is based on a downsloping or less than perfectly elastic product demand curve.

**Ratio of Resource Cost to Total Cost** *The larger the proportion of total production costs accounted for by a resource, the greater the elasticity of demand for that resource.* In the extreme, if labour cost is the only production cost, then a 20 percent increase in wage rates will shift all the firm's cost curves upward by 20 percent. If product demand is elastic, this substantial increase in costs will cause a relatively large decline in sales and a sharp decline in the amount of labour demanded. So labour demand is highly elastic. But if labour cost is only 50 percent of production cost, then a 20 percent increase in wage rates will increase costs by only 10 percent. With the same elasticity of product demand, this will cause a relatively small decline in sales and therefore in the amount of labour demanded. In this case the demand for labour is much less elastic. ***(Key Question 3)***

**15-2**

**QUICK REVIEW**

- A resource demand curve will shift because of changes in product demand, changes in the productivity of the resource, and changes in the prices of other inputs.
- If resources A and B are substitutable, a decline in the price of A will decrease the demand for B provided the substitution effect exceeds the output effect. But if the output effect exceeds the substitution effect, the demand for B will increase.
- If resources C and D are complements, a decline in the price of C will increase the demand for D.

- Elasticity of resource demand measures the extent to which producers change the quantity of a resource they hire when its price changes.
- The elasticity of resource demand will be less the more rapid the decline in marginal product, the smaller the number of substitutes, the smaller the elasticity of product demand, and the smaller the proportion of total cost accounted for by the resource.

## OPTIMAL COMBINATION OF RESOURCES

Thus far we have considered one variable input, usually labour. But in the long run firms can vary the amounts of all the resources they use. That's why we need to consider what combination of resources a firm will choose when *all* its inputs are variable. While our analysis is based on two resources, it can be extended to any number of inputs.

We will consider two interrelated questions:

1. What combination of resources will minimize costs at a specific level of output?
2. What combination of resources will maximize profit?

### The Least-Cost Rule

A firm is producing a specific output with the **least-cost combination of resources** *when the last dollar spent on each resource yields the same marginal product*. That is, the cost of any output is minimized when the ratios of marginal product to price of the last units of resources used are the same for each resource. In competitive resource markets, recall, marginal resource cost is the market resource price; the firm can hire as many or as few units of the resource as it wants at that price. Then, with just two resources, labour and capital, a competitive firm minimizes its total cost of a specific output when

$$\frac{\text{Marginal product of labour } (\text{MP}_L)}{\text{Price of labour } (P_L)} = \frac{\text{Marginal product of capital } (\text{MP}_C)}{\text{Price of capital } (P_C)} \quad (1)$$

Throughout, we will refer to the marginal products of labour and capital as $\text{MP}_L$ and $\text{MP}_C$, respectively. The price of labour will be symbolized by $P_L$ and the price of capital by $P_C$.

A concrete example shows why fulfilling the condition in equation (1) means least-cost production. Suppose the prices of capital and labour are both $1 per unit but capital and labour are currently employed in such amounts that the marginal product of labour is 10 and the marginal product of capital is 5. Our equation immediately tells us this is *not* the least costly combination of resources:

$$\frac{\text{MP}_L = 10}{P_L = \$1} > \frac{\text{MP}_C = 5}{P_C = \$1}$$

Suppose the firm spends $1 less on capital and shifts that dollar to labour. It loses 5 units of output produced by the last dollar's worth of capital, but it gains 10 units of output from the extra dollar's worth of labour. Net output increases by 5 (= 10 – 5) units for the same total cost. More such shifting of dollars from capital to labour will push the firm *down* along its MP curve for labour and *up* along its MP curve for capital, increasing output and moving the firm towards a position of equilibrium where equation (1) is fulfilled. At that equilibrium position, the MP per dollar for the last unit of both labour and capital might be, for example, 7. And the firm will be producing a greater output for the same (original) cost.

Whenever the same total resource cost can result in a greater total output, the cost per unit—and therefore the total cost of any specific level of output—can be reduced. Being able to produce a *larger* output with a *specific* total cost is the same as being able to produce a *specific* output with a *smaller* total cost. If the firm in our example buys $1 less of capital, its output will fall by 5 units. If it spends only $.50 of that dollar on labour, the firm will increase its output by a compensating 5 units (= $\frac{1}{2}$ of the MP per dollar). Then the firm will realize the same total output at a $.50 lower total cost.

The cost of producing any specific output can be reduced as long as equation (1) does not hold. But when dollars have been shifted among capital and labour to the point where equation (1) holds, no additional changes in the use of capital and labour will reduce costs further. The firm is now producing that output using the least-cost combination of capital and labour.

*All the long-run cost curves developed in Chapter 9 and used thereafter assume that the least-cost combi-*

*nation of inputs has been realized at each level of output.* Any firm that combines resources in violation of the least-cost rule would have a higher-than-necessary average total cost at each level of output. That is, it would incur *X-inefficiency*, as discussed in Figure 11-7.

The producer's least-cost rule is analogous to the consumer's utility-maximizing rule in Chapter 8. In achieving the utility-maximizing combination of goods, the consumer considers both his or her preferences as reflected in diminishing-marginal-utility data and the prices of the various products. Similarly, in achieving the cost-minimizing combination of resources, the producer considers both the marginal product data and the price (costs) of the various resources.

## The Profit-Maximizing Rule

Minimizing cost is not sufficient for maximizing profit. A firm can produce any level of output in the least costly way by applying equation (1). But there is only *one* unique level of output that maximizes profit. Our earlier analysis of product markets showed that this profit-maximizing output occurs where marginal revenue equals marginal cost (MR = MC). Near the beginning of this chapter, we determined that we could write this profit-maximizing condition as MRP = MRC as it relates to resource inputs.

In a purely competitive resource market the marginal resource cost (MRC) is exactly equal to the resource price $P$. Thus, for any competitive resource market, we have as our profit-maximizing equation

$$\text{MRP (resource)} = P \text{ (resource)}$$

This condition must hold for every variable resource, and in the long run all resources are variable. In competitive markets, a firm will therefore achieve its **profit-maximizing combination of resources** when each resource is employed to the point at which its marginal revenue product equals its price. For two resources, labour and capital, we need both

$$P_L = \text{MRP}_L \text{ and } P_C = \text{MRP}_C$$

We can combine these conditions by dividing both sides of each equation by their respective prices and equating the results to get

$$\frac{\text{MRP}_L}{P_L} = \frac{\text{MRP}_C}{P_C} = 1 \qquad (2)$$

Note in equation (2) that it is not sufficient that the MRPs of the two resources be proportionate to their prices; the MRPs must be equal to their prices and the ratios therefore equal to 1. For example, if $\text{MRP}_L = \$15$, $P_L = \$5$, $\text{MRP}_C = \$9$, and $P_C = \$3$, the firm is underemploying both capital and labour even though the ratios of MRP to resource price are identical for both resources. The firm can expand its profit by hiring additional amounts of both capital and labour until it moves down their downsloping MRP curves to the points at which $\text{MRP}_L = \$5$ and $\text{MRP}_C = \$3$. The ratios will then be 5/5 and 3/3 and equal to 1.

The profit-maximizing position in equation (2) includes the cost-minimizing condition of equation (1). That is, if a firm is maximizing profit according to equation (2), then it must be using the least-cost combination of inputs to do so. However, the converse is not true: a firm operating at least cost according to equation (1) may not be operating at the output that maximizes its profit.

## Numerical Illustration

A numerical illustration will help you understand the least-cost and profit-maximizing rules. In columns 2, 3, 2′, and 3′ in Table 15-5, we show the total products and marginal products for various amounts of labour and capital that are assumed to be the only inputs needed in producing some product, say, key chains. Both inputs are subject to diminishing returns.

We also assume that labour and capital are supplied in competitive resource markets at \$8 and \$12, respectively, and that key chains sell competitively at \$2 per unit. For both labour and capital we can determine the total revenue associated with each input level by multiplying total product by the \$2 product price. These data are shown in columns 4 and 4′. They allow us to calculate the marginal revenue product of each successive input of labour and capital as shown in columns 5 and 5′ respectively.

**Producing at Least Cost** What is the least-cost combination of labour and capital to use in producing, say, 50 units of output? The answer, which we can obtain by trial and error, is 3 units of labour and 2 units of capital. Columns 2 and 2′ indicate that this combination of labour and capital does,

**TABLE 15-5 Data for finding the least-cost and profit-maximizing combination of labour and capital***

| LABOUR (PRICE = $8) | | | | | CAPITAL (PRICE = $12) | | | | |
|---|---|---|---|---|---|---|---|---|---|
| (1) Quantity | (2) Total product (output) | (3) Marginal product | (4) Total revenue | (5) Marginal revenue product | (1′) Quantity | (2′) Total product (output) | (3′) Marginal product | (4′) Total revenue | (5′) Marginal revenue product |
| 0 | 0 | | $ 0 | | 0 | 0 | | $ 0 | |
| 1 | 12 | 12 | 24 | 24 | 1 | 13 | 13 | 26 | 26 |
| 2 | 22 | 10 | 44 | 20 | 2 | 22 | 9 | 44 | 18 |
| 3 | 28 | 6 | 56 | 12 | **3** | 28 | 6 | 56 | **12** |
| 4 | 33 | 5 | 66 | 10 | 4 | 32 | 4 | 64 | 8 |
| **5** | 37 | 4 | 74 | **8** | 5 | 35 | 3 | 70 | 6 |
| 6 | 40 | 3 | 80 | 6 | 6 | 37 | 2 | 74 | 4 |
| 7 | 42 | 2 | 84 | 4 | 7 | 38 | 1 | 76 | 2 |

*To simplify, it is assumed in this table that the productivity of each resource is independent of the quantity of the other. For example, the total and marginal product of labour is assumed not to vary with the quantity of capital employed.

indeed, result in the required 50 (= 28 + 22) units of output. Now, note from columns 3 and 3′ that hiring 3 units of labour gives us $MP_L/P_L = 6/8 = 3/4$ and hiring 2 units of capital gives us $MP_C/P_C = 9/12 = 3/4$, so equation (1) is fulfilled. How can we verify that costs are actually minimized? First, we see that the total cost of employing 3 units of labour and 2 of capital is $48 [= (3 × $8) + (2 × $12)].

Other combinations of labour and capital will also yield 50 units of output, but at a higher cost than $48. For example, 5 units of labour and 1 unit of capital will produce 50 (= 37 + 13) units, but total cost is higher, at $52 [= (5 × $8) + (1 × $12)]. This comes as no surprise because 5 units of labour and 1 unit of capital violate the least-cost rule—$MP_L/P_L = 4/8 > MP_C/P_C = 13/12$. Only that combination (3 units of labour and 2 units of capital) that minimizes total cost will satisfy equation (1). All other combinations capable of producing 50 units of output violate the cost-minimizing rule, and therefore cost more than $48.

**Maximizing Profit** Will 50 units of output maximize the firm's profit? No, because the profit-maximizing terms of equation (2) are not satisfied when the firm employs 3 units of labour and 2 of capital. To maximize profit, each input should be employed until its price equals its marginal revenue product. But for 3 units of labour, labour's MRP in column 5 is $12 while its price is only $8. This means the firm could increase its profit by hiring more labour. Similarly, for 2 units of capital, we see in column 5′ that capital's MRP is $18 and its price is only $12. This indicates that more capital should also be employed. By producing only 50 units of output (even though they are produced at least cost), labour and capital are being used in less-than-profit-maximizing amounts. The firm needs to expand its employment of labour and capital, thereby increasing its output.

Table 15-5 shows that the MRPs of labour and capital are equal to their prices, so that equation (2) is fulfilled, when the firm is employing 5 units of labour and 3 units of capital. This is therefore the profit-maximizing combination of inputs.[2] The firm's total cost will be $76, made up of $40 (= 4 × $8) of labour and $36 (= 3 × $12) of capital. Total revenue will be $130, found either by multiplying the total output of 65 (= 37 + 28) by the $2 product price or by summing the total revenues attributable to labour ($74) and to capital ($56). The difference between total revenue and total cost in this instance is $54 (= $130 – $76). You should experiment with other combinations of labour and capital to demonstrate that they yield an economic profit of less than $54.

Note that the profit-maximizing combination of 5 units of labour and 3 units of capital is also a

[2] Because we are dealing with discrete (nonfractional) units of the two outputs here, the use of 4 units of labour and 2 units of capital is equally profitable. The fifth unit of labour's MRP and its price (cost) are equal at $8, so that the fifth labour unit neither adds to nor subtracts from the firm's profit; similarly, the third unit of capital has no effect on profit.

least-cost combination for this particular level of output. Using these resource amounts satisfies the least-cost requirement of equation (1) in that $MP_L/P_L = 4/8 = 1/2$ and $MP_C/P_C = 6/12 = 1/2$. ***(Key Questions 4 and 5)***

## MARGINAL PRODUCTIVITY THEORY OF INCOME DISTRIBUTION

Our discussion of resource pricing is the cornerstone of the controversial view that fairness and economic justice are one of the outcomes of a competitive market economy. Table 15-5 tells us, in effect, that labour receives an income payment (wage) equal to the marginal contribution it makes to the firm's output and thus its revenue. Bluntly stated, labour is paid what it is economically worth. So, too, are the owners of the other resources. In this **marginal productivity theory of income distribution**, labour and other resources are paid according to their contributions to society's output. Therefore, if you are willing to accept the ethical proposition "To each according to what he or she creates," rewards based on marginal revenue product seem to provide a fair and equitable distribution of society's income.

This all sounds fair, but there are serious criticisms of this theory of income distribution:

1. **INEQUALITY** Critics argue that the distribution of income resulting from payment according to marginal productivity may be highly unequal because productive resources are very unequally distributed in the first place. Aside from their differences in genetic endowments, individuals encounter substantially different opportunities to enhance their productivity through education and training. Some people may not be able to participate in production at all because of mental or physical handicaps, and they would obtain *no* income under a system of distribution based solely on marginal productivity. Ownership of property resources is also highly unequal. Many landlords obtain their property by inheritance rather than through their own productive effort. Hence, income from inherited property resources conflicts with the "To each according to what he or she creates" idea. This reasoning calls for government policies that modify the income distributions made strictly according to marginal productivity.
2. **MARKET IMPERFECTIONS** The marginal productivity theory rests on the assumptions of competitive markets. Yet labour markets, for example, are riddled with imperfections, as you will see in Chapter 16. Some employers exert pricing power in hiring workers. And some workers, through labour unions, professional associations, and occupational licensing laws, wield monopoly power in selling their services. Even the process of collective bargaining over wages suggests a power struggle over the division of income. In this struggle market forces—and income shares based on marginal productivity—may get pushed into the background. In addition, discrimination in the labour market can distort earnings patterns. In short, because of real-world market imperfections, wage rates and other resource prices frequently are *not* based solely on contributions to output.

## The Last Word

### INPUT SUBSTITUTION: THE CASE OF ATMs

**Banks are using more automatic teller machines (ATMs) and employing fewer human tellers.**

FROM THIS CHAPTER YOU KNOW THAT A FIRM achieves its least-cost combination of inputs when the last dollar it spends on each input makes the same contribution to total output. This raises an interesting real-world question: What happens when technological advance makes available a new, highly productive capital good for which MP/P is greater than for other inputs, say a particular type of labour? The answer is that the least-cost mix of resources abruptly changes and the firm responds accordingly. If the new capital is a substitute for labour (rather than a complement), the firm replaces the particular type of labour with the new capital. *That is exactly what is happening in the banking industry, in which ATMs are replacing human bank tellers.*

ATMs made their debut about 25 years ago when Diebold, a U.S. firm, introduced the product. Today, Diebold and NCR (also a U.S. firm) dominate global sales, with the Japanese firm Fujitsu being a distant third. The number of ATMs and their usage have exploded, and currently there are more than 17,000 ATMs in Canada. Since 1992 alone, banks have added more than 150,000 *new* ATMs around the globe.

In 1985 there were only 2,400 ATMs across Canada. The growth of ATM transactions mirrors the explosive growth of the machines. In 1990 there were 239 million ATM transactions worth $100 million; by 1996 over 1 billion ATM transactions took place in Canada, worth over $300 billion.

ATMs are highly productive: A single machine can handle hundreds of transactions daily, thousands weekly, and millions over the course of several years. ATMs can handle not only cash withdrawals, they also accept deposits and facilitate switches of funds between various accounts. Although ATMs are expensive for banks to buy and install, they are available 24 hours a day, and their cost- per transaction is one-fourth the cost for human tellers. They rarely get "held up," and they do not quit their jobs (turnover among human tellers is nearly 50 percent per year). Moreover, ATMs are highly convenient; unlike human tellers, they are located not only at banks but also at busy street corners, workplaces, universities, and shopping malls. The same bank card that allows you to withdraw cash from your local ATM also allows you to withdraw pounds from an ATM in London, England, yen from an ATM in Tokyo, and even rubles from an ATM in Moscow. (All this, of course, assumes that you have money in your chequing account.)

In the terminology of this chapter, the more productive, lower priced ATMs have reduced the demand for a substitute in production—human tellers. Between 1990 and 1995, almost 3,000 human tellers lost their jobs, and half the remaining tellers could lose their jobs by the end of the next decade. Where will they go? Most will eventually move to other occupations. Although the lives of individual tellers are disrupted, society clearly wins. Society gets cheaper, more convenient banking services *and* more of the other goods that these "freed-up" labour resources help produce. ■

*Source:* Based partly on Ben Craig, "Where Have All the Tellers Gone?" *Economic Commentary* (Federal Reserve Bank of Cleveland), Apr. 15, 1997; and statistics provided by the Canadian Bankers Association.

## CHAPTER SUMMARY

1. Resource prices are a determinant of money incomes, and they simultaneously ration resources to various industries and firms.
2. The demand for any resource is derived from the product it helps produce. That means the demand for a resource will depend on its productivity and the market value (price) of the good it is producing.
3. Marginal revenue product is the extra revenue a firm obtains when it employs 1 more unit of a resource. The marginal revenue product curve for any resource is the demand curve for that resource. This follows because the firm equates resource price and MRP in determining its profit-maximizing level of resource employment. Thus each point on the MRP curve indicates how many resource units the firm will hire at a specific resource price.
4. The firm's demand curve for a resource slopes downward because the marginal product of additional units declines in accordance with the law of diminishing returns. When a firm is selling in an imperfectly competitive market, the resource demand curve falls for a second reason: Product price must be reduced for the firm to sell a larger output. The market demand curve for a resource can be derived by summing horizontally the demand curves of all firms hiring that resource.

5. The demand curve for a resource will shift as the result of **a** a change in the demand for, and therefore the price of, the product the resource is producing; **b** changes in the productivity of the resource; and **c** changes in the prices of other resources.

6. If resources A and B are substitutable for each other, a decline in the price of A will decrease the demand for B provided the substitution effect is greater than the output effect. But if the output effect exceeds the substitution effect, a decline in the price of A will increase the demand for B.

7. If resources C and D are complementary or jointly demanded, there is only an output effect; a change in the price of C will change the demand for D in the opposite direction.

8. The elasticity of demand for a resource measures the responsiveness of producers to a change in the resource's price. The coefficient of the elasticity of resource demand is

$$E_{rd} = \frac{\text{Percentage change in resource quantity}}{\text{Percentage change in resource price}}$$

When $E_{rd}$ is greater than 1, resource demand is elastic; when $E_{rd}$ is less than 1, resource demand is inelastic; and when $E_{rd}$ equals 1, resource demand is unit-elastic.

9. The elasticity of demand for a resource will be greater **a** the more slowly the marginal product of the resource declines, **b** the larger the number of good substitute resources available, **c** the greater the elasticity of demand for the product, and **d** the larger the proportion of total production costs attributable to the resource.

10. Any specific level of output will be produced with the least costly combination of variable resources when the marginal product per dollar's worth of each input is the same, that is, when

$$\frac{\text{MP of labour}}{\text{Price of labour}} = \frac{\text{MP of capital}}{\text{Price of capital}}$$

11. A firm is employing the profit-maximizing combination of resources when each resource is used to the point where its marginal revenue product equals its price. In terms of labour and capital, this occurs when the MRP of labour equals the price of labour and the MRP of capital equals the price of capital, that is, when

$$\frac{\text{MRP of labour}}{\text{Price of labour}} = \frac{\text{MRP of capital}}{\text{Price of capital}} = 1$$

12. The marginal productivity theory of income distribution holds that all resources are paid what they are economically worth: their marginal contribution to output. Critics assert that such an income distribution is too unequal and that real-world market imperfections result in pay above and below marginal contributions to output.

## TERMS AND CONCEPTS

derived demand
marginal product
marginal revenue product
marginal resource cost
MRP = MRC rule
substitution effect
output effect
elasticity of resource demand
least-cost combination of resources
profit-maximizing combination of resources
marginal productivity theory of income distribution

## STUDY QUESTIONS

1. What is the significance of resource pricing? Explain how the factors determining resource demand differ from those underlying product demand. Explain the meaning and significance of the fact that the demand for a resource is a *derived* demand. Why do resource demand curves slope downward?

2. KEY QUESTION *Complete the following labour demand table for a firm that is hiring labour competitively and selling its product in a competitive market.*

| Units of labour | Total product | Marginal product | Product price | Total revenue | Marginal revenue product |
|---|---|---|---|---|---|
| 0 | 0 | | $2 | $____ | |
| | | ____ | | | $____ |
| 1 | 17 | | 2 | ____ | |
| | | ____ | | | ____ |
| 2 | 31 | | 2 | ____ | |
| | | ____ | | | ____ |
| 3 | 43 | | 2 | ____ | |
| | | ____ | | | ____ |
| 4 | 53 | | 2 | ____ | |
| | | ____ | | | ____ |
| 5 | 60 | | 2 | ____ | |
| | | ____ | | | ____ |
| 6 | 65 | | 2 | ____ | |

**a.** *How many workers will the firm hire if the market wage rate is $27.95? $19.95? Explain why the firm will not hire a larger or smaller number of units of labour at each of these wage rates.*

**b.** *Show in schedule form and graphically the labour demand curve of this firm.*

**c.** *Now redetermine the firm's demand curve for labour, assuming that it is selling in an imperfectly competitive market and that, although it can sell 17 units at $2.20 per unit, it must lower product price by 5 cents to sell the marginal product of each successive labour unit. Compare this demand curve with that derived in question 2b. Which curve is more elastic? Explain.*

3. KEY QUESTION *What factors determine the elasticity of resource demand? What effect will each of the following have on the elasticity or the location of the demand for resource C, which is being used to produce commodity X? Where there is any uncertainty as to the outcome, specify the causes of that uncertainty.*

**a.** *An increase in the demand for product X.*

**b.** *An increase in the price of substitute resource D.*

**c.** *An increase in the number of resources substitutable for C in producing X.*

**d.** *A technological improvement in the capital equipment with which resource C is combined.*

**e.** *A decline in the price of complementary resource E.*

**f.** *A decline in the elasticity of demand for product X due to a decline in the competitiveness of the product market.*

4. KEY QUESTION *Suppose the productivity of capital and labour are as shown below. The output of these resources sells in a purely competitive market for $1 per unit. Both capital and labour are hired under purely competitive conditions at $3 and $1, respectively.*

| Units of capital | MP of capital | Units of labour | MP of labour |
|---|---|---|---|
| 0 | | 0 | |
| | 24 | | 11 |
| 1 | | 1 | |
| | 21 | | 9 |
| 2 | | 2 | |
| | 18 | | 8 |
| 3 | | 3 | |
| | 15 | | 7 |
| 4 | | 4 | |
| | 9 | | 6 |
| 5 | | 5 | |
| | 6 | | 4 |
| 6 | | 6 | |
| | 3 | | 1 |
| 7 | | 7 | |
| | 1 | | $\frac{1}{2}$ |
| 8 | | 8 | |

**a.** *What is the least-cost combination of labour and capital the firm should employ in producing 80 units of output? Explain.*

**b.** *What is the profit-maximizing combination of labour/capital the firm should use? Explain. What is the resulting level of output? What is the economic profit?*

**c.** *When the firm employs the profit-maximizing combination of labour and capital determined in 5b, is this combination also the least costly way of producing the profit-maximizing output? Explain.*

5. KEY QUESTION *In each of the following four cases $MRP_L$ and $MRP_C$ refer to the marginal revenue products of labour and capital, respectively, and $P_L$ and $P_C$ refer to their prices. Indicate in each case whether the conditions are consistent with maximum profits for the firm. If not, state which resource(s) should be used in larger amounts and which resource(s) should be used in smaller amounts.*
   **a.** $MRP_L = \$8$; $P_L = \$4$; $MRP_C = \$8$; $P_C = \$4$
   **b.** $MRP_L = \$10$; $P_L = \$12$; $MRP_C = \$14$; $P_C = \$9$
   **c.** $MRP_L = \$6$; $P_L = \$6$; $MRP_C = \$12$; $P_C = \$12$
   **d.** $MRP_L = \$22$; $P_L = \$26$; $MRP_C = \$16$; $P_C = \$19$

6. **(The Last Word)** Explain the economics of the substitution of ATMs for human tellers. Some banks are beginning to assess transaction fees when customers use human tellers rather than ATMs. What are these banks trying to accomplish?

7. WEB-BASED QUESTION **Textile Workers and Computer Workers—Sunrise or Sunset Occupations?** The demand for resources is a derived demand, derived from the products or services that resources help produce. Search the U.S. Bureau of Labor Statistics stats.bls.gov/search/search.asp using the keyword "textiles" for the current Occupational Outlook for textile, apparel, and furnishings occupations. Next, search using "computer" for the Occupational Outlook for computer scientists and systems analysts and for computer and peripheral equipment operators. What is the job outlook for the three occupations? Why do they differ? Do both computer occupations have the same job outlook? Do you expect the results to be similar in Canada?

16

CHAPTER

# Wage Determination and Discrimination

THE MOST IMPORTANT PRICE YOU WILL ENCOUNTER in your lifetime will likely be your hourly wage rate. Together with your annual hours of work, this price will be critical in determining your economic well-being. The following facts and questions may therefore be of interest to you:

- Fact: Real wages have increased historically in Canada but have stagnated during the past two decades. *Question:* What forces account for these trends?
- Fact: More than 13 million of us go to work each day in Canada. We work at an amazing variety of jobs, for thousands of different firms. *Question:* How do employers determine what wage to pay and how many workers to employ?
- Fact: Union workers generally receive higher wages than nonunion workers in the same occupation. *Question:* How do unions obtain this wage advantage?
- Fact: The average salary for major league baseball players in 1997 was over $1 million compared with about $45,000 for teachers. *Question:* What causes differences in wages and earnings?
- Fact: Most people are paid a certain hourly wage rate or an annual salary. But others are paid by the number of units of output produced or receive commissions and royalties. *Question:* What is the rationale for such varied compensation schemes?

**IN THIS CHAPTER YOU WILL LEARN:**

That wages are determined by demand and supply forces.

•

About the effects of monopoly power on the demand and supply of labour.

•

The pros and cons of a minimum wage.

•

The effect of unions on the wage rate.

•

The effects of labour market discrimination.

Having explored the major factors underlying resource demand, we now bring resource supply into our analysis. The supply of labour, land, capital, and entrepreneurial ability—interacting with the demand for these resources—explains how wages, rents, interest, and profits are determined. We discuss wages first because of their importance as a basic source of income for most households: nearly three-fourths of the domestic income arises as wages and salaries.

More specifically, our first goal is to understand how the general level of wage rates comes about in Canada. Then we develop several models that help explain how wage rates are determined in particular labour markets. Next, we look at the effects of unions on wages and discuss the economic impacts of the minimum-wage law. Finally, we examine the reasons for the great differences in wages among different jobs, and then we explore some compensation schemes that link pay to worker performance.

## The Big Picture

CHAPTER 15 LOOKED AT THE THEORY OF resource demand; resources include land, labour, capital, and entrepreneurial talent. This chapter focuses specifically on the demand and supply for labour and how wages are determined. If the labour market is competitive, then equilibrium wages in each market are the result of many buyers and sellers of labour services. But if there are impediments to supply and demand forces in the labour market, wages will diverge from their competitive rates.

As you read this chapter, keep the following points in mind:

- **Key Concept 3** is discussed.
- In a competitive market, the amount of labour employed and the wage rate are determined by supply and demand conditions.
- There are often impediments to competitive market forces in labour markets, among them, unions and market power of buyers of labour services.
- There are also other labour market imperfections that help explain wage differences paid on identical jobs. ■

## LABOUR, WAGES, AND EARNINGS

Economists use the term "labour" broadly to apply to (1) workers in the popular sense of the term, that is, blue- and white-collar workers of all varieties; (2) professional people such as lawyers, physicians, dentists, and teachers; and (3) owners of small businesses, including barbers, plumbers, television repairers, and a host of retailers, who provide labour in operating their own businesses.

*Wages*, and *wage rates*, are the price paid for labour. Wages may take the form of weekly or monthly salaries, bonuses, royalties, or commissions, but unless otherwise noted, we will use "wage" to mean the wage rate per unit of time—per hour, per day, and so forth. This will remind us that a wage rate is a price paid per unit of labour services. It will also let us distinguish between the *wage rate* and labour *earnings*, the latter being determined by multiplying the number of hours worked per week, per month, or per year by the hourly wage or wage rate.

We will also distinguish between nominal wages and real wages. A **nominal wage** is the amount of *money* received per hour, per day, and so on. A **real wage** is the quantity of goods and services a person can get with nominal wages; real wages are the "purchasing power" of nominal wages.

Your real wage depends on your nominal wage and the prices of the goods and services you purchase. Suppose you receive an 8 percent increase in your nominal wage during a certain year but in that same year the price level increases by 5 percent. Then your real wage has increased by only 3 percent (= 8 percent *minus* 5 percent). Unless otherwise indicated, we will assume that the level of product prices is constant so that our discussions involve only real wages.

## GENERAL LEVEL OF WAGES

Wages differ among nations, regions, occupations, and individuals. Wage rates are much higher in Canada than in China or India. They are higher in western Canada than in eastern Canada. Plumbers are paid less than NHL hockey players. And physician Adam may earn twice as much as physician Bennett for the same number of hours of work. Wage rates also differ by gender, race, and ethnic background.

The general level of wages, like the general level of prices, is a composite concept that includes a wide range of different wage rates. It includes the wages of bakers, barbers, baseball players, and brain surgeons, but it is not the wage of any real person. Nevertheless, such an average wage is useful for comparing international and interregional wages.

International wage comparisons are admittedly complex because wages are paid in different currencies and productivity varies from country to country. But data such as those in Global Perspective 16-1 suggest that the general level of real wages in Canada is relatively high—although not the highest globally.

The simplest explanation for high real wages in Canada and other industrially advanced economies (referred to hereafter as *advanced economies*) is that the demand for labour in these nations is quite large relative to the supply of labour.

## Role of Productivity

We know that the demand for labour—or for any other resource—depends on productivity. In general, the greater the productivity of labour, the greater the demand for it. And if the total supply of labour is fixed, then the stronger the labour demand, the higher the average level of real wages. The demand for labour in Canada and the other major advanced economies has been strong because it is highly productive. There are several reasons for this high productivity:

1. **PLENTIFUL CAPITAL** Workers in the advanced economies have access to large amounts of capital equipment in the production process. The total physical capital (machinery and buildings) available per worker in Canada is one of the highest in the world.
2. **ACCESS TO ABUNDANT NATURAL RESOURCES** In advanced economies, natural resources tend to be abundant in relation to the size of the labour force. These resources either are available domestically or are imported from abroad. Canada, for example, is richly endowed with arable land, mineral resources, and sources of energy for industry. The fact that Canadian workers have large amounts of high-quality natural resources to work with is perhaps most evident in agriculture, where, historically, the growth of productivity has been highly impressive.
3. **ADVANCED TECHNOLOGY** The level of technological progress is generally high in advanced economies. Workers in these economies not only use *more* capital equipment but also use *technologically superior* equipment, compared with the vast majority of workers worldwide. Similarly, work methods in the advanced economies are steadily being improved through scientific study and research.

### 16-1 GLOBAL PERSPECTIVE

**Hourly wages of production workers, selected nations**

Wage differentials are pronounced worldwide. The data shown here indicate that hourly compensation in Canada is not as high as in a number of European nations. It is important to note, however, that the prices of goods and services vary greatly among nations, and the process of converting foreign wages into dollars does not fully reflect these differences.

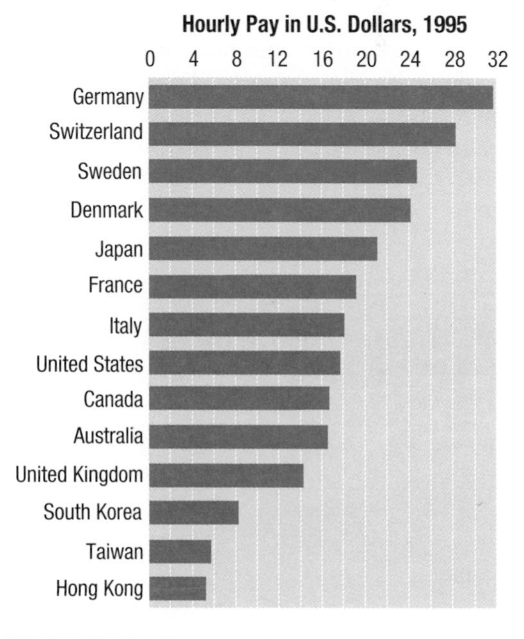


*Source:* U.S. Bureau of Labor Statistics, 1997.

4. **LABOUR QUALITY** The health, vigour, education, and training of workers in advanced economies are generally superior to those in developing nations. This means that, even with the same quantity and quality of natural and capital resources, workers in advanced economies tend to be more efficient than many of their foreign counterparts.
5. **INTANGIBLE FACTORS** Less tangible factors also may underlie the high productivity in some of the advanced economies. In Canada, for example, such factors include (a) the efficiency and flexibility of Canadian management; (b) a business, social, and political envi-

ronment that emphasizes production and productivity; and (c) the vast size of the North American market, which provides the opportunity for firms to realize mass-production economies.

## Real Wages and Productivity

The dependence of real hourly wages on the productivity level is implied by Figure 16-1, which shows the close long-run relationship between output per labour-hour and real hourly wages in Canada. Because real income and real output are two ways of viewing the same thing, *real income (earnings) per worker can increase only at about the same rate as output per worker*. When workers produce more real output per hour, more real income is available to distribute to them for each hour worked. The simplest example is Robinson Crusoe alone on an island: The number of coconuts he can pick per hour *is exactly* his real wage per hour. Then, too, Crusoe is his own entrepreneur. Since no one supplies him with property resources (land, capital), he receives as "income" *all* the coconuts he picks in an hour.

In the real world, however, suppliers of land, capital, and entrepreneurial talent also share in the income from production. Real wages therefore need not rise in lockstep with productivity increases over short spans of time. Nevertheless, our generalization holds true: Over very long periods, productivity and real wages travel similar upward paths.

**FIGURE 16-1 Output per hour and real average hourly earnings, all business-sector industries**

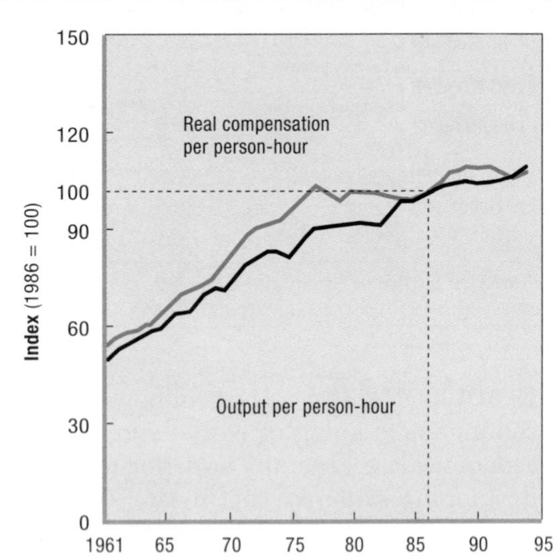


Over a long period of years there has been a close relationship between output per worker-hour and real hourly earnings.

Source: *Statistics Canada, Aggregate Productivity Measures*, 1994 Table 1. Adapted from "System of National Accounts: Aggregate Productivity Measures," Catalogue No. 15-204, 1993, Table 1.

## Secular Growth of Real Wages

Basic supply and demand analysis helps explain the long-term trend of real wage growth in Canada. The Canadian labour force has grown significantly over the decades, increasing the supply of labour. But, as a result of the productivity-increasing factors discussed previously, labour demand has increased *more rapidly* than labour supply. Several such increases in labour supply and labour demand are shown in Figure 16-2. The result has been a long-run, or *secular*, increase in wage rates and employment.

## Recent Stagnation of Real Wage Growth

Figure 16-2 might mislead you to think that real wages rise at a continuous, steady rate. But hourly

**FIGURE 16-2 The secular trend of real wages in Canada**

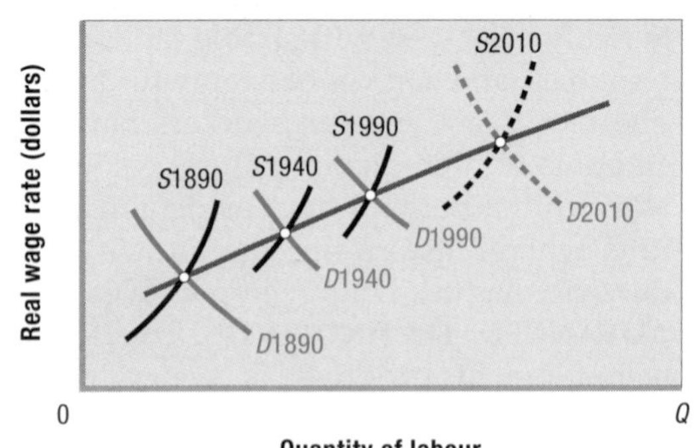


The productivity of Canadian labour has increased substantially in the long run, causing the demand for labour *D* to shift rightward (increase) more rapidly than increases in the supply of labour *S*. The result has been increases in real wages.

wages rise more rapidly in some periods than in others. Of particular importance, real hourly wages in Canada have been relatively stagnant in the 1980s and 1990s. Why so?

**Slower Productivity Growth** The first reason for the recent stagnation of real wage growth is that productivity has grown less rapidly in the past two decades than previously. This productivity slowdown is thought to have resulted from a combination of these factors:

1. A diminished rate of capital accumulation
2. An overburdened infrastructure—that is, an inadequate expansion of highways, bridges, transit systems, school systems, and airports to keep pace with population growth
3. The rapid expansion of employment and output in service industries, where productivity gains tend to be slow
4. The deterioration of labour-force skills due to a declining quality of education
5. A surge in the size of the work force, associated with large numbers of "baby boomers," immigrants, and married women
6. Management strategies that stress short-term profitability at the expense of R&D and to the detriment of innovative labour-relations programs that might increase productivity

**Downward Wage Pressure** But there is more to the recent stagnation of real wage growth than slower productivity growth. Economists do not fully understand the reasons, but the following two factors may be at work.

**GLOBALIZATION OF PRODUCTION** Today, much production can be transferred from high-wage advanced economies to developing countries where workers are paid less. As it relates to Canada, this possibility has the effect of expanding greatly the supply of less skilled workers available to Canadian firms. This increased labour supply pulls down the real wages of less skilled Canadian workers, who in essence compete for jobs with workers in lower-wage nations. If Canadian workers do not compete, they may lose their jobs when production is relocated to those nations. In fact, the real wages of less skilled Canadian workers have declined in the past two decades.

**STATISTICAL ILLUSION?** Many economists claim that much of the alleged stagnation of real wages is a "statistical illusion." Average hourly earnings include only wage and salary compensation, not fringe benefits or contributions for social insurance. Because these fringe benefits have been increasing faster than wages and salaries, average hourly earnings understate compensation growth.

Also, critics say that current measures of inflation used in Canada overstate by about 1 percentage point per year the actual rises in prices faced by workers in the past two decades. (This overstatement arises for several technical reasons: shifts in spending away from products whose prices have risen; failure to account for rapid price declines on new products; quality improvements not reflected in prices; and expansion of discount pricing and shopping.) If overstatement of inflation has occurred, then nominal wage increases have been overly adjusted downward in calculating real wage increases.

## A PURELY COMPETITIVE LABOUR MARKET

We now turn from the general level of wages to specific wage rates. What determines the wage rate paid for some specific type of labour? Demand and supply analysis again is revealing. Let's begin by examining labour demand and labour supply in a **purely competitive labour market**. In this type of market:

1. Many firms compete with one another in hiring a specific type of labour.
2. Numerous qualified workers with identical skills independently supply this type of labour.
3. "Wage-taker" behaviour pertains to both individual firms and individual workers; neither can exert any control over the market wage rate.

### Market Demand for Labour

Suppose many—say, 200—firms demand a particular type of semiskilled or skilled labour. These firms need not be in the same industry; industries are defined in terms of the products they produce and not the resources they employ. Thus, firms producing wood-frame furniture, wood windows and doors, and wood cabinets will all demand carpenters. The total, or market, labour demand curve for the labour service in question is found by summing horizontally the labour demand curves (the marginal-revenue product curves) of the individual firms, as suggested in ***Figure 16-3 (Key Graph)***. The horizontal summing of the 200 labour demand curves like *d* in Figure 16-3a yields the market labour demand curve *D* in Figure 16-3b.

## Market Supply of Labour

On the supply side of the labour market, we assume there is no union; workers compete individually for available jobs. The supply curve for each type of labour slopes upward, indicating that employers as a group must pay higher wage rates to obtain more workers. This is so because firms must bid these workers away from other industries, occupations, and localities. Within limits, workers have alternative job opportunities; that is, they may work in other industries in the same locality, or they may work in their current occupations in different cities or provinces, or they may work in other occupations. Firms wanting to hire these workers must pay higher wage rates to attract more of them away from the alternative job opportunities. Similarly, higher wages are necessary to induce individuals who are not currently in the labour force—those doing household activities or enjoying leisure—to seek employment. Assuming that wages are constant in other labour markets, higher wages in a particular labour market entice more workers to offer their labour services in that market. In Figure 16-3b, this fact is confirmed by the upsloping market supply of labour curve *S*.

## Labour Market Equilibrium

The equilibrium wage rate and level of employment for this type of labour are determined by the intersection of the market labour demand and supply curves. In Figure 16-3b the equilibrium wage rate is $W_c$ ($6), and the number of workers hired is $Q_c$ (1,000). To the individual firm the market wage rate $W_c$ is given. Each of the many firms employs such a small fraction of the total available supply of this type of labour that none can influence the wage rate. The supply of this labour is perfectly elastic to the individual firm, as shown by horizontal line *s* in Figure 16-3a.

Each individual firm will find it profitable to hire this type of labour up to the point at which marginal revenue product is equal to marginal resource cost. This is merely an application of the MRP = MRC rule developed in Chapter 15. (In fact, the demand curve in Figure 16-3a is based on Table 15-1.)

As Table 16-1 indicates, when a resource's price is given to the individual competitive firm, the marginal cost of that resource (MRC) is constant and equal to the resource price. In particular here, MRC *is constant and equal to the wage rate*. Each additional worker hired adds precisely his or her own wage rate ($6 in this case) to the firm's total resource cost. So the firm in a purely competitive labour market maximizes its profit by hiring workers to the point at which its wage rate equals MRP. In Figure 16-3a this "typical" firm will hire $q_c$ (5) workers, paying each of them the market wage rate $W_c$ ($6).

A firm's total revenue from employing a particular number of labour units can be found by summing their MRPs. For example, if a firm employs 3 labour units with marginal revenue products of $7, $6, and $5, respectively, then the firm's total revenue is $18 (= $7 + $6 + $5). In Figure 16-3a, where we are not restricted to whole units of labour, total revenue is represented by area $0abc$ under the MRP curve to the left of $q_c$. And what area represents the firm's total cost, including a normal profit? Answer: For $q_c$ units, the same area—$0abc$. The green rectangle represents the firm's total wage cost ($0q_c \times 0W_c$). The grey triangle (total revenue minus total wage cost) represents the firm's nonlabour costs—its payments to land, capital, and entrepreneurship. Thus, total cost (wages plus other income payments) equals total revenue. Again we are reminded that a purely

**TABLE 16-1 The supply of labour: pure competition in the hire of labour**

| (1) Units of labour | (2) Wage rate | (3) Total labour cost (wage bill) | (4) Marginal resource (labour) cost |
|---|---|---|---|
| 0 | $6 | $ 0 | |
| | | | $6 |
| 1 | 6 | 6 | |
| | | | 6 |
| 2 | 6 | 12 | |
| | | | 6 |
| 3 | 6 | 18 | |
| | | | 6 |
| 4 | 6 | 24 | |
| | | | 6 |
| 5 | 6 | 30 | |
| | | | 6 |
| 6 | 6 | 36 | |

## KEY GRAPH

**FIGURE 16-3 The supply of, and demand for, labour in (a) a single competitive firm and (b) a purely competitive labour market**

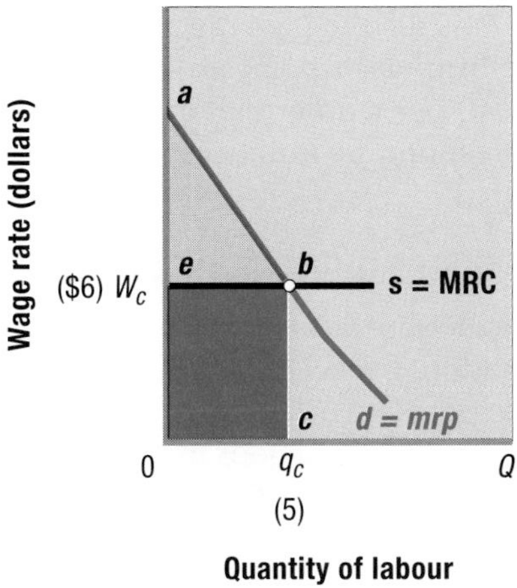


**(a) Individual firm**

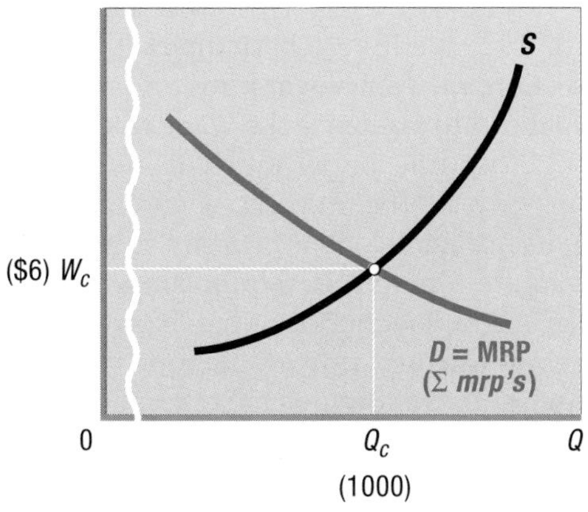


**(b) Market**

In a purely competitive labour market (b) the equilibrium wage rate $W_c$ and number of workers $Q_c$ are determined by labour supply *S* and labour demand *D*. Because this market wage rate is given to the individual firm (a) hiring in this market, its labour supply curve *s* = MRC is perfectly elastic. Its labour demand curve is its MRP curve (here labelled *mrp*). The firm maximizes its profit by hiring workers up to where MRP = MRC. Area 0*abc* represents both the firm's total revenue and its total cost. The green area is its total wage cost; the grey area is nonlabour costs—that is, its payments to the suppliers of land, capital, and entrepreneurship.

### 16-3

### QUICK QUIZ

1. The supply of labour curve *S* slopes upward in graph (b) because:
   - **(a)** the law of diminishing marginal utility applies.
   - **(b)** the law of diminishing returns applies.
   - **(c)** workers can afford to "buy" more leisure when their wage rates rise.
   - **(d)** higher wages are needed to attract workers away from other labour markets, household activities, and leisure.
2. This firm's labour demand curve *d* in graph (a) slopes downward because:
   - **(a)** the law of diminishing marginal utility applies.
   - **(b)** the law of diminishing returns applies.
   - **(c)** the firm must lower its price to sell additional units of its product.
   - **(d)** the firm is a competitive employer, not a monopsonist.
3. In employing five workers, the firm represented in graph (a):
   - **(a)** has a total wage cost of $6,000.
   - **(b)** is adhering to the general principle of undertaking all actions for which the marginal benefit exceeds the marginal cost.
   - **(c)** uses less labour than would be ideal from society's perspective.
   - **(d)** experiences increasing marginal returns.
4. A rightward shift of the labour supply curve in graph (b) would shift curve:
   - **(a)** *d* = *mrp* leftward in graph (a).
   - **(b)** *d* = *mrp* rightward in graph (a).
   - **(c)** *s* = *MRC* upward in graph (a).
   - **(d)** *s* = *MRC* downward in graph (a).

**Answers:** 1. (d); 2. (b); 3. (b); 4. (d)

competitive firm breaks even, earning only a normal profit. ***(Key Questions 3 and 4)***

## MONOPSONY MODEL

In the purely competitive labour market of the previous section, each employer hires too small an amount of labour to influence the wage rate. Each firm can hire as little or as much labour as it needs, but only at the market wage rate, as reflected in its horizontal labour supply curve. The situation is quite different in **monopsony**, a market in which an employer of resources has monopolistic buying (hiring) power. Labour market monopsony has the following characteristics:

1. There is only a single buyer of a particular kind of labour.
2. This type of labour is relatively immobile, either geographically or because workers would have to acquire new skills.
3. The firm is a "wage maker" in that the wage rate it must pay varies directly with the number of workers it employs.

In its pure form, the monopsonistic power of an employer is virtually complete because there is only one major employer in a labour market. For example, the economies of some towns and cities depend almost entirely on one major firm. A copper-mining company may be the basic source of employment in a remote British Columbia town. A textile mill in Quebec's Eastern Townships, a Gatineau paper mill, or a Newfoundland fish processor may provide a large proportion of the employment in the area.

In other cases *oligopsony* may prevail: three or four firms may each hire a large portion of the supply of labour in a particular market. Our study of oligopoly correctly suggests there is a stronger tendency for oligopsonists to act in concert—much like a single monopsonist—in hiring labour.

### Upsloping Labour Supply to Firm

When a firm hires most of the available supply of a particular type of labour, its decision to employ more or fewer workers affects the wage rate paid to that labour. Specifically, *if a firm is large in relation to the labour market, it will have to pay a higher wage rate to obtain more labour*. For simplicity, suppose there is only one employer of a particular type of labour in a certain geographic area. In this extreme case, the labour supply curve to that firm and the total supply curve for the labour market are identical. This supply curve is upsloping, indicating that the firm must pay a higher wage rate to attract more workers. The supply curve, *S* in Figure 16-4, is also the average-cost-of-labour curve for the firm; each point on it indicates the wage rate (cost) per worker that must be paid to attract the corresponding number of workers.

### MRC Higher than the Wage Rate

When a monopsonist pays a higher wage to attract an additional worker, it must pay that higher wage to all the workers it currently employs at a lower wage. If not, labour morale will deteriorate, and the employer will be plagued with labour unrest because of wage-rate differences existing for the same job. Paying a uniform wage to all workers means that the cost of an extra worker—the marginal resource (labour) cost (MRC)—is the sum of that worker's wage rate and the amount necessary to bring the wage rate of all current workers up to the new wage level.

Table 16-2 illustrates this point. One worker can be hired at a wage rate of $6. But hiring a sec-

**FIGURE 16-4 The wage rate and level of employment in a monopsonistic labour market**

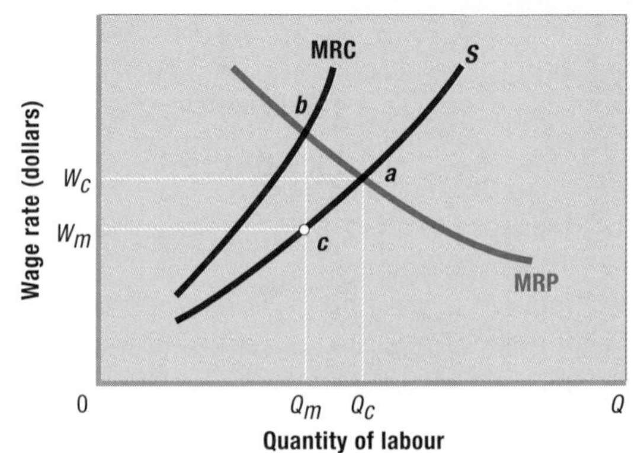


In a monopsonistic labour market the employer's marginal resource (labour) cost curve (MRC) lies above the labour supply curve *S*. Equating MRC with MRP at point *b*, the monopsonist will hire $Q_m$ workers (compared with $Q_c$ under competition) and pay wage rate $W_m$ (compared with the competitive wage $W_c$).

ond worker forces the firm to pay a higher wage rate of $7. The marginal resource (labour) cost of the second worker is $8—the $7 paid to the second worker plus a $1 raise for the first worker. From another viewpoint, total labour cost is now $14 (= 2 × $7), up from $6. So the MRC of the second worker is $8 (= $14 – $6)—not just the $7 wage rate paid to the second worker. Similarly, the marginal labour cost of the third worker is $10—the $8 that must be paid to attract this worker from alternative employment plus $1 raises—from $7 to $8—for the first two workers.

The important point is that *to the monopsonist, marginal resource (labour) cost exceeds the wage rate.* Graphically, the MRC curve lies above the average-cost-of-labour curve, or labour supply curve *S*, as is clearly shown in Figure 16-4.

**TABLE 16-2 The supply of labour: monopsony in the hire of labour**

| (1) Units of labour | (2) Wage rate | (3) Total labour cost (wage bill) | (4) Marginal resource (labour) cost |
|---|---|---|---|
| 0 | $ 5 | $ 0 | |
| | | | $ 6 |
| 1 | 6 | 6 | |
| | | | 8 |
| 2 | 7 | 14 | |
| | | | 10 |
| 3 | 8 | 24 | |
| | | | 12 |
| 4 | 9 | 36 | |
| | | | 14 |
| 5 | 10 | 50 | |
| | | | 16 |
| 6 | 11 | 66 | |

## Equilibrium Wage and Employment

How much labour will the monopsonist hire and what wage rate will it pay? To maximize profit, it will employ the quantity of labour $Q_m$ in Figure 16-4 because at that quantity MRC and MRP are equal (point b).[1] The monopsonist next determines how much it must pay to attract these $Q_m$ workers. From the supply curve *S*, specifically point *c*, it sees that it must pay wage rate $W_m$. Clearly, it need not pay a wage equal to MRP; it can attract exactly the number of workers it wants ($Q_m$) with wage rate $W_m$. That is what it will pay.

Contrast these results with those that a competitive labour market would yield. With competition in the hire of labour, the level of employment would be greater (at $Q_c$) and the wage rate would be higher (at $W_c$). *Other things equal, the monopsonist maximizes its profit by hiring a smaller number of workers and thereby paying a less-than-competitive wage rate.*[2] Society gets a smaller output, and workers get a wage rate that is less by *bc* than their marginal revenue product. Just as a monopolistic seller finds it profitable to restrict product output to realize an above-competitive price for its goods, so the monopsonistic employer of resources finds it profitable to restrict employment to depress wage rates and therefore costs, that is, to realize below-competitive wage rates.[3]

**Examples** Monopsonistic labour market outcomes are not common in the Canadian economy. There are typically many potential employers for most workers, particularly when these workers are occupationally and geographically mobile. Also, unions tend to counteract monopsony power in labour markets. Nevertheless, economists have found evidence of monopsony in such diverse labour markets as those for nurses, professional athletes, public school teachers, newspaper employees, and some building trades workers.

[1] The fact that MRC exceeds resource price when resources are hired or purchased under imperfectly competitive (monopsonistic) conditions calls for adjustments in Chapter 15's least-cost and profit-maximizing rules for hiring resources. [See equations (1) and (2) in the "Optimal Combination of Resources" section of Chapter 15.] Specifically, we must substitute MRC for resource price in the denominators of our two equations. That is, with imperfect competition in the hiring of both labour and capital, equation (1) becomes

$$\frac{MP_L}{MRC_L} = \frac{MP_C}{MRC_C} \qquad (1')$$

and equation (2) is restated as

$$\frac{MRP_L}{MRC_L} = \frac{MRP_C}{MRC_C} = 1 \qquad (2')$$

In fact, equations (1) and (2) can be regarded as special cases of (1′) and (2′) in which firms happen to be hiring under purely competitive conditions and resource price is therefore equal to, and can be substituted for, marginal resource cost.

[2] This is analogous to the monopolist's restricting output as it sets product price and output on the basis of marginal revenue, not product demand. In this instance, resource price is set on the basis of marginal labour (resource) cost, not resource supply.

[3] Will a monopsonistic employer also be a monopolistic seller in the product market? Perhaps, but not necessarily. The Eastern Township textile mill may be a monopsonistic employer yet face severe domestic and foreign competition in selling its product. In other cases—for example, the automobile and steel industries—firms have both monopsonistic and monopolistic (oligopolistic) power.

In the case of nurses the major employers in most locales are a relatively small number of hospitals. Further, the highly specialized skills of nurses are not readily transferable to other occupations. It has been found in accordance with the monopsony model that, other things equal, the smaller the number of hospitals in a town or city (that is, the greater the degree of monopsony), the lower the beginning salaries of nurses.

Although *potential* employers for professional athletes are quite numerous, those employers historically have used ingenious devices to limit competition in the hire of labour. The National Hockey League and the Canadian Football League have established rules that tie a player to one team and prevent him from selling his talents to the highest bidder on the open (competitive) market. In particular, through the new-player draft, the team that selects or "drafts" a player has the exclusive right to bargain a contract with that player. Further, the so-called reserve clause in each player's contract gives his team the exclusive right to purchase his services for the next season. Recently, new agreements that provide "free agency" to certain experienced players have made the labour markets for professional athletes more competitive, but collusive monopsony persists.

Empirical studies have shown that prior to 1976 baseball players (despite very high salaries) were paid substantially less than their estimated MRPs, which is, of course, consistent with Figure 16-4. However, since 1976, players have been allowed to become "free agents"—that is, to sell their services to any interested team—after their sixth season of play. A comparison of the salaries of current free agents with their estimated MRPs indicates that competition among teams for free agents has brought their salaries and MRPs into close accord, as our competitive model suggests. ***(Key Question 6)***

**16-1**

**QUICK REVIEW**

- Real wages have increased historically in Canada because labour demand has increased relative to labour supply.
- Over the long term, real wages per worker have increased at approximately the same rate as worker productivity.
- The competitive employer is a "wage taker" and employs workers at the point where the wage rate (= MRC) equals MRP.
- The labour supply curve to a monopsonist is upsloping, causing MRC to exceed the wage rate for each worker. Other things equal, the monopsonist, hiring where MRC = MRP, will employ fewer workers and pay a lower wage rate than would a purely competitive employer.

## THREE UNION MODELS

Thus far, we have assumed that workers compete with each other in selling their labour services. In some labour markets, though, workers sell their labour services collectively through unions. To view the economic impact of unions in the simplest context, let's first suppose a union is formed in an otherwise competitive labour market. That is, a union is now bargaining with a relatively large number of employers. It seeks many goals, the most important of which is to raise wage rates. This objective can be pursued in several ways.

### Demand-Enhancement Model

From the union's viewpoint, the most desirable technique for raising wage rates is to increase the demand for labour. As shown in Figure 16-5, an increase in the demand for labour will result in *both* higher wage rates and more jobs. The relative sizes of these increases will depend on the elasticity of labour supply.

A union might increase labour demand by altering one or more of the determinants of labour demand. Specifically, a union can attempt to increase the demand for the product or service it is producing, enhance labour productivity, or alter the prices of other inputs.

1. **INCREASE PRODUCT DEMAND** Unions may attempt to increase the demand for the products they help produce—and thus increase the derived demand for their own labour services—by advertising, political lobbying, or requiring redundant labour.

   Union television ads urging consumers to "buy the union label" are relevant. Historically, the International Ladies Garment Work-

**FIGURE 16-5 Unions and the demand for labour**

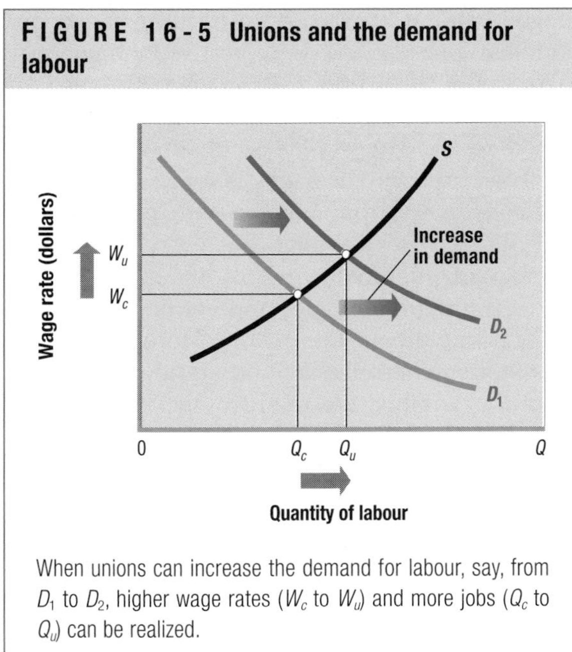


When unions can increase the demand for labour, say, from $D_1$ to $D_2$, higher wage rates ($W_c$ to $W_u$) and more jobs ($Q_c$ to $Q_u$) can be realized.

ers Union (ILGWU) has joined with its employers to finance advertising campaigns to bolster demand for products.

On the political front we see construction unions lobbying for new highway or urban renewal projects. Teachers' unions and associations push for increased public spending on education. And some unions have vigorously supported their employers in seeking protective tariffs or import quotas designed to exclude competing foreign products. Both the steelworkers and the automobile workers have sought such forms of protection. They recognize that a decline in the supply of imported cars through tariffs or negotiated international agreements will increase import prices, thus increasing the demand for highly substitutable North American-made autos. This will boost the derived demand for North American auto workers.

Some unions have sought to expand the demand for labour by forcing make-work, or "featherbedding," rules on employers. It took a Canada-wide strike in the 1950s before the railways were able to drop firemen from freight-yard diesels—firemen who had had no fire to tend since the days of the steam locomotives.

2. **INCREASE PRODUCTIVITY** Many decisions affecting labour productivity—for example, decisions concerning the quantity and quality of real capital used by workers—are made unilaterally by management. However, there is a growing interest in establishing joint labour-management committees designed to increase labour productivity.
3. **CHANGE PRICES OF OTHER INPUTS** Unions can enhance the demand for their labour by increasing the prices of substitute resources. For example, unions—whose workers are generally paid significantly more than the minimum wage—strongly support increases in the minimum wage. One alleged reason for this backing is that unions want to increase the price of substitutable low-wage, nonunion labour. A higher minimum wage for nonunion workers will deter employers from substituting them for union workers, bolstering the demand for union workers.

   Similarly, unions can increase the demand for their labour by supporting public actions that *reduce* the price of a complementary resource. Unions in industries using large amounts of energy might actively oppose rate increases proposed by electric or natural gas utilities. Where labour and energy are complementary, an energy price increase might reduce the demand for labour through Chapter 15's output effect.

   Unions recognize that their ability to influence the demand for labour is very limited. As many of our illustrations imply, unions frequently must try to *prevent declines* in labour demand rather than *cause increases.* Hence, it is not surprising that union efforts to increase wage rates have concentrated on the supply side of the labour market.

## Exclusive or Craft Union Model

Unions can boost wage rates by reducing the supply of labour. Historically, organized labour has favoured policies restricting the supply of labour to the Canadian economy as a whole to raise the general level of wages. Labour unions have in the past supported legislation that has (1) restricted immigration, (2) reduced child labour, (3) encouraged compulsory retirement, and (4) enforced a shorter workweek.

More relevant to our discussion, specific types of workers have adopted, through unions, techniques designed to restrict their numbers. This is especially true of *craft unions*—unions that are made up of workers of a specific skill, such as carpenters or bricklayers or plumbers. These unions have frequently forced employers to agree to hire only union workers, giving the union virtually complete control of the supply of labour. Then, by following restrictive membership policies—long apprenticeships, very high initiation fees, limits on new memberships—the unions have caused an artificial restriction of the labour supply. As indicated in Figure 16-6, this results in higher wage rates. This approach to achieving wage increases is called **exclusive unionism**. Higher wages result from excluding workers from the union and therefore from the supply of labour.

**Occupational licensing** is another means of restricting the supply of specific kinds of labour. Here a group of workers in an occupation will pressure provincial or municipal governments to pass a law that provides that, say, barbers (or physicians, plumbers, cosmetologists, egg graders, pest controllers) can practise their trade only if they meet certain specified requirements. These requirements might include level of education, amount of work experience, the passing of an examination, and personal characteristics ("the practitioner must be of good moral character"). The licensing board administering the law is typically dominated by members of the licensed occupation. The result is self-regulation that often leads to policies that serve only to restrict entry to the occupation.

The purpose of licensing is supposedly to protect consumers from incompetent practitioners, and this is a worthy goal. But by restricting the number of qualified workers, it also results in above-competitive wages and earnings for those in the occupation (Figure 16-6). Moreover, licensing requirements often include a residency requirement that inhibits the interprovincial movement of qualified workers. Some 200 occupations are now licensed in Canada.

**FIGURE 16-6 Exclusive or craft unionism**

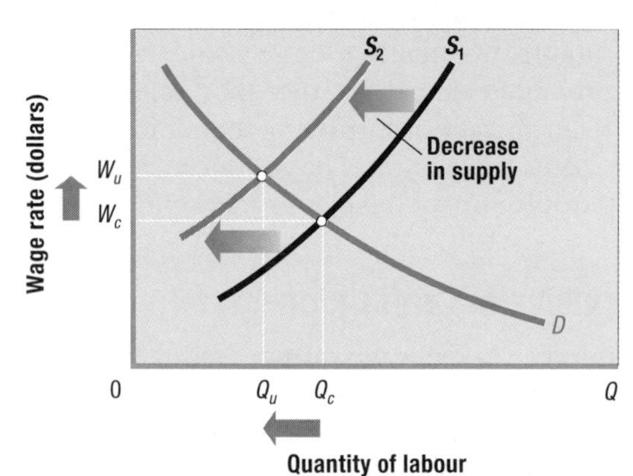


By reducing the supply of labour (say, from $S_1$ to $S_2$) through the use of restrictive membership policies, exclusive unions achieve higher wage rates ($W_c$ to $W_u$). However, restriction of the labour supply also reduces the number of workers employed ($Q_c$ to $Q_u$).

## Inclusive or Industrial Union Model

Most unions, however, do not attempt to limit their membership. On the contrary, they seek to organize all available workers. This is characteristic of the so-called *industrial unions*—unions, such as the automobile workers and steelworkers, which seek all unskilled, semiskilled, and skilled workers in an industry as members. A union can afford to be exclusive when its members are skilled craftspersons for whom there are few substitute workers. But a union composed of unskilled and semiskilled workers would be hurting itself by limiting its membership; that would create numerous highly substitutable *nonunion* workers who would be available for employment.

If an industrial union includes virtually all available workers in its membership, firms will be under great pressure to agree to union wage demands. By going on strike, the union could deprive those firms of their entire labour supply.

This **inclusive unionism** is illustrated in Figure 16-7. Initially, the competitive equilibrium wage rate is $W_c$ and the level of employment is $Q_c$. Now suppose an industrial union is formed and it imposes a higher, above-equilibrium wage rate of, say, $W_u$. This wage rate $W_u$ creates a pefectly elastic labour supply over the range *ae* in Figure 16-7. If employers hire any number of workers in this range, the union-imposed wage rate is effective and must be paid or the union will supply no labour at all—the firms will be faced with a strike. If the employers decide it is better to pay this higher wage rate than to suffer a strike, they will cut back on employment from $Q_c$ to $Q_u$.

**FIGURE 16-7 Inclusive or industrial unionism**

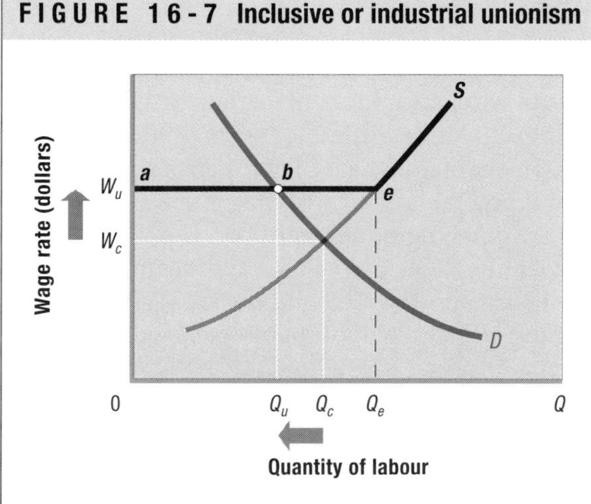


By organizing virtually all available workers to control the supply of labour, inclusive industrial unions may impose a wage rate, such as $W_u$, which is above the competitive wage rate $W_c$. The effect is to change the labour supply curve from *S* to *aeS*. At wage rate $W_u$, employers will cut employment from $Q_c$ to $Q_u$.

By agreeing to the union's $W_u$ wage demand, individual employers become wage takers. Because labour supply is perfectly elastic over range *ae*, the marginal resource (labour) cost is equal to the wage rate $W_u$ over this range. The $Q_u$ level of employment results from employers' equating this MRC (now equal to the *wage rate*) with MRP according to our profit-maximizing rule.

Note from point *e* on labour supply curve *S* that $Q_e$ workers desire employment at wage $W_u$. But as indicated by point *b* on labour demand curve *D*, only $Q_u$ workers are hired. The result is a surplus of labour in the amount $Q_e - Q_u$ (also shown by distance *eb*). Without the union—that is, in a purely competitive labour market—this surplus of unemployed workers would result in lower wages. Specifically, the wage rate would fall to the equilibrium level $W_c$, where the quantity of labour supplied equals the quantity of labour demanded (each $Q_c$). But this doesn't happen because workers are acting collectively through their union. Workers cannot individually offer to work for less than $W_u$; nor can employers contractually pay less than that wage rate.

## Wage Increases and Unemployment

Have unions been successful in raising the wages of their members? Evidence suggests that union members on the average achieve a 10 to 15 percent wage advantage over nonunion workers.

As Figures 16-6 and 16-7 suggest, the wage-raising actions of both exclusive and inclusive unionism reduce employment. A union's success in achieving above-equilibrium wage rates is thus tempered by an accompanying decline in the number of workers employed. This unemployment effect acts as a restraining influence on union wage demands. A union cannot expect to maintain solidarity within its ranks if it seeks a wage rate so high that joblessness will result for, say, 20 or 30 percent of its members.

The unemployment effect of union wage increases might be reduced in two ways:

1. **GROWTH** The normal growth of the economy increases the demand for most kinds of labour through time. This continual rightward shift of the labour demand curves in Figures 16-6 and 16-7 could offset, or more than offset, the unemployment effects associated with the indicated wage increases. Then union wage increases would tend to decrease the rate of growth of job opportunities but not the firm's total employment.
2. **ELASTICITY** The size of the unemployment effect will depend on the elasticity of demand for labour. The more inelastic the demand, the smaller the amount of unemployment accompanying a given wage-rate increase. And, if unions have sufficient bargaining strength, they *may* obtain provisions in their collective bargaining agreements that reduce the substitutability of other inputs for labour and thereby reduce the elasticity of demand for union labour. For example, a union may force employers to accept rules blocking the introduction of new machinery and equipment. Or the union may bargain successfully for severance or layoff pay, which increases the cost to the firm of substituting capital for labour when wage rates are increased. Similarly, the union might gain a contract provision prohibiting the firm from subcontracting production to non-union (lower-wage) firms or relocating work to low-wage workers overseas, thereby restricting the substitution of cheaper labour for union workers.

For these and other reasons the unemployment restraint on union wage demands may be less pressing than our exclusive and inclusive union models suggest.

## BILATERAL MONOPOLY MODEL

Suppose a strong industrial union is formed in a labour market that is monopsonistic rather than competitive. In other words, we combine the monopsony model with the inclusive unionism model. The result is **bilateral monopoly**. The union is a monopolistic "seller" of labour that controls labour supply and can influence wage rates, but it faces a monopsonistic employer (or combination of oligopsonistic employers) of labour that can also affect wages by altering its employment. This is not an extreme or special case. In such industries as steel, automobile, meatpacking, and farm machinery, "big labour"—one huge industrial union—bargains with "big business"—a few industrial giants.

### Indeterminate Outcome of Bilateral Monopoly

This situation is shown in Figure 16-8, which superimposes Figure 16-7 on 16-4. The monopsonistic employer will seek the below-competitive-equilibrium wage rate $W_m$, and the union presumably will press for some above-competitive-equilibrium wage rate such as $W_u$. Which will result? We cannot say with certainty. The outcome is "logically indeterminate" since economic theory does not explain what will happen at the collective bargaining table. We can expect the wage outcome to lie somewhere between $W_m$ and $W_u$. Beyond that, about all we can say is that the party with the most bargaining power and the most effective bargaining strategy will probably get a wage closer to the one it seeks.

**FIGURE 16-8 Bilateral monopoly in the labour market**

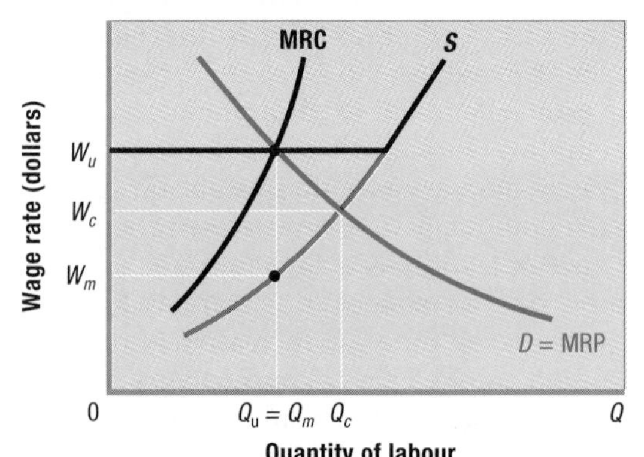


A monopsonist seeks to hire $Q_m$ workers (where MRC = MRP) and pay wage rate $W_m$ corresponding to $Q_m$ labour on labour supply curve $S$. The inclusive union it faces seeks the above-equilibrium wage rate $W_u$. The actual outcome cannot be predicted by economic theory.

### Desirability of Bilateral Monopoly

The wage and employment outcomes in this situation might be more socially desirable than the term "bilateral monopoly" would imply. The monopoly on one side of the market *might* in effect cancel out the monopoly on the other side, yielding competitive or near-competitive results. If either the union or management prevailed in this market—that is, if the actual wage rate were determined at either $W_u$ or $W_m$—employment would be restricted to $Q_m$ (where MRP = MRC), which is below the competitive level.

But now suppose the monopoly power of the union roughly offsets the monopsony power of management, and a bargained wage rate of $W_c$, which is the competitive wage, is agreed upon. Once management accepts this wage rate, its incentive to restrict employment disappears; no longer can it depress wage rates by restricting employment. Instead, management hires at the most profitable resource quantity, where the bargained wage rate $W_c$ (which is now the firm's MRC) is equal to the MRP. It hires $Q_c$ workers. Thus, with monopoly on both sides of the labour market, it is possible that the resulting wage rate and level of employment will be closer to competitive levels than would be the case if monopoly existed on only one side of the market. ***(Key Question 7)***

**16-2**

**QUICK REVIEW**

- In the demand-enhancement union model, a union increases the wage rate by increasing labour demand through actions that increase product demand, raise labour productivity, or alter the prices of related inputs.

- In the exclusive (craft) union model, a union increases wage rates by artificially restricting labour supply, say, through long apprenticeships or occupational licensing.
- In the inclusive (industrial) union model, a union raises the wage rate by gaining control over a firm's labour supply and threatening to withhold labour via a strike unless a negotiated wage is obtained.
- Bilateral monopoly occurs in a labour market where a monopsonist bargains with an inclusive, or industrial, union. Wage and employment outcomes are determined by collective bargaining in this situation.

## THE MINIMUM-WAGE CONTROVERSY

Both the federal and provincial governments have enacted **minimum wage** legislation. In 1998 the minimum wage was $4 an hour at the federal level. The provincial minimum wage ranged from under $5 per hour in Newfoundland and Prince Edward Island to over $7 per hour in British Columbia. Roughly 80 percent of all nonsupervisory workers are covered by the minimum wage law. Our analysis of union efforts to increase wages raises the question of how effective a minimum wage is as an anti-poverty device.

### Case Against the Minimum Wage

Critics, reasoning in terms of Figure 16-7, contend that an above-equilibrium minimum wage (say, $W_u$) will simply push employers back up their labour demand curves, causing them to hire fewer workers. The higher labour costs may even force some firms out of business. And some of the poor, low-wage workers whom the minimum wage was designed to help will find themselves out of work! Critics say a worker who is unemployed at a minimum wage of $4.00 per hour is clearly worse off than he or she would be if employed at a market wage rate of, say, $3.50 per hour.

A second criticism of the minimum wage is that it is "poorly targeted" as an antipoverty device. It is designed to provide a "living wage" that will allow less-skilled workers to earn enough for them and their families to escape poverty. However, critics point out that the primary impact of the minimum wage is on teenage workers, many of whom are part of relatively affluent families.

### Case for the Minimum Wage

Advocates say critics analyze the impact of the minimum wage in an unrealistic context. Figure 16-7, advocates claim, assumes a competitive and static market. But in a more real monopsonistic labour market (Figure 16-8), the minimum wage can increase wage rates without causing unemployment. Indeed, a higher minimum wage may even produce more jobs by eliminating the monopsonistic employer's motive for restricting employment.

Also, an effective minimum wage may increase labour productivity; that would shift the labour demand curve to the right and offset any unemployment that the minimum wage might cause.

But how might a minimum wage increase productivity? First, a minimum wage may have a *shock effect* on employers. Firms using low-wage workers may be using those workers inefficiently; the higher wage rates imposed by the minimum wage would presumably shock these firms into using labour more efficiently, and so the productivity of labour would increase. Second, some argue that higher wages would increase the real incomes and therefore the health, vigour, and motivation of workers, making them more productive.

### Evidence and Conclusions

Which view is correct? The consensus of the many research studies of the minimum wage is that it does cause some unemployment, particularly among teenage (16- to 19-year-old) workers. It is estimated that a 10 percent increase in the minimum wage will reduce teenage employment by 1 to 3 percent. Young adults (age 20 to 24) are also adversely affected; a 10 percent increase in the minimum wage will reduce employment for this group by 1 percent or less. Visible minorities and women, who are overrepresented in low-wage occupations, tend to suffer larger declines in employment than white males. Nevertheless, those who remain employed receive higher incomes and may escape poverty. The overall antipoverty effect of the minimum wage is thus an ambivalent one. Those who lose their jobs fall deeper into poverty; those who remain employed may escape poverty.

## WAGE DIFFERENTIALS

Why do some corporate executives and professional athletes get paid $5,000,000 or more per year while laundry workers and retail clerks receive $14,000 or $15,000 per year? Although these wage differences are obviously some of the most extreme, **wage differentials** are common, as Table 16-3 shows. Our objective now is to provide some insight as to why these differentials exist.

Once again the forces of supply and demand provide a general answer. If the supply of a particular type of labour is great in relation to the demand for it, the resulting wage rate will be low. But if demand is great and the supply relatively small, the wage will be high. Although it is a good starting point, this supply and demand explanation is not particularly revealing. To discover *why* supply and demand conditions differ in various labour markets, we must probe the factors underlying the supply of and demand for particular types of labour.

If (1) all workers were homogeneous, (2) all jobs were equally attractive to workers, and (3) labour markets were perfectly competitive, all workers would receive precisely the same wage rate. This is not a startling statement. It suggests that in an economy having one type of labour and in effect one type of job, competition would result in a single wage rate for all workers. The statement is important only because it suggests reasons why wage rates do differ in practice: (1) Workers are not homogeneous. They differ in abilities and in education and training and, as a result, fit into a number of distinct occupational groups. (2) Jobs vary in attractiveness; the nonmonetary aspects of various jobs are not the same. (3) Labour markets do not work perfectly.

**TABLE 16-3 Average hourly wages in selected industries, 1998**

| Industry | Average hourly earnings (paid by the hour) |
|---|---|
| Goods-producing industries | $17.36 |
| Service-producing industries | 13.32 |
| Logging and forestry | 18.46 |
| Mining, quarrying, and oil wells | 22.40 |
| Manufacturing | 16.64 |
| Construction | 18.39 |
| Transportation, communication, and other utilities | 19.10 |
| Trade | 11.36 |
| Finance, insurance, and real estate | 13.20 |
| Community business and personal service | 13.40 |
| Industrial aggregate | 14.75 |

*Source:* Statistics Canada, *Employment, Earnings, and Hours*, April, 1998 (Ottawa, July, 1998).

## Noncompeting Groups

Workers are not homogeneous; they differ in their mental and physical capacities *and* in their education and training. At any time the labour force is made up of many **noncompeting groups** of workers; workers from one group do not qualify for occupations of another group.

### Ability

Few workers have the ability to be brain surgeons, concert violinists, research chemists, entertainers, or professional athletes. The result is that supplies of these particular types of labour are very small in relation to the demand for them, and consequently their wages are high. These and similar groups do not compete with one another or with other skilled or semiskilled workers. The violinist does not compete with the surgeon, nor does the surgeon compete with either the violinist or the professional athlete.

The concept of noncompeting groups is flexible; it can be applied to various subgroups and even to specific individuals in a particular group. Some especially skilled lawyers can command higher fees than their run-of-the-mill colleagues. Shaquille O'Neal, Hakeem Olajuwon, Michael Jordan, and a few others demand and get salaries many times more than the average professional basketball player. A handful of top corporate executives earn 10 to 20 times as much as the average chief executive officer (CEO). In each of these cases, less talented colleagues are only imperfect substitutes.

### Education and Training

Noncompeting groups—and therefore wage differentials—also exist because of differing amounts of investment in human capital. A **human capital investment** *is an expenditure on education or training that improves the skills and therefore the productivity of workers.* Like expenditures on machinery and equipment, expenditures on education or training that increase a worker's productivity can be regarded as investments. In both cases, current costs are incurred with the intention that these costs will lead to a greater *future* flow of earnings.

Although education yields higher incomes, it also has costs. A community college or university education involves not only direct costs (tuition, fees, books) but also indirect or opportunity costs (forgone earnings). Does the higher pay received by more educated workers compensate for these costs? The answer is "yes." Rates of return are estimated to be 10 to 13 percent for investments in secondary education and 8 to 12 percent for college and university education. One generally accepted estimate is that each year of schooling raises a worker's wage by about 8 percent. Also, in recent years the pay gap between college and university graduates and high school graduates has increased sharply.

## Compensating Differences

If the workers in a particular noncompeting group are equally capable of performing several different jobs, you might expect the wage rates to be identical for all these jobs. Not so. A group of high school graduates may be equally capable of becoming salesclerks or unskilled construction workers. But these jobs pay different wages. In virtually all locales, construction labourers receive higher wages than salesclerks.

This difference results from differences in the *nonmonetary aspects* of the two jobs. The construction job involves dirty hands, a sore back, the hazard of accidents, and irregular employment, both seasonally and cyclically. The retail sales job means clean clothing, pleasant air-conditioned surroundings, and little fear of injury or layoff. Other things equal, it is easy to see why workers would rather pick up a credit card than a shovel. So construction firms must pay higher wages than retailers to compensate for the unattractive nonmonetary aspects of construction jobs. These wage differentials are called **compensating differences** because they must be paid to compensate for nonmonetary differences in various jobs.

## Market Imperfections

The notions of noncompeting groups and differences in nonmonetary aspects of jobs explain many of the wage differentials in the economy. Other persistent differentials result from several types of market imperfections that impede workers from moving from their current jobs to take higher-paying jobs.

**Lack of Job Information** Workers may simply not be aware of job opportunities and wage rates in other geographic areas and in other jobs for which they qualify. Consequently, the flow of qualified labour from lower-paying to higher-paying jobs—and thus the adjustments in labour supply—may not be sufficient to equalize wages within occupations.

**Geographic Immobility** Workers take root geographically. Many are reluctant to move to new places; to leave friends, relatives, and associates; to force their children to change schools; to sell their houses; and to incur the costs and inconveniences of adjusting to a new job and a new community. As Adam Smith noted over two centuries ago, "A [person] is of all sorts of luggage the most difficult to be transported." The reluctance or inability of workers to move allows geographic wage differentials within the same occupation to persist.

**Unions and Government Restraints** Wage differentials may be reinforced by artificial restrictions on mobility imposed by unions and government. We have noted that craft unions find it to their advantage to restrict membership. After all, if carpenters and bricklayers become too plentiful, the wages they can command will decline. Thus the low-paid non-union carpenter of Edmonton, Alberta may be willing to move to Vancouver in the pursuit of higher wages. But her chances for successfully doing so are slim. She may be unable to get a union card; no card means no job. Similarly, an optometrist or lawyer qualified to practise in one province may not meet licensing requirements of other provinces, so his or her ability to move geographically is limited. Other artificial barriers involve pension plans and seniority rights that might be jeopardized by leaving current employment for another job.

**Discrimination** Despite legislation to the contrary, discrimination often results in women and minority workers being paid less than white men doing virtually identical work. Also, women and minorities may be crowded into certain low-paying occupations, driving down wages there and raising them elsewhere. If discrimination keeps qualified women and minorities from taking these higher-paying jobs, then differences in pay among these occupations can persist.

A final point: Typically, all three considerations—noncompeting groups, nonmonetary differences, and market imperfections—come into play in explaining actual wage differentials. For example, the differential between the wages of a physician and a construction worker is largely explainable on the basis of noncompeting groups. Physicians fall into a noncompeting group where, because of mental and financial requisites to entry, the supply of labour is small in relation to demand and wages are therefore high. In construction work, where mental and financial prerequisites are much less significant, the supply of labour is great in relation to demand and wages are low when compared with those of physicians. However, were it not for the unpleasantness of the construction worker's job and the fact that his craft union pursues restrictive membership policies, the differential would probably be even greater.

## PAY FOR PERFORMANCE

The models of wage determination presented in this chapter presume that worker pay is always a standard amount for each hour's work, for example, $15 per hour. But pay schemes are often more complex than that in composition and in purpose. For example, many workers receive annual salaries rather than hourly pay. Many workers also receive fringe benefits: life insurance, paid vacation, paid sick-leave days, pension contributions, and so on. Finally, some pay plans are designed to elicit a desired level of performance from workers. This last aspect of pay requires further elaboration.

### The Principal-Agent Problem Revisited

In Chapter 5 we identified the *principal-agent problem* as it relates to possible differences in the interests of corporate stockholders (principals) and the executives (agents) they hire. This problem extends to all workers. Firms hire workers because they are needed to help produce the goods and services that the firms sell for a profit. Workers are the firms' agents; they are hired to advance the interest (profit) of the firms. The *principals* are the firms; they hire agents to advance their goals. Firms and workers have a common self-interest: they both want the firm to survive and thrive. That will ensure profit for the firm and continued employment and wage income for the workers.

But the interests of the firm and of workers are not *identical*. A principal-agent problem arises when those interests diverge. Workers may seek to increase their utility by shirking on the job, that is, by providing less than agreed-upon worker effort or by taking unauthorized work breaks. Workers may improve their well-being by increasing their leisure—during paid work hours—without forfeiting income. The night security guard in a warehouse may leave work early or spend time reading a novel rather than making the assigned rounds. A salaried manager may spend much time out of the office, visiting with friends, rather than attending to company business.

Firms (principals) have a profit incentive to reduce or eliminate shirking. One option is to monitor workers, but monitoring is difficult and costly. Hiring another worker to supervise or monitor our security guard might double the cost of having a secure warehouse. Another way of resolving a principal-agent problem is through some sort of **incentive pay plan** that ties worker compensation (pay) more closely to worker output or performance. Such incentive pay schemes include piece rates, commissions and royalties, bonuses and profit sharing, and efficiency wages.

**Piece Rates** Piece rates are pay or compensation paid in proportion to the number of units of output a worker produces. If a principal pays fruit pickers by the bushel or typists by the page, it need not be concerned with shirking or monitoring costs.

**Commissions or Royalties** Unlike piece rates which link pay to units of output, commissions and royalties tie pay to the value of sales. Employees who sell products or services—including real estate agents, insurance agents, stockbrokers, and retail salespersons—commonly receive *commissions* that are computed as a percentage of the monetary value of their sales. Recording artists and authors are paid *royalties*, computed as a certain percentage of sales revenues from their works (and we thank you). These types of pay align the financial interests of the salespeople or creative artists with the profit interest of the firms.

**Bonuses and Profit Sharing** Bonuses are payments beyond one's annual salary that are based on some factor such as the performance of the individual worker, a group of workers, or the overall firm. A professional baseball player may receive bonuses for a high batting average, the number of home runs hit, or the number of runs batted in. A business manager may receive a bonus based on the profitability of her or his unit. Profit-sharing plans allocate a percentage of a firm's profit to its employees. Such plans, for example, have in recent years resulted in large annual payments to many Canadian auto workers.

**Efficiency Wages** The notion of *efficiency wages* suggests employers might get greater effort from their workers by paying them relatively high, above-equilibrium wage rates. Glance back at Figure 16-3, which shows a competitive labour market where the equilibrium wage rate is $6. What if an employer decides to pay an above-equilibrium wage of $7 per hour? Rather than put the firm at a cost disadvantage compared with rival firms paying only $6, the higher wage *might* improve worker effort and productivity so unit labour costs actually fell. For example, if each worker produces 10 units of output per hour at the $7 wage rate compared with only 6 units at the $6 wage rate, unit labour costs will be only $.70 (= $7 ÷ 10) for the high-wage firm as opposed to $1.00 (= $6 ÷ 6) for firms paying the equilibrium wage.

An above-equilibrium wage can enhance worker efficiency in several ways. The higher wage permits the firm to attract higher-quality workers. Worker morale should be higher. Turnover should be lower, resulting in a more experienced work force, greater worker productivity, and lower recruitment and training costs. Because the opportunity cost of losing a higher-wage job is greater, workers are more likely to put forth their best efforts with less supervision and monitoring. In fact, efficiency wage payments have proved effective for many employers.

### Addenda: Negative Side Effects

Pay for performance can help overcome the principal-agent problem and enhance worker productivity. But such plans require careful design since they sometimes have negative side effects. Here are just a few examples:

1. The rapid production pace that piece rates elicit may result in poor product quality. It may also compromise the safety of workers. These outcomes can be costly to the firm over the long run.
2. Commissions may cause some salespeople to engage in questionable or even fraudulent sales practices, such as making exaggerated claims about products or recommending unneeded repairs. These practices can hurt the employer by leading to private lawsuits or government legal action.
3. Bonuses based on personal performance may disrupt the close cooperation needed for maximum team production. A professional basketball player who receives a bonus for points scored may be reluctant to pass the ball to teammates.
4. Since profit sharing is usually tied to the performance of the entire firm, less energetic workers can "free-ride" by obtaining their profit share on the basis of others' hard work.
5. There may be a downside to the reduced turnover resulting from above-market wages: Firms paying efficiency wages have fewer opportunities to hire *new* workers, yet this so-called new blood sometimes energizes a workplace.

**16-3**

**QUICK REVIEW**

- Proponents of the minimum wage argue it is needed to assist the working poor and counter monopsony where it might exist; critics say it is poorly targeted and reduces employment.
- Wage differentials are attributable in general to the forces of supply and demand, influenced by differences in workers' skills and nonmonetary differences in jobs. But several labour market imperfections also play a role.
- As it applies to labour, the principal-agent problem is one of workers pursuing their own interests to the detriment of the employer's profit objective.
- Pay-for-performance plans (piece rates, commissions, royalties, bonuses, profit sharing, and efficiency wages) are designed to improve worker productivity by overcoming the principal-agent problem.

## MORE ON THE ECONOMIC EFFECTS OF UNIONS

What effects do unions have on the economy? Do unions raise wages? Do they increase or diminish economic efficiency?

## The Union Wage Advantage

The three union models (see Figures 16-5, 16-6, and 16-7 and the accompanying discussions) all imply that unions are capable of raising wages. Has unionization really done so?

Empirical research overwhelmingly suggests that unions do raise the wages of their members relative to those of comparable nonunion workers, although the size of the union wage advantage varies according to occupation, industry, race, and gender. The consensus estimate is that the overall union wage advantage is about 10 to 15 percent. On the other hand, unions have had little impact on the *average* level of real wages received by Canadian workers taken as a whole.

These two conclusions (higher union pay, no overall impact) may seem inconsistent, but they are not. The higher union wages apply to only about 31 percent of the labour force. Moreover, these wages may come at the expense of lower wages for some nonunion workers. As you will see (in Figure 16-9), higher wages in unionized labour markets may cause employers to hire fewer workers. The workers who are left unemployed may seek employment in nonunion labour markets. The resulting increase in the supply of labour in the nonunion labour markets reduces wage rates there. The net result may be no change in the average level of wages.

The long-run relationship between productivity and the average level of real wages shown previously in Figure 16-1 suggests that unions have little power to raise the average real wage over long periods of time. But Figure 16-1 is an average relationship; it is therefore compatible with the idea that certain groups of (union) workers get higher relative wages while other (nonunion) workers simultaneously get lower real wages.

### 16-2 GLOBAL PERSPECTIVE

**Union membership as a percentage of the employed labour force, selected nations**

Compared with the percentages unionized in most other industrialized nations, union membership in Canada is close to levels in many European nations.

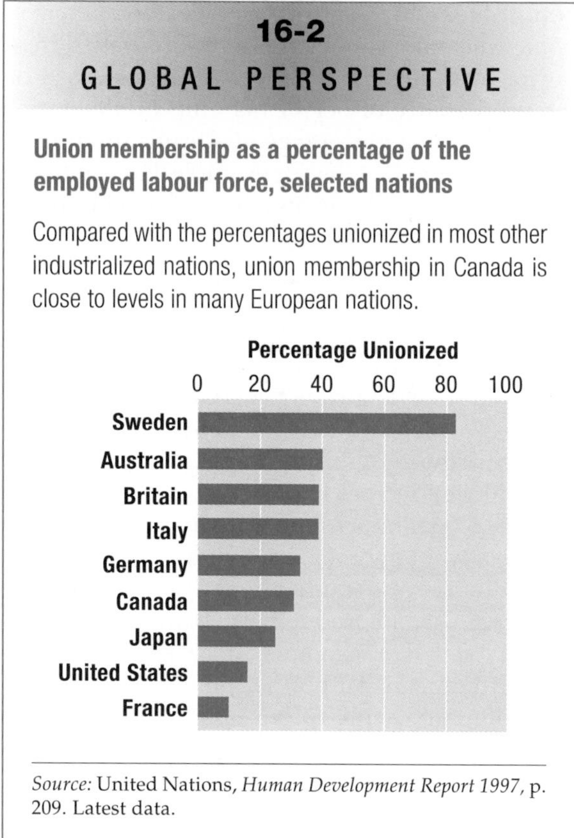


*Source:* United Nations, *Human Development Report 1997*, p. 209. Latest data.

## Efficiency and Productivity

Do labour unions increase or decrease efficiency and productivity? There is much disagreement on this question, but we can consider some of the ways unions might affect efficiency, both negatively and positively.

**Negative View** There are three ways unions might exert a negative impact on productivity and efficiency.

**LOSSES VIA FEATHERBEDDING AND WORK RULES** Some unions undoubtedly have diminished efficiency by engaging in "make-work" or "featherbedding" practices and resisting the introduction of output-increasing machinery and equipment. These productivity-reducing practices often appear in periods of technological change. Unions might reduce efficiency by establishing work rules and practices that impede putting the most productive workers in particular jobs. Under seniority rules, for example, workers may be promoted for their employment tenure rather than for their ability to perform the available job with the greatest efficiency. Also, unions might restrict the kinds of tasks workers may perform. Contract provisions may prohibit sheet-metal workers or bricklayers from doing the simple carpentry work often associated with their jobs. Observance of such rules means, in this instance, that firms must hire unneeded and underused carpenters. Finally, critics of unions contend that union contracts often chip away at managerial prerogatives to establish work schedules, determine production targets, introduce new technology, and make other decisions contributing to productive efficiency.

**LOSSES VIA STRIKES** A second way unions may adversely affect efficiency is through strikes. If union and management reach an impasse in their negotiations, a strike will result and the firm's production will cease for the strike's duration. The firm will forgo sales and profit; workers will sacrifice income; and the economy may lose output.

Statistics on strike activity suggest that strikes are rare and the associated aggregate economic losses are less than might be expected. Many strikes last only a few days. The amount of work time lost each year because of strikes is the equivalent of four hours per worker per year, which is less than 5 minutes per worker per week.

However, the economic costs associated with strikes may be greater or less than is suggested by the amount of work time lost. The costs may be *greater* if strikes disrupt production in nonstruck firms that either provide inputs to or buy goods and services from the struck firm. Example: An extended strike in the auto industry might reduce output and cause layoffs in firms producing, say, glass, tires, paints, and fabrics used in producing cars. It may also reduce sales and cause layoffs in auto dealerships.

On the other hand, the costs of strikes may be *less* than is implied by the work-time lost by strikers if nonstruck firms increase their output to offset the loss of production by struck firms. While the output of General Motors declines when its workers strike, auto buyers may shift their demand to Ford, Honda, or Chrysler, which will respond by increasing their employment and output. Thus, although GM and its employees are hurt by a strike, society as a whole may experience little or no decline in employment, real output, and income.

**LOSSES VIA LABOUR MISALLOCATION** A more subtle way in which unions might adversely affect efficiency is through the union wage advantage itself. Figure 16-9 shows (for simplicity) identical labour demand curves for a unionized sector and a nonunionized sector of the market for some particular kind of labour. We assume there is pure competition in both the product market and all resource markets.

If there were no union in either sector initially, the wage rate that would result from the competitive hiring of labour would be $W_n$, while $N_1$ work-

**FIGURE 16-9 The effects of the union wage advantage on the allocation of labour**

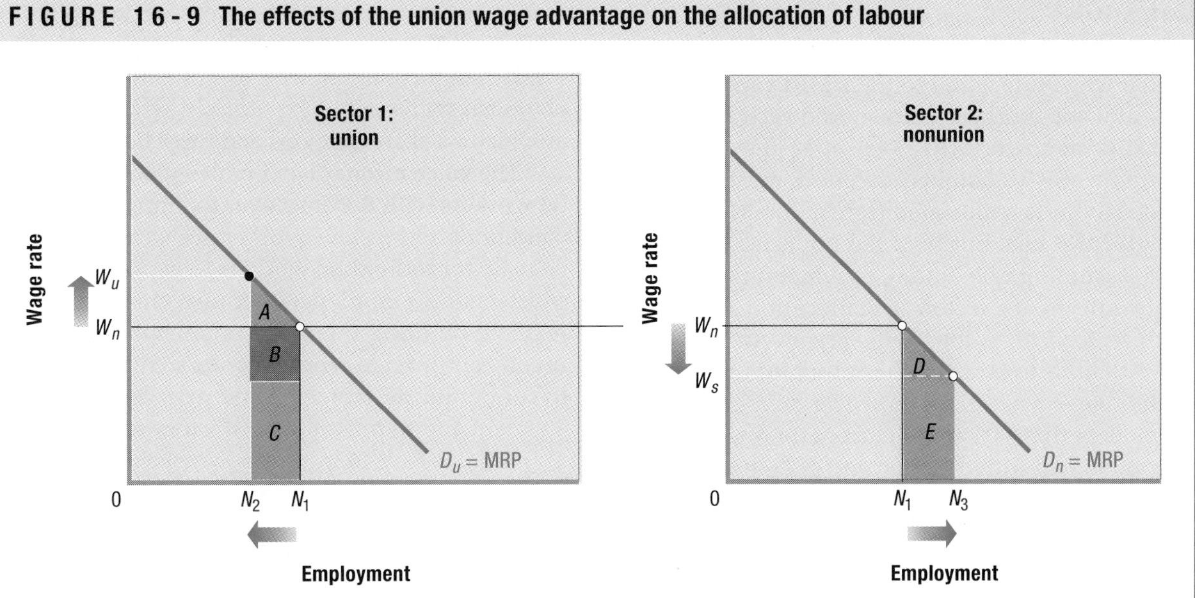


The higher wage $W_u$ that the union receives in sector 1 causes the displacement of $N_1N_2$ workers. The re-employment of these workers in sector 2 increases employment from $N_1$ to $N_3$ and reduces the wage rate there from $W_n$ to $W_s$. The associated loss of output in the union sector is area $A + B + C$, while the gain in the nonunion sector is only $D + E$. The net loss of output is area $B$. This loss of output suggests that the union wage advantage has resulted in a misallocation of labour and a decline in economic efficiency.

ers would be hired in each sector. Now suppose workers form a union in sector 1 and succeed in increasing the wage rate from $W_n$ to $W_u$. As a consequence, $N_1N_2$ workers lose their jobs in the union sector. Assume that they all move to nonunion sector 2, where they are employed. This increase in labour supply (not shown) in the nonunion sector increases the quantity of labour supplied there from $N_1$ to $N_3$, reducing the wage rate from $W_n$ to $W_s$.

Recall that the labour demand curves reflect the marginal revenue products (MRPs) of workers or, in other words, the contribution each additional worker makes to domestic output. This means that the area $A + B + C$ in the union sector represents the sum of the MRPs—the total contribution to domestic output—of the workers displaced by the wage increase achieved by the union. The re-employment of these workers in nonunion sector 2 results in an increase in domestic output indicated by the area $D + E$. Because the area $A + B + C$ exceeds area $D + E$, there is a net loss of domestic output. More precisely, because $A = D$ and $C = E$, the net loss attributable to the union wage advantage is represented by area $B$. Since the same amount of employed labour is now producing a smaller output, labour is being misallocated and inefficiently used.

From a slightly different perspective, after the shift of $N_1N_2$ workers from the union sector to the nonunion sector has occurred, workers will be paid a wage rate equal to their MRPs in both sectors. But the workers who shifted sectors will be working at lower-MRP jobs after the shift. An economy always obtains a larger domestic output when labour is reallocated from a low-MRP use to a high-MRP use. But here the opposite occurred. And assuming the union can maintain the $W_u$ wage rate in its sector, a reallocation of labour from sector 2 to sector 1 will *never* occur.

Attempts to estimate the output loss associated with unions' wage gains, however, suggest the loss is small: perhaps 0.2 to 0.4 percent (or one-fifth of 1 percent to two-fifths of 1 percent) of domestic product. In 1997 this cost would be about $1.7 to $3.4 billion, or $57 to $114 per person. ***(Key Question 12)***

### Positive View

Other economists take the position that, on balance, unions make a positive contribution to efficiency and productivity.

**LONGER-RUN POSITIVE IMPACTS: THE SHOCK EFFECT** A wage increase won by a union may have a *shock effect* on affected firms, causing them in the long run to substitute capital for labour and in the very long run to implement productivity-increasing technologies. When faced with higher production costs due to the union wage increase, employers will be motivated to reduce costs by using more machinery and by seeking improved production techniques that use less of both labour and capital per unit of output. In fact, if the product market is reasonably competitive, a unionized firm with labour costs 10 to 15 percent higher than nonunionized competitors will not survive over long periods unless productivity can be raised. Hence, union wage pressure may generate managerial actions that increase worker productivity and justify the higher union wages. If so, the overall economy benefits.

**REDUCED WORKER TURNOVER** Unions may also contribute to raising productivity within firms through reduced worker turnover and improved worker security. A union functions as a **collective voice** for its members by taking their side in resolving disputes and bettering working conditions.

If a group of workers are dissatisfied with their conditions of employment, they can respond in either of two ways: through the "exit mechanism" or through the "voice mechanism." With the **exit mechanism**, workers leave their current jobs in search of better ones as a way of reacting to undesirable employers and working conditions; it relies on the labour market. The use of this mechanism obviously increases *worker turnover*, which is the rate at which workers quit jobs and must be replaced.

The **voice mechanism** involves communication by workers with the employer to improve working conditions and resolve worker grievances. It might be risky for individual workers to express their dissatisfaction to employers because employers may retaliate by firing them as "troublemakers." But a union can provide workers with a collective voice to communicate problems and grievances to management and to press for satisfactory resolutions.

Unions may help reduce worker turnover in two ways:

1. Unions provide the voice mechanism as a substitute for the exit mechanism. They use communication to correct job dissatisfactions that otherwise would be "resolved" by workers through the exit mechanism of changing jobs.
2. The union wage advantage is a deterrent to job change. Higher wages make unionized firms more attractive places to work.

Compared with the rates at nonunion firms, the *quit rate* (resignation rate) for union workers is 31 to 65 percent lower, depending on the industry. A lower quit rate increases efficiency because it gives a firm a more experienced, and thus a more productive, workforce. Also, having fewer resignations reduces the firm's recruitment, screening, and hiring costs. Finally, reduced turnover makes employers more willing to invest in the training (and therefore the productivity) of their workers. If a worker quits or "exits" at the end of, say, a year's training, the employer will get no return from providing that training. But lower turnover increases the likelihood that the employer will receive a return on the training it provides, thereby increasing its willingness to upgrade its workforce.

**INCREASED INFORMAL TRAINING** Much productivity-increasing training is transmitted informally. Workers who are more skilled may share their experience with less skilled workers on the job, during lunch, or during coffee breaks. However, a more skilled senior worker may want to conceal his or her knowledge from less skilled junior workers, who might become competitors for the skilled worker's job. Because of union insistence on the use of seniority in such matters as promotion and layoff, worker security is enhanced and this problem is overcome. With this security, senior workers are more willing to pass on their job knowledge and skills to new or subordinate workers. This informal training enhances the quality and productivity of the firm's workforce.

**Mixed Research Findings** Many studies have tried to measure the effect of unionization on productivity, but their results are inconclusive. For every study that finds a positive union effect on productivity, another study using different methodology or data concludes there is a negative effect. At present there simply is no generally accepted conclusion regarding the overall impact of unions on productivity.

**16-4**

**QUICK REVIEW**

- Union wages average about 10 to 15 percent higher than comparable non-union wages.
- Union work rules, strikes, and the misallocation of labour associated with the union wage advantage are ways by which unions may reduce efficiency.
- Unions may enhance productivity by causing a shock effect, by reducing worker turnover, and by providing the worker security that is a prerequisite to informal on-the-job training.

## LABOUR MARKET DISCRIMINATION

Broadly defined, **labour market discrimination** occurs when equivalent labour resources are paid or treated differently even though their productive contributions are equal. These differences result from a combination of nondiscriminatory and discriminatory factors. For example, studies indicate that about one-half the differences in *earnings* between men and women can be explained by such nondiscriminatory factors as differences in education, age, training, industry and occupation, union membership, location, work experience, continuity of work, and health. (Of course, some of these factors may be influenced by discrimination.) The other half is *an unexplained difference*, the bulk of which economists attribute to discrimination.

In labour market discrimination, certain groups of people are accorded inferior treatment with respect to hiring, occupational access, education and training, promotion, wage rates, or working conditions even though they have the same abilities, education and training, and experience as the more preferred groups. People who practise discrimination are said to exhibit a *prejudice* or *bias* against the targets of their discrimination.

### Types of Discrimination

Labour market discrimination can take several forms:

1. **Wage discrimination** occurs when women or members of minorities are paid less than white males for doing the same work. This kind of discrimination is declining because of its explicitness and the fact that it clearly violates federal and provincial labour laws. But wage discrimination can be subtle and difficult to detect. For example, women and minorities sometimes find that their job classi-

fications carry lower pay than job classifications held by white males, even though they are performing essentially the same tasks.

2. **Employment discrimination** takes place when women or minority workers receive inferior treatment in hiring, promotions, assignments, temporary layoffs, and permanent discharges. This type of discrimination also encompasses sexual and racial harassment—demeaning treatment in the workplace by coworkers or administrators.
3. **Occupational discrimination** occurs when women or minority workers are arbitrarily restricted or prohibited from entering the more desirable, higher-paying occupations. Businesswomen have found it difficult to break through the "glass ceiling" which keeps them from moving up to executive ranks. Visible minoirites in executive and sales positions are relatively few. In addition, skilled and unionized work such as electrical work, bricklaying, and plumbing do not have high minority representation.
4. **Human-capital discrimination** occurs when women or members of visible minorities do not have the same access to productivity-enhancing investments in education and training as white males. Example: The lower average educational attainment of visible minorities has reduced their opportunities in the labour market.

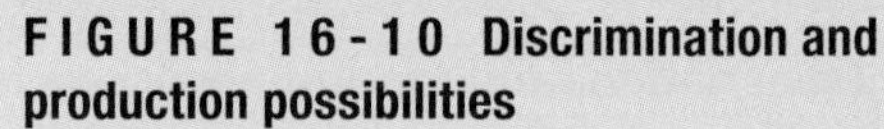
**FIGURE 16-10 Discrimination and production possibilities**

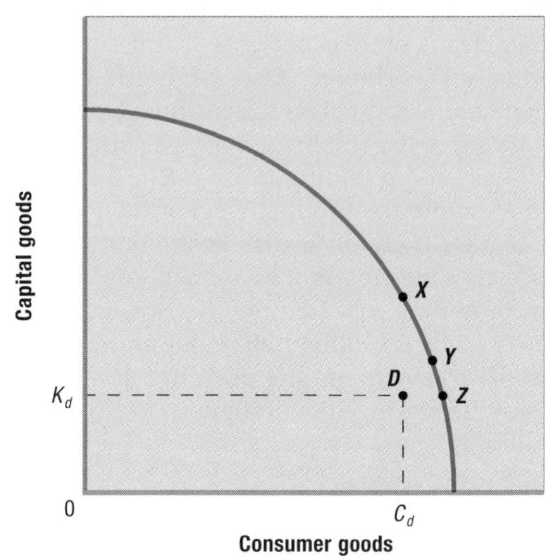


Discrimination represents a failure to achieve productive efficiency. The cost of discrimination to society is the sacrificed output associated with a point such as *D* inside the nation's production possibilities curve, compared with points such as *X*, *Y*, and *Z* on the curve.

## Costs of Discrimination

Discrimination imposes costs on those who are discriminated against. The groups that discriminate get the good jobs and the better pay that are withheld from the targets of their discrimination. But discrimination does more than simply transfer benefits from women and visible minorities to men and whites. Where it exists, discrimination actually *diminishes* the economy's output and income; like any other artificial barrier to free competition, it decreases economic efficiency and reduces production. By arbitrarily blocking certain qualified groups of people from high-productivity (and thus high-wage) jobs, discrimination prevents them from making their maximum contribution to the society's output, income, and well-being.

The effects of discrimination can be depicted as a point inside the economy's production possibilities curve, such as point *D* in Figure 16-10. At such a point, the economy obtains some combination of capital and consumption goods—here, $K_d + C_d$—which is less desirable than combinations represented by points such as *X*, *Y*, or *Z* on the curve. By preventing the economy from achieving productive efficiency, discrimination reduces the nation's real output and income. Very rough estimates suggest the Canadian economy would gain about $20 billion per year by ending gender discrimination.

# ECONOMIC ANALYSIS OF DISCRIMINATION

Prejudice reflects complex, multifaceted, and deeply ingrained beliefs and attitudes. Thus, economics can contribute some insights into discrimination but no detailed explanations. With this caution in mind, let's look deeper at the economics of discrimination.

## Taste-for-Discrimination Model

The **taste-for-discrimination model** examines prejudice by using the emotion-free language of demand theory. It views discrimination as resulting from a preference or *taste* for which the discriminator is willing to pay. The model assumes that, for whatever reason, prejudiced people experience a subjective or psychic cost—a *disutility*—whenever they must interact with those they are biased against. Consequently, they are willing to pay a certain "price" to avoid interactions with the nonpreferred group. The size of this price depends directly on the degree of prejudice.

The taste-for-discrimination model is general since it can be applied to race, gender, age, and religion. But our discussion focuses on *employer discrimination*, in which employers discriminate against nonpreferred workers. For concreteness, we will look at a white employer discriminating against visible minority workers.

**Discrimination Coefficient** A prejudiced white employer behaves as if employing visible minority workers adds a cost. The amount of this cost—this disutility—is reflected in a **discrimination coefficient**, $d$, measured in monetary units. Because the employer is not prejudiced against whites, the cost of employing a white worker is the white wage rate, $W_w$. However, the employer's perceived "cost" of employing a visible minority worker is the black worker's wage rate, $W_b$, *plus* the cost $d$ involved in the employer's prejudice, or $W_b + d$.

The prejudiced white employer will have no preference between visible minority and white workers when the total cost per worker is the same, that is, when $W_w = W_b + d$. Suppose the market wage rate for whites is $10 and the monetary value of the disutility the employer attaches to hiring members of visible minorities is $2 (that is, $d$ = $2). This employer will be indifferent between hiring members of visible minorities and whites only when the wage rate of visible minorities is $8 since at this wage the perceived cost of hiring either a white or a visible minority worker is $10:

$10 white wage = $8 visible minority wage + $2 discrimination coefficient

*It follows that our prejudiced white employer will hire visible minorities only if their wage rate is sufficiently below that of whites.* By "sufficiently" we mean at least the amount of the discrimination coefficient.

The greater a white employer's taste for discrimination as reflected in the value of $d$, the larger the difference between white wages and the lower wages at which visible minorities will be hired. A "colour-blind" employer whose $d$ is $0 will hire equally productive visible minorities and whites impartially if their wages are the same. A blatantly prejudiced white employer whose $d$ is infinity will refuse to hire visible minorities, even if the visible minority wage is zero.

Most prejudiced white employers will not refuse to hire visible minorities under all conditions. They will, in fact, *prefer* to hire visible minorities if the actual white-visible minority wage difference in the market exceeds the value of $d$. In our example, if whites can be hired at $10 and equally productive visible minorities at only $7.50, the biased white employer will hire visible minorities. That employer is willing to pay a wage difference of up to $2 per hour for whites to satisfy his or her bias, but no more. At the $2.50 actual difference, the employer will hire visible minorities.

Conversely, if whites can be hired at $10 and visible minorities at $8.50, whites will be hired. Again, the biased employer is willing to pay a wage difference of up to $2 for whites; a $1.50 actual difference means that hiring whites is a "bargain" for this employer.

**Prejudice and the Market Visible Minority-White Wage Ratio** For a particular supply of visible minority workers, the *actual* visible minority-white wage ratio—the ratio determined in the labour market—will depend on the collective prejudice of white employers. To see why, consider Figure 16-11, which shows a labour market for *visible minority* workers. Initially, suppose the relevant labour demand curve is $D_1$, so the equilibrium visible minority wage is $8 and the equilibrium level of visible minority employment is 6 million. If we assume that the *white* wage (not shown) is $10, then the initial visible minority-white wage ratio is .80 (= $8/$10).

Now assume that prejudice against visible minority workers increases—that is, the collective $d$ of white employers rises. An increase in $d$ means an increase in the perceived cost of visible minority labour at each visible minority wage rate, and that reduces the demand for visible minority labour, say, from $D_1$ to $D_2$. The visible minority wage rate falls from $8 to $6 in the market, and the level of visible minority employment declines from 6 million to 2 million. *The increase in white employer prejudice reduces the visible minority wage rate and thus the actual visible minority-white wage*

**FIGURE 16-11 The visible minority wage and employment level in the taste-for-discrimination model**

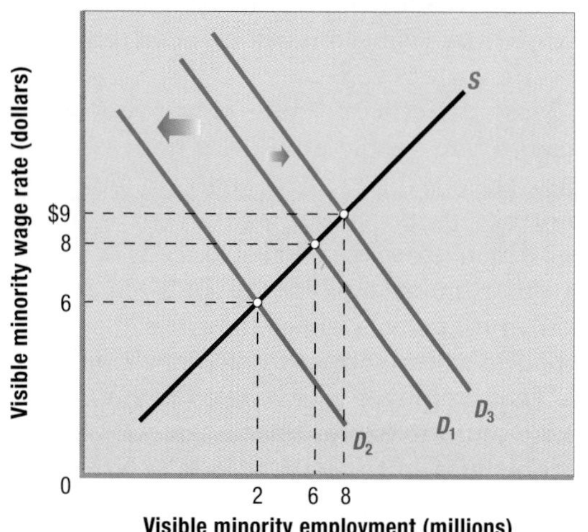


An increase in prejudice by white employers as reflected in higher discrimination coefficients would decrease the demand for visible minority workers, here from $D_1$ to $D_2$, and reduce the visible minority wage rate and level of visible minority employment. Not shown, this drop in the visible minority wage rate would lower the visible minority-white wage ratio. In contrast, if prejudice were reduced such that discrimination coefficients of employers declined, the demand for visible minority labour would increase, as from $D_1$ to $D_3$, boosting the visible minority wage rate and level of employment. The higher visible minority wage rate would increase the visible minority-white wage ratio.

*ratio.* If the white wage rate remains at $10, the new visible minority-white ratio is .6 (= $6/$10).

Conversely, suppose social attitudes change such that white employers become less biased and their discrimination coefficient as a group declines. This decreases the perceived cost of visible minority labour at each visible minority wage rate, so the demand for visible minority labour increases, as from $D_1$ to $D_3$. In this case, the visible minority wage rate rises to $9, and employment of visible minority workers increases to 8 million. *The decrease in white employer prejudice increases the visible minority wage rate and thus the actual visible minority-white wage ratio.* If the white wage remains at $10, the new visible minority-white wage ratio is .9 (= $9/$10).

**Competition and Discrimination** The taste-for-discrimination model suggests that competition will reduce discrimination in the very long run, as follows: The actual visible minority-white wage difference for equally productive workers—say, $2—allows nondiscriminators to hire visible minorities for less than whites. Firms that hire visible minority workers will therefore have lower actual wage costs per unit of output and lower average total costs than will the firms that discriminate. These lower costs will allow nondiscriminators to underprice discriminating competitors, eventually driving them out of the market.

But critics of this implication of the taste-for-discrimination model note that progress in eliminating racial discrimination has been modest. Discrimination based on race has persisted in Canada and other market economies decade after decade. To explain why, economists have proposed alternative models. ***(Key Question 15)***

## Statistical Discrimination

A second theory of discrimination centres on the concept of **statistical discrimination**, in which *people are judged on the basis of the average characteristics of the group to which they belong, rather than on their own personal characteristics or productivity.* The uniqueness of this theory is that discriminatory outcomes are possible even where there is no prejudice.

**Basic Idea** Suppose you are given a complex, but solvable, mathematical problem and told you will get $1 million in cash if you can find a student on campus to solve it. The catch is that you have only 15 minutes, are restricted to the campus area, and must approach students one at a time. Who among the thousands of students—all strangers—would you approach first? Obviously, you would like to select a mathematics, physics, or engineering major. Would you select a man or a woman? A white, black, or Asian student? If gender or race plays *any* role in your selection, you have engaged in statistical discrimination.

**Labour Market Example** How does statistical discrimination work in labour markets? Employers with job openings want to hire the most productive workers available. Their personnel departments collect information concerning each job applicant, including age, education, and prior work experience. They may supplement this information with pre-employment tests, whose results they feel are helpful indicators of potential job performance. But it is very expensive to collect detailed information about a job applicant, and it is difficult to predict job performance from limited data. Consequently, some employers looking for inexpensive information may consider average characteristics of women and minorities in determining whom to hire. In thus practising statistical discrimination, employers are not satisfying some taste for discrimination but, rather, are using gender, race, or ethnic background as a very crude indicator of production-related attributes of workers that are not easily discernible.

Example: Suppose an employer who plans to invest heavily in training a worker knows that on average women are less likely to be career-oriented than men, more likely to quit work to care for young children, and more likely to refuse geographical transfers. Thus, on average, the return on the employer's investment will be less for a woman than for a man. All else equal, when choosing between two job applicants—one a woman and the other a man—this employer will likely hire the man.

Note what is happening here. Average characteristics for a *group* are being applied to *individual* members of that group. The employer is falsely assuming that *each and every* woman worker has the same employment tendencies as the *average* woman. This stereotyping means that numerous women who are career-oriented, plan to work when they have families, and are flexible as to geographical transfers will be discriminated against.

**Profitable, Undesirable, but Not Malicious** The firm practising statistical discrimination is not being malicious in its hiring behaviour (although it may be violating antidiscrimination laws). The decisions it makes will be rational and profitable because *on average* its hiring decisions will likely be correct. Nevertheless, many people suffer because of statistical discrimination since it blocks the economic betterment of capable people. And since it is profitable, statistical discrimination can persist.

## Occupational Segregation: The Crowding Model

The practice of **occupational segregation**—*the crowding of women, visible minorities, and certain ethnic groups into less desirable, lower-paying occupations*—is still apparent in the Canadian economy. Statistics indicate that women are disproportionately concentrated in a limited number of occupations such as teaching, nursing, and secretarial and clerical jobs. Visible minorities are crowded into low-paying jobs such as those of laundry workers, cleaners and household aides, hospital orderlies, agricultural workers, and other manual labourers.

Let's look at a model of occupational segregation, using women and men as an example.

**The Model** The character and income consequences of occupational discrimination are revealed through a labour supply and demand model. We make the following assumptions:

1. The labour force is equally divided between men and women workers. Let's say there are 6 million male and 6 million female workers.
2. The economy comprises three occupations, X, Y, and Z, with identical labour demand curves as shown in Figure 16-12.
3. Men and women have the same labour force characteristics; each of the three occupations could be filled equally by men or women.

**Effects of Crowding** Suppose that, as a consequence of discrimination, the 6 million women are excluded from occupations X and Y and crowded into occupation Z, where they earn wage *W*. Men distribute themselves equally among occupations X and Y, meaning that 3 million male workers are in each occupation and have a common wage of M. (If we assume there are no barriers to mobility between X and Y, any initially different distribution of males between X and Y would result in a wage differential between the two occupations. This would prompt labour shifts from the low- to the high-wage occupation until an equal distribution occurred.)

Because women are crowded into occupation Z, their wage rate *W* is much lower than *M*. Because of the discrimination, this is an equilibrium situation. The occupational barrier means women *cannot* reallocate themselves to occupations X and Y in pursuit of a higher wage.

The result is a loss of output for society. To see this, recall again that labour demand reflects labour's marginal revenue product, which is labour's contribution to domestic output. Thus, the grey areas for occupations X and Y in Figure 16-12 show the *decrease* in domestic output—the market value of the marginal output—caused by subtracting 1 million women from each of these

**FIGURE 16-12 The economics of occupational segregation**

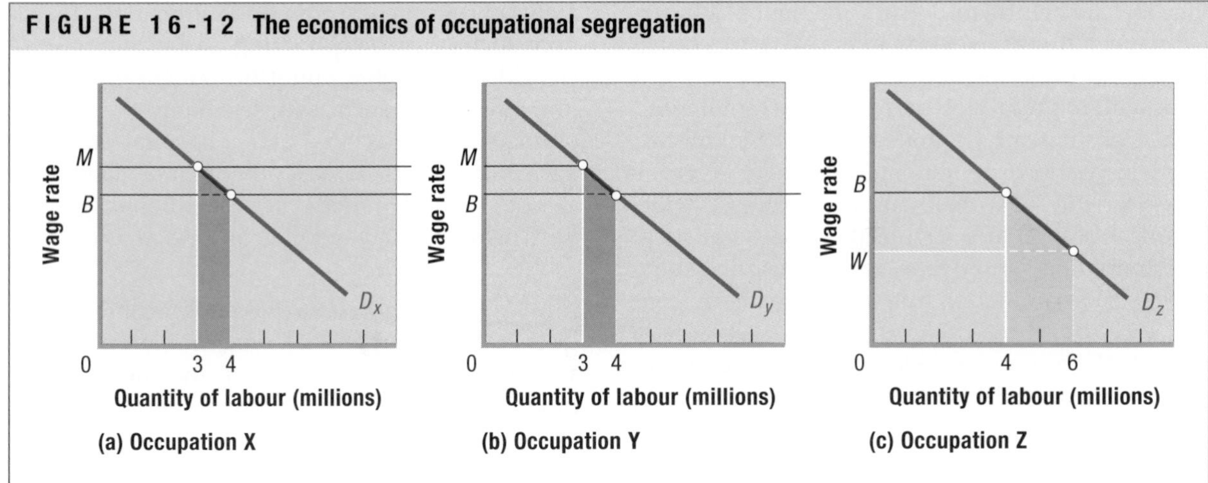


By crowding women into one occupation, men enjoy high wage rates of *M* in occupations X and Y, while women receive low wages of *W* in occupation Z. The elimination of discrimination will equalize wage rates at *B* and result in a net increase in the nation's output.

occupations. Similarly, the pale grey area for occupation Z shows the *increase* in domestic output caused by moving 2 million women into occupation Z. Although society gains the added output represented by the pale grey area in occupation Z, it loses the output represented by the sum of the two grey areas in occupations X and Y. This output loss exceeds the output gain, producing a net output loss for society.

**Eliminating Occupational Segregation** Now assume that through legislation or sweeping changes in social attitudes, discrimination disappears. Women, attracted by higher wage rates, shift from occupation Z to X and Y; 1 million women move into X and another 1 million move into Y, leaving 4 million workers in Z and eliminating occupational segregation. At that point 4 million workers are in each occupation, and wage rates in all three occupations are equal, here at *B*. This wage equality eliminates the incentive for further reallocations of labour.

The new, nondiscriminatory equilibrium clearly benefits women, who now receive higher wages; it hurts men, who now receive lower wages. But women were initially harmed and men benefited through discrimination; thus, removing discrimination corrects that situation.

Society also gains. The elimination of occupational segregation reverses the net output loss just discussed. Adding 1 million women to each of occupations X and Y in Figure 16-12 *increases* domestic output by the sum of the two grey areas. The *decrease* in domestic output caused by losing 2 million women from occupation Z is shown by the pale grey area. The sum of the two increases in domestic output in X and Y exceeds the decrease in domestic output in Z. Women workers move from occupation Z, where their contribution to domestic output (their MRP) is low, to occupations X and Y, where their contribution to domestic output is high. Thus society gains a more efficient allocation of resources when discrimination, an occupational barrier, is removed. (In terms of Figure 16-10, society moves from a point inside its production possibilities curve to a point closer to, or on, the curve.)

Example: The easing of occupational barriers has led to a surge of women gaining advanced degrees in some high-paying professions. In recent years, for instance, the percentage of law degrees and medical degrees awarded to women has exceeded 40 percent, compared with less than 10 percent in 1970. ***(Key Question 17)***

**16-5**

**QUICK REVIEW**

- Discrimination reduces domestic output and occurs when workers who have the same abilities, education, training, and experience as other workers receive inferior treatment with respect to hiring, occupational access, promotion, or wages.
- Nondiscriminatory factors explain about one-half of the gender and racial earnings gaps; most

of the remaining one-half is thought to reflect discrimination.

- The taste-for-discrimination model sees discrimination as representing a preference or "taste" for which the discriminator is willing to pay.
- The theory of statistical discrimination says that employers often wrongly judge *individuals* on the basis of average *group* characteristics rather than on personal characteristics, thus harming those discriminated against.
- The crowding model of discrimination suggests that when women and minorities are systematically excluded from high-paying occupations and crowded into low-paying ones, their wages and society's domestic output are reduced.

## ANTIDISCRIMINATION POLICIES AND ISSUES

Government might attack the problems of discrimination in several ways. One indirect policy is to promote a strong, growing economy. An expanding demand for products increases the demand for all workers. When the economy is at or near full employment, prejudiced employers must pay higher and higher wages to entice preferred workers away from other employers. Many—and perhaps most—such employers will likely decide that their taste for discrimination is not worth the cost. Tight labour markets also help overcome stereotyping. Once they obtain good jobs in tight labour markets, women and minorities have an opportunity to show they can do the work as well as white males.

A second indirect antidiscrimination policy is to improve the education and training opportunities of women and minorities. As an example, upgrading the quantity and quality of schooling received by visible minorities will make them more competitive with whites for higher-paying positions.

The third way of reducing discrimination is through direct governmental intervention. The federal and most provincial governments have outlawed certain practices in hiring, promotion, and compensation and have required that government contractors take affirmative action to ensure that women and minorities are hired at least up to their proportions of the labour force.

### The Affirmative Action Controversy

Let's consider the last item. **Affirmative action** consists of special efforts by employers to increase employment and promotion opportunities for groups that have suffered past discrimination and continue to experience discrimination. To say that affirmative action has stirred controversy is to make an understatement. There are strong arguments for and against this approach to remedying discrimination.

**In Support of Affirmative Action** Those who support affirmative action say that historically women and minorities have been forced to carry the extra burden of discrimination in their attempt to achieve economic success. Thus, they find themselves far behind white males, who have been preferred workers. Merely removing the discrimination burden does nothing to close the present socioeconomic gap. Something more than equal opportunity—preferential treatment—is necessary to counter the inherent bias in favour of white men if women and minorities are to catch up.

Supporters of affirmative action argue that job discrimination is so pervasive that it will persist for decades if society is content to accept only marginal antidiscriminatory changes in employment practices. Moreover, such changes are hampered by the fact that white males have achieved seniority that protects them from layoffs and places the burden of unemployment disproportionately on women and minorities. And women and minorities have been discriminated against in acquiring human capital—the education and job training needed to compete on equal terms with white males. Discrimination has supposedly become so highly institutionalized that extraordinary countermeasures are required.

Those who accept this line of reasoning endorse affirmative action and other forms of preferential treatment as appropriate means for hastening the elimination of discrimination. In this view, affirmative action is not only a path towards social equity but also a good national strategy for enhancing efficiency and economic growth since it brings formerly excluded groups directly into the productive economic mainstream.

**Opposing View** Those against affirmative action claim that preferential treatment frequently has forced employers to hire less qualified women and visible minority workers and therefore has *impaired* economic efficiency. Critics also say that quotas and preferential treatment are a form of **reverse discrimination**. Preferential treatment and discrimination, they say, are simply two views of the same thing: to show preference for a is to discriminate against b.

Some opponents of affirmative action go further, contending that policies that give preferential treatment to disadvantaged groups have actually worked to these groups' long-term detriment. Such policies, say critics, have placed many persons in positions where their skill deficiencies become evident to their employers and coworkers. This has two effects, both negative: First, majority workers who have been passed over for jobs or promotions resent the groups who are given special treatment. Second, the highly qualified women and minority members of the workforce, who have no need of preferential treatment, mistakenly get stereotyped by others as "affirmative action hires." In this view, continuing racial tension not only reflects the long legacy of discrimination but also the more recent ill-conceived policies designed to end it.

## 16-6 QUICK REVIEW

- In Canada federal and provincial legislation has outlawed wage and employment discrimination based on race, colour, religion, gender, and national origin.
- Affirmative action programs are designed to overcome past and present discrimination by giving preferences to women and visible minorities; they are highly controversial and recently have come under attack by those who feel they reflect reverse discrimination.

## In The Media

# Reality Bites: No Diploma, No Job Offers

BRUCE LITTLE

The economy has been creating jobs for almost three years now, but a very large group of Canadians has been getting almost nothing out of the recovery. They're easy to spot because they lack something employers increasingly demand—solid educational credentials.

A new iron law is taking over in the workplace.

If you have completed some form of postsecondary education —a university degree, a community-college diploma, a training certificate—you're going to get a job. If you have anything less, you won't.

Last year, the economy added 277,000 jobs, its best showing since 1989. Look who got them: For those with a high-school edu-

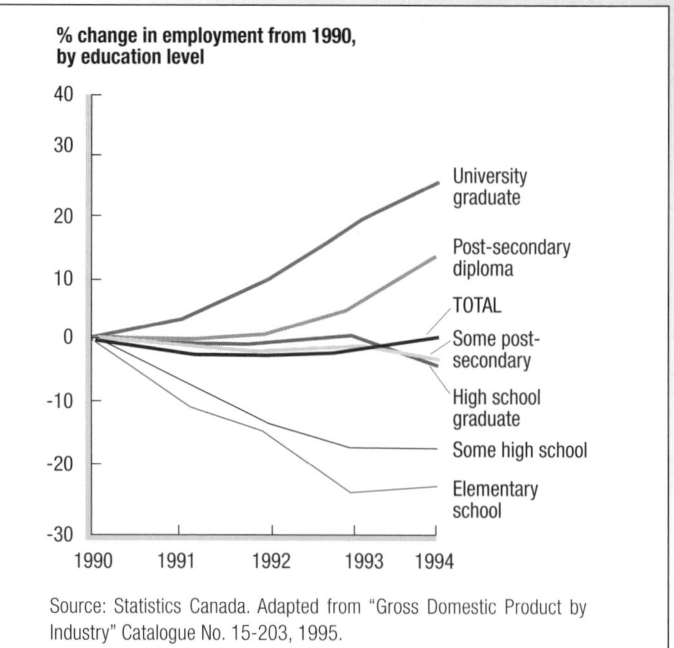


Source: Statistics Canada. Adapted from "Gross Domestic Product by Industry" Catalogue No. 15-203, 1995.

cation or less, 145,000 jobs disappeared. For those with a postsecondary education, 422,000 jobs opened up. That means 99.3 per cent of people entering the labour force with a degree or diploma found work.

As the accompanying chart shows, the door has closed on job seekers who have failed to go beyond high school. When you look at the overall job market, the path of recession and recovery is clear. From 1990 to 1992, total employment fell 323,000; from 1992 to 1994, employment climbed by 450,000. Last year, we were 127,000 jobs ahead of 1990.

Now zero in on what happened to people according to their schooling from 1990 to 1994:

- University graduates never missed a beat. For them, employment increased 483,000, a gain of 25 per cent.
- Those with a postsecondary diploma or certificate saw little job growth during the recession, but have cashed in during the recovery. By last year, they were 474,000 jobs ahead of 1990, a 14-per-cent increase.
- Those with some postsecondary schooling, but no certificate, lost 36,000 jobs over the four years, a 3-per-cent drop.
- High-school graduates held their own during the recession and first year of the recovery, but were shut out in 1994. Employment for that group was down 120,000—4 per cent—from 1990.
- Canadians with some high school to their credit fared badly throughout, losing 445,000 jobs, more than 17 per cent of the work slots open to them in 1990.
- The hardest hit were people with only an elementary-school education. For them, employment fell 229,000, a decline of 23 per cent.

Regular readers will recognize this chart as one we've run before. Two years ago, it appeared that the recession was having a disproportionate impact on the less educated, but even then, Philip Cross, Statistics Canada's chief of current analysis, was flagging the fact that a historic shift in the labour market was under way.

It's even clearer now that he was dead on. If the recession was tough on the less educated, the recovery has been even harder; they know companies are hiring, but they don't have the certified skills to get any of the jobs.

Look at it this way. From 1990 to 1994, the economy created about 957,000 jobs for people with that essential piece of paper attesting to their postsecondary-school achievements. At the same time, it destroyed 830,000 jobs for people with anything less.

In a 13.3-million-person job market, that's a massive change over such a short period. Last year, people with a postsecondary certificate of some kind held 48 per cent of all jobs, up from 41 per cent in 1990. The share of jobs available to those who didn't finish high school fell to 21 from 27 per cent. Those with a high-school diploma and some postsecondary schooling had the rest.

These rapidly changing shares underline the fundamental transformation of the work world in recent years. The spread of computers has been wiping out low-skilled clerical and blue-collar jobs. As companies have brought more sophisticated information technology into their offices and factories, they've been able to make do with fewer workers. At the same time, they've had to upgrade the skills of the people they kept; otherwise, their workers wouldn't be able to get the most out of the new equipment.

*Source: Globe and Mail*, March 13, 1995 p. A9. Reprinted with permission.

## THE STORY IN BRIEF

The author marshals statistical evidence indicating the more education and/or training you have, the more success you will have in the job market, both in pay and stability of employment.

## THE ECONOMICS BEHIND THE STORY

- Firms want to maximize profits; they select employees who will help them in this endeavour.
- Technological advances have made it possible to replace employees in jobs with low levels of education and/or training requirements. The new jobs being created in Canada in the last decade of the twentieth century are going overwhelmingly to those with a postsecondary diploma or degree who have either the necessary skills or the educational background to easily acquire those skills. Between 1990 and 1994 almost a million jobs were created, requiring postsecondary-school education; over 800,000 low-skilled jobs were lost.
- How do the education and/or training of a person affect the wage he or she commands on the job market? In your answer be sure to include the impact of supply and demand forces in a given labour market. ■

## The Last Word

### ORCHESTRATING IMPARTIALITY

**Have "blind" musical auditions, in which "screens" are used to hide the identity of candidates, affected the success of women in obtaining positions in major symphony orchestras?**

THERE HAVE LONG BEEN ALLEGATIONS OF discrimination against women in the hiring process in some occupations. But such discrimination is usually difficult to demonstrate. Economists Claudia Goldin and Cecilia Rouse* spotted a unique opportunity for testing such discrimination as it relates to major symphony orchestras. In the past, orchestras relied on their musical directors to extend invitations to candidates, audition them, and handpick new members. Concerned with the potential for bias, in the 1970s and 1980s orchestras altered the process in two ways. First, orchestra members were included as judges, and, second, orchestras began open competitions using "blind" auditions with a physical "screen" (usually a room divider) to conceal the identity of the candidates. (These blind auditions, however, did *not* extend to the final competition in most orchestras.) Did the change in procedures increase the probability of women being hired?

To answer this question, Goldin and Rouse gained access to orchestral management files to examine auditions for eight major orchestras. These records contained the names of all candidates and identified those who advanced to the next round, including the ultimate winner of the competition. The researchers then looked for women in the sample who had "competed" in auditions both before and after the introduction of the blind screening.

There was a strong suspicion of bias against women in hiring musicians for the nation's finest orchestras. These positions are highly desirable, not only because they are prestigious but also because they offer high pay (often more than $75,000 annually). In 1970 only 5 percent of the members of the top five orchestras in North America were women, and many music directors publicly suggested that women players, in general, have less musical talent.

The change to screens provided direct evidence of past discrimination. The screens increased by 50 percent the probability that a woman would be advanced from the preliminary rounds. The screens also greatly increased the likelihood that a woman would be selected in the final round. Without the screens, about 10 percent of all hires were women, but with the screens about 35 percent were women. Today, about 25 percent of the membership of top symphony orchestras are women, in contrast to 5 percent in 1970. The screens explain from 25 to 45 percent of the increases in the proportion of women in the orchestras studied.

Was the past discrimination in hiring an example of *statistical discrimination* based on, say, a presumption of greater turnover by women or more leaves for medical (including maternity) or other reasons? To answer that question, Goldin and Rouse examined information on turnover and leaves of orchestra members for the period 1960 to 1996. They found that neither differed by gender, so leaves and turnover should *not* have influenced hiring decisions.

Instead, the discrimination in hiring seemed to reflect a *taste-for-discrimination* by musical directors. Male musical directors apparently had a positive discrimination coefficient *d*. At the fixed (union-determined) wage, they simply preferred male musicians, at women's expense. ■

*Claudia Goldin and Cecilia Rouse, "Orchestrating Impartiality: The Impact of 'Blind' Auditions on Female Musicians," National Bureau of Economic Research, Working Paper 5903, January 1997.

## CHAPTER SUMMARY

1. The term "labour" encompasses all people who work for pay. The *wage rate* is the price paid per unit of time for labour. Labour *earnings* comprise total pay and are found by multiplying the number of hours worked by the hourly

wage rate. The nominal *wage rate* is the amount of money received per unit of time; the real wage rate is the purchasing power of the nominal wage.

2. The long-run growth of real hourly earnings—the average real wage—roughly matches that of productivity, with both increasing over the long run. But real wage growth has stagnated since 1982, due to **a** a slowdown in productivity growth and **b** real wage growth that has not kept pace with productivity growth.
3. Global comparisons show that real wages in Canada are relatively high, but not the highest, internationally. High real wages in the advanced industrial countries stem largely from high labour productivity.
4. Specific wage rates depend on the structure of the particular labour market. In a competitive labour market, the equilibrium wage rate and level of employment are determined at the intersection of the labour supply curve and labour demand curve. For the individual firm, the market wage rate establishes a horizontal labour supply curve, meaning that the wage rate equals the firm's constant marginal resource cost. The firm hires workers to the point where its MRP equals this MRC.
5. Under monopsony the marginal resource cost curve lies above the resource supply curve because the monopsonist must bid up the wage rate to hire extra workers and must pay that higher wage rate to *all* workers. The monopsonist hires fewer workers than are hired under competitive conditions, pays less-than-competitive wage rates (has lower labour costs), and thus obtains greater profit.
6. A union may raise competitive wage rates by **a** increasing the derived demand for labour, **b** restricting the supply of labour through exclusive unionism, or **c** directly enforcing an above-equilibrium wage rate through inclusive unionism.
7. In many industries the labour market takes the form of bilateral monopoly, in which a strong union "sells" labour to a monopsonistic employer. The wage rate outcome of this labour market model depends on union and employer bargaining power.
8. On average, unionized workers realize wage rates 10 to 15 percent higher than comparable nonunion workers.
9. Economists disagree about the desirability of the minimum wage as an anti-poverty mechanism. While it causes unemployment for some low-income workers, it raises the incomes of others who retain their jobs.
10. Wage differentials are largely explainable in terms of **a** noncompeting groups arising from differences in the capacities and education of different groups of workers; **b** compensating wage differences, that is, wage differences that must be paid to offset nonmonetary differences in jobs; and **c** market imperfections in the form of lack of job information, geographical immobility, union and government restraints, and discrimination.
11. The principal-agent problem arises when workers shirk—provide less-than-expected effort. Firms may combat this by monitoring workers or by creating incentive pay schemes that link worker compensation to effort.
12. There is disagreement about whether unions increase or decrease efficiency and productivity. The negative view cites **a** inefficiencies associated with featherbedding and union-imposed work rules, **b** loss of output through strikes, and **c** the misallocation of labour caused by the union wage advantage. The positive view holds that **a** through the shock effect, union wage pressure spurs technological advance and mechanization of the production process; **b** as collective-voice institutions, unions contribute to rising productivity by reducing labour turnover; and **c** the enhanced security of union workers increases their willingness to teach their skills to less experienced workers.
13. Discrimination relating to the labour market occurs when women or minorities having the same abilities, education, training, and experience as men or white workers are given inferior treatment with respect to hiring, occupational choice, education and training, promotion, and wage rates. Forms of discrimination are wage discrimination, employment discrimination, occupational discrimination, and human capital discrimination. Discrimination redistributes national income and, by creating inefficiencies, diminishes its size.
14. In the taste-for-discrimination model, some white employers have a preference for discrimination, measured by a discrimination coefficient *d*. Prejudiced white employers will hire visible minority workers only if their wages are at least *d* dollars below those of whites. The model indicates that declines in the discrimination coefficients of white employers will increase the demand for visible minority workers, raising the visible minority wage rate and the ratio of visible minority to white wages. It also suggests that competition may eliminate discrimination in the long run.
15. Statistical discrimination occurs when employers base employment decisions about *individuals* on the average characteristics of *groups* of workers. This can lead to discrimination against individuals even in the absence of prejudice.

16. The crowding model of occupational segregation indicates how white males gain higher earnings at the expense of women and minorities who are confined to a limited number of occupations. The model shows that discrimination also causes a net loss of domestic output.

17. Those who support affirmative action say it is needed to help women and minorities compensate for decades of discrimination. Opponents say affirmative action causes economic inefficiency and reverse discrimination.

## TERMS AND CONCEPTS

nominal and real wage
purely competitive labour market
monopsony
exclusive unionism
occupational licensing
inclusive unionism
bilateral monopoly
minimum wage
wage differentials
noncompeting groups
human capital investment
compensating differences
incentive pay plan
collective voice
exit mechanism
voice mechanism
labour market discrimination
wage discrimination
employment discrimination
occupational discrimination
human-capital discrimination
taste-for-discrimination model
discrimination coefficient
statistical discrimination
occupational segregation
affirmative action
reverse discrimination

## STUDY QUESTIONS

1. Explain why the general level of wages is high in Canada and other industrially advanced countries. What is the most important single factor underlying the long-run increase in average real wage rates in Canada?

2. What factors might explain the stagnation of real wages in Canada in the past two decades?

3. KEY QUESTION *Describe wage determination in a labour market in which workers are unorganized and many firms actively compete for the services of labour. Show this situation graphically, using $W_1$ to indicate the equilibrium wage rate and $Q_1$ to show the number of workers hired by the firm as a group. Show the labour supply curve of the individual firm and compare it with that of the total market. Why the differences? In the diagram representing the firm, identify total revenue, total wage cost, and revenue available for the payment of nonlabour resources.*

4. KEY QUESTION *Complete the following labour supply table for a firm hiring labour competitively:*

| Units of labour | Wage rate | Total labour cost (wage bill) | Marginal resource (labour) cost |
|---|---|---|---|
| 0 | $14 | $_____ | |
| | | | $_____ |
| 1 | 14 | _____ | |
| | | | _____ |
| 2 | 14 | _____ | |
| | | | _____ |
| 3 | 14 | _____ | |
| | | | _____ |
| 4 | 14 | _____ | |
| | | | _____ |
| 5 | 14 | _____ | |
| | | | _____ |
| 6 | 14 | _____ | |

**a.** *Show graphically the labour supply and marginal resource (labour) cost curves for this firm. Explain the relationship of these curves to one another.*

**b.** *Plot the labour demand data of question 2 in Chapter 15 on the same graph as (a). What is the equilibrium wage rate and level of employment? Explain.*

**5.** Suppose the formerly competing firms of question 3 form an employers' association that hires labour as a monopsonist would. Describe verbally the effect on wage rates and employment. Adjust the graph you drew for question 3, showing the monopsonistic wage rate and employment level as $W_2$ and $Q_2$, respectively. Using this monopsony model, explain why hospital administrators sometimes complain about a "shortage" of nurses. How might such a "shortage" be corrected?

**6.** KEY QUESTION *Assume a firm is a monopsonist that can hire its first worker for $6 but must increase the wage rate by $3 to attract each successive worker. Draw the firm's labour supply and marginal labour cost curves and explain their relationships to one another. On the same graph, plot the labour demand data of question 2 in Chapter 15. What is the equilibrium wage rate and level of employment? Why do these differ from your answer to question 4?*

**7.** KEY QUESTION *Assume a monopsonistic employer is paying a wage rate of $W_m$ and hiring $Q_m$ workers, as indicated in Figure 16-8. Now suppose an industrial union is formed and it forces the employer to accept a wage rate of $W_c$. Explain verbally and graphically why in this instance the higher wage rate will be accompanied by an increase in the number of workers hired.*

**8.** On average, do union workers receive higher wages than comparable nonunion workers?

**9.** "Many of the lowest-paid people in society—for example, short-order cooks—also have relatively poor working conditions. Hence, the notion of compensating wage differentials is disproved." Do you agree? Explain.

**10.** What is meant by investment in human capital? Use this concept to explain **a** wage differentials, and **b** the long-run rise of real wage rates in Canada.

**11.** What is the principal-agent problem? Have you ever worked in a setting where this problem has arisen? If so, do you think increased monitoring would have eliminated the problem? Why don't firms simply hire more supervisors to eliminate shirking?

**12.** KEY QUESTION *What is the estimated size of the union wage advantage? How might this advantage diminish the efficiency with which labour resources are allocated?*

**13.** Explain the logic of each of the following statements:

**a.** By constraining the decisions of management, unions reduce efficiency and productivity growth.

**b.** As collective-voice institutions, unions increase productivity by reducing worker turnover, inducing managerial efficiency, and enhancing worker security.

**14.** Explain how discrimination reduces domestic output and income. Demonstrate this loss using production possibilities analysis.

**15.** KEY QUESTION *The labour demand and supply data in the table below relate to a single occupation. Use them to answer the questions that follow. Base your answers on the taste-for-discrimination model.*

| Quantity of visible minority labour demanded, thousands | Visible minority wage rate | Quantity of visible minority labour supplied, thousands |
|---|---|---|
| 24 | $16 | 52 |
| 30 | 14 | 44 |
| 36 | 12 | 36 |
| 42 | 10 | 28 |
| 48 | 8 | 20 |

**a.** *Plot the labour demand and supply curves for visible minority workers in this occupation.*

**b.** *What are the equilibrium visible minority wage rate and quantity of visible minority employment?*

**c.** *Suppose the white wage rate in this occupation is $16. What is the visible minority-to-white wage ratio?*

**d.** *Suppose a particular employer has a discrimination coefficient d of $5 per hour. Will that employer hire visible minority or white workers at the visible minority-white wage ratio indicated in part (c)? Explain.*

**e.** *Suppose employers as a group become less prejudiced against visible minorities and demand 14 more units of visible minority labour at each wage rate in the table. What are the new equilibrium visible minority wage rate and level of employment? Does the visible minority-white wage ratio rise or fall? Explain.*

**f.** *Suppose visible minorities as a group increase their labour services in this occupation, collectively offering 14 more units of labour at each wage rate. Disregarding the changes indicated in part (e), what are the new equilibrium visible minority wage rate and level of employment? Does the visible minority-white wage ratio rise, or does it fall?*

**16.** Males under the age of 25 must pay far higher auto insurance premiums than females in this age group. How does this fact relate to statistical discrimination? Statistical discrimination implies that discrimination can persist indefinitely, while the taste-for-discrimination model suggests that competition might reduce discrimination in the long run. Explain the difference.

**17.** KEY QUESTION *Use a demand and supply model to explain the impact of occupational segregation or "crowding" on the relative wage rates and earnings of men and women. Who gains and who loses from the elimination of occupational segregation? Is there a net gain or net loss to society? Explain.*

**18.** "Current affirmative action programs are based on the belief that to overcome discrimination, we must practise discrimination. That perverse logic has created a system that undermines the fundamental values it was intended to protect." Do you agree? Why or why not?

**19.** Suppose Ann and Becky are applicants to your university and that they have *identical* academic admission qualifications. Ann is a member of a visible minority, growing up in a public housing development; Becky is white, growing up in a wealthy area of the city. You can admit only one of the two. Which person would you admit and why? Now suppose that *Ann* is white and *Becky* is a member of a visible minority, *all else equal.* Does this change your selection? Why or why not?

**20.** **(The Last Word)** What two types of discrimination are represented by the discrimination evidenced in this chapter's Last Word?

**21.** WEB-BASED QUESTION **Top Sports Salaries in Football, Basketball, and Baseball—Is There Equality?** In poll after poll, professional football has been called one of the country's most popular sports. It commands millions from TV contracts. Yet the top football salaries pale in comparison with the mega contracts players in other professional sports sign. Use the major sports sites www.espn.sportszone.com/, www.cnnsi.com/, and www.cbs.sportsline.com/ to identify the top yearly salary in the National Football League, the National Hockey League, the National Basketball Association, and the Major Baseball Leagues. Which league has the highest salaried player? Speculate as to why. What is the difference between productivity on the field and the productivity of business revenue which the game generates?

## CHAPTER 17

# Rent, Interest, and Profit

WE BEGAN THE PREVIOUS CHAPTER WITH SOME facts and questions about wages. We do the same here for three other sources of income: rent, interest, and profit.

- Fact: In urban areas such as Toronto or Vancouver, a hectare of land may sell for more than $30 million. In Tokyo, a hectare of land can sell for more than $85 million. A hectare of desert may cost $700,000 along the Las Vegas casino strip, while a hectare of land in the middle of the Nevada desert can be purchased for as little as $50. *Question:* How do land prices and rents get established?
- Fact: If you put money in a one-year Guaranteed Investment Certificate (GIC) in early 1991, you probably received an interest rate of 7 percent. One year later that GIC paid only 6 percent interest. In early 1998 the interest rate on this type of GIC was 3.7 percent. *Question:* What factors determine interest rates and cause those rates to change?
- Fact: The news media continually document the annual profit and loss performance of firms and industries. In 1996, Canadian Pacific's profit was up 201 percent from the year earlier, Bell Canada Enterprises had a 47 percent profit increase, and Nortel's profit increased by 32 percent. Meanwhile, Seagram's profit declined by 94 percent, Falconbridge's profit was down 26 percent, and Inco's profit was down 21 percent. All these firms were profitable, but a few major firms (Corel, Apple Computer) suffered losses in 1996. *Questions:* What are the sources of profits and losses? What functions do they serve? What causes profits and losses of individual firms to change over time?

Our emphasis in Chapter 16 was on labour markets; wages account for about three-fourths of Canadian domestic income. In this chapter we focus on rent, interest, and profit, which make up the remaining one-fourth of national income.

**IN THIS CHAPTER YOU WILL LEARN:**

How the price of land is determined.

•

How the interest rate is determined.

•

What profit is, and how profits, along with losses, allocates resources among alternative uses in an economy.

•

What the share of income going to each of the factors of production is in Canada.

## The Big Picture

THIS CHAPTER LOOKS AT THE EMPLOYMENT and pricing of the remaining factors of production: land, capital, and entrepreneurial talent. The main principles set out in Chapter 15 about demand still apply. Supply factors are now introduced; they, along with demand factors, determine the "price" of land, capital, and entrepreneurship, and the amounts employed.

As you read this chapter, keep the following points in mind:

- Land rents are determined by specific supply and demand conditions. Differential rents allocate land among alternative uses.
- Interest is the price paid for the use of money (capital). The interest rate is determined by the supply and demand of loanable funds. The interest rate allocates capital among alternative uses.
- The "price" paid for entrepreneurship is profit; economic profit results from **a** the bearing of uninsurable risk, **b** innovation, and **c** monopoly power. Profit allocates entrepreneurship among alternative industries. ■

## ECONOMIC RENT

To most people "rent" means the money one must pay for a two-bedroom apartment or a dormitory room. To the business executive "rent" is a payment made for the use of a factory building, machine, or warehouse facility. These common definitions of rent can be confusing and ambiguous. Dormitory room rent, for example, may include other payments as well—interest on money the university borrowed to finance the dormitory, wages for custodial services, utility payments, and so on.

Economists use "rent" in a narrower sense. **Economic rent** *is the price paid for the use of land and other natural resources that are completely fixed in total supply.* The unique supply conditions of land and other natural resources—their fixed overall supply—make rental payments distinguishable from wage, interest, and profit payments.

Let's examine this idea and some of its implications through supply and demand analysis. We first assume that all land is of the same grade or quality; each arable (tillable) hectare of land is as productive as every other hectare. Suppose, too, that all land has a single use: producing corn. And also assume that land is rented in a competitive market in which many corn farmers are demanding land and many landowners are offering land in the market.

In Figure 17-1, curve $S$ represents the supply of arable farmland available in the economy as a whole, and $D_2$ the demand of farmers for use of that land. As with all economic resources, this demand is derived from the demand for the product being produced. The demand curve for land is downsloping because of diminishing returns and because, for farmers as a group, product price must be reduced to sell additional units of output.

### Perfectly Inelastic Supply

The unique feature of our analysis is on the supply side. For all practical purposes the supply of land is perfectly inelastic, as reflected in supply curve $S$. Land has no production cost; it is a "free and nonreproducible gift of nature." The economy has only so much land, and that is that. Of course, within limits any parcel of land can be made more usable by clearing, drainage, and irrigation. But these are capital improvements and not changes in the amount of land itself. Also, these increases in the usability of land affect only a small fraction of the total amount of land and do not change the basic fact that land and other natural resources are virtually fixed in supply.

### Changes in Demand

Because the supply of land is fixed, demand is the only active determinant of land rent; supply is

**FIGURE 17-1 The determination of land rent**

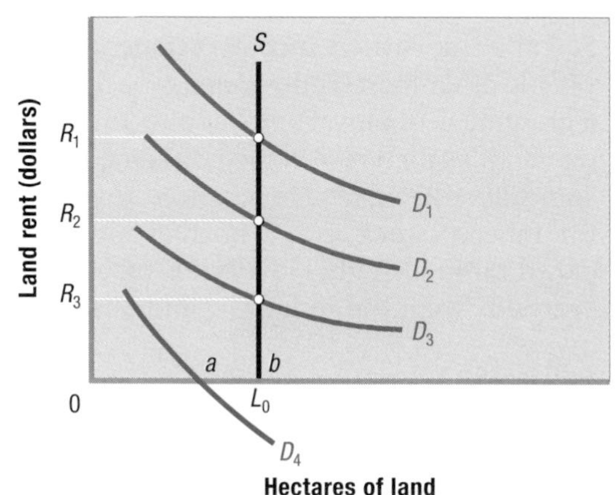


Because the supply $S$ of land (and other natural resources) is perfectly inelastic, demand is the sole active determinant of land rent. An increase in demand from $D_2$ to $D_1$ or a decrease in demand from $D_2$ to $D_3$ will cause a considerable change in rent: from $R_2$ to $R_1$ in the first instance and from $R_2$ to $R_3$ in the second. But the amount of land supplied will remain at $L_0$. If demand is very weak ($D_4$) relative to supply, land will be a "free good," commanding no rent.

passive. And what determines the demand for land? The factors discussed in Chapter 15: the price of the product grown on the land, the productivity of land (which depends in part on the quantity and quality of the resources with which land is combined), and the prices of the other resources that are combined with land.

If the demand for land in Figure 17-1 should increase from $D_2$ to $D_1$, land rent would increase from $R_2$ to $R_1$. On the other hand, if the demand for land declined from $D_2$ to $D_3$, land rent would fall from $R_2$ to $R_3$. But, in either case, the amount of land supplied would remain the same at $L_0$. Changes in economic rent can have no effect on the amount of land available since the supply of land cannot be augmented. If the demand for land were only $D_4$, land rent would be zero. Land would be a *free good*—one whose demand is so weak relative to supply that there is an excess supply of it even if the market price is zero. In Figure 17-1, this excess supply is shown as distance $b - a$ at rent of zero. This situation was approximated in the free-land era of Canadian history.

Figure 17-1 helps explain the high Japanese land prices noted at the start of this chapter. Japan's population is 120 million, roughly four times that of Canada. Japan's land area, however, is only about 4 percent that of Canada. Additionally, habitable land in Japan is roughly 1/40th that of Canada. Knowing land is in such short supply, we can see why 1 square metre of land in central Tokyo was priced at about $375,000 in 1997.

## Land Rent: A Surplus Payment

The perfectly inelastic supply of land must be contrasted with the relatively elastic supply of capital, such as apartment buildings, machinery, and warehouses. In the long run, capital is *not* fixed in total supply. A higher price gives entrepreneurs the incentive to construct and offer larger quantities of these property resources. Conversely, a decline in price induces suppliers to allow existing facilities to depreciate and not be replaced. The supply curves of these nonland resources are upsloping, meaning the prices paid to such resources provide an **incentive function**. A high price provides an incentive to offer more of the resource; a low price, an incentive to offer less.

Not so with land. Rent serves no incentive function because the total supply of land is fixed. Whether rent is $10,000, $500, $1, or $0 per hectare, the same amount of land is available to society for use in production. For this reason economists consider rent to be a *surplus payment* that is not necessary to ensure that land is available to the economy as a whole.

## A Single Tax on Land

If land is a free gift of nature, costs nothing to produce, and would be available even without rental payments, why should rent be paid to those who by historical accident, by inheritance, or by crook happen to be landowners? Socialists have long argued that all land rents are unearned incomes. They argue land should be nationalized—owned by the state—so that any payments for its use can be used by the government to further the well-being of the entire population rather than being used by a landowning minority.

**Henry George's Proposal** In the United States, criticism of rental payments has taken the form of a **single-tax movement**, which gained much support in the late nineteenth century. Spearheaded by Henry George's provocative book *Progress and Poverty* (1879), this reform movement maintained that economic rent could be taxed away without impairing the available supply of land or, therefore, the productive potential of the economy as a whole.

George observed that as population grew and the geographic frontier closed, landowners enjoyed larger and larger rents from their landholdings. These increasing rents were the result of a growing demand for a resource whose supply was perfectly inelastic. Some landlords were receiving fabulously high incomes not through their productive effort but solely from holding advantageously located land. George stated that these increases in land rent belonged to the economy; he held that land rents should be heavily taxed and the revenue spent for public uses.

George held that there was no reason to tax away, say, only 50 percent of the landowner's unearned rental income. Why not take 70 or 90 or 99 percent? In seeking popular support for his ideas on land taxation, George proposed that taxes on rental income be the *only* tax levied by government.

George's case for taxing land was based not only on equity or fairness but also on efficiency. That is, a tax on land is efficient because, unlike virtually every other tax, it does not alter the use of the resource. A tax on wages reduces after-tax wages and can weaken incentives to work; an individual who decides to work for a \$6 before-tax wage may decide to quit and go on welfare when an income tax reduces the wage to an after-tax \$4.50. Similarly, a property tax on buildings lowers returns to investors in such property and might cause some to look for other investments. But no such reallocations of resources occur when land is taxed. The most profitable use of land before it is taxed remains the most profitable use after a tax is imposed. Of course, a landlord could withdraw land from production when a tax is imposed, but this would mean no rental income at all. Some rental income, no matter how small, is better than none.

**Criticisms** Critics of the single tax on land say:

1. Current levels of government spending are such that a land tax alone would not bring in enough revenue; it cannot be considered realistically as a *single* tax.
2. Most income payments involve two or more elements of interest, rent, wages, and profits. Land is typically improved in some way, and economic rent cannot be readily disentangled from payments for these improvements. In practice, it would be difficult to determine how much of any specific income payment is actually economic rent.
3. So-called unearned income accrues to many people other than landowners, especially with a growing economy. For example, consider the *capital gains* income received by someone who, some 20 or 25 years ago, chanced to purchase (or inherit) stock in a firm that has experienced rapid growth. How is this income more "earned" than the rental income of the landowner?
4. Historically, a piece of land is likely to have changed ownership many times. Former owners may have been the beneficiaries of past increases in the value of the land (and in land rent). It is hardly fair to place a heavy tax on current owners who paid the competitive market price for the land.

## Productivity Differences and Rent Differences

Thus far we have assumed all units of land are of the same grade. This is plainly not so. Different pieces of land vary greatly in productivity, depending on soil fertility and such climatic factors as rainfall and temperature. These factors explain, for example, why soil in Southern Ontario is extremely well suited to corn production, the Prairies are much less well suited, and the Yukon is incapable of corn production. Such productivity differences are reflected in resource demand and prices. Competitive bidding by farmers will establish a high rent for the very productive Ontario land; less productive Prairie land will command a much lower rent; and land in the Yukon perhaps will command no rent at all.

Location may be equally important in explaining differences in land rent. Other things equal, renters will pay more for a unit of land that is strategically located with respect to materials, labour, and customers than for a unit of land whose location is remote from these things. Examples: the enormously high land rents in large metropolitan areas and at the bases of major alpine ski areas.

The rent differentials arising from quality differences in land can be seen by viewing Figure 17-1 from a slightly different perspective. Suppose, as before, that only corn can be produced on four grades of land, each of which is available in the fixed amount $L_0$. When combined with identical amounts of labour, capital, and entrepreneurial talent, the productivity or, more specifically, the marginal revenue product of each of the four grades of land is reflected in demand curves $D_1$, $D_2$, $D_3$, and $D_4$. Grade 1 land is the most productive, as shown by $D_1$, while grade 4 is the least productive, as shown by $D_4$. The resulting economic rents for grades 1, 2, and 3 land will be $R_1$, $R_2$, and $R_3$, respectively; the rent differential will mirror the differences in productivity of the three grades of land. Grade 4 land is so poor in quality that, given its supply $S$, farmers won't pay to use it. It will be a free good because it is not sufficiently scarce in relation to the demand for it to command a price and a rent.

### Alternative Uses of Land

We have also supposed that land has only one use. Actually, we know that land normally has alternative uses. A hectare of Ontario farmland may be useful in raising not only corn but also wheat, oats, barley, and cattle; or it may be used for a house, highway, or factory site. This tells us that a particular use of land involves an opportunity cost—the forgone production from the next best use of the resource. Where there are alternative uses, individual firms must pay rent to cover these opportunity costs if they are to secure the use of land for their particular purposes. To individual firms rent is a cost of production, just like wages and interest.

Recall that, as viewed by society, economic rent is *not* a cost. Society would have the same amount of land with or without the payment of economic rent. From society's perspective, economic rent is a *surplus payment* above that needed for society to gain the use of a resource. But individual firms *do* need to pay rent to attract land resources away from alternative uses; for firms, rental payments are a *cost*. ***(Key Question 2)***

#### 17-1
#### QUICK REVIEW

- Economic rent is the price paid for resources such as land whose supply is perfectly inelastic.
- Land rent is a surplus payment because land would be available to society even if this rent were not paid.
- The surplus nature of land rent was the basis for Henry George's single-tax movement.
- Differential rents allocate land among alternative uses.

## INTEREST

*Interest is the price paid for the use of money.* It is, in essence, the amount of money that must be paid for the use of $1 for 1 year.

1. **Interest is stated as a percentage.** Interest is paid in kind; that is, money (interest) is paid for the loan of money. For that reason, interest is typically stated as a percentage of the amount of money borrowed rather than as a dollar amount. It is less clumsy to say that interest is "12 percent annually" than to say that interest is "$120 per year per $1,000." Also, stating interest as a percentage makes it easier to compare interest paid on loans of different amounts. By expressing interest as a percentage, we can immediately compare an interest payment of, say, $432 per year per $2,880 with one of $1,800 per year per $12,000. Both interest payments are 15 percent per year, which is not obvious from the actual dollar figures. This interest of 15 percent per year is referred to as a 15 percent interest *rate*.
2. **Money is not a resource.** Money is *not* an economic resource. As coins, paper currency, or chequing accounts, money is not productive; it cannot produce goods and services. However, businesses "buy" the use of money because it can be used to acquire capital goods—factories, machinery, warehouses, and so on. These facilities clearly do contribute to production. Thus, in "hiring" the use of money capital, business executives are often indirectly buying the use of real capital goods.

### Loanable Funds Theory of Interest

In *macroeconomics* the interest rate is viewed through the lens of the economy's total supply of and demand for money. But since our present focus is microeconomics, it will be useful to consider a more micro-based theory of interest here. Specifically, the **loanable funds theory of interest** explains the interest rate not in terms of the total supply of and demand for money but, rather, in terms of the supply of and demand for *funds available for lending (and borrowing)*. As shown in Figure 17-2, the equilibrium interest rate (here, 8 percent) is the rate at which the quantities of loanable funds supplied and demanded are equal.

**FIGURE 17-2 The market for loanable funds**

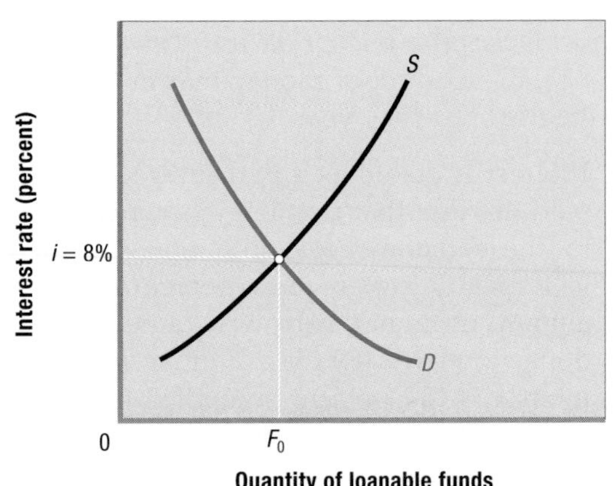


The upsloping supply curve *S* for loanable funds reflects the idea that at higher interest rates, households will defer more of their present consumption (save more) making more funds available for lending. The downsloping demand curve *D* for loanable funds indicates that businesses will borrow more at lower interest rates than at higher interest rates. At the equilibrium interest rate (here, 8 percent) the quantities of loanable funds lent and borrowed are equal (here, $F_0$ each).

Let's first consider the loanable funds theory in a simplified form. Specifically, assume households or consumers are the sole suppliers of loanable funds and businesses are the only demanders. Also suppose that lending occurs directly between households and businesses; there are no intermediate financial institutions.

**Supply of Loanable Funds** The supply of loanable funds is represented as curve *S* in Figure 17-2. Its upward slope indicates that households will make available a larger quantity of funds at high interest rates than at low interest rates. Most people prefer to use their incomes to purchase pleasurable goods and services *today*, rather than delay purchases to sometime in the *future*. For people to delay consumption—that is, to increase their saving—they must be "bribed" or compensated by an interest payment. The larger the amount of this payment, the greater the deferral of household consumption and thus the greater the amount of money made available for loans.

There is disagreement among economists as to how much the quantity of loanable funds made available by suppliers changes in response to changes in the interest rate. Most economists view saving as being relatively insensitive to changes in the interest rate. The supply curve of loanable funds may therefore be more inelastic than implied by *S* in Figure 17-2.

**Demand for Loanable Funds** Businesses borrow loanable funds primarily to add to their stocks of capital goods—new plants or warehouses, machinery, and equipment. Suppose a firm wants to buy a machine that will increase output and sales such that its total revenue will rise by \$110 for the year. Also assume the machine costs \$100 and has a useful life of just 1 year. Comparing the \$10 earned beyond the cost of the machine with the \$100 cost, we find that the *expected rate of return* on this investment is 10 percent (= \$10/\$100) for the 1 year.

To determine whether the investment is profitable and should be made, the firm must compare the interest rate—the price of loanable funds—with the 10 percent expected rate of return. If funds can be borrowed at some rate less than the rate of return, say, at 8 percent, as in Figure 17-2, then the investment is profitable and should be undertaken. But if funds are available only at an interest rate above the 10 percent rate of return, say, at 14 percent, this investment is unprofitable and should not be made.

Why is the demand for loanable funds downsloping, as in Figure 17-2? At higher interest rates fewer investment projects will be profitable to businesses, and hence a smaller quantity of loanable funds will be demanded. At lower interest rates, more investment projects will be profitable, and therefore more loanable funds will be demanded. Indeed, we have just seen in our example that it is profitable to purchase the \$100 machine if funds can be borrowed at 8 percent but not if the firm must borrow at 14 percent.

## Extending the Model

We now make this simple model more realistic in several ways.

**Financial Institutions** Households rarely lend their savings directly to the businesses that are borrowing funds for investment. Instead, households place their savings in chartered banks (and other financial institutions). The banks pay interest to savers to attract loanable funds and in turn lend these funds to businesses. Businesses borrow the funds from the banks, paying them interest for the use of the money. Financial institutions profit by charging borrowers higher interest rates than the interest rates they pay savers. Both these interest rates, however, are based on the supply of and demand for loanable funds.

**Changes in Supply** Anything that causes households to be more thrifty will prompt them to save more at each interest rate, shifting the supply curve rightward. For example, if interest earned on savings were suddenly exempted from taxation, we would expect the supply of loanable funds to increase and the equilibrium interest rate to decrease.

Conversely, a decline in thriftiness would shift the supply-of-loanable-funds curve leftward and increase the equilibrium interest rate. Illustration: If government expanded social insurance to more fully cover the costs of retirement, the incentives of households to save might diminish.

**Changes in Demand** On the demand side, anything that increases the rates of return on potential investments will increase the demand for loanable funds. Let's return to our earlier example, where a firm would receive additional revenue of $110 by purchasing a $100 machine and, therefore, would realize a 10 percent return on investment. What factors might increase or decrease the rate of return? Suppose a technological advance raises the productivity of the machine so that it increases the firm's total revenue by $120 rather than $110. The rate of return is now 20 percent, not 10 percent. Before the technological advance the firm would have demanded zero loanable funds at, say, an interest rate of 14 percent. But now it will demand $100 of loanable funds at that interest rate, meaning the demand curve for loanable funds has been shifted to the right.

Similarly, an increase in consumer demand for the firm's product will increase the price of its product. So even though the productivity of the machine is unchanged, its potential revenue will rise from $110 to perhaps $120, increasing its rate of return from 10 to 20 percent. Again the firm will be willing to borrow more than previously at our presumed 8 or 14 percent interest rate, implying that the demand curve for loanable funds has shifted rightward. This shift in demand increases the equilibrium interest rate.

Conversely, a decline in productivity or in the price of the firm's product would shift the demand curve for loanable funds leftward, reducing the equilibrium interest rate.

**Other Participants** We must recognize there are more participants on both the demand and supply sides of the loanable funds market. For example, while households are suppliers of loanable funds, many are also demanders of those funds. Households borrow to finance large purchases such as housing, automobiles, furniture, and household appliances. Governments are also on the demand side of the loanable funds market when they borrow to finance budgetary deficits. Similarly, businesses that have revenues in excess of their current expenditures may offer some of those revenues in the market for loanable funds. Thus, like households, businesses operate on both the supply and demand sides of the market.

Finally, if you have studied macroeconomics, you will recall that banks and other financial institutions not only gather and make available the savings of households but also *create* funds through the lending process. This bank creation of money is another source of loanable funds. ***(Key Question 4)***

## Range of Interest Rates

Although economists often speak in terms of a single interest rate, there are in reality a number of interest rates. Table 17-1 lists several interest rates often referred to in the media. These rates range from 5 to 16 percent. Why the differences?

1. **RISK** Loans to different borrowers for different purposes carry varying degrees of risk. The greater the chance that the borrower will not repay the loan, the more interest the lender will charge to compensate for this risk.
2. **MATURITY** The time length or *maturity* of a loan also affects the interest rate. Other things equal, longer-term loans command higher interest rates than shorter-term loans. The long-term lender suffers the inconvenience and possible financial sacrifice of forgoing alternative uses for his or her money for a greater period of time.
3. **LOAN SIZE** If there are two loans of equal maturity and risk, the interest rate on the smaller of the two loans usually will be higher. The costs of issuing a large loan and a small loan are about the same in dollars, but the cost is greater as a percentage of the smaller loan.

**TABLE 17-1 Selected interest rates, September, 1998**

| Type of interest rate | Annual percentage |
|---|---|
| 10-year Government of Canada bond | 5.54 |
| 8-year New Brunswick bond | 5.77 |
| 24-year B.C. Telephone bond | 6.23 |
| 9-year Thompson Corporation bond | 6.10 |
| 5-year closed mortgage | 7.4 |
| 91-day Treasury bill (Government of Canada) | 4.88 |
| Prime rate (rate charged by banks to their best corporate customers) | 7.50 |
| Visa interest rate | 16.50 |

4. **MARKET IMPERFECTIONS** Market imperfections also explain some interest-rate differentials. The small-town chartered bank branch that monopolizes local lending may charge high interest rates on consumer loans because households find it inconvenient and costly to "shop around" at chartered banks in somewhat distant cities. The large corporation, on the other hand, can survey a number of rival lenders to float a new bond issue and secure the lowest obtainable rate.

## Pure Rate of Interest

Economists talk of "the" interest rate to simplify the cluster of rates (Table 17-1). When they do so, they usually have in mind the **pure rate of interest**. The pure rate is best approximated by the interest paid on long-term, virtually riskless securities such as long-term bonds of the government of Canada. This interest payment can be thought of as being made solely for the use of money over an extended time period, because risk and administrative costs are negligible and the interest rate on these bonds is not distorted by market imperfections. In fall 1998 the pure rate of interest in Canada was 5.5 percent.

## Role of the Interest Rate

The interest rate is a critical price; it affects both the *level* and the *composition* of investment goods production, as well as the *amount* of R&D spending.

**Interest and Total Output** A lower equilibrium interest rate encourages more borrowing by businesses for investment. Total spending in the economy therefore rises, and if the economy has unused resources, so does total output. Conversely, a higher equilibrium interest rate discourages business borrowing for investment, reducing investment and total spending. Such a decrease in spending may be desirable if an economy is experiencing inflation.

Government often manipulates the interest rate to try to expand investment and output, on the one hand, or reduce investment and inflation, on the other. If you have studied macroeconomics, you know that government affects the interest rate by changing the supply of money. Increases in the money supply increase the supply of loanable funds, causing the equilibrium interest rate to fall. This boosts investment spending and expands the economy. In contrast, decreases in the money supply decrease the supply of loanable funds, boosting the equilibrium interest rate. As a result, investment is constrained and so is the economy.

**Interest and the Allocation of Capital** Prices are rationing devices. The interest rate is no exception; it rations the available supply of loanable funds to investment projects whose rate of return or expected profitability is sufficiently high to allow payment of the going interest rate.

If, say, the computer industry expects to earn a return of 12 percent on the money it invests in physical capital and it can secure the required funds at an interest rate of 8 percent, it can borrow and expand its physical capital. If the expected rate of return on additional capital in the steel industry is only 6 percent, that industry will find it unprofitable to expand its capital at 8 percent interest. The interest rate allocates money, and ultimately physical capital, to those industries in which it will be most productive and therefore most profitable. Such an allocation of capital goods is in the interest of society as a whole.

But the interest rate does not perfectly ration capital to its most productive uses. Large oligopolistic borrowers are in a better position than competitive borrowers to pass interest costs on to consumers because they are able to change prices by controlling output. Also, the size and prestige of large industrial concerns may help them obtain funds on more favourable terms than can less-well-known firms with superior profit expectations.

**Interest and the Level and Composition of R&D Spending** Recall from Chapter 13 that like the investment decision, the decision on how much to spend on R&D depends on the cost of borrowing funds in relationship to the expected rate of return. Other things equal, the *lower* the interest rate—that is, the less the cost of borrowing funds for R&D—the greater the amount of R&D spending that is profitable. The *higher* the interest rate, the less the amount of R&D spending.

Also, the interest rate allocates R&D funds to those firms and industries for which the expected rate of return on R&D is the greatest. Ace Microcircuits may have an expected rate of return of 16 percent on an R&D project, while Glow Paints has a 2 percent expected rate of return on its project. With the interest rate at 8 percent, loanable funds will flow to Ace, not to Glow. Society will benefit by having R&D spending allocated to projects with sufficiently high expected rates of return to justify using scarce resources for R&D rather than for other purposes.

**Nominal and Real Interest Rates** This discussion of the role of the interest rate in the investment and R&D decisions assumes no inflation. If inflation occurs, we must distinguish between nominal and real *interest rates*, just like we needed to distinguish between nominal and real *wages* in the previous chapter. The **nominal interest rate** is the rate of interest expressed in dollars of current value. The **real interest rate** is the rate of interest expressed in purchasing power—dollars of inflation-adjusted value. (For a comparison of *nominal* interest rates on bank loans in selected countries, see Global Perspective 17-1.)

An example will clarify this distinction. Suppose the nominal interest rate and rate of inflation are both 10 percent. If you borrow $100, you must pay back $110 a year from now. However, because of 10 percent inflation, each of these 110 dollars will be worth 10 percent less. Thus, the real value or purchasing power of your $110 at the end of the year is only $100. In inflation-adjusted dollars you are borrowing $100 and at year's end paying back $100. While the nominal interest rate is 10 percent, the real interest rate is zero. We determine this by subtracting the 10 percent inflation rate from the 10 percent nominal interest rate.

It is the real interest rate, not the nominal rate, that affects investment and R&D decisions. *(Key Question 6)*

**17-1**
**GLOBAL PERSPECTIVE**

**Nominal interest rates on bank loans, selected nations**

These data show the interest rates that banks in various countries charged their prime customers in 1995. Because these are nominal rates, much of the variation reflects differences in rates of inflation.

**Nominal Interest Rate**

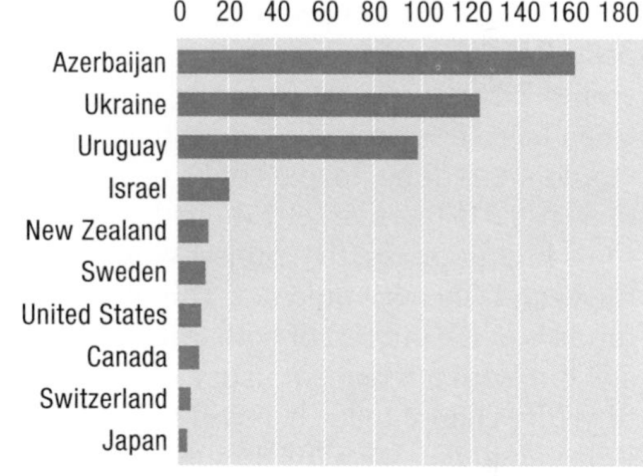


*Source:* World Development Report, 1997, pp. 216–217.

## Application: Usury Laws

A number of states in the United States have passed **usury laws** that specify a maximum interest rate at which loans can be made. The purpose is to hold down the interest cost of borrowing, particularly for low-income borrowers. ("Usury" simply means exorbitant interest.)

We can assess the impact of such legislation with the help of Figure 17-2. The equilibrium interest rate there is 8 percent, but suppose a usury law specifies that lenders cannot charge more than 6 percent. The effects are as follows:

1. **NONMARKET RATIONING** At 6 percent the quantity of loanable funds demanded exceeds the quantity supplied: there is a shortage of loanable funds. The market interest rate no longer can ration the available loanable funds to borrowers, so lenders (banks) have to do the rationing. We can expect them to make loans only to the most creditworthy borrowers (mainly wealthy, high-income people), which defeats the goal of the usury law. Low-income, riskier borrowers are excluded from the mar-

ket and may be forced to turn to loan sharks who charge illegally high interest rates.

2. **GAINERS AND LOSERS** Credit-worthy borrowers gain from usury laws because they pay below-market interest rates. Lenders (ultimately bank shareholders) are losers, receiving 6 percent rather than 8 percent on each dollar loaned.
3. **INEFFICIENCY** We just discussed how the equilibrium interest rate allocates money to the investments and R&D projects whose expected rate of return is greatest. Under usury laws, funds are much less likely to be allocated by banks to the most productive projects. Suppose Wilson has a project so promising she would pay 8 percent for funds to finance it. Chen has a less promising investment, and he would be willing to pay only 6 percent for financing. If the market rationed funds, Wilson's highly productive project would receive funds and Chen's would not. This allocation of funds is in the interest of both Wilson and society. But with a 6 percent usury rate, there is a fifty-fifty chance that Chen will be funded and Wilson will not. Legal maximum interest rates may ration funds to less productive investments or R&D projects.

**17-2**

**QUICK REVIEW**

- Interest is the price paid for the use of money.
- In the loanable funds model, the equilibrium interest rate is determined by the demand for and supply of loanable funds.
- There is a range of interest rates that is influenced by risk, maturity, loan size, taxability, and market imperfections.
- The equilibrium interest rate affects the total level of investment and therefore the levels of total spending and total output; it also allocates money and real capital to specific industries and firms. Similarly, the interest rate affects the level and composition of R&D spending.
- Usury laws that establish an interest-rate ceiling below the market interest rate may **a** deny credit to low-income people, **b** subsidize high-income borrowers and penalize lenders, and **c** diminish the efficiency with which loanable funds are allocated to investment and R&D projects.

## ECONOMIC PROFIT

As with rent, economists define profit narrowly. To accountants, "profit" is what remains of a firm's total revenue after it has paid individuals and other firms for the materials, capital, and labour they have supplied to the firm. To the economist, this definition overstates profit. The difficulty is that the accountant's view of profit considers only **explicit costs**: payments made by the firm to outsiders. It ignores **implicit costs**: the monetary income the firm sacrifices when it uses resources that it owns, rather than supplying those resources to the market. The economist considers implicit costs to be opportunity costs, and hence to be real costs that must be accounted for in determining profit. **Economic**, or **pure, profit** is what remains after all costs—both explicit and implicit costs, the latter including a normal profit—have been subtracted from a firm's total revenue. Economic profit may be either positive or negative (a loss).

For example, suppose a certain person owns her own bagel shop, including the land, building, and equipment, and also provides her own labour. As economists see it, she grossly overstates the economic profit if she merely subtracts from her total revenue her payments to outsiders for, say, baking ingredients, electricity, and insurance. She has not yet subtracted the cost of the resources *she* has contributed. Those costs are the rent, interest, and wage payments she could have received by making her land, labour, and capital resources available for alternative uses. They are her implicit costs, and they must be taken into account in determining her economic profit. She certainly would have to pay these costs if outsiders supplied these resources to her bagel shop.

### Role of the Entrepreneur

The economist views profit as the return to a very special type of human resource: entrepreneurial ability. We know from previous chapters that the entrepreneur (1) combines resources to produce a good or service, (2) makes basic, nonroutine policy decisions for the firm, (3) introduces innovations in the form of new products or production processes, and (4) bears the economic risks associated with all these functions.

Part of the entrepreneur's return is a **normal profit**. This is the minimum payment necessary to retain the entrepreneur in the current line of production. We saw in Chapter 9 that normal profit is a cost—the cost of using entrepreneurial ability for a particular purpose. We saw also that a firm's total revenue may exceed its total cost; the excess revenue above all costs is its economic profit. This residual profit also goes to the entrepreneur. The entrepreneur is the *residual claimant*: the resource that receives what is left after all costs are paid.

Why should there be residual profit? We next examine three possible reasons, two relating to the risks involved in business and one based on monopoly power.

## Sources of Economic Profit

Let's first construct an artificial economic environment where economic profit would be zero. Then, by noting how the real world differs from this environment, we will see where economic profit arises.

We begin with a purely competitive economy, and we make it also a static economy. A **static economy** is one in which the basic forces—such as resource supplies, technological knowledge, and consumer tastes—are constant and unchanging. As a result, all cost and supply data on the one hand, and all demand and revenue data on the other, are also constant.

Given the nature of these data, the economic future is *perfectly foreseeable*; there is no *uncertainty*. The outcome of any price or production policy can be *accurately predicted*. Furthermore, no product or production process is ever improved. Under pure competition any economic profit or loss that might have existed in an industry will disappear with the entry or exit of firms in the long run. All costs, explicit and implicit, are just covered in the long run, so there is no economic profit in our static economy.

The notion of zero economic profit in a static competitive economy suggests that profit is linked to the dynamic nature of a real-world market system and its accompanying uncertainty. Moreover, it indicates that economic profit may arise from a source other than the directing, innovating, and risk-bearing functions of the entrepreneur. That source is the presence of some amount of monopoly power.

**Risk and Profit** In a real, dynamic economy the future is not predictable; it is uncertain. This means the entrepreneur must assume risks. Economic profit can be thought of in part as a reward for assuming these risks.

In linking economic profit with uncertainty and risk bearing, we must distinguish between risks that are insurable and those that are not. Some types of risks—fire, floods, theft, and accidents to employees—are measurable; that is, their frequency of occurrence can be estimated accurately. Firms can avoid losses due to **insurable risks** by paying an annual fee (an insurance premium) to an insurance company. The entrepreneur need not bear such risks.

However, the entrepreneur must bear the **uninsurable risks** of business, and it is those risks that are a potential source of economic profit. The uninsurable risks are mainly the uncontrollable and unpredictable changes in the demand and supply conditions facing the firm (and hence its revenues and costs). Uninsurable risks may stem from three general sources:

1. **CHANGES IN THE GENERAL ECONOMIC ENVIRONMENT** A downturn in business (a recession), for example, can lead to greatly reduced demand, sales, and revenues, and thus to business losses. A prosperous firm can suffer these losses through no fault of its own.
2. **CHANGES IN THE STRUCTURE OF THE ECONOMY** Consumer tastes, technology, and resource availability and prices change constantly in the real world, bringing changes in production costs and revenues. For example, an airline earning economic profit one year may find its profit plunging the next due to a significant increase in the price of jet fuel.
3. **CHANGES IN GOVERNMENT POLICY** A newly instituted regulation, the removal of a tariff, or a change in national defence policy may significantly alter the cost and revenue data of the affected industry and firms.

Regardless of how such revenue and cost changes may come about, they are risks that the firm and entrepreneur must take to be in business. *Economic profit in a real, dynamic economy may be compensation for taking those risks.*

**Innovations and Profit** The uncertainties we just discussed are external to the firm, meaning they are beyond the control of the individual firm or industry. One other dynamic feature of a market economy—innovation—occurs at the initiative of the entrepreneur. Business firms deliberately introduce new methods of production to affect their costs favourably and new products to affect their revenues favourably. The entrepreneur purposely undertakes to upset existing cost and revenue data in a way that hopefully will be profitable.

But again, uncertainty enters the picture. Despite exhaustive market surveys, new products or modifications of existing products may be economic failures. Similarly, of the many new novels, textbooks, movies, and compact discs appearing every year, only a handful garner large profits. Nor is it known with certainty whether new production machinery will actually yield projected cost economies. Thus, innovations undertaken by entrepreneurs entail uncertainty and the possibility of losses, not just the potential for increased profit. *Economic profit in an innovative economy may be compensation for dealing with the uncertainty of innovation.*

**Monopoly and Profit** Thus far, we have linked economic profit with the uncertainties surrounding (1) the dynamic environment to which enterprises are exposed, and (2) the dynamic business processes they initiate themselves. *The existence of monopoly in some form is a final source of economic profit.* Because a monopolist can restrict output and deter entry, it may persistently enjoy above-competitive prices and economic profit if demand is strong relative to cost.

Economic uncertainty and monopoly are closely intertwined as sources of economic profit. A firm with some monopoly power can reduce business risk, or at least manipulate it enough to reduce its adverse effects, and thus increase and prolong economic profit. Furthermore, a firm can use innovation as a source of monopoly power and a means of sustaining itself and its economic profit.

An important distinction between profit stemming from uncertainty and that from monopoly has to do with the social desirability of these two sources of profit. Bearing business risk and undertaking innovation in an uncertain economic environment are socially desirable functions. Obtaining monopoly profit is not so socially desirable. This profit typically is founded on reduced output, above-competitive prices, and economic inefficiency. ***(Key Question 8)***

### Functions of Profit

Economic profit is the main energizer of the market economy. It influences both the level of economic output and the allocation of resources among alternative uses.

**Profit and Total Output** It is the expectation of economic profit that induces firms to innovate. Their innovation stimulates new investment, increasing total output and employment. Thus, through innovation, it is the pursuit of profit that underlies economic growth.

**Profit and Resource Allocation** Profit is also effective in allocating resources among alternative lines of production. Entrepreneurs seek profit and shun losses. The occurrence of economic profit in an industry is a signal that society wants that particular industry to expand. It attracts resources from industries that are not profitable. But profit rewards are more than an inducement for an industry to expand; they also attract the financing firms in that industry need for expansion. In contrast, losses penalize businesses that fail to adjust their productive efforts to the goods and services most preferred by customers. They signal society's desire for the afflicted industries to contract.

Profits and losses do not, however, result in an allocation of resources perfectly attuned to consumer preferences. The presence of monopoly, for example, impedes the shiftability of firms and resources from industry to industry in response to economic profit.

**17-3**

**QUICK REVIEW**

- Pure or economic profit is what remains after all explicit and implicit costs (including a normal profit) are subtracted from a firm's total revenue.
- Economic profit has three sources: the bearing of uninsurable risk, the uncertainty of innovation, and monopoly power.
- Profit and profit expectations affect the levels of investment, total spending, and domestic output; profit and loss also allocate resources among alternative uses.

## INCOME SHARES

Our discussion in this and the previous chapter would not be complete without a brief re-examination of how Canadian domestic income is distributed among wages, rent, interest, and profit.

**TABLE 17-2 Relative shares of domestic income, 1926–1994 (selected years or period averages of shares for individual years)**

| (1) Year or period | (2) Wages, salaries, and supplementary labour income | (3) Corporation profits before taxes | (4) Interest and miscellaneous investment income | (5) Accrued net income of farmers from farm production | (6) Net income of nonfarm unincorporated business including rent | (7) Inventory valuation adjustment | (8) Net domestic income at factor cost |
|---|---|---|---|---|---|---|---|
| 1926 | 55.3% | 11.4% | 3.2% | 14.1% | 14.9% | 1.1% | 100% |
| 1927–28 | 55.5 | 12.5 | 3.4 | 13.1 | 15.2 | 0.3 | 100 |
| 1929 | 60.0 | 12.9 | 3.7 | 8.0 | 15.7 | −0.3 | 100 |
| 1932 | 69.3 | 4.1 | 4.5 | 3.6 | 14.7 | 3.8 | 100 |
| 1933 | 70.2 | 9.7 | 4.3 | 2.6 | 14.1 | −0.9 | 100 |
| 1937 | 62.6 | 15.6 | 3.1 | 6.9 | 13.9 | −2.1 | 100 |
| 1941 | 61.9 | 18.1 | 2.8 | 7.0 | 12.6 | −2.4 | 100 |
| 1945 | 63.4 | 13.1 | 2.7 | 9.2 | 12.0 | −0.4 | 100 |
| 1951 | 60.7 | 17.9 | 2.5 | 10.5 | 12.0 | −3.6 | 100 |
| 1957–60 | 67.0 | 13.7 | 3.9 | 3.6 | 12.0 | −0.2 | 100 |
| 1961–65 | 67.7 | 14.2 | 4.3 | 3.6 | 10.6 | −0.3 | 100 |
| 1966–70 | 70.9 | 13.5 | 4.7 | 2.7 | 8.8 | −0.6 | 100 |
| 1971 | 73.0 | 12.2 | 5.5 | 2.0 | 8.2 | −0.9 | 100 |
| 1973 | 70.6 | 16.0 | 5.7 | 3.0 | 7.2 | −2.5 | 100 |
| 1975 | 71.2 | 14.8 | 7.1 | 2.9 | 6.0 | −2.0 | 100 |
| 1976 | 71.9 | 13.4 | 8.0 | 2.2 | 5.9 | −1.4 | 100 |
| 1979 | 69.3 | 16.4 | 10.7 | 1.7 | 5.4 | −3.5 | 100 |
| 1982 | 72.7 | 9.2 | 12.2 | 1.2 | 5.8 | −1.1 | 100 |
| 1990 | 72.6 | 8.7 | 11.1 | 0.6 | 7.0 | −0.0 | 100 |
| 1994 | 73.5 | 10.0 | 10.1 | 0.4 | 6.9 | −0.9 | 100 |
| 1997 | 74.9 | 12.0 | 7.2 | 0.2 | 8.2 | −2.5 | 100 |

Source: 1926–1982: Statistics Canada, *National Income and Expenditure Accounts*, Annual estimates 1926–1986, Table 70; for other years Statistics Canada, *National Income and Expenditure Accounts*. For updates, visit Statistics Canada at www.statcan.ca/english/Pgdb/Economy/Economic/econ03.htm

Let's look at Table 17-2. Although the income categories shown in this table do not neatly fit the economic definitions of wages, rent, interest, and profits, they do provide insights about income shares in Canada. Note the dominant role of the labour resource and thus labour income in the Canadian economy. Even with labour income defined narrowly as "wages and salaries," labour receives about 75 percent of national income. But some economists contend that proprietors' income (the sum of columns 5 and 6) is largely composed of implicit wages and salaries and therefore should be added to the "wages and salaries" category to determine labour income. When we use this broad definition, *labour's share* rises to over 80 percent of domestic income, a percentage that has been remarkably stable in Canada since 1926. That leaves about 20 percent for capitalists in the form of rent, interest, and profit—a relatively small share considering we call the Canadian economy a capitalist system.

# The Last Word

## DETERMINING THE PRICE OF CREDIT

**A variety of lending practices can cause the effective interest rate to be quite different from what it appears to be.**

BORROWING AND LENDING—RECEIVING AND granting credit—are a way of life. Individuals receive credit when they negotiate a mortgage loan and when they use their credit cards. Individuals make loans when they open a savings account in a chartered bank or buy a government bond.

It is sometimes difficult to determine exactly how much interest we pay and receive when we borrow and lend. Let's suppose that you borrow $10,000 which you agree to repay plus $1,000 of interest at the end of one year. In this instance, the interest rate is 10 percent per year. To determine the interest rate *i*, we compare the interest paid with the amount borrowed:

$$i = \frac{\$1,000}{\$10,000} = 10\%$$

But in some cases a lender, say, a bank, will *discount* the interest payment at the time the loan is made. Thus, instead of giving the borrower $10,000, the bank discounts the $1,000 interest payment in advance, giving the borrower only $9,000. This increases the interest rate:

$$i = \frac{\$1,000}{\$9,000} = 11\%$$

While the absolute amount of interest paid is the same, in this second case the borrower has only $9,000 available for the year.

An even more subtle point is that, to simplify their calculations, many financial institutions assume a 360-day year (twelve 30-day months). This means the borrower has the use of the lender's funds for 5 days less than the normal year. This use of a "short year" also increases the actual interest rate paid by the borrower.

The interest rate paid can change dramatically if a loan is repaid in instalments. Suppose a bank lends you $10,000 and charges interest in the amount of $1,000 to be paid at the end of the year. But the loan contract requires that you repay the $10,000 loan in 12 equal monthly instalments. In effect, then, the average amount of the loan outstanding during the year is only $5,000. Hence:

$$i = \frac{\$1,000}{\$5,000} = 20\%$$

Here interest is paid on the total amount of the loan ($10,000) rather than on the outstanding balance (which averages $5,000 for the year), making for a much higher interest rate.

Another factor that influences the effective interest rate is whether interest is *compounded*. Suppose you deposit $10,000 in a savings account that pays a 10 percent interest rate compounded semiannually. In other words, interest is paid on your "loan" to the bank twice a year. At the end of the first six months, $500 of interest (10 percent of $10,000 for half a year) is added to your account. At the end of the year, interest is calculated on $10,500 so that the second interest payment is $525 (10 percent of $10,500 for half a year). Thus:

$$i = \frac{\$1,025}{\$10,000} = 10.25\%$$

This means that a bank advertising a 10 percent interest rate compounded semiannually is actually paying more interest to its customers than a competitor paying a simple (noncompounded) interest rate of 10.20 percent.

"Let the borrower beware" is a fitting motto in the world of credit. ■

# CHAPTER SUMMARY

1. Economic rent is the price paid for the use of land and other natural resources whose total supplies are fixed.

2. Rent is a surplus payment that is socially unnecessary since land would be available to the economy even without rental payments. The idea of land rent as a surplus payment gave rise to the single-tax movement of the late 1800s.

3. Differences in land rent result from differences in the fertility and climatic features of the land and differences in location.

4. Although land rent is a surplus payment rather than a cost to the economy as a whole, to individual firms and industries, rental payments are correctly regarded as costs. These payments must be made to gain the use of land, which has alternative uses.

5. Interest is the price paid for the use of money. In the loanable funds theory, the equilibrium interest rate is determined by the demand for and supply of loanable funds. Other things equal, changes in the supply of loanable funds cause the equilibrium interest rate to move in the opposite direction from the change in supply; changes in the demand for loanable funds cause the equilibrium interest rate to move in the same direction as the change in demand.

6. Interest rates vary in size because loans differ as to risk, maturity, and amount, market imperfections cause additional variations. The *pure rate of interest* is the interest rate on long-term, virtually riskless, Government of Canada long-term bonds.

7. The equilibrium interest rate influences the level of investment and helps ration financial and physical capital to specific firms and industries. Similarly, this rate influences the size and composition of R&D spending. The *real interest rate*, not the nominal rate, is critical to investment and R&D decisions.

8. Although designed to make funds available to low-income borrowers, usury laws tend to allocate credit to high-income persons, subsidize high-income borrowers at the expense of lenders, and lessen the efficiency with which loanable funds are allocated.

9. Economic, or pure, profit is the difference between a firm's total revenue and the sum of its explicit and implicit costs, the latter including a normal profit. Profit accrues to entrepreneurs for assuming the uninsurable risks associated with organizing and directing economic resources and for innovating. Profit also results from monopoly power.

10. Profit expectations influence innovating and investment activities and therefore the economy's levels of employment and economic growth. The basic function of profits and losses, however, is to induce that allocation of resources most in accord with the tastes of consumers.

11. The largest share of national income—about 75 percent—goes to labour, a share narrowly defined as "wages and salaries." When labour's share is more broadly defined to include "proprietors' income," it rises to about 80 percent of domestic income. So-defined, labour's share has been remarkably stable since 1926.

## TERMS AND CONCEPTS

economic rent
incentive function
single-tax movement
loanable funds theory of interest
pure rate of interest
nominal interest rate
real interest rate
usury laws
explicit costs
implicit costs
economic or pure profit
normal profit
static economy
insurable risks
uninsurable risks

## STUDY QUESTIONS

1. How does the economist's use of the term "rent" differ from everyday usage? Explain: "Though rent need not be paid by society to make land available, rental payments are very useful in guiding land into the most productive uses."

2. KEY QUESTION *Explain why economic rent is a surplus payment when viewed by the economy as a whole but a cost of production from the standpoint of individual firms and industries. Explain: "Rent performs no 'incentive function' in the economy."*

3. If money is not an economic resource, why is interest paid and received for its use? What considerations account for interest rates differing greatly on various types of loans? Use these considerations to explain the relative sizes of the interest rates on the following:
   a. A 10-year $1,000 government bond
   b. A $20 pawnshop loan
   c. A 30-year mortgage loan on a $97,000 house
   d. A 24-month $12,000 chartered bank loan to finance an automobile
   e. A 60-day $100 loan from a personal finance company

4. KEY QUESTION *Why is the supply of loanable funds upsloping? Why is the demand for loanable funds downsloping? Explain the equilibrium interest rate. List some factors that might cause it to change.*

5. What are the major economic functions of the interest rate? How might the fact that many businesses finance their investment activities internally affect the efficiency with which the interest rate performs its functions?

6. KEY QUESTION *Distinguish between nominal and real interest rates. Which is more relevant in making investment and R&D decisions? If the nominal interest rate is 12 percent and the inflation rate is 8 percent, what is the real rate of interest?*

7. Usury laws that put below-equilibrium ceilings on interest rates make credit available to poor people who could not otherwise afford to borrow. Critics contend that it is poor people who are most likely to be hurt by such laws. Which view is correct?

8. KEY QUESTION *How do the concepts of accounting profit and economic profit differ? Why is economic profit smaller than accounting profit? What are the three basic sources of economic profit? Classify each of the following according to those sources:*
   a. *A firm's profit from developing and patenting a ballpoint pen containing a permanent ink cartridge*
   b. *A restaurant's profit that results from construction of a new highway past its door*
   c. *The profit received by a firm due to an unanticipated change in consumer tastes*

9. Why is the distinction between insurable and uninsurable risks significant for the theory of profit? Carefully evaluate: "All economic profit can be traced to either uncertainty or the desire to avoid it." What are the major functions of economic profit?

10. Explain the absence of economic profit in a purely competitive, static economy. Realizing that the major function of profit is to allocate resources according to consumer preferences, describe the allocation of resources in such an economy.

11. What is the rent, interest, and profit share of domestic income if proprietors' income is included within the labour (wage) share? Has the capitalists' share (proprietors' income included as wages) increased, decreased, or stayed about the same since 1926?

12. **(The Last Word)** Assume you borrow $5,000 and pay back the $5,000 plus $250 in interest at the end of the year. Assuming no inflation, what is the real interest rate? What would the interest rate be if the $250 of interest had been discounted at the time the loan was made? What would the interest rate be if you were required to repay the loan in 12 equal monthly installments?

13. WEB-BASED QUESTION **What's the Real Interest Today?** The real interest rate is the nominal rate less the rate of inflation. Assume the Consumer Price Index (CPI) is a proxy for the inflation rate and one-year Treasury Bill rates represent the nominal interest rate. Find the current CPI at www.statcan.ca/english/econoind/cpia.htm, and then subtract it from the current one-year Treasury Bill rate www.bank-banque-canada.ca/pdf/monmrt.pdf. Repeat the process for the one-month Treasury Bills and the CPI rate of change for the past one month. Is there a difference between the 1-month and the 12-month real interest rates? If so, why is there a difference?

CHAPTER 18

# Income Inequality and Poverty

THERE IS SIGNIFICANT INCOME INEQUALITY IN Canada, and the incidence of poverty rose in the 1990s as recession persisted in some parts of the country.

The issue of income inequality has come to the fore as the after-tax real family income stagnated over the course of the 1980s, having increased a meagre 0.5 percent compared with a 22 percent increase during the 1970s, 34 percent in the 1960s, and 27 percent in the 1950s.

Even more troubling is the fact that child poverty is on the rise, particularly in the "have" provinces of Ontario and British Columbia. Statistics Canada estimated that in 1996 30 percent of the nation's children—almost 1.5 million children—under 18 were poor.

The question of how income should be distributed is controversial. Should the national income and wealth in Canada be more equally distributed than it is now? Or, in language of Chapter 3, is society making the proper responses to the "For whom" question? In discussing this issue, we begin by surveying some basic facts about the distribution of income in Canada. Next, we consider the major causes of income inequality. Third, we examine the debate over income inequality and the tradeoff between equality and efficiency. Fourth, we look at poverty in Canada, and finally, we consider public policy regarding income redistribution and welfare.

**IN THIS CHAPTER YOU WILL LEARN:**

- The facts about income inequality in Canada and how to measure it.
- The causes of income inequality.
- That there is a tradeoff between income equality and economic efficiency.
- The distinction between absolute and relative poverty.
- About the extent of relative poverty in Canada.
- About Canada's income maintenance system.

## The Big Picture

A PERSISTENT PROBLEM AFFLICTING ALL MARKET economies is unequal distribution of income. Some people command very high wages while others earn a wage that can barely pay for the absolute necessities of life. This chapter explains why there is such unequal distribution of the fruits of society's output of goods and services. Unfortunately, there are signs that income inequality is growing in Canada in the last decade of the twentieth century.

You may well ask why not simply legislate that everyone have an equal weekly or monthly income. The problem has to do with incentive to work and take on risk. We will discuss the tradeoff between equality of income and getting the most out of scarce resources.

As you read this chapter, keep the following points in mind:

- **Key Concepts 4** and **7** are discussed.
- Income inequality is caused by a variety of factors.
- A more equal distribution of income after a certain point can be accompanied by a reduction in the incentive to get the most out of limited resources.
- Poverty has both social and economic cost. It greatly increases suffering and impedes those who are poor from making an economic contribution to society because they cannot find work or do not have the required skills to get existing jobs. ■

## FACTS ABOUT INCOME INEQUALITY

How equally—or unequally—is income distributed in Canada? How wide is the gulf between rich and poor? Has the degree of income inequality increased or lessened over time?

### Personal Income Distribution

Average income in Canada is among the highest in the world. The average income for all families was about $56,629 in 1996. But this average tells us nothing about income equality or inequality. We must also examine how income is distributed around the average. In Table 18-1 we find that 2.3 percent of all families received less than $10,000 a year in 1996; 5.5 percent of all families received less than $20,000 per year. At the top of the income pyramid, we find that 23.8 percent of the families had incomes of $75,000 or more per year. These figures suggest *considerable* **income inequality** *in Canada.*

### Trends in Income Inequality

Over time economic growth has raised Canadian incomes. In *absolute* dollar amounts, the entire distribution of income has been moving upward. But, has this changed the *relative* distribution of income—that is, the income of one group compared to another? Incomes can move up in absolute terms and the degree of relative inequality may or may not be affected. Table 18-2 shows the relative distribution of income over time. We divide the total number of income receivers into five numerically equal groups, or *quintiles,* and show the percentage of total personal (before tax) income received by each in selected years.

*The relative distribution of income has been basically stable since 1951,* when Statistics Canada began its detailed family-income surveys. Since 1951 the richest fifth of all Canadian families has received nine or ten times as much income as the poorest fifth.

Global Perspective 18-1 compares income inequality in Canada (here by individuals, not families) with that in several other nations. Income inequality tends to be highest in developing nations.

### Causes of Growing Inequality

Growing Canadian income inequality in the past three decades has attracted the attention of many scholars, who have suggested three major interrelated explanations:

1. **GREATER DEMAND FOR HIGHLY SKILLED WORKERS** Perhaps the most significant contributor to growing income inequality has been an increasing demand for workers who are highly skilled and well educated. Many

**TABLE 18-1 The distribution of personal income by families and unattached individuals, 1996**

(a)

| (1) Personal income class | (2) Percent of all families in this class | (3) Percent of all unattached individuals in this class | (4) Percent of all families and unattached individuals in this class | (5) Percent of all families in this class and all lower classes | (6) Percent of all unattached individuals in this class and all lower classes | (7) Percent of all families and unattached individuals in this class and all lower classes |
|---|---|---|---|---|---|---|
| Under $10,000 | 2.3 | 17.8 | 7.3 | 2.3 | 17.8 | 7.3 |
| $10,000 to $14,999 | 4.2 | 21.8 | 9.9 | 6.5 | 39.6 | 17.2 |
| $15,000 to $19,999 | 5.5 | 13.6 | 8.1 | 12.0 | 53.2 | 25.3 |
| $20,000 to $29,999 | 13.5 | 17.5 | 14.8 | 25.5 | 70.7 | 40.1 |
| $30,000 to $49,999 | 25.2 | 19.9 | 23.6 | 50.7 | 90.6 | 63.7 |
| $50,000 to $74,999 | 25.5 | 9.3 | 19.5 | 76.2 | 100.0 | 83.2 |
| $75,000 and over | 23.8 | | 16.8 | 100.0 | | 100.0 |
| | 100.0 | 100.0 | 100.0 | | | |

(b)

| | Families | Unattached individuals | Families & unattached individuals |
|---|---|---|---|
| Average 1996 income | $ 56,629 | $ 24,433 | $ 46,272 |
| Median 1996 income | $ 49,411 | $ 18,354 | $ 37,669 |
| 1996 population | 8,317,000 | 3,944,000 | 12,261,000 |

*Source:* Statistics Canada, *Income Distributions by Size in Canada, 1996* (Ottawa, December 1997), Tables 1, 24, and 34. Adapted from "Income Distributions by Size in Canada, 1996," Catalogue No. 13-207, December 1997, Tables 1, 24, and 34.

firms have restructured their production methods in ways that require more highly skilled, better-educated workers. Also, several industries requiring highly skilled workers have recently emerged or expanded greatly, such as computer software development, business consulting, biotechnology, health care, and advanced communications systems. Because highly skilled workers remain relatively scarce, their wages have been bid up, so the wage differences between them and less skilled workers have increased.

2. **DEMOGRAPHIC CHANGES** The entrance of large numbers of less experienced and less skilled "baby boomers" into the labour force in the 1970s and 1980s may have contributed to greater income inequality. Because younger workers tend to earn less income than older workers, their growing numbers contribute to income inequality. There has also been a growing tendency for men and women with high

**TABLE 18-2 Percentage of total before-tax and after-tax income received by each one-fifth of families and unattached individuals**

| | BEFORE TAX | | | AFTER TAX |
|---|---|---|---|---|
| Quintile | 1951 | 1965 | 1995 | 1996 |
| Lowest 20% | 4.4 | 4.4 | 4.6 | 5.7 |
| Second 20% | 11.2 | 11.8 | 10.0 | 11.5 |
| Third 20% | 18.3 | 18.0 | 16.3 | 17.2 |
| Fourth 20% | 23.3 | 24.5 | 24.7 | 24.5 |
| Highest 20% | 42.8 | 41.4 | 44.5 | 41.1 |
| | 100.0 | 100.0 | 100.0 | 100.0 |

*Source:* Statistics Canada, *Income Distributions: Incomes of Non-Farm Families and Individuals in Canada, 1951–1965* (Ottawa, 1969); *Income Distributions by Size in Canada, 1996* (Ottawa, 1997); and *Income After Taxes, Distributions by Size in Canada, 1995* (Ottawa, 1997), Table 26. Adapted from "Income Distributions, Incomes and Non-Farm Families and Individuals in Canada, 1951–1965," Catalogue No. 13-529; "Income Distributions by Size in Canada, 1996," Catalogue No. 13-207; and "Income After Tax, Distributions by Size in Canada, 1995," Catalogue No. 13-210.

## 18-1 GLOBAL PERSPECTIVE

**Percentage of total income received by top one-fifth of income receivers, selected nations**

The share of income going to the highest 20 percent of income receivers varies among nations. Frequently, income is less equally shared in poor nations than in rich ones.

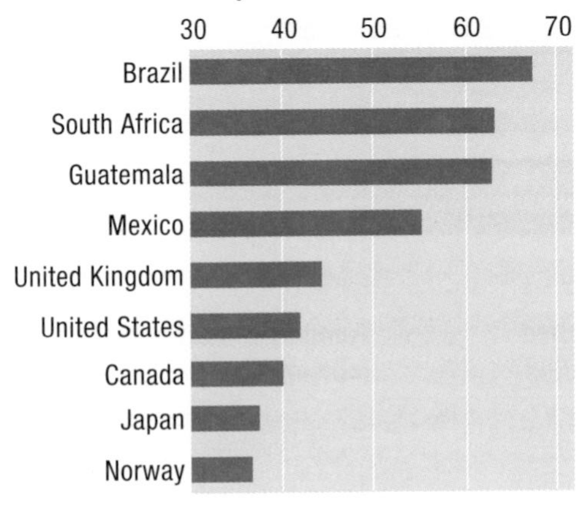


*Source: World Development Report*, 1997, pp. 222–223.

earnings potential to marry each other, thus increasing family income among the highest-income quintiles. Finally, the number of families headed by single or divorced women has increased greatly. This has increased income inequality because many such families lack a second wage earner, and women tend to receive low wage earnings or, in some cases, no wage earnings at all.

3. **INTERNATIONAL TRADE AND IMMIGRATION** Other factors are also at work. More *international competition* from imports in the 1970s and 1980s reduced the demand for and employment of less skilled (but highly paid) workers in such industries as automobile and steel. The decline in such jobs reduced the average wage for less skilled workers. It also swelled the ranks of workers in already low-paying industries, placing further downward pressure on wages in those industries. Similarly, the transfer of jobs to lower-wage workers in developing countries has exerted downward wage pressure on less skilled workers in Canada. Also, an upsurge in *immigration* of unskilled workers has increased the number of low-income families in Canada.

Two cautions: First, when we note growing income inequality, we are *not* saying that the "rich are getting richer and the poor are getting poorer" in terms of absolute income. Both the rich and the poor are getting richer. Rather, what has happened is that, while incomes grew in all quintiles, growth was fastest in the top quintile. Second, increased income inequality is *not* solely a Canadian phenomenon. The recent move towards greater inequality has also occurred in several other industrially advanced nations.

## The Lorenz Curve

The degree of inequality in income distribution can be shown with a **Lorenz curve**. In Figure 18-1, we plot the cumulative percentage of families on the horizontal axis and the percentage of income they obtain on the vertical axis. The diagonal line

**FIGURE 18-1 The Lorenz curve**

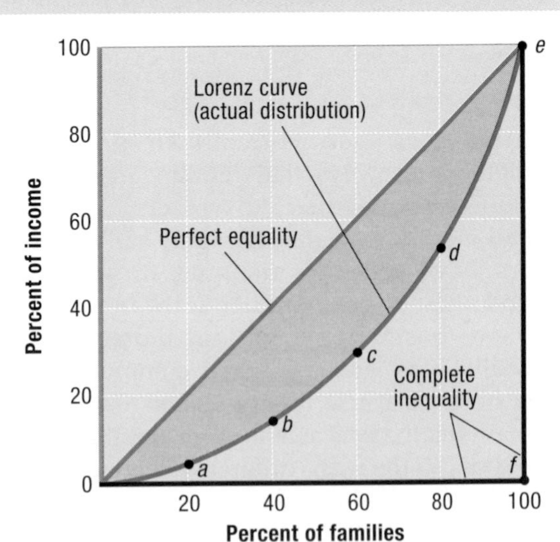


The Lorenz curve is a graph of the percentage of total income obtained by cumulative percentages of families. It is a convenient means of visualizing the degree of income inequality. Specifically, the area between the diagonal (the line of perfect equality) and the Lorenz curve represents the degree of inequality in the Canadian distribution of total income.

$0e$ represents a *perfectly equal distribution of income* because each of its points indicates that a particular percentage of families receive that same percentage of income. In other words, points representing 20 percent of all families receiving 20 percent of total income, 40 percent receiving 40 percent, 60 percent receiving 60 percent, and so on, all lie on the diagonal line.

By plotting the 1996 quintile data from Table 18-2, we obtain the Lorenz curve for that year to help us visualize the actual distribution of income. Observe from point *a* that the bottom 20 percent of all families received 5.7 percent of the after-tax income; the bottom 40 percent received 17.2 percent (= 5.7 + 11.5) as shown by point *b*; and so forth. The grey area between the diagonal line and the Lorenz curve, determined by the extent to which the Lorenz curve sags away from the diagonal, indicates the degree of income inequality. If the actual income distribution were perfectly equal, the Lorenz curve and the diagonal would coincide and the grey gap would disappear.

At the opposite extreme is a situation of complete inequality, where all families but one have zero income. In this case the Lorenz curve would coincide with the horizontal axis from 0 to point *f* (at 0 percent of income), then move immediately up from *f* to point *e* along the vertical axis (indicating that a single family has 100 percent of the income). The entire area below the diagonal line—area $0ef$—would indicate this extreme degree of inequality.

The Lorenz curve can be used to contrast the distribution of income at different points in time, among different groups (for example, native-born and recent immigrants), before and after taxes and transfer payments are taken into account, or between different countries. The Lorenz curve has not shifted significantly since World War II. Comparisons with other countries suggest that the distribution of income in Canada is quite similar to most other industrially advanced countries. ***(Key Question 2)***

## INCOME MOBILITY: THE TIME DIMENSION

There is a major limitation of the income data we have used thus far: The income accounting period of one year is too short to be very meaningful. Because the Statistics Canada data portray the distribution of income in only a single year, they may conceal a more equal distribution over a few years, a decade, or even a lifetime. If Brad earns \$1,000 in year 1 and \$100,000 in year 2, while Jenny earns \$100,000 in year 1 and only \$1,000 in year 2, do we have income inequality? The answer depends on the period of measurement. Annual data would reveal great income inequality, but there is complete equality over the two-year period.

This is important because there is evidence to suggest considerable "churning around" in the distribution of income over time. In fact, for most income receivers, income starts at a relatively low level, reaches a peak during middle age, and then declines. It follows that if all people receive exactly the same stream of income over their lifetimes, considerable income inequality would still exist in any specific year because of age differences. In any single year, the young and old would receive low incomes while the middle-aged received high incomes.

If we change from a "snapshot" view of income distribution in a single year to a "time exposure" portraying incomes over much longer periods, we find considerable movement of income receivers among income classes. This correctly suggests that income is more equally distributed over a 5-, 10-, 20-year period than in a single year. Such movement of individuals or families from one income quintile to another over time is called **income mobility.**

In short, there is significant individual and family income mobility over time; for many people, "low income" and "high income" are not permanent conditions. Also, the longer the time period considered, the more equal the distribution of income.

## EFFECT OF GOVERNMENT REDISTRIBUTION

The figures of Table 18-1 show the distribution of *nominal* income and include not only wages, salaries, dividends, and interest but also all *cash transfer payments* such as employment insurance benefits and welfare payments to families with dependent children. The data are *before taxes* and therefore do not account for the effects of personal income and payroll taxes that are levied directly on income receivers. Nor do they include in-kind or **noncash transfers** that provide specified goods or services rather than cash. Noncash transfers include such things as subsidized public housing and dental care.

What impact would the use of a broader income concept—one that included both taxes and noncash transfers—have on income distribution data? As Table 18-2 shows, because our overall tax system is only modestly progressive, after-tax data reveal only slightly less inequality. Noncash transfers, however, are significant for the poorest quintile and their inclusion would diminish the degree of inequality.

## CAUSES OF INCOME INEQUALITY

There are several causes of income inequality in Canada. In general, we note that the market system is an impersonal mechanism. It has no conscience or ethical standards concerning what is an "equitable" or "just" distribution of income. The basic environment of the capitalist economy is permissive of a high degree of income inequality since it rewards individuals on the basis of their contributions to society's output.

More specifically, the factors contributing to income inequality include those discussed below.

### Ability Differences

People have different mental, physical, and aesthetic talents. Some people have inherited the exceptional mental qualities essential to such high-paying fields as medicine, corporate leadership, and law. Some people are blessed with the physical capacity and coordination to become highly paid professional athletes. A few have the talent to become great artists or musicians or have the beauty to become top fashion models. Others have very weak mental endowments and work in low-paying occupations or are incapable of earning income at all. Most people's intelligence and skills fall somewhere in between.

### Education and Training

Native ability, alone, rarely produces high income; people must develop and refine their capabilities through education and training. Individuals differ significantly in the amounts of education and training they obtain and thus in their capacities to earn income. These differences may be a matter of choice: Chin enters the labour force after graduating from high school, while Rodriguez takes a job after earning a university degree. On the other hand, the differences may be involuntary: Chin and her parents may simply be unable to finance a university education.

People also get varying degrees of on-the-job training, which also contributes to income inequality. Some workers learn valuable new skills each year on the job and therefore experience significant income growth over time; others get little or no on-the-job training and earn no more at age 50 than at age 30. Moreover, firms tend to select for advanced on-the-job training those workers who have the most formal education. This added training magnifies the education-based income differences between less educated and more educated individuals.

### Discrimination

Simple supply and demand analysis suggests how discrimination—in this case, labour market discrimination—generates income inequality. Suppose that discrimination restricts racial and ethnic minorities (or women) to low-paying occupations. This means that the supplies of labour will be great relative to demand in these occupations; wages and incomes will be low. Conversely, discrimination means that whites (or men) do not face as much competition in the occupations in which they are predominant. Thus, labour supply is artificially limited relative to demand in these occupations, with the result that wages and incomes are high.

### Tastes and Risks

Incomes also differ because of differences in tastes for market work relative to nonmarket activities as well as differences in tastes for types of work. People who choose to stay home with children, work part-time, or retire early have less income than people who make the opposite choices. Those willing to take arduous, unpleasant jobs—for example, underground mining or heavy construction—or to work long hours with great intensity will tend to earn more. Individuals also differ in their willingness to assume risk. We refer here not only to the auto race driver or the professional boxer but to the entrepreneur who assumes risk.

Although many entrepreneurs fail, those who develop successful new products or services often realize very substantial incomes.

### Unequal Distribution of Wealth

Income is a *flow*; it represents a stream of wage and salary earnings, along with rent, interest, and profits, as depicted in Chapter 2's circular flow diagram. In contrast, wealth is a *stock*, reflecting at a particular moment the financial and real assets an individual has accumulated over time. A retired person may have very little income, yet a home, mutual fund shares, and a pension plan can add up to considerable wealth. A new university or college graduate may be earning a substantial income as an accountant, middle manager, or engineer but has yet to accumulate significant wealth.

In fact, the ownership of wealth in Canada is very unequal. This inequality of wealth leads to inequality in rent, interest, and dividends, which in turn contributes to income inequality. Those who own more machinery, real estate, farmland, stocks and bonds, and savings accounts obviously receive greater income from that ownership than people with less or no such wealth.

### Market Power

The ability to "rig the market" on one's own behalf is one factor that contributes to income inequality. For example, certain unions and professional groups have adopted policies limiting the supplies of their services, thereby boosting the incomes of those "on the inside." Also, legislation that requires occupational licensing for, say, hunting guides, barbers, or beauticians can exert market power favouring the licensed groups. In product markets, "rigging the market" means gaining or enhancing monopoly power, which means greater profit and thus greater income to the firms' owners.

### Luck, Connections, and Misfortune

Other forces also play roles in producing income inequality. Luck and "being in the right place at the right time" have caused individuals to stumble into fortunes. Discovering oil on a ranch, owning land along a proposed freeway interchange, and hiring the right press agent have accounted for some high incomes. Personal contacts and political connections are other potential routes to attaining high income.

In contrast, economic misfortunes such as prolonged illness, serious accident, death of the family breadwinner, or unemployment may plunge a family into the low range of income. The burden of such misfortune is borne very unevenly by the population and thus contributes to income inequality. ***(Key Question 4)***

**18-1**

**QUICK REVIEW**

- Income inequality in Canada has increased in the last decade; currently the top fifth of all families receive 44.5 percent of before-tax income, and the bottom fifth receives 4.6 percent.
- The Lorenz curve depicts income inequality graphically by comparing percentages of total families and percentages of total income.
- The distribution of income is less unequal over longer time periods.
- Government taxes and transfers significantly reduce income inequality by redistributing income from higher-income groups to lower-income groups; the bulk of this redistribution is from transfer payments.
- Differences in ability, education and training, tastes for market work versus nonmarket activities, property ownership, and market power—along with discrimination and luck—help explain income inequality.

## EQUALITY VERSUS EFFICIENCY

The critical policy issue concerning income inequality is how much is necessary and justified. While there is no general agreement on the amount, we can learn much by exploring the cases for and against greater equality.

### The Case for Equality: Maximizing Total Utility

*The basic argument for an equal distribution of income is that income equality maximizes total consumer satisfaction (utility).* The rationale for this argument is shown in Figure 18-2, in which we assume that the money incomes of two individuals, Anderson and Brooks, are subject to diminishing marginal utility. In any time period, income receivers spend the first dollars received on products they value

**FIGURE 18-2 The utility-maximizing distribution of income**

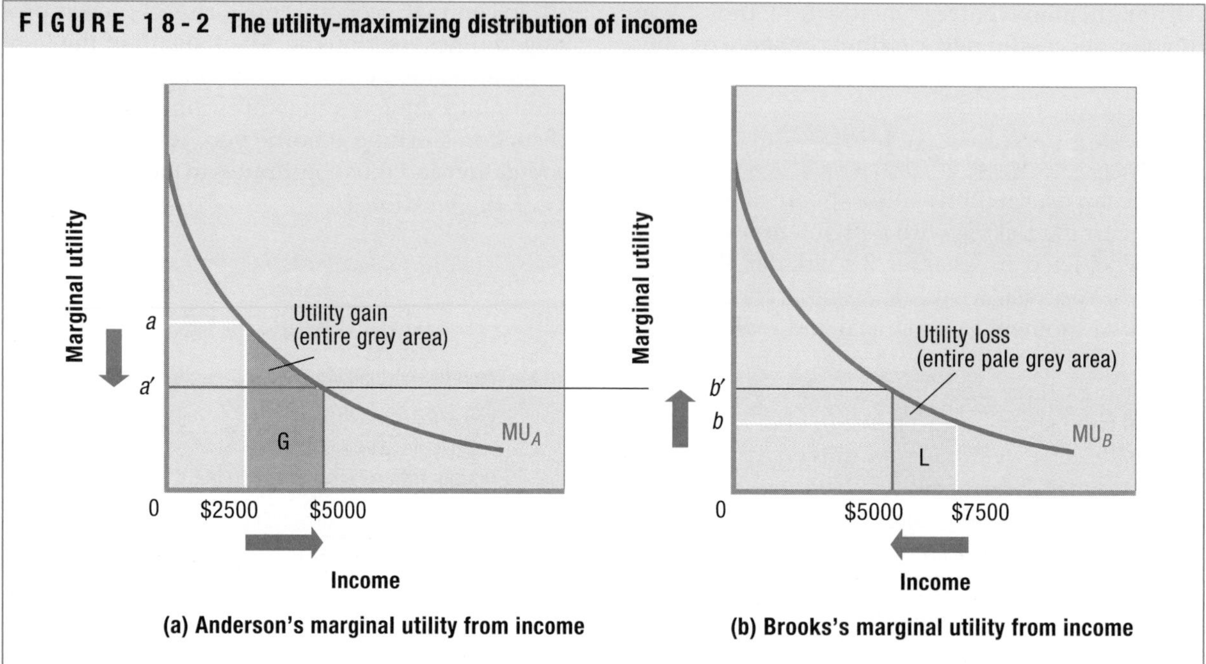


**(a) Anderson's marginal utility from income**

**(b) Brooks's marginal utility from income**

With identical marginal-utility-of-income curves $MU_A$ and $MU_B$, Anderson and Brooks will maximize their combined utility when any amount of income (say, $10,000) is equally distributed. If income is unequally distributed (say, $2,500 to Anderson and $7,500 to Brooks), the marginal utility derived from the last dollar will be greater for Anderson than for Brooks, and a redistribution towards equality will result in a net increase in total utility. The utility gained by equalizing income at $5,000 each, shown by area G in panel (a), exceeds the utility lost, indicated by area L in (b).

most—products whose marginal utility is high. As their most pressing wants become satisfied, consumers then spend additional dollars of income on less important, lower-marginal-utility goods. The identical diminishing *marginal utility from income curves* ($MU_A$ and $MU_B$ in the figure) reflect the assumption that Anderson and Brooks have the same capacity to derive utility from income.

Now suppose there is $10,000 worth of income (output) to be distributed between Anderson and Brooks. According to proponents of income equality, the optimal distribution is an equal distribution, which causes the marginal utility of the last dollar spent to be the same for both persons. We can prove this by demonstrating that if the income distribution is initially unequal, then distributing income more equally can increase the combined utility of the two individuals.

Suppose the $10,000 of income initially is distributed unequally, with Anderson getting $2,500 and Brooks $7,500. The marginal utility, *a*, from the last dollar received by Anderson is high, and the marginal utility, *b*, from Brooks's last dollar of income is low. If a single dollar of income is shifted from Brooks to Anderson—that is, towards greater equality—then Anderson's utility increases by *a* and Brooks's utility decreases by *b*. The combined utility then increases by *a* minus *b* (Anderson's large gain minus Brooks's small loss). The transfer of another dollar from Brooks to Anderson again increases their combined utility, this time by a slightly smaller amount. Continued transfer of dollars from Brooks to Anderson increases their combined utility until the income is evenly distributed and both receive $5,000. At that time their marginal utilities from the last dollar of income are equal (at *a′* and *b′*), and any further income redistribution beyond the $2,500 already transferred would begin to create inequality and decrease their combined utility.

The area under the MU curve, and to the left of the individual's particular level of income, represents the total utility of that income. Therefore, as a result of the transfer of the $2,500, Anderson has gained utility represented by the grey area G, and Brooks has lost utility represented by the pale grey area L. Area G is obviously greater than area L, so income equality yields greater combined total utility than income inequality.

### The Case for Inequality: Incentives and Efficiency

Although the logic of the argument for equality is sound, critics attack its fundamental assumption that there is some fixed amount of income to be distributed. Critics of income equality argue that *the way in which income is distributed is an important determinant of the amount of income that is produced and is available for distribution.*

Suppose once again in Figure 18-2 that Anderson earns $2,500 and Brooks earns $7,500. In moving towards equality, society (government) must *tax* away some of Brooks's income and *transfer* it to Anderson. This tax and transfer process diminishes the income rewards of high-income Brooks and raises the income rewards of low-income Anderson; in so doing, it reduces the incentives of both to *earn* high incomes. Why should high-income Brooks work hard, save and invest, or undertake entrepreneurial risks when the rewards from such activities will be reduced by taxation? And why should low-income Anderson be motivated to increase his income through market activities when government stands ready to transfer income to him? Taxes are a reduction in the rewards from increased productive effort; redistribution through transfers is a reward for diminished effort.

In the extreme, imagine a situation in which government levies a 100 percent tax on income and distributes the tax revenue equally to its citizenry. Why would anyone work hard? Why would anyone work at all? Why would anyone assume business risk? Or why would anyone save (forgo current consumption) to invest? The economic incentives to "get ahead" will have been removed, which would in turn greatly reduce society's total production and income. In other words, the way the income pie is distributed affects the size of that pie. The basic argument for income inequality is that inequality is essential to maintain incentives to produce output and income—to get the pie baked year after year.

### The Equality-Efficiency Tradeoff

The essence of this income equality-inequality debate is that there is a fundamental **tradeoff between equality and efficiency**. The problem for a society that is inclined towards equality is to redistribute income in a way that minimizes the adverse effects on economic efficiency. Consider this *leaky-bucket analogy*. Assume society agrees to shift income from the rich to the poor. But the money must be carried from affluent to indigent in a leaky bucket. The leak represents an efficiency loss—the loss of output and income—caused by the harmful effects of the redistribution on incentives to work, to save and invest, and to accept entrepreneurial risk. The leak also reflects the fact that resources must be diverted to the bureaucracies that administer the redistribution system.

How much leakage will society accept and still agree to the redistribution? If cutting the income pie into more equal slices shrinks the pie, what amount of shrinkage will society tolerate? Is a loss of 1 cent on each redistributed dollar acceptable? Five cents? Twenty-five cents? Fifty cents? This is the basic question in any debate over the ideal size of a nation's income-maintenance programs.

## THE ECONOMICS OF POVERTY

Many people are less concerned with the larger question of income distribution than they are with the more specific issue of inadequate income. Armed with some background information on income inequality, let's now turn to the poverty problem. How extensive is poverty in Canada? What are the characteristics of the poor? And what is the best strategy to lessen poverty?

### Definition of Poverty

Poverty does not lend itself to precise definition. But it helps to distinguish between absolute and relative poverty. **Absolute poverty** occurs when the basic material needs—food, clothing, and shelter—of an individual or family are not met. **Relative poverty** refers to an individual's or family's low income relative to others in society. While a family's basic material needs may be met, it would still be considered poor if its income relative to others is much lower.

While it is possible to eradicate absolute poverty, relative poverty will probably always be around, at least in a market economy, where some individuals are able to earn much more than others.

A family's needs have many determinants: its size, its health, the ages of its members, and so forth. Its means include currently earned income, transfer payments, past savings, property owned, and so on. Statistics Canada uses a (revised 1992) "low income cut-off": families that spend 54.7 percent or more of their income on food, shelter, and clothing are considered to be below the cut-off. In 1986 14.5 percent of families and 40.8 percent of unattached individuals were considered to be living in poverty in Canada.

## Who Are the Poor?

Unfortunately for purposes of public policy, the poor are heterogeneous: they can be found in all geographic regions; they are whites, non-whites, and native peoples; they include large numbers of both rural and urban people; they are both old and young.

Yet, despite this pervasiveness, poverty is far from randomly distributed, as Table 18-3 demonstrates. An aging widow with four years of schooling living in an Atlantic town and prevented from seeking paid work by her four under-16 children still at home—well, she is likely to be poor. And when her children have left home and, she is over

**TABLE 18-3 Incidence of low income by selected characteristics, 1996**

| | ESTIMATED PERCENTAGE BELOW LOW INCOME CUT-OFF* | |
|---|---|---|
| | Families | Unattached individuals |
| All families and unattached individuals | 14.5% | 40.2% |
| By region —Atlantic provinces | 14.7 | 40.2 |
| —Quebec | 17.1 | 48.3 |
| By age of household head —24 and under | 42.1 | 63.7 |
| —25 to 34 years | 20.9 | 29.5 |
| —65 and over | 8.7 | 47.9 |
| By sex of household head—female | 43.5 | 46.6 |
| By marital status of household head—neither married nor single** | 31.8 | 41.7 |
| By weeks worked —none | 29.6 | 60.4 |
| —1–9 weeks | 47.4 | 81.3 |
| —10–19 weeks | 33.9 | 70.9 |
| —20–29 weeks | 22.7 | 59.8 |
| —30–39 weeks | 16.7 | 41.5 |
| —40–48 weeks | 16.9 | 31.0 |
| —49–52 weeks | 6.0 | 14.3 |
| By education of household head—0–8 years of school | 18.6 | 61.0 |
| —some secondary | 20.8 | 50.6 |
| By origin of household head—Canadian born | 13.0 | 38.9 |
| —non-Canadian born | 20.9 | 47.8 |
| By number of children younger than 16 years—none | 11.9 | 40.2 |
| —1 | 24.3 | — |
| —2 | 24.5 | — |
| —3 or more | 32.4 | — |

*As defined on p. 42 of the source, families that on average spent 54.7% or more of their income on food, shelter, and clothing were considered to be in straitened circumstances and, therefore, below the 1992 low income cut-off. According to this criterion, it is estimated that 5.3 million persons were below the low income cut-off in 1996. These represent 17.9% of the covered population, of whom 1,498,000 were children under 18 years of age.

**Divorced, separated, widowed.

*Source:* Statistics Canada, *Income Distribution by Size in Canada, 1996* (Ottawa, 1997), Table 67.

70, her fortunes look no brighter. The strong correlation shown in Table 18-3 between working few weeks in the year and being poor is expected. However, note that 6 percent of families and 14.3 percent of unattached individuals who worked 49 to 52 weeks were still poor.

The high poverty rates for children are especially disturbing because in a very real sense poverty breeds poverty. Poor children are at greater risk for a range of long-term problems, including poor health and inadequate education, crime, drugs, and teenage pregnancy. Many of today's impoverished will reach adulthood unhealthy, illiterate, and unemployable. The increased concentration of poverty among children bodes poorly for reducing poverty in the future.

From our discussion of income mobility, we know that there is considerable movement out of poverty. Just over half of those who are in poverty one year will remain below the poverty line the next year. On the other hand, poverty is much more persistent for some groups, in particular families headed by women, those with little education and few labour market skills, and those who are dysfunctional because of drugs, alcoholism, or mental illness.

## The "Invisible" Poor

These facts and figures on the extent and character of poverty may be difficult to accept. After all, ours is an affluent society. How do we square the depressing statistics on poverty with everyday observations of abundance? The answer lies mainly in the fact that much Canadian poverty is hidden; it is largely invisible.

There are three reasons for this invisibility. First, a sizable proportion of the people in the poverty pool change from year to year. Research has shown that as many as one-half of those in poverty are poor for only one or two years before successfully climbing out of poverty. Many of these people are not visible as permanently downtrodden and needy. Second, the "permanently poor" are increasingly isolated. Poverty persists in the slums and ghettos of large cities and is not readily visible from the expressway or commuter train. Similarly, rural poverty and the chronically depressed areas of eastern Quebec and the Atlantic provinces are also off the beaten path. Third, and perhaps most important, the poor are politically invisible. They often do not have interest groups fighting the various levels of governments for their rights.

## THE INCOME MAINTENANCE SYSTEM

The existence of a wide variety of income-maintenance programs is evidence that alleviation of poverty has been accepted as a legitimate goal of public policy. In recent years, income-maintenance programs have involved substantial monetary outlays and large numbers of beneficiaries. About one-half of the federal government's 1998–99 expenditures were transfer payments. The government estimated these $70 billion of expenditures would be disbursed as shown in Table 18-4. It should be noted, however, that the bulk of these transfers go to the non-poor, and only a few of these programs are specifically targeted at the poor.

**TABLE 18-4 Federal government transfer payments**

| Program | Estimated expenditures, fiscal year ending March 31, 1999, millions of dollars |
|---|---|
| *Major transfers to other levels of government:* | |
| Fiscal Equalization | 8,482 |
| Canada Health and Social Transfers | 11,626 |
| Territorial governments | 1,134 |
| Alternative payments for standing programs | (2,241) |
| Other | (424) |
| *Subtotal: major transfers to other levels of government* | 18,577 |
| *Major transfers to persons:* | |
| Elderly Benefits | |
| —Old Age Security | 17,714 |
| —Guaranteed Income Supplement | 4,817 |
| —Spouses Allowance | 386 |
| *Subtotal: elderly benefits* | 22,917 |
| Employment Insurance | 12,560 |
| *Subtotal: major transfers to persons* | 35,477 |
| Other transfer payments and subsidies | 15,791 |
| **Total transfer payments*** | **69,845** |

*Excludes National Defence transfer payments.
*Source:* Government of Canada, *1998–1999 Estimates, Part I: The Government Expenditure Plan and Part II: The Main Estimates* (Ottawa: Supply and Services Canada, 1998).

In addition to all these programs, there is the **Canada Pension Plan (CPP)**—funded by obligatory employee and employer contributions.[1] It increases each year by the percentage increase in the cost of living in the previous year.

The **Old Age Security (OAS)** pension is paid on application at age 65 to everyone resident in Canada for 40 years or for at least 10 years immediately before attaining the age of 65. The **Guaranteed Income Supplement (GIS)** is paid on application, subject to a means test, to those receiving the OAS pension but who have an income below a certain level. Considerably more than half of Canadians over 65 draw the GIS. Both the OAS pension and the GIS are increased every three months by the percentage increase in the cost of living in the previous three months.

**Employment insurance** (EI) was started in 1940 to insure *workers* against the hazards of losing their jobs. Certainly it has lessened the misery of the very large number of involuntarily unemployed during recessionary periods. In the early 1970s, unemployment insurance benefits were greatly increased so that there was created a positive incentive for *marginal* workers to enter the labour force, not to work, but to qualify for benefits. In 1977, benefits were decreased slightly while qualifying for them was made more difficult. By the early 1990s the federal government tightened the rules to qualify for EI, as it coped with mounting deficits. By mid-1998 the number of persons paid EI had fallen significantly.

**18-2**

**QUICK REVIEW**

- The fundamental argument for income equality is that it maximizes total utility by equalizing the marginal utility of the last dollar of income received by all people.
- The basic argument for income inequality is that it is necessary as an economic incentive for production.
- By government standards, over 5 million Canadians, or 17.9 percent of the population, live in poverty.
- The Canadian income maintenance system includes both social insurance programs and public assistance (welfare) programs.

[1] The Quebec Pension Plan, for residents of that province, is similar.

## WELFARE: GOALS AND CONFLICTS

An ideal public assistance (welfare) program should simultaneously achieve three goals. First, the plan should be effective in getting individuals and families out of poverty. Second, it should provide adequate incentives for able-bodied, nonretired people to work. Third, the plan's cost should be "reasonable." Unfortunately, these three goals conflict, causing tradeoffs and necessitating compromises. To understand this, consider the three hypothetical welfare plans shown in Table 18-5.

### Common Features

Let's first examine the two common elements in each of the three plans (and in real-world public assistance plans). First, there is a *minimum annual income* that government will provide if the family has no earned income. Second, each plan has a *benefit-reduction rate*, which is the rate at which benefits are reduced or "lost" as a result of earned income.

Consider plan 1. The minimum annual income provided by government is $8,000, and the benefit-reduction rate is 50 percent. If a family earns no income, it will receive cash transfer payments totalling $8,000. If it earns $4,000, it will lose $2,000 ($4,000 of earnings *times* the 50 percent benefit-reduction rate) of transfer payments; its total income will then be $10,000 (= $4,000 of earnings *plus* $6,000 of transfer payments). If $8,000 is earned, transfer payments will fall to $4,000, and so on. Note that at an income of $16,000, transfer payments are zero. The level of earned income at which the transfer payments disappear is called the *break-even income*.

We might criticize plan 1 on the grounds that a 50 percent benefit-reduction rate is too high and therefore does not provide sufficient incentives to work. As earned income increases, the loss of transfer payments constitutes a "tax" on earnings. Some people may choose not to work when they lose 50 cents of each extra dollar earned. Thus in plan 2 the $8,000 minimum income is retained, but the benefit-reduction rate is reduced to 25 percent. But note that the break-even level of income increases to $32,000, so many more families would now qualify for transfer payments. Furthermore, a family with any earned income under $32,000 will receive a larger total transfer payment. For both reasons, a reduction of the benefit-loss rate to

**TABLE 18-5 Tradeoffs among goals: three public assistance plans**

| PLAN 1 ($8,000 MINIMUM INCOME AND 50% BENEFIT-REDUCTION RATE) | | | PLAN 2 ($8,000 MINIMUM INCOME AND 25% BENEFIT-REDUCTION RATE) | | | PLAN 3 ($12,000 MINIMUM INCOME AND 50% BENEFIT-REDUCTION RATE) | | |
|---|---|---|---|---|---|---|---|---|
| Earned income | Transfer payment | Total income | Earned income | Transfer payment | Total income | Earned income | Transfer payment | Total income |
| $ 0 | $8,000 | $ 8,000 | $ 0 | $8,000 | $ 8,000 | $ 0 | $12,000 | $12,000 |
| 4,000 | 6,000 | 10,000 | 8,000 | 6,000 | 14,000 | 8,000 | 8,000 | 16,000 |
| 8,000 | 4,000 | 12,000 | 16,000 | 4,000 | 20,000 | 16,000 | 4,000 | 20,000 |
| 12,000 | 2,000 | 14,000 | 24,000 | 2,000 | 26,000 | 24,000* | 12,000 | 24,000 |
| 16,000* | 0 | 16,000 | 32,000* | 0 | 32,000 | | | |

*Indicates break-even income. Determined by dividing the minimum income by the benefit-reduction rate.

enhance work incentives will raise the cost of the income-maintenance plan.

After examining plans 1 and 2, we might argue that the $8,000 minimum annual income is too low—it does not get families out of poverty. Plan 3 raises the minimum income to $12,000 and retains the 50 percent benefit-reduction rate of plan 1. While plan 3 does a better job of raising the incomes of the poor, it too yields a higher break-even income than plan 1 and therefore will be more costly. Also, if the $12,000 income guarantee of plan 3 were coupled with plan 2's 25 percent benefit-reduction rate to strengthen work incentives, the break-even income level would shoot up to $48,000 and add even more to the costs of the public assistance program.

## Conflicts Among Goals

Our discussion points clearly to the conflicting goals of eliminating poverty, maintaining work incentives, and holding down program costs.

Plan 1, with a low minimum income and a high benefit-reduction rate, keeps cost down. But the low minimum income means that this plan is not very effective in eliminating poverty, and the high benefit-reduction rate weakens work incentives.

In comparison, plan 2 has a lower benefit-reduction rate and therefore stronger work incentives. But it is more costly because it sets a higher break-even income and therefore pays benefits to more families.

Compared with plan 1, plan 3 has a higher minimum income and is more effective in eliminating poverty. While work incentives are the same as those in plan 1, the higher guaranteed income in plan 3 makes the plan more costly. ***(Key Question 10)***

## Welfare: Criticism and Reform 

There is no doubt the social insurance system—as well as local welfare, public housing, rent subsidies, minimum-wage legislation, agricultural subsidies, free dental treatment and drugs for those on welfare, private transfers through charities, veterans' benefits, and pensions—provides important means of alleviating poverty. Nevertheless, the system, broadly defined, has been subject to a wide variety of criticisms.

1. **LACK OF WORK INCENTIVES** It is argued that many programs impair incentives to work. For example, many people on welfare would actually lose money by going to work. Since $1 of benefits is often lost for every $1 earned, there is no incentive to become a productive member of society. Moreover, a family going off welfare loses its right to free dental care and free medicine. Thus, the individual or family can be worse off by working.

   Similarly, employment insurance benefits allow unemployed workers to seek a new job at a more leisurely pace, contributing to both the volume and duration of unemployment. Also, growing welfare benefits are financed by higher and higher taxes on the more productive, higher-income members of society, thereby weakening their incentives to work, take risks, and invest.

2. **ABUSES AND INEQUITIES** Many income-maintenance programs often benefit those who are *not* needy. This is particularly the case with unemployment insurance. The extension of coverage has induced many secondary income earners—those not primarily responsible for the family's income—to enter the labour force. Some of these people, as mentioned above, work barely long enough to qualify for unemployment insurance benefits. Other secondary income earners, while having an honest attachment to the labour force, on losing their jobs involuntarily, have no need of employment insurance benefits because of the continuing high income of the primary income earner. However, it is true that there are many families where the earnings of each spouse are so low that both must work to have a decent living standard for the family. But it is precisely those people who work, pay taxes, and make employment insurance contributions on their minimum wage incomes who are most victimized by someone's spouse drawing more in unneeded benefits than these working poor make in their unpleasant jobs.
3. **ADMINISTRATIVE INEFFICIENCY** Critics charge that the growth of our welfare programs has created a clumsy and inefficient system, characterized by red tape and dependent on a huge bureaucracy for its administration. As such, administration costs account for large portions of the total budget of many programs.
4. **DEPENDENCY** Critics say that long-term welfare payments create "a culture of poverty" which is actually detrimental to individuals and families because it creates dependency on the government, robbing family members of motivation and dignity.
5. **DIVISIVENESS** Welfare programs foster social divisiveness between people working and people receiving welfare. For example, working mothers with small children may wonder why poor mothers receiving welfare should not also work for their money.

## In The Media

# Gap Grows Between Rich, Poor

Booming economy does little for bottom fifth of families, Statscan study says

BY ALANNA MITCHELL
THE GLOBE AND MAIL

The gap between Canada's haves and have-nots has widened dramatically, becoming by some measures the starkest in about a generation, Statistics Canada says.

And it has happened despite robust growth in the economy last year.

"Normally in years like this when the economy has been relatively strong, you'd expect that income distribution would be getting more equal," said economist Gordon Betcherman of Canadian

**FOR RICHER, POORER**

**Average total family income by quintile, constant 1996 dollars.**

| | 1st | 2nd | 3rd | 4th | 5th |
|---|---|---|---|---|---|
| 1993 | $17,486 | $33,095 | $48,521 | $66,487 | $110,185 |
| 1994 | 17,935 | 34,234 | 49,803 | 67,570 | 111,398 |
| 1995 | 17,882 | 33,741 | 48,864 | 67,144 | 112,822 |
| 1996 | 17,334 | 33,564 | 49,310 | 68,063 | 114,874 |
| **Percentage Change 1995–96** | | | | | |
| | −3.1 | −0.5 | +0.9 | +1.4 | +1.8 |

*Source: Statistics Canada*

Policy Research Networks in Ottawa. "But we're seeing the opposite, even in a year like 1996."

The Statscan study, Income Distributions by Size in Canada, published yesterday, examined 35,000 households last April. It found that the poorest one-fifth of families were getting even poorer. On average, they had lost 3.1 per cent of their total family income in 1996.

For the bottom fifth, average income fell to $17,334 from $17,882 the year before, in constant 1996 dollars. This group lost out both in earned income and in government subsidies. These figures are adjusted to strip out the effects of inflation.

But the richest fifth of Canada's families were getting even richer. Their average income rose to $114,874 from $112,822 in constant dollars, a gain of 1.8 per cent in the year after adjusting for inflation.

In fact, since the recession ended, the average income of Canada's richest fifth of families has grown steadily, rising almost $4,700 in real spending power since 1993. That's an increase of 4.3 per cent.

Over the same period, the family income of the poorest Canadian families rose once and then fell for two years in a row for an overall loss of $152.

*Source: Globe and Mail*, December 23, 1997, pp. A1 and A10. Reprinted with permission from the *Globe and Mail*.

## THE STORY IN BRIEF

The gap between the haves and have-nots keeps increasing in Canada to levels not seen in a generation.

## THE ECONOMICS BEHIND THE STORY

- The distribution of income in Canada worsened. The poorest are getting poorer, losing 3.1 percent of their income, while the top quintile gained 1.8 percent.
- The deterioration in the distribution of income occurred despite a growing economy.
- Give some reasons why the poor are getting poorer, and the rich are getting richer. Is complete equality of income feasible? What is the tradeoff? ■

# CHAPTER SUMMARY

1. The distribution of income in Canada reflects considerable inequality. Before taxes, the top 20 percent of families earn 44.5 percent of total income, while the bottom 20 percent earn only 4.6 percent.
2. The Lorenz curve shows the percentage of total income received by each percentage of families. The extent of the gap between the Lorenz curve and a line of total equality illustrates the degree of income inequality.
3. Recognizing that the positions of individual families in the distribution of income change over time *and* incorporating the effects of noncash transfers and taxes would reveal less income inequality than do standard census data. Government transfers (cash and noncash) greatly lessen the degree of income inequality; taxes also reduce inequality, but not nearly as much as transfers.
4. Absolute poverty occurs when the basic material needs are not met. Relative poverty refers to an individual or family's low income relative to the rest of society. Absolute poverty can be eradicated, but relative poverty is much more difficult to resolve.
5. Causes of income inequality include differences in abilities, education and training, and job tastes, along with discrimination, inequality in the distribution of wealth, and an unequal distribution of market power.
6. The basic argument for income equality is that it maximizes consumer satisfaction (total utility) from a particular level of total income. The main argument for income inequality is that it provides the incentives to work, invest, and assume risk; it is necessary for the production of output that, in turn, creates income that is then available for distribution.

7. Current statistics suggest that about 18 percent of the country lives in poverty. Poverty is concentrated among the poorly educated, the aged, and families headed by women.

8. Our present income maintenance system is made up of social insurance programs (Canada Pension Plan and unemployment insurance benefits), universal programs (Old Age Security Pension), and public assistance or welfare programs. The present welfare programs have been criticized as being administratively inefficient, fraught with inequities, and detrimental to work incentives. Some economists believe that a negative income tax would provide a superior income maintenance system.

## TERMS AND CONCEPTS

income inequality
Lorenz curve
income mobility
noncash transfers
equality-efficiency trade-off
absolute poverty
relative poverty
Canada Pension Plan
Old Age Security
Guaranteed Income Supplement
employment insurance benefits

## STUDY QUESTIONS

1. Using quintiles, briefly summarize the degree of income inequality in Canada.
2. KEY QESTION *Assume Al, Beth, Carol, David, and Ed receive incomes of $500, $250, $125, $75, and $50 respectively. Construct and interpret a Lorenz curve for this five-person economy. What percentage of total income is received by the richest quintile and by the poorest quintile?*
3. Why is the lifetime distribution of income more equal than the distribution in any specific year?
4. KEY QUESTION *Briefly discuss the major causes of income inequality. With respect to income inequality, is there any difference between inheriting property and inheriting a high IQ? Explain.*
5. Use the "leaky-bucket analogy" to discuss the equality-efficiency tradeoff.
6. Should a nation's income be distributed to its members according to their contributions to the production of that total income or according to the members' needs? Should society attempt to equalize income or economic opportunities? Are the issues of "equity" and "equality" in the distribution of income synonymous? To what degree, if any, is income inequality equitable?
7. Analyze in detail: "There need be no tradeoff between equality and efficiency. An 'efficient' economy that yields an income distribution that many regard as unfair may cause those with meagre income rewards to become discouraged and stop trying. Hence, efficiency is undermined. A fairer distribution of rewards may generate a higher average productive effort on the part of the population, thereby enhancing efficiency. If people think they are playing a fair economic game and this belief causes them to try harder, an economy with an equitable income distribution may be efficient as well."
8. Comment on or explain:
   - **a.** "To endow everyone with equal income will certainly make for very unequal enjoyment and satisfaction."
   - **b.** "Equality is a 'superior good': the richer we become, the more of it we can afford."
   - **c.** "The mob goes in search of bread, and the means it employs is generally to wreck the bakeries."
   - **d.** "Under our welfare system we have foolishly clung to the notion that employment and receipt of assistance must be mutually exclusive."
   - **e.** "Some freedoms may be more important in the long run than freedom from want on the part of every individual."

f. "Capitalism and democracy are really a most improbable mixture. Maybe that is why they need each other—to put some rationality into equality and some humanity into efficiency."

g. "The incentives created by the attempt to bring about a more equal distribution of income are in conflict with the incentives needed to generate increased income."

9. What are the major criticisms of our present income maintenance system?

10. KEY QUESTION *The following table contains three hypothetic public assistance plans.*

| **PLAN ONE** | | | **PLAN TWO** | | | **PLAN THREE** | | |
|---|---|---|---|---|---|---|---|---|
| **Earned income** | **Transfer payment** | **Total income** | **Earned income** | **Transfer payment** | **Total income** | **Earned income** | **Transfer payment** | **Total income** |
| $ 0 | $4,000 | $4,000 | $ 0 | $4,000 | $ 4,000 | $ 0 | $8,000 | $ 8,000 |
| 2,000 | 3,000 | 5,000 | 4,000 | 3,000 | 7,000 | 4,000 | 6,000 | 10,000 |
| 4,000 | 2,000 | 6,000 | 8,000 | 2,000 | 10,000 | 8,000 | 4,000 | 12,000 |
| 6,000 | 1,000 | 7,000 | 12,000 | 1,000 | 13,000 | 12,000 | 2,000 | 14,000 |

a. *Determine the minimum income, the benefit-reduction rate, and the break-even income for each plan.*

b. *Which plan is the most costly? The least costly? Which plan is the most effective in reducing poverty? The least effective? Which plan embodies the strongest disincentive to work? The weakest disincentive to work?*

c. *Use your answers in part b to explain the following statement: "The dilemma of public assistance is that you cannot bring families up to the poverty level and simultaneously preserve work incentives and minimize program costs."*

11. WEB-BASED QUESTION **Is Poverty on the Rise?** Statistics Canada www.statcan.ca/english/Pgdb/People/Families/famil41.htm compiles information about low income in Canada. Use that site to answer the following questions: **a** Is the percentage of the population living below Statistics Canada's Low Income Cut-offs higher or lower than in the previous year reported? Compared to a decade earlier? **b** Is the poverty rate (in percent) higher or lower than the previous year for the general population and children under 18 and the elderly?

# Microeconomics of Government and the Gains from Trade

PART 4

CHAPTER 19

# Government and Market Failure: Public Goods, Externalities, and Information Problems

THE ECONOMIC ACTIVITIES OF GOVERNMENT AFFECT your well-being every day. If you attend a community college or university, taxpayers subsidize your education. When you receive a cheque from your part-time or summer job, you see deductions for income and social insurance taxes. The beef in your Big Mac has been examined by government inspectors to prevent contamination and ensure quality. Laws requiring seat belts, motorcycle helmets, and the sprinkler system in your dormitory are all government mandates. If you are a woman, a member of a minority group, or a person with a disability, legislation has been designed to reduce discrimination and enhance your education and employment opportunities.

In this chapter and in Chapter 20 we examine the microeconomics of government. We begin by returning to the topic of *market failure* introduced in Chapter 5. In particular, marginal analysis permits us to provide a fuller discussion of public goods and externalities. Our discussion of externalities in turn facilitates an extensive discussion of pollution and pollution policies. We then examine information failures in the private sector to determine their implications for government participation in the economy. In Chapter 20 our discussion of the microeconomics of government continues with an analysis of potential government inefficiencies—so-called *government failure*—and the economics of taxation.

**IN THIS CHAPTER YOU WILL LEARN:**

That when markets fail, there is a role for government intervention in a market economy.

•

To distinguish between a public and private good.

•

How to determine the optimal amount of a public good.

•

The nature of externalities and the ways of dealing with them.

•

About the cost of information.

## The Big Picture

THROUGHOUT THIS BOOK WE HAVE EXTOLLED the great virtues of markets in getting the most out of the available limited resources and producing those goods and services society wants most. But while markets have these wonderful virtues, they sometimes fail to do their job. As noted in Chapter 5, markets fail in the case of public goods; it is impossible to exclude those not paying for a public good from consuming it. Some people will consume a public good and try to avoid paying for it. Markets also fail when there are third party effects—a firm producing product X but polluting the air in the process will impose a cost on those living in the vicinity. The market price of product X, moreover, will not reflect the cost the pollution inflicts on those who suffer its effect. Another case of market failure discussed in this chapter is information failures. The pure competitive market model assumes perfect information. In the absence of such an ideal state, markets will not bring about productive and allocative efficiency.

As you read this chapter, keep the following points in mind:

- **Key Concepts 3, 6,** and **7** are discussed.
- It will be helpful to re-read the parts of Chapter 5 dealing with public good and externalities to refresh your memory of their definitions.
- The function of markets is to coordinate production and consumption decisions in a world of limited resources and unlimited wants. You will better appreciate the notion of "market failure"—instances when it fails to fulfil this function—if you remind yourself of the function of markets. ■

## PUBLIC GOODS: EXTENDING THE ANALYSIS

Recall from Chapter 5 that a private good is divisible; it comes in units small enough to be afforded by individual buyers. It is also subject to the exclusion principle: people unwilling or unable to pay for the product are barred from obtaining its benefits. Because of these characteristics, the demand for a private good gets expressed in the marketplace, and profit-seeking suppliers satisfy this demand. In contrast, a public good is indivisible and does *not* fit the exclusion principle; once the good is provided, the producer cannot stop nonpayers from obtaining the benefits. Consequently, the demand for the good gets understated in the marketplace, and firms lack a profit incentive to offer it for sale. If it is to exist, government must provide it. Two very simple examples will help clarify the distinction between a private and a public good.

The market demand for a private good is the horizontal summation of the demand curves representing all individual buyers (review Table 4-2 and Figure 4-2). Suppose there are just two people in society who enjoy hot dogs, which cost $.80 each to produce. If Adams wants to buy 3 hot dogs at $1 each and Benson wants to buy 2 hot dogs at that same price, the market demand curve will reflect that 5 hot dogs are demanded at a $1 price. A seller charging $1 for each hot dog can gain $5 of revenue and earn $1 of profit ($5 of total revenue minus $4 of cost).

It is different with public goods. Suppose an enterprising sculptor creates a permanent piece of art costing $600 and places it in the town square. Also suppose that Adams gets $300 of enjoyment from the art and Benson gets $400. Sensing this enjoyment—and hoping to make a profit—the sculptor approaches Adams for a donation equal to his satisfaction. Adams lies and says that, unfortunately, he doesn't much like the art. The artist then tries Benson, hoping to get $400 or so. Same deal: Benson professes not to like the art either. Adams and Benson have become *free riders*. Although feeling a bit guilty, both reason that it makes no sense to pay for something when you can receive the benefits without paying for them. The artist is a quick learner; he vows not to try anything like *that* again.

Generalization: Because of the free-rider problem, the *market* demand for a public good is nonexistent or significantly understated. *Where a producer cannot exclude nonpayers from receiving the benefits from a good, it is difficult, if not impossible, for the producer to profitably offer the good for sale.* Government will have to provide it.

## Determining the Demand for Public Goods

If consumers need not reveal their true demand for a public good in the marketplace, then how can the optimal amount of that good be determined? The answer is that government has to try to estimate the demand for a public good through surveys or public votes. Suppose Adams and Benson are the only two people in the society, and their marginal willingness to pay for a public good, this time national defence, is as shown in columns 1 and 2 and columns 1 and 3 in Table 19-1. Economists might have discovered these schedules through a survey asking hypothetical questions about how much each citizen is willing to pay for various types and amounts of public goods rather than go without them.

Notice that the schedules in Table 19-1 are price-quantity schedules, implying that they are demand schedules. Rather than depicting demand in the usual way—the quantity of a product someone is willing to buy at each possible price—these schedules show the price someone is willing to pay for the marginal unit of each possible quantity. That is, Adams is willing to pay $4 for the first unit of the public good, $3 for the second, $2 for the third, and so on.

Suppose government produces 1 unit of this public good. Because the exclusion principle does not apply, Adams's consumption of the good does not preclude Benson from also consuming it, and vice versa. So both consume the good, and neither volunteers to pay for it. But from Table 19-1 we can find the amount these two people would be willing to pay, together, rather than do without this 1 unit of the good. Columns 1 and 2 show that Adams would be willing to pay $4 for the first unit of the public good; columns 1 and 3 show that Benson would be willing to pay $5 for it. So the two people are jointly willing to pay $9 (= $4 + $5) for this unit.

For the second unit of the public good, the collective price they are willing to pay is $7 (= $3 from Adams plus $4 from Benson); for the third unit they will pay $5 (= $2 plus $3); and so on. By finding the collective willingness to pay for each additional unit (column 4), we can construct a collective demand schedule (willingness-to-pay schedule) for the public good. Here we are *not* adding the *quantities demanded at each possible price*, as when we determine the market demand for a private good. Instead, we are *adding the prices that people are willing to pay for the last unit of the public good at each possible quantity demanded.*

Figure 19-1 shows the same adding procedure graphically, using the data from Table 19-1. Note that we sum Adams's and Benson's willingness-to-pay curves vertically to derive the collective willingness-to-pay curve (demand curve). The height of the collective demand curve $D_c$ at 2 units of output, for example, is $7, the sum of the amounts that Adams and Benson are each willing to pay for the second unit (= $3 + $4). Likewise, the height of the collective demand curve at 4 units of the public good is $3 (= $1 + $2).

What does it mean in Figure 19-1a that, for example, Adams is willing to pay $3 for the second unit of the public good? It means that Adams expects to receive $3 of extra benefit or utility from that unit. And we know from the law of diminishing marginal utility that successive units of any good yield less and less added benefit. This is also true for public goods, explaining the downward slope of Adams's willingness-to-pay curve, as well as Benson's curve, and the collective demand curve. These curves, in essence, are marginal-*benefit* curves. ***(Key Question 1)***

**TABLE 19-1 Demand for a public good, two individuals**

| (1) Quantity | (2) Adams's willingness to pay (price) | | (3) Benson's willingness to pay (price) | | (4) Collective willingness to pay (price) |
|---|---|---|---|---|---|
| 1 | $4 | + | $5 | = | $9 |
| 2 | 3 | + | 4 | = | 7 |
| 3 | 2 | + | 3 | = | 5 |
| 4 | 1 | + | 2 | = | 3 |
| 5 | 0 | + | 1 | = | 1 |

## Supply of Public Goods

The supply curve for any good, private or public, is its marginal-cost curve. Marginal cost rises as

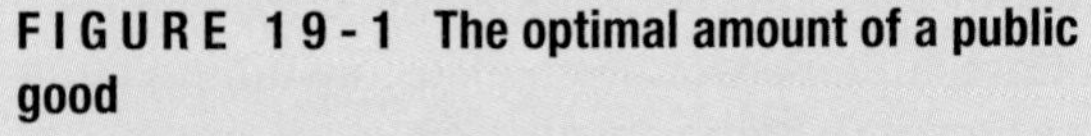

**FIGURE 19-1 The optimal amount of a public good**

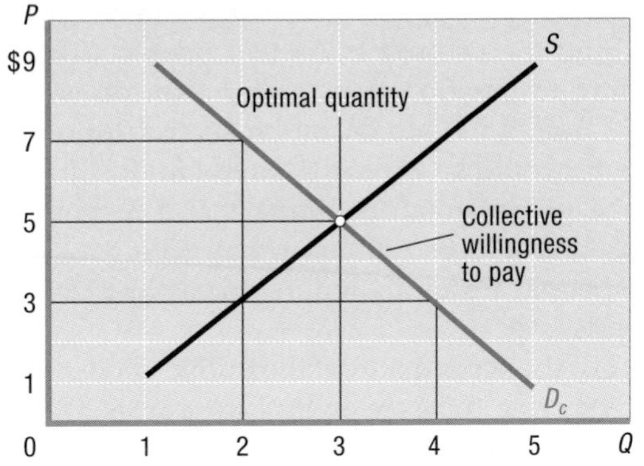


(c) Collective demand and supply

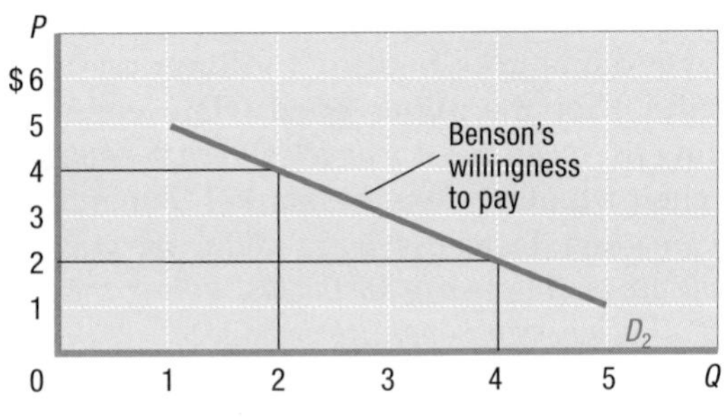


(b) Benson

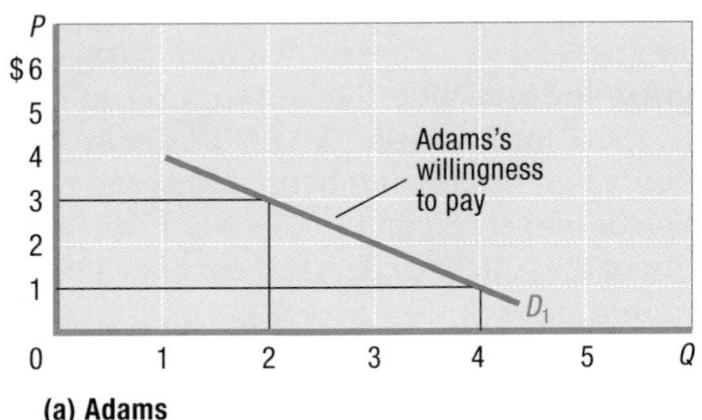


(a) Adams

The collective demand curve $D_c$ for the public good shown in (c) is found by summing vertically the individual demand curves $D_1$ and $D_2$ exhibited in (a) and (b). Government should provide 3 units of the public good because at that quantity the combined marginal benefit, as measured by the citizens' willingness to pay for the last unit (shown by $D_c$), equals the good's marginal cost (shown by $S$).

more of a good is produced. The reason is the law of diminishing returns, which applies whether a society is making missiles (a public good) or mufflers (a private good). In the short run, government has fixed resources (public capital) with which to "produce" public goods such as national defence. As it adds more units of a variable resource (labour) to these fixed resources, marginal product eventually rises at a diminishing rate. That means marginal cost rises, explaining why curve *S* in Figure 19-1c slopes upward.

## Optimal Quantity of a Public Good

We can now determine the optimal quantity of the public good. The collective demand curve $D_c$ in Figure 19-1c measures society's marginal benefit of each unit of this particular good. The supply curve *S* in that figure measures society's marginal cost of each unit. The optimal quantity of this public good occurs where marginal benefit equals marginal cost, or where the two curves intersect. In Figure 19-1c we see that the optimal quantity of the public good is 3 units—at the intersection of supply and demand. There the collective willingness to pay for the last (third) unit—the marginal benefit—just matches that unit's marginal cost ($5 = $5). As we saw in Chapter 2, equating marginal benefit and marginal cost allocates society's resources most efficiently. ***(Key Question 2)***

## Benefit-Cost Analysis

The above example suggests a practical means, called **benefit-cost analysis**, for deciding whether to provide a particular public good and how much of it to provide. Like our example, it involves a comparison of marginal benefits and marginal costs.

**Concept** Suppose government is contemplating a flood-control project. Because the economy's resources are limited, any decision to use more resources in the public sector will mean fewer resources for the private sector. There will be both a benefit and a cost. The benefit is the extra satisfaction resulting from the output of more public goods; the cost is the loss of satisfaction resulting from the accompanying decline in the production of private goods. Should the needed resources be shifted from the private to the public sector? The answer is "yes" if the benefit from the extra public goods exceeds the cost resulting from having fewer private goods. The answer is "no" if the cost of the forgone private goods is greater than the benefit associated with the extra public goods.

But benefit-cost analysis can indicate more than whether a public program is worth doing. It can also help government decide on the extent to which a project should be pursued. Real economic questions cannot usually be answered simply by "yes" or "no" but, rather, are matters of "how much" or "how little."

**Illustration** There is no doubt that a flood-control project is a public good since the exclusion principle is not readily applicable. Should government undertake a flood-control project in a particular river valley? If so, what is the proper size or scope for the project?

Table 19-2 lists a series of increasingly ambitious and increasingly costly flood-control plans for the valley. The extent to which government should undertake flood control depends on the costs and benefits. The costs are largely the costs of constructing and maintaining levees and reservoirs; the benefits are reduced flood damage.

The table shows that total annual benefit (column 4) exceeds total annual cost (column 2) for each plan, indicating that a flood-control project on this river is economically justifiable. We can see this directly in column 6, where total annual costs (column 2) are subtracted from total annual benefits (column 4).

But the question of optimal size or scope for this project remains. Comparing the additional, or marginal, cost and the additional, or marginal, benefit relating to each plan determines the answer. The guideline is essentially the one we just established: Increase an activity or project or output as long as the marginal benefit (column 5) exceeds the marginal cost (column 3). Stop the activity at, or as close as possible to, the point at which the marginal benefit equals the marginal cost.

In this case plan C—the medium-size reservoir—is the best plan. Plans A and B are too modest; in both cases the marginal benefit exceeds the marginal cost. Plan D's marginal cost ($12,000) exceeds the marginal benefit ($7,000) and therefore cannot be justified; it overallocates resources to the project. Plan C is closest to the optimum since its marginal benefit still exceeds marginal cost but approaches the MB = MC ideal.

This **marginal benefit = marginal cost rule** actually tells us which plan provides the maximum excess of total benefits over total costs—in other words, the plan that yields the maximum net benefit to society. You can confirm directly in column 6 that the maximum net benefit (of $7,000) is associated with plan C.

Benefit-cost analysis shatters the myth that "economy in government" and "reduced government spending" are synonymous. "Economy" is concerned with using scarce resources efficiently. If the cost of a proposed government program exceeds its benefits, then the proposed public program should *not* be undertaken. But if the benefits exceed the cost, then it would be uneconomical or "wasteful" not to spend on that government program. Economy in government does *not* mean minimization of public spending. It means allocating resources between the private and public sectors to achieve maximum net benefit. ***(Key Question 3)***

**TABLE 19-2 Benefit-cost analysis for a flood-control project**

| (1) Plan | (2) Total annual cost of project | (3) Marginal cost | (4) Total annual benefit (reduction in damage) | (5) Marginal benefit | (6) Net benefit or (4) – (2) |
|---|---|---|---|---|---|
| Without protection | $ 0 | | $ 0 | | $ 0 |
| | | $ 3,000 | | $ 6,000 | |
| A: Levees | 3,000 | | 6,000 | | 3,000 |
| | | 7,000 | | 10,000 | |
| B: Small reservoir | 10,000 | | 16,000 | | 6,000 |
| | | 8,000 | | 9,000 | |
| C: Medium reservoir | 18,000 | | 25,000 | | 7,000 |
| | | 12,000 | | 7,000 | |
| D: Large reservoir | 30,000 | | 32,000 | | 2,000 |

*Source:* Adopted from Otto Eckstein, *Public Finance,* 3d ed. (Englewood Cliffs, NJ: Prentice-Hall, 1973), p. 23. Used with permission.

**19-1**

**QUICK REVIEW**

- The demand (marginal-benefit) curve for a public good is found by vertically adding the prices that all members of the society are willing to pay for the last unit of output at various output levels.
- The optimal social amount of a public good is the amount at which the marginal benefit and marginal cost of the good are equal.
- Benefit-cost analysis is the method of evaluating alternative projects or sizes of projects by comparing marginal benefits and marginal cost and applying the MB = MC rule.

## EXTERNALITIES REVISITED

We return now to Chapter 5's discussion of government policies designed to correct the market failures we call externalities, or spillovers. Recall that a spillover is a cost or benefit accruing to an individual or group—a third party—that is external to a market transaction. An example of a spillover cost or *negative externality* is the cost of breathing polluted air; an example of a spillover benefit or *positive externality* is the benefit of having everyone else inoculated against some communicable disease. When there are spillover costs, an overproduction of the related product occurs and there is an overallocation of resources to this product. Conversely, underproduction and underallocation of resources result when spillover benefits are present. We can demonstrate both graphically.

### Spillover Costs

Figure 19-2a illustrates how spillover costs affect the allocation of resources. When spillover costs occur—when producers shift some of their costs onto the community—producers' marginal costs are lower than otherwise. So their supply curves do not include or "capture" all the costs associated with production of their goods. Thus a polluting producer's supply curve—*S* in Figure 19-2a—understates the total cost of production: the producer's supply curve lies to the right of (or below) the full-cost supply curve $S_t$, which would include the spillover cost. Through polluting and thus transferring cost to society, the firm enjoys lower production costs and has the supply curve *S*.

The outcome is shown in Figure 19-2a, where equilibrium output $Q_e$ is *larger* than the optimal output $Q_o$. This means that resources are overallocated to the production of this commodity; too many units of it are produced.

### Spillover Benefits

Figure 19-2b shows the impact of spillover benefits on resource allocation. When spillover benefits occur, the market demand curve *D* lies to the left of (or below) the full-benefits demand curve. That

**FIGURE 19-2 Spillover costs and spillover benefits**

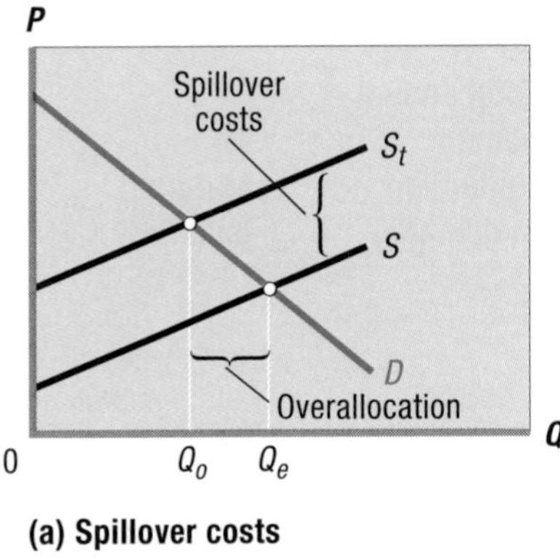


**(a) Spillover costs**

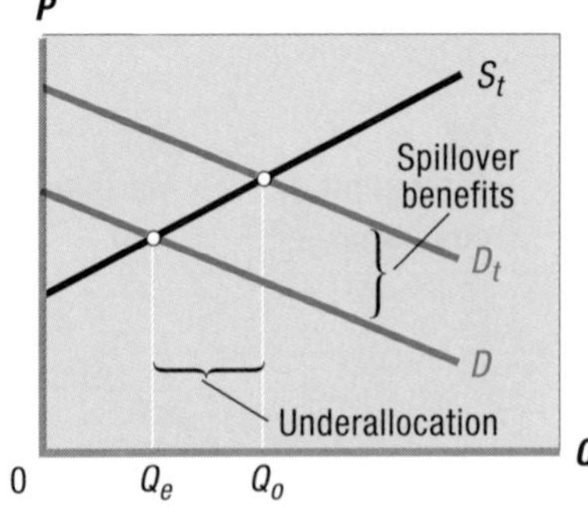


**(b) Spillover benefits**

(a) With spillover costs borne by society, the producers' supply curve *S* is to the right of (below) the full-cost curve $S_t$. Consequently, the equilibrium output $Q_e$ is greater than the optimal output $Q_o$. (b) When spillover benefits accrue to society, the market demand curve *D* is to the left of (below) the full-benefit demand curve $D_t$. As a result, the equilibrium output $Q_e$ is less than the optimal output $Q_o$.

is, $D$ does not include the spillover benefits of the product, whereas $D_t$ does. Consider inoculations against a communicable disease. Watson and Weinberg benefit when they get vaccinated, but so do their associates Alvarez and Anderson, who are now less likely to contract the disease from them. The market demand curve reflects only the direct, private benefits to Watson and Weinberg. It does not reflect the spillover benefits—the positive externalities—to Alvarez and Anderson, which are included in $D_t$.

The outcome is that the equilibrium output $Q_e$ is less than the optimal output $Q_o$. The market fails to produce enough vaccinations; resources are underallocated to this product.

Economists have explored several approaches to the problems of spillover costs and benefits. We will look first at situations where government intervention is not needed and then at some government solutions.

## Individual Bargaining: Coase Theorem

In the **Coase theorem**, conceived by Ronald Coase, government is not needed to remedy spillover costs or benefits where (1) property ownership is clearly defined, (2) the number of people involved is small, and (3) bargaining costs are negligible. Under these circumstances government should confine its role to encouraging bargaining between affected individuals or groups. Property rights place a price tag on an externality, creating opportunity costs for all parties. Because the economic self-interests of the parties are at stake, bargaining will enable them to find a mutually acceptable solution to the externality problem.

**Example** Suppose the owner of a large parcel of forestland is considering a plan to clear-cut (totally level) thousands of hectares of mature fir trees. The complication is that the forest surrounds a lake with a popular resort on its shore. The resort is on land owned by the resort. The unspoiled beauty of the general area attracts vacationers from all over the nation to the resort, and the resort owner is against the clear-cutting. Should provincial or local government intervene to allow or prevent the tree cutting?

According to the Coase theorem, the forest owner and the resort owner can resolve this situation without government intervention. As long as *one* of the parties to the dispute has property rights to what is at issue, an incentive will exist for *both* parties to negotiate a solution acceptable to each. In our example, the owner of the timberland holds the property rights to the land to be logged and thus has the right to clear-cut it. The owner of the resort therefore has an economic incentive to negotiate with the forest owner to reduce the logging impact. Excessive logging of the forest surrounding the resort will reduce tourism and revenues to the resort owner.

But what is the economic incentive to the forest owner to negotiate with the resort owner? The answer draws directly on the idea of opportunity cost. One cost incurred in logging the forest is the forgone payment, which the forest owner could obtain from the resort owner for agreeing not to clear-cut the fir trees. The resort owner might be willing to make a lump-sum or annual payment to the owner of the forest to avoid or minimize the spillover cost. Or perhaps the resort owner will be willing to buy the forested land to prevent the logging. As viewed by the forest owner, a payment for not clear-cutting or a purchase price above the market value of the land is an *opportunity cost* of logging the land.

It is likely that both parties would regard a negotiated agreement as better than clear-cutting the firs.

**Limitations** Unfortunately, many externalities involve large numbers of affected parties, high bargaining costs, and community property such as air and water. In these situations private bargaining cannot be used as a remedy. As an example, the acid-rain problem in Canada and the United States affects millions of people in both nations. The vast number of affected parties could not independently negotiate an agreement to remedy this problem. Instead, we must rely on the two governments to represent the millions of affected parties and find an acceptable solution.

Nevertheless, the Coase theorem reminds us that in many situations bargaining can be useful in remedying spillover costs and spillover benefits.

## Liability Rules and Lawsuits

Although private negotiation may not be a realistic solution to many externality problems, clearly established property rights may help in another way. Government has established a framework of laws that define private property and protect it from damage done by other parties. These laws—

and the damage recovery system to which they give rise—permit those suffering spillover costs to sue for compensation.

Suppose the Ajax Degreaser Company regularly dumps leaky barrels containing solvents into a nearby canyon owned by Bar Q ranch. Bar Q eventually discovers this dump site and, after tracing the drums to Ajax, immediately contacts its lawyer. Soon after, Bar Q sues Ajax. Not only will Ajax have to pay for the cleanup; it may also have to pay Bar Q additional damages for ruining its property.

Clearly defined property rights and government liability laws thus help remedy some externality problems. They do so directly by forcing the perpetrator of the harmful externality to pay damages to those injured. They do so indirectly by discouraging firms and individuals from generating spillover costs, for fear of being sued. It is not surprising, then, that many spillovers do *not* involve private property but rather property held in common by society. It is the *public* bodies of water, the *public* lands, and the public air, where ownership is less clear, which often bear the brunt of spillovers.

Caveat: Like private negotiations, private lawsuits to resolve externalities have their own limitations. Large legal fees and major time delays in the court system are commonplace. Also, the uncertainty associated with the court outcome reduces the effectiveness of this approach. Will the court accept your claim that your emphysema has resulted from the smoke emitted by the factory next door, or will it conclude that your ailment is unrelated to the plant's pollution? Can you prove that a specific firm in the area is the source of the contamination of your well? What happens to Bar Q's suit if Ajax Degreaser goes out of business during the litigation?

## Government Intervention

Government intervention may be needed to achieve economic efficiency when externalities affect large numbers of people or when community interests are at stake. Direct controls and taxes can be used to counter spillover costs; government may provide subsidies or public goods to deal with spillover benefits.

**Direct Controls** The direct way to reduce spillover costs due to a certain activity is to pass legislation placing limits on that activity. Such direct controls force the offending firms to incur the actual costs associated with the offending activity. To date, this approach has dominated public policy in Canada. Clean-air legislation limits the amounts of nitrogen oxide, particulates, and other substances factories can emit into the air. Clean-water legislation limits the amount of heavy metals, detergents, and other pollutants firms can discharge into rivers and bays. Toxic-waste laws dictate special procedures and dump sites for disposing of contaminated soil and solvents. Violations of these laws mean fines and, in some cases, imprisonment.

Direct controls raise the marginal cost of production, since the firms must operate and maintain pollution-control equipment. The supply curve $S$ in Figure 19-3b, which does not reflect the spillover costs, shifts leftward (upward) to the full-cost supply curve, $S_t$. Product price increases, equilibrium output falls from $Q_e$ to $Q_o$, and the initial overallocation of resources shown in Figure 19-3a is corrected.

**Specific Taxes** A second policy approach to spillover costs is to levy taxes or charges specifically on the related good. For example, the government has placed a manufacturing excise tax on chlorofluorocarbons (CFCs) which deplete the stratospheric ozone layer protecting the earth from excessive solar ultraviolet radiation. (CFCs are used widely as a coolant in refrigeration, a blowing agent for foam, and a solvent in the electronics industry.) Facing such an excise tax, manufacturers must decide whether to pay the tax or expend additional funds to purchase or develop substitute products. In either case, the tax raises the marginal cost of producing CFCs, shifting the private supply curve for this product leftward (or upward).

In Figure 19-3b, a tax equal to $T$ per unit increases the firm's marginal cost, shifting the supply curve from $S$ to $S_t$. The equilibrium price increases, and the equilibrium output declines from $Q_e$ to the economically efficient level $Q_o$. The initial overallocation of resources is eliminated.

**Subsidies and Government Provision** Where spillover benefits are large and diffuse, as in our earlier example of inoculations, government has three options for correcting the underallocation of resources:

1. **SUBSIDIES TO BUYERS** Figure 19-4a again shows the supply-demand situation for spill-

**FIGURE 19-3 Correcting for spillover costs (negative externalities)**

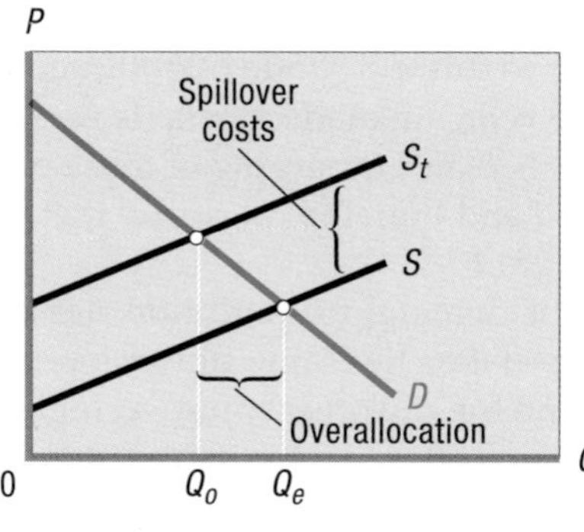


**(a) Spillover costs**

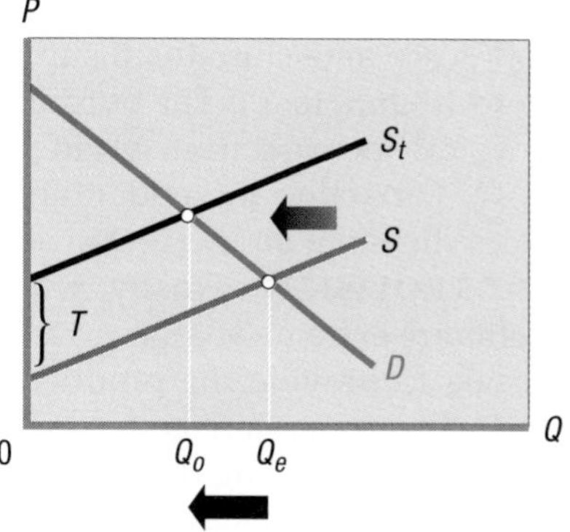


**(b) Correcting the overallocation of resources via direct controls or via a tax**

(a) Spillover costs result in an overallocation of resources. (b) This overallocation can be corrected in two ways: (1) use of direct controls, which would shift the supply curve from $S$ to $S_t$ and reduce output from $Q_e$ to $Q_o$; or (2) imposition of a specific tax $T$, which would also shift the supply curve from $S$ to $S_t$, eliminating the over allocation of resources.

over benefits. Government could correct the underallocation of resources—say, to inoculations—by subsidizing consumers of the product. It could give each new mother in Canada a discount coupon to be used to obtain a series of inoculations for her child. The coupon would reduce the "price" to the mother by, say, 50 percent. As shown in Figure 19-4b, this program would shift the demand curve for inoculations from the too low $D$ to $D_t$. The number of inoculations would rise from $Q_e$ to the economically optimal $Q_o$, eliminating the underallocation of resources shown in Figure 19-4a.

2. **SUBSIDIES TO PRODUCERS** A subsidy to producers is a specific tax in reverse; taxes impose an extra cost on producers, while sub-

**FIGURE 19-4 Correcting for spillover benefits (positive externalities)**

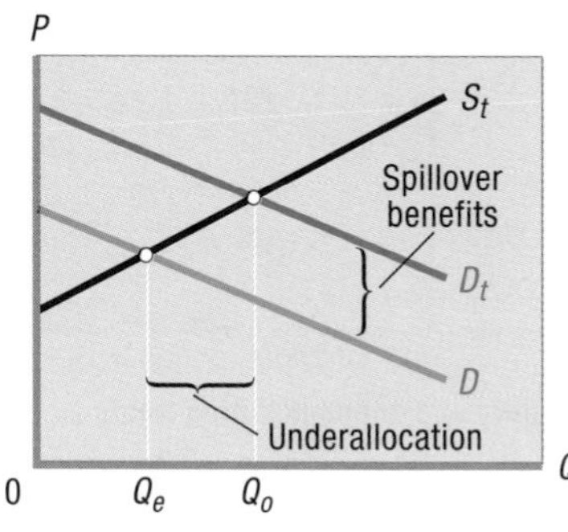


**(a) Spillover benefits**

**(b) Correcting the underallocation of resources via a subsidy to consumers**

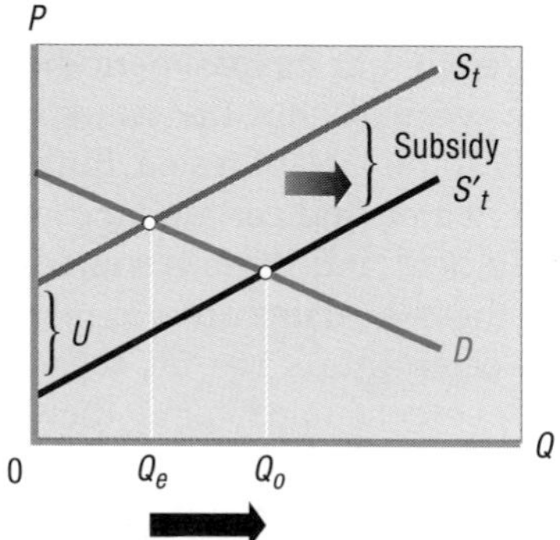


**(c) Correcting the underallocation of resources via a subsidy to producers**

(a) Spillover benefits result in an underallocation of resources. (b) This underallocation can be corrected by a subsidy to consumers, which shifts market demand from $D$ to $D_t$ and increases output from $Q_e$ to $Q_o$. (c) Alternatively, the underallocation can be eliminated by providing producers with a subsidy of $U$, which shifts their supply curve from $S_t$ to $S'_t$, raising output from $Q_e$ to $Q_o$.

sidies reduce producers' costs. As shown in Figure 19-4c, a subsidy of *U* per inoculation to physicians and medical clinics would reduce their marginal costs and shift their supply curve rightward from $S_t$ to $S'_t$. The output of inoculations would increase from $Q_e$ to the optimal level $Q_o$, correcting the underallocation of resources shown in Figure 19-4a.

3. **GOVERNMENT PROVISION** Finally, where spillover benefits are extremely large, government may decide to provide the product as a public good. The Canadian government largely eradicated the crippling disease polio by administering free vaccines to all children. India ended smallpox by paying people in rural areas to come to public clinics to have their children vaccinated. ***(Key Question 4)***

## A Market for Externality Rights 

One novel policy approach to spillover costs involves only limited government action. The idea is that government would create a **market for externality rights**. We confine our discussion to pollution, although this approach might also be used with other externalities.

The air, rivers, lakes, oceans, and public lands, such as parks and streets, are all objects for pollution because the *rights* to use these resources are held "in common" by society. No private individual or institution has an incentive to maintain the purity or quality of these resources because no one has the right to realize a monetary return from doing so.

We maintain the property we own—we paint and repair our homes periodically—in part because we will gain the value of these improvements at the time of resale. But as long as "rights" to air, water, and certain land resources are commonly held and these resources are freely available, there is no incentive to maintain them or use them carefully. As a result, these natural resources are "overconsumed" and thereby polluted. But would they be overconsumed and polluted if there were a cost to pollute them—and a market for the right to pollute?

### Operation of the Market

In this approach, an appropriate pollution-control agency determines the amount of pollutants that can be discharged into the water or air of a specific region annually while maintaining the water or air quality at some acceptable level. The agency may determine that 500 tonnes of pollutants can be discharged into Metropolitan Lake and "recycled" by nature each year. Then 500 pollution rights, each entitling the owner to dump 1 tonne of pollutants into the lake in one year, are made available for sale to producers each year. The supply of these pollution rights is fixed and therefore perfectly inelastic, as shown in Figure 19-5.

The demand for pollution rights—$D_{1999}$ in the figure—takes the same downsloping form as the demand for any other input. At higher prices there is less pollution, as polluters either stop polluting or pollute less by acquiring pollution-abatement equipment. An equilibrium market price for pollution rights, here $100, will be determined at which the environment-preserving quantity of pollution rights is rationed to polluters. Figure 19-5 shows that without this market—that is, if the use of the lake as a dump site for pollutants were free—750 tonnes of pollutants would be discharged into the lake; it would be "overconsumed," or polluted, in the amount of 250 tonnes.

Over time, as human and business populations expand, demand will increase, as from $D_{1999}$ to $D_{2009}$. *Without* a market for pollution rights, pol-

**FIGURE 19-5 The market for pollution rights**

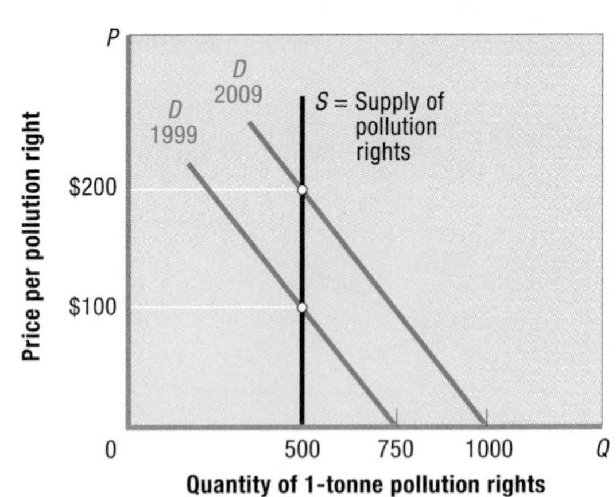



The supply of pollution rights *S* is set by government, which determines that a specific body of water can safely recycle 500 tonnes of waste. In 1999, the demand for pollution rights is $D_{1999}$ and the 1-tonne price is $100. The quantity of pollution is 500 tonnes, not the 750 tonnes it would have been without the pollution rights. Over time, the demand for pollution rights increases to $D_{2009}$ and the 1-tonne price rises to $200. But the amount of pollution stays at 500 tonnes, rather than rising to 1,000 tonnes.

lution in 2009 would be 1,000 tonnes, 500 tonnes beyond what can be assimilated by nature. *With* the market for pollution rights, the price would rise from $100 to $200 and the amount of pollutants would remain at 500 tonnes—the amount the lake can recycle.

**Advantages** This scheme has several advantages over direct controls. Most important, it reduces society's costs by allowing pollution rights to be bought and sold. Suppose it costs Acme Pulp Mill $20 a year to reduce a specific noxious discharge by 1 tonne while it costs Zemo Chemicals $8,000 a year to accomplish the same 1-tonne reduction. Also assume that Zemo wants to expand production, but doing so will increase its pollution discharge by 1 tonne.

Without a market for pollution rights, Zemo would have to use $8,000 of society's scarce resources to keep the 1-tonne pollution discharge from occurring. But with a market for pollution rights, Zemo has a better option: it buys 1 tonne of pollution rights for the $100 price shown in Figure 19-5. Acme is willing to sell Zemo 1 tonne of pollution rights for $100 because that amount is more than Acme's $20 cost of reducing its pollution by 1 tonne. Zemo increases its discharge by 1 tonne; Acme reduces its discharge by 1 tonne. Zemo benefits (by $8,000 – $100), Acme benefits (by $100 – $20), and society benefits (by $8,000 – $20). Rather than using $8,000 of its scarce resources to hold the discharge at the specified level, society uses $20 of these resources.

Market-based plans have other advantages. Potential polluters have a monetary incentive not to pollute: they must pay for the rights to pollute. Conservation groups can fight pollution by buying up and withholding pollution rights, reducing actual pollution below governmentally determined standards. As the demand for pollution rights increases over time, the growing revenue from the sale of a fixed quantity of pollution rights could be devoted to environmental improvement. At the same time, the rising price of pollution rights should stimulate the search for improved pollution-control techniques.

Administrative and political problems have kept governments in Canada from replacing direct controls—uniform emission limits—with a full-scale market for pollution rights. But such markets *have* emerged for air-pollution rights in the United States. Also in the United States, a system of pollution rights, or "tradeable emission allowances," was established as part of a plan to reduce the sulphur dioxide emitted by coal-burning public utilities. These firms are the major source of acid rain.

Table 19-3 reviews the methods for correcting externalities, and we urge you to study it.

## Society's Optimal Amount of Externality Reduction

Negative externalities such as pollution reduce the utility of those affected, rather than increase it. These spillovers are not economic goods but "economic bads." If something is bad, shouldn't society eliminate it? Why should society allow firms or municipalities to discharge *any* impure waste into public waterways or emit *any* pollution into our air?

Reducing a negative externality has a "price." Society must decide how much of a reduction it wants to "buy." Totally eliminating pollution might not be desirable, even if it were technologically fea-

**TABLE 19-3 Methods for dealing with externalities**

| Problem | Resource allocation outcome | Ways to correct |
|---|---|---|
| Spillover costs (negative externalities) | Overallocation of resources | 1. Individual bargaining<br>2. Liability rules and lawsuits<br>3. Tax on producers<br>4. Direct controls<br>5. Market for externality rights |
| Spillover benefits (positive externalities) | Underallocation of resources | 1. Individual bargaining<br>2. Subsidy to consumers<br>3. Subsidy to producers<br>4. Government provision |

sible. Because of the law of diminishing returns, cleaning up the last 10 percent of pollutants from an industrial smokestack normally is far more costly than cleaning up the previous 10 percent. Eliminating that 10 percent is likely more costly than cleaning up the prior 10 percent, and so on.

The marginal cost (MC) to the firm and hence to society—the opportunity cost of the extra resources used—rises as more and more pollution is reduced. At some point MC may rise so high that it exceeds society's marginal benefit (MB) of further pollution abatement (reduction). Additional actions to reduce pollution will therefore lower society's well-being; total cost will rise more than total benefit.

**MC, MB, and Equilibrium Quantity** Figure 19-6 shows both the rising marginal-cost curve, MC, for pollution reduction and the downsloping marginal-benefit curve, MB, for this outcome. MB slopes downward because of the law of diminishing marginal utility: The more pollution reduction society accomplishes, the lower the utility (and benefit) of the next unit of pollution reduction.

The **optimal reduction of an externality** occurs where society's marginal benefit and marginal cost of reducing that externality are equal (MB = MC). In Figure 19-6 this optimal amount of pollution abatement is $Q_1$ units. When MB exceeds MC, additional abatement moves society towards economic efficiency; the added benefit of cleaner air or water exceeds the benefit of any alternative use of the required resources. When MC exceeds MB, additional abatement reduces economic efficiency; there would be greater benefits from using resources in some other way than to further reduce pollution.

In reality, it is difficult to measure the marginal costs and benefits of pollution control. Nevertheless, Figure 19-6 is useful in demonstrating that some pollution may be economically efficient. This is so not because pollution is desirable but because beyond some level of control, further abatement may reduce our net well-being.

**Shifts in Locations of Curves** The locations of the marginal-cost and marginal-benefit curves in Figure 19-6 are not forever fixed; they can, and probably do, shift over time. For example, suppose the technology of pollution-control equipment improves noticeably. We would expect the cost of pollution abatement to fall, society's MC curve to shift rightward, and the optimal level of abatement to rise. As another example, suppose society wants cleaner air and water because of new information about the adverse health effects of pollution. The MB curve in Figure 19-6 would shift rightward, and the optimal level of pollution control would increase beyond $Q_1$. You can test your understanding of these statements by drawing the new MC and MB curves in Figure 19-6. ***(Key Question 7)***

**FIGURE 19-6 Society's optimal amount of pollution abatement**

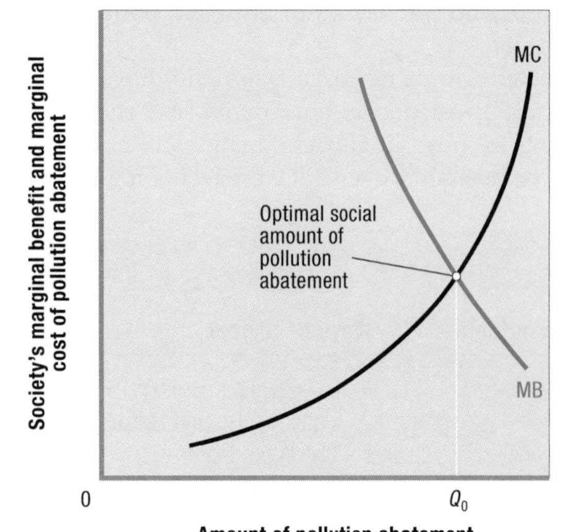


The optimal amount of externality reduction—in this case pollution abatement—occurs at $Q_0$ where society's marginal cost and marginal benefit of reducing the externality are equal.

### 19-2 QUICK REVIEW

- Policies for coping with the overallocation of resources caused by spillover costs are **a** private bargaining, **b** liability rules and lawsuits, **c** direct controls, **d** specific taxes, and **e** markets for externality rights.
- Policies for correcting the underallocation of resources associated with spillover benefits are **a** private bargaining, **b** subsidies to producers, **c** subsidies to consumers, and **d** government provision.
- The optimal amount of negative-externality reduction occurs where society's marginal cost and marginal benefit of reducing the externality are equal.

## A CLOSER LOOK AT POLLUTION

Pollution, the most acute external cost facing industrial society, provides a relevant illustration of several of the concepts just discussed.

### Dimensions of the Problem

There are many dimensions to the pollution problem. Canada alone has identified several thousand major industrial sources of air pollution, which contribute to lung cancer, emphysema, pneumonia, and other respiratory diseases. Municipal and industrial sewers severely pollute many of the Canadian rivers, lakes, and bays. Solid-waste disposal has become an acute problem for many cities as the most readily available dump sites have been filled and everyone says "not in my backyard" to new dumps or incinerators. The Canadian government has identified toxic-waste disposal sites across the country. Oil spills continue to occur, creating various degrees of environmental damage.

Global aspects of environmental pollution are equally disturbing. Russia, along with the former communist region of eastern Europe (Poland, eastern Germany, and so on) are so polluted that it will take decades to clean them up. Some scientists contend that the concentrations of industry, people, structures, and concrete that constitute cities are creating air and heat pollution sufficient to cause potential global warming through the so-called *greenhouse effect*.

### Causes: The Law of Conservation of Matter and Energy

The root of the pollution problem can be envisioned through the **law of conservation of matter and energy**. This law holds that matter can be transformed to other matter or into energy but can never vanish. All inputs (fuels, raw materials, water, and so forth) used in the economy's production processes will ultimately result in an equivalent amount of waste. For example, unless it is continuously recycled, the cotton found in a T-shirt ultimately will be abandoned in a closet, buried in a dump, or burned in an incinerator. Even if it is burned, it will not truly vanish; instead, it will be transformed into heat, smoke, and ash.

Fortunately, the ecological system has a self-generating capacity that allows it, within limits, to absorb or recycle such waste. But the volume of waste now outruns this absorptive capacity.

Why has this happened? Why do Canada and most other nations have pollution problems? There are many reasons, but four stand out.

**Population Growth** One reason is population growth and the accompanying greater density of population. An ecological system that can accommodate 50 to 100 million people may begin to break down under the pressure of 200 or 300 million.

**Rising Per Capita Consumption** As economies grow, each person consumes and disposes of more output. Unfortunately, a rising GDP (gross domestic product) means a rising "GDG" ("gross domestic garbage"). A higher standard of living permits Canadians to own millions of motor vehicles. But autos and trucks pollute the air and give rise to the problem of disposing of hundreds of thousands junked vehicles annually. Additionally, millions of tires hit Canadian scrap heaps each year.

But we must not overgeneralize. Although solid waste increases with GDP, this is not so for all pollutants. Because expanded national income enables countries to "buy" cleaner air and water through pollution-control measures, airborne concentrations of smoke (fine particles), heavier particles, and sulphur dioxide on average tend to decline when GDP grows beyond a threshold level of about $5,000 per capita. Nevertheless, there is no doubt that industrialization itself—and the resulting increase in GDP—has brought with it serious pollution problems.

**Technological Change** Some kinds of technological change have contributed to pollution. The development and widespread use of "throw-away" containers made of virtually indestructible aluminum or plastics have added to the solid-waste problem. Some detergent soap products have been highly resistant to decomposition or recycling. Nuclear energy has brought with it nuclear-waste products that must be stored and monitored for centuries.

**The "Tragedy of the Commons" and Incentives** The so-called tragedy of the commons is the tendency for society to overuse and thus abuse *common resources* to which no one holds property rights. A common pasture in which anyone can graze cattle will quickly be overgrazed, since each rancher has an incentive to graze as many cattle as possible. Similarly, commonly owned resources such as rivers, lakes, oceans, and the air get used beyond their capacities to absorb pollution. Profit-seeking manufacturers will choose the least-cost combination of inputs and bear only unavoidable costs. If they can dump waste chemicals into rivers and lakes rather than pay for proper disposal, businesses might well be inclined to do so. Firms will discharge smoke into the air if they can, rather than purchase expensive abatement facilities. Even governments—federal, provincial, and municipal—often discharge inadequately treated waste into rivers, lakes, or oceans because it is cheap and convenient to do so. Many individuals avoid the costs of proper refuse pickup and disposal by burning their garbage or dumping it in the woods.

The problem is mainly one of incentives. There is no incentive to incur internal costs associated with reducing or eliminating pollution when these costs can be transferred externally to the commons—to society at large. The fallacy of composition also comes into play. Each person and firm reasons that their individual contribution to pollution is so small that it is of little or no overall consequence. But their actions, multiplied by hundreds, thousands, or millions, overwhelm the absorptive capacity of the common resources. Society ends up with a pollution problem.

**Trading of Pollution Rights** Antipollution policies in Canada have been a mixture of direct and specific taxes levied by the federal and provincial governments. Although not yet tried in Canada, legislation in the United States allows trading of air-pollution rights. The American Clean Air Act of 1990 established a limited market for pollution rights, similar to that shown in Figure 19-5, by allowing utilities to trade *emission credits* provided by government. Utilities can obtain credits by reducing sulphur dioxide emissions by more than the specified amount. They can then sell their emission credits to other utilities that find it less costly to buy the credits than install additional pollution-control equipment.

This buying and selling of sulphur dioxide emission credits complements earlier air pollution policies that also permitted the exchange of pollution rights. The U.S. Environmental Protection Agency (EPA) now allows firms to exchange pollution rights internally and externally.

Polluters are allowed to transfer air pollution internally between individual sources within their plants. That is, as long as it meets the overall pollution standard assigned to it, a firm may increase one source of pollution by offsetting it with reduced pollution from another part of its operations.

The EPA also permits external trading of pollution rights. It has set targets for reducing air pollution in regions where the minimum standards are not being met. Previously, new pollution sources could not enter these regions unless existing polluters went out of business. In the last 15 years, the EPA has allowed firms that reduce their pollution below set standards to sell their pollution rights to other firms. A new firm desiring to locate in the Los Angeles area, for example, might be able to buy rights to emit 20 tonnes of nitrous oxide annually from an existing firm that has reduced its emissions below its allowable limit. The price of emission rights depends on their supply and demand.

A growing market for such rights has emerged, greatly expanded by the acid-rain provisions of the Clean Air Act.

**Progress Against Air Pollution** Clean-air laws and antipollution efforts by businesses and governments have reduced major air pollutants by almost 30 percent over the past 25 years, despite an almost doubling in the size of the economy. Lead concentration fell by nearly 80 percent from 1986 to 1995, mainly because of the phase-out of leaded gasoline. In that same period, concentrations of both sulphur dioxide (the major source of acid rain) and carbon monoxide declined by nearly 40 percent. Since 1987, nitrogen dioxide has declined by 14 percent; smog has decreased by 6 percent; and particulates (dust, soot, and dirt) have dropped 22 percent.

## Solid-Waste Disposal and Recycling

Nowhere is the law of conservation of matter and energy more apparent than in solid-waste disposal (Global Perspective 19-1). The millions of tonnes of garbage that accumulate annually in Canadian landfills have become a growing externality problem. Landfills in southern Ontario are either completely full or rapidly filling up.

On the receiving end, people in rural areas near newly expanding dumps are understandably

## 19-1 GLOBAL PERSPECTIVE

### Solid waste per capita, selected nations

Industrially advanced nations generate large amounts of solid waste each day, including by-products from mining, manufacturing, and other industries, as well as household trash. Solid waste per capita varies among industrial nations largely because of the different mixes of products produced and consumed.

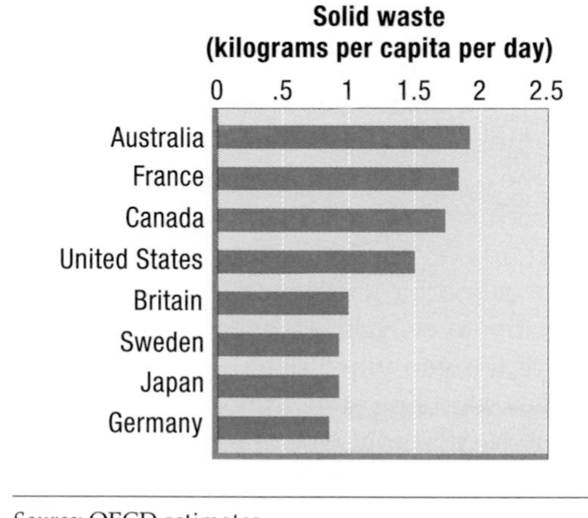


*Source:* OECD estimates

upset about the increased truck traffic on their roads and highways and growing mounds of smelly garbage in local dumps. Also, some landfills are producing serious water-supply pollution.

The high opportunity cost of urban and suburban land and the negative externalities created by dumps make landfills increasingly expensive. An alternative policy is to incinerate garbage in plants that produce electricity. But people object to having garbage incinerators—a source of truck traffic and air pollution—close to their homes. Is there a better solution to the growing problem of solid waste?

Although garbage dumps and incinerators remain the primary garbage disposal methods, recycling is receiving increased attention.

**Market for Recyclable Inputs** We can examine the incentives for recycling using Figure 19-7a, which shows the demand and supply curves for some recyclable product, say, glass.

The demand for recyclable glass derives from manufacturers that use recycled glass as a resource in producing new glass. This demand curve slopes downward, telling us that manufacturers will increase their purchases of recyclable glass as its price falls.

The location of the demand curve in Figure 19-7a depends partly on the demand for the products

**FIGURE 19-7 The economics of recycling**

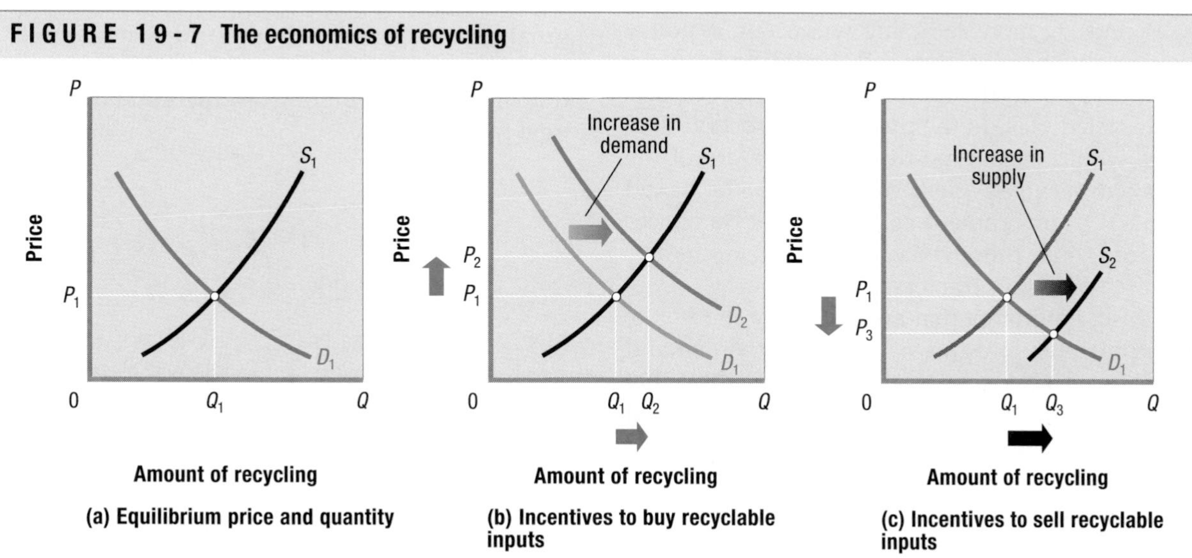


(a) The equilibrium price and amount of materials recycled are determined by supply $S_1$ and demand $D_1$. (b) Policies that increase the incentives for producers to buy recyclable inputs shift the demand curve rightward, say, to $D_2$, and raise both the equilibrium price and the amount of recycling. (c) Policies that encourage households to recycle shift the supply curve rightward, say, to $S_2$, and expand the equilibrium amount of recycling. These policies, however, also reduce the equilibrium price of the recycled inputs.

for which the recycled glass is used. The greater the demand for these products, the greater the demand for the recyclable input. The location of the curve also depends on the technology and thus the cost of using original raw materials rather than recycled glass in the production process. The more costly it is to use original materials relative to recycled glass, the farther to the right will be the demand curve for recyclable glass.

The supply curve for recyclable glass slopes upward in the typical fashion because higher prices increase the incentive for households to recycle. The location of the supply curve depends on such factors as the attitudes of households towards recycling and the cost to them of alternative disposal.

The equilibrium price $P_1$ and quantity $Q_1$ in Figure 19-7a are determined at the intersection of the supply and demand curves. At price $P_1$ the market clears; there is neither a shortage nor a surplus of recyclable glass.

**Policy** Suppose government wants to encourage recycling as an alternative to land dumps or incineration. It could do this in one of two ways.

**DEMAND INCENTIVES** Government could increase recycling by increasing the demand for recycled inputs. If the demand curve in Figure 19-7b shifts from $D_1$ rightward to $D_2$, the equilibrium price and quantity of recycled glass will increase to $P_2$ and $Q_2$; more recycling will occur. A policy that might increase demand would be to place specific taxes on the inputs that are substitutable for recycled glass in the production process. Such taxes would encourage firms to use more of the untaxed recycled glass and less of the taxed inputs. Or government could shift its purchases towards goods produced with recycled inputs and require that its contractors do the same.

Also, environmental awareness by the public can contribute to rightward shifts of the demand curve for recycled resources. Many large firms that produce waste-intensive goods have concluded that it is in their interest to support recycling, for fear of a consumer backlash against their products. Examples: Procter & Gamble (disposable diapers) and McDonald's (packaging of fast foods) have undertaken multimillion-dollar campaigns to use recycled plastic and paper.

**SUPPLY INCENTIVES** As shown in Figure 19-7c, government can also increase recycling by shifting the supply curve rightward, as from $S_1$ to $S_2$. The equilibrium price would fall from $P_1$ to $P_3$, but the equilibrium quantity—in this case recyclable glass—would rise from $Q_1$ to $Q_3$. That is, more recycling would occur. Many local governments have implemented specific policies that fit within this framework. For example, they encourage recycling by providing curbside pickup of recyclable goods such as glass, aluminum cans, and newspapers.

In a few cases, supply incentives for recyclables have been so effective that the price of a recycled item has fallen to zero. You can envision this outcome by shifting the supply curve in Figure 19-7c farther rightward. Some cities now are *paying* users of recycled inputs such as mixed paper to truck them away from the recycling centre, meaning that these items have a negative price. If the cost of paying firms to take away recyclable products is lower than the cost of alternative methods, even such paid-for recycling will promote economic efficiency. However, if it is more costly to recycle garbage than to bury or incinerate it, even when externalities are considered, such recycling will *reduce* efficiency rather than increase it. Again we are reminded that there can be either too little *or* too much of a good thing.

Government's task is to find the optimal amount of recycling compared with the alternative disposal of garbage. It can do this by estimating and comparing the marginal benefit and marginal cost of recycling. And, incidentally, consumers as a group can reduce the accumulation of garbage by buying products that have minimal packaging.

**19-3**

**QUICK REVIEW**

- The ultimate reason for pollution is the law of conservation of matter and energy, which holds that matter can be transformed into other matter or into energy but cannot vanish.
- Society's pollution problem has largely resulted from increasing population, rising per-capita consumption, certain changes in technology, and the so-called tragedy of the commons.
- Government can encourage recycling through demand and supply incentives; its task is to determine the optimal amount of recycling.

## INFORMATION FAILURES 

Thus far we have added new detail and insights concerning two types of market failure: public goods and externalities. There is another, more subtle, market failure. This one results when either buyers or sellers have incomplete or inaccurate information and their cost of obtaining better information is prohibitive. Technically stated, this market failure occurs because of **asymmetric information**—unequal knowledge possessed by the parties to a market transaction. Buyers and sellers do not have identical information about price, quality, or some other aspect of the good or service.

Sufficient market information normally is available to ensure that goods and services are produced and purchased efficiently. But in some cases, inadequate information makes it difficult to distinguish trustworthy from untrustworthy sellers or trustworthy from untrustworthy buyers. In these markets, society's scarce resources may not be used efficiently, implying that government should intervene by increasing the information available to the market participants. Under rarer circumstances government may itself supply a good for which information problems have prohibited efficient production.

### Inadequate Information Involving Sellers

Inadequate information about sellers and their products can cause market failure in the form of underallocation of resources. Examining the markets for gasoline and for the services of surgeons will show us how this comes about.

**Example: Gasoline Market** Assume an absurd situation: Suppose there is no system of weights and measures established by law, no government inspection of gasoline pumps, and no law against false advertising. Each gas station can use whatever measure it chooses; it can define a litre of gas as it pleases. A station can advertise that its gas is 87 octane when in fact it is only 75. It can rig its pumps to indicate it is providing more gas than the amount being delivered.

Obviously, the consumer's cost of obtaining reliable information under these conditions is exceptionally high, if not prohibitive. Each consumer would have to buy samples of gas from various gas stations, have them tested for octane level, and pour gas samples into a measuring device to see how each station has calibrated its pump. Also, the consumer would need to use a hand calculator to check that the pump is correctly multiplying the price per litre by the number of litres pumped. And these activities would have to be repeated regularly, since a station owner could alter the product quality and the accuracy of the pump at will.

Because of the high costs of obtaining information about the seller, many customers would opt out of this chaotic market. One tankful of a 50 percent solution of gasoline and water would be enough to discourage most motorists from further driving. More realistically, the conditions in this market would encourage consumers to vote for political candidates who promise to provide a governmental solution. The oil companies and honest gasoline stations would not object to this government intervention. They would realize that accurate information, by enabling this market to work, would expand their total sales and profit.

Government has in fact intervened in the market for gasoline and other markets with similar potential information difficulties. It has established a system of weights and measures, employed inspectors to check the accuracy of gasoline pumps, and passed laws against fraudulent claims and misleading advertising. There can be no doubt that these government activities have produced net benefits for society.

**Example: Licensing of Surgeons** Suppose now that anyone can hang out a shingle and claim to be a surgeon, much as anyone can become a house painter. The market would eventually sort out the true surgeons from those who are "learning by doing" or are fly-by-night operators who move into and out of an area. As people died from unsuccessful surgery, lawsuits for malpractice eventually would eliminate the medical imposters. People needing surgery for themselves or their loved ones could obtain information from newspaper reports or from people who have undergone similar operations.

But this process of obtaining information for those needing surgery would take considerable time and would impose unacceptably high human and economic costs. There is a fundamental difference between getting an amateurish paint job on one's house and being on the receiving end of heart surgery by a bogus physician. The marginal cost of obtaining information about sellers in the surgery market would be excessively high. The risk of proceeding without good information would result in much less surgery than desirable—an underallocation of resources to surgery.

Government has remedied this market failure through a system of qualifying tests and licensing. The licensing provides consumers with inexpensive information about a service they only infrequently buy. Government has taken a similar role in several other areas of the economy. For example, it approves new medicines, regulates the securities industry, and requires warnings on containers of potentially hazardous substances. It also requires warning labels on cigarette packages and disseminates information about communicable diseases. And it issues warnings about unsafe toys and inspects restaurants for health-related violations.

## Inadequate Information About Buyers

Just as inadequate information about sellers can keep markets from achieving economic efficiency, so can inadequate information about buyers. The buyers may be consumers buying products or firms buying resources.

**Moral Hazard Problem** Private markets may underallocate resources to a particular good or service for which there is a severe **moral hazard problem**. *The moral hazard problem is the tendency of one party to a contract to alter her or his behaviour after the contract is signed in ways that could be costly to the other party.*

To understand this problem, suppose a firm offers an insurance policy that pays a set amount of money per month to people who suffer divorces. The attraction of this insurance is that it pools the economic risk of divorce among thousands of people and, in particular, protects spouses and children from the economic hardship that divorce often brings. Unfortunately, the moral hazard problem reduces the likelihood that insurance companies can profitably provide this type of insurance.

After taking out this insurance, some people will alter their behaviour in ways that impose heavy costs on the insurer. For example, married couples would have less of an incentive to get along and to iron out marital difficulties. At the extreme, some people might be motivated to obtain a divorce, collect the insurance, and then live together. The insurance could promote *more* divorces, the very outcome it protects against. The moral hazard problem would force the insurer to charge such high premiums for this insurance that few policies would be bought. If the insurer could identify in advance those people most prone to alter their behaviour, the firm could exclude them from buying it. But the firm's marginal cost of getting this information is too high compared with the marginal benefit. Thus, this market fails.

Divorce insurance is not available in the marketplace. But society recognizes the benefits of insuring against the hardships of divorce. It has corrected for this underallocation of "hardship insurance" through child-support laws that dictate payments—when the economic circumstances warrant—to the spouse who retains the children. Alimony laws also play a role.

Since, unlike private firms, government does not have to earn a profit when supplying services, it provides "divorce insurance" of sorts through Mother's Allowance payments. If a divorce leaves a spouse with children destitute, the family is eligible for these payments. Government intervention does not eliminate the moral hazard problem; instead, it offsets the problem's adverse effects.

The moral hazard problem has numerous applications. Several are used here to reinforce your understanding of the basic principle:

1. Drivers may be less cautious because they have car insurance.
2. Medical malpractice insurance may increase the amount of malpractice.
3. Guaranteed contracts for professional athletes may reduce the quality of their performances.
4. Employment insurance may lead some workers to shirk.
5. Government insurance on bank deposits may encourage banks to make risky loans.

**Adverse Selection Problem** Another information problem resulting from inadequate information about buyers is the **adverse selection problem**. *The adverse selection problem arises when information known by the first party to a contract is not known by the second and, as a result, the second party incurs major costs.* Unlike the moral hazard problem, which arises *after* a person signs a contract, the adverse selection problem arises *at the time* a person signs a contract.

In insurance, the adverse selection problem is that people most likely to need insurance payouts are those who will buy insurance. For example, those in poorest health will seek to buy the most generous life insurance policies. Or, at the extreme, a person planning to hire an arsonist to "torch" his failing business has an incentive to buy fire insurance.

Our hypothetical divorce insurance sheds further light on the adverse selection problem. If the insurance firm sets the premiums on the basis of the average divorce rate, many married couples who are about to obtain a divorce will buy insurance. An insurance premium based on average probabilities will make a great insurance buy for those about to get divorced. Meanwhile, those in highly stable marriages will not buy it.

The adverse selection problem thus tends to eliminate the pooling of low and high risks, which is the basis for profitable insurance. Insurance rates then must be so high that few people would want to (or be able to) buy this insurance.

Where private firms underprovide insurance because of information problems, government often establishes some type of social insurance. Government can require everyone in a particular group to take the insurance and thereby can overcome the adverse selection problem. Example: Although the social insurance system in Canada is partly an insurance and partly a welfare program, in its broadest sense it is insurance against poverty during old age. The social insurance program requires nearly universal participation: People who are most likely to need the minimum benefits that social insurance provides are automatically participants in the program. So, too, are those not likely to need the benefits. There is, then, no adverse selection problem.

**Workplace Safety** The labour market also provides an example of how inadequate information about buyers (employers) can produce market failures.

For several reasons employers have an economic incentive to provide safe workplaces. A safe workplace reduces the amount of disruption of the production process created by job accidents and lowers the costs of recruiting, screening, training, and retaining new workers. It also reduces a firm's worker compensation insurance premiums (legally required insurance against job injuries).

But a safe workplace is expensive: Safe equipment, protective gear, and slower paces of work all entail costs. The firm will decide how much safety to provide by comparing its marginal cost and marginal benefit of providing a safer workplace. Will this amount of job safety achieve economic efficiency, as well as maximize the firm's profit?

The answer is "yes" if the labour and product markets are competitive and workers are fully aware of the job risks at various places of employment. With full information, workers will avoid employers having unsafe workplaces. The supply of labour to these establishments will be greatly restricted, forcing them to boost their wages to attract a work force. The higher wages will then give these employers an incentive to provide increased workplace safety; safer workplaces will reduce wage expenses. Only firms that find it very costly to provide safer workplaces will choose to pay high compensating wage differentials rather than reduce workplace hazards.

But a serious problem arises when workers *do not know* that particular occupations or workplaces are unsafe. Because information involving the buyer—that is, about the employer and the workplace—is inadequate, the firm *may not* need to pay a wage premium to attract its work force. Its incentive to remove safety hazards therefore will be diminished, and its profit-maximizing level of workplace safety will be less than economically desirable. In brief, the labour market will fail because of asymmetric information—in this case, sellers (workers) having less information than buyers (employers).

Government has several options for remedying this information problem:

1. It can directly provide information to workers about the injury experience of various employers, much like it publishes the on-time performance of the various airlines.
2. It can require that firms provide information to workers about known workplace hazards.
3. It can establish standards of workplace safety and enforce them through inspection and penalties.

The federal government has mainly employed the "standards and enforcement" approach to improve workplace safety, but some critics contend that an "information" strategy might be less costly and more effective. ***(Key Question 11)***

## Qualification

People have found many ingenious ways to overcome information difficulties without government intervention. For example, many firms offer product warranties to overcome the lack of information about themselves and their products. Franchising also helps overcome this problem. When you visit McDonald's or Holiday Inn, you know precisely what you are going to get, as opposed to stopping at Bob's Hamburger Shop or the Bates Motel.

Also, some private firms and organizations specialize in providing information to buyers and sellers. *Consumer Reports* provides product information; labour unions collect and disseminate information about job safety; and credit bureaus provide information to insurance companies. Brokers, bonding agencies, and intermediaries also provide information to clients.

However, economists agree that the private sector cannot remedy all information problems. In some situations, government intervention is desirable to promote an efficient allocation of society's scarce resources.

### 19-4 QUICK REVIEW

- Asymmetric information is a source of potential market failure, causing society's scarce resources to be allocated inefficiently.
- Inadequate information about sellers and their products may lead to an underallocation of resources to those products.
- The moral hazard problem is the tendency of one party to a contract to alter its behaviour in ways that are costly to the other party; for example, a person who buys insurance may willingly incur added risk.
- The adverse selection problem arises when one party to a contract has less information than the other party and incurs a cost because of that asymmetrical information. For example, an insurance company offering "no-medical-exam-required" life insurance policies may attract customers who have life-threatening diseases.

## In The Media

# Property Rights Only Answer for Fishery

TERENCE CORCORAN

The monumental failure of government management of the Canadian fishery is now a well-known national scandal. Decades of destructive policies—subsidies, massive income support, generous licencing arrangements and forced overcapacity—produced wild expansion of fishing and ultimately the decimation of a large part of the industry and most of the fish. Less well known is what actions are needed to turn the industry into a healthy, market-driven, profit-making segment of the economy. The best option, now in place in a few pioneering nations and parts of Canada, is to expand private property rights into the oceans.

The thought of applying property rights to fish brings howls of protest from those who believe that the oceans are a common resource that must forever remain in the public domain. The fear is that owners of property rights would plunder the fish to extinction—a strange worry given the global experience with the free-for-all of common ownership.

The largest applications of property rights principles to ocean fishing have occurred in Iceland and New Zealand, where the commercial fisheries have been allocated to private interests. Under the system, generically known as individual transferable quotas or ITQs, the rights to fish are acquired and remain the property of the owner. The rights can be bought and sold, their prices fluctuating with market demand and supply conditions. They are long-term (essentially permanent) rights to fish based on species and areas.

Iceland and New Zealand have different regulations on quota ownership. New Zealand, for example, discourages foreign ownership of ITQs but has allowed heavy concentration of ownership in the hands of about half a dozen major companies. In Iceland, ITQs are widely owned, reflecting the structure of the country's fishery. In both countries, however, the

ITQs are divisible and transferable, which means that the owner can sell, swap or lease all or part of his quota.

In principle, ownership regulations should be kept to a minimum, allowing the market to set the value of fishing rights. The freer the rights to trade and set prices, the more accurate the signals and the more efficient the market will be.

ITQs do not remove government from the process, at least not initially, although the opportunity exists to eventually get government out of the business altogether. In the meantime, governments still seem to be needed to determine the total amount of fish that can be removed under quota. Setting the total allowable catch (TAC), however, is really a technical matter to be decided by biologists.

Determining the allowable catch is roughly equivalent to defining the boundaries of a land property, or delineating mineral rights. If the allowable catch is 20,000 tonnes, and the quota owner is entitled to 10 per cent of the catch, the property is defined and its value can be based on the value of 2,000 tonnes of fish. The market price of a quota, however, would incorporate many complex and longer-term considerations. For example, if the outlook for stocks in coming years appeared to be improving, then the current value of the quota would rise.

ITQs help bring the discipline of property rights to the fishery. The owners of the quotas have a vested interest in conservation. Professor Peter Pearse of the University of British Columbia, a leading advocate of tradeable quotas, wrote recently that "fishers who find themselves with secure, defined shares of the productive capacity of a fish stock soon realize they have a common interest in protecting and enhancing it, and begin to co-operate in management, regulation and enforcement."

Ownership responsibility is the real benefit from the introduction of property rights principles. Quota owners have a direct financial and investment incentive to preserve and increase the long-term supply of fish. Under the common property system, the incentive is for a free-for-all rush to see who can get the most fish out of the fishery in the shortest period of time before they are all gone.

There are no government subsidies to the Iceland and New Zealand fisheries, which are self-supporting, market driven and profitable. Fishermen have an incentive to minimize their costs, and reports are that for the most part, fish quality has improved and overfishing has been eliminated.

Introducing property rights to the fishery is not without its own conflicts: Who should be given ITQs? Should they be sold or distributed to people who have historically fished a species in an area? How should the system be enforced? But these are essentially technical issues. In the past, for example, it would have been impossible to monitor fishing fleets to enforce property rights, but with satellite technology, poachers are easily detected.

When the fish were abundant, the need for property rights never seemed relevant. But as the global scarcity of fish grows, and the common property approach collapses, the application of property rights becomes the only solution.

*Source: Globe and Mail,* March 16, 1995, p. B2. Reprinted with permission from the *Globe and Mail.*

## THE STORY IN BRIEF

The writer advocates the application of property rights to Canadian ocean fishing to resolve the problem of overfishing. The property right would be transferable through a market in which one could purchase and sell the right to fish a specific quantity of fish.

## THE ECONOMICS BEHIND THE STORY

- Common property rights to fishing the ocean lead to over-fishing, threatening the very survival of the fish stock. This occurs because there is no incentive for those fishing to cooperate in regulating and enforcing fishing quotas. Each person fishing figures that what he or she won't take from the fishing ground, the next person will. Why not take as much as possible? If everyone follows this behaviour, eventually the fish stock will be decimated.
- With the assignment of property rights, through individual transferable quotas (ITQ), a person has to purchase the right to take a specific amount of fish per time period, say, one year. If everyone holding those rights depletes the stock of fish, their ITQ will be worthless. Thus there is an incentive to protect the fishing ground as if it were your own.
- In the seventeenth and eighteenth centuries, Canadian beaver pelts became a precious commodity because of the high price they could fetch in Europe, where they were used in the making of felt hats. The beaver population in Canada soon dwindled as trapping of beavers increased in intensity. Some scholars attribute the dwindling of the beaver population to the absence of property rights. If this is so, explain how ITQs could have helped to stop the dwindling Canadian beaver population. ■

# The Last Word

## USED CARS: THE MARKET FOR "LEMONS"

**Asymmetric product information could result in markets in which sellers offer only defective goods.**

A NEW CAR LOSES MUCH OF ITS MARKET value as the buyer drives it off the dealer's sales lot. Physical depreciation cannot explain this large loss of value since the same new car can sit on the dealer's lot for weeks, or even months, and retain its value.

One explanation of this paradox rests on the idea of asymmetric information about *used* cars.* Auto owners have much more knowledge about the mechanical condition of their vehicles than do potential buyers of used cars. At the time of the purchase, individual buyers of used cars find it difficult to distinguish between so-called lemons—defective cars—and vehicles of the same make and model that operate perfectly. Therefore, a single price emerges for used cars of the same year, make, and model whether they are lemons or high-quality vehicles. This price roughly reflects the average quality of the vehicles, influenced by the proportion of lemons to high-quality cars. The higher the proportion of lemons, the lower are the prices of used cars.

An adverse selection problem now becomes evident. Owners of lemons have an incentive to sell their cars to unsuspecting buyers, while owners of high-quality autos will wish to keep their cars. Therefore, most used cars on the market will be of lower quality than the same car models that are *not* for sale. As people become aware of this, the demand for used cars will decline and prices of used cars will fall. These lower prices will further reduce the incentive of owners of high-quality used cars to offer them for sale. At the extreme, only lemons will appear on the market; *poor-quality products will drive out high-quality products.*

This suggests a solution to our paradox. Once a buyer drives a new car away from the dealership, the auto's value becomes the value set in the used car lemons market. This is true even though the probability is high that the new car is of high quality.

The instantaneous loss of new-car value would be even greater were it not for several factors. Because new-car warranties are transferable to used-car buyers, purchasers of low-mileage late-model cars are protected against costly repairs. Thus, the demand for these vehicles rises. Also, prospective buyers can distinguish good cars from lemons by hiring mechanics to perform inspections. Moreover, sellers can signal potential buyers that their cars are not lemons through ads such as "Must sell, transferred abroad" or "Divorce forces sale." Of course, the buyer must determine the truth of these claims. Also, auto rental companies routinely sell high-quality, late-model cars, increasing the ratio of good used cars to lemons.

Government also plays a role in solving the market failure evident in the lemons market. Many provinces have "lemon laws" that force auto dealers to take back defective new cars. Dealers cannot offer these lemons for sale in the used-car market until completing all needed repairs. Also, some provinces require dealers to either offer warranties on used cars or state that a car is offered "as is." The latter designation clues the buyer that the car may be defective.

In brief, both private and governmental actions reduce the lemons problem. Nevertheless, the principle is applicable to a wide variety of used products such as autos, computers, and cameras, which are complex and occasionally defective. Buying any of these used products remains a somewhat risky transaction. ■

*The classic article on this topic is George A. Akerlof's "The Market for 'Lemons': Qualitative Uncertainty and the Market Mechanism," *Quarterly Journal of Economics*, August 1970, pp. 488–500.

# CHAPTER SUMMARY

1. Graphically, the collective demand curve for a particular public good can be found by summing *vertically* each of the individual demand curves for that good. The demand curve resulting from this process indicates the collective willingness to pay for the last unit of any given amount of the public good.
2. The optimal quantity of a public good occurs where the combined willingness to pay for the last unit—the marginal benefit of the good—equals the good's marginal cost.
3. Benefit-cost analysis can provide guidance as to the economic desirability and most efficient scope of public goods output.
4. Spillovers or externalities cause the equilibrium output of certain goods to vary from the optimal output. Spillover costs (negative externalities) result in an overallocation of resources that can be corrected by legislation or specific taxes. Spillover benefits (positive externalities) are accompanied by an underallocation of resources that can be corrected by subsidies to consumers, subsidies to producers, or government provision.
5. According to the Coase theorem, private bargaining is capable of solving potential externality problems where **a** the property rights are clearly defined, **b** the number of people involved is small, and **c** bargaining costs are negligible.
6. Clearly established property rights and liability rules permit some spillover costs to be prevented or remedied through private lawsuits. Lawsuits, however, can be costly, time-consuming, and uncertain as to their results.
7. Direct controls and specific taxes can improve resource allocation in situations where negative externalities affect many people and community resources. Both direct controls (example: smokestack emission standards) and specific taxes (example: taxes on firms producing toxic chemicals) increase production costs and hence product price. As product price rises, the externality is reduced since less of the output is bought and sold.
8. Markets for pollution rights, where people can buy and sell the right to discharge a fixed amount of pollution, put a price on pollution and encourage firms to reduce or eliminate it.
9. The optimal social amount of externality abatement occurs where society's marginal cost and marginal benefit of reducing the externality are equal. This optimal amount of pollution abatement is likely to be less than a 100 percent reduction. Changes in technology or changes in society's attitudes about pollution can affect the optimal amount of pollution abatement.
10. The law of conservation of matter and energy is at the heart of the pollution problem. Matter can be transformed into other matter or into energy but does not disappear. If not recycled, all production will ultimately end up as waste. More immediate causes of pollution are a growing population, rising per-person consumption, some new technologies, and the tendency to overuse and abuse resources owned in common.
11. Recycling is a recent response to the growing garbage disposal problem. The equilibrium price and quantity of recyclable inputs depend on their demand and supply. Government can encourage recycling through either demand or supply incentives.
12. Asymmetric information between sellers and buyers can cause markets to fail. The moral hazard problem occurs when people alter their behaviour after they sign a contract, imposing costs on the other party. The adverse selection problem occurs when one party to a contract takes advantage of the other party's inadequate information, resulting in an unanticipated loss to the latter party.

# TERMS AND CONCEPTS

benefit-cost analysis
marginal benefit = marginal cost rule
Coase theorem
market for externality rights
optimal reduction of an externality
law of conservation of matter and energy
asymmetric information
moral hazard problem
adverse selection problem

# STUDY QUESTIONS

1. KEY QUESTION *Based on the following three individual demand schedules for a particular good, and assuming these three people are the only ones in the society, determine* **a** *the market demand schedule on the assumption that the good is a private good, and* **b** *the collective demand schedule on the assumption that the good is a public good. Explain the differences, if any, in your schedules.*

| INDIVIDUAL 1 | | INDIVIDUAL 2 | | INDIVIDUAL 3 | |
|---|---|---|---|---|---|
| $P$ | $Q_d$ | $P$ | $Q_d$ | $P$ | $Q_d$ |
| $8 | 0 | $8 | 1 | $8 | 0 |
| 7 | 0 | 7 | 2 | 7 | 0 |
| 6 | 0 | 6 | 3 | 6 | 1 |
| 5 | 1 | 5 | 4 | 5 | 2 |
| 4 | 2 | 4 | 5 | 4 | 3 |
| 3 | 3 | 3 | 6 | 3 | 4 |
| 2 | 4 | 2 | 7 | 2 | 5 |
| 1 | 5 | 1 | 8 | 1 | 6 |

2. KEY QUESTION *Use your demand schedule for a public good, determined in question 1, and the following supply schedule to ascertain the optimal quantity of this public good. Why is this the optimal quantity?*

| $P$ | $Q_s$ |
|---|---|
| $19 | 10 |
| 16 | 8 |
| 13 | 6 |
| 10 | 4 |
| 7 | 2 |
| 4 | 1 |

3. KEY QUESTION *The following table shows the total costs and total benefits in billions for four different antipollution programs of increasing scope. Which program should be undertaken? Why?*

| Program | Total cost | Total benefit |
|---|---|---|
| A | $ 3 | $ 7 |
| B | 7 | 12 |
| C | 12 | 16 |
| D | 18 | 19 |

4. KEY QUESTION *Why are spillover costs and spillover benefits also called negative and positive externalities? Show graphically how a tax can correct for a spillover cost and a subsidy to producers can correct for a spillover benefit. How does a subsidy to consumers differ from a subsidy to producers in correcting for a spillover benefit?*

5. An apple grower's orchard provides nectar to a neighbour's bees, while the beekeeper's bees help the apple grower by pollinating the apple blossoms. Use Figure 19-2b to explain why this situation might lead to an underallocation of resources to apple growing and to beekeeping. How might this underallocation get resolved via the means suggested by the Coase theorem?

6. Explain: "Without a market for pollution rights, dumping pollutants into the air or water is costless; in the presence of the right to buy and sell pollution rights, dumping pollution creates an opportunity cost for the polluter." What is the significance of this opportunity cost to the search for better technology to reduce pollution?

7. KEY QUESTION *Explain the following statement, using the MB curve in Figure 19-6 to illustrate: "The optimal amount of pollution abatement for some substances, say, water from storm drains, is very low; the optimal amount of abatement for other substances, say, cyanide poison, is close to 100 percent."*

8. Relate the law of conservation of matter and energy to **a** the air pollution problem and **b** the solid-waste disposal problem. What is the "tragedy of the commons," as it relates to pollution?

9. Explain why there may be insufficient recycling of products when the externalities associated with landfills and garbage incinerators are not considered. What demand and supply incentives might government provide to promote more recycling? Explain how there could be too much recycling in some situations.

10. Why is it in the interest of new home buyers *and* builders of new homes to have government building codes and building inspectors?

11. KEY QUESTION *Place an M beside those items in the following list that describe a moral hazard problem and an A beside those that describe an adverse selection problem.*
    **a.** *A person with a terminal illness buys several life insurance policies through the mail.*
    **b.** *A person drives carelessly because he or she has automobile insurance.*
    **c.** *A person who intends to "torch" his warehouse takes out a large fire insurance policy.*
    **d.** *A professional athlete who has a guaranteed contract fails to stay in shape during the off-season.*
    **e.** *A woman anticipating having a large family takes a job with a firm that offers exceptional child-care benefits.*

14. **(The Last Word)** Explain how the prices of used cars are affected by **a** asymmetric information and **b** adverse selection.

15. WEB-BASED QUESTION **Clean Water and Government Intervention** Government can use direct controls in the form of legislation to reduce negative externalities such as water pollution. Environment Canada www.doe.ca/envpriorities/cleanwater_e.htm is responsible for getting environmental results on clean water. What success(es) has Environment Canada had? What is it doing now?

## CHAPTER 20

# Public Choice Theory and Taxation

WHY ARE SO MANY PEOPLE DISENCHANTED WITH—even distrustful of—government? One reason is the apparent failure of costly government programs to resolve socioeconomic ills. For example, even after billions of dollars have been spent on the problem, widespread poverty in Canada remains. Our farm programs were designed to save the family farm; instead, they have subsidized large corporate farms that, in turn, have driven family farms out of business. While per-pupil spending has gone upward in Canadian public education, the academic performance of Canadian students on standardized tests compares unfavourably with that of students in many other nations.

There are charges that government agencies have become bogged down in paperwork; that the public bureaucracy produces trivial regulations and great duplication of effort; that obsolete programs persist; that various agencies work at cross purposes; and so on.

Just as there are failures in the private sector's market system, the above suggests there are also deficiencies within the public sector. In this chapter we examine some of those shortcomings. We begin with two topics from **public choice theory**—the economic analysis of government decision making. First, we examine the problem society has in revealing its true preferences through majority voting; then we discuss so-called *government failure*—the idea that certain characteristics of the public sector keep it from promoting an efficient allocation of resources. Next we shift to **public finance**—the study of public expenditures and revenues. There, we examine taxes and tax incidence to see how taxes are apportioned in Canada, analyze inefficiencies arising through taxation, and discuss two proposed types of tax reforms.

The chapter ends with a very brief discussion of conservative and liberal stances on government and economic freedom.

**IN THIS CHAPTER YOU WILL LEARN:**

- That majority voting can produce inefficient voting outcomes.
- Why public sector failure occurs.
- The connection between elasticity and tax incidence.
- About the efficiency cost of taxes.
- About the Canadian tax system.

## The Big Picture

THIS CHAPTER IS ABOUT PUBLIC CHOICE THEORY, the economic analysis of how governments make decisions. We know how decisions are made by firms and consumers in a market economy, but government decisions are based on different criteria. Democratic governments have to make decisions reflecting majority wants. Because these decisions fail to incorporate the preferences of each individual voter, majority voting may produce inefficient economic outcomes. Moreover, majority voting may not be able consistently to rank society's preferences for public goods and services. Finally, there may be significant divergence between "sound economics" and "good politics"; rather than getting the most out of limited resources and giving the public what it wants most, the public sector may fail to do so because of the power of special interest groups, opportunism by politicians, and simple bureaucratic inefficiency.

As you read this chapter, keep the following points in mind:

- **Key Concepts 6** and **7** are discussed.
- We live in a world of limited resources but unlimited wants. The theory of public choice must be understood within these two fundamental facts.
- By definition, democratic governments have to make decisions that reflect the wishes of the majority. But gauging the wishes of millions of people is not easy, and since utility is a subjective criterion, decisions will never please everyone.
- The difficulty of gauging the desires of millions of people can lead to some group trying to exert its choice on the rest by claiming that its wishes are those of the rest of society. ■

## REVEALING PREFERENCES THROUGH MAJORITY VOTING

Which public goods should government produce and in what amounts? In what circumstances and through what methods should government intervene to correct for externalities? How should the tax burden of financing government be apportioned?

Decisions like these are made collectively in Canada through a democratic process relying heavily on majority voting. Candidates for office offer alternative policy packages, and citizens elect people who they think will make the best decisions on their collective behalf. Voters "retire" officials who do not adequately represent their collective wishes and elect persons they think do. Also, citizens periodically have opportunities at the provincial and municipal levels to vote directly on public expenditures or new legislation.

This democratic process generally works well at revealing society's true preferences, but it has shortcomings. Just as the market sometimes fails to allocate resources efficiently, the system of voting sometimes produces inefficiencies and inconsistencies.

### Inefficient Voting Outcomes

Providing a public good that has a total benefit greater than its total cost will add to society's well-being. Unfortunately, majority voting does not always produce such an economically efficient outcome. Voters may defeat a proposal to provide a public good even though it may yield total benefits exceeding its total cost. Conversely, it is possible that majority voting could result in the provision of a public good costing more than the benefits it yields.

**Illustration: Inefficient "No" Vote** Suppose government can provide a public good, say, national defence, at a total expense of $900. Also, assume there are only three individuals—Adams, Benson, and Conrad—in the society and they will share the $900 tax expense equally, each paying $300 of tax if the proposed good is provided. Suppose, as illustrated in Figure 20-1a, that Adams is willing to pay $700 to have this good; Benson, $250; and Conrad, $200.

What will be the result if a majority vote determines whether this good will be provided? Although people do not always vote strictly accord-

**FIGURE 20-1 Inefficient voting outcomes**

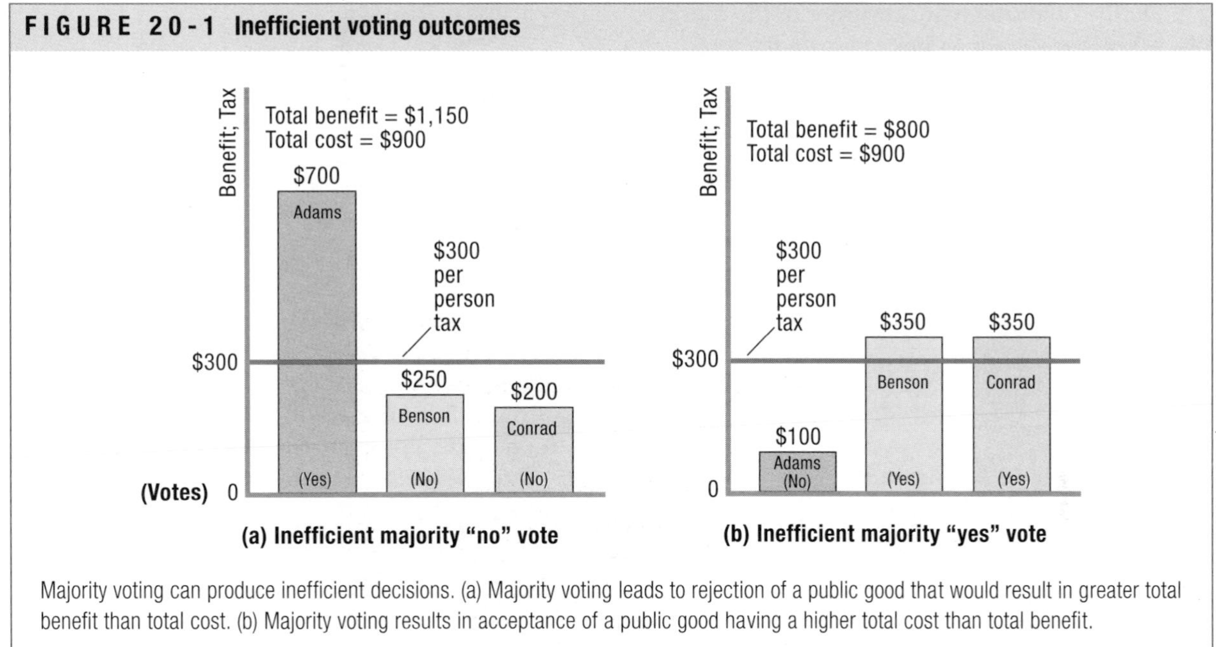


Majority voting can produce inefficient decisions. (a) Majority voting leads to rejection of a public good that would result in greater total benefit than total cost. (b) Majority voting results in acceptance of a public good having a higher total cost than total benefit.

ing to their own economic interest, it is likely Benson and Conrad will vote "no" because they will incur tax expenses of $300 each while gaining benefits of only $250 and $200, respectively. Adams will vote "yes." So the majority vote will defeat the proposal even though the total benefit of $1,150 (= $700 for Adams + $250 for Benson + $200 for Conrad) exceeds the total cost of $900. Resources should be devoted to this good, but they will not be.

**Illustration: Inefficient "Yes" Vote** We can also construct an example in which the majority favours a public good even though its total cost exceeds its total benefit. Figure 20-1b shows the details. Again, Adams, Benson, and Conrad will equally share the $900 cost of the public good; they will each be taxed $300. But now Adams is only willing to pay $100 for the public good, rather than forgo it. Meanwhile, Benson and Conrad are willing to pay $350 each. They will vote for the public good; Adams will vote against it. The majority vote will provide a public good costing $900 that produces total benefits of only $800 (= $100 for Adams + $350 for Benson + $350 for Conrad). Society's resources will be inefficiently allocated to this public good.

**Conclusion** The point of our examples is that an inefficiency may occur as either an overproduction or an underproduction of a specific public good, and therefore as an overallocation or underallocation of resources for that particular use. In Chapter 19 we saw that government can improve economic efficiency by providing public goods that the market system will not make available. Now we have extended that analysis to reveal that government might fail to provide some public goods whose production is economically justifiable while providing other goods that are not economically warranted.

In our examples, each person has only a single vote, no matter how much he or she might gain or lose from a public good. In the first example (inefficient "no" vote), Adams would be willing to purchase a vote from either Benson or Conrad if buying votes were legal. That way Adams could be assured of obtaining the national defence he so highly values. But buying votes is illegal, so many people with strong preferences for certain public goods may have to go without them.

When individual consumers have a strong preference for a specific *private good*, they usually can find it in the marketplace even though it may be unpopular with the majority of consumers. A consumer can buy beef tongue, liver, and squid in some supermarkets, although it is doubtful that these products would be available if majority voting stocked the shelves. But a person cannot easily "buy" a *public good* such as national defence once the majority has decided against it.

On the other hand, a consumer in the marketplace can decide *not* to buy a particular product, even a popular one. But although you may not want national defence, you must "buy" it through your tax payments when it is favoured by the majority.

Conclusion: *Because it fails to incorporate the strength of the preferences of the individual voter, majority voting may produce economically inefficient outcomes.*

### Interest Groups and Logrolling

There are avenues for resolving the just-mentioned inefficiencies associated with majority voting. Two examples follow.

**INTEREST GROUPS** Those who have a strong preference for a public good may band together into interest groups and use advertisements, mailings, and direct persuasion to convince others of the merits of that public good. Adams might try to persuade Benson and Conrad that it is in their best interest to vote for national defence—that national defence is much more valuable to them than their $250 and $200 valuations. Such appeals are common in democratic politics.

**POLITICAL LOGROLLING** **Logrolling**—the trading of votes to secure favourable outcomes—can also turn an inefficient outcome into an efficient one. In our first example (Figure 20-1a), perhaps Benson has a strong preference for a different public good, say, a new road, which Adams and Conrad do not think is worth the tax expense. That would provide an opportunity for Adams and Benson to trade votes to ensure provision of both national defence and the new road. That is, Adams and Benson would each vote "yes" on both measures. Adams would get the national defence and Benson would get the road. Without the logrolling, both public goods would have been rejected. Moreover, the logrolling will add to society's well-being if, as was true for national defence, the road creates a greater overall benefit than cost.

But logrolling need not increase economic efficiency. Even if national defence and the road each cost more than the total benefit it produces, both might still be provided because of the vote trading. Adams and Benson might still engage in logrolling if each expects to secure a sufficient net gain from her or his favoured public good, even though the gains would come at the clear expense of Conrad.

*Logrolling can either increase or diminish economic efficiency, depending on the circumstances.*

## Paradox of Voting

Another difficulty with majority voting is the **paradox of voting**, *a situation in which society may not be able to rank its preferences consistently through paired-choice majority voting.*

### Preferences

Consider Table 20-1, in which we again assume a community of three voters: Adams, Benson, and Conrad. Suppose the community has three alternative public goods from which to choose: national defence, a road, and a weather warning system. We expect that each member of the community prefers the three alternatives in a certain order. For example, one person might prefer national defence to a road, and a road to a weather warning system. We can attempt to determine the preferences of the community through paired-choice majority voting. Specifically, a vote can be held between any two of the public goods, and the winner of that vote can then be matched against the third public good in another vote.

The three goods and the assumed individual preferences of the three voters are listed in the top part of Table 20-1. It indicates that Adams prefers national defence to the road and the road to the weather warning system. This implies also that Adams prefers national defence to the weather warning system. Benson values the road more

**TABLE 20-1 Paradox of voting**

| | PREFERENCES | | |
|---|---|---|---|
| **Public Good** | **Adams** | **Benson** | **Conrad** |
| National defence | 1st choice | 3d choice | 2d choice |
| Road | 2d choice | 1st choice | 3d choice |
| Weather warning system | 3d choice | 2d choice | 1st choice |

| **Election** | **Voting outcomes: winner** |
|---|---|
| **1.** National defence vs. road | National defence (preferred by Adams and Conrad) |
| **2.** Road vs. weather warning system | Road (preferred by Adams and Benson) |
| **3.** National defence vs. weather warning system | Weather warning system (preferred by Benson and Conrad) |

than the weather warning system and the warning system more than national defence. Conrad's order of preference is weather warning system, national defence, and road.

**Voting Outcomes** The lower part of Table 20-1 shows the outcomes of three hypothetical elections decided through majority vote. In the first, national defence wins against the road because a majority of voters (Adams and Conrad) prefer national defence to the road. In the second election, to see whether this community wants a road or a weather warning system, a majority of voters (Adams and Benson) prefer the road.

We have determined that the majority of people in this community prefer national defence to a road *and* prefer a road to a weather warning system. It seems logical to conclude that the community prefers national defence to a weather warning system. But it does not!

To demonstrate this conclusion, we hold a direct election between national defence and the weather warning system. Row (3) shows that a majority of voters (Benson and Conrad) prefer the weather warning system to national defence. As listed in Table 20-1, then, the three paired-choice majority votes imply that this community is irrational: it seems to prefer national defence to a road *and* a road to a weather warning system, but would rather have a weather warning system than national defence.

The problem is not irrational community preferences but rather a flawed procedure for determining those preferences. We see that the outcome from paired-choice majority voting may depend on the order in which the votes are taken up. Under some circumstances majority voting fails to make *consistent* choices that reflect the community's underlying preferences. As a consequence, government may find it difficult to provide the "correct" public goods by acting in accordance with majority voting. Important note: This critique is *not* to suggest there is some better procedure. Majority voting is much more likely to reflect community preferences than decisions by, say, dictators or groups of self-appointed leaders. ***(Key Question 2)***

## Median-Voter Model

One final aspect of majority voting reveals insights into real-world phenomena. The **median-voter model** suggests that *under majority rule the median voter will in a sense determine the outcomes of elections.* The median voter is the person holding the middle position on an issue: half the other voters have stronger preferences for a public good, amount of taxation, or degree of government regulation, and half have weaker—or negative—preferences. The extreme voters on each side of an issue prefer the median choice rather than the other extreme position, so the median voter's choice predominates.

**Example** Suppose a society composed of Adams, Benson, and Conrad has reached agreement that as a society it needs a weather warning system. Each independently is to submit a total dollar amount he or she thinks should be spent on the warning system, assuming each will be taxed one-third of that amount. An election will determine the size of the system. Because each person can be expected to vote for his or her own proposal, no majority will occur if all the proposals are placed on the ballot at the same time. Thus, the group decides on a paired-choice vote: they will first vote between two of the proposals and then match the winner of that vote against the remaining proposal.

The three proposals are as follows: Adams desires a $400 system; Benson wants an $800 system; Conrad opts for a $300 system. Which proposal will win? The median-voter model suggests it will be the $400 proposal submitted by the median voter, Adams. Half the other voters favour a more costly system; half favour a less costly system. To understand why the $400 system will be the outcome, let's conduct the two elections.

First, suppose that the $400 proposal is matched against the $800 proposal. Adams naturally votes for her $400 proposal, and Benson votes for his own $800 proposal. But Conrad—who proposed a $300 expenditure for the warning system—votes for the $400 proposal because it is closer to his own. So Adams's $400 proposal is selected by a 2-to-1 majority vote.

Next, we match the $400 proposal against the $300 proposal. Again the $400 proposal wins, because it gets a vote from Adams and one from Benson, who proposed the $800 expenditure and for that reason prefers a $400 expenditure to a $300 one. Adams—the median voter in this case—in a sense is the person who has decided the level of expenditure on a weather warning system for this society.

**Real-World Applicability** Although our illustration is a simple one, this idea explains much. We *do* note a tendency for public choices to match most closely the median view. Political candidates, for example, take one set of positions to win the nomination of their political parties; in so doing, they tend to appeal to the median voter *within their party* to get the nomination. They then shift their views more closely to the political centre when they square off against opponents from the opposite political party. In effect, they redirect their appeal towards the median voter *within the total population*. They also try to label their opponents as being too liberal, or too conservative, and out of touch with the "mainstream." And they conduct polls and adjust their positions on issues accordingly.

**Implications** The median-voter model has two important implications:

1. Many people will be dissatisfied by the extent of government involvement in the economy. The size of government will largely be determined by the median preference, leaving many people desiring a much larger, or a much smaller, public sector. In the marketplace you can buy zero zucchinis, 2 zucchinis, or 200 zucchinis, depending on how much you enjoy them. In the public sector you get the number of hospitals and provincial highways the median voter prefers.
2. Some people may "vote with their feet" by moving into political jurisdictions where the median voter's preferences are closer to their own. Someone may move from the city to a suburb where the level of government services, and therefore taxes, is lower. Or they may move into an area known for its excellent, but expensive, school system.

For these reasons, and because our personal preferences for government activity are not static, the median preference shifts over time. Also, information about people's preferences is imperfect, leaving much room for politicians to misjudge the true median position. ***(Key Question 3)***

## PUBLIC SECTOR FAILURE

We have seen that the economic results of the marketplace are not always satisfactory and that government actions can help. Economists agree that government has a legitimate function in dealing with instances of *market failure*. They advocate the use of benefit-cost analysis to make efficient decisions, including adjustments for widespread spillover costs and benefits, provision of public goods and services, appropriate market information, and so on.

But as implied in our discussion of voting problems, the economic functions of government are not always performed effectively and efficiently. In fact, there may be inherent shortcomings within the public sector that keep it from promoting economic efficiency. These shortcomings may result in so-called **public sector failure**—inefficient operation of the public sector in an economic sense. Let's consider some sources of government inefficiency.

### Special Interests and Rent Seeking

Casual reflection suggests there may be a significant gap between "sound economics" and "good politics." Sound economics calls for the public sector to pursue various programs as long as marginal benefits exceed marginal costs. Good politics, however, suggests that politicians support programs and policies that will maximize their chance of getting elected and staying in office. This gap may result in government promoting the goals of groups of voters that have special interests to the detriment of the larger public. In the process, economic inefficiency can result.

**Special-Interest Effect** Efficient public decision making is often impaired by the **special-interest effect**. This is any outcome of the political process whereby *a small number of people obtain a government program or policy that gives them large gains at the expense of a much greater number of persons who individually suffer small losses.*

The small group of potential beneficiaries are well informed and highly vocal on the issue in question; they press politicians for approval. The large numbers facing very small individual losses are generally uninformed on this issue. Politicians feel they will lose the support of the small special-interest group that backs the issue if they legislate against it but will *not* lose the support of the large group of uninformed voters, who will likely evaluate them on other issues in which these voters have a stronger interest.

The special-interest effect is also evident in so-called *pork-barrel politics*, which involves securing a government project yielding benefits mainly to a single political district and its political representative. In this case, the special-interest group is made up of local constituents, while the larger group consists of relatively uninformed taxpayers scattered across a much larger geographic area. Politicians clearly have a strong incentive to secure public goods ("pork") for local constituents. These goods win political favour; they are highly valued by constituents and paid for mainly by the much larger group of relatively uninformed taxpayers.

Finally, a politician's inclination to support the smaller group of special beneficiaries is enhanced because special-interest groups are often quite willing to help finance the campaigns of "right-minded" politicians and politicians who "bring home the pork." The result is that politicians may support special-interest programs and projects that are not justifiable on economic grounds.

**Rent-Seeking Behaviour** The appeal to government for special benefits at taxpayers' or someone else's expense is called **rent-seeking**. To economists, "rent" is a payment beyond that necessary to keep a resource supplied in its current use. Corporations, trade associations, labour unions, and professional organizations employ vast resources to secure favourable government policies that result in rent—higher profit or income than would occur under competitive market conditions. Government is *able* to dispense such rent directly or indirectly through laws, rules, hiring, and purchases. Elected officials are *willing* to provide such rent because they want to be responsive to key constituents, who in turn help them remain in office.

Here are some examples of "rent-providing" legislation or policies: tariffs on foreign products that limit competition and raise prices to consumers; tax breaks that benefit specific corporations; public works projects that create union jobs but cost more than the benefits they yield; occupational licensing that goes beyond what is needed to protect consumers; and large subsidies to farmers by taxpayers. None of these is justified by economic efficiency.

## Clear Benefits, Hidden Costs

Some critics say vote-seeking politicians will not objectively weigh all costs and benefits of various programs, as economic rationality demands, in deciding which to support and which to reject. Because political officeholders must seek voter support every few years, they favour programs with immediate and clear-cut benefits and with vague or deferred costs. Conversely, politicians will reject programs with immediate and easily identifiable costs but with long-term, less measurable benefits.

Such biases can lead politicians to reject economically justifiable programs and to accept programs that are economically irrational. Example: A proposal to construct and expand mass-transit systems in large metropolitan areas may be economically rational on the basis of benefit-cost analysis. But if (1) the program is to be financed by immediate increases in highly visible income or sales taxes and (2) benefits will occur years from now when the project is completed, the vote-seeking politician may oppose the program.

Assume, on the other hand, that a program of provincial transfers to municipal police forces is not justifiable on the basis of benefit-cost analysis. But if the cost is deferred through deficit financing, the program's modest benefits may seem so large that it gains approval.

## Limited and Bundled Choice

Some public choice theorists say the political process forces citizens and their elected representatives to be less selective in choosing public goods and services than they are in choosing private goods and services.

In the marketplace, the citizen as a consumer can exactly satisfy personal preferences by buying certain goods and not buying others. However, in the public sector the citizen as a voter is confronted with, say, only two or three candidates for an office, each representing a different "bundle" of programs (public goods and services). None of these bundles of public goods is likely to exactly fit the preferences of any particular voter. Yet the voter must choose one of them. The candidate who comes closest to voter Smith's preference may endorse national dental insurance, increases in social security benefits, subsidies to tobacco farmers, and tariffs on imported goods. Smith will likely vote for this candidate even though Smith may oppose tobacco subsidies.

In other words, the voter must take the bad with the good. In the public sector, people are forced to "buy" goods and services they do not want. It is as if, in going to a sporting-goods store, you were forced to buy an unwanted pool cue to get a wanted pair of running shoes. This is a situation where resources are not being used efficiently to best satisfy consumer wants. In this sense, the provision of public goods and services is inherently inefficient.

Parliament is confronted with a similar limited-choice, bundled-goods problem. Legislation often combines hundreds, even thousands, of spending items into a single bill. Many of these spending items may be completely unrelated to the main purpose of the legislation. Yet members of Parliament must vote the entire package—yea or nay. Unlike consumers in the marketplace, they cannot be selective. ***(Key Question 4)***

## Bureaucracy and Inefficiency

Some economists contend that public agencies are generally less efficient than private businesses. The reason is *not* that lazy and incompetent workers somehow end up in the public sector, while ambitious and capable people gravitate to the private sector. Rather, it is that the market system creates incentives and pressures for internal efficiency that are absent in the public sector. Private enterprises have a clear goal—profit. Whether a private firm is in a competitive or monopolistic market, efficient management means lower costs and enlarged profit. The increased profit not only benefits the firm's owners but enhances the promotion prospects of managers. Moreover, part of the managers' pay may be tied to profit via profit-sharing plans and bonuses. There is no similar identifiable gain to government agencies and their managers—no counterpart to profit—that creates a strong incentive to achieve efficiency.

The market system imposes a very obvious test of performance on private firms: the test of profit and loss. An efficient firm is profitable and therefore successful; it survives, prospers, and grows. An inefficient firm is unprofitable and unsuccessful; it declines and in time goes bankrupt and ceases to exist. But there is no similar, clear-cut test that assesses the efficiency or inefficiency of public agencies. How can anyone determine whether a public hydroelectricity provider, a university, a local fire department, the Ministry of Agriculture, or the Ministry of Indian Affairs and Northern Development is operating efficiently?

Cynics even argue that a public agency that uses its resources inefficiently is likely to survive and grow! In the private sector, inefficiency and monetary loss lead to the abandonment of certain activities or products or even firms. But government, they say, does not like to abandon activities in which it has failed. Some suggest that the typical response of government to a program's failure is to double its budget and staff. This means public sector inefficiency just continues on a larger scale.

Furthermore, economists assert that government employees, together with the special-interest groups they serve, often gain sufficient political clout to block attempts to pare down or eliminate their agencies. Politicians attempting to reduce the size of the federal bureaucracies such as those relating to agriculture, health, human resource development, and national defence will incur sizable political risk, since bureaucrats and special-interest groups will team up to defeat them.

Finally, critics point out that there is a tendency for government bureaucracy to justify continued employment by looking for and eventually finding new problems to solve. Perhaps it is not surprising that social "problems," as defined by government, tend to persist or even expand.

## Imperfect Institutions

It is possible to argue that these criticisms of public sector efficiency are exaggerated and cynical. Perhaps so. Nevertheless, they do tend to shatter the concept of a benevolent government that responds with precision and efficiency to the wants of its citizens. The market system of the private sector is far from perfectly efficient. Government's economic function is mainly to correct the market system's shortcomings. But the public sector is also subject to deficiencies in fulfilling its economic function. "The relevant comparison is not between perfect markets and imperfect governments, nor between faulty markets and all-knowing, rational, benevolent governments, but between inevitably imperfect institutions."[1]

Because the market system and public agencies are both imperfect, it can sometimes be difficult to determine whether a particular activity can be performed with greater success in the private sector or the public sector. It is easy to reach agreement on opposite extremes: national defence must lie with the public sector, while corn production can best be accomplished by the private sector. But what about health insurance? Parks and recreation areas? Fire protection? Garbage collection? Housing? Education? It is very hard to assess every good or service and to say absolutely that it should be assigned to either the public sector or the pri-

[1] Otto Eckstein, *Public Finance*, 3d ed. (Englewood Cliffs, N.J.: Prentice-Hall, Inc., 1973), p. 17.

vate sector. Evidence: All the goods and services just mentioned are provided to varying degrees by both private enterprises and public agencies.

**20-1**

**QUICK REVIEW**

- Majority voting can produce voting outcomes that are inefficient; projects having greater total benefits than total costs can be defeated and projects having greater total costs than total benefits can be approved.
- The paradox of voting occurs where voting by majority rule does not provide a consistent ranking of society's preferences for public goods and services.
- The median-voter model suggests that under majority rule the voter having the middle preference will determine the outcome of an election.
- Public sector failure allegedly occurs because of rent seeking, pressure by special-interest groups, shortsighted political behaviour, limited and bundled choices, and bureaucratic inefficiency.

## APPORTIONING THE TAX BURDEN

We now turn from the difficulties of making collective decisions about public goods to the difficulties of deciding how those goods should be financed.

The characteristics of public goods make it difficult to measure precisely how their benefits are apportioned among individuals and institutions. We cannot accurately determine how much citizen Mildred Moore benefits from military installations, a network of highways, a public school system, the national weather bureau, and local police and fire protection.

The situation is different in regard to paying for those benefits. Studies do reveal with reasonable clarity how the overall tax burden is apportioned. (By "tax burden," we mean the total cost of taxes imposed on society.) This apportionment question affects each of us. The overall level of taxes is important, but the average citizen is much more concerned with his or her part of the overall tax burden.

### Benefits Received versus Ability to Pay

There are two basic philosophies on how the economy's tax burden should be apportioned.

**Benefits-Received Principle** The **benefits-received principle** of taxation asserts that households and businesses should purchase the goods and services of government in the same way they buy other commodities. Those who benefit most from government-supplied goods or services should pay the taxes necessary to finance them. A few public goods are now financed on this basis. Money collected as gasoline taxes is typically used to finance highway construction and repairs. Thus, people who benefit from good roads pay the cost of those roads. Difficulties immediately arise, however, when we consider widespread application of the benefits-received principle.

1. How will government determine the benefits individual households and businesses receive from national defence, education, and police and fire protection? Recall that public goods provide widespread spillover benefits and that the exclusion principle does not apply. Even in the seemingly straightforward case of highway financing it is difficult to measure benefits. Individual car owners benefit in different degrees from good roads. But others also benefit. For example, businesses benefit because good roads bring customers to them.
2. The benefits-received principle cannot logically be applied to income redistribution programs. It would be absurd and self-defeating to ask poor families to pay the taxes needed to finance their welfare payments. It would be ridiculous to think of taxing only unemployed workers to finance the unemployment compensation payments they receive.

**Ability-to-Pay Principle** The **ability-to-pay principle** of taxation asserts that the tax burden should be apportioned according to taxpayers' income and wealth. In Canada it means that individuals and businesses with larger incomes should pay more taxes—both absolutely and relatively—than those with smaller incomes.

What is the rationale of ability-to-pay taxation? Proponents argue that each additional dollar of income received by a household yields a smaller amount of satisfaction or marginal utility when it is spent. Because consumers act rationally, the first dollars of income received in any period of time will be spent on high-urgency goods yielding the greatest marginal utility. Successive dollars of income will go for less urgently needed goods and finally for trivial goods and services. This means a dollar taken through taxes from a poor person who has few dollars represents a greater utility sacrifice than a dollar taken by taxes from the rich person who has many dollars. To balance the sacrifices that taxes impose on income receivers, taxes should be apportioned according to the amount of income a taxpayer receives.

This argument is appealing, but application problems crop up here too. Although we might agree that the household earning $100,000 per year has a greater ability to pay taxes than a household receiving $10,000, we don't know exactly how much more ability to pay the first family has. Should the wealthier family pay the *same percentage* of its larger income—and hence a larger absolute amount—as taxes? Or should the richer family be made to pay a larger fraction of this income as taxes? And how much larger should that fraction be?

There is no scientific way of measuring someone's ability to pay taxes—and that's the main problem. In practice, the solution hinges on guesswork, the tax views of the political party in power, expediency, and how urgently the government needs revenue.

## Progressive, Proportional, and Regressive Taxes

Any discussion of taxation leads ultimately to the question of tax rates. Recall that an *average tax rate* is the total tax paid divided by some base against which the tax is compared.

**Definitions** Taxes are classified as progressive, proportional, or regressive, depending on the relationship between tax rates and taxpayer *incomes*. We focus on incomes because all taxes—whether on income or on a product or a building or parcel of land—are ultimately paid out of someone's income.

1. A tax is **progressive** if its average rate *increases* as income increases. Such a tax claims not only a larger absolute (dollar) amount but also a larger percentage of income as income increases.
2. A tax is **regressive** if its average rate *declines* as income increases. Such a tax takes a smaller proportion of income as income increases. A regressive tax may or may not take a larger absolute amount of income as income increases.
3. A tax is **proportional** if its average rate *remains the same* regardless of the size of income.

We can illustrate these ideas with the personal income tax. Suppose tax rates are such that a household pays 10 percent of its income in taxes regardless of the size of its income. This is a proportional income tax.

Now suppose the rate structure is such that a household with an annual taxable income of less than $10,000 pays 5 percent in income taxes; a household with an income of $10,000 to $20,000 pays 10 percent; one with an income of $20,000 to $30,000 income pays 15 percent; and so forth. This is a *progressive* income tax.

Finally, suppose the rate declines as taxable income rises: you pay 15 percent if you earn less than $10,000; 10 percent if you earn $10,000 to $20,000; 5 percent if you earn $20,000 to $30,000; and so forth. This is a *regressive* income tax.

In general, progressive taxes are those that fall most heavily on the rich; regressive taxes are those that fall most heavily on the poor. ***(Key Question 7)***

**Applications** Let's examine the progressivity, or regressivity, of several taxes.

**PERSONAL INCOME TAX** The federal *personal income tax* is progressive, with marginal tax rates —those assessed on *additional* income—ranging from 24 to 54 percent, depending on income level and the province one lives in. The fact that individuals can deduct from income contributions to their registered retirement savings plan (RRSP) tends to make the tax less progressive than these marginal rates suggest. Nevertheless, average tax rates rise with income.

**SALES TAXES** At first thought, a general sales tax with, say, a 3 percent rate would seem to be proportional. But in fact it is regressive with respect to income. A larger portion of a poor person's income is exposed to the tax than is the case for a rich person; the rich pay no tax on the part of income that is saved, whereas the poor are unable to save. Example: "Poor" Smith has an income of $15,000 and spends it all. "Rich" Jones has an income of $300,000 but spends only $200,000. Assuming a 3 percent sales tax applies to all expenditures of each individual, we find that Smith pays $450 (3 percent of $15,000) in sales taxes and Jones pays $6,000 (3 percent of $200,000). But Smith pays $450/$15,000 or 3 percent of income as sales taxes, while Jones pays $6,000/$300,000 or 2 percent of income. The general sales tax therefore is regressive.

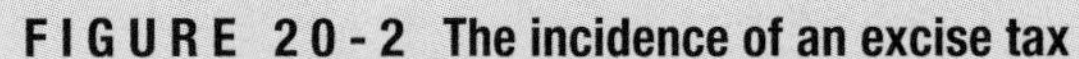

**FIGURE 20-2 The incidence of an excise tax**

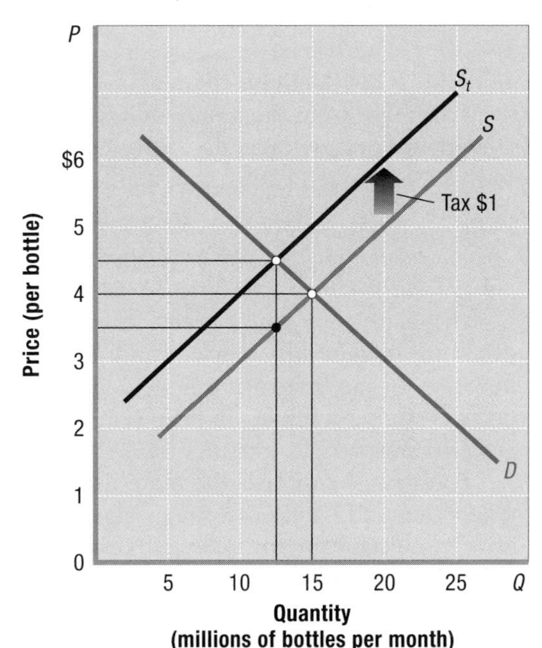


An excise tax of a specified amount, here $1 per unit, shifts the supply curve upward by the amount of the tax per unit: the vertical distance between $S$ and $S_t$. This results in a higher price (here $4.50) to consumers and lower after-tax price (here $3.50) to producers. Thus, consumers and producers share the burden of the tax in some proportion (here equally at $.50 per unit).

**CORPORATE INCOME TAX** The *corporate income tax* is essentially a proportional tax with a flat 28 percent tax rate. But this assumes that corporation owners (shareholders) bear the tax. Some tax experts argue that at least part of the tax is passed through to consumers in the form of higher product prices. To the extent that this occurs, the tax is like a sales tax and thus regressive.

**PROPERTY TAXES** Most economists conclude that *property taxes* on buildings are regressive for the same reasons as are sales taxes. First, property owners add the tax to the rents that tenants are charged. Second, property taxes, as a percentage of income, are higher for poor families than for rich families because the poor must spend a larger proportion of their incomes for housing. This alleged regressivity of property taxes may be increased by differences in property-tax rates from locality to locality. In general, property-tax rates are higher in poorer areas, to make up for lower property values.

## TAX INCIDENCE AND EFFICIENCY LOSS

Determining whether a particular tax is progressive, proportional, or regressive is complicated because taxes are not always paid by those on whom they are levied. We therefore need to locate as best we can the final resting place of a tax, or the **tax incidence**. The tools of elasticity of supply and demand will help. We will focus on a hypothetical excise tax on wine levied on producers. Do the producers really pay this tax, or do they shift it to wine consumers?

### Elasticity and Tax Incidence

In Figure 20-2, $S$ and $D$ represent the pre-tax market for a certain domestic wine; the no-tax equilibrium price and quantity are $4 per bottle and 15 million bottles. If government levies an excise tax of $1 per bottle at the winery, who actually pays it?

**Division of Burden** Since government places the tax on the sellers (suppliers), the tax can be viewed as an addition to the marginal cost of the product. Now sellers must get $1 more for each bottle to receive the same per-unit profit they were getting before the tax. While sellers are willing to offer, for example, 5 million bottles of untaxed wine at $1 per bottle, they must now receive $3 per bottle—$2 plus the $1 tax—to offer the same 5 million bottles. The tax shifts the supply curve upward (leftward) as shown in Figure 20-2, where $S_t$ is the "after-tax" supply curve.

The after-tax equilibrium price is $4.50 per bottle, whereas the before-tax price was $4.00. So, in this case, half the $1 tax is paid by consumers as a higher price; the other half must be paid by producers in the form of a lower after-tax per-unit revenue. That is, after remitting the $1 tax per unit to government, producers receive $3.50, or 50 cents less than the $4.00 before-tax price. In this instance, consumers and producers share the burden of the tax equally; producers shift half the tax to consumers in the form of a higher price and bear the other half themselves.

Note also that the equilibrium quantity decreases as a result of the tax levy and the higher price it imposes on consumers. In Figure 20-2, that decline in quantity is from 15 million bottles to 12.5 million bottles per month.

**Elasticities** If the elasticities of demand and supply were different from those shown in Figure 20-2, the incidence of tax would also be different. Two generalizations are relevant.

1. *With a specific supply, the more inelastic the demand for the product, the larger the portion of the tax shifted to consumers.* To verify this, sketch graphically the extreme cases where demand is perfectly elastic and perfectly inelastic. In the first case the incidence of the tax is entirely on sellers; in the second, the tax is shifted entirely to consumers.

   Figure 20-3 contrasts the more usual cases where demand is either relatively elastic or relatively inelastic in the relevant price range. With elastic demand (Figure 20-3a), a small portion of the tax ($P_e - P_1$) is shifted to consumers and most of the tax ($P_1 - P_a$) is borne by the producers. With inelastic demand (Figure 20-3b), most of the tax ($P_i - P_1$) is shifted to consumers and only a small amount ($P_1 - P_b$) is paid by producers. In both graphs the per-unit tax is represented by the *vertical* distance between $S_t$ and $S$.

   Note also that the decline in equilibrium quantity ($Q_1 - Q_2$) is smaller when demand is more inelastic. This is the basis of our previous applications of the elasticity concept: Revenue-seeking legislatures place heavy excise taxes on liquor, cigarettes, automobile tires, telephone service, and other products whose demands are inelastic. Since demand for these products is relatively inelastic, the tax doesn't reduce sales much, so the tax revenue stays high.
2. *With a specific demand, the more inelastic the supply, the larger the portion of the tax borne by producers.* When supply is elastic (Figure 20-4a), most of the tax ($P_e - P_1$) is shifted to consumers and only a small portion ($P_1 - P_a$) is borne by sellers. But where supply is inelastic (Figure 20-4b), the reverse is true; the major portion of the tax ($P_1 - P_b$) falls on sellers, and a relatively small amount ($P_i - P_1$) is shifted to buyers. The equilibrium quantity also declines less with an inelastic supply than it does with an elastic supply.

   Gold is an example of a product with an inelastic supply and therefore one where the burden of an excise tax would mainly fall on producers. On the other hand, because the supply of baseballs is elastic, producers would pass on to consumers much of an excise tax on baseballs.

## Efficiency Loss of a Tax

We just observed that an excise tax levied on producers typically is borne partly by producers and

**FIGURE 20-3 Demand elasticity and the incidence of an excise tax**

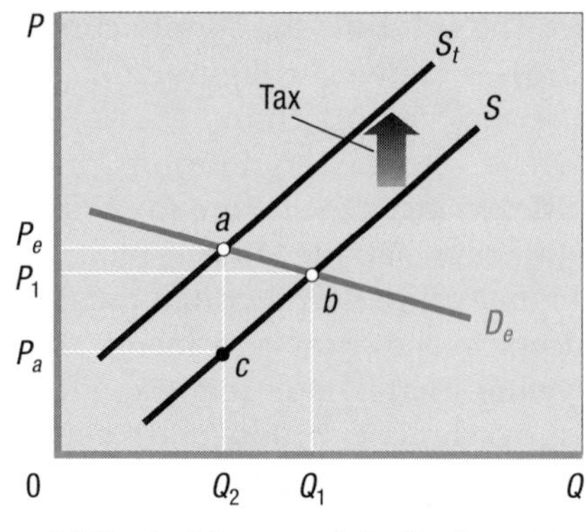


**(a) Tax incidence and elastic demand**

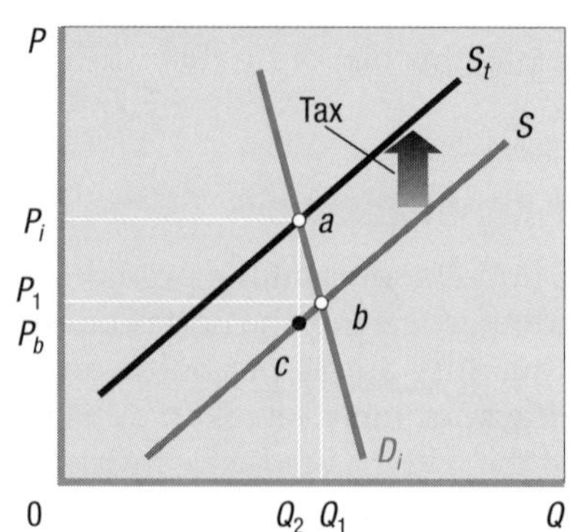


**(b) Tax incidence and inelastic demand**

(a) If demand is elastic in the relevant price range, price rises modestly ($P_1$ to $P_e$) when an excise tax is levied. Hence, the producer bears most of the tax burden. (b) If demand is inelastic, the price to the buyer increases substantially ($P_1$ to $P_i$) and most of the tax is shifted to consumers.

**FIGURE 20-4 Supply elasticity and the incidence of an excise tax**

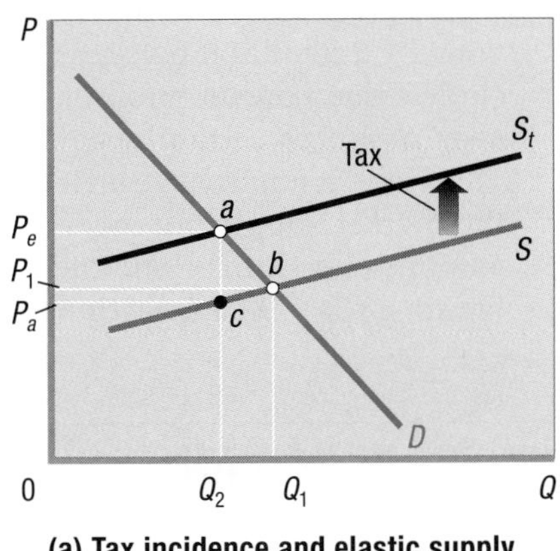


**(a) Tax incidence and elastic supply**

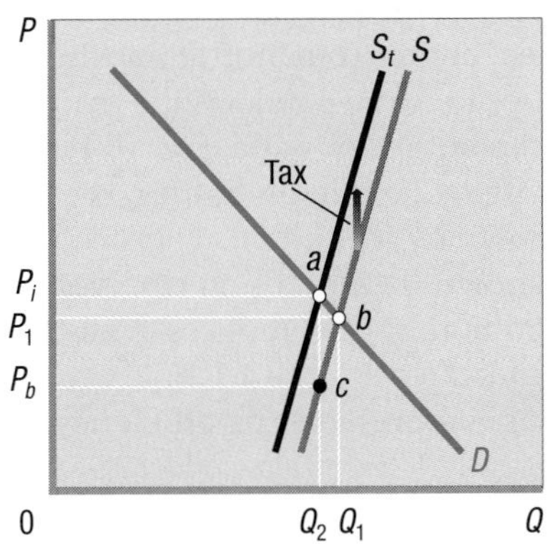


**(b) Tax incidence and inelastic supply**

(a) With elastic supply an excise tax results in a large price increase ($P_1$ to $P_e$) and the tax is therefore paid mainly by consumers. (b) If supply is inelastic, the price rise is small ($P_1$ to $P_i$) and sellers bear most of the tax.

**FIGURE 20-5 Efficiency loss of a tax**

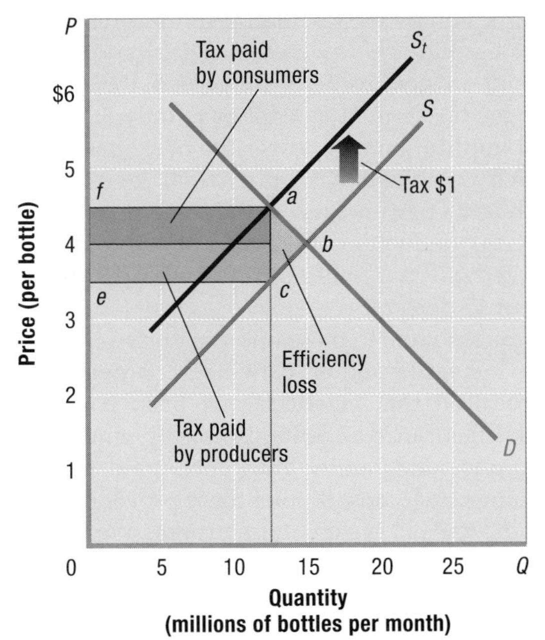


The levy of a $1 tax per bottle of wine increases the price per bottle from $4 to $4.50 and reduces the equilibrium quantity from 15 million to 12.5 million. Tax revenue to governments is $12.5 million (area *efac*). The efficiency loss of the tax arises from the 2.5 million decline in output; the amount of this loss is shown as triangle *abc*.

partly by consumers. Let's now look more closely at the overall economic effect of the excise tax. We will use Figure 20-5, which is identical to Figure 20-2 but contains additional detail needed for our discussion.

**Tax Revenues** In our example, a $1 excise tax on wine increases the market price from $4 to $4.50 per bottle and reduces the equilibrium quantity from 15 million bottles to 12.5 million. Government tax revenue is $12.5 million (= $1 × 12.5 million bottles), an amount shown as the rectangle *efac* in Figure 20-5. The elasticities of supply and demand in this case are such that consumers and producers each pay half this total amount, or $6.25 million apiece (= $.50 × 12.5 million bottles). Government uses this $12.5 million of tax revenue to provide public goods and services. So this transfer of dollars from consumers and producers to government involves no loss of well-being to society.

**Efficiency Loss** The $1 tax on wine does more than require consumers and producers to pay $12.5 million of taxes; *it also reduces the equilibrium amount of wine produced and consumed by 2.5 million bottles.* The fact that 2.5 million more bottles of wine were demanded and supplied before the tax means those 2.5 million bottles provided benefits in excess of their production costs. We can see this from the following analysis.

Segment *ab* of demand curve *D* in Figure 20-5 indicates the willingness to pay—the marginal benefit—associated with each of the 2.5 million bottles consumed before (but not after) the tax. Segment *cb* of supply curve *S* reflects the marginal cost of each of the bottles of wine. For all but the very last one of these 2.5 million bottles, the marginal benefit (shown by a point on *ab*) exceeds the marginal cost (shown by a point on *cb*). Not producing all 2.5 million bottles reduces well-being by an amount indicated by the triangle *abc*. The area of this triangle represents the **efficiency loss of the tax** (also called the *deadweight loss* of the tax). *This loss is society's sacrifice of net benefit because the tax reduces production and consumption of the product below their levels of economic efficiency where marginal benefit and marginal cost are equal.*

**Role of Elasticities** Most taxes create some degree of efficiency loss; how much depends on the supply and demand elasticities. Glancing back at Figure 20-3, we see that the efficiency loss area *abc* is greater in Figure 20-3a, where demand is relatively elastic, than in Figure 20-3b, where demand is relatively inelastic. Similarly, area *abc* is greater in Figure 20-4a than in Figure 20-4b, indicating a larger efficiency loss where supply is more elastic. *Other things equal, the greater the elasticities of supply and demand, the greater the efficiency loss of a particular tax.*

Two taxes yielding equal revenues do not necessarily impose equal costs on society. Government must keep this fact in mind in designing a tax system to finance beneficial public goods and services. In general, it should minimize the efficiency loss of the tax system in raising any specific dollar amount of tax revenue.

**Qualifications** We must acknowledge, however, that there may be other tax goals just as important—or even more important—than minimizing efficiency losses from taxes. Here are two examples:

1. **REDISTRIBUTIVE GOALS** Government may wish to impose progressive taxes as a way to redistribute income. The 10 percent excise tax placed on selected luxuries would be a case in point. Because the demand for luxuries is elastic, efficiency losses from this tax could be substantial. However, if the benefits from the redistribution effects of this tax would exceed the efficiency losses then a government would go ahead with such a tax.
2. **REDUCING NEGATIVE EXTERNALITIES** Government may have intended the $1 tax on wine in Figure 20-5 to reduce consumption of wine by 2.5 million bottles. It may have concluded that consumption of alcoholic beverages produces certain negative externalities. Therefore, it might have levied this tax to shift the market supply curve so as to reduce the amount of resources allocated to wine (as in Figure 20-3b). ***(Key Question 9)***

## RECENT CANADIAN TAX REFORM

The Canadian tax system has undergone two major changes in the last several years. These are (a) the 1987 Tax Reform and (b) the **Goods and Services Tax** (GST). It must be kept in mind that we refer to the federal government only; each province also levies a number of taxes, some in conjunction with the federal government.

### The 1987 Tax Reform

Spurred on by the tax reform in the United States that significantly lowered marginal tax rates, the Canadian government simplified the personal income tax from 11 categories to only 3. The general implication is to lower the marginal tax rate, which combined with provincial levies was as high as 64 percent, and at the same time to eliminate tax deductions in favour of tax credits. The top federal marginal tax rate has come down to about 45 percent.

Subsequent to these reforms the federal surtax was increased and a "claw-back" provision was introduced that in effect took back part of the social insurance benefits, primarily employment insurance and family allowance, paid to higher income Canadians. Both of these provisions made the income tax system more progressive.

### The GST

The controversy surrounding the introduction of the GST was unprecedented. Much of the dispute arose because of misunderstandings and a concerted and highly publicized effort by the official opposition in Parliament, the Liberal Party, to defeat the legislation.

The GST is similar to a **value-added tax** (VAT). It is much like a sales tax, except that it applies only to the difference between the value of a firm's sales and the value of its purchases from other firms. This is done by allowing firms a tax credit equal to the taxes paid on their inputs. Most European nations currrently use VATs as a source of revenue. This is reflected in Global Perspective 20-1.

The GST replaced the federal sales tax, which was levied primarily on manufactured goods and was as high as 13 percent on some products. The GST at present stands at 7 percent and is levied on a much broader base that includes both goods and services. The only exemptions are agricultural and fish products, prescription drugs, and medical devices.

An important feature of the GST is that exports are exempt since producers can claim a credit equal to the taxes paid on the inputs used to produce the product. Moreover, imported goods are subject to the GST, so they are at no particular advantage compared to domestically produced goods.

**20-1**
**GLOBAL PERSPECTIVE**

**Taxes on goods and services as a percentage of total tax revenues, selected nations**

Compared to its major trading partner, the United States, Canada relies more heavily on goods and services taxes (sales taxes, value-added taxes, and specific excise taxes). Canada's rates are closer to European Union countries.

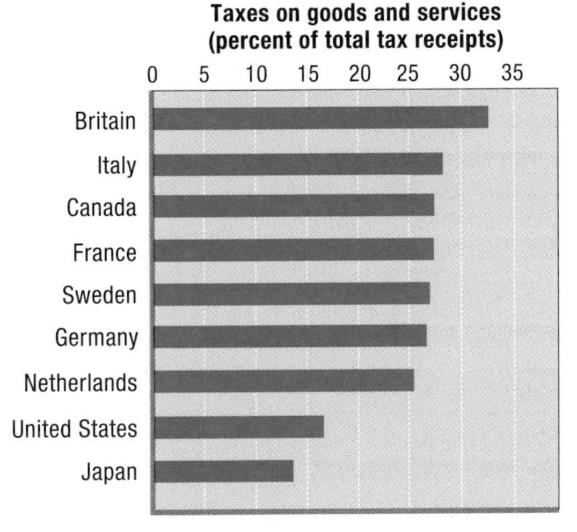


*Source: Statistical Abstract of the United States*, 1997, p. 844.

The GST's implementation on January 1, 1991, coincided with the country slipping into a recession. Many quickly jumped to the conclusion that the GST at least aggravated, if it was not the cause of, the recession. The government claims the GST will be revenue neutral: it will raise revenues just offset by the elimination of the federal sales tax.

There appears to be a consensus among economists that the GST is an improvement over the old federal sales tax since it introduces fewer distortions to the price of goods and services. For our exporters it is a definite advantage. Moreover, those in the lower income brackets receive a tax credit. Thus, it is not as regressive as some critics claim.

## THE ISSUE OF FREEDOM

We end our discussion of government decision making by considering an elusive question: What is the relationship between the role and size of the public sector and individual freedom? Although no attempt is made here to explore this issue in depth, let's outline two divergent views.

### The Conservative Position

Many conservative economists believe that, in addition to the economic costs of any expansion of the public sector, there is also a cost in the form of diminished individual freedom. Here's why.

First, there is the "power corrupts" argument. "Freedom is a rare and delicate plant ... history confirms that the great threat to freedom is the concentration of power ... by concentrating power in political hands, [government] is ... a threat to freedom."[2]

Second, we can be selective in the market system of the private sector, using our income to buy precisely what we choose and rejecting unwanted commodities. But, as noted, in the public sector—even assuming a high level of political democracy—conformity and coercion are inherent. If the majority decides in favour of certain governmental actions—to build a reservoir, to establish dental insurance, to provide a guaranteed annual income—the minority must conform. The "use of political channels, while inevitable, tends to strain the social cohesion essential for a stable society."[3]

[2] Milton Friedman, *Capitalism and Freedom* (Chicago: The University of Chicago Press, 1962), p. 2.
[3] Ibid., p. 23.

Because decisions can be rendered selectively by individuals through markets, the need for conformity and coercion is lessened and this "strain" reduced. The scope of government should be strictly limited.

Finally, the power and activities of government should be dispersed and decentralized.

### The Liberal Stance

But liberal economists are sceptical of the conservative position. They say the conservative view is based on the **fallacy of limited decisions**. Conservatives implicitly assume that during any particular period there is a limited, or fixed, number of decisions to be made in the operation of the economy. If government makes more of these decisions in performing its stated functions, the private sector of the economy will necessarily have fewer "free" decisions or choices to make. This is considered to be flawed reasoning. By sponsoring the production of public goods, government is *extending* the range of free choice by permitting society to enjoy goods and services that would not be available without governmental provision.

We can argue it is largely through the economic functions of government that we have freed ourselves in some measure from ignorance, unemployment, poverty, disease, crime, discrimination, and other ills. In providing most public goods, government does not typically undertake production itself, but rather purchases these goods through private enterprise. When government decides to build a highway, private firms are given the responsibility of making many specific decisions and choices in connection with carrying out this decision.

A noted economist has summarized the liberal view in these pointed words:

> Traffic lights coerce me and limit my freedom. Yet in the midst of a traffic jam on the unopen road, was I really "free" before there were lights? And has the algebraic total of freedom, for me or the representative motorist or the group as a whole, been increased or decreased by the introduction of well-engineered stop lights? Stop lights, you know, are also go lights.... When we introduce the traffic light, we have, although the arch individualist may not like the new order, by cooperation and coercion created by ourselves greater freedom.[4]

[4] Paul A. Samuelson, "Personal Freedoms and Economic Freedoms in the Mixed Economy," in Earl F. Cheit (ed.), *The Business Establishment* (New York: John Wiley & Sons, Inc., 1964), p. 219.

## CHAPTER SUMMARY

1. Majority voting creates a possibility of **a** an underallocation or overallocation of resources to a particular public good, and **b** inconsistent voting outcomes. The median-voter model predicts that, under majority rule, the person holding the middle position on an issue will in a sense determine the election outcome.
2. Public choice theorists cite a number of reasons that government might be inefficient in providing public goods and services. **a** There are strong reasons for politicians to support special-interest legislation. **b** Public choice may be biased in favour of programs with immediate and clear-cut benefits and difficult-to-identify costs *and* against programs with immediate and easily identified costs and vague or deferred benefits. **c** Citizens as voters and government representatives face limited bundle choices as to public goods and services; whereas consumers in the private sector can be highly selective. **d** Government bureaucracies have less incentive to operate efficiently than do private businesses.
3. The benefits-received principle of taxation is that those who receive the benefits of goods and services provided by government should pay the taxes required to finance them. The ability-to-pay principle is that those who have greater income should be taxed absolutely and relatively more than those who have less income.
4. The federal personal income tax is progressive. The flat-rate federal corporate income tax is regressive. General sales and property taxes are regressive.
5. Excise taxes affect supply and therefore equilibrium price and quantity. The more inelastic the demand for a product, the greater the proportion of the tax shifted to consumers. The greater the inelasticity of supply, the larger the proportion of tax borne by the seller.

6. Taxation involves loss of some output whose marginal benefit exceeds its marginal cost. The more elastic the supply and demand curves, the greater is this efficiency loss of a particular tax.

7. Sales taxes are likely to be shifted; personal income taxes are not. Specific excise taxes may or may not be shifted to consumers, depending on the elasticities of demand and supply. There is disagreement as to whether corporate income taxes are shifted. The incidence of property taxes depends primarily on whether the property is owner- or tenant-occupied.

8. The 1987 federal tax reform simplified income taxes and lowered the marginal tax rate.

9. The GST is similar to a value-added tax. It is more favourable than the federal sales tax it replaced because it introduces fewer distortions, exports are exempt, and imports will compete on equal footing with domestic goods.

10. Conservatives believe that individual freedom necessarily shrinks as government grows in size or power; liberals believe it does not.

## TERMS AND CONCEPTS

public choice theory
public finance
logrolling
paradox of voting
median-voter model
public sector failure
special-interest effect
rent-seeking behaviour
benefits-received principle
ability-to-pay principle
progressive tax
regressive tax
proportional tax
tax incidence
efficiency loss of a tax
Goods and Services Tax
value-added tax
fallacy of limited decisions

## STUDY QUESTIONS

1. Explain how affirmative and negative majority votes can sometimes lead to inefficient allocations of resources to public goods. Is this problem likely to be greater under a benefits-received or an ability-to-pay tax system? Use the information in Figures 20-1(a) and 20-1(b) to show how society might be better off if Adams were allowed to buy votes.

2. KEY QUESTION *Explain the paradox of voting through reference to the accompanying table that shows the ranking of three public goods by voters Larry, Curley, and Moe.*

| Public good | Larry | Curley | Moe |
|---|---|---|---|
| Courthouse | 2nd choice | 1st choice | 3rd choice |
| School | 3rd choice | 2nd choice | 1st choice |
| Park | 1st choice | 3rd choice | 2nd choice |

3. KEY QUESTION *Suppose that there are only five people in a society and that each favours one of the five flood-control options shown in Table 19-2 (include no protection as one of the options). Explain which of these flood-control options will be selected using a majority rule. Will this option be the optimal size of the project from an economic perspective?*

4. KEY QUESTION *How does the problem of limited and bundled choices in the public sector relate to economic efficiency? Why are public bureaucracies alleged to be less efficient than private enterprises?*

5. Explain: "Politicians would make more rational economic decisions if they weren't running for re-election every few years." Do you favour term limits for elected officials?

6. Distinguish between the benefits-received and the ability-to-pay principles of taxation. Which philosophy is more evident in our present tax structure? Justify your answer. To which principle of taxation do you subscribe? Why?

7. KEY QUESTION *Suppose a tax is such that an individual with an income of $10,000 pays $2,000 of tax; a person with an income of $20,000 pays $3,000 of tax; a person with an income of $30,000 pays $4,000 of tax, and so forth. What is each person's average tax rate? Is this tax regressive, proportional, or progressive?*

8. What is meant by a progressive tax? A regressive tax? A proportional tax? Comment on the progressivity or regressivity of each of the following taxes, indicating in each case your assumption concerning tax incidence:
   **a.** The federal personal income tax
   **b.** A 7 percent general sales tax
   **c.** A federal excise tax on automobile tires
   **d.** A municipal property tax on real estate
   **e.** The federal corporate income tax

9. KEY QUESTION *What is the incidence of an excise tax when demand is highly inelastic? Elastic? What effect does the elasticity of supply have on the incidence of an excise tax? What is the efficiency loss of a tax and how does it relate to elasticity of demand and supply?*

10. Advanced Analysis: Suppose that the equation for the demand curve for some product $X$ is $P = 8 - .6Q$ and the supply curve is $P = 2 + .4Q$. What is the equilibrium price and quantity? Now suppose that an excise tax is imposed on $X$ such that the new supply equation is $P = 4 + .4Q$. How much tax revenue will this excise tax yield the government? Graph the curves and label the area of the graph that represents the tax collection TC and the area that represents the efficiency loss of the tax EL. Briefly explain why area EL is the efficiency loss of the tax.

11. WEB-BASED QUESTION **Bureaucracy and Inefficiency—Canada Post versus FEDEX** Some economists contend that public agencies generally are less efficient than private businesses. Federal Express www.fedex.com competes directly with Canada Post www.Canadapost.ca for delivery of express mail and packages. Assume you need to send an express letter and a package from your address to either Halifax or Vancouver. Based on their interactive rate and options calculators, which service is more competitive as to price and delivery? Does a lower rate with greater delivery options mean greater efficiency? Why or why not?

21

CHAPTER

# Canadian Agriculture: Economics and Policy

IN THIS CHAPTER YOU WILL LEARN:

That in the short run there is significant price and income instability in the agricultural sector.

Why agriculture is a declining industry.

The effects of subsidies and price supports and ceilings in agriculture.

About recent agricultural policy reforms in Canada.

CANADIAN AGRICULTURE IS ECONOMICALLY important for a number of reasons:

- Agriculture is one of the nation's largest industries. Consumers spend about 15 percent of their after-tax income on food and other farm products. If we include the processing, wholesale, and retail sector, agriculture accounts for about 20 percent of Canada's GDP and employs about 3 percent of the nation's labour force.
- Agriculture is a sector that—in the absence of government farm programs—is a real-world example of Chapter 10's pure-competition model. The industry consists of many firms selling virtually standardized products and can be understood by applying the demand and supply tools of competitive markets.
- Farm products provide evidence of the intended and unintended effects of government policies that interfere with the forces of supply and demand.
- Agriculture reflects the increasing globalization of markets. In recent decades the economic ups and downs of Canadian agriculture have been closely tied to its ability to gain access to world markets.
- Farm policies are excellent illustrations of Chapter 20's special-interest effect and rent-seeking behaviour.

In this chapter we examine the problems within agriculture that have resulted in government intervention, the forms that intervention has taken and some of its results, and recent major changes in farm policy.

## The Big Picture

THIS CHAPTER IS THE APPLICATION OF microeconomic theory to analyze the problems of the agricultural sector. Given that without food we would certainly perish, agriculture has always held our intense interest. The very necessity of agriculture to the sustaining of life has also often led to policies that have not served the interest of consumers. We have witnessed continual government intervention in agriculture through efforts to keep agricultural commodity prices from falling below certain levels, and heavy subsidization of certain crops. While the intentions of these policies were honourable, the outcome has often been inefficiencies, waste, and price distortions.

As you read this chapter, keep the following points in mind:

- Some of agriculture's problems are short-run, others are irreversible and long-run phenomenon.
- Historically, the major problem has been to produce more agricultural commodities. Ironically, in the late twentieth century, the main problem is an overabundance of agricultural output.
- Technological improvements have greatly increased the productivity of agriculture. ■

## ECONOMICS OF AGRICULTURE

Over the years, farmers have faced severely fluctuating prices and periodically low incomes. There are actually two separate problems: the **short-run farm problem** of year-to-year fluctuations of farm prices and incomes, and the **long-run farm problem** of agriculture's being a declining industry.

### Short-Run Problem: Price and Income Instability

The short-run farm problem is the result of (1) an inelastic demand for agricultural products, combined with (2) fluctuations in farm output and (3) shifts of the demand curve for farm products.

**Inelastic Demand for Agricultural Products** In most developed societies, the price elasticity of demand for agricultural products is low. For farm products in the aggregate, the elasticity coefficient is between .20 and .25. These figures suggest that the prices of agricultural products would have to fall by 40 to 50 percent for consumers to increase their purchases by a mere 10 percent. Consumers apparently put a low value on additional farm output compared with alternative goods.

Why is this so? Recall that the basic determinant of elasticity of demand is substitutability. When the price of a product falls, the consumer tends to substitute *that* product for other products whose prices presumably have not fallen. But in relatively wealthy societies this "substitution effect" is very modest for food. People do not switch from three meals a day to, say, five or six meals a day in response to a decline in the relative prices of farm products. An individual's capacity to substitute food for other products is subject to very real biological constraints.

The inelasticity of agricultural demand can also be understood in terms of diminishing marginal utility. In a wealthy society, the population is generally well fed and well clothed; it is relatively saturated with the food and fibre of agriculture. Therefore, additional farm output involves rapidly diminishing marginal utility. Thus it takes very large price cuts to induce small increases in consumption.

**Fluctuations in Output** Farm output tends to fluctuate from year to year, mainly because farmers have limited control over their output. Floods, droughts, unexpected frost, insect damage, and similar disasters can mean poor crops, while an excellent growing season may mean bumper crops. Natural phenomena are beyond the control of farmers, yet they exert an important influence on output.

In addition to these natural phenomena, it is the highly competitive nature of agriculture that makes it difficult for farmers to form huge combi-

**FIGURE 21-1 The effect of output changes on farm prices and income**

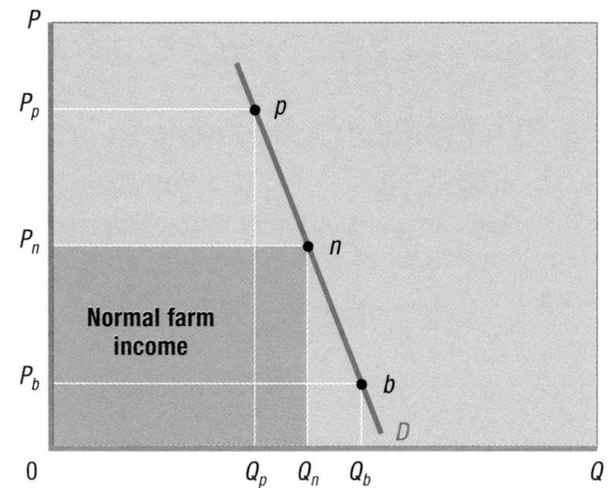


Because of the inelasticity of demand for farm products, a relatively small change in output (from $Q_n$ to $Q_p$ or $Q_b$) will cause a relatively large change in farm prices (from $P_n$ to $P_p$ or to $P_b$). Farm income will change from the green area to $0P_ppQ_n$ or $0P_bbQ_b$).

nations to control production. If the thousands of widely scattered and independent producers happen to plant an unusually large or an abnormally small portion of their land one year, an extra-large or very small farm output will result even if the growing season is normal.

Curve *D* in Figure 21-1 depicts the inelastic demand for agricultural products. Combining this demand with the instability of farm production, we can see why farm prices and incomes are unstable. Even if the market demand for agriculture products remains fixed at *D*, its price inelasticity will magnify small output changes into relatively large changes in farm prices and income. For example, assume that a "normal" crop of $Q_n$ results in a "normal" price of $P_n$ and a "normal" farm income represented by the green rectangle. A bumper crop or a poor crop will cause large deviations from these normal prices and incomes because of the inelasticity of demand.

If a good growing season occurs, the resulting bumper crop of $Q_b$ will reduce farm income to that of area $0P_bbQ_b$. When demand is inelastic, an increase in the quantity sold will be accompanied by a *more than* proportionate decline in price. The net result is that total revenue, that is, total farm income, will decline disproportionately.

Similarly, a poor crop caused by, say, drought will boost total farm income to that represented by area $0P_ppQ_p$. A decline in output will cause a *more than* proportionate increase in price—and in income—when demand is inelastic. Ironically, for farmers as a group, a poor crop may be a blessing, and a bumper crop a hardship. Conclusion: *With a stable market demand for farm products, the inelasticity of that demand will turn relatively small changes in output into relatively larger changes in farm prices and income.*

**Fluctuations in Domestic Demand** The third factor in the short-run instability of farm income has to do with shifts in the demand curve for agricultural products. Suppose that somehow agricultural output is stabilized at the "normal" level of $Q_n$ in Figure 21-2. Now, because of the inelasticity of the demand for farm products, short-run changes in the demand for these products—prompted perhaps by cyclical changes in the nation's total income—will cause markedly different prices and incomes to be associated with this fixed level of output.

A slight drop in demand from $D_1$ to $D_2$ will reduce farm income from area $0P_1aQ_n$ to $0P_2bQ_n$. That is, a relatively small decline in demand gives

**FIGURE 21-2 The effect of demand shifts on farm prices and income**

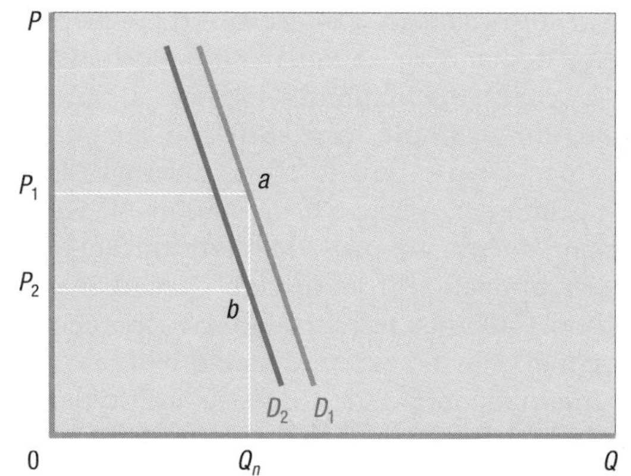


Because of the highly inelastic demand for agricultural products, a small shift in demand (from $D_1$ to $D_2$) will cause drastically different levels of farm prices ($P_1$ to $P_2$) and farm income (area $0P_1aQ_n$ to area $0P_2bQ_n$) to be associated with a fixed level of production $Q_n$.

farmers a drastically reduced money reward for the same amount of farm output. Conversely, a slight increase in demand—as from $D_2$ to $D_1$—will bring an equally sharp increase in farm income for the same volume of output. Again, large price and income changes occur because demand is inelastic.

It is tempting to argue that the sharp declines in farm prices that accompany a decrease in demand will cause many farmers to close down in the short run, reducing total output and alleviating the price-income declines. But farm production is relatively insensitive to price changes because farmers' fixed costs are high compared with their variable costs. Interest, rent, tax, and mortgage payments on land, buildings, and equipment are the major costs faced by the farmer. These are fixed charges. Furthermore, the labour supply of farmers and their families can also be regarded as a fixed cost. As long as they stay on their farms, farmers cannot reduce their costs by firing themselves. Their variable costs are the costs of the small amounts of extra help they may employ, as well as expenditures for seed, fertilizer, and fuel. As a result of their high proportion of fixed costs, farmers are usually better off working their land than they are sitting idle and attempting to pay their fixed costs out of pocket.

**Unstable Foreign Demand** Canadian agriculture's dependence on world markets is another source of demand volatility—and hence of income instability. The incomes of Canadian farmers are sensitive to changes in weather and crop production *in other countries*: Better crops there mean less foreign demand for Canadian farm products. Similarly, cyclical fluctuations in incomes in Europe or Japan, for example, can shift the demand for Canadian farm products. So can changes in foreign economic policies. If the nations of western Europe decide to provide their farmers with greater protection from foreign (Canadian) competition, Canadian farmers will have less access to those markets and export demand will fall.

International politics can also add to demand instability. Changes in the international value of the dollar can be critical. Depreciation of the dollar in the 1970s increased the demand for Canadian farm products (which became cheaper to foreigners), while appreciation of the dollar decreased foreign demand for U.S. farm products in the early 1980s.

To summarize: The increasing relative importance of exports has increased the short-run instability of the demand for Canadian farm products. Farm exports are affected not only by weather, income fluctuations, and economic policies abroad but also by international politics and changes in the international value of the dollar. ***(Key Question 1)***

## Long-Run Problem: A Declining Industry

We must add two other characteristics of agricultural markets to price inelasticity of demand to explain why agriculture has been a declining industry:

1. Over time the supply of farm products has increased rapidly because of technological progress.
2. The demand for farm products has increased slowly because it is inelastic with respect to income.

**Technology and Supply Increases** A rapid rate of technological advance, particularly since World War I, has significantly increased the supply of agricultural products. This technological progress has many roots: the electrification and mechanization of farms, improved techniques of land management and soil conservation, irrigation, development of hybrid crops, availability of improved fertilizers and insecticides, and improvements in breeding and care of livestock. The amount of capital used per worker increased 15 times between 1930 and 1980, permitting a fivefold increase in the amount of land cultivated per farmer. The simplest measure of these advances is the increasing number of people that a single farmer's output will support. In 1846 each farmworker produced enough food and fibre to support 15 people. By 1997 each farmer produced enough to support over 90 people. Unquestionably, physical productivity in agriculture has risen spectacularly; since World War II, it has advanced at a rate *twice* as fast as that in the nonfarm economy.

Most of the technological advances in agriculture have *not* been initiated by farmers but rather are the result of government-sponsored programs of research and education and the work of farm machinery producers. Experimental farms, provincial agricultural representatives, educational pamphlets issued by the federal and provincial departments of agriculture, and the research departments of farm machinery, pesticide, and fertilizer producers are the primary sources of technological advance in Canadian agriculture.

**Lagging Demand** Increases in demand for agricultural products have failed to keep pace with technologically caused increases in their supply. The reason lies in the two major determinants of agricultural demand—income and population.

**INCOME INELASTIC DEMAND** In developing countries, consumers must devote most of their meagre incomes to agricultural products—food and clothing—to sustain themselves. But as income expands beyond subsistence and the problem of hunger diminishes, consumers increase their outlays on food at ever-declining rates. Once consumers' stomachs are filled, they turn to the amenities of life that manufacturing and services, not agriculture, provide. Economic growth in Canada has boosted average per-capita income far beyond the level of subsistence. As a result, *increases in the incomes of Canadian consumers lead to less-than-proportionate increases in spending on farm products.*

In economic terms, the demand for farm products is *income-inelastic*; it is quite insensitive to increases in income. Estimates indicate that a 10 percent increase in real per-capita after-tax income means at most an increase of only 2 percent in consumption of farm products. Certain farm products—for example, cabbages and lard—may be inferior goods. As income increases, purchases of these products may actually *decrease*.

**FIGURE 21-3 A graphical depiction of the long-run farm problem**

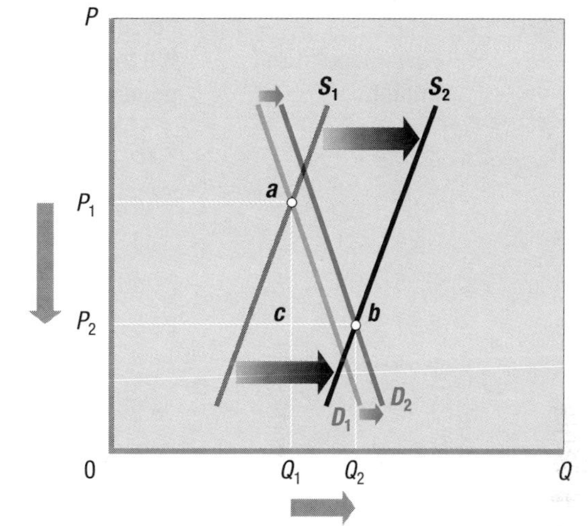


In the long run, increases in the demand for farm products (from $D_1$ to $D_2$) have not kept pace with the increases in supply (from $S_1$ to $S_2$) that technological advances have permitted. Because agricultural demand is inelastic, these shifts have tended to depress farm prices (from $P_1$ to $P_2$) and reduce farm income (from $0P_1aQ_1$ to $0P_2bQ_2$) while increasing output only modestly (from $Q_1$ to $Q_2$).

**Population Growth** Once a minimum income level is reached, each individual consumer's intake of food and fibre becomes relatively fixed. Thus subsequent increases in demand depend on growth in the number of consumers. In most advanced nations, the demand for farm products increases at a rate roughly equal to the rate of population growth. None the less, the resulting overall increase in the purchase of farm products has not been nearly large enough to match increases in farm output.

**Graphical Portrayal** The combination of an inelastic and slowly increasing demand for agricultural products with a rapidly increasing supply puts strong downward pressure on farm prices and income. This is illustrated in Figure 21-3, where a large increase in agricultural supply is shown with a very modest increase in demand. Because of the inelastic demand, these shifts result in a sharp decline in farm prices, accompanied by a relatively small increase in output. Farm income therefore declines. On the graph, we see that farm income before the increases in demand and supply (measured by rectangle $0P_1aQ_1$) exceeds farm income after these increases ($0P_2bQ_2$). *Because of an inelastic demand for farm products, an increase in supply of such products relative to demand creates a persistent downward pressure on farm income.*

**Consequences** The actual consequences over time have been those predicted by the pure-competition model. Because of the demand and supply conditions just outlined, many small, high-cost farms that cannot benefit from scale economies or productivity gains cannot operate profitably. In the long run, financial losses in agriculture have triggered a massive exodus of labour to other sectors of the economy, as shown by Table 21-1. They have also caused a major consolidation of smaller farms into larger ones. A person farming, say, 240 hectares of corn three decades ago is today likely to be farming two or three times that number today. Huge corporate firms called *agribusinesses* have emerged in some parts of agri-

**TABLE 21-1 The declining farm population, selected years, 1920-1996**

| Year | Farm population, millions | Percentage of the total population |
|---|---|---|
| 1920 | 3.18 | 36.6 |
| 1929 | 3.26 | 32.2 |
| 1933 | 3.24 | 30.3 |
| 1941 | 3.15 | 27.4 |
| 1951 | 2.91 | 20.8 |
| 1961 | 2.13 | 11.7 |
| 1971 | 1.49 | 6.9 |
| 1981 | 1.08 | 4.4 |
| 1991 | 0.88* | 3.2 |
| 1996 | 0.89* | 3.0 |

*Estimate based on size of agricultural labour force.
*Source:* O.J. Firestone, *Canada's Economic Development 1867–1953* (London: Bowes & Bowes, 1958), p. 60, Statistics Canada, Census of Canada, 1931–1991, and Statistics Canada, Census of Canada 1996.

culture such as potatoes, beef, fruits, vegetables, and poultry.

As a consequence of outmigration and consolidation, net farm income per farm household has increased relative to nonfarm income. Currently, average incomes of farm households and nonfarm households are very similar. ***(Key Question 3)***

As Global Perspective 21-1 shows, poor nations have much higher percentages of their labour forces in agriculture than do Canada and other industrialized nations.

**21-1**
**QUICK REVIEW**

- Agricultural prices and income are volatile in the short run because an inelastic demand translates small changes in farm output and demand into relatively larger changes in prices and income.
- Technological progress has generated large increases in supplies of farm products over time.
- Increases in demand for farm products have been modest in Canada because demand is inelastic with respect to income and because population growth has been modest.
- The combination of large increases in supply and small increases in demand has made Canadian agriculture a declining industry.

## ECONOMICS OF FARM POLICY

Government has subsidized Canadian agriculture since the 1930s. The "farm program" includes (1) support for farm prices, income, and output; (2) soil and water conservation; (3) agricultural research; (4) farm credit; (5) crop insurance; and (6) subsidized sale of farm products in world markets. However, the typical Canadian farmer and the

**21-1**
**GLOBAL PERSPECTIVE**

**Percentage of labour force in agriculture, selected nations**

Rich nations have much smaller percentages of their labour forces in agriculture than do poor nations. Because their work forces are so heavily committed to producing the food and fibre needed for their populations, poor nations have relatively less labour available to produce housing, schools, autos, and the other goods and services that contribute to a high standard of living.

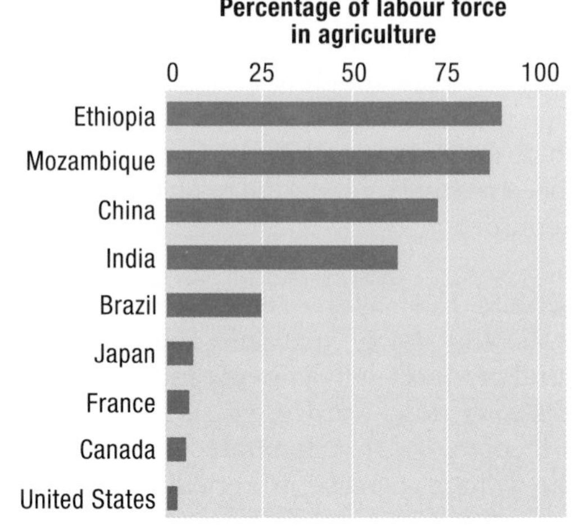


*Source: World Development Report, 1997.* Latest data.

average politician both have viewed the farm program primarily as one to prop up prices and income, and it is this "price-support" (subsidies) aspect of farm policy that we will explore. You need to know about the purposes and outcomes of farm subsidies. Between 1990 and 1996, Canadian farmers received an average of $1.1 billion of such subsidies each year. (As indicated in Global Perspective 21-2, farm subsidies are common globally.)

### Rationale for Farm Subsidies

A variety of arguments have been made over the years to justify farm subsidies:

1. Although their products are needed, many farmers are comparatively poor; they should therefore receive higher prices and incomes through public help.
2. Farming—and particularly the "family farm" —is a fundamental Canadian institution and should be nurtured as a way of life.
3. Farmers are subject to extraordinary hazards —floods, droughts, and insects—which other industries do not face. For the most part, farmers cannot fully insure themselves against these disasters.
4. While farmers face purely competitive markets for their outputs, they buy inputs of fertilizer, farm machinery, and gasoline from industries that have considerable market power. While these industries have an ability to control their prices, farmers are at the "mercy of the market" in selling their output. The supporters of subsidies argue that agriculture warrants public aid in order to offset the disadvantageous terms of trade that result.

**21-2**
**GLOBAL PERSPECTIVE**

**Agricultural subsidies, selected nations**

While Canadian farmers receive about 43 percent of their incomes as government subsidies, farmers in other nations receive an even greater percentage.

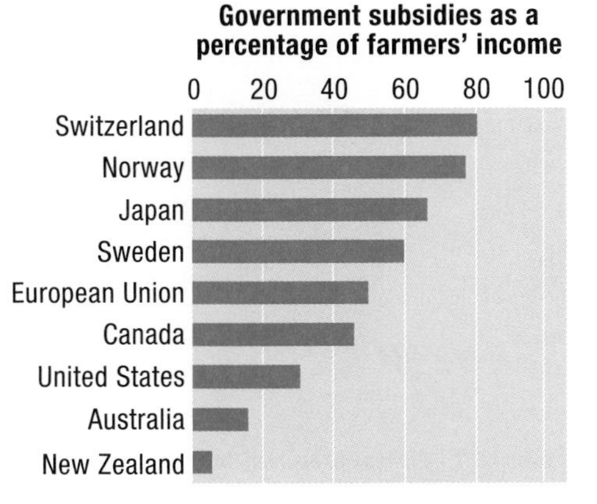


*Source:* Organization for Economic Cooperation and Development.

## THE ECONOMICS OF PRICE SUPPORTS

Canadian agricultural policy in the past has aimed at stabilizing agricultural prices at levels that result in higher incomes to farmers. The main tools used in agricultural stabilization policy are marketing boards and price supports.

### Marketing Boards

There are two types of agricultural marketing boards. One aims to increase prices by regulating supply, the other acts as a marketing agency for producers.

**Historical Background** During the Great Depression of the 1930s, many farmers believed they were no match for the concentrated agribusiness with which they dealt. The general belief was that the small farmer faced low offer-to-buy prices by processors, and farmers could not successfully withhold their produce to force up the price. The political pressure from farmers led to the passing of the Natural Products Marketing Act in 1934, which set up the Federal Marketing Board. This board could delegate its power to local producers' boards, its most important power being controlling sales of agricultural products.

The federal law was struck down by the courts on the grounds that regulation of trade *within* came under provincial jurisdiction. Several provinces, starting with British Columbia in 1936 and Ontario in 1937, passed laws allowing already functioning marketing boards to continue under provincial authority. By 1940 all provinces had farm marketing legislation in force except for Quebec, which passed such legislation in 1956. The main purpose of these marketing boards was *supply management*:

the maintenance of prices at board-determined levels through control of product supply.

In 1935 the **Canadian Wheat Marketing Board** was created. As of 1998 it still had complete control over the price and marketing of western wheat. When farmers deliver their wheat to the Wheat Board, they receive an initial payment per bushel that is 75 percent of the expected average selling price. This is in effect a floor price and is set low enough that the Wheat Board is reasonably certain to be able to sell the wheat at least at that price. The producers subsequently get the full average selling price the Wheat Board is able to get on the domestic and international markets, less transportation costs, storage costs, and administrative Wheat Board expenses. Farmers get the average price the Wheat Board is able to realize over the course of the year. A farmer thus does not have to worry what the price is the day the crop is delivered to the Wheat Board.

Marketing boards aim to stabilize agricultural prices at a level that insures higher incomes to farmers. This can be accomplished through price supports.

There are two basic methods of supporting prices above their market equilibrium values: (1) offers to purchase and (2) deficiency payments.

## Offers to Purchase

A marketing board can increase farm income by ensuring that the price farmers get for their produce does not fall below a specified minimum. In Figure 21-4(a) let's assume that the *floor price*—or, as it is commonly called, the **support price**—is $P_s$. Then the major effects are as follows:

1. **SURPLUS OUTPUT** The most obvious result is product surplus. Consumers are willing to purchase only $Q_o$ units at the supported price, while farmers will supply $Q_s$ units. What about the unpurchased surplus ($Q_s - Q_c$) that results? The government must buy it to make the above-equilibrium support price effective. These large accumulated surpluses are undesirable on two counts. First, their very existence indicates a misallocation of the economy's resources. Government-held surpluses mean that the economy is devoting too many resources to the production of commodities that, *at existing supported prices*, are not wanted by consumers. Second, the storing of surplus products is expensive, adding to the cost of the farm program and, ultimately, to the consumer's tax bill. For example, in the late 1950s the federal government accumulated over 100

**FIGURE 21-4 Price supports and crop restriction**

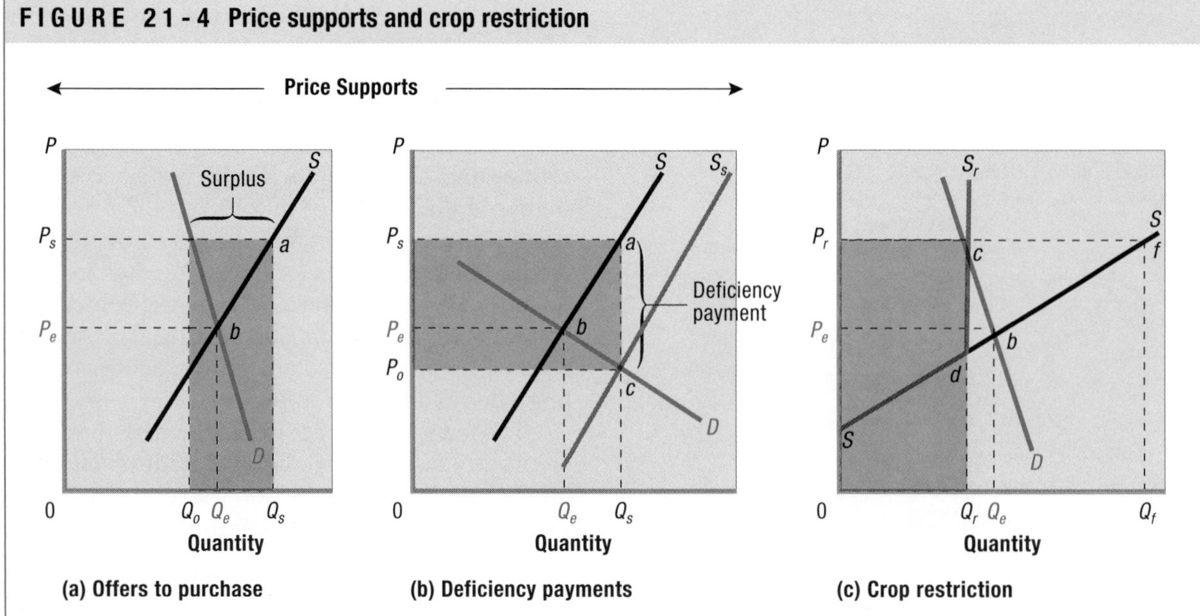


(a) Offers to purchase result in surpluses. (b) Deficiency payments or subsidies do not result in surpluses. (c) Crop restriction results in neither surpluses nor government payments. All costs (the higher price) are borne by consumers.

million pounds (45 million kilograms) of butter as it tried to maintain an above-equilibrium price. The solution was to convert the butter into butter oil, which the government then sold abroad at half the butter price.

2. **CONSUMERS' LOSS** Consumers "lose" in two ways. They pay a higher price ($P_s$ rather than $P_e$) and consume less ($Q_o$ rather than $Q_e$) of the product. They also pay higher taxes to finance the government's purchase of the surplus. In Figure 21-4(a), this added tax burden will amount to the surplus output $Q_o - Q_s$, multiplied by its price, $P_s$. Storage costs add to this tax burden. Unfortunately, the burden of higher food prices falls disproportionately on the poor because they spend a larger portion of their incomes on food.
3. **FARMERS GAIN** Farmers gain from price supports. In Figure 21-4(a), gross receipts rise from the free market level of $0P_ebQ_e$ to the larger supported level of area $0P_saQ_s$.

## Deficiency Payments

Deficiency payments are subsidies that make up the difference between the market price and the government-supported price; they work as follows: In Figure 21-4(b) suppose that the support price is $P_s$. Also, as before, at price $P_s$ farmers expand production from $Q_e$ to $Q_s$. However, with demand as shown by $D$, consumers will only buy $Q_s$ if the price is $P_o$. The government arranges for this to be the market price by simply subsidizing production by the amount $P_o - P_s$. The government makes a deficiency payment to each producer equal to $P_o - P_s$ times the quantity sold.

The total consumer expenditure is $0P_ocQ_s$, total government expenditure is $P_oP_sac$ = deficiency payment times $Q_s$. The producers are still on the original supply curve $S$. However, $S_s$ is the supply curve as seen by the consumer and is created by the government subsidy or deficiency payment. When we analyze the economic effect of these payments, two considerations arise.

**Elasticity of Supply and Demand** The incidence of the subsidy, like the sales tax, depends on the elasticity of the supply and demand curves. In Figure 21-4(b), the combined effects of the elastic demand curve in the price range $P_oP_s$ and the inelastic supply curve result in the subsidy going mostly to the producer: the producer gets $P_eS_s$ of the deficiency payment, the consumer only $P_eP_o$. The effect of elasticity on the incidence of a subsidy is precisely the same as that of a sales tax.

## Comparing Offers to Purchase and Deficiency Payments

Assuming, as we have done, that $P_s$ is the same in both Figures 21-4(a) and (b), farmers will benefit equally from the two programs: their total income will be $0P_saQ_s$ in each case. Consumers prefer **deficiency payments** since they receive a large amount of output, $Q_s$, at a low price, $P_o$. This compares with a high price, $P_s$, and small quantity, $Q_o$, under a program of offers to purchase. But when the subsidies of taxpayers to farmers (the shaded areas) are taken into account, we find that total payments by the public (consumption expenditures plus tax-financed subsidies) to farmers are identical under both programs: $0P_saQ_s$.

Offers to purchase and deficiency payments have one important difference. Offers to purchase result in government-held surpluses that can be costly to store. While it might be desirable to have some reserve stocks as a buffer against a year or two of crop failures, it is quite another matter for government to spend hundreds of millions a year simply to store large surpluses of farm commodities.

**Overallocation of Resources** There is a more subtle cost in *both* offers to purchase and deficiency payments. Society loses because price supports contribute to economic inefficiency by encouraging an overallocation of resources to agriculture. A price floor ($P_s$) attracts more resources to the agricultural sector than would the free market price ($P_e$). In terms of Chapter 10's pure competition model, the market supply curve in Figure 21-4 represents the marginal costs of all farmers producing this product at various outputs $Q_o$. An efficient allocation of resources occurs where the market price ($P_e$) is equal to marginal costs and that is at point $b$. The output $Q_e$ reflects that efficient allocation of resources. In contrast, the output $Q_s$ associated with the price support $P_s$ represents an overallocation of resources. A misallocation of resources between agriculture and the rest of the economy imposes a cost on society.

**Environmental Costs** We know from Figure 21-4 that price supports motivate additional production. Although some of this extra output may require additional land, much of the added production comes from greater use of fertilizer and pesticides. Unfortunately, pesticides and fertilizers are also poisons that may pollute the environment (for example, groundwater) and pose health risks to farmworkers and to consumers as residues in food. Research shows a positive relationship between the level of price-support subsidies and the use of agri-chemicals.

Farm policy may also cause environmental problems in less obvious ways. First, farmers benefit from price supports only when they use their land consistently for a specific crop such as corn or wheat. This creates a disincentive to practise crop rotation, which is a nonchemical technique for controlling pests. Farm policy thus encourages the substitution of chemical for nonchemical pest control.

Second, we know from the concept of derived demand that an increase in the price of a product will increase the demand for relevant inputs. In particular, price supports for farm products increase the demand for land. And the land that farmers bring into farm production is often environmentally sensitive "marginal" land such as steeply sloped, highly erodable land or wetlands that provide wildlife habitat. Similarly, price supports result in the use of more water for irrigation, and the resulting runoff may contribute to soil erosion.

**International Costs** The costs of farm price supports go beyond those indicated by Figure 21-4. Price supports generate economic distortions that cross national boundaries. For example, price supports make the Canadian agricultural market attractive to foreign producers. But inflows of foreign agricultural products would increase supplies in Canada, aggravating the problem of surpluses. To prevent this from happening, Canada is likely to impose import barriers in the form of tariffs or quotas. These barriers often restrict the output of more efficient foreign producers, while simultaneously encouraging more output from less efficient Canadian producers. The result is a less efficient use of world agricultural resources.

Similarly, as Canada and other industrially advanced countries with similar agricultural programs dump surplus farm products on world markets, the prices of such products are depressed. Developing countries—heavily dependent on world commodity markets for their incomes—are hurt because their export earnings are reduced. Thus, Canadian price supports for wheat production have imposed significant costs on Argentina, a major wheat exporter. ***(Key Question 7)***

## Coping with Surpluses: Crop Restrictions

Another method for increasing prices to farmers is to reduce the amount of land devoted to a specific crop.

Suppose in Figure 21-4(c) that the government wants to assure the producers price $P_r$. Neither offers to purchase nor deficiency payments would be appropriate because of the price *elastic supply*. An offer to purchase at price $P_r$ would result in a surplus of $Q_r - Q_f$, a greater amount than is bought for domestic consumption. A deficiency payment program makes even less sense, for there is simply no demand for quantity $0Q_f$ at any price.

The only sensible way for the government to ensure price $P_r$ in these circumstances is to impose **crop restriction**. With production restricted to $Q_r$ and with the inelastic demand as shown, price will rise to $P_r$. The supply curve, in effect, is no longer $S$, but $SdS_r$.

**21-2**

**QUICK REVIEW**

- Marketing boards aim to stabilize agricultural prices at levels that insure higher incomes to farmers.
- Price supports are government-imposed price floors (minimum prices) on selected farm products. Price supports can be achieved through **a** offers to purchase, **b** deficiency payments, or **c** crop restrictions.
- Price supports cause surplus production; raise farm income; increase food prices to consumers; and cause an overallocation of resources to agriculture.
- Domestic price supports encourage nations to erect trade barriers against imported farm products and to dump surplus farm products on world markets.

# CRITICISM, POLITICS, AND REFORM

Sixty years of experience with government price-support programs suggested that these programs were not working well. There was a growing feeling among economists and political leaders that the goals and techniques of farm policy needed to be reexamined and revised. Nevertheless, these programs maintained strong political support, for reasons we will address.

## Criticisms

Here are some of the key criticisms of agricultural subsidies that led to the recent reform:

**Symptoms, Not Causes** Our subsidy strategy towards agriculture is designed to treat symptoms, not causes. The root cause of the farm problem has been a misallocation of resources between agriculture and the rest of the economy. Historically, the problem has been one of too many farmers. The effect or symptom of this misallocation of resources was relatively low farm incomes. For the most part, public policy in agriculture has been oriented towards supporting farm prices and incomes rather than towards alleviating the resource allocation problem that is the fundamental cause of these relatively low farm incomes.

Further, price-income supports have kept people in agriculture who would otherwise have moved to a nonfarm occupation. Thus, the price-income orientation of the farm programs has slowed the reallocation of resources necessary to resolve the long-run farm problem.

**Misguided Subsidies** Price-income support programs have most benefited those farmers who least need government assistance. If the goal of our farm program is bolstering low farm incomes, it follows that any program of government aid should be aimed at farmers at the bottom of the farm income distribution scale. But the poor, small-output farmer does not produce and sell enough in the market to get much aid from price supports. It is the large farm that reaps the benefits by virtue of its large output. If public policy must be designed to supplement farm incomes, a strong case can be made for targeting those benefits to those farmers in most need.

An income-support program should be geared to *people*, not *products*. Many economists say that, on equity grounds, direct income subsidies to poor farmers are highly preferable to indirect price support subsidies, which go mainly to large and prosperous farmers.

A related point concerns land values. The price and income benefits that various farm programs provide are eventually capitalized into higher farmland values. By making crops more valuable, price supports have made the land itself more valuable. Sometimes this is helpful to farmers, but often it is not. To the extent that farmers rent their farmland, price supports become a subsidy to people who are *not* actively engaged in farming.

The quota system has a similar effect with regard to young would-be farmers. Before becoming dairy farmers, for example, they must buy milk quotas from retiring farmers. An adequate quota can easily cost $100,000. The interest payments on this become a permanent fixed cost that for the young farmer may very well eliminate the benefit of the higher price for milk brought about by the quota system. This applies with even greater force in the poultry business: the average value of an egg quota in Ontario is about $250,000.

**Policy Contradictions** Because farm policy has many objectives, it often leads to contradictions. Subsidized research is aimed at increasing farm productivity and increasing the supply of farm products, while crop restriction programs require that farmers take land out of production to reduce supply. Price supports for crops mean increased feed costs for ranchers and high consumer prices for animal products. Tobacco farmers are subsidized at a time when serious health problems are associated with tobacco consumption. Conservation programs call for setting aside land for wildlife habitat, while price supports provide incentives to bring such land into production.

## The Politics of Farm Policy

In view of these criticisms and inconsistencies, we might ask why Canada has continued its price-support program for so many decades. Why has it taken so long for government to restore free markets for some farm products? Why do price-support programs for such commodities still continue?

**Public Choice Theory Revisited** We can respond to these questions largely in terms of Chapter 20's public choice theory. Recall that *rent-seeking behaviour* occurs when a group (a labour union, firms in a specific industry, or farmers producing a particular crop) uses political means to transfer income or wealth to itself at the expense of another group or of society as a whole. The *special-interest* effect involves a program or policy from which a small group receives large benefits at the expense of a much larger group whose members individually suffer small losses. Both rent-seeking behaviour and the special-interest effect help explain the politics of farm subsidies.

Suppose a specific group of farmers, say, egg producers or dairy farmers, organize and establish a well-financed political action committee (PAC). The PAC's job is to promote government programs that will transfer income to the group (this is rent-seeking behaviour). The PAC vigorously lobbies Members of Parliament to enact or continue price supports and import quotas for eggs and milk. The PAC does this in part by making political contributions to sympathetic legislators. Although egg production is heavily concentrated in a few provinces, the PAC will also make contributions to Members of Parliament from other provinces to gain support.

But how can a small interest group successfully lobby to increase its own income at the expense of society as a whole? Because, even though the total cost of the group's programs might be considerable, the cost imposed on *each individual* taxpayer is small (this is the special-interest effect). Citizen-taxpayers are likely uninformed about and indifferent to these programs since they have little at stake. For example, unless you raise your own chickens to provide your family's egg supply, you probably have no idea how much these programs cost you as an individual taxpayer and consumer and therefore do not object when your Member of Parliament votes for, say, a price-support program for egg production. Thus, there is little or no counterlobbying to negate the PAC's efforts.

Public choice theory also tells us that politicians are more likely to favour programs having hidden costs. As you have seen, this is often true of farm programs. The discussion of Figure 21-4 showed that price supports involve not simply a transfer of money from taxpayer to farmer but costs that are hidden as higher food prices, storage costs for surplus output, costs of administering farm programs, and costs associated with both domestic and international misallocations of resources. While the direct cost of an egg subsidy program to taxpayers is small, the price increase provided by the program carries a hidden subsidy (cost) that is much larger. Because the cost of the program is largely indirect and hidden, the program is much more acceptable to politicians and the public than it would be if all costs were explicit.

**Changing Politics** In spite of rent seeking, special interests, and logrolling, a combination of factors has led to a change in the politics of farm subsidies, for several reasons.

**DECLINING POLITICAL SUPPORT** As the farm population has declined, agriculture's political power has also diminished. The farm population was about 30 percent of the general population in the 1930s, when many Canadian farm programs were established; now it is less than 3 percent. Urban congressional representatives are now a 9 to 1 majority over their rural colleagues. More and more politicians are critically examining farm programs for their effect on consumers' grocery bills as well as on farm incomes. Also, more farmers themselves resent the intrusion of the federal government into their farming decisions. Many rural Members of Parliament now support free-market agriculture.

**BUDGET DEFICITS** Continued pressure to balance the federal budget has brought farm subsidies under increased political scrutiny.

**WORLD TRADE CONSIDERATIONS** The new, more critical attitude towards farm subsidies has also resulted from Canada's lead in attempting to reduce barriers to world trade in agricultural products. The 15 nations of the European Union (EU) and many other nations support agricultural prices. To maintain high domestic prices, these nations restrict imports of foreign farm products. They do this by imposing tariffs (excise taxes) and quotas (specific limits on imports of foreign goods). They then try to rid themselves of domestic surpluses by subsidizing their exports into world markets.

The effects on Canada are that (1) trade barriers hinder Canadian farmers from selling to EU nations, and (2) subsidized exports from these other nations depress world prices for agricultural products, making world markets less attractive to Canadian farmers.

Perhaps most importantly, farm programs such as those in the EU and Canada distort both world agricultural trade and the international allocation of agricultural resources. Encouraged by artificially high prices, farmers in industrially advanced nations produce more farm output than

they would otherwise. The resulting surpluses flow into world markets where they depress prices. This means farmers in countries with no farm programs—often developing countries—face artificially low prices for their exports, and this signals them to produce less. Overall, the result is a shift in production away from what would occur on the basis of comparative advantage.

Recognizing these distortions, in 1994 the world's trading nations agreed to reduce farm price-support programs by 20 percent by the year 2000 and reduce tariffs and quotas on imported farm products by 15 percent. Canada made a strong case against price supports in these discussions, and its stance undoubtedly altered the domestic debate on whether supports should be continued within the country.

**21-3**

**QUICK REVIEW**

- Canadian farm policy has been heavily criticized for delaying the shift of resources away from farming, directing most subsidies to wealthier farmers, and being fraught with policy contradictions.
- The persistence of price supports can largely be explained in terms of rent-seeking behaviour, the special-interest effect, and other aspects of public choice theory.
- Recently, the politics of farm subsidies has changed due to the declining political clout of farmers, the need to address federal budget deficits, and world trade considerations.

## CHAPTER SUMMARY

1. In the short run, the highly inelastic nature of agricultural demand translates small changes in output and small shifts in domestic or foreign demand into large changes in prices and income.
2. Over the long run, rapid technological advance, together with a highly inelastic and relatively slow-growing demand for agricultural output, has caused agriculture to be a declining industry.
3. Historically, farm policy has been centred on price and based on the parity concept, which suggests that the relationship between prices received and paid by farmers should be constant over time.
4. The use of price floors or price supports has a number of economic effects: **a** Surplus production occurs; **b** the incomes of farmers are increased; **c** consumers pay higher prices for farm products; **d** an overallocation of resources to agriculture occurs; **e** society pays higher taxes to finance the purchase and storage of surplus output; **f** pollution increases because of the greater use of agri-chemicals and vulnerable land; and **g** other nations bear the costs associated with import barriers and depressed world agricultural prices.
5. Government has pursued with limited success programs to reduce agricultural supply and increase agricultural demand as a method of reducing the surpluses associated with price supports.
6. Economists have criticized farm policy for **a** confusing symptoms (low farm incomes) with causes (excess capacity), **b** providing the largest subsidies to high-income farmers, and **c** creating contradictions among specific farm programs.
7. The persistence of agricultural subsidies can be explained in terms of public choice theory and, in particular, in terms of rent-seeking behaviour, and the special-interest effect.
8. Political backing for price supports and crop restriction programs has eroded for several reasons: **a** The number of farmers, and thus their political clout, has declined dramatically relative to the number of urban consumers of farm products; **b** farm subsidies have received close scrutiny due to efforts to eliminate the federal budget deficit; **c** successful efforts by Canada to get other nations to reduce their farm subsidies have altered the domestic debate on the desirability of Canadian farm subsidies.

## TERMS AND CONCEPTS

short-run farm problem
long-run farm problem
Canadian Wheat Marketing Board
support price
deficiency payments
crop restriction

## STUDY QUESTIONS

1. KEY QUESTION *Carefully evaluate: "The supply and demand for agricultural products are such that small changes in agricultural supply result in drastic changes in prices. However, large changes in farm prices have modest effects on agricultural output." (Hint: A brief review of the distinction between supply and quantity supplied may be helpful.) Do exports increase or reduce the instability of demand for farm products? Explain.*
2. What relationship, if any, can you detect between the fact that the farmer's fixed costs of production are large and the fact that the supply of most agricultural products is generally inelastic? Be specific in your answer.
3. KEY QUESTION Explain how each of the following contributes to the farm problem: **a** the inelasticity of demand for farm products, **b** the rapid technological progress in farming, **c** the modest long-run growth in demand for farm commodities, and **d** the competitiveness of agriculture.
4. The key to efficient resource allocation is shifting resources from low-productivity to high-productivity uses. In view of the high and expanding physical productivity of agricultural resources, explain why many economists want to divert additional resources from farming to achieve allocative efficiency.
5. Explain and evaluate: "Industry complains of the higher taxes it must pay to finance subsidies to agriculture. Yet the trend of agricultural prices has been downward while industrial prices have been moving upward, suggesting that on balance agriculture is actually subsidizing industry."
6. "Because consumers as a whole must ultimately pay the total incomes received by farmers, it makes no real difference whether the income is paid through free farm markets or through price supports supplemented by subsidies financed out of tax revenue." Do you agree?
7. KEY QUESTION *Explain the economic effects of price supports. Explicitly include environmental and global impacts in your answer. On what grounds do economists contend that price supports cause a misallocation of resources?*
8. Use supply and demand curves to depict equilibrium price and output in a competitive market for some farm product. Then show how an above-equilibrium price floor (price support) would cause a surplus in this market. Demonstrate in your graph how government could reduce the surplus through a policy that **a** changes supply or **b** changes demand. Identify each of the following actual government policies as primarily affecting the supply of or the demand for a particular farm product: crop restriction, government buyout of dairy herds, export promotion.
9. Do you agree with each of the following statements? Explain why or why not.
   **a.** "The problem with Canadian agriculture is that there are too many farmers. This is not the fault of farmers but the fault of government programs."
   **b.** "The federal government ought to buy up Canadian farm surpluses and give them away to developing nations."
   **c.** "All industries would like government price supports if they could get them; agriculture got price supports *only* because of its strong political clout."
10. What are the effects of farm subsidies such as those of Canada and the European Union on **a** domestic agricultural prices, **b** world agricultural prices, and **c** the international allocation of agricultural resources?
11. Use public choice theory to explain the persistence of farm subsidies in the face of major criticisms of these subsidies.

CHAPTER 22

# The Gains from International Trade

THE WTO, TRADE DEFICITS AND SURPLUSES, dumping. Exchange rates, the EU, the G-7 nations. The IMF, official reserves, currency interventions. Capital flight, brain drains, the ruble. This is the language of international economics, and people across the globe are speaking it in newspapers, corporate offices, retail outlets, and union halls.

This chapter builds on Chapter 6, providing deeper analysis of international trade and protectionism. We begin by reviewing key facts about world trade, and then we look more closely at how international specialization based on comparative advantage can mutually benefit the participating nations. After using supply and demand analysis to examine equilibrium prices and quantities of imports and exports, we examine the economic impact of trade barriers such as tariffs and import quotas and evaluate the arguments for protectionism. Finally, we discuss the costs of protectionism and look at continuing controversies in international trade.

**IN THIS CHAPTER YOU WILL LEARN:**

The facts about Canada's international trade.

•

The distinction between absolute and comparative advantage.

•

That trading on the basis of comparative advantage results in gains to trading nations.

•

About trade barriers and their negative effects on nations' economic well-being.

## The Big Picture

THE ECONOMIZING PROBLEM CONSISTS OF limited resources, unlimited wants, and thus the need for choices. In a world of limited resources, if we can somehow get more output of goods and services from those resources, the constraints an individual or a society faces are less severe. One of the ways to get more output from the limited resources available is specialization. Adam Smith, the so-called father of economics, noticed the beneficial effect of specialization in the celebrated pin factory he talks about in *The Wealth of Nations.* Just as a factory can greatly increase its output if each person specializes, the world output of goods and services would increase if each nation specialized in those pursuits to which it is best suited. In technical terms, it should specialize in the line of production in which it enjoys a comparative advantage. Each nation would then import goods to satisfy its other needs. In this manner, each nation would be materially better off than if each tried to produce all the goods and services it consumes. These beneficial effects are the driving force behind the globalization of trade, such as manifested by the Canada–U.S. Free Trade Agreement (FTA), and the North American Free Trade Agreement (NAFTA).

As you read this chapter, keep the following points in mind:

- **Key Concepts 3** and **5** are discussed.
- It may be helpful for you to think of trading between two nations as similar to trading between two individuals. Each specializes in what he or she does best and then trades.
- The purpose of tariffs is to protect domestic industries from international competition. Tariff protection implies an inability to successfully compete with imports. Firms in the protected industries enjoy a level of profit higher than would be the case if they had to compete. Consumers lose because they have to pay higher prices for goods produced by the protected industries.
- Protecting domestic industry has an intuitive appeal, particularly in regards to "saving jobs." But ultimately, consumers and society at large will pay for the tariff protection through higher prices. Each of the jobs saved will be very costly. ■

## FACTS OF INTERNATIONAL TRADE

In Chapter 6 we presented a number of facts about international trade. Let's briefly review those facts and add a few others.

1. Exports of goods and services are 38 percent of Canadian GDP. The percentage is high by world standards; only the Netherlands, at 56 percent, is higher among the industrialized nations.
2. Canadian exports and imports have increased in volume and risen by more than a third as a percentage of GDP since 1965 (Figure 6-2).
3. In 1997 Canada had a $27 billion trade surplus, meaning that the export of goods exceeded the import of goods by this amount. But in that year Canada's imports of services exceeded its exports of services by $8 billion. Thus, the goods and services surplus was $19 billion.
4. Canada's principal commodity exports are automotive products, machinery and equipment, and forestry products. Its main imports are machinery and equipment and automotive products.
5. Like other advanced industrial nations, Canada imports some of the same categories of goods that it exports (Figure 6-3).
6. The bulk of Canadian export and import trade is with other industrially advanced nations, specifically the United States, nations of western Europe, and Japan (Figure 6-4).
7. Improved transportation and communications technologies, declines in tariffs, and peaceful relations among major industrial nations have all helped expand world trade since World War II.
8. Although trade is still dominated by industrially advanced nations, several new "players" have greatly increased their roles (Global Perspective 22-1). The four "Asian tigers" of

**22-1**
**GLOBAL PERSPECTIVE**

**Shares of world exports, selected nations**

The United States has the largest share of world exports, followed closely by Germany and Japan. Canada, a much smaller economy, represents over 4 percent of the world's exports. The seven largest export nations account for nearly 50 percent of world exports.

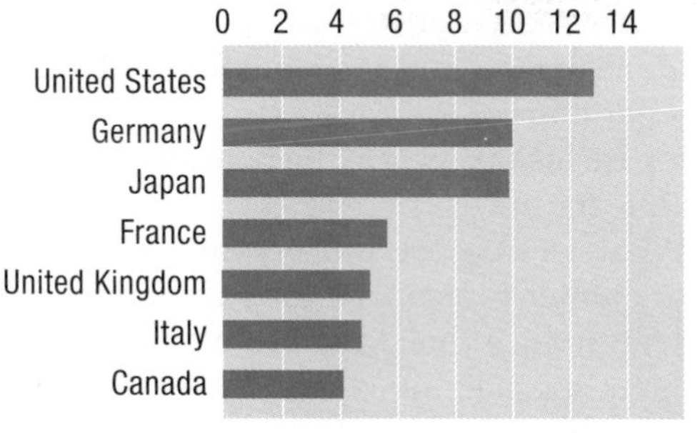


*Source:* Organization for Economic Cooperation and Development.

Hong Kong, Singapore, South Korea, and Taiwan have expanded their share of world trade from 3 percent in 1972 to nearly 10 percent today. China has emerged as a major new international trader, and the collapse of communism has led Eastern European nations and Russia to look globally for new trade partners.

9. International trade (and finance) link economies. Through trade, changes in economic conditions in one spot on the globe can quickly affect other places. Example: In early 1998, economists scaled back forecasts for economic growth in Canada and Europe because of economic problems in the Southeast Asian countries of Japan, South Korea, Indonesia, Malaysia, and the Philippines. Reduced purchases of Canadian and European imports mean lower Canadian and European exports and thus slower Canadian and European output growth.
10. International trade is often at the centre of international policy. Examples: The North American Free Trade Agreement (NAFTA), the conclusion of negotiations on the General Agreement on Tariffs and Trade (GATT).

With these facts in mind, let's look more closely at the economics of international trade.

## THE ECONOMIC BASIS FOR TRADE

In Chapter 6 we found that international trade is a way nations can specialize, increase the productivity of their resources, and realize a larger total output than otherwise. Sovereign nations, like individuals and regions of a nation, can gain by specializing in products they can produce with the greatest relative efficiency and by trading for goods they cannot produce efficiently.

This rationale for trade is correct, but a more detailed understanding is needed. The more complete answer to the question "Why do nations trade?" hinges on two points.

1. The distribution of economic resources—natural, human, and capital goods—among nations is uneven; nations are different in their endowments of economic resources.
2. Efficient production of various goods requires different technologies or combinations of resources.

The character and interaction of these two facts can be readily illustrated. Japan, for example, has a large, well-educated labour force; skilled labour is abundant and therefore inexpensive. Japan can produce efficiently (at low cost) a variety of goods whose design and production require much skilled labour: Cameras, transistor radios, and video recorders are examples of such **labour-intensive goods**.

In contrast, Australia has vast amounts of land compared with its human and capital resources and can inexpensively produce goods requiring much land; it produces such **land-intensive goods** as wheat, wool, and meat. Brazil has the soil, tropical climate, rainfall, and lots of unskilled labour needed for efficient, low-cost production of coffee.

Industrially advanced economies with relatively large amounts of capital can produce inexpensively those goods whose production requires much capital. Automobiles, agricultural equipment, machinery, and chemicals are such **capital-intensive goods**.

The distribution of both resources and technology among nations, however, is not forever fixed. When the distribution changes, the relative efficiency with which nations produce goods also changes. For example, in the past few decades South Korea has upgraded the quality of its labour force and has greatly expanded its stock of capital. Although South Korea was primarily an exporter of agricultural products and raw materials a half-century ago, it now exports large quantities of manufactured goods. Similarly, the new technologies that gave us synthetic fibres and synthetic rubber drastically altered the resource mix needed to produce these goods and changed the relative efficiency of nations in manufacturing them.

As national economies evolve, the size and quality of their labour forces may change, the volume and composition of their capital stocks may shift, new technologies will develop, and even the quality of land and quantity of natural resources may be altered. As these changes occur, the relative efficiency with which a nation can produce specific goods will also change.

## SPECIALIZATION AND COMPARATIVE ADVANTAGE

Let's now use the concept of comparative advantage to analyze the basis for international specialization and trade.

**The Basic Principle** The central concept underlying comparative advantage can be illustrated by posing a problem. Consider the case of a chartered accountant (CA) who, we will assume, is also a skilled house painter. Suppose the CA can paint her house in less time than the professional painter she is thinking of hiring. Also suppose the CA can earn $50 per hour doing her accounting and must pay the painter $15 per hour. It will take the accountant 30 hours to paint her house; the painter, 40 hours. Finally, assume the CA receives no special pleasure from painting.

Should the CA take time off from her accounting to paint her own house or should she hire the painter? The CA should hire the painter. Her opportunity cost of painting her house is $1,500 (= 30 hours × $50 per hour of sacrificed income). The cost of hiring the painter is only $600 (= 40 hours × $15 per hour paid to the painter). Although the CA is better at both accounting and painting, the CA's relative or comparative advantage lies in accounting. She will *lower her cost of getting her house painted* by specializing in accounting and using some of the proceeds to hire the house painter.

Note that the CA has **absolute advantage** in both accounting and painting; she can do accounting and paint more efficiently than our hypothetical house painter. Despite this, the CA should hire the house painter to paint her house because of her "comparative advantage."

Similarly, the house painter perhaps can reduce his cost of obtaining accounting services by specializing in painting and using some of his income to hire the CA. Suppose it would take the painter 10 hours to prepare his income tax, while the CA could handle this task in 2 hours. The house painter would sacrifice $150 of income (= 10 hours × $15 per hour of sacrificed time) to get a task done that he could hire out for $100 (= 2 hours × $50 per hour of the CA's time). By using the CA to prepare his tax return, the painter *lowers his cost of getting the tax return completed.*

What is true for our hypothetical CA and house painter is also true for two nations. Countries can reduce their cost of obtaining desirable goods by specializing where they have comparative advantages.

With this simple example in mind, let's turn to an international trade model to acquire an understanding of the gains from international specialization and trade.

### Two Isolated Nations

Suppose the world economy has just two nations, Canada and Brazil. Each can produce both steel and soybeans, but at differing levels of economic efficiency. Suppose Canadian and Brazilian domestic production possibilities curves for soybeans and steel are as shown in Figure 22-1a and b. Two characteristics of these production possibilities curves should be noted:

1. **CONSTANT COSTS** The "curves" are drawn as straight lines, in contrast to the concave-from-the-origin production possibilities frontiers introduced in Chapter 2. This means the law of increasing costs has been replaced with the assumption of constant costs. This simplifies our discussion and will not impair the validity of our analysis and conclusions. We later will consider the effect of the more realistic increasing costs.
2. **DIFFERENT COSTS** The production possibilities curves of Canada and Brazil are different, reflecting different resource mixes and differing levels of technological progress. Specifi-

**FIGURE 22-1 Production possibilities for Canada and Brazil**

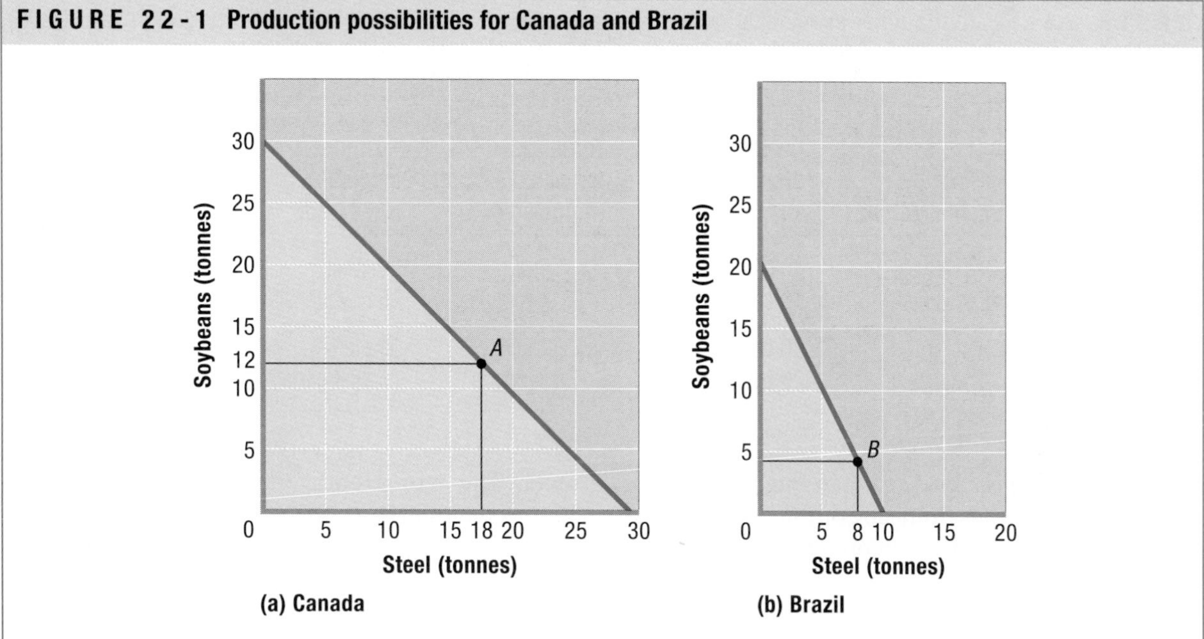


The two production possibilities lines show the amounts of soybeans and steel (a) Canada and (b) Brazil can produce domestically. The curves for both countries are straight lines because we are assuming constant costs. The different cost ratios, 1 steel = 1 soybean for Canada, and 1 steel = 2 soybeans for Brazil are reflected in the different slopes of the two lines.

cally, the opportunity costs of producing steel and soybeans differ between the two nations.

**Canada** In Figure 22-1a, with full employment, Canada will operate on its production possibilities curve. On that curve, it can increase its output of steel 30 tonnes by forgoing an output of 30 tonnes of soybeans. This means the slope of the production possibilities curve is –1 (= –30 soybeans/ +30 steel), implying that 1 tonne of steel can be obtained for every tonne of soybeans sacrificed. In Canada the domestic exchange ratio or **cost ratio** for the two products is 1 tonne of steel for 1 tonne of soybean, or

$$1\ S_t = 1\ S_{oy}$$

Canada can "exchange" a tonne of steel for a tonne of soybeans. Our constant-cost assumption means this exchange or opportunity cost equation prevails for all possible moves from one point to another along Canada's production possibilities curve.

**Brazil** Brazil's production possibilities curve in Figure 22-1b represents a different opportunity cost ratio. In Brazil 20 tonnes of soybeans must be given up to get 10 tonnes of steel. The slope of the production possibilities curve is –2 (= –20 soybeans/ +10 steel). This means that in Brazil the domestic cost ratio for the two goods is 1 tonne of steel for 2 tonnes of soybeans, or

$$1\ S_t = 2\ S_{oy}$$

3. **SELF-SUFFICIENCY** If Canada and Brazil are isolated and are to be self-sufficient, each must choose some output mix on its production possibilities curve. Assume point A in Figure 22-1a is the optimal output mix in Canada. The choice of this combination of 18 tonnes of steel and 12 tonnes of soybeans equates the marginal benefit and marginal cost of both goods. Suppose Brazil's optimal product mix is 8 tonnes of steel and 4 tonnes of soybeans, indicated by point *B* in Figure 22-1b. These choices are also reflected in column 1, Table 22-1.

## Specialization According to Comparative Advantage

With these different cost ratios, determining the product in which Canada and Brazil should specialize is as follows: The **principle of comparative advantage** says that *total output will be greatest when each good is produced by that nation that has the*

**TABLE 22-1 International specialization according to comparative advantage and the gains from trade (*in tonnes*)**

| Country | (1) Outputs before specialization | (2) Outputs after specialization | (3) Amounts exported (–) and imported (+) | (4) Outputs available after trade | (5) = (4) – (1) Gains from specialization and trade |
|---|---|---|---|---|---|
| Canada | 18 steel<br>12 soybeans | 30 steel<br>0 soybeans | –10 steel<br>+15 soybeans | 20 steel<br>15 soybeans | 2 steel<br>3 soybeans |
| Brazil | 8 steel<br>4 soybeans | 0 steel<br>20 soybeans | +10 steel<br>–15 soybeans | 10 steel<br>5 soybeans | 2 steel<br>1 soybeans |

*lowest domestic opportunity cost.* In our two-nation illustration, Canada's domestic opportunity cost is lower for steel. Canada need only forgo 1 tonne of soybeans to produce 1 tonne of steel, whereas Brazil must forgo 2 tonnes of soybeans for 1 tonne of steel. *Canada has a comparative (cost) advantage in steel and should specialize in steel production.* The "world" (Canada and Brazil) is *not* economizing in the use of its resources if a specific product (steel) is produced by a high-cost producer (Brazil) when it could have been produced by a low-cost producer (Canada). To have Brazil produce steel would mean that the world economy would have to give up more soybeans than is necessary to obtain a tonne of steel.

Brazil has the lower domestic opportunity cost for soybeans; it must sacrifice only $\frac{1}{2}$ tonne of steel in producing 1 tonne of soybeans, while Canada must forgo 1 tonne of steel in producing a tonne of soybeans. *Brazil has a comparative advantage in soybeans and should specialize in soybean production.*

*Economizing—using fixed quantities of scarce resources so as to obtain the greatest total output—requires that any particular good be produced by that nation having the lower domestic opportunity cost, or a comparative advantage.* Canada should produce steel and Brazil soybeans. Note that this conclusion holds even though Canada has an absolute advantage in both steel and soybeans.

In column 2 of Table 22-1 we can verify that specialized production in accordance with the principle of comparative advantage allows the world to get more output from given amounts of resources. By specializing completely in steel, Canada can produce 30 tonnes of steel and no soybeans: Brazil, by specializing completely in soybeans, produces 20 tonnes of soybeans and no steel. The world ends up with more steel—30 tonnes, compared with 26 (= 18 + 8) tonnes—*and* more soybeans—20 tonnes, compared with 16 (= 12 + 4) tonnes—than where there is self-sufficiency or unspecialized production.

## Terms of Trade

But consumers of each nation want *both* steel and soybeans. They can have both if the two nations trade or exchange the two products. But what will be the **terms of trade**? At what exchange ratio will Canada and Brazil trade steel and soybeans?

Because $1\ S_t = 1\ S_{oy}$ in Canada, Canada must get *more than* 1 tonne of soybeans for each tonne of steel exported or it will not pay Canada to export steel in exchange for Brazilian soybeans. Canada must get a better "price" (more soybeans) for its steel in the world market than it can get domestically, or there is no gain from trade and it will not occur.

Similarly, because $1\ S_t = 2\ S_{oy}$ in Brazil, Brazil must get 1 tonne of steel by exporting some amount *less than* 2 tonnes of soybeans. Brazil must pay a lower "price" for steel in the world market than it must pay domestically, or it will not want to trade. The international exchange ratio or *terms of trade* must lie somewhere between

$1\ S_t = 1\ S_{oy}$ (Canada's cost conditions)

and

$1\ S_t = 2\ S_{oy}$ (Brazil's cost conditions)

But where between these limits will the world exchange ratio fall? Canada will prefer a ratio close to $1\ S_t = 2\ S_{oy}$, say, $1\ S_t = 1\frac{3}{4}\ S_{oy}$. Canadians want to get a great deal of soybeans for each tonne of steel they export. Similarly, Brazil wants a rate near 1 $S_t$ = 1 $S_{oy}$, say 1 $S_t$ = $1\frac{1}{4}$ $S_{oy}$. Brazil wants to export as little soybeans as possible for each tonne of steel it receives in exchange. The exchange ratio or terms of trade determines how the gains from international specialization and trade are divided between the two nations.

The final exchange ratio depends on world supply and demand for the two products. If overall world demand for soybeans is weak relative to its supply and the demand for steel is strong relative to its supply, the price of soybeans will be lower and the price of steel higher. The exchange ratio will settle near the 1 $S_t$ = 2 $S_{oy}$ figure Canada prefers. Under the opposite world supply and demand conditions, the ratio will settle near the 1 $S_t$ = 1 $S_{oy}$ level favourable to Brazil. (We will take up the topic of equilibrium world prices later in this chapter.)

## Gains from Trade

Suppose the international exchange ratio or terms of trade is 1 $S_t$ = $1\frac{1}{2}$ $S_{oy}$. The possibility of trading on these terms permits each nation to supplement its domestic production possibilities line with a **trading possibilities line**. This can be seen in ***Figure 22-2 (Key Graph)***. A trading possibilities line shows the options that a nation has by specializing in one product and trading (exporting) its specialty to obtain the other product. The trading possibilities lines in Figure 22-2 are drawn on the assumption that both nations specialize based on comparative advantage—Canada specializes completely in steel (point *S* in Figure 22-2a) and Brazil completely in soybeans (at point *c* in Figure 22-2b).

### Improved Options

Now Canada is not constrained by its domestic production possibilities line, which requires it to give up 1 tonne of steel for every tonne of soybeans it wants as it moves up its domestic production possibilities line, say, from point *S*. Instead, Canada, through trade with Brazil, can get $1\frac{1}{2}$ tonnes of soybeans for every tonne of steel it exports to Brazil, so long as Brazil has soybeans to export. Trading possibility line *SC′* thus represents the 1 $S_t$ = $1\frac{1}{2}$ $S_{oy}$ trading ratio.

Similarly, Brazil, starting at, say, point *c*, no longer has to move down its domestic production possibilities curve, giving up 2 tonnes of soybeans for each tonne of steel it wants. It can now export just $1\frac{1}{2}$ tonnes of soybeans for each tonne of steel it wants by moving down its trading possibilities line *cs′*.

Specialization and trade create a new exchange ratio between steel and soybeans, reflected in a nation's trading possibilities line. This exchange ratio is superior for both nations to the self-sufficiency exchange ratio embodied in the production possibilities line of each. By specializing in steel and trading for Brazil's soybeans, Canada can obtain *more than* 1 tonne of soybeans for 1 tonne of steel. By specializing in soybeans and trading for Canada's steel, Brazil can get 1 tonne of steel for *less than* 2 tonnes of soybeans.

### Added Output

By specializing according to comparative advantage and trading for those goods produced in other nations with greater domestic efficiency, Canada and Brazil can realize combinations of steel and soybeans beyond their production possibilities boundaries. *Specialization according to comparative advantage results in a more efficient allocation of world resources, and larger outputs of both steel and soybeans are therefore available to both nations.*

Suppose that at the 1 $S_t$ = $1\frac{1}{2}$ $S_{oy}$ terms of trade, Canada exports 10 tonnes of steel to Brazil and in return Brazil exports 15 tonnes of soybeans to Canada. How do the new quantities of steel and soybeans available to the two nations compare with the optimal product mixes that existed before specialization and trade? Point *A* in Figure 22-2a reminds us that Canada chose 18 tonnes of steel and 12 tonnes of soybeans originally. But, by producing 30 tonnes of steel and no soybeans, and by trading 10 tonnes of steel for 15 tonnes of soybeans, Canada can obtain 20 tonnes of steel and 15 tonnes of soybeans. This new, superior combination of steel and soybeans is shown by point *A′* in Figure 22-2a. Compared with the nontrading figures of 18 tonnes of steel and 12 tonnes of soybeans, Canada's **gains from trade** are 2 tonnes of steel and 3 tonnes of soybeans.

Similarly, recall that Brazil's optimal product mix was 4 tonnes of soybeans and 8 tonnes of steel (point *B*) before specialization and trade. Now, by specializing in soybeans and trading—producing 20 tonnes of soybeans and no steel and exporting 15 tonnes of its soybeans in exchange for 10 tonnes of Canadian steel—Brazil can have 5 tonnes of soybeans and 10 tonnes of steel. This new position is indicated by point *B′* in Figure 22-2b. Brazil's gains from trade are 1 tonne of soybeans and 2 tonnes of steel.

*As a result of specialization and trade, both countries have more of both products.* Table 22-1 summarizes the transaction and outcomes. You should study it very carefully.

KEY GRAPH

**FIGURE 22-2 Trading possibilities lines and the gains from trade**

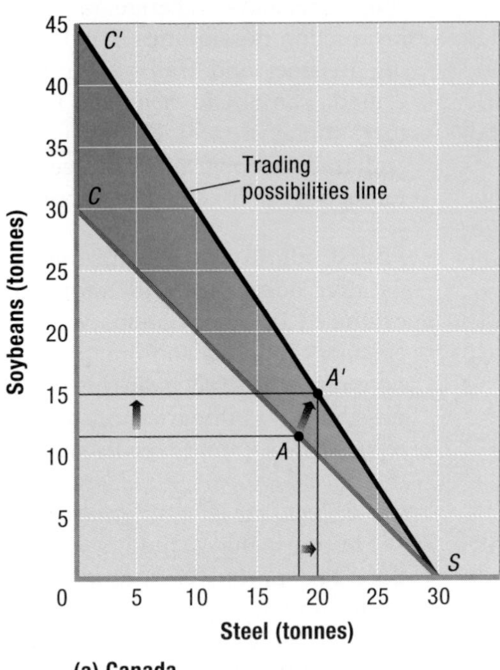

(a) Canada

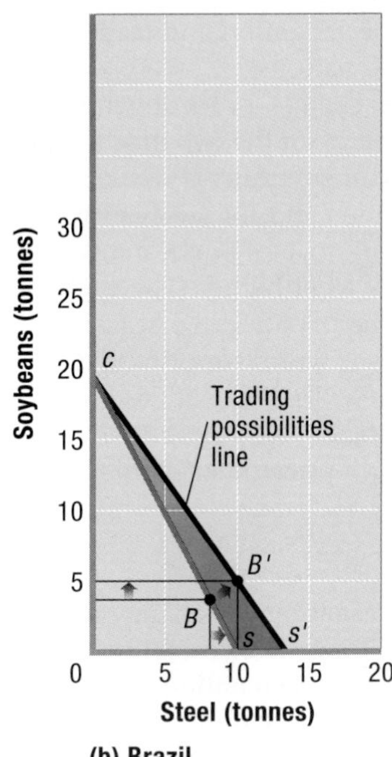

(b) Brazil

As a result of international specialization and trade, Canada and Brazil both can have levels of output higher than those attainable on their domestic production possibilities curves. (a) Canada can move from point A on its domestic production possibilities curve to, say, A′ on its trading possibilities line. (b) Brazil can move from B to B′.

## 22-2 QUICK QUIZ

1. The production possibilities curves in graphs (a) and (b) imply:
   - **(a)** increasing domestic opportunity costs.
   - **(b)** decreasing domestic opportunity costs.
   - **(c)** constant domestic opportunity costs.
   - **(d)** first decreasing, then increasing, domestic opportunity costs.
2. Before specialization, the domestic opportunity cost of producing 1 unit of steel is:
   - **(a)** 1 unit of soybeans in both Canada and Brazil.
   - **(b)** 1 unit of soybeans in Canada and 2 units of soybeans in Brazil.
   - **(c)** 2 units of soybeans in Canada and 1 unit of soybeans in Brazil.
   - **(d)** 1 unit of soybeans in Canada and $\frac{1}{2}$ unit of soybeans in Brazil.
3. After specialization and trade, the world output of steel and soybeans is:
   - **(a)** 20 tons of steel and 20 tons of soybeans.
   - **(b)** 45 tons of steel and 15 tons of soybeans.
   - **(c)** 30 tons of steel and 20 tons of soybeans.
   - **(d)** 10 tons of steel and 30 tons of soybeans.
4. After specialization and international trade:
   - **(a)** Canada can obtain units of soybeans at less cost than before trade.
   - **(b)** Brazil can obtain more than 20 tons of soybeans, if it so chooses.
   - **(c)** Canada no longer has a comparative advantage in producing steel.
   - **(d)** Brazil can benefit by prohibiting soybean imports from Canada.

**Answers:** 1. (c) 2. (b) 3. (c) 4. (a)

The fact that points $A'$ and $B'$ are economic positions superior to $A$ and $B$ is extremely important. Recall, from Chapter 2, that a nation can expand beyond its production possibilities boundary by (1) expanding the quantity and improving the quality of its resources or (2) realizing technological progress. We have now explained another way—international trade—for a nation to circumvent the output constraint imposed by its production possibilities curve. The effects of international specialization and trade are the equivalent of having more and better resources or discovering improved production techniques.

## Trade with Increasing Costs

To explain the basic principles underlying international trade, we simplified our analysis in several ways. For example, we limited discussion to two products and two nations. But multiproduct/multinational analysis yields the same conclusions. We also assumed constant opportunity costs (linear) production possibilities curves, which is a more substantive simplification. Let's consider the effect of allowing increasing opportunity costs (concave-from-the-origin production possibilities curves) to enter the picture.

Suppose that Canada and Brazil are initially at positions on their concave production possibilities curves where their domestic cost ratios are $1\ S_t = 1\ S_{oy}$ and $1\ S_t = 2\ S_{oy}$ as they were in our constant-cost analysis. As before, comparative advantage indicates that Canada should specialize in steel and Brazil in soybeans. But now, as Canada begins to expand steel production, its $1\ S_t = 1\ S_{oy}$ cost ratio will *fall*, it will have to sacrifice *more than* 1 tonne of soybeans to get 1 additional tonne of steel. Resources are no longer perfectly shiftable between alternative uses, as the constant-cost assumption implied. Resources less and less suited to steel production must be allocated to the Canadian steel industry in expanding steel output, and this means increasing costs—the sacrifice of larger and larger amounts of soybeans for each additional tonne of steel.

Similarly, Brazil, starting from its $1\ S_t = 2\ S_{oy}$ cost ratio position, expands soybean production. But as it does, it will find that its $1\ S_t = 2\ S_{oy}$ cost ratio begins to *rise*. Sacrificing a tonne of steel will free resources that can be used to produce something *less than* 2 tonnes of soybeans, because these transferred resources are less suitable to soybean production.

As the Canadian cost ratio falls from $1\ S_t = 1\ S_{oy}$ and Brazil's rises from $1\ S_t = 2\ S_{oy}$, a point will be reached where the cost ratios are equal in the two nations, perhaps at $1\ S_t = 1\tfrac{3}{4}\ S_{oy}$. At this point, the underlying basis for further specialization and trade—differing cost ratios—has disappeared. Most important, this point of equal cost ratios may be reached where Canada is still producing *some* soybeans along with its steel and Brazil is producing some steel along with its soybeans. *The primary effect of increasing costs is to make specialization less than complete.* For this reason we often find domestically produced products competing directly against identical or similar imported products within a particular economy. ***(Key Question 4)***

## The Case for Free Trade Restated

The case for free trade reduces to this one potent argument. *Through free trade based on the principle of comparative advantage, the world economy can achieve a more efficient allocation of resources and a higher level of material well-being than without free trade.* The resource mixes and technological knowledge of each country are somewhat different. Therefore each nation can produce particular commodities at different real costs. Each nation should produce goods for which its domestic opportunity costs are lower than the domestic opportunity cost of other nations, and exchange these specialties for products for which its domestic opportunity costs are high relative to those of other nations. If each nation does this, the world can realize the advantages of geographic and human specialization. The world— and each free-trading nation— can obtain a larger real income from the fixed supplies of resources available to it. Protection—barriers to free trade—lessens or eliminates gains from specialization. If nations cannot freely trade, they must shift resources from efficient (low-cost) to inefficient (high-cost) uses to satisfy their diverse wants.

One side benefit of free trade is that it promotes competition and deters monopoly. The increased competition from foreign firms forces domestic firms to adopt the lowest-cost production techniques. It also compels them to be innovative and progressive with respect to both product quality and production methods, thereby contributing to economic growth. And free trade provides consumers with a wider range of product choices. The reasons to favour free trade are essentially the same reasons that endorse competition.

A second side-benefit of free trade is that it links national interest and breaks down national animosities. Confronted with political disagreements, trading partners tend to negotiate rather than make war.

### 22-1 QUICK REVIEW

- International trade has always been important to Canada, and it is becoming increasingly so.
- International trade enables nations to specialize, enhance the productivity of their resources, and obtain a larger output.
- Comparative advantage means total world output will be greatest when each good is produced by that nation having the lowest domestic opportunity cost.
- Specialization is less than complete among nations because opportunity costs normally rise as any particular nation produces more of a particular good.

## SUPPLY AND DEMAND ANALYSIS OF EXPORTS AND IMPORTS

Supply and demand analysis helps us see how equilibrium prices and quantities of exports and imports are determined. The amount of a good or service that a nation will export or import depends on differences between equilibrium world and domestic prices. The equilibrium **world price** derives from the interaction of *world* supply and demand; it is the price at which the quantities supplied and demanded are equal globally. The equilibrium **domestic price** is determined by *domestic* supply and demand; it is the price that would prevail in a closed economy—one having no international trade. It is the price at which domestic supply and demand are equal.

Because of comparative advantages and disadvantages, no-trade domestic prices *may* or *may not* equal world equilibrium prices. When economies are opened for international trade, differences between world and domestic prices motivate exports or imports. To see how, let's now look at the international effects of such price differences in a simple two-nation world.

### Supply and Demand in Canada

Suppose the world consists of just Canada and the United States, each producing aluminum. There are no trade barriers such as tariffs and quotas. Also, to keep things simple, let's ignore international transportation costs.

Figure 22-3a shows the domestic supply curve $S_d$ and domestic demand curve $D_d$ for aluminum in Canada. The intersection of $S_d$ and $D_d$ determines the equilibrium domestic price is $1.25 per kilogram and the equilibrium domestic quantity of 100 million kilograms. The market clears at $1.25—there are no domestic surpluses nor shortages of aluminum.

But what if the Canadian economy is opened to world trade and the *world price* of aluminum is above or below this $1.25 domestic price?

**Canadian Export Supply** If the world aluminum price exceeds $1.25, Canadian firms will produce more than 100 million kilograms and export the excess domestic output to the rest of the world (United States). First, consider a world price of $1.50. We see from the supply curve $S_d$ that Canadian aluminum firms will produce 125 million kilograms of aluminum at that price. The demand curve $D_d$ tells us that Canadians will purchase only 75 million kilograms at $1.50. A domestic surplus of 50 million kilograms of aluminum will result. Canadian producers will export these 50 million kilograms at the $1.50 world price.

What if the world price is $1.75? The supply curve shows that Canadian firms will produce 150 million kilograms of aluminum, while the demand curve tells us that Canadian consumers will buy only 50 million kilograms. The domestic surplus of 100 million kilograms will be exported.

Towards the top of Figure 22-3b we plot on the horizontal scale the domestic surpluses—the Canadian exports—occurring at world prices above the $1.25 domestic equilibrium price. When the world and domestic prices are equal (= $1.25), the quantity of exports supplied is zero (point *a*). There is *no* surplus of domestic output to export. But when the world price is $1.50, Canadian firms export 50 million kilograms of surplus aluminum (point *b*). At a $1.75 world price, the domestic surplus of 100 million kilograms is exported (point *c*).

The Canadian **export supply curve**, found by connecting points such as *a*, *b*, and *c*, shows the amount of aluminum that Canadian producers will export at each world price above $1.25. This curve *slopes upward*, revealing a direct or positive relationship between the world price and amount of Canadian exports. *As world prices rise relative to domestic prices, Canadian exports increase.*

**FIGURE 22-3 Canadian export supply and import demand**

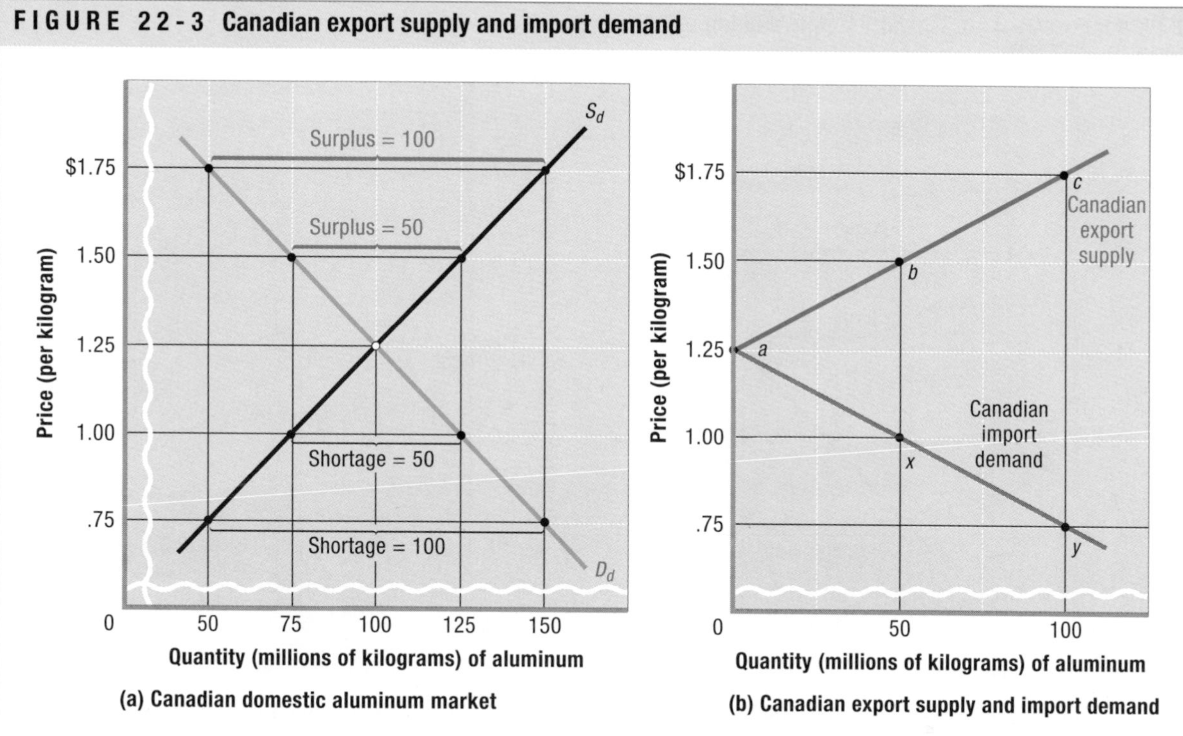


In (a) world prices above the $1.25 domestic price create domestic surpluses of aluminum. As shown by the export supply curve in (b), these surpluses are exported. Domestic shortages occur when the world price is below $1.25 (a). These shortages are met by importing aluminum (b). The export supply curve shows the direct relationship between world prices and Canadian exports; the import supply curve portrays the inverse relationship between world prices and Canadian imports.

**Canadian Import Demand** If the world price is below $1.25 Canada will end up importing aluminum. Consider a $1.00 world price. The supply curve in Figure 22-3a reveals at that price Canadian firms will produce only 75 million kilograms of aluminum. But the demand curve shows that Canadians want to buy 125 million kilograms at that price. The result is a domestic shortage of 50 million kilograms. To satisfy this shortage, 50 million kilograms of aluminum will be imported into Canada.

At an even lower $.75 world price, Canadian producers supply only 50 million kilograms. Because Canadian consumers want to buy 150 million kilograms, there is a domestic shortage of 100 million kilograms. Imports will flow to Canada to make up the difference. That is, at a $.75 world price Canadian firms supply 50 million kilograms and foreign firms supply 100 million kilograms.

In Figure 22-3b we plot the Canadian **import demand curve**. This *downsloping curve* shows the amounts of aluminum that will be imported at world prices below the $1.25 Canadian domestic price. The relationship between world prices and imports is inverse or negative. At a world price of $1.25, domestic output will satisfy Canadian demand; imports will be zero (point *a*). But at $1.00 Canadians will import 50 million kilograms of aluminum (point *x*); at $.75, they will import 100 million kilograms (point *y*). Connecting points *a*, *x*, and *y* yields a *downsloping* Canadian import demand curve. *It reveals that as world prices fall relative to domestic prices, Canadian imports increase.*

## Supply and Demand in the United States

We repeat our analysis in Figure 22-4, this time for the United States. (We have converted American dollar prices to Canadian dollar prices via the exchange rate.) Note that the domestic supply curve $S_d$ and demand curve $D_d$ for aluminum in the United States yield a domestic price of $1.00, which is $.25 lower than the $1.25 Canadian domestic price.

The analysis proceeds exactly as for Canada. If the world price is $1.00, Americans will neither export nor import aluminum (which gives us

**FIGURE 22-4 U.S. export supply and import demand**

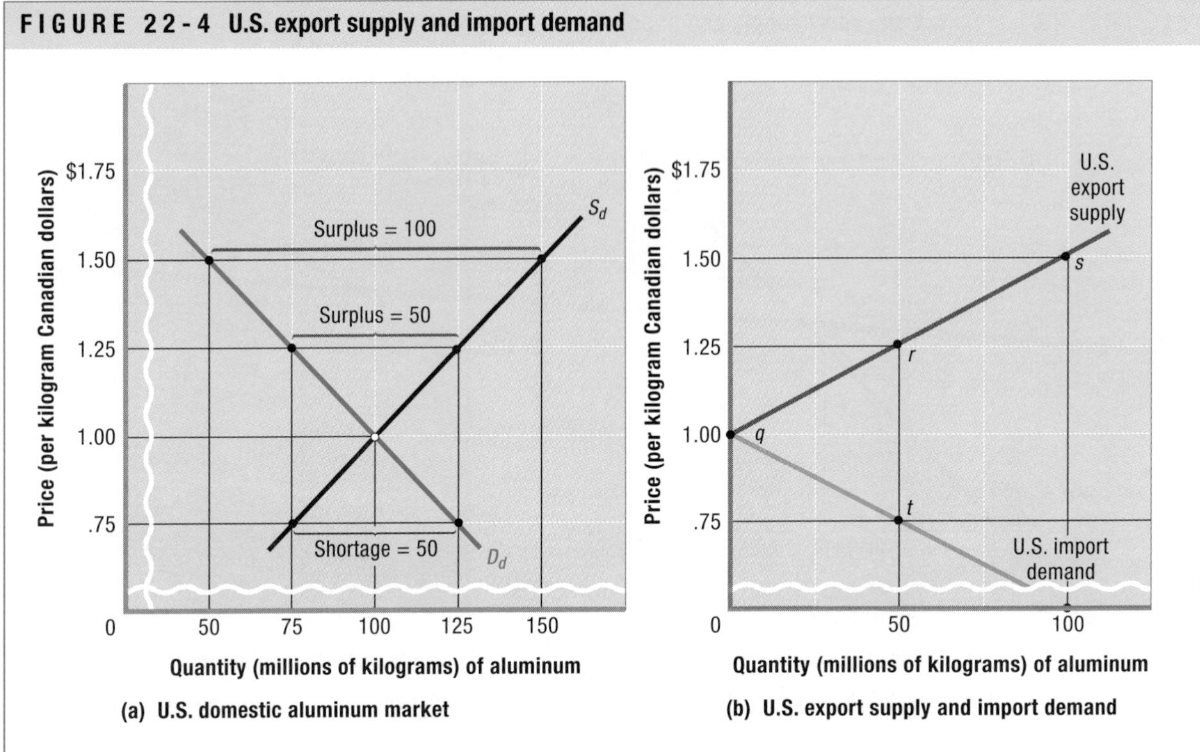


In (a) domestic production of aluminum in the United States exceeds domestic consumption at all world prices above the $1.00 domestic price. These domestic surpluses result in U.S. exports (b). When the domestic price falls below $1.00, domestic shortages occur (a) and imports flow to the United States (b). The U.S. export supply curve and import demand curve depict these relationships.

point $q$ in Figure 22-4b). At world prices above $1.00, American firms will produce more aluminum than American consumers will buy. The surplus will be exported. At a $1.25 world price, Figure 22-4a tells us that the United States will have and export a domestic surplus of 50 million kilograms (yielding point $r$). At $1.50 it will have and export a domestic surplus of 100 million kilograms (point $s$). Connecting these points yields the upsloping American *export supply curve* that reflects the domestic surpluses (and thus exports) occurring when the world price exceeds the $1.00 American domestic price.

Domestic shortages occur in the United States at world prices below $1.00. At a $.75 world price, Figure 22-4a shows that American consumers want to buy 125 million kilograms of aluminum but American firms will produce only 75 million kilograms. The shortage will bring 50 million kilograms of imports to Canada (point $t$ in Figure 22-4b). The American *import demand curve* in that figure shows American imports at world aluminum prices below the $1.00 American domestic price.

## Equilibrium World Price, Exports, and Imports

We now have the tools to determine the equilibrium world price of aluminum and the equilibrium world levels of exports and imports. Figure 22-5 combines the Canadian export supply curve and import demand curve in Figure 22-3b and the American export supply curve and import demand curve in Figure 22-4b. The two Canadian curves proceed rightward from the $1.25 domestic price; the two American curves proceed rightward from the $1.00 American domestic price. *International equilibrium occurs in this two-nation model where one nation's import demand curve intersects another nation's export supply curve.* In this case Canada's import demand curve intersects America's export supply curve at $e$. There, the world price of aluminum is $1.12. The American export supply curve indicates that the United States will export 25 million kilograms of aluminum at this price. Also at this price Canada will import 25 million kilograms from the United States, indicated

**FIGURE 22-5 Equilibrium world price and quantity of exports and imports**

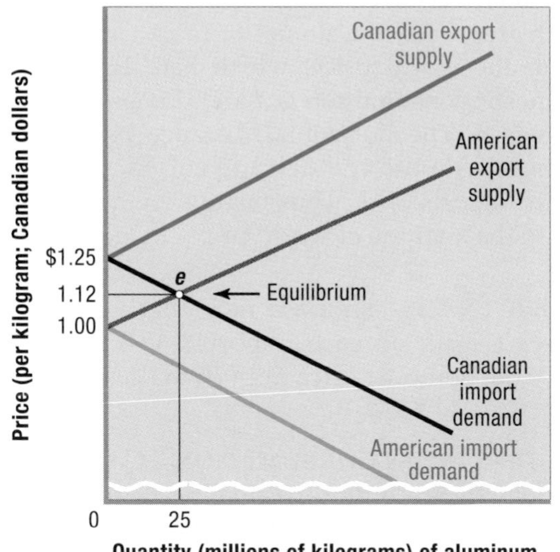


In a two-nation world, the equilibrium world price (= $1.12) is determined at the intersection of one nation's export supply curve and another nation's import demand curve. This intersection also decides the equilibrium volume of exports and imports. Here, the United States exports 25 million kilograms of aluminum to Canada.

by the Canadian import demand curve. The $1.12 world price equates the quantity of imports demanded and the quantity of exports supplied (= 25 million kilograms). Thus there will be world trade of 25 million kilograms of aluminum at $1.12 per kilogram.

Note that after trade, the single $1.12 world price will prevail in both Canada and the United States. *Only one price for a standardized commodity can persist in a highly competitive market.* With trade, all consumers can buy a kilogram of aluminum for $1.12 and all producers can sell it for that price. This world price means that Americans will pay more for aluminum with trade (= $1.12) than without it (= $1.00). The increased American output caused by trade raises American production costs and therefore the price of aluminum in the United States. Canadians, however, pay less for aluminum with trade (= $1.12) than without it (= $1.25). The Canadian gain comes from America's comparative cost advantage in producing aluminum.

Why would the United States willingly send 50 million kilograms of its aluminum output to Canada for consumption? Producing this output uses up scarce American resources and drives up the price of aluminum for Americans. Americans are willing to export aluminum to Canada because Americans can gain the means—the earnings of Canadian dollars—to import other goods, say, automobile parts, from Canada. American exports enable Americans to acquire imports that have greater value to Americans than the exported aluminum. American exports to Canada finance American imports from Canada. ***(Key Question 6)***

## TRADE BARRIERS

No matter how compelling the case for free trade, barriers to free trade *do* exist. Let's examine Chapter 6's list of trade impediments more closely.

1. **Tariffs** are excise taxes on imported goods; they may be imposed for purposes of revenue or to protect domestic firms.

   A **revenue tariff** is usually applied to a product not produced domestically, for example, coffee and bananas. Rates on revenue tariffs are modest; their purpose is to provide the federal government with revenues.

   A **protective tariff** is designed to shield domestic producers from foreign competition. Although protective tariffs are usually not high enough to stop importation of foreign goods, they put foreign producers at a competitive disadvantage in selling in domestic markets.
2. An **import quota** specifies the maximum amount of a commodity that may be imported in any period. Import quotas can more effectively retard international commerce than tariffs. A product might be imported in large quantities despite high tariffs; low import quotas completely prohibit imports once the quotas are filled.
3. A **nontariff barrier** (NTBs) is a licensing requirement, unreasonable standards pertaining to product quality and safety, or unnecessary red tape used to restrict imports. Japan and the European countries frequently require their domestic importers of foreign goods to obtain licences. By restricting the issuance of licences, imports can be restricted. Great Britain uses this barrier to bar the importation of coal.
4. A **voluntary export restriction** (VER) is a trade barrier by which foreign firms "volun-

tarily" limit the amount of their exports to a particular country. VERs, which have the effect of import quotas, are agreed to by exporters in the hope of avoiding more stringent trade barriers. Japanese auto manufacturers agreed to a VER on exports to Canada under the threat of the imposition of low import quotas.

Later in this chapter we will consider the specific arguments and appeals made to justify protection.

## Economic Impact of Tariffs

Once again we use supply and demand analysis—now to examine the economic effects of protective tariffs. Curves $D_d$ and $S_d$ in Figure 22-6 show domestic demand and supply for a product in which Canada has a comparative *dis*advantage, for example, video cassette recorders (VCRs). (Disregard $S_d + Q$ for now.) Without world trade, the domestic price and output would be $P_d$ and $q$ respectively.

**FIGURE 22-6 The economic effects of a protective tariff or an import quota**

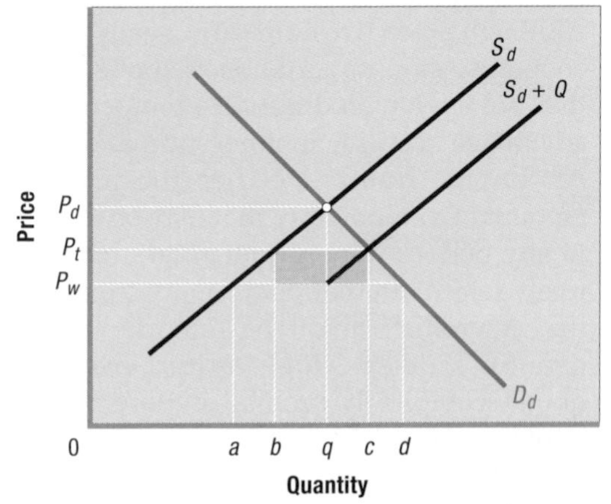


A tariff of $P_wP_t$ will reduce domestic consumption from *d* to *c*. Domestic producers will be able to sell more output (*b* rather than *a*) at a higher price ($P_t$ rather than $P_w$). Foreign exporters are injured because they are able to sell less output (*bc* rather than *ad*) in Canada. The shaded area represents the amount of tariffs paid by Canadian consumers. An import quota of *bc* units will have the same effects as the tariff, with one exception: the shaded area will go to foreign producers rather than to the Canadian government.

Assume now that the domestic economy is opened to world trade and that the Japanese, who have a comparative advantage in VCRs, begin to sell their recorders in Canada. We assume that with free trade the domestic price cannot differ from the world price, which here is $P_w$. At $P_w$ domestic consumption is *d* and domestic production is *a*. The horizontal distance between the domestic supply and demand curves at $P_w$ represents imports of *ad*. Thus far, our analysis is similar to the analysis of world prices in Figure 22-3.

**Direct Effects** Suppose now that Canada imposes a tariff on each imported VCR. This will raise the domestic price from $P_w$ to $P_t$ and has four effects.

1. **DECLINE IN CONSUMPTION** Consumption of video recorders in Canada will decline from *d* to *c* as the higher price moves buyers up and to the left along their demand curve. The tariff prompts consumers to buy fewer recorders and to reallocate a portion of their expenditures to less-desired substitute products. Canadian consumers are injured by the tariff, since they pay $P_wP_t$ more for each of the *c* units they now buy at price $P_t$.
2. **INCREASED DOMESTIC PRODUCTION** Canadian producers—who are *not* subject to the tariff—receive higher price $P_t$ per unit. Because this new price is higher than the pre-tariff or world price of $P_w$, the domestic VCR industry moves up and to the right along its supply curve $S_d$, increasing domestic output from *a* to *b*. Domestic producers thus enjoy both a higher price and expanded sales, which explains why domestic producers lobby for protective tariffs. But from a social point of view, the expanded domestic production of *ab* means that the tariff permits domestic producers of recorders to bid resources away from other, more efficient, Canadian industries.
3. **DECLINE IN IMPORTS** Japanese producers are hurt. Although the sale price of recorders is higher by $P_wP_t$, that amount accrues to the Canadian government, not to Japanese producers. The after-tariff world price, and thus the per-unit revenue to Japanese producers, remains at $P_w$, while the volume of Canadian imports (Japanese exports) falls from *ad* to *bc*.
4. **TARIFF REVENUE** The shaded rectangle indicates the amount of revenue that the tariff yields. Total revenue from the tariff is deter-

mined by multiplying the tariff, $P_wP_t$ per unit, by the number of imported recorders, *bc*. This tariff revenue is a transfer of income from consumers to government and does *not* represent any net change in the nation's economic well-being. The result is that government gains a portion of what consumers lose by paying more for VCRs.

**Indirect Effects** Tariffs have a subtle effect beyond what our supply and demand diagram can show. Because of diminished sales of VCRs in Canada, Japan will earn fewer dollars with which to buy Canadian exports. Canadian export industries—industries in which Canada has a comparative advantage—will cut production and release resources. These are highly efficient industries, as evidenced by their comparative advantage and ability to sell goods in world markets.

*Tariffs directly promote the expansion of inefficient industries that do not have a comparative advantage; they also indirectly cause contraction of relatively efficient industries that do have a comparative advantage.* This means tariffs cause resources to be shifted in the wrong direction. We know that specialization and world trade lead to more efficient use of world resources and greater world output. But protective tariffs reduce world trade. Therefore, tariffs also reduce efficiency and the world's real output.

### Economic Impact of Quotas

We noted previously that an import quota is a legal limit placed on the amount of some product that can be imported each year. The economic impact of quotas is similar to that of a tariff with one salient difference: While tariffs generate revenue for the Canadian government, a quota transfers that revenue to foreign producers.

Suppose in Figure 22-6 that, instead of imposing a tariff of $P_wP_t$ per unit, Canada prohibits any Japanese imports of VCRs in excess of *bc* units. In other words, an import quota of *bc* VCRs is imposed on Japan. We have deliberately chosen the size of this quota to be the same amount as imports would be under a $P_wP_t$ tariff so we are comparing "equivalent" situations. As a consequence of the quota, the supply of recorders is $S_d + Q$ in Canada. This consists of the domestic supply plus the constant amount *bc* (= *Q*), that importers will provide at each domestic price. The $S_d + Q$ supply curve does not exist below price $P_w$ because Japanese producers would not export VCRs to Canada at any price *below* $P_w$ when they can sell them to other countries at the world market price of $P_w$.

Most of the economic results are the same as with a tariff. VCR prices are higher ($P_t$ instead of $P_w$) because imports have been reduced from *ad* to *bc*. Domestic consumption of VCRs is down from *ad* to *bc*. Canadian producers enjoy both a higher price ($P_t$ rather than $P_w$) and increased sales (*b* rather than *a*).

The difference is that the price increase of $P_wP_t$ paid by Canadian consumers on imports of *bc*—the shaded area—no longer goes to Revenue Canada as tariff (tax) revenue, but flows to those Japanese firms that have acquired the rights to sell VCRs in Canada. Other things being the same, the economic effects of a tariff are better for Canadians than are those of a quota. A tariff generates government revenue, which can be used to cut other taxes or to finance public goods and services that benefit Canadians. In contrast, the higher price created by quotas results in additional revenue for foreign producers. ***(Key Question 7)***

## THE CASE FOR PROTECTION: A CRITICAL REVIEW

Despite the logic of specialization and trade, there are still protectionists in some union halls, corporate boardrooms, and Parliament. What arguments do protectionists make to justify trade barriers? How valid are these arguments?

### Military Self-Sufficiency Argument

The argument here is not economic but political-military: Protective tariffs are needed to preserve or strengthen industries that produce the materials essential for national defence. In an uncertain world, the political-military objectives (self-sufficiency) sometimes must take precedence over economic goals (efficiency in the use of world resources).

Unfortunately, it is difficult to measure and compare the benefit of increased national security against the cost of economic inefficiency when protective tariffs are imposed. The economist can only point out that there are economic costs when a nation levies tariffs to increase military self-sufficiency.

The self-sufficiency argument is open to serious abuse. Nearly every industry can claim that it makes direct or indirect contributions to national security and hence deserves protection from imports.

Are there not better ways than tariffs to provide needed strength in strategic industries? When it is achieved through tariffs, this self-sufficiency increases the domestic prices of the products of the protected industry. Thus only those consumers who buy the industry's products shoulder the cost of greater military security. A direct subsidy to strategic industries, financed out of general tax revenues, would distribute these costs more equitably.

## Increased Domestic Employment Argument

Arguing for a tariff to "save Canadian jobs" becomes fashionable as an economy encounters a recession. In an economy that engages in international trade, exports involve spending on domestic output and imports reflect spending to obtain part of another nation's output. So, in this argument, reducing imports will divert spending on another nation's output to spending on domestic output. Thus domestic output and employment will rise. But this argument has several shortcomings:

1. **JOB CREATION FROM IMPORTS** While imports may eliminate some Canadian jobs, they create others. Imports may have eliminated the jobs of some Canadian steel and textile workers in recent years, but other workers have gained jobs unloading ships and selling imported cars and imported electronic equipment. Import restrictions alter the composition of employment, but they may have little or no effect on the volume of employment.
2. **FALLACY OF COMPOSITION** All nations cannot simultaneously succeed in restricting imports while maintaining their exports; what is true for *one* nation is not true for *all* nations. The exports of one nation must be the imports of another nation. To the extent that one country is able to expand its economy through an excess of exports over imports, the resulting excess of imports over exports worsens another economy's unemployment problem. It is no wonder that tariffs and import quotas meant to achieve domestic full employment are called "beggar my neighbour" policies: They achieve short-run domestic goals by making trading partners poorer.
3. **POSSIBILITY OF RETALIATION** Nations adversely affected by tariffs and quotas are likely to retaliate, causing a "trade-barrier war" that will choke off trade and make all nations worse off. For example, when the United States, under the Smoot-Hawley Tariff Act of 1930, imposed the highest tariffs ever enacted, the action backfired miserably. Rather than increasing U.S. output, this tariff act only led to retaliatory restrictions by affected nations, including Canada. This trade war caused a further contraction of international trade and lowered the income and employment levels of all nations. As stated by an international trade expert:

   > A trade war in which countries restrict each other's exports in pursuit of some illusory advantage is not much like a real war. On the one hand, nobody gets killed. On the other, unlike real wars, it is almost impossible for anyone to win, since the main losers when a country imposes barriers to trade are not foreign exporters but domestic residents. In effect, a trade war is a conflict in which each country uses most of its ammunition to shoot itself in the foot.[1]
4. **LONG-RUN FEEDBACKS** In the long run, forcing an excess of exports over imports cannot exceed in raising domestic employment. It is through Canadian imports that foreign nations earn dollars for buying Canadian exports. In the long run a nation must import to export. The long-run impact of tariffs is not to increase domestic employment but at best to reallocate workers away from export industries and to protected domestic industries. This shift implies a less efficient allocation of resources.

## Diversification for Stability Argument

Highly specialized economies such as Saudi Arabia's (based on oil) and Cuba's (based on sugar) are very dependent on international markets for their incomes. In these economies, wars, international political developments, recessions abroad, and random fluctuations in world supply and

[1] Paul Krugman, *Peddling Prosperity* (New York: W. W. Norton & Co., 1994), p. 287.

demand for one or two particular goods can cause deep declines in export revenues and therefore in domestic income. Tariff and quota protection are allegedly needed in such nations to enable greater industrial diversification. That way, these economies will not be so dependent on exporting one or two products to obtain the other goods they need. Such goods will be available domestically, thereby providing greater domestic stability.

There is some truth in this diversification for stability argument. There are also two serious shortcomings:

1. The argument has little or no relevance to Canada and other advanced economies.
2. The economic costs of diversification may be great; for example, one-crop economies may be highly inefficient at manufacturing.

## Infant Industry Argument

The infant industry argument contends that protective tariffs are needed to allow new domestic industries to establish themselves. Temporarily shielding young domestic firms from the severe competition of more mature and more efficient foreign firms will give infant industries a chance to develop and become efficient producers.

This argument for protection rests on an alleged exception to the case for free trade. The exception is that young industries have not had, and if they face mature foreign competition will never have, the chance to make the long-run adjustments needed for larger scale and greater efficiency in production. In this view, tariff protection for such infant industries will correct a misallocation of world resources perpetuated by historically different levels of economic development between domestic and foreign industries.

### Counterarguments

There are some logical problems with this infant industry argument:

1. In the developing nations it is difficult to determine which industries are the infants that are capable of achieving economic maturity and therefore deserving protection.
2. Protective tariffs may persist even after industrial maturity has been realized.
3. Most economists believe that if infant industries are to be subsidized, there are better means than tariffs for doing it. Direct subsidies, for example, have the advantage of making explicit which industries are being aided and to what degree.

### Strategic Trade Policy

In recent years the infant industry argument has taken a modified form in advanced economies. Now proponents contend that government should use trade barriers to reduce the risk of investing in product development by domestic firms, particularly where advanced technology is involved. Firms protected from foreign competition can grow more rapidly and achieve greater economies of scale than unprotected foreign competitors. The protected firms can eventually dominate world markets because of their lower costs. Supposedly, dominance of world markets will enable the domestic firms to return high profits to the home nation. These profits will exceed the domestic sacrifices caused by trade barriers. Also, advances in high-technology industries are deemed beneficial because the advances achieved in one domestic industry often can be transferred to other domestic industries.

Japan and South Korea, in particular, have been accused of using this form of **strategic trade policy**. The problem with this strategy, and therefore this argument for tariffs, is that the nations put at a disadvantage by strategic trade policies tend to retaliate with tariffs of their own. The outcome may be higher tariffs worldwide, reductions of world trade, and the loss of potential gains from technological advances.

## Protection Against Dumping Argument

This argument contends that tariffs are needed to protect domestic firms from "dumping" by foreign producers. **Dumping** is the selling of excess goods in a foreign market at a price below cost. Economists cite two plausible reasons for this behaviour:

1. Firms may use dumping abroad to drive out domestic competitors there, thus obtaining monopoly power and monopoly prices and profits for the importing firm. The long-term economic profits resulting from this strategy may more than offset the earlier losses that accompany the below-cost sales.
2. Dumping may be a form of *price discrimination*, which is charging different prices to different customers even though costs are the same. The foreign seller may find it can maximize its profit by charging a high price in its monopolized domestic market while unloading its sur-

plus output at a lower price in Canada. The surplus output may be needed so the firm can obtain the overall per-unit cost saving associated with large-scale production. The higher profit in the home market more than makes up for the losses incurred on sales abroad.

Because dumping is a legitimate concern, many nations prohibit it. For example, where dumping is shown to injure Canadian firms, the federal government imposes tariffs called "antidumping duties" on the specific goods (see this chapter's In the Media). But there are relatively few documented cases of dumping each year, and those few cases do *not* justify widespread, permanent tariffs.

In fact, foreign producers argue that Canada uses dumping allegations and antidumping duties to restrict legitimate trade. Some foreign firms clearly can produce certain goods at substantially less per-unit cost than Canadian competitors. So, what may seem to be dumping actually is comparative advantage at work. If antidumping laws are abused, they can increase the price of imports and restrict competition in the Canadian market. This reduced competition can allow Canadian firms to raise prices at consumers' expense. And even where true dumping does occur, Canadian consumers gain from the lower-priced product, at least in the short run, much as they gain from a price war among Canadian producers.

## Cheap Foreign Labour Argument

The cheap foreign labour argument says that domestic firms and workers must be shielded from the ruinous competition of countries where wages are low. If protection is not provided, cheap imports will flood Canadian markets and the prices of Canadian goods—along with the wages of Canadian workers—will be pulled down. That is, the domestic living standards in Canada will be reduced.

This argument can be rebutted at several levels. The logic of the argument suggests that it is *not* mutually beneficial for rich and poor persons to trade with one another. However, that is not the case. A low-income farm worker may pick lettuce or tomatoes for a rich landowner, and both may benefit from the transaction. And Canadian consumers gain when they buy a Taiwanese-made pocket radio for $12 as opposed to a similar Canadian-made radio selling for $20.

Also, recall that gains from trade are based on comparative advantage, not on absolute advantage. Looking back at Figure 22-1, suppose Canada and Brazil have labour forces of exactly the same size. Noting the positions of the production possibilities curves, we observe that Canadian labour can produce more of *either* good. Thus, it is more productive. Because of this greater productivity, we can expect wages and living standards to be higher for Canadian labour. Brazil's less productive labour will receive lower wages.

The cheap foreign labour argument suggests that, to maintain our standard of living, Canada should not trade with low-wage Brazil. Suppose it does not. Will wages and living standards rise in Canada as a result? No. To obtain soybeans, Canada will have to reallocate a portion of its labour from its efficient steel industry to its inefficient soybean industry. As a result, the average productivity of Canadian labour will fall, as will real wages and living standards. The labour forces of *both* countries will have diminished standards of living because without specialization and trade they will have less output available to them. Compare column 4 with column 1 in Table 22-1 or points $A'$ and $B'$ with $A$ and $B$ in Figure 22-2 to confirm this point.

## A Summing Up

These many arguments for protection are not weighty. Under proper conditions, the infant-industry argument stands as a valid exception, justifiable on economic grounds. And on political-military grounds, the self-sufficiency argument can be used to validate some protection. But both arguments are open to severe overuse, and both neglect other ways of promoting industrial development and military self-sufficiency. Most other arguments are emotional appeals—half-truths and fallacies. These arguments see only the immediate and direct consequences of protective tariffs. They ignore the fact that in the long run a nation must import to export.

There is also compelling historical evidence suggesting that free trade has led to prosperity and growth and that protectionism has had the opposite effects. Here are several examples:

1. The Canadian Constitution forbids individual provinces from levying tariffs, and that makes Canada a huge free-trade area. Economic his-

torians cite this as a positive factor in the economic development of Canada.

2. Great Britain's shift towards freer international trade in the mid-nineteenth century was instrumental in its industrialization and growth at that time.
3. The creation of the Common Market in Europe after World War II eliminated tariffs among member nations. Economists agree that creation of this free-trade area, now the European Union, was a major ingredient in Western European prosperity.
4. The trend towards tariff reduction since the mid-1930s stimulated post-World War II expansion of the world economy.
5. The high tariffs imposed by the Smoot-Hawley Act of 1930 in the United States and the retaliation by most of the industrialized world worsened the Great Depression of the 1930s.
6. Studies of developing countries strongly suggest that those that have relied on import restrictions to protect their domestic industries have had slow growth compared to those pursuing more open economic policies (see Global Perspective 22-2).

## 22-2 GLOBAL PERSPECTIVE

**Growth per capita and level of trade protection**

Higher levels of trade protection in less developed nations are generally associated with lower levels of economic growth, as measured by average annual increases in output per person.

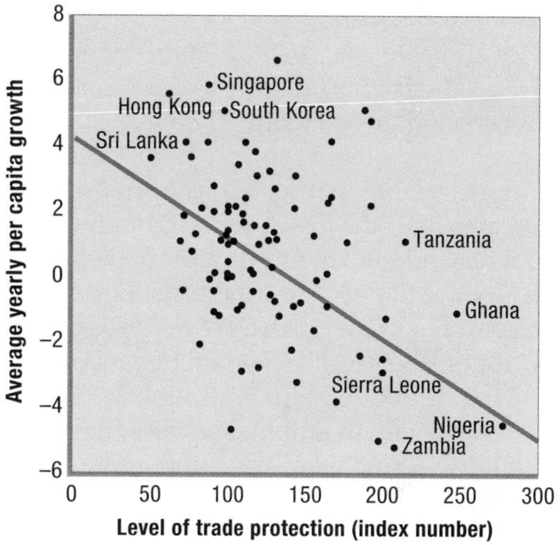


*Source:* David M. Gould, Graeme L. Woodbridge, and Roy J. Ruffin, "The Theory and Practice of International Trade," *Economic Review*, Federal Reserve Bank of Dallas, 4th Quarter, 1993, p. 3. Data are for 1976–1985.

## 22-2 QUICK REVIEW

- A nation will export a particular product if the world price exceeds the domestic price; it will import the product if the world price is less than the domestic price.
- In a two-country model, equilibrium world prices and equilibrium quantities of exports and imports occur where one nation's export supply curve intersects the other nation's import demand curve.
- Trade barriers include tariffs, import quotas, nontariff barriers, and voluntary export restrictions.
- A tariff on a product increases price, reduces consumption, increases domestic production, reduces imports, and generates tariff revenue for government; an import quota does the same, except a quota generates revenue for foreign producers rather than for the government imposing the quota.
- Most arguments for trade protection are special-interest pleas that, if followed, would create gains for protected industries and their workers at the expense of greater losses for the economy.

## COSTS OF PROTECTION

In spite of the weakness of most arguments for trade protection, Canada and most other countries continue to impose some protective measures. (These tariffs and quotas, however, are falling under terms of the recent world trade agreements.) How costly are trade protections to Canada?

### Cost to Society

Figure 22-6 shows that tariffs and quotas impose costs on domestic consumers, but provide gains to domestic producers, and in the case of tariffs, revenue to the federal government. The consumer cost of trade restrictions can be calculated by determining the effect they have on prices of protected goods. Protection will raise the price of a product in three ways.

1. The price of the imported product goes up.
2. The higher price of imports causes some consumers to shift their purchases to higher-priced domestically produced goods.
3. The prices of domestically produced goods rise because import competition has declined.

Studies indicate the costs to consumers of protected products substantially exceed the gains to producers and government. There is a sizable net cost or efficiency loss to society from trade protection. Furthermore, net losses from trade barriers are greater than the losses reported in most studies. Tariffs and quotas produce myriad costly, difficult-to-quantify secondary effects. For example, the import restraints on steel in the 1980s drove up the price of steel to all Canadian buyers of steel—including the Canadian automobile industry. Therefore Canadian automakers had higher costs than otherwise and were less competitive in world markets.

Finally, industries employ large amounts of economic resources to influence Parliament to pass and retain protectionist laws. Because these rent-seeking efforts divert resources away from more socially desirable purposes, trade restrictions impose that cost on society.

Conclusion: The gains that Canada's trade barriers create for protected industries and their workers come at the expense of much greater losses for the entire economy. The result is economic inefficiency.

### Impact on Income Distribution

Studies also show that import restrictions affect low-income families proportionately more than high-income families. Because tariffs and quotas act much like sales or excise taxes, these trade restrictions are highly regressive. That is, the "overcharge" associated with trade protection falls *as a percentage of income* as income increases. Example: Households pay more per year for clothing because of trade restrictions. Relative to their incomes, the burden of this protectionism is heavier for poorer households than for wealthier ones. ***(Key Question 11)***

## CANADIAN INTERNATIONAL TRADE POLICY

We now turn to Canadian trade policy, the results of these policies, and proposed alternatives.

### The National Policy

The general policy on which the present tariff structure of Canada was built was adopted shortly after Confederation. The **National Policy**, introduced in 1879, imposed high tariffs to protect Canada's manufacturing sector. Canada's manufacturing remained highly protected up to 1945. Tariffs on our manufactured goods have been falling ever since, but until very recently our manufacturing sector was highly protected.

If tariffs are economically undesirable, why has Parliament been willing to employ them? The answer lies in the political realities of tariff making and the special-interest effect. A small group of domestic producers who will receive large economic gains from tariffs and quotas will press vigorously for protection through well-financed political lobbyists. The large number of consumers who individually will have small losses imposed on them will be generally uninformed, and unorganized.

The public may be won over, not only by the vigour, but also by the apparent plausibility ("Cut imports and prevent domestic unemployment") and the patriotic ring ("Buy Canadian!") of the protectionists. Alleged tariff benefits are immediate and clear-cut to the public. The costs are obscure and widely dispersed over the economy. Moreover, the public is likely to stumble on the fallacy of composition: "If a quota on Japanese automobiles will preserve profits and employment in the Canadian automobile industry, how can it be detrimental to the economy as a whole?"

## GENERAL TRADE LIBERALIZATION

The across-the-board reduction of tariffs has come about because of various bilateral agreements Canada signed. By incorporating **most-favoured-nation clauses** in these agreements, the resulting tariff reductions not only apply to the specific nation negotiating with Canada, but would apply to all nations.

But bilateral (two-nation) negotiations were slow and cumbersome. This approach was broadened in 1947 when 23 nations, including Canada, signed the **General Agreement on Tariffs and Trade (GATT)**. GATT is based on three principles: (1) equal, nondiscriminatory treatment for all member nations; (2) the reduction of tariffs by *multilateral* negotiations; and (3) the elimination of import quotas. GATT is a forum for the negotiation of reductions in tariff barriers on a multilateral basis. There is little doubt that GATT has been an important force in the trend towards liberalized trade. Under its sponsorship, seven "rounds" of negotiations to reduce trade barriers have been completed in the post-World War II period.

In 1994 more than 120 of the world's nations successfully completed the eighth "round" of negotiation, of the Uruguay Round of the GATT. Provisions to be implemented between 1995 and 2005 included:

1. reduction of tariffs worldwide;
2. liberalization of rules that have impeded trade in services;
3. reduction of agricultural subsidies that have distorted the global pattern of trade in agricultural goods;
4. new protections for intellectual property (copyrights, patents, trademarks);
5. a phasing out of quotas on textiles and apparel, replacing them with gradually declining tariffs;
6. establishment of the World Trade Organization to oversee the provisions of the agreement and to resolve any disputes under the new rules.

When completed in 2005, GATT will boost the world's GDP by an estimated $6 trillion, or 8 percent.

## Economic Integration

Another development in trade liberalization has taken the form of **economic integration**—the joining of the markets of two or more nations into a free-trade zone. Three illustrations of economic integration are the European Union (EU)—also called the Common Market—the Canada–United States Free Trade Agreement (FTA), and the North American Free-Trade Agreement (NAFTA).

**The Common Market** The best example is the **European Union (EU)**—formerly called the European Economic Community. Begun in 1958 with six nations, the EU is now made up of 15 Western European nations—France, Germany, Italy, Belgium, the Netherlands, Luxembourg, Denmark, Ireland, United Kingdom, Greece, Spain, Portugal, Austria, Finland, and Sweden.

**Goals** The original Common Market calls for (1) the gradual abolition of tariffs and import quotas on all products traded among the participating nations, (2) establishment of a common system of tariffs applicable to all goods received from nations outside the EU, (3) free movement of capital and labour within the Common Market, (4) the creation of common policies with respect to other economic matters of joint concern, such as agriculture, transportation, and restrictive business practices. The EU has achieved most of these goals and is now a strong **trade bloc**.

**Results** Motives for creating the European Union were both political and economic. The economic motive was to gain the advantages of freer trade for members. While it is difficult to determine how much EU prosperity and growth have resulted from integration, integration has created mass markets essential to EU industries. The economies of large-scale production have permitted European industries to achieve the lower costs that small, localized markets have historically denied them.

Effects on nonmember nations such as Canada are less certain. A peaceful and increasingly prosperous EU makes member nations better potential customers for Canadian exports. But Canadian firms encounter tariffs that make it difficult to compete in EU markets. For example, before the establishment of the EU, Canadian, German, and French manufacturers all faced the same tariff in selling their products to, say, Belgium. However, with the establishment of internal free trade among EU members, Belgian tariffs on German Volkswagens and French Renaults fell to zero, but an external tariff still applies to all nonmember nations such as Canada. This puts Canadian firms and those of other nonmember nations at a competitive disadvantage.

By giving preferences to other countries within their free-trade zone, trade blocs such as the EU may reduce their trade with nonbloc members. Thus, the world loses some of the benefits of a completely open global trading system. Eliminating this disadvantage has been one of the motivations for promoting freer global trade through GATT.

## THE CANADA–U.S. FREE TRADE AGREEMENT

Other examples of economic integration are the **Canada–U.S. Free Trade Agreement (FTA)** enacted in 1989 and the North American Free Trade Agreement (NAFTA), which came into effect in 1995. More will be said about NAFTA below.

Although three-fourths of the trade between Canada and the United States was already free in 1988, the FTA accord was highly significant: It created the largest free-trade area in the world. Under terms of the agreement, all trade restrictions such as tariffs, quotas, and nontariff barriers would be eliminated by 1999. Canadian producers gained increased access to a market ten times the size of Canada, while U.S. consumers gained the advantage of lower-priced Canadian goods. In return, Canada cut its tariffs by more than the United States because Canadian tariffs were higher.

### The North American Free-Trade Zone

In 1993 Canada, Mexico, and the United States formed a trade bloc. The **North American Free Trade Agreement (NAFTA)** established a free-trade zone having about the same combined output as the EU, but a much larger geographical area. The agreement went into effect January 1, 1995. When fully implemented in 1999, the agreement is expected to generate $1 billion to $3 billion of annual gains for each nation.

Free trade with Mexico is even more controversial in Canada than is free trade with the United States. Critics fear a loss of Canadian jobs as firms move to Mexico to take advantage of lower wages and less stringent pollution and workplace safety regulations. Critics also are concerned that Japan and South Korea will build plants in Mexico to ship goods tariff-free through the United States and into Canada, further hurting domestic firms and workers.

Defenders of NAFTA reject these concerns and cite several strong arguments in its favour.

1. Specialization according to comparative advantage will enable Canada to obtain more total output from its scarce resources.
2. The reduction of high Mexican tariffs will increase Canadian exports to Mexico.
3. This free-trade zone will encourage worldwide investment in Mexico, enhancing Mexican productivity and national income. Mexican consumers will use some of that increased income to buy Canadian exports.
4. The resulting higher standard of living in Mexico will enable Mexico to afford more pollution-control equipment and to provide safer workplaces.
5. The loss of specific Canadian jobs to Mexico may have occurred anyway to low-wage countries such as South Korea, Taiwan, and Hong Kong. NAFTA will enable and encourage Canadian firms to be more efficient, enhancing their long-term competitiveness with firms in Japan and the European Union.

### Reasons for Joining NAFTA

It may appear that the world's nations are combining into potentially hostile trade blocs. But NAFTA constitutes a vehicle to negotiate reductions in trade barriers with the EU, Japan, and other trading countries. Access to the vast North American market is as important to the EU and Japan as is access to their markets by Canada, the United States, and Mexico. NAFTA gives Canada a lever in future trade negotiations with the EU and Japan. Conceivably, direct negotiations between NAFTA and the EU could eventually link the two free-trade zones. Japan and other major trading nations, not wishing to be left out of the world's wealthiest trade markets, would be forced to eliminate their high trade barriers—to open their domestic markets to additional imports. Nor do other nations and trade blocs want to be excluded from North America. Examples:

1. **APEC** In 1989 Canada and 16 other members of the Asia-Pacific Economic Cooperation (APEC) nations agreed to establish freer trade and more open investment over the next few decades. APEC nations are Australia, Brunei, Canada, Chile, Hong Kong, Indonesia, Japan, Malaysia, Mexico, New Zealand, the Philippines, Papua New Guinea, Singapore, South Korea, Taiwan, Thailand, and the United States.
2. **ADMISSION OF CHILE INTO NAFTA** At the invitation of Canada, Mexico, and the United States, Chile has agreed to become the fourth partner in NAFTA.

3. **MERCOSUR** The free-trade area encompassing Brazil, Argentina, Uruguay, and Paraguay—called Mercosur—is interested in linking up with NAFTA. So are other South American countries. The Canadian prime minister and 33 other prime ministers and presidents of Western hemisphere nations have agreed to begin negotiations on a free-trade area from "Alaska to Argentina."

Canada had defensive reasons to join in NAFTA. If it had chosen to exclude itself from the agreement, it would have been excluded from bilateral agreements between the United States and Mexico, to the detriment of Canadian exporters seeking access to the Mexican market. Even in the U.S. market, Canada could have ended up at a competitive disadvantage vis à vis Mexico in the American market.

Subsequent events to the signing of NAFTA have also pointed to another reason for joining NAFTA—trade liberalization that may eventually include the Western hemisphere. If, as it is likely, Chile officially joins NAFTA, there will undoubtedly be demands from other nations in the Western hemisphere to join in; many of these claims will probably be defensive actions in a bid not to be excluded.

## NAFTA's Strengthening of the Rules of Origin

NAFTA has strengthened the rules of origin to ensure a certain amount of North American content in goods produced and traded among Canada, United States, and Mexico. For example, a car built by Toyota in Ontario must have a specified minimum percentage of its parts produced in North America. This will in effect protect some producers against foreign competition.

Already disputes have arisen between the Canadian and U.S. governments over whether the Honda plant in Canada was meeting the content requirements on its automobiles shipped to the United States. While the rules of origin are clearer in NAFTA compared to the FTA, they will likely continue to be a source of dispute.

## NAFTA and Concerns About Environmental and Labour Laws

Critics of NAFTA were particularly vocal against Canada joining because of concern over the perceived less stringent regulations of Mexico's environmental and workplace safety regulations, which would put producers there at a huge competitive advantage when added to the lower wages in Mexico. These concerns were expressed equally strongly in both Canada and the United States over the course of negotiations.

Proponents of NAFTA pointed out that Mexico has adequate laws to protect the environment and workplace safety but these laws are not strongly enforced. Provisions in the agreement make it possible for Canada and the United States to demand Mexico enforce its own environmental and labour laws. Thus NAFTA ensures a higher compliance by its three members to laws that protect the environment and make the workplace safer for workers than in its absence.

Both critics and defenders of NAFTA agree on one point: It constitutes a powerful trade bloc to counter the European Union. Access to the vast North American market is as important to European Union nations as is access to the European market by Canada, the United States, and Mexico. Observers believe negotiations between the North American trade bloc and the European Union will follow, eventually resulting in a free-trade agreement between the two blocs.

Economists agree that the ideal free-trade area would be the world.

### 22-3 QUICK REVIEW

- The various "rounds" of the General Agreement on Tariffs and Trade (GATT) have established multinational reductions in tariffs and import quotas among the more than 120 member nations.
- The Uruguay Round of GATT that went into effect in 1995: **a** reduced tariffs worldwide; **b** liberalized rules impeding barriers to trade in services; **c** reduced agricultural subsidies; **d** created new protections for intellectual property; **e** phased out quotas on textiles and apparel; and **f** set up the World Trade Organization.
- The European Union (EU), the Canada-U.S. Free Trade Agreement (FTA), and the North American Free Trade Agreement (NAFTA) have reduced trade barriers by establishing large free-trade zones.

In The Media

# Gerber Faces Duty on Baby Food Imports

## Revenue Canada sides with Heinz

BY HEATHER SCOFFIELD
PARLIAMENTARY BUREAU

OTTAWA—Revenue Canada has decided to impose a provisional duty that averages 69 per cent on Gerber jarred baby food, saying the U.S. company is dumping its product in Canada.

The department said it agreed with a complaint from H.J. Heinz Co. of Canada Ltd., the only Canada-based producer of jarred baby food, that Gerber Products Co. of Michigan was selling its product at unfairly low prices, cutting into Heinz's profit and causing layoffs at its plant in Leamington, Ont.

"We want to stop the unfair trade practices. That's the main objective," said Ana Relyea, spokeswoman for Heinz in Toronto.

Food for tots is worth big bucks in Canada. Heinz estimates that the country's jarred baby food market is worth $60-million to $70-million a year. Heinz has a 78-per-cent market share, and Gerber has the other 22 per cent, Ms. Relyea said.

Gerber officials could not be reached for comment.

Revenue Canada began an investigation into Heinz's dumping claims in October, and found that jarred baby food from the United States was being sold in Canada at prices well below prices in the United States.

"There is a reasonable indication that the dumping has caused injury [to the Canadian industry]," the department said in its statement of reasons for the duty decision.

The department said it will continue its investigation to see if the duty should be permanent, and issue a final decision by the end of March. At the same time, the Canadian International Trade Tribunal will investigate to see if the dumped exports are harming Canadian production. The tribunal is to decide by April 29 if the duty should stick.

Gerber shut its Canadian baby food plant in Niagara Falls, Ont., in 1992. Since then, Heinz said, Gerber's imports have forced Heinz to lose sales and market share, to cut production and to lay off 57 out of 200 employees making baby food in Leamington.

In Ontario, where sales were hit the hardest, the price of Heinz jars of baby food has dropped to 43 cents from 49 cents four years ago, Ms. Relyea said.

"In order for us to compete, we've had to lower our prices too," she said.

She would not say whether Heinz planned to raise its prices because of the ruling.

H.J. Heinz Co. of Canada Ltd. is a private, wholly owned subsidiary of H.J. Heinz Co. of Pittsburgh.

The duty applies to all U.S. jarred baby food exports to Canada, but Gerber is the only U.S. company involved in the Canadian market for now, Revenue Canada said.



### THE STORY IN BRIEF

Revenue Canada imposed an import duty on the U.S. firm Gerber Product Company after it found that Gerber was dumping its jarred baby food in Canada.

### THE ECONOMICS BEHIND THE STORY

- H.J Heinz Company of Canada came under intense price pressure from Gerber as the U.S. firm aggressively cut the price of its jarred baby food. Heinz's profit declined, leading to layoffs. Heinz accused Gerber of dumping its jarred baby food.
- Revenue Canada found Gerber guilty of dumping; it sold its products at prices below those it charged in the United States. Such tactics are illegal under international law.
- Who benefited and who lost from the dumping of jarred baby food in Canada? How does an economist decide whether the dumping was on balance beneficial or detrimental to Canada's economic well-being? ■

# The Last Word

## PETITION OF THE CANDLEMAKERS, 1845

**The French economist Frédéric Bastiat (1801–1850) devastated the proponents of protectionism by satirically extending their reasoning to its logical and absurd conclusions.**

PETITION OF THE MANUFACTURERS OF CANDLES, Wax-lights, Lamps, Candlesticks, Street Lamps, Snuffers, Extinguishers, and of the Producers of Oil Tallow, Rosin, Alcohol, and, Generally, of Everything Connected with Lighting.

**TO MESSIEURS THE MEMBERS OF THE CHAMBER OF DEPUTIES.**

Gentlemen—You are on the right road. You reject abstract theories, and have little consideration for cheapness and plenty. Your chief care is the interest of the producer. You desire to emancipate him from external competition, and reserve the *national market for national industry*.

We are about to offer you an admirable opportunity of applying your—what shall we call it? your theory? No; nothing is more deceptive than theory; your doctrine? your system? your principle? but you dislike doctrines, you abhor systems, and as for principles, you deny that there are any in social economy: we shall say, then, your practice, your practice without theory and without principle.

We are suffering from the intolerable competition of a foreign rival, placed, it would seem, in a condition so far superior to ours for the production of light, that he absolutely inundates our national market with it at a price fabulously reduced. The moment he shows himself, our trade leaves us—all consumers apply to him; and a branch of native industry, having countless ramifications, is all at once rendered completely stagnant. This rival … is no other than the Sun.

What we pray for is, that it may please you to pass a law ordering the shutting up of all windows, skylights, dormerwindows, outside and inside shutters, curtains, blinds, bull's-eyes; in a word, of all openings, holes, chinks, clefts, and fissures, by or through which the light of the sun has been in use to enter houses, to the prejudice of the meritorious manufactures with which we flatter ourselves we have accommodated our country,—a country which, in gratitude, ought not to abandon us now to a strife so unequal.

If you shut up as much as possible all access to natural light, and create a demand for artificial light, which of our French manufactures will not be encouraged by it?

If more tallow is consumed, then there must be more oxen and sheep; and, consequently, we shall behold the multiplication of artificial meadows, meat, wool, hides, and, above all, manure, which is the basis and foundation of all agricultural wealth.

The same remark applies to navigation. Thousands of vessels will proceed to the whale fishery; and, in a short time, we shall possess a navy capable of maintaining the honour of France, and gratifying the patriotic aspirations of your petitioners, the undersigned candlemakers and others.

Only have the goodness to reflect, Gentlemen, and you will be convinced that there is, perhaps, no Frenchman, from the wealthy coalmaster to the humblest vendor of lucifer matches, whose lot will not be ameliorated by the success of this our petition. ■

Source: Frédéric Bastiat, *Economic Sophisms* (Edinburgh: Oliver and Boyd, Tweeddale Court, 1873) pp.49–53, abridged.

# CHAPTER SUMMARY

1. International trade is important to most nations, including Canada. Since 1965 our exports and imports have more than doubled as a percentage of GDP. Our major trading partner is the United States. Other major trading nations

are Germany, Japan, the Western European nations, and the newly industrialized Asia tigers (Hong Kong, Singapore, South Korea, and Taiwan).

2. World trade is based on two considerations: the uneven distribution of economic resources among nations, and the fact that efficient production of various goods requires particular techniques or combinations of resources.

3. Mutually advantageous specification and trade are possible between any two nations if they have different opportunity cost ratios for any two products. By specializing based on comparative advantage, nations can obtain larger real incomes with fixed amounts of resources. The terms of trade determine how this increase in world output is shared by the trading nations. Increasing (rather than constant) costs limits specialization and trade.

4. A nation's export supply curve shows the quantity of product it will export at world prices that exceed the domestic price—the price in a closed, no-international-trade economy. Its import demand curve reveals the quantity of a product it will import at world prices below the domestic price. In a two-nation model, the equilibrium world price and the equilibrium quantities of exports and imports occur where one nation's import supply curve intersects the other nation's export demand curve.

5. Trade barriers take the form of protective tariffs, quotas, nontariff barriers, and "voluntary" export restrictions. Supply and demand analysis reveals that protective tariffs and quotas increase the prices and reduce the quantities demanded of affected goods. Sales by foreign exporters diminish; domestic producers, however, enjoy higher prices and enlarged sales. Tariffs and quotas promote a less efficient allocation of domestic and world resources.

6. The strongest arguments for protection are the infant-industry and military self-sufficiency arguments. Most of the other arguments for protection are half-truths, emotional appeals, or fallacies that emphasize the immediate effects of trade barriers while ignoring long-run consequences. Numerous historical examples suggest that free trade promotes economic growth; protectionism does not.

7. Protectionism costs Canadian consumers substantial amounts annually. The cost to consumers for each job saved is far greater than the average salary paid. Consumer losses from trade restrictions greatly exceed producer and government gains, creating an efficiency loss to society.

8. Recent Canadian international trade policy entails **a** general liberalization of trade through NAFTA and GATT; **b** aggressive export promotion by government; and **c** bilateral negotiations over specific trade disputes.

9. The Uruguay Round of GATT negotiations, completed in 1993: **a** reduced tariffs; **b** liberalized trade in services; **c** reduced agricultural subsidies; **d** reduced pirating of intellectual property; **e** phased out import quotas on textiles and apparel; and **f** established the World Trade Organization, which replaces GATT.

10. Free-trade zones (trade blocs) may liberalize trade within regions but may also impede trade with nonbloc members. Three examples of free-trade arrangements are **a** the European Union (EU), formerly the European Community or "Common Market"; **b** the Canada-U.S. Free Trade Agreement (FTA); and **c** the North American Free Trade Agreement (NAFTA), comprising Canada, Mexico, and the United States, and later, Chile.

## TERMS AND CONCEPTS

labour-intensive goods
land-intensive goods
capital-intensive goods
absolute advantage
cost ratio
comparative advantage
terms of trade
trading possibilities line
gains from trade
world price
domestic price
export supply curve
import demand curve
revenue and protective tariffs
import quotas
nontariff barriers (NTBs)
voluntary export restrictions (VERs)
strategic trade policy
dumping
National Policy
most-favoured-nation clause
General Agreement on Tariffs and Trade (GATT)
economic integration
European Union (EU or Common Market)
trade bloc
Canada-U.S. Free Trade Agreement (FTA)
North American Free Trade Agreement (NAFTA)

## STUDY QUESTIONS

1. Quantitatively, how important is international trade to Canada relative to other nations?

2. Distinguish among land-, labour- and capital-intensive commodities, citing an example of each. What role do these distinctions play in explaining international trade?

3. Suppose nation A can produce 80 units of X by using all its resources to produce X and 60 units of Y by devoting all its resources to Y. Comparative figures for nation B are 60 of X and 60 of Y. Assuming constant costs, in which product should each nation specialize? Why? What are the limits of the terms of trade?

4. KEY QUESTION *The following are hypothetical production possibilities tables for New Zealand and Spain.*

**New Zealand's production possibilities table (millions of bushels)**

| PRODUCT | PRODUCTION ALTERNATIVES | | | |
|---|---|---|---|---|
| | A | B | C | D |
| Apples | 0 | 20 | 40 | 60 |
| Plums | 15 | 10 | 5 | 0 |

**Spain's production possibilities table (millions of bushels)**

| PRODUCT | PRODUCTION ALTERNATIVES | | | |
|---|---|---|---|---|
| | R | S | T | U |
| Apples | 0 | 20 | 40 | 60 |
| Plums | 60 | 40 | 20 | 0 |

*Plot the production possibilities data for each of the two countries separately. Referring to your graphs, determine:*

**a.** *Each country's cost ratio of producing plums and apples;*

**b.** *Which nation should specialize in which product;*

**c.** *The trading possibilities lines for each nation if the actual terms of trade are 1 plum for 2 apples. (Plot these lines on your graph.)*

**d.** *Suppose the optimum product mixes before specialization and trade were B in New Zealand and S in Spain. What are the gains from specialization and trade?*

5. "Canada can produce product X more efficiently than can Great Britain. Yet we import X from Great Britain." Explain.

6. KEY QUESTION *Refer to Figure 4-5. Assume the graph depicts Canada's domestic market for oats. How many bushels of oats, if any, will Canada export or import at a world price of $1, $2, $3, $4, and $5? Use this information to construct Canada's export supply curve and import demand curve for corn. Suppose the only other corn-producing nation is France, where the domestic price is $4. Why will the equilibrium world price be between $3 and $4? Who will export corn at this world price; who will import it?*

7. KEY QUESTION *Draw a domestic supply and demand diagram for a product in which Canada does not have a comparative advantage. Indicate the impact of foreign imports on domestic price and quantity. Now show a protective tariff that eliminates approximately one-half the assumed imports. Indicate the price-quantity effects of this tariff to* **a** *domestic consumers,* **b** *domestic producers, and* **c** *foreign exporters. How would the effects of a quota that creates the same amount of imports differ?*

8. "The most valid arguments for tariff protection are also the most easily abused." What are these particular arguments? Why are they susceptible to abuse? Evaluate the use of artificial trade barriers, such as tariffs and import quotas, as a means of achieving and maintaining full employment.

9. Evaluate the following statements:

   **a.** "Protective tariffs limit both the imports and the exports of the nation levying tariffs."

**b.** "The extensive application of protective tariffs destroys the ability of the international market system to allocate resources efficiently."

**c.** "Unemployment can often be reduced through tariff protection, but by the same token inefficiency typically increases."

**d.** "Foreign firms that 'dump' their products onto the Canadian market are in effect presenting the Canadian people with gifts."

**e.** "In view of the rapidity with which technological advance is dispersed around the world, free trade will inevitably yield structural maladjustments, unemployment and balance of payments problems for industrially advanced nations."

**f.** "Free trade can improve the composition and efficiency of domestic output. Only the Volkswagen forced Detroit to make a compact car, and only foreign success with the oxygen process forced Canadian steel firms to modernize."

**g.** "In the long run foreign trade is neutral with respect to total employment."

**10.** From 1981 to 1985 the Japanese agreed to a voluntary export restriction that reduced Canadian imports of Japanese automobiles by about 10 percent. What would you expect the short-run effects to have been on the Canadian and Japanese automobile industries? If this restriction were permanent, what would be its long-run effects in the two nations on **a** the allocation of resources, **b** the volume of employment, **c** the price level, and **d** the standard of living?

**11.** KEY QUESTION *What are the benefits and the costs of protectionist policies? Which are larger?*

**12.** What are NAFTA and GATT and how do they relate to international trade? What policies has the Canadian government recently used to promote our exports?

**13.** **(The Last Word)** What point is Bastiat trying to make with his petition of the candlemakers?

**14.** WEB-BASED QUESTION **Multilateral Trade Liberation—GATT and WTO** GATT (General Agreement on Tariffs and Trade) was founded in 1947 to reduce world trade barriers on a multilateral basis. GATT partners have to grant each other the best conditions they grant any of the other nations that have most favoured nation status. GATT was subsumed by the World Trade Organization (WTO) www.wto.org/ on January 1, 1995. Review how the WTO is trying to reduce trade barriers in two disparate industries: information technology and textiles; visit www.wto.org/wto/goods/goods.htm. What types of trade barriers are present in each industry? What timetable has been set for barrier reductions? Why is it more difficult to negotiate trade barrier reductions in textiles rather than information technology?

**15.** WEB-BASED QUESTION **Canada's Main Trading Partners** Statistics Canada www.statcan.ca/english/Pgdb/Economy/International/gblec02a.htm sets out Canada's main trading partners. Which country is our largest trading partner? Now visit www.statcan.ca/english/Pgdb/Economy/International/gblec04.htm to determine Canada's biggest export sector. What sector is a close second?

# Glossary

**Ability-to-pay principle** The idea that those who have greater income (or wealth) should pay a greater proportion of it as taxes than those who have less income (or wealth).

**Abstraction** Elimination of irrelevant and noneconomic facts to obtain an *economic* principle.

**Adjustable pegs** The device used in the *Bretton Woods system* to alter *exchange rates* in an orderly way to eliminate persistent payments deficits and surpluses. Each nation defined its monetary unit in terms of (pegged it to) gold or the dollar, kept the rate of exchange for its money stable in the short run, and adjusted its rate in the long run when faced with international payments disequilibrium.

**Adverse selection problem** A problem arising when information known to one party to a contract is not known to the other party, causing the latter to incur major costs. Example: Individuals who have the poorest health are more likely to buy health insurance.

**Advertising** A seller's activities in communicating its message about its product to potential buyers.

**Agricultural Stabilization Board** The federal agency established in 1958 to support the following commodities at not less than 90 percent of their average price over the previous five years, with adjustments according to production costs: cattle, hogs, and sheep; industrial milk and cream; and oats and barley not produced on the Prairies (where the *Canadian Wheat Board* has jurisdiction).

**Allocative efficiency** The apportionment of resources among firms and industries to obtain the production of the products most wanted by society (consumers); the output of each product at which its *marginal cost* and *price* or *marginal benefit* are equal.

**American Federation of Labor (AFL)** The American organization of affiliated *craft unions* formed in 1886.

**Anti-combines laws** Legislation that prohibits anticompetitive business activities such as price fixing, bid rigging, monopolization, and *tying contracts*. (*See also* Competition Act.)

**Applied economics** (*See* Policy economics.)

**Appreciation (of the dollar)** An increase in the value of the dollar relative to the currency of another nation so that a dollar buys a larger amount of the foreign currency and thus of foreign goods.

**"Asian tigers"** The newly industrialized and rapidly growing economies of Hong Kong, Singapore, South Korea, and Taiwan.

**Asset** Anything of monetary value owned by a firm or individual.

**Asymmetric information** A situation in which one party to a market transaction has much more information about a product or service than the other; the result may be an under- or overallocation of resources.

**Authoritarian capitalism** An economic system in which property resources are privately owned and government extensively directs and controls the economy.

**Average fixed cost** A firm's total *fixed cost* divided by output (the quantity of product produced).

**Average product** The total output produced per unit of a *resource* employed (total product divided by the quantity of that employed resource).

**Average revenue** Total revenue from the sale of a product divided by the quantity of the product sold (demanded); equal to the price at which the product is sold when all units of the product are sold at the same price.

**Average tax rate** Total tax paid divided by total (taxable) income, as a percentage.

**Average total cost** A firm's *total cost* divided by output (the quantity of product produced); equal to *average fixed cost* plus *average variable cost*.

**Average variable cost** A firm's total *variable cost* divided by output (the quantity of product produced).

**Backflows** The return of workers to the countries from which they originally migrated.

**Balance of payments** (*See* International balance of payments.)

**Balance of payments deficit** The amount by which the sum of the *balance on current account* and the *balance on the capital account* is negative in a year.

**Balance of payments surplus** The amount by which the sum of the *balance on current account* and the *balance on the capital account* is positive in a year.

**Balance on current account** The exports of goods and services of a nation less its imports of goods and services plus its *net investment income* and *net transfers* in a year.

**Balance on goods and services** The exports of goods and services of a nation less its imports of goods and services in a year.

**Balance on the capital account** The *capital inflows* of a nation less its *capital outflows.*

**Balance sheet** A statement of the *assets, liabilities*, and *net worth* of a firm or individual at some given time.

**Barrier to entry** Anything that artificially prevents the entry of firms into an industry.

**Barter** The exchange of one good or service for another good or service.

**Benefit-cost analysis** Comparing the *marginal benefits* of a government project or program with the *marginal costs* to decide whether to employ resources in that project or program and to what extent.

**Benefit-reduction rate** The percentage by which subsidy benefits in a *public assistance program* are reduced as earned income rises.

**Benefits-received principle** The idea that those who receive the benefits of goods and services provided by government should pay the taxes required to finance them.

**Bilateral monopoly** A market in which there is a single seller (*monopoly*) and a single buyer (*monopsony*).

**Bond** A financial device through which a borrower (a firm or government) is obligated to pay the principle and interest on a loan at a specific date in the future.

**Brain drain** The emigration of highly educated, highly skilled workers from a country.

**Break-even income** The level of disposable income at which households plan to consume (spend) all their income and to save none of it; also denotes that level of earned income at which subsidy payments become zero in an income transfer program.

**Break-even output** Any output at which a (competitive) firm's *total cost* and *total revenue* are equal; an output at which it has neither an *economic profit* nor a loss; at which it has only a normal profit.

**Bretton Woods system** The international monetary system developed after World War II in which *adjustable pegs* were employed, the *International Monetary Fund* helped to stabilize foreign exchange rates, and gold and the U.S. dollar were used as *international monetary reserves*.

**Budget deficit** The amount by which the expenditures of the federal government exceed its revenues in any year.

**Budget line** A line that shows the different combinations of two products a consumer can purchase with a specific money income, given the products' prices.

**Budget constraint** The limit that the size of a consumer's income (and the prices that must be paid for goods and services) imposes on the ability of that consumer to obtain goods and services.

**Budget surplus** The amount by which the revenues of the federal government exceed its expenditures in any year.

**Business firm** (*See* Firm.)

**Canada Assistance Plan** The federal Act under which the federal government makes funds available to the provinces for their programs of assistance to disabled and unemployed who are not entitled to employment insurance benefits, and other needy persons.

**Canada Deposit Insurance Corporation** Federal Crown Corporation that, for a fee payable by the chartered banks and federally chartered trust companies, insures their customers' deposits up to a limit of $60,000 per customer per bank or trust company.

**Canada Labour Code** The federal law of 1970 that consolidated previous legislation regulating employment practices, labour standards, and so on, in the federal jurisdiction.

**Canada Pension Plan** The compulsory, contributory, earnings-related federal pension plan that covers most employed members of the labour force between the ages of 18 and 65, and payable at the latter age; it came into effect in 1965; there is transferability between the Plan and the Quebec Pension Plan, which applies to the people of that province.

**Canada-United States Free Trade Agreement (FTA)** An accord that came into effect on January 1, 1989, to eliminate all *tariffs* between the two countries over the following ten years.

**Canadian Congress of Labour (CCL)** The federation of *industrial unions* formed in 1940 and affiliated with the Congress of Industrial Organizations; amalgamated into *Canadian Labour Congress* in 1956.

**Canadian International Development Agency (CIDA)** The federal agency responsible for the operation and administration of Canada's international development assistance programs of approximately $2.5 billion a year.

**Canadian Labour Congress (CLC)** The largest federation of *labour unions* in Canada, with 3 million members in international and national unions; founded in 1956 on the amalgamation of the *Canadian Congress of Labour* and the *Trades and Labour Congress of Canada.*

**Canadian Wheat Board** Federal Crown Corporation established in 1935, which does not own or operate grain-handling facilities but has complete control over the way western wheat is marketed and the price at which it is sold. The Board also acquired complete control of the supplies of all Prairie coarse grains in 1949.

**Capital** Human-made resources (buildings, machinery, and equipment) used to produce goods and services; goods that do not directly satisfy human wants; also called capital goods.

**Capital account** The section of a nation's *international balance of payments* statement in which the foreign purchases of assets in Canada (producing money *capital inflows*) and Canadian purchases of assets abroad (producing money *capital outflows* of that nation) are recorded.

**Capital account deficit** A negative *balance on the capital account.*

**Capital account surplus** A positive *balance on the capital account.*

**Capital gain** The gain realized when securities or properties are sold for a price greater than the price paid for them.

**Capital goods** (*See* Capital.)

**Capital inflow** The expenditures made by the residents of foreign nations to purchase real and financial capital from the residents of a nation.

**Capital-intensive commodity** A product that requires a relatively large amount of *capital* to produce.

**Capitalism** (*See* Pure capitalism.)

**Capital outflow** The expenditures made by the residents of a nation to purchase real and financial capital from the residents of foreign nations.

**Capital stock** The total available *capital* in a nation.

**Cartel** A formal agreement among firms in an industry to set the price of a product and the outputs of the individual firms or to divide the market for the product geographically.

**Causation** A relationship in which the occurrence of one or more events brings about another event.

**Ceiling price** (*See* Price ceiling.)

**Central economic planning** Government determination of the objectives of the economy and how resources will be directed to attain those objectives.

**Ceteris paribus assumption** (*See* "Other things equal" assumption.)

**Change in demand** A change in the *quantity demanded* of a good or service at every price; a shift of the *demand curve* to the left or right.

**Change in supply** A change in the *quantity supplied* of a good or service at every price; a shift of the *supply curve* to the left or right.

**Chartered bank** One of the 66 multibranched, privately owned, commercial, financial intermediaries that have received charters by Act of Parliament and that alone, with Quebec Savings Banks, may call themselves "banks"; and which accept *demand deposits.*

**Chartered banking system** All *chartered banks* as a group.

**Cheque clearing** The process by which funds are transferred from the *chequing accounts* of the writers of cheques to the chequing accounts of the recipients of the cheques; also called the "collection" of cheques.

**Chequing account** A *demand deposit* in a chartered bank.

**Circular flow model** The flow of resources from *households* to *firms* and of products from firms to households. These flows are accompanied by reverse flows of money from firms to households and from households to firms.

**Closed economy** An economy that neither exports nor imports goods and services.

**Closed shop** A place of employment where only workers who are already members of a labour union may be hired.

**Coase theorem** The idea first stated by economist Ronald Coase that spillover problems may be resolved through private negotiations of the affected parties.

**Coincidence of wants** A situation in which the good or service which one trader desires to obtain is the same as that which another trader desires to give up, and an item which the second trader wishes to acquire is the same as that which the first trader desires to surrender.

**COLA** (*See* Cost-of-living adjustment.)

**Collective bargaining** The negotiation of labour contracts between *labour unions* and *firms* or government entities.

**Collective voice** The function a *labour union* performs for its members as a group when it communicates their problems and grievances to management and presses management for a satisfactory resolution.

**Collusion** A situation in which firms act together and in agreement (collude) to fix prices, divide a market, or otherwise restrict competition.

**Combines Investigation Act** The federal Act, first passed in 1910, whose avowed aim is to prevent agreements to lessen competition unduly; amended and renamed the *Competition Act* in June 1986.

**Command economy** An economic system (method of organization) in which property resources are publicly owned and government uses *central economic planning* to direct and coordinate economic activities.

**Communism** (*See* Command economy.)

**Comparative advantage** A lower relative or comparative cost than another producer.

**Compensating differences** Differences in the *wages* received by workers in different jobs to compensate for nonmonetary differences in the jobs.

**Competing goods** (*See* Substitute goods.)

**Competition** The presence in a market of a large number of independent buyers and sellers competing with one another and the freedom of buyers and sellers to enter and leave the market.

**Competition Act** The Act that amended the *Combines Investigation Act* in June 1986 and, in so doing, renamed it the Competition Act.

**Competitive industry's short-run supply curve** The horizontal summation of the short-run supply curves of the *firms* in a purely competitive industry (see *Pure competition*); a curve that shows the total quantities offered for sale at various prices by the firms in an industry in the short run.

**Competitive labour market** A resource market in which a large number of (noncolluding) firms demand a particular type of labour supplied by a large number of nonunion workers.

**Complementary goods** Products and services that are used together; when the price of one falls the demand for the other increases (and conversely).

**Concentration ratio** The percentage of the total sales of an industry made by the four (or some other number) largest sellers in the industry.

**Confederation of National Trade Unions (CNTU)** The *labour union* federation that represents approximately 20 percent of Quebec's union members; established in 1921 as the Federation of Catholic Workers of Canada, it was later renamed the Canadian and Catholic Confederation of Labour; it adopted its present name and became nonconfessional in 1956.

**Conglomerate combination** A group of *plants* owned by a single *firm* and engaged at one or more stages in the production of different products (of products that do not compete with each other).

**Conglomerate merger** The merger of a *firm* in one *industry* with a firm in another industry or region (with a firm that is not a supplier, customer, or competitor).

**Constant-cost industry** An industry in which expansion by the entry of new firms has no effect on the prices firms in the industry must pay for resources and thus no effect on production costs.

**Consumer goods** Products and services that satisfy human wants directly.

**Consumer sovereignty** Determination by consumers of the types and quantities of goods and services that will be produced with the scarce resources of the economy; consumer direction of production through dollar votes.

**Consumer surplus** The difference between what a consumer (or consumers) is willing to pay for an additional unit of a product or service and its market price; the triangular area below the *demand curve* and above the market price.

**Consumption of fixed capital** Estimate of the amount of *capital* worn out or used up (consumed) in producing the *gross domestic product*; also called *depreciation*.

**Copyright** A legal protection provided to developers and publishers of books, computer software, videos, and musical compositions against copying of their works by others.

**Corporate income tax** A tax levied on the net income (profit) of corporations.

**Corporation** A legal entity ("person") chartered by a province or the federal government that is distinct and separate from the individuals who own it.

**Correlation** A systematic and dependable association between two sets of data (two kinds of events); does not itself indicate causation.

**Cost-of-living adjustment (COLA)** An automatic increase in the incomes (wages) of workers when inflation occurs; guaranteed by a collective bargaining contract between firms and workers.

**Cost ratio** An equality showing the number of units of two products that can be produced with the same resources; the cost ratio 1 corn = 3 olives shows that the resources required to produce 3 units of olives must be shifted to corn production to produce 1 unit of corn.

**Craft union** A *labour union* that limits its membership to workers with a particular skill (craft).

**Creative destruction** The hypothesis that the creation of new products and production methods simultaneously destroys the market power of existing monopolies.

**Credit** An accounting item that increases the value of an *asset* (such as the foreign money owned by the residents of a nation).

**Cross elasticity of demand** The ratio of the percentage change in *quantity demanded* of one good to the percentage change in the price of some other good. A positive coefficient indicates the two products are *substitute goods*; a negative coefficient indicates they are *complementary goods*.

**Crowding model of occupational discrimination** A model of labour markets suggesting that *occupational discrimination* has kept many women and minorities out of high-paying occupations and forced them into a limited number of low-paying occupations.

**Currency appreciation** (*See* Exchange rate appreciation.)

**Currency depreciation** (*See* Exchange rate depreciation.)

**Current account** The section in a nation's *international balance of payments* that records its exports and imports of goods and services, its *net investment income*, and its *net transfers*.

**Customary economy** (*See* Traditional economy.)

**Debit** An accounting item that decreases the value of an asset (such as the foreign money owned by the residents of a nation).

**Declining industry** An industry in which *economic profits* are negative (losses are incurred) and that will, therefore, decrease its output as firms leave it.

**Decreasing-cost industry** An industry in which expansion through the entry of firms decreases the prices firms in the industry must pay for resources and therefore decreases their production costs.

**Deduction** Reasoning from assumptions to conclusions; a method of reasoning that first develops a hypothesis (an assumption) and then tests the hypothesis with economic facts.

**Demand** A schedule showing the amounts of a good or service buyers (or a buyer) wish to purchase at various prices during some time period.

**Demand curve** A curve illustrating *demand*.

**Demand deposit** A deposit in a *chartered bank* against which cheques may be written for immediate payment; bank-created money.

**Dependent variable** A variable that changes as a consequence of a change in some other (independent) variable; the "effect" or outcome.

**Depreciation** (*See* Consumption of fixed capital.)

**Depreciation (of the dollar)** A decrease in the value of the dollar relative to another currency so that a dollar buys a smaller amount of the foreign currency and therefore of foreign goods.

**Derived demand** The demand for a resource that depends on the demand for the products it can be used to produce.

**Determinants of demand** Factors other than its price that determine the quantities demanded of a good or service.

**Determinants of supply** Factors other than its price that determine the quantities supplied of a good or service.

**Devaluation** A decrease in the governmentally defined value of a currency.

**Differentiated oligopoly** An *oligopoly* in which the firms produce a *differentiated product*.

**Differentiated product** A product that differs physically or in some other way from the similar products produced by other firms; a product such that buyers are not indifferent to the seller when the price charged by all sellers is the same.

**Diffusion** The spread of an *innovation* through its widespread imitation.

**Dilemma of regulation** The tradeoff a *regulatory agency* faces in setting the maximum legal price a monopolist may charge: *optimal social price* is below *average total cost* (and either bankrupts the *firm* or requires that it be subsidized), while the higher *fair-return price* does not produce *allocative efficiency*.

**Diminishing marginal returns** (*See* Law of diminishing returns.)

**Direct foreign investment** The building of new factories (or the purchase of existing capital) in a particular nation by corporations of other nations.

**Direct relationship** The relationship between two variables that change in the same direction, for example, product price and quantity supplied.

**Discrimination** According individuals or groups inferior treatment in hiring, occupational access, education and training, promotion, wage rates, or working conditions, even though they have the same abilities, education and skills, and work experience as other workers.

**Discrimination coefficient** A measure of the cost or disutility of prejudice; the monetary amount an employer is willing to pay to hire a preferred worker rather than a nonpreferred worker.

**Diseconomies of scale** Increase in the *average total cost* of producing a product as the *firm* expands the size of its *plant* (its output) in the *long run*.

**Disposable income** *Personal income* less personal taxes; income available for *personal consumption expenditures* and *personal saving*.

**Dividends** Payments by a corporation of all or part of its profit to its stockholders (the corporate owners).

**Division of labour** Dividing the work required to produce a product into a number of different tasks that are performed by different workers; *specialization* of workers.

**Dollar votes** The "votes" that consumers and entrepreneurs cast for the production of consumer and capital goods, respectively, when they purchase them in product and resource markets.

**Domestic capital formation** Addition to a nation's stock of *capital* by saving and investing part of its own domestic output.

**Domestic price** The price of a good or service within a country, determined by domestic demand and supply.

**Double taxation** The taxation of both corporate net income (profits) and the *dividends* paid from this net income when they become the personal income of households.

**Dumping** The sale of products below cost in a foreign country or below the prices charged at home.

**Durable good** A consumer good with an expected life (use) of three or more years.

**Dynamic efficiency** The development over time of less costly production techniques, improved products, and new products; technological progress.

## E

**Earnings** The money income received by a worker; equal to the *wage* (rate) multiplied by the amount of time worked.

**Economic analysis** Deriving *economic principles* from relevant economic facts.

**Economic concentration** A description or measure of the degree to which an industry is monopolistic or competitive. (*See* Concentration ratio.)

**Economic cost** A payment that must be made to obtain and retain the services of a *resource*; the income a firm must provide to a resource supplier to attract the resource away from an alternative use; equal to the quantity of other products that cannot be produced when resources are instead used to make a particular product.

**Economic efficiency** Obtaining the socially optimal amounts of goods and services using minimum necessary resources; entails both *productive efficiency* and *allocative efficiency*.

**Economic growth** (1) An outward shift in the *production possibilities curve* that results from an increase in resource quantity or quality or an improvement in *technology*; (2) an increase either in real output (*gross domestic product*) or in real output per capita.

**Economic integration** Cooperation among and the complete or partial unification of the economies of different nations; the elimination of barriers to trade among these nations; the bringing together of the markets in each of the separate economies to form one large (a common) market.

**Economic law** (*See* Economic principle.)

**Economic model** A simplified picture of economic reality; an abstract generalization.

**Economic perspective** A viewpoint that envisions individuals and institutions making rational decisions by comparing the marginal benefits and marginal costs associated with their actions.

**Economic policy** A course of action intended to correct or avoid a problem.

**Economic principle** A widely accepted generalization about the economic behaviour of individuals and institutions.

**Economic profit** The *total revenue* of a firm less all its *economic costs*; also called "pure profit" and "above normal profit."

**Economic regulation** (*See* Industrial regulation.)

**Economic rent** The price paid for the use of land and other natural resources, the supply of which is fixed (*perfectly inelastic*).

**Economic resources** The *land, labour, capital,* and *entrepreneurial ability* that are used in the production of goods and services; productive agents; factors of production.

**Economics** The social science dealing with the use of scarce resources to obtain the maximum satisfaction of society's virtually unlimited material wants.

**Economic theory** Deriving *economic principles* from relevant economic facts; an *economic principle.*

**Economic system** A particular set of institutional arrangements and a coordinating mechanism for solving the economizing problem; a method of organizing an economy; of which the *market economy, command economy,* and *traditional economy* are three general types.

**Economies of scale** Reductions in the *average total cost* of producing a product as the firm expands the size of plant (its output) in the *long run*; the economies of mass production.

**Economizing problem** The choices necessitated because society's material wants for goods and services are unlimited but the *resources* available to satisfy these wants are limited (scarce).

**Efficiency loss of a tax** The loss of net benefits to society because a tax reduces the production and consumption of a taxed good below the level of allocative efficiency.

**Efficient allocation of resources** That allocation of the resources of an economy among the production of different products that leads to the maximum satisfaction of the wants of consumers; producing the socially optimal mix of output with society's scarce resources.

**Efficiency wage** A wage that minimizes wage costs per unit of output.

**Elastic demand** Product or resource demand whose *price elasticity* is greater than 1; means the resulting change in *quantity demanded* is greater than the percentage change in *price.*

**Elasticity coefficient** The number obtained when the percentage change in *quantity demanded* (or supplied) is divided by the percentage change in the *price* of the commodity.

**Elasticity formula** (*See* Price elasticity of demand.)

**Elastic supply** Product or resource supply whose price elasticity is greater than 1; means the resulting change in quantity supplied is greater than the percentage change in price.

**Employment discrimination** Inferior treatment in hiring, promotions, work assignments, and such for a particular group of employees.

**Entrepreneurial ability** The human resources that combine the other resources to produce a product, make nonroutine decisions, innovate, and bear risks.

**Equality versus efficiency tradeoff** The decrease in *economic efficiency* that may accompany a decrease in *income inequality*; the presumption that some income inequality is required to achieve economic efficiency.

**Equilibrium price** The *price* in a competitive market at which the *quantity demanded* and the *quantity supplied* are equal; where there is neither a shortage nor a surplus; and where there is no tendency for price to rise or fall.

**Equilibrium quantity** (1) The quantity demanded and supplied at the equilibrium price in a competitive market; (2) the profit-maximizing output of a firm.

**Employment insurance** The insurance program that in Canada is financed by compulsory contributions from employers and employees and from the general tax revenues of the federal government with benefits (income) made available to insured workers who are unable to find jobs.

**European Union (EU)** An association of European nations initiated in 1958 that has eliminated tariffs and import quotas that existed among them, established common tariffs for goods imported from outside the member nations, allowed the free movement of labour and capital among them, and created other common economic policies.

**Excess capacity** Plant resources that are underused when imperfectly competitive firms produce less output than that associated with achieving minimum average total cost.

**Exchange control** (*See* Foreign exchange control.)

**Exchange rate** The *rate of exchange* of one nation's currency for another nation's currency.

**Exchange-rate appreciation** An increase in the value of a nation's currency in foreign exchange markets; an increase in the *rate of exchange* for foreign currencies.

**Exchange-rate depreciation** A decrease in the value of a nation's currency in foreign exchange markets; a decrease in the *rate of exchange* for foreign currencies.

**Exchange-rate determinant** Any factor other than the *rate of exchange* that determines a currency's demand and supply in the *foreign exchange market.*

**Excise tax** A tax levied on the production of a specific product or on the quantity of the product purchased.

**Exclusion principle** The ability to exclude those who do not pay for a product from receiving its benefits.

**Exclusive unionism** The practice of a labour union of restricting the supply of skilled union labour to increase the wages received by union members; the policies typically employed by a *craft union.*

**Exhaustive expenditure** An expenditure by government resulting directly in the employment of *economic resources* and in the absorption by government of the goods and services those resources produce; a *government purchase*.

**Exit mechanism** The process of leaving a job and searching for another one as a means of improving one's working conditions.

**Expanding industry** An industry whose firms earn *economic profits* and that experience an increase in output as new firms enter the industry.

**Expectations** The anticipations of consumers, firms, and others about future economic conditions.

**Expected rate of return** The increase in profit a firm anticipates it will obtain by purchasing capital (or engaging in research and development), expressed as a percentage of the total cost of the investment (or R&D) activity.

**Explicit cost** The monetary payment a *firm* must make to an outsider to obtain a *resource*.

**Export controls** The limitation or prohibition of the export of certain products on the basis of foreign policy or national security objectives.

**Exports** Goods and services produced in a nation and sold to customers in other nations.

**Export subsidies** Government payments to domestic producers to enable them to reduce the *price* of a good or service to foreign buyers.

**Export supply curve** An upsloping curve showing the amount of a product domestic firms will export at each *world price* above the *domestic price*.

**Export transactions** A sale of a good or service that increases the amount of foreign currency flowing to the citizens, firms, and governments of a nation.

**External benefit** (*See* Spillover benefit.)

**External cost** (*See* Spillover cost.)

**External debt** Private or public debt owed to foreign citizens, firms, and institutions.

**Externality** (*See* Spillover.)

**Factors of production** *Economic resources: land, capital, labour*, and *entrepreneurial ability*.

**Fair-return price** The price of a product that enables its producer to obtain a *normal profit* and that is equal to the *average total cost* of producing it.

**Fallacy of composition** Incorrectly reasoning that what is true for the individual (or part) is necessarily true for the group (or whole).

**Fallacy of limited decisions** The false notion that there are a limited number of economic decisions to be made so that, if government makes more decisions, there will be fewer private decisions to render.

**Farm problem** Technological advance, coupled with a price-inelastic and relatively constant demand, have made agriculture a *declining industry*; also, the tendency for farm income to fluctuate sharply from year to year.

**Farm products and marketing boards** The federal and provincial boards, numbering more than 100, that set marketing regulations for commodities ranging from asparagus to turkeys. The boards have the power to allocate quotas, set prices, issue licences, collect fees, and require that the commodity be marketed through them.

**Final goods and services** Goods and services that have been purchased for final use and not for resale or further processing or manufacturing.

**Financial capital** (*See* Money capital.)

**Firm** An organization that employs resources to produce a good or service for profit and owns and operates one or more *plants*.

**Fiscal federalism** The system of transfers (grants) by which the federal government shares its revenues with provincial and municipal governments.

**Fiscal policy** Changes in government spending and tax collections designed to achieve a full-employment and noninflationary domestic output; also called *discretionary fiscal policy*.

**Five fundamental economic questions** The five questions that every economy must answer: how much to produce, what to produce, how to produce it, how to divide the total output, and how to ensure economic flexibility.

**Fixed cost** Any cost that in total does not change when the *firm* changes its output; the cost of *fixed resources*.

**Fixed exchange rate** A *rate of exchange* that is set in some way and hence prevented from rising or falling with changes in currency supply and demand.

**Fixed resource** Any resource whose quantity cannot be changed by a firm in the *short run*.

**Flexible exchange rate** A *rate of exchange* determined by the international demand for and supply of a nation's money; a rate free to rise or fall (to float).

**Floating exchange rate** (*See* Flexible exchange rate.)

**Food and Drugs Act** The federal law enacted in 1920 as outgrowth of legislation dating back to 1875; subsequently amended, the Act and its Regulations now provide for controls over all foods, drugs, cosmetics, and medical devices sold in Canada.

**Foreign competition** (*See* Import competition.)

**Foreign exchange control** The control a government may exercise over the quantity of foreign currency demanded by its citizens and firms and over the *rates of exchange* in order to limit its *outpayments* to its *inpayments* (to eliminate a *payments deficit*).

**Foreign exchange market** A market in which the money (currency) of one nation can be used to purchase (can be exchanged for) the money of another nation.

**Foreign exchange rate** (*See* Rate of exchange.)

**Freedom of choice** The freedom of owners of property resources to employ or dispose of them as they see fit, of workers to enter any line of work for which they are qualified, and of consumers to spend their incomes in a manner that they think is appropriate.

**Freedom of enterprise** The freedom of *firms* to obtain economic resources, to use these resources to produce products of the firm's own choosing, and to sell their products in markets of their choice.

**Free-rider problem** The inability of potential providers of an economically desirable but indivisible good or service to obtain payment from those who benefit because the *exclusion principle* is not applicable.

**Free trade** The absence of artificial (government-imposed) barriers to trade among individuals and firms in different nations.

**Full employment** (1) Use of all available resources to produce want-satisfying goods and services. (2) The situation when the unemployment rate is equal to the full-employment unemployment rate and there is frictional and structural but no cyclical unemployment (and the real output of the economy equals its potential real output).

**Full production** Employment of available resources so that the maximum amount of (or total value of) goods and services is produced; occurs when both *productive efficiency* and *allocative efficiency* are realized.

**Functional distribution of income** The manner in which *national income* is divided among the functions performed to earn it (or the kinds of resources provided to earn it); the division of national income into wages and salaries, proprietors' income, corporate profits, interest, and rent.

**G-7 Nations** A group of seven major industrial nations (Canada, the United States, Japan, Germany, United Kingdom, France, and Italy) whose leaders meet regularly to discuss common economic problems and try to coordinate economic policies. (Recently has also included Russia, making it unofficially the G-8.)

**Gains from trade** The extra output that trading partners obtain through specialization of production and exchange of goods and services.

**Game theory** A means of analyzing the pricing behaviour of oligopolists using the theory of strategy associated with games such as chess and bridge.

**GDP** (*See* Gross domestic product.)

**General Agreement on Tariffs and Trade (GATT)** The international agreement reached in 1947 in which 23 nations agreed to give equal and nondiscriminatory treatment to the other nations, to reduce tariff rates by multi-national negotiations, and to eliminate *import quotas*. Now includes most nations and has become the *World Trade Organization*.

**Generalization** Statement of the nature of the relation between two or more sets of facts.

**Gold standard** A historical system of fixed exchange rates in which nations defined their currency in terms of gold, maintained a fixed relationship between their stock of gold and their money supplies, and allowed gold to be freely exported and imported.

**Government purchases** Disbursements of money by government for which government receives a currently produced good or service in return; the expenditures of all governments in the economy for *final goods and services*.

**Government transfer payment** The disbursement of money (or goods and services) by government for which government receives no currently produced good or service in return.

**Gross domestic product (GDP)** The total market value of all final goods and services produced in Canada in a particular year.

**Gross private domestic investment** Expenditures for newly produced *capital goods* (such as machinery, equipment, tools, and buildings) and for additions to inventories.

**Guaranteed annual income** The minimum income a family (or individual) would receive if a *negative income tax* were to be adopted.

**Guaranteed Income Supplement** A 1966 amendment to the *Old Age Security Act* provides for the payment of a full supplement to pensioners with no other income and a partial supplement to those with other, but still low, income.

**Guiding function of prices** The ability of price changes to bring about changes in the quantities of products and resources demanded and supplied.

## H

**Herfindahl index** A measure of the concentration and competitiveness of an industry; calculated as the sum of the squared percentage market shares of the individual firms.

**Homogeneous oligopoly** An *oligopoly* in which the firms produce a *standardized product*.

**Horizontal axis** The "left-right" or "west-east" axis on a graph or grid.

**Horizontal combination** A group of *plants* in the same stage of production that are owned by a single *firm*.

**Horizontal merger** The merger into a single firm of two firms producing the same product and selling it in the same geographical market.

**Household** An economic unit (of one or more persons) that provides the economy with resources and uses the income received to purchase goods and services that satisfy material wants.

**Human capital** The accumulation of prior investments in education, training, health, and other factors that increase productivity.

**Human-capital discrimination** The denial to members of particular groups of equal access to productivity-enhancing education and training.

**Human-capital investment** Any expenditure undertaken to improve the education, skills, health, or mobility of workers, with an expectation of greater productivity and thus a positive return on the investment.

**Hypothesis** A tentative, untested economic principle.

## I

**IMF** (*See* International Monetary Fund.)

**Immobility** The inability or unwillingness of a worker to move from one geographic area or occupation to another or from a lower-paying job to a higher-paying job.

**Imperfect competition** All market structures except *pure competition*; includes *monopoly, monopolistic competition*, and *oligopoly*.

**Implicit cost** The monetary income a *firm* sacrifices when it uses a resource it owns rather than supplying the resource in the market; equal to what the resource could have earned in the best-paying alternative employment.

**Import competition** The competition that domestic firms encounter from the products and services of foreign producers.

**Import demand curve** A downsloping curve showing the amount of a product that an economy will import at each *world price* below the *domestic price*.

**Import quota** A limit imposed by a nation on the quantity (or total value) of a good that may be imported during some period of time.

**Imports** Spending by individuals, *firms*, and governments for goods and services produced in foreign nations.

**Import transaction** The purchase of a good or service that decreases the amount of foreign money held by citizens, firms, and governments of a nation.

**Incentive function of price** The inducement that an increase in the price of a commodity gives to sellers to make more of it available (and conversely for a decrease in price); and the inducement that an increase in price offers to buyers to purchase smaller quantities (and conversely for a decrease in price).

**Incentive pay plan** A compensation structure that ties worker pay directly to performance. Such plans include piece rates, bonuses, commissions, and profit sharing.

**Inclusive unionism** The practice of a labour union of including as members all workers employed in an industry.

**Income effect** A change in the price of a product changes a consumer's *real income* (*purchasing power*) and thus the quantity of the product purchased.

**Income elasticity of demand** The ratio of the percentage change in the *quantity demanded* of a good to a percentage change in consumer income; measures the responsiveness of consumer purchases to income changes.

**Income inequality** The unequal distribution of an economy's total income among persons or families.

**Income-maintenance system** Government programs designed to eliminate poverty and reduce inequality in the distribution of income.

**Increase in demand** An increase in the *quantity demanded* of a good or service at every price; a shift of the *demand curve* to the right.

**Increase in supply** An increase in the *quantity supplied* of a good or service at every price; a shift of the *supply curve* to the right.

**Increasing-cost industry** An *industry* in which expansion through the entry of new firms increases the prices *firms* in the industry must pay for resources and therefore increases their production costs.

**Increasing marginal returns** An increase in the *marginal product* of a resource as successive units of the resource are employed.

**Independent goods** Products or services for which there is no relationship between the price of one and the demand for the other; when the price of one rises or falls, the demand for the other remains constant.

**Independent variable** The variable causing a change in some other (dependent) variable.

**Indifference curve** A curve showing the different combinations of two products that give a consumer the same satisfaction or *utility*.

**Indifference map** A set of *indifference curves*, each representing a different level of *utility*, and that together show the preferences of the consumer.

**Individual demand** The demand schedule or *demand curve* of a single buyer.

**Individual supply** The supply schedule or *supply curve* of a single seller.

**Induction** A method of reasoning that proceeds from facts to *generalization*.

**Industrial concentration** A situation in which a single firm or a small number of firms produces the major portion of an industry's output; fewness of producers within industries.

**Industrial Disputes Investigation Act** The 1907 law that marked the beginning of federal labour legislation; it required disputes in the federal jurisdiction to be submitted to a Board of Conciliation and Investigation; replaced by *Canada Labour Code*.

**Industrial policy** Any policy by which government takes a direct and active role in promoting specific firms or industries for purposes of expanding their output and achieving economic growth; called "technology policy" when its goal is to promote technological advance.

**Industrial regulation** The older and more traditional type of regulation in which government is concerned with the prices charged and the services provided the public in specific industries: in contrast to *social regulation*.

**Industrial union** A *labour union* that accepts as members all workers employed in a particular industry (or by a particular firm).

**Industry** A group of (one or more) *firms* that produces identical or similar products.

**Inelastic demand** Product or resource demand for which the *price elasticity coefficient* is less than 1; means the resulting percentage change in *quantity demanded* is less than the percentage change in *price*.

**Inelastic supply** Product or resource supply for which the price elasticity coefficient is less than 1; the percentage change in *quantity supplied* is less than the percentage change in *price*.

**Inferior good** A good or service whose consumption declines as income rises (and conversely), price remaining constant.

**Inflation** A rise in the general level of prices in an economy.

**Inflation premium** The component of the *nominal interest rate* that reflects anticipated inflation.

**Infrastructure** The capital goods usually provided by the *public sector* for the use of its citizens and firms (for example, highways, bridges, transit systems, wastewater treatment facilities, municipal water systems, and airports).

**Injunction** A court order directing a person or organization not to perform a certain act because the act would do irreparable damage to some other person or persons; a restraining order.

**Innovation** The first commercially successful introduction of a new product, the use of a new method of production, or the creation of a new form of business organization.

**Inpayments** The receipts of its own or foreign money that individuals, firms, and governments of one nation obtain from the sale of goods and services abroad, or as investment income, *remittances*, and *capitals inflows* from abroad.

**Insurable risk** An event that would result in a loss but whose frequency of occurrence can be estimated with considerable accuracy; insurance companies are willing to sell insurance against such losses.

**Interest** The payment made for the use of money (of borrowed funds).

**Interest income** Payments of income to those who supply the economy with *capital*.

**Interest rate** The annual rate at which interest is paid; a percentage of the borrowed amount.

**Interindustry competition** The competition for sales between the products of one industry and the products of another industry.

**Interlocking directorate** A situation where one or more members of the board of directors of a *corporation* are also on the board of directors of a competing corporation; and which is illegal in the United States—but not in Canada—when it tends to reduce competition among the corporations.

**International balance of payments** A summary of all the transactions that took place between the individuals, firms, and government unit of one nation and those in all other nations during a year.

**International balance of payments deficit** (*See* Balance of payments deficit.)

**International balance of payments surplus** (*See* Balance of payments surplus.)

**International Monetary Fund (IMF)** The international association of nations that was formed after World War II to make loans of foreign monies to nations with temporary *payments deficits* and, until the early 1970s, to administer the *adjustable pegs*; it now mainly makes loans to nations facing possible defaults on private and government loans.

**International value of the dollar** The price that must be paid in foreign currency (money) to obtain one Canadian dollar.

**Invention** The first discovery of a product or process through the use of imagination, ingenious thinking, and experimentation and the first proof that it will work.

**Inverse relationship** The relationship between two variables that change in opposite directions, for example, product price and quantity demanded.

**Inverted-U theory** A theory saying that, other things equal, *R&D* expenditures as a percentage of sales rise with industry concentration, reach a peak at a *concentration ratio* of about 50 percent, and then fall as concentration further increases.

**Investment** Spending for the production and accumulation of *capital* and additions to inventories.

**Investment goods** Same as *capital*.

**Investment in human capital** (*See* Human-capital investment.)

**Invisible hand** The tendency of firms and resource suppliers seeking to further their own self-interests in competitive markets to also promote the interest of society as a whole.

**Kinked demand curve** The demand curve for a noncollusive oligopolist, which is based on the assumption that rivals will follow a price decrease and will ignore a price increase.

**Labour** The physical and mental talents and efforts of people that are used to produce goods and services.

**Labour force** Persons 15 years of age and older who are not in institutions and who are employed or are unemployed (and seeking work).

**Labour force participation rate** The percentage of the working-age population that is actually in the *labour force*.

**Labour-intensive commodity** A product requiring a relatively large amount of *labour* to produce.

**Labour productivity** Total output divided by the quantity of labour employed to produce it; the *average product* of labour or output per worker per hour.

**Labour theory of value** The Marxian idea that the economic value of any commodity is determined solely by the amount of labour required to produce it.

**Labour union** A group of workers organized to advance the interests of the group (to increase wages, shorten the hours worked, improve working conditions, and so on).

**Laissez faire capitalism** (*See* Pure capitalism.)

**Land** Natural resources ("free gifts of nature") used to produce goods and services.

**Land-intensive commodity** A product requiring a relatively large amount of land to produce.

**Law of demand** The principle that, other things equal, an increase in a product's price will reduce the quantity of it demanded; and conversely for a decrease in price.

**Law of diminishing marginal utility** As a consumer increases the consumption of a good or service, the *marginal utility* obtained from each additional unit of the good or service decreases.

**Law of diminishing returns** As successive increments of a *variable resource* are added to a *fixed resource*, the *marginal product* of the *variable resource* will eventually decrease.

**Law of increasing opportunity costs** As the production of a good increases, the *opportunity cost* of producing an additional unit rises.

**Law of supply** The principle that, other things equal, an increase in the price of a product will increase the quantity of it supplied; and conversely for a price decrease.

**Least-cost combination of resources** The quantity of each resource a firm must employ in order to produce a particular output at the lowest total cost; the combination at which the ratio of the *marginal product* of a resource to its *marginal resource cost* (to its *price* if the resource is employed in a competitive market) is the same for the last dollar spent on each resource employed.

**Legal cartel theory of regulation** The hypothesis that some industries seek regulation or want to maintain regulation so they may form or maintain a legal *cartel*.

**Liability** A debt with a monetary value; an amount owed by a firm or an individual.

**Limited liability** Restriction of the maximum loss to a predetermined amount for the owners (stockholders) of a *corporation*; the maximum loss is the amount they paid for their shares of stock.

**Limited-liability company** An unincorporated business whose owners are protected by *limited liability*.

**Loanable funds** *Money* available for lending and borrowing.

**Loanable funds theory of interest** The concept that the supply of and demand for *loanable funds* determine the equilibrium rate of interest.

**Logrolling** The trading of votes by legislators to secure favourable outcomes on decisions concerning the provision of *public goods* and *quasipublic goods*.

**Long run** (1) In *microeconomics*, a period of time long enough to enable producers of a product to change the quantities of all the resources they employ; period in which all resources and costs are variable and no resources or costs are fixed. (2) In *macroeconomics*, a period sufficiently long for *nominal wages* and other input prices to change in response to a change in the nation's *price level*.

**Long-run competitive equilibrium** The price at which firms in *pure competition* neither obtain *economic profit* nor suffer losses in the *long run* and the total quantity demanded and supplied at that price are equal; a price equal to the minimum long-run *average total cost* of producing the product.

**Long-run farm problem** The tendency for agriculture to be a declining industry as technological progress increases supply relative to an inelastic and slowly increasing demand.

**Long-run supply** A schedule or curve showing the prices at which a *purely competitive industry* will make various quantities of the product available in the *long run*.

**Lorenz curve** A curve showing the distribution of income in an economy; the cumulated percentage of families (income receivers) is measured along the horizontal axis and cumulated percentage of income is measured along the vertical axis.

**Loss-minimizing case** The circumstances where a firm loses less than its *total cost*; when the price at which the firm can sell its product is less than *average total* but greater than *average variable cost*.

**Lotteries** Games of chance where people buy numbered tickets and winners are drawn by lot; a source of provincial government revenue.

**Macroeconomics** The part of economics concerned with the economy as a whole; with such major aggregates as the household, business, and governmental sectors; and with measures of the total economy.

**Managed floating exchange rate** An *exchange rate* that is allowed to change (float) as a result of changes in currency supply and demand but at times is altered (managed) by governments via their buying and selling of particular currencies.

**Marginal analysis** The comparison of marginal ("extra" or "additional") benefits and marginal costs, usually for decision making.

**Marginal benefit** The extra (additional) benefit of consuming one more unit of some good or service; the change in total benefit when one more unit is consumed.

**Marginal cost** The extra (additional) cost of producing one more unit of output; equal to the change in *total cost* divided by the change in output (and in the short run to the change in total *variable cost* divided by the change in output).

**Marginal labour cost** The amount total labour cost increases when a *firm* employs one additional unit of labour (the quantity of other resources employed remaining constant); equal to the change in the total cost of labour divided by the change in the quantity of labour employed.

**Marginal product** The additional output produced when one additional unit of a resource is employed (the quantity of all other resources employed remaining constant); equal to the change in total product divided by the change in the quantity of a resource employed.

**Marginal productivity theory of income distribution** The contention that the distribution of income is equitable when each unit of each resource receives a money payment equal to its marginal contribution to the firm's revenue (its *marginal revenue product*).

**Marginal rate of substitution** The rate at which a consumer is prepared to substitute one good for another (from a given combination of goods) and remain equally satisfied (have the same *total utility*); equal to the slope of a consumer's *indifference curve* at each point on the curve.

**Marginal resource cost** The amount the total cost of employing a *resource* increases when a firm employs one additional unit of the resource (the quantity of all other resource employed remaining constant); equal to the change in the *total cost* of the resource divided by the change in the quantity of the resource employed.

**Marginal revenue** The change in *total revenue* that results from the sale of one additional unit of a firm's product; equal to the change in total revenue divided by the change in the quantity of the product sold.

**Marginal-revenue–marginal-cost approach** A method of determining the total output at which *economic profit* is a maximum (or losses a minimum) by comparing the *marginal revenue* and the *marginal cost* of each additional unit of output.

**Marginal revenue product** The change in a firm's *total revenue* when it employs one additional unit of a resource (the quantity of all other resources employed remaining constant); equal to the change in total revenue divided by the change in the quantity of the resource employed.

**Marginal tax rate** The tax rate paid on each additional dollar of income.

**Marginal utility** The extra *utility* a consumer obtains from the consumption of one additional unit of a good or service; equal to the change in total utility divided by the change in the quantity consumed.

**Market** Any institution or mechanism that brings together buyers (demanders) and sellers (suppliers) of a particular good or service.

**Market demand** (*See* Total demand.)

**Market economy** An economy in which only the private decisions of consumers, resource suppliers, and firms determine how resources are allocated; the market system.

**Market failure** The failure of a market to bring about the allocation of resources that best satisfies the wants of society. In particular, the over- or underallocation of resources to the production of a particular good or service because of *spillovers* or informational problems and because markets fail to provide desired *public goods*.

**Market for externality rights** A market in which firms can buy rights to pollute the environment; the price of such rights is determined by the demand for the right to pollute and a *perfectly inelastic supply* of such rights (the latter determined by the quantity of pollution that the environment can assimilate).

**Market period** A period in which producers of a product are unable to change the quantity produced in response to a change in its price; in which there is a *perfectly inelastic supply*.

**Market socialism** An *economic system* (method of organization) in which property resources are publicly owned *and* markets and prices are used to direct and coordinate economic activities.

**Market system** All the product and resource markets of a *market economy* and the relationships among them; a method that allows the prices determined in these markets to allocate the economy's scarce resources and to communicate and coordinate the decisions made by consumers, firms, and resource suppliers.

**Median-voter model** The view that under majority rule the median (middle) voter will be in the dominant position to determine the outcome of an election.

**Medium of exchange** Items sellers generally accept and buyers generally use to pay for a good or service; *money*; a convenient means of exchanging goods and services without engaging in *barter*.

**Merger** The combination of two (or more) firms into a single firm.

**Microeconomics** The part of economics concerned with such individual units as *industries*, *firms*, and *households*; and with individual markets, particular prices, and specific goods and services.

**Minimum wage** The lowest *wage* employers may legally pay for an hour of work.

**Mixed capitalism** An economy in which both government and private decisions determine how resources are allocated.

**Monetary policy** A central bank's changing of the *money supply* to influence interest rates and assist the economy in achieving a full-employment, noninflationary level of total output.

**Money** Any item that generally is acceptable to sellers in exchange for goods and services.

**Money capital** Money available to purchase *capital*.

**Money interest rate** The *nominal interest rate*; the interest rate that includes an *inflationary premium* (if any).

**Money wage** (*See* Nominal wage.)

**Money wage rate** (*See* Nominal wage.)

**Monopolistic competition** A market structure in which many firms sell a *differentiated product*, into which entry is relatively easy, in which the firm has some control over its product price, and in which there is considerable *nonprice competition*.

**Monopoly** A market structure in which the number of sellers is so small that each seller is able to influence the total supply and the price of the good or service. (*See also* Pure monopoly.)

**Monopsony** A market structure in which there is only a single buyer of a good, service, or resource.

**Moral hazard problem** The possibility that individuals or institutions will change their behaviour as the result of a contract or agreement; for example, a bank whose deposits are insured against loss may make riskier loans and investments.

**Most-favoured-nation (MFN) status** An agreement by Canada to allow some other nation's *exports* into Canada at the lowest tariff level levied by Canada, then or at any later time.

**MR = MC rule** A firm will maximize its profit (or minimize its losses) by producing that output at which *marginal revenue* and *marginal cost* are equal, provided product price is equal to or greater than *average variable cost*.

**MRP = MRC rule** To maximize profit (or minimize losses) a firm should employ that quantity of a resource at which its *marginal revenue product* (MRP) is equal to its *marginal resource cost* (MRC), the latter being the wage rate in pure competition.

**Multinational corporation** A firm that owns production facilities in other countries and produces and sells its product abroad.

**Mutual interdependence** A situation in which a change in price strategy (or in some other strategy) by one firm will affect the sales and profits of another firm (or other firms); any firm that makes such a change can expect the other rivals to react to the change.

**Mutually exclusive goals** Two or more goals that conflict and cannot be achieved simultaneously.

**Natural monopoly** An industry in which *economies of scale* are so great the product can be produced by one firm at a lower average total cost than if the product were produced by more than one firm.

**Negative income tax** The proposal to subsidize families and individuals with money payments when their incomes fall below a *guaranteed annual income*; the negative tax would decrease as earned income increases. (*See* Benefit-reduction rate).

**Negative relationship** (*See* Inverse relationship.)

**Net export** *Exports* minus *imports*.

**Net investment income** The interest and dividend income received by the residents of a nation from residents of other nations less the interest and dividend payments made by the residents of that nation to the residents of other nations.

**Net private domestic investment** *Gross private domestic investment* less *consumption of fixed capital*; the addition to the nation's stock of *capital* during a year.

**Net taxes** The taxes collected by government less *government transfer payments*.

**Net transfers** The personal and *government transfer payments* made by one nation to residents of foreign nations, less the personal and government transfer payments received from residents of foreign nations.

**Net worth** The total *assets* less the total *liabilities* of a firm or an individual; the claims of the owners of a firm against its total assets.

**Nominal gross domestic output (GDP)** The *GDP* measured in terms of the price level at the time of measurement (unadjusted for changes in the price level).

**Nominal income** The number of dollars received by an individual or group for its resources during some period of time.

**Nominal interest rate** The interest rate expressed in terms of annual amounts currently charged for interest and not adjusted for inflation.

**Nominal wage** The amount of money received by a worker per unit of time (hour, day, etc.); money wage.

**Noncollusive oligopoly** An *oligopoly* in which the firms do not agree to act together in determining the price of the product and the output each firm will produce.

**Noncompeting groups** Groups of workers in the economy who do not compete with each other for employment because the skill and training of the workers in one group are substantially different from those in other groups.

**Nondurable good** A *consumer good* with an expected life (use) of less than three years.

**Nonexhaustive expenditure** An expenditure by government that does not result directly in the employment of economic resources or the production of goods and services; see *Government transfer payment*.

**Nonprice competition** Distinguishing one's product by means of *product differentiation* and then *advertising* the distinguished product to consumers.

**Nontariff barriers** All barriers other than *protective tariffs* that nations erect to impede international trade: include *import quotas*, licensing requirements, unreasonable product-quality standards, and unnecessary red tape in customs procedures.

**Normal good** A good or service whose consumption increases when income increases and falls when income decreases, price remaining constant.

**Normal profit** The payment made by a firm to obtain and retain *entrepreneurial ability*; the minimum income that entrepreneurial ability must receive to induce it to perform entrepreneurial functions for a firm.

**Normative economics** That part of economics involving value judgements about what the economy should be like; concerned with identifying economic goals and promoting them via public policies.

**North American Free Trade Agreement (NAFTA)** A 1993 agreement establishing, over a 15-year period, a free trade zone composed of Canada, Mexico, and the United States.

**Occupational discrimination** Arbitrary restriction of particular groups from entering the more desirable higher-paying occupations.

**Occupational licensing** The laws of provincial or municipal governments that require a worker to satisfy certain specified requirements and obtain a licence from a licensing board before engaging in a particular occupation.

**Occupational segregation** Crowding women or minorities into less desirable, lower-paying occupations.

**Official international reserves** The international monetary assets owned by the federal government and held in its behalf by the Bank of Canada in the Exchange Fund Account.

**Official reserves** (*See* Official international reserves.)

**Oligopoly** A market structure in which a few firms sell either a *standardized* or *differentiated product*, into which entry is difficult, in which the firm has limited control over product price because of *mutual interdependence* (except when there is collusion among firms), and in which there is typically nonprice competition.

**Oligopsony** A market in which there are only a few buyers.

**OPEC** An acronym for the *Organization of Petroleum Exporting Countries*.

**Open economy** An economy that exports and imports goods and services.

**Open shop** A place of employment in which the employer may hire nonunion workers and in which the workers need not become members of a *labour union*.

**Opportunity cost** The amount of other products that must be forgone or sacrificed to produce a unit of a product.

**Optimal social price** The price of a product that results in the most efficient allocation of an economy's resources and that is equal to the *marginal cost* of the last unit of the product produced.

**Organization of Petroleum Exporting Countries (OPEC)** The cartel formed in 1970 by 13 oil-producing countries to control the price and quantity of crude oil exported by its members, and which accounts for a large proportion of the world's export of oil.

**Other things equal assumption** The assumption that factors other than those being considered are held constant.

**Outpayments** The expenditures of its own or foreign currency that the individuals, firms, and governments of one nation make to purchase goods and services, for *remittances*, as investment income, and *capital outflows* abroad.

**Output effect** An increase in the price of one input will increase a firm's production costs and reduce its level of output, thus reducing the demand for other inputs; conversely for a decrease in the price of the input.

**Paradox of voting** A situation whereby paired-choice voting by majority rule fails to provide a consistent ranking of society's preferences for *public goods* or services.

**Partnership** An unincorporated firm owned and operated by two or more persons.

**Patent** An exclusive right to inventors to produce and sell a new product or machine for a set period of time.

**Payments deficit** (*See* Balance of payments deficit.)

**Payments surplus** (*See* Balance of payments surplus.)

**Per capita GDP** *Gross domestic product* (GDP) per person; the average GDP of a population.

**Per capita income** A nation's total income per person; the average income of a population.

**Perfectly elastic demand** Product or resource demand in which *quantity demanded* can be of any amount at a particular *price*; graphs as a horizontal *demand curve*.

**Perfectly elastic supply** Product or resource supply in which *quantity supplied* can be of any amount at a particular *price*; graphs as a horizontal *supply curve*.

**Perfectly inelastic demand** Product or resource demand in which *price* can be of any amount at a particular quantity of the product or resource demanded; *quantity demanded* does not respond to a change in price; graphs as a vertical *demand curve*.

**Perfectly inelastic supply** Product or resource supply in which *price* can be of any amount at a particular quantity of the product or resource demanded; *quantity supplied* does not respond to a change in price; graphs as a vertical *supply curve*.

**Personal consumption expenditures** The expenditures of *households* for *durable* and *nondurable consumer goods* and services.

**Personal distribution of income** The manner in which the economy's *personal* or *disposable income* is divided among different income classes or different households.

**Personal income** The earned and unearned income available to resource suppliers and others before the payment of *personal taxes*.

**Personal income tax** A tax levied on the *taxable income* of individuals, households, and unincorporated firms.

**Personal saving** The *personal income* of households less *personal taxes* and *personal consumption expenditures; disposable income* not spent for *consumer goods*.

**Per-unit production cost** The average production cost of a particular level of output; total input cost divided by units of output.

**Planned economy** An economy in which government determines how resources are allocated.

**Plant** A physical establishment that performs one or more functions in the production, fabrication, and distribution of goods and services.

**P = MC rule** A purely competitive firm will maximize its profit or minimize its loss by producing that output at which the *price* of the product is equal to *marginal cost*, provided that price is equal to or greater than *average variable cost* in the short run and equal to or greater than *average total cost* in the long run.

**Policy economics** The formulation of courses of action to bring about desired economic outcomes or to prevent undesired occurrences.

**Positive economics** The analysis of facts or data to establish scientific generalizations about economic behaviour.

**Positive relationship** Direct relationship between two variables.

***Post hoc, ergo propter hoc* fallacy** Incorrectly reasoning that when one event precedes another the first event must have caused the second event.

**Potential competition** New competitors that may be induced to enter an industry if firms now in that industry are receiving large *economic profits*.

**Poverty** A situation in which the basic needs of an individual or family exceed the means to satisfy them.

**Poverty rate** The percentage of the population with incomes below the official poverty income levels established by Statistics Canada.

**Price** The amount of money needed to buy a particular good, service, or resource.

**Price ceiling** A legally established maximum price for a good or service.

**Price discrimination** The selling of a product to different buyers at different prices when the price differences are not justified by differences in cost.

**Price elasticity of demand** The ratio of the percentage change in *quantity demanded* of a product or resource to the percentage change in its *price*; a measure of the responsiveness of buyers to a change in the price of a product or resource.

**Price elasticity of supply** The ratio of the percentage change in *quantity supplied* of a product or resource to the percentage change in its *price*; the responsiveness of producers to a change in the price of a product or resource.

**Price leadership** An informal method that firms in an *oligopoly* may employ to set the price of their product: one firm (the leader) is the first to announce a change in price, and the other firms (the followers) soon announce identical or similar changes.

**Price level** The weighted average of the *prices* paid for final goods and services produced in an economy.

**Price maker** A seller (or buyer) of a product or resource that is able to affect the product or resource price by changing the amount it sells (or buys).

**Price-level stability** A steadiness of the price level from one period to the next; zero or low annual inflation; also called "price stability."

**Price support** A minimum price that government allows sellers to receive for a good or service; a legally established or maintained minimum price.

**Price taker** A seller (or buyer) of a product or resource who is unable to affect the price at which a product or resource sells by changing the amount it sells (or buys).

**Price war** Successive and continued decreases in the prices charged by the firms in an oligopolistic industry; each firm lowers its price below rivals' prices, hoping to increase its sales and revenues at its rivals' expense.

**Principal-agent problem** A conflict of interest that occurs when agents (workers or managers) pursue their own objectives to the detriment of the principals' (stockholders) goals.

**Private good** A good or service that is subject to the *exclusion principle* and that is provided by privately owned firms to consumers who are willing to pay for it.

**Private property** The right of private persons and firms to obtain, own, control, employ, dispose of, and bequeath *land, capital*, and other property.

**Private sector** The *households* and business *firms* of the economy.

**Process innovation** The development and use of a new or improved production or distribution method.

**Product differentiation** A strategy in which one firm's product is distinguished from competing products by means of its design, related services, quality, location, or other attributes (except price).

**Product innovation** The development and sale of a new or improved product (or service).

**Production possibilities curve** A curve showing the different combinations of two goods or services that can be produced in a *full-employment, full-production* economy in which the available supplies of resources and technology are fixed.

**Productive efficiency** The production of a good in the least costly way; occurs when production takes place at the output at which *average total cost* is a minimum and at which *marginal product* per dollar's worth of input is the same for all inputs.

**Productivity** A measure of average output or real output per unit of input. For example, the productivity of labour may be found by dividing real output by hours of work.

**Product market** A market in which products are sold by *firms* and bought by *households*.

**Profit** The return to the resource entrepreneurial ability (see *Normal profit*); *total revenue* minus *total cost* (see *Economic profit*).

**Profit-maximizing combination of resources** The quantity of each resource a firm must employ to maximize its profit or minimize its loss; the combination in which the *marginal revenue product* of each resource is equal to its *marginal resource cost* (to its *price* if the resource is employed in a competitive market).

**Profit-sharing plan** A compensation device through which workers receive part of their pay in the form of a share of their employer's profit (if any).

**Progressive tax** A tax whose *average tax rate* increases as the taxpayer's income increases and decreases as the taxpayer's income decreases.

**Property tax** A tax on the value of property (*capital, land*, stocks and bonds, and other *assets*) owned by *firms* and *households*.

**Proportional tax** A tax whose *average tax rate* remains constant as the taxpayer's income increases or decreases.

**Proprietor's income** The net income of the owners of unincorporated firms (proprietorships and partnerships).

**Protective tariff** A *tariff* designed to shield domestic producers of a good or service from the competition of foreign producers.

**Public assistance programs** Government programs that pay benefits to those who are unable to earn income (because of permanent disabilities or because they have very low income and dependent children); financed by general tax revenues and viewed as public charity (rather than earned rights).

**Public choice theory** The economic analysis of collective and government decision making, politics, and the democratic process.

**Public finance** The branch of economics that analyzes government revenues and expenditures.

**Public good** A good or service that is indivisible and to which the *exclusion principle* does not apply; a good or service with these characteristics provided by government.

**Public interest theory of regulation** The presumption that the purpose of the regulation of an *industry* is to protect the public (consumers) from abuse of the power possessed by *natural monopolies*.

**Public sector** The part of the economy that contains all government entities; government.

**Public sector failure** Inefficiencies in resource allocation caused by problems in the operation of the public sector (government); occurs because of rent-seeking pressure by special-interest groups, short-sighted political behaviour, limited and bundled choices, and bureaucratic inefficiencies.

**Public utility** A firm that produces an essential good or service, has obtained from a government the right to be the sole supplier of the good or service in the area, and is regulated by that government to prevent the abuse of its monopoly power.

**Purchasing power** The amount of goods and services that a monetary unit of income can buy.

**Purchasing power parity** The idea that exchange rates between nations equate the purchasing power of various currencies; exchange rates between any two nations adjust to reflect the price-level differences between the countries.

**Pure capitalism** An economic system in which property resources are privately owned and markets and prices are used to direct and coordinate economic activities.

**Pure competition** A market structure in which a very large number of firms sell a *standardized product*, into which entry is very easy, in which the individual seller has no control over the product price, and in which there is no nonprice competition; a market characterized by a very large number of buyers and sellers.

**Pure monopoly** A market structure in which one firm sells a unique product, into which entry is blocked, in which the single firm has considerable control over product price, and in which *nonprice competition* may or may not be found.

**Pure profit** (*See* Economic profit.)

**Pure rate of interest** An essentially risk-free, long-term interest rate that is free of the influence of market imperfections.

**Quantity demanded** The amount of a good or service buyers (or a buyer) desire to purchase at a particular price during some period.

**Quantity supplied** The amount of a good or service producers (or a producer) offer to sell at a particular price during some period.

**Quasipublic good** A good or service to which the *exclusion principle* could apply but which has such a large *spillover benefit* that government sponsors its production to prevent an underallocation of resources.

**R&D** Research and development activities undertaken to bring about *technological progress*.

**Rate of exchange** The price paid in one's own money to acquire one unit of a foreign currency; the rate at which the money of one nation is exchanged for the money of another nation.

**Rate of return** The gain in net revenue divided by the cost of an investment or an R&D expenditure; expressed as a percentage.

**Rationing function of prices** The ability of market forces in a competitive market to equalize *quantity demanded* and *quantity supplied* and to eliminate shortages and surpluses via changes in prices.

**Real capital** (*See* Capital.)

**Real gross domestic product (GDP)** *Gross domestic product* adjusted for inflation; gross domestic product in a year divided by the *GDP deflator* for that year, expressed as a decimal.

**Real GDP** (*See* real gross domestic product.)

**Real income** The amount of goods and services that can be purchased with *nominal income* during some period of time; nominal income adjusted for inflation.

**Real interest rate** The interest rate expressed in dollars of constant value (adjusted for *inflation*); and equal to the *nominal interest rate* less the expected rate of inflation.

**Real wage** The amount of goods and services a worker can purchase with his or her *nominal wage*; the purchasing power of the nominal wage.

**Recession** A period of declining real GDP, accompanied by lower real income and higher unemployment.

**Regressive tax** A tax whose *average tax rate* decreases as the taxpayer's income increases, and increases as the taxpayer's income decreases.

**Regulatory agency** An agency, commission, or board established by the federal government or a provincial government to control the prices charged and the services offered by a natural monopoly.

**Remittance** A gift or grant; a payment for which no good or service is received in return; the funds sent by workers who have legally or illegally entered a foreign nation to their families in the nations from which they have migrated.

**Rental income** The payments (income) received by those who supply *land* to the economy.

**Rent-seeking behaviour** The actions by persons, firms, or unions to gain special benefits from government at the taxpayers' or someone else's expense.

**Resource market** A market in which *households* sell and *firms* buy resources or the services of resources.

**Revaluation** An increase in the governmentally defined value of its currency relative to other nations' currencies.

**Revenue tariff** A *tariff* designed to produce income for the federal government.

**Reverse discrimination** The view that the preferential treatment associated with *affirmative action* efforts constitutes discrimination against other groups.

**Roundabout production** The construction and use of *capital* to aid in the production of *consumer goods*.

**Rule of 70** A method for determining the number of years it will take for some measure to double, given its annual percentage increase. Example: To determine the number of years it will take for the *price level* to double; divide 70 by the annual rate of *inflation*.

**Sales tax** A tax levied on the cost (at retail) of a broad group of products.

**Saving** Disposable income not spent for consumer goods; equal to *disposable income* minus *personal consumption expenditures*.

**Scarce resources** The limited quantities of *land, capital, labour*, and *entrepreneurial ability* that are never sufficient to satisfy the virtually unlimited material wants of humans.

**Seasonal variations** Increases and decreases in the level of economic activity within a single year, caused by a change in the season.

**Secular trend** Long-term tendency; change in some variable over a very long period of years.

**Self-interest** That which each firm, property owner, worker, and consumer believes is best for itself and seeks to obtain.

**Seniority** The length of time a worker has been employed absolutely or relative to other workers; may be used to determine which workers will be laid off when there is insufficient work for them all, and who will be rehired when more work becomes available.

**Separation of ownership and control** The fact that different groups of people own a *corporation* (the stockholders) and manage it (the directors and officers).

**Service** An (intangible) act or use for which a consumer, firm, or government is willing to pay.

**Shirking** Actions by workers to increase their utility or well-being by neglecting or evading work.

**Shut-down case** The circumstance in which a firm would experience a loss greater than its total *fixed cost* if it were to produce any output greater than zero; alternatively, a situation in which a firm would cease to operate when the *price* at which it can sell its product is less than its *average variable cost*.

**Shortage** The amount by which the *quantity demanded* of a product exceeds the *quantity supplied* at a particular (below-equilibrium) price.

**Short run** (1) In microeconomics, a period of time in which producers are able to change the quantity of some but not all of the resources they employ; a period in which some resources (usually plant) are fixed and some are variable. (2) In macroeconomics, a period in which nominal wages and other input prices do not change in response to a change in the price level.

**Short-run supply curve** A supply curve that shows the quantity of a product a firm in a purely competitive industry will offer to sell at various prices in the *short run*; the portion of the firm's short-run marginal cost curve that lies above its *average variable cost* curve.

**Short-run competitive equilibrium** The price at which the total quantity of a product supplied in the *short run* in a purely competitive industry equals the total quantity of the product demanded and which is equal to or greater than *average variable cost*.

**Short-run farm problem** The sharp year-to-year changes in the prices of agricultural products and in the incomes of farmers.

**Slope of a line** The ratio of the vertical change (the rise or fall) to the horizontal change (the run) between any two points on a line. The slope of an upward-sloping line is positive, reflecting a direct relationship between two variables; the slope of a downward-sloping line is negative, reflecting an inverse relationship between two variables.

**Social insurance programs** The programs that replace some of the earnings lost when people retire or are temporarily unemployed, which are financed by deductions from individuals' earnings, and which are viewed as earned rights (rather than charity).

**Social regulation** The regulation by which government is concerned with the conditions under which goods and services are produced, their physical characteristics, and the impact of their production on society; in contrast to *industrial regulation*.

**Sole proprietorship** An unincorporated *firm* owned and operated by one person.

**Special economic zones** Regions of China open to foreign investment, private ownership, and relatively free international trade.

**Special-interest effect** Any result of government promotion of the interests (goals) of a small group at the expense of a much larger group.

**Specialization** The use of the resources of an individual, a firm, a region, or a nation to produce one or a few goods and services.

**Speculation** The activity of buying or selling with the motive of later reselling or rebuying for profit.

**Spillover** A benefit or cost from production or consumption, accruing without compensation to nonbuyers and nonsellers of the product. (*See* Spillover benefit; Spillover costs).

**Spillover benefit** A benefit obtained without compensation by third parties from the production or consumption of sellers or buyers. Example: A beekeeper benefits when a neighbouring farmer plants clover.

**Spillover cost** A cost imposed without compensation on third parties by the production or consumption of sellers or buyers. Example: A manufacturer dumps toxic chemicals into a river, killing the fish sport fishers seek.

**Standardized product** A product for which buyers are indifferent to the seller from whom they purchase it so long as the price charged by all sellers is the same; a product for which all units of the product are identical and thus perfect substitutes for each other.

**Startup (firm)** A new firm focused on creating and introducing a particular new product or employing a specific new production or distribution method.

**State-owned enterprises** Businesses that are owned by government; the major types of enterprises in Russia and China before their transitions to the market system.

**Statistical discrimination** Judging an individual on the basis of the average characteristic of the group to which the person belongs rather than on personal characteristics.

**Stock (corporate)** An ownership share in a corporation.

**Strategic trade policy** The use of trade barriers to reduce the risk inherent in product development by domestic firms, particularly that involving advanced technology.

**Strike** The withholding of labour services by an organized group of workers (a *labour union*).

**Subsidy** A payment of funds (or goods and services) by a government, firm, or household for which it receives no good or service in return; when made by a government, it is a *government transfer payment*.

**Substitute goods** Products or services that can be used in place of each other. When the price of one falls the demand for the other falls, and conversely with an increase of price.

**Substitution effect** (1) A change in the price of a *consumer good* changes the relative expensiveness of that good and hence changes the consumer's willingness to buy it rather than other goods. (2) The effect of a change in the price of a *resource* on the quantity of the resource employed by a firm, assuming no change in its output.

**Sunk cost** A cost that has been incurred and cannot be recovered.

**Superior good** (*See* Normal good.)

**Supply** A schedule showing the amounts of a good or service sellers (or a seller) will offer at various prices during some period.

**Supply curve** A curve illustrating *supply*.

**Surplus** The amount by which the *quantity supplied* of a product exceeds the *quantity demanded* at a specific (above-equilibrium) price.

**Surplus payment** A payment to a resource that is not required to ensure the availability of the resource, for example, land rent.

**Surplus value** A Marxian term; the amount by which the value of a worker's daily output exceeds the worker's daily wage; workers' output appropriated by capitalists as profit.

**Tacit collusion** Any method by an oligopolist to set prices and outputs that does not involve outright (or overt) *collusion*; *price leadership* is an example.

**Tariff** A tax imposed by a nation on an imported good.

**Taste-for-discrimination model** A theory of discrimination that views discrimination as a preference for which an employer is willing to pay.

**Tax** An involuntary payment of money (or goods and services) to a government by a *household* or *firm* for which the household or firm receives no good or service directly in return.

**Tax incidence** The person or group who ends up paying a tax.

**Tax subsidy** A grant in the form of reduced taxes through favourable tax treatment.

**Tax-transfer disincentives** Decreases in the incentives to work, save, invest, innovate, and take risks that allegedly result from high *marginal tax rates* and *transfer payments*.

**Technology** The body of knowledge and techniques that can be used to produce goods and services from *economic resources*.

**Technological progress** New and better goods and services and new and better ways of producing or distributing them.

**Terms of trade** The rate at which units of one product can be exchanged for units of another product; the price of a good or service; the amount of one good or service that must be given up to obtain one unit of another good or service.

**Theory of human capital** Generalization that *wage differentials* are the result of differences in the amount of *human-capital investment*, and that the incomes of lower paid workers are increased by increasing the amount of such investment.

**Total cost** The sum of *fixed cost* and *variable cost*.

**Total demand** The demand schedule or the *demand curve* of all buyers of a good or service; also called market demand.

**Total product** The total output of a particular good or service produced by a firm (or a group of firms or the entire economy).

**Total revenue** The total number of dollars received by a firm (or firms) from the sale of a product; equal to the total expenditures for the product produced by the firm (or firms); equal to the quantity sold (demanded) multiplied by the price at which it is sold.

**Total-revenue test** A test to determine elasticity of *demand* between any two prices: Demand is elastic if *total revenue* moves in the opposite direction as price; it is inelastic when it moves in the same direction as price; and it is of unitary elasticity when it does not change when price changes.

**Total spending** The total amount buyers of goods and services spend or plan to spend; also called *aggregate expenditures*.

**Total supply** The supply schedule or the supply curve of all sellers of a good or service; also called market supply.

**Total utility** The total amount of satisfaction derived from the consumption of a single product or a combination of products.

**Township and village enterprises** Privately owned rural manufacturing firms in China.

**Trade balance** The export of goods (or goods and services) of a nation less its imports of goods (or goods and services).

**Trade bloc** A group of nations that lowers or abolishes trade barriers among members. Examples include the *European Union* and the nations of the *North American Free Trade Agreement*.

**Trade controls** *Tariffs, export subsidies, import quotas*, and other means a nation may use to reduce *imports* and expand *exports*.

**Trade deficit** The amount by which a nation's *imports* of goods (or goods and services) exceed its *exports* of goods (or goods and services).

**Trademark** A legal protection that gives the originators of a product an exclusive right to use the brand name.

**Tradeoffs** The sacrifice of some or all of one economic goal, good, or service to achieve some other goal, good, or service.

**Trades and Labour Congress of Canada (TLC)** The federation of *craft unions* formed in 1886 and affiliated with the *American Federation of Labor*; amalgamated into the *Canadian Labour Congress* in 1956.

**Trade surplus** The amount by which a nation's exports of goods (or goods and services) exceed its imports of goods (or goods and services).

**Trading possibilities line** A line that shows the different combinations of two products an economy is able to obtain (consume) when it specializes in the production of one product and trades (exports) it to obtain the other product.

**Traditional economy** An economic system in which traditions and customs determine how the economy will use its scarce resources.

**Transfer payment** A payment of *money* (or goods and services) by a government to a *household* or *firm* for which the payer receives no good or service directly in return.

**Tying contract** A promise made by a buyer when allowed to purchase a product from a seller that it will purchase certain other products from the same seller.

**Underemployment** (1) Failure to produce the maximum amount of goods and services that can be produced from the resources employed; failure to achieve *full production*. (2) A situation in which workers are employed in positions requiring less than the amount of education and skill that they have.

**Undistributed corporate profits** After-tax corporate profits not distributed as dividends to stockholders; corporate or business saving; also called retained earnings.

**Unemployment** Failure to use all available *economic resources* to produce goods and services; failure of the economy to fully employ its *labour force*.

**Unemployment insurance** (*See* Employment Insurance.)

**Unemployment rate** The percentage of the *labour force* unemployed at any time.

**Uninsurable risk** An event that would result in a loss and whose occurrence is uncontrollable and unpredictable; insurance companies are not willing to sell insurance against such a loss.

**Union shop** A place of employment where the employer may hire either *labour union* members or nonmembers but where nonmembers must become members within a specified period of time or lose their jobs.

**Unit elasticity** Demand or supply for which the *elasticity coefficient* is equal to 1; means the percentage change in the quantity demanded or supplied is equal to the percentage change in price.

**Unit labour cost** Labour costs per unit of output; total labour cost divided by total output; also equal to the *nominal wage rate* divided by the *average product* of labour.

**Unlimited liability** Absence of any limits on the maximum amount which an individual (usually a business owner) may become legally required to pay.

**Unlimited wants** The insatiable desire of consumers for goods and services that will give them satisfaction or *utility*.

**Urban collectives** Chinese enterprises jointly owned by their managers and their workforces, located in urban areas.

**Uruguay Round** The eighth and most recent round of trade negotiations under *GATT* (now the *World Trade Organization*).

**Utility** The want-satisfying power of a good or service; the satisfaction or pleasure a consumer obtains from the consumption of a good or service (or from the consumption of a collection of goods and services).

**Utility-maximizing rule** To obtain the greatest *utility* the consumer should allocate *money income* so that the last dollar spent on each good or service yields the same marginal utility.

**Value added** The value of the product sold by a *firm* less the value of the products (materials) purchased and used by the firm to produce the product.

**Value-added tax** A tax imposed on the difference between the value of the products sold by a firm and the value of the goods purchased from other firms to produce the product.

**Value judgement** Opinion of what is desirable or undesirable; belief regarding what ought or ought not to be (regarding what is right or just and wrong or unjust).

**Variable cost** A cost that in total increases when the firm increases its output and decreases when it reduces its output.

**VAT** (*See* Value-added tax.)

**Vertical axis** The "up-down" or "north-south" axis on a graph or grid.

**Vertical combination** A group of *plants* engaged in different stages of the production of a final product and owned by a single *firm*.

**Vertical intercept** The point at which a line meets the vertical axis of a graph.

**Vertical merger** The merger of one or more *firms* engaged in different stages of the production of a final product.

**Very long run** A period in which *technology* can change and in which *firms* can introduce new products.

**Voluntary export restrictions** Voluntary limitations by countries or firms of their exports to a particular foreign nation to avoid enactment of formal trade barriers by that nation.

**Wage** The price paid for the use or services of *labour* per unit of time (per hour, per day, and so on).

**Wage differential** The difference between the *wage* received by one worker or group of workers and that received by another worker or group of workers.

**Wage discrimination** The payment of a lower wage to members of particular groups than to preferred workers for the same work.

**Wage rate** (*See* Wage.)

**Wages** The income of those who supply the economy with *labour*.

**Welfare programs** (*See* Public assistance programs.)

**World Bank** A bank that lends (and guarantees loans) to developing nations to help them increase their *capital stock* and thus achieve economic growth; formally, the International Bank for Reconstruction and Development.

**World price** The international market price of a good or service, determined by world demand and supply.

**World Trade Organization** An organization established in 1994 to replace *GATT* to oversee the provisions of the *Uruguay Round* and resolve any disputes stemming therefrom.

**X-inefficiency** Failure to produce any specific output at the lowest average (and total) cost possible.

# Index

## A

## E

Q